116566/10/94

E

$ 31.50

D1306147

Acronyms for Accounting and Disclosure Standards and Those Who Set Them

AICPA	American Institute of Certified Public Accountants
APB	Accounting Principles Board Opinion (e.g. APB 15)
ASC	Accounting Standards Committee (United Kingdom)
DM	Discussion Memorandum (usually FASB)
E	Exposure Draft (e.g. E32) issued by IASC
ED	Exposure Draft (proposed standard)
FASB	Financial Accounting Standards Board
FRS	Financial Reporting Standard (issued by ASC)
IASC	International Accounting Standards Committee
IAS	International Accounting Standard (e.g. IAS 31)
SAB	Staff Accounting Bulletin (e.g. SAB 88) issued by SEC
SEC	Securities and Exchange Commission
SFAC	Statement of Financial Accounting Concepts (e.g. SFAC 6) issued by FASB
SFAS	Statement of Financial Accounting Standards (e.g. SFAS 8) issued by FASB
SOP	Statement of Position, issued by AICPA

THE ANALYSIS AND USE OF FINANCIAL STATEMENTS

GERALD I. WHITE, CFA
Grace & White, Inc

ASHWINPAUL C. SONDHI, Ph.D.
Columbia Business School
Columbia University

DOV FRIED, Ph.D.
Stern School of Business
New York University

JOHN WILEY & SONS, INC

New York • Chichester • Brisbane • Toronto • Singapore

ACQUISITIONS EDITOR   Karen Hawkins
MARKETING MANAGER   Karen Allman
SENIOR PRODUCTION EDITOR   Micheline A. Frederick
TEXT AND COVER DESIGNER   Lee Goldstein
DESIGN SUPERVISOR   Karin Gerdes Kincheloe
MANUFACTURING MANAGER   Andrea Price
ILLUSTRATION COORDINATOR   Anna Melhorne

This book was set in Times Roman by ATLIS Graphics and
printed and bound by Malloy Lithographing.

Recognizing the importance of preserving what has been written, it is a
policy of John Wiley & Sons, Inc. to have books of enduring value published
in the United States printed on acid-free paper, and we exert our best
efforts to that end.

"Figure 1 of FASB Concepts Statement No. 2, *Qualitative
Characteristics of Accounting Information,* copyright by
Financial Accounting Standards Board, 401 Merritt 7,
P.O. Box 5116, Norwalk, Connecticut, 06856-5116,
U.S.A., is reprinted with permission. Copies of the
complete document are available from the FASB."

Printed in the United States of America

10 9 8 7 6 5 4 3 2 1

Printed and bound by Malloy Lithographing, Inc.

To Penny, Rachel, and our families and friends

PREFACE

The objective of this book is the presentation of financial statement analysis from the point of view of the primary users of financial statements: equity and credit analysts. The analysis and use of financial statements is not restricted to analysts, however. Managers, auditors, educators, and regulators can also benefit from the insights and analytic techniques presented in this text.

Corporate managers, and those training to be managers, require an understanding of how financial statements provide information regarding an enterprise. This book is intended for use as a university level textbook for MBA and advanced undergraduate financial statement analysis courses. In addition, it should help equip businesspeople to prepare, audit, or interpret financial information. Finally, the text is designed to be a useful reference for both neophytes and informed readers.

WHO SHOULD READ THIS BOOK?

We believe that our work will be valuable to numerous audiences. First, it will benefit the working financial analyst. Some of the areas covered (off balance sheet financing techniques, for example) are rarely covered either in the professional literature or in accounting textbooks. While many analysts are familiar with some of the techniques in this book, we believe that even the most experienced analyst will find fresh insights on financial reporting issues.

Financial analysis, in some cases, is nothing more than journalism. Analysts accept the financial statements and what management tells them at face value. Good analysis is hampered by the inadequacies of published financial data. Many analysts examine the trend of reporting earnings but are unable to go "behind the numbers" or beyond them. The analysis taught in most textbooks starts and ends with reported financial statements or computerized databases.

Our view is that good financial analysis requires the analyst to understand how financial statements are generated in order to *separate the economic process that generates the numbers from the accounting process that (sometimes) obscures it*. Such analysis requires the use of assumptions and approximations, as reported financial data are often inadequate. We may dislike the need to make assumptions, but most financial analysis depends on them. Good analysis also requires the recasting of reported data into other formats when the latter yield superior insights.

However, we do not believe that there are always simple solutions to analytic problems. There is, for example, no precisely correct or "optimal" leverage ratio; there are many possible ratios, depending on the goals of the analysis and the judgement of the analyst. Our view is that asking the right questions is more than half the battle. This text asks many questions, and suggests some answers.

Previous financial analysis books have been written from an academic point of view, stressing either an accounting or an empirical (data analysis) approach. While both financial reporting and empirical analysis are present in this text, they are integrated with, and subordinated to user oriented analysis. They are subjected to the test of relevance: how do they aid in the interpretation of financial statement data?

Most of the analysis presented is based on the financial statements of actual companies. While such analysis can be frustrating (due to inadequate data), we believe that financial analysis can be presented best in a real world setting. While "models" are sometimes required for exposition purposes (such as for the analysis of foreign operations), the principles learned are always applied to real company statements.

The end-of-chapter materials (all problems and solutions were written by the authors) are also largely based on real corporate data. Some problems are adapted from the Chartered Financial Analyst examination program. Readers and students need to apply the text material to actual financial statements and the problems are designed to test their ability to do so.

ORGANIZATION AND CONTENT

A few comments on the organization and content of the book may be helpful to both reader and instructor. As already stated, we have integrated accounting, economic theory, and empirical research into a financial analysis framework. In doing so, we realize that some topics may be more important to some readers than to others. For that reason some elementary material (e.g., the Comprehensive Review of the Financial Reporting Process in Chapter 1) and some advanced material (e.g., the Analysis of Oil and Gas Disclosures in Chapter 6) appears in appendices. Within chapters, we have organized some material into boxes that are available to interested readers without distracting those who are not.

As the globalization of financial markets continues apace, we include discussions and comparisons of relevant foreign and international (IASC) accounting standards throughout the text. Some of this material is in separate "international" sections but much of it is integrated. As the comparative analysis of companies using different accounting standards is an increasingly common concern, our goal is to help the user who must make an investment decisions despite the lack of comparability. In some cases (for example Chapter 12, Business Combinations), non-U.S. companies are used to illustrate international accounting differences.

The first four chapters introduce the essential elements of financial statement analysis. Chapter 1 provides the framework, including discussions of data sources and the roles of preparers, auditors, and standard setters in the financial reporting process. Appendix 1-A provides an introduction to financial statements. Appendix 1-B offers a guided tour of the financial statements of Deere, to acquaint readers with the primary source of data for analysis.

Chapter 2 describes the primary financial statements and discusses their role as inputs for analysis. Chapter 3 presents ratio analysis, suggesting both its advantages and its limits. Appendix 3-C is concerned with the most widely used (and often misunderstood) ratio: earnings per share. Chapter 4 reviews empirical research, emphasizing its implications for financial analysis.

Chapters 5 to 13 focus on specific areas of analysis, ranging from inventories to multinational corporations. Throughout these chapters our goal is to show how differences in accounting methods and estimates affect reported financial condition, results of operations (including cash flows), and ratios. In many cases, analytic techniques are used to restore comparability, enhancing the decision usefulness of financial data. Each chapter includes a discussion of international accounting differences and relevant empirical research findings.

Chapter 5 considers the analysis of inventories, where differing methods have far-reaching effects on financial data. Chapter 6 (Long-Lived Assets) addresses the capitalization versus expensing decision, differing methods of allocating capitalized costs to operations, and the thorny area of impairment and restructuring. Chapter 7 concerns income tax accounting, where three different standards have been used in recent years.

Chapter 8 is the first in a series of chapters analyzing long term liabilities, beginning with the various forms of debt. This chapter includes an extensive discussion of leases, the granddaddy of "off-balance-sheet" financing techniques, presented from both the lessor and lessee perspectives.

Chapter 9 considers pensions and other postemployment benefits, both of which were largely "off-balance-sheet" until new accounting standards were adopted in recent years. Chapter 10 covers a number of other "off-balance-sheet" activities and the important but often misunderstood subject of hedging.

The next three chapters focus on problems resulting from the combination of more than one enterprise. Chapter 11 considers the cost, mark-to-market, equity method, and consolidation issues resulting from intercorporate investments, including joint ventures. Chapter 12 presents the alternative methods of accounting for business combinations, as well as the analysis of leveraged buyout firms (LBOs) and spinoffs. Chapter 13 describes the impact of changing exchange rates on multinational firms and suggests how available data can be used to separate exchange rate and accounting effects from operating results.

Finally, Chapters 14 and 15 pull together the previous material. Chapter 14 demonstrates how financial data can be used to assess different forms of risk. Chapter 15 presents both asset-based and discounted cash flow valuation models, and relates their use to the material covered earlier in the text. The final section of the book considers forecasting models, for which financial data constitute the input.

ACKNOWLEDGEMENTS

We acknowledge the help of our many teachers, mentors, colleagues, and friends throughout our respective careers. In particular, we thank the late Oliver R. Grace and Professors Michael Schiff, George Sorter, Joshua Livnat, and Sanford C. Gunn.

Many colleagues and friends read parts of the manuscript during its preparation, offering us encouragement and constructive criticism. In particular we would like to thank Terry Arndt, CFA (Ball State University), Phil Malone, CFA (University of Mississippi), James B. Rosenwald III, CFA (Rosenwald Capital Management), Rolf Rundfelt (Bohlins), and Stephen Ryan (New York University).

Lawrence D. Brown (State University of New York), Carl Crego (Pace University), Gerald Lobo (Syracuse University), David Mielke (Marquette University), Haim Mozes (Fordham University), R.D. Nair (University of Wisconsin), David Smith (University of Dayton), and Walter Teets (University of Illinois), the reviewers of our manuscript, deserve special thanks for their valuable insights and suggestions. Many students at New York University and Columbia University field tested the manuscript and problems.

Research assistance was provided by Aryeh Glatter and Patricia D. McQueen, to whom we express our appreciation. Invaluable help in preparing the manuscript was provided by Kimberly Phillips and Shevon Nurse Estwick. Karen Hawkins, our Wiley editor, provided valuable encouragement throughout the writing and editing process. Micheline Frederick ably steered us through the rigors of the production process.

Despite the help provided by the many people mentioned, errors may remain, for which we accept full responsibility. Comments are welcome and should be directed to us in care of John Wiley & Sons.

GERALD I WHITE
ASHWINPAUL C. SONDHI
DOV FRIED

August 1993

CONTENTS

1. **FRAMEWORK FOR FINANCIAL STATEMENT ANALYSIS**   1

Introduction   2

Focus on Investment Decisions   4
Classes of Users, 4
Financial Information and Capital Markets, 5

The Financial Reporting System   6
General Principles and Measurement Rules, 6
The Securities and Exchange Commission, 7
Financial Accounting Standards Board, 9

Principal Financial Statements   12
The Balance Sheet, 12
The Income Statement, 15
The Statement of Cash Flows, 18
The Statement of Stockholders' Equity, 19
Footnotes, 20
Contingencies, 21
Supplementary Schedules, 22

Other Sources of Financial Reporting Information   22
Management Discussion and Analysis, 22
Other Data Sources, 23

Role of the Auditor   24
Reporting on Uncertainties, 25

International Accounting Standards   27
International Accounting Standards Committee, 28

European Financial Reporting Standards   29
SEC Requirements for Foreign Registrants   29
Multijurisdictional Disclosure System   30
Summary   31
Problems   31
Appendix 1-A: Review of the Financial Reporting Process   35
The Accounting Cycle   35
Financial Reporting at Formation Date, 37
First Year of Operations, 39
Entries Required for the Preparation of Financial Statements, 41
Closing Entries in the Preparation of the Income Statement, 41
Creation of the Statement of Cash Flows   45
Cash Flows from Operations, 45
Investment Cash Flows, 49
Financing Cash Flows, 49
Problems   50
Appendix 1-B: Deere & Company   56
Introduction   56
General Comments   56
Financial Summary   57
Letter to Stockholders   57
Business Review   58
Financial Statements   58
Consolidated Balance Sheet, 59
Financial Statement Footnotes, 63
Statement of Consolidated Income and Retained Earnings, 64

Statement of Consolidated Cash
  Flows, 65
**Management Discussion and
  Analysis** 65
Capital Resources and Liquidity, 66
Ten-Year Review 66

**2. FINANCIAL STATEMENTS: THE
  RAW DATA OF ANALYSIS** 113
Introduction 114
**Income, Cash Flows, and Assets:
  Definitions and Relationships** 115
The Accrual Concept of Income 116
Measurement and Classification Rules:
  Income Statement Components, 119
Thousand Trails: Introduction, 121
Accounting Income: Revenue and
  Expense Recognition, 124
Analysis of Cash Flow Information 131
Statement of Cash Flows: Classification
  Issues, 132
CFO: The Effect of Reporting
  Methods, 136
Transactional Analysis: Overview, 137
Relationship of the Cash Flow Statement
  and Income Statement, 138
**Thousand Trails: Income and Cash
  Flow Analysis** 150
Revenue Recognition by Thousand
  Trails, 150
Expense Recognition by Thousand
  Trails, 152
Thousand Trails: CFO and Free Cash
  Flows, 155
Thousand Trails: Balance Sheet
  Analysis, 157
Thousand Trails: Analytic Lessons, 158
Nonrecurring Items 159
Components of Nonrecurring
  Income, 159
The Analysis of Nonrecurring Items, 174
Summary and Concluding Remarks 179
Problems 179

**3. FOUNDATIONS OF RATIO AND
  FINANCIAL ANALYSIS** 197
Introduction 198
Purpose and Use of Ratios, 198
Ratios: Cautionary Notes, 199
Common-Size Statements 202
Discussion of Ratios by Category 206
Activity Analysis, 208
Liquidity Analysis, 212
Long-Term Debt and Solvency
  Analysis, 219
Profitability Analysis, 223
Ratios: An Integrated Analysis 231
Analysis of Firm Performance, 232
Economic Characteristics and
  Strategies, 236
Classification and Partitioning of
  Ratios, 245
Ratios: Patterns of Disclosure,
  Definition, and Use, 248
Summary 253
Problems 253
**Appendix 3-A: Estimating
  Operating Leverage** 267
**Appendix 3-B: Merck Financial
  Statements** 270
Appendix 3-C: Earnings per Share 272
Introduction 272
Simple Capital Structure, 273
Complex Capital Structure, 273
Computational Issues, 273
Adjustments for Convertibles Bonds and
  Preferred Stock, 275
Adjustments for Options and Warrants,
  276
Comprehensive Example of EPS
  Computation, 278
EPS Computations for Two-Class
  Securities, 278
Additional Disclosure Requirements, 282
Limitations of EPS Calculations, 282
International Differences, 283
Concluding Remarks 284
Problems 285

**4. EMPIRICAL RESEARCH:
IMPLICATIONS FOR FINANCIAL
STATEMENT ANALYSIS** 287

Introduction 288
The Classical Approach 290
Market-Based Research 291
Efficient Market Theory, 292
Modern Portfolio Theory, 293
Test of the Mechanistic Hypothesis
Versus the EMH, 295
The Ball and Brown Study, 297
Information Content Studies, 299
The Relationship Between Earnings and
Stock Returns, 300
Market-Based Research—Current
Status, 303
Market Anomalies, 309
Positive Accounting Research 312
Disclosure and Regulatory Requirements,
313
Agency Theory, 313
Direction of Current Research 319
Ball and Brown Revisited—Back to the
Future? 320
**Implications for Financial
Statement Analysis** 323
Problems 324

5. ANALYSIS OF INVENTORIES 331
Introduction 332
**Inventory and Cost of Goods Sold:
Basic Relationships** 332
Scenario 1: Stable Prices, 333
Scenario 2: Rising Prices, 333
**Comparison of Information Provided
by Alternative Methods** 335
Balance Sheet Information: Inventory
Account, 335
Income Statement Information: Cost of
Goods Sold, 335
**LIFO Versus FIFO: Income, Cash
Flow, and Working Capital
Effects** 339
Adjustment from LIFO to FIFO 342
Adjustment of Inventory Balances, 342

Adjustment of COGS from LIFO to
FIFO, 344
**Adjustment of Income to Current
Cost Income** 346
Financial Ratios: FIFO versus LIFO 349
Profitability: Gross Profit Margin, 351
Liquidity: Working Capital, 352
Activity: Inventory Turnover, 352
Solvency: Debt to Equity, 356
**LIFO: Reporting and Measurement
Issues** 356
Initial Adoption or Change to LIFO, 357
Change from LIFO, 357
LIFO Liquidations, 359
Declining Prices, 360
LIFO and Interim Reporting, 361
LIFO Inventory Methods, 364
Retail Inventory Methods, 365
**LIFO: A Historical and Empirical
Perspective** 366
Overview of FIFO/LIFO Choice, 366
The FIFO/LIFO Choice: Empirical
Studies, 368
Summary of FIFO/LIFO Choice, 376
**Concluding Comments on
Accounting for Inventories** 376
Non-U.S. Reporting Requirements 379
**Using Inventory Balances to Aid in
Forecasting** 380
Summary 382
Problems 382

**6. ANALYSIS OF LONG-LIVED
ASSETS** 393
Introduction 395
**I. Acquiring the Asset: The
Capitalization Decision** 395
**Capitalization Versus Expensing:
Conceptual Issues** 396
Financial Statement Effects, 398
Need for Analytic Adjustments, 403
Valuation Implications, 405
Other Valuation and Economic
Consequences, 406

**Capitalization Versus Expensing:
  General Issues**   **409**
Capitalization of Interest Costs, 409
Intangible Assets, 411
**Capitalization Versus Expensing:
  Industry Issues**   **414**
Regulated Utilities, 414
Accounting for Oil and Gas Exploration,
  416
**II. Accounting for Long-Lived
  Assets over their Useful Lives**   **424**
Introduction   **424**
Depreciation Methods   **425**
Depletion, 432
Amortization, 433
Depreciation Methods and
  Disclosures, 433
Impact of Depreciation Methods on
  Financial Statements, 434
Accelerated Depreciation and Taxes, 434
Inflation and Its Impact on
  Depreciation, 435
Changes in Depreciation Method, 439
Analysis of Fixed Asset Disclosures   **448**
Estimating Relative Age and Useful
  Lives, 452
Estimating the Age of Assets, 453
**III: Impairment of Long-Lived
  Assets**   **454**
Introduction   **454**
**Financial Statement Impact of
  Impairments**   **458**
Impairment of Oil and Gas
  Properties: Pennzoil, 455
Financial Statement Impact of
  Impairments, 458
**International Accounting
  Differences Affecting
  Long-Lived Assets**   **464**
Capitalization of Borrowing Costs, 465
Research and Development
  Expenditures, 465
Goodwill, 465
Oil and Gas Accounting, 466
Depreciation Methods, 466
Concluding Comments   **466**

Problems   **467**
**Appendix 6A Analysis of Oil and
  Gas Disclosures**   **480**
Disclosure of Physical Reserve
  Quantities, 480
Disclosure of Capitalized Costs, 482
Analysis of Finding Costs, 482
Disclosure of Present Value Data, 485
Using Present Value Disclosures, 488
Changes in Present Values, 490
**Appendix 6-B: Research and
  Development Partnerships**   **491**
Introduction, 491
Centocor: R&D Arrangements in
  Practice, 492
**Appendix 6-C: Analysis of Changing
  Prices Information**   **497**
Introduction, 497
Analysis of General Inflation, 497
Current Cost Method, 500
Adjusting Financial Statements for
  Changing Prices, 504
Using Constant Dollar Data, 506
Concluding Remarks, 507

7. ANALYSIS OF INCOME TAXES   **509**
Introduction   **510**
**Accounting for Income Taxes:
  Basic Issues**   **511**
**Deferred Taxes: Alternative
  Approaches**   **513**
APB 11: The Deferred Tax Method, 513
SFAS 96: The Liability Method, 520
SFAS 109: Modified Liability Method,
  531
Deferred Taxes: Analytical Issues   **536**
Liability or Unrecognized Income?, 000
Effective Tax Rates, 539
**Accounting for Taxes: Specialized
  Issues**   **541**
Temporary Versus Permanent
  Differences, 541
Treatment of Operating Losses, 541
Indefinite Reversals, 542
Accounting for Acquisitions, 543

**Financial Statement Presentation
and Disclosure Requirements** 544
**Usefulness of Analysis of Income
Taxes** 545
**Accounting Outside the United
States** 550
Conclusion 550
Problems 551

8. **ANALYSIS OF FINANCING
LIABILITIES** 561
   Introduction 562
   Balance Sheet Debt 563
   Current Liabilities, 563
   Long-Term Debt, 564
   Debt with Equity Features, 572
   Effects of Changes in Interest Rates, 575
   Retirement of Debt Prior to
   Maturity, 582
   Bond Covenants 583
   Nature of Covenants, 584
   Calculating Accounting-Based
   Constraints, 586
   Analysis of Deere's Covenants, 587
   Leases 589
   Incentives for Leasing, 589
   Lease Classification: Lessees, 592
   Lease Classification: Lessors, 592
   Financial Reporting by Lessees:
   Illustration, 594
   Financial Reporting by Lessors, 606
   Lease Accounting Outside the United
   States, 615
   Conclusion 615
   Problems 616

9. **PENSIONS AND OTHER
POSTEMPLOYMENT BENEFITS** 633
   Introduction 634
   Pension Plans 634
   Defined Contribution Pension Plans, 637
   Defined Benefit Pension Plans, 637
   Defined Benefit Pension Plans 638
   Estimating Benefit Obligations, 638

Factors Affecting Benefit
Obligations, 644
Pension Plan Assets, 646
**Accounting for Pensions Under
SFAS 87** 647
Computing Pension Cost, 647
Disclosure of Plan Status, 651
**Analysis of Pension Costs and
Liability** 652
Importance of Assumptions, 652
Pension Analysis: Plan Status and Plan
Costs, 654
Analyzing Pension Plan Disclosures 662
The General Motors Plan, 662
Estimating GM's Pension Status, 665
GM's Pension Costs, 667
Analysis of GM Pension Trends, 670
Estimating Future Pension Cost, 674
The Importance of Pension Plans
to GM, 677
Impact of Discontinuities 678
Acquisitions and Divestitures, 678
Curtailments and Settlements, 679
Termination of Overfunded Plans, 680
Non-U.S. Reporting Requirements 683
Other Postemployment Benefits 685
Estimating Health Care Benefits, 686
Computing Postretirement Benefit
Cost, 687
Disclosure of Plan Status, 688
Importance of Assumptions, 688
Transition Methods, 691
Analysis of General Electric, 696
Using SFAS 106 Disclosures, 699
Non-U.S. GAAP Treatment, 699
Summary 700
Problems 701

10. **THE ANALYSIS OF
OFF-BALANCE-SHEET
ACTIVITIES AND HEDGING
TRANSACTIONS** 713
    Introduction 714
    **I. OFF-BALANCE
    SHEET-FINANCING ACTIVITIES** 715

**Examples of Off-Balance-Sheet
Financing Techniques** 716
Accounts Receivable, 716
Inventories, 721
Commodity-Linked Bonds, 724
Fixed Assets, 725
Joint Ventures,725
Investments, 725
**Analysis of OBS Activities: Ashland
Oil** 727
II. HEDGING ACTIVITIES 733
Foreign Currency Transactions 733
Interest Rate Swaps 734
Options 735
**Comparison of Accounting for
Hedges, Options and Swaps** 735
Examples of Hedge Disclosures 735
**Disclosure Standards for Financial
Instruments** 738
Summary 740
Problems 741

**11. ANALYSIS OF INTERCORPORATE
INVESTMENTS** 761
Overview 762
Cost Methods 763
Marketable Equity Securities, 764
Analysis of Marketable Securities, 769
Summary of Analytical
Considerations, 783
U.S. Practice Compared to the Practices
of Major Foreign Countries, 784
Equity Method of Accounting 784
Conditions for Use, 784
Illustration, 785
Comparison of Equity Method and Cost
Method, 787
The Equity Method and Deferred
Taxes, 788
Equity Accounting and Analysis:
Concluding Comments, 789
Consolidation 790
Illustration, 790
Applicability of Consolidation, 794
Nonhomogeneous Subsidiaries, 795

Consolidation Practices Outside the
United States, 796
Comparison of Consolidation with
Equity Method, 796
Consolidated Versus Equity Method: The
Case of Deere, 797
Significance of Consolidation, 804
Analysis of Minority Interest 805
Analysis of Joint Ventures 806
Jointly Controlled Entities, 807
Alternatives to the Equity Method, 808
Use of the Alternatives to the Equity
Method in Practice, 809
Analysis of Segment Data 820
Geographic Segment Reporting, 821
Analysis of Segment Data: Dow
Chemical, 822
Uses of Segment Data, 825
Segment Reporting in Practice, 826
Using Segment Data to Estimate
Consolidated Earnings and Risk, 826
**U.S. GAAP Compared to Major
Foreign Countries** 829
Proportionate Consolidation, 829
Segment Reporting, 829
Problems 830
**Appendix 11-A: Expanded Equity
versus Proportionate
Consolidation** 843

12. BUSINESS COMBINATIONS 845
Introduction 846
The Purchase Method 848
Illustration, 849
The Pooling of Interests Method 852
Conditions Necessary for Use, 852
Illustration, 853
Effects of Accounting Method 853
Comparison of Balance Sheets, 853
Comparison of Income Statements, 854
Effects on the Cash Flow Statement, 859
Impact of Accounting Method on
Ratios, 861
**Income Tax Effects of Business
Combinations** 862

**Analysis of a Pooling Method
    Acquisition: The Conagra-Golden
    Valley Merger   863**
Balance Sheet Under Pooling
    Method, 863
Balance Sheet Under Purchase
    Method, 866
Income Statement Under Pooling
    Method, 867
Income Statement Under Purchase
    Method, 870
Comparison of Financial Ratios, 872
Summary, 873
**Analysis of a Purchase Method
    Acquisition: Georgia Pacific's
    Purchase of Great Northern
    Nekoosa   873**
Balance Sheet Under Purchase
    Method, 873
Restating the GP-GNN Transaction to
    Pooling, 875
Income Statement Under Pooling
    Method, 877
Effects on Balance Sheet, 878
Effects on Cash Flow Statement, 878
Comparison of Financial Ratios, 882
Using Pro Forma Information, 883
Summary, 885
**Analysis of International Differences:
    The Smithkline Beecham Merger   885**
The Merged Balance Sheet, 886
Differences in Accounting Methods, 886
Comparison of Stockholders' Equity, 888
Restatement of the Balance Sheet, 890
Income Statement Effects, 891
Restatement of the Income
    Statement, 896
Comparison of Financial Ratios, 898
Summary, 898
International Differences in Accounting
    for Business Combinations, 898
Choosing the Acquisition Method   899
Income Maximization as Motivation for
    the Pooling/Purchase Choice, 901
Market Reaction and the
    Pooling/Purchase Choice, 903

Other Factors Influencing Mergers, Bid
    Premia, and the Pooling/Purchase
    Choice, 905
Summary, 909
The Analysis of Goodwill   909
Goodwill and the Income Statement, 910
Push Down Accounting   910
Push Down in Practice: The GM-Hughes
    Transaction, 911
Impact on the Balance Sheet, 912
Impact on the Income Statement, 912
Effect on Cash Flows, 913
Effect on Financial Ratios, 913
Push-Down Summed Up, 914
**Leveraged Buyouts: Duracell
    International   914**
Balance Sheet Effects, 915
Income Statement Effects, 915
Comparing Buyout Firms with
    Others, 918
Spinoffs   919
Analysis of Spinoffs, 919
Reasons for Investment in Spinoffs, 920
The Spinoff of ESCO Electronics, 921
**Corporate Reorganization and
    Revaluation   922**
Quasi-Reorganizations, 922
Miscellaneous Restructuring
    Methods, 923
Summary   923
Problems   924

**13. ANALYSIS OF MULTINATIONAL
    OPERATIONS   941**
Introduction   942
Basic Accounting Issues   943
FASB's First Attempt: SFAS 8   943
**Foreign Currency Translation
    Under SFAS 52   944**
Treatment of Exchange Gains and
    Losses, 945
Role of the Functional Currency, 947
Remeasurement Versus Translation, 948
**Illustration of Translation and
    Remeasurement   950**

Translation, 950
Cumulative Translation Adjustment, 954
Remeasurement, 955
**Comparison of Translation and
  Remeasurement**   957
Income Statement Effects, 957
Balance Sheet Effects, 960
Impact on Financial Ratios, 960
Comparison of Ratios Under Translation
  and Remeasurement, 961
Comparison of Translated and Local
  Currency Ratios, 961
Impact on Reported Cash Flows   963
**Accounting Principles Used Outside
  of the United States**   966
Foreign Currency Translation, 966
Foreign Currency Transactions, 967
IASC Exposure Draft, 968
Case Studies of MNC Analysis   968
IBM Corp., 968
Alcoa, 982
**Analytic Difficulties Related
  to Foreign Operations**   987
Relationship Among Interest Rates,
  Inflation, and Exchange Rates, 987
Consistency in Reporting, 988
Economic Interpretation of Results, 990
Impact of SFAS 8 and SFAS 52 on
  Management and Investor
  Behavior, 993
Concluding Comments   995
Problems   996

14. **CREDIT AND RISK ANALYSIS**   1013
Introduction   1014
**I. CREDIT ANALYSIS: OBJECTIVES,
METHODOLOGY, AND USE**   1015
Objectives   1015
**Analysis of and Adjustments
  to Book Value**   1015
Adjustments to Assets, 1016
Adjustments to Liabilities, 1017
Credit Analysis of Deere   1019
Adjustments to Deere's Assets, 1019
Adjustments to Deere's Liabilities, 1024

Adjustments to Stockholders'
  Equity, 1027
Adjusted Book Value, 1027
Analysis of Deere's Capital
  Structure, 1027
Analysis of Cash Flow, 1029
**II. ACCOUNTING- AND
FINANCE-BASED MEASURES
OF RISK**   1037
Overview   1037
Earnings Variability and Its Components,
  1038
The Prediction of Bankruptcy   1046
Usefulness of Bankruptcy
  Prediction, 1046
Model Results, 1047
Bankruptcy Prediction and Cash
  Flows, 1054
Concluding Comments, 1055
The Prediction of Debt Risk   1055
The Prediction of Bond Ratings, 1055
Usefulness of Bond Ratings
  Prediction, 1059
The Significance of the
  Ratings—Another Look, 1064
The Prediction of Equity Risk   1066
Importance and Usefulness of
  Beta (β_e), 1067
Review of Theoretical and Empirical
  Findings, 1068
Summary of Research, 1079
Concluding Comments   1079
Problems   1080

15. **VALUATION AND
FORECASTING**   1093
Introduction   1094
VALUATION MODELS   1095
Overview of Models   1095
Asset-Based Valuation Models   1096
Market Price and Book Value:
  Theoretical Considerations, 1097
Book Value: Measurement Issues, 1097
Tobin's Q Ratio, 1099

Stability and Growth of Book Value, 1099

Discounted Cash Flow Valuation Models **1101**

Dividend-Based Models, 1102

Earnings-Based Models, 1104

Free Cash Flow Approach to Valuation, 1114

Dividends, Earnings, or Free Cash Flows?, 1117

Valuation: Empirical Results and Additional Considerations, 1118

Effects of Nonrecurring Income and Differing Accounting Policies, 1122

FORECASTING MODELS AND TIME SERIES PROPERTIES OF EARNINGS **1129**

Forecasting Models **1129**

Extrapolative Models, 1129

Index Models, 1132

Forecasting Using Disaggregated Data, 1133

Comparison with Financial Analysts' Forecasts **1136**

Analyst Forecasts: Some Caveats, 1142

Summary **1143**

Problems **1144**

Appendix 15-A Multistage Growth Models **1157**

Valuing a Nondividend-Paying Firm, 1158

Shifting Growth Rate Patterns, 1158

Glossary **1161**

Present Value Tables **1164**

Bibliography **1173**

Index **1184**

1

FRAMEWORK FOR FINANCIAL STATEMENT ANALYSIS

INTRODUCTION

FOCUS ON INVESTMENT DECISIONS
Classes of Users
Financial Information and Capital Markets

THE FINANCIAL REPORTING SYSTEM
General Principles and Measurement Rules
The Securities and Exchange Commission
Financial Accounting Standards Board
   FASB Conceptual Framework

PRINCIPAL FINANCIAL STATEMENTS
The Balance Sheet
   Elements of the Balance Sheet
   Format and Classification
   The Measurement of Assets and Liabilities
The Income Statement
   Elements of the Income Statement
   Format and Classification
   Components of Net Income
The Statement of Cash Flows
The Statement of Stockholders' Equity
Footnotes
Contingencies
Supplementary Schedules

OTHER SOURCES OF FINANCIAL REPORTING INFORMATION
Management Discussion and Analysis
Other Data Sources

ROLE OF THE AUDITOR
Reporting on Uncertainties

INTERNATIONAL ACCOUNTING STANDARDS
International Accounting Standards Committee

EUROPEAN FINANCIAL REPORTING STANDARDS

SEC REQUIREMENTS FOR FOREIGN REGISTRANTS

MULTIJURISDICTIONAL DISCLOSURE SYSTEM

SUMMARY

APPENDIX 1-A: REVIEW OF THE FINANCIAL REPORTING PROCESS

THE ACCOUNTING CYCLE
Financial Reporting at Formation Date
First Year of Operations

1

Entries Required for the Preparation of Financial Statements

Closing Entries in the Preparation of the Income Statement

CREATION OF THE STATEMENT OF CASH FLOWS
Cash Flows from Operations
Investment Cash Flows
Financing Cash Flows

APPENDIX 1-B: DEERE & COMPANY

INTRODUCTION

GENERAL COMMENTS

FINANCIAL SUMMARY

LETTER TO STOCKHOLDERS

BUSINESS REVIEW

FINANCIAL STATEMENTS
Consolidated Balance Sheet
Current Assets
Noncurrent Assets
Current Liabilities
Noncurrent Liabilities
Stockholders' Equity
Financial Statement Footnotes
Stock Compensation Plans
Commitments and Contingencies
Statement of Consolidated Income and Retained Earnings
Statement of Consolidated Cash Flows

MANAGEMENT DISCUSSION AND ANALYSIS
Capital Resources and Liquidity

TEN-YEAR REVIEW

INTRODUCTION

Why are financial statements useful? Because they help investors and creditors make better economic decisions.

The goal of this book is to show why the previous statement is true. To that end, we have designed this book to lead the financial statement user through the labyrinth of financial reporting. Because of the selective reporting of economic events by the accounting system, compounded by noncomparable accounting methods and estimates, financial statements are, at best, only an approximation of economic reality. The tendency to delay accounting recognition means that financial statements tend to lag reality as well.

We will examine the impact on financial statements of differential application of accounting methods and estimates, with particular emphasis on the effect of accounting choices on reported earnings, stockholders' equity, cash flow, and various measures of corporate performance (including, but not limited to, financial ratios). We will also stress the use of cash flow analysis to evaluate the financial health of an enterprise.

The United States has the most complex financial reporting system in the world. Detailed accounting principles combined with supplementary disclosure requirements result in extensive financial information regarding the enterprise. In some cases, the financial statements and footnotes add up to dozens of pages.

In an ideal world, the user of financial statements could focus only on the bottom lines of financial reporting: net income and stockholders' equity. If financial statements were completely comparable from company to company, consistent over time, and if they always fully reflected the economic position of the firm, financial statement analysis would not be needed to make sound investment decisions. Our financial reporting system is not, however, perfect. One reason is that economic events and accounting entries do not correspond precisely; they diverge across the dimensions of timing, recognition, and measurement.

Economic events and accounting recognition of those events frequently take place at different times. One example of this phenomenon is the recognition of capital gains and losses only upon sale in most cases. Appreciation of a real estate investment, which took place over a period of many years, for example, will receive income statement recognition only in the period management chooses for its disposal.[1]

Similarly, an impairment write-down of fixed assets will be reported, most of the time, in a fiscal period of management's choice. The period of recognition will be *neither* the period in which the impairment took place *nor* the period of sale or disposal. Accounting for discontinued operations, in the same manner, results in recognition of any loss in a period different from when the loss occurred or the disposal is consummated.

In addition, many economic events do not receive accounting recognition. Most contracts, for example, are not reflected in financial statements when entered into. Yet they might be highly significant to the company's present and future financial condition. Some contracts, such as leases, may be recognized in the financial statements by some companies but disclosed only in footnotes by others.

Further, generally accepted accounting principles (GAAP) permit economic events that do receive accounting recognition to be recognized in different ways by different financial statement preparers. Inventory and depreciation of fixed assets are only two of the significant areas where comparability may be lacking.

Financial reports often contain supplementary data that, while not included in the statements themselves, help the financial statement user to interpret the statements or adjust measures of corporate performance (such as financial ratios) to make them more comparable across companies, consistent over time, and more representative of economic reality. When making adjustments to financial statements, we will seek to discern substance from form and exploit the information contained in footnotes and supplementary schedules of data in the annual report and SEC 10-K filings. The analytic treatment of "off-balance-sheet" financing activities is a good example of this process.

Finally, information from outside the financial reporting process can be used to make financial data more useful. Estimating the effects of changing prices on corporate performance, for example, may require the use of price data from outside sources.

---

[1]However, in countries (such as the United Kingdom) where periodic asset revaluation is permitted, balance sheet recognition of market value changes may occur much sooner.

This chapter provides a framework for the study of financial statement analysis. This framework consists of the users being served, the information system available to them, and the institutional structure within which they interact. Each of these components is introduced in this chapter.

FOCUS ON INVESTMENT DECISIONS

The focus of this book is on the concepts and techniques of financial analysis employed by users of financial statements who are external to the company. Principal emphasis is on the financial statements of companies whose securities are publicly traded. The techniques described are generally applicable to the analysis of financial statements prepared according to U.S. GAAP. However, we will also discuss the pronouncements of the International Accounting Standards Committee (IASC), compare them to U.S. GAAP, and where relevant, provide brief discussions of foreign reporting standards.

The common characteristic of external users is their general lack of authority to prescribe the information they want from an enterprise. They depend on general-purpose external financial reports provided by management. The objectives of these external users are aptly described by the Financial Accounting Standards Board (FASB) in its Statement of Financial Accounting Concepts (SFAC) 1, Objectives of Financial Reporting by Business Enterprises:

INFORMATION USEFUL IN INVESTMENT AND CREDIT DECISIONS

Financial reporting should provide information that is useful to present and potential investors and creditors and other users in making rational investment, credit, and similar decisions. The information should be comprehensible to those who have a reasonable understanding of business and economic activities and are willing to study the information with reasonable diligence.[2]

Classes of Users

External users of financial information encompass a wide range of interests but can be classified into three general groups:

1. Investors, both creditors and equity investors
2. Government (the executive and legislative branches), regulatory bodies, tax authorities
3. The general public and special interest groups, labor unions, consumer groups, and so on

Each of these groups of users has a particular objective in financial statement analysis, but, as the FASB stated, the *primary users are equity investors and creditors*. However, the information supplied to investors and creditors is likely to be generally

---

[2]SFAC 1, para. 34.

useful to other user groups as well. Hence financial accounting standards are geared to the purposes and perceptions of investors and creditors. That is the group for whom the analytical techniques in this book are intended.

The underlying objective of financial analysis is the comparative measurement of risk and return to make investment or credit decisions. These decisions require estimates of the future, be it a month, a year, or a decade. General-purpose financial statements, which describe the past, provide one basis for projecting future earnings and cash flows. Many of the techniques used in this analytical process are broadly applicable to all types of decisions, but there are also specialized techniques concerned with specific investment interests or, in other words, risks and returns specific to one class of investors.

The equity investor is primarily interested in the long-term earning power of the company, its ability to grow, and, ultimately, its ability to pay dividends. Since the equity investor bears the residual risk in an enterprise, the required analysis is the most comprehensive of any user and encompasses techniques employed by all other external users. Because the residual risk is the largest and most volatile, the equity investor must focus attention on the measurement of comparative risks and on the diversification of these risks in investment portfolios.

Creditors employ somewhat different analytical approaches. Short-term creditors, such as banks and trade creditors, place more emphasis on the immediate liquidity of the business because they seek an early payback of their investment. Long-term investors in bonds, such as insurance companies and pension funds, are primarily concerned with the long-term asset position and earning power of the company. They seek assurance of the payment of interest and the capability of retiring or refunding the obligation at maturity. Creditor risks are usually smaller than equity risks and may be more easily quantifiable.

More subordinated or junior creditors, especially in the case of "high-yield" or other highly leveraged investments, however, bear risks similar to those of equity investors and may find analytic techniques normally applied to equity investments more relevant than those employed by creditors.

Financial Information and Capital Markets

The issue of the usefulness of accounting information in the decision-making processes of investors and creditors has been the subject of much academic research during the last 25 years. This research has examined in great detail the impact and interrelationship of accounting information, standards, and policies on financial markets. At times, the conclusions of the research are highly critical of the accounting standard-setting process and of the utility of financial analysis. This criticism, it should be noted, is based on research results evaluated on an aggregate or average level in a capital market setting. These findings do not negate the usefulness of financial analysis of individual securities that may be mispriced or for decisions made outside a capital market setting.[3]

Some researchers argue that the information is of little or no value to investors except insofar as it aids the prediction of a firm's risk characteristics. To a great extent, this line of reasoning is influenced by the finance literature and the prevalent acceptance of the efficient market hypothesis. Others argue that the impact of accounting is not so

---

[3]Examples include acquisitions and credit decisions made by banks or other institutional lenders.

much in its information content per se, but rather in the "economic consequences" to the firm resulting from contracts[4] (implicit or explicit) that are based on or driven by accounting-determined variables.

By and large, the early conclusions of the academic literature have proven to be somewhat premature. Researchers have demonstrated that the interplay between markets and information is richer and more sophisticated than originally thought. In fact, the trend in research is now to incorporate fundamental analysis techniques in model development and research design.

Various research trends and relevant economic considerations are discussed throughout the book with varying emphasis from topic to topic. Chapter 4 is devoted entirely to a review of the major strands of empirical research in order to set the stage for subsequent discussions of other topics, where appropriate, within chapters. Throughout the text we focus on what the analyst can learn from the research and how its implications are relevant to analysis.

THE FINANCIAL REPORTING SYSTEM

It may be useful to know a little about the conceptual bases and the preparation of financial statements. They are issued by corporate management, which is responsible for their form and content. It is management that selects accounting methods, compiles accounting data, and prepares the financial statements. For smaller companies, portions of the preparation work may be carried out by auditors.

The accounting process or financial reporting system, which generates financial information for external users, encompasses four principal financial statements:

- Balance sheet (statement of financial position)
- Income statement (statement of earnings)
- Statement of cash flows
- Statement of stockholders' equity

Examples of these statements are the exhibits in Appendix 1-A and Appendix 1-B. These four financial statements, augmented by footnotes and supplementary data, are interrelated. Collectively, they are intended to provide relevant, reliable, and timely information essential to making investment, credit, and similar decisions, thus meeting the objectives of financial reporting.

General Principles and Measurement Rules

Financial statements provide information about the assets and liabilities of the firm and the income and cash flows generated by the firm. The impacts of transactions and other events are recorded in the relevant financial statement. The balance sheet shows assets, liabilities, and the equity account; the income statement reflects revenues, expenses, and

---

[4]Management compensation contracts and covenants contained in debt agreements are two examples of such contracts.

gains and losses; the statement of cash flows includes operating, investing, and financing inflows and outflows; and the statement of stockholders' equity reports capital transactions with owners. Many transactions are reflected in more than one statement so that the entire set is required to evaluate the total impact.

The financial reporting system is based on data generated from *accounting events*. Only events meeting certain criteria are recognized in accounting, primarily exchange transactions—normally the exchange of cash (or another asset) for a different asset or to create or settle a liability. Accounting events may also include the passage of time (e.g., accrual of interest) and the impact of contractual arrangements (e.g., leases). The financial reporting system also recognizes selected external or economic events including some market value changes. However, many market value changes and contractual arrangements are disclosed only in the footnotes or in supplementary schedules.

However, the exchange of cash is not sufficient for the recognition of revenue and expense events. Under *accrual accounting*, revenues are recognized when goods are delivered or services are performed and expenses are recorded as services are used, rather than when cash is collected or expenditures incurred for these transactions. Accrual accounting rests on the *matching principle,* which says that performance can be measured only if the related revenues and costs are accounted for in the same period.

Financial statements are prepared using a monetary unit to quantify (measure) the operations of the firm. Transactions are generally measured at their *historical cost*, the amount of cash or other resources exchanged for the asset or liability; changes in value subsequent to acquisition are usually ignored. The advantage of historical cost is that it is objective and verifiable. Its utility declines as specific prices or the general price level changes; as a result, the Securities and Exchange Commission (SEC) and the Financial Accounting Standards Board (FASB) are considering disclosure and accounting changes. In 1991 the FASB issued SFAS 107 requiring disclosure of the market values of certain financial instruments.

Financial reporting also relies on the *going concern* assumption, that the firm will continue in operation for the foreseeable future. The alternative would be to assume liquidation or sale of the firm, which would require a different measure of assets and liabilities. Only by assuming normal future operations is it possible, for example, to depreciate fixed assets over their useful life rather than valuing them at their estimated disposal value.

The Securities and Exchange Commission

In the United States, the form and content of the financial statements of companies whose securities are publicly traded are governed by the Securities and Exchange Commission through its regulation S-X. A listing of SEC-required filings is contained in Exhibit 1-1.

While the SEC has delegated much of this responsibility to the FASB, it frequently adds its own requirements. For example, the SEC-mandated *Management Discussion and Analysis* (MD&A) often provides helpful information regarding past operating results and current financial position. In such areas as segment data, leases, the effects of changing prices, and disclosure of oil and gas reserves, SEC-required disclosures preceded FASB action.

EXHIBIT 1-1
Corporate Filings — Securities and Exchange Commission

10-K Annual Report

Contents   (partial listing)
Business of Company
Properties
Legal Proceedings
Management Discussion and Analysis
Changes or Disagreement with Auditors
Financial Statements and Footnotes
Investee Financial Statements (where applicable)
Parent Company Financial Statements (where applicable)

Schedules:
I: Investments in Marketable Securities and Other Securities
II: Amounts Receivable from Related Parties and Underwriters, Promoters, and Employees Other Than Related Parties
III: Condensed Financial Information
IV: Indebtedness of and to Related Parties—Not Current
V: Fixed Assets
VI: Accumulated Depreciation
VII: Guarantees of Securities of Other Issuers
VIII: Bad Debt and Other Valuation Accounts
IX: Short-Term Borrowings
X: Supplementary Income Statement Information (Includes expenditures for advertising, maintenance, and real estate taxes.)
XI: Real Estate and Accumulated Depreciation
XII: Mortgage Loans on Real Estate
XIII: Other Investments
XIV: Supplementary Information Concerning Property-Casualty Insurance Operations

Due Date: 3 months following end of fiscal year.

10-Q Quarterly Report

Contents   Financial Statements
Management Discussion and Analysis

Due Date: 45 days following end of fiscal quarter. Not required for fourth quarter of fiscal year.

8-K Current Reports

Contents   (used to report important events)
Change in Control
Acquisitions and Divestitures
Bankruptcy
Change in Auditors
Resignation of Directors

Due Date: 15 days following event.

The financial statements, related footnotes, and supplementary data are presented both in filings with the SEC and in the annual reports to stockholders. SEC filings often contain valuable information not presented in reports to stockholders. Quarterly financial reports and SEC 10-Q filings, both of which contain abbreviated financial statements, may be reviewed but are rarely audited.[5]

Financial Accounting Standards Board

The Financial Accounting Standards Board is a nongovernmental body with seven full-time members. The Board sets accounting standards for all companies issuing audited financial statements. Because of Rule 203 of the American Institute of Certified Public Accountants (AICPA), all FASB pronouncements are considered authoritative; new FASB Statements immediately become part of GAAP. Prior to creation of the FASB in 1973, accounting standards were set by an AICPA committee known as the Accounting Principles Board (APB). Many APB Opinions remain part of GAAP.[6]

Because the SEC recognizes FASB Statements as authoritative (as it recognized APB Opinions prior to 1973), there is only one set of generally accepted accounting principles applicable to the United States. There are a few instances (earnings per share, for example) where nonpublic companies are exempted from certain GAAP requirements. Generally speaking, however, all audited statements are prepared using the same financial reporting framework.

The FASB is an independent body whose members are required to sever all ties with previous employers. While historically most Board members have been former auditors, some have come from the corporate world, government service, and academia. There has been one financial analyst (Frank Block, CFA, who served from 1979 to 1985) on the Board.

Before issuing a new Statement of Financial Accounting Standards (SFAS), the FASB staff often works with a task force—composed of public accountants, representatives from industry, academics, regulators, and financial statement users—to develop a Discussion Memorandum on relevant issues for public comment. The staff uses comments received and public hearings to prepare an Exposure Draft (a proposed standard) for public comment. Because of the Board's due process rules, there is extensive dissemination of its agenda. Any rulemaking by the SEC will also normally be

---

[5]In 1989, the SEC issued a concepts release seeking comments on a proposal to require timely reviews by independent auditors of interim period registration statements and quarterly filings. No action has been taken to date.

[6]FASB Statements and Interpretations, Accounting Principles Board (APB) Opinions, and AICPA Accounting Research Bulletins constitute the highest level of authority in the hierarchy of accounting principles. These are followed in descending order of authority by FASB Technical Bulletins, cleared AICPA Industry Audit and Accounting Guides, and AICPA Statements of Position at Level B. ("Cleared" means that the FASB has not objected to the issuance of the guide or statement of position.) Positions of the FASB Emerging Issues Task Force and cleared AcSEC Practice Bulletins constitute Level C, followed by AICPA accounting interpretations, question-and-answer guides published by the FASB staff, uncleared AICPA Statements of Position, and uncleared AICPA Industry Audit and Accounting guides.

The lowest authoritative level encompasses accounting literature, including FASB Concepts Statements, APB Statements, AICPA Issues Papers, IASC Statements, and so on.

preceded by a request for comments on a proposed set of rules. Thus it is possible to anticipate new accounting and disclosure standards well in advance of their issuance and implementation.

FASB Conceptual Framework

When the FASB started setting standards, it realized that its task could be eased by creation of a conceptual framework, or "constitution," and it has since issued six Concepts Statements. Reviewing these statements helps in understanding the framework the FASB uses to set standards. Many critics of the FASB view the conceptual framework as a failure.[7] They state that the definitions are unduly vague and that the Board has repeatedly deferred difficult decisions (such as how to measure income). Others believe that the conceptual framework has helped the Board set better standards. For the analyst, the conceptual framework is an important building block in understanding the information provided by financial statements.

We have already addressed Statement of Financial Accounting Concepts (SFAC) 1, which sets forth the objectives of financial reporting. SFAC 2 is concerned with Qualitative Characteristics of Accounting Information. These characteristics are shown in Figure 1-1, which is reproduced from the statement. A brief discussion follows.[8]

Qualitative Characteristics of Accounting Information. Analysts' concern with the qualitative characteristics of accounting information derives from the need for information that facilitates comparison of firms using alternative reporting methods, and that is useful for decision making. While some of these characteristics are self-evident, others require some explanation. We will start with relevance and reliability, which are key characteristics from the analyst point of view.

Relevance is defined as "the capacity of information to make a difference in a decision . . . ."[9] In practice, of course, the relevance of information depends on the decision maker. To a technical analyst (chartist), all financial data are irrelevant. For fundamental analysts, the relevance of information varies with the method of analysis (emphasis on income statement, cash flow, balance sheet, etc.).

Timeliness is an important aspect of relevance. Information loses value rapidly in the financial world. Market prices are predicated on estimates of the future; data on the past are helpful in making projections. But as time passes, and the future becomes the present, past data become increasingly irrelevant.

Reliability encompasses *verifiability*, *representational faithfulness*, and *neutrality*. The first two elements (verifiability and representational faithfulness) are concerned with whether financial data have been measured accurately and they are what they purport to be. Data without these characteristics cannot be relied upon in making investment decisions.

---

[7]For example, see David Solomons, "The FASB's Conceptual Framework: An Evaluation, *Journal of Accountancy*, June 1986, pp. 114–124.

[8]SFAC 3, Elements of Financial Statements of Business Enterprises, has been superseded by SFAC 6, Elements of Financial Statements, which is discussed in detail in subsequent sections of this chapter. The topics covered by SFAC 4, Objectives of Financial Reporting by Nonbusiness organizations, are beyond the scope of this text. The remaining concepts statement, SFAC 5, Recognition and Measurement in Financial Statements of Business Enterprises, is addressed elsewhere in this chapter.

[9]SFAC 2, Glossary.

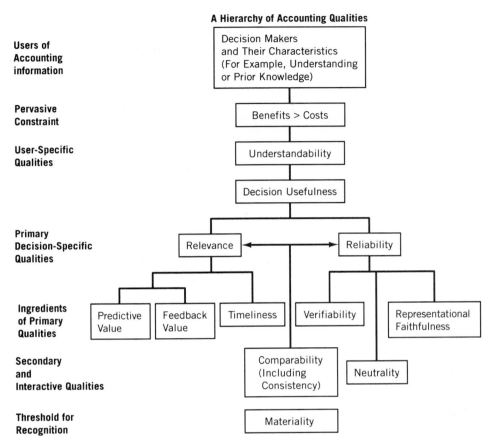

FIGURE 1-1 A Hierarchy of Accounting Qualities.
Source: Figure 1 of FASB Concepts Statement No. 2, *Qualitative Characteristics of Accounting Information*, copyright by Financial Accounting Standards Board, Norwalk, CT.

Neutrality is concerned with whether financial statement data are biased. When the FASB proposes new standards, it is frequently the object of complaints that companies will be adversely affected by the standard. The principle of neutrality states that the Board should consider only the relevance and reliability of the data, not any possible economic impact.

Unfortunately, relevance and reliability tend to be opposing qualities. For example, the audit process improves the reliability of data, but at the cost of timeliness. For that reason financial statement users have generally not supported the auditing of quarterly data, believing that the time delay does not compensate for the improved quality of data.

Relevance and reliability also clash strongly in a number of accounting areas. Probably, the best example is market value data. Information on the current market value of investments can be highly relevant (see discussion in Chapter 11) but may be accurate (reliable) only to a limited extent. Yet historical cost, while highly reliable, may have little relevance. It is the old argument as to whether it is better to be "precisely wrong" or "approximately right."

Analysts have generally opted for "approximately right." They have supported the disclosure of supplementary data in such areas as natural resources (SFAS 69, Chapter 6), off-balance-sheet financing (Chapter 10), and segment data (SFAS 14, Chapter 11). Auditors and preparers, more concerned with reliability (and with legal liability), have often opposed the inclusion of less reliable data in the financial statements.

Consistency and comparability are also key characteristics of accounting information from the analyst perspective. *Consistency* refers to use of the same accounting principles over time. A broader term, *comparability*, refers to all comparisons among companies.

Consistency is affected by new accounting standards, and by voluntary changes in accounting principles and estimates. Accounting changes hinder the comparison of operating results between periods when the accounting principles used to measure those results differ. As the transition provisions of new accounting standards vary, it is frequently difficult to obtain a consistent time series of earnings properly adjusted for such changes. For voluntary changes (such as depreciation methods and lives), the effect of the change is generally disclosed only for the year of the change.

Comparability is a pervasive problem in financial analysis. Companies are free to choose among different accounting methods and estimates in a variety of areas, making comparisons of different enterprises difficult or impossible. While the FASB has narrowed the differences somewhat in recent years, new types of transactions (such as securitization of assets) constantly create new sources of noncomparability. Even when accounting differences do not exist, however, comparability may be missing because of real differences between the firms (e.g., one has foreign operations and the other does not).

PRINCIPAL FINANCIAL STATEMENTS

The preceding sections have described the general principles and measurement rules of the basic accounting process applicable to financial reporting in the United States. The role of standard-setting bodies (the SEC and the FASB) and the latter's conceptual framework that guides this process was also examined along with the qualitative characteristics of accounting information. This section provides a detailed discussion of the output of this system: the different financial statements, footnotes, and supplementary data. Appendix 1-A contains a review of the basics of financial reporting.

The Balance Sheet

The *balance sheet (statement of financial position)* reports major categories and amounts of assets, liabilities (claims on those assets), and stockholders' equity and their interrelationships at a specific point in time, generally, at the end of each quarter and the end of the year in the United States.

Elements of the Balance Sheet

SFAC 6 discusses the elements of financial statements. While this statement also deals with nonprofit organizations, we will restrict our comments to business enterprises.

Assets are defined in SFAC 6 as

> probable future economic benefits obtained or controlled by a particular entity as a result of past transactions or events. (Paragraph 25)

This definition seems to be noncontroversial. Its weakness is its lack of reference to risk. It seems to us that an enterprise that retains the risks of ownership still "owns" the asset. This issue is important, for example, as it relates to the sale of assets (such as accounts receivable, see Chapter 10) when the seller retains some risk of loss.

Liabilities are defined, similarly, as

> probable future sacrifices of economic benefits arising from present obligations of a particular entity to transfer assets or provide services to other entities in the future as a result of past transactions or events. (Paragraph 35)

Again, the definition reads well. Yet it permits the nonrecognition of contractual obligations such as operating leases (see Chapter 8). The interpretation of "present obligation" and "result of past transactions or events" is key to accounting for all such contracts; some believe that only payments immediately due as a consequence of completed transactions create liabilities. Others believe that long-term contracts should be recognized as long-term liabilities.

Equity is therefore

> the residual interest in the net assets of an entity that remains after deducting its liabilities. (Paragraph 49)

In practice, some financial instruments have characteristics of both liabilities and equities, making them difficult to categorize. Convertible debt and redeemable preferreds are two common examples that we will examine in Chapter 8.

Format and Classification

The major categories of assets, liabilities, and equities are classified according to liquidity, that is, their expected use in operations or conversion to cash in the case of assets and time to maturity for liabilities. Assets expected to be converted to cash or used within one year (or one operating cycle, even if longer than one year) are classified as current assets. Current liabilities include obligations the firm expects to settle within one year or an operating cycle.

Assets expected to provide benefits and services over periods longer than one year and liabilities to be repaid after one year are classified as long-term assets and liabilities. Tangible assets and liabilities are generally reported before intangibles and other assets and liabilities with more uncertain measurement attributes.

This classification scheme is used in the development of ratios and other financial indices used in financial analysis. The analysis of liquidity, for example, relies on the current–noncurrent distinction. In recent years, however, the distinction has become somewhat arbitrary as differences between short-term and long-term investments and debt are sometimes difficult to discern.

The most liquid assets, cash and cash equivalents, precede marketable equity securities, receivables, inventories, and prepaid expenses in the current asset section of the balance sheet. Long-lived assets, including property, plant, and equipment, investments in affiliated companies, and intangible assets such as brand names, patents, copyrights, and goodwill are reported as noncurrent assets.

Short-term bank and other debt, current portion of long-term debt and capitalized leases, accounts payable to suppliers, accrued liabilities (amounts owed to employees and others), interest, and taxes payable are classified as current liabilities. Long-term debt, capitalized lease obligations, pension obligations, and other "liabilities" (such as deferred income taxes and minority interest in the net assets of consolidated affiliates) constitute commonly observed noncurrent liabilities.

Stockholders' equity (the residual interest in the firm) also lists components in order of their priority in liquidation with any preference (preferred) stock listed before common stock, treasury stock, and reinvested earnings. This section may also include valuation accounts related to foreign subsidiaries and noncurrent investments.

The Measurement of Assets and Liabilities

Most components of the balance sheet are reported at historical cost, that is, the exchange price at acquisition date.[10] In some cases (accounts receivable, for example), valuation allowances (reserve for bad debts) adjust the reported amount to an approximation of net realizable value. Lower of cost or market rules may, however, require that market values be reflected when they are below cost.[11] In general, however, market values are *not* reflected in the balance sheet prior to realization (sale or other transaction).[12]

Recoveries (reversal of previous write-downs) to the original acquisition cost are allowed in the case of marketable equity securities but not for inventories. Declines in the carrying amounts of long-term assets are also recognized, but firms have substantially more discretion in recognizing impairments of long-lived assets.[13]

Certain assets and liabilities are reported at their market value in such industries as insurance and financial services.[14] Reporting realizable values for certain assets and the maturity or liquidation values for some liabilities incorporates significant judgment, discretion, and estimates. Examples include the allowance for uncollectible receivables and liability for warranties. The allowance for uncollectibles is an estimate of bad debts that is reported as a deduction from the gross receivables balance and is called a "contra" account. (Accumulated depreciation is also a contra account since it accumulates the

---

[10]Some exceptions to this general rule follow: assets acquired in nonmonetary exchange transactions are reported at adjusted fair market values, capitalized leases are reflected at the present value of contractually determined cash flows, and certain liabilities may be reflected at negotiated amounts in a troubled debt restructuring.

[11]For more discussion, see Chapter 5 (Inventories) and Chapter 11 (Marketable Securities).

[12]The concept of realization is discussed in Chapter 2.

[13]See Chapter 6.

[14]Companies also record assets and liabilities acquired in a purchase method acquisition at fair market value. However, acquisitions meeting the pooling method of accounting criteria do not result in the recognition of market values of the acquired firm's assets and liabilities. See Chapter 12 for a comparative analysis of the differences between these two methods of accounting for acquisitions.

periodic depreciation, that is, use of long-lived assets.) Some changes in assets or liabilities are accumulated in "adjunct" accounts, such as premium on bonds payable that records the excess of the bond's issue price over its face value.

The contra and adjunct accounts allow firms to report both the original, historical cost (e.g., gross plant assets) and the net carrying amount (plant assets net of accumulated depreciation). They also reflect management's estimate of realizable values of the underlying assets, for example, receivables net of the allowance for bad debts. However, these are *accounting estimates* of realizable values and generally do not reflect market values.[15]

Finally, the assets and liabilities of foreign affiliates are reported at amounts translated from other currencies at the exchange rate prevailing on the financial statement date or a combination of this current rate and specific historical rates for certain components.[16]

The balance sheet does not report all assets and liabilities of the firm, but reflects only those meeting specific recognition criteria.[17] Some assets and liabilities meet some of these criteria but may not be measurable (see discussion of contingencies later in this chapter). In other cases measurement may not be sufficiently reliable to warrant inclusion in the financial statements. As discussed in the preceding section, those assets and liabilities that are included are measured using a mixture of historical cost and market (or quasi-market) values.

Some intangible assets have extremely uncertain or hard-to-measure benefits, for example, brand names, and they are recognized only when acquired in a purchase method acquisition. Similarly, a liability may exist as a result of a lawsuit, but, because it is not reliably measurable, it would be disclosed in footnotes (see, for example, the footnote on commitments and contingencies in Deere's financial statements in Appendix 1-B) but not recognized in the financial statements.

The balance sheet does not report the value of the assets, liabilities, or equity of the firm, although the information provided can be useful in the development of estimates of the market value of the firm or its securities.

The Income Statement

The *income statement (statement of earnings)* reports on the performance of the firm, the result of its operating activities. It explains some but not all of the changes in the assets, liabilities, and equity of the firm between two consecutive balance sheets. The definition of income is based upon the use of the accrual concept of earnings.

---

[15]The level of and trends in the allowance for uncollectibles may, however, provide information useful in assessing market values of the receivables, the firm's credit policies and the adequacy of its revenue recognition methods.

[16]See Chapter 13.

[17]SFAC 5, Recognition and Measurement in Financial Statements of Business Enterprises" (FASB 1984), requires financial statement recognition when four basic criteria are met:

Definition: The item qualifies as an element (e.g., asset or liability) of financial statements.

Measurability: It has a reliably measurable relevant attribute.

Relevance: The information provided by the item can make a difference in user decisions.

Reliability: The information is representationally faithful, verifiable and neutral.

Recognition is subject to cost/benefit and materiality constraints.

The preparation of the income statement is governed by the matching principle, which states that performance can be measured only if related revenues and costs are accounted for during the same time period. This requires the recognition of expenses incurred to generate revenues in the same period as the related revenues. For example, the cost of a machine is recognized as an expense (it is depreciated) over its useful life (as it is used in production) rather than as an expense in the period it is purchased.[18]

Elements of the Income Statement

Revenues are defined in SFAC 6 as

> inflows . . . of an entity . . . from delivering or producing goods, rendering services, or other activities that constitute the entity's ongoing major or central operations. (Paragraph 78)

Expenses are defined as

> outflows . . . from delivering or producing goods, rendering services, or carrying out other activities that constitute the entity's ongoing major or central operations. (Paragraph 80)

These definitions explicity exclude *gains* and *losses,* defined as

> increases (decreases) in equity (net assets) from peripheral or incidental transactions. . . . (Paragraph 82)

Gains or losses are, therefore, nonoperating events. Examples would include gains and losses from asset sales, lawsuits, and changes in market values (including currency rates).

These definitions are, like the others in SFAC 6, easy to accept as stated. The difficulties come in practice. For example, investment activities may be "central" to a financial institution but "peripheral" to a manufacturing company. More problematic would be a write-down of inventories due to obsolescence: Is this an expense or a loss? To some extent the distinction between revenue and expense on the one hand and gains and losses on the other is a precurser of the controversy over "extraordinary items." From the analyst's point of view, disclosure is more important than classification; analysts prefer to make their own distinctions between operating and nonoperating events in many instances. From the point of view of database users, however, the outcome of the debate may be important.

Comprehensive Income The notion of *comprehensive income* is perhaps the most innovative (and potentially most useful) concept in SFAC 6. It is defined as

---

[18]Note that no depreciation expense would be recorded if the products manufactured were not sold in the period the machine was used; the cost of using the machine would be added to work in process or finished goods inventories and carried on the balance sheet as an asset until the goods are sold.

the change in equity . . . from transactions . . . from nonowner sources. It includes all changes in equity during a period except those resulting from investments by owners and distributions to owners. (Paragraph 70)

While the comprehensive income concept has yet to be incorporated directly in an FASB standard, it has several obvious applications. Financial statements contain increasing numbers of valuation adjustments—foreign currency translation, market values of investments, and minimum pension liability are but three commonly found. Such adjustments, and the plethora of "restructuring" and other "nonrecurring" items, make it difficult to discern the operating results of an enterprise. The concept of comprehensive income holds a solution to this problem.

Changes in carrying amounts of assets and liabilities could be accounted for as part of comprehensive income, but kept outside of "income from continuing operations," which most analysts use as the best guide to future earnings of an enterprise. It remains to be seen whether the FASB develops this concept into a mechanism with operational usefulness.

Format and Classification

The income statement reports revenues generated by the sales of goods and services from a firm's primary, recurring operations. These revenues are followed[19] by income from other activities, such as interest or dividends from investments, income of unconsolidated affiliates, and gains or losses on sales or disposal of assets.

The costs and expenses incurred in the process of generating these revenues and other income are reported in the order of their relationship to the underlying revenues. The cost of manufacturing or merchandising the goods sold is reported first since it can be directly related to the volume of sales. Indirect costs of selling and administrative activities, payments to employees, research and development expenditures, and interest costs follow. Unusual or infrequent items, such as gains and losses from the sale or impairment of assets or investments, are discussed in Chapter 2. Income tax expense is usually the final deduction before arriving at net income from continuing operations.

The income statement effects of discontinued operations are segregated and reported net of taxes to emphasize the fact that they will not contribute to future revenues and income. The net of tax effect of "extraordinary items" is also reported separately because they are incidental to the firm's operating activities, unusual in nature, and not expected to be a normal, recurring component of income and cash flows.

Finally, the income statement separately reports the cumulative effect of accounting changes since they are unrelated to the period's income or operating activities and rarely have any impact on cash flows.[20] Footnotes provide detailed information on both

---

[19]The format of the income statement is not fixed by GAAP, with the exception of the issues discussed in APB 30. Actual formats used may vary, especially in the treatment of such items as the equity in earnings of affiliates and nonoperating income and expense. In some cases, income statement detail appears in the footnotes to the financial statements.

[20]Cash flows are not affected by financial reporting changes unless the firm changes methods on its tax return. A switch to or from the LIFO method for inventories must be made on both the financial statements and the tax return. See the discussion in Chapter 5. Also see Chapter 7 for the analysis of income taxes.

mandatory and voluntary changes in accounting methods, which must be analyzed to evaluate the impact on trends in reported earnings. A typical income statement format is depicted here:

	Revenues
+	Other income and revenues
−	Expenses
=	Recurring continuing operations
±	Unusual or infrequent items
=	Pretax earnings from continuing operations
−	Provision for taxes (income tax expense)
=	After-tax income from continuing operations*
±	Discontinued operations (net of tax effects)*
±	Extraordinary items (net of tax effects)*
±	Cumulative effect of accounting changes (net of tax effects)*
=	Net income*

*Per share amounts are reported for each of these items.

Components of Net Income

Many "non-recurring" items disclosed separately on the income statement are discretionary from two perspectives. First, the timing of the occurrence (e.g., sale or disposal of an asset or the discontinuation of a segment) is subject to management discretion. Second, accounting guidelines also leave the classification of the item (as recurring, unusual, or extraordinary) to the judgment of management. These issues are examined in greater detail in Chapter 2, where we comment on their implications for analysis.

The Statement of Cash Flows

The *statement of cash flows* reports the cash receipts and outflows in the period of their occurrence, classified as to operating, investing, and financing activities. It also provides supplementary disclosures about noncash investing and financing activities. Cash flow data also help explain changes in consecutive balance sheets and supplement the information provided by the income statement.

SFAS 95, Statement of Cash Flows (1987), defines *investing cash flows* as those resulting from

- Acquisition or sale of property, plant, and equipment.
- Acquisition or sale of a subsidiary or segment.
- Purchase or sale of investments in other firms.

Similarly, *financing cash flows* are those resulting from

- Issuance or retirement of debt and equity securities.
- Dividends paid to stockholders.

The standard requires gross rather than net reporting of significant investing and financing activities, thereby providing improved disclosure. For example, the acquisition of property must be shown separately from the sale of property.

Significant noncash investing and financing (such as leases of plant assets) activities must be disclosed separately within the cash flow statement or in a footnote elsewhere in the financial statements. Complex investment and financing transactions sometimes involve combinations of cash, debt, and other resources—these separate but integral components must be reported separately.

Cash from Operations includes the cash effects of all transactions that do not meet the definition of investing or financing. In effect, they are the cash flow consequences of the revenue-producing activities of the firm. They may be reported either directly, using major categories of gross cash receipts and payments, or indirectly by providing a reconciliation of net income to net cash flow from operating activities.[21] The *indirect method* also requires separate disclosure of the cash outflows for income taxes and interest within the statement or elsewhere in the financial statements.

Firms using the *direct method* are also required to provide this reconciliation, which includes separate disclosure of the changes in operating assets and liabilities. These changes are particularly informative when a firm acquires another firm or some operations from another entity. Under those circumstances changes in asset accounts include both operating and investment components. For example, the change in inventories will include both the operating change and the increase due to the addition of inventories of the acquired firm.

SFAS 95 requires that translated local currency cash flows be used to consolidate the cash flows of foreign subsidiaries and affiliates. Thus the parent currency statement reflects the same cash flow relationships as those in the local currency. Otherwise, cash flow data for foreign operations would contain a mixture of operating and exchange rate effects.[22]

The Statement of Stockholders' Equity

This statement reports the amounts and sources of changes in equity from capital transactions with owners and may include the following components:

- Preferred shares
- Common shares (at par or stated value)
- Additional paid-in capital

[21]On average, only 15 firms out of 600 surveyed annually by the AICPA in *Accounting Trends and Techniques* have reported using the direct method.

[22]For example, the difference between the translated inventory balances in successive balance sheets reflects purchases and sale of inventory in addition to the impact of fluctuations in exchange rates on the translated balances. This phenomenon is discussed in more detail in Chapter 13.

- Retained earnings
- Treasury shares (repurchased equity)
- Valuation allowance (marketable equity securities)
- Cumulative translation allowance (foreign operations)

Equity events and transactions are generally recognized as they occur, but capital market developments have created significant measurement and classification problems in transactions with owners.[23]

The firm usually records the issuance of preferred and common stock at par (or stated) value and the amounts received in excess of par as additional paid-in capital. Repurchases or retirements of common stock may be reported as treasury shares, a contra account, that reflects a reduction in common stock outstanding. Retained (reinvested) earnings, which increase with income and decline with dividend declarations, are also reported. Finally, this statement also includes adjustments made in a quasi-reorganization (see Chapter 12).

The valuation allowance for noncurrent investments and the cumulative foreign currency translation adjustment result from selective recognition of market value changes (see Chapter 11) and exchange rate changes (see Chapter 13), respectively.

Footnotes

Information provided in the financial statements is augmented by footnotes and other supplementary disclosures. Generally, the data provided are required by either GAAP (FASB standards) or by regulatory authorities (SEC). They are designed to allow users to improve assessments of the amounts, timing, and uncertainty of the estimates reported in the financial statements. Some supplementary information is provided voluntarily by management.

Financial statement footnotes are an integral part of those statements and provide substantial amounts of supplementary data, such as the operations of major segments of the firm's business, the financial position of retirement plans, and off-balance-sheet obligations.

Footnotes also provide information about the accounting methods, assumptions, and estimates used by management to develop the data reported in the financial statements. Companies provide a broad statement of accounting policies used and augment this disclosure with footnotes on specific components of the financial statements. Relevant additional information is often provided in supplementary schedules, some of which are required by the SEC in 10-K filings (see Exhibit 1-1). The financial statements and footnotes in the annual report and the SEC 10-K filings are audited, whereas the supplementary data may not be audited.

Footnotes also provide a detailed discussion of, and additional disclosure related to fixed assets, inventories, taxes, pensions, other postemployment benefits, debt, compensation plans, and other elements of the financial statements.

---

[23]The FASB is currently engaged in several projects related to significant problems in this area. The effects of reorganizations and new basis accounting proposals are discussed in Chapter 12. A brief commentary on the FASB's project on Consolidation Policy and Procedures is provided in Chapter 11. Another project concerns distinguishing debt from equity.

For example, footnote disclosures provide details about applicable interest rates, maturity schedules, and contractual terms for outstanding debt. Similarly, footnotes describe the conditions under which obligations were recognized from lawsuits and other loss contingencies and provide information on those loss contingencies where recognition of losses or liabilities has not taken place.

Firms often report the market value of investment and marketable securities in parentheses to the related account balances in the balance sheet. Separate schedules in the SEC 10-K filings provide additional information on the securities in the portfolio, and, in some cases, the amounts of different securities held may also be disclosed (see Exhibits 11-3 and 11-5 in Chapter 11 for examples of these disclosures).

Parenthetical disclosure of the allowance for uncollectibles provides additional information about the realizability of the underlying receivables; these data are sometimes relegated to footnotes. SEC 10-K filings provide data on bad-debt and other valuation accounts. Finally, other disclosures provide data on significant customers, sales to related parties, and export sales.

Contingencies

Footnotes often contain disclosures relating to contingent[24] losses. Firms are required to accrue a loss (recognize a liability) if *both* of the following conditions are met:

1. It is probable that assets have been impaired or a liability has been incurred.
2. The amount of the loss can be reasonably estimated.

If the loss amount lies within a range, the firm may report either the lower end of the range or the most likely amount.

SFAS 5 defines *probable* events as those "more likely than not" to occur, suggesting that a probability of more than 50% requires recognition of a loss. However, in practice, firms generally report contingencies as losses only when the probability of loss is significantly higher.

Footnote disclosure of (unrecognized) loss contingencies is required when it is reasonably possible (more than remote but less than probable) that a loss has been incurred or when it is probable that a loss has occurred but the amount cannot be reasonably estimated. The standard provides an extensive discussion of loss contingencies.

The recognition and measurement of loss contingencies is problematic because it involves judgment and is subjective at best. External analysis is hampered by the paucity of data, as disclosures are often vague. Expanded disclosure requirements and the SEC's MD&A are the best sources of information.

Significant problem areas include litigation, expropriation, self-insurance, debt guarantees, repurchase agreements, take-or-pay contracts, and throughput arrangements. In later chapters we provide discussion of analytical techniques applicable to many of these contingencies and examples of losses recognized in the financial statements as well as others disclosed only in footnotes.

---

[24]The FASB defines a contingency as an "existing condition, situation, or set of circumstance involving uncertainty as to possible gain or loss" (SFAS 5, Para. 1).

Supplementary Schedules

In some cases additional information about the assets and liabilities of a firm is provided within the financial statements and footnotes, or as supplementary data outside the financial statements. For example, oil and gas companies provide additional data on their exploration activities, quantities of and types of reserves, and the present value of cash flows expected from those reserves (see Chapter 6).

Significant price level changes during the 1970s resulted in the requirement for supplemental disclosure of their impact; this disclosure is now voluntary. (See Appendix 6-C.)

Companies also disclose sales revenue, operating income, and other data for major business segments (see Chapter 11) and by geographic areas (see Chapter 13). They also provide additional information about export sales.

Because of the increased use (and complexity) of financial instruments by both financial and nonfinancial firms, required disclosures in this area are growing. Disclosures of risk exposures (SFAS 105, 1990) and market values (SFAS 107, 1991) are increasing. As discussed in Chapter 11, we expect the use of market values to increase in coming years.

OTHER SOURCES OF FINANCIAL REPORTING INFORMATION

Stockholder reports often contain useful supplementary financial and statistical data as well as management comments. The Management Discussion and Analysis required by the SEC may appear in either reports to stockholders or in SEC filings. In some cases the stockholder report is included ("incorporated by reference") in the SEC filing, or vice versa. A brief discussion of the contents of the MD&A is provided followed by a discussion of other sources of financial reporting information.

Management Discussion and Analysis

Companies with publicly traded securities have been required, since 1968,[25] to provide discussion of earnings in the MD&A section. The financial statements of Deere in Appendix 1-B are one example. In 1980,[26] the SEC expanded the requirements to a comprehensive, broad-based discussion and analysis of the financial statements to encourage more meaningful disclosure.

The MD&A is required to discuss

- Results of operations, including discussion of trends in sales and in categories of expense.
- Capital resources and liquidity, including discussion of cash flow trends.
- Outlook based on known trends.

[25]Securities Act Release No. 4936, December 9, 1968 (33 FR 18617), and Securities Act Release No. 5520, August 14, 1974 (39 FR 31894).
[26]Securities Act Release No. 6231, September 2, 1980 (45 FR 63630).

As many companies, in the past, complied with these requirements in a purely mechanical way, the Commission has placed increasing emphasis on this requirement in recent years and has insisted on better disclosures. In 1988, the SEC evaluated compliance with MD&A disclosures of 359 companies in 24 industries, and in 1989 it issued an interpretive release providing additional guidance on compliance in the following areas:

1. Prospective information and *required* discussion of significant effects of currently known trends, events, and uncertainties, for example, decline in market share or impact of inventory obsolescence. Firms may *voluntarily* disclose forward-looking data that anticipates trends or events.

2. Liquidity and capital resources: firms are expected to use cash flow statements to analyze liquidity; provide a balanced discussion of operating, financing, and investing cash flows; and discuss transactions or events with material current or expected long-term liquidity implications.

3. Discussion of discontinued operations, extraordinary items, and other "unusual or infrequent" events with current or expected material effects on financial condition or results of operations.

4. Extensive disclosures in interim financial statements in keeping with the obligation to update MD&A disclosures periodically.

5. Disclosure of a segment's disproportionate need for cash flows or contribution to revenues or profits. Also, disclosure of any restrictions on a free flow of funds between segments.

This additional guidance and stricter review may improve compliance and augment information available to external users.

Other Data Sources

Many companies prepare periodic "fact books" containing additional financial and operational data. Corporate press releases also provide new information on a timely basis. Computerized services (e.g., The Dow Jones News Retrieval System) provide databases of corporate releases and other business news. In addition, many companies hold periodic meetings or conference telephone calls to keep the financial community apprised of recent developments regarding the company. In between such meetings, or in lieu thereof, a company officer may be designated to answer questions and provide additional data to analysts following the company.

Industry data and other information about a company also may be obtained from sources outside the company. Trade publications, the general business press, computerized databases, investment research reports, and the publications of competitors are among the sources that may supplement company-originated financial data. A comprehensive analysis of a company requires use of all these sources of information.

When reviewing corporate reports to stockholders and other publications, it is important to remember that they are written by management. Annual reports are often viewed as public relations or sales materials and are intended to impress customers, suppliers, and employees, as well as stockholders. As a result, they must be read with at least some degree of skepticism. Only the financial statements (including footnotes and other disclosures labeled "audited") are independently reviewed and attested to by outside auditors.

ROLE OF THE AUDITOR

The auditor (independent certified public accountant) is responsible for seeing that the financial statements issued conform with generally accepted accounting principles. Thus the auditor must agree that the management's choice of accounting principles is appropriate and that any estimates are reasonable. The auditor will also perform checks of the company's accounting and internal control systems, confirm assets and liabilities, and generally try to assure that there are no material errors in the financial statements. The auditor will often review interim reports and "unaudited" portions of the annual report. While hired by the company (often through the audit committee of the board of directors), the auditor is supposed to be independent of management and to serve the stockholders and other users of the financial statements.

Audited financial statements are always accompanied by the auditor's report, often referred to as an "opinion." Because of the "boilerplate" nature of these reports, there is a tendency to skip over them when reviewing financial statements. Failure to read this report, however, may cause the financial analyst to miss significant information.

Exhibit 1-2 is the independent auditor's report issued by Deloitte & Touche after its audit of Deere & Company for fiscal 1990. The first three paragraphs of the report are standard and are required by Statement of Auditing Standards (SAS) 58, Reports on Audited Financial Statements,[27] which addresses the audit report in which auditors express their opinion on the financial statements developed by management. It clarifies the scope of the assurance provided by the auditors and briefly describes the audit work. The first three paragraphs tell us the following:

Paragraph 1: While the financial statements are prepared by Deere's management, and are the responsibility of management, the auditor has performed an independent review of the statements.

Paragraph 2: The audit has been conducted using generally accepted auditing standards (GAAS) that require the auditor to provide "reasonable assurance" that there are no *material* errors in the financial statements. The auditor does *not* guarantee that the statements are free from error or that no fraud is present. The auditor has performed tests of the company's accounting system designed to ensure that the statements are accurate.

Paragraph 3: The financial statements of Deere are prepared in accordance with GAAP. The auditor is satisfied that the accounting principles chosen and the estimates employed are reasonable.

---

[27]Auditing Standards Board (ASB) of the American Institute of Certified Public Accountants, 1989.

EXHIBIT 1-2. DELOITTE & TOUCHE
An Independent Auditor's Report

Deere & Company:

We have audited the accompanying consolidated balance sheets of Deere & Company and subsidiaries as of October 31, 1990 and 1989 and the related statements of consolidated income and of consolidated cash flows for each of the three years in the period ended October 31, 1990. These financial statements are the responsibility of the company's management. Our responsibility is to express an opinion on these financial statements based on our audits.

We conducted our audits in accordance with generally accepted auditing standards. Those standards require that we plan and perform the audit to obtain reasonable assurance about whether the financial statements are free of material misstatement. An audit includes examining, on a test basis, evidence supporting the amounts and disclosures in the financial statements. An audit also includes assessing the accounting principles used and significant estimates made by management, as well as evaluating the overall financial statement presentation. We believe that our audits provide a reasonable basis for our opinion.

In our opinion, such consolidated financial statements present fairly, in all material respects, the financial position of Deere & Company and subsidiaries at October 31, 1990 and 1989 and the results of their operations and their cash flows for each of the three years in the period ended October 31, 1990 in conformity with generally accepted accounting principles.

As discussed in the Notes to Consolidated Financial Statements, in 1990 the company recognized in the consolidated balance sheet its additional minimum pension liability, as required by Statement of Financial Accounting Standards No. 87. In 1988, the company changed its method of accounting for income taxes, to conform with Statement of Financial Accounting Standards No. 96.

Chicago, Illinois
December 5, 1990

Source: Deere & Co., 1990 Annual Report.

These three paragraphs (sometimes presented as one or two paragraphs) should always be present in an audited set of GAAP financial statements.

SAS 58 also requires the addition of an explanatory paragraph to the auditors' report when accounting methods have not been used consistently among periods. In the case of Deere, Paragraph 4 tells us that the company adopted SFAS 96 (Income Taxes) in 1988 and implemented the "minimum liability" provision of SFAS 87 (Pensions) in 1990.

Reporting on Uncertainties

In some cases, the new SAS requires the addition of an explanatory paragraph (following the third or "opinion" paragraph) that reports and describes material uncertainties affecting the financial statements, and it references the footnote(s) to the financial statements that further detail those uncertainties. The auditor's report on material uncertainties depends on the probability of material loss due to uncertainty. If the probability of a loss is remote, the auditor issues a standard, unqualified opinion.

An explanatory paragraph is required when a material loss is probable and the amount of the loss cannot be reasonably estimated. Exhibit 1-3 contains examples of three types of report paragraphs:

1. For Bolt Technology, doubt regarding the "going concern" assumption that underlies the preparation of financial statements

---

EXHIBIT 1-3. UNCERTAINTY PARAGRAPHS
Independent Auditor's Reports

Bolt Technology Corporation

The accompanying consolidated financial statements have been prepared assuming that Bolt Technology Corporation and subsidiaries will continue as a going concern. As discussed further in Note 1, the Company has sustained significant continuing losses over the past five years, and as a result, the operations and the assets of the Company have been substantially reduced. The ability of the Company to continue in existence as a going concern and to realize the carrying value of its assets in the normal course of business is dependent upon its ability to obtain sufficient cash flows from operations or from other sources of financing in order to meet the financial covenants of its existing debt agreement and to return to profitable operations. The consolidated financial statements do not include any adjustments relating to the recoverability and classification of recorded asset amounts or the amounts and classification of liabilities that might be necessary should the Company be unable to continue as a going concern.

ADDSCO Industries, Inc.

As discussed in the notes to financial statements, the net amounts of recoveries from certain contracts, the reversion amount from the termination of the bargaining pension plan of Alabama Dry Dock and Shipbuilding Corporation, and the potential liability from workers' compensation claims depend on future events, the result of which the ultimate outcome is uncertain.

In our opinion, except for the effects, if any, of such adjustments as might have been required had the outcome of the uncertainties discussed in the preceding paragraph been known, the consolidated financial statements referred to above present fairly, in all material respects, the financial position of ADDSCO Industries, Inc. and consolidated subsidiaries at June 30, 1989 and 1988 and the results of their operations and their cash flows for each of the years in the three-year period ended June 30, 1989 in conformity with generally accepted accounting principles.

Green Tree Acceptance, Inc

Note J to the consolidated financial statements discusses the Midwest Federal litigation, institutional purchasers' lawsuits, and a shareholder lawsuit. The ultimate outcome of these lawsuits cannot presently be determined. Accordingly, no provision for any liability that may result upon adjudication has been made in the accompanying financial statements.

Source: Annual reports.

2. For ADDSCO Industries, uncertainty regarding the valuation or realization of assets

3. For Green Tree Acceptance, uncertainty due to litigation

Whenever the auditors' report contains any of the three types of disclosures just listed, or the consistency exception, the financial statements should be examined closely. Note that "subject to" and "except for" disclosures no longer appear in auditors' reports; they have been replaced by the language (SAS 58) discussed earlier, effective in 1989.

The first category is the most serious. A "going concern" qualification suggests doubt as to whether the firm can continue in business. It may be that the firm requires financing due to losses or a lack of liquidity. This paragraph should be viewed as the equivalent of a flashing red light.

The other two categories suggest problems that are significant, but may not threaten the firm's existence. In these cases, an explanatory paragraph may be included at the auditors' discretion when a material loss is reasonably possible. The decision depends on whether the probability of loss is closer to remote (unlikely) or to probable (likely) and on the magnitude of the possible loss.

The auditor also performs other services less visible to readers of financial statements. The auditor will usually examine the internal control system of the company and report any weaknesses to management or to the audit committee of the board of directors. The report to the audit committee will sometimes also contain information regarding significant audit adjustments, unusual transactions, disagreements with management, or serious audit difficulties. This report is generally not available to outside financial statement users. The ASB[28] issued two new standards dealing with these reports.

Changes in auditors have become more frequent in recent years. In most cases changes are due to an effort to reduce audit costs or to personality issues. At times, however, they result from disagreements regarding the application of accounting principles. When an auditor is willing to lose a client because of such a disagreement, the financial analyst should exercise extreme caution with respect to the financial statements of the company in question.

INTERNATIONAL ACCOUNTING STANDARDS

Growing international trade, multinational industrial and financial enterprises, and increasingly global markets for capital have significantly expanded investment opportunities. Thus investors need to be able to analyze both domestic and foreign companies. However, there is no internationally accepted set of accounting standards. Further, as accounting standards are established separately in each country, it is difficult to generalize. The differences in accounting and reporting standards make it difficult to compare investments in U.S. companies with those in other countries.

---

[28]For a detailed discussion, see R. S. Roussey, E. L. Ten Eyck, and M. Blanco-Best, "Three New SASs: Closing the Communications Gap," *Journal of Accountancy,* December 1988, pp. 44–52.

Financial reporting requirements in different countries are a function of tax regulations, corporate law, the comparative significance of capital markets and financial institutions in industrial development, and cultural differences across countries. However, as capital markets and international investments expand, the need for international accounting standards is obvious.

International Accounting Standards Committee

The International Accounting Standards Committee, established in 1973, attempts to harmonize (conform) the accounting standards of different nations. The IASC is a nongovernmental body with representatives from the national accounting federations of a number of nations as well as representatives of other groups (including two financial analysts). Without any enforcement mechanism in place, the IASC had to strive for consensus, and, as a result, most of its standards were broad, allowing several alternatives. Starting in 1989, with increasing support from the International Organization of Securities Commissions (IOSCO), the IASC has become more aggressive in limiting accounting alternatives.

As of November 1, 1992, the IASC has issued 31 international accounting standards (IAS) and is expected to issue an additional 13 standards (mostly amendments of prior standards) by the end of 1993. It has also issued a Framework for the Preparation and Presentation of Financial Statements, which is used in reviewing existing standards and in the development of future IAS. This framework is also used to promote harmonization of regulations and standard setting by providing a basis for reducing the number of alternative accounting treatments permitted by the IASC.

In 1989, the IASC issued Exposure Draft 32 (E32), Comparability of Financial Statements, which dealt with 29 accounting issues. E32 was designed to eliminate all but one accounting treatment where the alternatives represented a free choice for similar transactions and events and to ensure that alternative treatments are used only under different circumstances. In some cases, E32 identified *benchmark* (preferred) and *allowed alternative* standards. Where the allowed alternative was used, firms were to be required to reconcile reported net income and stockholders' equity to amounts determined using the preferred treatment. In 1990, the IASC revised E32, and 21 proposals contained in the original E32 were incorporated in the IAS without substantive changes.

The IASC has largely "caught up" with the FASB. In the early 1990s the IASC issued standards dealing with issues such as joint ventures and financial instruments that the FASB has yet to resolve. Despite the handicaps of part-time members, a limited budget, and the need to achieve consensus among a large (and diverse) membership, the IASC has emerged as a rival source of accounting standards. Individual IASC standards are discussed in each chapter of this text as appropriate.

On the other hand, IASC lacks an enforcement mechanism. Neither the SEC nor the regulator of any other major industrial country has required adoption of IASC standards.[29] As capital markets continue to become more international in scope, the need for universal accounting standards grows. Various attempts have been made to harmonize

[29]However, IOSCO which consists of the SEC and many foreign regulatory bodies has been encouraging the IASC to complete its comparability project, and it is possible that IASC standards will be mandated in the future.

accounting standards over the last few years; the SEC's efforts and some developments in Europe are the most prominent and are discussed next.

EUROPEAN FINANCIAL REPORTING STANDARDS

Financial reporting requirements in Europe differ from those in the United States and other countries because of differences in their economies, relevance of local commercial law to the development of reporting standards, comparative importance of capital markets and banks as a source of financing, and the degree to which tax laws influence financial reporting.

Within the European Economic Community (EEC) attempts have been made to reduce reporting differences. The Fourth Directive (1978) attempted to provide a framework for a common level of disclosure with an emphasis on accounting rules and measurement (valuation) methods. The directive permits some options as to format and required content of the balance sheet and income statement and does not mandate a cash flow statement. The directive was a preliminary attempt at harmonization, and its adoption followed the passage of the directive into law in each member country.

The Fédération des Experts Comptables Européens (FEE) conducted and published a survey of financial statements of companies in the member states of the EEC. It suggested that a substantial degree of conformity has been achieved in the format of statements and major categories of accounts in the financial statements. Accounting for deferred taxes, leases, pensions, and foreign currency translation remains far from uniform; these differences may persist because of varying levels of economic development in the member countries.

In 1983, the EEC issued the Seventh Directive with an effective date of January 1, 1990. The new standards are similar to international practice, particularly as to the requirement for consolidated financial statements. The level of compliance and the impact on financial statement analysis were observable from 1991 onward when the first statements prepared under the seventh directive were published.

SEC REQUIREMENTS FOR FOREIGN REGISTRANTS

Foreign issuers may sell their securities in the United States by registering with the SEC and are subject to substantially the same reporting requirements as their domestic counterparts. Except for foreign governments and issuers of American Depositary Receipts (ADRs),[30] foreign issuers may elect to file the registration and reporting forms used by domestic issuers (see Exhibit 1-1). However, filing requirements for foreign firms are generally less stringent, requiring reporting on foreign forms 20-F (similar to 10-K) and 6-K (similar to 8-K). ADRs may be registered on either Form F-6 or Form 20-F and are exempt from Form 6-K requirements.

---

[30]ADRs are depository shares representing a specified number of shares and are issued against the deposit of a foreign issuer's securities. ADRs must be registered on Form F-6 unless another registration form is more appropriate.

Form 20-F filings are commonly used by foreign issuers thereby making them exempt from requirements to file proxies and insider trading reports. Form 20-F annual reports are due six months after the fiscal year end, quarterly reports are optional, and relatively little business and segment data disclosure is required.

Form 20-F filers must identify reporting principles used, identify material variations from U.S. GAAP, and reconcile reported income and stockholders' equity to U.S. GAAP. These reconciliations provide insights into the differences in reporting requirements across countries and the tasks involved in developing universal financial reporting standards. (See Chapter 12 for an example of the analysis of and the utility of data provided in Form 20-F reconciliations.)

The SEC issued Staff Accounting Bulletin (SAB) 88 in August 1990 clarifying disclosures and quantitative reconciliations required by Item 17 of Form 20-F. The new guidance requires some additional disclosures regarding pension obligations (SFAS 87) and financial instruments (SFAS 105) in the MD&A. However, SAB 88 does not mandate disclosures required by U.S. GAAP or the SEC but not by the foreign issuer's local GAAP.[31]

MULTIJURISDICTIONAL DISCLOSURE SYSTEM

In 1991, to facilitate efficient international capital formation and growth, and to harmonize disclosure standards, the SEC entered into an agreement, the multijurisdictional disclosure system (MJDS), with Canadian regulators. Under this agreement large Canadian companies can issue certain classes of securities in the United States using financial statements prepared according to Canadian GAAP (and vice versa.)[32] Reconciliation to U.S. GAAP is generally required, as specified in SEC Form 20-F, for filings made prior to July 1, 1993. Subsequent filings will not require reconciliation, unless the SEC changes these rules.

The United States and Canada have similar financial reporting standards, but Canada requires substantially less disclosure. Discussions with several European countries along the same lines have taken place. However, European GAAP is quite different, and the development of similar agreements with the European community would appear to be more difficult than the current MJDS with Canada.

Thus it seems likely that the further internationalization of the securities markets requires a common set of accounting standards. As the IASC continues to establish a credible set of standards, those standards become the only candidate for "world GAAP." Major IASC standards and significantly different (from U.S. GAAP) foreign standards will be discussed in the appropriate chapters of this book.

---

[31]See "Implications of SEC Staff Accounting Bulletin 88 for Foreign Registrants," by R. Dieter and J. A. Heyman, *Journal of Accountancy,* August 1991, pp. 121–125.

[32]*Multijurisdictional Disclosure and Modifications to the Current Registration and Reporting System for Canadian Issuers,* Securities Act Release No. 6902, June 21, 1991.

SUMMARY

Chapter 1 is intended to provide an informational background for the study of financial statement analysis. We have examined the sources of financial data and the institutional framework in which accounting and disclosure standards are set. In addition, we have provided a general guide to the contents of the financial statements and the roles played by statement preparers and auditors. Finally, we have touched upon research that examines the relationship between financial information and financial markets. In Chapter 2, we will build upon this informational framework by addressing the goals and methods of the analysis of financial statements.

Chapter 1

Problems

1. [Conceptual basis for accounting standards] In February 1993, the Chinese Ministry of Finance awarded a contract to develop accounting standards for China. Assume that you are employed on that project. Discuss how the standards to be developed would be affected by:

   (i) Decisions regarding which financial statement users are most important.

   (ii) The choice between relevance and reliability.

   (iii) The importance placed on comparability.

   (iv) Political, legal, and cultural factors.

2. [Conceptual basis for accounting standards] Explain why accounting standards might be different if they were established by:

   (i) Short-term lenders such as banks.

   (ii) Long-term equity investors.

   (iii) Tax authorities.

   (iv) Corporate managers.

3. [Basic accounting concepts] Describe the relationship between the matching principle and the accrual method of accounting in the preparation of financial statements.

4. [Basic accounting concepts] Describe why the going concern assumption is important in the preparation of financial statements.

5. [Sources of information] Contrast investors in public companies with those in private companies with respect to access to financial and other information useful for investment decisions.

6. [Sources of information] Contrast investors in public companies in the United States with those in foreign countries with respect to access to financial and other information useful for investment decisions.

7. [Sources of accounting standards] Contrast the roles of the Financial Accounting Standards Board and the Securities and Exchange Commission in the setting of accounting standards for American companies.

8. [Basic accounting concepts] Explain why the definitions of assets and liabilities affect accounting standards and, therefore, the preparation of financial statements.

9. [Basic accounting concepts] Explain why the distinction between liabilities and equity is important to investors and creditors.

10. [Basic accounting concepts] Explain why the difference between historical cost and market value affects the relevance and reliability of financial statement data.

11. [Basic accounting concepts] Contrast the role of contra accounts and adjunct accounts in financial statements.

12. [Basic accounting concepts]

A. Contrast gains and losses with revenues and expenses. Explain why the distinction is important for financial analysis.

B. Define "comprehensive income" and explain how that concept might make financial statements more useful for financial analysis.

13. [Basic concepts] Differentiate among extraordinary items, nonrecurring items, and recurring income. Explain why the distinctions are important for financial analysis.

14. [Basic concepts] Explain why cash flows are classified into three categories. Discuss the usefulness of each category.

15. [Basic concepts] Differentiate between financial statement footnotes and supplementary schedules as sources of financial data.

16. [Basic concepts] Discuss the SEC's requirements for Management Discussion and Analysis and explain how MD&A disclosures can be useful for financial analysis.

17. [Role of auditor] You are reviewing a company's financial statements. Its auditor has issued an unqualified opinion regarding the financial statements. Discuss what that opinion tells you about:

    (i) Possible changes in accounting principles.

    (ii) Possible changes in accounting estimates.

    (iii) The existence of significant risks regarding the future operations of the company.

    (iv) The possibility that the financial statements are fraudulent.

18. [Role of auditor, accounting changes] Exhibit 1P-1 contains an extract from the auditor's report and footnotes of Deere's fiscal 1992 annual report.

A. Discuss whether the auditor's report should have referred to the change in accounting principle. Your answer should include both reasons why and reasons why not.

EXHIBIT 1P-1. DEERE
Extracts from Financial Statements

Independent Auditors' Report

Deloitte & Touche

Deere & Company:

We have audited the accompanying consolidated balance sheets of Deere & Company and subsidiaries as of October 31, 1992 and 1991 and the related statements of consolidated income and of consolidated cash flows for each of the three years in the period ended October 31, 1992. These financial statements are the responsibility of the company's management. Our responsibility is to express an opinion on these financial statements based on our audits.

We conducted our audits in accordance with generally accepted auditing standards. Those standards require that we plan and perform the audit to obtain reasonable assurance about whether the financial statements are free of material misstatement. An audit includes examining, on a test basis, evidence supporting the amounts and disclosures in the financial statements. An audit also includes assessing the accounting principles used and significant estimates made by management, as well as evaluating the overall financial statement presentation. We believe that our audits provide a reasonable basis for our opinion.

In our opinion, such consolidated financial statements present fairly, in all material respects, the financial position of Deere & Company and subsidiaries at October 31, 1992 and 1991 and the results of their operations and their cash flows for each of the three years in the period ended October 31, 1992 in conformity with generally accepted accounting principles.

Chicago, Illinois
December 9, 1992

Excerpt from Footnote on Income Tax

In the second quarter of 1992, the company adopted FASB Statement No. 109, "Accounting for Income Taxes". There was no cumulative effect of adoption or current effect on continuing operations mainly because the company had previously adopted FASB Statement No. 96, "Accounting for Income Taxes", in 1988.

Source: Deere *1992 Annual Report.*

B. Discuss why knowledge of the change in accounting principle is important for analysis purposes despite its immaterial effect on 1992 results.

19. [Role of auditor] Compare the role of the auditor with that of the financial statement preparer (firm being audited) in preparation of the firm's financial statements.

20. [Sources of information] Discuss the importance to investors of the controversy over the conditions under which companies may issue securities in foreign jurisdictions.

21. [Contingencies; 1988 CFA adapted] Bonnywill Auto produced 10,000 Fiery models. On December 31, 19X2, the company's engineers discovered a possible fire hazard for this model. The probability of fire is estimated at 0.00009. If a fire occurs, the company's liability is estimated at $100,000 per occurrence, plus or minus $30,000. When answering the following questions, show any calculations.

A. Describe the most likely treatment of this contingency in Bonnywill's 19X2 financial statements.

B. Suggest an alternative treatment that would portray the liability more accurately.

22. [Contingencies] Consider two firms that self-insure for workers' compensation losses. Assume that the annual probability of a claim is 1 in 1000 for each firm and that each claim has an expected value of $10,000.

A. Firm A has 3 employees.

B. Firm B has 10,000 employees.

Discuss how each firm should account for its liability for workers' compensation benefits. If there is any difference in your answers, explain why.

23. [Basic concepts]

A. Explain what is meant by "discontinued operations." Explain both the advantages and disadvantages of segregating the results of discontinued operations from those of continuing operations.

B. Explain why discontinued *portions* of segments are *not* treated as discontinued operations. Discuss the effect of this difference in treatment on the financial statements and explain why that difference can both help and hinder the analysis of operating results.

Appendix 1—A

Review of the Financial Reporting Process

THE ACCOUNTING CYCLE

The objective of this appendix is to provide a comprehensive review of the basic financial reporting process. It is designed for readers with only a perfunctory knowledge of accounting. However, it will provide a useful review as well as insights for more advanced readers, particularly when used in conjunction with Appendix 1–B. Box 1A-1 provides a brief summary of the mechanics of the accounting process.

BOX 1A-1
Mechanics of the Accounting Process

The financial statements provide information about the assets (resources) of the firm and the claims of suppliers of capital (creditors and stockholders) used to obtain these resources. The accounting process used to develop these statements is designed to maintain the fundamental accounting relationship expressed as the balance sheet equation:

Assets (A) = Liabilities (L) + Stockholders' Equity (E)

where the claims of creditors are represented by liabilities (L) and those of stockholders (owners) by stockholders' equity (E). The assets reported on the balance sheet are either purchased by the firm or generated through operations; they are financed, directly or indirectly, by the creditors and stockholders of the firm.

Transactions and events that generate any one of the three effects in Column 'D' will unbalance the equation as the left side will be greater than the right side (A > L + E). Similarly, any one of the three effects in the column labeled 'C' will unbalance the equation, with the right side becoming greater than the left side (A < L + E).

Column 'D'	Column 'C'
A increase relative to L + E	L + E increase relative to A
1. Increase in Assets	1. Decrease in Assets
2. Decrease in Liabilities	2. Increase in Liabilities
3. Decrease in Equity	3. Increase in Equity

Therefore, in order to maintain the balance, every accounting event must be recorded with (at least) one effect from Column 'D' and[1] *(at least) one effect from Column 'C'.* These effects are called *debits* (column 'D') and *credits* (column 'C') respectively. Transactions which affect the income statement also fit within this model if we recall that revenues (expenses) increase (decrease) net income and hence stockholder's equity.

---

[1] Hence the name, double-entry bookkeeping.

35

Journal Entries

Accounting events are recorded by *journal entries* and *T-accounts*. For example, the first event for the WSF company is recorded with the following journal entry:

	Debit	Credit
(1) (Asset) Cash	$5,000,000	
(Stockholders' equity) Common Stock		
—Par Value		$1,000,000
—Additional Paid-in Capital		$4,000,000

The asset account, cash, is increased (debited) and the stockholders' equity account, common stock, is increased (credited). The positioning of the entries is made to correspond with the side (left or right) of the equation affected.

Adjusting and Closing Entries

The accounting process recognizes changes in asset, liability, and equity accounts as a result of accounting or exchange transactions. The accrual process also mandates the recognition of revenues and expenses arising from the use of services (e.g., electricity) or assets (e.g., depreciation expense), prepayments or receipts of cash before services are provided (e.g., advances), estimates such as bad debt expense, and the passage of time as in the recognition of interest expense.

The final step in the process closes out (summarizes) all revenue and expense accounts to the income summary account, creating the *income statement*.

T-Accounts

Journal entries record individual events. Account balances are maintained by means of T-accounts. Entries that increase the left (right) side of the balance sheet equation are entered on the left (right) side of the T-account. The first event journalized above is entered into the T-accounts as shown below ($000s):

Asset		Liability		Stockholders' Equity	
+	−	−	+	−	+
Debit	Credit	Debit	Credit	Debit	Credit
(1) 5,000					1,000 (1)
					4,000 (1)

Each asset, liability, and equity account is given its own T-account. At the end of the period, the entries on each side of the T-account are aggregated and the differences between the '+' and '−' sides are recorded as the balance. These balances are used to prepare the *balance sheet* at the end of the period.

The T-accounts for revenues and expenses are used to develop the income statement. These are "temporary" accounts as their balances are not carried forward to the next accounting period. They are instead set to zero at the end of each period, that is, "closed" to the income summary account to facilitate the creation of the income statement.

Changes in balance sheet accounts and the income statement for the period are used to generate the *cash flow statement*. This process is demonstrated later in this appendix for the WSF company.

Financial Reporting at Formation Date

Our example begins with the formation of a business enterprise, WSF Company, on December 31, 1992, and follows it for one year to illustrate the recognition, measurement, and reporting of transactions and events over that period. Six events occurring on the formation date are given. These are used to create the balance sheet as of December 31, 1992, which becomes the beginning balance sheet for 1993. The statement is depicted in Exhibit 1A-2.

1. WSF issues, for $5 per share, 1 million shares of common stock with a par value of $1 per share.

2. It sells $2.5 million (face value) of bonds, to pay interest semiannually, on January 1 and July 1 of each year, at an annual rate of 10%. The bonds are sold at par (100% of face value), netting the firm $2.5 million.

3. WSF purchases a warehouse building for $3.5 million, paid in cash.

4. The firm enters into a 3-year lease for a retail store located in a shopping mall at an annual rent of $120,000. A payment of $50,000 is due on January 1, 1993, and the remaining $70,000 of the annual rent is due in two installments payable on June 30 and December 31, 1993.

5. The firm purchases goods for inventory at a cost of $850,000 payable in 30 days. The firm's supplier also promises delivery of $300,000 of additional inventory on January 15, 1993.

6. The retail store is staffed with employees expected to report for work on January 1, 1993. Employment contracts are signed on December 31, 1992.

December 31, 1992, Balance Sheet Recognition ($)

	Assets			=	Liabilities	+	Equities
1.	Cash $5,000,000			=			Common Stock $5,000,000
2.	$2,500,000			=	Bonds Payable $2,500,000		
	$7,500,000			=	$2,500,000	+	$5,000,000
3.	(3,500,000)	+	Buildings $3,500,000	=			
	$4,000,000	+	$3,500,000	=	$2,500,000	+	$5,000,000
4.	No effect.						
5A.			Inventory $ 850,000	=	Accounts Payable $ 850,000		
5B.	No effect.						
6.	No effect.						

Totals:

Cash + Inventory + Buildings	=	Accounts Payable + Bonds Payable + Common Stock
$4,000,000 + $850,000 + $3,500,000	=	$850,000 + $2,500,000 + $5,000,000
= $8,350,000	=	$8,350,000

Journal Entries, December 31, 1992*

1. Cash $5,000,000
        Common Stock
          —Par Value $1,000,000
          —Additional Paid-in Capital $4,000,000
2. Cash $2,500,000
        Bonds Payable $2,500,000
3. Buildings $3,500,000
        Cash $3,500,000
4. No entry since first payment is due on January 1, 1993, and later. No performance occurs on this date, only an exchange of promises to provide the use of a building in return for specified payments.
5A. Inventory $850,000
        Accounts Payable $ 850,000
5B. No entry. The promised delivery will occur on January 15, 1993. There is no recognition on December 31, 1992, because there is no performance, only an exchange of promises.
6. No entry. Employment contracts are signed, but payments will be made only as services are provided.

*See ledgers, T-accounts.

T-Accounts, December 31, 1992

Cash

Beginning Balance	-0-	
Operating Cash Flows	-0-	
Investing Cash Flows		3,500,000 (3)
Financing (1) 5,000,000		
Cash Flows (2) 2,500,000		
Ending Balance	4,000,000	

Inventory

B.B.	-0-	
(5A)	850,000	
E.B.	850,000	

Accounts Payable

	-0- B.B.
	850,000 (5A)
	850,000 E.B.

Buildings

B.B.	-0-	
(3)	3,500,000	
E.B.	3,500,000	

Bonds Payable

	-0- B.B.
	2,500,000 (2)
	2,500,000 E.B.

Common Stock

	-0- B.B.
	1,000,000 (1)
	1,000,000 E.B.

Additional Paid-in Capital

	-0- B.B.
	4,000,000 (1)
	4,000,000 E.B.

Note: These T-accounts are used to generate the balance sheet as of December 31, 1992 (see Exhibit 1A-2).

First Year of Operations

1993 Transactions and Events

1. The initial rental payment for the retail store is made on January 1, 1993.
2. The firm receives the inventory promised on January 15 and is billed for the goods.
3. Additional inventory purchases for the year cost $975,000; total payments to suppliers of merchandise are $1,750,000.
4. Total sales for the year are $2,775,000, including $250,000 in cash and the remainder on credit. The store also receives $175,000 for deliveries to be made in the first quarter of 1994. The cost of the merchandise sold is $1,700,000.
5. During the year, collections from credit customers are $2,250,000.
6. Other operating expenditures include

Salaries	$140,000
Advertising	85,000
Utilities and supplies	85,000
	$310,000

   At the end of the year, WSF owes its employees $12,000 in salaries, and it owes other suppliers $38,000; all these expenditures and obligations relate to services used during 1993.

7. Balance of rent payments made June 30 and December 31, 1993.
8. Interest payment on bonds made on July 1, 1993.
9. On January 15, 1993, WSF purchases 10% of the outstanding common stock of a supplier, JL, Inc., for $710,000. On December 31, 1993, the market value of this investment has risen to $850,000.
10. On June 30, 1993, WSF declares a dividend of 3.5 cents per share, payable on July 20, 1993, and on December 31, 1993, it declares a dividend of 3.5 cents per share, payable on January 20, 1994.

Journal Entries

These entries record all the exchange transactions that occurred during 1993.

1/1/93:

1.	Prepaid Rent	50,000	
	Cash		50,000
	Initial payment of rent for the retail store.		

1/15/93 and later:

2.	Inventory	300,000	
	Accounts Payable		300,000
	Receipt of inventory on January 15.		

3A. Inventory   975,000
    Accounts Payable   975,000
    Additional inventory purchases over the year.

3B. Accounts Payable   1,750,000
    Cash   1,750,000
    Payments made to suppliers of merchandise during 1993.

4A. Cash   425,000
    Accounts Receivable   2,525,000
      Sales Revenue   2,775,000
      Advances from Customers.   175,000
    Total sales during 1993 and advances from customers.

4B. Cost of Goods Sold   1,700,000
    Inventory   1,700,000
    Cost of sales revenue recorded in 4A; see discussion of the matching concept in Chapter 1.

5. Cash   2,250,000
    Accounts Receivable   2,250,000
    Cash collections from customers during the year.

6. Operating Expense   360,000
    Cash   310,000
    Accrued Liabilities   50,000
    Recognition of operating expense for the year.

7. Prepaid rent   70,000
    Cash   70,000
    (The June and December installments are reported on a combined basis; they would normally be recorded separately as they were made.)

8. Interest expense   125,000
    Cash   125,000
    (Semiannual interest at 10%; $0.1 \times 2,500,000 \times 0.5$; represents the July 1, 1993, payment.)

9. Investment in Affiliates (JL, Inc.)   710,000
    Cash   710,000
    Purchase of supplier's common stock.

10A. Dividends Declared (Retained Earnings)   35,000
    Dividends Payable   35,000

10B. Dividends Payable   35,000
    Cash   35,000
    Records June 30 declaration and subsequent July 20 payment of dividends.

10C. Dividends Declared (Retained Earnings)   35,000
    Dividends Payable   35,000
    Records December 31 declaration of dividends.

Entries Required for the Preparation of Financial Statements

These entries record services used during the period and reflect events not resulting from exchange transactions occurring in 1993. They reflect the application of the accrual basis and the matching principle in the preparation of 1993 financial statements.

(A)	Depreciation Expense	175,000	
	Accumulated Depreciation		175,000

Recognition of Depreciation Expense (Straight-line depreciation; 20-year estimated life; salvage value is zero; for 1 year: $3,500,000 \div 20$.)

(B)	Rent Expense	120,000	
	Prepaid Rent		120,000

(Total annual rent = 120,000.)

(C)	Interest Expense	125,000	
	Interest Payable		125,000

(Semiannual interest due $1/1/94 = 0.1 \times 2,500,000 \times 0.5 = 125,000$.)

(D)	Bad-Debt Expense	50,500	
	Allowance for Uncollectibles		50,500

(WSF estimates uncollectibles at 2% of credit sales.)
($.02 \times 2,525,000 = 50,500$.)

Closing Entries in the Preparation of the Income Statement

All temporary accounts of revenues, expenses, etc., related to 1993 are closed out to the income summary, used to prepare the income statement.

(E)	Sales Revenue	2,775,000	
	Income Summary		2,775,000
(F)	Income Summary	50,500	
	Bad-Debt Expense		50,500
(G)	Income Summary	2,605,000	
	Cost of Goods Sold		1,700,000
	Operating Expense		360,000
	Depreciation Expense		175,000
	Rent Expense		120,000
	Interest Expense		250,000

(These closing entries may be recorded separately; they are combined here for illustration.)

(H)	Tax Expense	40,630	
	Taxes Payable		40,630

(34% of $119,500)

(I)	Income Summary	40,630	
	Tax Expense		40,630
(J)	Income Summary	78,870	
	Retained Earnings		78,870

These entries are used directly to create the WSF income statement for the year ended December 31, 1993, as shown in Exhibit 1A-1.

T-Accounts, December 31, 1993

Cash

Beginning Balance 12/31/92	4,000,000		
(4A)	425,000	50,000	(1)
(5)	2,250,000	1,750,000	(3B)
		310,000	(6)
		70,000	(7)
		125,000	(8)
Operating Cash Flows	370,000		
		710,000	(9)
Investing Cash Flows			
Financing Cash Flows		35,000	(10B)
Ending Balance	3,625,000		

Inventory

B.B.	850,000	1,700,000	(4B)
(2)	300,000		
(3A)	975,000		
E.B.	425,000		

Accounts Receivable

B.B.	-0-		
(4A)	2,525,000	2,250,000	(5)
E.B.	275,000		

Prepaid Rent

B.B.	-0-		
(1)	50,000		
(7)	70,000	120,000	(B)
E.B.	-0-		

Allowance for Uncollectibles

		-0-	B.B.
		50,500	(D)
		50,500	E.B.

Accounts Payable

		850,000	B.B.
(3B)	1,750,000	300,000	(2)
		975,000	(3A)
		375,000	E.B.

Advances from Customers

		-0-	B.B.
		175,000	(4A)
		175,000	E.B.

Accumulated Depreciation

		-0-	B.B.
		175,000	(A)
		175,000	E.B.

Accrued Liabilities

		-0-	B.B.
		50,000	(6)
		50,000	E.B.

Investment in JL, Inc.

B.B.	-0-		
(9)	710,000		
E.B.	710,000		

Interest Payable

		125,000	(C)
		125,000	E.B.

Retained Earnings

		-0-	B.B.
(10A)	35,000		
(10C)	35,000	78,870	(J)
		8,870	E.B.

Dividends Payable

		-0-	B.B.
(10B)	35,000	35,000	(10A)
		35,000	(10C)
		35,000	E.B.

Taxes Payable

		-0-	B.B.
		40,630	(H)
		40,630	E.B.

Bonds Payable

		2,500,000	B.B.
		-0-	
		2,500,000	E.B.

Common Stock

		1,000,000	B.B.
		-0-	
		1,000,000	E.B.

Buildings

B.B.	3,500,000		
	-0-		
E.B.	3,500,000		

Additional Paid-in Capital

		4,000,000	B.B.
		-0-	
		4,000,000	E.B.

	Sales Revenue					Cost of Goods Sold				Operating Expenses		
(E)	2,775,000	2,775,000	(4A)	(4B)	1,700,000	1,700,000	(G)	(6)	360,000	360,000	(G)

	Interest Expense				Depreciation Expense				Rent Expense		
(8)	125,000			(A)	175,000	175,000	(G)	(B)	120,000	120,000	(G)
(C)	125,000	250,000	(G)								

	Bad-Debt Expense					Tax Expense		
(D)	50,500	50,500	(F)	(H)	40,630	40,630	(I)

Income Summary

(F)	50,500	2,775,000	(E)
(G)	1,700,000		
(G)	360,000		
(G)	250,000		
(G)	175,000		
(G)	120,000		
(I)	40,630		
(J)	78,870		

Note: These T-accounts are used to prepare the 1993 income statement and balance sheet.

EXHIBIT 1A-1. THE WSF COMPANY
Income Statement, for Year Ended December 31, 1993

Sales revenue			$ 2,775,000
Less: Bad debts			(50,500)
Net sales			$ 2,724,500
Less: Cost of goods sold			(1,700,000)
Gross margin			$ 1,024,500
Less: Operating expense	$360,000		
Depreciation expense	175,000		
Rent expense	120,000		
Interest expense	250,000		
			(905,000)
Income before taxes			119,500
Tax expense			(40,630)
Net income			$ 78,870

Statement of Retained Earnings

Beginning balance, January 1, 1993	$	0
Net income		78,870
Dividends declared		(70,000)
Ending balance, December 31, 1993	$	8,870

EXHIBIT 1A-2. THE WSF COMPANY
Balance Sheet, at December 31, 1992–1993

	1992	1993
Assets		
Cash	$4,000,000	$3,625,000
Accounts receivable (less allowance for uncollectibles of $50,500 on December 31, 1993 and $0 on December 31, 1992)	0	224,500
Inventory	850,000	425,000
Prepaid rent	0	0
Current assets	$4,850,000	$4,274,500
Investment in affiliates	0	710,000
Buildings	3,500,000	3,500,000
Less: Accumulated depreciation	0	(175,000)
Long-term assets	$3,500,000	$4,035,000
Total assets	$8,350,000	$8,309,500
Liabilities		
Advances from customers	$ 0	$ 175,000
Accounts payable	850,000	375,000
Accrued liabilities	0	50,000
Interest payable	0	125,000
Taxes payable	0	40,630
Dividends payable	0	35,000
Current liabilities	$ 850,000	$ 800,630
Bonds Payable	2,500,000	2,500,000
Total liabilities	$3,350,000	$3,300,630
Common stock	1,000,000	1,000,000
Additional paid-in capital	4,000,000	4,000,000
Retained earnings	0	8,870
Stockholders' equity	$5,000,000	$5,008,870
Total liabilities and equities	$8,350,000	$8,309,500

CREATION OF THE STATEMENT OF CASH FLOWS

The statement of cash flows is conceptually simple: it is intended to show all the cash inflows and outflows of the firm during the period. However, as the cash flow statement must combine cash flows that are recognized on the balance sheet (purchases of assets, for example) and the income statement (cash received from the sale of goods, for example), it is computationally more difficult.

Preparation of this statement is further complicated by differences between the time cash flows occur and when they are recognized as revenues or expenses. The accrual process (income statement recognition) is subject to management judgment, assumptions, and various estimates that affect both time series and cross-sectional analyses.

The WSF company statement of cash flows for the year ended December 31, 1993 (see Exhibit 1A-4), reflects a careful categorization of cash flows as mandated by SFAS 95, discussed in Chapter 1 using the transactional analysis[1] method (see Exhibit 1A-3). This technique can be used to create a statement of cash flows for firms that do not prepare such statements in accordance with SFAS 95.[2] It also allows conversion of the indirect method cash flow from operations to the direct method. More important, it is useful in reorganizing the statement of cash flows to suit analytic and decision objectives. It reflects the gross cash flows, reporting separately gross cash collections and the outflows incurred to generate those cash inflows. These gross cash flows facilitate analyses of the firm's operations and its ability to meet current and planned cash flow requirements.

One objective of transactional analysis is to understand the relationship between accrual accounting events and their cash impact. A second goal is to classify cash flows among operating, financing, and investing activities as required by SFAS 95. That standard allows firms to use either the direct or the indirect method to report operating cash flows. In the absence of acquisitions, divestitures, and significant foreign operations,[3] the indirect method simply recasts the income statement and the balance sheet, providing little new information or insight into a firm's cash generating ability.

Cash Flows from Operations

The principal component of cash flows from operations (CFO) is the cash collections for the period. We shall start with WSF net sales in 1993 of $2,724,500. Some sales have been recognized, although cash has not yet been received, generating accounts receivable. Conversely, some cash has been received (and recorded as advances), but revenue has not yet been earned. By modifying net sales, deducting the increase in accounts receivable, and adding the increase in advances, we arrive at cash collections.

---

[1]See Ashwinpaul, C. Sondhi, George H. Sorter, and Gerald I. White, "Transactional Analysis," *Financial Analysts Journal* (September/October 1987); "Cash Flow Redefined: FAS 95 and Security Analysis," *Financial Analysts Journal*, (November/December 1988), by the same authors links the transactional analysis method to cash flow statements required by SFAS 95.

[2]Most non-U.S. companies do not prepare such statements.

[3]These activities require a segregation of the operating and nonoperating effects that are combined in such reported balance sheet accounts as inventories, receivables, and payables. See the discussion and illustration of the statement of cash flows for A.M. Castle in Chapter 2.

EXHIBIT 1A-3. THE WSF COMPANY
Transactional Analysis for the Year Ended December 31, 1993
($ thousands)

Account	Income Statement	Balance Sheet 12/31/92	Balance Sheet 12/31/93	Balance Sheet Change	Cash Effect +	Cash Effect −
Net Sales	2724.5				2724.5	
Receivables		0	224.5	+224.5		224.5
Advances		0	175	+175	175.0	
Cash Collections					2675.0	
COGS	(1700.0)					1700.0
Inventory		850	425	−425	425	
A/C Payable		850	375	−475		475.0
Cash Inputs						1750.0
Operating Expense	(360.0)					360.0
Rent Expense	(120.0)					120.0
Accrued Liabilities		0	50	+50	50.0	
Cash Expenses						430.0
Tax Expense	(40.63)					40.63
Tax Payable		0	40.63	+40.63	40.63	
Cash Taxes Paid						0
Interest Expense	(250.0)					250.0
Interest Payable		0	125	+125	125.0	
Cash Interest Paid						125.0
Depreciation Expense	(175.0)					175.0
Plant, Property, and Equipment, Net		3500	3325	−175	175.0	
Cash Investment						0
Investment in Affiliates		0	710	+710		710.0
Cash Invested in Affiliates						710.0
Net Income	78.87					
Dividends Declared	(70.0)					70.0
Dividends Payable		0	35	+35	35.0	
Cash Dividends Paid						35.0

EXHIBIT 1A-4. THE WSF COMPANY
Statement of Cash Flows for the Year Ended December 31, 1993

Direct Method

Cash Collections		$ 2,675,000
Less: Cash inputs	$1,750,000	
Cash expenses (rent, operating)	430,000	
Cash interest	125,000	
		(2,305,000)
Cash Flows from Operations		$ 370,000
Investment in affiliate	710,000	
Investment cash flow		(710,000)
Dividends paid	35,000	
Financing cash flow		(35,000)
Net cash flow		$ (375,000)
Cash balance, as of December 31		
1993	$3,625,000	
1992	4,000,000	
Net change		$ (375,000)

Indirect Method

Net income		78,870
Add: Noncash expenses		
Depreciation expense		175,000
		$ 253,870
Changes in operating accounts		
(Incr.) in receivables	(224,500)	
Decr. in inventories	425,000	
(Decr.) in accounts payable	(475,000)	
Incr. in accrued liabilities	50,000	
Incr. in interest payable	125,000	
Incr. in taxes payable	40,630	
Incr. in advances from customers	175,000	
		116,130
Cash Flows from Operations		$ 370,000

Note: Investing and financing cash flows are identical to those reported under the direct method.

The firm would also provide a separate footnote on cash payments for interest and taxes. The WSF Company paid $125,000 in interest, but it made no tax payments during the year ended December 31, 1993.

This is the amount of cash actually received during the period as a result of sales activities, regardless of when revenues were earned.

The next stage requires the determination of the cash outflows incurred to generate the cash collections computed. The first component is the cash outflow for inputs into the manufacturing or retailing process. Cost of goods sold (COGS) is modified in similiar fashion to arrive at cash inputs. Once again there are two modifications: we subtract the decrease in inventory (cash outflow was in prior period) and add the decrease in accounts payable (cash flow in the current period for goods received in prior period). The cash outflow for inputs is not affected by the inventory valuation method used by the firm, facilitating comparison across firms.[4]

The remaining income statement accounts are similarly modified to their cash analogs to determine the cash outflows for salaries, administrative expenses, and research and development expenditures among others. In each case, the goal is to link the income statement account with related balance sheet accounts. By related, we mean that the balance sheet account contains cash flows that either have been recognized in that income statement category (accruals and payables) or will be recognized in the future (prepaid). As disclosures are often inadequate to do this precisely, educated guesses and approximations may be necessary. For example, we assume that accounts payable relate only to the purchase of inventory; in many cases they will also relate to the purchase of investments.[5]

Transactions and events that are nonrecurring or peripheral to the basic activities of the firm are combined into a miscellaneous category, which also includes the cash impact of transactions for which the financial statements and the footnotes do not provide information enabling more precise classification. The objective is to develop a classification scheme that is consistent over time and comparable across firms. However, constant review is essential because of discretionary and mandatory changes in reporting methods and changes in a firm's operations and capital structure.

We must also adjust balance sheet and income statement accounts when information is available to do so. For example, some companies include depreciation expense in COGS but disclose the amount separately; in such cases we must reduce COGS by the amount of depreciation expense and create a "depreciation expense" account to estimate correctly cash invested in property. The reported depreciation expense should also be verified by reference to Schedule VI of the SEC 10-K filing. This schedule provides details of the components of the change in accumulated depreciation for the period, including effects of acquisitions, divestitures, and foreign operations. Sometimes footnote data provide breakdowns of aggregated balance sheet accounts, permitting finer breakdowns of assets and liabilities. *The transactional analysis method requires that each balance sheet change and each income statement accounts be analyzed except cash.*

---

[4]The net cash flow from operations under the indirect method is similarly unaffected by the inventory method. However, the indirect method does not separately report the cash outflow for inputs.

[5]Under SFAS 95, cash flows must be categorized correctly as operating, financing, or investing.

Investment Cash Flows

The primary component of investment cash flows is the capital expenditure for long-term assets such as plant and machinery. This amount may be calculated net or gross of proceeds on sales of these assets. The cash flows from such sales are considered investment cash flows regardless of whether they are netted in capital expenditures. However, trends in gross capital expenditures may contain useful insights into management plans. Segment disclosures should be monitored for differential investment patterns.

Other components of this category include cash flows from investments in joint venture and equity method affiliates and long-term investments in securities (see Chapter 11 for a detailed discussion of these issues). The cash flow consequences of acquisitions and divestitures must also be reported in this category. Footnote disclosures (when available) should be used to segregate operating assets and liabilities obtained (relinquished) in acquisitions (divestitures). This separation is necessary to ensure accurate measurements of CFO. (See Chapter 12 for a discussion of this issue.)

Financing Cash Flows

Inflows from additional borrowing, repayments of debt, dividend payments, and equity financing are all components of financing cash flow. Equity financing is determined by analyzing the change in stockholders' equity, breaking out the effects of

- Net income
- Dividends declared
- Shares issued or repurchased
- Changes in valuation accounts included in equity

Once this is done, every change in the balance sheet has been included (net income is included by incorporating each of its components) except cash. The net cash flow must, by definition, be equal to the change in cash. This identity provides a check on computations. (There is an additional check: make sure that the income statement components used in the transactional analysis add up to net income.)

The last step is to summarize the cash flows from operations, financing, and investing activities. The result is a statement of cash flows. The statement of cash flows for WSF for 1993 is shown in Exhibit 1A-4.

This exhibit also contains a statement of cash flows for WSF using the indirect method. This is the method most often used in annual reports. It differs from the statement of cash flows in terms of how cash flow from operations is computed. Under the indirect method, the starting point is the net income. Two types of adjustments are then made to net income to arrive at cash from operations:

1. all "non-cash" expenses (revenues) are added (subtracted).
2a. increases (decreases) in balances of operating asset accounts are subtracted (added).

b. increases (decreases) in balances of operating liability accounts are added (subtracted).

These adjustments are examined in greater detail in Chapter 2. The chapter provides an illustration of the reconciliation of the direct and indirect methods and a discussion of the analysis of cash flow statements.

Appendix 1–A

Problems

1. [Review of accounting cycle] The balance sheet for Mamont for the year ended December 31, 19X0, follows. Using the list of events for 19X1 prepare the balance sheet, income statement, and statement of cash flows for the year ended December 31, 19X1.

MAMONT COMPANY
Balance Sheet, at December 31, 19X0

Cash	$ 34	Accounts payable	$104
Accounts receivable	365	Income tax payable	81
Inventory	227	Short-term debt	181
Current assets	$626	Current liabilities	$366
		Long-term debt	48
		Total liabilities	$414
Property, plant, and equipment	120		
Less: Accumulated depreciation	(40)		
Net property	$ 80	Common stock	81
		Retained earnings	211
			$292
Total assets	$706	Total liabilities and equity	$706

Mamont Company: 19X1 Events

1. The company purchased $881 of inventory on account.

2. Sales for the year were $1265.

3. Depreciation expense was $10.

4. Interest of $19 was paid on the company's long- and short-term debt.

5. The company obtained short-term financing of $65 and repaid $2 of long-term debt.

6. Mamont issued new stock for $5.

7. The company received $1210 from customers during the year.

    8. Inventory sold during the year had cost the company $843.

    9. Income tax expense for the year was $33; $19 was paid.

    10. Dividends declared and paid were $21.

    11. New equipment costing $17 was purchased and paid for.

    12. The company repurchased some of its own common stock for $14.

    13. Operating expenses paid during the year were $320.

    14. The company paid $867 of its accounts payable during 19X1.

2. [Impact of events on financial statements] A company begins operations on June 1 with zero retained earnings. The following events occurred during the month:

    1. Merchandise was purchased for $50,000.

    2. Half this merchandise was sold for $75,000.

    3. Rent of $9000 for three months was paid in advance on June 1.

    4. Wages for June of $5000 will be paid on July 1.

    5. Common stock was sold for $200,000 on June 8.

    6. A cash dividend of $7000 was declared on June 20, to be paid on July 15.

Determine the balance in retained earnings on June 30.

3. [Impact of events on financial statements] The following events occurred during the accounting period:

    1. Goods that cost $80,000 were sold for $130,000.

    2. Factory equipment was depreciated by $15,000.

    3. Office equipment was depreciated by $7000.

    4. Materials costing $2000 were placed into production.

    5. A cash dividend was declared.

    6. The company provided consulting services to a client and charged the client $20,000 for these services.

    7. The company rented office space for which it paid $8,000.

    8. Retained earnings increased by $24,000.

Determine the amount of the cash dividend.

4. [Impact of events on financial statements] From the information that follows determine the balance of the Arda Company's cash account at the close of 1992.

    1. Cash from operations during 1992 totaled $600,000.

    2. Plant and equipment purchases were $100,000. The company's policy is to finance all such purchases with long-term notes.

    3. Long-term notes increased by $200,000.

    4. Accounts receivable decreased by $45,000 during 1992.

    5. The 1991 year-end cash balance was $2,000,000.

    6. Dividends of $60,000 were declared; dividends of $80,000 were paid.

7. No common stock was bought or sold during the year.

8. Depreciation expense was $40,000. The accumulated depreciation account increased by $30,000 as a fully depreciated asset was scrapped.

5. [Deriving events from financial statements]

A. Sales for the Aspen Company in 19X0 were $100,000. The company's pricing policy was to charge a 25% profit margin over the cost of inventory. Accounts payable decreased by $30,000 and the inventory account fell by $60,000 during the year. Calculate the payments made for inventory purchases.

B. During 19X1, the retained earnings account of the Ace Company increased by $10,000. The dividends payable account decreased by $8000 over the same period. Net income was $12,000. Determine the dividends paid during 19X1.

C. The BFF Company had depreciation expense of $30,000 for the year. No new assets were purchased. Net property, plant, and equipment decreased by $50,000, and the balance of accumulated depreciation decreased by $40,000 for the year. Calculate the original cost and accumulated depreciation of the assets disposed of during the year.

6. [Financial statement relationships] The balance sheet and statement of cash flows of the Morano Company for the two years ended December 31, 19X7, follow:

MORANO COMPANY
Balance Sheet, at December 31, 19X6–19X7

	19X6	19X7
Cash	$ 80,000	$120,000
Accounts receivable	55,000	80,000
Inventory	75,000	90,000
Prepaid rent	5,000	0
Property, plant, and equipment	100,000	80,000
Less: Accumulated depreciation	(30,000)	(30,000)
Total assets	$285,000	$340,000
Accounts payable (inventory)	$ 55,000	$ 65,000
Tax payable	40,000	50,000
Wages payable	0	10,000
Dividends payable	30,000	40,000
Common stock	90,000	100,000
Retained earnings	70,000	75,000
Total liabilities and equity	$285,000	$340,000

MORANO COMPANY
Statement of Cash Flows, 19X7

Cash flow from operations:	
From customers	$?
For suppliers	(100,000)
For taxes	(20,000)
For salaries	(50,000)
For rent	(15,000)
	$?
Cash flow from investment	
Sale of property, plant, and equipment*	10,000
Cash flow from financing	
Sale of stock	10,000
Dividends	(20,000)
Change in cash	$?

*No gain or loss was realized on the sale of property, plant, and equipment.

A. Determine:

1. Dividends declared.
2. Inventory purchased.
3. Monthly rent.
4. Cash receipts from customers.
5. Income for 19X7.
6. Cash from operations for 19X7.
7. Original cost of property, plant, and equipment sold.

B. Prepare an income statement for the Morano Co. for 19X7.

7. [Financial statement relationships] From the balance sheets and additional information provided for the Ashber Company:

A. Determine the following for 19X2:

1. Inventory purchases
2. Dividends paid
3. Additions to plant and equipment
4. Net income
5. Sales revenue
6. Monthly rent

7. Interest rate on bond (assume any new borrowings were made at December 31, 19X2)

B. Prepare a statement of cash flows for 19X2.

ASHBER COMPANY
Balance Sheet, at December 31, 19X1–19X2

	19X1	19X2
Cash	$185,000	$120,000
Accounts receivable	80,000	150,000
Inventory	120,000	80,000
Plant and equipment	180,000	200,000
Less: accumulated depreciation	(40,000)	(50,000)
Total assets	$525,000	$500,000
Accounts payable	120,000	110,000
Rent payable	0	40,000
Dividend payable	5,000	0
Bond payable	20,000	30,000
Common stock	200,000	220,000
Retained earnings	180,000	100,000
Total liabilities and equity	$525,000	$500,000

Additional information:

	19X2 Expenses
Cost of goods sold	$100,000
Wage expense	80,000
Rent expense	60,000
Depreciation expense	10,000
Interest expense	2,000
	$252,000

Dividend of $50,000 was declared.

8. [Preparation of statement of cash flows] Prepare a statement of cash flows for year 2 using the balance sheet, income statement, and additional information provided for the GHS Company.

GHS COMPANY
Balance Sheet, at December 31

	Year 1	Year 2
Cash	$101,000	$113,000
Accounts receivable	70,000	75,000
Less: Allowance for doubtful accounts	?	?
Inventory	50,000	60,000
Prepaid rent	3,000	0
Property, plant, and equipment	100,000	110,000
Accumulated depreciation	(30,000)	(30,000)
Total assets	$?	$?
Accounts payable, merchandise	$ 40,000	$ 20,000
Accounts payable, services	50,000	40,000
Rent payable	0	6,000
Interest payable	1,000	1,000
Long-term debt	100,000	120,000
Common stock	80,000	90,000
Retained earnings	20,000	50,000
Total liabilities and equity	$291,000	$327,000

GHS COMPANY
Income statement, for Year Ended December 31

	Year 2
Sales	$?
Bad-debt expense	2,000
	$?
Cost of goods sold	90,000
Operating expenses	30,000
Rent expense	?
Interest expense	12,000
Depreciation expense	1,000
Loss on disposal of property	1,000
Net income	$?

Additional information:

1. Newly acquired property cost $25,000.
2. Dividends declared were $12,000.
3. Bad-debt expense is calculated as 1% of sales.

Deere & Company

INTRODUCTION

The primary objective of this appendix is to introduce readers to corporate annual reports. Financial statements, footnotes, supplementary schedules, and data outside of the financial statements provide significant information about a firm's business activities, the environment in which those activities are conducted, and the financial condition and operating results.

This appendix is intended as a guide to financial statements for readers who need a practical reference to augment their study of financial reporting and its uses. Thus it should be read in conjunction with Chapters 1 and 2 and Appendix 1A.

Deere manufactures, distributes, and finances a wide range of agricultural and industrial equipment and power machinery. It also provides credit, insurance, and health care products and services to other businesses and the public. This diversity in operations allows a discussion of many different reporting requirements, some of which are relatively recent.

These requirements are illustrated with specific reference to the financial sections of Deere's 1988 (portions only) and 1991 annual reports, contained in Exhibit 1B-1 and 1B-2, respectively. These sections will be the basis of the balance of this appendix. They also will be used to illustrate specific points of analysis and as the basis for some problems in various chapters of this book.

GENERAL COMMENTS

The annual report is used to disseminate financial information about the firm, including its financial condition and results of operations. It is an important, even critical, means of communication between a firm and its various constituencies, among them investors, creditors, suppliers, customers, current and potential employees, and regulators. This communications function may result in a public relations emphasis that detracts from the basic financial reporting objectives of the annual report.

Interim (quarterly) reports are unaudited and even less rigorous; management has substantially greater discretion as to the information provided.[1] Most foreign countries

---

[1]For this reason, the 10-Q quarterly reports filed with the Securities and Exchange Commission should always be obtained. While these reports do not have the same level of detail as annual reports (10-K), they almost always contain more detail than the quarterly report to shareholders.

do not require quarterly reports, a few (for example, the United Kingdom and Japan) mandate the publication of semiannual reports, but standards are not well specified, and the resulting reports may not be comparable over time or across firms.

FINANCIAL SUMMARY

The vast majority of firms provide a table that highlights their financial condition at the report date and the results of its operations for the period and for previous years. Deere's annual reports are typical: the *1988 Annual Report* contains three years of data (1986–1988) and the *1991 Annual Report* provides information for five years (1987–1991).

Deere's 1988 financial summary begins with net sales for the three years, broken down between the two major segments of operations: farm and industrial equipment. The 1991 summary does not provide that breakdown, reporting only total equipment sales. However, net income, assets, and other data are reported separately for Deere's financial units, perhaps because of the change in reporting method discussed shortly.

The financial summary reports income from continuing operations, net income, and dividends declared and paid. Selected ratios are also disclosed: Deere reports net income as a percentage of sales and beginning stockholders' equity. Firms may also disclose other relevant indices of their financial condition. Deere reports outlays for research and development, capital expenditures, employment costs, and number of employees. Working capital, total assets, debt, equity, and common shares outstanding are also shown.

The financial summary data are a useful indicator of results and trends, but they are not designed to provide more than a glance at selected measures. Because its contents are largely discretionary, the summary does not substitute for the detailed analysis required for investment decisions.

LETTER TO STOCKHOLDERS

Periodic reports facilitate communication between the firm and its owners, the stockholders. Managements, typically the chairman and/or president, use these reports to inform stockholders of the period's major events that had a material impact on its financial condition, operations, and prospects.

The letter may provide information on economic and strategic events not reported in the financial statements. Deere's 1991 report (the letter to stockholders is not reproduced here), for example, discusses new labor agreements that are not financial events but are significant to future operating results. The 1988 letter (not reproduced) discusses unusual weather conditions that affected Deere's sales of farm equipment.

Letters to stockholders may also highlight significant achievements or challenges, In 1991, Deere discusses the growth and increasing importance of its credit and insurance operations. The continuing impact of the poor economy, reflected in the operating loss and the restructuring charges, is also discussed. These disclosures mirror the 1988 letter wherein Deere reports the growth of its credit and insurance units and the challenges presented by the economy.

BUSINESS REVIEW

The annual report also usually provides a detailed review of the firm's business segments, corporate developments, and relevant domestic and international business and economic trends. This segment of the annual report should be scanned for useful information, but it does not generally reward readers with any significant insights. The firm's discussion of business and its competition in the SEC 10-K filings is often more informative.

The remainder of the annual report is of more direct interest to analysts and investors: it contains the financial statements, footnotes, and related disclosures that are discussed in the remaining sections of this appendix. We begin with a commentary on individual financial statements followed by the Management Discussion and Analysis and conclude with a brief discussion of other data provided in the annual report.

FINANCIAL STATEMENTS

Firms are required to present a balance sheet (statement of financial position), income statement, statement of cash flows, statement of retained earnings and stockholders' equity, footnotes, and supplementary schedules comprising a complete financial report.

Each of these reporting elements is discussed in the paragraphs that follow. However, some preliminary comments are required to delineate the basic principles used in these statements. Deere's reports have been prepared by its management using GAAP, that is, U.S. generally accepted accounting principles. The primary methods used are discussed in the Summary of Significant Accounting Policies (SSAP), which follows the statements.

In 1988, Deere's SSAP states that the transactions of all wholly owned subsidiaries, *except* the retail finance, leasing, insurance, and health care subsidiaries, are consolidated in the financial statements. The exclusion of some wholly owned units was based on the "nonhomogeneous" exemption; the operations of these units were considered to be so different from manufacturing operations of the firm that consolidation would obscure rather than provide useful information. These units were reported under the equity method: Deere reported its share of their net assets and earnings.[2]

In 1991, Deere has consolidated all majority-owned subsidiaries. The changed reporting method reflects Deere's application (since 1989) of Statement of Financial Accounting Standards (SFAS) 94, Consolidation of All Majority-Owned Subsidiaries. Because Deere uses an October 31 fiscal year end, and because the new reporting

---

[2]See Chapter 11 for a complete discussion of consolidation, the equity method, and related issues summarized here.

standards were effective for fiscal years ending after December 15, 1988, it was able to postpone its adoption of the new standard until fiscal 1989.[3]

In Deere's 1988 report, separate footnotes provide a condensed balance sheet, income statement, and review of the insurance and retail finance subsidiaries. This summarized information allowed users to consolidate the wholly owned finance subsidiaries of firms like Deere. Consolidation of all wholly owned subsidiaries in the 1991 report facilitates the analysis of Deere and provides some additional footnote disclosure.

However, consolidation also obscures data on the assets and liabilities of the finance units, reducing the effectiveness of some analytical techniques. The cash flows, asset and liability structures, and income statements have different characteristics and trends compared to those of industrial companies. Footnote disclosures in the 1991 report provide some but not all of this information.

The 1991 report provides both consolidated and separate balance sheets for the equipment unit (with financial services on the equity basis) and the financial services subsidiaries. Note that only the net assets of the financial services unit are reported in the balance sheet of the equipment unit; the consolidated balance sheet shows all the assets and liabilities of the finance unit. For example, the equipment unit reports long-term borrowings of $1018 million on December 31, 1991, under the equity method while the consolidated balance sheet shows long-term debt of $2206 million, reflecting the addition of $1189 million of debt of the financial services unit. Disclosure of both consolidated and disaggregated data is very useful but is not always available.

Consolidated Balance Sheet

Balance sheets report Deere's assets, liabilities, and stockholders' equity at each fiscal year end. Firms must provide at least two consecutive balance sheets to facilitate the determination of changes over the year. These changes should be analyzed in conjunction with the income statement and statement of cash flows for the year.

Deere's 1988 balance sheet is typical of manufacturing companies. Assets and liabilities are classified between current and long-term (noncurrent) categories. Note that the 1991 balance sheet is no longer classified, although the order is virtually unchanged, reflecting the consolidation of Deere's financial operations. (Balance sheets of financial firms are generally not presented in a classified format; see Deere's 1988 footnote disclosure of the finance units' balance sheet.)

Current Assets

In the 1988 balance sheet, cash balances, the most liquid of current assets, are reported first. Short-term investments are reported next; Deere states that cost approximates market value, and no separate parenthetical or footnote disclosure of actual market value is provided.

The next current asset account is refundable income taxes, the expected benefits of tax loss and tax credit carryforwards. Receivables from unconsolidated subsidiaries and

---

[3]Financial statement effects of significant mandatory reporting changes on "early" adopters can provide information about the impact on firms such as Deere, which do not adopt the new standard until a later date.

affiliates are reported next, segregated from trade and finance receivables. Advances and loans to affiliates are quite different in nature from receivables generated by sales transactions.

Trade receivables are Deere's most significant current asset as befits a firm that must provide dealer and customer financing; it even considers financing as a separate business segment. Deere segregates receivables from sales to dealers and those generated from direct sales to customers. Retail notes are reported net of deferred finance (interest) income. A footnote discusses the terms of financing provided.

The nature and risks of these categories of receivables merit the separate disclosure and analyses of risks, and collectibility should reflect these differences.[4] The firm also discloses amounts of receivables sold each year, uncollected balances on receivables sold previously, and its exposure to repurchase obligations. Trends in these sales and obligations are important indicators of credit quality and should be monitored.

Equipment on operating or short-term leases is reported as a component of current assets. The balance sheet and footnotes provide the required information, including the portions owned and financed by the manufacturing and finance units. The footnote also reports the depreciation expense, accumulated depreciation, future payments, and the time period over which these inflows are expected.

The last component of current assets is inventory, all of which relates to the manufacturing unit. The accounting method used (see Chapter 5) and the amounts of inventories held as raw materials, supplies, work in process, and finished equipment and parts are reported in footnotes, and the adjustment to their last-in, first-out (LIFO) cost is also reported in the footnote.

The footnote discloses the different cost and valuation methods used, primarily LIFO in the United States and first-in, first-out (FIFO) in other countries. Current assets reflect a mixture of different cost methods; depending on the accounting method used, current costs or market values may be used or reported parenthetically or in footnotes.

In Deere's 1991 balance sheet, there is no separate classification of current assets. However, the same asset accounts are present, and the order is approximately the same.

Note that short-term investments are not reported separately in the 1991 balance sheet but may have been reported as a component of cash and cash equivalents.[5] The marketable securities shown in the 1991 balance sheet are the long-term investments of Deere's insurance and health care subsidiaries. A footnote contains details regarding this portfolio.

Noncurrent Assets

The major long-term asset reported by Deere is property and equipment, both in 1988 (reported at cost and net of accumulated depreciation) and 1991 (only net amount shown). Details of land, buildings, machinery, equipment, dies and parts, and construction in progress included in this category are contained in footnotes.

---

[4]The 1988 and 1991 footnotes on receivables are instructive: the 1991 footnote contains much more information because the receivables of the (now consolidated) finance subsidiaries are included.

[5]Under the provisions of SFAS 95, which became effective in 1988, risk-free marketable securities with maturities of less than three months are aggregated with cash for reporting purposes. In some countries (but not in the United States), cash may also be net of overdrafts.

Those footnotes also indicate the firm's policy of capitalizing expansion and replacement expenditures; they are recorded as assets when acquired and are expensed as used in operations. Repairs and maintenance costs are expensed as incurred. Depreciation methods and expense for each year are also disclosed.

The reported capital expenditures for the period include assets purchased for cash as well as leased property and capitalized interest. The cash flow information footnote provides information on capital expenditures not requiring cash. For firms capitalizing interest, the amount will appear either on the face of the income statement or in a footnote. Many of these issues are discussed in Chapter 6.

The economic substance of some leasing arrangements is often equivalent to an installment purchase, and GAAP mandates capitalization (recognition as a long-term asset) of the present value of the periodic lease payments in such cases. Other leases (operating leases) do not receive balance sheet recognition. Footnotes provide data regarding both capital and operating leases.[6]

Investments in unconsolidated, equity method affiliates[7] are reported at Deere's investment in the net assets, that is, original cost plus its share of their undistributed earnings. The relevant accounting policy and cash flow effects are also detailed in the SSAP, which states that foreign equipment affiliates are included. The carrying amounts are also affected by the foreign currency translation methods used.

The physical, tangible assets listed are followed in the 1991 balance sheet by two intangible assets. The first, goodwill, resulted from the acquisitions of Funk Manufacturing in 1989 and SABO in 1991, both purchased at prices in excess of the fair market value of their tangible assets, requiring the allocation of the excess purchase price to goodwill.[8] The second intangible is a pension intangible asset that resulted from recognition of the minimum pension liability as required by SFAS 87.[9]

The reader should note that carrying amounts for various long-term assets depend on management's choice of accounting methods, assumptions, and estimates. The classification of assets in the order of liquidity, tangibility, and risk is also relevant to the development and use of financial ratios.

Current Liabilities

In 1988, Deere's current liabilities include short-term notes payable, primarily commercial paper. A footnote discloses the credit lines (separately and jointly) available to the different units of the firm. The most important disclosure involves the restrictions imposed by the credit lines. In 1988, Deere's finance unit was required to maintain a minimum ratio of earnings to interest costs and was subject to other limitations on the amount of debt relative to equity. These restrictions are designed to protect lenders.

The 1991 footnote reports the amounts of interest rate swap and interest cap agreements that serve as hedges of the firm's exposure to interest rate changes. The firm

---

[6]See Chapter 8 for comparison of capital and operating leases and their effect on financial statements.
[7]See Chapter 11 for discussion of equity method.
[8]See Chapter 12 for discussion of the purchase method of accounting.
[9]The minimum pension liability represents the excess of the accumulated benefit obligation (present value of pension benefits earned to date) over plan assets and accruals (see Chapter 9).

states that the credit (probability of default by the counterparty) and market risks (impact of changes in rates) are not significant.[10]

Both the 1988 and 1991 balance sheets report payables to unconsolidated subsidiaries and affiliates (which in 1991 reflect only the amounts owed to the less than 50% owned units). The 1988 balance includes liabilities to wholly owned finance subsidiaries that are excluded in 1991 because they are now fully consolidated.

Accounts payable and accrued expenses include Deere's short-term obligations to suppliers and employees.[11] Dividends payable reflect dividends declared but not paid as of year end. The final component of current liabilities, income tax payable, is the amount owed at the end of the period. In this case, it also includes deferred taxes, the effect of timing differences in revenue, and expense recognition between tax returns and financial statements.[12]

Liabilities in 1991 include insurance and health care claims and reserves, which represent future policy benefits and unpaid losses of those units. The 1988 balance sheet does not include these liabilities because these subsidiaries were reported under the equity method.

Noncurrent Liabilities

Long-term debt (see Chapter 8) consists of the domestic and foreign borrowings of Deere and its finance units. In 1988, the finance affiliates' debt was not included since the units were reported under the equity method; only the net assets were shown in Deere's balance sheet. The firm reports capitalized lease obligations as a component of noncurrent debt. Credit balances of deferred income taxes and pension accruals are among the other liabilities included here.

The footnote on long-term debt details the categories of borrowings in order of their priority in liquidation and time to maturity, and the repayment schedules for the next five years. In both 1988 and 1991, restrictions in the borrowing agreements required Deere to maintain minimum working capital and consolidated net worth and restricted its use of retained earnings for dividend payments and repurchases of common stock.

Lease obligation disclosures include payment schedules for the next five years, total payments thereafter on both operating and capitalized leases, and the present value of capitalized lease payments. No present value disclosures are provided for operating leases.

The current portion of capital lease payments (principal due in next year) has been included in "accounts payable and accrued expenses," but it should be segregated for the analysis of liquidity and leverage. Rental expense recorded under operating leases is also disclosed; note that these expenses are a fixed cost and should be treated as such in ratio analysis.

Firms often raise capital using hybrid securities with debt and equity characteristics. Common examples include convertible debt or preferred stock and mandatorily redeem-

---

[10]These disclosures are required by SFAS 105 (1991), which is discussed in greater detail in Chapters 10 and 14.

[11]A footnote provides a breakdown of this category (reproduced for 1991 only).

[12]See Chapter 7.

able preferred stock. These securities are listed after noncurrent debt but prior to stockholders' equity.

Stockholders' Equity

This section reports the number of preferred and common shares authorized and the amount currently outstanding. Most firms issue par value stock, and that amount is disclosed here. The excess of the issue price above par is reported as additional paid-in capital (APIC). The par and additional amounts have little economic significance except in some jurisdictions where they may be the basis for taxes.

The treasury stock account reflects the firm's purchases of its own shares. Such repurchases are reflected at cost; when treasury shares are retired, the excess cost over par value reduces APIC.

The equity section also includes the cumulative translation adjustment (CTA), which reports the accumulated effect of translating foreign currency transactions and the accounts of foreign affiliates.[13] The CTA footnote also discloses Deere's hedges of currency exposure on its foreign investments, current and expected inventory purchases, and short-term debt.

The final component of the equity section is retained earnings, the cumulative undistributed earnings of the firm. Footnotes disclose any restrictions on dividend payments or stock repurchases, another form of protection for creditors since it guarantees a minimum, continuing equity investment in the firm.

Financial Statement Footnotes

Some footnotes provide information on balance sheet components like receivables and debt as previously discussed. Other footnotes contain information on events that have not been recognized on the balance sheet. A brief discussion of these footnotes follows.

Stock Compensation Plans

Deere reports restricted stock plans, options for key employees, and employee stock purchase and savings plans. The Financial Accounting Standards Board has undertaken a project that may result in greater financial statement impact for these plans. These disclosures generally have greater significance for young, high-growth firms that use such plans to attract and retain key employees.

Commitments and Contingencies

Some footnotes provide information on unresolved litigation, warranties and guarantees on products and financing transactions, contingent liabilities resulting from recourse agreements on sales of receivables and guarantees of the debt of affiliates, and commitments for construction and capital expenditures. These contingencies do not meet recognition criteria for the balance sheet, but the disclosures should be evaluated for potential impacts on future earnings, cash flows, and leverage.

---

[13]See Chapter 13 for analysis of foreign operations.

Statement of Consolidated Income and Retained Earnings

Deere's 1988 and 1991 income statements, like the balance sheets for those years, reflect the contrasting perspectives of the equity and consolidation methods. The 1988 income statement reports net sales and finance and interest income earned, with supporting disclosure of revenue recognition methods in the SSAP. Sales are reported net of returns and allowances. Foreign exchange gains and miscellaneous income are also reported.

Generally, sales are recognized when products are shipped to dealers. There is a time lag between Deere's recognition of sales (to dealers) and final sales (by dealers) to customers. In such cases, one should analyze the growth of sales and dealer receivables carefully. The provision for doubtful accounts is disclosed separately, but it has been reported as a component of selling expense.

An important feature of the 1988 income statement is the reporting of the (posttax) equity in net income of the financial service, insurance, and health care affiliates. Summarized income statements are provided in the footnotes.

The 1991 report contains both consolidated and equity method income statements for the equipment operations and a separate income statement for the financial services subsidiaries. Note that finance and interest income is earned mainly by the financial services unit for which it represents revenue. The revenues and expenses of the financial services units have been included in the consolidated income statement. Some items are exclusively originated by the equipment unit (cost of goods sold) or the insurance units (premium revenues). Note that interest is the primary expense for the finance unit.

The 1991 consolidated income statement includes insurance and health care claims and benefits. These expenses, and the interest expense reported by the financial services unit, were not reported in Deere's 1988 income statement, which contained only the net income of these unconsolidated affiliates. As previously noted, details of these unconsolidated operations were disclosed as supplementary data.

The 1991 income statement reports restructuring costs, resulting from closing plants and reducing employment costs. The footnote disclosure is perfunctory, and the management discussion and analysis does not provide useful additional information.[14]

The 1988 income statement reflects two new reporting requirements adopted that year. First, the firm changed its income tax accounting method. Under the new method,[15] deferred tax balances were remeasured to reflect current tax rates rather than rates for the period in which the timing differences originated. The entire impact was on the deferred taxes of the financial services unit. The gain from adoption of the new standard was reported separately in the income statement.

While not highlighted in the income statement, in 1988 Deere also adopted the provisions of SFAS 87 for its foreign pension plans.[16] Adoption of the standard required additional footnote disclosures but had no significant impact on reported income. This change was reported only in the SSAP and pension footnotes.

In both 1991 and 1988, Deere reports health care and life insurance costs for retired employees; Deere expenses these costs as incurred. A footnote in the *1991 Annual*

---

[14]See Chapter 6 for discussion of impairment and other "restructuring" charges.

[15]SFAS 96, discussed in Chapter 7.

[16]See Chapter 9 for the analysis of pension and other postretirement benefit plans.

Report discusses the impact of SFAS 106, which requires accrual accounting for these plans and which must be adopted by Deere no later than fiscal 1994.

Statement of Consolidated Cash Flows

Deere adopted SFAS 95, Statement of Cash Flows, in 1988. However, like the vast majority of companies, Deere uses the indirect method to report cash flows. In 1988, it reported net income of $315 million and cash flows from operations (CFO) of $97 million. The indirect method computes CFO by adjusting net income for (1) noncash items such as depreciation expense, deferred income taxes, and the undistributed income of unconsolidated subsidiaries[17] and (2) the changes in the operating accounts, including receivables, inventories, and payables. In 1988, both receivables and inventories balances increased substantially contributing to the low CFO relative to reported income.

The 1991 statement of cash flows shows CFO of $613 million despite a loss of $20 million because of decreases in receivables and inventory and the addback of noncash restructuring costs. Note that when the financial units are reported under the equity method, the CFO is $438 million, or $175 million lower. The difference can be traced to receivables. Deere treats credit receivables as investing activities increasing CFO; in 1991 the firm invested (net) $907 million in credit receivables.

Turning to financing cash flow, most borrowing was done by the finance units; the equipment segment reported net outflows of $5 million, whereas the finance unit raised nearly $800 million. Deere also provides a separate footnote on cash flow that reports the cash outflow for interest and taxes paid, as well as Deere's noncash investing and financing activities. This footnote also reports the assumption of liabilities as a result of Deere's acquisition of two firms that year.

MANAGEMENT DISCUSSION AND ANALYSIS

Public companies in the United States must provide a detailed financial review in a section called Management Discussion and Analysis (MD&A). This section usually begins with a description of the firm's primary business and segments. In 1991 Deere reports four segments, one of which is financial services, now consolidated. Thus consolidation has the added benefit of significant discussion of factors that affect the success of this segment's operations; the MD&A adds information on planning and strategic issues as well.

The MD&A's business and segment review details net sales by segment and by major domestic and foreign markets. Trends in and changing reliance on different segments and markets can provide signals of future prospects. This summary review is followed by a narrative discussion of market (economic and business) conditions and their expected impact on the firm's operations and market share prospects.

The MD&A contains a detailed discussion of operating results with a breakdown of net sales and revenues by market augmented with a similar analysis of operating and net

[17]The undistributed earnings added back represent the portion of Deere's equity in income of unconsolidated affiliates (a component of Deere's net income) that was not received as dividends.

income. Unusual factors are detailed. From the 1988 MD&A we have reproduced paragraphs dealing with the effect of work stoppages, the change in tax methods, LIFO liquidations,[18] and costs of early retirement. The 1991 MD&A contains a similar discussion of "nonrecurring" items.

The reader may want to eliminate the impact of these items from income reported for these periods.[19] But it must be noted that they also have implications for the future. The change in method of accounting for income taxes affects future income tax expense. LIFO liquidations should be evaluated for indications of changes in demand or technology. Early retirement costs may be unusual, but the reader will note that such costs were incurred in both 1987 and 1991.

Discussions of operating results by industry segments and geographic area are also informative. The MD&A discussion supplements the extensive segment disclosures required by SFAS 14 (see Chapter 11), contained in a footnote.

The MD&A is expected to contain forward-looking information. Readers can therefore expect to see discussion of economic trends and expected changes in markets. Such disclosures can help analysts forecast future profitability. They may also alert the reader to important issues such as labor negotiations, expiring patents, and new products.

Capital Resources and Liquidity

The MD&A also focuses on the balance sheet and statement of cash flows in its evaluation of capital resources and liquidity. This section incorporates a discussion of operating, investing, and financing cash flows; that is, it provides information on the firm's cash generating ability. The 1991 MD&A notes the fundamental differences between the characteristics of the cash flows of its different segments and provides a separate discussion of capital resources and liquidity for these segments.

A detailed analysis of changes in operating and long-term investments is provided. For example, in the 1991 Deere reports its investment in inventory, current and expected future capital outlays, and the increasing financing needs of its receivables portfolio. This discussion should be read in conjunction with other footnotes detailing the constraints on borrowing and the limitations on available lines of credit.

TEN-YEAR REVIEW

The 1988 Deere financial statements conclude with a 10-year summary of both the balance sheet and income statement. Such summaries can be most helpful for analysis, provided the user is aware of the pitfalls.

The advantage is clearly stated. Especially for a cyclical company such as Deere, an evaluation of firm performance should encompass at least one full economic cycle to see how revenues, earnings, cash flows, and ratios behave over the cycle. Such insights are

---

[18]LIFO liquidations occur when firms reduce inventory, bringing old (lower-cost) layers into cost of goods sold and inflating reported income. See the inventory footnote for additional discussion.

[19]See Chapter 15 for an extensive discussion of the treatment of Deere's "nonrecurring" items. Chapter 2 contains a more general discussion of this topic.

also important when predicting the impact of the analyst's economic assumptions on future earnings and liquidity. Eleven years of data are considered optimal, as they permit the calculation of 10-year growth rates (which can be subdivided into shorter time periods as well).

There are, however, risks in using these data without deeper analysis. The data shown for prior years may not be the data actually reported for those years. Prior years may have been restated for acquisitions (pooling method), dispositions (discontinued operations), or retroactive accounting changes.

While Deere did not have significant acquisition or disposition activity during the 1980s, there was a significant accounting change: the consolidation of financial subsidiaries required by SFAS 94. When the new standard was applied in fiscal 1989, the company restated previously reported data.

Thus data in the 1991 summary[20] have been restated (1985–1988) from that originally reported. While some data are not affected (earnings per share and book value per share, for example), balance sheet and income statement data are significantly different. The summary does not refer to this restatement.

Other accounting changes that have sometimes been adopted with retroactive effect include income taxes (see Chapter 7) and fixed assets (see Chapter 6). Accounting changes can also have pervasive impact on future reported operating results, as discussed in the specific chapters.

Firms that restate prior periods for acquisitions or discontinued operations provide even greater challenges. Restatement does provide past data on the same set of operations now comprising the firm. However, restatement includes (acquired) operations that were not managed by the firm and excludes (discontinued) operations that were managed by the firm. Thus restated data should be used cautiously to predict future performance.

Finally, the importance of reading financial statement footnotes cannot be overemphasized. In addition to highlighting accounting changes, acquisitions, and dispositions, footnotes are essential to the proper interpretation of financial data.

---

[20]The *1991 Annual Report* contains only a seven-year summary (1985–1991). It is possible that the company presented only seven years of data because of the cost of restating data for years prior to 1985 for the consolidation of its financial subsidiaries.

EXHIBIT 1B-1. DEERE & COMPANY
Extracts from Financial Statements, Year Ended October 31, 1988

Financial Review

MANAGEMENT'S DISCUSSION AND ANALYSIS (UNAUDITED)

Results of Operations for the Years Ended October 31, 1988, 1987 and 1986

1988 Compared with 1987

Worldwide net income in 1988 was $315 million or $4.32 per share on a fully diluted basis compared with a net loss of $99 million or $1.46 per share in 1987. Last year's results reflect the severe effects of the work stoppage which virtually shut down the company's United States agricultural and industrial equipment factories throughout the entire first quarter of 1987, resulting in a first quarter 1987 net loss of $193 million or $2.84 per share.

Net income in 1988 benefited by $41 million from the utilization of tax-loss carryforwards. Conversely, the net loss incurred in 1987 was increased by the company's inability to recognize approximately $23 million of income tax benefits associated with tax-loss carryforwards.

Results in both years were also affected by certain non-recurring and unusual items. In the first quarter of 1988, the company adopted new accounting rules for income taxes, which resulted in our unconsolidated retail finance, leasing and insurance subsidiaries recording one-time gains totaling $29 million or $.42 per share. Results in 1987 benefited on an after-tax basis by $14 million or $.21 per share from the reduction of inventories valued on a last-in, first-out (LIFO) basis. As part of the company's ongoing cost reduction efforts, an after-tax provision of $25 million or $.37 per share was made in 1987 for separation and early retirement allowances relating to employment reductions. Excluding these non-recurring and unusual items, net income would have been $286 million or $3.90 per share on a fully diluted basis in 1988 and the 1987 net loss would have been $88 million or $1.30 per share.

1987 Compared with 1986

Results in both years were also affected by certain non-recurring and unusual items. Results in 1987 and 1986 benefited on an after-tax basis by $14 million or $.21 per share and $54 million or $.80 per share, respectively, from the reduction of inventories valued on a LIFO basis. As part of the company's ongoing cost reduction efforts, provisions were made for separation and early retirement allowances relating to employment reductions and for the restructuring of certain manufacturing operations. These provisions in 1987 and 1986 were $25 million or $.37 per share and $58 million or $.85 per share, respectively. Excluding these non-recurring and unusual items, the net loss would have been $88 million or $1.30 per share in 1987 and $226 million or $3.33 per share in 1986.

The consolidated group incurred a net loss of $193 million in 1987 compared with a net loss of $309 million in 1986. Results for both years reflect the effects of the work stoppage, which was the principal reason for consolidated group net losses of $157 million in the fourth quarter of 1986 and $211 million in the first quarter of 1987. Both years were also adversely affected by very low capacity utilization and high levels of sales incentive costs. Operating results improved substantially in 1987 because of higher North American farm and industrial equipment sales and production volumes, improved operating efficiency in North America and better price realization, although sales incentives remained high.

INDEPENDENT AUDITORS' REPORT

Deloitte
Haskins+Sells

Deere & Company:

We have audited the accompanying consolidated balance sheets of Deere & Company and subsidiaries as of October 31, 1988 and 1987 and the related statements of consolidated income and retained earnings and of consolidated cash flows for each of the three years in the period ended October 31, 1988. These financial statements are the responsibility of the company's management. Our responsibility is to express an opinion on these financial statements based on our audits.

We conducted our audits in accordance with generally accepted auditing standards. These standards require that we plan and perform the audit to obtain reasonable assurance about whether the financial statements are free of material misstatement. An audit includes examining, on a test basis, evidence supporting the amounts and disclosures in the financial statements. An audit also includes assessing the accounting principles used and significant estimates made by management, as well as evaluating the overall financial statement presentation. We believe that our audits provide a reasonable basis for our opinion.

In our opinion, the accompanying financial statements present fairly, in all material respects, the financial position of Deere & Company and subsidiaries at October 31, 1988 and 1987 and the results of their operations and their cash flows for each of the three years in the period ended October 31, 1988 in conformity with generally accepted accounting principles.

As discussed on page 47 of the Notes to Consolidated Financial Statements, the company changed its method of accounting for income taxes in 1988 to conform with Statement of Financial Accounting Standards No. 96.

Deloitte Haskins & Sells

200 East Randolph Drive
Chicago, Illinois 60601
December 6, 1988

EXHIBIT 1B-1. *(Continued)*

Deere & Company

STATEMENT OF CONSOLIDATED INCOME AND RETAINED EARNINGS

(In thousands of dollars except per share amounts)	1988	Year Ended October 31 1987	1986
Sales and Other Income			
Net sales	$5,364,810	$4,134,534	$3,516,289
Finance and interest income earned (includes net interest received from unconsolidated subsidiaries and affiliates of $1,785 in 1988, $6,331 in 1987 and $8,039 in 1986)	66,131	96,254	89,300
Foreign exchange gain	532	1,232	
Miscellaneous income	22,933	21,390	19,554
Total	5,454,406	4,253,410	3,625,143
Less			
Cost of goods sold	4,366,640	3,668,563	3,270,670
Research and development expenses	215,916	213,830	224,743
Selling, administrative and general expenses	495,315	487,587	508,208
Interest expense	160,792	185,973	203,769
Foreign exchange loss			6,507
Miscellaneous charges	3,016	3,306	3,939
Total	5,241,679	4,559,259	4,217,836
Income (Loss) of Consolidated Group Before Income Taxes	212,727	(305,849)	(592,693)
Provision (credit) for income taxes	32,953	(112,681)	(283,936)
Income (Loss) of Consolidated Group	179,774	(193,168)	(308,757)
Equity in Net Income (Loss) of Unconsolidated Subsidiaries and Affiliates			
Retail finance and leasing subsidiaries	64,648	51,773	54,212
Insurance subsidiaries	37,116	37,872	37,007
Other	5,157	4,504	(11,734)
Total before change in accounting	106,921	94,149	79,485
Change in accounting for income taxes	28,744		
Total	135,665	94,149	79,485
Net Income (Loss)	$ 315,439	$ (99,019)	$ (229,272)
Income per share before change in accounting— $4.06 primary and $3.90 fully diluted in 1988			
Change in accounting for income taxes per share— $.42 in 1988			
Net income (loss) per share— $4.48 primary and $4.32 fully diluted in 1988; $(1.46) in 1987; and $(3.38) in 1986			
Deduct			
Cash dividends declared	(46,885)	(16,962)	(50,881)
Dividends per share—$.65 in 1988, $.25 in 1987 and $.75 in 1986			
Other adjustments to retained earnings	(26)	(96)	(5)
Retained Earnings at Beginning of Year	1,480,918	1,596,995	1,877,153
Retained Earnings at End of Year	$1,749,446	$1,480,918	$1,596,995

The information on pages 31 through 51 is an integral part of this statement.

EXHIBIT 1B-1. *(Continued)*

Deere & Company

CONSOLIDATED BALANCE SHEET

| (In thousands of dollars except per share amounts) | October 31 | |
ASSETS	1988	1987
Current Assets		
Cash	$ 36,248	$ 49,817
Short-term investments—at cost which approximates market value	12,742	66,567
Refundable income taxes	3,178	16,258
Receivables from unconsolidated subsidiaries and affiliates	46,699	29,139
Trade receivables:		
Dealer accounts and notes	2,311,083	2,115,746
Retail notes (less deferred finance income of $911 in 1988 and $1,348 in 1987)	25,334	26,492
Total	2,336,417	2,142,238
Less allowances for doubtful accounts	28,078	31,731
Trade receivables—net	2,308,339	2,110,507
Inventories	708,277	464,977
Total current assets	3,115,483	2,737,265
Property and Equipment—at cost	3,056,442	2,942,641
Less accumulated depreciation	2,063,237	1,960,459
Property and equipment—net	993,205	982,182
Investments in and Advances to Unconsolidated Subsidiaries and Affiliates	1,052,847	975,702
Other Assets	33,427	21,346
Deferred Charges	50,292	43,376
Total	$5,245,254	$4,759,871
LIABILITIES AND STOCKHOLDERS' EQUITY		
Current Liabilities		
Notes payable	$ 455,462	$ 342,075
Current maturities of long-term debt	21,132	13,387
Payables to unconsolidated subsidiaries and affiliates	30,763	74,554
Accounts payable and accrued expenses	1,121,925	1,036,842
Dividends payable	14,911	4,248
Accrued taxes (including deferred income taxes of $17,761 in 1988 and $14,103 in 1987)	84,131	58,272
Total current liabilities	1,728,324	1,529,378
Noncurrent Liabilities		
Long-term debt	804,587	1,051,513
Capital lease obligations	12,357	10,475
Pension accruals and other liabilities	229,380	238,926
Deferred income taxes	14,431	9,450
Stockholders' Equity		
Common stock, $1 par value (authorized—200,000,000 shares;		
issued—74,790,190 shares in 1988 and 68,186,467 in 1987) at stated value	760,491	496,563
Retained earnings	1,749,446	1,480,918
Cumulative translation adjustment	(51,037)	(54,627)
Total	2,458,900	1,922,854
Less common stock in treasury, 174,927 shares, at cost	2,725	2,725
Total stockholders' equity	2,456,175	1,920,129
Total	$5,245,254	$4,759,871

The information on pages 31 through 51 is an integral part of this statement.

EXHIBIT 1B-1. *(Continued)*

Deere & Company

STATEMENT OF CONSOLIDATED CASH FLOWS

(In thousands of dollars)	Year Ended October 31 1988	1987	1986
Cash Flows from Operating Activities			
Net income (loss)	$315,439	$ (99,019)	$ (229,272)
Adjustments to reconcile net income (loss) to net cash provided by operating activities:			
Provision for depreciation	187,523	183,972	202,291
Undistributed earnings of unconsolidated subsidiaries and affiliates	(58,710)	(54,547)	(43,197)
Provision for deferred income taxes	9,197	(118,213)	(249,582)
Changes in assets and liabilities:			
Receivables	(192,996)	9,014	700,539
Inventories	(242,910)	73,792	80,983
Accounts payable and accrued expenses	97,109	108,440	(114,723)
Other	(16,980)	235,662	(62,490)
Net cash provided by operating activities	97,672	339,101	284,549
Cash Flows from Investing Activities			
Purchase of property and equipment	(204,489)	(191,130)	(208,833)
Sale to finance subsidiary of John Deere products leased to customers			93,020
Reorganization of United States retail finance operations		86,292	
Increase in investment in foreign subsidiary			(27,076)
Tax benefits related to operations of unconsolidated subsidiaries			(10,100)
Other	(14,420)	45,086	43,909
Net cash used for investment activities	(218,909)	(59,752)	(109,080)
Cash Flows from Financing Activities			
Proceeds from common stock issued for stock options	33,481	3,587	473
Proceeds from long-term debt			274,381
Increase (decrease) in notes payable	91,645	(86,001)	(176,483)
Payments on long-term debt	(24,149)	(230,337)	(113,962)
Dividends paid	(36,222)	(21,198)	(59,345)
Other	(7,351)	(10,890)	(11,457)
Net cash provided by (used for) financing activities	57,404	(344,839)	(86,393)
Effect of Exchange Rate Changes on Cash	(3,561)	217	4,758
Net increase (decrease) in cash and cash equivalents	(67,394)	(65,273)	93,834
Cash and cash equivalents at beginning of year	116,384	181,657	87,823
Cash and cash equivalents at end of year	$ 48,990	$116,384	$181,657

The information on pages 31 through 51 is an integral part of this statement.

RETAIL FINANCE AND LEASING SUBSIDIARIES

Condensed combined financial information of the retail finance and leasing subsidiaries in millions of dollars follows:

Financial Position	October 31 1988	1987
Short-term investments—at cost which approximates market	$ 164.9	$ 190.9
Amounts due from Deere & Company		74.6
Net retail notes and wholesale receivables	2,620.5	2,374.3
Net investment in leases	355.7	424.0
Other assets	132.3	108.1
Total assets	$3,273.4	$3,171.9
Notes payable—due within one year	$1,720.4	$1,628.1
Amounts due Deere & Company	37.1	17.1
Other liabilities	218.0	269.8
Long-term debt	589.8	597.7
Stockholder's equity	708.1	659.2
Total liabilities and stockholder's equity	$3,273.4	$3,171.9

Summary of Operations	Year Ended October 31 1988	1987	1986
Earned finance and rental income	$385.5	$305.7	$324.3
Expenses:			
Interest	180.1	152.7	175.8
Insurance	19.8	17.5	22.6
Depreciation	17.3	22.5	7.1
Operating, administrative and other	68.7	28.6	28.6
Provision for income taxes	35.0	32.6	36.0
Total	320.9	253.9	270.1
Income before change in accounting	64.6	51.8	54.2
Change in accounting for income taxes	25.0		
Net income	$ 89.6	$ 51.8	$ 54.2

EXHIBIT 1B-1. *(Continued)*

Notes To Consolidated Financial Statements

SUMMARY OF SIGNIFICANT ACCOUNTING POLICIES

Following are significant accounting policies in addition to those included in the following notes to the consolidated financial statements.

All wholly-owned subsidiaries, except for the retail finance, leasing, insurance and health care subsidiaries, are consolidated in these financial statements. The company records its investment in each unconsolidated subsidiary (more than 50 percent ownership) and affiliated company (20-50 percent ownership) at the related equity in the net assets of such subsidiary or affiliate. Consolidated retained earnings at October 31, 1988 includes undistributed earnings of the unconsolidated subsidiaries of $605 million and undistributed earnings of the affiliates of $33 million. Dividends from unconsolidated subsidiaries in 1988, 1987 and 1986 were $77 million, $48 million and $35 million, respectively. Dividends from affiliates were $.4 million in 1988 and $1 million in 1986.

Sales are generally recorded by the company when products and service parts are shipped to independent dealers. Provisions for sales incentives and returns and allowances are made at the time of sale or at inception of the incentive programs. There is a time lag, which varies based on the timing and level of retail demand, between the date the company records a sale and when the dealer sells the equipment to a retail customer.

In the first quarter of 1988, the company adopted for all significant foreign pension plans Financial Accounting Standards Board (FASB) Statement No. 87, Employers' Accounting for Pensions, and FASB Statement No. 88, Employers' Accounting for Settlements and Curtailments of Defined Benefit Pension Plans and for Termination Benefits. These standards were previously adopted in the fourth quarter of 1986 for the company's United States pension plans.

In the first quarter of 1988, the company adopted FASB Statement No. 96, Accounting for Income Taxes. Financial statements for previous years were not restated. See "Income Taxes", on page 47, for further information.

In the fourth quarter of 1988, the company adopted FASB Statement No. 95, Statement of Cash Flows. The statement of cash flows replaces the statement of changes in financial position. Information for 1987 and 1986 has been restated.

In May 1988, the company and Hitachi Construction Machinery Company of Japan entered into an agreement and formed a 50-50 joint venture for the manufacture of hydraulic excavators in the United States for distribution in North, Central and South America. The current excavator lines of the company and Hitachi will continue to be marketed to the company's dealers through the existing distribution system. They will also be marketed to Hitachi dealers through the existing Hitachi distribution system, which is now part of the joint venture.

Certain amounts for prior years have been reclassified to conform with 1988 financial statement presentations.

The credit agreements contain provisions requiring net working capital (the excess of consolidated current assets over consolidated current liabilities), excluding loans under the credit agreements, to be not less than $950 million, and requiring consolidated tangible net worth to be not less than $1,600 million. Indenture agreements relating to certain of the company's debenture issues also contain provisions limiting the amount of retained earnings available for payment of dividends and purchase or redemption of the company's common stock. Under the most restrictive terms of these provisions, $437 million of the consolidated retained earnings balance of $1,749 million at October 31, 1988 was free of restrictions as to payment of dividends or acquisition of the company's common stock.

TRADE RECEIVABLES

Dealer accounts and notes receivable at October 31, 1988 totaled $2,311 million, $187 million of which were notes. At October 31, 1987, dealer accounts and notes were $2,116 million, $191 million of which were notes. The ratios of worldwide receivables from dealers to the last 12 months' net sales were 43 percent, 51 percent and 60 percent at October 31, 1988, 1987 and 1986, respectively.

Trade receivables arise from sales to dealers of John Deere products and are secured largely by the related equipment. Generally, terms to dealers require payments as the equipment which secures the indebtedness is sold to retail customers. Interest is charged on balances outstanding after certain interest-free periods, which range from 6 to 9 months for industrial equipment, 9 months for agricultural tractors, and from 9 to 24 months for most other equipment.

All receivables from dealers have been classified as current assets based on the average collection period which is less than twelve months. The collection period for receivables from dealers decreased in 1988 and 1987. During recent years prior to 1987, the collection period had increased because of the decline in agricultural equipment retail sales, but still averaged less than twelve months. The portion of outstanding trade receivables at October 31, 1988 that will be collected in the next twelve months depends largely upon the amount of related goods sold by dealers to retail customers. As of October 31, 1988 and 1987, the percentage of total receivables outstanding for periods exceeding twelve months was 9 percent and 14 percent, respectively.

Retail notes included in the consolidated balance sheet at October 31, 1988 and 1987 represented retail notes of overseas farm and industrial equipment customers. Retail notes were $25 million at October 31, 1988, one percent of which mature in more than one year. At October 31, 1987, retail notes were $26 million, two percent of which matured in more than one year. All of Deere & Company's retail notes receivable include finance charges based on the company's finance charge rate in effect at the time the respective notes were acquired or, for variable-rate notes, the current rate applicable from month to month on such notes. Almost all retail notes acquired from farm and industrial equipment customers in the United States and Canada are sold to the retail finance subsidiaries. Comments regarding those subsidiaries appear on page 38.

The company sold to other financial institutions retail notes receivable having unpaid balances at the time of sale of $23 million in 1988, $41 million in 1987 and $25 million in 1986. At October 31, 1988 and 1987, the unpaid balances of receivables previously sold were $23 million and $29 million, respectively.

The components of net periodic pension cost and the significant assumptions for the United States plans consisted of the following in percents and millions of dollars:

	1988	1987	1986
Service cost	$ 44	$ 51	$ 37
Interest cost	191	180	165
Return on assets	(292)	58	(446)
Net amortization and deferral	93	(254)	248
Net cost	$ 36	$ 35	$ 4
Discount rates for obligations	9.3%	9.5%	8.5%
Discount rates for expenses	9.5%	8.5%	9.6%
Assumed rates of compensation increases	6.3%	6.3%	6.1%
Expected long-term rates of return	9.7%	9.7%	9.7%

The reconciliation of the funded status of the United States plans in millions of dollars follows:

	October 31			
	1988		1987	
	Assets Exceed Accumu-lated Benefits	Accumu-lated Benefits Exceed Assets	Assets Exceed Accumu-lated Benefits	Accumu-lated Benefits Exceed Assets
Actuarial present value of benefit obligations				
Vested benefit obligation	$ (839)	$ (859)	$ (804)	$ (780)
Nonvested benefit obligation	(85)	(163)	(75)	(130)
Accumulated benefit obligation	(924)	(1,022)	(879)	(910)
Excess of projected benefit obligation over accumulated benefit obligation	(268)	(55)	(234)	(38)
Projected benefit obligation	(1,192)	(1,077)	(1,113)	(948)
Plan assets at fair value	1,284	899	1,209	834
Projected benefit obligation (in excess of) or less than plan assets	92	(178)	96	(114)
Unrecognized net gain	(35)	(8)	(24)	(24)
Prior service cost not yet recognized in net periodic pension cost		156		115
Remaining unrecognized transition net asset from Nov. 1, 1985	(163)	(34)	(175)	(38)
Unfunded accrued pension cost recognized in the consolidated balance sheet	$ (106)	$ (64)	$ (103)	$ (61)

The components of net periodic pension cost and the significant assumptions for the foreign plans consisted of the following in percents and millions of dollars:

	1988
Service cost	$ 8
Interest cost	16
Return on assets	(8)
Net amortization and deferral	2
Net cost	$18
Discount rates for obligations	7.0-9.5%
Discount rates for expenses	7.0-9.5%
Assumed rates of compensation increases	4.0-7.0%
Expected long-term rate of return	9.5%

The reconciliation of the funded status of the foreign plans in millions of dollars follows:

	October 31 1988	
	Assets Exceed Accumulated Benefits	Accumulated Benefits Exceed Assets
Actuarial present value of benefit obligations		
Vested benefit obligation	$(47)	$(129)
Nonvested benefit obligation	(2)	(6)
Accumulated benefit obligation	(49)	(135)
Excess of projected benefit obligation over accumulated benefit obligation	(10)	(31)
Projected benefit obligation	(59)	(166)
Plan assets at fair value	97	
Projected benefit obligation (in excess of) or less than plan assets	38	(166)
Unrecognized net gain	(6)	(4)
Remaining unrecognized transition net (asset) obligation from November 1, 1987	(32)	68
Unfunded accrued pension cost recognized in the consolidated balance sheet	$ 0	$(102)

PENSION AND OTHER RETIREMENT BENEFITS

The company has several pension plans covering substantially all of its United States employees and employees in certain foreign countries. The United States plans and significant foreign plans in Canada, Germany and France are defined benefit plans in which the benefits are based primarily on years of service and employee compensation near retirement. It is the company's policy to fund its United States plans according to the 1974 Employee Retirement Income Security Act (ERISA). In Canada and France, the company's funding is in accordance with local laws and income tax regulations, while the German pension plan is unfunded. Plan assets in the United States, Canada and France consist primarily of common stocks, common trust funds, government securities and corporate debt securities.

In 1988, the company adopted for all significant foreign plans FASB Statement No. 87, Employers' Accounting for Pensions. This standard was previously adopted in 1986 for the company's United States plans. For years prior to 1988, pension expense for foreign plans is reported under the previous accounting principles.

EXHIBIT 1B-1. *(Continued)*

Deere & Company

TEN-YEAR SUMMARY OF CONSOLIDATED INCOME AND RETAINED EARNINGS

(In thousands of dollars except per share amounts)	1988	1987	1986
Sales and Other Income			
Farm equipment sales	$4,202,721	$3,223,216	$2,648,594
Industrial equipment sales	1,162,089	911,318	867,695
Total net sales	5,364,810	4,134,534	3,516,289
Finance and interest income earned	66,131	96,254	89,300
Foreign exchange gain	532	1,232	
Miscellaneous income	22,933	21,390	19,554
Total	5,454,406	4,253,410	3,625,143
Less			
Cost of goods sold	4,366,640	3,668,563	3,270,670
Research and development expenses	215,916	213,830	224,743
Selling, administrative and general expenses	495,315	487,587	508,208
Interest expense	160,792	185,973	203,769
Financial support to John Deere Credit Company			
Foreign exchange loss			6,507
Miscellaneous charges	3,016	3,306	3,939
Total	5,241,679	4,559,259	4,217,836
Income (Loss) of Consolidated Group Before Income Taxes	212,727	(305,849)	(592,693)
Provision (credit) for income taxes	32,953	(112,681)	(283,936)
Income (Loss) of Consolidated Group	179,774	(193,168)	(308,757)
Equity in Net Income of Unconsolidated			
Subsidiaries and Affiliates before Change in Accounting	106,921	94,149	79,485
Change in Accounting for Income Taxes	28,744		
Total Equity Income	135,665	94,149	79,485
Net Income (Loss) for the Year	$ 315,439	$ (99,019)	$ (229,272)
Deduct			
Cash dividends declared	(46,885)	(16,962)	(50,881)
Other adjustments to retained earnings	(26)	(96)	(5)
Retained Earnings at Beginning of Year	1,480,918	1,596,995	1,877,153
Retained Earnings at End of Year	$1,749,446	$1,480,918	$1,596,995
Net income (loss) per share	$4.48	$(1.46)	$(3.38)
Net income (loss) per share assuming full dilution	$4.32	$(1.46)	$(3.38)
Dividends declared per share	$.65	$.25	$.75
Dividends paid per share	$.51¼	$.31¼	$.87½
Average number of common shares outstanding (in thousands)	70,488	67,897	67,867
Other Statistical Data			
Additions to property and equipment	$ 185,009	$ 170,557	$ 172,717
Provision for depreciation	$ 180,138	$ 184,403	$ 191,095
Number of employees (at year end)	38,268	37,931	37,793

EXHIBIT 1B-1. *(Continued)*

	Year Ended October 31						
1985	1984	1983	1982	1981	1980	1979
$3,118,257	$3,504,780	$3,313,560	$4,033,514	$4,665,035	$4,488,815	$3,936,346
942,391	894,388	654,374	574,712	781,685	981,010	996,758
4,060,648	4,399,168	3,967,934	4,608,226	5,446,720	5,469,825	4,933,104
86,678	115,893	99,309	97,853	91,209	65,355	69,377
			46,870	61,789	10,717	540
23,662	37,592	49,547	17,593	21,112	16,847	12,423
4,170,988	4,552,653	4,116,790	4,770,542	5,620,830	5,562,744	5,015,444
3,386,850	3,629,272	3,317,241	3,853,446	4,306,638	4,373,334	3,822,878
222,763	227,561	212,224	242,459	239,960	231,195	188,139
476,186	469,540	445,025	479,827	482,586	464,496	416,030
199,320	234,609	229,868	266,581	232,042	189,696	95,525
				74,000		
12,024	2,573	4,365				
3,073	3,650	6,131	8,501	5,241	4,286	3,900
4,300,216	4,567,205	4,214,854	4,850,814	5,340,467	5,263,007	4,526,472
(129,228)	(14,552)	(98,064)	(80,272)	280,363	299,737	488,972
(64,498)	(35,923)	(46,431)	(40,821)	119,909	115,658	214,871
(64,730)	21,371	(51,633)	(39,451)	160,454	184,079	274,101
95,235	83,573	74,918	92,349	90,540	44,192	36,536
95,235	83,573	74,918	92,349	90,540	44,192	36,536
$ 30,505	$ 104,944	$ 23,285	$ 52,898	$ 250,994	$ 228,271	$ 310,637
(67,820)	(67,772)	(50,771)	(118,401)	(133,055)	(116,004)	(98,709)
(56)	(96)	(34)	(37)	(413)		
1,914,524	1,877,448	1,904,968	1,970,508	1,852,982	1,740,715	1,528,787
$1,877,153	$1,914,524	$1,877,448	$1,904,968	$1,970,508	$1,852,982	$1,740,715
$.45	$1.55	$.34	$.78	$3.79	$3.72	$5.12
$.45	$1.55	$.34	$.78	$3.74	$3.59	$4.90
$1.00	$1.00	$.75	$1.75	$1.97½	$1.87½	$1.62½
$1.00	$1.00	$.75	$2.00	$1.95	$1.85	$1.55
67,833	67,786	67,698	67,629	66,300	61,390	60,690
$ 144,196	$ 88,663	$ 80,081	$ 129,964	$ 303,379	$ 392,665	$ 266,267
$ 183,689	$ 191,467	$ 193,519	$ 196,779	$ 177,444	$ 144,528	$ 119,467
40,509	43,011	45,728	48,372	60,857	61,039	65,392

EXHIBIT 1B-1. *(Continued)*

Deere & Company

TEN-YEAR SUMMARY OF CONSOLIDATED BALANCE SHEETS

(In thousands of dollars except per share amounts)

ASSETS	1988	1987	1986
Current Assets			
Cash	$ 36,248	$ 49,817	$ 69,703
Short-term investments—at cost which approximates market value	12,742	66,567	111,954
Refundable income taxes	3,178	16,258	6,699
Receivables from unconsolidated subsidiaries and affiliates	46,699	29,139	210,936
Trade receivables—net	2,308,339	2,110,507	2,079,318
Inventories	708,277	464,977	482,630
Total current assets	3,115,483	2,737,265	2,961,240
Property and Equipment—at cost	3,056,442	2,942,641	2,767,109
Less accumulated depreciation	2,063,237	1,960,459	1,816,053
Property and equipment—net	993,205	982,182	951,056
Investments in and Advances to Unconsolidated			
Subsidiaries and Affiliates	1,052,847	975,702	987,535
Other Assets	33,427	21,346	33,756
Deferred Charges	50,292	43,376	40,680
Total	$5,245,254	$4,759,871	$4,974,267

LIABILITIES AND STOCKHOLDERS' EQUITY	1988	1987	1986
Current Liabilities			
Notes payable	$ 455,462	$ 342,075	$ 383,454
Current maturities of long-term debt	21,132	13,387	12,078
Payables to unconsolidated subsidiaries and affiliates	30,763	74,554	
Accounts payable, accrued expenses and dividends payable	1,136,836	1,041,090	1,002,943
Accrued taxes	84,131	58,272	110,942
Total current liabilities	1,728,324	1,529,378	1,509,417
Noncurrent Liabilities			
Long-term debt	804,587	1,051,513	1,279,506
Capital lease obligations	12,357	10,475	10,554
Pension accruals and other liabilities	229,380	238,926	162,532
Deferred income taxes	14,431	9,450	12,981
Stockholders' Equity			
Common stock issued, at stated value	760,491	496,563	492,013
Retained earnings	1,749,446	1,480,918	1,596,995
Cumulative translation adjustment	(51,037)	(54,627)	(87,006)
Less common stock in treasury, at cost	(2,725)	(2,725)	(2,725)
Total stockholders' equity	2,456,175	1,920,129	1,999,277
Total	$5,245,254	$4,759,871	$4,974,267
Book value per share	$32.92	$28.23	$29.46

EXHIBIT 1B-1. *(Continued)*

	October 31					
1985	1984	1983	1982	1981	1980	1979
$ 35,402	$ 35,943	$ 56,574	$ 48,101	$ 57,213	$ 69,089	$ 50,600
52,421	5,380	158,310	4,268	10,998	512	2,759
5,266	4,232	62,736	75,204	13,437	71,049	
144,746	242,082	167,883	215,934	236,428	241,576	356,879
2,749,393	2,846,960	2,723,633	2,660,897	2,374,393	2,093,272	1,401,615
447,370	539,897	632,497	760,945	872,045	877,465	885,603
3,434,598	3,674,494	3,801,633	3,765,349	3,564,514	3,352,963	2,697,456
2,629,193	2,484,074	2,482,833	2,525,951	2,446,359	2,093,671	1,739,524
1,613,331	1,451,468	1,328,018	1,197,891	1,038,021	844,835	750,683
1,015,862	1,032,606	1,154,815	1,328,060	1,408,338	1,248,836	988,841
941,963	888,240	826,528	781,233	657,884	548,992	448,814
25,168	62,481	60,034	16,812	18,323	14,196	14,755
44,636	39,475	37,002	44,225	34,818	37,437	29,366
$5,462,227	$5,697,296	$5,880,012	$5,935,679	$5,683,877	$5,202,424	$4,179,232
$ 520,570	$ 567,783	$ 712,186	$ 952,027	$ 678,501	$ 723,914	$ 179,946
16,351	157,833	9,244	17,727	14,843	17,770	21,937
1,043,893	1,142,759	1,124,799	1,120,930	1,320,163	1,188,345	1,070,741
332,896	350,322	305,229	304,886	291,001	224,945	192,440
1,913,710	2,218,697	2,151,458	2,395,570	2,304,508	2,154,974	1,465,064
1,110,087	972,185	1,180,295	897,682	676,147	702,335	618,762
19,575	21,875	23,971	16,296	20,409	22,074	21,451
109,715	85,638	63,661	52,950	63,359	62,226	58,250
50,524	108,073	184,660	184,985	169,868	127,397	49,007
491,419	490,336	487,879	485,953	482,433	283,791	229,338
1,877,153	1,914,524	1,877,448	1,904,968	1,970,508	1,852,982	1,740,715
(107,231)	(111,307)	(86,635)				
(2,725)	(2,725)	(2,725)	(2,725)	(3,355)	(3,355)	(3,355)
2,258,616	2,290,828	2,275,967	2,388,196	2,449,586	2,133,418	1,966,698
$5,462,227	$5,697,296	$5,880,012	$5,935,679	$5,683,877	$5,202,424	$4,179,232
$33.29	$33.78	$33.60	$35.29	$36.29	$34.13	$32.34

Source: Deere & Company, 1988 Annual Report.

EXHIBIT 1B-2. DEERE & COMPANY
Financial Statements, Year Ended October 31, 1991

Deere & Company 1991 Annual Report
Financial Summary

Millions of dollars except per share amounts	1991	1990	1989	1988	1987
NET SALES AND REVENUES					
Net sales of equipment	$ 5,848	$ 6,779	$ 6,234	$ 5,365	$ 4,135
Net sales and revenues	$ 7,055	$ 7,875	$ 7,220	$ 6,237	$ 4,854
INCOME AND DIVIDENDS					
Net income (loss):					
Equipment operations	$ (132)*	$ 284	$ 248	$ 180	$ (193)
Credit subsidiaries	84	81	76	89**	52
Insurance and health care subsidiaries and affiliates	28	41	48	41**	36
Other affiliates		5	8	5	6
Total	$ (20)*	$ 411	$ 380	$ 315**	$ (99)
Return on beginning stockholders' equity	(.7)%	14.8%	15.5%	16.4%	(5.0)%
Return on net sales:					
Equipment operations	(2.2)%	4.2%	4.0%	3.4%	(4.7)%
Total	(.3)%	6.1%	6.1%	5.9%	(2.4)%
Per share:					
Net income (loss)–fully diluted	$ (.27)*	$ 5.42	$ 5.06	$ 4.32**	$ (1.46)
Dividends declared	$ 2.00	$ 2.00	$ 1.30	$ .65	$ .25
Stock price range	38^1/_2-57^3/_8$	37^5/_8-78^3/_8$	$44-64$^1/_4$	$ 27-50$^1/_2$	$ 22$^1/_4$-43
ASSETS					
Equipment operations	$ 5,590	$ 5,597	$ 4,717	$ 4,195	$ 3,802
Credit subsidiaries	4,929	4,059	3,532	3,267	3,081
Insurance and health care subsidiaries	1,130	1,008	896	802	683
Total	$ 11,649	$ 10,664	$ 9,145	$ 8,264	$ 7,566
Capital expenditures–Equipment operations	$ 295	$ 288	$ 182	$ 175	$ 164
Net property and equipment–Equipment operations	$ 1,220	$ 1,134	$ 982	$ 944	$ 958
STOCKHOLDERS' EQUITY					
Ending stockholders' equity	$ 2,836	$ 3,008	$ 2,780	$ 2,456	$ 1,920
Book value per share	$ 37.20	$ 39.52	$ 36.76	$ 32.92	$ 28.23
EMPLOYMENT AT YEAR END					
United States and Canada	27,100	28,500	28,600	28,200	27,700
Overseas	9,400	10,000	10,300	10,100	10,200
Total	36,500	38,500	38,900	38,300	37,900

*Includes restructuring costs of $120 million or $1.58 per share. See page 47 for comments regarding restructuring costs.
**Includes the benefit from a change in accounting for income taxes of $29 million or $.42 per share for the company, which is comprised of benefits of $25 million for the credit subsidiaries and $4 million for the insurance subsidiaries.

EXHIBIT 1B-2. *(Continued)*

Deere & Company

Statement of Consolidated Income

	CONSOLIDATED (Deere & Company and Consolidated Subsidiaries)		
	Year Ended October 31		
(In millions of dollars except per share amounts)	1991	1990	1989
Net Sales and Revenues			
Net sales of equipment	$5,847.8	$6,778.7	$6,233.9
Finance and interest income	654.4	592.7	550.5
Insurance and health care premiums	444.1	384.2	342.9
Investment income	87.9	86.0	75.7
Other income	21.0	33.4	16.8
Total	7,055.2	7,875.0	7,219.8
Costs and Expenses			
Cost of goods sold	4,894.2	5,424.1	5,025.0
Research and development expenses	279.3	263.5	234.1
Selling, administrative and general expenses	839.6	792.3	697.3
Interest expense	450.0	435.2	406.6
Insurance and health care claims and benefits	405.5	334.5	292.7
Other operating expenses	30.9	37.9	25.0
Restructuring costs	181.9		
Total	7,081.4	7,287.5	6,680.7
Income (Loss) of Consolidated Group			
Before Income Taxes	(26.2)	587.5	539.1
Provision (credit) for income taxes	(5.2)	182.0	167.0
Income (Loss) of Consolidated Group	(21.0)	405.5	372.1
Equity in Income (Loss) of Unconsolidated Subsidiaries and Affiliates			
Credit			
Insurance and health care	1.3		
Other	(.5)	5.6	8.1
Total	.8	5.6	8.1
Net Income (Loss)	$ (20.2)	$ 411.1	$ 380.2
Per Share Data			
Net income (loss) per share, primary and fully diluted	$ (.27)	$ 5.42	$ 5.06
Dividends declared	$ 2.00	$ 2.00	$ 1.30

EXHIBIT 1B-2. *(Continued)*

EQUIPMENT OPERATIONS (Deere & Company with Financial Services on the Equity Basis)			FINANCIAL SERVICES		
Year Ended October 31			Year Ended October 31		
1991	1990	1989	1991	1990	1989
$5,847.8	$6,778.7	$6,233.9			
116.3	111.9	101.0	$ 540.8	$ 483.5	$452.4
			568.4	492.3	440.7
			88.1	86.1	75.9
21.2	19.4	15.2	6.9	21.3	9.4
5,985.3	6,910.0	6,350.1	1,204.2	1,083.2	978.4
4,903.9	5,429.8	5,035.7			
279.3	263.5	234.1			
599.1	588.5	533.0	256.4	219.8	179.3
192.7	190.6	173.6	260.1	247.4	236.1
			511.2	428.2	372.6
17.5	24.3	10.3	13.5	13.6	14.7
181.9					
6,174.4	6,496.7	5,986.7	1,041.2	909.0	802.7
(189.1)	413.3	363.4	163.0	174.2	175.7
(57.6)	129.5	115.3	52.5	52.5	51.7
(131.5)	283.8	248.1	110.5	121.7	124.0
83.5	80.6	76.0			
28.3	41.1	48.0	1.3		
(.5)	5.6	8.1			
111.3	127.3	132.1	1.3		
$ (20.2)	$ 411.1	$ 380.2	$ 111.8	$ 121.7	$124.0

The "Consolidated" (Deere & Company and Consolidated Subsidiaries) data in this statement conform with the requirements of FASB Statement No. 94. In the supplemental consolidating data in this statement "Equipment Operations" (Deere & Company with Financial Services on the Equity Basis) reflect the basis of consolidation described on page 46 of the notes to the consolidated financial statements. The consolidated group data in the "Equipment Operations" income statement reflect the results of the agricultural equipment, industrial equipment and lawn and grounds care equipment operations. The supplemental "Financial Services" consolidating data in this statement include Deere & Company's credit, insurance and health care subsidiaries. Transactions between the "Equipment Operations" and "Financial Services" have been eliminated to arrive at the "Consolidated" data.

The information on pages 35 through 58 is an integral part of this statement.

EXHIBIT 1B-2. *(Continued)*

Deere & Company

Consolidated Balance Sheet

	CONSOLIDATED (Deere & Company and Consolidated Subsidiaries)	
	October 31	
(In millions of dollars except per share amounts) ASSETS	1991	1990
Cash and cash equivalents	$ 278.5	$ 185.4
Marketable securities carried at cost	856.6	801.0
Receivables from unconsolidated subsidiaries and affiliates	17.8	3.0
Dealer accounts and notes receivable – net	2,966.6	3,099.9
Credit receivables – net	4,745.6	3,895.8
Other receivables	108.9	141.5
Equipment on operating leases – net	184.8	181.4
Inventories	538.1	677.7
Property and equipment – net	1,235.2	1,149.4
Investments in unconsolidated subsidiaries and affiliates	106.0	84.6
Intangible assets – net	371.5	239.7
Other assets	133.2	81.1
Deferred income taxes	17.0	12.3
Deferred charges	89.6	111.5
Total	$11,649.4	$10,664.3
LIABILITIES AND STOCKHOLDERS' EQUITY		
LIABILITIES		
Short-term borrowings	$ 3,471.1	$ 2,892.5
Payables to unconsolidated subsidiaries and affiliates	5.5	28.1
Accounts payable and accrued expenses	1,803.6	1,722.4
Insurance and health care claims and reserves	491.1	444.2
Accrued taxes	84.8	66.2
Deferred income taxes	75.4	171.7
Long-term borrowings	2,206.3	1,785.9
Pension accruals and other liabilities	675.8	545.7
Total liabilities	8,813.6	7,656.7
STOCKHOLDERS' EQUITY		
Common stock, $1 par value (authorized – 200,000,000 shares; issued – 76,443,138 shares in 1991 and 76,310,441 shares in 1990)		
at stated value	838.7	831.4
Retained earnings	2,119.0	2,291.3
Minimum pension liability adjustment	(86.4)	(88.2)
Cumulative translation adjustment	(16.4)	(11.8)
Unamortized restricted stock compensation	(6.5)	(5.0)
Common stock in treasury, 208,370 shares in 1991 and 203,253 shares in 1990, at cost	(12.6)	(10.1)
Total stockholders' equity	2,835.8	3,007.6
Total	$11,649.4	$10,664.3

The "Consolidated" (Deere & Company and Consolidated Subsidiaries) data in this statement conform with the requirements of FASB Statement No. 94. In the supplemental consolidating data in this statement "Equipment Operations" (Deere & Company with Financial Services on the Equity Basis) reflect the basis of consolidation described on page 46 of the notes to the consolidated financial statements. The supplemental "Financial Services" consolidating data in this statement include Deere & Company's credit, insurance and health care subsidiaries. Transactions between the "Equipment Operations" and "Financial Services" have been eliminated to arrive at the "Consolidated" data.

The information on pages 35 through 58 is an integral part of this statement.

EXHIBIT 1B-2. *(Continued)*

EQUIPMENT OPERATIONS (Deere & Company with Financial Services on the Equity Basis)		FINANCIAL SERVICES	
October 31		October 31	
1991	1990	1991	1990
$ 99.1	$ 25.7	$ 179.4	$ 159.7
		856.6	801.0
200.5	74.5	10.0	
2,966.6	3,099.9		
75.0	64.9	4,670.6	3,830.9
	42.0	110.3	101.0
98.4	102.5	86.4	78.9
538.1	677.7		
1,219.6	1,134.5	15.6	14.9
1,221.7	1,187.4	28.0	
345.9	224.3	25.6	15.4
108.3	61.8	24.9	19.3
		37.5	18.4
53.4	75.9	36.2	35.6
$ 6,926.6	$ 6,771.1	$ 6,081.1	$ 5,075.1
$ 880.8	$ 850.3	$ 2,590.3	$ 2,042.2
5.5	28.1	192.8	71.5
1,334.2	1,297.1	470.8	426.9
		491.1	444.2
83.6	64.0	1.2	2.2
95.9	177.8		
1,017.8	803.7	1,188.5	982.2
673.0	542.5	2.8	3.2
4,090.8	3,763.5	4,937.5	3,972.4
838.7	831.4	196.0	184.0
2,119.0	2,291.3	936.7	911.2
(86.4)	(88.2)		
(16.4)	(11.8)	10.9	7.5
(6.5)	(5.0)		
(12.6)	(10.1)		
2,835.8	3,007.6	1,143.6	1,102.7
$ 6,926.6	$ 6,771.1	$ 6,081.1	$ 5,075.1

EXHIBIT 1B-2. *(Continued)*

Deere & Company

Statement of Consolidated Cash Flows

(In millions of dollars)	CONSOLIDATED (Deere & Company and Consolidated Subsidiaries) Year Ended October 31		
	1991	1990	1989
Cash Flows from Operating Activities			
Net income (loss)	$ (20.2)	$ 411.1	$ 380.2
Adjustments to reconcile net income (loss) to net cash provided by (used for) operating activities:			
Provision for doubtful receivables	69.6	56.6	27.1
Provision for depreciation	209.2	203.8	192.9
Provision for restructuring costs	181.9		
Undistributed earnings of unconsolidated subsidiaries and affiliates	(2.7)	2.8	(6.9)
Provision (credit) for deferred income taxes	(100.1)	57.7	91.8
Changes in assets and liabilities:			
Receivables	87.9	(486.3)	(315.9)
Inventories	134.8	67.6	4.2
Accounts payable and accrued expenses	(65.0)	(38.7)	41.4
Insurance and health care claims and reserves	34.7	52.5	32.0
Other	82.9	70.0	(28.1)
Net cash provided by operating activities	613.0	397.1	418.7
Cash Flows from Investing Activities			
Collections of credit receivables	2,623.9	2,217.1	2,160.7
Proceeds from sales of credit receivables	6.0	590.3	293.4
Proceeds from sales of marketable securities	136.3	118.9	259.7
Proceeds from sales of equipment on operating leases	32.4	36.8	27.8
Cost of credit receivables acquired	(3,537.3)	(3,367.9)	(2,793.4)
Purchases of marketable securities	(200.6)	(192.9)	(319.9)
Purchases of property and equipment	(298.0)	(292.1)	(181.1)
Cost of operating leases acquired	(53.9)	(83.4)	(91.3)
Acquisition of businesses	(87.4)		(86.8)
Other	(.4)	5.0	(1.3)
Net cash used for investing activities	(1,379.0)	(968.2)	(732.2)
Cash Flows from Financing Activities			
Increase (decrease) in short-term borrowings	453.2	578.9	(127.3)
Change in intercompany receivables/payables			
Proceeds from issuance of long-term borrowings	776.5	492.1	746.0
Principal payments on long-term borrowings	(204.8)	(381.2)	(287.5)
Dividends paid	(152.3)	(140.3)	(86.2)
Other	(12.0)	2.8	7.0
Net cash provided by (used for) financing activities	860.6	552.3	252.0
Effect of Exchange Rate Changes on Cash	(1.5)	.4	(.7)
Net Increase (Decrease) in Cash and Cash Equivalents	93.1	(18.4)	(62.2)
Cash and Cash Equivalents at Beginning of Year	185.4	203.8	266.0
Cash and Cash Equivalents at End of Year	$ 278.5	$ 185.4	$ 203.8

The "Consolidated" (Deere & Company and Consolidated Subsidiaries) data in this statement conform with the requirements of FASB Statement No. 94. In the supplemental consolidating data in this statement "Equipment Operations" (Deere & Company with Financial Services on the Equity Basis) reflect the basis of consolidation described on page 46 of the notes to the consolidated financial statements. The supplemental "Financial Services" consolidating data in this statement include Deere & Company's credit,

EXHIBIT 1B-2. *(Continued)*

	EQUIPMENT OPERATIONS (Deere & Company with Financial Services on the Equity Basis)			FINANCIAL SERVICES		
	Year Ended October 31				Year Ended October 31	
1991	1990	1989	1991	1990	1989
$ (20.2)	$ 411.1	$ 380.2	$ 111.8	$ 121.7	$ 124.0
1.9	6.3	.3	67.6	50.3	26.8
192.2	186.6	175.2	17.0	17.2	17.8
181.9					
(26.8)	(39.1)	(62.2)	(1.1)		
(80.9)	89.2	115.5	(19.2)	(31.5)	(23.7)
106.6	(468.7)	(297.1)	(18.6)	(17.6)	(19.1)
134.8	67.6	4.2			
(117.3)	(81.9)	(6.6)	52.2	43.1	48.9
			34.7	52.5	32.0
95.9	64.9	(4.0)	(13.0)	5.1	(18.8)
468.1	236.0	305.5	231.4	240.8	187.9
61.5	59.8	49.4	2,562.4	2,157.3	2,111.3
6.0	11.5	11.8	27.4	603.8	303.2
			136.3	118.9	259.7
12.2	10.3	5.7	20.2	26.5	22.1
(76.3)	(77.8)	(70.6)	(3,488.3)	(3,315.1)	(2,744.3)
			(200.6)	(192.9)	(320.0)
(295.2)	(287.9)	(175.6)	(2.8)	(4.2)	(5.4)
(12.5)	(39.8)	(52.1)	(41.4)	(43.6)	(39.2)
(71.1)		(86.8)	(16.3)		
(12.8)	4.8	(1.4)	.4	.2	
(388.2)	(319.1)	(319.6)	(1,002.7)	(649.1)	(412.6)
133.2	111.9	27.3	319.9	467.0	(154.6)
(121.2)	64.0	(87.1)	121.2	(63.5)	81.1
350.2	175.4	198.5	426.3	316.7	547.5
(202.9)	(161.6)	(36.9)	(1.9)	(219.6)	(250.5)
(152.3)	(140.3)	(86.2)	(86.5)	(79.7)	(68.7)
(12.0)	2.3	6.9	12.0		
(5.0)	51.7	22.5	791.0	420.9	154.8
(1.5)	.4	(.7)			
73.4	(31.0)	7.7	19.7	12.6	(69.9)
25.7	56.7	49.0	159.7	147.1	217.0
$ 99.1	$ 25.7	$ 56.7	$ 179.4	$ 159.7	$ 147.1

insurance and health care subsidiaries. Transactions between the "Equipment Operations" and "Financial Services" have been eliminated to arrive at the "Consolidated" data. The information on pages 35 through 58 is an integral part of this statement.

EXHIBIT 1B-2. *(Continued)*

Report of Management

The consolidated financial statements and other financial information of Deere & Company in this report were prepared by management, which is responsible for their contents. They reflect amounts based upon management's best estimates and informed judgments. In management's opinion, the financial statements present fairly the financial position, results of operations and cash flows of the company in conformity with generally accepted accounting principles.

The company maintains a system of internal accounting controls and procedures which is intended, consistent with reasonable cost, to provide reasonable assurance that transactions are executed as authorized, that they are properly recorded to produce reliable financial records, and that accountability for assets is maintained. The accounting controls and procedures are supported by careful selection and training of personnel, examinations by an internal auditing department and a continuing management commitment to the integrity of the system.

The financial statements have been audited to the extent required by generally accepted auditing standards by Deloitte & Touche, independent auditors. The independent auditors have evaluated the company's internal control structure and performed tests of procedures and accounting records in connection with the issuance of their report on the fairness of the financial statements.

The Board of Directors has appointed an Audit Review Committee composed entirely of directors who are not employees of the company. The Audit Review Committee meets with representatives of management, the internal auditing department and the independent auditors, both separately and jointly. The Committee discusses with the independent auditors and approves in advance the scope of the audit, reviews with the independent auditors the financial statements and their audit report, consults with the internal audit staff and reviews management's administration of the system of internal accounting controls. The Committee reports to the Board on its activities and findings.

Independent Auditors' Report

Deloitte & Touche

Deere & Company:

We have audited the accompanying consolidated balance sheets of Deere & Company and subsidiaries as of October 31, 1991 and 1990 and the related statements of consolidated income and of consolidated cash flows for each of the three years in the period ended October 31, 1991. These financial statements are the responsibility of the company's management. Our responsibility is to express an opinion on these financial statements based on our audits.

We conducted our audits in accordance with generally accepted auditing standards. Those standards require that we plan and perform the audit to obtain reasonable assurance about whether the financial statements are free of material misstatement. An audit includes examining, on a test basis, evidence supporting the amounts and disclosures in the financial statements. An audit also includes assessing the accounting principles used and significant estimates made by management, as well as evaluating the overall financial statement presentation. We believe that our audits provide a reasonable basis for our opinion.

In our opinion, such consolidated financial statements present fairly, in all material respects, the financial position of Deere & Company and subsidiaries at October 31, 1991 and 1990 and the results of their operations and their cash flows for each of the three years in the period ended October 31, 1991 in conformity with generally accepted accounting principles.

As discussed in the Notes to Consolidated Financial Statements, in 1990 the company recognized in the consolidated balance sheet its additional minimum pension liability, as required by Statement of Financial Accounting Standards No. 87.

Deloitte & Touche

Chicago, Illinois
December 11, 1991

EXHIBIT 1B-2. *(Continued)*

Management's Discussion and Analysis

Deere & Company's consolidated financial statements result from consolidation of the company's agricultural equipment, industrial equipment and lawn and grounds care equipment businesses with its Financial Services businesses. The consolidation procedure is explained on page 46 in the notes to the consolidated financial statements. The notes explain how the terms "Equipment Operations", "Financial Services" and "Consolidated" are used in this report to help readers understand the data presented. These terms are used in Management's Discussion and Analysis for clarification or emphasis.

Results of Operations for the Years Ended October 31, 1991, 1990 and 1989 [Unaudited]

BUSINESS AND SEGMENT DESCRIPTION
Deere & Company and its subsidiaries manufacture, distribute and finance a full range of agricultural equipment, a broad range of industrial equipment and a variety of lawn and grounds care equipment. The company also provides credit, insurance and health care products for businesses and the general public.

In prior years, the company's business segment disclosures reflected a farm equipment segment which included both agricultural equipment and lawn and grounds care equipment operations. In 1991, the company reorganized the corporate and marketing structures of its agricultural and lawn and grounds care businesses. As a result of those changes and the continued development of the lawn and grounds care operations as an increasingly important part of the company's total business, the agricultural equipment and lawn and grounds care equipment operations have been realigned into separate segments. Segment information for prior periods has been reclassified to conform to the current presentation. The company's operations are now categorized into five business segments.

The company's worldwide agricultural equipment segment manufactures and distributes a full range of equipment used in commercial farming–including tractors; tillage, soil preparation, planting and harvesting machinery; and crop handling equipment.

The company's worldwide industrial equipment segment manufactures and distributes a broad range of machines used in construction, earthmoving and forestry–backhoe loaders; crawler dozers and loaders; four-wheel-drive loaders; scrapers; motor graders; wheel and crawler excavators; log skidders; feller bunchers and rough terrain forklifts. This segment also includes the manufacture and distribution of engines and drivetrain components for the OEM market.

The company's worldwide lawn and grounds care equipment segment manufactures and distributes equipment for commercial and residential uses–including small tractors for lawn, garden and utility purposes; riding and walk-behind mowers; golf course equipment; utility transport vehicles; snowblowers; and other outdoor power products.

The products produced by the agricultural, industrial and lawn and grounds care equipment segments are marketed primarily through independent retail dealer networks.

The company's credit segment, which operates in the United States and Canada, purchases and finances retail notes (retail installment sales and loan contracts) from John Deere's equipment sales branches in the United States and Canada. The notes are acquired by the sales branches through John Deere retail dealers and originate in connection with retail sales by dealers of new John Deere equipment and used equipment. The credit segment also purchases and finances retail notes unrelated to John Deere equipment, representing primarily recreational vehicle and recreational marine product notes acquired from independent dealers of that equipment (non-Deere retail notes). The credit subsidiaries also lease John Deere equipment to retail customers, finance and service unsecured revolving charge accounts acquired from merchants in the agricultural and lawn and grounds care retail markets, and provide wholesale financing for recreational vehicles and John Deere engine inventories held by dealers of those products.

The company's insurance and health care segment issues policies in the United States and Canada primarily for: (1) a general line of property and casualty insurance to dealers and to the general public; (2) group accident and health insurance for employees of participating John Deere dealers; (3) group life and group accident and health insurance for employees of the company; (4) life and annuity products to the general public; and (5) credit physical damage insurance and credit life insurance in connection with certain retail sales of John Deere products financed by the credit subsidiaries. This segment also provides health management programs and related administrative services in the United States to corporate customers and employees of Deere & Company.

SUMMARY

(In millions of dollars except per share amounts)	1991	1990	1989
NET SALES AND REVENUES			
Net sales:			
Agricultural equipment	$4,054	$4,519	$4,109
Industrial equipment	1,014	1,348	1,310
Lawn and grounds care equipment	780	912	815
Total net sales	5,848	6,779	6,234
Financial Services revenues	1,078	973	879
Other revenues	129	123	107
Total net sales and revenues	$7,055	$7,875	$7,220
Net income (loss)	$ (20)*	$ 411	$ 380
Net income (loss) per share– fully diluted	$ (.27)*	$ 5.42	$ 5.06

*Includes restructuring costs of $120 million or $1.58 per share. See page 47 for comments regarding restructuring costs.

NET SALES BY MAJOR MARKETS	1991	1990	1989
United States	$3,968	$4,777	$4,332
Canada	381	448	481
Europe, Africa and Middle East	1,148	1,158	1,074
Central and South America	171	149	159
Asia–Pacific Region	180	247	188
Total	$5,848	$6,779	$6,234

EXHIBIT 1B-2. *(Continued)*

Net sales of service parts and accessories, which are included in the previous totals, amounted to $1,243 million in 1991, $1,222 million in 1990 and $1,174 million in 1989.

1991 Compared with 1990 (Unaudited)

MARKET CONDITIONS

North American agricultural economic conditions were less favorable in 1991 than in 1990. Agricultural commodity exports declined in 1991 due to large overseas grain supplies and a drop in demand by major importing countries, resulting in lower commodity prices. Livestock prices also declined from 1990 levels and drought conditions were experienced across a large area of the corn belt. As a result of these developments along with reduced government farm subsidies, total 1991 United States farm cash receipts and net cash income are expected to decline from last year's record levels, but will still be at a relatively high historic level. These conditions caused farmers to become more cautious in making new product purchase decisions. North American retail sales of John Deere agricultural equipment increased slightly in the 1991 fiscal year compared with last year.

The economic recession in North America during 1991 resulted in a significant decline in housing starts and non-residential construction compared with last year. Additionally, demand for equipment used in forestry production was lower in 1991, and public sector spending for construction equipment also declined. As a result, North American retail sales of industrial and construction equipment for the industry and John Deere were significantly below 1990 volumes.

North American retail sales of John Deere lawn and grounds care equipment were somewhat lower than in 1990, as consumer spending for durable goods declined and dry weather conditions affected sales across a large part of the Midwest.

Outside the United States and Canada, retail sales of John Deere agricultural equipment were lower than last year's level, due primarily to recessionary pressures and economic uncertainties facing farmers in the European Economic Community and Australia. Overseas demand for the company's industrial equipment declined, while retail sales of lawn and grounds care products improved modestly in 1991 compared with the prior year.

The company's credit operations experienced additional growth in 1991 as an increased proportion of John Deere agricultural equipment retail sales was financed by the company. Revolving charge accounts financed also experienced growth during the current year. Primarily due to recessionary pressures affecting purchases of recreational marine products combined with the utilization of more selective retail note acquisition criteria, acquisitions of non-Deere retail notes were significantly lower in 1991 compared with the previous year. Insurance and health care premium volumes increased this year compared with 1990, even though soft market conditions prevailed in the property/casualty insurance industry.

OPERATING RESULTS

Deere & Company's operating results for 1991 reflect the effects of producing at a significantly lower volume than last year in response to weak retail demand and to facilitate reduction of company and dealers' inventories. These inventories were reduced by $273 million during the year. Additionally, sales discounts and allowances were much higher this year mainly due to extremely competitive conditions in all of the company's markets.

The company's total worldwide net sales and revenues, which include net sales of equipment and revenues from the credit, insurance and health care operations, declined 10 percent to $7,055 million in 1991 compared with net sales and revenues of $7,875 million in 1990.

Worldwide net sales to dealers of John Deere agricultural equipment decreased 10 percent to $4,054 million in 1991 from last year's volume of $4,519 million. Worldwide industrial equipment net sales of $1,014 million declined 25 percent from $1,348 million last year. Net sales of lawn and grounds care equipment totaled $780 million in 1991 compared with $912 million last year, representing a decrease of 14 percent. The physical volume of the company's worldwide sales to dealers decreased approximately 15 percent in 1991. Worldwide production tonnage of all John Deere products in 1991 was 17 percent lower than last year.

Net sales to dealers of John Deere equipment in the United States and Canada decreased 17 percent to $4,349 million compared with $5,225 million in 1990. Net sales of equipment overseas totaled $1,499 million, a decrease of four percent compared with last year's net sales of $1,554 million. Excluding the effects of price increases and changes in currency relationships, the physical volume of overseas sales was approximately seven percent lower in 1991 than in 1990.

Finance and interest income increased 10 percent to $654 million in 1991 compared with $593 million last year, while insurance and health care premiums increased 16 percent to $444 million in the current year compared with $384 million in 1990.

The company incurred a worldwide net loss of $20 million or $.27 per share in 1991 compared with net income of $411 million or $5.42 per share in 1990. The company's worldwide equipment operations, which exclude income from the credit, insurance and health care operations, incurred a net loss of $132 million in 1991 compared with net income of $284 million last year. Fourth quarter restructuring charges of $120 million or $1.58 per share, discussed below, adversely affected 1991 results. The decline in earnings this year was caused mainly by the lower production and sales volumes combined with higher sales discounts and allowances. Reflecting the effects of lower volumes, increased sales discounts and allowances affecting net sales and higher manufacturing cost levels this year, the worldwide ratio of cost of goods sold to net sales increased to 83.9 percent in 1991 compared with 80.1 percent last year, despite the benefit from the reduction of inventories valued on a last-in, first-out (LIFO) basis.

Worldwide net income and results of the Equipment Operations in 1991 were affected by certain non-recurring or unusual

EXHIBIT 1B-2. *(Continued)*

items. During the fourth quarter of 1991, the company initiated plans to reduce costs and rationalize operations, both in North America and overseas. This resulted in a fourth quarter after-tax provision for restructuring costs of $120 million or $1.58 per share, representing costs of employment reductions and the closure of a ductile iron foundry. Excluding this one-time charge, 1991 worldwide net income would have been $100 million, and the Equipment Operations net loss would have been $12 million. However, results in 1991 benefited by $84 million or $1.11 per share from the reduction of LIFO inventories. Additional information is presented on page 52 of the notes to the consolidated financial statements.

Net income of the company's credit subsidiaries totaled $84 million in 1991 compared with $81 million last year. Net income from insurance and health care operations was $28 million in 1991 compared with $41 million last year. Additional information is presented in the discussion of "Credit Operations" and "Insurance and Health Care Operations" on pages 40 through 42.

In December 1990, the Financial Accounting Standards Board (FASB) issued Statement No. 106, Employers' Accounting for Postretirement Benefits Other Than Pensions. This statement must be adopted no later than the company's 1994 fiscal year, and generally requires the accrual of retiree health care and other postretirement benefits during employees' years of active service. Deere & Company currently expenses the costs of these benefits when paid.

Upon adoption, the new standard requires the recognition of a transition obligation which represents that portion of future retiree benefit costs related to service already rendered by both active and retired employees up to the date of adoption. This initial liability can be either recognized immediately as a one-time charge to earnings in the year of adoption, or amortized through charges to earnings over a 20-year period. Although Deere & Company continues to evaluate the impact of this new standard, the company's preliminary estimates of the transition obligation range from $1.2 billion to $1.7 billion. Preliminary estimates of incremental annual expense for Deere & Company and its consolidated subsidiaries following adoption range from $60 million (if the entire transition obligation were recognized in the year of adoption) to $200 million (if the transition obligation were accrued over a 20-year period). The foregoing amounts have been reduced by income tax benefits expected to be recognized in accordance with a FASB exposure draft of a new accounting standard. These preliminary estimates are subject to change and are dependent upon a number of variables including future medical inflation rates, health care trends, benefit plan changes, the discount factor used in determining the initial liability, when the standard is adopted, whether the transition obligation is recognized immediately or amortized over 20 years, whether or not the tax benefits are in fact available, etc.

Although implementation of the standard is expected to have an adverse effect on Deere & Company's future reported net income, it will not affect the company's cash flows because the company plans to continue paying the cost of post-employment benefits when incurred. The company has not determined when the statement will be adopted or how the transition obligation will be recognized.

BUSINESS SEGMENT AND GEOGRAPHIC AREA RESULTS
The following discussion of operating results by industry segment and geographic area relates to information beginning on page 43. Operating profit is defined as income before interest expense, foreign exchange gains and losses, income taxes and certain corporate expenses, except for the operating profit of the credit segment, which includes the effect of interest expense.

Operating profit of the worldwide agricultural equipment segment declined significantly in 1991 to $123 million compared with $472 million in 1990. This decline was caused primarily by the 10 percent decrease in worldwide agricultural equipment sales to dealers, a 14 percent decrease in production tonnage and significantly higher levels of sales discounts and allowances during the year. Additionally, the agricultural equipment operations incurred pretax restructuring charges of $128 million in 1991. However, pretax benefits from the reduction of LIFO inventories totaled $102 million this year.

Operating profit of the North American agricultural equipment operations was substantially lower in the current year compared with 1990, resulting from lower production and sales volumes, increased sales discounts and allowances and restructuring charges. However, results benefited from the reduction of LIFO inventories. Sales to dealers decreased 12 percent in 1991 compared with 1990, and production tonnage was 14 percent lower this year.

The overseas agricultural equipment operations incurred an operating loss in 1991 compared with an operating profit in 1990. Overseas agricultural equipment sales to dealers declined seven percent in 1991, and production was 13 percent lower than last year. Operating performance in the current year was also unfavorably affected by higher sales discounts and allowances, increased operating cost and expense levels and restructuring charges, but benefited from the reduction of LIFO inventories.

The worldwide industrial equipment operations incurred an operating loss of $131 million in 1991 compared with operating profit of $63 million in 1990. Volumes were significantly lower this year, sales discounts and allowances and operating expense levels were relatively higher and restructuring charges totaled $44 million. However, LIFO inventory benefits were $14 million in the current year. Industrial equipment sales to dealers declined 25 percent in 1991, and production was 26 percent lower. However, dealer inventories of industrial equipment were reduced by $94 million during the year.

The worldwide lawn and grounds care equipment operations earned an operating profit of $24 million in 1991 compared with $106 million in 1990. Lawn and grounds care equipment sales to dealers declined 14 percent in 1991, production was down 27 percent and sales discounts and allowances were higher. In addition to the negative

EXHIBIT 1B-2. *(Continued)*

effects of substantially lower volumes, restructuring charges were $10 million in 1991. However, LIFO inventory benefits totaled $12 million in the current year. Dealer inventories of lawn and grounds care equipment were reduced by $64 million in 1991.

The combined operating profit of the credit, insurance and health care business segments declined to $164 million in 1991 from $175 million in 1990, as a result of lower insurance earnings. Additional information on these businesses is presented in the discussion of "Credit Operations" and "Insurance and Health Care Operations" on pages 40 through 42.

On a geographic basis, the United States and Canadian equipment operations earned $26 million in 1991 compared with an operating profit of $552 million last year. Lower volumes and higher sales discounts and allowances in all of the company's businesses along with restructuring costs of $162 million caused this decrease. However, LIFO inventory benefits were $104 million this year. Total United States and Canadian net sales to dealers declined 17 percent from 1990, while production was 18 percent lower than last year's level. North American dealers' inventories were reduced by $114 million during 1991.

The overseas equipment operations incurred an operating loss of $10 million in 1991 compared with an operating profit of $89 million last year. This decline was caused mainly by the previously discussed depressed results of the overseas agricultural equipment operations. Additionally, restructuring charges of $20 million were incurred this year. Benefits from the reduction of LIFO inventories totaled $24 million in 1991. Total overseas sales declined four percent in 1991 and production was 13 percent lower than last year. Overseas dealers' inventories decreased $53 million during the year.

OUTLOOK

Although the economic fundamentals of North American agriculture remain relatively strong, the company expects farmers to remain cautious in making new product purchase decisions in 1992. It is expected that large shipments of grain to the Soviet Union and China will help support world grain and oil-seed prices next year. Additionally, interest rates are expected to remain low and reduced government program set-asides are expected to permit eight million acres to be brought back into production in 1992. However, farmers' net cash income is expected to drop modestly in 1992 as a result of lower livestock prices, reduced government payments and higher expense levels. As a result of these factors, domestic agricultural machinery retail sales are expected to remain near 1991 levels.

The North American economy is expected to emerge from the recession in 1992, but at a much slower rate than in previous recoveries. Domestic retail sales of both industrial equipment and lawn and grounds care equipment are expected to gradually respond to such an upturn. In overseas markets, retail demand for all John Deere product lines is expected to approximate the level achieved in 1991.

Because of the uncertain outlook for the company's businesses, initial 1992 worldwide production, in tons, is scheduled to be about the same as the company's actual 1991 output. Agricultural equipment production is scheduled to be down modestly from last year, but offset by increases in lawn and grounds care equipment and industrial equipment schedules. Brief factory shutdowns have again been scheduled throughout the year to facilitate the low production volumes. These production levels are expected to result in further reductions in dealer and company inventories during 1992.

Margins of the company's Equipment Operations are expected to remain under pressure in 1992 due to the low volumes and continued strong price competition. Although first quarter 1992 production is expected to be approximately three percent higher than production in last year's extremely depressed first quarter, several of the company's factories will be shut down for one- to two-week periods in addition to the normal holiday shutdowns. As a result, the Equipment Operations are expected to incur a loss in the normally seasonally weak first quarter of 1992.

1990 Compared with 1989 (Unaudited)

MARKET CONDITIONS

North American agricultural economic conditions were favorable in 1990. Generally good weather conditions existed in major crop producing areas, facilitating higher production in 1990. Total North American industry retail sales of agricultural equipment increased for the 1990 fiscal year compared with 1989. Retail sales of John Deere agricultural equipment also improved for the entire year. However, despite continuing favorable agricultural fundamentals, agricultural equipment retail sales were lower in the fourth quarter of 1990 compared with 1989's final quarter. Outside the United States and Canada, retail sales of John Deere agricultural equipment were slightly higher in 1990.

The generally slower economic conditions caused industry retail sales of industrial and construction equipment in North America to be lower in 1990 compared with 1989's relatively strong level. However, North American retail sales of John Deere construction and forestry equipment were somewhat higher in 1990 compared with 1989. Overseas retail sales of industrial equipment declined in 1990.

As a result of slower economic growth in the United States and Canada and reduced consumer confidence and spending, retail sales of the company's lawn and grounds care equipment were lower in 1990. As the recessionary pressures became more intense and widespread in the latter part of the fiscal year, retail sales declined significantly from the comparable period in 1989. Overseas demand for lawn and grounds care equipment increased again in 1990.

The company's credit operations experienced additional growth in 1990 as higher overall retail sales of John Deere equipment coupled with an increase in the proportion of John Deere retail note acquisitions in relation to retail sales resulted in an increase in acquisitions of John Deere equipment retail notes. Insurance and health care premium volumes increased in 1990 compared with 1989.

EXHIBIT 1B-2. *(Continued)*

OPERATING RESULTS

Deere & Company's total worldwide net sales and revenues increased nine percent to $7,875 million in 1990 compared with $7,220 million in 1989. Worldwide net sales to dealers of John Deere agricultural equipment increased 10 percent to $4,519 million in 1990 from 1989's volume of $4,109 million. Worldwide industrial equipment net sales of $1,348 million increased three percent from $1,310 million in 1989. Worldwide net sales of lawn and grounds care equipment increased 12 percent to $912 million in 1990 from $815 million in 1989. The physical volume of the company's worldwide sales to dealers increased approximately four percent in 1990. Worldwide production tonnage of all John Deere products in 1990 was four percent higher than in 1989.

Net sales to dealers of John Deere equipment in the United States and Canada increased nine percent to $5,225 million compared with $4,813 million in 1989. Net sales of equipment overseas totaled $1,554 million, an increase of nine percent compared with 1989's net sales of $1,421 million. Excluding the effects of price increases and changes in currency relationships, the physical volume of overseas sales was approximately one percent lower in 1990 than in 1989.

Finance and interest income increased eight percent to $593 million in 1990 compared with $550 million in 1989, while insurance and health care premiums increased 12 percent to $384 million in 1990 compared with $343 million in 1989.

Worldwide net income in 1990 increased eight percent to $411 million or $5.42 per share compared with income of $380 million or $5.06 per share in 1989. The company's worldwide equipment operations had net income of $284 million in 1990, up 14 percent from income of $248 million in 1989. The improved operating results in 1990 were attributable to the company's North American agricultural equipment and lawn and grounds care equipment operations, and resulted primarily from higher sales and production volumes and improved operating efficiency. These gains were partially offset by lower earnings of the industrial equipment and overseas businesses. The ratio of the company's cost of goods sold to net sales was 80.1 percent in 1990 compared with 80.8 percent in 1989. This improvement relates to the North American operations. North American production tonnage was seven percent higher in 1990 than in 1989. Additionally, North American operating efficiency improved in 1990, and 1989's operations were affected by new product start-up expenses. However, the overseas operations' 1990 cost ratio increased over 1989 due to lower production, higher cost levels and a less favorable mix of sales.

The Equipment Operations' research and development expenses increased 13 percent in 1990 compared with 1989. These higher expense levels resulted mainly from the development of new products. Additionally, changes in foreign currency values in relation to the United States dollar caused some of the increase. The Equipment Operations' selling, administrative and general expenses increased 10 percent in 1990 compared with 1989. Although North American expense levels increased moderately in 1990, overseas expenses were higher due to increased marketing and advertising efforts, higher overall employment costs and, as previously mentioned, changes in foreign currency values.

Net income of the company's credit subsidiaries totaled $81 million in 1990 compared with net income of $76 million in 1989. Net income from insurance and health care operations was $41 million in 1990 compared with net income of $48 million in 1989. Additional information is presented in the discussion of "Credit Operations" and "Insurance and Health Care Operations" on pages 40 through 42.

BUSINESS SEGMENT AND GEOGRAPHIC AREA RESULTS

Operating profit of the worldwide agricultural equipment segment increased significantly in 1990 to $472 million compared with $399 million in 1989, benefiting from higher North American agricultural equipment volume. Worldwide agricultural equipment sales to dealers increased 10 percent from 1989, and production was up three percent from the level in 1989. North American agricultural equipment sales to dealers increased 10 percent over 1989, while production was up seven percent. Operating profit of the North American agricultural equipment division was up substantially compared with 1989. The 1990 results benefited from increased production and sales volumes and improved operating efficiency, offset to a certain extent by higher sales discounts and allowances. Operating profit from the overseas agricultural equipment business was lower in 1990 compared with 1989's strong results, due to lower production and higher cost and expense levels. Overseas agricultural equipment sales to dealers increased nine percent in 1990, while production was seven percent lower than in 1989.

Worldwide industrial equipment operating profit declined to $63 million in 1990 from $103 million in 1989, mainly as a result of higher sales incentive costs in 1990. Industrial equipment sales to dealers and production each increased three percent in 1990 compared with 1989's respective volumes.

Worldwide lawn and grounds care equipment operating profit increased considerably in 1990 to $106 million compared with $55 million in 1989. Sales to dealers of lawn and grounds care equipment increased 12 percent in 1990 and production was up 17 percent from 1989's level, while sales discounts and allowances were at a lower level in 1990. The lawn and grounds care results in 1989 were affected by extremely low volumes of production and sales to dealers coupled with higher sales incentive costs, as dealers reduced their excess inventories, and by the effects of a four-week strike at the company's factory in Wisconsin.

The combined operating profit of the credit, insurance and health care business segments declined slightly in 1990 to $175 million from $176 million in 1989.

On a geographic basis, United States and Canadian equipment operating profit was $552 million in 1990 compared with $446 million in 1989. This increase resulted mainly from the previously-described improved performance of the North American agricultural equipment and lawn and grounds care equipment operations. Total

EXHIBIT 1B-2. *(Continued)*

United States and Canadian net sales to dealers increased nine percent over 1989, while production was seven percent higher than in the prior year.

The overseas equipment operations produced an operating profit of $89 million in 1990 compared with $111 million in 1989. This decline resulted mainly from lower production and higher cost and expense levels. Total overseas sales increased nine percent over 1989, while production declined seven percent in 1990.

Credit Operations

Deere & Company's credit subsidiaries consist of John Deere Credit Company and its subsidiaries in the United States and John Deere Finance Limited in Canada. John Deere Credit Company's subsidiaries include John Deere Capital Corporation (Capital Corporation). The credit operations bear all credit risk, net of recovery from withholdings from dealers, and perform all servicing and collection functions on retail notes and leases on John Deere products acquired by the credit subsidiaries from the Equipment Operations. The Equipment Operations receive compensation from the United States credit operations for originating retail notes and leases. The Equipment Operations are reimbursed by the credit operations for staff support and other administrative services at estimated cost, and for credit lines provided by Deere & Company based on utilization of the lines. The credit subsidiaries receive compensation from the Equipment Operations approximately equal to the normal net finance income on retail notes for periods during which finance charges have been waived or reduced.

Condensed combined financial information of the credit subsidiaries in millions of dollars follows:

Financial Position	October 31	
	1991	1990
Cash and cash equivalents	$ 119	$ 98
Credit receivables and leases:		
Deere retail notes	3,370	2,672
Non-Deere retail notes	924	789
Revolving charge accounts	240	199
Financing leases	127	161
Wholesale notes	91	81
Equipment on operating leases	86	79
Total credit receivables and leases	4,838	3,981
Less allowance for credit losses	81	71
Total–net	4,757	3,910
Net property and other assets	75	62
Total assets	$4,951	$4,070

Financial Position	October 31	
	1991	1990
Short-term borrowings	$2,590	$2,042
Payables to Deere & Company	176	56
Deposits withheld from dealers and merchants	115	107
Other liabilities	112	128
Long-term borrowings	1,188	982
Stockholder's equity	770	755
Total liabilities and stockholder's equity	$4,951	$4,070

Summary of Operations	Year Ended October 31		
	1991	1990	1989
Finance and interest income	$548	$505	$462
Expenses:			
Interest	260	247	236
Selling, administrative and general	73	68	56
Provision for credit losses	68	50	27
Insurance	3	6	12
Depreciation	14	14	15
Total	418	385	346
Income before provision for income taxes	130	120	116
Provision for income taxes	46	39	40
Net income	$ 84	$ 81	$ 76

During 1991, net retail notes acquired by the credit subsidiaries totaled $2,684 million, a three percent increase compared with 1990 acquisitions of $2,601 million. Acquisitions of non-Deere retail notes accounted for 12 percent of total note acquisitions in 1991 and 15 percent in 1990. Acquisitions of John Deere equipment notes increased in the current year. Increased agricultural equipment retail note acquisitions resulted primarily from an increase in the proportion of John Deere agricultural equipment retail sales that were financed by the credit subsidiaries. This increase was offset to a certain extent by lower retail sales and related note acquisitions of industrial equipment and lawn and grounds care equipment in 1991 due to the overall recessionary environment in North America. Acquisitions of non-Deere retail notes were significantly lower in the current year, due mainly to lower industry retail sales of recreational marine products and more selective note acquisition criteria utilized by the credit subsidiaries.

Revolving charge accounts receivable increased by $41 million this year primarily due to the introduction in 1991 of a major purchase finance option for lawn and grounds care equipment, an increase in revolving charge account volume and an increase in the number of active credit card accounts during the past 12 months. The average balance of total net credit receivables and leases financed was 21 percent higher in 1991 compared with last year.

During 1990, $579 million of proceeds were received from the sale of Deere retail notes to other financial institutions. Retail notes were not sold in 1991. The net unpaid balance of retail notes sold was $242 million at October 31, 1991 compared with $521 million at October 31, 1990.

EXHIBIT 1B-2. *(Continued)*

Net income of the credit operations was $84 million in 1991 compared with $81 million in 1990 and $76 million in 1989. The ratio of earnings before fixed charges to fixed charges was 1.50 to 1 in 1991, 1.48 to 1 in 1990 and 1.49 to 1 in 1989. Net income in the current year benefited from a larger volume of receivables and leases financed and improved financing margins. Finance and interest income increased nine percent in 1991 compared with 1990, while interest expense increased five percent. Partially offsetting these improvements were increases in the provision for credit losses and administrative and operating expenses. The increase in the provision for credit losses resulted mainly from increased receivable and lease write-offs and a higher allowance for credit losses due to growth in the receivable and lease portfolio. Although increased write-offs affected all receivable categories, the largest write-offs related to the non-Deere portfolio, resulting from recessionary pressures affecting customers and lower resale values of repossessed equipment. Administrative and operating expenses increased in 1991 primarily due to the larger portfolio financed. Results in 1990 benefited from net after-tax gains on sales of retail notes to other financial institutions.

The higher net income in 1990 compared with 1989 resulted mainly from higher margins earned on a larger average volume of total net receivables and leases financed, increased gains on sales of retail notes to other financial institutions, lower insurance expense incurred on financed equipment and a lower effective income tax rate. Finance and interest income increased nine percent in 1990 compared with 1989. Partially offsetting these improvements was a significant increase in the provision for credit losses and higher administrative and operating expenses in 1990. The increase in the provision for credit losses was primarily due to the continued growth of the retail note portfolio and significantly higher write-offs of uncollectible non-Deere retail notes.

The total face value of retail note and lease installments 60 days or more past-due was $23 million at October 31, 1991 compared with $19 million at October 31, 1990. These past-due installments represented .40 percent of the unpaid face value of retail notes and leases held at October 31, 1991 and .39 percent at October 31, 1990. The total amount of revolving charge accounts past due 60 days or more was $8.5 million at October 31, 1991 compared with $7.0 million at October 31, 1990. These past due accounts represented 3.5 percent of the revolving charge accounts receivable held at the end of 1991 and 1990. The allowance for credit losses represented 1.68 percent and 1.79 percent, respectively, of the unpaid balance of total net receivables and leases financed at October 31, 1991 and 1990. Deposits withheld from dealers and merchants, which amounted to $115 million at October 31, 1991, also provide for potential non-collectibility.

Deere & Company has expressed an intention of conducting business with the Capital Corporation on such terms that its ratio of earnings before fixed charges to fixed charges will not be less than 1.05 to 1 for each fiscal quarter. These arrangements are not intended to make Deere & Company responsible for the payment of obligations of this credit subsidiary.

Insurance and Health Care Operations

Deere & Company's insurance subsidiaries consist of John Deere Insurance Group, Inc. and its subsidiaries in the United States and John Deere Insurance Company of Canada. John Deere Health Care, Inc., through its health care management subsidiary, Heritage National Healthplan, provides health programs and administrative services for companies located in Illinois, Iowa, Wisconsin and Tennessee. At October 31, 1991, 192,000 individuals were enrolled in these programs, of which approximately 67,000 were Deere & Company employees, retirees and their dependents.

Condensed combined financial information of the insurance and health care operations in millions of dollars follows:

	October 31	
Financial Position	1991	1990
Cash	$ 60	$ 62
Marketable securities carried at cost	857	801
Other assets	214	147
Total assets	$1,131	$1,010
Claims and reserves	$ 494	$ 443
Unearned premiums	116	114
Other liabilities	148	105
Stockholder's equity	373	348
Total liabilities and stockholder's equity	$1,131	$1,010

	Year Ended October 31		
Summary of Operations	1991	1990	1989
Premiums	$576	$505	$454
Investment income	88	87	76
Total revenues	664	592	530
Expenses:			
Claims and benefits	517	439	385
Selling, administrative and general	114	98	85
Total	631	537	470
Income before provision for income taxes	33	55	60
Provision for income taxes	6	14	12
Income of consolidated group	27	41	48
Equity in income of unconsolidated affiliate	1		
Net income	$ 28	$ 41	$ 48

Insurance premium revenue of $30 million in 1991, $31 million in 1990 and $29 million in 1989 and health care premium revenue of $102 million in 1991, $90 million in 1990 and $82 million in 1989 related to coverages provided to Deere & Company and its subsidiaries.

Net income of the insurance and health care operations totaled $28 million in 1991 compared with $41 million in 1990 and $48 million in 1989. The decrease in 1991 net income compared with last year resulted from a decline in insurance income. Although premium

EXHIBIT 1B-2. *(Continued)*

volumes increased, insurance income was adversely affected by underwriting losses in the company's property/casualty insurance lines, reflecting continued soft market conditions and deteriorating worker's compensation results, in common with overall performance by the insurance industry. Health care income increased in 1991 as a result of higher volumes, improved underwriting performance and higher investment income. Insurance and health care premiums increased 14 percent in 1991, while insurance and health care claims and policy benefits increased 18 percent from last year.

The decrease in 1990 net income compared with 1989 resulted from a decline in insurance underwriting income and a higher effective income tax rate, partially offset by increased investment income and improved health care margins. The lower underwriting income included the effects of an unusually high number of large property/casualty claims. Insurance and health care premiums increased 11 percent in 1990, while claims and policy benefits increased 14 percent from 1989.

Capital Resources and Liquidity (Unaudited)

The discussion of capital resources and liquidity focuses on the balance sheet and statement of cash flows. The nature of the company's Equipment Operations and Financial Services businesses are so different that most of the asset, liability and cash flow categories do not lend themselves to simple combination. Additionally, the fundamental differences between these businesses are reflected in different financial measurements commonly used by investors, rating agencies and financial analysts. In recognition of these differences and to provide clarity with respect to the analyses of the capital resources and liquidity of these different businesses, the following discussion has been organized to discuss separately, where appropriate, the company's Equipment Operations, Financial Services operations and the consolidated totals.

EQUIPMENT OPERATIONS

The company's equipment businesses are capital intensive and are subject to large seasonal variations in financing requirements for receivables from dealers and inventories. Accordingly, to the extent necessary, funds provided from operations are supplemented from external borrowing sources.

Despite a significant decline in income, cash flows from operating activities were higher in 1991 compared with 1990, mainly as a result of decreases in receivables and inventories this year compared with a significant increase in receivables during 1990. Cash flows from operating activities, which include dividends of $87 million received from the Financial Services subsidiaries, totaled $468 million in 1991. Total proceeds from additional net borrowings were $281 million during 1991. The aggregate amount of these cash flows was used primarily to fund expenditures for property and equipment of $295 million, the payment of dividends to stockholders of $152 million, an increase in receivables from Financial Services subsidiaries of $121 million, $71

million for the acquisition of a European lawn and grounds care company and a $73 million increase in cash and cash equivalents.

Over the last three years, operating activities have provided an aggregate of $1,010 million in cash, which includes dividends of $235 million received from the Financial Services subsidiaries. Total additional net borrowings have provided $595 million during this three-year period. The aggregate amount of these cash flows were used mainly to fund expenditures for property and equipment of $759 million, stockholders' dividends of $379 million, acquisitions of businesses of $158 million and an increase in receivables from Financial Services subsidiaries of $144 million.

Net dealer accounts and notes receivable result mainly from sales to dealers of equipment that is being carried in their inventories. Total dealer receivables decreased by $167 million during 1991. North American agricultural equipment dealer receivables increased $37 million during the year, mainly as a result of higher used goods inventories. North American industrial equipment dealer receivables decreased by $93 million during 1991, while North American lawn and grounds care equipment receivables declined by $58 million. Total overseas dealer receivables were $53 million lower than one year ago. The ratios of worldwide net dealer accounts and notes receivable at October 31 to fiscal year net sales were 51 percent in 1991, 46 percent in 1990, 41 percent in 1989 and 43 percent in 1988.

The collection period for receivables from dealers averages less than 12 months. The percentage of receivables outstanding for a period exceeding 12 months was 16 percent at October 31, 1991 compared with 10 percent at October 31, 1990 and nine percent at October 31, 1989.

Company-owned inventories decreased by $140 million in 1991 mainly as a result of lower production levels and continued improvement in inventory management practices.

Capital expenditures were $295 million in 1991 compared with $288 million in 1990 and $182 million in 1989. It is currently estimated that capital expenditures for 1992 will be approximately $290 million. As in recent years, the 1992 expenditures will be primarily for new product and operations improvement programs.

Total interest-bearing debt of the Equipment Operations was $1,899 million at the end of 1991 compared with $1,654 million at the end of 1990 and $1,463 million at the end of 1989. The ratio of total debt to total capital (total interest-bearing debt and stockholders' equity) at the end of 1991, 1990, and 1989 was 40.1 percent, 35.5 percent and 34.5 percent, respectively.

The average short-term borrowings and the weighted average interest rate incurred thereon during 1991, excluding the current portion of long-term borrowings, were $1,201 million and 8.7 percent, respectively, compared with $937 million and 10.2 percent, respectively, in 1990. During 1989, average short-term borrowings were $960 million with an average interest rate of 9.9 percent.

In 1991, Deere & Company issued $150 million of 8-1/4% notes due in 1996 and $201 million of medium-term notes. Additional information on these borrowings is included in the "Long-Term Borrowings" note on pages 54 through 55.

EXHIBIT 1B-2. *(Continued)*

FINANCIAL SERVICES

The Financial Services credit subsidiaries rely on their ability to raise substantial amounts of funds to finance their receivable and lease port-folios. Their primary sources of funds for this purpose is a combination of borrowings and equity capital. Additionally, in 1989 and 1990, the Capital Corporation sold substantial amounts of retail notes to other financial institutions, although none were sold in 1991. The insurance and health care operations generate their funds through internal opera-tions and have no external borrowings.

Cash flows from the company's Financial Services operating activities were $231 million in 1991. Net cash used for investing activi-ties totaled $1,003 million in 1991, resulting mainly from an increase in credit receivables financed. The cost of credit receivables acquired exceeded collections by $926 million in 1991. Cash provided by financing activities totaled $791 million in 1991, resulting mainly from a net increase in outside borrowings of $744 million and an increase in payables to the Equipment Operations of $121 million, partially offset by $87 million of dividends paid to the Equipment Operations. The aggregate cash provided by operating and financing activities was used to finance the net increase in credit receivables and leases during 1991. Within the Financial Services operations, the positive cash flows from insurance and health care operations were primarily invested in mar-ketable securities.

Over the past three years, the Financial Services operating activities have provided $660 million in cash, total proceeds from addi-tional borrowings were $1,451 million and payables to the Equipment Operations have increased by $139 million. These amounts, along with a decrease in cash of $38 million, have been used mainly to fund an increase of $1,838 million in the credit receivable and lease portfolios, an increase of $199 million in marketable securities and $235 million of dividends to the Equipment Operations.

Marketable securities carried at cost consist primarily of debt securities held by the insurance and health care operations in support of their obligations to policyholders. The $56 million increase in 1991 resulted primarily from the continuing growth in the insurance and health care operations.

Net credit receivables increased by $840 million in 1991 compared with 1990. The discussion of "Credit Operations" on pages 40 through 41, and pages 51 through 52 of the notes to the consolidated financial statements provide detailed information on these receivables.

Total interest-bearing debt of the credit subsidiaries was $3,779 million at the end of 1991 compared with $3,024 million at the end of 1990 and $2,461 million at the end of 1989. Strong capital posi-tions for both the credit and insurance operations continued during 1991. The credit subsidiaries' ratio of total interest-bearing debt to total stockholders' equity was 4.9 to 1 at the end of 1991 compared with 4.0 to 1 at the end of 1990 and 3.3 to 1 at the end of 1989.

The average short-term borrowings of the credit subsidiaries and the weighted average interest rate incurred thereon during 1991, excluding the current portion of long-term borrowings, were $2,135 million and 7.3 percent, respectively, compared with $1,809 million

and 8.9 percent, respectively, in 1990. During 1989, average short-term borrowings were $1,631 million with an average interest rate of 9.6 percent.

In 1991, the Capital Corporation issued $150 million of 7.40% notes due in 1993 and $276 million of medium-term notes. Additional information on these borrowings is included in the "Long-Term Borrowings" note on pages 54 and 55.

The Capital Corporation has an agreement with a financial institution providing the Capital Corporation with the right to sell retail notes from time to time through June 1992, provided the net unpaid value of all retail notes sold does not exceed $400 million. The Capital Corporation sold retail notes under this agreement, and under two similar facilities, receiving proceeds of $579 million in 1990. The Capital Corporation did not sell any retail notes in 1991. At October 31, 1991, the Capital Corporation had the right under this agreement to sell additional retail notes having a net unpaid value of approximately $320 million. Additional sales of retail notes may be made in the future.

CONSOLIDATED

Deere & Company maintains unsecured lines of credit with various banks in North America and overseas. Some of the lines are maintained jointly by the company and its wholly-owned credit subsidiaries. Worldwide lines of credit totaled $3,962 million at October 31, 1991, $832 million of which were unused. For the purpose of computing unused credit lines, total short-term borrowings, excluding the current portion of long-term borrowings, were considered to constitute utiliza-tion. Included in the total credit lines are three long-term credit agree-ment commitments totaling $3,213 million.

Stockholders' equity was $2,836 million at October 31, 1991 compared with $3,008 million and $2,780 million at October 31, 1990 and 1989, respectively. The decrease in 1991 resulted primarily from the net loss of $20 million and dividends declared of $152 million.

Industry Segment and Geographic Area Data for the Years Ended October 31, 1991, 1990 and 1989

Because of integrated manufacturing operations and common adminis-trative and marketing support, a substantial number of allocations must be made to determine industry segment and geographic area data. Intersegment sales and revenues represent sales of components, insur-ance and health care premiums, and finance charges. Interarea sales rep-resent sales of complete machines, service parts and components to units in other geographic areas. Intersegment sales and revenues are generally priced at market prices, and interarea sales are generally priced at cost plus a share of total operating profit. Overseas operations are defined to include all activities of divisions, subsidiaries and affiliated companies conducted outside the United States and Canada.

EXHIBIT 1B-2. *(Continued)*

Information relating to operations by industry segment in millions of dollars follows. Comments relating to this data are included in Management's Discussion and Analysis.

Industry Segments	1991	1990	1989
Net sales and revenues			
Unaffiliated customers:			
Agricultural equipment net sales...........	$4,054	$4,519	$4,109
Industrial equipment net sales..............	1,014	1,348	1,310
Lawn and grounds care equipment			
net sales...........	780	912	815
Credit revenues	547	504	460
Insurance and health care revenues	531	469	419
Total...........	6,926	7,752	7,113
Intersegment:			
Agricultural equipment net sales...........	85	117	120
Industrial equipment net sales..............	54	57	47
Credit revenues	1	1	2
Insurance and health care revenues	133	123	111
Total...........	273	298	280
Unaffiliated customers and intersegment:			
Agricultural equipment net sales...........	4,139	4,636	4,229
Industrial equipment net sales..............	1,068	1,405	1,357
Lawn and grounds care equipment			
net sales...........	780	912	815
Credit revenues	548	505	462
Insurance and health care revenues	664	592	530
Elimination of intersegment..................	(273)	(298)	(280)
Total...........	6,926	7,752	7,113
Other revenues	129	123	107
Consolidated net sales and			
revenues	$7,055	$7,875	$7,220
Operating profit (loss)			
Agricultural equipment	$ 123 *	$ 472	$ 399
Industrial equipment	(131)*	63	103
Lawn and grounds care equipment	24 *	106	55
Credit**	130	120	116
Insurance and health care**	34	55	60
Total operating profit..................	180	816	733
Other income and (expense)			
Interest income–net..................	14	9	15
Interest expense–net..................	(191)	(188)	(172)
Foreign exchange gain (loss)..................	1	(10)	(1)
Corporate expenses–net	(29)	(34)	(28)
Income taxes	5	(182)	(167)
Total	(200)	(405)	(353)
Net income (loss)	$ (20)	$ 411	$ 380

* Operating profit (loss) of the agricultural equipment, industrial equipment and lawn and grounds care equipment business segments in 1991 include restructuring costs of $128 million, $44 million and $10 million, respectively.

**Operating profit of the credit business segment includes the effect of interest expense, which is the largest element of its operating costs. Operating profit of the insurance and health care business segment includes investment income.

Industry Segments	1991	1990	1989
Identifiable assets			
Agricultural equipment	$ 3,500	$ 3,481	$2,833
Industrial equipment	1,205	1,287	1,133
Lawn and grounds care equipment	770	744	665
Credit.........	4,929	4,059	3,532
Insurance and health care	1,130	1,008	896
Corporate	115	85	86
Total.........	$11,649	$10,664	$9,145
Capital additions			
Agricultural equipment	$233	$216	$138
Industrial equipment	37	48	39
Lawn and grounds care equipment	33	25	28
Credit.........	1	2	3
Insurance and health care	2	2	2
Total	$306	$293	$210
Depreciation expense			
Agricultural equipment	$134	$127	$123
Industrial equipment	33	28	27
Lawn and grounds care equipment	18	17	16
Credit.........	2	2	1
Insurance and health care	2	2	2
Corporate	1	1	1
Total	$190	$177	$170

The company views and has historically disclosed its operations as consisting of two geographic areas, the United States and Canada, and overseas, shown below. The percentages shown in the captions for net sales and revenues, operating profit (loss) and identifiable assets indicate the approximate proportion of each amount that relates to either the United States only or to the company's Europe, Africa and Middle East division, the only overseas area deemed to be significant for disclosure purposes. The percentages are based upon a three-year average for 1991, 1990 and 1989.

Geographic Areas	1991	1990	1989
Net sales and revenues			
Unaffiliated customers:			
United States and Canada:			
Equipment net sales (91%).............	$4,349	$5,225	$4,813
Financial Services revenues (94%)..	1,078	973	879
Total	5,427	6,198	5,692
Overseas net sales (77%)	1,499	1,554	1,421
Total	6,926	7,752	7,113
Interarea:			
United States and Canada			
equipment net sales	411	386	424
Overseas net sales	299	382	310
Total.........	$ 710	$ 768	$ 734

(Continued)

EXHIBIT 1B-2. *(Continued)*

Geographic Areas	1991	1990	1989
Unaffiliated customers and interarea:			
United States and Canada:			
Equipment net sales	$4,760	$5,611	$5,237
Financial Services revenues	1,078	973	879
Total	5,838	6,584	6,116
Overseas net sales	1,798	1,936	1,731
Elimination of interarea	(710)	(768)	(734)
Total	6,926	7,752	7,113
Other revenues	129	123	107
Consolidated net sales and			
revenues	$7,055	$7,875	$7,220

Operating profit (loss)	1991	1990	1989
United States and Canada:			
Equipment operations (93%)	$ 26 *	$552	$446
Financial Services (90%)	164	175	176
Total	190	727	622
Overseas equipment operations (70%)	(10)*	89	111
Total operating profit	$180	$816	$733

* Operating profit (loss) of the United States and Canada equipment operations and the overseas equipment operations in 1991 include restructuring costs of $162 million and $20 million, respectively.

Identifiable assets	1991	1990	1989
United States and Canada:			
Equipment operations (91%)	$ 4,221	$ 4,299	$3,602
Financial Services (92%)	6,059	5,067	4,428
Total	10,280	9,366	8,030
Overseas equipment operations (81%)	1,254	1,213	1,029
Corporate	115	85	86
Total	$11,649	$10,664	$9,145

Capital additions	1991	1990	1989
United States and Canada:			
Equipment operations	$183	$198	$165
Financial Services	3	4	5
Total	186	202	170
Overseas equipment operations	120	91	40
Total	$306	$293	$210

Depreciation expense	1991	1990	1989
United States and Canada:			
Equipment operations	$138	$130	$129
Financial Services	4	4	3
Total	142	134	132
Overseas equipment operations	47	42	37
Corporate	1	1	1
Total	$190	$177	$170

Geographic Areas	1991	1990	1989
Number of employees			
United States and Canada:			
Equipment operations	24,800	26,300	26,700
Financial Services	2,300	2,200	1,900
Total	27,100	28,500	28,600
Overseas equipment operations	9,400	10,000	10,300
Total	36,500	38,500	38,900

Total exports from the United States were $713 million in 1991, $758 million in 1990 and $779 million in 1989. Exports decreased in 1991 and 1990 due to lower demand in Canada, Europe and Australia. Exports from the Europe, Africa and Middle East division were $416 million in 1991, $515 million in 1990 and $420 million in 1989.

Fourth Quarter Summary (Unaudited)

Condensed financial information, shown on a consolidated basis only, for the fourth quarter in millions of dollars follows:

	1991	1990
Net sales:		
Agricultural equipment	$1,080	$1,258
Industrial equipment	272	320
Lawn and grounds care equipment	232	193
Total net sales	1,584	1,771
Financial Services revenues	281	258
Other revenues	37	35
Total net sales and revenues	1,902	2,064
Total costs and expenses	2,013	1,974
Income (loss) of consolidated group before income taxes	(111)*	90
Provision (credit) for income taxes	(29)	17
Income (loss) of consolidated group	(82)*	73
Equity in income of unconsolidated affiliates	1	1
Net income (loss)	$ (81)*	$ 74
Net income (loss) per share	$(1.07)*	$ .98

*Includes pretax restructuring costs of $182 million ($120 million or $1.58 per share after taxes).

Net sales by geographic area	1991	1990
United States and Canada	$1,185	$1,333
Overseas	399	438
Total	$1,584	$1,771

North American retail sales of John Deere agricultural equipment were slightly higher during the fourth quarter of 1991 compared with last year's final quarter. In concert with general economic conditions, retail sales of John Deere industrial equipment and lawn and grounds care equipment declined below 1990 volumes during the final quarter of 1991. Demand for John Deere products overseas was higher than in last year's fourth quarter.

EXHIBIT 1B-2. *(Continued)*

A worldwide net loss of $81 million or $1.07 per share was incurred in the fourth quarter of 1991 compared with net income of $74 million or $.98 per share in last year's final quarter. Fourth quarter 1991 results include after-tax restructuring costs of $120 million or $1.58 per share, representing costs of employment reductions and the closure of a foundry. Excluding the one-time charges, fourth quarter net income would have been $39 million in 1991. However, results for the current quarter benefited by $65 million from the reduction of LIFO-valued inventories. Excluding the non-recurring charges, operating results for the quarter reflect the effects of producing at a significantly lower volume than last year in response to weak retail demand and to facilitate the reduction of company and dealers' inventories. Additionally, sales discounts and allowances were much higher, mainly due to extremely competitive conditions in all the company's markets. Net equipment sales were 11 percent lower than in the fourth quarter last year, while production tonnage was down 10 percent.

The worldwide Equipment Operations incurred a net loss of $103 million this year compared with net income of $40 million in the fourth quarter of 1990. Excluding the restructuring costs, the Equipment Operations would have earned $17 million for the quarter. The Equipment Operations benefited by $65 million from the reduction of LIFO-valued inventories. Net income of the credit operations was $21 million in the fourth quarter of both 1991 and 1990. The insurance and health care operations incurred a loss of $1 million in the quarter compared with net income of $12 million in the fourth quarter of 1990. Health care operations showed good improvement, but the insurance subsidiaries incurred a net loss in the fourth quarter this year due to underwriting losses in the property/casualty business.

Notes To Consolidated Financial Statements

Summary of Significant Accounting Policies

Following are significant accounting policies in addition to those included in other notes to the consolidated financial statements.

The consolidated financial statements represent the consolidations of all companies in which Deere & Company has a majority ownership. Deere & Company records its investment in each unconsolidated affiliated company (20 to 50 percent ownership) at its related equity in the net assets of such affiliate. Other investments (less than 20 percent ownership) are recorded at cost. Unconsolidated subsidiaries and affiliates at October 31, 1991 consisted primarily of equipment affiliates in Brazil, Mexico and the United States, and a United States reinsurance affiliate. Consolidated retained earnings at October 31, 1991 include undistributed earnings of the unconsolidated affiliates of $33 million. Dividends from unconsolidated affiliates were $6 million in 1991, $8 million in 1990 and $1 million in 1989.

In 1989, the company adopted Financial Accounting Standards Board (FASB) Statement No. 94, Consolidation of All Majority-owned Subsidiaries. In order to preserve as much as possible the identity of the principal financial data and related measurements to which stockholders and others have become accustomed over the years, consolidated financial statements and some information in the notes and commentary relating thereto are presented in a format which includes data grouped as follows:

Equipment Operations –These data reflect the pre-1989 basis of consolidation, which includes Financial Services on the equity basis. The consolidated group data in the Equipment Operations' income statement reflect the results of the company's agricultural equipment, industrial equipment and lawn and grounds care equipment operations. Where appropriate, for clarification or emphasis, these consolidated group data are also referred to as "Equipment Operations".

Financial Services –These data include Deere & Company's credit, insurance and health care subsidiaries, which consist of John Deere Credit Company, John Deere Finance Limited (Canada), John Deere Insurance Group, John Deere Insurance Company of Canada and John Deere Health Care, Inc. These subsidiaries and their respective subsidiaries are consolidated in the Financial Services data with the effect of transactions among them eliminated to arrive at this consolidated presentation.

Consolidated –These data represent the consolidation of the Equipment Operations and Financial Services in conformity with FASB Statement No. 94. The effect of transactions between the "Equipment Operations" and "Financial Services" have been eliminated to arrive at the consolidated totals. References in this report to "Deere & Company" or "the company" refer to the entire enterprise.

Sales of equipment and service parts are generally recorded by the company when they are shipped to independent dealers. Provisions for sales incentives and returns and allowances are made at the time of sale or at inception of the incentive programs. There is a time lag, which varies based on the timing and level of retail demand, between the dates when the company records sales to dealers and when

EXHIBIT 1B-2. *(Continued)*

dealers sell the equipment to retail customers.

Retail notes receivable include unearned finance income in the face amount of the notes, which is amortized into income over the lives of the notes on the effective-yield basis. Unearned finance income on variable-rate notes is adjusted monthly based on fluctuations in the base rate of a specified bank. Financing leases receivable include unearned lease income, the excess of the gross lease receivable plus the estimated residual value over the cost of the equipment, which is recognized as revenue over the lease terms on the effective-yield basis. Rental payments applicable to equipment on operating leases are recorded as income on a straight-line method over the lease terms. These leased assets are recorded at cost and depreciated on a straight-line method over the terms of the leases. Origination costs incurred in the acquisition of retail notes and leases are deferred and amortized into income over the expected lives of the affected receivables on the effective-yield basis. Interest charged to revolving charge account customers and on wholesale receivables is based on the balances outstanding.

Insurance and health care premiums are generally recognized as earned over the terms of the related policies. Insurance and health care claims and reserves include liabilities for unpaid claims and future policy benefits. Policy acquisition costs, such as commissions, premium taxes and certain other underwriting expenses, which vary with the production of business, are deferred and amortized over the terms of the related policies. The liability for unpaid claims and claims adjustment expenses is based on estimated costs of settling the claims using past experience adjusted for current trends. The liability for future policy benefits on traditional life insurance policies is based on the mortality, interest and withdrawal assumptions prevailing at the time the policies are issued. The liability for universal life type contracts is the total of the policyholder accumulated funds. Investment yields used in calculating future policyholder benefits and universal life account values range from six percent to 13 percent.

In September 1991, Deere & Company purchased for $75 million a majority interest in SABO Maschinenfabrik AG (SABO) of Germany, which produces lawn and grounds care products for European markets at facilities in Germany and the Netherlands.

During the 1991 fiscal year, the company's insurance subsidiaries purchased $16 million of additional shares of common stock in Re Capital Corporation, which increased the company's ownership percentage from nine percent to 25 percent. As a result, during 1991, this investment was recorded as an investment in unconsolidated affiliates. Also in 1991, the insurance subsidiaries acquired the business of the Integral Insurance Company for $14 million.

Certain amounts for prior years have been reclassified to conform with 1991 financial statement presentations.

Restructuring Costs

During the fourth quarter of 1991, the company initiated plans to reduce costs and rationalize operations, both in North America and overseas. This resulted in a fourth quarter pretax provision of $182 million ($120 million or $1.58 per share after income taxes), representing costs of employment reductions and the closure of a ductile iron foundry.

Pension and Other Retirement Benefits

The company has several pension plans covering substantially all of its United States employees and employees in certain foreign countries. The United States plans and significant foreign plans in Canada, Germany and France are defined benefit plans in which the benefits are based primarily on years of service and employee compensation near retirement. It is the company's policy to fund its United States plans according to the 1974 Employee Retirement Income Security Act (ERISA) and income tax regulations. In Canada and France, the company's funding is in accordance with local laws and income tax regulations, while the German pension plan is unfunded. Plan assets in the United States, Canada and France consist primarily of common stocks, common trust funds, government securities and corporate debt securities.

Provisions of FASB Statement No. 87 require the company to record a minimum pension liability relating to certain unfunded pension obligations, establish an intangible asset relating thereto and reduce stockholders' equity. At October 31, 1991, this minimum pension liability was remeasured, as required by the Statement. As a result, the minimum pension liability was adjusted from $305 million at October 31, 1990 to $380 million at October 31, 1991; the related intangible asset was adjusted from $171 million to $249 million; and the amount by which stockholders' equity had been reduced was adjusted from $88 million to $86 million (net of applicable deferred income taxes of $46 million in 1990 and $45 million in 1991). The adjustment in the minimum pension liability at October 31, 1991 resulted mainly from an increase in pension fund liabilities due to changes in plan benefits and a decrease in the discount rate. This increase was partially offset by an increase in pension fund assets due to favorable investment experience during 1991.

The expense of all pension plans was $94 million in 1991, $80 million in 1990 and $68 million in 1989. In 1991, pension expense increased by $22 million from service experience, retiree experience and certain actuarial assumption changes, which was partially offset by a reduction of $5 million from the utilization of a higher discount rate and a reduction of $3 million from favorable investment experience. In 1990, pension expense increased by $17 million from the utilization of a lower discount rate and by $8 million due to changes in plan benefits, experience and exchange rates. These increases were partially offset by a reduction of $13 million resulting from favorable investment experience.

The components of net periodic pension cost and the significant assumptions for the United States plans consisted of the following

EXHIBIT 1B-2. *(Continued)*

in millions of dollars and in percents:

	1991	1990	1989
Service cost	$ 64	$ 65	$ 51
Interest cost	231	213	203
Return on assets	(622)	200	(393)
Net amortization and deferral	400	(419)	190
Net cost	$ 73	$ 59	$ 51
Discount rates for obligations	8.3%	9.0%	8.5%
Discount rates for expenses	9.0%	8.5%	9.3%
Assumed rates of compensation increases	6.3%	6.3%	6.3%
Expected long-term rates of return	9.7%	9.7%	9.7%

A reconciliation of the funded status of the United States plans at October 31 in millions of dollars follows:

	1991		1990	
	Assets Exceed Accumulated Benefits	Accumulated Benefits Exceed Assets	Assets Exceed Accumulated Benefits	Accumulated Benefits Exceed Assets
Actuarial present value of benefit obligations				
Vested benefit obligation	$(1,257)	$(1,387)	$ (892)	$(1,008)
Nonvested benefit obligation	(101)	(186)	(114)	(230)
Accumulated benefit obligation	(1,358)	(1,573)	(1,006)	(1,238)
Excess of projected benefit obligation over accumulated benefit obligation	(351)	(27)	(345)	(28)
Projected benefit obligation	(1,709)	(1,600)	(1,351)	(1,266)
Plan assets at fair value	1,495	1,185	1,220	911
Projected benefit obligation (in excess of) or less than plan assets	(214)	(415)	(131)	(355)
Unrecognized net loss	91	182	153	192
Prior service cost not yet recognized in net periodic pension cost	1	224	1	140
Remaining unrecognized transition net asset from November 1, 1985	(103)	(20)	(141)	(27)
Adjustment required to recognize minimum liability		(359)		(277)
Pension liability recognized in the consolidated balance sheet	$ (225)	$ (388)	$ (118)	$ (327)

The components of net periodic pension cost and the significant assumptions for the foreign plans consisted of the following in millions of dollars and in percents:

	1991	1990	1989
Service cost	$ 9	$ 9	$ 7
Interest cost	21	19	17
Return on assets	(14)	(10)	(11)
Net amortization and deferral	5	3	4
Net cost	$ 21	$ 21	$ 17
Discount rates for obligations	7.0 - 9.3%	7.0 - 9.8%	7.0 - 8.5%
Discount rates for expenses	7.0 - 9.8%	7.0 - 8.5%	7.0 - 9.5%
Assumed rates of compensation increases	4.0 - 7.0%	4.0 - 7.3%	4.0 - 7.0%
Expected long-term rates of return	7.0 - 9.8%	7.0 - 8.5%	7.0 - 9.5%

A reconciliation of the funded status of the foreign plans at October 31 in millions of dollars follows:

	1991		1990	
	Assets Exceed Accumulated Benefits	Accumulated Benefits Exceed Assets	Assets Exceed Accumulated Benefits	Accumulated Benefits Exceed Assets
Actuarial present value of benefit obligations				
Vested benefit obligation	$(65)	$(183)	$(56)	$(185)
Nonvested benefit obligation		(4)		(4)
Accumulated benefit obligation	(65)	(187)	(56)	(189)
Excess of projected benefit obligation over accumulated benefit obligation	(10)	(40)	(10)	(41)
Projected benefit obligation	(75)	(227)	(66)	(230)
Plan assets at fair value	128		115	
Projected benefit obligation (in excess of) or less than plan assets	53	(227)	49	(230)
Unrecognized net (gain) loss	(12)	3	(11)	
Remaining unrecognized transition net (asset) obligation from November 1, 1987	(27)	58	(29)	69
Adjustment required to recognize minimum liability		(21)		(28)
Prepaid pension asset (pension liability) recognized in the consolidated balance sheet	$ 14	$(187)	$ 9	$(189)

EXHIBIT 1B-2. *(Continued)*

In addition to providing pension benefits, the company provides certain health care and life insurance benefits for retired employees. Substantially all of the company's United States and Canadian employees may become eligible for these benefits if they reach retirement age while still working for the company. These benefits are either self-insured or are provided through the company's insurance and health care subsidiaries. The company recognizes the cost of the self-insured benefits as the claims are incurred and recognizes the cost of the benefits provided through the insurance and health care subsidiaries by expensing the annual premiums. The cost of health care benefits for retired United States and Canadian employees in 1991, 1990 and 1989 was $71 million, $60 million and $55 million, respectively; and the cost of life insurance benefits for retired employees was $7 million in 1991 and $6 million in both 1990 and 1989.

Most retirees outside the United States and Canada are covered by governmental health care programs, and the company's cost is not significant.

In December 1990, the FASB issued Statement No. 106, Employers' Accounting for Postretirement Benefits Other Than Pensions. This statement must be adopted no later than the company's 1994 fiscal year, and generally requires the accrual of retiree health care and other postretirement benefits during employees' years of active service. Deere & Company currently expenses the costs of these benefits when paid.

Upon adoption, the new standard requires the recognition of a transition obligation which represents that portion of future retiree benefit costs related to service already rendered by both active and retired employees up to the date of adoption. This initial liability can either be recognized immediately as a one-time charge to earnings in the year of adoption, or amortized through charges to earnings over a 20-year period. Although Deere & Company continues to evaluate the impact of this new standard, the company's preliminary estimates of the transition obligation range from $1.2 billion to $1.7 billion. Preliminary estimates of incremental annual expense for Deere & Company and its consolidated subsidiaries following adoption range from $60 million (if the entire transition obligation were recognized in the year of adoption) to $200 million (if the transition obligation were accrued over a 20-year period). The foregoing amounts have been reduced by income tax benefits expected to be recognized in accordance with a FASB exposure draft of a new accounting standard. These preliminary estimates are subject to change and are dependent upon a number of variables including future medical inflation rates, health care trends, benefit plan changes, the discount factor used in determining the initial liability, when the standard is adopted, whether the transition obligation is recognized immediately or amortized over 20 years, whether or not the tax benefits are in fact available, etc.

Although implementation of the standard is expected to have an adverse effect on Deere & Company's future reported net income, it will not affect the company's cash flows because the company plans to continue paying the cost of post-employment benefits when incurred. The company has not determined when the statement will be adopted or how the transition obligation will be recognized.

Income Taxes

Income (loss) before income taxes in millions of dollars based upon the locations of the company's operations follow:

	1991	1990	1989
Equipment Operations			
United States operations	$(162)	$366	$233
Foreign operations	(27)	47	130
Total	(189)	413	363
Financial Services			
United States operations	143	153	159
Foreign operations	20	22	17
Total	163	175	176
Consolidated			
United States operations	(19)	519	392
Foreign operations	(7)	69	147
Total	$ (26)	$588	$539

Certain overseas operations are branches of Deere & Company and are therefore subject to United States as well as foreign income tax regulations. The above analysis of pretax income (loss) and the following analysis of the income tax provision (credit) by taxing jurisdiction are therefore not directly related.

The provision (credit) for income taxes by location of the taxing jurisdiction and by significant component consisted of the following in millions of dollars:

	1991	1990	1989
Equipment Operations			
Current:			
United States:			
Federal	$ 4	$ 20	$ 30
State	11	5	7
Foreign	8	15	25
Total current	23	40	62
Deferred:			
United States:			
Federal	(74)	86	58
State	(5)	2	(5)
Foreign	(2)	1	
Total deferred	(81)	89	53
Total	(58)	129	115
Financial Services			
Current:			
United States:			
Federal	61	76	66
State	2	2	2
Foreign	9	6	8
Total current	72	84	76
Deferred United States federal	(19)	(31)	(24)
Total	53	53	52
Consolidated provision (credit) for income taxes	$ (5)	$182	$167

EXHIBIT 1B-2. *(Continued)*

A comparison of the statutory and effective income tax provision (credit) and reasons for related differences in millions of dollars follows:

	1991	1990	1989
United States federal income tax provision (credit) at a statutory rate of 34 percent	$ (9)	$200	$183
Equipment Operations			
Increase (decrease) resulting from:			
Taxes on foreign income which differ from the United States statutory rate	6	5	(4)
Realization of benefits of tax-loss and tax-credit carryforwards	(2)	(17)	(2)
Other adjustments – net............................	3	1	(2)
Total..	7	(11)	(8)
Financial Services			
Increase (decrease) resulting from:			
Tax exempt investment income	(6)	(7)	(8)
Realization of benefits of tax-loss carryforwards..........................		(4)	
Other adjustments–net..............................	3	4	
Total..	(3)	(7)	(8)
Consolidated provision (credit) for income taxes...............................	$ (5)	$182	$167

Deferred income taxes arise because there are certain items that are treated differently for financial accounting than for income tax reporting purposes. An analysis of the deferred income tax liability at October 31 in millions of dollars follows:

	1991	1990
Equipment Operations		
Deferred installment sales income	$281	$321
Tax over book depreciation	88	81
Accrual for sales allowances.....................	(134)	(113)
Minimum pension liability adjustment.	(45)	(46)
Accrual for vacation pay	(26)	(18)
Accrual for restructuring costs	(12)	
Allowances for doubtful receivables	(6)	(6)
Other items..	(50)	(41)
Total................................	96	178
Financial Services		
Deferred retail note finance income.	2	6
Deferred lease income	4	5
Allowances for doubtful receivables and leases.................................	(27)	(22)
Other items..		5
Total................................	(21)	(6)
Consolidated deferred income tax liability...................................	$ 75	$172

At October 31, 1991, accumulated earnings in certain overseas subsidiaries and affiliates totaled $364 million for which no provision for United States income taxes or foreign withholding taxes has been made, because it is expected that such earnings will be reinvested overseas indefinitely. Determination of the amount of unrecognized deferred tax liability on these unremitted earnings is not practicable. The amount of withholding taxes that would be payable upon remittance of those earnings would be $33 million.

Deere & Company files a consolidated federal income tax return in the United States which includes certain wholly-owned Financial Services subsidiaries, primarily John Deere Capital Corporation, Deere Credit, Inc. and the health care subsidiaries. These subsidiaries account for income taxes generally as if they filed separate income tax returns. Deere & Company's insurance subsidiaries file separate federal income tax returns.

During 1991, 1990 and 1989, the company recognized $2 million, $21 million and $2 million, respectively, of income tax benefits relating to tax-loss and tax-credit carryforwards from previous years. At October 31, 1991, certain foreign tax-loss carryforwards were available which have not been recognized as tax benefits.

Marketable Securities

Marketable securities are held by the insurance and health care subsidiaries. Fixed maturities, consisting of corporate bonds, government bonds and certificates of deposit, are carried at amortized cost and generally held to maturity. Equity securities, consisting of common and preferred stocks, are carried at cost.

The value of marketable securities at October 31 in millions of dollars follows:

| | 1991 | | 1990 | |
	Carrying Value	Market Value	Carrying Value	Market Value
Fixed maturities........................	$780	$837	$711	$732
Equity securities........................	65	65	80	72
Other	12	14	10	9
Marketable securities..........	$857	$916	$801	$813

The carrying value and market value of fixed maturities at October 31, 1991 in millions of dollars follows:

	Carrying Value	Gross Unrealized Gains	Gross Unrealized Losses	Market Value
United States government and its agencies	$217	$ 16		$233
States and municipalities.........	196	17		213
Corporate.................................	350	25	$ 3	372
Other	17	2		19
Fixed maturities	$780	$ 60	$ 3	$837

EXHIBIT 1B-2. *(Continued)*

The contractual maturities of fixed maturities at October 31, 1991 in millions of dollars follows:

	Carrying Value	Market Value
Due in one year or less	$ 31	$ 31
Due after one year through five years	119	121
Due after five years through 10 years	152	163
Due after 10 years	478	522
Fixed maturities	$780	$837

Actual maturities may differ from contractual maturities because some borrowers have the right to call or prepay obligations. Proceeds from the sales of fixed maturities during 1991 were $91 million. Gross gains of $12 million and gross losses of $4 million were realized on those sales.

Dealer Accounts and Notes Receivable

Dealer accounts and notes receivable at October 31 consisted of the following in millions of dollars:

	1991	1990
Dealer accounts and notes:		
Agricultural	$1,746	$1,755
Industrial	587	681
Lawn and grounds care	475	539
Total	2,808	2,975
Other receivables	178	146
Total	2,986	3,121
Less allowance for doubtful receivables	19	21
Dealer accounts and notes receivable–net	$2,967	$3,100

At October 31, 1991 and 1990, dealer notes included above were $457 million and $354 million, respectively.

Dealer accounts and notes receivable arise primarily from sales to dealers of John Deere agricultural, industrial and lawn and grounds care equipment. The company retains as collateral a security interest in the equipment associated with these receivables. Generally, terms to dealers require payments as the equipment which secures the indebtedness is sold to retail customers. Interest is charged on balances outstanding after certain interest-free periods, which range from six to nine months for industrial equipment, nine months for agricultural tractors, and from nine to 24 months for most other equipment.

Dealer accounts and notes receivable have significant concentrations of credit risk in the agricultural, industrial and lawn and grounds care business sectors. At October 31, 1991 and 1990, the portions of these net receivables related to the agricultural equipment business were approximately 62 percent and 59 percent, those related to the industrial equipment business were approximately 21 percent and 23 percent, and those related to the lawn and grounds care equipment business were 17 percent and 18 percent, respectively. On a geographic basis, there is not a disproportionate concentration of credit risk in any area.

Credit Receivables

Credit receivables at October 31 consisted of the following in millions of dollars:

	1991	1990
Retail notes:		
John Deere equipment:		
Agricultural	$3,216	$2,402
Industrial	591	594
Lawn and grounds care	237	256
Non-Deere equipment	1,545	1,401
Total	5,589	4,653
Revolving charge accounts	240	199
Financing leases	207	237
Wholesale notes	91	81
Total credit receivables	6,127	5,170
Less:		
Unearned finance income:		
Deere notes	652	560
Non-Deere notes	621	612
Financing leases	27	31
Total	1,300	1,203
Allowance for doubtful receivables	81	71
Credit receivables–net	$4,746	$3,896

Credit receivables have significant concentrations of credit risk in the agricultural, industrial, lawn and grounds care, and recreational (non-Deere equipment) business sectors. At October 31, 1991 and 1990, the portions of credit receivables related to the agricultural equipment business were 60 percent and 56 percent, those related to the industrial equipment business were 12 percent and 14 percent, those related to the lawn and grounds care equipment business were seven percent and eight percent, and those related to the recreational equipment business were 21 percent and 22 percent, respectively. On a geographic basis, there is not a disproportionate concentration of credit risk in any area. The company retains as collateral a security interest in the equipment associated with retail notes and leases.

Credit receivable installments, including unearned finance income, at October 31 are scheduled as follows in millions of dollars:

	1991	1990
Due in months:		
0-12	$1,961	$1,637
13-24	1,381	1,176
25-36	1,006	833
37-48	675	522
49-60	385	320
Thereafter	719	682
Total	$6,127	$5,170

EXHIBIT 1B-2. *(Continued)*

The maximum maturities for retail notes are generally six years for agricultural equipment, five years for industrial equipment, six years for lawn and grounds care equipment and 15 years for non-Deere equipment. The maximum term for financing leases is five years, while the maximum maturity for wholesale notes is 12 months.

The company's United States credit subsidiary, John Deere Capital Corporation, and certain foreign subsidiaries sold retail notes to other financial institutions and received proceeds at the time of sale of $6 million in 1991, $590 million in 1990 and $294 million in 1989. At October 31, 1991 and 1990, the net unpaid balances of retail notes previously sold were $247 million and $534 million, respectively. The company is subject to a limited repurchase obligation which had a maximum exposure of $26 million and $62 million at October 31, 1991 and 1990, respectively. The retail notes sold are collateralized by security agreements on the related machinery sold to the customers. There is a minimal amount of credit and market risk due to monthly adjustments to the sale price of retail notes. There is no anticipated credit risk related to nonperformance by the counterparties.

The allowance for doubtful credit receivables represented 1.68 percent and 1.80 percent of credit receivables outstanding at October 31, 1991 and 1990, respectively. In addition, at October 31, 1991 and 1990, the company's credit subsidiaries had $115 million and $107 million, respectively, of deposits withheld from dealers and merchants available for potential credit losses. An analysis of the allowance for doubtful credit receivables follows in millions of dollars:

	1991	1990	1989
Balance, beginning of the year	$ 71	$ 58	$ 47
Provision charged to operations	68	50	27
Amounts written off	(58)	(37)	(20)
Transfers			4
Balance, end of the year	$ 81	$ 71	$ 58

Allowances for doubtful credit receivables are maintained in amounts considered appropriate in relation to the receivables and leases outstanding based on estimated collectibility and collection experience. The significantly higher provisions and write-offs in 1991 and 1990 resulted from an increase in credit receivables and leases financed and higher write-offs of uncollectible receivables and leases, particularly non-Deere related notes. The total "Provision for doubtful receivables" is included in the "Statement of Consolidated Cash Flows" on pages 32 and 33.

Equipment on Operating Leases

Operating leases arise from the lease of John Deere equipment to retail customers in the United States and Canada. Initial lease terms range from 12 to 60 months. The net value of John Deere equipment on operating leases was $185 million and $181 million at October 31, 1991 and 1990, respectively. Of these leases, at October 31, 1991, $98 million was financed by the Equipment Operations and $87 million by John Deere Credit Company. The accumulated depreciation on this equipment was $50 million and $48 million at October 31, 1991 and 1990, respectively. The corresponding depreciation expense was $28 million in 1991, $27 million in 1990 and $23 million in 1989.

Future payments to be received on operating leases totaled $133 million at October 31, 1991 and are scheduled as follows: 1992–$49, 1993–$40, 1994–$28, 1995–$14 and 1996–$2.

Inventories

Substantially all inventories owned by Deere & Company and its United States equipment subsidiaries are valued at cost on the "last-in, first-out" (LIFO) method. Remaining inventories are generally valued at the lower of cost, on the "first-in, first-out" (FIFO) basis, or market. The value of gross inventories on the LIFO basis represented 80 percent and 77 percent of worldwide gross inventories at current cost value on October 31, 1991 and 1990, respectively.

Under the LIFO inventory method, cost of goods sold ordinarily reflects current production costs thus providing a matching of current costs and current revenues in the income statement. However, when LIFO-valued inventories decline, as they did in 1991, lower costs that prevailed in prior years are matched against current year revenues, resulting in higher reported net income. The 1991 LIFO inventory benefit totaled $128 million ($84 million or $1.11 per share after income taxes).

Raw material, work-in-process and finished goods inventories at October 31, 1991 totaled $538 million on a LIFO-value basis compared with $678 million one year ago. If all inventories had been valued on a current cost basis, which approximates FIFO value, estimated inventories by major classification at October 31 in millions of dollars would have been as follows:

	1991	1990
Raw materials and supplies	$ 219	$ 252
Work-in-process	348	360
Finished machines and parts	1,088	1,187
Total current cost value	1,655	1,799
Adjustment to LIFO basis	1,117	1,121
Inventories	$ 538	$ 678

Property and Depreciation

Property and equipment additions, which exclude acquisitions of businesses, were $306 million in 1991 compared with $293 million in 1990. Additions for 1991 included $298 million for capital expenditures, $6 million for leased property under capital leases and $2 million for capitalization of interest. Additions for 1990 included $292 million for capital expenditures and $1 million for leased property under capital leases. Of the 1991 capital expenditures, $177 million were in the United States and Canada, $118 million were overseas and $3 million were incurred by the Financial Services subsidiaries.

EXHIBIT 1B-2. *(Continued)*

A summary of consolidated property and equipment at October 31 in millions of dollars follows:

	1991	1990
Land	$ 40	$ 39
Buildings and building equipment	771	763
Machinery and equipment	1,877	1,832
Dies, patterns, tools, etc	359	364
All other	389	365
Construction in progress	121	82
Total	3,557	3,445
Less accumulated depreciation	2,322	2,296
Property and equipment–net	$1,235	$1,149

Leased property under capital leases amounting to $42 million at October 31, 1991 and 1990 is included primarily in machinery and equipment and all other.

Property and equipment expenditures for new and revised products, increased capacity and the replacement or major renewal of significant items of property and equipment are capitalized. Expenditures for maintenance, repairs and minor renewals are generally charged to expense as incurred.

Depreciation amounted to $190 million in 1991, $177 million in 1990 and $170 million in 1989. Most of the company's property and equipment is depreciated using the straight-line method for financial accounting purposes. Depreciation for United States federal income tax purposes is computed using accelerated depreciation methods.

It is not expected that the cost of compliance with foreseeable environmental requirements will have a material effect on the company's financial position or operating results.

Intangible Assets

Consolidated net intangible assets totaled $371 million and $240 million at October 31, 1991 and 1990, respectively. The Equipment Operations' balance of $346 million at October 31, 1991 consisted primarily of $249 million related to the minimum pension liability required by FASB Statement No. 87 and unamortized goodwill, which resulted from the purchase cost of assets acquired exceeding their fair value. The intangible pension asset increased by $78 million during 1991, while goodwill increased by $53 million mainly as a result of the acquisition of SABO.

Intangible assets, excluding the intangible pension asset, are being amortized over 25 years or less, and the accumulated amortization was $40 million and $36 million at October 31, 1991 and 1990, respectively. The intangible pension asset is remeasured and adjusted at least annually.

Short-Term Borrowings

Short-term borrowings at October 31 consisted of the following in millions of dollars:

	1991	1990
Equipment Operations		
Commercial paper	$ 594	$ 284
Notes payable to banks	165	375
Long-term borrowings due within one year	122	192
Total	881	851
Financial Services		
Commercial paper	2,122	2,017
Notes payable to banks	248	23
Long-term borrowings due within one year	220	2
Total	2,590	2,042
Consolidated short-term borrowings	$3,471	$2,893

All of the Financial Services short-term borrowings represent obligations of the credit subsidiaries.

Unsecured lines of credit available from United States and foreign banks were $3,962 million at October 31, 1991. Of these credit lines, $3,060 million were available to both the Equipment Operations and the credit subsidiaries. At October 31, 1991, $832 million of the worldwide lines of credit were unused. For the purpose of computing the unused credit lines, total short-term borrowings, excluding the current portion of long-term borrowings, were considered to constitute utilization.

Included in the above lines of credit are three long-term committed credit agreements expiring on various dates through December 1994 for an aggregate maximum amount of $3,213 million. Of this amount, $713 million is available to the Canadian operations and $2,500 million is available in the United States or other countries. Each agreement is extendable. Annual facility fees on the credit agreements are 0.125 percent.

Certain of these credit agreements have various requirements of John Deere Capital Corporation, including the maintenance of its consolidated ratio of earnings before fixed charges to fixed charges at not less than 1.05 to 1 for each fiscal quarter. In addition, the Capital Corporation's ratio of senior debt to total stockholder's equity plus subordinated debt may not be more than 8 to 1 at the end of any fiscal quarter. The credit agreements also contain provisions requiring Deere & Company to maintain a consolidated tangible net worth of $1,600 million.

The company's credit subsidiaries have entered into interest rate swap and interest rate cap agreements to hedge their interest rate exposure in amounts corresponding to a portion of their short-term borrowings. At October 31, 1991 and 1990, the total notional principal

EXHIBIT 1B-2. *(Continued)*

amounts of fixed interest rate swap agreements were $284 million and $176 million, having fixed rates of 8.8 percent to 11.3 percent, terminating in up to 43 months and 38 months, respectively. The total notional principal amounts of interest rate cap agreements at October 31, 1991 and 1990 were $181 million and $201 million, having capped rates of 8.0 percent to 9.0 percent, terminating in up to 40 months and 52 months, respectively. The differential to be paid or received on all swap and cap agreements is accrued as interest rates change and is recognized over the lives of the agreements. The credit and market risk under these agreements is not considered to be significant.

Accounts Payable and Accrued Expenses

Accounts payable and accrued expenses at October 31 consisted of the following in millions of dollars:

	1991	1990
Equipment Operations		
Accounts payable:		
Trade	$ 569	$ 536
Dividends payable	38	38
Capital lease obligations	18	21
Other	29	31
Accrued expenses:		
Employee benefits	144	157
Dealer commissions	123	123
Other	413	391
Total	1,334	1,297
Financial Services		
Accounts payable:		
Deposits withheld from dealers and merchants	115	107
Other	52	67
Accrued expenses:		
Unearned premiums	110	101
Unpaid loss adjustment expenses	49	37
Interest payable	44	36
Other	101	79
Total	471	427
Intercompany eliminations	(1)	(2)
Consolidated accounts payable and accrued expenses	$1,804	$1,722

Insurance and Health Care Claims and Reserves

Insurance and health care claims and reserves were $491 million and $444 million at October 31, 1991 and 1990, respectively. These liabilities represent future policy benefits, unpaid losses and experience rated refunds related to the insurance and health care operations.

Long-Term Borrowings

Long-term borrowings at October 31 consisted of the following in millions of dollars:

	1991	1990
Equipment Operations		
Notes and Debentures:		
5.40% debentures due 1992		$ 17
8.60% notes due 1992		100
Medium-term notes due 1993 - 2006: Average interest rate of 8.9% as of year end 1991 and 9.5% as of year end 1990	$ 272	75
Foreign borrowings due 1993 - 1997: Average interest rate of 8.2% as of year end 1991 and 8.4% as of year end 1990	9	10
8-1/4% notes due 1996	150	
9-1/8% notes due 1996	100	100
8.45% debentures due 2000	60	60
5-1/2% convertible subordinated debentures due 2001, convertible into common stock of Deere & Company at $32.75 per share	2	4
8% debentures due 2002	126	139
Adjustable Rate Senior Notes due 2002: Interest rate of 8.7% as of year end 1991 and 10.1% as of year end 1990	100	100
8.95% debentures due 2019	199	199
Total	1,018	804
Financial Services		
Notes and Debentures:		
Medium-term notes due 1992 - 1995: Average interest rate of 7.4% as of year end 1991 and 8.7% as of year end 1990	253	192
7.40% notes due 1993: Swapped to variable interest rate of 5.2% as of year end 1991	150	
9% notes due 1993	124	124
Floating rate notes due 1993: Interest rate of 5.9% as of year end 1991 and 8.1% as of year end 1990	9	9
11-5/8% notes due 1995: Swapped to variable interest rate of 5.2% as of year end 1991 and 8.0% as of year end 1990	150	150
7-1/2% debentures due 1998	50	50
5% Swiss franc bonds due 1999: Swapped to variable interest rate of 5.7% as of year end 1991 and 8.5% as of year end 1990	97	97
Total notes and debentures	$ 833	$ 622

(Continued)

EXHIBIT 1B-2. *(Continued)*

	1991	1990
Subordinated Debt:		
9-5/8% subordinated notes due 1998: Swapped to variable interest rate of 5.8% as of year end 1991 and 8.5% as of year end 1990.	$ 150	$ 150
9.35% subordinated debentures due 2003	55	60
8-5/8% subordinated debentures due 2019: Swapped to variable interest rate of 5.1% as of year end 1991	150	150
Total subordinated debt	355	360
Total	1,188	982
Consolidated long-term borrowings	$2,206	$1,786

All of the Financial Services long-term borrowings represent obligations of John Deere Capital Corporation.

The Capital Corporation has entered into interest rate swap agreements with independent parties that change the effective rate of interest on certain long-term borrowings to a variable rate based on specified United States commercial paper rate indices. The above table reflects the effective year-end variable interest rates relating to these swap agreements. A Swiss franc to United States dollar currency swap agreement is also associated with the Swiss franc bonds in the table. The notional principal amounts and maturity dates of these swap agreements are the same as the principal amounts and maturities of the related borrowings. In addition, the Capital Corporation in 1991 entered into interest rate cap agreements associated with medium-term notes. The total notional principal amount of these cap agreements is $125 million, terminating in up to 46 months. The credit and market risk under these agreements is not considered to be significant.

The approximate amounts of the Equipment Operations' long-term borrowings maturing and sinking fund payments required in each of the next five years in millions of dollars are as follows: 1992–$122, 1993–$35, 1994–$50, 1995–$30 and 1996–$347. The approximate amounts of John Deere Capital Corporation's long-term borrowings maturing and sinking fund payments required in each of the next five years in millions of dollars are as follows: 1992–$220, 1993–$448, 1994–$69, 1995–$193 and 1996–$7.

Certain of the company's current credit agreements contain provisions requiring the maintenance of a minimum consolidated tangible net worth. Under these provisions, $864 million of the consolidated retained earnings balance of $2,119 million at October 31, 1991 was free of restrictions as to payment of dividends or acquisition of the company's common stock.

Leases

The company leases certain computer equipment, lift trucks and other property. The present values of future minimum lease payments relating to leased assets deemed to be capital leases as determined from the lease contract provisions are capitalized. Capitalized amounts are amortized over either the lives of the leases or the normal depreciable lives of the leased assets. All other leases are defined as operating leases. Lease expenses relating to operating leases are charged to rental expense as incurred.

At October 31, 1991, future minimum lease payments under capital leases totaled $21 million as follows: 1992–$8, 1993–$7, 1994–$3, 1995–$1, 1996–$1, later years–$1. Total rental expense for operating leases during 1991 was $49 million compared with $45 million in both 1990 and 1989. At October 31, 1991, future minimum lease payments under operating leases amounted to $68 million as follows: 1992–$25, 1993–$18, 1994–$10, 1995–$5, 1996–$4, later years–$6.

Commitments and Contingent Liabilities

On October 31, 1991, the company was contingently liable for recourse of approximately $26 million on credit receivables sold to financial institutions by both the Financial Services and Equipment Operations. In addition, certain foreign subsidiaries have pledged assets with a balance sheet value of $52 million as collateral for bank advances of $6 million. Also, at October 31, 1991, the company had commitments of approximately $92 million for construction and acquisition of property and equipment.

The company is subject to various unresolved legal actions which arise in the ordinary course of its business. The most prevalent of such actions relate to product liability and retail credit matters. While amounts claimed may be substantial and the ultimate liability with respect to such litigation cannot be determined at this time, the company believes that the ultimate outcome of these matters will not have a material adverse effect on the company's consolidated financial position.

Capital Stock

The calculation of net income per share is based on the average number of shares outstanding during the year. The calculation of net income per share assuming full dilution recognizes the dilutive effect of the assumed exercise of stock appreciation rights and stock options, and conversion of convertible debentures. The calculation also reflects adjustment for interest expense relating to the convertible debentures, net of applicable income taxes.

EXHIBIT 1B-2. *(Continued)*

Changes in the common stock account in 1989, 1990 and 1991 were as follows:

	Number of Shares Issued	Amount (in millions)
Balance at October 31, 1988	74,790,190	$761
Stock options exercised	737,058	31
Debenture conversions	220,924	7
Other		2
Balance at October 31, 1989	75,748,172	801
Stock options exercised	529,616	26
Debenture conversions	32,653	1
Other		3
Balance at October 31, 1990	76,310,441	831
Stock options exercised	55,210	2
Debenture conversions	77,487	3
Other		3
Balance at October 31, 1991	76,443,138	$839

The company is authorized to issue 3,000,000 shares of preferred stock, none of which has been issued.

The major changes during 1991 affecting common stock in treasury included the acquisition of 70,300 shares of treasury stock at a total cost of $4 million. In addition, 65,183 shares of treasury stock at original cost of $1 million were issued under the restricted stock plan.

Restricted Stock

Changes in the unamortized restricted stock compensation account since adoption of the Plan were as follows:

	Number of Shares Granted	Amount (in millions)
Granted during 1989	52,970	$ 3
Outstanding at October 31, 1989	52,970	3
Granted	52,428	4
Amortized and vested	(10,272)	(2)
Canceled	(424)	
Outstanding at October 31, 1990	94,702	5
Granted	65,183	3
Amortized and vested	(4,791)	(2)
Outstanding at October 31, 1991	155,094	$ 6

In 1989, the stockholders approved a restricted stock plan for key employees of the company. Under the Plan, 750,000 shares may be granted as restricted stock. The company will establish the period of restriction for each award and hold the restricted stock during the restriction period, while the employee will receive any dividends and vote the restricted stock. No award may be made under the Plan providing for restrictions that lapse after October 31, 1999.

The market value of the restricted stock at the time of grant is recorded as unamortized restricted stock compensation in a separate component of stockholders' equity. This compensation is amortized to expense evenly over the period of restriction, which is currently four years. At October 31, 1991, 579,843 shares remained available for award under the Plan.

Stock Options

Options for the purchase of the company's common stock are issued to officers and other key employees under stock option plans as approved by stockholders. Options outstanding at October 31, 1991 generally become exercisable one year after the date of grant and are exercisable up to 10 years after the date of grant.

In February 1991, stockholders of the company approved the 1991 John Deere Stock Option Plan, which authorizes the grant of options to key employees for the purchase of 6,500,000 shares of common stock. The stock option plan includes authority to grant stock appreciation rights, either concurrently with the grant of options or subsequently, and to accept stock of the company in payment for shares under the plan. Both incentive options and options not entitled to incentive stock option treatment (nonstatutory options) may be granted under the Plan. At October 31, 1991, 6,500,000 shares remained available for the granting of options.

During the last three fiscal years, changes in shares under option were as follows:

	Shares	Option Price Per Share
Outstanding at October 31, 1988	1,779,833	$23.31 - $41.81
Granted	499,513	$46.81
Exercised	(737,058)	$23.31 - $46.81
Expired or cancelled	(138,862)	$23.31 - $46.81
Outstanding at October 31, 1989	1,403,426	$23.31 - $46.81
Granted	431,718	$60.06
Exercised	(529,616)	$23.31 - $60.06
Expired or cancelled	(154,181)	$23.31 - $60.06
Outstanding at October 31, 1990	1,151,347	$23.31 - $60.06
Granted	597,152	$45.31
Exercised	(55,210)	$23.31 - $46.81
Expired or cancelled	(16,661)	$26.38 - $60.06
Outstanding at October 31, 1991	1,676,628	$23.31 - $60.06

For options outstanding at October 31, 1991, the average exercise price was $45.57 per share and expiration dates ranged from November 1992 to December 2000. Of the outstanding options, 235,932 may be exercised in the form of stock appreciation rights.

EXHIBIT 1B-2. *(Continued)*

Employee Stock Purchase and Savings Plans

The company maintains the following significant plans for eligible employees:

John Deere Savings and Investment Plan,
for salaried employees
John Deere Stock Purchase Plan, for salaried employees
John Deere Tax Deferred Savings Plan,
for hourly and incentive paid employees

Company contributions under these plans were $22 million in 1991, $23 million in 1990 and $12 million in 1989.

Retained Earnings

An analysis of the company's retained earnings follows in millions of dollars:

	1991	1990	1989
Balance, beginning of the year	$2,291	$2,032	$1,749
Net income (loss)	(20)	411	380
Dividends declared	(152)	(152)	(97)
Balance, end of the year	$2,119	$2,291	$2,032

Cumulative Translation Adjustment

An analysis of the company's cumulative translation adjustment follows in millions of dollars:

	1991	1990	1989
Balance, beginning of the year	$ 12	$ 48	$ 51
Translation adjustments for the year.	7	(40)	(4)
Income taxes applicable to translation adjustments	(3)	4	1
Balance, end of the year	$ 16	$ 12	$ 48

The company has entered into foreign exchange contracts and options in order to hedge the currency exposure of certain foreign investments, inventory, short-term borrowings and expected inventory purchases. The foreign exchange contract gains or losses are accrued as foreign exchange rates change, and the contract premiums are amortized over the terms of the foreign exchange contracts. The option premiums and any gains are deferred and recorded as part of the cost of future inventory purchases. At October 31, 1991 and 1990, the company had foreign exchange contracts maturing in up to five months and four months for $406 million and $506 million, respectively. At October 31, 1991 and 1990, the company had options maturing in up to 24 months and 36 months for $106 million and $150 million, respectively. The credit and market risk under these agreements is not considered to be significant.

Cash Flow Information

For purposes of the statement of consolidated cash flows, the company considers investments with original maturities of three months or less to be cash equivalents.

Cash payments for interest and income taxes consisted of the following in millions of dollars:

	1991	1990	1989
Interest:			
Equipment Operations	$191	$193	$179
Financial Services	250	235	215
Intercompany eliminations	(3)	(3)	(3)
Consolidated	$438	$425	$391
Income taxes:			
Equipment Operations	$ 11	$136	$ 65
Financial Services	74	85	74
Intercompany eliminations	(56)	(63)	(54)
Consolidated	$ 29	$158	$ 85

Non-cash investing and financing activities which are not included in the cash flow statement for 1991, 1990 and 1989 included additions to property and equipment from increases in capital lease obligations of $6 million, $1 million and $23 million, respectively. Deere & Company assumed liabilities in 1991 of $22 million from the purchase of SABO and $14 million from the acquisition of the business of Integral Insurance Company. The additional investment in Re Capital Corporation in 1991, which increased the insurance subsidiaries' ownership to 25 percent, resulted in a reclassification of $10 million from "Marketable securities carried at cost" to "Investments in unconsolidated subsidiaries and affiliates". In conjunction with the purchase of Funk Manufacturing Company in 1989, Deere & Company assumed liabilities of $13 million.

Supplemental 1991 and 1990 Quarterly Information (Unaudited)

Common stock per share sales prices from New York Stock Exchange composite transactions quotations follow:

	First Quarter	Second Quarter	Third Quarter	Fourth Quarter
1991 Market price				
High	$51.75	$56.50	$57.00	$57.38
Low	38.50	46.50	48.25	46.88
1990 Market price				
High	$66.13	$78.13	$78.38	$73.13
Low	52.75	64.88	66.63	37.63

EXHIBIT 1B-2. *(Continued)*

Quarterly information with respect to net sales and revenues and earnings is shown in the following schedule. Such information is shown in millions of dollars except for per share amounts.

	First Quarter	Second Quarter	Third Quarter	Fourth Quarter
1991				
Net sales and revenues	$1,438	$1,925	$1,790	$1,902
Income (loss) before income taxes	(64)	103	46	(111)*
Net income (loss)	(43)	73	31	(81)*
Net income (loss) per share	(.57)	.96	.41	(1.07)*
Dividends declared per share	.50	.50	.50	.50
Dividends paid per share	.50	.50	.50	.50
1990				
Net sales and revenues	$1,640	$2,118	$2,053	$2,064
Income before income taxes	116	214	168	90
Net income	79	144	114	74
Net income per share	1.04	1.90	1.50	.98
Dividends declared per share	.50	.50	.50	.50
Dividends paid per share	.35	.50	.50	.50

*Includes pretax restructuring costs of $182 million ($120 million or $1.58 per share after taxes).

At October 31, 1991, there were 25,581 holders of record of the company's $1 par value common stock and 33 holders of record of the company's 5-1/2% convertible subordinated debentures due 2001.

Dividend

A quarterly dividend of $.50 per share was declared at the Board of Directors' meeting held on December 11, 1991, payable on February 3, 1992.

EXHIBIT 1B-2. *(Continued)*

Deere & Company

Summary of Consolidated Income and Retained Earnings

(In millions of dollars except per share amounts)	1991	1990	1989	1988	1987	1986	1985
				Year Ended October 31			
Net Sales and Revenues							
Agricultural equipment net sales	$4,054.6	$4,518.8	$4,109.3	$3,347.6	$2,308.9	$1,898.6	$2,541.9
Industrial equipment net sales	1,014.0	1,348.3	1,310.3	1,162.1	911.3	867.7	942.4
Lawn and grounds care equipment net sales	779.2	911.6	814.3	855.1	914.3	750.0	576.3
Net sales of equipment	5,847.8	6,778.7	6,233.9	5,364.8	4,134.5	3,516.3	4,060.6
Finance and interest income	654.4	592.7	550.5	441.9	389.3	396.1	406.8
Insurance and health care premiums	444.1	384.2	342.9	347.8	246.9	203.6	142.8
Investment income	87.9	86.0	75.7	62.0	60.4	54.2	41.3
Other income	21.0	33.4	16.8	21.0	22.7	26.0	25.5
Total	7,055.2	7,875.0	7,219.8	6,237.5	4,853.8	4,196.2	4,677.0
Costs and Expenses							
Cost of goods sold	4,894.2	5,424.1	5,025.0	4,355.1	3,637.4	3,212.6	3,350.1
Research and development expenses	279.3	263.5	234.1	215.9	213.2	223.6	219.0
Selling, administrative and general expenses	839.6	792.3	697.3	666.3	582.9	561.5	554.7
Interest expense	450.0	435.2	406.6	332.5	328.8	370.9	358.4
Insurance and health care claims and benefits	405.5	334.5	292.7	290.8	207.9	169.9	125.1
Other operating expenses	30.9	37.9	25.0	15.9	19.5	17.6	25.3
Restructuring costs	181.9				39.5	95.4	40.7
Total	7,081.4	7,287.5	6,680.7	5,876.5	5,029.2	4,651.5	4,673.3
Income (Loss) of Consolidated Group Before Income Taxes	(26.2)	587.5	539.1	361.0	(175.4)	(455.3)	3.7
Provision (credit) for income taxes	(5.2)	182.0	167.0	79.2	(70.6)	(236.7)	(17.4)
Income (Loss) of Consolidated Group	(21.0)	405.5	372.1	281.8	(104.8)	(218.6)	21.1
Equity in Income (Loss) of Unconsolidated Affiliates	.8	5.6	8.1	4.9	5.8	(10.7)	9.4
Change in Accounting for Income Taxes				28.7			
Net Income (Loss) for the Year	$ (20.2)	$ 411.1	$ 380.2	$ 315.4	$ (99.0)	$ (229.3)	$ 30.5
Cash Dividends Declared and Other Adjustments	(152.1)	(151.7)	(97.7)	(46.9)	(17.1)	(50.9)	(67.8)
Retained Earnings at Beginning of Year	2,291.3	2,031.9	1,749.4	1,480.9	1,597.0	1,877.2	1,914.5
Retained Earnings at End of Year	$2,119.0	$2,291.3	$2,031.9	$1,749.4	$1,480.9	$1,597.0	$1,877.2
Net income (loss) per share	$ (.27)	$ 5.42	$ 5.06	$ 4.48	$ (1.46)	$ (3.38)	$ .45
Net income (loss) per share assuming full dilution	$ (.27)	$ 5.42	$ 5.06	$ 4.32	$ (1.46)	$ (3.38)	$ .45
Dividends declared per share	$ 2.00	$ 2.00	$ 1.30	$ .65	$ .25	$ .75	$ 1.00
Dividends paid per share	$ 2.00	$ 1.85	$ 1.15	$ .51¼	$ .31¼	$ .87½	$ 1.00
Average number of common shares outstanding (in thousands)	76,164	75,883	75,167	70,488	67,897	67,867	67,833
Other Statistical Data							
Capital expenditures	$ 298.2	$ 291.5	$ 186.3	$ 179.8	$ 165.8	$ 172.9	$ 131.3
Provision for depreciation	$ 190.1	$ 176.8	$ 170.3	$ 182.3	$ 185.7	$ 192.3	$ 184.5
Number of employees (at year end)	36,469	38,493	38,954	38,268	37,931	37,793	40,509

EXHIBIT 1B-2. *(Continued)*

Deere & Company

Summary of Consolidated Balance Sheets

(In millions of dollars except per share amounts) Assets	1991	1990	1989	October 31 1988	1987	1986	1985
Cash and cash equivalents	$ 278.5	$ 185.4	$ 203.8	$ 266.0	$ 371.7	$ 465.9	$ 171.9
Marketable securities carried at cost	856.6	801.0	725.3	662.1	535.8	482.1	409.3
Receivables from unconsolidated affiliates	17.8	3.0	5.3	.3	3.3	.2	52.8
Dealer accounts and notes receivable – net	2,966.6	3,099.9	2,586.9	2,283.0	2,084.0	2,057.0	2,635.8
Credit receivables – net	4,745.6	3,895.8	3,358.4	3,019.4	2,763.4	2,844.7	3,015.3
Other receivables	108.9	141.5	97.2	71.2	78.5	53.4	38.5
Equipment on operating leases – net	184.8	181.4	160.2	119.9	125.4	136.5	119.8
Inventories	538.1	677.7	711.2	708.3	465.0	482.6	447.4
Property and equipment – net	1,235.2	1,149.4	996.6	956.1	965.2	956.3	937.9
Investments in unconsolidated affiliates	106.0	84.6	71.3	52.5	43.9	37.5	41.1
Intangible assets – net	371.5	239.7	72.0	22.6	26.3	29.7	33.2
Other assets	133.2	81.1	52.2	25.7	29.0	44.1	38.7
Deferred income taxes	17.0	12.3					
Deferred charges	89.6	111.5	105.0	76.6	74.2	65.7	62.8
Total	$11,649.4	$10,664.3	$9,145.4	$8,263.7	$7,565.7	$7,655.7	$8,004.5
Liabilities and Stockholders' Equity							
Liabilities							
Short-term borrowings	$ 3,471.1	$ 2,892.5	$2,248.6	$2,197.0	$1,983.6	$1,739.0	$2,074.1
Payables to unconsolidated affiliates	5.5	28.1	15.0	30.8		.6	
Accounts payable and accrued expenses	1,803.6	1,722.4	1,579.0	1,453.1	1,319.5	1,163.3	1,180.6
Insurance and health care claims and reserves	491.1	444.2	391.4	359.2	295.4	252.2	215.3
Accrued taxes	84.8	66.2	75.1	74.6	43.4	60.1	50.7
Deferred income taxes	75.4	171.7	148.2	69.1	115.6	183.5	436.8
Long-term borrowings	2,206.3	1,785.9	1,675.6	1,394.3	1,649.2	2,092.2	1,678.7
Pension accruals and other liabilities	675.8	545.7	232.2	229.4	238.9	162.5	109.7
Total liabilities	8,813.6	7,656.7	6,365.1	5,807.5	5,645.6	5,656.4	5,745.9
Stockholders' Equity							
Common stock issued, at stated value	838.7	831.4	800.8	760.5	496.5	492.0	491.4
Retained earnings	2,119.0	2,291.3	2,031.9	1,749.4	1,480.9	1,597.0	1,877.2
Minimum pension liability adjustment	(86.4)	(88.2)					
Cumulative translation adjustment	(16.4)	(11.8)	(47.6)	(51.0)	(54.6)	(87.0)	(107.3)
Unamortized restricted stock compensation	(6.5)	(5.0)	(2.9)				
Common stock in treasury, at cost	(12.6)	(10.1)	(1.9)	(2.7)	(2.7)	(2.7)	(2.7)
Total stockholders' equity	2,835.8	3,007.6	2,780.3	2,456.2	1,920.1	1,999.3	2,258.6
Total	$11,649.4	$10,664.3	$9,145.4	$8,263.7	$7,565.7	$7,655.7	$8,004.5
Book value per share	$ 37.20	$ 39.52	$ 36.76	$ 32.92	$ 28.23	$ 29.46	$ 33.29

Source: Deere & Company, 1991 Annual Report

2

FINANCIAL STATEMENTS: THE RAW DATA OF ANALYSIS

INTRODUCTION

INCOME, CASH FLOWS, AND ASSETS: DEFINITIONS AND RELATIONSHIPS

THE ACCRUAL CONCEPT OF INCOME

Measurement and Classification Rules: Income Statement Components

Thousand Trails: Introduction

Accounting Income: Revenue and Expense Recognition

Departures from the Sales Basis of Revenue Recognition

Percentage-of-Completion and Completed Contract Methods

Comparison of Completed Contract and Percentage of Completion

Installment Method

Cost Recovery Method

Summary of Revenue Recognition Methods

ANALYSIS OF CASH FLOW INFORMATION

Statement of Cash Flows: Classification Issues

Cash Flows From Investments

Free Cash Flows

Interest and Dividends Received

Interest Paid

Noncash Transactions

CFO: The Effect of Reporting Methods

Transactional Analysis: Overview

Relationship of the Cash Flow Statement and Income Statement

Income, Cash Flow, and the Going Concern Assumption

Income, Cash Flow, and the Choice of Accounting Policies

Income, Cash Flow, and Liquidity

THOUSAND TRAILS: INCOME AND CASH FLOW ANALYSIS

Revenue Recognition by Thousand Trails

Expense Recognition by Thousand Trails

Thousand Trails: CFO and Free Cash Flows

Thousand Trails: Balance Sheet Analysis

Thousand Trails: Analytic Lessons

NONRECURRING ITEMS

Components of Nonrecurring Income

Unusual or Infrequent Items

Extraordinary Items

Discontinued Operations

Accounting Changes

Prior Period Adjustments

113

INTRODUCTION

The primary objective of this book is to assist financial statement users to develop skills needed to analyze and use financial statement data in making rational investment, credit, and similar decisions. As discussed in Chapter 1, the primary objective of financial reporting is to provide information that is useful in making such decisions and facilitates assessments of the amount, timing, and uncertainty of cash flows. Financial reporting is also designed to provide information about a firm's assets (economic resources), liabilities (claims on those resources), owners' equity, and the impact of transactions and events that change those resources and the related claims on those resources.

The current financial reporting system falls short of these objectives as the task is inherently impossible given the diverse requirements of the multitude of users of financial statements. The standard-setting process is often unduly influenced by practical and political rather than conceptual and economic considerations; even on a conceptual level there is often a lack of consensus as to the reporting needs of a given user.

However, financial statements are not devoid of valuable information. On the contrary, they contain a wealth of information that users can tailor to their specific needs. To do so, they need to understand what information is provided by financial statements and what is lacking. In addition, users must be able to arrange the information provided in the statements in a manner consistent with the objectives of the analysis. Reporting methods, measurement techniques, and the method of presentation of financial information can all be criticized in many cases; good analysis requires skepticism.

The comparison of the risk and return characteristics of alternative investments is an important objective of financial analysis. Risk and return measures are based on projections of future earnings and cash flows and assessments of the assets and liabilities of entities. How should earnings and cash flows be defined? Are they simply the numbers provided by financial statements? In practice, earnings and cash flow estimates are superior when historical financial statement data are adjusted to suit the requirements of the specific decision under consideration. Users need to understand what financial statements tell them about net assets, income, and cash flows and their interrelationships to develop the information required to make optimal investment, credit, and other decisions.

Comprehensive financial analysis, therefore, requires a thorough understanding of the financial reporting system and its output. Chapter 1 provided a general overview of the accounting process, the reporting system, and their product: the financial statements.

This chapter takes us to the next step. It provides an introduction to (1) relevant information that can be derived from the financial statements and (2) the analytical techniques needed to generate this information. Although we discuss the full set of financial statements, our focus is on the income and cash flow statements with an emphasis on integrated analyses. We use Thousand Trails, Inc. to illustrate these issues throughout this chapter.

INCOME, CASH FLOWS, AND ASSETS: DEFINITIONS AND RELATIONSHIPS

This section introduces several conceptual definitions of "income" and measures of cash flows and assets. The relationship between these concepts of income and "accounting income" reported by the current financial reporting system is then explored.

In a world of certainty,[1] the interrelationship of income, cash flow, and assets is captured through the concept of *economic earnings*, defined as net cash flow plus the change in market value of the firm's assets. The market value of the firm's assets in a world of certainty is equivalent to the present value of their future cash flows discounted at the (risk-free) rate, r. For a two-period model, if cash flow equals $100 in each period and $r = 5\%$, the value of the asset at the

$$\text{Beginning of period 1} = \$100/(1.05) + \$100/(1.05)^2 = \$185.94$$
$$\text{Beginning of period 2} = \qquad\qquad \$100/(1.05) = \$95.24$$

and economic earnings equals cash flow plus the change[2] in asset value:

$$\text{For period 1: } \$100 + (\$95.24 - \$185.94) = \$9.30$$
$$\text{For period 2: } \$100 + (\$0 \qquad - \$95.24) = \$4.76$$

Note that economic income in each year is equal to the rate of return times the opening value of the assets.[3] Equivalently, one can view the market value at the beginning of the period as equal to a (constant) multiple of earnings with the multiple equal to $1/r$.[4]

However, in the real, but uncertain, world, these neat relationships are not so easy to come by. Future cash flows and interest rates are not known with certainty. Market prices of some assets are more reliably determinable than are those of others[5] and when known may not easily be related to the present value of generally unknown, estimated future cash flows discounted at estimated interest rates. Note that these estimates are also a function of varied expectations of different decision makers. Moreover, market

---

[1]This would include perfect financial markets.

[2]The change in asset value in this example is often referred to as economic depreciation (see Chapter 6).

[3]For year 1, $0.05 \times 185.94 = 9.30$; for year 2, $0.05 \times 95.24 = 4.76$.

[4]In this case the price/earnings multiple is 20 (1/0.05).

[5]Some assets are heavily traded on regulated markets (common stock of companies like IBM and General Electric), others may be thinly traded (certain stocks trading over the counter or relatively new financial instruments like interest rate swaps), and still others have very limited secondary markets from which verifiable prices can be obtained (most manufacturing equipment).

value may be defined in various and often inconsistent ways, for example, as replacement cost that may not be equivalent to liquidating value. In a world of uncertainty, income (however defined) can, at best, serve as a proxy for economic income. To this end, economists, analysts, and others have developed a number of analytic definitions of earnings.

Distributable earnings are defined as the amount of earnings that can be paid out as dividends without changing the value of the firm. This concept is derived from the Hicksian definition of income:

> the amount that a person can consume during a period of time and be as well off at the end of that time as at the beginning.[6]

A related measure, *sustainable income*, refers to the level of income that can be sustained in the future given the firm's stock of capital investment (e.g., fixed assets and inventory). Another construct, *permanent earnings*, is used by analysts for valuation purposes.[7] It reflects the amount that can normally be earned each period given the firm's assets and is equivalent to the market value of those assets times the firm's required rate of return. Similar to economic earnings, it is the base to which a multiple is applied to arrive at a "fair price."[8]

All these definitions attempt, in some fashion, to mirror economic earnings. The interrelationships between these definitions and economic income and some of the difficulties inherent in applying them are discussed in greater detail in Box 2-1.

As the discussion in the box indicates, applying these definitions to the concept of economic earnings is not always a straightforward proposition. Furthermore, due to problems with measurement and asset valuation alluded to earlier, operationalizing these concepts in practice can be extremely difficult.

As a result of these difficulties, the financial reporting concept of income—*accounting income*—is quite different. The analyst, therefore, needs to evaluate accounting income and its relationship to the income concepts just discussed with respect to the needs of the decision at hand.

Accounting income is measured on the basis of the *accrual concept* and is useful for the information[9] it provides about the ability of the enterprise to generate future cash flows. It is not, a priori, equivalent to any of the definitions discussed earlier.

THE ACCRUAL CONCEPT OF INCOME

Accounting and economic income are similar in that both define income as the sum of cash flows and changes in net assets. However, in financial reporting, the determination of

---

[6]J.R. Hicks, *Value and Capital* (2nd Edition Oxford: Chaundon Press, 1946), p. 176
[7]*Normalized earnings* and *earnings power* are similar concepts.
[8]The price/earnings ratio used by analysts exploits this conceptual relationship.
[9]Beaver (1989) refers to this as the "informational perspective" of accounting earnings.

BOX 2-1
Elaboration of Conceptual Income, Cash Flow, and Asset Relationships

In the discussion that follows, we assume that all "income" is paid out as dividends, allowing us to avoid consideration of the issue of reinvestment of income in the firm.

Case A

Assume that a firm possesses an asset that is purchased at the beginning of each period for $10 and is sold at the end of each period, at a markup of 20%, for $12. Further, assume that the markup of 20% is equivalent to the interest (discount) rate.* Under these conditions, the market value of the firm at the beginning of the period will be equal to the $10 paid for the asset. The market value of $10 can be derived in a single- or multiperiod context.

In a one-period context, the discounted value of the end of period cash flow is equal to $12/1.20 = $10. *In a multiperiod context,* for each period the firm will use $10 to replace the asset, leaving $2 of income. The present value of $2 per period earned for an infinite period is equal to $2/0.20 = $10.

The economic earnings of the firm will be equal to the cash flow of $2 ($12–10) as the market value of the firm will remain at $10 over the period and this level of earnings is the expected level of earnings in the future. As this calculation is identical each period, the distributable income is $2, since paying out $2 will not change the value of the firm. Similarly, sustainable income is also $2, the amount that can be distributed without altering the firm's level of operations, that is, buying and selling one asset per period. Finally, since the value of the firm is $10, the permanent earnings concept will also give rise to income of $2 (0.2 × $10). The economic, distributable, sustainable, and permanent earnings are all identical.

In the next case, by introducing uncertainty and changing one assumption, the problem becomes much more complex.

Case B

Assume that during one period, the amount that can be received for the asset suddenly increases to $13.20. Accordingly, the price of the asset should also increase as its one-period present value is now $13.20/1.20 = $11.00. Thus, if the firm replaces the asset at the end of that period, economic earnings will equal $2.20 of cash flow ($13.20 − $11.00) plus a $1.00 increase in the market value of the firm (from $10.00 to $11.00), for a total of $3.20.

If the firm does not replace the asset in its entirety (assuming the asset is divisible) but only purchases $10.00 of the now more expensive asset, its net cash flows will be $3.20 ($13.20 − $10.00). Since the market value of its assets stays at $10.00, the economic earnings are unchanged at $3.20.

We can now pose the following question: What are the expected earnings of the firm given the change in the value of the asset? It is clearly not $3.20. If the firm retains the original level of *physical* assets now valued at $11.00, the expected earnings are $2.20 (20% of $11.00). If the firm retains the original level of *monetary* assets of $10.00, the expected earnings are $2.00 (20% of $10.00). Note that economic earnings now has two components: earnings of $2.20 generated by operations and a *holding gain* of $1.00. The holding gain is a consequence of owning an asset while its market value increases. It is a "one-time" occurrence and cannot be expected to recur. The earnings generated by continuing operations, however, are of a "permanent" nature and can be expected to continue into the future given the level of physical assets.†

What happens to the other definitions of income under this scenario? To maintain the initial wealth level of $10.00, *distributable income* is $3.20, equivalent to economic earnings. However, *sustainable income,* the future earnings level that the firm is capable of achieving, is only $2.00 (assuming that $3.20 is distributed).

However, if we assume that the firm maintains the same physical level of assets and consider the Hicksian definition of income in terms of the physical measure of assets, both distributable and sustainable income would equal $2.20. Similarly, *permanent earnings* will depend on whether the firm retains its original physical asset base (whose value is now $11.00), or whether it retains its original monetary asset base of $10.00. In the former case, permanent earnings is $2.20; in the latter it will be $2.00.

The neat mappings from one definition to another do not hold anymore as they become situation specific.

---

*Under conditions of certainty, the rate of return earned on the asset (the 20% markup) will be equal to the prevailing interest rate.

†See Chapter 15, Box 1, for further elaboration as to the differing valuation implications of permanent and transitory earnings components.

- Which cash flows are included in income and when,
- Which changes in asset values are to be included in income, and
- How and when the selected changes in asset values are measured

is bound by the accounting rules and principles that make up generally accepted accounting principles (GAAP).

An important assumption of the accrual concept of earnings is that information about future cash flows can be derived from other sources in addition to historical cash flows:

Information about enterprise earnings based on accrual accounting generally provides a better indication of an enterprise's present and continuing ability to generate cash flows than information limited to the financial effects of cash receipts and payments.[10]

Reported income under the accrual concept provides a measure of the firm's current operating performance.[11] Accounting income is not solely based on current period actual cash flows. Rather cash inflows and outflows are recognized as a part of income in their "appropriate" accounting periods, that is, as services are provided and used rather than as cash is collected or expenditures incurred. Appropriate means the period that "best" indicates the firm's present and continuing ability to generate future cash flows.

Consider case A in Box 2-1. In that example, an item is sold for $12 in period 1 and replaced at a cost of $10. If we assume that the sale is on credit and that cash will

---

[10]SFAC 1, "Objectives of Financial Reporting by Business Enterprises" (November, 1978) p. ix.

[11]Reported accounting income often includes nonoperating or extraordinary items. Certain realized gains (inventory profits and recovery of unrealized losses on short-term investments) and selected unrealized losses (declines in the market value of short-term investments) are included in current operating income, whereas other realized gains and losses (from early retirement of debt) are reported as extraordinary items. Unrealized holding gains (due to changes in the market or fair values of assets and liabilities) are not recognized in the financial statements.

be collected in the following period, the actual cash outflow in period 1 is −$10, the cost of replacing the asset. Under accrual accounting, the revenue (expected future cash flow) is recognized at the time of sale, and income is $2. Which is a better indicator of the earning power of the firm and its ability to generate future cash flows: −$10 or $2? The accrual concept, which reports income of $2 in keeping with its objective of providing such forward-looking information, is better than pure cash flow accounting.

The accrual basis of accounting, therefore, allocates many cash flows to time periods other than those in which they occur. Accrual accounting principles are, fundamentally, the decision rules that tell preparers of financial statements how to perform that allocation function to recognize the revenue and expense consequences of cash flows and other events in the appropriate time period.

Over the life of the firm, income and cash flows converge. They differ only as to timing of recognition. The reallocation of cash flows to other accounting periods is both the strength and the weakness of the accrual method. It is a strength in that it results in more meaningful measurement of current operating performance (income statement) and a better indicator of future operating performance and earnings power. If accrual accounting did not exist, financial analysts would have to invent it.[12] The reallocation is a weakness in that accruals are subject to management discretion and require estimates that can and do change over time. The impact of real changes and those stemming from management choices are thus confounded. We return to a discussion of this aspect shortly.

In addition to the accrual accounting basis, the determination of accounting earnings (as opposed to the concepts of economic earnings discussed earlier) is governed by

1. General principles and measurement rules underlying all accounting transactions and events.
2. Specific rules to determine revenue and expense recognition.

The impact of these two factors on income reported by the accrual accounting process is the focus of the next section. The objective is to discuss the classifications used in the income statement and evaluate their ability to provide information needed to make investment and credit decisions.

Measurement and Classification Rules: Income Statement Components

From an analyst's perspective the need for data with predictive ability implies that earnings resulting from a firm's recurring operating activities are considered the best indicators of future earnings. In the (typical) income statement format reproduced here

---

[12]This occasionally happens. Because of the deficiencies of (cash-based) regulatory accounting in the insurance industry, analysts developed methods of analysis in the 1960s that eventually were adopted as GAAP by the industry. More recently, German analysts developed their own method of adjusting tax-based income statements.

from Chapter 1, the first set of numbers presented—pretax earnings from *recurring continuing operations*[13] or, on a posttax basis, income from continuing operations after adjustment for "unusual or infrequent items" (after tax)—would be the primary focus of analysis.

	Revenues
+	Other income and revenues
−	Expenses
=	Recurring continuing operations
±	Unusual or infrequent items
=	Pretax earnings from continuing operations
−	Provision for taxes (income tax expense)
=	After-tax income from continuing operations*
±	Discontinued operations (net of tax effects)*
±	Extraordinary items (net of tax effects)*
±	Cumulative effect of accounting changes (net of tax effects)*
=	Net income*

*Per share amounts are reported for each of the items followed by an asterisk.

The predictive ability of income numbers is enhanced by excluding the impact of transitory or random components, which are not directly related to operating activities and are generally more volatile in nature. Segregation of the results of normal, recurring operations from the effects of "nonrecurring" or "extraordinary" items facilitates the forecasting of future earnings and cash flows. In terms of the definitions of income discussed earlier (and elaborated on in Box 2-1), transitory gains or losses would not be regarded as components of permanent, or sustainable income. The concept of recurring income is similar to permanent or sustainable income in the sense that it is persistent; i.e., its level or rate of growth is predictable, and cash flows will eventually ensue at the predicted levels and rates of growth.

The historical cost–based approach underlying GAAP results in rules that exclude most unrealized holding gains or losses (increases/decreases in the market value of assets and liabilities held by the firm).[14] Recognition of these gains/losses must await the disposal of the assets and the early retirement or settlement of the liabilities. All realized holding gains/losses are included in income. Depending on their nature, they may be included as part of operating income or given separate disclosure. However, as will be illustrated, operational definitions of "operating," "nonrecurring," and "extraordinary"

---

[13]As stated in footnote 11, although unrealized holding gains do not appear on the income statement, realized holding gains (including gains on inventories and operating fixed assets) are included in reported income. These gains are often not disclosed separately from operating income. Further discussion of the relevance of this issue is left to future chapters.

[14]See footnote 11.

are elusive. Accounting standards setters have struggled with this issue for decades. Ultimately, the analyst must evaluate the role of nonrecurring items, whether they are called extraordinary, unusual, or something else, in the prediction of earnings power.[15]

Financial reporting defines nonrecurring in terms of *the type of event* itself. For analysis purposes, however, the important issue is whether the amount of so-called "nonrecurring" income or loss in a given year is a good predictor of future income or loss. For example, for some firms, a gain or loss from the sale of fixed assets will be rare; the amount reported will have no predictive value. Other firms retire fixed assets each year and regularly report gains or losses (consider a car rental company, for example, that retires part of its fleet of cars each year). In the latter case, the analytic issue is whether this year's income or loss from the sale of retired property is higher or lower than the "normal" amount.

The goal of *analysis of the income statement* is to derive an effective measure of future earnings and cash flows and, therefore, exclude components of reported income (regardless of their accounting label) that reduce its *predictive ability*.

The predictive ability objective does not mean that financial analysis of the income (or other) statements is simply an exercise in the extrapolation of previous trends. Rather, all financial statement information should be viewed as part of a database that provides information about future prospects and opportunities facing the firm. For example, an increase in the sale of cameras provides useful information not only for forecasts of future camera sales but also to estimate revenues of related products; that is, sales of film and film development services. Similarly, nonrecurring items can also provide such information. Gains from asset sales may be nonrecurring. However, their implications for the firm's future are apparent if we consider how the cash generated by the sale will be utilized and in what manner, if at all, the productive capacity represented by the asset will be replaced. We shall return to the analysis of nonrecurring items later in the chapter. With the goal of predictive ability in mind, we now examine the case of Thousand Trails.

Thousand Trails: Introduction

Thousand Trails owned and operated private membership resort campgrounds (preserves) in the United States and Canada. Memberships allowed a member's family an unlimited number of visits to any of the company's present or proposed campgrounds for an initial membership fee and annual dues. Memberships could be used over the lifetime of the member and passed on to heirs (transfer limited to one generation). They did not convey ownership interest in the company or its preserves. The company was not contractually obligated to provide additional campgrounds or to provide additional facilities at existing sites. The company, however, did promise (and planned) to develop and operate additional sites.

In addition to membership sales, the company earned income from (1) interest on installment receivables generated by membership sales and (2) annual dues paid by existing members. Membership sales, however, were by far the primary source (approximately two-thirds) of Thousand Trails' income and are the focus of our analysis.

[15]We will return to this question when we discuss the quality of earnings and valuation in Chapters 14 and 15.

Thousand Trails' net income (see income statement, Exhibit 2-1) increased almost fourfold (from $3.3 million to $12 million) in the period 1981 to 1983. Most of the increase was attributable to the high growth rate of membership sales, which increased by 40% in each of the years 1982 and 1983. Income from membership sales increased almost three times over the same period.

From a valuation perspective, the first question is whether such growth rates are sustainable. In most cases they are not; all markets reach saturation eventually. For every company that maintains a very high growth rate year after year (Wal-Mart, for example), there are others that fail to sustain earlier high rates of growth. The current growth rate of sales and income must be tempered, in most cases, to recognize the expected slower future growth rate. The estimation of future growth rates requires data from outside of the financial statements and is beyond the scope of this text.

Our analysis of Thousand Trails must, however, take into account this factor. Given the "lifetime" nature of membership sales, customers do not return for second purchases, and future membership sales are purely a function of demographics and population trends. Once saturation is reached, the company's main source of income would be annual dues rather than membership sales. Thus, for "long-run" analytic purposes, we must recognize that the annual dues component of income is more important than is income from membership sales, which had historically been the most prominent factor.

This does not mean that historical membership sales are irrelevant. On the contrary, they are the primary inputs in estimating the level of future annual membership dues. This underscores the use of financial statements in general, and the income statement in particular, as (part of) a database used to predict the company's future.

The long run is not the only focus of analysis. As 1981–1983 earnings show, a firm can report substantial income in the short or intermediate term until a saturation point is reached. One objective of analysis is to estimate the future cash flows that will be generated by membership sales as well as the effects on the company when growth flattens out. To do so requires an analysis of the "quality" of Thousand Trails' earnings:

1. Are reported amounts of revenue, expense, and income reliable?
2. How well do they forecast future cash flows (that is, will reported receivables be collected)?

We will return to these issues and the analysis of Thousand Trails after

1. Discussing the general principles underlying revenue and expense recognition.
2. Considering the optimal use of information contained in the cash flow statement (separately and in conjunction with the income statement).

Presentation of the general principles will help us analyze the "quality" of reported income. The second step will provide insights into the relationship between income and cash flows in keeping with our contention that financial statements are best utilized when the information from various statements and footnotes are integrated.

EXHIBIT 2-1. THOUSAND TRAILS, INC. AND SUBSIDIARIES
Consolidated Statements of Earnings

Year ended December 31,	1983	1982	1981
Membership Sales	$79,971,000	$56,454,000	$40,006,000
Costs Attributable to Membership Sales:			
Marketing expenses	35,209,000	24,892,000	19,831,000
Preserve land and improvement costs	13,047,000	8,389,000	5,753,000
General and administrative expenses	11,827,000	8,612,000	7,141,000
Provision for doubtful accounts	3,977,000	2,241,000	1,866,000
	64,060,000	44,134,000	34,591,000
Income From Membership Sales	15,911,000	12,320,000	5,415,000
Preserve Operations:			
Membership dues	7,355,000	4,982,000	3,304,000
Trading post and other sales	2,749,000	2,015,000	1,482,000
	10,104,000	6,997,000	4,786,000
Less—			
Cost of trading post sales	2,400,000	1,839,000	1,346,000
Maintenance and operations expense	5,709,000	3,860,000	2,560,000
General and administrative expenses	1,506,000	973,000	711,000
	9,615,000	6,672,000	4,617,000
Income From Preserve Operations	489,000	325,000	169,000
Other Income (Expense):			
Interest income	10,147,000	6,622,000	4,153,000
Interest expense	(3,957,000)	(4,203,000)	(3,213,000)
Other	42,000	35,000	(147,000)
	6,232,000	2,454,000	793,000
Earnings Before Deferred Income Taxes	22,632,000	15,099,000	6,377,000
Deferred Income Taxes	10,628,000	7,338,000	3,050,000
Net Earnings	$12,004,000	$ 7,761,000	$ 3,327,000
Net Earnings Per Share:			
Primary	$1.85	$1.45	$.71
Fully diluted	$1.81	$1.34	$.68

Source: Thousand Trails, Inc., 1983 Annual Report

Accounting Income: Revenue and Expense Recognition

Under accrual accounting, revenue recognition involves questions of both timing and measurement:

1. When should revenue be recognized?
2. How much revenue should be recognized?

The responses to these questions determine the amount and timing of revenue recognition. The application of the "matching principle" relates expense recognition to revenue recognition.[16]

Statement of Financial Accounting Concepts (SFAC) 5, Recognition and Measurement in Financial Statements of Business Enterprises, specifies two conditions that must be met for revenue recognition to take place. These conditions are (1) completion of the earnings process and (2) its realization or assurance of realizability.

To satisfy the first condition, the firm must have provided all or virtually all of the goods or services for which it is to be paid, and it must be possible to measure the total expected cost of providing the goods or services; that is, the seller has no significant contingent obligation. If, for example, the seller was obligated to provide future services but was unable to estimate the cost of doing so, this condition would not be satisfied.

Recognition also requires a second condition: the quantification of cash or assets expected to be received for services provided. Reliable measurement encompasses the realizability (collectibility) of the proceeds of sale. If the seller were unable to make a reasonable estimate of the probability of nonpayment, realization would not be assured, and the second condition would not be satisfied.

The general revenue recognition rule includes this concept of realizability: revenue, measured as the amount expected to be collected, can be recognized when goods or services have been provided and their cost can be reliably determined.

The amount of revenues to be recognized at any given point in time is measured as

$$\frac{\text{Services provided to date}}{\text{Total expected services}} \times \text{Total expected inflow}$$

Note that the computation determines the amount of revenue that can be recognized *cumulatively* over time. Revenue reported for the current period is the cumulative total less revenues previously recognized.

The most common case is revenue recognition at the time of sale. Goods or services have been provided, and the sale is for cash or to customers whose ability to pay has been established.[17]

---

[16]Direct costs, such as cost of goods sold, are recognized in proportion to revenue recognized under accrual accounting. Note that cost of goods sold may also include depreciation expense or other capitalized expenditures such as overhead. However, certain expenses cannot be directly related to revenues and must be recognized using different principles. Some, called period costs (e.g., advertising costs), are expensed as incurred. Other costs are recognized as time passes, for example, interest costs. Finally, some costs may be based on other criteria, for example, taxes on income.

[17]In some cases, sales are made with repurchase agreements. If the risks or benefits (or both) of ownership are retained by the "seller," the transaction is, in economic substance, a consignment rather than a completed sale. See Chapter 10 for a discussion of transfers of receivables with recourse.

Magazine publishers receive subscription payments in advance; the receipts represent an obligation to provide delivery of periodic issues. Revenues are recognized in proportion to issues delivered. Revenues from credit card fees are also recognized as advances from customers and then as revenues as the right to use the cards expires over time. Revenues on equipment or property leases are recognized as time passes or based on usage (copier rental is sometimes based on a per copy charge). These examples show that performance can be measured in terms of the expenditure of cash, the passage of time, or the provision of service to the customer.

Departures from the Sales Basis of Revenue Recognition

Revenues may be recognized prior to sale or delivery when the earnings process is substantially complete and the proceeds of sale can be reasonably determined. For example, revenue may be recognized at the completion of production in the case of certain agricultural products with highly organized and liquid markets or, in the case of long-term construction contracts, as production takes place.

Alternatively, revenues may not be recognized even at the time of sale when there is significant uncertainty regarding the seller's ability to collect the sales price (the resulting accounts receivable) or estimate costs. Either the installment method or the more extreme cost recovery method, both discussed shortly, must be used in such cases.

Percentage-of-Completion and Completed Contract Methods

The *percentage-of-completion method* recognizes revenues and costs in proportion to the work completed; production activity is considered the critical event signaling completion of the earnings process rather than delivery or cash collections. The percentage-of-completion method is used for long-term projects when reliable estimates of production completed, revenues, and costs are available.

The *completed contract method* recognizes revenues and expenses only at the end of the contract. It must be used when any one of the conditions (specified for the percentage-of-completion method) is not met, generally when no contract exists or estimates of selling prices or collectibility are not reliable. It must be used for short-term contracts.[18]

The percentage-of-completion method usually measures progress using engineering estimates or ratios of costs incurred to expected total costs. The method may overstate revenues and gross profit if expenditures are recognized earlier than they contribute to completed work, for example, when the costs of raw materials and advance payments to subcontractors are included in the determination of work completed. When estimates of revenue or costs change, there is a "catch-up" effect on the earnings of the period in which the change in estimate is made. That effect is recognized currently as a change in accounting estimate, and the earnings of prior periods are not restated. Whenever there

---

[18]SFAS 56 (FASB, 1982) emphasizes that percentage-of-completion and completed contract are not "intended to be free-choice alternatives under either Accounting Research Bulletin 45 (ARB 45) or AICPA Statement of Position 81-1 (SOP 81-1)." ARB 45 states that percentage-of-completion is preferable when estimates of costs to complete and degree of completion are reliable. SOP 81-1 reiterates this position.

is an estimated loss on a contract, that loss must be recognized when the amount can be estimated.

Comparison of Completed Contract and Percentage of Completion

Exhibit 2-2 provides a comparison between percentage-of-completion and completed contract revenue recognition methods. The assumptions are stated first.

Part A compares the revenues, expenses, and income reported under each method for each year. Computations for the percentage-of-completion method are based on the assumption that the expenditures reflect the work completed. In 1992, 12.5% of the contract price is recognized as revenue to reflect that amount of work completed. The same percentage (12.5%) of the expected total income[19] is recognized as income for 1992. This pattern is repeated as long as the actual results mirror expectations.

The *completed contract method* recognizes revenues, expenses, and income only at the end of the contract period. The first three periods report no expense, revenue, or income. Expenditures during these periods are reported as inventory and cash receipts as advances from customers.

As a result, the different methods result in different recognition patterns for periodic revenue, expense, and income, but total revenue, expense, and income over the life of the transaction are identical under both methods.

The percentage-of-completion method provides both a better measure of operating activity and a more informative disclosure of the status of incomplete contracts. Given constant growth, the two methods will eventually produce identical results.[20] However, since the business world is rarely in a steady state of equilibrium, *the former method reports income earlier and is a better indicator of trends in growth and earning power.* Detailed disclosure of contracts in progress under the completed contract method would alleviate some of the problems but is unlikely to be as informative as the other method.

Part B shows the balance sheet and cash flow statement effects of the two methods. The most important result here is that during the first three years the completed contract method reports higher assets since construction in process is reported as inventory. Cash flows, however, are identical under both approaches.

Because the percentage-of-completion method recognizes revenues during the life of the contract, inventory is replaced by receivables that are collected. Since cash flow is unaffected by the choice of method, the completed contract method reports larger total assets because it accumulates inventory. However, the completed contract method reports lower equity (net assets) since no income is recognized until the end of the contract. *These differences are critical when comparing the size, return on assets, and return on equity ratios for European and Japanese construction firms with their U.S. competitors because foreign firms generally use the completed contract method.*[21]

Part C depicts the impact of a change in estimate. The example assumes that the

---

[19]Using the same percentage for revenue and income is, of course, equivalent to using the same rate for expense recognition as well.

[20]Income recognized from contracts completed in each period would be equal to the income recognized from the partial completion of contracts in process.

[21]However, German and Japanese regulators have recommended the use of the percentage-of-completion method in recent years.

EXHIBIT 2-2. JUSTIN CORPORATION
Comparison of Percentage-of-Completion and Completed Contract Revenue Recognition Methods

In 1992, Justin Corp. entered into a construction project with the following terms:

Total contract price	$6,000,000
Total expected cost	$4,800,000

Actual production costs over the duration of the contract and cash inflow information is provided as follows (in $ thousands):

	1992	1993	1994	1995
Costs incurred				
Current year	$ 600	$1200	$1800	$1200
Cumulative	600	1800	3600	4800
Estimated *remaining* costs to complete				
(as of December 31)	4200	3000	1200	0
Cash received during the year	1500	1500	1500	1500

A. Income Statement (in $ thousands)

	Percentage-of-Completion Method			Completed Contract Method		
	Revenue	Expense	Income	Revenue	Expense	Income
1992	$ 750*	$ 600	$ 150	$ 0	$ 0	$ 0
1993	1500†	1200	300	0	0	0
1994	2250‡	1800	450	0	0	0
1995	1500§	1200	300	6000	4800	1200
Total	$6000	$4800	$1200	6000	4800	$1200

* $\dfrac{\$600}{\$4800} \times \$6000 = \$750.$

† $\dfrac{(\$600 + \$1200)}{\$4800} \times \$6000 = \$2250 - \$750 = \$1500.$

‡ $\dfrac{(\$600 + \$1200 + \$1800)}{\$4800} \times \$6000 = \$4500 - \$2250 = \$2250.$

§ $\dfrac{(\$600 + \$1200 + \$1800 + \$1200)}{\$4800} \times \$6000 = \$6000 - \$4500 = \$1500.$

B. Balance Sheet and Cash Flow (in $ thousands)

Percentage-of-Completion Method

	Assets	=	Liabilities	+	Equity
	Cash	=	Advances	+	Retained Earnings
1992					
Cash received	$ 1500		$ 1500		
Revenue			(750)		$ 750
Costs incurred	(600)				(600)
Year-end balances	$ 900	=	$ 750	+	$ 150

EXHIBIT 2-2. *(Continued)*

	Assets	=	Liabilities	+	Equity
	Cash	=	Advances	+	Retained Earnings
1993					
Cash received	1500		1500		
Revenue			(1500)		1500
Costs incurred	(1200)				(1200)
Year-end balances	$ 1200	=	$ 750	+	$ 450
1994					
Cash received	1500		1500		
Revenue			(2250)		2250
Costs incurred	(1800)	=			(1800)
Year-end balances	$ 900		$ 0	+	$ 900
1995					
Cash received	1500		1500		
Revenue			(1500)		1500
Costs incurred	(1200)				(1200)
Year-end balances	$ 1200	=	$ 0	+	$ 1200

Completed Contract Method

	Assets			=	Liabilities	+	Equity	
	Cash	+	Inventory	=	Advances	+	Retained Earnings	
1992								
Cash received	$ 1500				$ 1500			
Costs incurred	(600)		$ 600					
Year-end balances	$ 900	+	$ 600	=	$ 1500	+	$	0
1993								
Cash received	1500				1500			
Costs incurred	(1200)		1200					
Year-end balances	$ 1200	+	$ 1800	=	$ 3000	+		0
1994								
Cash received	1500				1500			
Costs incurred	(1800)		1800					
Year-end balances	$ 900	+	$ 3600	=	$ 4500	+		0
1995								
Cash received	1500				1500			
Costs incurred	(1200)		1200					
Revenue					(6000)		6000	
Expense			(4800)				(4800)	
Year-end balances	$ 1200	+	$ 0	=	$ 0	+	$ 1200	

EXHIBIT 2-2. *(Continued)*

C. Change in Estimated Cost to Complete

On December 31, 1994, Justin Corp. determines that the total cost of the project will be $5400, making remaining costs to complete $1800, an increase of $600 from the original estimate. This changes *both* revenue and expense for 1994 under the percentage-of-completion method. The adjustment is made on a cumulative basis; revenue and expense reported for previous years are *not* restated.

Cumulative revenue recognized is

$$\frac{\$3600 \text{ (cumulative costs incurred)}}{\$5400 \text{ (revised total cost)}} \times \$6000 \text{ (estimated revenue)}$$

= $4000, of which $2250 was recognized as revenue in 1992 and 1993

Therefore, $1750 ($4000 − $2250) is recognized as revenue for 1994.

Cumulative expense recognized is $3600, the total incurred. Expense recognized for 1994 remains unchanged at $1800. As a result, income recognized in 1994 is

$1750 − $1800 = ($50) Loss

This loss reflects *both* the income on the portion of the contract completed during 1994 ($200) *and* the loss resulting from the overestimation of project in 1992 and 1993 ($250 loss).*

Revised Income Statements (in $ thousands)

	Percentage-of-Completion Method			Completed Contract Method		
	Revenue	Expense	Income	Revenue	Expense	Income
1992	$ 750	$ 600	$150	$ 0	$ 0	$ 0
1993	1500	1200	300	0	0	0
1994	1750	1800	(50)	0	0	0
Subtotal	$4000	$3600	$400			
1995	2000	1800	200	6000	5400	600
Total	$6000	$5400	$600	$6000	$5400	$600

*Using the revised estimate of cost to complete, year-by-year revenue, expense, and income would have been (in $ thousands):

Year	Revenue	Expense	Income
1992	$ 667	$ 600	$ 67
1993	1333	1200	133
1994	2000	1800	200
Total	$4000	$3600	$400

estimate of cost to complete is increased at the end of the third year (1994). This increase is recognized in 1994, and that year's loss reflects the income on work completed during the period offset by the impact of the change in estimate. Note that the cumulative income correctly reflects the degree of completion using the revised cost estimate.[22]

Similarly, if the firm estimated the remaining cost to complete the project at $2,750,000 at the end of 1994, the expected loss of $350,000 would be recognized in that year. The previously recognized earnings would be offset and the full contract loss would be recognized in 1994, the year in which it can be estimated, even though some of that loss will be incurred in 1995.

An interesting comparison of the completed contract and percentage-of-completion methods can be found later in the chapter. Newcor Company changed its accounting method from the completed contract method to the percentage-of-completion method in 1991. In doing so, the company had to restate its income statements for the previous three years. Both sets of statements are presented in Exhibit 2-13. Note that both sales and net income are more stable when restated to the percentage-of-completion method.

Installment Method of Revenue Recognition

Revenues cannot be recognized at the time of sale or delivery when there is substantial uncertainty regarding the seller's ability to realize the revenue or if there is no reasonable basis to estimate collectibility of the sales price. *The installment method* recognizes gross profit in proportion to cash collections, resulting in delayed recognition as compared with full recognition at the time of sale.

Until recently, use of the installment method was substantially limited to tax accounting. The 1986 tax reforms restricted its use in tax accounting, and its use in financial reporting is now limited to reporting asset sales and real estate transactions.

Cost Recovery Method

Revenue recognition on sale or delivery is also precluded when the costs to provide goods or services cannot be reasonably determined, for example, in the development of raw land. This occurs when completion of the sale is dependent on expenditures to be made in the future (e.g., roads) and it is impossible to estimate the amount of those expenditures (which may depend on zoning or environmental factors).

Generally, in these cases, there is also substantial uncertainty about realization since the customers' investment may be minor (small down payment with nonrecourse financing provided by the seller) and future collections (realization) may be uncertain. In view of these uncertainties, the *cost recovery method* requires that all cash receipts be accounted for as a recovery of costs. Only after all costs are recovered can profit be recognized under this method. The cost recovery method is not allowed for tax purposes.

The installment or cost recovery methods may be used to recognize franchise revenues when revenue is collectible over an extended period and there is no reasonable

---

[22]The firm has completed two-thirds ($3600 of costs incurred to date out of total expected costs of $5400) of the work on the project and at the end of the year will have recognized $400 or two-thirds of expected income of $600 ($150 in 1992, $300 in 1993, and a loss of $50 in 1994).

basis to estimate collectibility.[23] These methods may also be used, under specific circumstances, in real estate sales and retail land sales.[24]

Summary of Revenue Recognition Methods

The preceding discussion reflects the conceptual bases of different revenue recognition methods. From the analyst's point of view, it is important to be aware of the assumptions underlying the different methods both for comparison purposes and for the implications for future cash flows. The percentage-of-completion method for long-term contracts accrues revenues in proportion to services performed and the firm's assessment of the realizability of those revenues. This method highlights the relationship among the income statement (reported revenues), balance sheet (resulting receivables), and the cash flow statement (current collections). It is designed to provide a measure of current operating performance and facilitate forecasts of future performance and expected future cash flows.

The completed contract method lies at the other extreme since it recognizes revenues and expenses only when the contract has been completed. The analyst's reliance on the statement of cash flows may be greatest under this method.

The installment and cost recovery methods are used when there is uncertainty regarding the collectibility of future cash flows. The installment method is similar to the percentage-of-completion method for contracts in that it reports earnings in stages (as funds are received). The cost recovery method is similar to the completed contract method in that it postpones income recognition (but not recognition of revenue and expense) until all uncertainties have been eliminated. However, note that the balance sheet effects of the installment and cost recovery methods are different from those shown in Exhibit 2-2.

Whichever method is used, the analyst needs to monitor the cash flow statement and its relationship to the income statement. Before turning to a discussion of Thousand Trails' revenue recognition methods, we examine the cash flow statement.

Our discussion of the cash flow statement follows two paths. First, we examine the statement itself and discuss the implications and pitfalls of the information inherent in the present classification scheme. A method to recast the statements will be demonstrated. Second, we explore how the cash flow statement can and should be used in conjunction with the income statement.

ANALYSIS OF CASH FLOW INFORMATION

Accrual accounting rules determine the amount and timing of revenue and expense recognition and therefore the determination of periodic income. This process requires the allocation of cash flows to periods other than those in which they occur and in some cases obscures the cash impact of transactions and events. The resulting financial statements may produce income and net worth data that are not comparable since it is

---

[23]See SFAS 45, Accounting for Franchise Fee Revenue, Para. 6 (FASB, 1981).
[24]See SFAS 66, Accounting for Sales of Real Estate (FASB, 1982).

difficult to determine the extent to which differences across companies are induced by accounting or management choice or reflect real economic differences.

Given analysts' need for information about the amount, timing, and uncertainty of cash flows, these drawbacks serve to underscore the need for the statement of cash flows, which provides information about

1. A firm's ability to generate cash flows from operations.
2. The cash consequences of investing and financing decisions.

The latter contain insights regarding the capital markets' assessment of the firm's prospects (the availability and the relative cost of debt and equity capital) and management's decisions regarding expansion. Trends in these cash flows also provide information regarding the firm's ability to sustain (and increase) cash flows generated from current operations.

Statement of Cash Flows: Classification Issues

Statement of Financial Accounting Standards (SFAS) 95 requires that all cash flows reported by a firm be classified as operating, financing, or investing in nature. Such classification is essential to the analysis of cash flow data. Cash flow from operations provides information about the amount of cash generated by the firm from its sales of goods and services. While negative cash flows from operations are expected in some circumstances (rapid growth, for example), in the normal case positive operating cash flows are essential for long-run survival. Internally generated funds can be used for payment of dividends, repayment of loans, the replacement of existing capacity, or growth.

Investing cash flow reflects the cost of noncurrent assets such as plant and equipment and acquisitions of entire businesses. These outlays are needed to maintain a firm's current operating capacity as well as to provide capacity for future growth.

Financing cash flow provides information about the sources of externally generated funds of the firm. It reflects the firm's capital structure (debt versus equity), returns to shareholders in the form of dividends, and the incurrence and repayment of debt.

While it is important to classify cash flows into these categories, we must recognize that classification guidelines are arbitrary by their nature; the resulting data must therefore be adjusted or interpreted rather than accepted without question. The classification guidelines of SFAS 95 create problems for users of the cash flow statement in the following areas:

1. Classification of cash flows from investments
2. Classification of interest and dividends received
3. Classification of interest paid
4. Noncash transactions

We discuss each of these issues in turn.

Cash Flows From Investments

Consider the components of cash flow from operations in the following simple example:

Net income	$30,000
+ Depreciation (noncash expense)	5,000
= Funds from operations	$35,000
+ Decrease in inventory	15,000
= Cash from operations	$50,000

The first adjustment to income adds back "noncash" expenses and the result equals funds from operations (FFO). Cash from operations (CFO) is determined by adjusting FFO for changes in operating accounts. Note that the term "funds" in FFO (which was the focus of most "cash flow" statements prior to SFAS 95) is defined to include all current assets and liabilities. Whether "funds" are held as cash, receivables, or inventory is irrelevant under this definition. Funds (working capital) were long regarded as an appropriate measure of liquidity because near-cash current accounts were considered to be surrogates for cash. However, the concept of "funds" has limited relevance for analysis, and its limitations were increasingly recognized in the late 1970s and early 1980s.[25]

The cash flow statement adds both depreciation expense and the decrease in inventory to net income to arrive at cash from operations. But the nature of these addbacks is not identical. On the one hand, both adjustments reflect outlays of cash that occurred in prior periods but are recognized in income in the current period. Both must be "reversed" to arrive at CFO for the current period. Depreciation allocates the cost of fixed assets to the period in which they are used; cost of goods sold allocates the cost of inventory to the period the inventory is actually sold.

The difference between the two adjustments is the classification of the initial cash outlays. In the strictest sense both initial outlays were for investments; in one case the firm invested in fixed assets; in the other it invested in inventories. The latter, however, is classified as an operating cash outflow,[26] deducted from CFO in the period of the initial outlay and added back to income when expensed to avoid double counting.

The original investment in fixed assets was reported as an investment cash outflow, and its allocation (depreciation expense) is added back to income because it is never

---

[25]The credit crunch and high-interest-rate environment of the 1970s made liquidity and cash itself more critical—greater emphasis was placed on shortening the cash generating cycle of the firm's operations, leading to the decline of working capital and funds as indicators of liquidity. As will be noted shortly, two major components of working capital—receivables and inventories—need careful evaluation as both FFO and income can increase with little or no cash generated if the receivables increase without a corresponding increase in collections or inventories increase because they are not being sold. The W. T. Grant bankruptcy is a classic example of increasing working capital and income but declining cash. See the analysis of W. T. Grant's cash cycle in Chapter 3. Also see Largay and Stickney (1980). Furthermore, CFO is favored because reported FFO varies more readily with accounting methods used but actual cash flows are less prone to manipulation.

[26]An exception occurs when inventory is acquired as part of an acquisition (Chapter 12).

classified as an operating flow, but always as an investment flow.[27] The following implications of the difference between these two adjustments are worth noting:

1. Cash from operations does not include a charge for use of the firm's operating capacity. Cash required to provide for the replacement of the productive capacity or physical plant used up in operations during the period is not included in CFO.

2. Firms reporting positive CFO may be doing poorly unless the CFO (generated and retained) has been sufficient to replace the productive capacity used to generate the operating cash flow.

3. Identical firms with equal capital intensity will report different CFOs when one firm leases plant assets and the other owns its assets. The leasing firm reports lower CFO because lease rentals are reflected as operating expenditures (operating cash flows) while the other firm's expenditures are reported as investment cash flows.[28]

4. Outflows for inventory may also be excluded from CFO. If inventories are included in the acquisition of another entity, the cash outflow is treated as part of investing cash flow. What makes this example intriguing is that the proceeds from sale of such "purchased" inventory are included in CFO, distorting reported CFO as it shows only the benefits obtained and not the costs of the purchase.

In addition, it is important to note that the term "investment" is not precisely defined. Hertz, for example, classifies its investment in rental cars as operating cash flows. For analytic purposes, it can be argued that cash flows associated with the purchase and sale of rental cars should be treated differently from other operating cash flows. Conversely, firms with finance subsidiaries generally classify their cash flows related to finance receivables as investment cash flows. Such receivables, it can be argued (see analysis of Deere in Chapter 14) are accounts receivable, whose collection of and investment in should be treated as operating cash flows.

Free Cash Flows

The first three differences suggest the need for a charge to CFO to provide for the use and acquisition of plant capacity, regardless of whether it is owned or rented. The last underscores the need to evaluate cash flows from acquisitions with care. *Free cash flow*, a term that has gained increasing popularity among analysts, should reflect a charge for use of capacity and can be defined as CFO less cash outlays for the replacement of operating capacity.

For the computation of free cash flow, investment cash flows should be segregated into those for expansion as opposed to those made to maintain current productive,

---

[27]The distinction between adding back to avoid double counting or because of nonclassification as an operating item can perhaps best be seen if we consider what happens to the current period cash outflows for inventory and plant assets acquired and used during the period. For inventory, no adjustment is required. The current period allocation of the investment in plant assets (depreciation expense) must be added back as the outflow has been recorded as an investing cash outflow.

[28]See Chapter 8 for a detailed discussion of the financial statement impacts of the lease versus buy decision.

operating capacity.[29] Free cash flow, under this definition, is the amount available to finance planned expansion, reduce debt, pay dividends, or repurchase equity.[30] If historical cost depreciation expense provided a good measure of the use of productive capacity,[31] net income and free cash flow would be identical.[32]

In practice, it is difficult to separate investing cash flows into expansion and replacement, and free cash flow may be computed by deducting all investment in fixed assets from CFO. In this case free cash flow becomes equivalent to the amount available or needed for the financing activities of the company. As will be noted in Chapter 15, this alternative definition of free cash flow is useful as an input in certain valuation models.

Interest and Dividends Received

Firms also receive income and cash flows from investments in other firms, as well as from operating activities. Interest and dividends received from such investments are classified under SFAS 95 as operating cash flows. *As a result, the return on capital is separated from return of capital.*[33] Analysis would be facilitated if the two returns were combined to report cash flow to and from investees. More important, the reclassification of after-tax dividend and interest from operating to investing cash flows would have the advantage of reporting operating cash flows that reflect only the operating activities of the firm's core business.[34]

Interest Paid

Interest payments are classified as operating cash outflows under SFAS 95. Such payments, however, are the result of corporate structure and leverage decisions, and they reflect financing rather than operating risk. The reported CFO of two firms with different capital structures are not comparable because returns to creditors (interest) are included in CFO while returns to stockholders (dividends) are reported in financing cash flow. For analytic purposes, therefore, interest payments (after tax to reflect the cash flow benefits of tax deductibility) should be classified as financing cash flows. The resulting operating

[29]The International Accounting Standards Committee's new standard on cash flow statements recommends this disclosure.

[30]This argument revives the original motivation for depreciation expense and its relationship to net income, the segregation from income of an amount sufficient to replace capacity used. The remainder would be available for distribution to owners, leaving the firm as well off as before. See Chapter 14 for further discussion of the concept of free cash flow.

[31]However, depreciation in financial reporting is defined as a rational and systematic allocation of historical costs to operations. Given changes in price level and technology, it is unlikely that depreciation expense would provide a good indicator of the amount of productive capacity used up during a period. For further discussion of this problem, see Appendix 6C, Analysis of Changing Prices Information.

[32]Net income and free cash flow would be identical only under a restrictive set of assumptions: zero growth and the absence of changes in operating accounts, other noncash revenues or expenses, and gains or losses.

[33]Only the nominal (cash) return (dividend or interest received) is reported as an operating cash flow; the real (total) return (which includes capital gain or loss) is split between operating and investing cash flow.

[34]However, investments and joint ventures are often operating in nature. Such investments may assist in current and future operations, require significant financing commitments, and allow varying degrees of control over the cash flows generated by the investee. This problem, discussed at great length in Chapter 11, highlights the problems of generalized classification schemes.

cash flow is independent of the firm's capitalization, facilitating comparative analyses of firms with different capital structures.

Noncash Transactions

Firms often undertake investing and financing activities that do not require explicit outlays of cash. For example, a building may be acquired by assuming a mortgage. Under current disclosure rules, such transactions do not appear as cash from financing or investing activities but are given separate disclosure as "Significant Noncash Financing and Investment Activities."

For analytic purposes, however, this transaction is identical to the issuance of a bond to a third party, using the proceeds to acquire the building. The "noncash" transaction reflects both a financing and investing activity and should be included in each category. For example, in a valuation model based on free cash flows, noncash transactions must be included in the computation of free cash flows. What is important is information about the firm's cash requirements for investing activities, not just the method of financing.

A related implication of the classification issue is the subject of the next section. Reported income, we have seen, can be manipulated by accounting choices. What about CFO?

CFO: The Effect of Reporting Methods

Net cash flow (change in cash and cash equivalents during the period) measures real flows. However, its components, including CFO, are not "pure" measures but, rather, accounting constructs that can be variously defined.

CFO can be manipulated by reporting methods that affect the classification of cash flows among operating, investing, and financing categories. That is, if one accounting method results in classification of the cash flow as investing and another method results in classification of the same cash flow as operating, then reported CFO will differ depending on the method chosen.[35]

Capitalization of costs, for example, may lead to classification of cash outflows as investing cash flows, whereas they would be reported as operating cash flows if they were expensed immediately.[36] A good example is provided in Chapter 6 in its comparison of full cost (FC) and successful efforts (SE) reporting methods used in the oil and gas industry. The costs of dry holes are capitalized (expensed) under the FC (SE) method. The costs of dry holes are reported as investment cash flows under the FC method and as operating cash outflows under the SE method.

Cumulative net income (over the life of the investment) will be equal under both methods, but cumulative reported CFO will not because the cash flow is reported in two different categories and the differences never reverse as they are classification and not timing differences.

---

[35]However, note that CFO is not affected by the timing differences generated by revenue and expense recognition methods.

[36]This effect depends on the cash flow classification of the capitalized amount. Overhead capitalized in inventory, for example, will not change reported CFO because changes in inventory are also included in CFO. Overhead capitalized in fixed assets, however, will result in reclassification of the outflow from operating to investing cash flow.

Similarly, the classification of a lease as a capital or operating lease (see Chapter 8) also generates a difference in CFOs. All cash outflows under the operating lease method are reported as operating cash outflows. Lease payments under capital leases, however, are allocated between operating (interest component) and financing cash flows (principal repayment). The difference grows over time as interest declines and principal repayment increases.[37]

Other examples exist as we shall demonstrate throughout the book. It is, therefore, important to be aware that the cash flow statement, as other financial statements, is based on assumptions and arbitrary accounting rules. Knowledge of these assumptions and rules allows the analyst to make adjustments when necessary for good analysis. In the next section we describe an analytic technique useful for such adjustments.

Transactional Analysis: Overview

Transactional analysis is a method of preparing cash flow statements for analytic purposes. See Appendix 1A for a detailed example. This method makes it possible to examine the components of cash from operations, providing insights not available from the indirect method cash flow statement. Using the previous example, we have the following indirect presentation of cash from operations:

Net income	$30,000
+ Depreciation (noncash expense)	5,000
= Funds from operations	$35,000
+ Decrease in inventory	15,000
= Cash from operations	$50,000

This presentation format, unfortunately, does not provide information as to the elements that make up the cash flows. Any one of the following income statements would yield the identical presentation of CFO.

	Scenario		
	1	2	3
Sales	$80,000	$60,000	$100,000
Dividends received	0	20,000	0
Total revenues	$80,000	$80,000	$100,000
Cost of goods sold	45,000	45,000	60,000
Interest expense	0	0	5,000
Depreciation	5,000	5,000	5,000
Total expenses	$50,000	$50,000	$ 70,000
Net income	$30,000	$30,000	$ 30,000

[37]However, as discussed before, interest payments should not be reported as operating cash flows. Their treatment as financing cash flows would increase the discrepancy in CFO between the two methods, and as before, the difference would never reverse.

The three different scenarios, of course, reflect some of the problems with the current classifications of cash flow discussed earlier. In scenarios 2 and 3, operations (sale of goods and services) are confounded with investment (dividends received) and financing (interest expense) activities, respectively. Under the direct method, although cash flows from operations would also be reported as $50,000, the detail provided therein would make it easy to separate the various cash flow components and segregate cash flows that are actually operating in nature from those that are investing and financing.

	Scenario		
	1	2	3
Cash from customers	$80,000	$60,000	$100,000
Cash paid to suppliers	30,000	30,000	45,000
Subtotal	$50,000	$30,000	$ 55,000
Interest paid	0	0	(5,000)
Dividends received	0	20,000	0
Cash from operations	$50,000	$50,000	$ 50,000

Furthermore, the direct method provides information useful for trend analysis. It is worthwhile knowing, for example, whether CFO is increasing because receipts are increasing or because payments are decreasing. The direct method of cash flows provides more information in this respect. An analyst should be able to convert an indirect cash flow statement to a direct one. Transactional analysis allows for a better understanding of all the cash generating activities (not only operations) of the firm independent of how they have been classified. Box 2-2 contains such an analysis of cash flow statements over a five-year period (1987–1991) for the A.M. Castle company. The transactional analysis methodology showing how to effect this conversion is illustrated in Exhibit 2-3 for 1990 data obtained from Exhibit 2-4.

Relationship of the Cash Flow Statement and Income Statement

Accrual accounting does have its weaknesses. It is subject to pervasive accounting assumptions such as the going concern assumption. Because periodic statements must be prepared, estimates of the revenues earned and costs incurred during the reporting interval are required. These estimates require management judgment and estimates that are subject to modification as more information about the operating cycle becomes available. Accruals are, therefore, susceptible to manipulation by management's choice of accounting policies and estimates. Furthermore, accrual accounting fails to provide adequate information about the liquidity of the firm and long-term solvency. Some of these problems can be alleviated by the use of the cash flow statement in conjunction with the income statement.

Cash flow statements provide information about the amount and timing of the components of income and the firm's ability to realize reported asset balances (and repay liabilities). Neither the statement of cash flows nor the income statement alone contain

EXHIBIT 2-3. A. M. CASTLE
Conversion of Indirect Statement of Cash Flows to Direct Method, for Year Ended December 31, 1990

Sales	$ 478,856	
Provision for bad debts	790	
Decrease in accounts receivable	3,818	
Cash collections		$ 483,464
Cost of materials	(363,577)	
Increase in inventories	(13,592)	
Decrease in accounts payable	(11,709)	
Cash material cost		(388,878)
Operating expense	(97,449)	
Decrease in accrued liabilities*	(233)	
Decrease in accrued payroll	(3,034)	
Decrease in prepaid expense	555	
Gain on property	(17)	
Vested stock award	321	
Cash operating expense		(99,857)
Interest expense	(6,832)	
Increase in accrued interest†	508	
Interest paid		(6,324)
Income tax expense	(2,655)	
Decrease in current deferred tax	(524)	
Increase in deferred income tax	71	
Decrease in other accrued tax‡	(8)	
Income tax paid		(3,116)
Cash from operations		$ (14,711)

*Reported change (cash flow)	$ 267
Interest accrued†	(508)
Income tax accrued‡	8
Adjusted change	$(233)

We assume that the undisclosed interest and tax accruals are included in accrued liabilities.

   †Deduced. Since both interest expense and interest paid are disclosed, the difference must be due to a change in accrued interest payable.

   ‡Deduced. Income tax paid is disclosed. The disclosed balance sheet changes do not fully account for the difference between income tax expense and income tax paid. Therefore, there must be an undisclosed accrual.

Explanation:

   Following the transactional analysis methodology in Appendix 1A to Chapter 1, we relate each income statement account to its corresponding balance sheet account(s). The goal is to replace each income statement accrual with its cash flow equivalent. A. M. Castle's financial statements are contained in Exhibit 2-4.

   It is important to note that we use the cash flows shown in the indirect method statement of cash flows rather than the balance sheet changes. Because Castle acquired Norton Steel in 1990, the balance sheet changes include both the operating change for the year and the effect of the acquisition (see Chapter 12 for more detailed discussion of the impact of acquisitions on reported

EXHIBIT 2-3. *(Continued)*

cash flows). If Castle's foreign operations were more significant, exchange rate changes would further distort the balance sheet changes (see Chapter 13).

Because we used the balance sheet changes resulting only from operating activities, the direct method cash flow is not distorted by either the acquisition or (any) effect of currency changes. It is, therefore, an accurate portrayal of Castle's operating cash flow.

EXHIBIT 2-4. A.M. Castle
Consolidated Statements of Income

Dollars in thousands, except per share data	Years Ended December 31,		
	1991	1990	1989
Net sales	$436,441	$478,856	$501,118
Cost of material sold	331,093	363,577	380,659
Gross profit on sales	105,348	115,279	120,459
Expenses			
Operating expenses	92,848	97,449	96,679
Depreciation	5,273	5,215	4,378
Interest expense, net	6,848	6,832	5,134
	104,969	109,496	106,191
Income before income taxes	379	5,783	14,268
Income taxes (Notes 1 and 3)			
Federal—currently payable	298	1,786	4,621
—deferred	(146)	367	(25)
State	26	502	1,022
	178	2,655	5,618
Net income	201	3,128	8,650
Net income per share	$ .03	$ .43	$ 1.20

Consolidated Statements of Cash Flows

(Dollars in thousands)	Years Ended December 31,		
	1991	1990	1989
Cash flows from operating activities			
Net income	$ 201	$ 3,128	$ 8,650
Adjustments to reconcile net income to net cash provided from (used by) operating activities			
Depreciation	5,273	5,215	4,378
Provision for bad debts	522	790	860

EXHIBIT 2-4. *(Continued)*

(Dollars in thousands)	Years Ended December 31,		
	1991	1990	1989
Gain on sale of facilities/equipment	(635)	(17)	(72)
Increase in deferred taxes	728	71	445
(Increase) decrease in prepaid expenses and other assets	(1,173)	555	(1,953)
Vested portion of restricted stock awards	64	321	169
Cash provided from operating activities before changes in current accounts, net of effects of acquisition	4,980	10,063	12,477
(Increase) decrease in current assets/liabilities			
Accounts receivable	4,479	3,818	7,068
Inventories	25,601	(13,592)	9,790
Accounts payable	(7,541)	(11,709)	(1,074)
Accrued payroll and employee benefits	(1,701)	(3,034)	(3,322)
Accrued liabilities	91	267	43
Current deferred income taxes	(834)	(524)	(249)
Net (increase) decrease in current assets/liabilities	20,095	(24,774)	12,256
Net cash provided from (used by) operating activities	25,075	(14,711)	24,733
Cash flows from investing activities			
Acquisition of Norton Steel Co. Ltd.	—	(2,529)	—
Proceeds from sales of facilities/equipment	5,490	34	196
Capital expenditures	(3,305)	(13,390)	(10,381)
Net cash provided from (used by) investing activities	2,185	(15,885)	(10,185)
Cash flows from financing activities			
Net borrowing under line-of-credit agreements	(11,700)	11,400	500
Proceeds from issuance of long-term debt	201	29,875	—
Repayment of Norton Steel Co. Ltd. short-term debt	—	(3,400)	—
Repayments of long-term debt	(11,830)	(3,908)	(10,187)
Proceeds from issuance of stock	25	50	40
Dividends paid	(3,927)	(4,931)	(4,640)
Fractional shares repurchased	—	—	(8)
Net cash provided from (used by) financing activities	(27,231)	29,086	(14,295)
Net increase (decrease) in cash	29	(1,510)	253
Cash—beginning of year	302	1,812	1,559
Cash—end of year	$ 331	$ 302	$ 1,812

EXHIBIT 2-4. *(Continued)*

	Years Ended December 31,		
(Dollars in thousands)	1991	1990	1989
Supplemental disclosures of cash flow information			
Cash paid during the year for—			
Interest (net of amount capitalized)	$ 7,340	$ 6,324	$ 4,886
Income taxes	$ 283	$ 3,116	$ 5,423

Consolidated Balance Sheets

	Years Ended December 31,		
(Dollars in thousands)	1991	1990	1989
Assets			
Current assets			
Cash	$ 331	$ 302	$ 1,812
Accounts receivable, less allowances of $600	44,564	49,043	51,068
Inventories—principally on last-in, first-out basis (latest cost higher by approximately $51,200 in 1991, $57,200 in 1990 and $62,900 in 1989)	88,292	113,893	96,299
Total current assets	133,187	163,238	149,179
Prepaid expenses and other assets	9,813	8,640	7,798
Property, plant and equipment, at cost			
Land	4,115	4,115	3,687
Buildings	34,688	33,893	26,896
Machinery and equipment	54,653	59,340	52,531
	93,456	97,348	83,114
Less—accumulated depreciation	46,041	42,583	37,839
	47,415	54,765	45,275
Total assets	$190,415	$226,643	$202,252
Liabilities and stockholders' equity			
Current liabilities			
Accounts payable	$ 37,374	$ 44,915	$ 53,520
Accrued payroll and employee benefits	3,742	5,443	8,477
Accrued liabilities	3,715	3,624	3,101
Short-term debt	200	11,900	500
Current deferred income taxes	2,501	3,335	3,907
Current portion of long-term debt	5,925	4,107	3,846
Total current liabilities	53,457	73,324	73,351
Long-term debt, less current portion	63,278	76,725	51,019

EXHIBIT 2-4. *(Continued)*

(Dollars in thousands)	Years Ended December 31,		
	1991	1990	1989
Deferred income taxes	9,010	8,282	8,138
Stockholders' equity			
Common stock, without par value	21,813	21,364	20,648
Earnings reinvested in the business	44,717	48,443	50,246
Cumulative translation adjustment	(5)	—	—
Treasury stock, at cost	(1,855)	(1,495)	(1,150)
Total stockholders' equity	64,670	68,312	69,744
Total liabilities and stockholders' equity	$190,415	$226,643	$202,252

Source: A.M. Castle 1991 Annual Report

BOX 2-2. A. M. CASTLE
Analysis of Cash Flow, 1987–1991 (in $ thousands)

	1987	1988	1989	1990	1991
Cash collections	$ 364,224	$ 487,448	$ 509,046	$ 483,464	$ 441,442
Cash material cost	(268,890)	(408,664)	(371,943)	(388,878)	(313,033)
Cash operating expense	(71,947)	(85,066)	(102,062)	(99,857)	(95,711)
Interest paid	(3,433)	(5,135)	(4,886)	(6,324)	(7,340)
Income tax paid	(5,018)	(7,870)	(5,422)	(3,116)	(283)
Cash from operations	$ 14,936	$ (19,287)	$ 24,733	$ (14,711)	$ 25,075
Capital expenditures	(2,605)	(7,816)	(10,381)	(13,390)	(3,305)
Proceeds from property sales	1,888	503	196	34	5,490
Acquisitions	—	—	—	(2,529)	—
Cash from investment	$ (717)	$ (7,313)	$ (10,185)	$ (15,885)	$ 2,185
Net change in debt	(10,816)	28,184	(9,687)	33,967	(23,329)
Net issue of equity	204	21	32	50	25
Dividends paid	(3,040)	(3,442)	(4,640)	(4,931)	(3,927)
Cash from financing	$ (13,652)	$ 24,763	$ (14,295)	$ 29,086	$ (27,231)
Net change in cash	$ 567	$ (1,837)	$ 253	$ (1,510)	$ 29
Ratios					
Cash material/cash collections	0.738	0.839	0.730	0.804	0.709
Cash operations/cash collections	0.198	0.174	0.200	0.207	0.217
Cost of materials/net sales*	0.750	0.751	0.760	0.759	0.759
Operating expense/net sales*	0.199	0.185	0.193	0.204	0.213

*Based on income statement data. See Exhibit 2-4 for data for 1989–1991.

Discussion

We present a direct method cash flow statement for A. M. Castle for the five years 1987–1991. For each year the methodology described in Exhibit 2-3 was used.

Castle is a metals wholesaler. Its revenues and earnings are heavily influenced by the business cycle. As steel products account for 70% of sales, steel prices also impact reported sales and cash flows. As Castle accounts for inventories using the LIFO method (see Chapter 5), price changes are largely excluded from reported income. From the income statements shown, we can see that Castle's earnings are cyclical although the company reported earnings for each year.

Because of this cyclicality, we start by looking at cash flows over the entire five-year period:

Cash from operations			$ 30,746
Capital expenditures	$(37,497)		
Property sales	8,111		
Acquisitions	(2,529)		
Cash from investment (reported)		$(31,915)	
Less: reclassification of sale-leaseback		(5,317)	
Cash from investment (adjusted)			(37,232)
Net change in debt	$ 18,319		
Net issue of equity	332		
Dividends paid	(19,980)		
Cash from financing (reported)		(1,329)	
Less: reclassification of sale-leaseback		5,317	
Cash from financing (adjusted)			3,988
Net change in cash			$ (2,498)

Aggregate cash from operations was approximately $31 million, although CFO was negative for two of the five years. Total capital expenditures were $37 million, suggesting that free cash flow was negative. Before adopting this conclusion, however, we would question management to see how much of capital spending over the five-year period represented expansion rather than replacement of capacity. Given the lack of sales growth, we shall, for purposes of this discussion, assume that none of the capital expenditure was for expansion. The 1990 acquisition, however, would be considered a cash outflow for expansion.

Turning to financing cash flow, we see that Castle paid dividends of $20 million over the five-year period while increasing debt by $18 million. Reclassification of the sale/leaseback transaction† changes the debt increase to more than $23 million.

In rough terms, therefore, it appears that Castle's operating cash flow was insufficient to cover capital expenditures necessary to maintain its operating capacity. The shortfall and cash dividend payments were financed by an increase in debt. Long- and short-term debt increased from less than $45 million at the end of 1986 (87% of stockholders' equity) to more than $63 million (98% of equity) five years later.

Looking at the components of CFO, we see that cash material cost has been highly variable relative to cash collections. While accrual-based cost of materials has been quite stable (75–76% of sales), the cash basis ratio has ranged from 71% to 84% over the five-year period. Swings in inventory levels and prices (which do affect cash flows, even when LIFO is used for accrual purposes) create that volatility. That volatility may explain why Castle has substantial lines of credit.

---

†Proceeds from sales of property were $8 million over the five-year period, but most of that resulted from a 1991 sale and leaseback transaction. The proceeds of that sale are really a financing transaction and should not be considered a reduction of cash for investment. This is another case where good analysis requires the reclassification of reported cash flows.

BOX 2-3
Accrual Income Versus Cash Flow: Some Empirical Evidence

Empirical results provide consistent evidence that, given cash flows from operations, accruals provide incremental information.* Bernard (1989) notes that such results demonstrate that "increases in accruals, including receivables and inventory, translate on average into increases in expected future cash flows."

Evidence that both earnings and cash flow information numbers are useful to investors† is provided by Bowen, Burgstahler, and Daley (1987), who compared market reaction to cash flows,‡ funds from operations, and net income. They found that both cash flows and net income provided incremental information to the market. Specifically, they found that after controlling for earnings, cash flow data had incremental information, and separately, after controlling for the information provided by CFO, they found that earnings provided incremental information. However, they found that FFO did not provide any additional information over that contained in earnings.

Bernard and Stober (1989), however, argue that cash flow results may not be consistent across all years and that the variation in results may be caused by using models that do not capture the specific implications of any particular company or situation. They suggest that "further progress in this line of research will require a better understanding of the economic context in which the implications of detailed earnings components are interpreted."§ Livnat and Zarowin (1990) do provide some evidence that, although aggregated CFO does not provide additional informational content, individual cash components from operations as well as individual components of financing cash flows do provide incremental information.||

---

*See, for example Judy Rayburn, "The Association of Operating Cash Flow And Accruals With Security Returns," *Journal of Accounting Research* (Supplement 1986) and G. Peter Wilson, "The Relative Information Content Of Accruals And Cash Flows: Combined Evidence At The Earnings Announcement And Annual Report Release Date": *Journal of Accounting Research* (Supplement 1986), in addition to Robert M. Bowen, David Burgstahler, and Lane A. Daley, "The Incremental Information Content of Accrual Versus Cash Flows," *The Accounting Review* (October 1987), discussed shortly.

†In Chapter 4, we provide a more detailed look at and critique of the nature of the "information content" line of empirical research.

‡They examined both CFO and cash flows after investments.

§Victor Bernard and Thomas Stober, "The Nature and Amount of Information in Cash Flows and Accruals," *The Accounting Review* (October 1989), p. 648.

||This does not mean that cash flow information is superior as the relevant comparison would have to be individual components of accrual income.

---

sufficient information for decision making. (See Box 2-3 for some empirical evidence in this respect.) Income statement data must be combined with cash flows for insights into the firm's ability to realize reported revenues and expenses and thereby assist the analyst in the development of other valuation-relevant income measures.

Cash flow is relatively (but not completely) free of the drawbacks of the accrual concept. It is less likely to be affected by variations in accounting principles and estimates,[38] making it more useful than reported income in assessing liquidity and solvency. The next section discusses three areas where cash flow statements can and

---

[38]However, variations in methods and estimates used on tax returns affect cash flows and therefore liquidity and solvency.

should be used together with information from the income statement to assess the cash generating ability of a firm.

Income, Cash Flow, and the Going Concern Assumption

As noted earlier, income numbers based on accrual accounting are presumed to be good predictors of future cash flows. That predictive ability is subject to a number of implicit assumptions, most important, the going concern assumption. The classification of inventories as assets rather than as expenses implicitly assumes that they will be sold in the normal course of business to generate cash. Similarly, recognition of credit sales and the valuation of receivables assume that the firm will continue to operate normally.

When the going concern assumption is subject to doubt, recognition and valuation can no longer be taken for granted. The value of inventory and receivables declines sharply when they must be liquidated. Long-term assets (especially intangibles and other assets with little or no value in a nonoperating framework) also must be reexamined when the going concern assumption is questioned.

Figure 2-1 shows the income and cash flow patterns of W. T. Grant in the years preceding its bankruptcy. Note that income was positive in the decade prior to

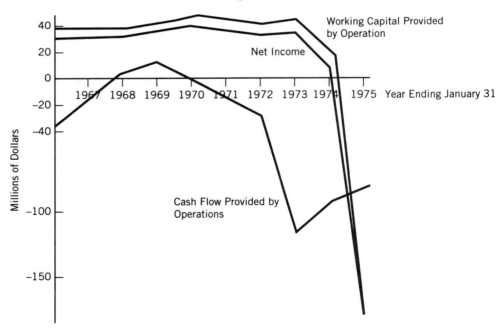

W.T. Grant Company Net Income, Working Capital and Cash Flow From Operations
For Fiscal Years Ending January 31, 1966 to 1975

Source: James A. Largay, III and Clyde P. Stickney, Financial Analysts Journal, July - August 1980, Vol. 36, No.4

FIGURE 2-1 Trends of Net Income and Cash Flow Prior to Bankruptcy: W.T. Grant

bankruptcy. Cash flows from operations, on the other hand, were negative. Thus income failed as a predictor of future cash flows. In fact, examples such as W. T. Grant helped lead to the adoption of SFAS 95, which requires the preparation of the cash flow statement in its present form. Previously, financial statements used funds or working capital flows (inventories and receivables were components of funds) as surrogates for cash flows.[39] Note that in the W. T. Grant case, the funds flow surrogate did not work. Although income was recorded, collections of receivables showed a substantial decline, and purchased inventories were not sold, which increased outstanding debt. *The statement of cash flows serves as a "check" on the assumptions inherent in the income statement.*

Figure 2-1 compares the bottom-line characteristics of the income and cash flow numbers. To find out why income failed as a predictor of cash generating ability (uncollected receivables or unsold inventories) requires a comparison of amounts recorded as sales and cost of goods sold on the income statement with the pattern of cash collections from customers and cash paid for inventories on the cash flow statement. These latter amounts would require a direct method cash flow statement. We provide such a comparison shortly in the discussion of the second beneficial use of cash flow statements.

Income, Cash Flow, and the Choice of Accounting Policies

Consider the income statements for the three companies presented in Exhibit 2-5. They are based on the example illustrated in Exhibit 2-2.

These three income patterns differ only because of the choice of accounting policy. The selected policies convey information as to management's expectations and its other objectives or incentives. In case A, income is recognized on the basis of future expectations as to eventual completion of a project, and the firm shows positive income each year. In case B, a conservative management recognizes income only when the project is completed, and the income statement indicates no operations (except for the buildup of costs) during the first three years. Finally, in case C, management assumes that eventual collectibility of the revenues is uncertain and thus does not recognize profit until after all costs are recovered.

Are the net income numbers different because the firms' activities differ or because accounting methods and assumptions of managers differ? *Use of the cash flow statement in this context allows the analyst to distinguish between the actual events that have occurred and the accounting assumptions that have been used to represent these events.* This is not to say that the assumptions are wrong. They may provide useful information. It is important, however, to disclose the interrelationship between these events and financial reporting choices.

A check of the cash flow statement on the indirect method shows that cash from operations is identical for all three companies. Further, using transactional analysis, one can derive cash flow on the direct method basis, further highlighting that the companies are identical in terms of the activities undertaken. Cash collected and cash disbursed are identical for all three companies. They differ only with respect to the information provided in the income statement.

[39]To some extent, this measure (net income plus depreciation) is still used as a surrogate for cash flow.

EXHIBIT 2-5
Derivation of Cash from Operations Under Alternative Accounting Methods

Indirect Method

Company A: Percentage of Completion

Year	1	2	3	4
Revenue	$ 750	$ 1500	$ 2250	$ 1500
Expense	(600)	(1200)	(1800)	(1200)
Net income	$ 150	$ 300	$ 450	$ 300
Add: Increase in advances	750	0	(750)	0
Cash from operations	$ 900	$ 300	$ (300)	$ 300

Company B: Completed Contract

Revenue	$ 0	$ 0	$ 0	$ 6000
Expense	0	0	0	(4800)
Net income	$ 0	$ 0	$ 0	$ 1200
Add: Increase in advances	1500	1500	1500	(4500)
Subtract: Increase in inventory	(600)	(1200)	(1800)	3600
Cash from operations	$ 900	$ 300	$ (300)	$ 300

Company C: Cost Recovery

Revenue	$ 600	$ 1200	$ 1800	$ 2400
Expense	(600)	(1200)	(1800)	(1200)
Net income	$ 0	$ 0	$ 0	$ 1200
Add: Increase in advances	900	300	(300)	(900)
Cash from operations	$ 900	$ 300	$ (300)	$ 300

Direct Method: Identical for All Three Companies

Cash collections*	$1500	$ 1500	$ 1500	$ 1500
Cash disbursements†	(600)	(1200)	(1800)	(1200)
Cash from operations	$ 900	$ 300	$ (300)	$ 300

*Cash collections = revenue + increase in advances (e.g., for year 1, Company A = $750 + $750; Company B = 0 + $1500; and Company C = $600 + $900).

†Cash disbursements = expense + increase in inventory (e.g., for year 1, Company A and Company C = $600 + $0; Company B = $0 + $600).

This information is a function of different assumptions reflected in differing accounting policies. To a great extent, the cash flow statement is less subject to manipulation (by accounting policies related to the timing of revenue and expense recognition) than the income statement and hence can be analyzed to see the extent to which variations in firm income reflect real differences or the impact of differences in assumptions, accounting methods, and estimates. However, the cash flow statement is affected by other choices such as capitalization and expensing as discussed previously.

Income, Cash Flow, and Liquidity

Figure 2–2 presents a comparison of the trends in cash flows and income for a hypothetical firm. The pattern is very similar to that of Figure 2–1 and the W. T. Grant Company. However, unlike W. T. Grant, the going concern assumption does not create problems. Rather, the company is simply growing too fast. As it must pay for inventories before they are sold and cannot collect sales proceeds until some time after the sale, there is a gap between the expenditures and receipts. The income statement would show a strong growth pattern that would be indicative of a sustainable ability to generate cash flows in the future, assuming the firm survives.

Potential liquidity problems would be highlighted by *the cash flow statement, which provides information as the firm's liquidity and the firm's ability to generate funds internally to finance its growth.* This example highlights the importance of using both statements. Reliance on the cash flow statement or income statement by itself may not allow an assessent of the underlying strength of the company. That strength may be reflected in the income statement, which, however, does not reveal the liquidity dangers facing the company. Armed with our analyses of the cash flow statement along with our previous discussion of revenue recognition methods, we now turn to an evaluation of Thousand Trails. This will allow us to demonstrate many of the analytic points raised in the chapter thus far.

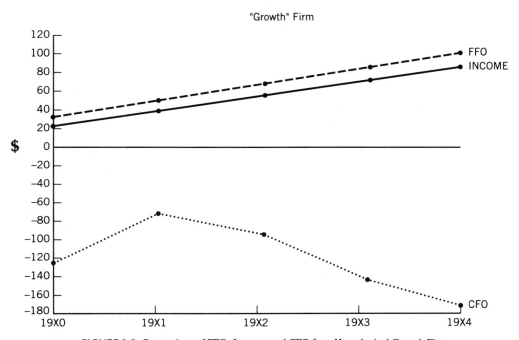

FIGURE 2-2 Comparison of FFO, Income, and CFO for a Hypothetical Growth Firm.

THOUSAND TRAILS: INCOME AND CASH FLOW ANALYSIS

The statement of changes in financial position (see Exhibit 2-6) provided by Thousand Trails was required prior to the adoption of SFAS 95. That the CFO definition used by Thousand Trails differs from that specified by SFAS 95 illustrates our earlier point that the definition of CFO is arbitrary. It is the information contained in financial statements, not their format, that determines their usefulness. Fortunately, Thousand Trails used the direct method, allowing separate comparison of its pattern of revenue growth with its cash inflows and of its expenses with cash outflows.

Revenue Recognition by Thousand Trails

Thousand Trails' reported CFO lagged reported income (see Exhibit 2-1). Given the growth in Thousand Trails' income and revenue, this phenomenon may have been purely a function of Thousand Trails' growth.

Thousand Trails' revenue recognition footnote states

> The Company sells memberships for cash or on installment contracts. Revenues are recorded in full upon execution of membership agreements. Installment sales require a down payment of at least 10% of the sales price. All marketing costs and an allowance for estimated contract collection losses (based on historical loss occurrence rates) are recorded currently.

Did Thousand Trails' method of revenue recognition meet the required criteria; that is,

1. Had Thousand Trails provided all or substantially all the service to its customers?
2. Was cash collectibility reasonably assured?

With respect to criterion 1, it can be argued that part of the lure of membership was the accessibility to both current and *future* campgrounds promised by Thousand Trails. Thus Thousand Trails' service was complete only when these campgrounds materialized. This point is, however, not relevant. Under the terms of the membership sales agreement, however, no refunds were available once memberships were sold, even if future campsites were not completed. Thus this criterion suggests that revenue recognition was appropriate.

The second criterion is more problematic. The footnote indicates that revenue was recognized in full for both cash and installment sales as long as a down payment of 10% was received. Other footnotes indicate that installment sales had terms of 24 to 84 months with an average term of 61 months. Thus the lag between CFO and income raises the following questions:

What percentage of sales was made for cash?

For installment sales, what was the creditworthiness of the customers and what were the terms of payment?

EXHIBIT 2-6. THOUSAND TRAILS, INC. AND SUBSIDIARIES
Consolidated Statements of Changes in Financial Position, 1981–1983

Year ended December 31,	1983	1982	1981
Operations:			
Cash received—			
Membership sales	$ 27,738,000	$ 22,582,000	$18,003,000
Collections on contracts receivable,			
including interest	28,619,000	19,278,000	13,258,000
Dues and preserve revenues	10,507,000	7,336,000	5,133,000
Other	211,000	133,000	(69,000)
	67,075,000	49,329,000	36,325,000
Cash expended—			
Marketing expenses	34,211,000	23,211,000	19,983,000
General and administrative expenses	11,788,000	7,739,000	7,130,000
Preserve maintenance and operations	9,001,000	6,127,000	4,571,000
Principal payments on debt related to			
preserve properties	4,337,000	3,744,000	2,032,000
Interest expense	3,957,000	4,203,000	3,213,000
	63,294,000	45,024,000	36,929,000
Cash provided by (used in) operations			
before preserve improvements	3,781,000	4,305,000	(604,000)
Cash expended for preserve improvements	(18,391,000)	(11,275,000)	(6,837,000)
Cash used in operations	(14,610,000)	(6,970,000)	(7,441,000)
Other Sources (Uses) of Cash:			
Issuance of common stock	17,756,000	4,161,000	10,000
Proceeds of borrowings collateralized by			
contracts receivable	851,000	8,646,000	9,069,000
Principal payments on notes payable and			
credit line arrangements	(1,109,000)	(735,000)	(743,000)
Acquisition of preferred stock		(3,000,000)	
Purchase of construction and operating			
equipment, net of related borrowings of			
$1,388,000, $1,072,000 and			
$1,588,000	(2,943,000)	(1,490,000)	(789,000)
Other, net	122,000	(81,000)	(566,000)
	14,677,000	7,501,000	6,981,000
Increase (Decrease) in Cash	67,000	531,000	(460,000)
Cash:			
Beginning of year	703,000	172,000	632,000
End of year	$ 770,000	$ 703,000	$ 172,000

Source: Thousand Trails, Inc., 1983 Annual Report.

These questions, in addition to having relevance for criterion 2, also reopen consideration of criterion 1. While it is true that the company did not have to refund any monies collected if customers canceled, at the same time, it had no recourse in terms of collecting any unpaid balances upon cancellation. Thus, if customers stopped paying (effectively canceling their memberships), previously recognized revenues might have to be reversed.

Further insights on these issues can be obtained from a disaggregation of the cash flow statement.

Membership Sales: Comparison of Revenue Recognized and Cash Inflows (in $ millions)

	1981	1982	1983
Revenue	$ 40.0	$ 56.5	$ 80.0
Cash inflow*	(27.1)	(35.3)	(46.2)
Difference	$ 12.9	$ 21.2	$ 33.8

*Defined as the sum of cash received from membership sales plus collections on contracts receivable, less interest income. Thus, for 1983, cash inflow = $27.7 + $28.6 − $10.1 = $34.2 million. (We have made the simplifying assumptions that interest income all relates to membership contracts and is received in cash.)

The annual difference between revenues and cash inflows grew from year to year. Furthermore, even on a lagged basis, the difference was growing. Collections in 1982 ($35.3 million) were less than revenue recognized in 1981 ($40.0 million); similarly, in 1983 ($46.2 million versus $56.5 million). The lag grew on both an absolute ($4.8 million versus $10.4 million) and percentage (12% versus 18%) basis.

Thus the key issue for the analyst goes beyond the "narrow" focus of whether or not Thousand Trails was in technical compliance with GAAP revenue recognition methods. What is more important is the answer to the following question: Would the revenues recognized eventually be collected and how well did the company's earnings predict future cash flows?

We will return to these issues after examining Thousand Trails' method of recognizing expenses.

Expense Recognition by Thousand Trails

Thousand Trails incurred two types of expenditures in generating sales of memberships: (1) marketing costs and (2) preserve development costs. Marketing costs were charged to expense as incurred. Preserve development costs were treated as stated in the revenue recognition footnote:

Operating preserve land and improvement costs, including the estimated costs to complete preserves in accordance with the Company's development plans, are aggregated by geographical region and recorded as a cost of membership sales based upon the ratio of actual memberships sold within each region to the total memberships planned by the Company to be available for sale within the region

For expense recognition, Thousand Trails used a percentage-of-completion method and allocated (actual and planned) costs to expenses based upon the portion of actual to planned sales. Note that this method differs from the one discussed in the context of Exhibit 2-2. In that case the customer for the project had already contracted for it. For Thousand Trails, the customer had still to be found. The accompanying table presents the difference between the expenses reported by Thousand Trails and the cash outflows for preserve improvements. In all years, cash outflows exceed expense recognition.

Preserve Improvement Costs: Comparison of Expense Recognized and Cash Outflows, 1981–1983

	1981	1982	1983
Expense	$5.8	$ 8.4	$13.0
Cash outflow*	(6.8)	(11.3)	(18.4)
Difference	($1.0)	($ 2.9)	($ 5.4)

*Defined as cash expended for preserve improvements

The appropriateness of this method was clearly a function of whether the planned sales would occur. The revenue recognition footnote indicates that

As of December 31, 1983, the Company had 51,000 members which represented approximately one-third of the total planned memberships for sale on its 36 operating preserves.

Note that management forecast that total memberships (based on existing preserves) would be three times the current level. Management forecasts used as accounting inputs must be examined carefully as misestimation, whether purposeful or not, may have significant effects on reported earnings and asset values. Taken together with Thousand Trails' revenue recognition methods, the following picture emerges.

Thousand Trails attempted to have the best of both worlds. It made large outlays for preserve improvements based on optimistic estimates of future cash flows. But some current cash outflows were capitalized (deferred to future periods), while all estimated future cash inflows were recognized as revenue immediately.

Moving beyond the issue of whether this accounting complied with GAAP, the implications of the cash flow gap should be clear. Analysis suggests that Thousand Trails' past growth rates were untenable. The only way to maintain the growth rate of income would have been to continue making sales at the same rate as in the past. These sales would require new campgrounds, which would result in further cash outlays and deferral of costs. This cycle assumed, to some extent, the existence of a large untapped market. Even if this market existed, the cash flow (liquidity) constraint would eventually overwhelm the company.

The analysis, although not yet complete, demonstrates the use of cash flow information in conjunction with the income statement. Thousand Trails' reported CFO from 1981 through 1983 was negative, although reported income was positive. The differences relate to all three factors discussed earlier.

1. Assuming for the moment that the growth rate could be maintained, the negative *CFO indicated potential liquidity and solvency problems* as Thousand Trails continually accessed capital markets to achieve that growth. Given its increasing cash needs, there was increased risk that the company would approach its borrowing capacity.

2. *The difference between reported CFO and reported income was a function of Thousand Trails' choice of accounting policies.* Thousand Trails took an "aggressive" position in recognizing revenues (and expenses). Sales were recognized in full, although only a portion was collected. Given the long collection period, there was a built-in lag between present cash outflows and future cash inflows. Expenses, on the other hand, were deferred to periods following the cash outlay. Thus reported income was not a good indicator of near-term cash flows. It (again assuming that forecast growth could be achieved) might have been a good indicator of long-term cash flows.

3. *The disparity between CFO and income raised the question as to the validity of the going concern assumption.* From the revenue point of view we can ask whether the assumption of eventual cash collectibility was tenable? There was some doubt as to whether the cash would eventually be collected; thus the CFO acts as a "check" on reported revenues. Additionally, Thousand Trails' expense recognition methods hinged on these eventual sales. If these sales did not materialize, then *the expenditures already made* would have to be written off against membership sales made to date. The unallocated expenditures of $43.8 million by themselves would wipe out the firm's retained earnings of $30.9 million (both at December 31, 1983).

This analysis does not provide all the answers, but it does provide direction for the analyst in searching for other information with respect to the company. In particular, for Thousand Trails two questions (raised earlier) still need further exploration:

1. Did a market exist for the membership sales forecast by the company? Note it took at least three years to reach a level of 50,000. How long would it take to reach its forecast of 100,000 more members on its current campgrounds? The increase in memberships was dependent to some extent on new campgrounds being opened, which, again would require expansion of the market. The answer to this question exists outside the financial reports. Demographic and population trends, competition, and other factors would need to be examined. What the

financial statements tell you is the impact on the company if the growth rates are (not) feasible.

2. How creditworthy were its customers? The company ran minimum credit checks on its customers before it booked a sale. Although this information was not available in the financial statements, its impact on Thousand Trails was considerable.

Thousand Trails: CFO and Free Cash Flows

A large portion of the cash outflows reported by Thousand Trails related to expenditures for "preserve improvements." This cost reflected the transformation of undeveloped land into land suitable for campgrounds. Does this item represent an investing or operating outflow? A strong argument can be made that preserve improvements costs are investments given their long-term nature. They would be conceptually similar to the costs incurred in building a hotel or apartment building. On the other hand, unlike property, plant, and equipment, which produce the product to be sold, the preserves are similar to an operating item such as inventory as it is the preserves themselves (or access to them) that are being sold.

The statement of changes prepared by Thousand Trails (prior to SFAS 95) classified "preserve improvements" as operating cash flows. Perhaps, under a strict reading of SFAS 95, they would have been reported as investing cash flows. If that were the case, CFO would be positive! This does seem somewhat capricious for a "pure" number.

Upon further reflection, however, it should be clear that the classification of a given cash flow is irrelevant; what is important is the implication. Analysts can (and should) reclassify cash flows if the resulting data provides better analytic insights. In the case of Thousand Trails, the need to expand and improve campgrounds was a constant cash drain. It is this cash requirement that should be the focus of the analysis.

Focusing on the cash requirements of Thousand Trails allows us to expand our analysis and address a final issue. In addition to preserve improvements, Thousand Trails made additional outlays for the preserves themselves as it continued to expand. From the balance sheet (Exhibit 2-7), we can compute the following *increase in the investment in preserves* during 1983:

Operating preserves (land and improvements)*	$26.1 million
Preserves under development	4.3
Total increase	$30.4 million

*Before deductions for "costs applicable to membership sales."

Of this $30 million increase, Thousand Trails only reported $18.4 million as cash expended for preserve improvements. The remaining expenditure did not appear in the cash flow statement at all. We can infer that the remaining increase represents preserves acquired for debt (noncash transactions). In addition, the statement of changes data suggest a significant decline in debt during 1983, yet the balance sheet shows a

EXHIBIT 2-7. THOUSAND TRAILS, INC. AND SUBSIDIARIES
Consolidated Balance Sheets

Assets December 31,	1983	1982
Current Assets:		
Cash	$ 770,000	$ 703,000
Current portion of notes, contracts and accounts receivable—		
Membership contracts	20,382,000	13,568,000
Other	1,558,000	1,025,000
	21,940,000	14,593,000
Allowance for doubtful accounts	(1,111,000)	(646,000)
	20,829,000	13,947,000
Inventory and prepaid expenses	2,067,000	1,331,000
Total Current Assets	23,666,000	15,981,000
Notes, Contracts and Accounts Receivable, less current portion		
Membership contracts	66,740,000	42,546,000
Real estate contracts	732,000	788,000
Other	218,000	179,000
	67,690,000	43,513,000
Allowance for doubtful accounts	(3,638,000)	(2,025,000)
	64,052,000	41,488,000
Operating Preserves:		
Land	17,702,000	12,347,000
Improvements	64,580,000	43,820,000
	82,282,000	56,167,000
Costs applicable membership sales	(38,466,000)	(25,427,000)
	43,816,000	30,740,000
Preserves Under Development, at cost	6,592,000	2,244,000
Investment in Real Estate, at cost	2,773,000	2,793,000
Construction and Operating Equipment, net of accumulated depreciation of $3,174,000 and $2,085,000	5,293,000	3,480,000
Other Assets, at cost	5,575,000	5,573,000
	$151,767,000	$102,299,000

Liabilities and Shareholders' Equity December 31,	1983	1982
Current Liabilities:		
Accounts payable	$ 2,415,000	$ 1,836,000
Accrued salaries	3,714,000	1,949,000
Prepaid membership dues	1,887,000	1,064,000
Other liabilities	1,180,000	1,289,000
Current portion of long-term debt	5,896,000	4,350,000
Deferred income taxes	7,026,000	4,513,000
Total Current Liabilities	22,118,000	15,001,000
Long-Term Debt, less current portion	47,343,000	43,112,000
Deferred Income Taxes	22,007,000	13,992,000
Commitments and Contingencies (Note G)		
Shareholders' Equity:		
Common stock, no par value	29,358,000	11,252,000
Retained earnings	30,941,000	18,942,000
	60,299,000	30,194,000
	$151,767,000	$102,299,000

Source: Thousand Trails, Inc. 1983 Annual Report

significant increase. Footnote data (not reproduced here) confirm that Thousand Trails acquired preserves by incurring debt.

Under SFAS 95, such transactions would again not appear in the cash flow statement directly. Rather, they would be given separate disclosure as "Significant Noncash Financing and Investment Activities." For analytic purposes, however, these amounts need to be considered when analyzing the free cash flows and solvency of a company. It is interesting to note that Thousand Trails classifies the payments on such debt (see $4.3 million—Principal payments on debt related to preserve properties) as part of cash from operations.

Our analysis goes a step farther. As we have argued that the cost of acquiring preserves should be considered an operating outflow, the debt incurred to acquire preserves should be included in that outflow. Thus we would argue that Thousand Trails' operating cash flow was significantly worse than the $14 million outflow actually reported for 1983, perhaps it was as much as $26 million.

As the analysis indicates, it is important to use all financial data; no single statement provides all the needed information. The relationship between cash flow from operations and net income is one of timing. The income statement reflects the firm's operations but does not provide information about the extent to which the firm's cash and liquidity needs are generated internally. Free cash flow does provide that information. The cash flow statement also segregates the impact of the components of the income statement on short-term liquidity and long-run cash flow needs by providing a breakdown between operating and nonoperating cash flows. The income statement, cash flow statement, and the discussion of liquidity and capital resources in the MD&A can be used to develop inferences regarding a firm's cash generating ability and its future cash needs.[40]

Thousand Trails: Balance Sheet Analysis

Our analysis would not be complete without consideration of the balance sheet (Exhibit 2-7). Although this discussion will be short, it will serve to underscore the interlocking nature of the financial statements.

Assets (see discussion in Chapter 1) represent economic resources that provide future benefits. Consistent with a long-run "going concern" perspective of the firm, these future benefits can be their earnings generating ability or their cash collectibility. Fixed assets and inventory, for example, are assets primarily because they help generate future sales. Receivables, on the other hand, which arise after the earnings generating process has been completed, are forecasts of cash collections.

When the going concern assumption no longer holds (such as in liquidation), the future benefit can be defined only in terms of cash collectibility. If anticipated future sales do not materialize and a ready market for the assets does not exist, then the carrying value of the assets should be viewed as nothing more than unexpired costs; "expenses waiting to happen." When there is no expectation of future revenues, there is nothing to "match" those expenses against, and the carrying amount of the assets will be overstated.

---

[40]The CFO should not be interpreted as a measure of a firm's profitability. Positive cash flows from operations can occur during periods of losses from operations, and vice versa. Short-term cash flow deficiencies as well as shortages of funds for capital expenditures can result in bankruptcy.

Therefore, defining an asset in terms of future benefits makes its value depend on the firm's future earning power and cash generating ability. Income and cash flow statements tell us how well the firm has performed in the past. The balance sheet closes the loop by providing information as to which assets are available to generate earnings and cash flows in the future.

The assets shown on Thousand Trails' December 31, 1983, balance sheet fell primarily into two categories. Approximately 85% of Thousand Trails' assets of $151.8 million consisted of receivables (56%) and operating preserves (29%):

		% of Total Assets
Receivables (net of allowance)		
Current	$20.8 million	13.7%
Noncurrent	64.1	42.2%
Total	$84.9 million	55.9%
Operating preserves	$43.8 million	28.8%

Receivables are an asset to the extent that they will result in the collection of cash. The service has already been provided; conversion to cash is now awaited. Operating preserves are assets if they have potential to provide services in the future. Our previous income and cash flow analysis questions both these assumptions. To some extent, these assets existed only as a function of Thousand Trails' revenue and expense recognition rules. For the operating preserves to be an asset, nearly three times the then level of memberships would have to be reached. With respect to receivables, both the creditworthiness of the customers and the limits to growth raise some questions as to the ultimate cash collectibility.

Liquidation analysis also provides a dreary picture. If the firm were liquidated, the receivables would not be collected as membership sales were made without recourse. For the operating preserves, although the land may have had some market value (for alternative uses), most of the carrying cost was for improvements. These have value only if used as campgrounds, which, we have already pointed out, depended on the achievement of optimistic assumptions.

Thousand Trails: Analytic Lessons

Reported revenues of Thousand Trails rose by nearly 50% in 1984 but by only 14% in 1985. Net income increased by more than 50% in 1984 but fell by 95% in 1985. Large revenue declines in 1986 and 1987 were accompanied by large reported losses. At its peak price in 1984, Thousand Trails' common stock had a total market value of approximately $200 million (more than three times stated equity). By November 1986, that market value had shrunk by 90%. While the company escaped bankruptcy, its publicly traded bonds went into default.

The collapse of Thousand Trails may appear, with the benefit of hindsight, to have been easily predictable. Yet many professional investors owned shares in the company.

Were investors who lost money in Thousand Trails just unlucky? We would suggest that they relied on the steady growth of reported earnings and failed to analyze the company. The lessons to be learned from Thousand Trails are as follows:

1. Always examine the revenue recognition policies of a firm. Revenues not accompanied by cash inflows should be considered suspect, especially when the disparity persists for a long time period.

2. Always examine how expenses are recognized. Be wary of firms that capitalize expenditures that appear to be current period expenses, especially when capitalization is based on optimistic assumptions.

3. Analyze the company's cash inflows and outflows and their trend. Ultimately, returns to creditors and investors must come from cash flow. Reclassify cash flows when that improves comparability or otherwise facilitates analysis.

4. Study the balance sheet. Be sure that the "assets" meet at least one of the criteria previously discussed. There should be reasonable assurance that the assets contribute to the generation of income and cash flows of the firm either through future operations or by direct conversion to cash.

5. Use all the financial data available, all three financial statements, footnotes, and any supplementary disclosures. Treat the financial reporting system as a database, intended to help you make better decisions.

NONRECURRING ITEMS

While not an issue in the analysis of Thousand Trails, nonrecurring items do affect the analysis of many firms. We have previously noted that, when estimating a firm's "earning power," analysts should exclude items that are unusual and nonrecurring in nature. However, this does not mean that all such items should be ignored. In this section, we will discuss the extent to which nonrecurring items may provide useful information.

Components of Nonrecurring Income

The income statement format previously described contains four classifications that fall under the general category of nonrecurring:

1. Unusual or Infrequent Items
2. Extraordinary Items
3. Discontinued Operations
4. Accounting Changes

The first of these appears "above the line" as a component of continuing operations and is presented on a pretax basis. The other items are "below the line," not a part of continuing operations, and are presented net of tax. We first describe these classifications and then turn to a discussion of their analytic implications.

Unusual or Infrequent Items

Transactions or events that are *either unusual in nature or infrequent in occurrence but not both* may be disclosed separately (as a single-line item) as a component of income from continuing operations. However, they cannot be reported net of tax in the income statement. The tax impact may be disclosed in a separate footnote. Common examples are:

1. Gains or losses from disposal of a portion of a business segment.
2. Gains or losses from sales of assets or investments in affiliates or subsidiaries.
3. Losses from environmental disasters, ineligible for treatment as extraordinary items.
4. Impairments, write-offs, write-downs, and restructuring costs. (See Chapter 6 for a detailed discussion.)

Exhibit 2-8 provides two examples of unusual gains: one (Acme Steel) from the settlement of a bankruptcy claim and the other (USG) from the sale of a building in 1990

EXHIBIT 2-8
Two Examples of Nonrecurring/Unusual Gains

ACME STEEL COMPANY

	1990	1989	1988
		(in thousands)	
Net sales	$446,046	$439,412	$412,453
Costs and expenses:			
Cost of products sold	396,726	375,902	347,505
Depreciation expense	12,540	11,624	10,455
Gross profit	36,776	51,886	54,493
Selling and administrative expense	28,028	25,751	22,858
Operating income	8,748	26,135	31,635
Unusual income item—Wabush settlement	4,005	—	—
Interest expense—net	4,178	2,116	271
Other income (expense)—net	813	2,107	(382)
Income before income taxes and extraordinary credit	9,388	26,126	30,982

EXHIBIT 2-8. *(Continued)*

NOTES TO CONSOLIDATED FINANCIAL STATEMENTS

Unusual Income Item:

Results for 1990 include a pre-tax gain of $4 million arising from the settlement of a bankruptcy claim filed by Wabush Iron Company on behalf of Acme Steel and the other participants in an iron ore mining joint venture. The claim was filed against Wheeling-Pittsburgh Steel, a former participant that filed for bankruptcy in 1985. All proceeds have been invested at the iron ore operation to fund its required capital expenditure program to control air emissions.

USG CORPORATION

	1990	1989	1988
	(in millions)		
Net sales	$1,915	$2,007	$2,070
Cost of products sold	1,499	1,506	1,536
Gross Profit	416	501	534
Selling and administrative expenses	203	209	223
Recapitalization and restructuring expenses	18	—	20
Operating Profit	195	292	291
Interest expense	292	297	178
Interest income	(8)	(10)	(13)
Other expenses, net	5	15	16
Nonrecurring gains	(34)	(33)	—
Earnings/(Loss) from Continuing Operations Before Taxes on Income	(60)	23	110

SIGNIFICANT ACCOUNTING POLICIES AND PRACTICES

Nonrecurring Gains

In January 1990, a nonrecurring pre-tax gain of $34 million was recorded on the sale of USG's corporate headquarters building at 101 South Wacker Drive in Chicago. This gain was calculated after deducting $9 million as a reserve against which lease payments made by the Corporation while occupying the 101 South Wacker facility are being charged. The Corporation will continue to lease office space in this building until it moves to new leased offices scheduled for completion in 1992. Proceeds from this transaction were used to reduce debt.

In March 1989, a pre-tax gain of $16 million was recorded on an insurance settlement following a favorable U.S. Appellate Court ruling. This ruling upheld a U.S. Federal District Court judgment in September 1987 which obligated the insurance carrier to pay the Corporation approximately $25 million for claims stemming from the November 1984 subsidence of a mine shaft at United State Gypsum Company's Plasterco, Virginia, gypsum board plant. In April 1989, the Corporation received a payment of $35 million, which included approximately $10 million in pre- and post-judgment interest.

In June 1989, a pre-tax gain of $11 million was recorded on the sale of United State Gypsum Company's construction metal business which had been treated as a continuing operation in the consolidated financial statements. The sale, which was part of the 1988 plan of recapitalization and restructuring, included five plants and the production equipment from another location in Torrance, California. The disposal of the assets of this business was completed in November 1989 with the sale of the Torrance land. A pre-tax gain of $6 million was recorded on the latter transaction.

and from an insurance settlement and sale of a business unit the previous year. Exhibit 2-9 depicts one unusual loss due to a terminated acquisition attempt reported in 1990 by Ball Corp. In 1988, the firm recorded unusual losses from the discontinuation of an operation and write-downs of equipment. Also, in Exhibit 2-9 Coors reports unusual losses from the potential costs of repairing environmental damage at a landfill in one year and write-downs the previous year. The pretax effects of these items are included in the income statement; footnotes disclose the posttax impact.

EXHIBIT 2-9
Two Examples of Nonrecurring/Unusual Losses

BALL CORPORATION

	1990	1989	1988
	(in millions)		
Net sales	$1,357.2	$1,224.4	$1,073.0
Costs and expenses			
Cost of sales	1,165.2	1,078.5	911.3
Selling, general and administrative expenses	97.4	84.2	87.2
Unusual items	9.1	—	24.1
Interest expense	22.2	20.3	10.7
	1,293.9	1,183.0	1,033.3
Income before taxes on income and cumulative effect of accounting change	63.3	39.4	39.7

NOTES TO CONSOLIDATED FINANCIAL STATEMENTS

Unusual Items

The $9.1 million cost of the company's proposed 1990 acquisition of the European packaging interests of Continental Can Europe, Inc. which was terminated, was charged to fourth quarter 1990 results of operations with an after tax effect of $5.6 million or 26 cents per share.

In December 1988, the company recorded unusual charges of $30.0 million ($18.6 million or 80 cents per share after tax) including a provision of $18.3 million ($11.3 million or 49 cents per share after tax) for the cost of exiting the blow molded, coextruded plastic bottle business. Operating losses of this business were $2.9 million in 1988. A charge of $8.6 million ($5.3 million or 23 cents per share after tax) was made for the write-down of certain metal container production equipment removed from service as part of plant modernization programs. Other individually insignificant items totaling $3.1 million ($2.0 million or eight cents per share after tax) were charged to results of operations.

During the first quarter of 1988, the company sold its remaining investment in Constar International at a gain of approximately $5.9 million ($3.6 million or 16 cents per share after tax).

EXHIBIT 2-9. *(Continued)*

ADOLPH COORS COMPANY

	1990	1989	1988
		(In thousands)	
Sales	$2,050,110	$1,934,337	$1,680,968
Less—federal and state beer			
excise taxes	186,756	170,467	159,271
Net sales	1,863,354	1,763,870	1,521,697
Costs and expenses:			
Cost of goods sold	1,273,840	1,232,028	1,021,084
Marketing, general and			
administrative	462,911	433,435	408,348
Research and project			
development	22,219	22,991	22,723
Special charge (Note 7)	30,000	—	—
Asset write-downs	—	41,670	—
Total operating expenses	1,788,970	1,730,124	1,452,155
Operating income	74,384	33,746	69,542

NOTES TO CONSOLIDATED FINANCIAL STATEMENTS

Note 7: Special Charge and Asset Write-Downs

Included in 1990 is a special pre-tax charge of $30,000,000 for potential costs related to remediation of the Lowry Landfill Superfund site. The Company has received notice from the U.S. Environmental Protection Agency that it is a "potentially responsible party" under the Comprehensive Environmental Response Compensation and Liability Act (as amended by the Superfund Amendment and Reauthorization Act) and may be required to share in the cost of study and any clean-up of the Lowry Landfill Superfund site. The impact of this charge on 1990 net earnings was $18,600,000, or $0.50 per share. The ultimate remediation methods and appropriate allocation of costs for Lowry are not yet final. The Company, in cooperation with certain other users of the landfill, is vigorously studying the site in an effort to understand the scope of the problem and recommend appropriate remedies.

Included in 1989 is a charge of $41,670,000 representing the excess of net book value over estimated recoverable value for certain assets. The impact of this charge on 1989 net earnings was $26,232,000, or $0.71 per share. The Company decided to offer for sale certain natural gas properties as market conditions made it uneconomical for the Company to produce based on its investment in these properties. In addition, the Company discontinued mining operations at its Keenesburg, Colorado, coal mine because of the availability of attractive long-term coal supply contracts. The Company also wrote off the cost of certain budgetary engineering studies for projects no longer considered feasible and wrote down assets used in a snack food business. The snack food business was sold during 1990.

Source: Reprinted with Permission from Accounting Trends and Techniques, 1991 Edition. Copyright 1991, American Institute of Certified Public Accountants (New York, N.Y.)

Extraordinary Items

APB 9 (1966) defined extraordinary items broadly, and the standard was interpreted to include such categories as asset sales, impairments, and devaluation. Because of unsatisfactory experience, the APB revisited the issues, and APB 30 (1973) restricted the definition of extraordinary and created the income statement format discussed earlier and still used under U.S. GAAP. APB 30 defines extraordinary items as transactions and events that are *unusual in nature and infrequent in occurrence and that are material in amount*. The criteria are applied with reference to the firm, comparable firms in the same industry, and the operating environment. Extraordinary items must be reported separately, net of income tax. Firms are also required to report per share amounts for these items and are encouraged to provide additional footnote disclosures.

Common examples of extraordinary items are:

1. Losses due to foreign government expropriation of assets.
2. Gains or losses on qualifying[41] "early" retirement of debt.
3. Benefits of tax loss carryforwards (prior to adoption of SFAS 96 and SFAS 109. (See Chapter 7 for details.)

The last two of these examples involve mandatory reporting requirements, where no judgment is involved.[42] The eligibility of losses from environmental disasters like hurricanes or earthquakes for extraordinary treatment may be a function of geographic location. Hurricanes might, for example, be considered normal and recurring in Florida, but not in Canada.

Exhibit 2-10, from an AICPA survey, shows trends in reporting extraordinary items. With the exception of 1987, the number of companies reporting extraordinary items has not changed significantly. Note that the data for the period 1974–1977 (following the adoption of APB 30) show similar results. Use of tax loss carryforwards and debt extinguishment remain the most common items.

Exhibit 2-11 contains two disclosures of extraordinary items. The first is from DSC Communications Corp., which reports offsetting gains from debt repurchases ($7.5 million) and costs of litigation ($7.7 million). It is also a good example of the classification and timing issues. The lawsuit was related to a mandatory restatement of the firm's financial statements; gains or losses from most litigation are reported as unusual (but not extraordinary) items. (In Exhibit 2-8, Acme Steel reports the settlement of a lawsuit as an unusual gain, not as an extraordinary item.) The second example in Exhibit 2-11 is from Flowers Industries and involves a loss from a divestiture required by the Federal Trade Commission.

---

[41]Gains and losses on early retirement of debt are considered extraordinary except for those related to sinking fund requirements (SFAS 4, 1975).

[42]Although management controls the timing of the "early" retirement and selects reporting methods for taxes that can accelerate or delay the recognition of deductible expenses.

EXHIBIT 2-10
Trends in Reporting Extraordinary Items, 1974–1991

	Number of Companies				
	1987	1988	1989	1990	1991
Nature					
Debt extinguishments	53	26	16	36	33
Operating loss carryforwards	80	35	26	24	20
Litigation settlements	2	6	3	2	1
Other	9	6	9	5	4
Total extraordinary items	144	73	54	67	58
Number of companies					
Presenting extraordinary items	127	67	49	63	55
Not presenting extraordinary items	473	533	551	537	545
Total companies	600	600	600	600	600

Source: Reprinted with Permission from Accounting Trends and Techniques, 1992 Edition. Copyright 1992, American Institute of Certified Public Accountants (New York, N.Y.)

	Number of Companies			
	1974	1975	1976	1977
Nature				
Operating loss carryforwards and other tax adjustments	55	31	52	38
Major casualties	N/C	N/C	N/C	6
Debt extinguishments	—	9	5	5
Other	27	11	24	8
Total extraordinary items	82	51	81	57
Number of companies				
Presenting extraordinary items	75	49	69	51
Not presenting extraordinary items	525	551	531	549
Total companies	600	600	600	600

N/C – Not compiled.
Source: Reprinted with Permission from Accounting Trends and Techniques, 1978 Edition. Copyright 1978, American Institute of Certified Public Accountants, (New York, N.Y.)

EXHIBIT 2-11
Two Disclosures of Extraordinary Items

Litigation Settlement

DSC COMMUNICATIONS CORPORATION

	1990	1989	1988
		(In thousands)	
Income from continuing operations before extraordinary items	$20,331	$34,164	$20,015
Discontinued operations, net of income taxes:			
Loss from operations	—	—	(1,003)
Estimated loss on disposal	—	(840)	(7,300)
Loss from discontinued operations	—	(840)	(8,303)
Extraordinary items, net	(209)	—	856
Net income	$20,122	$33,324	$12,568

NOTES TO CONSOLIDATED FINANCIAL STATEMENTS

Extraordinary Items, Net

The net extraordinary items for 1990 and 1988 were comprised of the following (in thousands):

	1990	1988
Gains from purchases of subordinated convertible debentures, net of income tax of $1,537 in 1990, and $90 in 1988	$ 7,506	$856
Cost of settlement of shareholder litigation, net of income tax benefit of $1,540	(7,715)	—
Extraordinary items, net	$ (209)	$856

The extraordinary gains resulted from purchases of the Company's subordinated convertible debentures at market prices lower than face value (see "Long-Term Debt").

During 1990, the Company settled a shareholder suit originally filed in 1985, that arose out of the Company's voluntary restatement of its financial statements for certain periods in 1984 and 1985. The total settlement was for approximately $30,000,000 with approximately $21,000,000 being contributed by the company's insurance carrier and other defendants.

EXHIBIT 2-11. *(Continued)*

FTC-Ordered Divestiture

FLOWERS INDUSTRIES, INC.

	1990	1989	1988
	(In thousands)		
Income before extraordinary item and cumulative effect of a change in accounting principles	$34,253	$29,552	$41,476
Extraordinary loss on FTC ordered divestiture, net of tax benefit of $4,045 (Note 3)	(4,955)		
Cumulative effect on prior years of a change in accounting for income taxes			1,757
Net income	$29,298	$29,552	$43,233

NOTES TO CONSOLIDATED FINANCIAL STATEMENTS

Note 3. Extraordinary Item—Divestiture of Operating Facilities

Pursuant to an order issued by the Federal Trade Commission ("FTC") as discussed in Note 12, the Company sold its production facilities and transferred or licensed its trademarks in Gadsden, Alabama, and High Point, North Carolina on October 17, 1989. An extraordinary loss on this FTC ordered divestiture of $4,955,000, net of applicable income tax benefit of $4,045,000, is reflected in the accompanying consolidated statement of income.

Source: Reprinted with Permission from Accounting Trends and Techniques, 1991 Edition. Copyright 1991, American Institute of Certified Public Accountants (New York, N.Y.)

Discontinued Operations

The discontinuation or sale of a business segment usually indicates that its markets or prospects are inadequate or uncertain, its contribution to earnings and cash flows is not satisfactory, it is no longer considered by management to be a strategic fit, or simply that it can be sold at a significant profit.

Operating income and any gains or losses (net of taxes) from such segments are segregated in the income statement, since these activities will not contribute to income and cash flows in the future. As in the case of extraordinary items, this segregation makes reported income more useful for analysis.

A business segment is defined as a "component of an entity whose activities represent a separate major line of business or class of customer" (APB 30, Para. 13). Subsidiaries and investees also qualify as separate segments.

The assets, results of operations, and investing and financing activities of business segments must be separable from the assets, results of operations, and other activities of the firm to qualify for treatment as discontinued operations. APB 30 states that the separation must be possible physically and operationally, and for financial reporting purposes.

Once management develops or adopts a formal plan for the sale or disposal of a segment (the "measurement date"), the operations of the segment are segregated within the income statement. The firm reports the income or loss from operations of the discontinued segment on a net basis. Sales and expenses of discontinued operations are usually shown in a footnote.

A second component reflects both the income or loss from operations during the "phase-out" period, that is, from the measurement date to the disposal date,[43] and any gain or loss on sale or disposal. However, a gain on disposal (net of operating losses during the phase-out period) can be reported only after disposal, that is, when realized. If there is an estimated loss on disposal, it would be reported immediately.

These measurement rules are also applied when only a portion of a business segment, example, a factory, a plant, or a group of machines, is to be sold, disposed of, or abandoned. The gain or loss must be reported pretax as a separate component of income from continuing operations[44] rather than as discontinued operations. Firms are encouraged to disclose separately the affected assets and liabilities on the balance sheet.

An example of the income statement reporting of discontinued operations appears in Exhibit 2-12, which reproduces the income statement and partial footnotes of the Heico Corporation. The income statement shows the two components of the required disclosure of discontinued operations. Note that the sales and operating losses of the laboratory products segment have been *excluded* from reported sales and income from continuing operations. Previously reported sales and earnings have been restated to exclude the discontinued segment.

Note 2 of the financial statements shows that Heico entered into an agreement to sell the segment in December 1989, recorded a provision for the loss that year, and then recognized an additional loss when the sale was completed during the first quarter of 1990. It also provides summary disclosure of the net assets and operating results of the discontinued segment.

In addition, Heico's Note 3 discloses information regarding several "nonrecurring" costs related to a proxy contest and restructuring costs. The total pretax costs reported in a separate line as a component of operating costs and expenses were

Costs of the proxy contest	$ 717,000
Settlement with stockholders	855,000
Restructuring costs	500,000
Total	$2,072,000

---

[43]The disposal date is the date the sale is finalized or the operations are shut down if the segment is to be abandoned or discontinued.

[44]See Accounting Interpretations of APB 30 (AICPA, November 1973). However, the income or loss from operations from the beginning of the year to the measurement date is not always segregated on the income statement. Some firms provide footnote disclosure of this datum for all years presented. The income or loss during the phase-out period and the gain or loss on sale or disposal, is included in income from continuing operations.

EXHIBIT 2-12
Disclosure of Discontinued Operations

HEICO CORPORATION AND SUBSIDIARIES
Notes to Consolidated Financial Statements
for the years ended October 31, 1990, 1989 and 1988

NOTE 2 – DISCONTINUED OPERATIONS – SALE OF LABORATORY PRODUCTS SEGMENT

In March 1990, the Company completed the sale of the stock of its various laboratory products segment subsidiaries to Varlen Corporation for $11.5 million cash consideration and the assumption of related liabilities of $4.7 million. In fiscal 1989, the Company recorded a $5.6 million provision representing an estimated loss pursuant to the terms of a letter of intent entered into with Varlen in December 1989. The sale, as consummated, resulted in an additional charge of $2,480,000, or $.78 per share, in the first quarter of fiscal 1990. The sale resulted in capital losses aggregating approximately $7 million which can be used to offset any capital gains realized over the next five years.

The results of operations of the laboratory products segment have been reported as discontinued operations for the three-year period ended October 31, 1990 and reported separately from the results of continuing operations. The 1990 and 1989 provisions for loss on disposal of the laboratory products segment include a provision for fiscal 1990 operating losses prior to disposition of $159,000 and $400,000, respectively.

The Company's net investment in the laboratory products segment at October 31, 1989, after reduction for the $5.6 million estimated loss on disposal, is included in current assets. A summary of the net assets as of October 31, 1989 follows:

Trade accounts receivable, net	$ 3,832,000
Inventories	9,496,000
Other current assets	91,000
Property, plant and equipment, net	5,140,000
Intangible assets, net	3,955,000
Other assets	131,000
Current liabilities	(1,774,000)
Long-term debt	(2,897,000)
Deferred income taxes	(214,000)
Provision for loss on disposal	(5,600,000)
	$ 12,160,000

Summary operating results for the laboratory products segment are as follows:

	Period from November 1, 1989 through disposal (March 5, 1990)	Fiscal Year Ended October 31	
		1989	1988
Net sales	$ 6,013,000	$ 20,599,000	$ 20,236,000
Operating loss	$ (770,000)	$ (951,000)	$ (856,000)
Loss, net of income taxes	$ (559,000)	$ (769,000)	$ (746,000)

With the discontinuance of the laboratory products segment, the Company's operations are within a single business segment, the aviation and defense products industry.

NOTE 3 – NON-RECURRING CHARGES

During fiscal 1989, the Company incurred the costs of a proxy contest relating to the election of directors and the subsequent litigation contesting that election aggregating $717,000. In December 1989, a settlement was reached whereby, among other things, the Company and its insurers agreed to reimburse the plaintiff shareholder group for certain expenses in connection with the proxy contest and litigation. A provision of $855,000 for the costs associated with the settlement was recorded in the fiscal 1989 financial statements.

In October 1989, the Company announced restructuring plans to further integrate the operations of its aviation and defense products subsidiaries. A $500,000 provision was charged against income in the fourth quarter of 1989 to cover the expenses associated with this plan. These expenses together with the charges discussed in the preceding paragraph have been set forth separately in the Consolidated Statements of Income for fiscal 1989 as non-recurring charges. These non-recurring charges adversely affected income from continuing operations and the net loss by $1,316,000, or $.41 per share, in fiscal 1989.

HEICO CORPORATION AND SUBSIDIARIES
CONSOLIDATED STATEMENTS OF INCOME
For the years ended October 31, 1990, 1989 and 1988

	1990	1989	1988
Net sales	$26,239,000	$26,473,000	$22,925,000
Operating costs and expenses:			
Cost of products and services sold	19,165,000	17,239,000	13,600,000
Selling, general and administrative expenses	5,205,000	5,291,000	5,100,000
Non-recurring charges	–	2,072,000	–
Total operating costs and expenses	24,370,000	24,602,000	18,700,000
Income from operations	1,869,000	1,871,000	4,225,000
Interest expense	(181,000)	(131,000)	(173,000)
Interest and other income	970,000	751,000	788,000
Income from continuing operations before income taxes	2,658,000	2,491,000	4,840,000
Income taxes	697,000	770,000	1,608,000
Income from continuing operations	1,961,000	1,721,000	3,232,000
Discontinued operations (Note 2):			
(Loss) from operations of discontinued laboratory products segment (less applicable tax benefits of $442,000 in 1989 and $407,000 in 1988)	–	(769,000)	(746,000)
(Loss) on disposal of laboratory products segment (includes a provision for operating losses prior to disposition of $159,000 in fiscal 1990 and $400,000 in fiscal 1989)	(2,480,000)	(5,600,000)	–
Net income (loss)	$ (519,000)	$ (4,648,000)	$ 2,486,000
Income per share from continuing operations	$ .66	$ .54	$1.00
Net income (loss) per share	$(.17)	$(1.45)	$ .77
Weighted average number of common and common-equivalent shares outstanding	2,992,947	3,213,355	3,237,488

See notes to consolidated financial statements.

Source: Heico Corp. 1990 Annual Report.

The note shows that the posttax effect was a loss of $1,316,000 or $0.41 per share for 1989. Note the differences in the location on the income statement and footnote disclosures for this category of nonrecurring items in contrast to that of discontinued operations.

The preceding discussion of extraordinary items, unusual gains and losses, and discontinued operations illustrates the difficulty of deciding what constitutes income from continuing operations. In developing an estimate of a firm's "earning power," analysts would normally exclude all items that are unusual or nonrecurring in nature. Yet such events seem to recur, more so in some companies than others. Some companies seem to be "accident prone," although each "accident" is different. To exclude all unusual or nonrecurring items would make such a company look better than it should. All gains and losses do, after all, affect the wealth of the firm.[45]

Accounting standard setters cannot draw "bright lines" that are adequate to separate clearly "unusual" items. In practice, gains tend to wind up "above the line" in continuing operations, while losses are often shown "below the line" as extraordinary. In addition, disclosure is not always sufficient. In some cases the Management Discussion and Analysis in SEC Form 10-K may provide more information on unusual items than the financial statements themselves.

Accounting Changes

Accounting changes fall into two general categories: those undertaken voluntarily by the firm and those mandated by new accounting standards. Generally, these changes do not have direct cash flow consequences.

The change from one acceptable accounting method to another acceptable method is reported in the period of change. Any cumulative impact on *prior periods* is reported net of taxes after extraordinary items and discontinued operations on the income statement.[46] Firms are required to provide footnote disclosure of the impact of the change on current period operations (and on prior periods, if restated) and their justification for the change. However, accounting changes also affect future operating results. That impact is rarely disclosed but can sometimes be estimated. Accounting changes are dealt with frequently in the remaining chapters of the text.

APB 20 identifies several exceptions to the general treatment. These are:

1. Change from LIFO to another inventory method. (See Chapter 5.)
2. Change to or from the full cost method. (See Chapter 6.)
3. Change to or from the percentage-of-completion method.
4. Change in accounting methods prior to an initial public offering.

Similarly, a change in accounting principle from an incorrect to an acceptable accounting method is treated as an error, and its impact is reported as a prior period adjustment. These exceptions require retroactive restatement for all years presented.

---

[45]See Chapter 15 for a discussion of the analytic treatment of Deere's nonrecurring items.

[46]The cumulative impact makes the assumption that the new method had been used in all past periods and is therefore the difference between previously reported income and income computed under the new method.

Part A of Exhibit 2-13 provides Newcor, Inc.'s 1991 income statement and an excerpt from the company's MD&A, which contains a brief description of its revenue and expense recognition methods. Part B reproduces excerpts from a news release issued by the firm in February 1992 that contains a restatement of its 1987–1991 income statements from the completed contract to the percentage-of-completion method. Part C shows the restated income statements for 1989–1991.

EXHIBIT 2-13. NEWCOR, INC.
Consolidated Statements of Income

A. Income Statement (Completed Contract Method)

for the years ended October 31	1991	1990	1989
Sales	$98,747,000	$79,865,000	$100,436,000
Costs and expenses:			
Cost of sales	76,872,000	64,211,000	83,884,000
Selling, general, and administrative	12,536,000	11,123,000	10,418,000
Interest	2,017,000	1,895,000	2,131,000
Closedown of operation in Canada	—	1,188,000	—
	91,425,000	78,417,000	96,433,000
Income before income taxes	7,322,000	1,448,000	4,003,000
Provision for income taxes	2,294,000	233,000	908,000
Net income	$ 5,028,000	$ 1,215,000	$ 3,095,000
Net income per share of common stock	$ 1.55	$ 0.37	$ 0.95

Newcor, Inc. is organized into two business segments: special machines and precision machined parts. Special machines are custom designed and sold individually on a made-to-order basis or incorporated into complete systems. Revenue and costs for special machines are determined under the completed contract method of accounting, which can result in significant fluctuations in sales and net income between accounting periods. In addition, the cyclical nature of this segment can result in sharp changes in the order backlog, working capital, and bank borrowings.

Source: Part A is from Newcor, Inc., *1991 Annual Report.*

B. News Release

Newcor, Inc., Troy, Michigan, February 18, 1992. Richard A. Smith, Newcor, Inc. President and Chief Executive Officer, announced today that the company has adopted the percentage of completion method of accounting for revenue and costs associated with long-term contracts within the company's special machinery segment. In the opinion of management, with concurrence from the company's outside auditors, the percentage of completion method of accounting is the preferable method for reporting the financial results of the special machinery segment. The percentage of completion method of accounting will be implemented in the first quarter of fiscal 1992. In all prior years, the completed contract method of accounting was utilized to determine revenue and costs.

EXHIBIT 2-13. *(Continued)*

C. *Restated Income Statements (Percentage of Completion Method)*

	For the Fiscal Years ended October 31		
	1991	1990	1989
Sales	$89,309,000	$92,160,000	$95,974,000
Costs and expenses:			
Cost of sales	69,225,000	74,203,000	79,473,000
Selling, general, and administrative	12,491,000	11,307,000	10,517,000
Interest	2,017,000	1,895,000	2,131,000
Closedown of operation in Canada	—	1,188,000	—
	83,733,000	88,593,000	92,121,000
Income before income taxes	5,576,000	3,567,000	3,853,000
Provision for income taxes	1,700,000	953,000	857,000
Net income	$ 3,876,000	$ 2,614,000	$ 2,996,000
Net income per share of common stock	$ 1.19	$ 0.81	$ 0.92

Source: Parts B and C are from Newcor, Inc., press release, February 18, 1992.

Prior Period Adjustments

Certain transactions are not reported as components of current period income, but are recorded as adjustments directly to retained earnings. Under APB 9, managements had some flexibility and reported as prior period adjustments such items as litigation costs and income tax settlements.

SFAS 16, Prior Period Adjustments, restricted this treatment to accounting errors and adjustments due to realization of tax benefit carryforwards of purchased subsidiaries.[47] Some accounting changes also involve adjustments to prior period retained earnings.

Exhibit 2-14 contains disclosures regarding a prior period adjustment for an error; inventories had been overstated and certain operating costs understated. Vicorp discloses the gross amount, tax effect, and impact on net income, facilitating adjustment of the historical series of data and earnings forecasts. Footnote 11 of Vicorp's financial statements shows the adjustment from the reported 1989 (1990) earnings per share (EPS) of $0.91 ($1.42) to the adjusted EPS of $0.73 ($1.18)—substantial changes for both years.

---

[47]SFAS 96 and 109 require that these tax benefits be included in reported income (see Chapter 7).

EXHIBIT 2-14. VICORP RESTAURANTS, INC.
Disclosures of a Prior Period Adjustment for an Error

A. Note 2: Prior Period Adjustment

In October 1990, the Company became aware of and investigated irregularities in the accounts of its production and distribution division. The investigation disclosed that a group of accountants concealed and failed to properly account for certain variances in the Company's cost system. As a result, the Company determined that a restatement of 1989 consolidated financial statements was appropriate. The effect of the restatement was to decrease inventories and to increase restaurant operating costs $1,894,000. After income tax effect of $209,000, the restatement reduced net income for 1989 by $1,685,000. As previously reported, net income for 1989 was $9,810,000 and earnings per share was $0.91. See Note 11 for a restatement of 1990 and 1989 fiscal quarters.

B. Note 11: Quarterly Financial Data (Unaudited)

The quarterly data for the first three quarters of 1990 and all of 1989 have been restated for the adjustment discussed in Note 2. The Company's quarterly results of operations as originally reported and as restated are summarized as follows (in thousands, except per share data):

	Quarter ended		Revenues	Restaurant operating income	Net income	Earnings per common and common equivalent share
1990	February 18	As reported	$115,906	$11,803	$3,313	$.31
		Adjustment		1,147	1,021	.11
		Restated	115,906	10,656	2,292	.20
	May 13	As reported	93,644	10,717	4,382	.42
		Adjustment		745	663	.06
		Restated	93,644	9,972	3,719	.36
	August 5	As reported	93,427	10,779	4,260	.41
		Adjustment		732	652	.07
		Restated	93,427	10,047	3,608	.34
	October 28	As reported	91,439	8,961	2,958	.28
	February 19	As reported	$105,354	$ 9,913	$1,849	$.16
		Adjustment		576	513	.06
		Restated	105,354	9,337	1,336	.10
	May 14	As reported	83,891	8,752	2,237	.21
		Adjustment		489	434	.05
		Restated	83,891	8,263	1,803	.16

EXHIBIT 2-14. *(Continued)*

Quarter ended		Revenues	Restaurant operating income	Net income	Earnings per common and common equivalent share
1989					
August 6	As reported	84,601	8,818	2,636	.25
	Adjustment		404	360	.04
	Restated	84,601	8,414	2,276	.21
October 29	As reported	85,310	9,569	3,088	.29
	Adjustment		425	378	.03
	Restated	85,310	9,144	2,710	.26

Source: Vicorp Restaurants, *1990 Annual Report.*

The Analysis of Nonrecurring Items

Current Versus Future Cash Flow Impact

Nonrecurring items with cash flow consequences do affect the wealth of the firm. However, they should still be segregated because valuation implications differ from recurring income. The analyst must distinguish between components of income that have cash flow implications only for the current period and those that provide forward-looking information. As outlined in Box 2-1 and discussed in greater detail in our chapter on valuation (Chapter 15), components that are truly nonrecurring have only a one-shot dollar-for-dollar effect on value, whereas the multiple for recurring income is greater.

In analyzing such items, it must also be recognized that they are not all alike. That is, although the sale of assets, divisions, or segments may not be part of continuing operations, such sales may recur, albeit sporadically. Recurring and nonrecurring are not two distinct categories but rather a continuum. The objective, therefore, is to place each item in its appropriate place on the spectrum.

Implications for Continuing Operations

For nonrecurring events, including those that may not have cash flow effects, it is also important to distinguish between the information provided by the amount reported on the income statement and the information provided by the event itself. A plant closing and the write-off of its book value are one example. The relevant cash flow occurred in the past, and it is only now being "written off." Thus the value implications from the amount reported on the income statement are nonexistent. The event itself may, however, convey relevant information about the firm's continuing operations and its level of future sales, earnings, and cash flows.

Management Discretion and Earnings Manipulation

In forming estimates of earnings trends, the analyst must also be wary of the discretionary nature of the income statement. Many of the items requiring separate disclosure on the income statement are discretionary from two perspectives. First, the timing of the occurrence (e.g., the disposal of an asset or the discontinuation of a segment) is to a great extent at management's discretion.

Second, accounting guidelines may also leave the classification of the item as ordinary, unusual, or extraordinary to the discretion of management. Additionally, managers can alter reported income statement trends by changing their accounting methods. It is difficult to adjust for this kind of discontinuity, as in many cases there is no disclosure (except in the aggregate) of the effects on individual prior periods.

The discretionary nature of income has led to examination of the degree of management manipulation of earnings under one or more of the following guises:

1. Classification of good news/bad news
2. Income smoothing
3. Big bath behavior
4. Accounting changes

Classification of Good News/Bad News. Management has some incentive to report good news "above the line" as part of continuing operations and bad news "below the line" as extraordinary or discontinued operations. For example, the determination of whether the component of the firm sold meets the definition of a segment and hence is given "below-the-line" treatment as income from discontinued operations is to some extent at the discretion of management. As SFAS 14 notes,

> determination of enterprise industry segments must depend to a considerable extent on the judgment of the management of the enterprise.[48]

This ambiguity allows for the possibility that management may take advantage of the situation. A study by Rapaccioli and Schiff (1991) shows results consistent with that behavior. Their results are presented in Exhibit 2-15. Based on a sample of 504 disposals carried out in 1985–1986, they found that approximately 60% of the cases were accorded the more favorable treatment with gains (61%) being reported above the line and losses (57%) reported below the line.

Income Smoothing. Since investors favor firms with stable earnings, firms are tempted to depress earnings in good years (defer gains or recognize losses) and inflate earnings in bad years (recognize gains or defer losses). Ronen and Sadan (1981) demonstrate that managements can and do engage in such smoothing behavior by engaging in either intertemporal smoothing and/or classificatory smoothing. Intertemporal smoothing refers to selection of the timing of events such as research and

[48]SFAS 14, Para. 12.

EXHIBIT 2-15

Percentages of Gains and Losses from the Sale of Business Components Reported Above-the-line and Below-the-line for 1985–1986

	% of Sales Reported Above-the-line	% of Sales Reported Below-the-line
Gain	61%	43%
Loss	39%	57%

Source: Rapacciolli, Donna and Allen Schiff, "Reporting Segment Sales Under APB Opininon No. 30", *Accounting Horizons* (December 1991), pp. 53–59. Table 1 (p. 55).

development, repairs and maintenance, and asset disposals. In addition, the choice of accounting method (e.g., capitalization or expensing) allocates the item over time and is another manifestation of intertemporal smoothing. Classificatory smoothing refers to smoothing by choice of classification of an item as either ordinary income, income from continuing operations, and/or extraordinary income.[49]

It should be noted that Ronen and Sadan argue that smoothing is not necessarily "bad." Rather, by engaging in smoothing, management may be aiding predictive ability by conveying information as to the future prospects of the firm.[50] Similar arguments have been made recently by Moses (1987).

"Big Bath" Accounting. Under "big bath" behavior (in somewhat of a contrast to income smoothing behavior), it is hypothesized that in "bad" years, management will take additional losses in the hope that by taking all losses at one time they will "clear the decks" once and for all. The implicit assumption is that this will lead to increased profits in the future.

The "big bath" phenomenon is more widely believed in the financial press than in the academic literature. Copeland and Moore (1972) reported that the behavior was not as widespread as one might believe. Similarly, Elliott and Shaw (1988) found that analysts' forecasts following large write-offs are not consistent with behavior hypothesized by the "big bath" theory. Rather than increasing the forecast following the write-off, indicating a "clearing of the deck," they tend to decrease the forecast. Fried et al. (1989) report that a firm taking an asset write-down in one year is likely to take

[49]Because of the looser classification standards in the United Kingdom, the distinction between ("above-the-line") exceptional items and ("below-the-line") extraordinary items became a major reporting issue in that country. Financial Reporting Standard (FRS) 3, which became effective for fiscal years ending after June 22, 1993, virtually eliminates extraordinary items under U.K. GAAP.

[50]Gonedes (1978), testing for such signaling behavior, however, found that extraordinary items did not convey any incremental information above that of contemporaneously reported income numbers. This result was somewhat of a contradiction to an earlier study by Gonedes (1975), where he found that special items did convey information to investors. In reconciling the two studies, Gonedes (1978, p. 74) notes that the latter study included only those items reported "below the line" as extraordinary items whereas the earlier study included both "extraordinary" items and items for which separate disclosure is recommended or required whenever material amounts are involved—even though those other items are not supposed to be labeled "extraordinary" according to GAAP.

another one soon after. This is inconsistent with "big bath" behavior, which argues that firms would tend to overestimate rather than underestimate the size and amounts of write-offs.[51]

Accounting Changes. Regardless of whether an accounting change is undertaken voluntarily by the firm or mandated by accounting rule changes, it does not have any direct cash flow consequences[52] for a U.S. company. Thus such changes can be viewed as a form of earnings manipulation. Empirical research has studied these changes extensively, focusing on the stock market reaction to these changes and on managerial motivations for undertaking the change. We shall refer to many of those studies in later chapters.

[51]See discussion of impairment in Chapter 6 for more details of these results.

[52]The FIFO to LIFO change being the major exception in the United States (see Chapter 5).

EXHIBIT 2-16
Type of Change in Accounting Method by Year (1976–1984)

Type of Changes	1976	1977	1978	1979	1980	1981	1982	1983	1984	Total
Voluntary Changes										
FIFO to LIFO	9	5	22	26	34	12	4	2	2	116
Other to LIFO	1	1	4	4	2	2	1	0	1	16
Def. to FT-ITC[a]	0	0	5	4	2	2	5	0	2	20
Acc. to SL deprec.[b]	0	0	1	0	2	5	1	0	0	9
Other depreciation	1	1	1	0	3	1	6	5	3	21
Pension	1	0	0	0	1	1	1	4	2	10
Capitalize to Expense	0	0	2	1	2	2	0	0	0	7
Expense to Capitalize	1	0	3	3	2	4	2	1	0	16
Revenue Recognition	1	1	2	4	0	3	4	2	1	18
Miscellaneous Voluntary	1	5	6	7	8	7	6	8	4	52
Total Voluntary	15	13	46	49	56	39	30	22	15	285
Mandatory Changes										
SFAS No. 13—Leases	0	7	14	0	0	0	0	0	0	21
SFAS No. 34—Interest Capitalization	0	0	0	29	51	3	0	0	0	83
SFAS No. 43-Vacation Accruals	0	0	0	0	10	35	5	0	0	50
SFAS No. 52—Foreign Currency	0	0	0	0	0	94	40	9	0	143
Miscellaneous Mandatory	5	0	2	6	2	3	6	4	2	30
Total Mandatory	5	7	16	35	63	135	51	13	2	327
Total Changes	20	20	62	84	119	174	81	35	17	612

[a]Change from deferral to flow through method of accounting for investment tax credit.

[b]Change from accelerated to straight line method of depreciation.

Source: Elliott, John A. and Donna R. Philbrick, Accounting Changes and Earnings Predictability, *The Accounting Review* (January 1990), pp. 157–174. Table 2 (p. 161).

Elliott and Philbrick (1990) examined the effects of accounting changes on earnings predictability. They examined both voluntary and mandated changes and partitioned their sample on the basis of whether analysts, prior to making their forecasts, had disclosure as to the change. Their study indicates that accounting changes are relatively frequent. In the period 1976 to 1984, 1273 firms had accounting changes large enough to generate a consistency exception in the audit opinion. From this set of firms, they were able to obtain relevant data on 612 accounting changes.

These changes are listed in Exhibit 2-16 by year of occurrence and type of change and in Exhibit 2-17 in terms of their effect on income. Not surprisingly, they found that

EXHIBIT 2-17
Income Effects of Changes in Accounting Method by Type of Change (1976–1984)

	Number of Firms	Average EPS[a] Effect of the Change		Number (%) of Cases in Which Change Increases Income	
		Mean	Median		
Voluntary Changes					
FIFO to LIFO	116	−0.0977	−0.0666	5	4.3%
Other to LIFO	16	−0.0795	−0.0832	2	12.5%
Def. to FT-ITC	20	0.1275	0.0596	18	90.0%
ACC. to SL deprec.	9	0.0509	0.0260	9	100.0%
Other depreciation	21	0.2216	0.0609	15	71.4%
Pension	11	0.1244	0.0761	8	72.7%
Capitalize to Expense	7	−0.0793	−0.0448	2	28.5%
Expense to Capitalize	17	0.1207	0.0442	12	70.6%
Revenue Recognition	18	0.0165	0.0238	11	61.1%
Miscellaneous Voluntary	52	0.0992	0.0479	35	67.3%
Total Voluntary	285	0.0098	−0.0234	118	41.0%
Mandatory Changes					
SFAS No. 13—Leases	21	−0.0018	0.0000	2	9.5%
SFAS No. 34—Interest Capitalization	83	0.1667	0.0579	79	95.2%
SFAS No. 43—Vacation Accruals	50	−0.0016	0.0000	4	8.0%
SFAS No. 52—Foreign Currency	143	0.4133[b]	0.0900	118	82.5%
Miscellaneous Mandatory	30	0.1795	0.0093	17	56.7%
Total Mandatory	327	0.2392	0.0404	220	67.3%
Total All Changes	612	0.1324	0.0155	337	55.0%

[a]Impact of change in accounting method on change year EPS divided by Annual Report EPS before the Accounting Change. A positive value indicates an increase in earnings.

[b]Three cases larger than three standard deviations from the mean account for the high mean value. With these omitted the mean is 0.1493.

Source: Elliott, John A. and Donna R. Philbrick, Accounting Changes and Earnings Predictability, *The Accounting Review* (January 1990), pp. 157–174. Table 3 (p. 162).

analysts have difficulty in forecasting earnings in the year of the change. The difficulty is more pronounced for mandatory changes for which there was no prior information as to the change. Interestingly, however, they found that, when analysts did not have prior information as to the change, their forecast revisions tended to be in the opposite direction of the effect of the accounting change; for example, a downward forecast revision tended to be associated with an accounting change that increased income. This behavior, the authors concluded, was consistent with management using accounting changes to manipulate or smooth earnings.

SUMMARY AND CONCLUDING REMARKS

The financial statements are interrelated and must be used together to obtain all relevant information and to facilitate good financial analysis. For example, the income statement reports current sales and earnings that can be used, with past trends, to develop forecasts of future earnings and assessments of firm value. Investment decisions should be based on forecasts of future earnings and cash flows. Thus the ability to realize earnings, that is, convert reported sales to cash, is equally important. Such information can be obtained only from the balance sheet and the cash flow statement.

But amounts and trends of reported earnings and cash flows are also important indicators of the firm's ability to realize asset values reported in the balance sheet (receivables resulting from sales or fixed assets expected to generate sales). Thus income statement and cash flow data are needed to evaluate the financial position (assets and liabilities) of the firm.

In the next chapter we examine financial statement ratios, used as shorthand indicators of firm performance. While some of these ratios use data from only one financial statement (debt/equity ratio), others use data from several statements (all turnover ratios). Sound investment decisions, based on the comparative assessment of alternative investments, require use of all three financial statements as well as footnote and supplementary disclosures.

In the following chapter, we examine trends in empirical research to gain insight into the information content of financial data. Starting in Chapter 5, we examine areas of financial reporting more specifically, seeking to apply the general principles articulated in this chapter.

Chapter 2

Problems

Problems 1–9 are concerned with revenue recognition methods.

   1. Describe the conditions under which revenue would be recognized:

      (i) At the time of production, but prior to sale.

      (ii) At the time of sale, but prior to cash collection.

      (iii) Only when cash collection has occurred.

2. [1989 CFA adapted] In October 1993, the Terry Company ships a new product to retailers.

A. Discuss how each of the following conditions would affect the timing of revenue recognition as reflected in its financial statements for the year ended December 31, 1993.

> **(i)** Retailers are not required to pay for the product until January 31, 1994.
>
> **(ii)** Retailers have an unlimited right to return unsold product. As the product is new, the company cannot reliably estimate the return rate.

B. Discuss which balance sheet accounts would be misstated if the Terry Company accelerates revenue recognition contrary to the economic substance of the transaction implied by conditions A(i) and A(ii).

3. [1992 CFA adapted]

A. Compare the volatility of reported earnings over the life of a contract between the completed contract and percentage-of-completion accounting methods.

B. Discuss the difference in volatility when a firm has many contracts.

C. Discuss how the volatility discussed in parts A and B impacts the usefulness of the information provided by the statement of cash flows.

4. Compare the effect during the contract period of the completed contract and percentage-of-completion methods of accounting on the level and trend of reported:

> **(i)** Revenues and cost of goods sold.
>
> **(ii)** Earnings.
>
> **(iii)** Operating cash flows.
>
> **(iv)** Accounts receivable, total current assets, and total long-term assets

5. [1988 CFA adapted] James Construction enters into a contract in 19X5 to build a tunnel at a cost of $11 million. The company estimates that the total cost of the project will be $10 million and that it will take three years to complete. Actual costs incurred and billings are as follows:

Year	Costs Incurred	Billings
19X5	$ 2.5 million	$ 2.0 million
19X6	4.0	3.5
19X7	3.5	5.5
Totals	$10.0 million	$11.0 million

A. Calculate James Construction's reported sales, operating profit, and operating cash flows for each year using the percentage-of-completion method of accounting.

B. Calculate James' reported sales, operating profit, and operating cash flows for each year using the completed contract method of accounting.

C. Assume that, just prior to the end of 19X6, the estimated cost to complete the tunnel increases to $11 million, with that additional $1 million of cost to be incurred in 19X7. Under that assumption, calculate 19X6 sales and operating profit for the project assuming use of the percentage-of-completion method.

D. Using your answers to parts A–C, discuss the advantages and disadvantages of the two accounting methods from the point of view of the financial analyst.

6. On April 1, 19X0, Pine Construction enters into a fixed price contract to construct an apartment building for $6 million. Pine uses the percentage-of-completion method. Information related to the contract follows:

	December 31, 19X0	December 31, 19X1
Percentage of completion	20%	60%
Estimated total construction cost	$4,500,000	$4,800,000
Income recognized to date	$ 300,000	$ 720,000

A. Calculate the following for both 19X0 and 19X1:

    (i) Revenue recognized

    (ii) Costs incurred

B. Assume that during 19X1, Pine purchases and pays for $0.3 million of products and services that will be used in construction during 19X2. What is the impact of these expenditures on Pine's revenue recognition for 19X1?

7. [Revenue recognition methods, income and cash flow effects] The Able, Baker, Charlie, and David companies are identical in every respect except for their revenue recognition methods:

    1. Able recognizes sales when an order is received.

    2. Baker recognizes sales at time of production.

    3. Charlie recognizes sales at the time of shipment.

    4. David recognizes sales when cash is collected.

After the first year of operations, Charlie's closing inventory was $30,000 and accounts receivable was $50,000. Backorders, for which production had not yet started, were $10,000. Charlie recognized sales for the year of $100,000.

A. Assuming that each company charges a markup of 100% over cost, fill in the following table:

	Able	Baker	Charlie	David
Sales			$100,000	
Cost of goods sold				
Net income				

B. Ignoring income taxes, which company will have the largest cash balance at year end?

C. Which company will report the largest cash from operations?

8. [Effect of revenue recognition methods on bonus] The Kwai Co. has obtained a contract to build a bridge over the Celluloid River. The bridge will take three years to construct and will require cash outflows by Kwai of $1.0 million, $0.5 million, and $0.5 million in years 1, 2, and 3, respectively. Kwai will receive the $3 million contract price in three equal installments of $1 million.

As manager of this project you have three revenue recognition choices:

    1. Completed contract

    2. Percentage of completion

    3. Installment basis

A. Assume that your objective is to maximize the present value (discount rate is 12%) of your bonus. Bonus payments are made at the end of each year. Which accounting method would you choose if the bonus were based on:

    (i) 10% of annual income.

    (ii) 10% of annual revenue.

    (iii) 10% of cash flows from operations.

For each case, explain your reasoning.

B. Assume that bonuses are calculated on an annual basis but paid only when the bridge is completed. Explain how your anwers to part A would change.

Note: This problem can be solved without calculations. The answer can be deduced with some thought and inspection of the data.

9. Exhibit 2–13 in the text presents three years of income statements for Newcor, Inc., as originally reported (completed contract basis) and restated (percentage-of-completion basis).

A. On the completed contract basis, Newcor shows an increase in revenues of 24% from 1990 to 1991. On the percentage-of-completion basis, it shows a decrease of 3%. Explain this difference.

B. Newcor's total revenues recognized over the period 1989–1991 are greater under the completed contract basis, although the percentage-of-completion method generally recognizes revenues sooner. Explain why.

C. Discuss the trend in Newcor's gross profit margin (sales less cost of sales) over the period 1989 to 1991. Explain why the change in accounting method affected that trend. Which accounting method provides the earlier signal of changes in firm profitability?

D. Discuss the effects of the change in accounting method on Newcor's balance sheet. Your answer should focus on the inventory, accounts receivable, and advances from customers accounts.

E. Discuss the effects of the change in accounting method on the three components of Newcor's statement of cash flows.

F. Discuss whether the cash flow effects in part E are the same for all accounting changes.

10. [Revenue and expense recognition, cash flow analysis] The accrual concept results in recognition of revenue at the time a sale is made. However, as some customers will surely default, an allowance must be made for bad debts. The Stengel Company showed the following pattern of sales, bad-debt expense, and net receivables for 19X1–19X5 (in millions of dollars):

	19X1	19X2	19X3	19X4	19X5
Sales	$140	$150	$165	$175	$195
Bad-debt expense	7	7	8	10	10
Net receivables*	40	50	60	75	95
Net receivables* at 19X0 = 30					

*At year end.

A. Calculate the cash collected from customers each year from 19X1 to 19X2.

B. Based on the pattern of sales, net receivables, and cash collections in part A, discuss the adequacy of the provision for bad debts.

11. [Cash flow; 1992 CFA adapted] The cash flow data of Palomba Pizza Stores for the year ended December 31, 1991 is as follows:

Cash payment of dividends	$(35,000)
Purchase of land	(14,000)
Cash payments for interest	(10,000)
Cash payments for salaries	(45,000)
Sale of equipment	38,000
Retirement of common stock	(25,000)
Purchase of equipment	(30,000)
Cash payments to suppliers	(85,000)
Cash collections from customers	250,000
Cash at December 31, 1990	50,000

A. Prepare a statement of cash flows for Palomba for 1991. Classify cash flows as required by SFAS 95.

B. Discuss, from an analyst's viewpoint, the purpose of classifying cash flows into the three categories used in part A.

C. Discuss whether any of the cash flows should be classified differently.

D. Discuss the significance of the change in cash during 1991 as an indicator of Palomba's performance.

12. [Cash flow, transactional analysis; 1990 CFA adapted] The following financial statements are from the *19X2 Annual Report* of Niagara Company:

Income Statement, for Year Ended December 31, 19X2

Sales	$1000
Cost of goods sold	(650)
Depreciation expense	(100)
Sales and general expense	(100)
Interest expense	(50)
Income tax expense	(40)
Net income	$ 60

Balance Sheets, at December 31, 19X1–19X2

	19X1	19X2
Assets		
Cash	$ 50	$ 60
Accounts receivable	500	520
Inventory	750	770
Current assets	$1300	$1350
Fixed assets (net)	500	550
Total assets	$1800	$1900
Liabilities and equity		
Notes payable to banks	$ 100	$ 75
Accounts payable	590	615
Interest payable	10	20
Current liabilities	$ 700	$ 710
Long-term debt	300	350
Deferred income tax	300	310
Capital stock	400	400
Retained earnings	100	130
Total liabilities and equity	$1800	$1900

Prepare a statement of cash flows for the year ended December 31, 19X2. Use the direct method.

13. [Cash flow and income analysis] The financial statements of M company and G Company are contained in Exhibit 2P-1.

A. Derive the 19X4 income statement for the G Company.

B. Derive the 19X4 cash receipts and disbursements for the M Company.

C. Convert the schedules of cash receipts and disbursements for the years 19X0–19X4 for both G Company and M Company to statements of cash flows segregating the cash from operations, financing, and investment. Use the direct method.

D. As a bank loan officer, would you prefer to lend to G Company or M Company? Justify your answer.

EXHIBIT 2P-1. M COMPANY
Comparative Balance Sheets, at December 31, 19X0–19X4 (in $ thousands)

	19X0	19X1	19X2	19X3	19X4
Cash	$ 34	$ 35	$ 50	$ 30	$ 46
Accounts receivable	365	420	477	545	599
Inventory	227	265	304	405	458
Current assets	$626	$720	$831	$ 980	$1103
Plant, property, and equipment	120	137	174	204	237
Less: Accumulated depreciation	(40)	(50)	(61)	(73)	(87)
Total assets	$706	$807	$944	$1111	$1253
Accounts payable	$104	$118	$125	$ 113	$ 104
Taxes payable	81	95	113	130	133
Short-term debt	181	246	238	391	453
Current liabilities	$366	$459	$476	$ 634	$ 690
Long-term debt	48	46	143	143	239
Total liabilities	$414	$505	$619	$ 777	$ 929
Common stock	81	72	80	73	76
Retained earnings	211	230	245	261	248
Total equity	$292	$302	$325	$ 334	$ 324
Total liabilities and equity	$706	$807	$944	$1111	$1253

M COMPANY
Income Statements, for Years Ended 19X0–19X4 (in $ thousands)

	19X0	19X1	19X2	19X3	19X4
Sales	$1220	$1265	$1384	$1655	$1861
Cost of goods sold	818	843	931	1125	1277
Operating expenses	298	320	363	434	504
Depreciation	9	10	11	12	14
Interest	15	19	16	21	51
Taxes	38	33	27	26	6
Total expenses	$1178	$1225	$1348	$1618	$1852
Net income	$ 42	$ 40	$ 36	$ 37	$ 9

EXHIBIT 2P-1. *(Continued)*

M COMPANY
Cash Receipts and Disbursements, 19X0–19X4 (in $ thousands)

	19X0	19X1	19X2	19X3	19X4
Cash Receipts from					
From customers	$1165	$1210	$1327	$1587	$?
Issue of stock	5	5	8	3	?
Short-term debt	64	65	—	153	?
Long-term debt	—	—	100	—	?
Total receipts	$1234	$1280	$1435	$1743	$?
Cash Disbursements for					
Cost of goods sold and operating expenses	1130	1187	1326	1672	?
Dividends	20	21	21	21	?
Taxes	23	19	9	9	?
Interest	15	19	16	21	?
Plant, property, and equipment purchase	14	17	37	30	?
Repurchase of stock	22	14	—	10	?
Repayment of long-term debt	2	2	3	—	?
Repayment of short-term debt	—	—	8	—	?
Total disbursements	$1226	$1279	$1420	$1763	$?
Change in cash	$8	$1	$15	$(20)	$?

G COMPANY
Comparative Balance Sheets, at December 31, 19X0–19X4 (in $ thousands)

	19X0	19X1	19X2	19X3	19X4
Cash	$ 28	$ 32	$ 35	$ 54	$ 19
Accounts receivable	249	321	419	549	711
Inventory	303	391	510	672	873
Current assets	$580	$744	$ 964	$1275	$1603
Property, plant, and equipment	200	200	220	230	230
Less: Accumulated depreciation	(10)	(20)	(32)	(46)	(61)
Total assets	$770	$924	$1152	$1459	$1772
Accounts payable	$102	$134	$ 177	$ 235	$ 309
Income tax payable	20	25	36	38	45
Short-term debt	138	190	281	284	344
Current liabilities	$260	$349	$ 494	$ 557	$ 698
Long-term debt	40	63	83	208	258
Total liabilities	$300	$412	$ 577	$ 765	$ 956

EXHIBIT 2P-1. *(Continued)*

	19X0	19X1	19X2	19X3	19X4
Common stock	440	440	445	490	520
Retained earnings	30	72	130	204	296
Total equity	$470	$512	$ 575	$ 694	$ 816
Total liabilities and equity	$770	$924	$1152	$1459	$1772

G COMPANY
Income Statements for Years Ended 19X0–19X4 (in $ thousands)

	19X0	19X1	19X2	19X3	19X4
Sales	$1339	$1731	$2261	$2939	$?
Cost of goods sold	1039	1334	1743	2267	?
Operating expenses	243	312	398	524	?
Depreciation	10	10	12	14	?
Interest	11	13	23	29	?
Taxes	13	20	27	31	?
Total expenses	$1316	$1689	$2203	$2865	$?
Net income	$ 23	$ 42	$ 58	$ 74	$?

G COMPANY
Cash Receipts and Disbursements, 19X0–19X4 (in $ thousands)

	19X0	19X1	19X2	19X3	19X4
Cash Receipts from					
Customers	$1110	$1659	$2163	$2809	$3679
Issue of stock	10	—	5	45	30
Short-term debt	80	52	91	3	60
Long-term debt	40	23	20	125	50
Total receipts	$1240	$1734	$2279	$2982	$3819
Cash Disbursements for					
Cost of goods sold and operating expenses	1214	1702	2217	2895	3778
Dividends	—	—	—	—	—
Taxes	13	15	16	29	35
Interest	11	13	23	29	41
Plant, property, and equipment purchase	—	—	20	10	—
Repurchase of common stock	—	—	—	—	—
Repayment of long-term debt	—	—	—	—	—
Repayment of short-term debt	—	—	—	—	—
Total disbursements	$1238	$1730	$2276	$2963	$3854
Change in cash	$ 2	$ 4	$ 3	$ 19	$ (35)

14. [Cash flow, conversion of indirect to direct method] Exhibit 2P-2 contains balance sheets, income statements, and cash flow statements for Mercantile Stores, a department store company, for the two years ended January 31, 1992. The statement of cash flows is prepared using the indirect method as permitted by SFAS 95.

A. Using the data in Exhibit 2P-2, prepare a statement of cash flow from operations, using the direct method, for the year ended January 31, 1992.

B. Discuss the usefulness of the direct method statement, with particular emphasis on insights not provided by the income statement and indirect method cash flow statement.

15. [Cash flow statement—relationship to other statements] Exhibit 2–4 in the text contains financial statements for A. M. Castle for the years 1989–1991.

A. In 1990, Castle acquired Norton Steel. Estimate the impact of the acquisition on the following components of operating working capital:

  (i) Accounts receivable

  (ii) Inventory

  (iii) Accounts payable

B. Estimate the amount of property, plant, and equipment purchased in the acquisition.

C. In 1991, Castle's income declined. Its CFO, however, increased dramatically.

  (i) Explain how this difference occurred.

  (ii) Explain how the acquisition of Norton may have affected the trend in CFO.

16. [Cash flows, free cash flows; 1989 CFA adapted] In October 1988, Philip Morris announced an unsolicited cash tender offer for all the 124 million outstanding shares of Kraft at $90 per share. Kraft subsequently accepted a $106-per-share all-cash offer from Philip Morris. Following the completion of the acquisition of Kraft, Philip Morris released its 1988 year-end financial statements.

A. Prepare a statement of cash flows for Philip Morris Companies based on the format utilized in SFAS 95 using only the actual 1988 financial data contained in Exhibit 2P-3.

(Important Note: The acquisition of Kraft requires that you remove the assets acquired and liabilities incurred as a result of that acquisition from the balance sheet changes used to prepare the statement of cash flows. Philip Morris paid $11.383 billion for Kraft, net of cash acquired. A breakdown of the purchase is contained in Exhibit 2P-3.)

B. Based on your answer to part A, compute Philip Morris' free cash flow for 1988, and discuss how free cash flow may impact the Company's future earnings and financial condition.

C. In the Philip Morris cash flow statement prepared in part A, the cost of Kraft's inventories and receivables acquired by Philip Morris was classified as cash from investment rather than cash from operations. Discuss how this classification may distort the trend in CFO, and state under what conditions this distortion will occur.

EXHIBIT 2P-2. MERCANTILE STORES
Consolidated Balance Sheets

in thousands January 31,	1992	1991
Assets		
Current Assets:		
Cash and cash equivalents	$ 122,458	$ 44,655
Receivables:		
Customer	606,189	626,656
Other	50,239	40,944
Inventories	381,406	393,304
Deferred income taxes	6,470	6,668
Other current assets	3,846	4,515
Total Current Assets	1,170,608	1,116,742
Investments and Other Noncurrent Assets	40,928	35,192
Property and Equipment:		
Land	17,640	17,640
Building and improvements	396,473	377,832
Fixtures	243,307	223,114
Leased property	65,525	61,001
	722,945	679,587
Less accumulated depreciation	261,382	234,891
Property and equipment-net	461,563	444,696
Total	$1,673,099	$1,596,630

See Notes to Consolidated Financial Statements

EXHIBIT 2P-2. *(Continued)*

in thousands January 31,	1992	1991
Liabilities and Stockholders' Equity		
Current Liabilities:		
Current maturities of long-term debt	$ 7,030	$ 7,985
Note payable	6,401	—
Accounts payable	86,414	88,112
Other current liabilities	44,628	46,379
Accrued income taxes	18,192	18,465
Accrued payroll	19,160	21,307
Total Current Liabilities	181,825	182,248
Long-term Debt	207,150	207,906
Due to Affiliated Companies	17,792	17,372
Deferred Income Taxes	7,217	6,520
Other Long-term Liabilities	8,067	8,453
Stockholders' Equity:		
Common Stock–$.14 2/3 par value, issued 36,887,475 shares, outstanding 36,844,050 (after deducting 43,425 treasury shares)	5,403	5,403
Additional paid-in capital	6,018	6,018
Retained earnings	1,239,627	1,162,710
Total Stockholders' Equity	1,251,048	1,174,131
Total	$1,673,099	$1,596,630

EXHIBIT 2P-2. *(Continued)*
Statements of Consolidated Income and Retained Earnings

in thousands January 31,	1992	1991	1990
Net Sales	$2,442,425	$2,367,210	$2,312,802
Cost, Expenses and Other Income:			
Cost of goods sold (including occupancy and central buying expenses)	1,720,947	1,670,555	1,594,849
Selling, general and administrative expenses	546,682	527,467	502,537
Provision for relocation	—	—	10,000
Interest expense	23,390	23,422	22,818
Interest income	(4,511)	(4,160)	(4,289)
Other income	(30,485)	(29,186)	(26,156)
	2,256,023	2,188,098	2,099,759
Income Before Income Taxes	186,402	179,112	213,043
Income Taxes:			
Currently payable	71,468	85,327	99,845
Deferred	895	(29,829)	(17,145)
	72,363	55,498	82,700
Net Income	$ 114,039	$ 123,614	$ 130,343
Retained Earnings at Beginning of Year	1,162,710	1,065,900	969,454
	1,276,749	1,189,514	1,099,797
Dividends Declared (1)	37,122	26,804	33,897
Retained Earnings at End of Year	$1,239,627	$1,162,710	$1,065,900
Net Income per Share	$ 3.10	$ 3.36	$ 3.54
(1) Dividends Paid	$ 37,122	$ 35,278	$ 32,792

See Notes to Consolidated Financial Statements

EXHIBIT 2P-2. *(Continued)*
Statements of Consolidated Cash Flows

in thousands January 31,	1992	1991	1990
Cash Flows from Operating Activities:			
Net Income	$114,039	$123,614	$130,343
Adjustments to reconcile net income			
to net cash provided by operating activities:			
Depreciation and amortization	70,607	63,158	54,478
Deferred taxes	895	(29,829)	(17,145)
Provision for relocation	—	—	10,000
Equity in unremitted earnings of affiliated companies	(931)	(1,840)	(1,873)
Net pension benefit	(4,256)	(6,248)	(4,468)
Change in inventories	11,898	15	(31,282)
Change in accounts receivable	11,172	(22,967)	(19,434)
Change in accounts payable	(1,698)	(4,634)	8,206
Net change in other working capital items	(2,854)	(17,921)	(6,276)
Net cash provided by operating activities	198,872	103,348	122,549
Cash Flows from Investing Activities:			
Cash payments for property and equipment	(79,931)	(82,944)	(97,196)
Net change in other noncurrent assets			
and liabilities	(1,163)	(3,719)	(190)
Net change in notes receivable	—	(165)	249
Net cash used in investing activities	(81,094)	(86,828)	(97,137)
Cash Flows from Financing Activities:			
Payments of long-term debt	(9,254)	(7,860)	(8,194)
Increase in note payable	6,401	—	—
Dividends paid	(37,122)	(35,278)	(32,792)
Net cash used in financing activities	(39,975)	(43,138)	(40,986)
Net increase (decrease) in cash and cash equivalents	77,803	(26,618)	(15,574)
Cash and cash equivalents at beginning of year	44,655	71,273	86,847
Cash and cash equivalents at end of year	$122,458	$ 44,655	$ 71,273
Supplemental Cash Flow Information:			
Interest paid	$ 23,397	$ 23,453	$ 22,865
Income taxes paid	$ 71,741	$100,440	$103,019
Noncash Investing and Financing Activities:			
Leases capitalized	$ 7,543	$ 16,681	$ 10,073

See Notes to Consolidated Financial Statements
Source: Mercantile Stores 1991 Annual Report

EXHIBIT 2P-3. PHILIP MORRIS COMPANIES, INC.
Balance Sheets, at December 31, 1987–1988 (in $ millions)

	1987	1988
Assets		
Cash and cash equivalents	$ 90	$ 168
Accounts receivable	2,065	2,222
Inventories	4,154	5,384
Current assets	$ 6,309	$ 7,774
Property, plant, and equipment (net)	6,582	8,648
Goodwill (net)	4,052	15,071
Investments	3,665	3,260
Total assets	$20,608	$34,753
Liabilities and Stockholders' Equity		
Short-term debt	$ 1,440	$ 1,259
Accounts payable	791	1,777
Accrued liabilities	2,277	3,848
Income taxes payable	727	1,089
Dividends payable	213	260
Current liabilities	$ 5,448	$ 8,233
Long-term debt	6,293	17,122
Deferred income taxes	2,044	1,719
Stockholders' equity	6,823	7,679
Total liabilities and stockholders' equity	$20,608	$34,753

PHILIP MORRIS COMPANIES, INC.
Income Statement, for Year Ended December 31, 1988 (in $ millions)

Sales	$ 31,742
Cost of goods sold	(12,156)
Selling and administrative expenses	(14,410)
Depreciation expense	(654)
Goodwill amortization	(125)
Interest expense	(670)
Pretax income	$ 3,727
Income tax expense	(1,390)
Net income	$ 2,337

Dividends declared $941 million

EXHIBIT 2P-3. *(Continued)*

PHILIP MORRIS PURCHASE OF KRAFT
Allocation of Purchase Price (in $ millions)

Accounts receivable	$ 758
Inventories	1,232
Property, plant, and equipment	1,740
Goodwill	10,361
Short-term debt	(700)
Accounts payable	(578)
Accrued liabilities	(530)
Long-term debt	(900)
Purchase price (net of cash acquired)	$11,383

17. [Cash flow from operations, free cash flows] Hertz is the world's largest provider of rented cars and trucks. Extracts from its statement of cash flows follow:

Cash Flows of Hertz Corp.

	1989	1990	1991
Net income	108	89	48
Depreciation of revenue equipment	475	530	497
Depreciation of property	57	69	75
Self-insurance and other accruals	100	85	122
Purchases of revenue equipment	(3003)	(4024)	(4016)
Sales of revenue equipment	2354	3434	3784
Changes in operating assets and liabilities (net)	(141)	13	(118)
Payment of self-insurance claims	(67)	(104)	(106)
Cash flow from operations	$ (117)	$ 92	$ 286
Cash flow for investing	(133)	(79)	(72)
Net change in debt	241	(4)	(84)
Dividends paid	(90)	(64)	(62)
Cash flow from financing	$ 151	$ (68)	$ (146)
Effect of foreign exchange rates	1	11	0
Net increase (decrease) in cash	$ (98)	$ (44)	$ 68

Source: Hertz Corp. 1991 Annual Report

Note that Hertz includes purchases and sales of revenue equipment (cars and trucks to be rented) in cash flow from operations.

A. Recompute cash flow from operations, classifying purchases and sales of revenue equipment as investing cash flows.

B. Compare the trend of cash flow from operations as reported with the trend after reclassification.

C. Recompute cash flow for investing, classifying purchases and sales of revenue equipment as investing cash flows.

D. Compare the trend of cash flow for investing as reported with the trend after reclassification.

E. Which classification provides the better measure of cash flow from operations for Hertz? Define and compute a useful measure of free cash flow for Hertz. State your assumptions.

F. Assume that Hertz leases (rather than purchasing) some of its rental cars and trucks. Discuss the impact of leasing (rather than buying) on cash flow from operations as reported by Hertz.

G. Discuss the impact of leasing on cash flow from operations assuming that purchases of revenue equipment are reported as cash flows from investing.

[Hint for parts F and G: Think of leasing and buying as expensing and capitalizing, respectively.]

3

FOUNDATIONS OF RATIO AND FINANCIAL ANALYSIS

INTRODUCTION
Purpose and Use of Ratios
Ratios: Cautionary Notes
Economic Assumptions
Benchmarks
Timing and Window Dressing
Negative Numbers
Accounting Methods

COMMON-SIZE STATEMENTS

DISCUSSION OF RATIOS BY CATEGORY
Activity Analysis
Short-Term (Operating) Activity Ratios
Long-Term (Investment) Activity Ratios
Liquidity Analysis
Length of Cash Cycle
Working Capital Ratios and Defensive Interval
Long-Term Debt and Solvency Analysis
Debt Covenants
Capitalization Table and Debt Ratios
Interest Coverage Ratios
Capital Expenditure and Cash Flow from Operations to Debt Ratios
Profitability Analysis
Return on Sales

Return on Investment
Profitability and Cash Flows
Operating and Financial Leverage

RATIOS: AN INTEGRATED ANALYSIS
Analysis of Firm Performance
Disaggregation of ROA
Disaggregation of ROE and Its Relationship to ROA
Economic Characteristics and Strategies
Competing Strategies
Product Life Cycle
Interindustry Economic Factors
Classification and Partitions of Ratios
Ratios: Patterns of Disclosure, Definitions, and Use
Perceived Importance and Classification
Disclosure of Ratios
Industry Norms as Benchmarks

SUMMARY

APPENDIX 3–A: ESTIMATING OPERATING LEVERAGE

APPENDIX 3–B: MERCK-CONDENSED FINANCIAL STATEMENTS

APPENDIX 3–C: EARNINGS PER SHARE

INTRODUCTION

Traditional ratio analysis is primarily designed to meet the informational needs of equity investors and creditors. The objective of ratio analysis is the comparative measurement of risk and return, facilitating intelligent investment and credit decisions.

Investment decisions range from an evaluation of risk and return over time for a particular investment (e.g., the common stock of General Electric) to a comparison among classes of investments (e.g., stocks or bonds compared with real estate). Alternatively, the investor may be interested in a cross-sectional analysis, that is, comparing risk and return across all firms in the pharmaceutical industry at a specific point in time.

The informational needs and appropriate analytical techniques needed for specific investment and credit decisions are a function of the decision maker's time horizon. Short-term bank and trade creditors are interested in the immediate liquidity of the firm. Longer-term creditors (e.g., bondholders) are interested in the long-term asset position, solvency, and earning power of the firm. Their focus is to minimize risk and ensure that resources are available to assure payment of interest and principal obligations.

Equity investors are primarily interested in the long-term earning power of the firm. By bearing the residual risk (which can be defined as the return from operations after all claims from suppliers and creditors have been satisfied), the equity investor requires a return commensurate to that risk. The residual risk, being highly volatile, is difficult to quantify as is the equity investor's time horizon. Thus analysis by the equity investor needs to be the most comprehensive, and it subsumes the analysis carried out by other users.

Purpose and Use of Ratios

A pervasive problem when comparing a firm's performance over time or with other firms is changes in the firm's size over time and the different sizes of firms with which it is compared. One approach to this problem is to use *common-size statements* in which the various components of the financial statements are standardized by expressing them as a percentage of some base. For example, different components of the balance sheet can be reflected as a percentage of total assets; similarly, revenues and expenses can be computed as a percentage of total sales, and, on the direct method cash flow statement, cash collections may serve as the base for the components of cash flow from operations.

Ratios, in general, involve a process of standardization. They can be used to standardize reporting methods, financial statements, and other relevant variables, allowing for comparisons over time and cross sectionally between firms. The second purpose of ratios, however, is the more important and meaningful one. Ratios measure a firm's crucial relationships by relating inputs (costs) with outputs (benefits) and facilitate comparisons of these relationships over time and across firms.

Four broad categories of analysis measure such relationships:

1. *Activity analysis:* Evaluates the levels of output generated by the assets employed by the firm.

2. *Liquidity analysis:* Measures the adequacy of a firm's cash resources to meet its near-term cash obligations.

3. *Long-term debt and solvency analysis:* Examines the firm's capital structure in terms of the mix of its financing sources and the ability of the firm to satisfy its longer-term debt and investment obligations.

4. *Profitability analysis:* Measures the net income of the firm relative to its revenues and capital.

As will become apparent in the discussions that follow, the categories are not distinct but rather are interrelated. Thus profitability affects solvency, and the efficiency with which assets are used (as measured by activity analysis) impacts the analysis of profitability.

In measuring these relationships, ratios provide a profile of a firm and its management's operating, financial, and investment decisions. Thus an intelligent analysis of the ratios can provide insight into a firm's economic characteristics and competitive strategies.

Common-size statements permit standardization and provide the analyst with insights of this nature. For example, significant changes in net income over time may be traced to variations in cost of goods sold (COGS) or labor costs as a percentage of sales. Moreover, differences over time in a single firm or between firms due to managements' operating, financing, and investing decisions and external economic factors are highlighted by common-size statements.

Ratios: Cautionary Notes

The analysis of these economic differences is an important objective of financial analysis. This section will discuss some important caveats that must be considered when incorporating ratios as part of an overall financial analysis. For explanatory purposes, the discussion at times will use specific ratios as examples, although these ratios have not as yet been formally defined. However, some cautionary points are relevant prior to a comprehensive discussion of ratios, as many of the points raised apply in a pervasive manner to all ratios, even those not directly addressed.

Economic Assumptions

Ratio analysis is designed to eliminate size differences across firms and over time, thus allowing for more meaningful comparisons. Implicit in this statement and in the overall construction of ratios is the *proportionality assumption* that the relationship between numerator and denominator should be similar irrespective of size. This assumption is problematic, as it ignores the existence of fixed costs. When there are fixed costs, changes in profits are not proportional to changes in sales.

Similarly, even in the absence of a fixed component, the implicit assumption of a linear relationship between numerator and denominator may be incorrect. For example, use of the inventory turnover ratio, COGS/inventory, implies a constant relationship between volume of sales and inventory levels. Management science theory, however, indicates that the optimum relationship is nonlinear and inventory levels may be proportional to the square root of demand. Thus a doubling in demand should result in inventory increasing 40% (approximately) and a subsequent 40% increase in the turnover ratio. *The inventory turnover ratio is clearly not size independent.*[1]

Benchmarks

Ratios, even when well specified, may suffer from lack of an appropriate benchmark to indicate an optimal level. Thus, to a great extent, evaluation of the ratio depends on the question being posed by the analyst. For example, from the point of view of a short-term credit extender, a high liquidity ratio may be a positive indicator. However, from the perspective of cash or working capital management, it may indicate that the firm has too much idle cash and is not managing its resources well.

Using an industry average[2] as the benchmark may be useful for intraindustry analysis but not for interindustry analysis. Furthermore, even for intraindustry analysis, the benchmark may have limited usefulness if the whole industry or major firms in that industry are doing poorly.

Timing and Window Dressing

Data used to compute ratios are available only at specific points in time, primarily when financial statements are issued. For annual reports, these points in time correspond to the end of a firm's operating cycle, and the reported levels of assets and liabilities generally do not reflect the firm's level of normal operations. As a result, certain ratios will not reflect the actual (short-term) operating relationships, especially in the case of seasonal businesses. For example, inventories and accounts payable will most likely be below the average operating levels. Reference to interim statements is one way of alleviating this problem.

The timing issue leads to another problem. Transactions at year end by management can lead to manipulation of the ratios to show them in a more favorable light (window dressing). For example, a firm with a current ratio (current assets/current liabilities) of 1.5 ($300/$200) can increase it to 2.0 ($200/$100) by simply using cash of $100 to reduce accounts payable immediately prior to the period's end.

Generally, any ratio where a transaction affects the numerator and denominator can be manipulated as follows. If the ratio is greater than 1, it can be increased by a transaction that subtracts the same amount from both numerator and denominator. If it is less than 1, it can be increased by a transaction that adds the same amount to both numerator and denominator.[3]

Negative Numbers

Two examples will serve to illustrate the care that must be taken in ratio analysis when negative numbers occur.

---

[1]See Chapter 5 for a more detailed discussion of this issue.

[2]See the last section of the chapter where we discuss databases that provide information as to industry averages.

[3]To decrease the ratio, for ratios greater (less) than 1, the same amount is added to (subtracted from) the numerator and denominator.

$$\text{Example 1} \quad \text{Return on Equity (ROE)} = \frac{\text{Income}}{\text{Equity}}$$

Co. A: Income = $ 10,000 Equity = $ 100,000 ROE = 10%
Co. B: Income = $(10,000) Equity = $(100,000) ROE = 10%

Looking only at the ratios without the underlying data can clearly lead to the wrong conclusions. Before the reader protests that such a mistake is unlikely as the "negative effect" would be immediately noticeable, one need only point out that much financial and ratio analysis today is computer generated. Unless the program is well written, such mistakes are bound to be overlooked.

$$\text{Example 2} \quad \text{Dividend Payout Ratio} = \frac{\text{Dividend}}{\text{Income}}$$

Co. A: Dividend = $10,000   Income = $50,000   Payout ratio = 20%
Co. B: Dividend = 10,000   Income = 30,000   Payout ratio = 33%
Co. C: Dividend = 10,000   Income = (50,000) Payout ratio = (20%)

A ranking of these firms by payout ratio from highest to lowest would list them as B, A, and C. However, the payout ratio is intended to measure the extent to which income is paid to shareholders as opposed to being retained in the business. For the same size of dividend, the lower the income, the larger the proportion paid out (higher payout ratio). As the income approaches zero, the ratio approaches infinity. The payment of dividends despite negative income clearly indicates a high proportion of income being paid out to shareholders. Thus, in reality, Company C has the highest payout ratio.

Accounting Methods

Accounting conventions and choice of accounting methods can greatly affect income and balance sheet accounts. In addition, as described in Chapter 2, even "pure" numbers such as cash flows from operations can be affected by accounting methods and definitions. Thus ratios resulting from differing accounting methods will not be comparable either across firms or over time. To interpret such ratios, one needs to know how to convert from one accounting method to another. A strong understanding of accounting rules and a judicious eye for information contained in the notes to financial statements is a must for this type of analysis. The impact of accounting methods on ratios will be left to subsequent chapters dealing with the specific accounting issues.

The balance of this chapter will discuss ratios primarily in narrative form. Exhibits 3-4, 3-6, 3-7, 3-8, and 3-10 through 3-13 will illustrate the calculation of the ratios with a brief analysis using the financial statements of Merck, a leading firm in the pharmaceutical industry. Summarized financial statements of Merck are presented in Appendix B to this chapter. In addition, for comparative purposes, reference will occasionally be made to the financial statements and ratios of Pfizer and Schering-Plough, two of Merck's competitors.

The calculations presented in these exhibits are based on numbers taken directly from the financial statements without any adjustments. In one sense, therefore, the exhibits are intended for illustrative purposes only. The nature of the adjustments that are necessary will become clearer as we progress through the book. On the other hand, it is our position that ratios are not to be viewed as an end unto themselves but rather as a starting point for further analysis. The ratios highlight where further investigation and adjustment may be needed. In that sense, ratios calculated on raw data also serve a useful purpose.

COMMON-SIZE STATEMENTS

The purpose of this section is to illustrate the use of common-size statements (1) to identify important economic characteristics, any differences stemming from reporting choices and operating, investing, and financing decisions made by management, and competitive strengths or drawbacks of a given firm or comparable firms and (2) to highlight factors that require further analysis. This is the first step in a comprehensive ratio analysis: common-size statements should not be used simply to provide a scaling factor for standardization, but rather *to develop insights into the economic characteristics of different industries and of different firms in the same industry*.

The analysis of common-size statements is based on data presented in Exhibits 3-1 and 3-2. Exhibit 3-1 compares the 1990 balance sheets and income statements for Merck, Pfizer, and Schering-Plough. The data in the exhibit is presented both in actual terms and on a common-size basis. Exhibit 3-2 presents a comparison of common-size balance sheets and income statements of the pharmaceutical industry and selected other industries. For the balance sheets, the scaling factor is total assets; for the income statements, it is sales.

Any meaningful comparison of the performance of the three companies based on the actual reported numbers poses some difficulty even though Merck and Pfizer are roughly equivalent in size as measured by assets or sales; Schering-Plough is considerably smaller. Comparing, for example, Merck and Pfizer's net income of $1,781 million and $801 million, respectively, with Schering-Plough's $565 million does not provide much insight unless the numbers are scaled by relating them to the level of sales.

The common-size balance sheets and income statements provide such insight. Merck's net income is highest as a percentage of sales as well as in absolute terms, indicating superior profitability. However, Pfizer's net income as a percentage of sales is lower than that of Schering-Plough even though the actual dollar amount of net income is higher.

The components of the income statement further highlight the relative characteristics of the three firms. Exhibit 3-2 indicates that, as compared with other industries, the drugs and medicine industry cost of sales as a percentage of sales is relatively low. Similar patterns are apparent for the three companies in Exhibit 3-1. Sales are approximately three to four times cost of goods sold.

The high markup over manufacturing costs is a function of a need to compensate for the up-front cost (and risk) of research and development. The pharmaceutical industry invests heavily in research and development as evidenced by the relatively high percentage (10–11%) shown by all three companies. In addition, the relative inelasticity of demand for medicine coupled with the monopoly power associated with a patented drug provides the economic basis that enables pharmaceutical companies to enjoy the relatively high return on sales.

Moving past these general similarities, we find that Pfizer's cost of goods sold percentage is substantially higher than that of the other two companies. This is due to the

EXHIBIT 3-1
Comparative Income Statements and Balance Sheets, 1990 Data.

A. Comparative Balance Sheets

	As Reported ($ millions)			Common Size		
	Merck	Pfizer	Schering-Plough	Merck	Pfizer	Schering-Plough
Cash	$ 806	$ 870	$ 742	10%	10%	18%
Short-term investment	391	783	178	5%	9%	4%
Accounts receivable	1346	1377	467	17%	15%	11%
Inventories	893	1143	358	11%	13%	9%
Prepaid expenses	331	263	255	4%	3%	6%
Current assets	$3767	$4436	$2000	47%	49%	49%
Long-term loans	1012	1423	514	13%	16%	13%
Net property, plant, and equipment	2721	2608	1284	34%	29%	31%
Other assets	530	585	305	7%	6%	7%
Total assets	$8030	$9052	$4103	100%	100%	100%
Short-term debt	793	1499	783	10%	17%	19%
Accounts payable	1138	734	343	14%	8%	8%
Income tax payable	679	308	223	8%	3%	5%
Other current liabilities	217	576	181	3%	6%	4%
Current liabilities	$2827	$3117	$1530	35%	34%	37%
Long-term debt	124	193	183	2%	2%	4%
Deferred taxes	695	352	172	9%	4%	4%
Other noncurrent liabilities	549	298	137	7%	4%	3%
Total liabilities	$4195	$3960	$2022	52%	44%	49%
Common stock	167	351	279	2%	4%	7%
Retained earnings	6387	4510	2818	80%	50%	69%
Treasury stock	(2719)	(25)	(945)	(34%)	0%	(23%)
Currency translation adjustment	0	256	(71)	0%	3%	(2%)
Total equity	$3835	$5092	$2081	48%	56%	51%
Total liabilities and equity	$8030	$9052	$4103	100%	100%	100%

EXHIBIT 3-1. *(Continued)*

	B. *Comparative Income Statements* As Reported ($ millions)			Common Size		
	Merck	Pfizer	Schering-Plough	Merck	Pfizer	Schering-Plough
Sales	$7672	$6406	$3323	100%	100%	100%
Cost of goods sold	1778	2259	801	23%	35%	24%
Selling, general, and administrative expenses	2388	2453	1419	31%	38%	43%
Research and development	854	640	380	11%	10%	11%
Income from operations	$2652	$1054	$ 723	35%	16%	22%
Other income	47	45	46	1%	1%	1%
Income before taxes	2699	1099	769	35%	17%	23%
Provision for taxes	(918)	(298)	(204)	(12%)	(5%)	(6%)
Net income	$1781	$ 801	$ 565	23%	13%	17%

Note: Numbers may not add due to rounding.
Source: adapted from Annual Reports, 1990.

fact that, unlike Merck and Schering-Plough, which are primarily producers of ethical drug and consumer health products (including over-the-counter drugs), 15% of Pfizer's sales come from its other divisions such as Specialty Minerals and Chemicals. Exhibit 3-2 shows that the markup enjoyed by the chemical industry, for example, is not as high as for the pharmaceutical industry. Hence, on a weighted average basis, Pfizer can be expected to show a higher cost of goods sold percentage. Finally, Schering-Plough's relatively high selling, general, and administrative (SG&A) expense may be due to the fact that a greater proportion of its sales are from its consumer products division. Sales of these products require a different marketing strategy and generate higher selling costs than do those of pharmaceuticals.

The balance sheet comparison exhibits similar proportions of current assets and current liabilities. The components of working capital raise an intriguing question as to why Schering-Plough has the highest percentages of both cash and short-term debt (18–19%). Why doesn't the company use its "excess" cash to pay off the "excess" debt?[4]

All three companies have low levels of long-term debt (2–4%). Pfizer's relatively high equity position (56%) resulted from Pfizer retaining its income, while the other firms have engaged heavily in common stock repurchase programs. (Note the amount of treasury stock in each company's equity section.) Generally, however, the balance sheets of the three companies show similar structures.

Industry comparisons using the data in Exhibit 3-2, however, show that balance sheet compositions differ widely from industry to industry. The two retailer categories, for example, show (as would be expected) considerably lower receivables and higher

---

[4]One possible answer is that the cash and debt are located in different subsidiaries or tax jurisdictions and transfer of the cash to repay the debt would have unfavorable tax consequences.

EXHIBIT 3-2
Common-Size Balance Sheets and Income Statements Industry Comparisons, 1990

	Retailers		Manufacturers					
	Groceries	Department Stores	Rubber and Plastic Footwear	Pulp and Paper	Drugs and Medicine	Chemicals	Iron and Steel	Petroleum Refining
A. Comparative Balance Sheets								
Cash and equivalents	11%	6%	6%	7%	10%	10%	6%	7%
Trade receivables	5%	16%	29%	25%	24%	26%	30%	21%
Inventory	35%	47%	24%	21%	28%	22%	20%	19%
Other	2%	2%	2%	3%	2%	2%	2%	3%
Current assets	53%	71%	61%	55%	63%	60%	58%	49%
Fixed assets (net)	35%	22%	30%	37%	27%	29%	36%	43%
Intangibles	2%	1%	2%	1%	4%	2%	1%	0%
Other	11%	6%	7%	6%	7%	10%	6%	7%
Total assets	100%	100%	100%	100%	100%	100%	100%	100%
Notes payable	6%	10%	10%	7%	9%	8%	9%	9%
Current, portion of long-term debt	5%	3%	4%	3%	4%	4%	5%	5%
Trade payables	21%	14%	14%	16%	16%	17%	15%	16%
Income tax payables	1%	1%	1%	1%	1%	1%	1%	1%
Other	8%	9%	7%	6%	8%	8%	9%	8%
Current liabilities	41%	37%	36%	34%	37%	37%	38%	41%
Long-term debt	26%	17%	16%	21%	13%	13%	21%	13%
Deferred taxes	0%	1%	1%	3%	1%	1%	1%	2%
Other noncurrent liabilities	2%	2%	3%	3%	3%	3%	5%	2%
Total liabilities	69%	58%	56%	61%	54%	54%	65%	59%
Equity	31%	42%	45%	39%	46%	46%	35%	41%
Total liabilities and equity	100%	100%	100%	100%	100%	100%	100%	100%
B. Comparative Income Statements								
Sales	100%	100%	100%	100%	100%	100%	100%	100%
Cost of sales	77%	64%	73%	76%	58%	68%	79%	80%
Gross profit	23%	36%	27%	24%	42%	32%	21%	20%
Operating expense	22%	35%	22%	17%	35%	26%	16%	16%
Operating profit	1%	1%	5%	7%	7%	6%	5%	4%
Other expenses	0%	0%	1%	2%	1%	1%	2%	2%
Profit before tax	1%	1%	4%	5%	6%	5%	3%	2%

Source: "Reprinted with permission, copyright Robert Morris Associates 1990. Data adapted from the ALL SIZES column appearing in 1990 *Annual Statement Studies*." RMA cautions that the Studies be regarded only as a general guideline and not as an absolute industry norm. This is due to limited samples within categories, the categorization of companies by their primary Standard Industrial Classification (SIC) number only, and different methods of operations by companies within the same industry. For these reasons, RMA recommends that the figures be used only as general guidelines in addition to other methods of financial analysis.

inventory balances than manufacturers. Within the manufacturing industries, petroleum refining, iron and steel, and pulp and paper have the highest proportion of fixed assets. This is due to a combination of two factors: (1) the investment in physical plant and (2) the natural resources these industries possess. These differences do not indicate that one industry is "better" than the other but, rather, are a reflection of the industries' operating environment.

Common-size statements can also be used to compare the performance of companies over time. Exhibit 3-3 shows actual and common-size income statements for Merck over the four-year period 1987–1990. Sales increased by 52% from $5061 million to $7672 million. Profits, however, nearly doubled from $906 million to $1,781 million. The common-size statements indicate that most of the improvement resulted from a 20% improvement in manufacturing costs, as cost of goods sold declined from 29% to 23% of sales. SG&A also declined relative to sales, but to a lesser degree. In addition, the declines seem to have ended in 1989, with no additional improvement in 1990.

Exhibit 3-3B illustrates a common-size statement useful for trend analysis. For this statement, a base year is chosen, and subsequent year data are calculated as percentages of the base year data. This statement confirms our previous observation of the impact of declines in cost of goods sold relative to sales on net income. Although sales increased by 52% from 1987 to 1990, COGS increased by only 23% over that same period. In the last year, however, the trend seems to have stabilized, as most of the increase in COGS occurred in 1990.[5]

Changes in balance sheet components can also be analyzed over time. Similarly, analyses discussed in Exhibits 3-1 through 3-3 can be applied to cash flow statements. The insights obtained from these analyses of common-size statements facilitate detailed analysis of the firm and comparative analysis of firms—issues discussed in the following sections.

DISCUSSION OF RATIOS BY CATEGORY

The ratios presented in the paragraphs that follow and their mode of calculation are neither exhaustive nor uniquely "correct." The definition of many ratios is not standardized[6] and may vary from analyst to analyst, textbook to textbook, and annual report to annual report.[7] Not all such variations are logical or useful; we believe that the ratios presented in this book meet both these criteria.

The analyst's primary focus should be on the relationships indicated by various ratios, not on the details of the calculations. As we proceed through the book, many adjustments to and modifications of these basic ratios will be suggested.

---

[5]This does not mean that manufacturing costs were out of line in 1990. Actually, the 15% increase in cost of goods sold from 1989 to 1990 was below the percentage increase in sales. Thus, the increase was in line with the firm's growth that year.

[6]In this chapter when one of the components of the ratio comes from the balance sheet and the other from the income or cash flow statement, the balance sheet number is an average of the beginning and ending balances. An exception is the cash flow from operations to debt ratio. Other sources may use the beginning or ending balances for all "mixed" ratios.

[7]See, for example, the Gibson papers (1982, 1987) discussed in the section in this chapter entitled "Ratios: Patterns of Disclosure, Definitions and Use."

EXHIBIT 3-3. Comparative Income Statements
Merck, 1987–1990

A. Income Statements

	As Reported (in $ millions)				Common Size Income Statements As a % of Total Sales			
	1987	1988	1989	1990	1987	1988	1989	1990
Sales	$5061	$5940	$6551	$7672	100%	100%	100%	100%
Cost of goods sold	1443	1526	1550	1778	29%	26%	24%	23%
Selling, general, and administrative expenses	1682	1878	2013	2388	33%	32%	31%	31%
Research and development	566	669	751	854	11%	11%	11%	11%
Income from operations	$1370	$1867	$2237	$2652	27%	31%	34%	35%
Other income	35	4	47	47	1%	0%	1%	1%
Income before taxes	1405	1871	2284	2699	28%	31%	35%	35%
Provision for taxes	499	664	788	918	10%	11%	12%	12%
	$ 906	$1207	$1496	$1781	18%	20%	23%	23%

B. Income Statements

	As Reported (in $ millions)				Common Size Income Statements As % of 1987 Level			
	1987	1988	1989	1990	1987	1988	1989	1990
Sales	$5061	$5940	$6551	$7672	100%	117%	129%	152%
Cost of goods sold	1443	1526	1550	1778	100%	106%	107%	123%
Selling, general, and administrative expenses	1682	1878	2013	2388	100%	112%	120%	142%
Research and development	566	669	751	854	100%	118%	133%	151%
Income from operations	$1370	$1867	$2237	$2652	100%	136%	163%	194%
Other income	35	4	47	47	100%	11%	134%	134%
Income before taxes	1405	1871	2284	2699	100%	133%	163%	192%
Provision for taxes	499	664	788	918	100%	133%	158%	184%
	$ 906	$1207	$1496	$1781	100%	133%	165%	197%

Source: Annual Reports, 1987–1990

Activity Analysis

To carry out operations, a firm needs to invest in both short-term (inventory and accounts receivable) and long-term (property, plant, and equipment) assets. Activity ratios describe the relationship between the firm's level of operations (usually defined as sales) and the assets needed to sustain the activity.

The higher the ratio, the more efficient the firm's operations, as relatively fewer assets are required to maintain a given level of operations (sales). Monitoring the trends in these ratios over time and in comparison to other firms in the industry can point out potential trouble spots or opportunities. Further, although these ratios do not measure profitability or liquidity directly, they are, ultimately, important factors affecting those performance indicators.

Activity ratios can also be used to forecast a firm's capital requirements (both operating and long term). Increases in sales will require investments in additional assets. Activity ratios enable the analyst to forecast these requirements and to assess the firm's ability to acquire the assets needed to sustain the forecasted growth.

Short-Term (Operating) Activity Ratios

The inventory turnover ratio, defined as

$$\text{Inventory turnover} = \frac{\text{Cost of goods sold}}{\text{Average inventory}}$$

provides an indicator of the efficiency of the firm's inventory management. A higher ratio is an indicator that inventory does not languish in warehouses or on the shelves but rather "turns over" rapidly as it moves quickly from time of acquisition to sale.

The inverse of this ratio can be used to calculate the average number of days inventory is held until it is sold:[8]

$$\text{Average number of days inventory in stock} = \frac{365}{\text{Inventory turnover}}$$

The receivable turnover ratio and the average number of days that receivables are outstanding can be calculated similarly as

$$\text{Receivables turnover} = \frac{\text{Sales}}{\text{Average receivables}}$$

and

$$\text{Average number of days receivables are outstanding} = \frac{365}{\text{Receivable turnover}}$$

---

[8]For manufacturing firms the calculation is not as straightforward. See the discussion in Box 3–1.

These ratios (1) measure the effectiveness of the firm's credit policies and (2) indicate the level of investment in receivables needed to maintain the firm's level of sales.

When computing receivables turnover, care should be taken to include only trade receivables, excluding receivables related to financing and investment activities. Adjustments may also be necessary if the firm has sold receivables during the period.[9]

The working capital turnover ratio, defined as

$$\text{Working capital turnover} = \frac{\text{Sales}}{\text{Average working capital}}$$

is a summary ratio that reflects the amount of working capital needed to maintain a given level of sales. In using this measure, only operating items should be included. Short-term debt, marketable securities, and excess cash should be excluded.

In Chapter 1, it was noted that the going concern assumption is a basic tenet of accrual accounting. To defer the recording of inventory cost until the item is sold and to recognize sales prior to cash collection, we must assume that the inventories will be sold and the receivables will be collected.

Similarly, the ability to use working capital as a proxy for cash flows (and liquidity—see the next section) is contingent upon this assumption. The turnover ratios provide information as to how well this assumption holds up. Lower turnover ratios, indicating longer shelf life for inventory and slower collection of receivables, could be indicators of a cutback in demand for a firm's products or of sales to customers whose ability to pay is uncertain. This might signal one or more of the following:

1. The firm's income is overstated.
2. Future production cutbacks may be required.
3. Potential liquidity problems may exist.

Long-Term (Investment) Activity Ratios

The fixed asset turnover ratio measures the efficiency of (long-term) capital investment. The ratio, defined as

$$\text{Fixed assets turnover} = \frac{\text{Sales}}{\text{Average fixed assets}}$$

reflects the level of sales maintained or generated by investments in productive capacity.

Analysis of this ratio must consider changes in its level over time that can be a function of a number of subtle factors. First, sales growth is continuous, albeit at varying rates. Increases in capacity to meet that sales growth, however, are discrete, depending on the addition of new factories, warehouses, stores, and so forth.

The combination of these factors, as Figure 3-1 shows, results in an erratic turnover ratio. The life cycle of a company or product includes a number of stages: start-up,

[9]See Chapter 10 for a discussion of this issue.

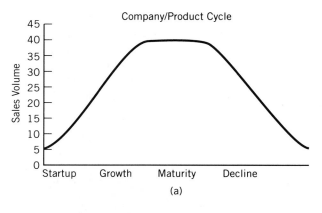

(a)

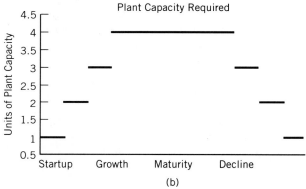

(b)

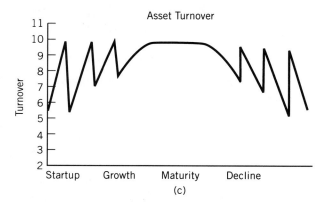

(c)

Asset Turnover Ratio Over Firm Life Cycle

FIGURE 3-1 Asset Turnover and Capacity Requirements

EXHIBIT 3-4. ACTIVITY ANALYSIS
Merck, 1988–1990

	1988	1989	1990
Inventory turnover	2.32	2.16	2.13
# of days	158	169	172
Accounts receivable turnover	5.66	5.72	5.87
# of days	65	64	62
Fixed asset turnover	2.96	3.00	3.06
Total asset turnover	1.01	1.02	1.04

1990 Calculations ($ millions)

$$\text{Inventory turnover} = \frac{\text{COGS}}{\text{Avg inventory}} = \frac{1778}{\frac{1}{2}(780 + 893)} = 2.13$$

$$\text{Average number of days inventory in stock} = \frac{365}{2.13} = 172 \text{ days}$$

$$\text{Accounts receivable turnover} = \frac{\text{Sales}}{\text{Avg A/R}} = \frac{7672}{\frac{1}{2}(1266 + 1346)} = 5.87$$

$$\text{Average number of days receivables outstanding} = \frac{365}{\text{A/R turnover}} = \frac{365}{5.87} = 62 \text{ days}$$

$$\text{Fixed asset turnover} = \frac{\text{Sales}}{\text{Avg fixed assets}} = \frac{7672}{\frac{1}{2}(2293 + 2721)} = 3.06$$

$$\text{Total asset turnover} = \frac{\text{Sales}}{\text{Avg assets}} = \frac{7672}{\frac{1}{2}(6757 + 8030)} = 1.04$$

Comments: Merck is a manufacturing firm. Therefore, the calculation for number of days is an approximation based on the information available in the statements without reference to the footnotes. For 1990, using the breakdown available in the footnotes and calculating the number of days for finished goods inventory separately from the number of days for raw material and work in process resulted in a calculation of 185 days (7% higher). Overall inventory turnover has decreased, whereas the accounts receivable turnover has increased contributing to a relatively stable total asset turnover.

Source: Data from Merck Annual Reports.
*See Appendix 3B for 1989–1990 data.

growth, maturity (steady state), and decline. Start-up companies' initial turnover may be low, as their level of operations is below their productive capacity. As sales grow, however, turnover will improve continually until the limits of the firm's initial capacity are reached. However, the increase in capital investment needed to maintain the growth will then impact unfavorably on that ratio until the firm's growth satisfies the new capacity. This process will continue until the firm matures and its sales and capacity level off, only to reverse when the firm enters its decline stage.

Additional problems can result from the timing of a firm's purchase of assets. Two firms with similar operating efficiencies, having the same productive capacity and the same level of sales, may show differing ratios depending on when their assets were acquired. The firm with the older assets would show a higher turnover ratio, as the accumulated depreciation would tend to lower the carrying value of that firm's assets. Similarly, for any firm, the accumulation of depreciation expense would result in an improving ratio (faster if the firm uses accelerated depreciation methods or short depreciable lives) even if actual efficiency did not change.

An offsetting and complicating factor is that the productivity of assets also depends on their acquisition date. Newer assets, while purchased at higher prices, probably operate more efficiently. The use of gross (before depreciation) rather than net fixed assets would alleviate this shortcoming. However, due to inflation, more recently acquired assets tend to be more expensive and thus distort the comparison of firms with older assets versus those with newer assets. A valuation basis other than historical cost would be needed to make the comparison more meaningful.

An overall activity measure relates sales to total assets:

$$\textbf{Total asset turnover} = \frac{\textbf{Sales}}{\textbf{Average total assets}}$$

This relationship provides a measure of overall investment efficiency by aggregating the joint impact of both short- and long-term assets. An important use of this comprehensive measure will be presented in a subsequent section of this chapter.

Liquidity Analysis

Liquidity analysis is used by short-term lenders such as suppliers and creditors to assess the risk level and ability of a firm to meet its current obligations. Satisfying these obligations requires the use of the cash resources available as of the balance sheet date and the cash to be generated through the operating cycle of the firm.

Figure 3-2 is a schematic representation of the operating cycle of a firm. The firm purchases or manufactures inventory, requiring an outlay of cash and/or the creation of trade payables debt. Sale of inventory generates receivables that, when collected, are used to satisfy the payables, and the cycle is begun again. The ability to repeat this cycle on a continuous basis depends on the firm's short-term cash generating ability and liquidity.

Length of Cash Cycle

One indicator of short-term liquidity uses the activity ratios as a liquidity measure. The inverse of the inventory and accounts receivable (A/R) turnover ratios indicates the number of days it takes until inventory is sold and then the number of days until the receivables (generated by those sales) are converted to cash. Thus, for a *merchandising* firm, the sum of these two numbers indicates the length of the firm's operating cycle, that is, the number of days it takes for inventory to be converted to cash. Schematically, this amount is represented by the circumference of the circle in Figure 3-2. If a firm operates without credit, it also represents the number of days cash is tied up.

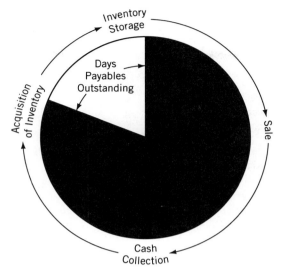

Shaded Area Circumference = Cash Cycle

FIGURE 3-2 Operating and Cash Cycles (Shaded area = cash cycle)

To the extent a firm obtains credit, the length of the cash (operating) cycle is reduced. The inverse of the accounts payable turnover ratio is equal to

$$\text{Average number of days payables outstanding} = \frac{365 \times \text{Average accounts payable}}{\text{Purchases}}$$

reflecting the number of days it takes until the payables are settled.[10]

Subtracting this measure from the time interval it takes to convert inventory to cash represents the firm's cash operating cycle, that is, the number of days a company's cash is tied up by its current operating cycle (the circumference of the shaded portion of the circle in Figure 3-2). This measure captures the interrelationship of sales, collections, and trade credit in a manner that the individual numbers may not. (See Richards and Laughlin (1980) for an extended discussion.)[11]

Exhibit 3-5 presents the components of the cash operating cycle for the W. T. Grant Company in the five years leading up to its bankruptcy. Note that the deterioration of the individual components is not that pronounced. The trend in the overall cash cycle is, however, unmistakable.

[10]Purchases are computed by adding COGS to ending inventory and subtracting opening inventory.

[11]The inverse of the working capital turnover ratio (times 365) is also used sometimes as a crude approximation of the cash cycle.

EXHIBIT 3-5. ANALYSIS OF W. T. GRANT
Operating and Cash Cycle Preceding Bankruptcy

	1970	1971	1972	1973	1974
A. Turnover Ratios					
Inventory	4.6	4.2	4.0	4.2	3.9
Accounts receivable	5.3	5.2	4.9	5.3	5.0
Accounts payable	6.5	6.2	6.2	8.3	10.5
B. Average Number of Days					
Inventory in stock	79	86	90	86	93
Receivables in stock	69	71	74	69	73
Operating cycle	148	157	164	155	166
Payables outstanding	56	59	59	44	35
Cash operating cycle	92	98	105	111	131

Comments: In 1973 the firm's inventory and receivables turnover improved, reducing the length of the operating cycle. However, at the same time, perhaps causing Grant to tighten up, Grant's creditors drastically reduced their credit terms, resulting in an overall longer cash cycle.

Source: Calculated from W. T. Grant's Annual Reports (1970–1974).

For a *manufacturing* firm further refinements and approximations may be necessary to calculate the length of the operating and cash cycle.[12] They are discussed in Box 3-1.

Working Capital Ratios and Defensive Intervals

The concept of working capital relies on the classification of assets and liabilities into "current" and "noncurrent" categories. The traditional definition of current assets and liabilities is based on a maturity of less than one year or (if longer) the operating cycle of the company.

In the typical balance sheet we find five categories of current assets

1. Cash and cash equivalents
2. Marketable securities
3. Accounts receivable
4. Inventories
5. Prepaid expenses

and three categories of current liabilities

1. Short-term debt
2. Accounts payable
3. Accrued liabilities

[12]The refinements are needed only when the activity ratios are viewed in terms of measuring length of time. When the ratio is being used to measure the amount of inventory needed to "support" a given level of sales then the composite measure [COGS/average (total) inventory] is still appropriate.

BOX 3-1
Estimating the Operating and Cash Cycle for a Manufacturing Firm

A merchandising firm holds only one type of inventory—finished goods inventory. Consequently, the inventory turnover ratio need measure only one time stage; the time it takes from when the inventory is bought until it is sold. For a manufacturing firm, on the other hand, inventory can wait through three stages:

1. As raw material, from purchase to beginning of production
2. As work in process, over the length of the production cycle
3. As finished goods, from completion of production until its sale

It is only in the last stage as finished goods that it is comparable to a merchandising firm and the inventory turnover ratio, COGS/average finished goods inventory, can be used to reflect the length of time from when inventory is completed until it is sold.

To arrive at the length of time inventory is in the production cycle (stage 2), the calculation would be

$$365 \times \frac{\text{Average work in process inventory}}{\text{Cost of goods manufactured}}$$

For the length of time it takes for raw material to enter production the calculation is

$$365 \times \frac{\text{Average raw material inventory}}{\text{Raw material used}}$$

The breakdown among finished goods, work in process, and raw materials inventory is available in the notes to financial statements. Cost of goods manufactured can be calculated from financial statements as cost of goods sold + ending (finished goods) inventory − beginning (finished goods) inventory. However, the amount of material used in production is rarely available making the calculation of the length of stage 1 infeasible. Some approximations are possible. The first involves calculating the combined length of stage 1 and 2 as

$$365 \times \frac{\text{Average (work in process and raw material) inventory}}{\text{Cost of goods manufactured}}$$

The accuracy of the approximation depends on the proportion of the various inventories and the degree to which the individual ratios differ. Another (less accurate but perhaps simpler) approximation ignores this whole discussion and uses the composite turnover ratio thereby mirroring the merchandising firm:

$$365 \times \frac{\text{Average (total) inventory}}{\text{Cost of goods sold}}$$

By definition, each current asset and liability has a maturity (the expected date of conversion to cash for an asset; the expected date of liquidation of cash for a liability) of less than one year. However, in practice the line between current and noncurrent has blurred in recent years.

The ratios used in short-term liquidity analysis evaluate the adequacy of the firm's cash resources relative to its cash obligations. Its cash resources can be measured by (1) the firm's current cash balance and potential sources of cash or (2) its (net) cash flows from operations, whereas the firm's cash obligations can be measured by either (1) its current obligations or (2) the cash outflows arising from operations. The following table summarizes the combinations commonly used in measuring the relationship between resources and obligations.

	Numerator Cash Resources	Denominator Cash Obligations
Level	Current assets	Current liabilities
Flow	Cash inflows from operations	Cash outflows from operations

Conceptually, the ratios differ in whether *levels* (amounts shown on the balance sheet) or *flows* (cash inflows and outflows) are used to gauge the relationships.

The first three ratios to be described compare different measures of the present level of cash resources with the present level of obligations. The current ratio uses all current assets to define cash resources: inventory and accounts receivable convert to cash as they move through the operating cycle (see Figure 3-2):

$$\text{Current ratio} = \frac{\text{Current assets}}{\text{Current liabilities}}$$

A more conservative measure of liquidity, the quick ratio, is defined as

$$\text{Quick ratio} = \frac{\text{Cash + Marketable securities + Accounts receivable}}{\text{Current liabilities}}$$

It excludes inventory from cash resources, recognizing that the conversion of inventory to cash is less certain both in terms of timing and amount.[13] The other assets in the numerator are "quick assets" because they can be more quickly converted to cash. Using Figure 3-2, the quick ratio requires an initial movement along the operating cycle toward cash before counting an item as cash.

Finally, the cash ratio, defined as

$$\text{Cash ratio} = \frac{\text{Cash + Marketable securities}}{\text{Current liabilities}}$$

is the most conservative of these measures as it includes only actual cash and cash equivalent balances to measure cash resources.

The use of the current (or quick) ratio implicitly assumes that the current assets will eventually be converted to cash. Realistically, however, it is not anticipated that firms will actually liquidate their current assets to pay down their current liabilities. Certain

---

[13]It should be noted that for actively traded commodities such as oil, metals, or wheat, the inventory balances can be considered very liquid and thus should also be included in the quick ratio for the appropriate industries.

levels of inventories and receivables, as well as payables and accruals (which finance inventories and receivables), are always needed to maintain operations. If all current assets and liabilities are liquidated, then, in effect, the firm has ceased operations. Rather it is assumed, as suggested earlier in our schematic of a firm's operating cycle, that the process of generating inventories, collecting receivables, and so on is ongoing. These ratios therefore measure the "margin of safety" provided by the cash resources relative to obligations.

Liquidity analysis is not independent of activity analysis. Poor receivables or inventory turnover limits the usefulness of the current and quick ratios, as the reported amounts of these components of current assets may not truly represent sources of liquidity. Obsolete inventory or uncollectible receivables are unlikely to be sources of cash. Thus short-term liquidity ratios should be examined in conjunction with turnover ratios.

The cash flow from operations ratio, defined as

$$\frac{\text{Cash flow from}}{\text{operations ratio}} = \frac{\text{Cash flow from operations}}{\text{Current liabilities}}$$

addresses the issues of actual convertibility to cash, turnover, and the need for minimum levels of working capital (cash) to maintain operations by measuring liquidity through a comparison of actual cash flows (instead of current and potential cash resources) with current liabilities.

An important limitation of the preceding analysis of liquidity ratios is the absence of an economic or "real-world" interpretation of those measures. Unlike the cash cycle liquidity measure, which reflects the number of days cash is tied up in the firm's operating cycle, it is difficult to react intuitively to a current ratio of 1.5.

The defensive interval is one tool that provides an intuitive "feel" for a firm's liquidity, albeit a most conservative one. It compares the currently available "quick" sources of cash (cash, marketable securities, and accounts receivable) with the estimated outflows needed to operate the firm: projected expenditures. There are various forms of the defensive interval as well as various methods one can use to arrive at the projected expenditures.[14] We present here only the basic form:

$$\textbf{Defensive interval} = 365 \times \frac{\text{Cash + Marketable securities + Accounts receivable}}{\text{Projected expenditures}}$$

The calculation of the defensive interval for Merck (Exhibit 3-6) uses current year income statement data as the estimate of projected expenditures. This measure is essentially a "worst case" scenario that tells us for how many days the firm could maintain its present level of operations with its present cash resources but without the generation of any additional revenues.

---

[14]Details can be found in Sorter and Benston (1960). The most conservative variation, the "no credit" interval, is the number of days the firm could survive if its trade credit was cut off. In this version, accounts payable are subtracted from the numerator.

EXHIBIT 3-6. LIQUIDITY ANALYSIS
Merck, 1988–1990

	1988	1989	1990
Average number of days of inventory in stock*	158	169	172
+ Receivables outstanding*	65	64	62
Length of operating cycle	222	233	234
− Payables outstanding	209	193	200
Length of cash cycle	13	40	34
Current ratio	1.77	1.79	1.33
Quick ratio	1.35	1.26	0.90
Cash ratio	0.45	0.36	0.29
Cash from operations ratio	0.73	0.72	0.73
Defensive interval in days	243	215	195

1990 Calculations ($ *millions*):

$$\text{Purchases} = \text{COGS} + \text{Change in inventory}$$
$$= 1778 + (893 - 780) \qquad\qquad\qquad = 1891$$

$$\text{Average number of days payable outstanding} = 365 \times \frac{\text{Avg A/P}}{\text{Purchases}} = \frac{\tfrac{1}{2}(937 + 1138)}{1891} = 200$$

$$\text{Current ratio} = \frac{\text{Current Assets}}{\text{Current Liabilities}} = \frac{3767}{2827} = 1.33$$

$$\text{Quick ratio} = \frac{\text{Cash + Marketable Securities + A/R}}{\text{Current Liabilities}} = \frac{806 + 391 + 1346}{2827} = 0.90$$

$$\text{Cash ratio} = \frac{\text{Cash + Marketable Securities}}{\text{Current Liabilities}} = \frac{806 + 391}{2827} = 0.42$$

$$\text{Cash from operations ratio} = \frac{\text{CFO}}{\text{Current Liabilities}} = \frac{2055}{2827} = 0.73$$

$$\text{Defensive interval} =$$
$$365 \times \frac{\text{Cash + Marketable Securities + A/R}}{\text{Projected Expenditures}} = 365 \times \frac{806 + 391 + 1346}{4766} = 195 \text{ days}$$

Comments: Projected expenditures calculated as sum of cost of goods sold, selling and administrative expenses + research and development after subtracting depreciation = 1778 + 2388 + 854 − 254 = 4766. The depreciation amount was obtained directly from Merck's statements and is not provided in the Appendix.

The most striking aspect is the length of time Merck's payables are outstanding. This requires further investigation as to whether Merck actually has over six months to pay its creditors or whether the data (accounts payable) includes other than regular operating amounts, for example, purchases of equipment.

*See Appendix 3B for data. Average number of days of inventory in stock and receivables outstanding were computed in Exhibit 3–4.

Long-Term Debt and Solvency Analysis

The analysis of a firm's capital structure is essential to evaluate its long-term risk and return prospects. Leveraged firms accrue excess returns to their shareholders so long as the rate of return on the investments financed by debt is greater than the cost of debt. The benefits of financial leverage bring additional risks, however, in the form of fixed costs that adversely affect profitability (see next section) if demand declines. Moreover, the priority of interest and debt claims can have a severe negative impact on a firm when adversity strikes. The inability to meet these obligations can lead to default and possibly bankruptcy.

Debt Covenants

To protect themselves, long-term creditors often impose restrictions on the borrowing company's ability to incur additional debt as well as on dividend payments. The debt covenants that control these activities are often expressed in terms of working capital, cumulative profitability, and net worth. It is, therefore, important to monitor the maintenance of various ratios to ensure that their levels are in compliance with the debt covenant specifications. Violations of debt covenants are frequently an "event of default" under loan agreements, making the debt due immediately. When covenants are violated, therefore, borrowers must either repay the debt (not usually possible) or obtain waivers from lenders. Such waivers often require additional collateral, restrictions on firm operations, or higher interest rates.[15]

Capitalization Table and Debt Ratios

A firm's financing is obtained from debt and equity. The greater the proportion of debt relative to equity, the greater the risk to the firm as a whole. Exhibit 3-7 presents capitalization tables taken from the balance sheets of Merck. Two important factors should be noted: (1) the relative debt levels themselves and (2) the trend over time in the proportion of debt to equity.

Debt ratios are expressed either as

$$\text{Debt to total capital} = \frac{\text{Total debt (current and long term)}}{\text{Total capital (debt + equity)}}$$

or, equivalently,

$$\text{Debt to equity} = \frac{\text{Total debt}}{\text{Total equity}}$$

[15]The relationship between debt covenants and ratios is explored in greater detail in Chapter 8.

The definition of short-term debt may or may not include operating (trade) debt (accounts payable and accrued liabilities). The argument for excluding it, and *using only short-term debt financing* (as we do in the capitalization table of Exhibit 3-7), is that operating debt is part of the normal operations of a firm and as such it does not reflect a firm's external financing decisions. It should be noted, however, that many lenders use a definition of debt that includes all liabilities.

EXHIBIT 3-7. LONG-TERM DEBT AND SOLVENCY ANALYSIS
Merck, 1988–1990

	1988	1989	1990
Capitalization Table		($ millions)	
Short-term debt	459	327	793
Long-term debt	143	118	124
Total debt	602	545	917
Common stock	146	153	167
Retained earnings	4580	5394	6387
Treasury stock	(1870)	(2026)	(2719)
Total equity	2856	3521	3834
Total capital	3458	4065	4751
Debt			
to equity	0.21	0.13	0.24
to capital	0.17	0.11	0.19
Debt (including trade)			
to equity	0.67	0.55	0.71
to capital	0.40	0.35	0.42
Times interest earned	25	44	40
Capital expenditure ratio	3.72	3.19	3.06
CFO to debt	2.30	2.53	2.24

1990 Calculations* ($ millions):

$$\text{Debt to equity} = \frac{\text{Debt}}{\text{Equity}} = \frac{917}{3834} = 0.24$$

$$\text{Debt to capital} = \frac{\text{Total debt}}{\text{Total capital}} = \frac{917}{4751} = 0.19$$

Including trade

$$\text{Debt to equity} = \frac{\text{Trade payables} + \text{Debt}}{\text{Total equity}} = \frac{1138 + 679 + 917}{3834} = 0.71$$

EXHIBIT 3-7. *(Continued)*

$$\text{Debt to capital} = \frac{\text{Trade payables} + \text{Debt}}{\text{Total capital}} = \frac{1138 + 679 + 917}{1138 + 679 + 4751} = 0.42$$

$$\text{Times interest earned} = \frac{\text{EBIT}}{\text{Interest}} = \frac{2769}{70} = 40$$

$$\text{Capital expenditure ratio} = \frac{\text{CFO}}{\text{Capital expenditures}} = \frac{2056}{671} = 3.06$$

$$\text{CFO to debt} = \frac{\text{CFO}}{\text{Debt}} = \frac{2056}{917} = 2.24$$

Merck's capital structure is very sound. Its debt ratios are low, and the ratios that monitor its ability to carry the debt (times interest earned, capital expenditure ratio, and CFO to debt) are all comfortably high. Similar to Exhibit 3-6, the only issue that comes up relates to the trade payables. When they are included, the debt ratios are not as attractive.

*See Appendix 3B for data.

The higher the debt ratio, the riskier the firm. As with other ratios, however, industry factors play an important role both in the level of debt as well as the nature of the debt—whether short or long term, variable or fixed, and the relative proportion of different maturities. Capital-intensive industries tend to have high levels of debt needed to finance their property, plant, and equipment. Moreover, the debt should be long term to match the horizon of the assets acquired.

An interesting measurement issue concerns the use of book or market values in the computation of debt ratios. Market values of both debt and equity are available or can readily be estimated, and their use can often make the ratio a more useful analytical tool.

The use of market values may produce contradictory results. A firm that is perceived to be a poor credit risk may have its debt discounted to a market value well below face amount. Depending on how the market values the firm's equity relative to the debt, the resultant ratio may actually show an "acceptable" level of leverage. A useful ratio to use in conjunction with book- or market-based debt ratios is one that compares debt at book value to equity capital measured at market:

Total debt at book value

Equity at market

If the market value of equity is higher than the book value, the foregoing ratio will be lower than the book value measure of the debt-to-equity ratio.[16] This is an indicator that perceptions of the firm's earning power are positive and that conditions are favorable

[16]The analysis assumes that all debt has been included. See Chapter 10 for a discussion of off-balance-sheet financing techniques.

in terms of both the firm's current debt position and/or its ability to raise additional debt. If this ratio, however, is higher than the book value debt-to-equity measure, it could be a signal of deteriorating credit conditions for the firm.

Defining debt or equity is not always straightforward. The existence of leases (whether capitalized or operating), other off-balance-sheet transactions such as contractual obligations not accorded accounting recognition, deferred taxes, financial instruments with debt *and* equity characteristics, and various forms of innovative financing techniques must all be considered when making these calculations. These issues are discussed in Chapters 7, 8 and 10.

Interest Coverage Ratios

The capitalization ratios examine the capital structure of the firm and thereby indirectly the ability to meet current or additional debt obligations. A more direct measure of the ability to meet interest payments is

$$\text{Times interest earned} = \frac{\text{Earnings before interest and taxes (EBIT)}}{\text{Interest expense}}$$

This ratio, often referred to as the "interest coverage ratio," indicates the degree of protection available to creditors by measuring the extent to which earnings available for interest "covers" required interest payments. A more comprehensive measure, the fixed charge coverage ratio, includes all fixed charges arising from a firm's debt commitments:

$$\text{Fixed charge coverage} = \frac{\text{Earnings before fixed charges and taxes}}{\text{Fixed charges}}$$

Fixed charges are defined as contractually committed periodic interest and principal payments on leases as well as funded debt. Variations of these ratios use adjusted operating cash flows—cash from operations (CFO) + interest (fixed charge) payments + tax payments—as the numerator:

$$\text{Times interest earned (cash basis)} = \frac{\text{Adjusted operating cash flow}}{\text{Interest expense}}$$

$$\text{Fixed charge coverage ratio (cash basis)} = \frac{\text{Adjusted operating cash flow}}{\text{Fixed charges}}$$

Capital Expenditure and Cash Flow from Operations-to-Debt Ratios

In addition to servicing debt, internally generated cash flows are also needed for purposes of investment. The interest coverage ratio(s) do not take this aspect into consideration. Cash flow from operations, as noted in Chapter 2, is calculated without any deduction for the cost of operating capacity. Net income, with its provision for depreciation, reflects the use of assets. However, even with minimal inflation rates, over their relatively long service life, replacement costs of these assets tend to be significantly higher, and historical cost depreciation cannot adequately account for their replacement.[17] Neither net income nor cash from operations, of course, makes any provision for the capital required for growth.

A firm's long-term solvency is a function of (1) its ability to finance the replacement and expansion of its investment in productive capacity and (2) the amount of cash left for debt repayment after paying for capital investments.

The capital expenditure ratio

$$\text{Capital expenditure ratio} = \frac{\text{Cash from operations}}{\text{Capital expenditures}}$$

measures the relationship between the firm's cash generating ability and its investment expenditures. To the extent that the ratio exceeds 1, it indicates the amount of money the firm has left for debt after payment for capital expenditures.

The CFO-to-debt[18] ratio

$$\text{CFO to debt} = \frac{\text{CFO}}{\text{Total debt}}$$

similarly provides information as to the amount of principal current CFO can cover. Low CFO-to-debt ratios could signal a long-term solvency problem as the firm is not able to generate enough cash internally to repay its debt.

Profitability Analysis

Stockholders invest in the expectation that the firm will earn profits. Profits are also required to ensure the firm's long-term growth and staying power. A firm's profitability can be measured in several differing but interrelated dimensions. First, there is the relationship of a firm's profits to sales, that is, what is the residual return to the firm per sales dollar? The second type of measure, return on investment (ROI)—quantified as return on total assets (ROA) or return on equity (ROE), relates profits to the investment required to generate them. We briefly define these measures and then elaborate on their use in financial statement analysis.

---

[17]See Chapter 6 and its appendix 6–C for a discussion of these issues.

[18]As with other ratios using debt, the definition of debt can vary whether the focus is short- or long-term debt and whether trade debt is to be included.

Return on Sales

One measure of a firm's profitability is the relationship between the firm's costs and its sales. The greater a firm's ability to control costs in relation to its revenues, the more its earnings power is enhanced. A common-size income statement can provide detailed information as to the ratio of each of the component cost items to sales. In addition, six summary ratios listed next measure the relationship between different measures of profitability and sales.

1. The gross margin captures the relationship between sales and manufacturing costs:

$$\text{Gross margin} = \frac{\text{Gross profit}}{\text{Sales}}$$

2. The operating margin, calculated as

$$\text{Operating margin} = \frac{\text{Operating income}}{\text{Sales}}$$

provides information about a firm's profitability from the operations of its "core" business without regard to
   a. investment policy (e.g., income from affiliates or gains/losses arising from sale of assets)
   b. financing policy (interest expense)
   c. tax position
3. A profit margin measure that is independent of both the firm's financing and tax position is the

$$\frac{\text{Margin before}}{\text{interest and tax}} = \frac{\text{Earnings before interest and tax}}{\text{Sales}}$$

4. The pretax margin is calculated after financing costs (interest) but prior to income taxes:

$$\text{Pretax margin} = \frac{\text{Earnings before tax (EBT)}}{\text{Sales}}$$

5. Finally the overall profit margin is net of all expenses:

$$\text{Profit margin} = \frac{\text{Net income}}{\text{Sales}}$$

These ratios can be computed directly from a firm's financial statements.

6. Another useful profitability measure is the contribution margin ratio, defined as

$$\text{Contribution margin} = \frac{\text{Contribution}}{\text{Sales}}$$

where contribution = sales − variable costs.

The contribution margin ratio, however, cannot be computed directly from a firm's financial statements as information as to the breakdown between fixed and variable costs is not provided therein. It can, however, be estimated as is illustrated in appendix 3–A.

Return on Investment

ROI measures are computed with return measured before financing costs or before both financing and taxes. The first, return on assets (ROA), measures the operating efficiency of the firm without regard to its financial structure. The return is defined as net income prior to the cost of financing and is computed by adding back the (after-tax) interest cost:[19]

$$\text{Return on assets} = \frac{\text{Net income} + \text{After-tax interest cost}}{\text{Average total assets}}$$

A variation of the ROA ratio uses pretax earnings as the return measure, thereby bypassing not only the firm's financing policy but its tax position as well:

$$\frac{\text{Earnings before interest and taxes}}{\text{Average total assets}}$$

It should be noted that the ROA measure is sometimes computed "after interest" as either net income or EBT over assets. Preinterest measures of profitability facilitate the comparison of firms with different degrees of leverage. Using postinterest measures of profit negates this advantage and makes leveraged firms appear less profitable by charging earnings for payments (interest) to some capital providers (lenders) but not others (stockholders). Ratios that use total assets in the denominator should include total earnings (before interest) in the numerator. As interest is tax deductible, interest payments must be tax effected when a posttax measure of profits is used.

The second commonly used ROI measure focuses on the returns accruing to the residual owners of the firm—common shareholders:

$$\text{Return on common equity (ROCE)} = \frac{\text{Net income} - \text{Preferred dividends}}{\text{Average common equity}}$$

[19]The after-tax interest cost is calculated by multiplying the interest cost by $(1 - T)$, where T is the firm's marginal tax rate.

A more general definition of this relationship computes the return on total stockholders' equity:

$$\textbf{Return on (total) equity (ROE)} = \frac{\textbf{Net income}}{\textbf{Average total equity}}$$

The relationship between ROA and ROE can be understood in terms of the firm's relationship to its creditors and shareholders. As reflected in Figure 3-3, the creditors and shareholders provide the capital needed by the firm to acquire the assets needed for the business. In return, they expect to be rewarded with their share in the firm's profits.

The ROA measure can be interpreted in two different ways. First, it is an indicator of management's operating efficiency: how well management is using the assets at its disposal to generate profits. Alternatively, it can be viewed as the total return accruing to the providers of capital, independent of the source of capital.

The ROCE measure reflects returns to the firm's common shareholders and is calculated after deducting the returns paid to the creditors (interest) and other providers of equity capital (preferred shareholders).

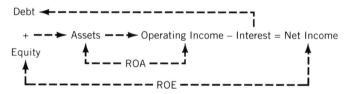

FIGURE 3-3 Relationship of ROA and ROE to Providers of Investment Base

Profitability and Cash Flows

Profitability ratios have traditionally been measured using accrual-based income measures, and this is how we have defined and illustrated them in Exhibit 3-8. Given the emphasis on cash flows in recent years, however, many of the foregoing ratios should also be calculated on a cash flow basis. This would require a cash flow statement calculated by the direct method (at least for the component profitability ratios such as gross margin and operating margin). Empirical evidence exists (see discussion of Gombola and Ketz, 1983, that follows) that indicates that such cash flow–based ratios have different properties from traditional profitability measures.

Operating and Financial Leverage

Profitability ratios, which imply that profits are proportional to sales, in some sense belie the true relationship among costs, sales, and profits. Generally, a doubling of sales would not be expected to result in a doubling of income. This would occur *only* if all expenses were variable. Conceptually, expenses can be classified into variable (*V*) and

EXHIBIT 3-8. PROFITABILITY ANALYSIS
Merck, 1988–1990

	1988	1989	1990
Gross margin	0.74	0.76	0.77
Operating margin	0.31	0.34	0.35
Preinterest and tax margin	0.33	0.36	0.36
Pretax margin	0.32	0.35	0.35
Profit margin	0.20	0.23	0.23
ROA (preinterest)			
After tax	0.21	0.24	0.24
Pretax	0.33	0.36	0.37
ROE			
After tax	0.49	0.47	0.48
Pretax	0.75	0.72	0.73

1990 Calculations* ($ millions)

The return on sales and margin figures can be calculated directly from the common-size statements of Exhibits 3-1 and 3-3.

ROA Preinterest

$$\text{After tax} = \frac{\text{Net income} + [\text{Interest }(1 - \text{Tax rate})]}{\text{Average assets}} = \frac{1781 + [70(1 - 0.34)]}{7394} = 0.24$$

$$\text{Pretax} = \frac{\text{EBIT}}{\text{Average assets}} = \frac{2769}{7394} = 0.37$$

ROE

$$\text{After tax} = \frac{\text{Net income}}{\text{Average equity}} = \frac{1781}{3677} = 0.48$$

$$\text{Pretax} = \frac{\text{EBT}}{\text{Average equity}} = \frac{2699}{3677} = 0.73$$

Note: Average assets = 0.5 × ($6757 million + $8030 million) = $7394 million; average equity = 0.5 × ($3521 million + $3834 million) = $3677 million.

Trends in profit margins were discussed in the section on "Common-Size Statements." Trends in ROA/ROE are discussed in the section covering Exhibits 3-10, 3-12, and 3-13.

*See Appendix 3–B for data.

fixed (F) components. Variable expenses tend to be operating in nature, whereas fixed costs tend to be the result of operating, investing, and financing decisions.[20]

The mix of variable and fixed operating cost components in a firm's cost structure to a large extent reflects the industry in which the firm operates. Fixed investing and financing costs depend upon the asset intensity of the firm's operations and (somewhat related) on the amount of debt financing used by the firm.

A firm's leverage can be defined as the proportion of fixed costs in its overall cost structure, which can be subdivided into two portions: fixed operating costs that reflect operating leverage, that is, the proportion of fixed operating costs to variable costs, and fixed financing costs that impart financial leverage.

The general notion of leverage is one of trading risk for return. Increases in fixed costs are risky because at lower levels of demand, as in recessionary periods, fixed costs must still be met, depressing the firm's income. At higher levels of demand, during periods of growth, the fixed costs are spread over a larger base, thus enhancing profitability. These concepts can be illustrated with the numeric example in Exhibit 3-9.

Operating Leverage. Part A of Exhibit 3-9 illustrates the notion of operating leverage. At sales of 100 (scenario B), Company V and Company F have the identical return on sales of 20% and ROA (= ROE) of 10%. The return on sales is constant for Company V, since its operating costs are completely variable. Changes in net income are directly proportional to changes in demand—a 50% increase in sales to 150 results in a 50% increase in income to 30.

Company F's profitability, on the other hand, varies by more than changes in demand. A 50% change in demand results in a change of 150% in net income. At lower levels of demand, the fixed costs must still be met, thereby reducing the firm's profitability drastically. At higher levels of demand, the fixed costs are spread over a larger volume, greatly increasing the profitability of the firm. Because of the existence of fixed costs, the return on sales does not remain constant with volume.

The trade-off of fixed for variable costs implied by operating leverage is a risk/return trade-off. Capital-intensive firms tend to have high fixed costs due to their investments in plant and equipment. In recessionary times with lower levels of sales volume, these firms tend to fare worse. In expansionary times, on the other hand, when sales volume increases, these firms do very well.

The contribution margin ratio is a useful measure in assessing the effects of operating leverage on the firm's profitability. It can be restated as

$$\frac{\text{Contribution}}{\text{margin ratio}} = \frac{\text{Contribution}}{\text{Sales}} = 1 - \frac{\text{Variable costs}}{\text{Sales}}$$

This ratio indicates the *incremental profit resulting from a given dollar change of sales*. For Company V, this ratio is 20% (1 − 80%), and for Company F it is 60% (1 −

---

[20]Recent changes in financial markets have created investing and financing transactions with variable payment streams, that is, lease payments tied to revenues and adjustable rate loans. These payments may have both variable and fixed components.

EXHIBIT 3-9
Illustration of Operating, Financial, and Total Leverage Effects

General Assumptions

	Company V	Company F
Fixed costs	$ 0	$ 40
Variable costs/sales	80%	40%
Assets	$200	$200

A. Assume 0% Financing, Debt $0, Equity $200

	No Leverage Company V			Operating Leverage Company F		
Scenario	A	B	C	A	B	C
Sales	$50	$100	$150	$50	$100	$150
Variable cost	40	80	120	20	40	60
Contribution	$10	$ 20	$ 30	$30	$ 60	$ 90
Fixed cost	0	0	0	40	40	40
Operating income	$10	$ 20	$ 30	($10)	$ 20	$ 50
Return						
On sales	20%	20%	20%	(20%)	20%	33%
On assets	5%	10%	15%	(5%)	10%	25%
On equity	5%	10%	15%	(5%)	10%	25%

B. Assume 50% Financing, Debt 100, Equity 100, Interest rate = 5%

	Financial Leverage Company V			Total Leverage Company F		
Scenario	A	B	C	A	B	C
Operating income	$10	$ 20	$ 30	($10)	$ 20	$ 50
Interest	5	5	5	5	5	5
Net income	$ 5	$ 15	$ 25	($15)	$ 15	$ 45
Return						
On assets	5%	10%	15%	(5%)	10%	25%
On equity	5%	15%	25%	(15%)	15%	45%

40%). Thus, for Company V (Company F), a change of $50 in sales results in a change of 20% × 50 = $10 (60% × 50 = $30) in profit.

The operating leverage effect (OLE) can then be defined as

$$\text{OLE} = \frac{\text{Contribution margin ratio}}{\text{Return on sales}} = \frac{\text{Contribution}}{\text{Operating income}}$$

and is the relative proportion of contribution margin to operating income. The OLE can be used to estimate *the percentage change in income and ROA for a given percentage change in sales volume:*

% Change in income (ROA) = OLE × % Change in sales

When OLE is greater than 1, operating leverage exists. It should be noted that this measure of operating leverage[21] is not constant across all levels of activity. Rather, the *OLE is a relative measure and varies with the level of sales.*

For Company V, the OLE is equal to 1, across all scenarios, because its costs are completely variable. Thus, for Company V, a given percentage change in sales results in equivalent percentage changes in income and ROA.

For Company F, however, the OLE varies: it is equal to 3 (60%/20%) for scenario B. A 50% change in sales (to scenario A or scenario C) will result in a threefold percentage change (3 × 50% = 150%) in income and ROA.

Using scenario C as the base starting point, however, results in an OLE measure of 1.8 (60%/33%). A 33% drop in sales from scenario C to scenario B (150 to 100) results in a 60% (1.8 × 33%) drop in income (50 to 20) and ROA.[22]

Financial Leverage. It is also possible to measure the effects of financial leverage. From the point of view of the common shareholders, financial leverage is, like operating leverage, a risk and return trade-off. The financial leverage trade-off is one of taking on the risk of fixed financing costs anticipating that higher returns will accrue to the common shareholders at higher levels of demand. In part B we assume that each company is 50% financed by debt and that interest costs = 5 (5% interest rate).

Focusing on Company V first (which has no operating leverage), changes in net income are now proportionally higher than changes in demand; changes of 50% in volume are accompanied by changes of 67% in profit and ROE. (Note that ROA, because it is computed *before* interest expense, is unaffected by the existence of financial leverage.)

The financial leverage effect (FLE) is measured by relating operating income to net income:

$$\text{FLE} = \frac{\text{Operating income}}{\text{Net income}}$$

---

[21]Similarly, the measure for financial leverage discussed shortly is also variable, dependent on the starting point.

[22]In all cases, ROE is identical to ROA, as we have assumed no financing in panel A.

The FLE for Company V is (at scenario B) $20/15 = 1.33$. Thus a 50% shift in sales (and operating income) results in a 67% ($1.333 \times 50\%$) shift in income and ROE (from 15 to 25).

For Company F, the changes in income relative to the change in demand are even higher. Here, the effects of both operating and financial leverage work together, giving a total leverage effect (TLE) equal to the product of the individual leverage effects:

$$\text{TLE} = \text{OLE} \times \text{FLE} = \frac{\text{Contribution}}{\text{Net income}}$$

$$\text{TLE} = 3 \times 1.333 = 4$$

For Company F, the 50% change in sales (from 100 to 150) results in a 200% ($4 \times 50\%$) change in income and ROE (from 15 to 45). This suggests that firms with high operating leverage take on high financial leverage only at their peril. Traditionally, high debt ratios have been considered acceptable only for firms with low operating leverage or with stable operations (such as public utilities), where the risk of combining operating and financial leverage was minimal. In recent years, however, financial leverage has been applied to companies with high operating leverage as well (airlines, for example), resulting in financial distress or even bankruptcy during periods of economic adversity.[23]

RATIOS: AN INTEGRATED ANALYSIS

The ratios surveyed in this chapter are used to measure such diverse aspects of an enterprise's performance as its liquidity, solvency, profitability, and efficiency of operations (activity ratios). The preceding discussion of ratios has focused on their individual characteristics. Comprehensive analysis requires a review of the interrelationships among ratios, resulting from the following factors:

1. *Economic relationships:* The underlying economics of a firm result in elements of the financial statements moving in tandem. For example, higher sales are generally associated with higher investment in working capital components such as receivables and inventory. Ratios comprising these various elements would be correlated.

2. *Overlap of components:* A cursory examination of the ratios examined indicates that the components of many ratios overlap. This overlap may result from ratios containing an identical term in the numerator or denominator or because a term in one ratio is a subset of a component of another ratio.[24]

[23]The growth in off-balance-sheet financing can be partly explained by the desire by firms to report lower levels of operating and financial leverage. By reflecting leased assets under operating leases, for example, firms report rental expense only and avoid the recognition of debt and related interest costs. Thus it is important to adjust all ratios for operating leases and other forms of off-balance-sheet financing (see Chapters 8 and 10).

[24]An example of the first type is the appearance of sales in various activity ratios and profitability ratios. Examples of the second type are cash being a part of quick assets, which in turn are a part of current assets, and so on.

In a similar vein, the total assets turnover ratio is essentially a (weighted) aggregation of the individual turnover ratios. Ratios that aggregate other ratios can be expected to follow patterns over time similar to those of their components.

3. *Ratios as composites of other ratios:* Some ratios are related to other ratios across categories. For example, the return on assets ratio is a combination of a profitability and turnover ratio:

$$\frac{\text{Income}}{\text{Assets}} = \frac{\text{Income}}{\text{Sales}} \times \frac{\text{Sales}}{\text{Assets}}$$

Changes in either of the ratios on the right-hand side will affect return on assets as well.

The interrelationships among ratios have important implications for financial analysis. On the one hand, disaggregation of a ratio into its component elements allows us to gain insight into factors affecting a firm's performance. Further, ratio differences can highlight the economic characteristics and strategies of

- Firms in the same industry
- The same firm over time
- Firms in different industries

On the other hand, the relationships between ratios imply that one might be able to "ignore" some component ratios and use a composite or representative ratio to capture the information contained in other ratios. For example, in the ROA relationship earlier, the effect of the two ratios on the right side of the equation may be captured by the ROA ratio. For certain analytic purposes, this composite return on assets ratio may suffice.

Analysis of Firm Performance

This section will exploit some of the interrelationships to analyze a firm's performance by focusing on disaggregations of the overall profitability measures ROA and ROE.

Disaggregation of ROA

The return on assets ratio can be disaggregated as follows:

$$\text{ROA} = \text{Total asset turnover} \times \text{Return on sales}$$

$$= \frac{\text{Sales}}{\text{Assets}} \times \frac{\text{EBIT}}{\text{Sales}}$$

This disaggregation of ROA indicates that the firm's overall profitability is the product of an activity ratio and a profitability ratio. A low ROA, for example, can thus reflect either low turnover, indicating poor asset management, or low profit margins even when turnover is high. A combination of both is also possible.

EXHIBIT 3-10. DISAGGREGATION OF PRETAX ROA AND ROE
Merck, 1986–1990

	A. Return on Assets				B. Return on Equity		
	$\dfrac{\text{Profit}}{\text{Margin}}$ ×	$\dfrac{\text{Asset}}{\text{Turnover}}$ =	ROA		$\dfrac{\text{Return}}{\text{on Assets}}$ ×	Leverage =	ROE
	$\dfrac{\text{EBIT}}{\text{Sales}}$ ×	$\dfrac{\text{Sales}}{\text{Average total assets}}$ =	$\dfrac{\text{EBIT}}{\text{Average total assets}}$ −	$\dfrac{\text{Interest expense}}{\text{Average total assets}}$ =	$\dfrac{\text{EBT}}{\text{Average total assets}}$ ×	$\dfrac{\text{Average total assets}}{\text{Average common equity}}$ =	$\dfrac{\text{EBT}}{\text{Average common equity}}$
1986	27.08% ×	0.83	= 22.34% −	0.89%	= 21.45% ×	1.94	= 41.69%
1987	28.80% ×	0.94	= 27.10% −	1.05%	= 26.05% ×	2.32	= 60.34%
1988	32.79% ×	1.01	= 32.99% −	1.30%	= 31.69% ×	2.37	= 75.19%
1989	35.66% ×	1.02	= 36.26% −	0.82%	= 35.44% ×	2.02	= 71.60%
1990	36.08% ×	1.04	= 37.44% −	0.94%	= 36.50% ×	2.01	= 73.36%

Note: Numbers have been rounded.

The disaggregation can lead to analysis of a firm's performance (over time or with respect to that of other firms) in a hierarchical fashion. Changes or differences in ROA can be traced first to changes in activity and/or profitability. Such an analysis is presented in Exhibit 3-10 for Merck for the period 1986–1990. Note that profitability is measured by earnings before interest and taxes (EBIT). The use of EBIT rather than net income has the advantage of showing trends independent of the capital structure of the firm.

The analysis shows that the improvement in Merck's ROA resulted from gains in both asset turnover (activity) and profitability. Asset turnover rose by approximately one quarter (from 0.83 to 1.04), while profitability increased by approximately one-third (from 27% to 36%). These two effects compounded, resulting in an increase in ROA of 75% (from 22% to 37%) over the five-year period.

This analysis can be refined further by examining individual turnover ratios (Exhibit 3-4) and the elements of profitability (Exhibit 3-8). Exhibit 3-11 provides an overall summary of this hierarchical analysis.

Disaggregation of ROE and Its Relationship to ROA

The next logical step involves a detailed examination of the return on equity. From the perspective of equity analysis, net income is the measure of profitability, as only the residual (after interest expense, income taxes, etc.) belongs to the common stockholder.

Exhibit 3-9 suggests a characterization of the ROA and ROE relationship. Focusing on Company V, we find that at low levels of volume (scenario A) when ROA is equal to the 5% cost of debt, there are no benefits from financial leverage. However, as volume increases and ROA is greater than the cost of debt, then the excess return accrues to the

**EXHIBIT 3-11. DISAGGREGATION OF ROA INTO
BASIC COMPONENTS
Merck & Co.**

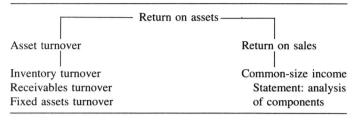

common shareholders. The relationship of ROE and ROA is thus a function of the proportion of debt used for financing and the relationship of the cost of that debt to the ROA. This can be formally expressed as

$$\text{ROE} = \text{ROA} + \left[(\text{ROA} - \text{Cost of debt}) \times \frac{\text{Debt}}{\text{Equity}} \right]$$

In effect, the benefits of financial leverage are a product of the excess returns earned on the firm's assets over the cost of debt[25] and the proportion of debt financing to equity financing. If there are no excess returns (i.e., ROA < cost of debt), then ROE will be less than ROA.

The relationship between ROA and ROE may also be expressed as

$$\text{ROE} = \left(\text{ROA} - \frac{\text{Interest cost}}{\text{Assets}} \right) \times \frac{\text{Assets}}{\text{Equity}}$$

Exhibit 3-10 (parts A and B) illustrates the ROA and ROE relationship on a pretax basis. Note that it is merely an extension of the ROA calculation deducting the interest component and multiplying by the assets/equity ratio.

The assets/equity ratio is a capital structure/financial leverage ratio indicating the degree to which assets are internally financed. The larger the ratio the more outside financing. It is equal[26] to 1 plus the debt/equity ratio where debt is defined as total liabilities. Thus, when we recall the categories making up the ROA ratio, the ROE relationship[27] can be shown to be a function of three of the four categories discussed. That is,

$$\text{ROE} = \text{Profitability ratio} \times \text{Activity ratio} \times \text{Solvency ratio}$$

$$= \frac{\text{Income}}{\text{Sales}} \times \frac{\text{Sales}}{\text{Assets}} \times \frac{\text{Assets}}{\text{Equity}}$$

[25]This relationship is, of course, just another manifestation of the financial leverage effect defined earlier as operating income/net income, where net income = operating income − interest costs.

[26]Recall that assets = liabilities (debt) + equity.

Exhibit 3-12 (part A) provides an analysis of Merck's ROE in terms of these three components for the years 1986–1990. An expanded hierarchical analysis can be carried out by examining the individual components (from Exhibits 3-4, 3-7, and 3-8) making up these categories. Exhibit 3-13 provides this hierarchical analysis of Merck's ROE for the years 1988–1990.

The analysis of the components of ROE, which is frequently known as the "duPont model," enables the analyst to discern the contribution of different factors to the change in ROE.

Looking at Exhibit 3-12, we can see that two of three components of ROE largely accounted for the increase in ROE. These are the same two components (profitability and asset turnover) that accounted for the increase in ROA; the only difference is that now we are looking at ROA on a postinterest and tax basis.

The third component, the ratio of assets to equity, showed only a nominal gain over the full 1986–1990 period, although it fluctuated during the period itself. Merck remained a relatively unleveraged company, despite large repurchases of its own shares.

While the three-component model shown is the standard duPont model, it can be developed further. In many cases it is worthwhile to look at the effect of interest payments or tax payments. To do so we must disaggregate the profitability ratio further as follows:[28]

$$\frac{\text{Net income}}{\text{EBT}} \times \frac{\text{EBT}}{\text{EBIT}} \times \frac{\text{EBIT}}{\text{Sales}} = \frac{\text{Net income}}{\text{Sales}}$$

yielding a five-way breakdown of ROE. This decomposition is presented in Exhibit 3-12 (part B) allowing the analyst to view the income tax burden (element one is 1 minus the tax rate) separately from the interest burden [element 2, which shows the percentage of

---

[27]A variation of the formulation for ROE is suggested by Selling and Stickney (1990). They disaggregate ROE as follows:

$$\text{ROE} = \text{ROA} \times \frac{\text{Assets}}{\text{Equity}} \times \frac{\text{Net income}}{\text{Operating income}}$$

The relationships to the right of the ROA term are clearly financial leverage ratios. The assets/equity ratio (the capital structure leverage) discussed earlier will always be greater than 1. Being greater than 1, the effect of the capital structure leverage is to increase ROE relative to ROA. The ratio of net income to operating income (the common earnings leverage), on the other hand, is equivalent to the inverse of the financial leverage effect defined earlier and will always be less than 1, tending to drive ROE below ROA. Whether ROE is greater or less than ROA depends on whether the effects of the capital structure leverage outweigh those of the common earnings leverage; do the returns from all the assets that accrue to the (common) shareholders (as reflected by the capital structure leverage) outweigh the cost of obtaining the outside financing (the common earnings leverage)?

[28]See, for example, Zvi Bodie, Alex Kane and Alan J. Marcus, *Investments* (Homewood, Ill.: Richard D. Irwin, 1989).

**EXHIBIT 3-12. DISAGGREGATION OF RETURN ON EQUITY (AFTER TAX)
Merck, 1986–1990**

A. Three-Component Disaggregation of ROE

	(Profitability	×	Turnover)			× Solvency =	ROE
	$\dfrac{\text{Net Income}}{\text{Sales}}$	×	$\dfrac{\text{Sales}}{\text{Average Total Assets}}$	=	$\dfrac{\text{Net Income}}{\text{Average Total Assets}}$	× $\dfrac{\text{Average Total Assets}}{\text{Average Common Equity}}$ =	$\dfrac{\text{Net Income}}{\text{Average Common Equity}}$
1986	16.37%	×	0.83	=	13.50%	× 1.94 =	26.25%
1987	17.91%	×	0.94	=	16.81%	× 2.32 =	38.92%
1988	20.32%	×	1.01	=	20.44%	× 2.37 =	48.54%
1989	22.83%	×	1.02	=	23.21%	× 2.02 =	46.90%
1990	23.22%	×	1.04	=	24.09%	× 2.01 =	48.44%

B. Five-Component Disaggregation of ROE

	(Profitability				×	Turnover)			× Solvency =	ROE
Effects of:	Taxes	Financing	Operations							
	$\dfrac{\text{Income}}{\text{EBT}}$	× $\dfrac{\text{EBT}}{\text{EBIT}}$	× $\dfrac{\text{EBIT}}{\text{Sales}}$	= $\dfrac{\text{Income}}{\text{Sales}}$	×	$\dfrac{\text{Sales}}{\text{Average Total Assets}}$	=	$\dfrac{\text{Net Income}}{\text{Average Total Assets}}$	× $\dfrac{\text{Average Total Assets}}{\text{Average Common Equity}}$ =	$\dfrac{\text{Net Income}}{\text{Average Common Equity}}$
1986	0.63 ×	0.96 ×	27.08% =	16.37% ×		0.83	=	13.50%	× 1.94 =	26.25%
1987	0.65 ×	0.96 ×	28.80% =	17.91% ×		0.94	=	16.81%	× 2.32 =	38.92%
1988	0.65 ×	0.96 ×	32.79% =	20.32% ×		1.01	=	20.44%	× 2.37 =	48.54%
1989	0.64 ×	1.00 ×	35.66% =	22.83% ×		1.02	=	23.21%	× 2.02 =	46.90%
1990	0.66 ×	0.97 ×	36.08% =	23.22% ×		1.04	=	24.09%	× 2.01 =	48.44%

EBIT that is (not) "lost" to debtholders] and each separately from operating profitability (EBIT/sales). While this analysis is not insightful for Merck, it is more helpful for highly leveraged firms or firms whose leverage or tax position is changing.

Economic Characteristics and Strategies

Competing Strategies

Firms (and industries) can often be differentiated by whether they employ a high-turnover/low-margin strategy or a low-turnover/high-margin strategy to generate profits. The high-turnover/low-margin firm operates by charging low prices to sell large

EXHIBIT 3-13. DISAGGREGATION OF ROE INTO BASIC COMPONENTS
Merck, 1988–1990

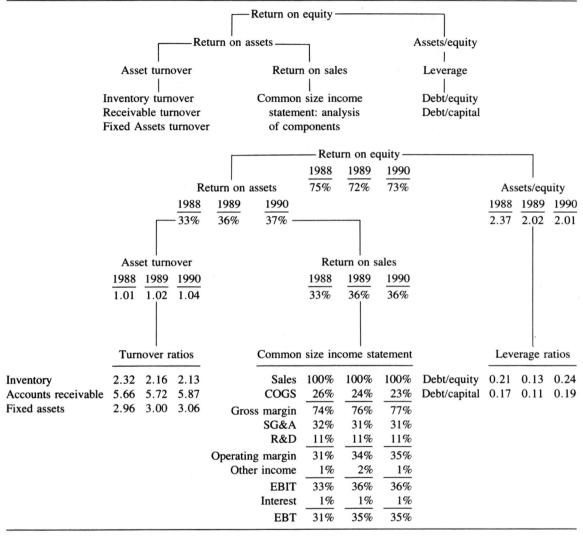

Note: Numbers have been rounded and may not agree with other Exhibits.

volumes of its product.[29] The low price results in a lower profit margin; to be successful, the firm must carefully control costs to ensure that profit margins do not get too low. This requires tight controls over both costs and investment as the firm strives to be a low-cost producer. The supermarket industry generally follows this strategy.

The low-turnover/high-margin firm, on the other hand, competes on a product differentiation basis. It attempts to make the product desirable to the consumer on the basis of attributes other than price. If successful, the firm is able to charge a (relatively) higher price and thus is profitable on the basis of its higher profit margin. Cost control is not as important as costs can generally be passed on to the customer through higher prices. Specialty (gourmet) food shops would follow this strategy by offering goods and service not generally available from supermarkets.

Product Life Cycle

The four stages of the product life cycle, a well-known concept in marketing research, can be used to forecast and understand changes over time in a firm's financial performance as it passes through various stages in the cycle. Figure 3-1 and our discussion of asset turnover ratios is one example of such an analysis.

Savich and Thompson (1978) present a breakdown, reproduced as Exhibit 3-14, of the impact of product cycle stages on balance sheet, income statement, and funds flow components.

Moving through the cycle we would expect to see the following pattern of ratios at the various stages:

1. *Start-up*
   a. High short-term activity ratios but low liquidity ratios. The explanation of this seemingly contradictory result is that, at the early stages, a firm's inventory levels as well as receivables are low. The company is cash "hungry" and cannot build these elements of working capital.
   b. Profits and cash from operations are very low (or even negative). Thus all ratios—profitability, solvency, and liquidity—with these numbers in the numerator will tend to be poor.
   c. Debt (both short and long term) will be high.

2. *Growth*
   a. Profits will start to grow, but CFO will lag behind as cash receipts will be based on past levels of sales, whereas disbursements will be geared toward higher future sales levels. Thus ratios based on income will tend to improve ahead of those based on cash flows.
   b. Investment in capacity will also rise, causing long-term activity (turnover) ratios to be low. At the same time, profit margins will not have reached their optimum

[29]Much of the discussion in this section is based on Selling, Thomas and Clyde Stickney, "The Effects of Business Environment and Strategy on a Firm's Rate of Return on Assets", Financial Analysts Journal (January-February 1989), pp. 43–52.

EXHIBIT 3-14
Characteristics of Product Life Cycle

| | A. Balance Sheet | | | |
	Start-up	Growth	Maturity	Harvest
Current Assets				
Cash	Starved	Hungry	Rich	Fair
Marketable securities	None	None	Use for idle cash	High
Accounts receivable	None	Factored-assigned	Stable	Collected before
Inventory	Low	Rising	Average	Declining
Property, Plant, and Equipment	Starting	Rising	Stable	Declining
Intangibles	Building	Stable	Write off	Written off
Current Liabilities				
Accounts payable	High	Stretched	Constant	Supplies like cash
Taxes payable	None	None due to carry-forwards	Level	High
Long-Term Liabilities	High	Moderate	Available	Pay off
Deferred Liabilities				
Taxes	Receivables due to net operating loss	Offset by carry-forwards	Delayed by accelerated depreciation	High payoff
Compensation	Offered	Taken	Used	Refused
Stockholders' Equity				
Common Stock	Low	Public offering	Used for options	Only leverage
Retained earnings	Deficit	Reinvested	Stable	Paid out
	B. Income Statement			
Sales	Low but rising	Rising fast	Level	Declining
Cost of Goods Sold				
Direct material	Lots of scrap	Rising	Search for efficiencies	Tied to sales
Direct labor	High per unit	Learning curve benefit	Dependent on union negotiations	Reduced considerably
Overhead Depreciation	High due to accelerated depreciation	Rising due to acquisitions	Stable	Low

EXHIBIT 3-14. *(Continued)*

	Start-up	*Growth*	*Maturity*	*Harvest*
Indirect labor	Minimal	Growing with labor force	Stable	Redirected
Taxes, property	Minimal	Growing with equipment	Depend on mill levy	Down
Utilities	Related to R&D	Growing with equipment	Stable	Reduced
Gross Profit	Fluctuating	% established	Smooth	Market bearing
Expenses Sales Compensation	Variable	Individual rewards	Group rewards	Fixed
Advertising	High	Rising	Stable	None
Travel and entertainment	Very high	Grows with sales force	Reduced	None
Market research	Very high	Leveling	Seek new markets	Accept defeat
General and administrative Salaries	Division management	Expanding with work force	Administrative	Reduced
Depreciation	Minimal	Growing with furniture	Stable	None
Research and development	Very high	Production oriented	Cost-reduction oriented	Look for new products
Income taxes	Negative	Rising	Stable	Declining
Distribution costs	Looking	Rising	Stable	Cut back
Accounting and information	Start-up costs	Formalizing	Stable	Looking for benefits
Insurance	Minimal	High	Constant and business interruption	Unnecessary
Earnings	Lowest	Good	Highest	Below average
Earnings per Share	Lowest	Average	Highest	Average

EXHIBIT 3-14. *(Continued)*

C. Funds Flow Analysis

Sources of Funds				
Net income	Low	Good	High	Declining
Long-term debt	High	Moderate	Capacity high but no new debt	None
Stock financing	Hesitant market	Lots of buyers	Looking for dividends	Sell out
Sales of property, plant, and equipment	None	None	Replacement	Extensive
Use of Funds				
Purchase of property, plant, and equipment	Mainly prototype	High	Replacement	None
Dividends	None	Little if any	Good	Extensive
Repayment of debt	None	None	High	Remainder
Treasury stock	None	None	For options	At deflated prices
Change in Cash	Negative	Not too bad	None	Very positive

Source: Savich, Richard S. and Laurence A. Thompson, "Resource Allocation within the Product Life Cycle," *MSU Business Topics* (Autumn 1978), pp. 35–44, Exhibit 2, p. 38; Exhibit 3, p. 39; Exhibit 4, p. 40.

as the expansion in productive capacity will not allow the full impact of operating leverage to take effect; the fixed costs incurred by the company will be high relative to the sales level. ROA, as a result, will tend to be low. Debt ratios will still be high. At the late stages of the company's growth, the ratios will tend to move toward the pattern realized in the maturity stage.

3. Maturity and 4. Decline (Harvest)

a. The firm will reach its long-run normal operating levels, as ratios will tend to move toward expected industry norms. Profit margins and turnover ratios will be high. Debt will be reduced relative to equity as more funds will be internally generated. Furthermore, these funds will not be needed for expansion. Liquidity will be high as CFO will have "caught" up to profits.

b. To some extent, as the firm begins the decline (harvest) stage, cash flows will lead profitability as cash flows resulting from past investments tend to be positive. Moreover, with a reduction in the asset base ROA measures may be at their highest as the firm first enters this last stage.

The product life cycle concept, although providing some useful insights, should not be overrated. The concept is primarily product based. Firms that survive build a portfolio

EXHIBIT 3-15
Illustration of Product Life Cycle

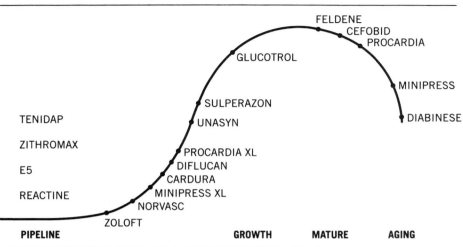

Source: Pfizer Inc. Annual Report, 1990, cover.

of products, continually introducing new ones. Thus, at any one time, a firm will most likely have products at each stage of the cycle. Defining the firm's "stage" depends on where the preponderance of its products are. Exhibit 3-15, from the cover of Pfizer's *1990 Annual Report,* provides a good illustration of this concept.

Interindustry Economic Factors

The earlier discussion of Exhibit 3-2 in the section on common-size statements, has demonstrated that interindustry economic differences and characteristics can be determined by examination of "industry norm" ratios.

The fact that industries differ by ROA, activity ratios, and profit margins is well known and documented. In comparing the means of 58 ratios for two broad-based industry classifications, manufacturing versus retail firms, Gombola and Ketz (1983) note that

> All of the income measures expressed as a percentage of sales are much smaller for retail firms than manufacturing firms. All of the turnover ratios show much higher values for retail firms than for manufacturing firms. Retail firms also tend to show less cash and fewer receivables than manufacturing firms as well as somewhat more debt than manufacturing firms.[30]

Selling and Stickney examined the ROAs for 22 industries over the period 1977–1986 as well as the components that make up ROA. Their results are reproduced in

---

[30]Gombola, Michael J. and J. Edward Ketz, "Financial Ratio Patterns in Retail and Manufacturing Organizations," *Financial Management* (Summer 1983), pp. 45–56.

Exhibit 3-16 and are plotted in Figure 3-4. The authors noted that an infinite number of different combinations of turnover and return on sales could result in the same overall ROA number (represented by the solid lines in Figure 3-4). For example, rubber manufacturers and grocery stores both have ROAs of 6.6%. Their turnover ratios and profit margins, however, differ significantly as noted by the different locations along the turnover and profit margin axes of Figure 3-4.

These differences, the authors note, can be explained first by the distinction between capital-intensive and noncapital-intensive industries. Capital-intensive industries tend to have low asset turnover and higher fixed costs. As a result, profit margins can fluctuate greatly due to the effects of operating leverage.

The microeconomic literature classifies firms' operating environments as ranging from monopolistic at one extreme to pure competition at the other. Monopolistic industries are characterized by high barriers to entry, high capital intensiveness, and relatively high profit margins. The capital intensity results in low turnover ratios and "excess" profits. In addition the barriers to entry, whether a result of regulation,

EXHIBIT 3-16
Distributions of ROA, Profit Margin, and Asset Turnover, Selected Industries

	ROA	Profit Margin	Asset Turnover
Publishing	11.5	8.7	1.41
Chemicals	9.0	7.0	1.40
Food processors	8.5	4.3	2.28
Paper	8.3	6.9	1.29
Metal products	7.8	5.3	1.53
Department stores	7.7	3.6	2.27
Telecommunications	7.0	16.1	0.49
Petroleum	6.9	5.3	1.47
Glass	6.8	6.3	1.07
Rubber	6.6	4.0	1.66
Grocery stores	6.6	1.5	5.00
Transportation equipment	6.4	4.0	1.69
Wholesale equipment	6.4	2.8	1.93
Engineering/architecture	6.4	4.1	1.89
Real estate	6.3	12.1	0.75
Apparel	6.3	3.4	1.80
Industrial equipment	5.6	3.8	1.38
Trucking	5.6	3.5	1.80
Textiles	5.3	3.1	1.64
Oil exploration	5.1	8.1	0.47
Lumber	5.1	3.1	2.10
Steel	4.0	3.3	1.25

Source: Selling, Thomas and Clyde Stickney, "The Effects of Business Environment and Strategy on a Firm's Rate of Return on Assets", *Financial Analysts Journal* (January–February 1989), pp. 43–52, Table IV, p. 51 (Adapted).

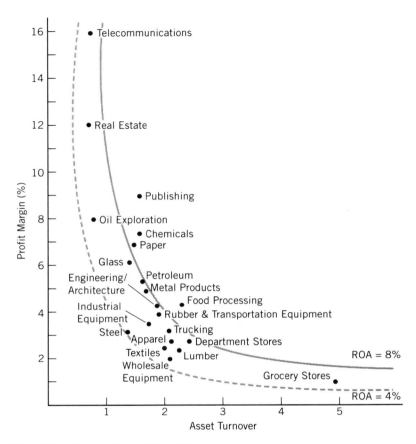

FIGURE 3-4 ROAs of Sample Firms, 1977–1986.
Source: Selling, Thomas and Clyde Stickney, "The Effects of Business Environment and Strategy on a Firm's Rate of Return on Assets," *Financial Analysts Journal* (January–February 1989), pp. 43–52, Figure 1, p. 48.

technology, or capital requirements, also give rise to "monopoly" profits. Pure competition, on the other hand, is characterized by low barriers to entry, low levels of capital intensity, and correspondingly low profit margins. Products are commoditylike in nature and do not lend themselves to product differentiation. Companies in these industries attempt to generate higher returns on the basis of increased efficiency and turnover.

Oligopolistic or multifirm industries, finally, have turnovers and profit margins characterized at the midpoint of the continuum. Selling and Stickney summarize the argument with the following table:

Capital Intensity	Nature of Competition	Strategies
High	Monopoly	High profit margin
Medium	Oligopolistic	Combination of profit margin and turnover
Low	Pure competition	High turnover

Source: Selling, Thomas and Clyde Stickney, "The Effects of Business Environment and Strategy on a Firm's Rate of Return on Assets," *Financial Analysts Journal* (January–February 1989), pp. 43–52, Table II, p. 47 (Adapted).

Classification and Partitioning of Ratios

The ratios provided in this chapter are by no means exhaustive, and a full list of the ratios available (and used) across these various categories would include close to 100 different ratios. One possible reason for the proliferation of ratios is that ratio analysis is used not only in (external) financial analysis but also as a tool in internal management analysis and evaluation.

Ratios designed for managerial analysis may not necessarily add any information to those already used for financial analysis as the needs of these users are not the same. Management may need detailed information about aspects of the firm to pinpoint and remedy specific "problem" areas. The financial analyst's needs, however, are more general and thus may be satisfied with a ratio that captures the effects of other ratios or is highly correlated with other ratios. Unfortunately, once a ratio is developed for one purpose, it tends to be used in ways never intended. Ratio analysis is an area where more may not necessarily be better.

Empirical work on ratios has generally progressed on two fronts. The first, which is the focus of this section, is descriptive: to examine the properties of and correlations among the ratios available in an attempt to find a manageable set of ratios suitable for analytic purposes. Finding such a parsimonious set can be very beneficial for financial analysis as it reduces the number of ratios that must be computed and monitored. The reduced set can be used for decision making directly (second approach that follows) or can act as a signal that would trigger further detailed analysis.

Building on these results (explicitly or implicitly), the second approach (described in Chapter 14) uses ratios as inputs in specific predictive models of risk in such areas as bankruptcy, bond ratings, and beta.

Horrigan (1965) examined the statistical properties of ratios and, as expected, found that many of the ratios were positively correlated with one another. That is, they tended to "move in tandem." In addition, some ratios, especially those with long-term components (e.g., long-term debt, fixed assets), were correlated over time. The primary factor explaining dispersion of ratios was found to be industry classification, although characteristics such as firm size, seasonality, and cyclical conditions also had an impact.

The existence of collinearity among ratios is a double-edged sword. As Horrigan stated,

> This presence of collinearity is both a blessing and a curse for financial ratio analysis. It means that only a small number of financial ratios are needed to capture most of the

information ratios can provide, but it also means that this small number must be selected very carefully.[31]

Using a small subset of ratios as representative of the whole set requires choosing ratios that are (1) highly correlated with those ratios excluded from the analysis and at the same time (2) not correlated with the other ratios in the subset. Condition 1 ensures that any information available from excluded ratios is captured, whereas condition 2 ensures no overlap and hence maximum information provided by the ratios included.

A number of studies, using multivariate statistical analysis tools such as factor analysis and principal components, have been carried out in an effort to find the subset(s) of ratios that meet these conditions. The reader will be spared the details of these statistical techniques. Their objective is, however, straightforward. They partition the ratios into groups such that the ratios within each group are highly correlated with one another but not with the ratios in the other groups. Each of these partitions is assumed to be affected by an underlying factor, the nature of which is not specified by the statistical model. Rather, the researcher or analyst, after examining the ratios grouped in a given partition, attempts to find the unifying theme descriptive of the underlying empirically derived factor.

The results of a study by Pinches, Eubank, Mingo, and Caruthers (PEMC, 1975) are presented in Exhibit 3-17. They examined 48 different ratios and found that they can be "explained" by 7 such empirical factors. These factors are consistent with the classifications used in our earlier discussions.

Exhibit 3-17 also lists, for each factor, the two "representative" ratios that the study found most closely depicts that classification. The utility of these results is that one need not deal with the full set of (48) ratios. One ratio for each factor can be chosen that will fully provide the incremental information present in that partition. The study was performed on data from the years 1966–1969. The results were found to be stable over the four-year period. Other studies using different sample firms, time periods, and sets of ratios ostensibly came up with alternative factor groupings. Chen and Shimerda (1981) reconcile the various studies and show that to a great extent the differences are one of nomenclature and are subsumed by the seven factors found in the PEMC studies.

These studies confined themselves to manufacturing firms. Johnson (1979), using data from 1972 and 1974, extended the analysis to retail as well as manufacturing firms. Although median ratios between the two groups differ significantly (as discussed earlier), Johnson found that the same seven "factors" delineated by PEMC for manufacturing companies were also descriptive of retail firms.

Gombola and Ketz (1983) using data from 1971–1980 also examined retail and manufacturing firms. Their analysis, however, added a new dimension in the analysis of the cash flows components of ratios. Previous studies estimated cash flows by simply adding depreciation to net income. The fact that these ratios were found to group together with profitability ratios

---

[31]Horrigan, James O., "Some Empirical Bases of Financial Ratio Analysis," *The Accounting Review* (July 1965), pp. 558–568.

EXHIBIT 3-17
Partitioning of Ratios

Return on Investment	Financial Leverage	Capital Turnover	Short-Term Liquidity	Cash Position	Inventory Turnover	Receivable Turnover
Total income/ Sales	Debt/Net plant	Cash flow/Sales	Current liabilities/	*Cash/Total assets	Current assets/	*Receivables/ inventory
Cash flow/Total assets	*Debt/Total capital	Current assets/ Total assets	Net worth	Cash/Current liabilities	Sales	Inventory/ Current
Cash flow/Net worth	Total liabilities/ Net worth	Quick assets/ Total assets	*Current assets/ Current liabilities	Cash/Sales	*Inventory/ Sales	assets
Total income/ Total assets	Total assets/Net worth	Net worth/Sales	Inventory/ Working	*Cash/Fund expenditures	Sales/ Working capital	*Receivables/ Sales
Net income/ Total assets	*Debt/Total assets	*Sales/Total assets	capital		*Cost of goods sold/ Inventory	Quick assets/ Sales
*Net income/ Net worth	Total liabilities/ Total assets	*Sales/Net plant	*Quick assets/ Current liabilities			
Earnings before interest and taxes/Total assets		Sales/Total capital	Current liabilities/ Total assets			
Earnings before interest and taxes/Sales						
Cash flow/Total capital						
*Total income/ Total capital						

*Indicates two most "representative" ratios for each factor.

Source: Reprinted by permission of the publisher from "The Hierarchical Classification of Financial Ratios," by George E. Pinches, A.A. Eubank, Kent A. Mingo, and J. Kent Caruthers, *Journal of Business Research*, pp. 295–310, Copyright October, 1975 by Elsevier Science Publishing Co., Inc., Table 5, p. 303.

could stem from the use of net income plus depreciation as a proxy for cash flow in all of these studies. Cash flow from operations, properly defined as cash receipts minus cash disbursements, is an accounting construct that differs markedly from profit. The empirical similarity between profitability measures using net income plus depreciation therefore suggests that net income plus depreciation might be measuring profitability instead of cash flow.[32]

Gombola and Ketz extended the ratios examined by PEMC with eight more properly defined cash ratios, four of which used cash flows in the numerator and four of which used working capital in the numerator. (The denominators were sales, equity, assets, and debt). In addition, for the two defensive interval ratios examined, they used actual *cash expenditures* in the denominator as well as the standard expenses (accrual based) from the income statement. (Cash and quick assets were used in the numerator.)

[32]Gombola and Ketz, p. 47.

They found that these new cash-based ratios did not group on the original seven factors. Rather, two additional factors appeared: *a cash flow factor* and *a cash expenditures factor*.

> The seven factors found by Pinches, Mingo and Caruthers for manufacturing firms correspond to seven specific factors studied in this paper. In addition to these seven factors two other factors appear in almost all years studied. One is a Cash Expenditures (defensive interval) factor and the other is a Cash Flow factor. In previous studies, measures of cash flow and defensive interval were calculated using proxies for cash flow and cash expenditures, namely net income plus depreciation and operating expenses, respectively. Appearance of separate factors for cash flow and cash expenditures point to the empirical materiality of accrual and deferral items other than depreciation as well as the empirical materiality of the difference between expenses and expenditures. *Such results should at least caution researchers or other users interested in cash flow performance using simple proxies for the cash flow construct or using expenses, an accrual concept, as a proxy for expenditures, a cash concept.*[33]

The cash flow and cash expenditure factors were also found to be important for retail firms. These results are consistent with our suggestion that ratios using income/expense flows should also be examined on a cash flow basis.

Ratios: Patterns of Disclosure, Definition, and Use

Before concluding this chapter, we would like to reiterate that the definitions and classifications of ratios used in our presentation are not set in stone. The proper definition of a ratio is not mandated, and there is wide diversity as to how ratios are defined, their relative importance, and even to which category (Is a turnover ratio a measure of activity, liquidity, or profitability?) a particular ratio belongs. This section will present some evidence with respect to these issues in terms of

1. How analysts classify and rank ratios
2. Which ratios are most commonly disclosed by firms
3. Publicly available industry norms

Perceived Importance and Classification

Exhibit 3-18 from a study by Gibson (1987) summarizes the responses of 52 chartered financial analysts (CFAs) who were asked to classify a set of 60 ratios in terms of whether they measure profitability, liquidity, or debt. Additionally, they were asked to rank (on a scale of 0 to 9) the relative importance of the ratios. Note that only for a handful of ratios is there a 100% agreement as to classification. In terms of relative importance by classification category, the analysts gave profitability ratios the highest significance rating followed by debt and then liquidity ratios.

---

[33]Ibid., pp. 54–55; emphasis added.

EXHIBIT 3-18
Classification and Ranking of Ratios by CFAs

% Classifying in Primary Classification	Ratio	Degree of Significance (0–9) by Primary Classification		
		Profitability	Debt	Liquidity
96%	Return on equity after tax	8.21		
69%	Earnings per share	7.58		
100%	Net profit margin after tax	7.52		
94%	Return on equity before tax	7.41		
100%	Net profit margin before tax	7.32		
92%	Fixed charges coverage		7.22	
96%	Quick ratio			7.10
92%	Times interest earned		7.06	
94%	Return on assets after tax	7.06		
85%	Debt/equity ratio		7.00	
94%	Return on total invested capital after tax	6.88		
57%	Degree of financial leverage		6.61	
85%	Long-term debt as a % of total invested capital		6.52	
96%	Total debt/Total assets		6.50	
63%	Total equity/Total assets		6.42	
92%	Return on total invested capital before tax	6.40		
58%	Degree of operating leverage	6.36		
100%	Current ratio			6.34
90%	Return on assets, before interest and tax	6.04		
92%	Return on assets before tax	6.00		
94%	Return on operating assets	5.96		
80%	Cash flow/Total debt		5.84	
54%	Days' sales in inventory			5.82
59%	Common equity as a % of total invested capital		5.62	
98%	Cash ratio			5.51
61%	Total asset turnover	5.50		
54%	Inventory turnover (times)			5.46
60%	Cash flow/current maturities of long-term debt		5.42	
69%	Accounts receivable turnover (times)			5.31
81%	Total debt as a % of net working capital		5.18	
74%	Accounts receivable turnover (days)			5.15
58%	Inventory turnover (days)			5.14
62%	Short-term debt as a % of total invested capital		5.08	
69%	Days' sales in receivables			5.02
65%	Sales/Operating assets	4.96		
52%	Net worth at market value/Total long-term liabilities		4.86	
80%	Cash/Total assets			4.74
82%	Current assets/Total assets			4.74
50%	Sales/Working capital	4.63		
91%	Quick assets/Total assets			4.56
55%	Current debt/Net worth		4.55	
58%	Retained earnings/Net income	4.49		

EXHIBIT 3-18. *(Continued)*

% Classifying in Primary Classification	Ratio	Degree of Significance (0–9) by Primary Classification		
		Profitability	Debt	Liquidity
64%	Sales/Fixed assets	4.25		
61%	Funded debt/Working capital		4.17	
53%	Sales/Net worth	4.04		
84%	Inventory/Working capital			4.02
92%	Return on working capital	4.02		
67%	Current debt/Inventory			3.56
88%	Inventory/Current assets			2.89

Source: Gibson, Charles H., "How Chartered Financial Analysts View Financial Ratios," *Financial Analysts Journal* (May–June 1987), pp. 74–76, Table 1, p. 75 (Adapted).

Disclosure of Ratios

Ratios are readily derived from financial statement information. There is no requirement for their explicit disclosure. When firms do disclose their ratios, the ratios disclosed are consistent with those perceived to be most important by the analysts. That is, ROA, ROE, profit margins, and solvency ratios such as debt to equity are disclosed most often. A number of studies have examined the nature of the disclosure of ratios provided in financial statements along two dimensions:

1. The (lack of) uniformity in their calculation
2. The motivation for voluntarily disclosing the ratio

Gibson (1982) documented wide disparity in how ratios were defined across a sample of 100 annual reports. The following table lists five such ratios and relevant statistics documenting the variability of definitions found in Gibson's study.

Ratio	Frequency of Appearance	Number of Variations	Frequency of Most Common Definition
Debt/Capital	23	11	7
Debt/Equity	19	6	7
Return/Equity	62	5	53
Profit Margin	58	8	40
Return/Capital	21	12	6

Williamson (1984) examined the 1978 annual reports of 141 *Fortune* 500 firms for voluntary disclosure of ratios. His purpose was to test if firms engaged in selective disclosure; that is, were the ratio values of reporting companies significantly different from (better than) those of nonreporting companies? The ratio values for the reporting companies and nonreporting companies were compared on three dimensions:

1. The ratio itself
2. The ratio's percentage deviation from the industry median
3. The percentage change in the ratio from the previous year

The results of the study are presented here for the first two dimensions.[34]

Ratio	Percentage Reporting
Significantly higher for reporting companies	
Return on equity	58%
Current ratio	51%
Return on sales	50%
No significant difference between reporting and nonreporting	
Debt/Assets	49%
Dividend payout	18%
Return on assets	16%
Inventory turnover	8%
Receivables turnover	7%
Times interest earned	6%
Asset turnover	6%
Working capital turnover	2%

The results indicate that there is evidence of selective disclosure for the three ratios that have the highest frequency of voluntary disclosure. Williamson's results incidentally also provide indirect evidence that the industry norm has relevance as a benchmark. The strongest results are consistent with the hypothesis that firms tend voluntarily to disclose a ratio the higher the ratio is above the industry norm.

Industry Norms as Benchmarks

Lev (1969) and more recently Frecka and Lee (1983) provide further evidence that industrywide norms have relevance as a benchmark. They found that ratios[35] of individual firms tend to converge toward the industrywide average.

---

[34]For the percentage change measure, only the return on equity proved to be significantly higher for the reporting companies.

[35]These ratios were calculated by Lev (1969) and Frecka and Lee (1983) from the firms' annual reports. They were not necessarily disclosed by the firms.

Two differing explanations are offered:

1. Managers view the industry norms as targets and "aim" their ratios accordingly. This is done by choice of accounting method, allocation of resources, or both.

2. Industrywide economic characteristics operate on the firm to "correct" deviations from the industry norm.

Industry norms may be calculated directly through the use of computerized databases such as Standard & Poor's Compustat Data Base. Alternatively, industry profiles are available from sources such as Robert Morris Associates (RMA) and Dun & Bradstreet's (D&B) *Industrial Handbook*. These sources provide common-size balance sheet, income statements, and selected ratios on an industry basis.

EXHIBIT 3-19
Industry Norm Ratios Available

	Robert Morris Associates	Dun & Bradstreet
A. Activity		
A/R turnover Collection period	Yes	Yes
Inventory turnover	COGS/Inventory	Sales/Inventory
Payable turnover	Yes	N/A
Working capital turnover	Yes	Yes
Fixed asset turnover	Yes	N/A
Total asset turnover	Sales/Assets	Assets/Sales
B. Liquidity		
Quick ratio	Yes	Yes
Current ratio	Yes	Yes
C. Debt and Solvency		
Interest coverage	Yes	Yes
Current liabilities/Net worth	N/A	Yes
Debt to equity	Yes	Yes
Fixed assets to equity	Fixed assets/Tangible net worth	Fixed assets/ Net worth
Cash flow to debt	(Net income + depreciation)/ Current portion long-term debt	N/A
Current liabilities/Inventory	N/A	Yes
D. Profitability		
Return on sales	N/A	Yes
Return on assets	EBT/Assets	Net income/Assets
Return on equity	EBT/Tangible net worth	EBT/Net worth
Depreciation/Sales	Yes	N/A
Officers', directors', owners' compensation/Sales	Yes	N/A

N/A – Not available.

Exhibit 3-19 presents a comparison of the ratios provided by each source. The ratios are presented in terms of the categories used in this chapter. Where the sources differ in their calculation of the ratios with respect to one another or as compared to the presentation suggested in the chapter, the ratios are defined explicitly. For example, for the profitability ratios, RMA calculates ROA[36] and ROE on a pretax basis, whereas D&B does it on an after-tax basis.

SUMMARY

The chapter provides an overview of ratios most commonly used in the analysis of financial statements. These ratios are generally classified as activity, liquidity, solvency, and profitability indicators and are designed to measure different aspects of a firm's operating, investment, and financing activities. The diverse ratio categories also provide insights into other, related activities, and this aspect is evaluated in an integrated analysis across relevant categories.

Ratios are used to standardize across firms and over time, facilitating comparative analysis. Although important, this aspect is secondary to the more useful function(s) of ratios. Ratios allow one to analyze the economic characteristics of a firm by matching the input/output cost/benefit trade-offs implicit in the numerator/denominator relationship. They are not intended to provide all the answers about a firm but rather to point to the relevant questions.

Throughout this book, we address the various questions these ratios point to and show how an understanding of the accounting process facilitates the required analysis.

[36]Somewhat surprisingly, but consistent with the CFA rankings, both calculate ROA on an "after-interest" basis.

Chapter 3

Problems

General Note: For ratios that are generally calculated on average data, use year-end data when prior year information is not available.

Problems 1–4 are based on the financial statements of Chicago Refrigerator, Inc. [Exhibit 3P-1].

1. [1986 CFA adapted] Calculate the following ratios for 19X5:

   A. Activity ratios

      1. Inventory turnover
      2. Accounts receivable turnover
      3. Fixed asset turnover
      4. Total asset turnover

EXHIBIT 3P-1. CHICAGO REFRIGERATOR INC.
Balance Sheet, at December 31, 19X4–19X5 ($ thousands)

	19X4	19X5
Assets		
Current assets		
Cash	$ 683	$ 325
Accounts receivable	1490	3599
Inventories	1415	2423
Prepaid expenses	15	13
Total current assets	$3603	$6360
Property, plant, equipment, gross	1498	2296
Less: Accumulated depreciation	(432)	(755)
Property, plant, equipment (net)	1066	1541
Other	123	157
Total assets	$4792	$8058
Liabilities		
Current liabilities		
Notes payable to bank	$ —	$ 875
Current portion of long-term debt	38	116
Accounts payable	485	933
Estimated income tax	588	472
Accrued expenses	576	586
Customer advance payments	34	963
Total current liabilities	$1721	$3945
Long-term debt	122	179
Other liabilities	81	131
Total liabilities	$1924	$4255
Shareholders' Equity		
Common stock	$ 550	$ 829
Preferred stock (10%)	500	450
Additional paid-in capital	450	575
Retained earnings	1368	1949
Total shareholders' equity	$2868	$3803
Total liabilities and shareholders' equity	$4792	$8058

EXHIBIT 3P-1. *(Continued)*

CHICAGO REFRIGERATOR, INC.
Income Statement, for years ended December 31, 19X4–19X5 ($ thousands)

	19X4	19X5
Net sales	$7570	$12,065
Other income (net)	261	345
Total revenues	$7831	$12,410
Cost of goods sold	$4850	$ 8,048
General administrative and marketing expense	1531	2,025
Interest expense	22	78
Total costs and expenses	$6403	$10,151
Net income before tax	$1428	$ 2,259
Income tax expense	628	994
Net income	$ 800	$ 1,265

CHICAGO REFRIGERATOR, INC.
Cash Flow Statement, 19X5

Cash from operations		$(256)
Cash for investments		(832)
Cash from financing		
Debt	$1060	
Issue of shares	354	
Dividends paid	(684)	
		730
Change in cash		$(358)

B. Liquidity ratios

  1. Length of operating cycle

  2. Length of cash cycle

  3. Current ratio

  4. Quick ratio

  5. Cash ratio

  6. CFO to current liabilities

  7. Defensive interval

C. Solvency ratios

  1. Debt to equity

  2. Debt to capital

   3. Times interest earned

   4. Capital expenditures ratio

   D. Profitability ratios

   1. Gross margin

   2. Operating income to sales

   3. Return on sales

   4. Return on assets

   5. Return on equity

2. [Disaggregation of ROE] Disaggregate the 19X5 return on equity of Chicago Refrigerator, Inc., using the three-component and five-component models.

3. [Effect of growth on ratios]

   A. Chicago Refrigerator grew considerably in 19X5, with total assets nearly doubling. Discuss how this rapid growth may have affected the ratios calculated in Problem 1 relative to those of the previous year.

   B. By calculating some ratios based on the average of opening and closing balances, we make the implicit assumption that changes in these accounts occurred uniformly throughout the year. Sometimes, however, the actual change occurs unevenly, perhaps due to an acquisition. In such cases, ratios based on averages will be distorted. Discuss how you would calculate the return on assets ratio if the growth in assets occurred:

   (i) At the beginning of the year.

   (ii) At the end of the first quarter.

   (iii) At the end of the second quarter.

   (iv) At the end of the fourth quarter.

4. [Operating and financial leverage, effects of growth]

   A. Estimate Chicago Refrigerator's fixed and variable costs for 19X5.

   B. Estimate Chicago Refrigerator's operating, financial, and total leverage effects for 19X4 and 19X5.

   C. Discuss how the company's rapid growth in 19X5 may have distorted the estimates calculated in parts A and B.

Problems 5 and 6 are based on the common-size statements presented in Exhibit 3P-2.

5. [Common-size statements—ratios] Using the common-size statements of company 1 in Exhibit 3P-2, calculate the following ratios:

   1. Inventory turnover

   2. Receivable turnover

   3. Length of operating cycle

EXHIBIT 3P-2
Common-Size Balance Sheets

Company	1	2	3	4	5	6	7	8	9
Cash and short-term investments	2%	13%	37%	1%	1%	3%	1%	22%	6%
Receivables	17	8	22	28	23	5	11	16	8
Inventory	15	52	15	23	14	2	2	0	5
Other current assets	6	0	5	1	4	2	2	1	0
Current assets	40%	73%	79%	53%	42%	12%	16%	39%	19%
Gross property	86	40	26	44	63	112	65	1	106
Less: Accumulated depreciation	(50)	(19)	(8)	(15)	(23)	(45)	(28)	0	(34)
Net property	36%	21%	18%	29%	40%	67%	37%	1%	72%
Investments	3	1	0	0	3	14	16	55	0
Intangibles and other	21	5	3	18	15	7	31	5	9
Total assets	100%	100%	100%	100%	100%	100%	100%	100%	100%
Trade payables	11	21	22	13	26	7	11	NA	20
Debt payable	4	0	3	6	4	6	2	46	4
Other current liabilities	9	43	0	0	1	4	1	16	8
Current liabilities	24%	64%	25%	19%	31%	17%	14%	62%	32%
Long-term debt	20	5	12	27	23	34	24	27	21
Other liabilities	16	0	1	21	16	12	13	5	12
Total liabilities	60%	69%	38%	67%	70%	63%	51%	94%	65%
Equity	40	31	62	33	30	37	49	6	35
Total liabilities and equity	100%	100%	100%	100%	100%	100%	100%	100%	100%

NA – Not available.

Common-Size Income Statements

Company	1	2	3	4	5	6	7	8	9
Revenues	100%	100%	100%	100%	100%	100%	100%	100%	100%
Cost of goods sold	58	81	58	63	52	0	59	0	0
Operating expenses	21	7	24	28	33	84	29	55	91
Research and development	7	5	9	0	1	NA	0	0	0
Advertising	3	0	3	2	5	NA	NA	0	2
Operating income	11%	7%	6%	7%	9%	16%	12%	45%	7%
Net interest expense	1	(1)	0	2	2	6	3	41	1
Income from continuing operations before tax	10%	8%	6%	5%	7%	10%	9%	4%	6%
Asset turnover ratio	0.96	1.12	0.94	1.38	1.82	0.45	0.96	0.15	0.96

NA – Not available.

  4. Length of cash cycle

  5. Fixed asset turnover ratio

  6. Cash ratio

  7. Quick ratio

  8. Current ratio

  9. Debt to equity

  10. Interest coverage

  11. EBIT/sales

  12. Sales/assets

  13. EBIT/assets

  14. EBT/assets

  15. Assets/equity

  16. EBT/equity

Hint: Ratios for which one component is derived from the balance sheet and the other from the income statement can be calculated by making use of the asset turnover ratio, which is given in Exhibit 3P-2.

  6. [Ratio analysis—industry characteristics] The nine companies in Exhibit 3P-2 are drawn from the following nine industries:

  A. Aerospace

  B. Airline

  C. Chemicals and drugs

  D. Computer software

  E. Consumer foods

  F. Department stores

  G. Consumer finance

  H. Newspaper publishing

  I. Electric utility

  A. Based on the common-size statements, match each company to its industry.

  B. Briefly discuss the balance sheet and income statement characteristics which enabled you to identify the industry to which each company belonged.

  7. [Ratio analysis—industry and economic benchmarks [1988 CFA adapted]

  A. Using the financial ratios contained in Exhibit 3P-3, analyze the relative credit position of:

  (i) The brewing industry compared with the S&P 400.

  (ii) Anheuser-Busch compared with the brewing industry.

  (iii) Anheuser-Busch compared with the S&P 400.

EXHIBIT 3P-3. THE BREWING INDUSTRY AND ANHEUSER-BUSCH COMPANIES, INC. (BUD)
Selected Financial Ratios for the S&P 400, 1982–1986

	1982			1983			1984			1985			1986		
	S&P 400	Brewing Industry	BUD	S&P 400	Brewing Industry	BUD	S&P 400	Brewing Industry	BUD	S&P 400	Brewing Industry	BUD	S&P 400	Brewing Industry	BUD
Current ratio	1.5	1.3	1.1	1.5	1.4	1.2	1.5	1.3	1.1	1.4	1.5	1.2	1.4	1.4	1.0
Quick ratio	0.9	0.7	0.4	0.9	0.8	0.7	0.8	0.7	0.5	0.8	1.0	0.6	0.7	0.8	0.4
Long-term debt/Total assets (%)	24	21	25	23	18	22	25	15	18	26	15	17	27	17	19
Total debt*/Total assets (%)	43	37	41	42	36	39	44	31	34	48	32	33	48	34	37
Times interest earned	4.0	7.2	12.2	4.6	7.5	12.7	4.8	7.6	13.3	4.2	10.1	14.9	3.6	11.0	9.8
Cash flow/long-term debt (%)	54	52	43	61	70	55	65	84	71	57	88	79	51	80	73
Cash flow/Total debt* (%)	23	29	26	25	35	32	25	39	38	20	40	40	20	38	38
Total asset turnover	1.2	1.2	1.2	1.2	1.4	1.4	1.2	1.5	1.6	1.2	1.3	1.5	1.1	1.3	1.4
Net profit margin (%)	3.95	5.36	6.3	4.42	5.58	5.8	4.77	5.12	6.0	3.84	5.73	6.3	3.75	6.16	6.17
Return on total assets (%)	4.64	6.46	7.4	5.10	7.98	8.0	5.80	7.47	8.7	4.41	7.66	8.7	3.97	7.90	8.89

*Total debt is defined as long-term debt plus current liabilities.

259

B. Evaluate the credit quality of Anheuser-Busch based upon the trend in financial ratios.

8. [Liquidity analysis] The working capital accounts of Queen Chana, a retailer, are as follows:

Year	19X1	19X2	19X3
Cash	$1,000	$ 1,500	$ 2,000
Accounts receivable	2,000	4,000	6,000
Inventory	2,000	4,500	8,000
Current assets	$5,000	$10,000	$16,000
Accounts payable	$2,000	$ 3,500	$ 4,500
Short-term debt	500	1,500	3,500
Current liabilities	$2,500	$ 5,000	$ 8,000

A. For years 19X1–19X3 calculate Queen Chana's:

  (i) Current ratio.

  (ii) Quick ratio.

  (iii) Cash ratio.

B. What other useful indicators of the firm's liquidity can you calculate from the data given?

C. Using the trend in the ratios calculated in part A and the indicators in part B, discuss the firm's liquidity.

D. What other information or ratios would help you confirm your analysis? What would you expect these ratios to show?

9. [Liquidity, profitability, and cash flow analysis—extension of Problem 13 of Chapter 2] In Problem 13 of Chapter 2, you were asked to analyze the liquidity of the M and G companies based on income and cash flow trends.

A. What ratios might you use to support the conclusions reached in Problem 13 of Chapter 2?

B. Calculate those ratios from Exhibit 2P-1 for the years 19X0–19X4.

C. Discuss how the ratios computed in part B affect the conclusions reached in Problem 13 of Chapter 2.

10. [ROE—duPont model, 1988 CFA adapted] Tennant, founded in 1870, has evolved into the leading producer of large-sized floor sweepers and scrubbers that are ridden by their operators. Currently, Tennant has approximately 50% of this specialized market and is a supplier to 90% of the *Fortune* 500 industrial companies. In 1983, the company established a minor position in the production and marketing of smaller "walk-behind" floor service equipment and also provides floor cleaning supplies and floor maintenance services. However, large floor maintenance equipment remains Tennant's core business. Use the duPont model to analyze the components of Tennant's return on equity to explain the change that has occurred in the company's return on equity over the 12 years ended in 1987. The five factors in the model are:

1. EBIT margin
2. Asset turnover
3. Interest burden
4. Financial leverage
5. Tax retention rate

   A. Compute ROE and *each* of these *five* factors for 1975, 1981, and 1987.

   B. Identify the individual component that had the greatest influence on the change in return on equity over this period and briefly explain the possible reasons for the changes in this component.

11. [Comprehensive review of ratios, operating and financial leverage, and financial statements] Company C and Company L operate in the same industry and have equal market shares. Their operating and financing characteristics differ as Company C has adopted newer manufacturing practices: it operates highly automated plants and maintains tight control of inventories consistent with just-in-time inventory techniques. To achieve these inventory levels, close coordination with suppliers and customers is needed; collections and payments are relatively prompt.

EXHIBIT 3P-4. TENNANT COMPANY
Selected Historic Operating and Balance Sheet Data at December 31, 1975, 1981, and 1987 (in $ thousands, except per share data)

	1975	1981	1987
Net sales	$47,909	$109,333	$166,924
Cost of goods sold	27,395	62,373	95,015
Gross profit	$20,514	$ 46,960	$ 71,909
Selling and general expenses	11,895	29,649	54,151
Earnings before interest and taxes	$ 8,619	$ 17,311	$ 17,758
Interest on long-term debt	0	53	248
Pre-tax income	$ 8,619	$ 17,258	$ 17,510
Income tax expense	4,190	7,655	7,692
Net income	$ 4,429	$ 9,603	$ 9,818
Total assets	$33,848	$ 63,555	$106,098
Stockholders' equity	25,722	46,593	69,516
Long-term debt	6	532	2,480
Common shares outstanding	5,654	5,402	5,320
Earnings per share	$ 0.78	$ 1.78	$ 1.85
Dividends per share	0.28	0.72	0.96
Book value per share	4.55	8.63	13.07

Financial data for 19X2 for Company C and Company L follow:

	Company C	Company L
Gross plant assets	$175,000	$65,000
Current ratio	9.475	3.592
Quick ratio	8.875	3.192
Return on equity	0.130	0.167
Cash from operations/ Current liabilities	5.275	0.942
Decline in receivables	($ 3,000)	($ 4,500)
Decline in inventory	0	($ 6,000)
Decline in accounts payable	0	($ 5,000)
Cash from operations	$ 52,750	$28,250
Cash from financing: decline in short-term debt	($ 1,000)	($ 5,000)
Cash for investment	0	0

Common-size statements for Companies C and L, prepared by your assistant, follow, but they are unidentified as to which company they belong. Sales in 19X2 for both companies were one-sixth less than in 19X1.

Common-Size Statements

	Company ?		Company ?	
	19X1	19X2	19X1	19X2
Sales	100.00%	100.00%	100.00%	100.00%
COGS	63.89	66.67	58.33	66.67
Selling, general, and administrative expenses	19.44	20.00	17.78	20.00
Interest	1.67	2.00	3.89	4.67
Taxes	3.75	2.83	5.00	2.17
	88.75%	91.50%	85.00%	93.50%
Net income	11.25%	8.50%	15.00%	6.50%

Finally, your assistant also computed the ratios shown for 19X2 (again unidentified as to company). In addition, the ratios are mixed up: some in column 1 belong to

Company C and some to Company L (similarly, the ratios in column 2 are a mixture of Company C and Company L):

	Column 1	Column 2
Inventory turnover	6.667	16.667
Receivable turnover	11.111	7.409
Payable turnover	25.000	4.444
Long-term debt to capital	0.195	0.429

When answering the following questions, round all numbers to the nearest $50.

A. Identify the common-size statements and each ratio with Company C or Company L. Briefly explain your reasoning.

B. Recreate the income statements for 19X1 and 19X2 for Company C and Company L.

C. Using the two years of data available, estimate for *each* company:

  (i) Level of fixed costs.

  (ii) Variable costs (as a percentage of sales).

D. The recession is expected to continue with a 20% drop in sales in 19X3. Forecast the 19X3 income statement for *each* company.

E. Comment briefly on the impact of operating and financing leverage on the 19X1–19X3 financial performance of the two firms.

12. [Extension of Problem 11]

A. For Company C *or* L re-create the balance sheet for 19X1 and 19X2. The balance sheet will have the following components:

Assets	Liabilities
Cash	Accounts payable
Accounts receivable	Short-term debt
Inventory	Long-term debt
Property, plant, and equipment	
Less: Accumulated depreciation	Shareholder's equity

B. For the same company selected forecast the balance sheet and cash from operations for 19X3. (Hint: use the ratios to make the required assumptions regarding levels of inventories, payables, and receivables.)

C. Assess the strength of the cash position and cash flows of the company analyzed.

13. [Relationship of ROE, ROA, leverage, and cost of debt] The Vac Company has an ROA of 10%. The company has no debt (not even trade liabilities). Its total assets are $1 million and its tax rate is 20%. The company is considering borrowing some money and using the proceeds to buy back outstanding stock. The bank has stated that the interest rate charged will depend on the level of bank debt according to the following schedule:

	Debt to Equity	Interest Rate
(1)	0.25	6%
(2)	0.50	8%
(3)	1.00	10%
(4)	1.50	12%
(5)	2.00	15%

A. Compute the company's current ROE.

B. Using the formula in the chapter that related ROE to ROA and interest costs, calculate the expected ROE for each level of debt.

C. Confirm your calculation for cases (1) and (5) by completing the following for each case.

1. Debt in dollars
2. Equity in dollars
3. Income before interest and taxes
4. Interest expense
5. Tax expense
6. Net income
7. Return on equity

D. What does this table imply about "optimal" levels of debt and limits to the use of leverage?

14. [Relationship of ROE, ROA, leverage, and cost of debt] Redo Problem 13 assuming that the company has trade payables of $200,000 and intends to maintain that level. Note that the debt-to-equity ratio in the schedule is calculated by excluding the trade payables; that is, debt is defined as bank debt only. [Hint: The formula used in part B will require adjustment of the interest cost as the trade payables carry a zero interest rate.]

15. [Profitability analysis] The financial statements of Harley-Davidson, Inc., for the period 1985–1990 are presented in Exhibit 3P-5. Harley-Davidson is considered one of the success stories of the last decade having introduced "world-class" management techniques to turn around the company. At the same time, however, an examination of the company's return on equity indicates that, after initial growth, the ratio stabilized and then declined.

EXHIBIT 3P-5. HARLEY-DAVIDSON INC.
Comparative Income Statements, for Years Ended 1985–1990 (in $ millions)

	1985	1986	1987	1988	1989	1990
Sales	$287.48	$295.32	$685.36	$757.38	$790.97	$864.60
Cost of goods sold	209.69	210.45	506.91	559.53	582.70	619.10
Selling, general, and administrative expense	57.34	60.06	104.14	111.91	127.61	144.27
Depreciation	7.53	8.72	14.86	15.73	14.23	16.45
Operating income after depreciation	$ 12.91	$ 16.10	$ 59.45	$ 70.20	$ 66.42	$ 84.78
Interest expense	(9.41)	(9.51)	(25.51)	(24.67)	(17.96)	(11.44)
Other income (expense)	(0.34)	0.75	0.52	4.38	4.54	(2.12)
Special items	0	0	(3.60)	(3.90)	0	(8.60)
Pretax income	$ 3.16	$ 7.33	$ 30.85	$ 46.01	$ 53.01	$ 62.62
Income tax expense	0.53	3.03	13.18	18.85	20.40	24.31
Income before extraordinary items	$ 2.64	$ 4.31	$ 17.67	$ 27.16	$ 32.61	$ 38.31
Extraordinary items and discontinued operations	7.32	0.56	3.54	(3.24)	0.33	(0.48)
Net income	$ 9.95	$ 4.87	$ 21.21	$ 23.91	$ 32.94	$ 37.83

HARLEY-DAVIDSON INC.
Comparative Balance Sheets, 1985–1990 (in $ millions)

	1985	1986	1987	1988	1989	1990
Assets						
Cash and short-term	$ 13.47	$ 27.85	$ 68.23	$ 52.36	$ 39.08	$ 14.00
Total receivables	27.31	36.46	34.42	47.15	45.56	51.90
Total inventories	28.87	78.63	83.75	97.66	87.54	109.88
Other current assets	3.24	5.81	11.51	14.12	15.49	20.91
Current assets	$ 72.89	$148.76	$197.90	$211.29	$187.67	$196.68
Gross property	55.82	116.53	137.43	159.49	176.83	212.70
Accumulated depreciation	(17.09)	(25.60)	(37.00)	(48.71)	(61.13)	(76.65)
Net property	$ 38.73	$ 90.93	$100.43	$110.79	$115.70	$136.05
Intangibles	0.00	82.11	74.16	70.21	66.19	63.08
Other assets	2.47	5.39	8.38	8.82	9.36	11.65
Total assets	$114.09	$327.20	$380.87	$401.11	$378.93	$407.47

EXHIBIT 3P-5. *(Continued)*

	1985	1986	1987	1988	1989	1990
Liabilities and Equity						
Current debt	$ 2.88	$ 18.09	$ 28.33	$ 33.23	$ 26.93	$ 23.86
Accounts payable	27.52	29.59	35.85	39.12	40.09	50.41
Income tax payable	0.00	8.22	12.41	4.07	7.63	9.59
Other current liabilities	26.25	52.92	57.08	59.97	61.70	62.67
Total current liabilities	$ 56.65	$108.82	$133.68	$136.39	$136.36	$146.53
Long-term debt	51.50	191.59	178.76	135.18	74.79	48.34
Other liabilities	1.32	0.62	0.64	3.31	5.27	9.19
Deferred income tax	0.00	0.00	4.87	4.59	6.25	4.63
Total liabilities	$109.47	$301.04	$317.96	$279.47	$222.68	$208.69
Stockholders' equity	$ 4.62	$ 26.16	$ 62.91	$121.65	$156.25	$198.77
Total liabilities and equity	$114.09	$327.20	$380.87	$401.11	$378.93	$407.47

Note: Numbers may not add due to rounding.

Analyze the factors (sales growth, efficient use of assets, cost control) contributing to Harley-Davidson's increased profitability. How do these factors explain the changes in ROE over the period 1985–1990?

Appendix 3—A

Estimating Operating Leverage

Throughout this appendix, we shall make use of the following notation:

$$S = \text{Sales}$$
$$F = \text{Fixed costs}$$
$$V = \text{Variable costs}$$
$$v = \text{Variable costs as a Percentage of Sales, that is, } V = vS$$
$$TC = \text{Total costs} = F + V = F + vS$$
$$NI = \text{Net income} = S - TC = S - F - vS = (1 - v)S - F$$
$$(1 - v)S = \text{Contribution}$$

In a deterministic world, where relationships are constant and not subject to random error, estimating the variable and fixed components of a firm's cost structure is straightforward. A plot of total costs against sales would yield a straight line. The equation of the line would be the equation for total cost; that is, $TC = F + vS$. The slope of the line, v, would be the variable cost percentage, and the (y-intercept) point of intersection of the line with the TC axis would be the fixed costs, F.

The exact values of v and F can be calculated by using any two adjacent periods, that is, years 1 and 2,

$$v = \frac{TC(\text{year 2}) - TC(\text{year 1})}{S(\text{year 2}) - S(\text{year 1})} \tag{3.A.1}$$

and then using any year

$$F = TC - vS \tag{3.A.2}$$

Unfortunately, real data are not deterministic, and actual cost structures are not as simplistic as described. The problems one encounters with real data are manifold, and we list some of them here:

- Fixed and variable costs are defined conceptually in terms of how costs change as a result of changes in output levels. Fixed costs can, however, change as a result of other factors; that is, a raise in rent or salary levels, general inflation, increases in property taxes and so on. Hence, changes in TC from one year to the next are not only a result of changes in V.

- The division between fixed and variable costs is only appropriate in the context of some relevant range. For example, rent may be considered a fixed cost as long as the firm's range of output falls within its capacity. When output exceeds capacity and new facilities are acquired, rent will increase as a result of changes in output.[1] Within a certain range, therefore, rent is a fixed cost; outside the range, it is variable. Here again, changes in TC from year to year are not only a result of changes in V.

- Variable costs vary with respect to changes in output as measured in units. Unfortunately, quantity data are rarely available, and estimates must be made based on sales dollars. To the extent that changes in prices affect total revenues, the estimate of v will be distorted. One possibility is to deflate revenues to a base year before carrying on further analysis. In addition, reference can be made to the Management Discussion and Analysis (MD&A), which sometimes provides information as to the relative effects of quantity and price changes on sales dollars.

- Our formulation assumes a linear relationship between costs and output. The relationship may, however, be nonlinear,[2] and the linear relationship imposed is at best an approximation.

Estimating operating leverage in this more complex world is a difficult but not insurmountable task. A number of techniques are possible. The best results would probably be obtained if a combination of techniques were used.

STEP 1   EXAMINE INDIVIDUAL COMPONENTS

An examination of the components that make up total cost can often provide some insight into the proportion of costs that are fixed or variable. Thus, for example, depreciation and rent expense may be assumed to be fixed, whereas cost of goods sold in a merchandising operation can readily be assumed to be variable. Similarly, for a manufacturing environment, the materials component and to some extent the labor cost component (if available) of cost of goods sold can be assumed to be variable. By segregating these identifiable items and estimating their current (next period) status separately,[3] the estimation procedure for the other cost components can be simplified.

---

[1]In economics, this is often expressed as a short-run/long-run dichotomy. In the short run, there are some fixed costs; in the long run, all costs are viewed as variable.

[2]See any introductory microeconomics textbook, which generally depicts the cost–output relationship as nonlinear.

[3]We note that the current status must be estimated separately as it would not suffice just to identify an item as fixed or variable and use its last known value as the next period estimate. Depreciation, for example, even if one identified it as fixed, could vary from year to year if straight-line depreciation were not being used. Similarly, if the firm undertook a major capital expansion, depreciation would be expected to increase whether or not the firm experienced changes in output.

STEP 2   USE REGRESSION ANALYSIS TO ESTIMATE *v*

After disaggregating the "known" fixed costs, the variable cost component, *v*, can be estimated by regression analysis. Regressing the remaining costs against sales will provide a regression equation of the form

$$\text{Costs} = a + b \text{ (sales)} + e$$

where *e* represents the error term and *a* and *b* represent the estimates of the fixed and variable cost components. It would usually be more meaningful to run the regression on the change in costs versus the change in sales. This would alleviate the autocorrelation problem usually found in time series data. In addition the intercept, *a*, would be able to incorporate changes in (fixed) costs due to factors other than volume such as inflation.

The regression estimation procedure assumes that cost structures do not change over the time period examined. As a control for this assumption, it would be useful to apply the following "check" procedure.

Treat the earnings as if they were deterministic and estimate a sequence of *v*'s using expression (3.A.1) for the years used in the regression study. If the *v*'s do not exhibit a trend and are fairly consistent, use the regression results. Otherwise, the best estimate of *v* may be the estimate obtained from the last two years' data using expression (3.A.1).

STEP 3   ESTIMATE FIXED COSTS

After obtaining the estimate of *v*, use expression (3.A.2) to obtain the estimate of fixed costs using the most recent year's data.

Appendix 3—B

Merck Financial Statements

Merck & Co., Inc.

COMPARATIVE BALANCE SHEETS

Assets	1987	1988	1989	1990
Cash	408	854	685	806
Short-term Investments	740	696	458	391
Accounts Receivable	1077	1023	1266	1346
Inventories	660	658	780	893
Prepaid Expenses	122	159	221	331
Current Assets	3007	3390	3410	3767
Investments	459	403	737	1012
Net PP&E	1948	2070	2293	2721
Other Assets	266	265	317	530
TOTAL ASSETS	5680	6128	6757	8030
Liabilities & Equity				
Short term debt	851	459	327	793
Accounts Payable	910	833	937	1138
Dividends Payable	105	147	178	217
Income Tax Payable	342	471	465	679
Current Liabilities	2208	1910	1907	2827
Long Term Debt	168	143	118	124
Deferred Taxes	652	676	701	695
Minority Interest	535	543	510	549
TOTAL LIABILITIES	3563	3272	3236	4195
Common Stock	152	146	153	167
Retained Earnings	3920	4580	5394	6387
Treasury Stock	(1955)	(1870)	(2026)	(2719)
TOTAL EQUITY	2117	2856	3521	3835
TOTAL LIABILITIES & EQUITY	5680	6128	6757	8030

Merck & Co., Inc.

COMPARATIVE INCOME AND CASH FLOW STATEMENTS

Income Statement

	1987	1988	1989	1990
Sales	5061	5940	6551	7672
Cost of Goods Sold	1443	1526	1550	1778
SG&A	1682	1878	2013	2388
Research & Development	566	669	751	854
Income from Operations	1370	1867	2237	2652
Interest Income	na	106	148	153
Interest Expense	na	(77)	(53)	(70)
Other income (deductions)	na	(25)	(48)	(36)
	35	4	47	47
Income before Taxes	1405	1871	2284	2699
Provision for Taxes	(499)	(664)	(788)	(918)
Net Income	906	1207	1496	1781

Statement of Cash Flows

	1987	1988	1989	1990
From Operations	1148	1387	1381	2056
From Investments				
Capital Expenditures	(254)	(373)	(433)	(671)
Other	(81)	267	(125)	(329)
	(335)	(106)	(558)	(1000)
From Financing				
Debt Financing	465	(386)	(154)	475
Treasury Stock Purchases	(1000)	0	(208)	(745)
Dividends Paid	(335)	(505)	(650)	(749)
Other	84	56	20	84
	(786)	(835)	(992)	(935)
Net Change in Cash	27	446	(169)	121

Appendix 3–C

Earnings per Share

INTRODUCTION

This appendix is designed to introduce users of financial statements to measurement and disclosure rules employed in reporting earnings per share (EPS). These rules are illustrated using both hypothetical examples and actual company reports.

Earnings per share is probably the most widely available and commonly used corporate performance statistic for publicly traded firms. It is used for comparative analyses of operating performance and valuation either directly or with market prices in the familiar form of price/earnings (P/E) ratios. The EPS and P/E ratios are generally available in the business section of most newspapers.

Current EPS reporting requirements are governed by Accounting Principles Board (APB) 15, Earnings per Share, with subsequent technical amendments provided by Financial Accounting Standards Board (FASB) Statements and *Technical Bulletins*. In addition, there are several American Institute of Certified Public Accountants (AICPA) "unofficial" interpretations of APB 15,[1] published in 1970 and 1971.

EPS measurement and disclosure rules are a function of the reporting firm's capital structure. A single EPS amount must be disclosed by firms with simple capital structures, and a dual presentation is required from firms with complex capital structures in keeping with the objective of reporting the potential dilution of earnings due to convertible securities and options.

For many companies, reported EPS is not simply income divided by the average number of outstanding shares. Companies whose capital structures include convertible debt (or options) must recognize the potential diltution of EPS upon conversion (exercise) of those securities. In order to account for this potential dilution, certain assumptions must be made with respect to (1) whether the conversion or exercise will actually take place and (2) how the proceeds of exercise will be used. Unfortunately, as we shall see, these assumptions are in many ways arbitrary and not necessarily tied to economic reality. Thus, for companies with complex or changing capital structures, both the level and trend of reported EPS must be carefully monitored.

---

[1] The AICPA interpretations cover some of the issues left unclear by APB 15. As these interpretations are "unofficial," they have not always been followed. See footnote 6 in Chapter 1, which details the five authoritative levels in the hierarchy of accounting principles. ("Unofficial" AICPA interpretations are classified as Level 4.)

SIMPLE CAPITAL STRUCTURE

APB 15 defines a simple capital structure as one that does not include any potentially dilutive convertible securities, options, warrants, or other contingent securities. These firms report a single EPS amount computed as

$$\text{EPS} = \frac{\textbf{Earnings available for common shareholders}}{\textbf{Weighted average number of common shares outstanding}}$$

$$= \frac{\textbf{Net Income} - \textbf{Preferred stock dividends}}{\textbf{Weighted average number of common shares outstanding}}$$

COMPLEX CAPITAL STRUCTURE

A complex capital structure includes potentially dilutive securities, and qualifying firms disclose a primary EPS that reflects some of the potential dilution and a fully diluted EPS that reports maximum dilution. The calculation of these two EPS numbers is described in the paragraphs that follow.

COMPUTATIONAL ISSUES

Earnings Available for Common Shareholders

The current period dividend on cumulative preferred stock must be deducted from net income (or added to a loss) even if it has not been declared to reflect accurately only the earnings available for distribution to common shareholders. Dividends (whether paid in cash or stock) on participating preferred shares must also be deducted.

Weighted Average Number of Common Shares Outstanding

The denominator of the EPS measure is the number of shares outstanding during each month weighted by the number of months those shares were outstanding.[2]

The denominator includes the impact of all stock dividends and stock splits effective during the period and those announced after the end of the reporting period (but before the financial statements are issued) as if they had been effective at the beginning of the reporting period. All prior periods presented must be restated to facilitate comparative analyses.

Shares issued in purchase method acquisitions (see Chapter 12) are included in the denominator only for the period after the acquisition date. Only the postacquisition date results of operations of the acquired firms are included in the numerator of the EPS computation. Note that no restatement of prior periods is permitted for purchase method acquisitions.

---

[2]EPS calculations may also be based on daily or weekly weighting.

The impact of the pooling method is quite different. Merged firms are considered combined entities for all years presented. The number of shares issued in the combination are assumed to have been outstanding for all periods presented, and the results of operations for the two firms are also combined for those periods in the EPS calculation.

Acquisitions and incentive compensation schemes often require the issuance of common shares if specific conditions, such as the passage of time, achievement of income levels, or specified market prices of the common stock, are met. Securities whose issuance depends solely on the passage of time are always included in the weighted average shares outstanding.

Additional shares to be issued are included in the computation of primary and fully diluted EPS if the required income levels or market prices have been reached at the end of the reporting period. When the issuance of additional shares depends on the achievement of earnings targets, and when it is likely that those targets will be achieved, the computation of fully diluted earnings per share includes *both* the incremental shares and the level of income assumed to have been achieved. These adjustments to the EPS measures are required even if the incremental shares are to be issued at a later date.[3]

Primary Earnings per Share

The first level of the dual EPS presentation required for firms with complex capital structures, primary earnings per share (PEPS), reflects only the expected dilution due to securities that derive a significant portion of their value from their conversion right. Such convertible securities are called common stock equivalents (CSEs).

Participating securities and two-class common stock are CSEs, even if they cannot be converted to common stocks if their terms allow them a share of earnings substantially equivalent to that of common shareholders.

PEPS are calculated as

$$\frac{\text{Net income available for common} + \text{Adjustments for CSEs}}{\text{Weighted average common shares} + \text{Weighted average CSE shares}}$$

Fully Diluted EPS

Convertible securities not qualifying as CSEs are called other potentially dilutive securities (OPDS), and their impact is included in the computation of fully diluted earnings per share (FDEPS) to reflect the maximum potential dilution.

Fully diluted EPS is defined as

$$\frac{\text{Net income available for common} + \text{Adjustments for CSEs and OPDS}}{\text{Weighted average common shares} + \text{Weighted average CSEs and OPDS}}$$

---

[3]See AICPA Accounting Interpretations 88-92 of APB 15.

Exceptions to Dilution Calculations

Only dilutive securities are included in EPS computations. If the EPS adjustment for any individual CSE or OPDS is antidilutive, that is, if it increases the earnings or decreases the loss per share, that security is excluded from the EPS calculation for that reporting period.

In addition, firms are required to report only the simple EPS if the FDEPS results in a dilution of less than 3% from the simple EPS. Note that the materiality test is applied in the aggregate to all dilutive securities, whereas the antidilutive exception is the result of an individual security test.

ADJUSTMENTS FOR CONVERTIBLE BONDS AND PREFERRED STOCK

Convertible securities are considered CSEs if their effective yield is less than two-thirds of the average Aa bond yield at the date of issuance. If dilutive, they are included in *both* PEPS and FDEPS. All other convertible securities are considered as OPDS. Their dilutive effect is only included in FDEPS.

The effective yield must be based on the stated annual interest or dividend payments and the effect of any premium or discount at issuance or due to call provisions. For adjustable rate securities, it incorporates scheduled adjustments based on information available at issuance. The Aa bond yield must be compared to the lowest yield to maturity, including the effect of call provisions.[4]

Convertible securities are permanently classified as either CSEs or OPDS at issuance. Subsequent changes in interest rates or market prices cannot affect the classification. When a newly issued convertible security is classified as a CSE, all outstanding (non-CSE) or subsequently issued securities with similar terms must also be classified as CSEs. Note that antidilutive securities must be excluded from EPS computations regardless of classification.

PEPS and FDEPS include dilutive CSEs, which are convertible within 5 years of the financial statement date. Convertible CSEs exercisable after 5 years but within 10 years of the statement date only enter FDEPS calculations.[5] However, conversion is not assumed for either PEPS or FDEPS if the conversion privilege is not effective within 10 years of the reporting period.

The adjustments for CSEs are based on the "if converted" method, which assumes that securities were converted[6] into common shares at the beginning of the period or on the date of issuance, whichever is later.

---

[4]See SFAS 85, Yield Test for Determining Whether a Convertible Security Is a Common Stock Equivalent (FASB, March 1985).

[5]Per AICPA Interpretation 28; see footnote 1.

[6]For PEPS, the earliest conversion rate should be used for securities with changing conversion rates over time. FDEPS is based on the conversion rate (applicable over the next 10 years) most favorable to the holder to reflect maximum potential dilution.

Illustration of the Two-thirds Rule

Assume that on July 1, 1993, a firm issues $1 million face amount of 10% (paid semiannually) convertible bonds for $1,197,928. Each $1000 bond is convertible into 25 common shares of $10 par value common shares. The bonds mature in 20 years. The average Aa bond yield on that date is 10%, and the firm's effective tax rate is 40%. All EPS calculations are shown for the year ended December 31, 1993.

The effective yield, 8% in this example,[7] is the rate at which the present value of the semiannual interest payments of $50,000 (0.05 × $1,000,000), and the face value of $1,000,000 is equal to the proceeds of $1,197,928. The effective yield is higher than two-thirds of the Aa yield (2/3 of 10% = 6.7%), so the bond does not qualify as a CSE. It is classified as an other potentially dilutive security. Thus conversion is assumed only for the calculation of FDEPS.

To calculate FDEPS, the numerator is adjusted by adding back the posttax bond interest expense.[8] On December 31, 1993, the convertible bonds have been outstanding for six months since issuance, and the semiannual interest expense at the effective interest rate is $47,917 (0.08 × $1,197,928 × 0.5). Since interest costs are tax deductible, only the net-of-tax amounts affect reported net income, and only $28,750 [(1 − 0.40) × ($47,917)] should be added back to income for the FDEPS calculation.

To adjust the denominator, 25,000 additional shares are assumed to be issued (25 shares for each $1000 bond or 25 × 1000). These are assumed outstanding for six months, making the denominator adjustment 12,500 shares on December 31, 1993.

ADJUSTMENTS FOR OPTIONS AND WARRANTS

Options and warrants are always CSEs since their conversion feature is the sole basis for their value. APB 15 uses the *treasury stock* method to calculate their impact on EPS. The method assumes that the proceeds of exercise of the options and warrants are used to purchase common shares on the open market. Only the incremental shares issued affect the denominator.[9]

The treasury stock method is applicable when the market price exceeds the exercise price for "substantially all"[10] of three consecutive months ending on the last month of the

---

[7]The sum of $1,197,928 is the present value of 40 (interest) payments of $50,000 each and a single (principal) payment of $1 million (to be paid 40 periods later) at a discount rate of 4%. This is equivalent to an annual rate of 8% with semiannual compounding. For a bond or redeemable preferred, the effective yield is the yield to maturity. For a nonredeemable preferred, the effective yield is the current yield. See Chapter 8 for a discussion of these calculations.

[8]In the case of convertible preferred, the total dividend would be added back since it is not deductible for tax purposes.

[9]A modified treasury stock method is used when the proceeds would result in the assumed repurchase of more than 20% of the outstanding common stock. Proceeds in excess of amounts needed to purchase 20% of the common are assumed to be used first to retire short-term debt and then long-term debt. Any balance is assumed invested in the purchase of government securities. If debt is assumed to be retired or government securities are assumed to be purchased, there will be a numerator effect in that income will be increased (or loss decreased) by the assumed decrease in interest expense or increased interest income.

[10]"Substantially all" refers to 11 of 13 weeks over the last 3 months. Similar rules apply to interim EPS. See AICPA Interpretation 63.

reporting period. PEPS calculations are based on the average market price and FDEPS on the higher of the end-of-period market price or average market price for the period. Options and warrants are included in EPS computations only if their effect is dilutive (that is, the maket price exceeds their exercise price).

If

MP = Market price (average if PEPS, higher of average or year end for FDEPS)
EP = Exercise price for the option or warrant
N = Number of shares issuable on exercise

the proceeds received upon exercise are $EP \times N$. The number of repurchased shares $R = (EP \times N)/MP$, and incremental shares

$$I = (N - R)$$
$$= \frac{MP - EP}{MP} \times N$$

Illustration of Treasury Stock Method

Assume that on December 31, 1992, a firm awards options to key managers that allow them to purchase 25,000 shares of common at an exercise price of $25 per share. Average MP = $27.50 per share. Year end or December 31, 1993 MP = $30 per share, which has been higher than the exercise price for substantially all of the last three months of 1993. All EPS calculations are for the year ended December 31, 1993. The adjustments needed to calculate primary earnings per share and fully diluted earnings per share are as follows:

PEPS: Shares issued when options exercised = 25,000
        Shares repurchased* = 22,727 (25,000 × $25.00/$27.50)
        Incremental shares = 25,000 − 22,727 = 2,273, which is the denominator
          adjustment

Using the formula,

$$I = \frac{(\$27.50 - \$25.00)}{\$27.50} \times 25{,}000 = 2{,}273$$

FDEPS: Shares issued when options exercised = 25,000
        Shares repurchased† = 20,833 (25,000 × $25.00/$30.00)
        Incremental shares = 25,000 − 20,833 = 4,167, which is the denominator
          adjustment

Using the formula,

$$I = \frac{(\$30 - \$25)}{\$30} \times 25{,}000 = 4{,}167$$

Note the higher number of incremental shares due to the use of the higher year-end price. This method yields a larger denominator and, consequently, lower EPS.

---

*Proceeds of exercise used to purchase shares at average price.
†Proceeds of exercise used to repurchase shares at (higher) end-of-year price.

COMPREHENSIVE EXAMPLE OF EPS COMPUTATION

Exhibit 3C-1 incorporates the adjustments for the convertible bond and options already discussed into an actual computation of earnings per share.

The following points require emphasis. First, since the convertible bond was not classified as a CSE at issuance, conversion is not assumed when computing primary EPS, but it is assumed for the fully diluted EPS.

Second, options are always CSEs, and they enter into the computation of both primary and fully diluted EPS. The difference is that, for the fully diluted calculation, the period-end price is used if higher (hence, more dilutive) than the period-average price.

These considerations are always modified, if necessary, by the requirement to exclude antidilutive securities (whether CSEs or not).

EPS COMPUTATIONS FOR TWO-CLASS SECURITIES

Some firms issue more than one class of common stock or other "participating" securities that are entitled to share in the dividends paid on common stock but generally do not possess voting rights. EPS computations for each class of nonconvertible[11] two-class securities are based on an allocation of earnings according to dividends paid and participation rights in undistributed earnings.

Exhibit 3C-2 contains an illustration of the two-class method, using excerpts from the *1991 Annual Report* of Greif Bros. Corporation. The firm has two classes of common; Note 4 describes the dividend and voting rights applicable to each class.

The firm reports its EPS under the two-class method (see Exhibit 3C-2) but also contends that no set of assumptions would fairly represent the interests of each class of stock. The exhibit also contains another EPS calculation based on a different set of assumptions (derived from Note 4). The resulting EPS reflects higher dilution because it assumes that all net income is distributed in the form of dividends. Because the two classes have relative dividend rights that differ from relative liquidation rights, the dividend payout ratio has a significant impact on EPS. The higher the actual payout ratio, the greater disparity between the EPS for the two classes. The ratio of $EPS_{Class\ B}$ to $EPS_{Class\ A}$ is 1.15 as actually reported, but 1.49 based on the alternative calculation.

---

[11] If shares of one class are convertible into shares of the other class, as is normally the case, the problem is simplified. EPS is computed based on the number of shares outstanding assuming conversion. While the AICPA Interpretations suggest that the "two-class method" should be used when it results in greater dilution, in practice this advice is not followed.

EXHIBIT 3C-1
Computation of Earnings Per Share

Assumptions:	1993 Net income	$500,000
	Average common shares	100,000

Convertible bond, issued July 1, 1993

	Face amount	$1,000,000
	Proceeds	$1,197,928
	Coupon	10% (semiannual)
	Convertible	25 shares per $1000 bond
	Aa bond rate	10%

Options on common stock, issued December 31, 1992

	Number of shares	25,000
	Exercise price	$25.00 per share
	Average price	$27.50 per share during 1993
	Year-end price	$30.00 per share at 12-31-93

Simple earnings per share:

$$\frac{\text{Net income}}{\text{Average common shares}} = \frac{\$500,000}{100,000} = \$5.00$$

Primary earnings per share:

$$\frac{\text{Net income + Interest adjustment (net of tax)*}}{\text{Average common shares + Additional shares†}}$$

$$\frac{\$500,000}{100,000 + 2,273} = \frac{\$500,000}{102,273} = \$4.89$$

Fully diluted earnings per share:

$$\frac{\text{Net income + Interest adjustment (net of tax)‡}}{\text{Average common shares + Additional shares§}}$$

$$\frac{\$500,000 + \$28,750}{100,000 + 12,500 + 4,167} = \frac{\$528,750}{116,667} = \$4.53$$

---

*No adjustment is required since the bonds are not CSEs.
†2,273 incremental shares from assumed exercise of options.
‡Interest expense = $ 47,917 [8% × $1,197,928 × ½ year]
  Tax effect   = (19,167) [40% × $47,917]
  Adjustment   = $ 28,750

§12,500 shares from assumed conversion of bonds, 4,167 incremental shares from assumed exercise of options.

EXHIBIT 3C-2. GREIF BROS. CORPORATION
Illustration of Two-Class Method

($ and shares in millions)	Years Ended October 31		
	1989	1990	1991
Net income	$26.923	$22.127	$22.244
Dividends paid:			
Class A	$ 3.044	$ 3.044	$ 3.044
Class B	5.625	5.591	5.536
Dividends per share of common stock			
Class A	$ 0.56	$ 0.56	$ 0.56
Class B	0.82	0.82	0.82
Average shares outstanding for 1991			
Class A			5.436
Class B			6.751

Based on the assumption that earnings are allocated to class A and class B common stock to the extent that dividends were actually paid for the year and the remainder are allocated as they would be received by shareholders in the event of liquidation, that is, equally to class A and class B shares, EPS would be

	1989	1990	1991*
Class A	$2.04	$1.66	$1.68
Class B	2.30	1.92	1.94

Due to the special characteristics of the company's two classes of stock (see Note 4 below), earnings per share can be calculated upon the basis of varying assumptions, none of which, in the opinion of management, would be free from the claim that it fails fully and accurately to represent the true interest of the shareholders of each class of stock and in the earnings retained for use in the business.

*Reported EPS amounts are based on the assumption that Greif's undistributed earnings would be equally shared by the shareholders of the two classes of stock:

$$\frac{\text{Undistributed earnings}}{\text{Class A and Class B shares}} = \frac{\$22.244 - \$8.580}{5.436 + 6.751} = \$1.12 \text{ per share}$$

Earnings per share	Class A	Class B
Dividends paid	$0.56	$0.82
Undistributed earnings	1.12	1.12
EPS	$1.68	$1.94

Note 4—Capital Stock and Retained Earnings (Excerpt)

Class A common stock is entitled to cumulative dividends of 2 cents a share per year after which class B common stock is entitled to noncumulative dividends up to 1 cent a share per year. Further distribution in any year must be in proportion of 1 cent for class A common stock to 1½ cents a share for class B common stock. The class A common stock shall have no voting power nor shall it be entitled to notice of meetings of the stockholders, all rights to vote and all voting power being

EXHIBIT 3C-2. *(Continued)*

vested exclusively in the class B common stock unless four quarterly cumulative dividends upon the class A common Stock are in arrears. There is no cumulative voting.

Source: Adapted from Greif Bros. *1991 Annual Report.*

Alternative Computation of EPS

Assumptions: Note 4 describes the terms under which earnings are allocated between the two classes of stock:

ClassA: 2 cents per share per year, followed by 1 cent per share per year for class B. Additional distributions are in proportion of 1 cent a share for class A to 1.5 cents per share for class B.

If we assume that all earnings are paid out in the form of dividends, then earnings per share would be as follows:

1991 net income		$22.244 million
Less: Actual dividends paid		
Class A	$3.044	
Class B	5.536	
		(8.580)
Undistributed earnings		$13.664 million

If each class B share is entitled to a dividend of 1½ cents for each 1 cent paid per class A share, then we can compute the number of "class A equivalent" shares as follows:

Class A: $5.436 \times 1 = \$ 5.4360$ million
Class B: $6.751 \times 1.5 = 10.1265$

Class A equivalents $= \$15.5625$ million

Undistributed earnings per class A equivalent share is equal to

$$\frac{13.664}{15.5625} = \$0.88$$

Undistributed earnings per class B shares is equal to

$$1.5 \times 0.88 = \$1.32$$

Thus, under this assumption, earnings per share for 1991 was

	Class A	Class B
Distributed earnings	$0.56	$0.82
Undistributed earnings	0.88	1.32
EPS	$1.44	$2.14

ADDITIONAL DISCLOSURE REQUIREMENTS

Firms must provide a summary of the rights of convertible securities to disclose possible equity dilution. Dividend and liquidation preferences, participation and voting rights, call prices and dates, conversion (or exercise) prices and dates, and sinking fund requirements must all be disclosed.

Conversion of CSEs (bonds or preferred stock) into common shares may not change the total capital of the firm. However, such conversions or the issuance of shares (exercise of options) can change the number of shares outstanding and the trends in reported EPS. The impact of these changes on primary EPS must be disclosed even if the event occurs after the close of the reporting period (but before the financial statements are issued). Disclosure is made under the assumption that the events occurred at the beginning of the reporting period. Retroactive disclosure is also encouraged to depict the trend in EPS.

The SEC requires separate disclosure of EPS calculations if they cannot be determined directly from the financial statements or other disclosures.[12] Separate disclosure of income or loss per common share (simple EPS) is required when it reflects a difference of 10% or more from income or loss per share, as this may significantly affect EPS trends.[13]

LIMITATIONS OF EPS CALCULATIONS

The calculation of EPS provides excellent insight into some of the serious limitations of financial reporting. CSE classification for convertibles is permanently decided on the basis of the Aa bond yield at the time of issuance, a benchmark that has all the virtues of historical cost accounting, as it is verifiable and objective. However, it does not consider the fact that changes in market prices affect the value of the conversion feature and changes the probability that conversion (dilution) will actually occur.

Further, the Aa bond yield is too low a benchmark for many firms; its use results in a higher probability of CSE classification for lower-rated firms than if the benchmark were A or Baa.

The assumptions behind the treasury stock method are also unrealistic in many cases. They mirror the actual impact of exercise only in rare cases.

Another problem is that EPS calculations do not distinguish among firms with different dividend payout policies. Firms with low dividend payout ratios will show higher earnings per share growth than will those with high payout ratios.[14] As a result, misleading conclusions can arise when firms with different dividend policies are compared.

Firm A, shown in Exhibit 3C-3, has a low dividend payout ratio of 10%. As a result of the reinvestment of earnings, there is steady growth in EPS as we have assumed no

---

[12]Item 601, Exhibit 11 of Regulation S-K. This exhibit is required even when the dilution is less than 3% and APB 15 would not require the dual presentation.

[13]See Staff Accounting Bulletin 64, Topic 6B-1.

[14]The payout ratio is an explicit factor in such valuation methods as the dividend discount model.

EXHIBIT 3C-3
Effect of Dividend Policy on Growth of Earnings per Share, 1988–1992

	1988	1989	1990	1991	1992
Firm A: Low dividend payout					
Net income ($000)	1000	1090	1188	1295	1411
Average shares (000)	1000	1000	1000	1000	1000
Earnings per share ($)	1.00	1.09	1.19	1.30	1.41
Dividends paid ($000)	100	109	119	130	141
Firm B; High dividend payout					
Net income ($000)	1000	1090	1188	1295	1411
Average shares (000)	1000	1090	1188	1295	1411
Earnings per share ($)	1.00	1.00	1.00	1.00	1.00
Dividends paid ($000)	1000	1090	1188	1295	1411
Stock issued ($000)	900	981	1069	1165	1270
Assumed price per share ($)	10.00	10.00	10.00	10.00	10.00
# shares issued (000)	90	98	107	116	127
Firm A compared to Firm B					
Ratio of earnings per share	1.00	1.09	1.19	1.30	1.41

issuance of new stock. Firm B, shown at the bottom of Exhibit 3C-3, is assumed to pay out all its net income in the form of dividends. To obtain the capital for growth, it sells new shares at the price indicated (for simplicity we assume a constant price-earnings ratio of 10). While both firms show the same (9%) growth of net income, Firm B shows no growth in EPS. The growth in shares outstanding is as rapid as the growth in earnings. The last line of the exhibit shows the widening differential between the earnings per share of the two firms.

While this example may appear unrealistic, it is a reasonable description of the plight of public utility companies (gas, electric, water) in the United States. To attract investors, firms pay out most of their earnings as dividends. To finance growth, firms must periodically sell additional common shares. As a result, EPS growth rates are quite low. These firms are trapped in a vicious cycle. If they reduced their dividend rates, their EPS growth rates would rise, and they might be considered growth companies rather than bond substitutes.[15]

INTERNATIONAL DIFFERENCES

Earnings per share computations and disclosure requirements under U.S. GAAP are more comprehensive than are those in other countries. U.K. and Canadian standards are closest in that they require firms to calculate basic and fully diluted EPS, which are

---

[15]A few utility companies have been successful in promoting themselves as growth companies by paying low dividends and/or stock dividends and retaining their earnings for growth.

similar to the primary and fully diluted EPS required in the United States. However, basic EPS does not include the effect of any potentially dilutive securities, as the U.K. and Canadian standards do not use the concept of common stock equivalents.

The dilutive impact of options and warrants is included only in fully diluted EPS, but neither country employs the treasury stock method used in the United States. Proceeds are assumed to be invested so as to generate a notional return, which is included in earnings when computing fully diluted earnings per share.

The most important international difference is that the computation of fully diluted earnings per share is not required in most countries. Comparisons of basic and primary EPS are also affected by the use of common stock equivalents in the United States but not in other countries. Finally, rights issues are common in other countries, and they are included in basic EPS. Rights issues at the current market price are treated as new issues of common stock, but a denominator adjustment is required for the bonus element when rights are issued below the current market price.

CONCLUDING REMARKS

Earnings per share is probably the most widely used indicator of corporate performance, yet most of those who use it do not understand how it is computed. Fewer still understand how it is affected by the issuance of convertibles, options, or other potentially dilutive securities. We have tried to remedy that deficiency in this appendix.

APB 15, like most accounting standards, is a set of arbitrary rules, and it sometimes provides data at variance with economic reality. When a convertible security has a conversion price close to or below the market price of the common shares, the "if converted" method is sound. Use of that method means that earnings per share will not be affected by the actual conversion. When the conversion price is well above the market price, then the probability of conversion may be remote. In this case the "if converted" method produces an unlikely "worst case" EPS, and for purposes of analysis the "nondiluted" EPS may be more useful. As we will argue repeatedly throughout this book, the role of the analyst clearly includes selecting the accounting data that best suit the purpose at hand and adjusting that data when necessary to make it more meaningful for analysis.

Appendix 3C

Problems

1. [Primary and fully diluted EPS calculations; CFA adapted] The following information is provided regarding the capital structure of WFA, Inc., at December 31, 1992:

Common shares outstanding on December 31, 1992	2,700,000
Weighted average common shares outstanding during 1992	2,500,000
Convertible bonds (issued December 31, 1989)	$12,000,000
(5% coupon, convertible into common shares at $30 per share)	
Convertible preferred shares (issued July 1, 1992)	70,000
($4.00 dividend per share, 5.5% effective yield, each share convertible into 5 common shares)	
Options outstanding at December 31, 1992	200,000
(exercise price $15 per share)	

WFA common shares on December 31, 1992, had a market price of $25. The weighted average market price per share for 1992 was $20.

1. The Aa corporate bond yield was:
   a. 8.5% at December 31, 1989.
   b. 7.5% at July 1, 1992.
   c. 7.0% at December 31, 1992.
2. Net income for 1992 was $6,500,000.
3. WFA's tax rate for 1992 was 40%.

A. Which securities are considered to be common stock equivalents? Explain why. Compute the number of common and common equivalent shares used to compute primary earnings per share for 1992.

B. Compute primary earnings per share for 1992.

C. Compute the number of common shares used to compute fully diluted earnings per share. Explain any differences between your answer and your answer to part A.

D. Compute fully diluted earnings per share for 1992. Explain any difference between the numerator (earnings) used to compute primary and fully diluted EPS.

E. Explain how your answers to parts A–D would change if:

(i) WAF's common share price were $30 at December 31, 1992.

(ii) the Aa bond rate were 9% at December 31, 1992.

F. WFA's 1992 results have been restated for a pooling acquisition made on March 31, 1992. WFA issued 240,000 shares and the acquired firm earned $600,000 in 1992 ($150,000 per quarter).

(i) Compute WFA's primary EPS for 1992 under the assumption that the acquisition had not been made.

(ii) Compute WFA's primary EPS for 1992 under the assumption that the acquisition was accounted for as a purchase (the shares are considered outstanding and the earnings of the acquired firm are included only for the period following the acquisition).

2. [1989 CFA adapted] Champion Lion Tamers had 2 million shares outstanding on December 31, 1987. On March 31, 1988, Champion pays a 10% stock dividend. On June 30, 1988, Champion sells $10 million of 5% convertible debentures, convertible into common shares at $5 per share. The Aa bond rate on the issue date was 8%. On September 30, 1988, Champion issues 800,000 warrants, exercisable at $5 per share. The market price of Champion shares was $8 on December 31, 1988; the average price for the fourth quarter of 1988 was $4.

A. Compute the number of common and common equivalent shares used to compute primary earnings per share for 1988.

B. Compute the number of shares used to compute fully diluted earnings per share for 1988.

C. Discuss how your answers to parts A and B would change under the following conditions:

(i) Champion's share price was $10 at December 31, 1988.

(ii) Champion's average share price for the fourth quarter of 1988 was $8.

(iii) The Aa bond rate at December 31, 1988 was 7%.

D. Discuss how your answers to parts A and B might change if Champion prepared its financial statements under non-U.S. accounting standards.

4

EMPIRICAL RESEARCH: IMPLICATIONS FOR FINANCIAL STATEMENT ANALYSIS

INTRODUCTION

THE CLASSICAL APPROACH

MARKET-BASED RESEARCH

Efficient Market Theory

Modern Portfolio Theory

Test of the Mechanistic Hypothesis Versus the EMH

The Ball and Brown Study

Information Content Studies

The Relationship Between Earnings and Stock Returns

Accounting Variable

Market-Based Variable

Test of the Relationship Between the Good News/Bad News Parameter and "Abnormal" Returns

Market-Based Research—Current Status

Critical Evaluation of Research Findings

Market Anomalies

POSITIVE ACCOUNTING RESEARCH

Disclosure and Regulatory Requirements

Agency Theory

The Bonus Plan Hypothesis

The Debt Covenant Hypothesis

The Political Cost Hypothesis

Summary of the Research

DIRECTION OF CURRENT RESEARCH

Ball and Brown Revisited—Back to the Future?

IMPLICATIONS FOR FINANCIAL STATEMENT ANALYSIS

INTRODUCTION

Accounting research has undergone tremendous changes in the last quarter century in objectives, methodology, and underlying philosophies. To a great extent, the changes mirrored (or, as some argue, merely followed) shifts in financial economic theory. This chapter presents an overview of the research. We will not try to review all this research here but rather will

- Characterize the nature of the research.
- Indicate where in the book the research has relevance and where it will be discussed in further detail.
- Summarize the important findings without getting bogged down in the detail. One study in each area will be used to demonstrate the nature of the research.

The goals of this chapter are to

1. Give the reader a general understanding of the underlying theory, objectives, methods, and results of major academic research in the area of financial accounting.
2. Provide some guidance as to the relevance of such research to the financial analysis process.

The first three sections of the chapter are devoted to an examination of three major approaches to accounting theory and research. Figure 4-1 presents these approaches schematically. In the first section we briefly review the classical approach to accounting theory prior to the mid-1960s and the framework still (largely) underlying existing accounting regulation. This approach attempts, using a purely theoretical perspective, to define an optimal or "most correct" accounting representation of some true (but unobservable) reality.

The second, and largest, section deals with what is commonly referred to as market-based accounting research. Criticizing the classical approach for its lack of testability, market-based research takes a more empirical, as well as user-oriented, perspective. Its primary focus is the market reaction to (or association with) accounting numbers. Observable relationships between earnings[1] and market returns are the basis upon which conclusions are to be drawn.

The "positive" accounting theory approach, described in the third section, also focuses on observable reactions to accounting numbers, but this is not its primary focus. As Figure 4-1 indicates, it broadens the perspective in two ways. First, in addition to the market, it includes other "environments" influenced by financial statements. These entail management compensation plans, debt agreements with creditors, and the host of regulatory bodies interacting with the firm. More important, it recognizes that since the financial statements impact these other "environments," there exist incentives for the

---

[1]We use the term earnings here and throughout the chapter in a generic sense. It is not intended to preclude other accounting variables examined by the research.

A. Classical Theory

```
          ┌─────────────────────┐
          │ Operating, Financing,│
          │   and Investment     │
          │     Decisions        │
          │      Events          │
          └─────────────────────┘
            ┆                  │
            ▼                  ▼
  ┌──────────────────┐  ┌──────────────────┐
  │ True Economic    │  │   Accounting     │
  │   Reality        │  │  Description     │
  │ (unobservable)   │  │                  │
  └──────────────────┘  └──────────────────┘
```

B. Market-Based Research

```
          ┌─────────────────────┐
          │ Operating, Financing,│
          │   and Investment     │
          │     Decisions        │
          │      Events          │
          └─────────────────────┘
                    ┆
                    ▼
          ┌──────────────────┐
          │   Accounting     │
          │  Description     │
          └──────────────────┘
                    ┆
                    ▼
          ┌──────────────────┐
          │   Information    │
          └──────────────────┘
                    │
                    ▼
          ┌──────────────────┐
          │  Market Reaction │
          └──────────────────┘
```

C. Positive Accounting

```
          ┌─────────────────────┐
          │ Operating, Financing,│
          │   and Investment     │◄───┐
          │     Decisions        │    │
          │      Events          │    │
          └─────────────────────┘    │
                    ┆                 │
                    ▼                 │
          ┌──────────────────┐        │
          │   Accounting     │◄───────┤
          │  Description     │        │
          └──────────────────┘        │
                    ┆                 │
                    ▼                 │
          ┌──────────────────┐        │
          │   Information    │        │
          └──────────────────┘        │
                    │                 │
                    ▼                 │
    ┌──────────────────────────────┐ │
    │      Market Reaction         │─┘
    │  Management Compensation     │
    │      Debt Covenants          │
    │   Regulatory Environment     │
    │         Other                │
    └──────────────────────────────┘
```

*Solid Line Indicates
Research Focus

FIGURE 4-1 Schematic Representation of Three Approaches to Accounting Theory and Research

accounting system to be used not only to measure the results of decisions but in turn to influence these decisions in the first place. This "feedback" interaction can influence both management operating decisions and their choice of accounting variables.

The three approaches can be described in terms of how they view the underlying economic reality of the firm. In the classical approach, an underlying reality exists, and it is the role of accounting to describe it. Market-based research, on the other hand, views reality as given by market value—"what you see is what you get" (WYSIWYG)—and accounting alternatives, a priori, really do not make any difference. The positive approach adds a new twist: accounting alternatives are what define and determine reality.

These approaches evolved over time both in response to the results generated by research undertaken to test the competing theories and by new developments in information economics and finance theory. As will be noted, the research began with much fanfare and promise, only to be tempered over time by both the economic (in)significance of the results and by reality, or what academics euphemistically call anomalies.

The concluding section of the chapter will be devoted to a discussion of the present direction of the research. This trend is characterized by a return to the examination of a priori linkages between financial statements and security valuation. This underlying structural or fundamental analysis,[2] in some respects, combines the direction of the classical approach with the empiricism of market-based research. This "neoclassical" approach is still in the embryonic stage. Given the experience of the last two decades, one is hesitant to make any prediction as to its ultimate success.

The discussion of this research, however, will lay the context within which this book is to be viewed. We argue that to be able to carry out any mode of analysis, one must know the underlying framework of financial statements. The resulting number, whether bottom-line earnings or some other component, cannot be taken at face value without considering the context. Doing so requires synthesis of the lessons learned from all the approaches to accounting research together with a thorough understanding of the information provided in the statements.

THE CLASSICAL APPROACH

Classical accounting theory approaches issues from a normative point of view. Accounting methods and technologies are evaluated in terms of how close the information provided comes to some preconceived "true" picture or status of the firm. In this approach the ideal picture is viewed as being determinable within the accounting system itself. Notions such as economic profit and its relationship to accounting income are the focus of debate. Thus much discussion (without consensus) ensues over topics such as current cost versus replacement cost versus historical cost accounting frameworks.

---

[2]The term structural for modeling the a priori linkages can be traced to Ryan (1988). Using fundamental (or financial statement) analysis to classify the research can be attributed to empirical studies by Ou and Penman (1989), Ou (1990) and Penman (1991, 1992).

The approach is one of deducing correct procedures from a stated set of concepts, principles, and objectives. Implicit in this approach is a view that users of financial statements accept (and react to) the statements at face value, and thus great importance is attached to ensure the preparation of statements that reflect this elusive true financial picture[3] of the firm. Moreover, as the nature of users' reaction to the information in financial statements is deemed to be predictable, no explicit effort is made to examine, empirically or otherwise, the interrelationship between financial statements and users' motivations and/or reaction to the information contained in the statements.

Concurrently with the early development of this approach to accounting theory, the teachings of Graham and Dodd reigned supreme in the academic and professional finance communities. In their world, stocks have "intrinsic value," and fundamental analysis using ratios and other financial analysis techniques could develop filter rules using data from financial statements that would identify those stocks that were over- or undervalued.

Simultaneously (and, perhaps, paradoxically), it was argued by some that, although determining the "true" financial picture was a worthwhile objective, since the accounting rules in use did not actually mirror the underlying "true" picture, the financial statements presented were meaningless and of no use to investors. A statement by Canning (1929) was often quoted in support of this viewpoint:

> What is set out as a measure of net income can never be supposed to be a fact in any sense at all except that it is the figure that results when the accountant has finished applying the procedures which he adopts.[4]

The classical approach fell out of favor in academic circles due to its lack of testability. It was argued that questions as to the usefulness of accounting information could be resolved only by observing the effects on financial statement users. The emphasis turned to empirical verification of the decision relevance of the information contained in accounting reports.

Accounting regulators never fully embraced this new approach to accounting theory.[5] Whether this was because they did not agree with it philosophically or because they felt that the results emanating from it had no practical implications is a matter of debate. It is important to note that existing accounting rules, which make up the body of procedures known as generally accepted accounting principles (GAAP), are greatly influenced by and are still a product of the classical approach. In the concluding section of this chapter, we will return to this point.

MARKET-BASED RESEARCH

Advances in finance theory in the mid- and late 1960s were the primary catalyst for the shift in accounting research described in this section. Academic accounting research

---

[3]This is equivalent to the concept of representational faithfulness discussed in Chapter 1.

[4]Canning, John B., *The Economics of Accountancy*, The Ronald Press Co., New York, 1929, p. 98

[5]There are some exceptions. For example, the change in the current cost disclosures required by Financial Accounting Standards Board No. 33 from mandatory to voluntary was partially a result of empirical evidence indicating that the market ignored the information.

shifted from the classical deductive approach to accounting problems to a more empirical approach that focused primarily on three issues:

1. What were users' reaction to financial statements?
2. Did alternative accounting methods make a difference in terms of users' reactions?
3. Given users' needs, could accounting policy and rules be set to maximize the utility to the user?

The two major advances in finance literature exerting influence over accounting theory in this period were the efficient market hypothesis and modern portfolio theory.

Efficient Market Theory

Underlying the new approach to accounting research and theory was the widespread interest in and increasing acceptance of one form or another of the efficient market hypothesis (EMH) in the academic and professional finance community. The EMH, as defined in Fama (1970), states that a market is efficient if security prices "fully reflect" the information available. "Fully reflecting" the information is taken to mean that knowledge of that information would not allow anyone to profit from it, as security prices already incorporate the information. Further, the information became impounded in the prices correctly and instantaneously as soon as it became known.

Information available was classified into three sets, and hence three forms of the EMH were propounded:

1. *The weak form:* The information set includes information about past securities prices only.
2. *The semistrong form:* The information set includes all publicly available information.
3. *The strong form:* The information set includes all information including privately held (inside) information.

Evidence in the finance literature during this period strongly supported the weak and semistrong forms. The weak form implied that using the past series of security prices to predict future prices was not possible. Hence, charting techniques (head and shoulder patterns, double tops, etc.) and other types of technical analysis were meaningless and unprofitable.

The information set used by the market under the semistrong form included all publicly available information such as financial statements, government reports, industry reports, and analysis. Two implications for accounting research, policy, and analysis flow from the semistrong form.

First, financial statements are not the sole source of information used to make investment decisions. Second, and more important, no trading advantages could accrue to users of financial statements as the information contained in them was instantaneously impounded in prices as soon as the information became public. This latter point was a direct attack on fundamental analysis—the mainstay of financial analysts who searched for stocks that were over- or undervalued relative to their intrinsic value. Graham himself was quoted as saying in 1976

> I am no longer an advocate of elaborate techniques of security analysis in order to find superior value opportunities. This was a rewarding activity, say, forty years ago . . . but the situation has changed a good deal since then. In the old days any well-trained security analyst could do a good professional job of selecting undervalued issues through detailed studies; *but in light of the enormous amount of research being carried out, I doubt whether in most cases such extensive efforts will generate sufficiently superior selections to justify their cost. To that very limited extent I'm on the side of the "efficient market" school of thought.*[6]

The ironic part of the argument (as indicated by the preceding quotation) is that it was the same analysts engaging in fundamental analysis looking for the bargains that ensured that there were no bargains to be found. Their research efforts resulted in prices that fully reflected all available information:

> this error takes the form of asserting that accounting data have no value. . . . The efficient market in no way leads to such implications. It may very well be that the publishing of financial statements data is precisely what makes the market as efficient as it is.[7]

The EMH also had implications for the setting of accounting standards. No longer did such standards have to be set with the intention of protecting the naive or unsophisticated investor. The existence of savvy analysts/investors, who ensured that prices correctly and instantaneously reflected available information, provided protection for the naive investor. Any trades made by such investors would be at a "fair" price.

Modern Portfolio Theory

The second trend in finance theory having an impact on accounting theory and research was modern portfolio theory (MPT), as embodied in the capital asset pricing model (CAPM). The CAPM characterized the relationship between expected returns and risk as

$$E(R_i) = R_f + \beta_i[E(R_m) - R_f]$$

Where

R_i = the rate of return on stock i

R_f = the risk-free rate of return

R_m = the rate of return on the market as a whole and

β_i = the "beta" of the ith firm that measures the co-movement of that firm's returns with that of the overall market

$E(*)$ = the expectation symbol representing the expected value

[6]The quotation is from John Train, *Money Masters* (New York: Harper & Row, 1987), emphasis added.

[7]Beaver, William, "What Should Be the FASB's Objectives?", *Journal of Accountancy*, (August 1973), pp. 49–56

The actual realized return is therefore (removing the expectation symbol $E(*)$)

$$R_i = R_f + \beta_i(R_m - R_f) + e_i$$

where *e is the unexpected or abnormal return*. In other words, e_i represents the portion of a stock's realized return above or below the expected return (given existing market conditions).

Under MPT, it was argued that while the relationship between risk and return holds insofar as higher risks are rewarded by higher (expected) returns, the relationship holds only for that portion of risk that cannot be diversified away. Risk is classified as either systematic or unsystematic. Systematic risk is that portion of the uncertainty faced by a firm that is due to common factors facing all firms in the economy and/or industry:[8] the business cycle, interest rates, inflation, and so on. Its measure under CAPM is the "beta" of the firm, β_i.

Unsystematic risk is the portion of uncertainty specific to a given firm. The unsystematic return is the return, e_i, accruing to the firm after accounting for the systematic effects. The unsystematic portion of risk could be diversified away by investors holding well-diversified portfolios. Thus, since it could be diversified away, there is no "reward" to investors for this portion of risk in terms of higher returns, that is, the expected abnormal return, $E(e_i) = 0$. The systematic risk, on the other hand, could not be diversified away and hence has to be compensated for by offering the investor a higher expected return.

MPT and the CAPM impacted accounting theory in a number of ways. First, it provided a ready model used to measure market returns and the reaction to earnings. Deviations from expected earnings could be shown to influence the realized rate of return or, more specifically, the unexpected portion (the abnormal return, e_i).

Second, it implied that since the expected return for a given firm did not depend on risks that could be diversified away, information regarding the outlook for a *specific* firm was irrelevant. The only thing that mattered was the systematic risk of the firm and its relationship to the total portfolio.

> In an efficient market, the usefulness of financial statement data to individual investors is not to find mispriced securities *since they are nonexistent. What then is the value, if any?* The value lies in the ability of financial statement data to aid in risk prediction.[9]

The use of accounting data to predict measures of risk thus became an avenue of accounting research with the evidence indicating that such data could be used to enhance the prediction of risk attributes such as beta. What is surprising is that this line of research, although promising, did not play a bigger role. A detailed review of this research is presented in Chapter 14, where overall risk and credit analysis is discussed.

---

[8]The single index model just defined only has provision for systematic risk on an economy wide basis. Multi-index models, however, could be constructed to capture industrywide effects.

[9]Beaver, "What Should Be the FASB's Objectives?" p. 55, emphasis added.

In addition to the prediction of risk measures, market-based research studies can be classified into the following categories:

1. Tests of the EMH versus the classical approach
2. Tests of the informational content of accounting alternatives
3. Tests of the earnings/return relationship

Test of the Mechanistic Hypothesis Versus the EMH

The mechanistic hypothesis, which is consistent with the classical approach to accounting theory, held that users of financial statements accept the information provided there at face value.[10] Implicit in this hypothesis is the assumption that users of financial statements do not access other sources of information and do not adjust financial statements for the effects of alternative accounting methods. Clearly, the mechanistic hypothesis stands as the antithesis to the EMH, which holds that current prices reflect all information available.

The mechanistic hypothesis was tested by examining the stock market reaction to changes in accounting methods that inflated income but had no cash flow effects. Specifically, firms that changed their depreciation method for financial reporting (but not for tax) purposes from accelerated to straight line (see Chapter 6 for discussion of these methods) were examined by both Archibald (1972) and Kaplan and Roll (1972). Since reported income increased as a result of the switch, under the mechanistic hypothesis, we should expect to see increases in stock prices, whereas the EMH would argue that the market would see through the changes as being purely artificial and no reaction should result.

The methodology, essentially,[11] consisted of measuring the abnormal return, e_i, around the time of the earnings announcement for the sample of firms that made the switch in accounting method. Under the mechanistic approach, we would expect to see $e_i > 0$, and under the EMH, we would expect to see $e_i = 0$. Figure 4-2 presents the results from the Kaplan and Roll study. Around the time of the earnings announcement, which occurs at week 30, both the cumulative abnormal return (CAR) and the abnormal return itself are insignificantly different from zero. About six weeks following the earnings announcement (week 36), a pronounced *negative* abnormal return occurs for the sample of firms. These results are inconsistent with the mechanistic hypothesis.[12]

---

[10]The mechanistic view was sometimes referred to as "functional fixation."

[11]The actual approach used in many studies was not strictly the CAPM but variations of it such as the market model. The CAPM is a theoretically derived model based on a number of specific assumptions as to the nature and structure of capital markets. The "market" model does not have elaborate underpinnings, but rather is based on the intuitive argument that returns of a firm are a function of common and firm-specific factors. The linear equation that describes such a relationship is

$$R_i = a_i + \beta_i R_m + e_i$$

where a_i and e_i measure the firm-specific factor and $\beta_i R_m$ measures the common factors. Again, the $E(e_i) = 0$. The similarities between this model and the CAPM should be clear.

[12]These results, while offering some support for the EMH, also pose some problems for it. A possible explanation for the negative abnormal returns is that those firms that made the change were experiencing

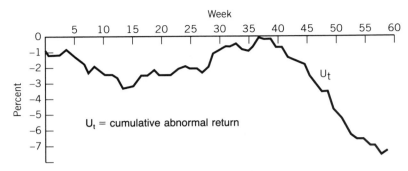

FIGURE 4-2 Kaplan and Roll Results. Source: Kaplan, Robert S. and Richard Roll, "Investor Evaluation of Accounting Information: Some Empirical Evidence" *Journal of Business,* 45 (April 1972) pp. 225–257, Figure 1, Panel C P. 239 (Adapted), ©University of Chicago.

Studies of this kind, motivated by tests of the mechanistic hypothesis versus the EMH, after a while became passé.[13] Although there was much disagreement as to what types of information markets reacted to, the general consensus[14] was that the market was not naive in the sense of following the earnings number blindly and could easily adjust the information provided accordingly.

> Many reporting issues are trivial. . . . The properties of such issues are twofold: (1) there is essentially no difference in cost to the firm of reporting either method. (2) There is essentially no cost to statement users in adjusting from one method to the other. In such cases there is a simple solution. Report one method, with sufficient footnote disclosure to permit adjustment to the other and let the market interpret implications of the data for security prices. . . . If there are no additional costs of disclosure to the firm, there is prima facie evidence that the item in question should be disclosed.[15]

On the other hand, studies of changes in accounting method did continue, but with other objectives in mind. Switches of first-in, first-out (FIFO) to last-in, first-out (LIFO) were studied extensively as these changes had real cash flow effects due to their tax consequences. These results are discussed in detail in our discussion of inventory

---

difficult times and management made the change in an attempt artificially to hide the effects of the bad times. It should be remembered that market efficiency does not mean that everyone (in this case, management) believes it is efficient. The negative reaction is, therefore, nothing more than the market reacting to the bad times as they occur. The problem for the EMH with these results is related to the fact that the negative reaction does not happen instantaneously at the time of the announcement and that it persists for a number of weeks (week 36 to week 60).

[13]Recently, however, in light of some of the anomalies associated with the EMH, the functional fixation hypothesis has returned in the form of the Extended Functional Fixation Hypothesis (see Hand (1990)). Under this guise, it is argued that there exist at least some unsophisticated investors on the margin who can and do affect prices.

[14]The general consensus here refers to the academic accounting community and sizable portions of the professional community. This is not to say that there did not exist accountants and accounting policymakers as well as managers themselves who did not believe that the market and investors needed to be protected from following the numbers blindly.

[15]Beaver, "What Should Be the FASB's Objectives?" p. 51

accounting (Chapter 5). In addition, positive accounting theory introduced motivations for accounting changes beyond those suggested by market-based accounting research. These motivations and related research will be elaborated on in the section dealing with positive accounting theory.[16]

The belief that the market does not follow numbers blindly led researchers to question how (if at all) markets react to accounting information. The methodology and philosophy underlying this mode of research can be understood best with an in-depth analysis of the seminal Ball and Brown (1968) study.

The Ball and Brown Study

The focus of the Ball and Brown study was to document whether an association existed between the price (returns) of a firm's securities and the accounting earnings of the firm. More precisely, using a sample of firms, they partitioned the firms into "good" news/"bad" news groupings. Based on the actual realization of a firm's earnings, a company is classified as having reported good (bad) news if the actual earnings realization was above (below) that predicted by a time series forecasting model. Then, acting as if this knowledge was known as far back as March of the year in question, two portfolios are constructed on the basis of the good news/bad news partitions.

The main finding of their study is reproduced here as Figure 4-3, which compares the cumulative abnormal returns realized over the year for the "good" news and "bad" news portfolios.[17] "Good" ("bad") news firms enjoyed, on average, abnormally positive (negative) returns as measured by e_i.

The figure shows unambiguously that firms whose earnings conveyed good news enjoyed abnormally better stock returns and vice versa for the firms whose earnings conveyed bad news. Hence, a clear (empirical) association between earnings and stock market reaction had been demonstrated.

These results, in addition to opening the door to future avenues of research, also raised many questions. As can be noted in Figure 4-3, the abnormal good/bad market reaction began close to a year prior to the publication of the good news/bad news contained in the annual reports. Further, there is little information content to the announcement per se. Ball and Brown estimated that approximately 80–85% of the abnormal market performance occurred prior to the publication of the annual report. This finding suggested that while earnings are meaningful in the sense that they are reflective of a firm's financial performance, by the time they are published, they may be redundant and have little or no impact.

> They demonstrate that the information contained in the annual income number is useful in that as actual income differs from expected income, the market typically has reacted in the same direction. . . .

---

[16]Mandatory switches caused by changes in accounting regulations, as opposed to voluntary switches instigated by management, are another avenue of research into the effects of changes in accounting policy; we will discuss such research in the next section.

[17]The graph depicts one (EPS, naive model) of the three variations of earnings examined by Ball and Brown.

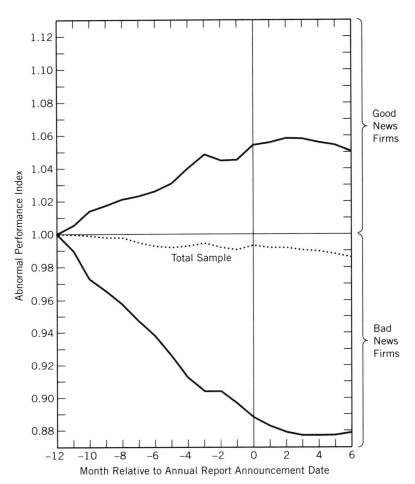

FIGURE 4-3 Ball and Brown Results. Source: Ball, Ray and Philip Brown, "An Empirical Evaluation of Accounting Income Numbers", *Journal of Accounting Research* (Autumn 1968) pp. 159–178, Figure 1, p. 169 (Adapted), reprinted with permission.

However, most of the information contained in reported income is anticipated by the market before the annual is released. In fact, anticipation is so accurate that the actual income number does not appear to cause any unusual jumps . . . in the announcement month.[18]

The anticipation of the accounting numbers raised the question as to the *timeliness of annual reports* and is indicative of the fact that the annual report is not the sole source of information available to the marketplace. Competing sources of information about the economy as a whole, the industry the firm operates in, and the firm itself are available from a multitude of sources such as government reports, industry associations, financial

[18]Ball, Ray and Philip Brown, "An Empirical Evaluation of Accounting Income Numbers", *Journal of Accounting Research* (Autumn 1968) pp. 159–178

analyst reports, and management announcements, not to mention the interim reports generated by the firm itself.

Ball and Brown triggered an explosion of empirical accounting research over the next two decades that can be roughly described as either studies of the information content of earnings or of the overall relationship between stock returns and reported earnings.

Information Content Studies

The results of the Ball and Brown study spurred a series of studies whose focus was an examination of the "information content" of accounting numbers, with information content measured by market reaction to the announced earnings number and its deviation from expectation. The procedure involved calculating the cumulative abnormal return resulting from alternative measures of earnings.

For example, Beaver and Dukes (1972) compared the informational content of earnings with and without the deferral of taxes. Others examined the information content of segment earnings, special items, capitalized leases, alternative accounting methods for oil and gas properties, and so on. These individual studies will be discussed in the chapters where the related accounting principles are presented.

At first, researchers tended to argue that, given a choice of accounting alternatives, the one that triggered the greatest market reaction, that is, had the most "information content," was the most desirable alternative. This notion was soon abandoned, not because it was felt that earnings and market reaction were unrelated, but rather because any change in market prices and/or purchase/sale of shares (regardless of price changes) resulted in some people being better off in relation to others. Thus deciding the best alternative necessarily involved judgments affecting social consequence and the general welfare, which were deemed to be "political" in nature and beyond the realm of academic research.[19]

> A second erroneous implication is, simply find out what method is most highly associated with security prices and report that method in the financial statements. As it stands it is incorrect for several reasons. One major reason is that such a simplified decision rule fails to consider the costs of providing the information. . . . Moreover, the choice among different accounting methods involves choosing among differing consequences. . . . Hence, some individuals may be better off under one method, while others may be better off under an alternative method. . . . The issue is one of social choice, which in general is an unresolvable problem.[20]

The reluctance to prescribe normative solutions did not diminish the quantity of research carried out in this area; it just shifted the emphasis. Recognition, however, was now

---

[19]In this way of thinking, intrinsic value, even if it existed, was not necessarily a standard by which to measure choice of accounting alternatives since somebody may "suffer" if the "truth" be known. An extensive rationale for this argument can be found in Gonedes and Dopuch (1974).

[20]Beaver, "What Should Be the FASB's Objectives?" p. 55. This position was something of a reversal for Beaver. In an earlier paper (1972, p. 321), Beaver took the position, consistent with the general approach of the time, that the accounting method most closely associated with security prices is the one that should be reported.

given to the implicit cost/benefit trade-offs resulting from any disclosure requirement. Some of the implications of viewing information as an economic commodity will be discussed in further detail later in this chapter.

The Relationship Between Earnings and Stock Returns

Studies of the earnings/return relationship was by far the most prevalent form of research as far as market-based studies are concerned. Organizing and classifying the nature of this research can be done best by reference to the Ball and Brown study. Their study included the following interrelated categories and subcategories, and we shall summarize the nature of the research along those lines.

1. Accounting variable
   a. Choice of the appropriate accounting variable
   b. Expectations of accounting variables
   c. Measurement of "good" news and "bad" news
2. Market-based variable
   a. Choice of market model
   b. Measurement of "abnormal" market performance
   c. Measurement period ("window") for market performance
3. Test of the relationship between the good news/bad news parameter and "abnormal" returns

A great deal of the research that followed explored the foregoing elements both in terms of variations of Ball and Brown's approach and as legitimate areas of research in their own right. Some of the research was broad in scope, testing many variations of the variables. In other cases, the research was merely a repetition of previous studies, with an emphasis on methodological refinements. All in all, the results of the research proved to be somewhat disappointing, with no major breakthroughs in terms of understanding the role of earnings in the stock return generating process. In addition, some of the research began to turn up evidence that seemed to contradict the semistrong form of market efficiency.

Accounting Variable

Choice of the Appropriate Accounting Variable. Ball and Brown used annual net income and earnings per share (EPS). Other researchers [e.g., Foster (1977), Bathe and Lorek (1984)] used the quarterly earnings report with similar results, indicating that the quarterly reports also possessed "information content." However, a number of studies (see Ball (1978) and Joy and Jones (1979) for surveys) began to document postannouncement drift wherein positive (negative) abnormal return patterns continued for some time after the announcement of good (bad) news quarterly earnings.

Gonedes (1975, 1978) and Ronen and Sadan (1981), among others, focused on the question of which definition of income was more important—operating income, income from continuing operations, or net income—by examining whether the inclusion of special, nonrecurring, or extraordinary items had any impact on security returns. The spate of restructuring and write-offs in the 1980s rekindled research in this area.

More recently, in line with the current focus on cash flows in accounting and finance, research has tended to examine the relative informational content of cash flow versus net income. As discussed in Chapter 2, the results do not generally demonstrate additional information in the cash flow number over that found in the accrual-based earnings number.

Finally, in response to criticisms, such as Lev's paper (1989) discussed shortly, that focusing on a single number such as earnings to explain return behavior was too simplistic, some studies examined the relationship between returns and various components of earnings (Lipe, 1986) and between returns and cash flow components (Livnat and Zarowin, 1990).

Expectations of Accounting Variables. Earnings forecasts play an important role in many finance valuation models and are thought to be of great interest to investors. An important by-product of the earnings/return relationship research, which soon became a major area of research in its own right, lay in the development and construction of earnings forecasting models. Simple and complex time series models, using annual and/or quarterly data, were compared against one other and with those generated by financial analysts and management to examine two independent but closely related questions:

1. Which forecasting model or forecast performed best in terms of predictive ability?
2. Which forecasting model or forecast most closely mirrored the market's expectations?

The first issue is discussed in greater detail in Chapter 15, where various forecasting models are described and compared.

Research into the second issue (also discussed in Chapter 15) suggests that financial analyst forecasts are a better surrogate of market expectations than are models based solely on the historical time series of reported income.[21] This superiority was attributed (Brown, Hagerman, Griffin and Zmijewski (1987)) to the fact that the analyst has available both a broader set of information upon which to base forecasts and more timely information.

The fact that "market" expectations coincide with that of financial analysts led researchers to examine whether financial analysts in some sense lead the market and whether the market derives its expectations from analyst forecasts. The results of such studies found that there was market reaction to changes in analysts forecasts, thus indicating that the answers to the research questions posed are affirmative. A study by Givoly and Lakonishok (1979), however, also indicated that abnormal returns could be earned by trading on revisions of analyst forecasts, again raising questions as to the efficiency of capital markets.

[21]O'Brien (1988), however, presents contradictory findings.

Measurement of Good News/Bad News. Refinements in this respect were primarily of a methodological nature. Ball and Brown defined good news/bad news simply on the basis of the direction of the forecast error, that is, whether the realized earnings number was above or below expectation. Beaver, Clarke, and Wright (1979) also took into consideration the magnitude of the error, weighting their portfolios by the size of the error. Other researchers (Rendelman, Jones and Latane (1982)) carried this a step further by weighting the forecast error by a measure of the earnings stream's overall variability. This latter paper also documented post announcement drift.

Market-Based Variable

Choice of Market Model.

Measurement of "Abnormal" Market Performance. Generally the market-based variable used was abnormal returns. Variations existed in terms of which security pricing model was used. The primary candidates were the CAPM and the "market" model.[22] Other researchers used control firms matched to the sample by size and industry classification and, instead of examining the abnormal return, compared the difference in actual returns between the control group and the sample under study. In addition, other studies focused on trading volume or risk measures such as total variance of the return and/or "beta."

The choice of an appropriate model is grounded to a great extent in the finance literature and is not the focus of this book. However, it should be noted that any test carried out of the earnings/return relationship is as much a test of the underlying asset pricing model as it is of the relationship itself. To the extent that these models do not accurately describe the market process, conclusions drawn from them are suspect.

Measurement Period ("Window") for Market Performance. Ball and Brown examined monthly returns over a full year. Other studies, depending on the issue under examination, used weekly (or daily) returns in the periods immediately surrounding the announcement.[23] The trade-off between using narrow (short) versus wide (long) windows is that in the former case there is less risk that the market could be reacting to information other than that being tested. Wider windows have the advantage of allowing for the possibility of information "leakage," thus implying earlier market reaction. In addition, and perhaps more important, it has been argued that the significance of a piece of information may at times not be known until a later date. Using too narrow a window would miss this reaction. The emergence of postannouncement drift, alluded to earlier,[24] made this issue take on greater importance.

[22]See footnote 11 for a description of the market model. In addition, some studies used other pricing models such as the Black–Scholes *option pricing model* and the *arbitrage pricing model*.

[23]Patell and Wolfson (1982, 1984) focused on the intraday measure of market reaction.

[24]See the accompanying discussion of *market anomalies*.

Test of the Relationship Between the Good News/Bad News Parameter and "Abnormal" Returns

Early studies, as we have discussed, grouped firms into good news/bad news portfolios by the sign and/or magnitude of the earnings forecast error. There was no explicit measurement (either theoretical or empirical) of the relationship between earnings and returns. Later studies explicitly related the response of stock returns to earnings by introduction of the earnings response coefficient (ERC).[25]

ERC studies tested for differential reactions across firms and for differential reactions to various components of earnings. Moreover, the ERC permitted testing of explicit relationships between prices and earnings as implied by finance valuation models. Studies of the ERC led to interest in the "persistence" issue, namely which components of earnings were permanent and hence had future implications for valuation and market reaction, and which were transitory and thus had differing implications for valuation and market reaction.

Chapter 15, which deals with earnings forecasts and valuation models, will discuss the ERC, issues of persistence, and their relationship to the price/earnings (P/E) ratio in greater detail.

Market-Based Research—Current Status

Market-based research at present is "on the ropes." The end of the 1980s triggered a number of "20-year" retrospectives of developments in the field since Ball and Brown's work. The consensus was not complimentary. In addition, cracks in the efficient market theory began to appear. This section will review the conclusions of two of these retrospective papers and also summarize the anomalies in the EMH. These have important insights and implications for financial statement analysis and the approach taken in this book.

Critical Evaluation of Research Findings

Lev, in a paper entitled "On the Usefulness of Earnings and Earnings Research: Lessons and Directions from Two Decades of Empirical Research,"[26] presented a review and assessment of this literature. His overall evaluation and critique of the research is not favorable:

> What is the incremental contribution of the recent methodological improvements in the returns/earnings research to our understanding of how and to what extent earnings are used by investors? What is the contribution . . . to the deliberations of accounting policymakers? The answer seems to be—very little.[27]

---

[25]The ERC itself was the coefficient (b) in the regression equation having the form $R = a + bE$, where R and E are a measure of returns and earnings, respectively.

[26]Lev, Baruch, "On the Usefulness of Earnings and Earnings Research: Lessons and Directions from Two Decades of Empirical Research" *Journal of Accounting Research* (Supplement 1989) pp. 153–192

[27]Ibid., p. 172.

He argues that when all is said and done, the earnings/return research paradigm leaves much to be desired.

> If one considers the persistence research, for example, the idea that investors react differently to the earnings of different firms and that such differential reaction is related to the future implications of earnings (persistence) is not particularly revealing.[28]

Bernard, in his review paper, "Capital Markets Research in Accounting During the 1980s: A Critical Review,"[29] points out that the research has been beneficial:

> Some impacts of the research are more subtle, but nevertheless important. Imagine what our view of the role of accounting information might be if Ball and Brown had found, as many predicted they would, that accounting earnings were completely uncorrelated with the information used by investors![30]

Notwithstanding the foregoing, however, he notes that pessimism about the research had set in by the mid-1970s[31] and further that

> The emphasis on methodology throughout the 1980s sharpened our tools in important ways but the "love affair" with sophisticated statistical techniques may have diverted our attention from more central problems of model specification. In the area of valuation, a substantial amount of work appears to be guided by the philosophy that the accounting system produces only one number—earnings—that tracks performance with error. As a result, we have probably overinvested in analyses of the details of the simple returns-earnings regression without considering a richer information set.[32]

Exhibit 4-1, reproduced from Lev, lists a number of papers that for the most part consist of methodological refinements of Ball and Brown's original paper. The refinements listed mirror the ones already described. The last column in the table provides data as to the R^2 found by these studies. (The R^2 measures the percentage of variation in returns explained by variations in earnings. A high R^2 would imply a strong earnings/return association.) On average, no more than 5% of the variation in returns can be explained by earnings. The relationship, while it may have *statistical significance*, at the same time, has little or no *economic significance*. It does not provide a meaningful explanation of the relationship between earnings and returns.

Lev proceeds to list a number of reasons for this failure and suggests directions for future research:

1. Researchers used earnings numbers as given and did not adjust them for accounting manipulations by managers, year-to-year random occurrences, or the inherent arbitrariness of many accounting measurement and valuation techniques.

[28]Ibid.
[29]Bernard, Victor L. "Capital Market Research During the 1980's: A Critical Review." in Thomas Frecka (ed.), *The State of Accounting Research As We Enter the 1990's,* (University of Illinois, 1989), pp. 72–120
[30]Ibid., p. 5.
[31]See Figure 4-6, which is from Bernard's working paper.
[32]Bernard, Victor L. "Capital Market Research During the 1980's: A Critical Review" (Working Paper) p. 53

EXHIBIT 4-1
Sample of Research (1980–88) on the Relationship Between Earnings and Stock Returns

Author/Reference	Sample Period	Return Variable	Earnings Variable	Earnings Expectations	Additional Independent Variables	Cross-Section or Time Series	"Window"	R^2
1. Hagerman et al., *JAR* (Autumn 1984)	1974–76	Residual returns	Quarterly *EPS*	Last-quarter *EPS*	None	C-S	Five days around announcement	0.05
2. Wilson, *JAR* (Supplement 1986)	1981–82	Residual returns	Earnings	Time-series predictions	Components of cash flows and accruals	C-S	Two days	0.02–0.05
3. Hughes and Ricks, *AR* (January 1987)	1979–84	Residual returns	Quarterly *EPS*	Analyst forecasts or previous *EPS*	Two independent variables; analyst and mechanical forecast errors	C-S	Two days	0.02 for entire sample; 0.06 when extreme forecast errors were dropped
4. Hopwood and McKeown, *JAR* (Spring 1985)	1973–78	Residual returns	*EPS*	Time-series model	Interim sales and expenses	C-S	One quarter	*EPS* = 0.04 Sales = 0.01 Expenses = 0.004
5. Beaver et al., *JAE* (March 1980)	1958–76	% change in price	*EPS*	Last year's *EPS*	None	C-S	Fiscal year	0.07 for individual securities 0.55–0.95 for portfolios
6. Bowen et al., *AR* (October 1987)	1972–81	Residual returns	Annual earnings	Last year's earnings	Cash flow components	C-S	Twelve months	0.04
7. Fried and Givoly, *JAE* (October 1982)	1969–79	Residual returns	*EPS*	Analyst forecasts or time-series forecasts	None	C-S	4/1–3/31	R = 0.33 for analyst forecasts; R = 0.27 for time-series forecasts
8. Freeman, *JAR* (Spring 1983)	1963–77	Residual returns	Change in profit to total assets, minus the industry change	—	Leads and lags of industry and price variable approximating current costs	C-S	Fiscal year	0.07 0.10

305

EXHIBIT 4-1. *(Continued)*

Author/Reference	Sample Period	Return Variable	Earnings Variable	Earnings Expectations	Additional Independent Variables	Cross-Section or Time Series	"Window"	R^2
9a. Jacobson, *AER* (June 1987)	1963–82	Raw returns	$ROI = \dfrac{\text{Net income}_t}{\text{Total assets}_{t-1}}$	—	—	C-S	12/31–12/31	0.02
9b. Jacobson, *AER* (June 1987)	1963–82	Residual returns	Residual ROI	—	—	C-S	12/31–12/31	0.05
10. Lustgarten, *JAE* (October 1982)	1976–77	Residual returns	Earnings	Last year's earnings	Replacement costs and sales	C-S	Ten months (−6 to +4 of fiscal year-end)	0.02–0.04 for earning alone; 0.05–0.09 for all three variables
11. Beaver et al., *JAE* (July 1982)	1977–78	Raw returns	Net income	Last year's income	Cash flows or inflationary gains	C-S	12/31–12/31	0.14–0.15
12. Lipe, *JAR* (Supplement 1986)	1977–80	Residual returns	*EPS*	Time series	Six earnings components	C-S	4/1–3/31	0.15
13. Hoskin et al., *JAR* (Supplement 1986)	1979–81	Residual returns	Fourth-quarter earnings to market value	Analyst's forecasts	A large number of additional disclosures	C-S	Two days	0.12–0.15
14. Rayburn, *JAR* (Supplement 1986)	1963–82	Residual returns	—	Time series	Components of earnings and cash flows	C-S	Annual	R^2 of annual regressions fluctuate from −0.002 to 0.28
15. Beaver et al., *JAE* (July 1982) for Easman et al. sample	1973–77	Raw returns	Net income	Last year's income	Inflationary gain	C-S	12/31–12/31	1973 = 0.04 1974 = 0.30 1975 = 0.05 1976 = 0.03 1977 = 0.23
16. Sepe, *AR* (July 1982)	1974–76	Residual returns	—	—	Various financial ratios, risk, and inflation-adjusted measures	C-S	Fiscal year	0.30
17. Ajinkya and Gift, *JAR* (Autumn 1984)	1970–77	Residual returns	Management forecasts	Analyst's forecasts	—	C-S	Month before forecast to March next year	0.05–0.17

EXHIBIT 4-1. (*Continued*)

Author/Reference	Sample Period	Return Variable	Earnings Variable	Earnings Expectations	Additional Independent Variables	Cross-Section or Time Series	"Window"	R^2
18. Imhoff and Lobo, *JAR* (Autumn 1984)	1977–78	Residual returns	Revisions in *IBES* forecasts	Last forecast	—	C-S	Month of forecast revision	0.01
19. Magliolo, *JAR* (Supplement 1986)	1979–83	Change in market value of firm	—	—	Reserve recognition data for oil and gas company	C-S	Annual	0.10–0.062

Source: Lev, Baruch, "On the Usefulness of Earnings and Earnings Research: Lessons and Directions from Two Decades of Empirical Research" *Journal of Accounting Research* (Supplement 1989) pp. 153–192, Table 1, p. 160–161, reprinted with permission.

AR = The Accounting Review.

JAR = Journal of Accounting Research.

JAE = Journal of Accounting and Economics.

no serious attempt is being made to question the quality of the reported earnings number. . . . While various deficiencies in earnings are obviously adjusted for by financial analysts and even in the media, most researchers . . . accept the reported numbers at face value.[33]

2. There is little or no knowledge as to how accounting information is disseminated in the marketplace; that is, what is it that financial analysts do with the information? Lev suggests that accounting research should study how analysts disseminate and use the information provided in financial statements:

> Research on the quality of earnings and other financial information items and on the way investors disseminate such information (namely, adjust for quality deficiencies) offers a promising extension. . . .
> Adjustments of reported data are an essential element of financial statement analysis or the information dissemination process in capital markets. However, surprisingly little is known about this important process.
> In general, the research line suggested here is aimed at understanding the use of financial data by investors. (a) What financial variables play a role in asset valuation? . . . (b) What are the specific adjustments made by analysts to reported data?[34]

What is remarkable and ironic about Lev's criticisms is that it suggests that accounting research has come full circle. The researchers, who have argued that use of fundamental or financial analysis is meaningless since the market is not fooled by the numbers, have carried out their experimentation and tests justifying their arguments by using the very same numbers that supposedly the market ignores and adjusts for.[35]

3. Lev proceeds to argue for a research emphasis on the quality of earnings that incorporates the effects of alternative GAAP measures on earnings and their relationship to valuation models. Elements of this paradigm include

- Measuring earnings/returns relationships on a portfolio basis may not be meaningful since analysts usually view firms on an individual rather than portfolio basis.
- Looking at the immediate effect of *a single period's* earnings on stock prices may not be as meaningful as averaging the earnings numbers over time.[36]
- The horizons studied should be extended; future year impacts should also be studied. This would require more careful analysis of valuation models as they relate to accounting and earnings.

[33]Lev, "On the Usefulness of Earnings and Earnings Research," pp. 175–176.

[34]Ibid., pp. 178–181.

[35]The rationale offered is that with large samples the noise resulting from nonadjustment would tend to be averaged away. This contention itself is subject to empirical verification as it would depend on whether or not the errors cancel or whether they are in some fashion systematically related. Subject to the evidence on this issue, it would seem that it is the researchers who suffer from functional fixation!

[36]To test for this, Lev examined the relationship of earnings and returns taken over a five-year period. He argued that over a longer period manipulations and smoothing tended to even out and earnings mirrored cash flows. The R^2 over this longer period proved to be 35%—seven times what the one-year numbers indicated.

- Earnings components used in the research should incorporate *all* possible adjustments, not just one at a time, to arrive at a more comprehensive and meaningful analysis.

Bernard echoes Lev's suggestions:

1) Progress will require that we end reliance on simple, naive models. . . . An injection of knowledge about the accounting system and fundamental analysis is necessary; . . .
2) It would frequently be useful to sacrifice large sample sizes and sophisticated statistics for the sake of achieving a deeper understanding of the relations among accounting variables, and between those variables and equity values. . . .
3) Further reliance on formal modelling would be fruitful.[37]

The relationship between these recommendations and the objectives laid out in the study of financial statement analysis can best be summed up in Lev's words:

Capital market research should, therefore, shift its focus to the role of accounting measurement rules in asset valuation. Such research involves both positive and normative aspects. Regarding the former, the proposed research is aimed at understanding the use of financial information by investors, that is, a *thorough investigation of the financial statement analysis process*. . . . The normative aspect . . . is aimed at filling a current void in financial economic modelling. Economic models posit a relation between generic financial variables (e.g., "income") and market values, leaving unspecified the nature of the financial variables. The research conjectures proposed above are aimed at adding a fundamental element to this relation—the impact of GAAP and GAAP alternatives on market values, via the impact of accounting techniques on the predictive power of financial variables."[38]

Market Anomalies

A number of anomalies exist that question the validity of the EMH and the conclusions drawn from the research described previously. Some of these anomalies are related to the relationship between earnings and returns, whereas others would seem to be purely market based. Additionally, some of the anomalies tend to overlap. For example, the Monday Effect and Postannouncement Drift are most pronounced for small size firms.

January Effect

Empirical evidence exists suggesting that markets typically perform extremely well during the month of January. This would seem to be a violation of the weak form of the EMH, as knowledge of this past pattern could lead to abnormal gains by buying stock at the end of December.

Monday Effect

After the weekend, prices tend to open lower, suggesting that an advantageous strategy would be to go short at the close on Friday and buy back one's position Monday morning.

[37]Bernard, "Capital Markets Research in Accounting During the 1980s," pp. 99–100.
[38]Lev, "On the Usefulness of Earnings and Earnings Research," pp. 185–186, emphasis added.

Size Effect

Firms that are smaller in terms of total assets or total capitalization tend to outperform the market even when risk is adjusted for. This suggests that a sound investment strategy would be to invest in a portfolio of smaller-sized firms.

Price/Earnings Ratio

Firms with low P/E ratios tend to outperform the market even when risk is adjusted for. This suggests a strategy of buying low-P/E-ratio firms.

Postannouncement Drift

The EMH holds that stock prices adjust instantaneously to new information. Evidence, however, exists that price changes persist for some time after the initial announcement.

The Briloff Effect

Professor Briloff is an outspoken critic of some accounting practices and in his *Barron's* column has analyzed the financial reports of some firms. In doing so, he is highly critical of their reporting practices. The firms he reports about typically suffer large price drops (see Figure 4-4) following publication. Since Briloff's analysis is based upon publicly available information, it would seem that the market price prior to Briloff's analysis did not fully reflect all the available information.

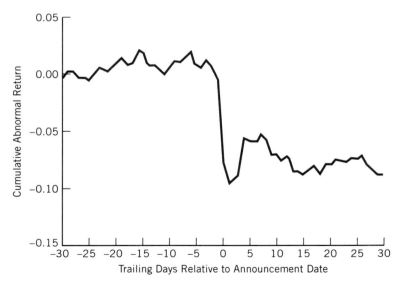

FIGURE 4-4 The Briloff Effect: Market Reaction for 28 Stocks. Source: Foster, George, "Briloff and the Capital Market", *Journal of Accounting Research* (Spring 1979), pp. 262–274, Figure 1, p. 266, reprinted with permission.

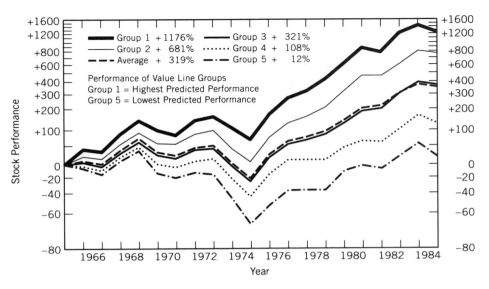

Record of Value Line Rankings for Timeliness April 16, 1965 – January 2, 1985
(Without Allowances for Changes in Rank)

FIGURE 4-5 Performance of Value Line Groups
Group 1 = Highest Predicted Performance Group 5 = Lowest Predicted Performance. Source: Value Line
Selections and Opinion (January 18, 1985, page 962)

Value Line

Figure 4-5 presents the performance of the stock groupings ranked by Value Line
Investment Services. The continued and consistent performance of these groupings,
relative to the market, imply that Value Line has been able to "beat the market."

While all the anomalies have implications for analysts, explanations of the size
effect, Briloff effect, and the Value Line results relate most directly to the role of
financial analysts in the capital markets. The size effect is often attributed to the fact that
smaller firms are not followed by analysts to the extent that larger firms are. Thus not all
the information available about these firms is immediately incorporated in the prices,
leaving room for abnormal returns to be earned by those who trade on the information
early enough. The excess returns on small-firm portfolios may also represent compensation for the cost and difficulty of analyzing underfollowed companies.

As a possible explanation of the Briloff effect, Foster noted that Briloff's *superior
accounting knowledge and analytical insights were in a sense nonpublic information,*
and hence capital market efficiency was not violated per se.

> This explanation is based on the argument that Briloff possesses superior skills and is able
> to earn a (competitive) return from using these skills. The so-called information market,
> rather than the capital market, is seen as the key to the results.[39]

[39]Foster, George, "Briloff and the Capital Market", *Journal of Accounting Research* (Spring 1979), pp.
262–274.

Value Line rankings are based on the performance of variables referred to as "earnings momentum" and "earnings surprise." The former relates to changes in quarterly earnings over time whereas the latter relates to the deviation between actual and forecasted earnings. Whether this qualifies as statistical or fundamental analysis is open for debate. The results, however, indicate that superior analysis can lead to results that outperform the market.

In summing up the evidence on efficient markets, we leave the reader with the following:

> The lesson is clear. An overly doctrinaire belief in efficient markets can paralyze the investor and make it appear that no research effort can be justified. This extreme view is probably unwarranted. There are enough anomalies in the empirical evidence to justify the search for underpriced securities that clearly goes on. The bulk of the evidence, however, suggests that any supposedly superior strategy should be taken with many grains of salt. The market is competitive *enough* that only differentially superior information or insight will earn money; the easy pickings have been picked.[40]

POSITIVE ACCOUNTING RESEARCH

Watts and Zimmermann (1990), the "fathers" of this line of research, noted that the term positive accounting research

> was used to distinguish research aimed at explanation and prediction from research whose objective was prescription. . . . A positive theory differs from a normative theory, though a positive theory can have normative implications once an objective function is specified.[41]

The positive accounting approach is sometimes referred to as "contracting theory" or as "the economic consequences of accounting" literature. These terms denote that accounting variables are not exogenous to the firm but are an integral part of the firm and its organizational structure. The information provided in the financial statements interacts with the firm's investment, production, and financing decisions as this information is the basis on which resources are allocated, management is compensated, debt restrictions are measured, and so on. Managements would, therefore, be expected to take into consideration financial information effects by changing their decisions and/or altering their choice of accounting methods. Operationally, the positive theory approach moved the focus away from observation of market reaction to accounting numbers to, as Figure 4-1C indicates, *a study of the incentives underlying management's behavior in terms of (1) their operating, investing, and financing decisions and (2) their choice of alternative accounting numbers.*

---

[40]Bodie, Zvi, Alex Kane and Alan J. Marcus, *Investments*, (Homewood Ill., Richard D. Irwin 1989) p. 371.

[41]Watts, Ross and Jerold L. Zimmerman, "Positive Accounting Theory: A Ten Year Perspective", *The Accounting Review* (January 1990) pp. 131–156.

Although both types of research fall into this paradigm, the "Rochester school," which popularized and applied to it the label of "positive accounting" (see Watts and Zimmerman, 1986) focused most of their attention on the second type.[42] Hence, studies as to incentives underlying choice of accounting methods are the most closely identified with positive accounting research.

Market studies also play a role, but that emphasis is secondary. Changes in accounting methods have an informational impact but are more significantly a result of the interaction of the alternative choice with the production-financing-investment opportunities of the firm. As the opportunity set changes, so does the appropriate informational environment. It is for this reason that mandated rather than voluntary choices of accounting method are perceived to have more of a market impact. Voluntary changes are anticipated or predictable as the firm itself changes. For example, as it changes its primary industry classification, it is likely to change its accounting policies. Since the change in industry emphasis is somewhat predictable, so is the change in accounting policy.

Impetus for this broadened approach was once again led by changes in the finance and economics literature.

Disclosure and Regulatory Requirements

Economists examining regulation and its effects began to question the belief that all regulation was motivated by concern with the public good and that regulation necessarily increased social welfare. Politicians and regulators were now viewed as being motivated by their own self-interest, and hence regulations propagated by them may have as their incentive the enhancement of this self-interest.

Disclosure requirements were also viewed in this light. The benefits from increased disclosure requirements were not automatically assumed to outweigh the costs. Moreover, it was argued (further elaborated on shortly) that there existed private incentives for firms to produce information so long as the cost of disseminating and producing the information did not outweigh its potential rewards. These cost/benefit trade-offs tended to make the choice between accounting alternatives not a moot point as had been suggested by the proponents of the EMH. Thus the question as to what motivated accounting choice still required explanation. Furthermore,

> Firms in the same industries tended to change procedures at the same time, just as at any given time firms in the same industry tend to use the same procedures. *This systematic behavior caused researchers to question the no-effects hypothesis.*[43]

Agency Theory

The agency theory literature also took as a starting point the argument that people were motivated by their own self-interest. Thus managers would take steps to maximize the value of the firm only if that was consistent with their own best interests. If managers

[42]Research on the effects of accounting on management's operating decisions, in fact, preceded the research on choice of accounting method. It had, however, not as yet been given any classification.

[43]Watts, Ross and Jerold L. Zimmerman, *Positive Accounting Theory,* (Englewood Cliffs, New Jersey Prentice-Hall 1986) p. 178, emphasis added.

could, moreover, *in the absence of a monitoring device*, enhance their well-being (1) by appropriating resources for themselves in addition to their agreed-upon compensation or (2) by shirking their duties, equity or debt investors could be reluctant to provide financing to the firm. Similarly, in the absence of a monitoring device, managers might engage in risk taking and other activities that would hurt the bondholder to the advantage of the equityholder. Thus a monitoring device is needed to ensure that the agreements or contracts between managers-shareholders-creditors are adhered to. The discussion leads to viewing a firm not as an independent entity but rather as a "nexus of contracts"[44] (explicit or implicit) between parties, each motivated by their own self-interest. The role of accounting in this scenario is to provide the monitoring device enabling the contracting process to function.

This approach to the accounting process views the financial statements as the means by which contracting parties measure, monitor, and enforce the objectives of the various contracts.[45] Thus, as mentioned in the introduction to this chapter, the accounting numbers do not merely describe reality—they in effect define reality, as real economic consequences flow from the numbers reported. Positive accounting research, it should be noted, does not exclude market-based research. Rather, its approach subsumes the market-based research as a component of an overall research paradigm.

> The hypothesis that accounting and auditing arose as a monitoring device for the firm's contracts contrasts with the common hypothesis that investors demand accounting reports as a source of information for investment and valuation decisions. The information hypothesis . . . asserts that investors demand information on current and future cash flows and the market value of assets and liabilities. . . .
>
> The two hypotheses are not mutually exclusive. Both the contract and information roles could exist at the same time. Information that enables individuals to determine certain contractual requirements have been met is often useful in valuing the firm's securities.[46]

The specific hypotheses flowing from the positive theory approach to accounting that are most often tested are the

- Bonus plan hypothesis
- Debt covenant or debt/equity hypothesis
- Political process hypothesis

The Bonus Plan Hypothesis

The "contract" between management and its shareholders concerns the performance expected from the manager and his or her level of compensation. Under *the bonus plan*

---

[44]This term can be traced to Jensen and Meckling (1976).

[45]Under this view the choice of accounting policy by management may not necessarily have "sinister" implications. The various parties view the accounting process as an efficient way to operate the firm. Otherwise, if there were no proper monitoring device, equity shareholders would be reluctant to hire managers (or they would pay them less). Thus, management has an incentive to have a "proper" monitoring system in place.

[46]Watts and Zimmerman, *Positive Accounting Theory,* pp. 197–198.

hypothesis, a contract exists between the owners and managers of the firm whereby the managers are compensated for how well they manage the firm. The financial statements are used (often explicitly under the terms of the firm's executive compensation plan) as the benchmark for the firm's performance. Thus it is in the best interest of the firm's management to choose "liberal" accounting policies to improve their own compensation.

The motivation for choosing liberal accounting policies under this approach is not posited in terms of "fooling" the market with all the ramifications and implications vis-à-vis the efficient market hypothesis. Rather, motivation is in terms of the increased management compensation resulting from higher reported earnings.[47]

At the same time, however, it is noted that more complicated applications of the bonus plan hypothesis are also possible:

> a bonus plan does not always give managers incentives to increase earnings. If, in the absence of accounting changes, earnings are below the minimum level required for payment of a bonus, managers have incentives to reduce earnings this year because no bonuses are likely to be paid. Taking such an "earnings bath" increases expected bonuses and profits in future years.[48]

An extension of this argument exists when managers find themselves above the maximum allowable under the compensation plan. There are no incentives to increase earnings. On the contrary, it may be worthwhile to take certain losses (as long as earnings remain above the maximum threshold) currently as opposed to future years. Healy (1985) provides some evidence on this effect. He found that owners tend to change their accounting policies based upon the incentives underlying their bonus plan and that these modifications are associated with the initial inception or modification of the plan. However, he also reports that managers do not seem to alter accounting policy if they are either below the minimum threshold or above the maximum ceiling for the current period.

The Debt Covenant Hypothesis

Bondholders and other creditors want to ensure repayment of their principal and interest. To protect themselves, they impose restrictions on the borrower as to dividends, share repurchases, and issuance of additional debt. These restrictions are often expressed in terms of accounting amounts and ratios. Typical covenants also call for the maintenance of acceptable levels of working capital, interest coverage, and net worth. Ratio tests may also be present.

Accounting choices can greatly affect these measures and consequently define whether a firm is in "technical default" of debt covenants. Under the debt covenant hypothesis, managers are motivated to choose accounting methods that minimize the likelihood that covenants would be violated. Operationally, this is often expressed as the debt/equity hypothesis that asserts that firms with higher debt/equity ratios tend to

---

[47]See footnote 45 which points out that the management compensation hypothesis is also consistent with an efficiency point of view and is not necessarily tied to "opportunistic" behavior on the part of managers.

[48]Watts and Zimmerman, "Positive Accounting Theory: A Ten Year Perspective", p. 139.

choose accounting policies that increase current income at the expense of future income.[49]

Political Cost Hypothesis

The previous discussion of regulation implied that the political process imposes costs on the firm. To the extent that politicians and regulators can enhance their (or their constituents') interests at the expense of others, they will do so. An important aspect of this process is the role of information and how it is perceived. If it is believed that a firm or an industry is taking advantage of the public and is making "obscene" profits (as has been charged during oil crises), then reported earnings will be examined to see if profits are excessive. This may result in pressures to reduce prices or impose a "windfall profits" tax.

Firms will thus be induced to choose accounting methods that will show lower profits so as to lower the political risk to them. For example, some oil companies reduced reported earnings in 1991 (during the period when oil prices were high because of the Kuwait crisis) by making provisions for environmental costs or asset impairment.

Similarly, accounting procedures that reduce reported income on the financial statements can be motivated by the desire to use those same methods on the tax returns. Even though alternative methods are permissible, it is less "embarrassing" to be paying little or no taxes if financial statement income is not too high. Utilities, on the other hand, whose revenues are determined on the basis of accounting rules, can be motivated to lobby for accounting rules that are most favorable from a rate-setting point of view.

The political cost hypothesis is often presented in the research literature as a size hypothesis. It is argued that large firms are most susceptible to political costs and pressures. Thus the larger the firm, the more likely it would be to choose accounting methods that would lower profits and hence lessen political pressures. One example might be the oil industry. Large firms uniformly use the successful efforts method (see Chapter 6), which tends to minimize reported earnings; among smaller firms the full cost method is more common.

Summary of the Research

Positive accounting research takes on a number of forms that we will describe from a general perspective. Details of specific studies will be provided in the chapters dealing with the relevant accounting issue.

Although our discussion of the three hypotheses focused on the choice of accounting method, the same hypotheses can be used to examine the effects of accounting numbers on management operating decisions. Thus, for example, the FASB's requirement (SFAS 2) that research and development costs be expensed rather than capitalized lowers reported earnings for many firms. This could induce a cutback in the amount of actual research and development work undertaken if managers felt that the lower earnings would hurt their compensation and/or imperil the status of the firm's bond covenants. A number of studies examining this issue are discussed in Chapter 6. Similarly, studies

---

[49]See Chapter 8 for a more elaborate description of the nature of bond covenants and research in the area.

dealing with the interaction of accounting methods and the incentives for mergers and acquisitions, pension plan terminations, and oil exploration are discussed in the chapters dealing with these topics.

Market-based studies exist that deal with mandated accounting changes in the oil and gas industry, purchase versus pooling accounting, and voluntary switches similar to the depreciation changes described earlier. The approach, however, differs because rather than just viewing the relationship as one of returns being a function of earnings, it is now posited that return reaction may vary across firms as a function of a number of variables in addition to earnings, such as debt/equity, size, and management compensation. Changes that increase earnings, for example, could result in positive market reaction for firms with high debt/equity ratios because the increase in income would permit wealth transfers from the firm's existing bondholders to equity shareholders as additional debt could be taken on without affecting the reported debt/equity ratio.

On the other hand, for large-sized firms, the increased income could increase the possibility of political costs, thus resulting in negative market reaction. Generally, research results were consistent, albeit weakly, with the predicted relationships for mandated accounting changes but not for voluntary ones. This finding is consistent with the theory described earlier.

The emphasis of positive accounting research was not market based. Most of the research dealt with explanations as to why firms chose certain accounting alternatives. We will briefly review one paper in the area to give the reader a "feel" for the nature of the research.

Zmijewski and Hagerman. The Zmijewski and Hagerman (ZH) study (1981) focused on explaining firms' choices with respect to four accounting alternatives that could increase or decrease reported net income:

	Income Effect	
Policy	Increase	Decrease
1. Inventory	FIFO	LIFO
2. Investment tax credit	Flow-through	Deferral
3. Pensions: Amortization of past service costs	> 30 years	< 30 years
4. Depreciation	Straight line	Accelerated

Source: Zmijewski, Mark and Robert Hagerman, "An Income Strategy Approach to the Positive Theory of Accounting Standard Setting/Choice," *Journal of Accounting and Economics* 3 (1981), pp. 129–149 Table 1 P. 135 (Summary Only)

For each choice—increasing (decreasing) income—a score of 1 (0) was assigned.[50] Thus a firm's score for income strategy could vary from 0 to 4. For the 300 firms in their sample, the distribution of the strategy scores is as follows:

[50]Other weighting schemes giving smaller weights to the pension and investment tax credit choices were also tested with results similar to the equal weighted scores reviewed here.

Number of Income Increasing Choices	Frequency	Percentage
Zero	10	3.33%
One	49	16.33%
Two	107	35.67%
Three	107	35.67%
Four	27	9.00%
	300	100.00%

Source: Zmijewski and Hagerman (1981)

To explain the choices, the following explanatory variables were used to test the underlying theory:

- *Bonus plan variable (B):* A score of 1 if the firm had a management compensation plan; 0 otherwise. Presence of a compensation plan was expected to increase the *strategy* score.
- *Debt variable (D):* The debt/assets ratio was used to measure the (relative) debt of the firm. The higher the debt, the greater the likelihood that the *strategy* score would be higher.
- *Political cost variables (P1, P2, P3, and P4):* Four variables were used to measure different aspects related to political pressure: size, industry concentration (indicating the degree of monopoly power), capital intensiveness and beta. Political cost variables were expected to decrease the frequency of choosing income-increasing alternatives.

The following equation[51] was then tested to determine the relationship between the strategy scores and the explanatory variables:

$$Strategy = c_0 + c_1 B + c_2 D + c_3 P1 + c_4 P2 + c_5 P3 + c_6 P4$$

Based on the theory, we would expect the coefficients (c_1 and c_2) of the bonus and debt variables to be positive but the coefficients for the political process variables ($c_3 - c_6$) to be negative. The results were consistent with the predicted relationships in terms of the signs of the coefficients, and the overall equation proved to be significant.

Other studies using similar modes of analysis focused on single-choice alternatives as opposed to the Zmijewski and Hagerman study, which examined multiple choices. In reviewing the research to date, Watts and Zimmermann contend that the results are generally consistent with the bonus plan, debt/equity, and political cost hypotheses. With respect to the political cost hypothesis,

---

[51]The method of analysis used was probit analysis, which is similar to regression analysis but is more appropriate when the dependent variable is discrete (i.e., in our case, it can only be one of five values).

however, the result only appears to hold for the largest firms and is driven by the oil and gas industry.[52]

Moreover, with echoes of Lev's analysis

> While bonus, debt and political process variables tend to be statistically significant . . . , in many studies the explanatory power (R^2) of the models is low.[53]

In their discussion of avenues for further research in the area, Watts and Zimmermann note that most of the studies have been concerned with incentives for management to behave opportunistically as these tend to be the most observable (and hence testable) phenomena. However, they argue that more work needs to be done in terms of strengthening the relationship between theory and empirical testing in determining whether management choices are made purely for opportunistic reasons or whether the choices are motivated by efficiency considerations inherent in the firm's organizational structure and/or industrial dynamics.

DIRECTION OF CURRENT RESEARCH

Bernard (1989) summarized the accounting research of the last quarter century by means of a cumulative abnormal return plot reproduced in Figure 4-6. The early promise of the market-based research (begun by Ball and Brown and Beaver) was soon tempered by the realization that the desirability of accounting principles could not be determined solely on the basis of information content considerations. The economic consequences or positive theory approach provided the next "high." However, "disillusionment" with this line of research resulted as scant evidence of economic consequences was found.[54]

This brings us to the present state and direction of research. It is difficult to categorize what is still evolving. It is, however, possible to describe some of its attributes.

Current research involves a return to principles of valuation. This trend evolved out of market-based research, and, in its initial stages, much of it was cast as a refinement of earlier information content types of studies. However, eventually a difference began to set in. The thrust was not one of attempting to define regulatory policy but rather to get a better understanding of the relationship among prices, earnings, and other accounting information. No longer were price or returns taken as given and accounting numbers just tested to justify their usefulness.[55] The emphasis shifted to the information derived from accounting data and its relationship to prices.

---

[52]Watts and Zimmerman, "Positive Accounting Theory: A Ten Year Perspective", p. 140.

[53]Ibid.

[54]Bernard, it should be noted, was specifically addressing evidence with respect to the area of capital market research and the positive (economic consequences) approach. As noted in the previous section, this is only one area of the overall positive accounting approach.

[55]As Penman (1992) notes when advocating the new direction for research: "Fundamental analysis, in contrast, involves the discovery of price without reference to price" (p. 466).

FIGURE 4-6 A "CAR Plot" for Capital Markets Research, 1968–1990. Source: Bernard, Victor L. "Capital Market Research During the 1980's: A Critical Review" (Working Paper) (1989), Figure 1 P. 3

Research on the diversity of the earnings response coefficient across firms led to a rethinking of basic price/earnings relationships. Evidence that prices could be used to forecast future earnings led to the (re)awareness (in research design) that prices react not only to changes in current earnings but also to changes in the expectations of future earnings. Consistent with these directions in the research were calls for a return to fundamental analysis. As Ou and Penman (1989) noted,

> There have been many claims of market efficiency with respect to "publicly available" information, but (astonishingly, when one considers the many tests of technical analysis) little research into the competing claim of fundamental analysis.[56]

In keeping with our approach, we will describe one study, Ou (1988), as indicative of this trend. We have chosen this study because its research design provides a contrast to the Ball and Brown study discussed at the beginning of the chapter.

Ball and Brown Revisited—Back to the Future?

The salient results of Ou's study are captured in Figure 4-7, which, similar to Ball and Brown, separates firms into good and bad news categories. The graphs marked E^+ and E^-, in fact, are replications of Ball and Brown's study and are based upon whether a

---

[56]Ou, Jane A. and Stephen Penman, "Financial Statement Analysis and the Prediction of Stock Returns" *Journal of Accounting and Economics* (November 1989), pp. 295–329.

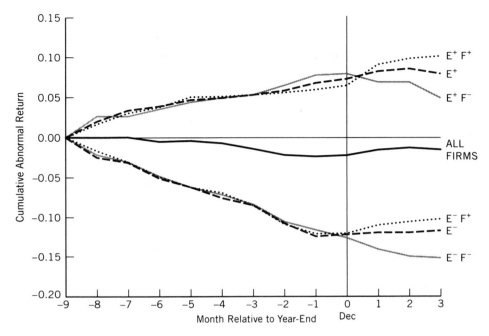

FIGURE 4-7 Ou's Results. Source: Ou, Jane A., "The Information Content of Nonearnings Accounting Numbers as Earnings Predictors", *Journal of Accounting Research* (Spring 1990) pp. 144–162, Figure 1, p. 158, reprinted with permission.

firm's realized earnings for the year were above (good news) or below (bad news) earnings predicted by a time series forecasting model.

Acting as if this knowledge were known as far back as March of the year in question, two portfolios are constructed on the basis of the good news/bad news partitions. The positive (negative) abnormal returns for the good (bad) news portfolios result in the E^+ and E^- graphs. These graphs indicate that earnings have informational content and that earnings are associated with prices. The assumption is that prices are supreme, and the question is whether earnings convey the same information. No more can be said as the portfolios were formed "as if" the knowledge with respect to the abnormal earnings was available in advance. Implications for valuation from this design are limited.[57]

The Ou study extended this analysis by partitioning the firms both on the basis of the realization of current year earnings and on the basis of a forecast of next year's earnings. They designed a model to predict whether the realization of the *next year's* earnings would be above (F^+ = good news) or below (F^- = bad news) the earnings forecast by a time series model. This resulted in the formation of four portfolios:

E^+F^+:   good news realized this year and good news predicted for next year

E^+F^-:   good news realized this year and bad news predicted for next year

[57] As Penman (1991) notes "Fundamental analysis concerns the measurement of investment worth and the "information perspective" is limited in providing insights about this" (p. 5).

E^-F^+:   bad news realized this year and good news predicted for next year

E^-F^-:   bad news realized this year and bad news predicted for next year

The forecast for the next year was in the form of a probability assessment as to whether next year's earnings would be above or below that predicted by a time series model. The variables that went into the model are as follows:[58]

1. Percentage growth in the ratio of inventory to total assets
2. Percentage growth in the total asset turnover (net sales/total assets)
3. Change in dividends per share relative to previous year
4. Percentage growth in depreciation expense
5. Percentage growth in the ratio of capital expenditures to total assets
6. Percentage growth in the previous year's ratio of capital expenditures to total assets
7. Return on equity
8. Change in return on equity relative to the previous year

These variables were culled from a list of 61 variables and are characteristic of those commonly used in financial statement or fundamental analysis. As the graph indicates, all the E^+ portfolios and all the E^- portfolios moved together until year end. Then, from January on, the F^+ portfolios (good news forecasts) moved upward, whereas the F^- (bad news forecasts) turned downward. The results indicate that the forecast model could be used successfully to predict (the direction) of future prices.

Ou's study is characterized by two attributes that differentiate it from previous market-based research studies. First, the analysis is not motivated by showing whether accounting information is associated on an ex post basis with market prices but rather whether the information can be used ex ante as a basis of valuation. Second, and consistent with this ex ante approach, Ou broadens the set of accounting information by utilizing "tools of fundamental analysis" in her research design.

It is worth noting that we refer to Ou's approach as utilizing tools of fundamental analysis rather than fundamental analysis itself. The utilization of the eight variables just introduced was done in a purely mechanical fashion. All firms and variables were subjected to identical statistical analysis. Fundamental analysis requires more in-depth analysis, the nature of which varies from firm to firm. If anything, however, this shortcoming biased her results downward, and more promising results may be obtainable with more in-depth analyses. An effort along these lines has been made by Lev and Thiagarajan (1991). They use fundamental variables commonly used by analysts to study whether these variables are associated with stock returns. A more detailed discussion of this paper is found in Chapter 15.

These papers are a beginning. As Bernard, in mapping out the future direction of this research stated

---

[58]Ou, Jane A., "The Information Content of Nonearnings Accounting Numbers as Earnings Predictors", *Journal of Accounting Research* (Spring 1990) pp. 144–162.

> there is much groundwork to be laid . . . moving to within-industry analyses, explicitly considering how the information conveyed by accounting numbers is conditioned on the accounting context, gaining a better understanding of the relations among accounting numbers before understanding price data, emphasizing economic interpretation more and statistics less—may be useful in laying that groundwork.[59]

We are in agreement with that point of view and believe that this book can be useful in laying that groundwork.

IMPLICATIONS FOR FINANCIAL STATEMENT ANALYSIS

The empirical studies reviewed put to rest a number of beliefs, some of which, with hindsight, may have been overly naive in the first place. Financial markets are not simplistic and do not react in a knee-jerk fashion to accounting information. On the contrary, the reactions seem to be complex enough that the vast methodological carpet bombing of the past 20 years has not been able to uncover them.

In fact, understanding the nature of the work of the financial analyst seems to be the future direction for much of this line of research. Analysts seem to be the driving force keeping the market intelligent, and evidence exists that they lead the market.[60] Moreover, it is acknowledged that "better" analysts can carve out worthwhile areas of expertise. The positive theory approach has contributed by pointing out that there are important contractual considerations that one cannot afford to ignore when examining accounting data.

The classical theory at the same time cannot be discarded. Even though one may disagree with the view that theory can dictate "correct" accounting policy, the fact remains that much of GAAP is based on the measurement of some theoretical construct. Thus, in analyzing financial statements, it is important to know the underlying principles that argued for a given treatment before interpreting or adjusting it to the analyst's own view. At the same time, however, there is a need to be aware that the relationships governing accounting information involve complex interactions among investors, managers, and regulators and that these interactions may have powerful implications. To repeat a previous citation:

> The bulk of the evidence, however, suggests that any supposedly superior strategy should be taken with many grains of salt. The market is competitive enough that *only differentially superior information or insight will earn money; the easy pickings have been picked.*[61]

In conclusion, accounting research has clearly *not* proven that financial analysis is a futile exercise. On the contrary, it is trying to get a better understanding of its modus operandi. While the financial markets have become increasingly sophisticated in recent

---

[59]Bernard, Victor L. "Capital Market Research During the 1980's: A Critical Review," p. 106

[60]More detailed discussion of analyst forecasts and other forecasting models will be presented in Chapter 15.

[61]Bodie et al., *Investments,* p. 371; emphasis added.

years, we believe that superior financial analysis is still rewarding. We advance three arguments for this belief:

1. An inability to understand the impact of alternative accounting methods places the investor at a competitive disadvantage in a world of increasingly sophisticated analytic techniques. Knowledge of the techniques may give him the advantage.

2. Particularly with respect to smaller, less intensively researched companies, market efficiency cannot be taken for granted.

3. Recent financial history provides many examples of companies where, at least in retrospect, the financial markets ignored warning signals, and those left "holding the bag" suffered significant financial losses. Investors in banks and other financial intermediaries are but one example of this phenomenon.

At the same time, one would be foolish to ignore the lessons learned from the research and theory reviewed. The answers will not be found by simply focusing on the statements themselves. An awareness of the environment of the firm and its management is needed for proper analysis. It is with this belief that we continue with the remaining chapters of this book.

Chapter 4

Problems

1. [Approaches to accounting standard setting] In Chapter 1 (see Figure 1–1) under the topic of "the hierarchy of accounting qualities" one of the elements discussed is the quality of neutrality.

> Neutrality is concerned with whether financial statement data are biased. When the FASB proposes new standards, it is frequently the object of complaints that companies will be adversely affected by the standard. The principle of neutrality states that the Board should consider only the relevance and reliability of the data, not any possible impact.

Contrast this approach to accounting standard setting with that taken:

1. By academics in drawing conclusions from "information content" studies.

2. By proponents of the "positive" approach to accounting theory.

2. [Predictability, "surprises," and information content] Suppose it were possible to evaluate the effects on stock prices of two information systems: Alpha and Gamma. Each produces two accounting reports. The second report of each system will be identical. Information system Alpha allows you to predict the second report more accurately than the Gamma system.

A. Which of the two systems do you believe to be a better information system?

B. Under which system would the second report show more "information content"?

C. What is the implication of your replies to parts A and B on the factors that must be considered when evaluating the usefulness of financial reporting systems?

D. Ingberman and Sorter in their paper, "The Role of Financial Statements in an Efficient Market" (Journal of Accounting, Auditing and Finance, 1978) suggest that:

> . . . financial statements are seldom the place in which significant firm-related events are initially reported. Instead, these statements help the investor to construct a forecasting model for future income and cash flows. During the period, firm-related events become known in various ways, and these are inserted into the forecasting model.

How does this view relate to your reply to parts A–C and on the approach used by information content studies?

3. [Implications of adjusting for general market conditions] Assume that new information arrived affecting all aspects of the economy. Under standard research procedures, using a model such as the capital asset pricing model to test for market reaction, what would the results show? What does this imply about the nature of conclusions that can be drawn from certain market studies? Can you think of any (mandated) accounting standards that may have had pervasive effects across many sectors of the economy?

4. [Accounting standard setting] It has been said by some that:

> Generally accepted accounting principles are anything but principled. How could they be? They are a product of a political process.

How would the proponents of the three approaches to accounting theory view this statement?

5. [Implications for analysis] WSF investment services has a policy of completing a "company profile" for each new company whose financial statements they intend to analyze. You have been hired by WSF as an instructor in their training program. For each item on the checklist, explain to a trainee what the relevance might be for financial analysis.

  1. Terms of labor contract

  2. Number of analysts following the company

  3. Details of management compensation plans

  4. Capitalization size

  5. The proportion of stock held by managers

  6. Industry classification

6. [Mandated accounting changes, economic consequences, market reaction] *Newsweek* magazine (January 11, 1993, p. 59) reports that a survey:

> found that two thirds of major corporations have curtailed retiree health plans or intend to in 1993.

The article attributes the curtailment of such benefits to:

> a change in the national accounting rules that, beginning this year, require companies to carry the cost of such benefits as liabilities on their balance sheets. Technically, the new rule is a hit only on paper. But critics say many companies are using it as an excuse to cut costs and renege on past promises to workers.

Evaluate the argument made in the *Newsweek* article in the context of the accounting theories discussed in the chapter. Consideration should be given to the following points:

A. How consistent is the article with the efficient market and/or positive theory views of accounting?

B. The possibility that firms were not aware of the magnitude of the health costs until the new accounting rule came into effect.

C. What market reaction might you expect to the

(i) new accounting rule?

(ii) subsequent balance sheet disclosures?

(iii) "results" of the survey?

D. Do curtailments of health plans around the time of the implementation of the new accounting rule necessarily show "economic consequences" of accounting rules?

7. [News releases, market reaction, and abnormal returns] Exhibit 4P-1 contains information as to:

1. Closing prices and news items/releases of three companies.

2. The performance of various market indices on February 24, 1993

A. Ignoring the news items for the moment, which of the three stocks do you believe exhibited abnormal returns? How would you go about determining whether that was the case?

B. The Amgen news item appeared after the market close. Thus the closing price and price change do not reflect the news. Is the sharp market reaction to the news an indication of market efficiency or does the lack of anticipation of the news indicate inefficiency? Can this same type of question be asked with respect to the price change in the last month of Dell Computer's shares?

C. The news items for Amgen and Dell imply that the price change was in reaction to the news reported. In the case of Deere, although that argument can be made, the article does not do so. For which of these news releases can you argue that the market reaction is associated with the news release?

D. In the case of Dell Computers, why is it particularly difficult to determine the "cause" of the market reaction?

E. Most research studies would test for the market reaction to an announcement coming after the close of the market on the basis of the market reaction of the following day. In the case of Amgen, its shares on February 25,

EXHIBIT 4P-1

February 24, 1993	Close	Change	Percent
Overall Averages			
Dow Jones Industrial Average	3356.50	+33.23	1.0%
S&P 500	440.87	+6.07	1.4%
NASDAQ Composite	662.46	+10.90	1.7%
Technology (Dow Jones)	331.14	+6.81	2.1%
Industry Group Performance			
Biotechnology	669.27	+34.50	5.4%
Computers	275.35	+3.00	1.1%
Heavy machinery	167.73	+4.73	2.9%
Closing Prices			
Amgen	46¼	+2¾	6.3%
Dell Computers	30⅛	−6⅛	−16.9%
Deere	50¾	+2½	5.2%

The following news items are from *The New York Times*, February 25, 1993, p. D3.

Amgen Shares Plummet After Profit Forecast

Shares of Amgen, Inc., a biotechnology company, plunged in after-hours trading yesterday after the company said it expected its first-quarter earnings to come in well below Wall Street expectations. Amgen made the disclosure after regular trading hours, when its shares had closed on NASDAQ at $46.25, up $2.75. But in the half-hour of after-hour trading, shares plummeted $9, to $37.25.

Amgen's chief financial officer, Lowell Sears, said the company had anticipated that earnings per share for the first quarter would be 10 to 15 percent lower than Wall Street's average estimate of 60 cents a share . . . .

Dell's Stock Price Plunges After Forecast
by Thomas C. Hayes

Dallas, Feb. 24—The stock of the Dell Computer Corporation plummeted nearly 17 percent today after analysts said an earnings projection for the current fiscal year raised worries that the fast-growing maker of personal computers had quietly reduced its long-term profit goal to below 5 percent of sales.

The projection by Dell's chief financial officer was part of the announcement that it had withdrawn an offering of four million new common shares because its stock price fell sharply recently and because declining interest rates made borrowing more attractive.

The earnings and revenue projections were interpreted as a sign of Dell's determination to expand in the months ahead a price war [sic] that has crimped its profitability and pushed smaller rivals into financial distress.

Dell's stock fell $6.125 today, to $30.125, on volume of more than 9.5 million shares—the heaviest in NASDAQ trading. The stock hit an all-time high of $49.875 only last month.

EXHIBIT 4P-1. *(Continued)*

Deere Plans to Expand Production This Year

Deere & Company, the world's largest producer of agricultural machinery, told shareholders yesterday at its annual meeting in Moline, Ill., that it would expand production this year for the first time since 1990. Hans W. Becherer, chairman and chief executive, said output would grow 5 percent this year, thanks to sharp reductions in inventories at dealers, renewed buying from American farmers and the appeal of new products. Growth would be even stronger, he said, but for declines in the European market, where debates about the level of farm price and production supports have made farmers cautious about investing in new machinery.

1993, the following day, closed at 37 down 9.25, or 20%. The Biotechnology index closed at 591.07 down 11.68%.

   (i) Under these circumstances why might a research study underestimate the effects of the earnings announcement?

   (ii) *The Wall Street Journal* reported that the weakest stocks in the biotechnology group (on February 25, 1993) were Amgen, Chiron, and Centocor. Chiron stock fell by 1.02% and Centocor was unchanged. How does this information affect your response to (i).

   F. These news items are examples of the flow of information about a company during the year. Assuming the projections implied by these news items prove to be true, what should the market reaction be when the financial statements are released? Do these news items make financial statements irrelevant?

   G. The Deere article does not deal with earnings but rather with production. Do financial statements have any relevance in the context of news items of this sort?

   8. [Disclosure, need for regulation] In describing the financial reporting environment, William H. Beaver (Financial Reporting: An Accounting Revolution, Prentice Hall, 1989) portrays an environment in which investors with (perhaps) limited access to or knowledge of financial information make use of financial intermediaries/analysts. These intermediaries provide information gathering as well as investment services and compete with each other in the information processing function. Managers and firms compete for investors' capital by producing and disseminating information to investors and their intermediaries. The information provided is, often, more timely than the annual report or SEC filings.

   Given this environment, Beaver suggests that there exist incentives for firms to produce information on their own in the absence of any regulation. Given this argument, discuss the need for regulators such as the SEC and the FASB to mandate the type and form of disclosure required.

[Note: The interested reader is referred to Chapter 7 of Beaver's book.]

9. [Regulatory accounting, market reaction, and economic consequences] Certain regulated industries such as utilities, banks, and insurance companies are subject to accounting rules, known as Regulatory Accounting Principles (RAP). These RAP rules, which can differ from GAAP, are the basis by which, for example, the permitted rate of profit is calculated. Additionally, for many of these industries, certain minimum net worth requirements must be met. RAP governs how these requirements are measured.

The following article, by Greg Steinmetz, appeared in *The Wall Street Journal* on January 8, 1993.

Certain Life Insurers Plan Reserves
for Real Estate Losses due to New Rule

Giant, policyholder-owned life insurance companies plan to set aside billions of dollars in coming months to cover potential losses from real estate holdings.

The actions do not signify further deterioration in the companies' real estate holdings, nor will they seriously weaken the companies' financial strength. Rather, they stem from an accounting change that affects already identified problems. The change will bring the insurers' reserves up to the levels already established by publicly traded insurers. . . .

. . . The new rules, established by the National Association of Insurance Commissioners, require companies to build reserves to a level determined by a complicated formula. Insurers have several years to build the reserve to their minimum requirement.

The new rules came in response to criticism that insurance accounting practices let insurers hide losses. The rules are also part of an effort to ward off federal regulation of insurance, which is now overseen by states.

In anticipation of the new rules, some insurers began to voluntarily put up real estate reserves in 1991.

A. Notwithstanding the manner in which the first paragraph was written, no actual cash is set aside in these reserves. They are merely accounting entries. Would proponents of the efficient market hypothesis view this accounting change as cosmetic? Should one expect the market to react when it first "heard" about the accounting change? Can you predict what the nature of the reaction might be?

B. Would one expect to see any market reaction around the time this article was published? In what direction?

C. Discuss the similarities between the implications of changes in RAP and the "positive accounting" approach to GAAP.

10. [Market "crashes" and efficient markets] On October 19, 1987, the Dow Jones Industrial Average dropped by over 500 points. Overall market value on the New York Stock Exchange stocks fell by close to 25% on that day. What are the implications of the crash for the efficient market theory?

5

ANALYSIS OF INVENTORIES

INTRODUCTION

INVENTORY AND COST OF GOODS SOLD: BASIC RELATIONSHIPS
Scenario 1: Stable Prices
Scenario 2: Rising Prices

COMPARISON OF INFORMATION PROVIDED BY ALTERNATIVE METHODS
Balance Sheet Information: Inventory Account
Income Statement Information: Cost of Goods Sold
Inventory Valuation: Lower of Cost or Market

LIFO VERSUS FIFO: INCOME, CASH FLOW, AND WORKING CAPITAL EFFECTS

ADJUSTMENT FROM LIFO TO FIFO
Adjustment of Inventory Balances
Adjustment of COGS from LIFO to FIFO

ADJUSTMENT OF INCOME TO CURRENT COST INCOME

FINANCIAL RATIOS: LIFO VERSUS FIFO
Profitability: Gross Profit Margin
Liquidity: Working Capital

Activity: Inventory Turnover
Inventory Theory and Turnover Ratios
Economic Order Quantity
Just in Time
The LIFO/FIFO Choice and Inventory Holding Policy
Solvency: Debt to Equity

LIFO: REPORTING AND MEASUREMENT ISSUES
Initial Adoption or Change to LIFO
Change from LIFO
LIFO Liquidations
Declining Prices
LIFO and Interim Reporting
LIFO Inventory Methods
Pooled Specific Goods Method
Dollar Value LIFO Method
Retail Inventory Methods

LIFO: A HISTORICAL AND EMPIRICAL PERSPECTIVE
Overview of FIFO/LIFO Choice
The FIFO/LIFO Choice: Empirical Studies
Summary of FIFO/LIFO Choice

CONCLUDING COMMENTS ON   USING INVENTORY BALANCES TO AID IN
ACCOUNTING FOR INVENTORIES   FORECASTING

NON-U.S. REPORTING REQUIREMENTS   SUMMARY

INTRODUCTION

In early August 1990, after the invasion of Kuwait by Iraq, the spot price of oil rose from approximately $20 a barrel to almost $30 a barrel. Simultaneously, the price of gasoline sold at the pump increased by 15% to 20%. Consumers and politicians were vociferous in their criticism of oil companies for immediately raising the price of gasoline sold at the retail level. They argued that the gasoline being sold had been refined from oil purchased at a price of $20 a barrel and hence raising the price of this "old" gasoline was unfair resulting in windfall profits.

The oil companies countered that since the market price of oil had risen, replacing the "old" oil would cost more and hence raising the price of gasoline was justified and reflective of current market conditions.

The accounting choice of last-in, first-out (LIFO) versus first-in, first-out (FIFO) for inventory and cost of goods sold (COGS) mirrors this debate as to the more appropriate measure of income. The choice affects the firm's income statement, balance sheet, and related ratios. Perhaps more important, the decision has real cash flow effects as taxes paid by the firm are affected by its choice of accounting method.

INVENTORY AND COST OF GOODS SOLD: BASIC RELATIONSHIPS

The inventory account is affected by two events: the purchase (or manufacture) of goods (P) and their subsequent sale $(COGS)$. The relationship between these events and the balance of beginning inventory (BI) and ending inventory (EI) can be expressed as

$$EI = BI + P - COGS \quad \text{or}$$
$$BI + P = COGS + EI$$

For any period, prior to the preparation of financial statements for the period, the left side of the equation is known: the beginning inventory plus purchases (cost of goods acquired for sale during the period). Preparation of the income statement and balance sheet for the period involves the allocation of these costs $(BI + P)$ between cost of goods sold and ending inventory. This process is illustrated under two scenarios:

Beginning inventory: 200 units @ $10/unit = $2000

Quarter	Purchases Units	Scenario 1: Stable Prices		Scenario 2: Rising Prices	
		Unit Cost	Purchases Dollars	Unit Cost	Purchases Dollars
1	100	$10	$1000	$11	$1100
2	150	$10	$1500	$12	$1800
3	150	$10	$1500	$13	$1950
4	100	$10	$1000	$14	$1400
Total	500		$5000		$6250
			$BI + P = $7000		$BI + P = $8250

Units sold: 100 units per quarter for a total of 400 units
Ending inventory: 300 units

Scenario 1: Stable Prices

Beginning inventory plus purchases equal $7000. Since unit costs are constant at $10 per unit and 400 units were sold, the cost of goods sold under any accounting method equals $4000 (400 × $10) and the cost of the 300 units in ending inventory equals $3000 (300 × $10).

$$BI + P = COGS + EI$$
$$\$2000 + \$5000 = \$4000 + \$3000$$

Unfortunately, stable prices are the exception rather than the norm, as costs and prices are constantly changing. Accounting for inventory and cost of goods sold in such an environment, as a result, becomes more complex but at the same time that much more interesting.

Scenario 2: Rising Prices

Beginning inventory plus purchases equal $8250. Unlike the case of stable prices, however, the cost of goods sold and the cost of ending inventory are not determinable without some assumptions as to the flow of costs. Essentially, three alternative assumptions are possible: *first-in, first-out; last-in, first-out;* and *weighted average cost*.

FIFO accounting assumes that the costs of items *first purchased* are deemed to be the costs of items *first sold* and these costs enter cost of goods sold; ending inventory is made up of the cost of the most recent items purchased.

At the opposite extreme is LIFO—last-in, first-out—accounting where items *last purchased* are assumed to be the ones *first sold* and the ending inventory is made up of the earliest costs incurred.

Finally, as its name implies, weighted average cost accounting uses the (same) average cost for both the items sold and those in closing inventory.

In our example, this would result in the following three alternative presentations on the income statement and balance sheet (the calculations are shown in Exhibit 5-1):

	BI	+	P	=	COGS	+	EI
FIFO	$2000	+	$6250	=	$4300	+	$3950
Weighted Average	$2000	+	$6250	=	$4714	+	$3536
LIFO	$2000	+	$6250	=	$5150	+	$3100

EXHIBIT 5-1. Allocation of Costs Under Different Inventory Methods, Scenario 2

A. FIFO

The 400 units sold (COGS) are assumed to carry the earliest costs incurred and the 300 units left in inventory carry the latest costs:

Cost of Goods Sold	Ending Inventory
200 @ $10 = $2000	100 @ $14 = $1400
100 @ $11 = $1100	150 @ $13 = $1950
100 @ $12 = $1200	50 @ $12 = $ 600
400 $4300	300 $3950

B. LIFO

The 400 units sold (COGS) are assumed to carry the latest costs incurred and the 300 units left in inventory carry the earliest costs:

Cost of Goods Sold	Ending Inventory
100 @ $14 = $1400	200 @ $10 = $2000
150 @ $13 = $1950	100 @ $11 = $1100
150 @ $12 = $1800	
400 $5150	300 $3100

C. Weighted Average

The total cost for the 700 units = $8250. On a per unit basis, this results in a weighted average unit cost of

$$\frac{\$8250}{700} = \$11.786$$

Cost of goods sold = 400 × $11.786 = $4714
Ending inventory   = 300 × $11.786 = $3536

COMPARISON OF INFORMATION PROVIDED BY ALTERNATIVE METHODS

This section compares the information provided by the three alternative accounting methods.

Balance Sheet Information: Inventory Account

The ending inventory consists of 300 units. At current replacement cost (i.e., the fourth quarter unit cost of $14), the inventory would have a carrying value of $4200. The FIFO inventory of $3950 comes closest to this amount, whereas the LIFO amount of $3100 is farthest from the current cost because FIFO allocates the earliest costs to cost of goods sold, leaving the most recent costs in ending inventory.

Conversely, LIFO accounting allocates the earliest (outdated) costs to ending inventory. In fact, the cost of ending inventory for many companies using LIFO may be decades old,[1] thus rendering the balance in the inventory account for a LIFO company virtually useless. In terms of information provided on the balance sheet, inventories based on FIFO are preferable to those presented under LIFO, as carrying values under FIFO most closely resemble current cost. In other words, FIFO provides a measure of inventory that is closer to its current (economic) value.

Income Statement Information: Cost of Goods Sold

Consider a situation where an item purchased for $6 is sold for $10 at a time when it costs $7 to replace it. Prior to replacement of the item (under any accounting method), reported income will be $4 ($10 − $6). However, if income is defined as the amount available for distribution to shareholders without impairing the firm's operations, then it can be argued that income is only $3, as $7 (not the original cost of $6) are needed to replace the item in inventory and continue operations. The $1 difference between the original cost of the item and the cost of replacement is referred to as a holding gain or inventory profit,[2] and there is strong debate as to whether this amount should be considered as income.[3]

In our hypothetical case, *only if the item were not replaced* would there be $10 to distribute to shareholders, indicating a profit of $4. Under a going concern assumption, however, firms that sell their inventory need to replenish it constantly for sales in the future. Thus income should be measured in terms of profits after providing for the replacement of inventory.

---

[1]For example, Caterpillar, Inc., states that the LIFO method "was first adopted for the major portion of inventories in 1950."

[2]Using the terminology of Chapter 2, economic income equals 4. As the holding gain is 1, sustainable income is 3.

[3]The situation is obviously similar to having purchased a home before a rapid increase in real estate prices and not being able to cash in on your good fortune because any replacement home would cost as much as the home you live in now.

In our example, the replacement cost of the items sold (using the unit cost for each quarter) is $5000[4] [(100 × $11) + (100 × $12) + (100 × $13) + (100 × $14)]. As generally accepted accounting principles (GAAP) are based on a historical cost framework, however, replacement cost accounting is not permitted. LIFO allocates the most recent purchase prices to cost of goods sold. The reported LIFO COGS of $5150 is, therefore, closest to the replacement cost, with the FIFO COGS of $4300 being farthest from this cost. For income statement purposes, LIFO is the most informative accounting method in that it provides a better measure of current income and future profitability.

This leaves us in something of a quandary, since FIFO provides the best measure for the balance sheet. The preceding discussion has also implied the use of a single method for all inventories; in practice, this is rarely the case as firms often use more than one inventory method. Firms may use different methods for their foreign operations since LIFO is rarely used in many countries, or they may use different methods in various business segments. This factor serves to disguise further the impact of reported inventory on the income statement and balance sheet.

However, from an analyst's perspective the choice between the different methods is not so grim.[5] Information is often available to permit restatement of financial statements from one method to the other. This methodology will be illustrated later in the chapter. Our discussion will now, however, turn to pragmatic differences between the two methods.

Before doing so, it is important to note that the FIFO/LIFO issue begins after the determination of costs to be included in inventory. In a manufacturing environment, as Box 5-1 illustrates, that determination itself can be affected by management choice. Furthermore, the carrying amount of inventory can also be affected by changes in market value as discussed below.

Inventory Valuation: Lower of Cost or Market

GAAP requires the use of the lower-of-cost-or-market-valuation basis (LCM) for inventories, with market value defined as replacement cost.[6] The LCM valuation basis follows the principle of conservatism (on both the balance sheet and income statement) since it recognizes losses or declines in market value as they occur, whereas increases are reported only when inventory is sold. Because tax-based LIFO is a cost (as opposed to LCM) method, firms using LIFO cannot recognize (and obtain tax benefits from) write-downs and declines in market value for tax purposes.

---

[4]If the computation is done on an annual basis, the replacement cost would be $5600 (400 × $14) using the most recent purchase price to measure replacement cost.

[5]The weighted average method falls someplace in between the FIFO and LIFO methods both in terms of the balance sheet and income statement. In some sense, therefore, it is seen by some as a compromise candidate. One can, however, alternatively argue that it is the worst of the three choices: unlike LIFO and FIFO, which provide good information on one financial statement, the weighted average method does not do so for any statement. Practically speaking, however, over time the weighted average method tends to be closer to FIFO than to LIFO, especially with regards to inventory costs on the balance sheet.

[6]However, replacement cost cannot exceed the net realizable value or be below the net realizable value less the normal profit margin.

BOX 5-1
Inventory Costing in a Manufacturing Environment

Accounting for inventories in a manufacturing environment adds another dimension to the problem of inventory costing. A merchandising operation has only one type of inventory; finished goods, and the costs of obtaining that inventory can be determined directly. They are the amounts charged by the supplier of the finished goods.

Manufacturing operations, on the other hand, carry three types of inventory;

1. Raw Material
2. Work in Process
3. Finished Goods

Costs included in the various stages of inventory are raw material costs and labor and overhead costs which are needed to transform the raw material into finished goods. Determining the amount of overhead costs, or indirect costs, poses the most problems. The magnitude of these problems can be appreciated if we consider the nature of some of the items included in (factory) overhead:

- supervisors' salaries
- rent of factory plant and equipment
- depreciation of factory plant and equipment
- utilities
- employee benefits such as pensions, health insurance, etc.
- repairs and maintenance
- engineering costs
- quality control

Let us consider the utility bill in a factory producing fifty different product lines. How much of the utility cost should be charged to each product line? Costs of this kind are *joint costs* and, in a multi-product environment, it is impossible to determine, a priori, how much of the cost should be charged or allocated to any given product. An estimated allocation method is required. As the amount charged to any one product line depends on the chosen allocation procedure, results can be somewhat arbitrary and capable of manipulation. That is, manufacturers can increase income by choosing an allocation scheme that charges more of the overhead costs to slow moving items. These costs then remain in inventory as an asset and their expense recognition is delayed until the products are sold.

A second aspect of this problem relates to the fixed nature of many of these costs. Items such as depreciation, rent, or supervisors' salaries will not increase (in the short run) with changes in production. Therefore, allocating their cost to products involves an averaging process that is subject to manipulation by changing levels of production. A simple example in a single product environment will illustrate this.

Assume a company has factory rent of $12,000 and it sells 10,000 units. If it only produces 10,000 units, the full $12,000 of factory rent will flow through Cost of Goods Sold (at a rate of $1.20/unit) and be expensed. If the company increases production to 12,000 units, then factory rent is charged at $1.00/unit. But if it sells only 10,000 units, then $2,000 of rent cost will remain in inventory and only $10,000 will be expensed as part of Cost of Goods Sold. The company has increased income by manipulating production rather than increasing sales.

It should be noted that although we speak of manipulation, it does not mean such manipulation must be willful. As the allocation method is by necessity based on estimation, any resultant income number is suspect because a different allocation method would have yielded a different income number. This inherent arbitrariness makes it imperative for the analyst to monitor

- the accounting policies used by different firms in the same industry; and
- the effects of fluctuations in production on COGS and reported income.

Finally, it must be noted that there does not exist uniformity as to which costs are charged to inventory (and then expensed when sold) and which costs are expensed as incurred. Schiff (1987) notes that although it is commonly suggested in accounting textbooks that fixed overhead costs must be allocated to inventory, in practice, many companies* have (historically) charged certain overhead costs directly to expense. Examples of such costs are depreciation, pension costs and property taxes. For companies that expense these costs, variations in production and inventory levels will not affect the amount expensed. It will always equal the amount incurred. However, in firms that allocate these costs to inventory, when inventory levels increase, the amount expensed will be less than the amount actually incurred with the difference remaining in inventory. On the balance sheet, those firms that capitalize more costs in inventory will have higher carrying values of inventory, working capital and equity balances. Unfortunately, not all companies disclose their practices in this respect. This can make comparisons between companies difficult.

In recent years, a number of firms that had been expensing such items have changed their inventory costing method and begun to capitalize them.† The motivation may be to conform to their method of tax accounting since the Tax Reform Act of 1986 limited the number of items that could be expensed directly. Alternatively, with the beginning of the recession at the end of the 1980s firms changed their method to improve reported income keeping some of their fixed costs off the income statement by capitalizing them.

Additionally, with the increased emphasis in recent years on improving their manufacturing process, many firms have been adjusting their method of inventory costing. This does not relate only to the issue of which items to include as part of inventory cost, but also to the allocation procedures used.

Exhibit 5-2 taken from the footnotes of the Binks Manufacturing Co. shows one company making two such changes in three years. This example only serves to underscore the subjective nature of cost allocations and the difficulty involved in the estimation of inventory costs in a manufacturing environment.

---

*The steel industry is one example noted by Schiff.

†Bartley and Chen (1992) report 27 companies that changed their inventory accounting method in this fashion in the two-year period 1986–1987. All of the changes resulted in an increase in income.

EXHIBIT 5-2. Example of Changes in Accounting of Overhead Costs

Binks Manufacturing Company

Consolidated Statements of Earnings

	December 1		
	1990	1989	1988
Earnings before cumulative effect of a change in accounting principle	$5,786,419	$9,607,196	$7,043,612
Cumulative effect to December 1, 1989 and December 1, 1987 of changing overhead recorded in inventory	930,000	—	375,000
Net earnings	$6,716,419	$9,607,196	$7,418,612

EXHIBIT 5-2. *(Continued)*

NOTES TO CONSOLIDATED FINANCIAL STATEMENTS

Note 2. Change in the Application of an Accounting Principle.

In the fourth quarter of 1990 the Company changed its method of applying overhead to inventory. Historically, the Parent company used a single overhead rate in valuing the ending inventory, determined by comparing the total manufacturing overhead expenses for the year with total direct labor costs for the year. In 1990 the Company performed an extensive study to precisely determine the manufacturing overhead to be applied to specific product lines.

The Company believes that the change in the application of this accounting principle is preferable because it provides a better determination of overhead costs in inventory and thus improves the matching of production costs with related revenues in reporting operating results.

The change in the application of this accounting principle resulted in an increase in net earnings of $930,000 (after reduction of income taxes of $570,000), reflecting the cumulative effect of this change for the periods prior to December 1, 1989. In accordance with generally accepted accounting principles, the cumulative effect of the change on prior years has been recorded in the first quarter of fiscal 1990. The effect of the change on the current year's net earnings before cumulative effect of a change in accounting principle is not material.

In accordance with generally accepted accounting principles, pro forma amounts, assuming the new accounting principle was applied retroactively, are presented below;

	1990	1989	1988
Net earnings	$5,786,000	$9,297,000	$7,605,000
Net earnings per share	1.97	3.22	2.67

In 1988 the Company changed its accounting procedures to include in inventory certain manufacturing overhead costs previously charged to operations as incurred. Such costs included in inventory are production engineering costs and costs incurred in transporting manufactured inventory to the point of sale. The Company believes this method is preferable because it more accurately reflects total product costs and improves the matching of cost of sales with related revenues in reporting operating results. The change in accounting procedure resulted in an increase in net earnings of 1988 of $375,000 (after reduction for income taxes of $225,000), reflecting the cumulative effect of this change for the periods prior to December 1, 1987.

Source: Binks Manufacturing Co. Annual Report (1990)

LIFO VERSUS FIFO: INCOME, CASH FLOW, AND WORKING CAPITAL EFFECTS

The foregoing examples illustrate that, in periods of rising prices and stable or increasing inventory quantities, the use of LIFO results in higher cost of goods sold expense and lower reported income. In the absence of income taxes, there would be no difference in cash flow. Cash flow would equal payments made for purchases and be independent of the accounting method used.

When LIFO is a permitted method for income taxes, however, lower income translates into lower taxes and thus higher cash flows. In the United States, unlike other accounting policy choices that allow differing methods of accounting for financial statements and for tax purposes, *IRS regulations require that the same method of inventory accounting used for tax purposes also be used for financial reporting*. From an economic perspective, given rising prices, LIFO is a good choice, as taxes will be lower and cash flows will be higher despite the lower reported income.[7]

In Chapter 3 (concerning ratios), it was noted that working capital is used as an expanded liquidity measure because it includes cash and near-cash assets. Inventory accounting can distort the working capital measure and lead to erroneous and contradictory conclusions. LIFO accounting results in higher cash flows, but it reports lower working capital because the inventory balances retain earlier (lower) costs and the cash saved is only a percentage (the marginal tax rate) of the difference in inventory values.

In periods of rising prices and stable or increasing inventory quantities, the impact of LIFO and FIFO on the financial statements can be summarized as

	LIFO	FIFO
Cost of goods sold	Higher	Lower
Income before taxes	Lower	Higher
Income taxes	Lower	Higher
Net income	Lower	Higher
Cash flows	**Higher**	**Lower**
Inventory balance	Lower	Higher
Working capital	Lower	Higher

Cash flow has been highlighted because it is the only figure with direct economic impact. The others are accounting constructs and their economic significance is indirect and informational.

Continuing with the previous numeric example, and assuming that 400 units were sold for $10,000 (average price of $25) and a tax rate of 40%, the above differences can be illustrated as follows. The income statements are

	FIFO	LIFO
Sales	$10,000	$10,000
COGS	4,300	5,150
Income before tax	$ 5,700	$ 4,850
Tax @ 40%	2,280	1,940
Net income	$ 3,420	$ 2,910

---

[7]The question of why, given the foregoing, all firms do not use LIFO will be considered later in the chapter.

Assuming sales are for cash and that payment for purchases and taxes are made immediately, then cash flows are

	FIFO	LIFO
Sales inflows	$10,000	$10,000
Purchases	6,250	6,250
Inflows before tax	$ 3,750	$ 3,750
Taxes paid	2,280	1,940
Net cash flows	$ 1,470	$ 1,810

Therefore, changes in balance sheet accounts are

Assets

	FIFO	LIFO
Cash*	$1470	$1810
Inventory†	1950	1100
Working capital	$3420	$2910

Liabilities and Owner's Equity

	FIFO	LIFO
Retained earnings‡	$3420	$2910

*Net cash flow for period.
†Purchases less COGS.
‡Net income for period.

The difference in net income of $510 and the difference in cash flows of $340 are related to the difference in COGS (equivalently the difference in inventory balances) of $850 as follows:

$$\text{Difference in income} = (1 - \text{Tax rate}) \times \text{Difference in COGS}$$
$$\$510 = \quad 0.6 \quad \times \$850$$

$$\text{Difference in cash flow} = \text{Tax rate} \quad \times \text{Difference in COGS}$$
$$\$340 = 0.4 \quad \times \$850$$

However, these differences are *in opposite directions* with higher income for the FIFO firm and higher cash flows for the LIFO firm. The difference in working capital is the net of the difference in inventory balance and cash flow:

$$\$510 = \$850 - \$340$$

This leads to misleading liquidity measures for the LIFO firm as its working capital is understated:[8] the increase in cash is more than offset by the understatement of inventory.

The next section describes the techniques used to adjust financial statements from LIFO to FIFO (and vice versa). The analyst can eliminate differences between firms due to accounting methods so that any remaining differences reflect economic and operating variations.

ADJUSTMENT FROM LIFO TO FIFO

Adjustment of Inventory Balances

Generally, LIFO inventory balances contain old and outdated costs with little or no relationship to current costs. To remedy this deficiency, we must adjust the inventory balances of firms using LIFO by the amount of the *LIFO reserve*. The LIFO reserve (usually found in the financial statement footnotes, but sometimes shown on the face of the balance sheet) is the difference between the inventory balance shown on the balance sheet and the amount that would have been reported had the firm used FIFO. We can express this as

$$\text{LIFO reserve} = \text{Inventory}_F - \text{Inventory}_L$$

or

$$\text{Inventory}_F = \text{Inventory}_L + \text{LIFO reserve}$$

(where the subscripts "F" and "L" represent the accounting methods FIFO and LIFO, respectively). Many firms refer to current or replacement costs, which approximate FIFO costs.

Example: Sun Company

Exhibit 5-3 contains extracts from the annual report of Sun Company, a large oil refiner, for the year ended December 31, 1991: details of current assets and portions of financial statement footnotes. Note that, with the 1991 change of accounting for the inventories of Suncor (Sun's Canadian subsidiary), the company uses LIFO for virtually all crude oil and refined product inventories. Exhibit 5-3A shows the adjustment of LIFO to FIFO inventory, adding the LIFO reserve to the LIFO inventory. Note that the LIFO reserve is large, meaning that the balance sheet carrying amount significantly understates inventories. This understatement is typical of firms whose products have risen in price and that have used LIFO for many years. In the case of Sun, LIFO cost is only 40% of FIFO cost;

---

[8]Johnson and Dhaliwal (1988) studied firms that abandoned LIFO in favor of FIFO. Their evidence suggested one possible motivation for the abandonment decision was to increase their reported working capital. Compared to firms that retained LIFO, the abandonment firms had less slack in the working capital constraints as defined by their debt covenants.

EXHIBIT 5-3. Inventory Disclosures

Sun Company

	December 31	
	1991	1990
	($ millions)	
Cash	$ 366	$ 279
Short-term investments	—	15
Accounts and notes receivable	814	1207
Inventories	514	582
Total current assets	$1694	2083
Total current liabilities	$1965	$2314
Net working capital	(271)	(231)

Effective January 1, 1991, Sun changed its method of accounting for the cost of crude oil and refined product inventories at Suncor from the FIFO method to the LIFO method. Sun believes that the use of the LIFO method better matches current costs with current revenues. The cumulative effect of this accounting change for years prior to 1991 is not determinable, nor are the pro forma effects of retroactive application of the LIFO method to prior years. This change decreased the 1991 net loss and net loss per share of common stock by $3 million and $0.03, respectively.

	December 31	
	1991	1990
	($ millions)	
Crude oil	$ 147	$ 200
Refined products	229	258
Materials, supplies, and other	138	124
	$ 514	$ 582

The cost of crude oil and refined products inventories is determined using the following accounting methods (Note 6):

	December 31	
	1991	1990
	($ millions)	
Crude oil:		
Last-in, first-out (LIFO)	$ 147	$ 154
First in, first-out (FIFO) or other	—	46
	$ 147	$ 200
Refined products:		
Last-in, first-out (LIFO)	$ 213	$ 152
First-in, first-out (FIFO) or other	16	106
	$ 229	$ 258

EXHIBIT 5-3. *(Continued)*

During 1990, Sun reduced certain inventory quantities which were valued at lower LIFO costs prevailing in prior years. The effect of this reduction was to increase 1990 net income and net income per share of common stock by $8 million and $0.07, respectively. The current replacement cost of all inventories valued at LIFO exceeded their carrying value by $536 million and $835 million at December 31, 1991 and 1990, respectively.

Source: Sun Company, *1991 Annual Report.*

EXHIBIT 5-3A. SUN COMPANY
Adjustment from LIFO to FIFO, 1988–1991

	December 31			
	1991	1990	1989	1988
	($ millions)			
Total Inventories (as reported)*	514	582	583	484
LIFO Reserve	536	835	641	497
Inventories at FIFO	1050	1417	1224	981
Crude Oil and Refined Products (as reported)†	360	306	298	156
LIFO Reserve	536	835	641	497
Inventory at FIFO	896	1141	939	653
Cost of Goods Sold (as reported)‡	8460	9529	7763	na
Less: Change in LIFO reserve: LIFO effect	(299)	194	144	na
Equals: Cost of Goods Sold at FIFO	8759	9335	7619	na

*See Exhibit 5-3 for components and inventory methods used.
†Portion of Sun's inventory carried at LIFO (see Exhibit 5-3).
‡From Sun's income statement, not shown in Exhibit 5-3.
na—not applicable.
Source: Sun Company, Annual Reports, 1989–1991

one year earlier (when oil prices were higher), the ratio of LIFO cost to FIFO cost was only 27%.

Adjustment of COGS from LIFO to FIFO

Cost of goods sold can be derived using the opening and closing inventory balances and purchases for the period:

$$COGS = BI + P - EI$$

Thus, to arrive at FIFO cost of goods sold ($COGS_F$), these figures need to be restated on a FIFO basis. The LIFO-to-FIFO adjustment in inventory balance was illustrated earlier. Purchases (which are not a function of the accounting method used) need not be adjusted and can be derived directly from the (opening and closing) inventory balances and cost of goods sold as stated in the financial statements:

$$P = COGS_L + EI_L - BI_L$$

Example: Sun Company

For Sun Company, purchases for 1991 can be calculated (in millions of dollars) as

$$P = \$8460 + \$514 - \$582$$
$$= \$8392$$

To convert COGS from LIFO to FIFO, we need restated inventories on a FIFO basis. These calculations are shown in Exhibit 5-3A.

Using 1991 purchases, as calculated, with the FIFO inventory amounts derived in Exhibit 5-3A yields 1991 cost of goods sold on a FIFO basis for Sun Company:

$$COGS_F = BI_F + P - EI_F$$
$$= \$1417 \text{ million} + \$8392 \text{ million} - \$1050 \text{ million} = \$8759 \text{ million}$$

Thus COGS on a FIFO basis is higher than on a LIFO basis by $299 million ($8759 million $-$ $8460 million). The astute reader will note that this amount is equal to the decrease in the LIFO reserve during the year ($835 million $-$ $536 million). This is no coincidence (see footnote 9), and the adjustment from LIFO-to-FIFO cost of goods sold can be made directly from the LIFO reserve accounts without going through the intermediate steps of calculating purchases and adjusting inventories. The direct adjustment is[9]

---

[9]For those with a more mathematical bent, this result can be proven as follows:

$$COGS_F = BI_F + P - EI_F \tag{1}$$

Similarly,

$$COGS_L = BI_L + P - EI_L \tag{2}$$

or

$$P = COGS_L + EI_L - BI_L \tag{3}$$

Substituting expression (3) for P in expression (1) (since the purchases, P, are identical for both accounting methods) and rearranging yields

$$COGS_F = COGS_L - [(EI_F - EI_L) - (BI_F - BI_L)] \tag{4}$$

Since the two terms in brackets—$(EI_F - EI_L)$ and $(BI_F - BI_L)$—on the right side of the equation are just the LIFO reserve at the end and beginning of the period, respectively, equation (4) can be expressed as

$$COGS_F = COGS_L - [(\text{LIFO reserve}_E - \text{LIFO reserve}_B)] \tag{5}$$

$$COGS_F = COGS_L - (\text{LIFO reserve}_E - \text{LIFO reserve}_B)$$
$$\$8759 \text{ million} = \$8460 \text{ million} - (\$536 \text{ million} - \$835 \text{ million})$$

where the subscripts "E" and "B" refer to ending (inventory) and beginning (inventory), respectively. The change in LIFO reserve during the year, sometimes called the *LIFO effect* for the year, is thus the difference between the COGS computed under the two methods.

Before leaving this discussion, several questions are in order. Most important, why does conversion to FIFO result in *higher* 1991 cost of goods sold when we normally expect $COGS_F$ to be *lower* than $COGS_L$? The second question is, why did the LIFO reserve decrease in 1991?

The answer to both questions is the same: oil prices decreased in 1991. This decrease reduced the difference between inventory cost on a LIFO basis and cost on a FIFO basis; the LIFO reserve, which represents this difference, is thus reduced.

Notice that the change to LIFO by Suncor (see footnote in Exhibit 5-3) *reduced* Sun's 1991 loss; it reduced COGS, again the opposite of what we would expect from a change to LIFO. The lesson here should be clear: *when prices are declining, LIFO produces lower COGS and, therefore, higher earnings*. In the case of Sun, use of the LIFO method reduced COGS by $299 million in 1991, increasing pretax earnings by an equal amount.

For 1990, however, the effect of LIFO was quite different. Sun's LIFO reserve increased by $194 million.[10] For 1990, we can compute that

$$COGS_F = COGS_L - (\text{LIFO reserve}_E - \text{LIFO reserve}_B)$$
$$\$9335 \text{ million} = \$9529 \text{ million} - (\$835 \text{ million} - \$641 \text{ million})$$

Thus in 1990, a year of rising prices, LIFO had the expected effect: $COGS_L$ was increased and pretax income reduced by the amount of the increase in the LIFO reserve.

ADJUSTMENT OF INCOME TO CURRENT COST INCOME

This section discusses the adjustment of COGS calculated on a FIFO basis to reflect current costs. It is important to distinguish between the adjustment of FIFO COGS to current costs and the recalculation of COGS "as if" the firm reported on a LIFO basis. Generally, LIFO COGS approximates current cost COGS as long as the firm does not deplete any of its opening inventory. In this case these two adjustment techniques produce equivalent results. When inventory quantities are reduced, however, further adjustment is required.

LIFO COGS and income will both be distorted when the firm reduces its opening inventory (known as a LIFO liquidation), as old costs will flow into the income statement and COGS no longer reflects the current cost of inventory sold. In the event of a LIFO liquidation, the "as if" recalculation does not provide a current cost adjustment, as COGS includes inventory costs from earlier years. As such, it is not relevant to an

---

[10]Despite a LIFO invasion of $8 million after tax (discussed later in the chapter).

assessment of expected future performance. The adjustment to current cost, however, is relevant. LIFO liquidations will be discussed in a subsequent section of the chapter. For the moment, therefore, we will ignore this problem and use the terms LIFO and current cost interchangeably. The reader should, however, keep this important caveat in mind.

For firms using FIFO, *only the adjustment of the FIFO cost of goods sold to LIFO cost of goods sold is relevant.* Adjustments of inventory balances to LIFO serve no purpose, as LIFO inventory costs are outdated and almost meaningless. However, information needed to adjust cost of goods sold to LIFO is not generally provided in the financial statements. An approximate adjustment, however, is often possible.[11]

This adjustment involves multiplying the opening inventory by the (specific) inflation rate and adding the product to $COGS_F$ to arrive at $COGS_L$. More formally,

$$COGS_L = COGS_F + (BI_F \times r)$$

where r is the *specific* inflation rate appropriate for the products in which the firm deals. A simple proof of this adjustment is presented in Box 5-2.

---

[11]A more detailed adjustment taking into consideration the firm's inventory turnover is possible. Falkenstein and Weil (1977) discuss the use of turnover, but note (p. 51 of their article) that estimates from the more basic procedure (used in this text) have always approximated the estimates from the more tedious methods.

BOX 5-2
Derivation of Current Cost Adjustment

The appropriateness of the approximation can be illustrated by the following "proof." Assume that a firm carries a *quantity Q* of inventory and that this quantity is equal to three months of inventory. The inventory level Q is replenished every three months. Assume further that the inflation rate over the year is equal to r. Finally, let P be the unit cost at which the opening inventory Q_0 was purchased at the end of the previous year. Thus the unit cost of the inventory at the end of the current year will equal $P(1 + r)$. The following illustrates the actual flow of goods purchased throughout the year.

$$\begin{aligned}
\text{Beginning inventory} &= Q_0 = \text{Sales during 1st quarter} \\
\text{End of 1st quarter purchase} &= Q_1 = \text{Sales during 2nd quarter} \\
\text{End of 2nd quarter purchase} &= Q_2 = \text{Sales during 3rd quarter} \\
\text{End of 3rd quarter purchase} &= Q_3 = \text{Sales during 4th quarter} \\
\text{End of 4th quarter purchase} &= Q_4 = \text{Ending inventory}
\end{aligned}$$

Under FIFO the cost of $Q_0, Q_1, Q_2,$ and Q_3 will appear in cost of goods sold. Under LIFO the cost of Q_1, Q_2, Q_3 and Q_4 will appear in cost of goods sold. Thus the difference between the two methods lies in the difference between the cost of the beginning (Q_0) and ending (Q_4) inventory. Hence the difference between LIFO and FIFO equals

$$Q_4 P(1 + r) - Q_0 P = Q_0 Pr$$

since the inventory quantity purchased each period is the same.

To the extent a firm's inventory purchasing policies are uniform, the adjustment suggested here will approximate the actual FIFO-to-LIFO (current cost) adjustment. The inflation rate needed for the adjustment is not a general producer or consumer price index, but rather should be the specific price index appropriate to the firm in question. (For a multi-industry firm, the calculation would have to be done on a segmented basis.) Many industry indices are readily available, published by the U.S. Department of Commerce. For companies whose inputs are commodities (oil, coffee, steel scrap), the spot price for the commodity may be used.

The example that follows illustrates an alternative basis for obtaining the specific price level change, derived from a competing (LIFO) firm in the same industry as the firm under examination.

Example: Amerada Hess

Exhibit 5-4 contains inventory and cost of goods sold data for Amerada Hess, a major oil producer and refiner, along with related footnotes. The firm uses the FIFO method for two-thirds of crude oil and refined product inventories and average cost for the balance.[12] Our objective is to adjust COGS for 1990 to a LIFO basis. There are two reasons for making this adjustment. One is to estimate the impact of changing oil prices on Amerada's sales and earnings; we wish to separate price effects from operating effects. The second reason is to compare Amerada with other firms in the oil industry using LIFO accounting. There are several ways to achieve our objective.

If the increase in specific price index (obtained, for example, from government statistics) for oil products was 20% in 1990, then the addition to FIFO cost of goods sold would be $190 million (0.20 × $950 million), where the latter is the inventory balance at the beginning of 1990). This $190 million, it should be noted, is the holding gain portion of the income reported under the FIFO method. Removing the holding gain from

---

[12]For simplicity, our analysis will assume that Amerada uses FIFO for all crude oil and refined product inventories.

EXHIBIT 5-4. AMERADA HESS
Crude Oil and Refined Product Inventories, December 31, 1988–1990

	1990	1989	1988
		($ millions)	
Closing inventory	$1243	$950	$754
Cost of goods sold	4709	3838	—

Inventories: Crude oil and refined product inventories are valued at the lower of cost or market value. Cost is determined on the first-in, first-out method for approximately two-thirds of the inventories and the average cost method for the remainder.

Inventories of materials and supplies are valued at or below cost

Source: Amerada Hess Annual Reports, 1989–1990.

income (adding it to cost of goods sold) results in a better measure of reported income (in millions):

Cost of goods sold (reported)	$4709
Adjustment for holding gain	190
COGS (approximate LIFO)	$4899

An alternative approach to arrive at the specific price index appropriate for the oil refining industry would be to examine the financial statements of a competing firm in that industry using LIFO. The LIFO reserve information presented earlier in Exhibit 5-3A for Sun Company can be used to approximate the effect of LIFO on Amerada Hess.

The 1990 change in Sun's LIFO reserve of $194 million ($835 million–$641 million) represents the increase in current costs during 1990. The specific inflation rate was, therefore,

$$\frac{\$194 \text{ million}}{\$939 \text{ million}} = 20.7\%$$

where $939 million is Sun's inventory balance (on a FIFO basis on December 31, 1989).

Since Amerada Hess is in the same industry, we can assume that it faced the same inflation rate, leaving us with an adjustment of

$$\$950 \text{ million} \times 0.207 = \$197 \text{ million}$$

to FIFO cost of goods sold, bringing Amerada Hess's cost of goods sold to $4906 million ($4709 million + $197 million).

Adjusting weighted average COGS (with subscript "w") to LIFO can be done in a similar fashion; the adjustment to opening inventory can be approximated[13] by one-half the (specific) inflation rate:

$$COGS_L = COGS_w + \left(BI_w \times \frac{r}{2}\right)$$

FINANCIAL RATIOS: FIFO VERSUS LIFO

Exhibit 5-5, based on a study by Dopuch and Pincus (1988), compares selected financial characteristics of FIFO and LIFO firms. The comparison is done first on the basis of amounts reported in financial statements (part A) and again after adjusting to the alternative accounting method (part B).

Using reported financial data, part A of the table indicates that, based upon median values, LIFO firms have higher turnover ratios, less inventory as a percentage of sales or

---

[13]When weighted average cost is used, the inventory turnover rate affects the adjustment.

EXHIBIT 5-5
Analysis of FIFO/LIFO Firms Based on Median Data, 1963–1981

A. Data as Reported

	LIFO	FIFO
COGS/Average inventory	4.97	3.88
Inventory/Sales	0.16	0.20
Inventory/Assets	0.21	0.29
C.V. inventory*	0.42	0.63
C.V. pretax income	0.74	0.79

B. FIFO Firms Adjusted to LIFO and LIFO Firms to FIFO

	FIFO to LIFO	LIFO to FIFO
COGS/Average inventory	4.72	4.03
Inventory/Sales	0.17	0.22
Inventory/Assets	0.25	0.24
C.V. Inventory	0.52	0.67
C.V. Pretax income	0.81	0.77

*C.V. is the coefficient of variation (standard deviation divided by the mean).
Source: Dopuch, Nicolas and Morton Pincus, "Evidence of the Choice of Inventory Accounting Methods: LIFO Versus FIFO", *Journal of Accounting Research* (Spring 1988), pp. 28–59, Tables 4 and 5, p. 44 (Adapted).

total assets, and lower variation in inventory levels and pretax income.[14] However, for the most part, these differences are not real operating differences but rather are differences due to the accounting choice. In part B the FIFO firms are adjusted to LIFO and the LIFO firms are adjusted to FIFO. The appropriate comparison can now be made with all firms using the same accounting method; that is, the numbers in part B should be compared with the numbers directly above them in part A.

Once the data are adjusted for accounting methods, the differences tend to disappear. For example, the inventory turnover ratio as reported is 4.97 for LIFO firms and 3.88 for FIFO firms—a difference of 1.09. After adjusting to the same method, the turnover ratios are

1. With all firms on FIFO, 4.03 for LIFO reporting firms and 3.88 for FIFO reporting firms—a difference of only 0.15.

2. With all firms on a LIFO basis, 4.97 versus 4.72, respectively—a difference of only 0.25

Similar patterns exist for the other variables.

With Exhibit 5-5 as prologue, we now focus on the distortions in measures of financial performance that result from the FIFO/LIFO choice.

---

[14]The variation in inventory and pretax income is measured by the coefficient of variation—standard deviation divided by the mean.

The LIFO/FIFO choice impacts reported profitability, liquidity, activity, and leverage ratios. For some ratios, LIFO provides a better measure, whereas for others, FIFO does. The LIFO-to-FIFO and FIFO-to-LIFO adjustment procedures discussed earlier, however, allow one to make the appropriate adjustments to arrive at the "correct" ratio no matter what is actually reported in a firm's financial statements. The general guideline is to use LIFO numbers for ratio components that are income related and FIFO-based data for components that are balance sheet related.

Profitability: Gross Profit Margin

An extension of the argument that LIFO better measures current income can be made with reference to gross profit margins. When input prices increase, firms pass along the added costs to customers. Moreover, they try to mark up not only those items purchased at the higher price but also all goods previously purchased. (This policy, it should be noted, is not rapacious but rather is economically defensible in terms of the argument made earlier that the real cost of an item sold is its replacement value.)

Thus, if the pricing policy of the firm in our opening example is to price by marking up cost by 100% (implying a gross profit margin of 50% of sales), the $10,000 of sales in our example would have been arrived at as follows:

Sales: 100 units per quarter for a total of 400 units
Sales price: determined as 100% markup over current costs

| Quarter | Unit | | Sales | |
	Cost	Price	Units	Dollars
1	$11	$22	100	2,200
2	$12	$24	100	2,400
3	$13	$26	100	2,600
4	$14	$28	100	2,800
Total			400	10,000

Gross profit margin under FIFO and LIFO would be

	Sales	−	COGS	=	Gross Profit	Percent
FIFO	$10,000	−	$4300	=	$5700	$5700/$10,000 = 57.0%
LIFO	$10,000	−	$5150	=	$4850	$4850/$10,000 = 48.5%

The gross profit margin, by measuring the profitability of current sales, also provides an indication of the potential future profitability of a firm. Clearly, FIFO net income (which includes holding gains resulting from rising prices) inflates expectations regarding the future profitability of the firm as future price rises (holding gains) may be smaller.

LIFO gives a more accurate rendering of the firm's future prospects by removing the impact of price changes. As noted earlier, the gross profit margin is more appropriately measured by LIFO. FIFO accounting, in times of rising (falling) prices, will tend to overstate (understate) it.

Liquidity: Working Capital

Working capital–based ratios are misstated under LIFO because, as we have already discussed, the inventory component of working capital carries outdated costs. As the purpose of the current ratio is to compare a firm's cash or near-cash assets and liabilities, clearly use of the current value of inventory (FIFO) results in the more appropriate measure.

Referring to Sun Company (Exhibit 5-3), the December 31, 1991 working capital and current ratio as reported are $(271) million and 0.86 ($1694 million/$1965 million), respectively. After adjusting LIFO inventory to current cost (FIFO) by adding the LIFO reserve of $536 million, current assets are $2230 million ($1694 million + $536 million) and adjusted working capital is $265 million ($2230 million − $1965 million), which converts negative working capital to a positive measure. The adjusted current ratio of 1.13 ($2230 million/$1965 million) is 31% higher than the unadjusted measure.

Activity: Inventory Turnover

Inventory turnover, defined in Chapter 3 as COGS/average inventory, is often meaningless for LIFO firms due to the mismatching of costs. The numerator represents current costs, whereas the denominator carries outdated historical costs. Thus the turnover ratio under LIFO will, when prices increase, trend higher irrespective of the trend of physical turnover.

This point is illustrated in Exhibit 5-6. We assume actual physical turnover of four times a year; that is, the average inventory is sufficient for one quarter. Further, it is assumed that costs increase 10% per quarter.

The FIFO inventory ratio is relatively unaffected by the change in price, and at 3.77 it is a rough approximation of the actual turnover of 4. The LIFO-based ratios of 5.11, 7.47, and 10.94 are, however, far from the actual measure of 4, and the discrepancy grows from year to year. Thus, to arrive at a reasonable approximation of the inventory turnover ratio for a LIFO firm, we must first convert to FIFO.

The preferred measure of inventory turnover is the one labeled "hybrid." It combines the two methods, using LIFO cost of goods sold in the numerator and FIFO inventory in the denominator. This approach provides the best matching of costs, as current costs are used in both numerator and denominator.

Referring once again to Sun Company (Exhibit 5-3A), the inventory turnover ratio (using total inventories) for 1990 is

$$\text{LIFO (reported):} \quad \frac{\$9529}{(\$582 \text{ million} + \$583 \text{ million})/2} = 16.36$$

EXHIBIT 5-6
Illustration of Turnover Ratio Under LIFO and FIFO

Year	Quarter	Purchases = Sales	Cost per Unit	Total		For Entire Year	
Opening inventory		100	$10.00	$1000			
1	1	100	$11.00	$1100	FIFO	COGS	$ 4,641
1	2	100	$12.10	$1210		Avg. inv.	$ 1,232
1	3	100	$13.31	$1331	LIFO	COGS	$ 5,105
1	4	100	$14.64	$1464		Avg. inv.	$ 1,000
2	1	100	$16.11	$1611	FIFO	COGS	$ 6,795
2	2	100	$17.72	$1772		Avg. inv.	$ 1,804
2	3	100	$19.49	$1949	LIFO	COGS	$ 7,474
2	4	100	$21.44	$2144		Avg. inv.	$ 1,000
3	1	100	$23.58	$2358	FIFO	COGS	$ 9,948
3	2	100	$25.94	$2594		Avg. inv.	$ 2,641
3	3	100	$28.53	$2853	LIFO	COGS	$10,943
3	4	100	$31.38	$3138		Avg. inv.	$ 1,000

Turnover Ratios

	Year 1	Year 2	Year 3
FIFO	3.77	3.77	3.77
LIFO	5.11	7.47	10.94
Hybrid	4.14	4.14	4.14

$$\text{FIFO (adjusted):} \quad \frac{\$9335}{(\$1417 \text{ million} + \$1224 \text{ million})/2} = 7.07$$

$$\text{Hybrid:} \quad \frac{\$9529}{(\$1417 \text{ million} + \$1224 \text{ million})/2} = 7.22$$

Note the decline in the ratio from that reported on a LIFO basis. The LIFO ratio implies very fast turnover that is overstated. The adjusted figures imply a less than two-month supply of inventory on hand rather than a less than one-month supply.

It should be noted that there is little difference between the ratio on a FIFO basis and on the more refined hybrid basis. This is empirically true in most situations, and for all practical purposes these two ratio calculations are equivalent as long as they are applied consistently over time.

We can compute inventory turnover for Amerada Hess for 1990, using the data in Exhibit 5-4:

$$\text{Inventory turnover (FIFO)} = \frac{\$4709 \text{ million}}{(\$950 \text{ million} + \$1243 \text{ million})/2} = 4.29$$

$$\text{Inventory turnover (hybrid)} = \frac{\$4906^{15} \text{ million}}{(\$950 \text{ million} + \$1243 \text{ million})/2} = 4.47$$

Comparing the inventory turnover ratio for Amerada to that of Sun, we can see the importance of making the calculation comparable. Using only the reported data (LIFO for Sun, FIFO for Amerada), it would appear that Sun turns its inventory almost four times faster (16.36 versus 4.29). Putting both on a FIFO basis, Sun still appears more efficient (7.07 versus 4.29), but the gap is smaller. (The hybrid calculations led to the same conclusion.) *Having made the ratios comparable (by eliminating the effect of different accounting methods), we now have a reasonable basis to look for other explanations for the difference in the ratio.*

Inventory Theory and Turnover Ratios

Computing the inventory turnover ratio implies that there is some standard against which to measure or that there is an optimal ratio. As for all turnover ratios, one's first instinct is to believe that higher is better, that more rapid inventory turnover indicates a more efficient use of capital. In practice, however, that assumption may be overly simplistic.

The management science literature has devoted much effort to the design of optimal inventory ordering policies. The traditional literature in the United States has focused on the economic order quantity (EOQ). More recently, in line with developments in Japanese management practices, focus has turned to just-in-time inventory policies. It is worthwhile to note the implications of these theories for the interpretation of the turnover ratio.

Economic Order Quantity

An implicit assumption (discussed in Chapter 3) in the construction and use of ratios for cross-sectional and time series comparisons is that the relationship between the numerator and denominator is linear. The inventory turnover ratio implies that as demand increases, the quantity of inventory on hand should increase proportionately. The EOQ model argues that the optimal level of inventory is proportionate to the square root of demand.

If, for example, demand (cost of goods sold) increases by four times, one would expect average inventory to double (2 = the square root of 4). Exhibit 5-7 indicates that as sales increase, we should expect a higher turnover ratio. The smaller a firm's sales, the lower its turnover ratio should be based on the EOQ. A high turnover ratio for such a firm would not be a sign of efficiency but, on the contrary, an indication that the firm was not managing its inventories in the most economic fashion.

---

[15]LIFO cost of goods sold estimated previously.

EXHIBIT 5-7
Economic Order Quantity

Assume that for a firm whose demand is 120 units annually, the optimal inventory quantity based on the EOQ model is 10, implying an inventory turnover ratio of 12 (120/10). Using the equation $Q = (2DS/H)^{1/2}$, where D is demand, S is setup cost, and H is holding cost, we can solve to get $S/H = 5/12$. Using this value for S/H, we can compute the EOQ (Q) for any level of demand (D).

Demand	EOQ	Turnover (Demand/EOQ)
600	22.36	26.83
480	20.00	24.00
240	14.14	16.97
120	**10.00**	**12.00**
60	7.07	8.50
30	6.00	5.00

Just in Time

Japanese management practices strive for the ideal that firms should not hold any inventory but rather should receive and ship orders "just in time" (JIT) as needed. Carried to its ultimate, this would argue for a turnover ratio approaching infinity or zero average inventory on hand. Hence, one would expect turnover ratios of Japanese firms to be considerably higher than those of American firms. To the extent that U.S. firms begin to adopt these practices, they can be expected to have higher turnover ratios in the future.

An interesting by-product of the trend toward JIT inventory is that it would render the FIFO/LIFO choice a meaningless one. If a firm has no inventories (or relatively small quantities), then there is little or no significant difference between FIFO and LIFO.[16]

The LIFO/FIFO Choice and Inventory Holding Policy

A final and important consideration is that the LIFO/FIFO choice can affect (and be affected by) a firm's actual inventory holding policy. Biddle (1980) found that LIFO firms tended to carry greater inventory balances (in terms of quantity) than comparably sized FIFO firms. This finding is in line with a number of factors:

1. The larger a firm's inventory balances, the larger its potential tax savings through the use of LIFO. Thus the higher inventory balances may be a result of the firm's production and operating environment and may explain why the firm chose LIFO in the first place.

[16]However, inventory may be carried by suppliers; if a firm owns or controls its suppliers, it may bear the residual risk that is usually borne by the suppliers. To be most useful and relevant, turnover ratios and other inventory measures should be based on consolidated financial statements where consolidation reflects economic rather than legal or regulatory control. Admittedly, such consolidation is not always feasible given the paucity of disclosure regarding such relationships. Further discussion of the issue of consolidation appears in Chapter 11.

2. The larger balances may be a result of LIFO as, once having chosen LIFO, firms attempt to get the most advantage from it by increasing their inventory balances.

3. To avoid LIFO liquidations and pay higher taxes, firms must buy (produce) as many goods as they sell each year. Thus for LIFO firms it is costly (in terms of taxes) to lower inventory levels.

It is interesting to note that Barlev et al. (1984), examining Canadian and Israeli firms that were not permitted to use LIFO but rather had an alternative tax adjustment for inflation, found that these firms also tended to have (larger) inventory balances, in line with the tax advantage relevant to them.

Solvency: Debt to Equity

Earlier it was argued that under LIFO the inventory balances are understated and should be adjusted upward by the amount of the LIFO reserve to reflect their current costs. By the same token, the equity or retained earnings of the firm should also be adjusted upward by the amount of the LIFO reserve.[17] The rationale for this is that the net worth of the firm is actually higher than reported because the firm owns inventory whose current value is higher than its carrying value.[18]

Effectively, the argument boils down to treating the inventory choice like other accounting choices that are subject to analytic adjustment. The fact that the Internal Revenue Service (IRS) does not allow the differing accounting methods should not tie the hands of the analyst. The valuation of a LIFO firm should not be reduced because it takes advantage of the tax savings inherent in LIFO.

LIFO: REPORTING AND MEASUREMENT ISSUES

This section examines certain important reporting and measurement issues that are a consequence of the use of LIFO for inventories. The unique tax and financial reporting conformity requirement that accompanies the use of LIFO generates some of these issues, whereas others are a result of the nature of the method, its application, and its impact on the financial statements.

---

[17]Lasman and Weil (1978) suggest that the LIFO reserve should not be adjusted for taxes unless a liquidation of LIFO layers is assumed. Further, as liquidations are reported in reverse LIFO order (latest layers are liquidated first), the largest gains reside in the earliest layers. Thus there is a low probability that the tax effect of "minor" liquidations will be significant and (assuming that the firm remains in business) extensive liquidations are unlikely, also arguing against tax adjustment. Note that firms have strong incentives to avoid liquidations that would result in significant tax payments.

[18]Using FIFO values for equity does not contradict our notion that the optimal choice for income presentation is LIFO. Referring back to the house example in footnote 3, the fact that your house doubled in value from $100,000 to $200,000 at a time when all houses doubled in value means that you do not benefit from selling the house as you will need the money to buy a replacement house. *The value (your equity) of your house is, nevertheless, $200,000.*

Initial Adoption or Change to LIFO

In the United States, GAAP do not require either retroactive restatement or the disclosure of any cumulative effect of a change to or initial adoption of LIFO and the change to LIFO is only made on a prospective basis. Generally, records necessary for the compilation of LIFO layers and the determination of cost of goods sold in prior years under the LIFO method would not be available.

The beginning inventory in the year of adoption is the base period inventory for subsequent LIFO computations. Because LIFO is a cost method, a switch from lower-of-cost-or-market (LCM) methods may require a write-up to the cost basis from the LCM, where a write-down to market value has been previously recorded. Generally, this adjustment is reported as other income and may offset decreases in income due to the adoption of LIFO. The change also has a cash effect since the LIFO book–tax conformity rule requires the addition of the (restored) write-downs to taxable income over a three-year period beginning with the adoption year. However, this requirement is not a significant economic disadvantage (in terms of cash flows), because write-down rules under non-LIFO methods have become considerably more restrictive over the years.

Required footnote disclosures include the impact of the adoption on the period's income before extraordinary items, net income, and related earning per share amounts. A brief explanation of the reasons for the change in method and the absence of any cumulative effect disclosures or retroactive adjustment must be provided.

Example: Quaker Oats. Effective July 1, 1988, Quaker Oats extended its use of the LIFO method to grocery products inventories, which had been valued using average cost (Exhibit 5-8). As a result of the change, the percentage of the company's inventories accounted for using LIFO rose from 29% to 65%, with the remainder at average cost (21%) or FIFO (14%).

Extension of the use of LIFO resulted in additional cost of goods sold of $25.6 million, reducing net income by $16 million or $0.20 per share for the fiscal year ended June 30, 1989. As Quaker reported earnings per share of $2.56 for that year, the extension of LIFO reduced reported earnings by 7.2% from the $2.76 that would have been reported without the accounting change.

Quaker also reported that its LIFO reserve rose from $24.0 million at June 30, 1988, to $60.1 million at June 30, 1989. Using the data on the effect of the accounting change, we see that the source of the increase in the LIFO reserve was

Balance, June 30, 1988	$24.0 million
LIFO effect fiscal 1989	10.5
LIFO effect, extension	25.6
Balance, June 30, 1989	$60.1 million

Change from LIFO

Changes from LIFO to other methods require a retroactive restatement of prior years to the new method. The cumulative effect is credited to retained earnings at the beginning

EXHIBIT 5-8. QUAKER OATS COMPANY
Notes to the Consolidated Financial Statements

Inventories. Inventories are valued at the lower of cost or market, using various cost methods, and include the cost of raw materials, labor, and overhead. The percentage of year-end inventories valued using each of the methods is as follows:

June 30	1989	1988	1987	1986
Average quarterly cost	21%	54%	52%	51%
Last-in, first-out (LIFO)	65%	29%	31%	21%
First-in, first-out (FIFO)	14%	17%	17%	28%

Effective July 1, 1988, the Company adopted the LIFO cost flow assumption for valuing the majority of remaining U.S. Grocery Products inventories. The Company believes that the use of the LIFO method better matches current costs with current revenues. The cumulative effect of this change on retained earnings at the beginning of the year is not determinable, nor are the pro forma effects of retroactive application of LIFO to prior years. The effect of this change on fiscal 1989 was to decrease net income by $16.0 million, or $0.20 per share.

If the LIFO method of valuing certain inventories were not used, total inventories would have been $60.1 million, $24.0 million and $14.6 million higher than reported at June 30, 1989, 1988, and 1987, respectively.

Source: Quaker Oats, 1989 and 1987 annual reports.

of the earliest restated year to avoid a misstatement of the current period's income. A change from LIFO requires Internal Revenue Service approval.[19] In addition, SEC regulations require a preferability letter from the firm's independent auditor stating its concurrence with and the rationale for the change.

The IRS considers changes from LIFO as a loss of tax deferral privileges, and the previous LIFO reserve becomes immediately taxable. Thus a change from LIFO brings significant tax and cash flow consequences and requires a comprehensive evaluation of the impact on operations and management incentives for the switch. (See the empirical section for a discussion of the capital market response to changes in accounting methods.)

The Chrysler Corporation provides an excellent example of this accounting change. In 1972, the firm switched to FIFO after using LIFO for 14 years. The retroactive adjustment to income was $53.5 million, and the tax consequences were significant. The firm's finances were strained at the time of the switch, and it was permitted by the IRS to spread the resulting tax liability over a number of years.

Given rising price levels and Chrysler's cash flow problems, why did the firm change methods? An increase in reported income (including the impact of the change in methods, the firm reported a loss of $7.6 million) may have been one incentive, but the unfavorable tax consequences were onerous. The firm may have switched primarily to

[19]Firms switching from LIFO to another method also agree not to switch back to LIFO for at least 10 years, except under "extraordinary circumstances."

avoid technical default on debt covenants;[20] FIFO allowed it to report significantly higher inventory balances and thereby to report higher working capital.

LIFO Liquidations

The discussion of LIFO in this chapter thus far has generally assumed that goods purchased in a period are at least as great (in quantity) as goods sold, so that inventory quantities are stable or increasing. When more goods are sold than are purchased, then goods held in opening inventory have to be sold to meet the excess demand. For LIFO companies, this is referred to as "dipping into or liquidating LIFO layers," and the phenomenon can lead to some strange results.

The cost of goods sold associated with the inventory reduction may be abnormally low and the gross profit margin abnormally high because the LIFO opening inventory carries old, *low* costs. For companies that have carried costs forward for many years, the degree of distortion from these "paper profits" can be quite large.

The increased income from LIFO liquidations results in higher taxes and lower cash flows as the taxes that have been avoided to date through the use of LIFO must now be paid. To defer taxes indefinitely, purchases (production) must always be greater than or equal to sales. (See Biddle, 1980, and the discussion of the impact of LIFO/FIFO on inventory purchases and holding policy.)

LIFO liquidations may be due to inventory reductions because of strikes, recession, or fall in demand for a particular product line. In the recessionary period at the end of the 1970s and the early 1980s, when many companies (notably those in the steel and related industries) were laying off workers and closing down plants, some of these same companies paradoxically reported respectable profits. Production cuts resulted in the liquidation of LIFO inventories, which, in many cases, dated back as far as World War II. The effects of the LIFO liquidation on these companies and other selected companies are presented in Exhibit 5-9.

Companies in Exhibit 5-9 experienced LIFO liquidations in more than one year. This result is consistent with that of Stober (1986), who examined 272 companies that experienced LIFO liquidations in the period 1979–1983. He found that over 60% had liquidations in more than one year and 33% experienced liquidations in three or more years. Furthermore, fully 85% of the latter occurrences happened in cases where a LIFO liquidation was disclosed one year earlier.

Thus a LIFO liquidation is often not a one-time, random occurrence but a signal that a company is entering an extended period of decline. Further evidence to this end has been documented by Davis et al. (1984), who found that liquidations were industry related, indicating a systematic effect, and by Fried, Schiff, and Sondhi (1989), who found that write-downs and/or restructurings are often preceded by LIFO liquidations.

The inventory footnote for Sun (Exhibit 5-3) reveals a small LIFO liquidation in 1990. Unfortunately, the amount is presented after tax so that the effect on the LIFO

---

[20]See Abdel-Khalik, Reiger and Reiter (1989), p. 167, who argue that improving working capital was the motivation for the Chrysler switch.

EXHIBIT 5-9
The Significance of LIFO Liquidation, 1980–1981

Company	Year	Net Income Before Taxes ($ millions)	LIFO Liquidation as a Percentage of Income
Bethlehem Steel	1980	$ 95	77%
Bethlehem Steel	1981	293	16
National Steel	1980	31	31
LTV Corp.	1980	161	31
Firestone Tire	1980	164	65
Firestone Tire	1981	189	13
American Can	1981	107	18
General Motors	1980	(1369)	16
General Motors	1981	(138)	39
U.S. Steel	1980	607	29

Source: Schiff, Allen, "The Other Side of LIFO" *Journal of Accountancy* (May 1983), pp. 120–121, Exhibit 1, p. 120.

reserve can be estimated only by estimating the applicable tax rate. In this case, however, the impact is small enough to ignore.

Declining Prices

The discussion until now generally has assumed rising price levels. In some industries (notably those that are technology related), input prices decline steadily over time; in others (mainly commodity based such as metals and petroleum), prices may fluctuate cyclically. The theoretical arguments as to which method provides better information still hold. LIFO provides the more recent costs on the income statement and outdated costs on the balance sheet. The direction of the differences, however, are reversed when prices decline. LIFO closing inventories are overstated, and FIFO cost of goods sold tends to be higher. The case of Sun for 1991, discussed earlier, illustrates what happens to a LIFO company when prices decline.

Thus the pragmatic incentives to use LIFO for tax purposes are lost when prices decline as LIFO will result in higher taxes and lower cash flow. In addition, companies whose inventories are subject to obsolescence often take advantage of the ability (not available under LIFO) to write down inventory to market value.

Declines in LIFO reserves occur when inventory costs are falling as the lower-cost current purchases enter reported LIFO COGS, decreasing the cost differences between LIFO and FIFO ending inventories. Such declines (the Sun case again illustrates this point) are *not* considered LIFO liquidations, and disclosure of their impact is not required.

Note that firms often use different inventory methods (or different pools, as discussed shortly) in different lines of business and may experience LIFO liquidations, reserve declines, and reserve increases simultaneously in different segments of their business.

EXHIBIT 5-10. GENERAL ELECTRIC COMPANY
Inventories, December 31, 1990–1991

	1990	1989
	($ millions)	
Raw materials and work in process	$ 5521	$ 5492
Finished goods	3281	3103
Unbilled shipments	184	249
	8986	8844
Less: Revaluation to LIFO	(2279)	(2189)
LIFO value of inventories	$ 6707	$ 6655

LIFO revaluations increased $90 million in 1990 compared with a $37 million decrease in 1989 and a $150 million increase in 1988. Included in these changes were decreases of $19 million, $68 million and $23 million (1990, 1989 and 1988, respectively) due to lower inventory levels. In each of the last three years, there was a current year expense for price increases.

Source: GE Annual Report, 1990.

Example: General Electric. Exhibit 5-10 contains excerpts from General Electric Company's 1990 financial statements. The inventory footnote reports a decrease in LIFO reserves (called "revaluation to LIFO" in the footnote) during 1989 and an increase in 1990. Both years include *decreases* in the reserves (LIFO liquidations) due to lower inventory levels and *increases* in the reserve as a result of price increases. We show the relationship as follows:

Change in reserve	= **Effect of price increases**	− **Liquidations**
1989: $(37) million =	**$31 million**	− **$68 million**
1990: $90 million =	**$109 million**	− **$19 million**

The decline in the LIFO reserve during 1989 was the net result of two different factors. One was a very small increase in prices ($31 million on $8712 million of inventory on a FIFO basis). The second factor was a reduction in the LIFO reserve due to a reduction in physical quantities in some segments. This second effect, which increased pretax earnings by $68 million, is the impact of LIFO liquidations.

In 1990, a larger current LIFO effect ($109 million) is partially offset by a LIFO liquidation of $19 million, resulting in a small net increase in the LIFO reserve.

LIFO and Interim Reporting

Technological changes, fluctuations in demand, and strikes may also result in a reduction in LIFO layers during the year. The application of LIFO during interim periods may result in substantial distortions (income statement and balance sheet) if the factors causing the LIFO liquidations are temporary and the layers will be replenished prior to year end.

The problem arises because the LIFO method of inventory accounting, like all tax-related accounting, is governed by results for the full year, which are used to file income tax returns. As a result, *interim period tax-related adjustments must be based on estimates of the year-end position.*

Financial reporting for interim periods is governed by APB Opinion 28. We focus here on its application to the LIFO inventory method. Opinion 28 provides for special inventory valuation procedures during interim periods when the firm experiences a LIFO liquidation during one or more of the first three quarters.

Permanent liquidations must be reported in the quarter of occurrence. However, temporary liquidations require the use of an estimated cost method when management believes that the liquidated layer(s) will be replenished before year end. Cost of goods sold for the quarter must include the estimated cost of replacing the temporary liquidation rather than the LIFO cost of the goods sold. The application of this method is illustrated using the following example:

Assumptions: All transactions occur during the second quarter
Beginning inventory (LIFO): 10 units @ \$10   **= \$100**
   LIFO reserve (@ \$20)   **= \$200**
   Inventory @ FIFO   **= \$300**
Purchases: 20 units @ \$30   **= \$600**
Goods available for sale   **= \$700**
Sales: 21 units @ \$40   **= \$840**

Management determines that the liquidation is temporary and expects the next purchase price (cost to replace) will be \$35. GAAP requires the use of \$35 rather than the cost of the liquidated layer. The COGS would be reported at

\$635 (20 units @ \$30 and 1 unit @ \$35)

Inventory would be reduced by

\$610 (20 units @ \$30 and 1 unit @ \$10)

The firm would recognize a current liability (called the LIFO base liquidation) for the difference of \$25, representing the fact that the firm has temporarily "borrowed" a unit from the base layer.[21] The next purchase of inventory is used to eliminate the current liability and replenish the LIFO base layer. This method eliminates the potential (temporary) distortion in reported gross profit and all income numbers due to temporary interim period liquidations.

Year-end LIFO liquidations are permanent reductions in LIFO layers, and the reported gross profit must include the impact of the reduction in LIFO reserves. If the foregoing scenario occurs during the fourth quarter, the firm would report COGS of \$610 [(20 × \$30) + (1 × \$10)] and separately disclose the impact of the LIFO liquidation on COGS and net income in the footnotes.

[21]An AICPA Task Force–issued paper, "Identification and Discussion of Certain Financial Accounting and Reporting Issues Concerning LIFO Inventories" (AICPA, 1984), suggests that the interim liquidation may be also be credited directly to inventories.

Example: Nucor. This example illustrates the impact of volatile prices and the procedures required for interim reporting. It is based on Nucor Corp., a steel and steel products manufacturer that uses the LIFO method of inventory accounting. Steel scrap is a major component of inventory cost, and as scrap prices can be volatile, Nucor must estimate its year-end position at the end of each interim period. That is, it must estimate what its physical inventory will be and what the price of scrap will be at year end to establish the appropriate LIFO reserve at the end of each interim period.

In 1981, scrap prices rose during the first part of the year, but declined in the second half. On a full year basis (the basis for LIFO as a tax-related computation), the LIFO reserve declined for 1981, reflecting a decline in the price of steel scrap. (At the end of 1981, the difference between the LIFO and FIFO cost of its inventory was lower than it had been one year earlier.)

During the first two quarters, Nucor assumed that scrap prices would be higher at the end of 1981 than one year earlier and accrued additional LIFO reserves. Because of the decline in steel scrap prices late in the year, these earlier accruals were reversed in the fourth quarter. The impact of the interim changes in the LIFO reserve can be seen in the following table:

Nucor Quarterly Results 1981

Quarter	I	II	III	IV	Year
			($ thousands)		
Pretax income	$13,087	$11,204	$ 4,637	$15,901	$44,829
LIFO effect	1,873	1,900	—	(5,134)	(1,361)
LIFO reserve (end of period) (12/31/80 = $23,727)	25,600	27,500	27,500	22,366	22,366

Source: Nucor annual and interim reports, 1981.

While the interim LIFO accruals (LIFO effect = change in reserve) were made in good faith, in retrospect we can see that they were incorrect and distorted operating results. To correct that distortion, we can (with perfect hindsight) reallocate the decrease in the LIFO reserve for the year so that an equal amount is credited to each interim period. We can obtain the "true" interim results by restating the LIFO impact as follows:

Quarter	I	II	III	IV	Year
			($ thousands)		
Pretax income	$13,087	$11,204	$4637	$15,901	$44,829
LIFO adjustment*	2,213	2,240	340	(4,793)	—
Adjusted pretax	$15,300	$13,444	$4977	$11,108	$44,829
% Change from reported	+16.9%	+20.0%	+7.3%	−30.1%	—

*Difference between original LIFO effect and "true" LIFO effect (one-fourth of annnual). For example, first quarter adjustment is $1,873 − (−$1,361/4).

The analysis indicates that management assumptions can play a major role in reported interim earnings and that the application of LIFO accounting to interim periods can result in large distortions in interim comparisons. This illustration also serves as an example of fourth quarter adjustments that have a significant impact on reported earnings and trends reflected during the previous three quarters.

LIFO Inventory Methods

The preceding discussions of inventory methods have implicitly assumed that the accounting procedures are applied to specific inventory items. The vast majority of manufacturing or retailing firms have far too many items in inventory to use specific item-based costing methods efficiently. The potential for LIFO liquidations and the resulting loss of tax benefits are additional deterrents to use of specific item methods. Various methods have been developed to alleviate these problems, and a brief discussion is provided below.

Pooled Specific Goods Method

Most firms *pool* "substantially identical" inventory items to measure unit costs and physical quantities. Pooling facilitates efficient inventory management, reducing recordkeeping costs. It also lowers the probability of LIFO liquidations relative to the specific item LIFO method, as reduced quantities of some items are offset by increased quantities of others. However, pooling does not eliminate liquidations and related increases in tax payments resulting from business interruptions, changes in demand, technology, production methods, or mix of raw materials.

Firms have substantial incentives to minimize the number of pools used: lower administrative costs and reduced probability of liquidations result from using fewer pools (increasing the number of items included in each pool). Alternatively, firms may report higher net income by increasing the number of pools.

For example, in 1982 the Stauffer Chemical Company, citing the objective of improved matching, changed the number of pools used from 8 to 280 and increased reported earnings by $16.5 million (13%). The firm reported higher income by liquidating a few newly defined pools and transferring inventories to FIFO method foreign subsidiaries. Securities and Exchange Commission (SEC) action eventually forced a restatement of the reported income and the pooling method.

Reeve and Stanga (1987) found that a majority of LIFO method companies use a single pool, generally defined by the natural business unit, and they use the same pooling method for financial reporting and taxes although conformity is not required. (While companies using LIFO for tax purposes must use LIFO for financial reporting purposes, different varieties of LIFO may be used.) The number of pools used was inversely related to the magnitude of tax benefits (companies with large tax savings from LIFO tended to use fewer pools).

Their survey also indicated that the retail industry used more pools (median of 6, with fewer than 7% using a single pool) than nonretailers (median of 3, one-third of the sample firms used one pool). They also reported substantial variation in the number of pools used within an industry and across all the firms in their sample. The impact on cash flows and financial statements suggests that analysts should carefully evaluate announcements of changes in LIFO pools to understand the impact of the change on reported earnings.

Dollar Value LIFO Methods

These methods are designed to reduce further the probability of LIFO liquidations by pooling a broader range of items. The pooling criterion is similarity of use, production method, or raw material in place of the restrictive "substantially identical" rule used in the specific goods method. Liquidations are also reduced because the method computes inventory amounts and layers in dollars rather than in quantities, facilitating the substitution of items in the pools.

Dollar value LIFO methods determine inventory balances by converting the ending inventory at year-end prices to base year prices and computing increases (or decreases) in inventory as the difference between the beginning and ending inventory at base year prices.

Increases, or "new layers," are added to the beginning inventory at current price levels using indices of price change over the period. Decreases are assumed to occur at and are liquidated at price levels prevailing when the layer was added to the inventory.

Most retailers use price indices developed and published by the Bureau of Labor Statistics. However, some firms use internally developed indices. The difference can be substantial.

For example, during 1990 K-Mart switched to internally generated indices (from the U.S. Department of Labor's Department Store Price Index) for its U.S. merchandise inventories. The financial statement footnote states the firm's belief that the internal index "results in a more accurate measurement of the impact of inflation on the prices of merchandise sold in its stores." The change reduced its COGS by $105 million (net of tax), increasing income by $0.52 per share (32.3% of reported income for the year).

Retail Inventory Methods

The specific goods method may also be too cumbersome for retailers (although this argument is difficult to sustain given advances in inventory management and computer technology) who often use an alternative, the retail method. Inventories are recorded at their retail values and converted to the cost basis using the cost-to-retail ratio:

$$\frac{\text{Beginning inventory plus purchases at cost}}{\text{Retail value of beginning inventory plus purchases}}$$

The conventional retail method approximates the lower of cost or market method by computing this ratio with net markups (net increases in the original retail price) included in the denominator (retail value of inventory). The LIFO retail method was developed to provide a better matching of current costs to revenues. The cost to retail ratio is computed by adjusting only the current period's purchases for *both* net markups and net markdowns (net decreases in price below the original sales price). Because the LIFO retail method uses only the current purchases (compared to the conventional retail method's use of beginning inventory plus purchases) during periods of rising prices, the cost-to-retail ratio will reflect higher prices than the ratio computed under the conventional retail method.

However, the LIFO retail method (depending on the existence of markdowns) may or may not report lower inventories (higher COGS) than the conventional retail method.

The dollar value retail LIFO method uses the ratios developed in the LIFO retail method but applies them to inventory balances adjusted for price level changes as in the dollar value LIFO method. Because of this indexing process, dollar value retail LIFO will result in lower ending inventories and higher COGS than will the LIFO retail method.

LIFO: A HISTORICAL AND EMPIRICAL PERSPECTIVE

Overview of FIFO/LIFO Choice

The American Institute of Certified Public Accountants' *Accounting Trends and Techniques* for 1990[22] presents data (Exhibit 5-11) as to the degree of current LIFO adoption. As indicated in part B, the adoption of LIFO is strongly affected by industry classification.

The incentives to use LIFO are powerful given the tax savings and cash flow advantages. Two interrelated[23] questions thus arise;

1. Why do some firms continue to use FIFO?
2. Are firms that switch to LIFO perceived as being "better off" by the market even though reported earnings may be lower?

Detailed discussion of studies which examined these two issues are presented shortly. Their main findings are relevant to the analyst as they provide evidence that the implications of the FIFO/LIFO choice are relatively complex and subtle and go beyond a lower taxes/higher income tradeoff.

Exhibit 5-14, for example, at the end of the discussion, provides a summary of reasons why firms opt to stay on FIFO. For a given firm, it is worthwhile knowing which of these motivations apply and thus whether the firm is "justified" in staying on FIFO or whether management is being inefficient (or perhaps self serving) by giving up a tax advantage.

Furthermore, the LIFO (or FIFO) choice itself may provide information about a firm's sensitivity to changing prices as well as other economic characteristics of the firm and its management. Thus, reaction to a switch may be a function of this other information rather than the tax advantage, This leads to the possibility that the reaction to a switch may vary (as Figure 5-1 indicates) depending on the time period estimated and/or the market and analysts understanding of the effects of inflation and/or the extent a change to LIFO can be anticipated.

[22]Annual Survey of Accounting Practices Followed in 600 Stockholders' Reports. American Institute of Certified Public Accountants.

[23]These questions are interrelated because if the market reacts (for whatever reason) negatively to a switch to LIFO, it may explain why some firms choose to remain on FIFO.

EXHIBIT 5-11
Extent to Which LIFO Has Been Adopted in the United States

A. Inventory Cost Determination, 1986–1990

	Number of Companies				
	1990	1989	1988	1987	1986
Methods					
FIFO	411	401	396	392	383
LIFO	366	366	379	393	393
Average cost	195	200	213	216	223
Other	44	48	50	49	53
Use of LIFO					
All inventories	20	26	20	18	23
50% or more of inventories	186	191	207	221	229
Less than 50% of inventories	92	99	90	86	74
Not determinable	68	50	62	68	67
Companies using LIFO	366	366	379	393	393

B. Industry Classification of Companies Using LIFO, 1988–1990

Industry	1990		1989		1988	
	No.	%*	No.	%*	No.	%*
Foods						
Meat products	3	50	4	57	5	71
Dairy products	1	50	1	50	1	50
Canning	2	50	2	50	2	50
Packaged and bulk	9	60	9	56	10	53
Baking	1	50	1	50	1	33
Sugar, confections	3	100	3	100	3	100
Beverages	7	100	7	100	7	100
Tobacco products	3	60	3	75	3	75
Textiles	16	69	14	67	16	70
Paper products	20	95	22	96	24	96
Printing, publishing	12	60	11	58	11	58
Chemicals	26	81	25	81	26	93
Drugs, cosmetics	15	58	14	56	17	57
Petroleum	26	87	26	90	27	90
Rubber products	7	88	7	88	8	80
Shoes—manufacturing, merchandising	6	75	6	75	6	86
Building						
Cement	3	60	2	50	1	25
Roofing, wallboard	6	86	7	78	7	78
Heating, plumbing	—	—	—	—	1	33
Other	11	66	10	59	11	65
Steel and iron	14	74	15	75	15	75
Metal—nonferrous	10	59	11	65	11	69

EXHIBIT 5-11. *(Continued)*

| | 1990 | | 1989 | | 1988 | |
Industry	No.	%*	No.	%*	No.	%*
Metal fabricating	17	85	19	90	18	95
Machinery	27	77	28	76	29	76
Electrical equipment, appliances	9	43	8	40	7	41
Electronic equipment	8	22	8	24	7	21
Business equipment	5	23	5	23	5	24
Containers	5	71	5	71	6	75
Autos and trucks	18	70	18	69	20	74
Aircraft and equipment, aerospace	4	33	4	33	5	38
Railway equipment, shipbuilding	1	20	1	20	1	20
Controls, instruments, medical equipment, watches and clocks	13	52	14	56	12	52
Merchandising:						
Department stores	4	100	4	100	4	100
Mail order stores, variety stores	2	100	2	100	2	100
Grocery stores	12	92	10	83	11	92
Other	5	62	5	62	4	67
Motion pictures, broadcasting	—	—	—	—	—	—
Widely diversified or not otherwise classified	35	44	35	43	35	45
Total companies	366	61	366	61	379	63

*Percentage of total number of companies for each industrial classification included in the survey.
Source: 1991 Accounting Trends & Techniques. American Institute of Certified Public Accountants.

The FIFO/LIFO Choice: Empirical Studies

There are several possible reasons for firms to stay on FIFO in addition to those related to LIFO liquidations and declining prices discussed previously. These include burdensome recordkeeping requirements, the inability to write down obsolete inventory, and the desire to maximize taxable income when using up a tax loss carryforward.

Other reasons offered relate to the desire to avoid the negative effect LIFO has on a firm's earnings. The motivations ascribed to this effect depend on whether (as discussed in Chapter 4) a market-based or financial contracting argument is used.

The market-based argument suggests that, whether or not the market is efficient and can see through the FIFO/LIFO numbers to the real economics behind them, as long as managers themselves believe that the market will be fooled by the lower earnings reported, there is a reluctance to use LIFO.

Alternatively, the financial contracting approach examines the impact of the FIFO/LIFO choice on management compensation and on debt covenant restrictions. The bonus plan hypothesis argues that the more a firm's compensation package for its top management is tied to income, the less likely it is for the firm to use LIFO accounting.

Managers may be reluctant to use LIFO if the resultant lower earnings will reduce their compensation.

The debt covenant hypothesis argues that the deleterious effect LIFO can have on a firm's reported income and ratios can increase the probability that a firm will violate its debt covenants with respect to working capital maintenance, net worth maintenance, income maintenance, and dividend payout ratio. Highly leveraged firms may be reluctant to use LIFO for that reason, notwithstanding the tax benefits.

Exhibit 5-12, taken from a study by Granof and Short (1984), found that over 70% of the companies that used FIFO did so because, for various reasons (including losses, tax loss carryforwards, etc.), they would not enjoy a material tax advantage if they switched to LIFO. Included in this number were the 15% of companies that preferred FIFO because they are in a declining cost environment. Another 20% of the companies preferred FIFO due to the high administrative costs involved in managing inventory levels from year to year (to avoid liquidations) that a LIFO environment entails. It is interesting to note that only about 10% of the respondents indicated that the lower reported earnings of LIFO played any role in their choice of accounting method.

More recently, as part of a larger study, Cushing and LeClere (1992) also conducted a survey asking both LIFO (32 firms) and FIFO (70 firms) to rank their reasons for their choice of inventory method. The results are presented in Exhibit 5-13. For LIFO firms,

EXHIBIT 5-12
Why Do Companies Reject LIFO? Summary of Responses

Explanation	Number	% of Total*
No expected tax benefits		
No required tax payment	34	16%
Declining prices	31	15
Rapid inventory turnover	30	14
Immaterial inventory	26	12
Miscellaneous tax related	38	17
	159	73%
Regulatory or other restrictions	26	12
Excessive cost		
High administrative costs	29	14
LIFO liquidation–related costs	12	6
	41	20%
Other adverse consequences		
Lower reported earnings	18	8
Bad accounting	7	3
	25	11%

*Percentage totals more than 100% as some companies offered more than one explanation.
Source: Granof, Michael H. and Daniel Short, "Why Do Companies Reject LIFO," *Journal of Accounting Auditing and Finance* (Summer 1984), pp. 323–333, Table 1, p. 327.

EXHIBIT 5-13
FIFO/LIFO Choice Survey Results

A. Reasons for Preferring LIFO to FIFO

Possible Reasons for Using LIFO	Response Code Number*				
	1	2	3	4	Average†
Tax/Cash Flow Reasons					
Lowers income taxes	27	5	0	0	1.16
Other Economic Consequences					
Increased reported earnings under FIFO could lead to unfair charges of excess profits	0	0	3	29	3.91
Orthodox Reasons					
Provides a better matching of costs and revenues	6	19	5	2	2.09
Conforms with other firms in the same industry	0	4	10	18	3.44

B. Reasons for Preferring FIFO to LIFO

Possible Reasons for Using FIFO	Response Code Number[a]				
	1	2	3	4	Average†
Tax/Cash Flow Reasons					
LIFO would not provide tax benefits	20	15	6	29	2.63
Concern about LIFO bookkeeping costs	4	17	18	31	3.09
Concern about possible liquidation of LIFO layers	6	7	14	43	3.34
Immateriality of inventories	9	2	5	54	3.49
Other Economic Consequences					
Concern about the effects on stock prices of reporting lower earnings under LIFO	13	14	9	34	2.91
Concern that debt convenants are based on FIFO-based accounting numbers	1	4	7	58	3.74
Orthodox reasons					
Better reflects the actual physical flow of inventories	20	19	13	18	2.41
Provides a more accurate inventory valuation in the balance sheet	11	32	11	16	2.46
Conforms with other firms in the same industry	5	12	11	42	3.29

*Per the questionnaire, response codes indicate the following:

  1 = The most important reason why we use LIFO (FIFO).

  2 = Not the most important reason why we use LIFO (FIFO), but an important reason, or at least an important advantage of using LIFO (FIFO).

  3 = Though an advantage of LIFO (FIFO), this reason is of minor importance to our choice of LIFO (FIFO).

  4 = Unimportant or irrelevant to our choice of LIFO (FIFO).

Note that three respondents did not follow directions and marked some reasons with an "X" while leaving others blank. In these cases, "X" was coded as 1, and "blank" as 4. Eleven other respondents coded some responses as instructed while leaving others blank; in these cases blanks were also coded as 4.

†Average is a weighted average of the responses.

Source: Cushing, Barry E. and Marc J. LeClere, "Evidence on the Determinants of Inventory Accounting Policy Choice," *The Accounting Review* (April 1992) pp. 355–366, Table 1, p. 357 (Adapted).

the overwhelming primary reason (response code = 1) given is the favorable tax effect. For FIFO firms, no single reason emerges as the most important; over half suggested various economic reasons (such as no tax effect, bookkeeping, liquidation) as their motivation. Twenty of the 70 firms (approximately 30%) indicated that LIFO did not provide them with any tax benefits. However, just as many stated that they chose FIFO because it was a "better accounting method" as it better reflected the physical flow of goods. Close to 40% indicated, as one of their two primary reasons, their concern about the lower earnings resulting from LIFO. These numbers are considerably higher than those reported in the Granof and Short survey.

These studies are but two of the many empirical studies that have focused on the LIFO/FIFO choice. The large number of studies on this issue is due to its richness. The choice has both income and (direct) cash flow consequences pulling in opposite directions. Moreover, the availability of data permitting adjustment from one method to another allows for "as if" comparisons in research design.

These studies for the most part focused on the impact of the choice on firms' financial performance both in terms of market reaction and management behavior and their effects on firms' financial statements. These studies and the hypotheses tested were affected both by the progression in academic accounting theory as well as the economic factors that caused a resurgence in the adoption of LIFO in the mid-1970s.

LIFO has been permitted in the United States since before World War II, and its rate of adoption understandably follows the rate of inflation. Its most recent resurgence in popularity was in the 1970s, when the rate of inflation reached the double-digit range. Approximately 400 companies made the FIFO to LIFO switch in 1974. This period coincided with heavy academic emphasis on market-based empirical research and the efficient market hypothesis, and the effect of the FIFO/LIFO switch was viewed as an ideal area for research.

It provided a situation where the functional fixation hypothesis could be tested to see whether

1. The market accepted financial statements as they were presented and thus viewed the switch unfavorably since income was depressed.

2. The market was efficient in the sense that it saw through the numbers and, on the contrary, viewed the switch positively since (from an economic perspective) the switch was beneficial as cash flows were increased.

The proponents of the efficient market hypothesis predicted that the market would see through the "cosmetic" aspects of the switch and react favorably to the cash flow effects.

Surprisingly, the results were not clear cut. Sunder (1973), examined a sample of firms which switched to LIFO in the period 1946–1966, and found that in the period leading up to the switch the firms experienced positive abnormal returns (see Figure 5-1A). At the time of the switch itself, the reaction was slightly negative or nonexistent as investors seemingly ignored the positive cash flow effects. Moreover, the beta risk of firms that switched to LIFO tended to increase in the months surrounding the switch.

This result was similar to that of Ball (1972), who examined the market reaction to various accounting changes, FIFO/LIFO included. The positive reaction in the year of

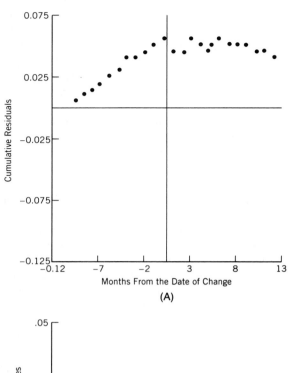

(A)

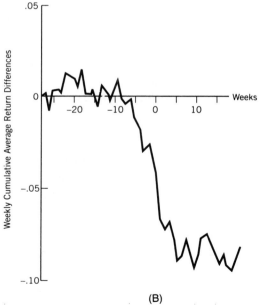

(B)

FIGURE 5-1 Abnormal Returns: Inventory Method Studies.

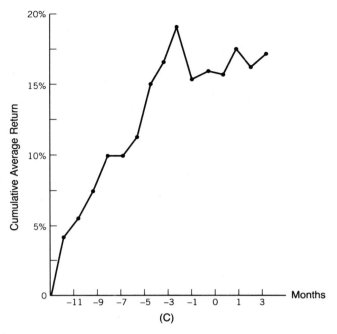

FIGURE 5-1 (Continued)

Sources: A (1946–1966 Adopters): Sunder, Shyam, "Relationship Between Accounting Changes And Stock Prices: Problems Of Measurement And Some Empirical Evidence," *Journal of Accounting Research* (Supplement 1973), pp. 1–45, Figure 2, p. 18. B (1974–1975 Adopters): Ricks, William E., "The Market's Response To The 1974 LIFO Adoption," *Journal of Accounting Research* (Autumn 1982), pp. 367–387, Figure 2, p. 378. C (1973–1982 Adopters): Biddle, Gary C. and Frederick W. Lindahl, "Stock Price Reactions to LIFO Adoptions: The Association Between Excess Returns and LIFO Tax Savings," *Journal of Accounting Research* (Autumn 1982), pp. 551–588, Figure 1, p. 569.

the switch was interpreted by some as a sign that the market had anticipated the switch and had already reacted prior to its actual announcement. Others felt that the firms that switched had been having "good" years, and could thus "afford" the negative impact of the switch, and that these studies suffered from a self-selection bias.

Subsequent studies such as Eggleton et al. (1976), Abdel-khalik and McKeown (1978), Brown (1980), and Ricks (1982) extended this research by controlling for earnings-related variables and by focusing on the large number of firms that switched in the 1974–1975 period. Generally, their results confirmed a negative market reaction in the year of the switch. Ricks, for example, used a control sample of non-LIFO adopters (matched on the basis of industry and "as if" earnings) and calculated the cumulative average return differences between the two groups. The results for weekly return differences around the preliminary earnings announcement date that are presented in Figure 5-1B clearly indicate a more positive reaction to firms that did not adopt LIFO. Although the lower returns were reversed within a year, the initial and prolonged negative reaction is difficult to understand. One explanation for this anomalous behavior was that those firms that switched to LIFO were the ones most affected by inflation. Thus the market was reacting negatively to the added risk (higher inflation) these firms were now perceived as bearing; hence the lower returns and the higher beta-risk measures.

The difficulty with this explanation is that the firms were matched by industry, and thus it is necessary to assume that these firms were somehow more adversely affected by inflation than other firms in the same industry. The Biddle and Ricks (1988) paper discussed shortly also found evidence consistent with this explanation. Implicitly, these studies provided an explanation as to why firms stayed on FIFO as they wanted to avoid the unfavorable market reaction resulting from the adoption of LIFO.

Biddle and Lindhal (1982) attempted to resolve some of these issues by arguing that the previous studies were flawed in that they did not consider the size of the tax savings as a result of adopting LIFO, but rather just classified firms on the basis of whether or not they had adopted LIFO. By including the magnitude of the tax savings, their study found a positive association (see Figure 5-1C) between the market reaction and the estimated tax savings.

> The results in this study are consistent with a cash-flow hypothesis which suggests that investor reactions to LIFO adoptions depend on the present value of tax-related cash-flow savings. After controlling for abnormal earnings performance, larger LIFO tax savings were found to be (cross-sectionally) associated with larger cumulative excess returns over the year in which a LIFO adoption (extension) first applied.[24]

Biddle and Lindhal's study covered 311 LIFO adopters from the period 1973–1980. The pattern of abnormal returns reported is similar to Sunder's findings (Figure 5-1A). Both Sunder and Biddle and Lindhal did not use a control group,[25] making their results not directly comparable to those of Ricks. However, the evidence would suggest that there was some systematic as yet unexplained factor affecting the 1974–1975 adoptions and that the research results were sensitive to the research design and the time horizon examined.

Biddle and Ricks (1988), using daily data, confirmed that there were

> negative excess returns around the preliminary dates of firms adopting LIFO in 1974. There is little evidence of significant excess returns (negative or positive) near the preliminary dates of firms adopting LIFO in other years.[26]

To explain the negative returns, they examined the analyst forecast errors for the 1974 LIFO adopters. They found that analysts significantly overestimated the earnings and did not fully appreciate the magnitude of the impact of inflation.[27] In other years,

---

[24]Biddle, Gary C. and Frederick W. Lindahl, "Stock Price Reactions to LIFO Adoptions: The Association Between Excess Returns and LIFO Tax Savings," *Journal of Accounting Research* (Autumn 1982 Part II) pp. 551–588.

[25]Biddle and Lindahl instead used the size of the tax saving as a "within-group" control.

[26]Biddle, Gary C. and William E. Ricks, "Analyst Forecast Errors and Stock Price Behavior Near the Earnings Announcement Dates of LIFO Adopters," *Journal of Accounting Research* (Autumn 1988) pp. 169–194.

[27]At that time, LIFO switches were relatively novel, and it took some time for analysts to "learn" the magnitude of the impact. That they did learn is evidenced by the improved earnings forecast errors for LIFO adopters in later years.

however, the error in analysts' forecasts for LIFO adopters was not significant. Furthermore, they found that the negative returns were positively correlated with the forecast error, indicating that the market as well as the analysts were surprised by the actual earnings realization. Thus the negative returns were due to the "surprise" when the markets realized that the impact of inflation was worse than they had originally expected. As the firms that adopted LIFO would presumably be the ones most likely to be affected by inflation, the negative "surprise" reaction hit them hardest. In later years, however, having learned from experience, the impact of inflation was more readily factored in.

Although these studies shed some light on the differential reaction to LIFO adopters, they still did not explain why some firms remained on FIFO. On the contrary, Biddle (1980) found

> surprising the finding that many firms have voluntarily paid tens of millions of dollars in additional income taxes by continuing to use FIFO rather than switching to LIFO.[28]

The contracting theories of accounting choice focused on this issue. Abdel-khalik (1985) examined the bonus plan hypothesis and its implicit corollary that management-controlled firms, in which ownership is widely held, are more likely to use FIFO than are owner-controlled firms. The rationale for this argument is that the more removed management is from ownership of the firm, the more the direct compensation to the manager becomes the primary motivator for the managers' actions rather than the wealth of the firm itself.

Thus the LIFO-induced tax savings become less important in the management-controlled firm. Evidence in support of this hypothesis was found as FIFO firms that were manager controlled had relatively higher income-based bonuses. On the other hand, evidence could not be found that differences in compensation plans were related to the FIFO/LIFO choice. In explaining this (non)finding, Abdel-khalik hypothesizes that either

> (1) firms switching to LIFO modify their compensation arrangements, or (2) as some executives have indicated to me, the FIFO-based income continues to be used in determining annual bonus.[29]

Hunt (1985) examined the bonus plan and debt covenant hypotheses. His results did not support the bonus plan hypothesis. Moreover, and in contrast to Abdel-khalik, he found that LIFO firms tended to be less owner controlled, which is contrary to expectations. Hunt, however, did find support for the debt covenant hypothesis especially with respect to the leverage and interest coverage ratios. His evidence also indicated a threshold in terms of dividend payout ratios above which firms are reluctant to use LIFO.

Dopuch and Pincus (1988) examined the bonus plan, debt covenant, and taxation

[28]Biddle, Gary C., "Accounting Methods and Management Decisions: The Case of Inventory Costing and Inventory Policy", *Journal of Accounting Research* (Supplement 1980), pp. 235–280.

[29]Abdel-Khalik, A. Rashad, "The Effect of LIFO-Switching And Firm Ownership on Executives Pay", *Journal of Accounting Research* (Autumn 1985), pp. 427–447.

hypotheses in one study and found that the taxation effect provided the best explanation for the FIFO/LIFO decision. They compared the holding gain that would have accrued to LIFO firms had they stayed on FIFO with the holding gain for firms that did use FIFO.

Their findings indicated that the holding gains tended to be larger for the LIFO firms, thus resulting in a more significant tax advantage for those firms. In addition, the holding gain tended to grow as they approached the switch date. Dopuch and Pincus argued that this indicated that

> the long-term FIFO firms in our sample have not been forgoing significant tax savings, in which case remaining on that method is certainly consistent with FIFO being an optimal tax choice, given other considerations. In contrast, long-term LIFO firms would have forgone significant tax savings. . . . Finally, using the long-term FIFO sample's average holding gains as a base, our change-firms' average holding gains became significantly larger than the FIFO average as they approached the year in which they switched, and this difference continued to grow subsequently.[30]

Further, Dopuch and Pincus argued that just as they had made the calculations relating to the increasing holding gains for the switch firms, financial analysts could also have made similar calculations and thus anticipate the switch. Thus the inconclusive findings of the market reaction studies could be a result of not taking into consideration the "advance warning" market agents had with regard to the switch.

More recently, Jennings et al. (1992) found evidence supporting this "advance warning" contention. They constructed a model that predicted which firms in the 1974–1975 period were more likely to adopt LIFO. The model accurately forecast adopting/nonadopting firms approximately two-thirds of the time. Furthermore, the prior probability of adoption affected the market reaction. Thus the less likely an adopting firm had been viewed as a likely candidate for adoption, the more *positive* the market reaction when it eventually adopted. Similarly, for firms that did not adopt, if they were originally viewed as likely candidates for adoption, the greater the *negative* reaction when the adoption did not materialize.

Summary of FIFO/LIFO Choice

A common finding in many of the inventory studies was that the choice of inventory method was closely related to industry and size factors, with larger firms opting for LIFO. The industry dimension is readily understood in terms of the similar production, operating, and inflation conditions facing firms in the same industry. The size factor has been explained in two ways. As noted, adoption of LIFO increases inventory management and control costs, which mitigates the benefit received from tax savings. For large-sized firms these costs are more readily absorbed and are viewed as being relatively smaller than the potential tax benefit. Others argue that the size effect is due to the fact that, for political reasons, larger firms tend to choose accounting methods that lower reported earnings.

---

[30]Dopuch, Nicholas and Morton Pincus, "Evidence of the Choice of Inventory Accounting Methods: LIFO Versus FIFO", *Journal of Accounting Research* (Spring 1988), pp. 28–59.

EXHIBIT 5-14
Variables Hypothesized to Affect FIFO-LIFO Choice

1. *Estimated tax savings* from use of LIFO expected to be larger for LIFO companies.

2. *Inventory materiality:* The larger a firm's inventory balance, the greater the incentive to use LIFO as the potential tax saving is larger.

3. *Tax loss carryforward:* The larger a firm's tax loss carryforward, the less incentive it has to use LIFO.

4. *Inventory variability:* The more variable a firm's inventory balance, the more likely it is to face inventory liquidations. This would tend to favor choosing FIFO over LIFO.

5. *Inventory obsolescence:* If a firm's inventory tends to become obsolete because of new product innovation, then the replacement of old products by new ones raises a difficult LIFO accounting question for which there is no authoritative answer. Such companies may prefer FIFO.

6. *Size as proxy for bookkeeping costs:* The larger the accounting costs required to use LIFO, the less likely a firm would choose LIFO. Larger firms would be able to absorb these costs more readily.

7. *Leverage:* Under the debt covenant hypothesis, firms with higher leverage would prefer FIFO as it would improve their debt/equity ratios.

8. *Current ratio:* Under the debt covenant hypothesis, firms with low current ratios would prefer FIFO, which improves their current ratio.

Source: Cushing, Barry E. and Marc J. LeClere, "Evidence on the Determinants of Inventory Accounting Policy Choice," *The Accounting Review* (April 1992) pp. 355–366, Table 4, p.363.

Exhibit 5-14, based on Cushing and LeClere (1992), serves as a useful summary of the findings relating to the FIFO/LIFO choice. The variables and the rationale behind their use are indicated in the table. Seven of the eight variables examined by them as explaining the FIFO/LIFO choice are significant in the direction predicted. The estimated tax savings are significantly greater for LIFO firms. Consistent with this, FIFO firms have higher average loss carryforwards. The inventory variability is higher for FIFO firms, increasing the chances of liquidation. FIFO firms tend to be smaller and more highly leveraged and have lower liquidity ratios. Similarly, the variable indicating the likelihood of inventory obsolescence is also significant. Only for the materiality measure are the results not statistically significant, although they are in the correct direction.

These variables are indicators of possible motivations as to why firms stay on FIFO. However, in summing up the research in this area,

> We continue to be relatively uninformed about these issues and know little about the real reasons that many firms do not switch to LIFO when it appears that they would benefit by positive tax savings.[31]

[31]Editor's Comments, *The Accounting Review* (Vol. 67: No. 2, April 1992), p. 319.

CONCLUDING COMMENTS ON ACCOUNTING FOR INVENTORIES

The choice of accounting method for inventories is one of the basic decisions made by nearly all companies engaged in the manufacturing and distribution of goods. The method chosen should result in the best measure of income and financial condition. However, as we have seen, no single method accomplishes this objective in most cases.

For companies operating in the United States, under conditions of rising prices, the cash flow advantage of LIFO usually dictates the choice of that method. When LIFO is not chosen, therefore, the first question should be: Why not? As the empirical work indicates, managers offer a number of reasons for not using LIFO, only some of which appear valid. Also, companies that should use LIFO but don't may not be attractive to investors.

In many cases, the analytical techniques presented in this chapter enable the analyst to approximate the effect of LIFO on a company using FIFO or average cost. Such analysis can result in estimates of both the cash savings forgone (relevant to the discussion in the previous paragraph) and the inclusion of holding gains in reported income.

Example: British Petroleum. Occasionally, managements make the required adjustments available. Exhibit 5-15 contains data from the 1990 annual report of British Petroleum (BP). Given the fluctuations in oil prices, holding gains and losses are a recurring feature of that company's income statement. As LIFO is generally not acceptable for income tax use outside of the United States, there is no incentive to use it for financial reporting.

The data in Exhibit 5-15 speak for themselves. Historical cost profit (before extraordinary items) approximately doubled from 1986 to 1990, with earnings per

EXHIBIT 5-15. BRITISH PETROLEUM
Comparison of Historic and Replacement Profit, 1986–1990

	1986	1987	1988	1989	1990
			(£ millions)		
Profit (historic)*	£817	£1391	£1210	£1744	£1676
Holding (gains)/losses	962	(83)	227	(383)	(472)
Profit (replacement)	£1779	£1308	£1437	£1361	£1204
	Pence per Ordinary Share				
Profit (historical)	14.9P	24.9P	20.0P	31.8P	31.3P
Dividends	11.7	12.5	13.5	14.9	16.0
Profit (replacement)	32.5	23.4	23.8	24.8	22.5

*Before extraordinary items.
Source: British Petroleum *1990 Annual Report.*

ordinary (common) share following suit. When holding gains and losses are excluded, however, a different picture emerges: replacement cost profit (before extraordinary items) has fallen by approximately one-third! The decline in operating earnings over this time period has been more than offset by inventory (stock) holding gains, replacing the large holding loss for 1986.

Referring back to our discussion of the meaning of income, it seems clear that replacement cost profit is a better measure of BP's earnings. Holding gains are not predictable. Moreover, such gains must be reinvested in inventory for the firm to remain in business.

British Petroleum increased its dividend rate by 37% over the period 1986–1990. Relative to reported (historical cost) profit, the dividend payout ratio has declined, making it appear that management has been "stingy" toward shareholders. But in light of the replacement cost profit trend, we believe that management can be accused of being overly generous.

What does the stock market think about reported profits? We note that, when BP reported that its profits quadrupled for the third quarter of 1990, the company was denounced in the House of Commons.[32] But the price of BP shares fell slightly, perhaps reflecting the fact that replacement cost profits actually declined.

While BP, subject to wide swings in the price of oil, may be an extreme case, it illustrates the necessity of analyzing the inventory accounting of a firm to understand the impact of changing prices on its earnings and net worth.

NON-U.S. REPORTING REQUIREMENTS

FIFO and the weighted average method are the most commonly used methods worldwide. The use of LIFO is essentially limited to companies in the United States, and the significant tax benefits this method can provide suggest that the method will continue to enjoy widespread acceptance. In Japan, LIFO is rarely used even though it is an acceptable method. Japanese standards do not require disclosure of LIFO reserves, reducing the analyst's ability to make some of the balance sheet adjustments discussed in this chapter.

LIFO is allowed but rarely used in France since the method may be used only in consolidated financial statements, not in the separate financial statements that are the norm. Although FIFO and weighted average are the most common methods in Italy and the Netherlands, LIFO is allowed, and it is used by a significant minority. Some Dutch firms use current cost (equivalent to LIFO) for inventories.

FIFO is the financial reporting method of choice for most firms in Canada and Spain; LIFO is allowed for financial reporting but not for taxes, which may account for its lack of popularity in these countries. In the United Kingdom, Statement of Standard Accounting Practice (SSAP) 9 holds that LIFO may not result in a true and fair valuation and, in addition, the method is not allowed for tax purposes.

---

[32]*The* (London) *Financial Times*, November 10, 1990.

Average cost is the most widely used method in Germany, although LIFO has been allowed for tax purposes since 1990, and it may change reporting habits. In October 1992, the IASC approved Exposure Draft (ED) 37 which revises International Accounting Standard (IAS) 2 designating FIFO and weighted average costs as the benchmark treatments and LIFO as the allowed alternative. Firms using LIFO will be required to provide FIFO/weighted average cost disclosures facilitating adjustments discussed in this chapter.

Inventories (other than LIFO) are reported at the lower of cost or market value; cost depends on the method used. Market is generally defined as net realizable value with specific limitations[33] in the United States; any write-down is determined on an item-by-item basis. The IASC's proposal, ED 37, limits itself to net realizable value (NRV), and it does not specify whether the cost versus NRV comparison should be made on an item-by-item basis or by groups of similar items. This proposal is in line with standards in most other countries.

USING INVENTORY BALANCES TO AID IN FORECASTING[34]

Changes in inventory balances can provide signals about a firm's future sales and earnings prospects. Unfortunately, two mutually exclusive but both convincing arguments can be made as to the direction of those future prospects. An unanticipated (from the analyst's perspective) increase in the inventory balance may signal either

- an unexpected decrease in demand causing an unplanned increase in inventory and signalling lower demand in the future; or[35]
- a (planned) increase of inventory levels by management as they anticipate higher demand for their product in the future.

Which condition prevails cannot be determined from the changes in the inventory account itself. Rather, the change itself acts as a signal for the analyst to investigate (using other sources of information) which condition is most likely for the company in question.[36]

The above discussion relates only to changes in finished goods inventory. In a manufacturing environment, changes in work in process inventory (and to some degree changes in raw materials inventory) indicate that management is increasing production to meet an increase in actual or anticipated orders. The balances in the inventory account (Exhibit 5-16) of BMC Industries Inc. for 1989–1990 illustrates this. Total inventory

---

[33]Generally, these limitations ensure that inventories are written down to approximately their current cost.

[34]See Bernard and Noel (1991) for a more elaborate discussion of the issues discussed in this section.

[35]Throughout this section, a distinction between demand and sales must be kept in mind. Lower demand can be associated with higher sales if a company, in response to lower demand, cuts prices thus stimulating sales.

[36]The analyst must also be sure that the change is not a result of a change in accounting method or management acquiring more inventory in an attempt to "beat" an anticipated price increase.

EXHIBIT 5-16. BMC INDUSTRIES
Increase in Work in Process Inventory as Indicator of Future Sales

A. Changes in Components of Inventory Account, 1989–1990

	1989	1990	% Increase
		($ millions)	
Raw material	$ 9.7	$13.1	35%
Work in process	4.7	13.3	180%
Finished goods	14.7	15.7	7%
Total	$29.2	$42.1	44%

B. Comparison of Quarterly Sales 1990 and 1991

Quarterly Sales

Quarter	1990	1991	% Change
First	$ 43.6	$ 44.5	2%
Second	46.1	62.2	35%
Third	39.2	42.5	8%
Fourth	46.1	54.0	17%
Total	$175.0	$203.2	16%

Source: BMC Industries, Annual Report (1990–1991)

increased by 44% but the bulk of the increase was due to a 180% change in the work in process component. This increase implies there was increased production in anticipation of future sales, which materialized in the second quarter of 1991 (Part B of Exhibit 5-16). After the second quarter, sales (and inventories) reverted to 'normal' levels. Generally, when such increases occur, the analyst must determine if the sales increase is "one shot" or signals an ongoing trend. Although both cases enhance the company's value; there is a difference in degree. In BMC's case, management stated in the 1990 MD&A that the build up in inventory was a result of a one time order for delivery in the second quarter of 1991.

On a more general level, Bernard and Noel (1991) examined whether changes in inventory could be used to forecast future sales and earnings. Their results are interesting because they indicated that the implications of inventory changes were not homogeneous for all firms, but differed between retailers and manufacturers. Even among manufacturers, the implications differed with respect to the nature of the component of inventory which changed.

For retailers, they found that increases in inventory signalled higher sales but lower earnings and profit margins. At first glance, this may seem paradoxical but the explanation is straightforward. Increases in inventory were usually a result of argument (1) above; a drop in demand resulted in increased inventory. To rid themselves of this unwanted "excess" inventory, retailers reduced prices to stimulate sales ("dumping" inventory). Therefore, sales increased but with lower earnings. These effects were generally short lived as the changes in sales dissipated over time.

For manufacturers, they found that increases in finished goods inventory indicated lower demand. Just as in the retail environment, these increases were followed by higher sales and lower earnings in the short-run as manufacturers dumped "unwanted" inventory. However, unlike retailers, in the long run (once the initial increase was worked down) the drop in demand persisted and future sales and earnings decreased. For raw materials and work in process, on the other hand, increases in inventory levels were consistent with higher demand and higher sales.

This concluding section of the chapter provides a different analytical application of information contained in financial reports. The lessons of the earlier sections, however, must not be forgotten. Any changes in inventory balances must take into consideration the inventory method used. Thus, for a LIFO company analysis of changes should be based on current cost inventory amounts. In addition, an effort should be made to ensure that the change in inventory balances is driven by quantity changes, not increased prices for the same inventory quantity.

SUMMARY

In an environment of changing prices, assumptions as to the flow of costs can affect reported income, balance sheet amounts and associated ratios. More important, the FIFO/LIFO choice, as a consequence of taxation, has real cash flow effects. The chapter compares the effects of the FIFO/LIFO choice along these dimensions and demonstrates how the analyst can adjust from one method to another. The effects of liquidations, interim reporting and inventory costing in a manufacturing environment are also explored. The motivations for firms to opt for one method over another as well as market reaction to these choices is also analyzed. After a comparison of US GAAP with those of other countries, the chapter concludes with a description of how changes in inventory balances can be used to aid in forecasting.

Chapter 5

Problems

1. [FIFO and LIFO: basic relationships] The Mogul Company, expecting that decreases in oil prices are only temporary, increases its monthly purchases as the price of oil decreases. During 19X8, its monthly oil purchases follow the pattern presented:

Quarter	Quantity (bbl)	Price/Barrel
First		
January	100,000	$25
February	100,000	25
March	100,000	25

Quarter	Quantity (bbl)	Price/Barrel
Second		
April	125,000	20
May	125,000	20
June	125,000	20
Third		
July	150,000	18
August	150,000	18
September	150,000	18
Fourth		
October	200,000	15
November	200,000	15
December	200,000	15

1. The company had no opening inventory.
2. Sales were 100,000 barrels *per month* for the period January–June and 150,000 *per month* for the period July–December.
3. Mogul uses the LIFO inventory method.
4. The company's tax rate is 40%.

A. Compute the difference in *each* of the following dollar amounts that Mogul would report under its present accounting method (LIFO) as compared with use of the FIFO method. [Note: The solution does not require long calculations; focus on the differences between FIFO and LIFO, not the actual levels.]

  (i) Inventory purchases

  (ii) Closing inventory

  (iii) Cost of goods sold

  (iv) Pretax income

  (v) Income tax expense

  (vi) Net income

  (vii) Cash flow from operations

  (viii) Working capital (end of year)

B. Assume that Mogul was forced to liquidate its inventory at year end. Discuss how the answers to part A would differ.

2. [Inventory methods, basic relationships, impact on turnover ratio] The Renemax Co. begins operations on December 31, 19X0, with $500 of inventory, enough for one month's (January 19X1) sales. During 19X1, the company maintains its inventory at one month's sales. Monthly sales (in units) are constant, and the company replenishes inventory each month.

At the end of 19X1, Renemax must choose an inventory method. The following additional information is available:

1. The cash flow difference between the FIFO and LIFO methods is $400. [Note: You do not know which is higher.]
2. Cost of goods sold is $12,000 using the weighted average method.
3. The company's tax rate is 40%.
4. Prices change only in one direction during the year.

A. Using the information provided, fill in the following blanks

	FIFO	Weighted Average	LIFO
Opening inventory	――――	――――	――――
Purchases	――――	――――	――――
Cost of goods sold	――――	12,000	――――
Closing inventory	――――	――――	――――
Inventory turnover (reported)	――――	――――	――――
Inventory turnover (actual)	――――	――――	――――

[Hint: To solve this problem, begin by considering that the firm's actual inventory turnover is 12. Use this insight to complete the blanks for the weighted average method. Then consider the effect of price changes on the amounts computed under the LIFO and FIFO methods.]

B. Compare the inventory turnover ratio reported under each method. Discuss which method provides the ratio that most accurately portrays the actual (physical) turnover.

C. Discuss the impact of the choice of accounting method on the components of and the total reported cash flow from operations.

3. [Inventory methods, basic relationships] The M & J Co. begins operations on January 1, 19X0, with the following balance sheet:

Cash	$10,000	Common stock	$10,000

During the year, the company maintains its inventory accounts on the FIFO basis. Before provision for income tax, the balance sheet at December 31, 19X0, is:

Cash	$ 5,000	Common stock	$10,000
Inventory	10,000	Pretax income	5,000
	$15,000		$15,000

M & J has sales in 19X0 of $25,000. On a *unit* basis, the company sells half of the *units* purchased during the year. Operating expenses (excluding COGS) are $12,000.

Prior to issuing financial statements, the company considers its choice of inventory method. Assume a tax rate of 40% and a dividend payout ratio of 50%.

A. Using the information provided, complete the following table:

	FIFO	Weighted Average	LIFO
Sales	$25,000	$25,000	$25,000
Cost of goods sold	———	———	———
Other expenses	12,000	12,000	12,000
Pretax income	———	———	———
Income tax expense	———	———	———
Net income	———	———	———
Retained earnings	———	———	———
Cash from operations	———	———	———
Closing cash balance	———	———	———
Closing inventory	10,000	———	———
Inventory purchases	———	———	———

B. Prepare a balance sheet for M & J at December 31, 19X0, assuming use of:

    (i) The LIFO inventory method.

   (ii) The weighted average method.

  (iii) The FIFO inventory method.

C. Discuss the advantages and disadvantages of *each* of the three possible choices of inventory method.

4. [Inventory costing for pricing purposes] The following paragraph was taken from the "Message to Stockholders" section of Driver-Harris Company's *1980 Annual Report*.

> We would like to call your attention to a major effect caused by inflation. Our results are significantly affected by the use of LIFO accounting. We believe that this method better reflects the results of operations in inflationary times, even though, had the FIFO method been used for inventory valuation, our 1980 results before income taxes would have been approximately $1,800,000 better. Unfortunately, some of our competitors throughout the world are still using the FIFO method, and thus tend to offer unrealistically low prices, based on outdated costs.

Discuss the validity of this paragraph.

5. [LIFO, FIFO, holding gains and comprehensive income; 1988 CFA adapted] The Quickie Rice Company sells Rice-O-Matics, a device that reduces the time required to prepare rice. Inventory at the beginning of the accounting period was one unit at $35. Two more units were purchased during the period, the first at $39 and the second at $43.

One unit was sold at $65. Replacement cost at the close of the accounting period was $46.

Calculate, on *both* a FIFO and LIFO basis, the company's

    (i) Ending inventory.

    (ii) Gross profit.

    (iii) Unrealized inventory holding gain.

    (iv) Comprehensive income (reported income plus unrealized holding gain).

Problems 6 and 7 are based on the following data, adapted from the financial statements of two firms in the automobile replacement parts industry.

Zenab Distributors, Balance Sheets, at December 31

	Year 1	Year 2
Cash	$ 500	$ 100
Accounts receivable (net)	8,100	8,300
Inventory	24,900	25,200
Current assets	$33,500	$33,600
Current liabilities	$11,600	$12,700

Zenab Distributors uses the LIFO method of accounting for 70% of its inventories; FIFO is used for the remainder. If all inventories were carried at FIFO, inventory would be higher by $3600 and $5100 in years 1 and 2, respectively.

Faybech Parts, Balance Sheets, at December 31

	Year 1	Year 2
Cash	$ 1,000	$ 600
Accounts receivable (net)	11,400	13,900
Inventory	22,300	30,300
Current assets	$34,700	$44,800
Current liabilities	$10,700	$12,200

Faybech Parts uses FIFO accounting for all inventories.

Income Statements, Year 2 (ended December 31)

	Zenab	Faybech
Sales	$92,700	$77,000
Cost of goods sold	61,300	52,000
Gross profit	$31,400	$25,000

Income Statements, Year 2 (ended December 31)

	Zenab	Faybech
Selling and general expense	26,400	21,500
Pretax income	$ 5,000	$ 3,500
Income tax expense	2,000	1,400
Net income	$ 3,000	$ 2,100

6. [Adjusting LIFO to FIFO and FIFO to LIFO/current cost] Using the financial data provided:

A. Calculate Zenab's cost of goods sold and pretax income on a FIFO basis.

B. Calculate Faybech's cost of goods sold and pretax income on a LIFO/current cost basis.

C. Discuss the circumstances under which income tax expense should be adjusted for when computing net income in parts A and B.

7. [LIFO versus FIFO; effect on ratios; adjusting ratios] **A.** Using the *reported* financial data, compute each of the following ratios for *both* Zenab and Faybech:

(i) Current ratio (years 1 and 2)

(ii) Inventory turnover (year 2)

(iii) Gross profit margin (year 2)

(iv) Pretax profit margin (EBT to sales) (year 2)

B. Briefly compare the performance of the two firms for year 2 based on the ratios computed in part A.

C. Compute each of the ratios in part A with both companies:

(i) on FIFO

(ii) on LIFO

(iii) using the hybrid method

D. Select the basis of comparison for *each* of the four ratios that you feel is most meaningful. Justify your choice.

8. [LIFO versus FIFO; effect on ratios; adjusting ratios; 1990 CFA adapted] The Zeta Corp. uses LIFO inventory accounting. The footnotes to the 19X4 financial statements contain the following data as of December 31:

	19X3	19X4
Raw materials	$392,675	$369,725
Finished products	401,325	377,075
Inventory on FIFO basis	$794,000	$746,800
Adjustment to LIFO basis	(46,000)	(50,000)
Inventory on LIFO basis	$748,000	$696,800

   1. The company has a marginal tax rate of 35%.

   2. Cost of goods sold for 19X4 is $3,800,000.

   3. Net income for 19X4 is $340,000.

   4. Return on equity for 19X4 is 4.6%.

   A. Calculate 19X4 net income for Zeta assuming that it used the FIFO inventory method.

   B. Calculate the company's inventory turnover ratio on both a FIFO and LIFO basis.

   C. Calculate Zeta'a return on equity on a FIFO basis. (Remember to adjust both the numerator and denominator.)

   D. Discuss the usefulness of the adjustments made in parts A, B, and C to a financial analyst.

   E. Describe alternative measures of inventory turnover and return on equity that would aid an understanding of Zeta's operating performance.

   9. [Estimating company specific inflation rates] Pope & Talbot, Inc.'s inventory footnote for 1991 states that:

> the portion of lumber and raw materials inventories determined using the last-in, first-out (LIFO) method aggregated $10,491,000 and $7,166,000 at December 31, 1991 and 1990, respectively. The cost of these LIFO inventories valued at the lower of average cost or market (which approximates current cost) at December 31, 1991 and 1990 was $16,141,000 and $11,480,000.

   A. Using the foregoing footnote data and the methodology described in the chapter, calculate the rate of price change experienced by Pope & Talbot during 1992.

   The behavior of the Lumber and Wood Products Price Index for the period December 1990 to December 1991 is:

Commodity Price Index
Lumber and Wood Products (1982 = 100)

December 1990	126.8		
January 1991	127.6	July	136.9
February	127.2	August	133.3
March	127.8	September	133.4
April	129.2	October	133.3
May	132.3	November	133.3
June	136.2	December	134.3

Source: Survey of Current Business, January 1992.

   B. Based on the Commodity Price Index data, calculate the rate of price change for lumber and wood products for 1991.

The methodology described in the chapter for estimating price level changes assumes that inventory levels do not change during the year. Pope & Talbot increased its inventory level considerably during the year.

C. Describe how the increase in Pope & Talbot's inventory levels during 1991 may have affected the estimate derived in part A.

D. Discuss other factors that may explain why the estimates derived in parts A and B differ.

10. [Adjusting for LIFO liquidations] The Jofen Company uses the LIFO inventory method. In 19X3, anticipating a downturn in demand, the company decided not to replenish inventory levels at year end. The ensuing LIFO liquidation increased *pretax income* by $300,000 over what it would have been had Jofen replaced units of inventory sold during the year. Ending inventory on December 31, 19X3, was $2,000,000, a reduction of $700,000 from the level at January 1, 19X3.

A. Compute the LIFO cost of inventory at January 1, 19X3.

B. Compute the additional purchases that would have been required to fully replenish inventories.

C. Describe the impact of the LIFO liquidation on reported cash flow from operations.

D. Describe how the foregoing data could be used to adjust reported income for 19X3.

E. Explain why net income as adjusted in part D would be more useful for financial analysis.

11. [Deere; Adjusting for alternative accounting methods; effects of liquidation] Deere reported a LIFO liquidation benefit of $128 million for 1991. Its reported inventory balances (80% LIFO and 20% FIFO) were:

	1990	1991
Total at current cost	$ 1799 million	$ 1655 million
Adjustment to LIFO basis	(1121)	(1117)
Total at LIFO	$ 678 million	$ 538 million
Cost of goods sold in 1991 was $4894 million.		

A. Compute Deere's 1991 COGS under the FIFO method.

B. *Excluding* the benefit of the LIFO liquidation, compute Deere's cost of goods sold for 1991 using:

    (i) Deere's current accounting method.

    (ii) FIFO for all inventories.

C. Calculate Deere's inventory purchases in 1991.

D. LIFO liquidations result from not buying (producing) enough inventory. Calculate the level of Deere's purchases required to avoid the liquidation.

E. Using your answers to parts A–D, estimate Deere's:

    (i) 1991 gross profit margin on equipment division sales of $5,848 million.

    (ii) 1991 inventory turnover ratio excluding all price change effects.

    (iii) Rate of change in price level for 1991.

F. Describe how you would use the inventory footnote data to adjust Deere's net worth (book value) to a current cost basis.

12. [Effect of using LIFO; decline in reserve] The New York Times Company inventory footnote is reproduced below:

Inventories as shown in the accompanying Consolidated Balance Sheets are composed of the following:

December 31, 1990–1991 (in $ thousands)

	1990	1991
Newsprint and magazine paper	$40,312	$33,393
Work in process	6,003	7,451
Total inventory	$46,315	$40,844

Utilization of the LIFO method reduced inventories as calculated on the FIFO method by approximately $3,619,000 and $7,882,000 at December 31, 1991 and 1990 respectively.

A. Calculate the effect on reported pretax income in 1991 of the use of LIFO by The New York Times Company.

B. Calculate the change in total reported inventory balances if The New York Times Company had used the FIFO method for 1990 and 1991.

C. State two possible reasons why The New York Times Company may not have had to report a LIFO liquidation effect for 1991 despite the inventory decline.

13. [Declines in inventory; choice of method] Control Data Corporation is a manufacturer of computer equipment. It uses FIFO or average cost for all inventories. Inventory levels for 1989 and 1990 (December 31) were:

	1989	1990
Finished goods	$ 84.1 million	$ 46.7 million
Work in process	38.5	49.3
Raw materials	122.4	86.0
Total	$245.0 million	$182.0 million

A. Suggest three factors that would explain *all or part* of the 1990 inventory decline.

B. Explain which of the factors in your answer to part A would justify Control Data's failure to use the LIFO inventory method.

C. Control Data states that

Costs incurred in placing developed standard commercial products into production are capitalized and amortized based upon the quantity of units shipped during an 18- to 24-month period after commencement of production.

Discuss how this policy affects trends in the company's cost of goods sold.

14. [Measuring operating performance in service economy] The inventory turnover ratio measures one aspect of a firm's operating efficiency. For companies that do not have significant inventories (i.e., service industries) this measure cannot be used. In some cases, even for firms that maintain inventory, the measure is inappropriate. Examples include:

- Airlines.
- Car rental firms.
- Private hospitals.

A. Explain why the inventory turnover ratio is not a useful measure for these industries.

B. Describe possible alternative measures of operating efficiency for companies in these industries.

15. [Effect of inventory methods on contracts] The Sechne Company has entered into a number of agreements in the past year. Certain consequences of these agreements depend on the firm's accounting numbers:

- *Management compensation plan:* Management bonuses are related to a weighted average of the firm's net income and cash from operations.
- *Bond indenture:* The agreement with lenders specifies that the firm must maintain a minimum level of working capital and that dividend payments to shareholders require a minimum level of retained earnings.
- *Labor contract:* Union employees have a profit-sharing plan that pays them a share of the firm's net income in excess of a minimum level.

Sechne's corporate controller is part of management, as well as a shareholder in the company. It is his job to select the accounting methods used for financial reporting. The methods chosen will determine how the firm complies with the foregoing agreements.

Discuss how these agreements may affect the controller's choice of inventory accounting methods for Sechne.

6

ANALYSIS OF LONG-LIVED ASSETS

INTRODUCTION

**I. ACQUIRING THE ASSET:
THE CAPITALIZATION DECISION**

**CAPITALIZATION VERSUS EXPENSING:
CONCEPTUAL ISSUES**

Research and Development
Advertising Costs
Oil and Gas Wells
Lease Versus Purchase
Financial Statement Effects
Income Variability
Levels of Profitability
Cash Flow from Operations
Leverage Ratios
Need for Analytic Adjustments
Valuation Implications
Other Valuation and Economic Consequences

**CAPITALIZATION VERSUS EXPENSING:
GENERAL ISSUES**

Capitalization of Interest Costs
Intangible Assets
Patents and Copyrights
Franchises and Licenses
Brands and Trademarks

Computer Software Development Costs
Research and Development Partnerships
Goodwill

**CAPITALIZATION VERSUS EXPENSING:
INDUSTRY ISSUES**

Regulated Utilities
Accounting for Oil and Gas Exploration
SFAS 69: Disclosures for Oil and Gas Firms
*Changing from Full Cost to Successful
Efforts: Pennzoil*

**II: ACCOUNTING FOR LONG-LIVED ASSETS
OVER THEIR USEFUL LIVES**

INTRODUCTION

DEPRECIATION METHODS

Annuity or Sinking Fund Depreciation
Straight-Line Depreciation
Accelerated Depreciation Methods
*Units-of-Production and Service Hours
Methods*
Group and Composite Depreciation Methods
Depletion
Amortization
Depreciation Methods and Disclosures

Impact of Depreciation Methods on Financial Statements

Accelerated Depreciation and Taxes

Inflation and Its Impact on Depreciation

Changes in Depreciation Method

Analysis of Depreciation Disclosures: General Motors

Change to Units-of-Production Depreciation: Ratliff Drilling

ANALYSIS OF FIXED ASSET DISCLOSURES

Estimating Relative Age and Useful Lives

Estimating the Age of Assets

III: IMPAIRMENT OF LONG-LIVED ASSETS

INTRODUCTION

Impairment of Oil and Gas Properties: Pennzoil

FINANCIAL STATEMENT IMPACT OF IMPAIRMENTS

INTERNATIONAL ACCOUNTING DIFFERENCES AFFECTING LONG-LIVED ASSETS

Capitalization of Borrowing Costs

Research and Development Expenditures

Goodwill

Oil and Gas Accounting

Depreciation Methods

CONCLUDING COMMENTS

APPENDIX 6A ANALYSIS OF OIL AND GAS DISCLOSURES

Disclosure of Physical Reserve Quantities

Disclosure of Capitalized Costs

Analysis of Finding Costs

Disclosure of Present Value Data

Using Present Value Disclosures

Changes in Present Values

APPENDIX 6B RESEARCH AND DEVELOPMENT PARTNERSHIPS

Introduction

Centocor: R&D Arrangements in Practice

APPENDIX 6C ANALYSIS OF CHANGING PRICES INFORMATION

Introduction

Analysis of General Inflation

Constant Dollar Method

Advantages of Constant Dollar Method

Disadvantage of Constant Dollar Method

Current Cost Method

Disadvantages of Current Cost

Accounting Series Release 190

SFAS 33 Requirements

Problems with SFAS 33 Disclosures

Problems with Current Cost Depreciation

Adjusting Financial Statements for Changing Prices

Adjustments to Fixed Assets

Using Current Cost Asset Values

Estimating and Using Current Cost Depreciation

Using Constant Dollar Data

Concluding Remarks

INTRODUCTION

This chapter deals with the long-lived operating assets of a firm that, unlike inventory, are not held for resale. They are used by the firm in its manufacturing, sales, and administrative operations and include tangible fixed assets (plant, machinery, and office facilities) as well as intangible assets such as computer software, patents, and trademarks.

This chapter has been organized to facilitate the examination of the financial reporting and analysis issues at three distinct stages:

1. When the assets are originally acquired
2. Over their useful lives
3. When they are disposed of, or written off when impaired or at the end of their useful lives

I. ACQUIRING THE ASSET: THE CAPITALIZATION DECISION

The costs of acquiring resources that provide services over more than one operating cycle are capitalized and carried as assets on the balance sheet. All costs incurred until the asset is ready for use must be capitalized, including the invoice price, applicable sales tax, freight and insurance costs incurred delivering the equipment, and any installation costs.

In general, application of these principles is clear. However, the conceptual merits of capitalization and expensing are debatable in the case of some components of and certain categories of acquisition cost. The decision to capitalize or expense interest during construction, software development costs, research and development costs, and exploration costs for oil and gas properties depends to some extent on management choice.

The choice affects the balance sheet, income and cash flow statements, and related ratios both in the year the choice is made and over the life of the asset. Management discretion can result in smoothing or manipulation of reported income, cash flows, and other measures of financial performance. Moreover, unlike some accounting choices that reverse or "even out" over time, effects of the decision to capitalize or expense may never reverse.

Part I is devoted to the controversial issue of capitalization versus expensing of expenditures for long-lived resources. We start with an overview of the conceptual issues and a review of the implications of capitalization for financial statement analysis. The remaining sections then examine the specific components and categories of cost where capitalization practices vary.

CAPITALIZATION VERSUS EXPENSING:
CONCEPTUAL ISSUES

The Financial Accounting Standards Board (FASB), in Statement of Financial Accounting Concepts (SFAC) 6, defines[1] accounting assets as probable future economic benefits. Analytically, the concept of long-lived assets can serve various purposes, representing:

1. Initial investment outlays
2. The property or holdings of a firm that represent its "wealth"
3. One of the inputs in the firm's production function

Corresponding to each of these alternatives is a context for evaluation of the firm:

1. *Profitability analysis:* Assets represent the initial investment (ROA measures the return on the firm's assets).
2. *Solvency analysis:* Assets measure the degree of protection available to creditors.
3. *Operational analysis:* Assets measure the degree of capital intensity of a firm and are used to evaluate the firm's operating efficiency and leverage.

The total assets reported by the firm provide one measure of the total investment when analyzing management's capital allocation decision as reflected by the return on assets. For debt analysis, assets reflect the security available to protect bondholders in the event of liquidation (e.g., debt/assets ratio). Finally, assets represent components of the firm's production function in the analysis of operating efficiency.

These different contexts may require differing definitions of what constitutes an asset. For example, leased machinery may not have been included as initial investments[2] and may not be available to bondholders for protection of their loans.[3] However, leased assets should be included when measuring capital intensity even though they have not been purchased.

Accounting rules for assets, unfortunately, do not have the flexibility to satisfy all contexts. Existing asset definitions must be evaluated and adjustments sometimes made. In many cases, particularly for intangible assets, the "correct" choice may not be clear cut. Moreover, measurement problems make it impractical to record certain items as assets. A few examples are presented to illustrate these issues.

Research and Development

Companies invest in research and development (R&D) because they expect the investment to result in future profits. However, absent a discovery, all the expenditures

---

[1]See Chapter 1 for discussion of SFAC 6.

[2]This argument, for the moment, ignores the conceptual basis for and analytical significance of lease capitalization. See Chapter 8 for a discussion of those issues.

[3]A lease can, however, be a valuable asset, whether capitalized or not, that can be sold to repay creditors.

may be wasted. Further, the value of any discovery may be unrelated to the amount spent on R&D. Finally, due to its ephemeral nature, R&D is generally unacceptable to creditors as security for loans.

Prior to 1975, firms were permitted to capitalize R&D costs. Statement of Financial Accounting Standards (SFAS) 2 (1974), however, required that virtually all[4] R&D costs be expensed and the amount disclosed. In effect, assets with uncertain future economic benefits were eliminated from the balance sheet. The impact on the financial statements of firms with significant R&D was substantial, and there is some evidence of a decrease in R&D expenditures as a result of this change in accounting principle. Notwithstanding SFAS 2, R&D expenditures are clearly investments in the economic sense, albeit risky ones.

Advertising Costs

Successful advertising campaigns can reap benefits for a firm in terms of brand loyalty for many years into the future. However, as with R&D, these benefits are uncertain and difficult to measure, and hence advertising costs are expensed as incurred. Thus, even though there are potential economic benefits, an asset is not recorded because of measurement problems.

Oil and Gas Wells

Oil and gas exploration often results in a number of dry holes[5] before yielding a "gusher." Until the art of prospecting is perfected, failures will remain an integral part of successful exploration. Thus the cost of dry holes can be considered as part of the cost of drilling productive ones. The same logic applies to the relationship between R&D and successful patents and, as in the case of R&D, the value of an oil discovery is frequently unrelated to the cost of drilling. The FASB, in SFAS 19, required (consistent with its treatment of R&D) that these costs be expensed. Under current accounting practice,[6] however, firms have the option of capitalizing the cost of dry holes (full cost method) or expensing them as they occur (successful efforts method). Although from the point of view of creditors, drilling costs per se offer no protection,[7] from an ROA perspective they are clearly investments on which a return must be earned.

Lease Versus Purchase

Consider two firms engaged in the same line of business. One buys the required assets and the other leases (rents) the same assets. Only the former has made a capital

---

[4]The main exception to the rule is when R&D is performed on a contract basis for unrelated entities. In this case the R&D is carried as an asset (similar to inventory) until completion of the contract. In addition, certain government-regulated entities can capitalize R&D expenses if they are deemed to be recoverable from future revenues. SFAS 71 (1982) governs the accounting for regulated enterprises.

[5]Dry holes and other technical terms used in the material on oil and gas exploration are defined in the glossary.

[6]Current practice is discussed in greater detail in a later section and Appendix 6-A to this chapter.

[7]Actual oil and gas reserves are frequently used to collaterize lending. It is the reserves, however, not the incurred costs, that have value.

investment and, from the creditor perspective, owns the assets. The other firm owns only the lease rights.

In economic terms, however, the firms are using the same mix of capital and labor. In this sense the firms are identical, and measurement of their return on assets and efficiency of operations should be made on a comparable basis, regardless of the differing form of ownership. The ownership costs should be similar, with total lease payments over the lease term approximating the acquisition and financing costs. The accounting and analysis of leases are covered in Chapter 8. Here we simply note that the form of ownership of an asset can greatly affect financial statement presentation even though operationally the firms are essentially identical.

The preceding examples illustrated some of the issues relevant to the capitalization versus expensing decision. We examine the impacts on reported financial performance next, with an emphasis on the critical implications for financial analysis.

Financial Statement Effects

Box 6-1 demonstrates, using a simple illustration, the effects of the capitalize versus expense choice on selected financial variables of two growing firms as they approach maturity ("steady state"). The following patterns emerge:

Income Variability:

Firms that capitalize costs and depreciate them over time will show "smoother" patterns of reported income (Figure 6-2). Firms that expense costs as incurred will tend to have greater variance in reported income. The variability of changes in income will tend to dampen as the firm reaches "steady state" (Figure 6-3A) and will be lower for larger firms (or those with other sources of income, Figure 6-3B).

BOX 6-1

Comparison of Financial Statement Effects: Capitalization Versus Expensing

For our illustration we consider two hypothetical firms, each with an asset base of $1000 on which it earns $150, which begin to grow. Growth requires the acquisition of an "asset," which has a three-year life. Each asset costs $100 and generates cash flows of $50 per year. The pattern of growth* (the number of assets acquired each year and the replacement of old assets) is illustrated in Figure 6-1.

Growth is assumed to continue for 15 years after which maturity is reached, and all subsequent acquisitions are for replacement only. We further assume that the asset cost may be capitalized or expensed at the discretion of management under the provisions of generally accepted accounting principles (GAAP). One firm capitalizes the acquisition cost; the other expenses it. The firms are otherwise operationally identical. Their reported income, cash flow from operations, and related ratios, however, will differ markedly.

Figure 6-2 compares the pattern of reported income. The "expensing" firm exhibits a fluctuating pattern of income growth through maturity, although the volatility (Figure 6-3A) dampens in later years as the firm becomes larger. The "capitalizing" firm, on the other hand, exhibits a smooth pattern of income growth. Similarly, for firms that are initially larger† (Figure 6-3B, based on the same growth pattern but assuming an opening asset base of $2000, earning $300), the fluctuations are not as great throughout the growth and maturity cycle because of the larger base.

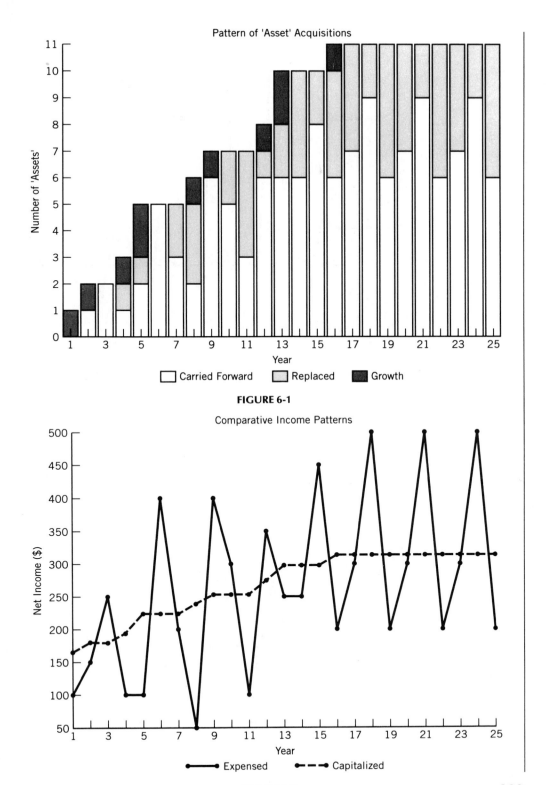

FIGURE 6-1

FIGURE 6-2

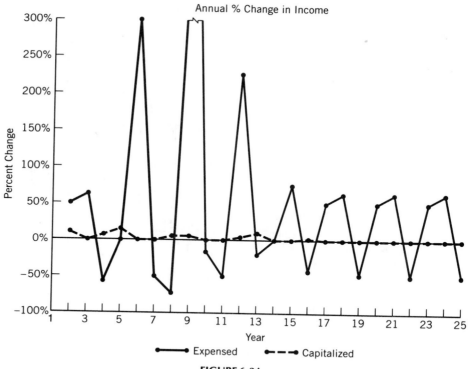

Annual % Change in Income

FIGURE 6-3A

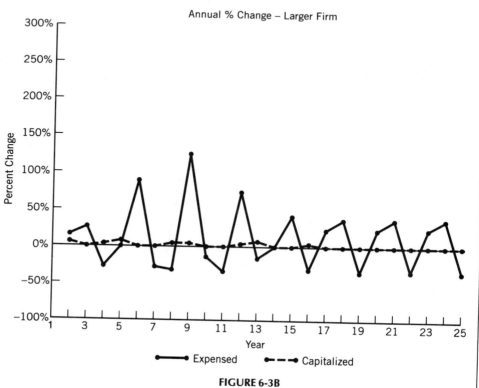

Annual % Change – Larger Firm

FIGURE 6-3B

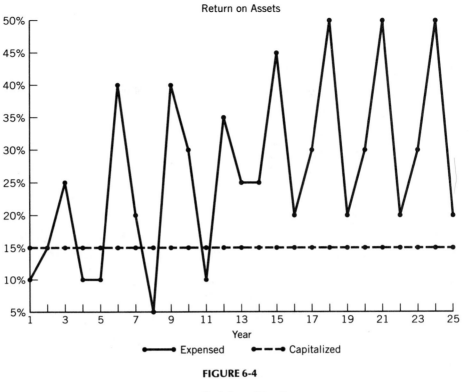

FIGURE 6-4

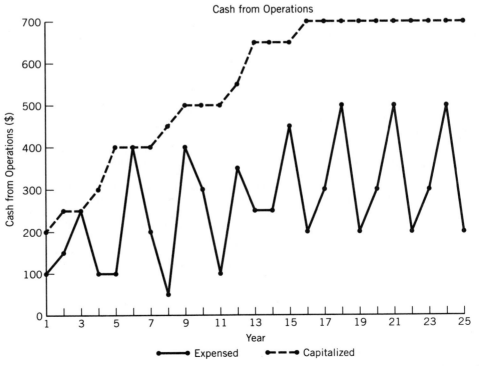

FIGURE 6-5

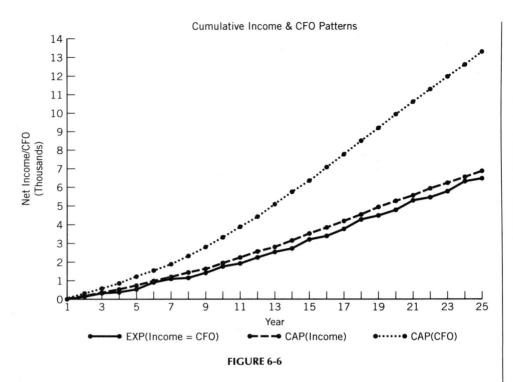

FIGURE 6-6

Figure 6-4 compares the return on assets ratio for the two firms. The choice of accounting method affects both the numerator and denominator of the ROA. The "expensing" firm, having fewer recorded assets, will have a smaller denominator, increasing its reported ROA. The numerator (earnings) is volatile, so that sometimes ROA increases but at other times decreases. At the early stage of growth, the "expensing" firm's ROA gyrates about that of the capitalizing firm but will initially tend to be lower. As the "expensing" firm grows larger, the fluctuations persist, but its ROA is higher because the effect of lower reported assets on the denominator dominates.

Figure 6-5 compares reported cash from operations for the capitalizing and expensing firms. The capitalizing firm always shows higher cash from operations; the difference increases and does not reverse over the life of the asset (see Figure 6-6).

---

*A variable growth rate is used in the illustration because it is more descriptive of reality (it has greater external validity). Any growth rate, other than a perfectly constant one, will create a similar pattern of differences between a capitalizing and expensing firm. At maturity or steady state, a constant growth rate generates identical (and constant) total expense for both firms. (ROA and cash flow from operations would still differ.)

†The term "larger" does not necessarily relate only to absolute size. It can also denote that the firm engages in other activities that offset the variability of the costs that are expensed.

Levels of Profitability:

The effects on profitability depend on how profit is measured. As the discussion on income variability implies, the effect on reported profits or return on sales depends on the actual pattern of expenditures. On the other hand, because expensing firms show lower assets (and equity) on the balance sheet, as the firm grows larger, their ROA/ROE measures are higher (Figure 6-4) when compared to firms that capitalize costs.

Cash Flow from Operations (CFO):

Reported net cash flow, unlike net income, should be immune to the choice of accounting alternatives.[8] However, the capitalization versus expensing decision has a significant impact on the components of cash flow—particularly CFO. As discussed in Chapter 2, the cash expenditure for capitalized assets is classified as investing cash flow and never flows through CFO.[9] Firms choosing to expense these outlays, however, treat the expenditures as components of CFO. Thus, CFO will always be higher for the capitalizing firm (Figure 6-5), and the cumulative difference (rather than reversing) will increase over time (Figure 6-6).

Leverage Ratios:

Expensing firms report lower assets and equity balances.[10] As a result, debt-to-equity and debt-to-assets solvency ratios will appear worse for expensing firms as compared to firms that capitalize the same costs.

Need for Analytic Adjustments

These differences are largely cosmetic and sometimes discretionary. Analysts must adjust reported numbers to facilitate analysis and comparisons. The pharmaceutical industry, for example, reports the highest ROA of all U.S. industries. Some suggest that this reflects a higher return for the risks inherent in R&D.[11] Others contend that the industry is guilty of taking advantage of people's misfortunes. To some degree, however, the high drug industry return on assets may be a result of the accounting method used for R&D. The fact that such costs must be expensed results in understatement of the denominator of the ROA measure, investment. Capitalizing R&D costs (treating them as an investment) might give a more accurate measure of ROA. Assets would increase and, even though net income might increase, the result may be to decrease ROA, bringing it closer to that of other industries. The data on Merck in Exhibit

---

[8]Ignoring any tax effects, of course.

[9]The ratio cash from operations/capital expenditures measures the degree to which internally generated funds of the firm finance the replacement of productive capacity and expansion. *Free cash flow,* the excess cash from operations, would be identical for both firms and would equal the CFO for the expensing firm, assuming that depreciation is also equal to the cost of replacing "used up" capacity that is equal to capital expenditures. (This equality also assumes that, as the firm is not growing, no investment in working capital is required.)

[10]These effects are not shown directly in Box 6-1. However, they can be deduced from the discussion of the return-on-investment (ROA/ROE) measures.

[11]Generally, industries with heavy research and development costs report higher ROAs. The arguments and adjustments put forth for Merck can be extended to other industries as well.

EXHIBIT 6-1. MERCK & CO.
Recomputation of Profitability Ratios Assuming Capitalization of R&D Expenditures, 1986–1990

Merck's income and total assets are recalculated assuming that R&D is capitalized and amortized over three-, five-, or seven-year periods.* Note that return on sales increases as the length of the amortization period increases. The effect on return on assets is the opposite as the denominator effect (higher assets) overwhelms the numerator effect (higher income). Thus ROA *decreases* with longer amortization periods.†

Return on Sales

Year	R&D Expensed as Reported	R&D Capitalized and Amortized over		
		3 Years	5 Years	7 Years
1986	16.4%	16.8%	17.1%	17.5%
1987	21.9	22.6	23.0	23.4
1988	29.2	30.1	30.6	31.0
1989	36.2	37.0	37.7	38.1
1990	43.1	43.9	44.7	45.3

Return on Assets

Year	R&D Expensed as Reported	R&D Capitalized and Amortized over		
		3 Years	5 Years	7 Years
1986	13.5%	12.7%	12.1%	11.7%
1987	16.8	15.8	15.0	14.4
1988	20.4	19.1	18.1	17.3
1989	23.2	21.4	20.2	19.3
1990	24.1	22.2	20.9	20.0

*Using five-year amortization for example, for 1990, add back to income the R&D expense for that year but subtract one-fifth of the sum of 1986 through 1990 R&D expenditures. Because Merck's R&D is growing, the net effect is to raise income. Assets are adjusted by adding four-fifths of 1990 R&D, three-fifths of 1989 R&D, two-fifths of 1988 R&D, and one-fifth of 1987 R&D to total assets. For simplicity, we ignore tax effects, which would reduce the impact of capitalization on reported income.

†One can also view these results as the disaggregation of ROA into return on sales and asset turnover. Although return on sales increases, the increased asset base with no change in sales reduces asset turnover.

Source: Based on R&D Expenditures reported in 1986–1990.

6-1 illustrate this point. Capitalizing R&D expenditures results in profitability, as measured by return on sales, increasing by up to 2 percentage points.[12] ROA, however, declines by up to 4 percentage points.

This example illustrates the analytic conversion of an "expense" to an "asset." At times, it may be more appropriate to go the other way—that is, convert a capitalized item to an expense.[13] Adjustment may be needed simply for comparative purposes, that is, to put two firms on the same footing.

[12]Although not illustrated, solvency ratios for Merck would also be improved as a result of the capitalization of R&D expense.

[13]Capitalized interest, discussed in a later section, is an example of such an adjustment.

Such adjustments may be required for reasons other than differences in accounting procedures. Firms in the same industry may vary in the extent to which they own their assets or lease them. Airlines, for example, may buy or lease airplanes. Similarly, retail store chains may differ in their policy of buying or leasing store space. These choices are conceptually similar to the (accounting) choice of capitalizing or expensing. Reported ROA numbers will be widely disparate; adjustments are required to achieve comparability.

Valuation Implications

The rationale for the expensing of expenditures for R&D and advertising is that it is difficult, if not impossible, to determine the future benefits associated with the expenditure. That may be true, but it does not follow that, for valuation purposes, these expenditures should be treated in the same way as other operating outflows. An outflow that is truly an expense reduces wealth. If the outflow will generate future cash flow, then it should not reduce wealth; it may actually increase it.

Chapter 15 discusses two types of valuation models: earnings based and asset based. Box 6-2 discusses how the capitalization decision affects these valuation models and presents empirical evidence that the market does not treat outflows in categories such as R&D, advertising, and oil and gas wells strictly as expenses but recognizes their asset characteristics.

BOX 6-2
Capitalization and Valuation

Consider the following simplified valuation model:

$$\text{Value} = p \times \text{Net inflows}$$

The model can be used to represent a (constant) discounted earnings model where net inflows represent revenue and expense flows and the coefficient p is simply the price/earnings (P/E) ratio. Disaggregating the net inflows into inflows and outflows yields

$$\text{Value} = p \times \text{Inflows} - p \times \text{Expense outflows} + b \times \text{Asset outflows}$$

where the asset outflows represent expenditures for such categories as R&D. If these outflows are actually expenses, then $b = -p$.

From a valuation perspective, the difference between asset and expense outflows should be whether the associated outflow has expected future benefits. An expense benefits only the period of occurrence, and the outlay reduces value by $-p$ times the outflow.* An asset outflow benefits future periods, and, in that case, we would not expect the coefficient p to be negative.† The closer b is to $-p$, the more the item in question can be considered an expense.

Bublitz and Ettredge (1989) compared the extent to which unexpected changes in advertising, R&D, and other expenses are valued by the market. Advertising was included because, like R&D, it is expected to provide benefits for more than one period, albeit for a shorter term. Thus they expected the coefficient for R&D to be larger (more positive) than the coefficient for advertising, with both of them being larger than the coefficient for other expenses. The results were mixed, but on balance they found "the evidence is consistent with a market assessment that advertising is short-lived while R&D is long-lived."‡

With respect to R&D, their results were consistent with Hirschey and Weygandt (1985) who found that the market valuation of R&D implies that it is an asset outflow. Hirschey and Weygandt also found that advertising had characteristics similar to a long-lived asset.

The valuation here uses a discounted earnings–based perspective. In the context of valuing R&D partnerships, Shevlin (1991) used an asset-based valuation model. In such a model, the value of the firm is defined as

$$\textbf{Value} = \textbf{Assets} - \textbf{Liabilities}$$

By including the expenditures for R&D as part of assets, Shevlin§ found that they contributed to value indicating that the market viewed these expenditures as assets. Moreover, the weighting given these expenditures was larger than that for other assets, indicating that the market is cognizant that the potential benefit from these expenditures is considerably greater than their book value.

Using a sample of oil and gas companies, Harris and Ohlson (1987) found that the market distinguished between successful efforts and full cost companies in a rational fashion. Book values of full cost companies were given less weight than were those of successful efforts companies. This by itself does not mean that one method is better than the other. It is only a reflection of one carrying perhaps "too many" assets and the other "too few." However, they did find that successful efforts book values have greater explanatory power than full cost book values, which, they contend, is consistent with a survey that indicated that analysts prefer successful efforts.‖

---

*The current benefits are reflected in the inflows.

†The asset outflows representing future benefits can be thought of as a growth component. In Chapter 15, we show that for a firm with growth, its value can be expressed as

$$\textbf{Value} = \frac{\textbf{E}}{\textbf{r}} + \left[\frac{1}{r}\left(\frac{r^* - r}{r - ar^*}\right)\right]\textbf{aE}$$

where E is earnings, r is the appropriate discount rate, r^* is the amount the firm earns on its investment, and aE is the amount the firm reinvests. In our example, $p = 1/r$ and b is the coefficient of the asset investment aE. That is, b is equal to the term in brackets. On the margin, it may be zero (if $r^* = r$) as the firm undertakes zero or break-even net present value investments.

‡Bruce Bublitz and Michael Ettredge, "The Information in Discretionary Outlays: Advertising, Research and Development," *The Accounting Review* (January 1989), pp. 108–124

§As will be noted later, in the section on R&D partnerships, Shevlin's valuation model is also interesting in that it viewed the R&D partnership in the context of an option pricing model.

‖Further discussion of valuation in the context of oil and gas accounting is provided later in the chapter, in the section on oil and gas accounting.

Other Valuation and Economic Consequences

Earlier we noted that differences in accounting methods are cosmetic. However, it must be recognized (in line with the "positive theory" approach[14]) that these differences can have real consequences. These may exist independently or create a form of chain reaction.

[14]See Chapter 4.

First, a firm's borrowing ability may be curtailed by unfavorable profitability or leverage ratios resulting from use of a particular accounting method. Second, to the extent that these ratios are affected by the level of a firm's expenditures for R&D, for example, a firm may curtail such expenditures, effectively scaling down its level of operations. Finally, whether or not managers actually reduce such expenditures, the fact that the market perceives such a possibility can give rise to negative market reaction.

Mandated accounting changes is one area where such effects can be examined. Such changes provide a "laboratory" environment permitting before and after comparisons. Box 6-3 reviews empirical evidence regarding mandated accounting changes for R&D and oil and gas accounting.

The research results indicate that even if an accounting change has no direct economic impact, the effects of the change on reported income can have real effects, such as the curtailment of expenditures and negative market reaction. Indirect effects may also be due to debt covenant constraints or the influence on management compensation contracts. In a similar vein, choices of accounting method may be motivated by variations in firm characteristics. Studies of this phenomenon are discussed in greater detail later, in the section on the oil and gas industry.

Clearly, a great deal of care must be exercised when assessing financial performance given management discretion as to the capitalize versus expense decision. The remainder of Part I is devoted to particular areas where this problem occurs. Some areas are pervasive and cut across all industries; others are industry specific.

BOX 6-3
Mandated Accounting Changes Economic
Consequences and Market Reaction

The capitalization versus expense issue has proved a fruitful area of empirical research. The issues examined provide interesting parallels between R&D and oil and gas accounting. In both cases mandated accounting changes favored expensing over capitalization (albeit in one case the standard was suspended). Proponents of capitalization argued that, in each case, the accounting change would lead to a reduction of risk-taking activities as the cost of risk taking would increase. Furthermore, preferences were related in a systematic fashion to firm characteristics. The empirical issues examined in this section are

- Economic consequences of mandated changes—impact on management behavior.
- Market reaction to mandated accounting changes.

Economic Consequences: Impact on Management Behavior

Any adverse effect of expensing R&D or exploration costs should be directly related to the level of expenditures on these items. Firms responding to the FASB Exposure Draft prior to SFAS 2 contended that the expensing requirement of the new standard would lead to a cutback in the level of R&D expenditures. Similar claims were made with respect to the provisions of SFAS 19 as it was asserted that the mandated switch to successful efforts accounting would reduce exploration and development expenditures. These claims played a major role in the eventual suspension of SFAS 19.

The new standards primarily affected smaller firms, as in both cases, larger firms generally used the expensing method.* Smaller companies feared that markets (at least private lenders) would focus on the effects on reported income (both amounts and variability). The change would thus impair their ability to raise capital.

As SFAS 19 was never implemented, the validity of these claims could not be verified. However, for SFAS 2, a number of studies attempted to verify whether or not the new standard curtailed R&D.

After a survey of chief financial officers of 131 companies engaged in R&D, Horwitz and Kolodny (1980) reported that

> In response to the question: "Do you believe that small firms reduced planned R&D expenditures as a consequence of SFAS 2?" 66.7 percent of firms with sales less than $10 million and 58.9 percent of firms with sales greater than $10 million answered affirmatively or possibly.†

Using a sample of small high-technology firms, they then found evidence that the actual levels of R&D expenditures dropped following the introduction of SFAS 2. In contrast, Dukes, Dyckman, and Elliott (1980), whose sample consisted of larger companies, found no evidence of curtailment of R&D subsequent to the adoption of SFAS 2.

In a subsequent study Elliott, Richardson, Dyckman and Dukes (1984) confirmed the finding that small companies that had previously capitalized R&D curtailed R&D expenditures after the issuance of SFAS 2. However, they noted that the downward trend in R&D expenditures for these companies had already begun years prior to the issuance of SFAS 2. Comparing the operating performance of the "capitalizers" with a control sample of firms that had always expensed R&D, they found that the operating performance of the "capitalizers" was worse. They conjectured that financial difficulties, rather than the accounting change, may have caused the curtailment of R&D. In fact, it could be argued that the original decision to capitalize R&D by these firms may have been motivated by an effort to improve reported financial performance in the face of financial stress.

Selto and Clouse (1985) approached the issue from a different perspective. They argued that firms would be likely to anticipate the effects of an accounting change such as SFAS 2 and adapt to it. Thus, if divisional managers would be motivated to reduce R&D expenditures because of the effect on their compensation (through earnings-based compensation plans), firms would adjust their compensation plans accordingly or, alternatively, take steps to centralize the R&D decision-making process. They found that although not all firms made such changes, those that did were the ones most likely to be affected by the provisions of SFAS 2. Thus, to the extent accounting changes have economic consequences, they may be manifested internally rather than externally.

Market Reaction

Vigeland (1981) found no market reaction to the mandated accounting change for R&D expenditures. There is little controversy with respect to this mandated accounting change. This is not true with respect to the mandated change(s) affecting accounting for oil and gas exploration. This issue spawned a cottage industry of research with studies examining the reaction to the announcement of the

1. SFAS 19 Exposure draft.
2. SFAS 19.
3. Accounting Series Release (ASR) 253, issued by the SEC, which suspended SFAS 19.

The research approach examined whether firms using the full cost method (FC) had negative (positive) returns when SFAS 19 (ASR 253) was announced. Generally negative reaction was found around the time of the announcement of the SFAS 19 Exposure Draft. Not everyone, however, agreed with its significance. Collins and Dent (1979) and Lev (1979) claimed that the results were statistically significant, whereas Dyckman and Smith (1979) argued that the market reaction was not statistically different from that experienced by firms using successful efforts (SE). The results were also found to be sensitive to the exact time period examined. In addition, at the time of the Exposure Draft announcement, there was "confounding" news affecting the oil industry. Thus, even when negative market reaction was found, its cause was not clear.

With respect to the ASR 253 announcement, Collins, Rozeff, and Salatka (1982), using a "reversal" methodology, compared the market reaction at the time the SFAS 19 Exposure Draft was announced with the reaction experienced when ASR 253 was announced. They found that there was a significant negative correlation for the FC firms; that is, negative reaction to the first announcement was followed by positive reaction to the subsequent (suspension) announcement.

These studies tested market reaction without considering any factors that might cause differential market reactions across firms due to differential impacts on income and equity. Such factors might include firm size, the relative importance of exploration, firm leverage, and the existence of debt covenants and accounting-based management compensation schemes. Collins, Rozeff, and Dhaliwal (1981) and Lys (1984) tested for such factors with some success. Collins and coworkers, for example, found that the degree of market reaction was related to (1) the size of the reduction in owner's equity that would result from SFAS 19, (2) the existence of debt convenants, and (3) management compensation schemes based on reported income.

*See Box 6-1 for discussion of the differential impact of the capitalize versus expense decision on large and small firms.

†Bertrand N. Horwitz and Richard Kolodny, "The Economic Effects of Involuntary Uniformity in the Financial Reporting of R&D Expenditures," *Journal of Accounting Research* (Supplement 1980), pp. 38–74.

CAPITALIZATION VERSUS EXPENSING: GENERAL ISSUES

Capitalization of Interest Costs

Companies often construct assets, such as new operating facilities, for their own use and capitalize costs incurred during construction until the assets are ready to be placed in service. When a company borrows to finance construction or has debt in its capital structure, the question arises as to whether interest cost should be capitalized or expensed.

SFAS 34 (1979) requires capitalization of such interest costs. When a specific borrowing is associated with the construction, the interest cost incurred on that borrowing is capitalized. If no specific borrowing is identifiable, the interest on the most recent debt (up to the amount invested in the project) is capitalized. In the absence of debt, there is no capitalization. SFAS 34 requires disclosure of the amount of interest capitalized. In October 1992, the International Accounting Standards Committee (IASC) approved IAS 23, Capitalization of Borrowing Costs, wherein expensing all borrowing costs is considered the benchmark treatment but also allowing capitalization of interest.

The argument for interest capitalization is that the cost of a self-constructed asset should be identical to the cost of one purchased after completion. In the latter case, the purchase price would presumably include the financing costs of the seller. Capitalization of interest for self-constructed assets, it is argued, replicates this process.

On the other hand, there are strong arguments against the capitalization of interest in general and against SFAS 34 in particular. On a conceptual level, one can argue that interest, as a financing cost, is different from the other costs of getting the asset ready for service. It results from a financing decision rather than an operating decision.

This argument is strengthened by the arbitrary nature of SFAS 34. Interest is capitalized only for selected assets and then only if the firm is leveraged. Capitalization of interest is required even if the debt was not incurred directly for the project in question. The rationale for this is that funds not required for construction could have been used to repay this debt. But the very same argument can be made for internally generated funds of a debt-free firm. The funds used could have otherwise been invested in interest-bearing securities and the forgone interest income viewed as part of the cost of the asset. Yet capitalization is prohibited in this case.

The result is that the carrying amount of a self-constructed asset is a function of the firm's financing decisions. It seems illogical that two identical assets, one financed by external funds and the other by internally available funds, should be carried at different costs. Further, the capitalization of interest creates a difference between earnings and cash flow.

For purposes of analysis, therefore, any capitalized interest should be removed from fixed assets and added to interest expense, lowering net income.

Capitalized interest also distorts the classification of cash flows. Interest capitalized as part of fixed assets will never be reported as cash from operations,[15] but as an investment outflow. To remedy this, the amount of interest capitalized should be added back to cash for investment and subtracted from CFO to achieve comparability with firms that do not capitalize interest. The cash flows for capitalized interest are then included with other interest payments.[16] The adjustment tends to be small for investment cash flow but more significant for interest expense and net income.

More important, the interest coverage ratio should be calculated with capitalized interest included in interest expense. Otherwise it will be distorted. Unfortunately, while the amount of interest capitalized in the current year must be disclosed, the amortization of previously capitalized interest (included in the fixed asset account) is usually not disclosed. Thus a completely accurate computation of interest expense assuming no capitalization may not always be possible.

The SFAS 95 requirement that *interest paid* be disclosed, makes it possible to compute interest coverage accurately (see Chapter 3) on a cash flow basis. However, as interest paid differs from interest expense by factors (mainly accruals) in addition to capitalization, this disclosure does not generally permit analysts to "undo" the capitalization of interest.[17]

---

[15]The effect of capitalization on cash from operations is discussed in Chapter 2. Figure 6-6 illustrates this.

[16]These interest payments would be treated as a deduction from cash from operations, consistent with SFAS 95. Alternatively, as we argue in Chapter 2, interest payments should be considered financing cash flows and thus excluded from any definition of free cash flow.

[17]If accruals such as interest payable are known, then such adjustment is possible.

One company that does disclose the amortization of capitalized interest is Corning Glass. In its *1990 Annual Report* the company reconciles interest expense to interest incurred (the amount that would be expensed if no interest was capitalized) as follows:

	December 31 ($ millions)		
	---	---	---
	1988	1989	1990
Interest incurred	$43.9	$ 53.0	$ 58.6
Interest capitalized	(7.5)	(13.0)	(10.5)
Amortization	4.6	4.5	5.9
Interest expense (net)	$41.0	$ 44.5	$ 54.0

Source: Corning Glass, *1990 Annual Report*.

While the impact of capitalized interest on Corning is not significant, this illustrates the principle involved. Interest incurred, whenever possible, should be substituted for interest expense in calculations calling for interest.

Intangible Assets

The capitalize versus expense issue is especially difficult when applied to such intangible resources and rights as patents, copyrights, licenses, franchises, brand names, goodwill, and increasingly the "look and feel" of computer software. Such intangibles sometimes constitute a substantial portion of the value of a firm. The variations in legal protection available for intellectual property and other intangible assets in many countries also makes assessments of value more difficult than for tangible assets. A brief discussion of capitalization is provided here; amortization is explained in Part II.

Patents and Copyrights

All costs incurred in developing patents and copyrights are expensed in conformity with the treatment of R&D costs. Only the legal fees incurred in registering internally developed patents and copyrights can be capitalized. The full acquisition cost is capitalized when such assets are purchased from other entities.

Patents have a legal life of 17 years under U.S. patent law; copyrights have a legal life of 50 years beyond the creator's life. However, these periods should be viewed as upper limits. Successful patented products invite competition and the development of comparable or improved products that can diminish the value of the patent or make it obsolete. In addition, there is often a gap between the time that a patent is registered and the time the product comes to market.

In the pharmaceutical industry, for example, even after a patent is registered, the product cannot be marketed until it obtains Food and Drug Administration approval. This process of approval takes, on average, five years.[18] An important consideration when analyzing companies and industries that are heavily dependent on patented or

---

[18]See, for example, "Drugmakers Under Attack," *Fortune*, July 29, 1991.

proprietary products is the remaining legal life of patents on existing products and the number of patents in the "pipeline."

Franchises and Licenses

Companies often sell the right to use their products, processes, management expertise, or their name to others for some negotiated time period or market. The franchisee or licensee can capitalize the cost of purchasing these rights.

Brands and Trademarks

The cost of acquiring brands and trademarks in arm's-length transactions can be capitalized. However, as in the case of other intangibles, U.S. GAAP limit the recognition of costs of brands or trademarks created by the firm. Companies in a few countries, notably, the United Kingdom and Australia, may report the value of brand names, whether created or purchased, as balance sheet assets.

Computer Software Development Costs

The growing proliferation of computer software companies in the 1980s led to the issuance of SFAS 86 (1985) to address the accounting for costs involved in the development of computer software. In line with the reporting requirements for R&D costs, SFAS 86 requires that all costs incurred in establishing the technological and/or economic feasibility of the software to be viewed as R&D costs and expensed as incurred.[19] Once economic feasibility has been established, subsequent costs are capitalized as part of product inventory and amortized based on product revenues or on a straight-line basis.

As external analysts, it is impossible to compare the capitalization decisions made by different companies. However, the SFAS 86 disclosures can be used to examine the impact of capitalization and to adjust reported income accordingly. For example, the following data were obtained from IBM's *1990 Annual Report:*

	December 31 ($ millions)		
	1989	1990	Change
Capitalized software costs (gross)	$ 8117	$ 9972	$ 1855
Accumulated amortization	(4824)	(5873)	(1049)
Capitalized software costs (net)	$ 3293	$ 4099	$ 806

Source: IBM, 1990 Annual Report.

[19]Notwithstanding the foregoing, for analytic purposes these costs are clearly indicative of initial investment outlays and should be so treated in profitability analysis.

Capitalized software (net) at December 31, 1990, is quite significant for IBM, accounting for 4.7% of total assets and 9.6% of stockholders' equity.

While the amortization of capitalized software cost is not broken out in IBM's income statement, the statement of cash flows does reveal for the year ended December 31, 1990,

Amortization of software*	$(1086) million
Investment in software	1892
Net increase in 1990	$806 million

*Notice that 1990 amortization does not equal the change in accumulated amortization. Also, 1990 investment does not equal the change in gross capitalized software. The difference in both cases ($37 million) probably represents the "retirement" of fully amortized software cost.

Source: IBM, 1990 Annual Report

These data can be used to calculate the effect of capitalizing software costs on IBM's reported earnings. If all costs had been expensed, pretax income would have been reduced by $806 million (1990 net increase) as the expensing of current year cost would be partly offset by the elimination of the amortization of past cost. Applying a 34% tax rate results in a change in net income of $532 million [806 × (1 − 0.34)] or $0.92 per share. As IBM earned $10.51 per share in 1990, expensing all software cost would have reduced reported income by 8.8%.

These disclosures also illustrate the impact of capitalization on reported cash flows. For 1990, IBM reported its investment in software as an *investing cash flow*. If the software costs had been expensed, they would have reduced IBM's *operating cash flow*. The capitalization of software development costs, therefore, increased IBM's reported CFO by $1892 million, the actual 1990 expenditures, as compared with CFO had those costs been expensed.

Research and Development Partnerships

SFAS 2 does not permit the capitalization of research and development costs. Companies, however, have found ways to defer the recognition of such costs. One method is the research and development partnership. These arrangements are discussed in Appendix 6-B.

Goodwill

The difference between the cost of an acquired firm and the fair market value of its assets is regarded as an intangible asset, goodwill. It represents the amount paid for the acquired firm's ability to earn excess profits or value that cannot be assigned to tangible assets like property. U.S. GAAP limit the recognition of goodwill to cases where it is acquired in purchase method transactions. (See Chapter 12.)

CAPITALIZATION VERSUS EXPENSING: INDUSTRY ISSUES

Regulated Utilities

Prior to the issuance of SFAS 34, almost all public utilities capitalized interest on construction work in progress. In fact, utilities tend to capitalize outflows rather than expense them. One reason for this behavior is that accounting rules have direct economic impact for utilities. Rates charged to their customers are to a great extent a function of accounting generated numbers.[20]

Regulators allow utilities to earn profits equal to a specified "allowable" rate of return on assets (rate base). Adding expenses to this allowable profit yields the rates they can charge their customers. Revenues are derived as follows:

$$\textbf{Revenues} = \textbf{Expenses} + (\textbf{Rate of return} \times \textbf{Rate base})$$

Using interest for a self-constructed asset as an example, Exhibit 6-2 shows the effects of the capitalization versus expense choice on a utility's revenues.[21] Expensing increases revenue immediately as the interest expense is recovered in the year incurred. Capitalizing results in the expense being recouped over time as depreciation of the additional "fixed asset." However, the total allowable profit is increased due to the fact that the asset base has been increased. Hence, although revenues are deferred, the total amount collected over the life of the asset is greater. As the average life of utility fixed assets (mainly generating plants) is quite long, the incentive to capitalize costs in fixed assets (increasing the rate base) is powerful.

In this example, the utility increases total revenues by $3000 over the five-year life of the asset by capitalizing $5000 of interest. The cause of the $3000 differential is that the utility not only recovers the $5000 capitalized but earns a return on the capitalized interest; that is, 12% $\times$ $5000 = $600 $\times$ 5 years = $3000. The net result of the trade-off between getting less revenue early but more total revenue over time depends on the utility's cost of capital. In our example, as long as the appropriate discount rate is less than 30%, it pays to capitalize the interest.[22]

It is interesting to note that the argument for capitalization is often one of fairness to customers, as capitalized costs are spread over time, in contrast to expensing, which would result in an immediate rate increase to ratepayers. As current customers do not (yet) benefit from investments in capacity growth, they should not bear the cost. This logic is also appealing to regulators who prefer to defer rate increases to future time

---

[20]For this reason, virtually all regulators that set rates also mandate the accounting principles followed by the companies that they regulate. This has given rise to so-called RAP (regulated accounting principles), which may differ materially from GAAP.

[21]The assumptions in Exhibit 6-2 are meant to be illustrative and were chosen for simplicity. Other bases (e.g., net assets) would give similar results.

[22]The differential cash flows are year 1, ($3400); year 2, $1600; year 3, $1600; year 4, $1600; year 5, $1600. This cash flow stream has a positive net present value at interest rates below (approximately) 30%.

EXHIBIT 6-2
Effect of Capitalization of Interest on a Utility's Revenue

Assumptions: Rate of return allowed on assets is 12%.
Cost of self-constructed asset is $100,000.
Asset has a 5-year useful life.
Interest rate on debt is 10%.
$5000 of first year interest is capitalizable.
Utility has no expenses other than depreciation and interest.

(A): Effects of Expensing

Asset base = $100,000

Allowable profit = 12% × $100,000 = $12,000

Year	Depreciation	Interest	Total Expense	Allowable Profit	Revenues
1	$ 20,000	$10,000	$ 30,000	$12,000	$ 42,000
2	20,000	10,000	30,000	12,000	42,000
3	20,000	10,000	30,000	12,000	42,000
4	20,000	10,000	30,000	12,000	42,000
5	20,000	10,000	30,000	12,000	42,000
Total	$100,000	$50,000	$150,000	$60,000	$210,000

(B): Effects of Capitalization

Asset base = $105,000

Allowable profit = 12% × $105,000 = $12,600

Year	Depreciation	Interest	Total Expense	Allowable Profit	Revenues
1	$ 21,000	$ 5,000	$ 26,000	$12,600	$ 38,600
2	21,000	10,000	31,000	12,600	43,600
3	21,000	10,000	31,000	12,600	43,600
4	21,000	10,000	31,000	12,600	43,600
5	21,000	10,000	31,000	12,600	43,600
Total	$105,000	$45,000	$150,000	$63,000	$213,000

periods. Logic and fairness aside, utilities have a direct economic incentive to capitalize, as our illustration shows.[23]

[23]This discussion assumes that the capitalized interest will, in fact be recovered from future revenues. In practice, "regulatory lag" often results in actual rates of return below the "allowable" rate of return. In addition, by capitalizing interest the recovery of that interest is delayed to a later period and thus the current period cash flow is reduced. For these reasons some utilities have successfully petitioned regulators to allow some portion of the interest on construction in progress to be recovered currently (expensed) rather than capitalized.

Accounting for Oil and Gas Exploration

Oil and gas accounting was one of the most controversial reporting issues in the late 1970s and early 1980s. In 1977, the FASB issued SFAS 19 requiring all firms to use *successful efforts* (SE) accounting, that is, expense all dry hole costs. Like the FASB's R&D reporting standard, this rule was conservative and eliminated assets with uncertain future benefits from the balance sheet. With the United States in the midst of an oil crisis, Congress and the Securities and Exchange Commission (SEC), fearing that the adoption of this rule would result in the curtailment of oil exploration (especially by smaller companies), forced the FASB to suspend SFAS 19 (SFAS 25, 1979). The SEC (ASR 253, 1978) permitted public companies to use either SE or full cost (FC) methods of accounting. The latter permits the capitalization of dry hole costs.

Exhibit 6-3 illustrates the difference between the SE[24] and FC methods of accounting for a productive oil well.

The choice of accounting method for oil and gas exploration has a significant impact on all financial statements and on many ratios as well. The balance sheet carrying amount of reserves, $4000, is higher under the FC method because of the inclusion of the cost of dry holes ($3000). The SE firm would carry its reserves at only $1000.

The reported profitability (both levels and trends over time) of production is also affected. The SE firm will show a net loss of $250 in year 1 but net income of $2750 per year for years 2 through 4, for a total net income of $8000. The FC firm shows constant net income of $2000 per year, again for a total of $8000 over the four years. The effect of the FC method is to defer (capitalize) exploration costs and, therefore, accelerate the recognition of profit.[25]

Cash from operations also differs. As in the example of Box 6-1, although the income difference reverses over time, the cash from operations difference does not. The cumulative cash from operations over the life of the well is higher for the FC firm by the cost of the capitalized dry holes ($12,000 − $9000 = $3000).

Box 6-4 presents empirical evidence as to how firms choose between the SE and FC methods. The illustration in Box 6-1 and the comparison in Exhibit 6-3 also help explain the choice of method.

Smaller firms tend to prefer full costing, whereas larger firms tend to be indifferent. For larger firms, with relatively stable exploration budgets and relatively constant success ratios (productive to total expenditures) across a "portfolio" of exploration projects, the year-to-year variability of dry hole expense is small. Amortization of past expenditures is large, reflecting a large reserve base. As a result, the difference between the two methods is small. Additionally, larger oil companies are often diversified into the refining and distribution segments of the oil business. Income from these sources dampen the variability of expenses resulting from the exploration segment. Large oil companies tend to use the SE method, which is perceived to be more conservative.[26]

---

[24]See the glossary for definitions of technical terms used in this section.

[25]The full cost method, however, does not permit unlimited capitalization of exploration costs. Impairment must be recognized when the carrying amount exceeds the present value of the reserves. See the discussion of impairment in Part III of this chapter.

[26]A more detailed analysis of the financial reporting effects of successful efforts versus full cost firms under different environments is discussed in Sunder (1976).

EXHIBIT 6-3
Comparison of Successful Efforts and Full Cost Impact on Net Income and Cash from Operations

Assumptions:

Cost of drilling well (dry or productive) is $1000. Four wells are drilled—one is productive, the other three are dry. The productive well has a four-year life, with revenues (net of cost of production) of $3000 per year.

Successful Efforts

Under successful efforts accounting, the $3000 spent on the dry holes is expensed immediately. Only the $1000 spent for the productive well is capitalized and amortized over its four-year life.

Year	1	2	3	4	Total
Net revenues	$ 3000	$3000	$3000	$3000	$12,000
Dry hole expense	(3000)	0	0	0	(3000)
Amortization	(250)	(250)	(250)	(250)	(1000)
Net income	$ (250)	$2750	$2750	$2750	$ 8000
Cash Flows					
Operations*	$ 0	$3000	$3000	$3000	$ 9000
Investment	(1000)	0	0	0	(1000)
Total	$(1000)	$3000	$3000	$3000	$ 8000

*Net revenues less dry hole expense.

Full Cost

Under the full cost method, the entire $4000 spent on drilling ($3000 for dry holes and $1000 for the productive well) is capitalized and amortized over the four-year life of the productive well.

Year	1	2	3	4	Total
Net revenues	$ 3000	$ 3000	$ 3000	$ 3000	$12,000
Amortization	(1000)	(1000)	(1000)	(1000)	(4000)
Net income	$ 2000	$ 2000	$ 2000	$ 2000	$ 8000
Cash Flows					
Operations*	$ 3000	$ 3000	$ 3000	$ 3000	$12,000
Investment	(4000)	0	0	0	(4000)
Total	$(1000)	$ 3000	$ 3000	$ 3000	$ 8000

*Net revenues.

For smaller companies, however, the difference in accounting methods can be considerable. Year-to-year variations in spending and success ratios means that dry hole expense can vary greatly. Under SE accounting, this variability is transmitted directly to the income statement. Further, smaller companies (especially if rapidly growing) have small reserve bases and low amortization of past capitalized costs. Dry hole costs from current drilling activities may even exceed the amortization of the capitalized costs of

---

BOX 6-4
Successful Efforts Versus Full Cost Choice of Methods: Empirical Evidence

A number of research studies* have examined characteristics of firms using successful efforts (SE) versus full cost (FC) accounting. Malmquist (1990) tested the relationship between the following characteristics and firm choice:

(1) Size

The larger the firm, the less likely it will choose full cost for several reasons. First, large firms prefer income-reducing alternatives such as successful efforts to avoid earning "windfall profits," especially when prices are rising, given the political sensitivity of energy prices.

Second, large firms have more drilling activities occurring simultaneously, creating a portfolio effect and thereby decreasing income variability. Third, in addition to the risks associated with exploration, oil companies are subject to the risks associated with marketing and refining. The larger the proportion of the firm's activities in marketing and refining, the lower the impact of successful efforts because its effect is limited to the income associated with exploration. As large firms tend to be more diversified, they have less incentive to opt for full costing.

Using sales as a proxy for size (political costs) and the ratio of exploration costs to market value as well as the ratio of production costs to market value to measure the various aspects related to size, Malmquist found them all to be significant in explaining the accounting choice. Higher sales and a larger proportion of production costs made the firm more likely to choose successful efforts. Conversely, the larger the exploration cost proportion, the more likely the firm was to choose full costing.

(2) Difficulty of Raising Capital in the Equity and Debt Markets

Successful efforts companies report lower assets than do FC companies. Therefore, securities underwriters may be hesitant (or find it difficult) to sell the securities of firms having low or negative net book value (equity) levels. Borrowing may also be more difficult for firms with high and variable debt/equity ratios. Moreover, for debt already in existence, there is a higher probability of technical violation of debt/equity-related debt covenants. Malmquist's study confirmed that firms with higher debt/equity ratios are less likely to choose successful efforts.

(3) Management Compensation Contracts

Earnings-based management compensation contracts are affected by the choice of accounting method. Opportunistic managers may choose full costing to increase the level of their compensation and decrease its variability. Malmquist notes "there are strong disincentives and limits placed on such behavior by the managerial labor market." No apparent relationship between the choice of accounting method and the presence of an earnings-based compensation contract was observed.

These results are consistent with some (but not all) of Deakin's (1989) findings. Analyzing firms that lobbied for full costing and the reasons given by those firms for lobbying, Deakin found that, on average, they had characteristics consistent with the stated reasons. The reasons given by the firms were:†

1. The expected impact on cost of capital and access to capital markets.
2. The potential of the proposed elimination of the full cost method to affect accounting income–based management incentive contracts.
3. The perceived effect on future drilling activity.
4. The effect on rate regulation.‡

To some extent, generalizing from Deakin's sample of companies, which lobbied for a particular accounting method to the general population of firms, is fraught with danger as the sample may be biased. Taking the time and effort to lobby can be an indication that these firms are the ones most likely to be affected by the choice. Thus Deakin's finding that the presence of management incentive contracts was associated with firms that lobbied for full cost in contrast to Malmquist, who did not find such a relationship, may reflect their different samples.

---

*See, for example, Steven Lilien and Victor Pastena, "Determinants of Intra-Method Choice in the Oil and Gas Industry", *Journal of Accounting and Economics* (1982), pp. 145–170 and Edward B. Deakin III "An Analysis of Differences Between Non-Major Oil Firms Using Successful Efforts And Full Cost Methods" *The Accounting Review* (October 1979), pp. 722–734.

†Edward B. Deakin III, "Rational Economic Behavior And Lobbying On Accounting Issues: Evidence From The Oil and Gas Industry" *The Accounting Review* (January 1989), pp. 137–151

‡The latter reason applied primarily to regulated companies that were required by rate-making authorities to use FC accounting procedures.

---

past drilling. Smaller companies are generally less diversified as they concentrate on exploration. Widely fluctuating patterns of earnings growth are a drawback for firms attempting to obtain external (equity or debt) financing. This problem is further exacerbated because, under successful efforts, the balance sheet shows lower assets and equity, thus hurting reported solvency ratios. As a result, smaller companies tend to use the FC method of accounting.

SFAS 69: Disclosures for Oil and Gas Firms

A major drawback of both accounting methods is the lack of correspondence between the reported cost of a producing oil or gas field and its value. While this is true of virtually all fixed assets, it is especially true of oil- and gas-producing assets because, even at the time of drilling, there may be little relationship between the expenditures and the results. An expenditure of millions of dollars can result in a dry hole. Alternatively, a small expenditure can result in a discovery of oil or gas worth many times its cost.

Neither method provides truly relevant data as to the value of reserves. This shortcoming is addressed by the extensive disclosure requirements of SFAS 69 (1982). These disclosures provide information about the physical quantity of the firm's reserves as well as the (discounted and undiscounted) cash flows expected from these reserves. Using Pennzoil, a large oil and gas producer, as an example, these disclosures are illustrated in Appendix 6-A. Somewhat surprisingly, however, the Harris and Ohlson (1987) study, discussed in Box 6-2, found that not only were net book value measures highly significant explanatory variables for the market valuation of oil and gas companies but that the book value measure dominated any of the other disclosures[27]

[27]A recent study, Greg Clinch and Joseph Magliolo, "Market Perceptions of Reserve Disclosures Under SAFS No. 69," *The Accounting Review* (October 1992), pp. 843–861, qualified some of these findings. Clinch and Magliolo argued that the value-relevance (informativeness) of the SFAS 69 data depended on the reliability investors attached to it. As the data were subject to constant revision, the reliability suffered. Thus they found that, although, on average, the reserve data were not perceived to be value-relevant by the market, production data were found to be informative. Production data, they argued, were more objective as they reflected actual actions taken by management rather than just estimates. Further, they found, for the subset of firms whose quantity estimates appeared more reliable (less revision of estimates), the proved reserve data were also value-relevant.

provided in the footnotes (such as the standardized present value or expected cash flow measures).[28]

When the price of oil causes the market value of the reserves to fall below book value, the SEC requires that companies using the FC method write down properties whose carrying cost exceeds the present value of future cash flows of the proved reserves attributable to that property. Companies using the SE method[29] are required to use the less stringent measure of *undiscounted* future cash flows. In the 1980s, when the price of oil fell drastically, companies that had previously chosen FC accounting to increase income were forced to take large write-offs, reducing reported income.

One method of avoiding such large write-offs was to change reporting methods from full cost to successful efforts. The impact of such a change on financial statements is illustrated using Pennzoil's 1988 data.

Changing from Full Cost to Successful Efforts: Pennzoil

Pennzoil switched from the FC method to the SE method effective June 30, 1988. Exhibit 6-4 shows that the capitalized cost of Pennzoil's oil and gas reserves on December 31, 1987, as reported in the *1987 Annual Report,* was $1832 million. It also shows that the (restated) capitalized cost (reported in the *1988 Annual Report*) was $1352 million, or 26% lower than the original reported amount.

This sharp decline reflects the change in method of accounting for oil and gas reserves, resulting in restatement of the previously reported 1987 data. The change was reported in the company's *1988 Annual Report,* in the footnote shown in Exhibit 6-4.

While the footnote is not explicit, comparison of data in the *1988 Annual Report* with that reported the previous year indicates that the company restated previously reported results at least back through 1984 and possibly earlier. The cumulative effect of the change (in excess of $300 million) is reported as an adjustment to previously reported retained earnings.

The change to or from the FC method is one of five cases where retroactive adjustment for accounting changes is mandatory; all prior years presented must be restated and the cumulative effect must be reported as an adjustment to the beginning retained earnings.[30]

---

[28]In a more recent paper, Harris and Ohlson (1990) questioned whether this result was due to historical costs actually having value relevance or whether the market was incorrectly focusing on the book values (functional fixation). As a result, what was being observed was a mispricing phenomenon. As preliminary evidence of mispricing, they found that abnormal riskless trading profits could be made by formulating a simple trading filter rule: rank firms on the basis of market value per barrel of reserves, and then create a zero investment portfolio by going long (short) those firms whose ranking fell below (above) the median.

This market inefficiency, combined with the conclusion that market prices are related to historical cost book values, is prima facie evidence that accounting information is value irrelevant as the market is incorrectly focusing on book values. Harris and Ohlson explored this question by creating a similar trading rule based on the portion of market value not explained by book values. They found that the abnormal profits were even greater under this second rule, indicating that, although the market was inefficient in its pricing, the source of the inefficiency was not historical accounting book values. On the contrary, they noted the results indicated the market would have been more efficient had it paid more attention to the historical cost information.

[29]See David B. Pariser and Pierre L. Titard, "Impairment of Oil and Gas Properties," *Journal of Accountancy* (December 1991), p. 52–62.

[30]See the discussion on accounting changes in Chapter 2 and see, for example, the change in income tax accounting by Amerada Hess described in Chapter 7.

EXHIBIT 6-4

Effect of Change from Full Cost to Successful Efforts, for Years Ended December 31, 1986–1988 (in millions)

The following table shows the aggregate capitalized costs related to oil- and gas-producing activities and related accumulated depreciation, depletion, and amortization.

	1986	1987	1988
From 1987 Annual Report—prior to change			
Capitalized costs			
Properties being amortized	$ 4356	$ 4469	
Properties not yet evaluated	295	332	
	$ 4651	$ 4801	
Accumulated depreciation, depletion, and amortization	(2765)	(2969)	
	$ 1886	$ 1832	
From 1988 Annual Report—after change			
Capitalized costs			
Proved properties		$ 2986	$ 2997
Unproved properties		354	293
		$ 3340	$ 3290
Accumulated depreciation, depletion, amortization, and valuation allowances		(1988)	(2399)
		$ 1352	$ 891

Pennzoil Co. Notes to Consolidated Financial Statements
Note 1

Oil and Gas Producing Activities and Depreciation, Depletion and Amortization—

Effective June 30, 1988 Pennzoil changed its method of accounting for oil and gas operations from the full cost method to the successful efforts method. In September 1988, Pennzoil filed an amendment to its 1987 Annual report on Form 10-K which reflected the restatement of the financial statements pursuant to this accounting change. Pennzoil's management concluded that the successful efforts method more appropriately reflects the mature nature of Pennzoil's oil and gas operations and enables investors and others to better compare Pennzoil to similar oil and gas companies, the majority of which follow the successful efforts method.

Under the successful efforts method, lease acquisition costs are capitalized. Significant unproved properties are reviewed periodically on a property-by-property basis to determine if there has been impairment of the carrying value, with any such impairment charged to exploration expense currently. All other unproved properties are generally aggregated and a portion of such costs estimated to be nonproductive, based on historical experience, is amortized on an average holding period basis.

Exploratory drilling costs are capitalized pending determination of proved reserves. If proved reserves are not discovered, the exploratory drilling costs are expensed. Other exploration costs are also expensed. All development costs are capitalized. Provision for depreciation, depletion and amortization is determined on a field-by-field basis using the unit-of-production method. The carrying amounts of proven properties are reviewed periodically and an impairment reserve is provided as conditions warrant.

EXHIBIT 6-4. *(Continued)*

The change in Pennzoil's accounting method increased 1988 net income by $44,354,000 or $1.14 per share, and 1987 net income by $2,136,000, or $.05 per share. The change decreased 1986 net income by $44,469,000, or $1.07 per share. As of December 31, 1987, retained earnings were reduced by $301,584,000 as a result of the accounting change.

Sulphur properties are generally depreciated and depleted on the unit-of-production method, except assets having an estimated life less than the estimated life of the mineral deposits, which are depreciated on the straight-line method.

All other properties are depreciated on straight-line or accelerated methods in amounts calculated to allocate the cost of properties over their estimated useful lives.

Source: Pennzoil annual reports, 1987–1988.

Adoption of the SE method of accounting requires the expensing of capitalized exploration expenditures, lowering reported income. On the other hand, the amortization of previously capitalized costs is also reduced, increasing reported earnings. The balance between increased expensing of current year expenditures and reduced amortization of past expenditures determines the net effect on earnings for any given year.

For example, a comparison of the restated 1986 data for the oil and gas production segment of Pennzoil with that originally reported shows the following differences:

1986 Oil and Gas Segment Data (in $ millions)

	Original	Restated	Decrease (Increase)
Capital expenditures	$ 159	$ 157	$ (2)
Depreciation, depletion, amortization	290	177	113
Estimated impact on operating income			(111)*
Reported operating income	38	(55)	(93)
Identifiable assets	2,025	1,539	486

*Estimated operating income increases by $111 million since capital expenditures (exploration costs capitalized) decrease by $2 million (increasing the amount expensed) but depreciation decreases by $113 million.

Apparently the change to successful efforts had little impact on the amount of 1986 cost capitalized. Pennzoil's expenditures for exploration were a small percentage of total capital expenditures;[31] apparently costs not meeting the successful efforts criteria were small.

The difference in depreciation, depletion, and amortization, however, is quite substantial, reflecting the sharp reduction in previously capitalized costs (notice the reduction in identifiable assets). These data can be used to estimate the impact of the accounting change on 1986 operating income, a net increase of $111 million.

---

[31]See Exhibit 6A-2 for data as to exploration costs and capital expenditures.

This calculation provides a good approximation of the disclosed effect of the accounting change on reported earnings. The discrepancy between the estimated impact ($111 million) and the actual change ($93 million) is probably due to differences in asset write-downs.

Why did Pennzoil make the accounting change? The reasons listed in the first paragraph of the footnote make sense. There may, however, have been an additional incentive for change. The "standardized measure" shows the net present value of the cash flows from the reserves using prices and costs prevalent at the date of the balance sheet. This standardized measure is a rough approximation of the current value of a company's reserves. (See Appendix 6-A for further details.) For Pennzoil, the "standardized measure" at the end of 1987 was $1081 million.[32] Compare this amount with the carrying value of oil and gas reserves as originally reported:

Standardized measure	$1081 million
Full cost carrying value (Exhibit 6-4)	1832

Even if the pretax standardized measure ($1407 million) was used, it is clear that the carrying value of the company's reserves was significantly above any possible measure of fair value. The company's opinion (included in Exhibit 6A-3) that "the estimated fair value of Pennzoil's oil and gas properties is in excess of the amounts set forth below" does not change that fact. These data suggest that the company was fearful that a large write-down of its properties would be required.

Adoption of the SE method resulted in a significant reduction in the carrying amount of the company's oil and gas reserves. Even so, the company took "impairment and abandonment" write-downs of $387 million in 1988.[33] The write-downs would have been much higher if not for the change to the successful efforts method.

As a result of the accounting change and impairment write-downs, Pennzoil's carrying amount was reduced to $891 million at the end of 1988, a reduction of 51% from the originally reported figure at the end of 1987. This reduced figure was comfortably below even the more conservative "standardized measure" of $1193 million at the end of 1988. As a result, the company was protected against the need for additional write-downs even if oil and gas prices declined further.

What was the effect of the accounting change on cash flow? Actual cash flow is unchanged as the change to the successful efforts method merely reallocates cash flows for financial reporting purposes. (For income tax purposes, Pennzoil, like other oil and gas companies, expenses the maximum allowable. The accounting change has no impact on tax return income.)

But components of reported cash flows are affected by the accounting change. We have already noted that reported capital expenditures are lower under the SE method. As illustrated in Exhibit 6-3, cash from operations appears to be higher when the FC method is used. While no restatement of Pennzoil's 1987 statement of cash flows is available (the

---

[32]See Exhibit 6A-3.

[33]An extraordinary gain of $1.7 billion from the settlement of litigation against Texaco, recognized in April 1988 enabled the company to take this charge against income without any dire effects on its balance sheet.

company adopted SFAS 95 in 1988), it should be clear that lower reported capital expenditures will be offset over time by lower reported operating cash flows. Once again, we see how the classification of cash flow components is affected by accounting choice.

The change to the SE method may cause a number of other changes in Pennzoil's present and future reported financial results, as suggested by Figures 6-2 through 6-6.

Summing up, Pennzoil's adoption of the successful efforts method had far-reaching effects on its financial statements, not only restating past results but changing future reported results as well. For a company with high fixed asset intensity, the capitalization versus expense decision is fundamental to the financial statements it prepares. Analysis of those statements requires an understanding of the impact of that decision.

II. ACCOUNTING FOR LONG-LIVED ASSETS OVER THEIR USEFUL LIVES

INTRODUCTION

The terms amortization, depletion, and depreciation are all used to denote the systematic allocation of the capitalized cost of an asset to income over its useful life. Depreciation, the most frequently used of these terms, is often used generically in discussions of the concept. Strictly speaking, depreciation refers to the allocation of the cost of tangible fixed assets, amortization is used when referring to the cost of intangible assets, and depletion applies to natural resource assets.

Accountants stress that the process of depreciation is one of allocation not valuation. *It is important, however, for analysts to differentiate between accounting depreciation and economic depreciation.* Whereas the accounting process may be purely allocative, the concept of depreciation also has economic meaning.

In Chapter 2 income was defined as the amount that can be distributed during the period without impairing the capacity of the firm. The cash flows generated by an asset over its life, therefore, cannot be considered income until provision is made for its replacement. These cash flows must be reduced by the amount it would take to replace the asset to determine the earnings generated by that asset.

This is the underlying principle of depreciation; profits would be overstated if no allowance were made for the replacement of the asset. The periodic depreciation expense, therefore, segregates a portion of cash flows for reinvestment, "protecting" that sum from being distributed as dividends and taxes.[34]

Continuing with this conceptual point of view, suppose an asset with a three-year life generates net cash flows of $100 per year and is purchased for $240. Over the life of the asset, income would be $60 ($300 − $240) as $240 would be required to replace the asset (assuming that the asset is worthless at the end of the three-year period and ignoring

---

[34]This should not be interpreted in the literal sense that specific monies equivalent to the periodic depreciation expense are set aside and earmarked for reinvestment but, rather, that the definition of income requires a subtraction for asset replacement.

EXHIBIT 6-5
Sinking Fund Depreciation

Year	(1) Opening Balance Asset	(2) Cash Flows	(3) Depreciation Expense	(4) = (2) − (3) Net Income	(5) = (4)/(1) Rate of Return
1	$240	$100	$ 71	$29	12%
2	169	100	80	20	12
3	89	100	89	11	12
Total		$300	$240	$60	

changes in price levels). Financial statements, however, report income annually, and it is necessary to determine how much income (or how much depreciation) to report each year. This requires the allocation of a portion of the multiperiod return to each period.

Generally, annual depreciation charges are designed to reflect fairly the portion of the multiperiod return earned in that year. The next section describes the depreciation methods used in financial reporting followed by a discussion of the impact of depreciation methods on financial statements. A separate analysis of accelerated depreciation methods used for income taxes is provided, followed by discussion of the interaction of inflation and depreciation methods. Analysis of financial statement depreciation disclosures, changes in depreciation methods, and a comprehensive examination of fixed asset disclosures round out the final section of Part II.

DEPRECIATION METHODS

Annuity or Sinking Fund Depreciation

From an economic perspective one can argue that the income reported each year should reflect the rate of return earned by the asset. For example, the asset just described generates a return of 12% over its three-year life.[35] To report a 12% return[36] for each year requires the pattern of depreciation shown in Exhibit 6-5.

Straight-line depreciation and the accelerated depreciation patterns discussed in the next section could be consistent with this notion of economic depreciation given a declining pattern of cash flows generated by the asset. For example, if cash flows followed the pattern in Exhibit 6-6, straight-line depreciation would be consistent with economic depreciation.

The pattern of depreciation shown in Exhibit 6-5, with the amount of depreciation increasing every year, is known as *annuity* or *sinking fund depreciation*. U.S. GAAP, however, do not permit this form of depreciation. In Canada, increasing charge methods

---

[35]The present value of a three-year annuity of $100 per year at 12% is (approximately) equal to $240.
[36]The rate of return in this example is calculated using the opening (not the average) asset balance.

EXHIBIT 6-6
Straight-line Depreciation with Declining Cash Flows

Year	(1) Opening Balance Asset	(2) Cash Flows	(3) Depreciation Expense	(4) = (2) − (3) Net Income	(5) = (4)/(1) Rate of Return
1	$240	$109	$ 80	$29	12%
2	160	99	80	19	12
3	80	90	80	10	12
Total		$298	$240	$58	

are used in the real estate industry and by a few utilities but they are not generally acceptable depreciation methods.[37]

Instead of depreciation patterns generating a constant rate of return, accountants generally use constant or declining expense depreciation patterns. These patterns, in some cases, may be justified by the matching principle. Generally, however, the actual pattern itself is arbitrary, the sole purpose being a systematic allocation of the asset cost over time.

Straight-Line Depreciation

Given the same asset, and the pattern of cash flows in Exhibit 6-5, accountants (using the matching principle) argue that since the revenues (cash flows of $100) generated by the asset each year are the same, the income shown each year should also be the same. The result of this line of reasoning is the pattern of depreciation expense exhibited in Exhibit 6-7.

Note that the annual rate of return increases from year to year and does not reflect the actual rate earned over the life of the asset. Under the matching principle, depreciation expense should be proportional to the revenue earned. The depreciation pattern depicted in Exhibit 6-7, with an equal expense each year, is known as *straight-line depreciation*.

Accelerated Depreciation Methods

The matching principle also supports accelerated depreciation patterns, with higher depreciation charges in early years and smaller ones in later years. First, benefits (revenues) from an asset may be higher in early years, declining in later years as efficiency falls (the asset wears out). The matching process requires that depreciation declines as benefits do.

---

[37]Canadian Pacific Limited, for example, uses the sinking fund method to account for buildings in its real estate and hotel segment. The depreciation policy footnote states that

This method will amortize the cost . . . in a series of annual installments increasing at the rate of 5% compounded annually. (*1990 Annual Report*)

EXHIBIT 6-7
Straight-line Depreciation with Constant Cash Flows

Year	(1) Opening Balance Asset	(2) Cash Flows	(3) Depreciation Expense	(4) = (2) − (3) Net Income	(5) = (4)/(1) Rate of Return
1	$240	$100	$ 80	$20	8.3%
2	160	100	80	20	12.5
3	80	100	80	20	25.0
Total		$300	$240	$60	

The second argument holds even if revenues are constant over time. Operating an asset requires maintenance and repairs over time, costs that tend to be lower early in the life of an asset and increase as the asset ages. Accelerated depreciation methods, it is argued, compensate for the rising trend of maintenance and repair costs so that total asset costs are level over the asset's life.

However, actual rates of decline in the efficiency of an asset are difficult if not impossible to forecast, and accelerated depreciation patterns are determined in practice by ad hoc (and somewhat arbitrary) procedures that systematically yield the desired pattern of higher depreciation amounts in earlier years.

The two most common accelerated methods are the sum-of-years'-digits (SYD) method and the double-declining-balance (DDB) method. A comparison of these methods with straight-line (SL) depreciation is presented in Exhibit 6-8, parts A–C. In the example used, the concept of salvage value, the estimated amount that the asset can be sold for at the end of its useful life, is introduced into the calculations.

Units-of-Production and Service Hours Methods

These methods depreciate assets in proportion to their actual usage rather than as a function of the passage of time. Thus, in busier years, more depreciation is recognized than in slow years. Both methods require an initial estimate of the total number of units of output (service hours) expected over the life of the machine. The methods differ in that the former uses output to measure asset usage, whereas the service hours method bases usage on hours worked.

Assume that the asset described in Exhibit 6-8 is expected to produce 60,000 units of output over its life and have a service life of 150,000 hours. The actual hours of service and output, and the resultant depreciation schedules, are presented in Exhibit 6-9.

These methods treat depreciation expense as a *variable rather than a fixed cost,* decreasing the volatility of reported earnings as compared to the straight-line method. In recent years a number of companies have adopted a hybrid depreciation method, combining features of the units-of-production and straight-line methods.

A significant drawback of these two methods occurs when the firm's productive capacity becomes obsolete as it loses business to more efficient competitors. As the units-of-production and service hour methods tend to decrease depreciation expense during periods of low production, the result will be an overstatement of reported income

EXHIBIT 6-8
Comparison of Straight-Line and Accelerated Depreciation Methods

Original cost $= \$18{,}000$
Salvage value $= \$3{,}000$
Depreciable life $\quad n = 5$

A. Straight-Line Depreciation

Depreciation in year i $= \dfrac{1}{n} \times$ (Original cost $-$ Salvage value)

Depreciation expense is constant each year; at the end of the five-year period, the net book value of the asset equals its salvage value of $3000.

Year	Rate	(Original Cost − Salvage Value)	Depreciation Expense	Accumulated Depreciation	Net Book Value
0					$18,000
1	1/5	$15,000	$ 3,000	$ 3,000	15,000
2	1/5	15,000	3,000	6,000	12,000
3	1/5	15,000	3,000	9,000	9,000
4	1/5	15,000	3,000	12,000	6,000
5	1/5	15,000	3,000	15,000	3,000
Total			$15,000		

B and C. Accelerated Depreciation Methods

B. Sum of Years' Digits

Depreciation in year i $= \dfrac{(n - i + 1)}{\text{SYD}} \times$ (Original cost $-$ Salvage value)

where SYD $= 1 + 2 + 3 + \cdots + n;$ the summation over the depreciable life of n years or simply SYD $= n(n + 1)/2$. For our example, $n = 5$;

SYD $= 1 + 2 + 3 + 4 + 5 = 15$ or, alternatively,

SYD $= \dfrac{(5)(5 + 1)}{2} = 15$

The rate of depreciation thus varies from year to year (as i varies) in reverse counting order of the years; that is, the pattern is 5/15, 4/15, 3/15, 2/15, and 1/15 and is depicted as follows:

Year	Rate	(Original Cost − Salvage Value)	Depreciation Expense	Accumulated Depreciation	Net Book Value
0					$18,000
1	5/15	$15,000	$ 5,000	$ 5,000	13,000
2	4/15	15,000	4,000	9,000	9,000
3	3/15	15,000	3,000	12,000	6,000
4	2/15	15,000	2,000	14,000	4,000
5	1/15	15,000	1,000	15,000	3,000
Total			$15,000		

EXHIBIT 6-8. *(Continued)*

C. Double Declining Balance

Depreciation in year $i = \dfrac{2}{n} \times$ (Original cost − Accumulated depreciation)

or

$\dfrac{2}{n} \times$ (Net book value)

The rate of $(2/n)$ is what gives the DDB method its name. The depreciation rate is double* the straight-line rate. The declining pattern occurs because the fixed rate is applied to an ever-decreasing asset balance (net book value),† and in our example it is calculated as

Year	Rate	Net Book Value	Depreciation Expense	Accumulated Depreciation	Net Book Value
0					$18,000
1	2/5	$18,000	$ 7,200	$ 7,200	10,800
2	2/5	10,800	4,320	11,520	6,480
3	2/5	6,480	2,592	14,112	3,888
4	NA	NA	888	15,000	3,000
5	NA	NA	0	15,000	3,000
Total			$15,000		

Note that in year 4 the DDB procedure is discontinued. This is because depreciation can be taken only until the salvage value is reached. Following DDB in year 4 and beyond would have reduced net book value below salvage. When the DDB method is applied to longer-lived assets, a switch to the straight-line method often occurs in later years, when the latter method results in higher depreciation expense.

NA – Not applicable.

*The double-declining-balance method is actually only one case of the family of declining-balance methods. The same principle can be applied to other multiples of the straight-line rate (e.g., 150% declining balance). Higher multiples result in more accelerated patterns of depreciation expense.

†Note that salvage value is not used to calculate depreciation under declining-balance methods but acts as a floor for net book value.

and asset values. The result is that, sooner or later, the firm will be forced to recognize the "impairment" (see discussion later in this chapter) of its productive capacity.

This danger is particularly acute for mature industries facing increased competition from new entrants or imports. *Competition frequently increases the rate of economic depreciation of fixed assets. Yet the corporate response is often to relieve the pressure on earnings by decreasing depreciation expense (either by lengthening lives or changing methods).*

Once impairment exists, companies report "restructuring" or similar charges to correct the overvaluation of fixed assets. Analysts often exclude such "nonrecurring" charges when evaluating corporate earnings. But to the extent that these charges represent an adjustment for past underdepreciation of assets, they correct a systematic

EXHIBIT 6-9
Service Hours and Units of Production Methods

Original cost = $18,000
Salvage value = $3,000

	Service Hours Method Expected service hours = 150,000 Cost/Service hour = $0.10*			Units of Production Method Expected output = 60,000 Cost/Unit of output = $0.25†		
Year	Hours Worked	Depreciation	Net Book Value	Units of Output	Depreciation	Net Book Value
0			$18,000			$18,000
1	40,000	$ 4,000	14,000	15,000	$ 3,750	14,250
2	35,000	3,500	10,500	16,000	4,000	10,250
3	45,000	4,500	6,000	20,000	5,000	5,250
4	20,000	2,000	4,000	10,000	2,250‡	3,000
5	40,000	1,000‡	3,000	12,500	0‡	3,000
Total		$15,000			$15,000	

*($18,000 − $3000)/150,000.
†($18,000 − $3000)/60,000.
‡Note that in both cases the asset is never depreciated below the salvage value even when actual usage exceeds estimated usage.

overstatement of past earnings. As past earnings are used to forecast the future, this issue should not be ignored.

On occasion, a company will recognize impairment of fixed assets gradually, by accelerating depreciation on a group of assets. From an analytic point of view, it is preferable for companies to recognize the impairment immediately rather than accelerate the depreciation of productive capacity in danger of becoming obsolete. Because the accounting concept of depreciation involves a systematic allocation of cost, its acceleration when the asset is impaired (and its use has declined or it has been temporarily idled) would not match costs and revenues and would misstate the earning power of the company.

Group and Composite Depreciation Methods

Depreciation methods described in the preceding sections are applicable to single assets; they may be impractical and uneconomic when firms use large numbers of similar assets in their operations. Group (composite) depreciation methods have been developed to allocate the costs of similar (dissimilar) assets using depreciation rates based on a weighted average of the service lives of the assets.

Gains or losses on disposal of these assets are not recognized separately; they are reported instead as a component of accumulated depreciation as is the carrying amount of the assets disposed of, sold, or retired. Firms may separately identify the effects of abnormal dispositions. However, group and composite methods may also obscure the existence of idled equipment.

EXHIBIT 6-10. DUPONT
Notes to Financial Statements, Note 1

Property, Plant and Equipment Property, plant and equipment (PP&E) is carried at cost and, except for petroleum and coal PP&E, is generally classified in depreciable groups and depreciated by accelerated methods that produce results similar to the sum-of-the-years' digits method. Depreciation rates range from 4 percent to 12 percent per annum on direct manufacturing facilities and from 2 percent to 10 percent per annum on other facilities; in some instances, appropriately higher or lower rates are used. Generally, for PP&E acquired prior to January 1, 1991, the gross carrying value of assets surrendered, retired, sold or otherwise disposed of is charged to accumulated depreciation and any salvage or other recovery therefrom is credited to accumulated depreciation. For disposals of PP&E acquired after December 31, 1990, the gross carrying value and related accumulated depreciation are removed from the accounts and included in determining gain or loss on such disposals.

Petroleum and coal PP&E, other than that described below, is depreciated on the straight-line method at various rates calculated to extinguish carrying values over estimated useful lives. Generally, when petroleum and coal PP&E is surrendered, retired, sold or otherwise disposed of, the gross carrying value is charged to accumulated depreciation, depletion and amortization; any salvage or other recovery therefrom is credited to accumulated depreciation, depletion and amortization.

Maintenance and repairs are charged to operations; replacements and betterments are capitalized.

Source: E. I. duPont de Nemours, *1991 Annual Report.*

Exhibit 6-10 contains an excerpt from duPont's 1991 "Summary of Significant Accounting Policies" and is representative of the information provided by companies using group depreciation. The firm discloses its policies in general terms, although its reference to the sum-of-the-years'-digits method is helpful. The range of rates is wide, limiting the analytical utility of the disclosure. duPont does not use group methods, however, for petroleum and coal fixed assets.

Note the change in accounting for assets retired or sold, applicable to plant, property, and equipment (PPE) depreciated in groups only. Prior to 1991, duPont did not recognize gains or losses from the disposition of fixed assets; the accumulated depreciation account was adjusted to reflect assets retired or sold. Thus fixed assets were never removed from the gross property account. Starting in 1991, however, gross property is reduced when assets are disposed of and gain or loss is recognized as the difference between proceeds received (if any) and the net book value of the assets in question.

There is no other disclosure in duPont's financial statements regarding the accounting change. The company does disclose $442 million of gains on asset sales in 1991 ($196 million in 1990), but without any indication of what the gain would have been under the 1990 accounting method.[38] The effect on future years will depend on whether duPont realizes gains or losses on fixed asset disposals.

---

[38]Having read (and understood) the accounting policy footnote, an analyst would have the ability to ask DuPont this question.

Exhibit 6-11 contains Georgia-Pacific's footnote regarding its accounting for fixed assets. Unlike duPont, which classifies its fixed assets into "depreciable groups," Georgia-Pacific uses composite depreciation combining dissimilar assets. The firm capitalizes replacements when retiring the replaced assets. Sales and dispositions are recognized through adjustments to the accumulated depreciation and asset accounts. Separate recognition in the income statement is provided only when the sales or dispositions are abnormal; this is a common feature of composite methods. Otherwise, Georgia-Pacific follows the disposition accounting used by duPont prior to its 1991 change.

EXHIBIT 6-11
Georgia-Pacific Corporation
Note 1

Property, Plant and Equipment   Property, plant and equipment are recorded at cost. Lease obligations for which the Corporation assumes substantially all the property rights and risks of ownership are capitalized. Replacements of major units of property are capitalized and the replaced properties are retired. Replacements of minor units of property and repairs and maintenance costs are charged to expense as incurred.

The majority of property, plant and equipment is depreciated using composite rates based upon estimated service lives. The ranges of composite rates for the principal classes are: land improvements—5% to 7%; buildings—3% to 5%; and machinery and equipment—5% to 20%. The remainder of property, plant and equipment is depreciated over the estimated useful life of the related asset using the straight-line method.

Under the composite method of depreciation, no gain or loss is recognized on normal property dispositions because the property cost is credited to the property accounts and charged to the accumulated depreciation accounts and any proceeds are credited to the accumulated depreciation accounts. However, when there are abnormal dispositions of property, the cost and related depreciation amounts are removed from the accounts and any gain or loss is reflected in income.

Source: Georgia-Pacific, *1990 Annual Report.*

Depletion

Financial reporting requirements for natural resources are similar to those for tangible assets. The carrying costs of natural resources include the costs of acquiring the land or mines and the costs of exploration and development of the resources. These costs may be capitalized or expensed as a function of the firm's accounting policies (such as successful efforts or full cost for oil and gas exploration). The development of natural resources often entails the use of machinery and equipment, generally depreciated using methods described in the preceding sections.

The carrying costs of natural resources (excluding costs of machinery and equipment used in extraction or production) are allocated to accounting periods using the units-of-production method. This method requires an initial estimate of the units of oil or gas, minerals, timber, et cetera in the resource base to compute a unit cost, which is then applied to the actual units produced, extracted or harvested. Pennzoil's disclosures

EXHIBIT 6-12
Depreciation Methods

	Number of Companies			
	1990	1989	1988	1987
Straight-line	560	562	563	559
Declining-balance................	38	40	44	44
Sum-of-the-years-digits	11	16	11	12
Accelerated method—not specified	69	69	70	76
Unit-of-production	50	50	53	51
Other	8	8	9	12

Source: Accounting Trends and Techniques, 1991 Edition, p.325. Copyright, 1991, American Institute of Certified Public Accountants. Reprinted with permission.

regarding depreciation and depletion, included in Exhibit 6-4, are typical for a natural resource company.

Amortization

Amortization of intangible assets may be based on useful lives as defined by law (e.g., patents) or regulation, or such assets may be depreciated over the period during which the firm expects to receive benefits from them. Companies use either straight-line or units-of-production methods. Goodwill and indefinite-term franchises and licenses may be amortized over periods not exceeding 40 years. However, goodwill[39] amortization is not deductible for tax purposes in the United States.

Depreciation Methods and Disclosures

As we have shown, the choice of depreciation method can greatly affect the pattern of reported income. Disclosure of the depreciation method used is required and can usually be found in the footnote listing accounting policies. Most American firms use straight-line depreciation, as can be seen from Exhibit 6-12.

The exhibit shows that in 1990, 560 of the 600 companies surveyed reported using this method. Accelerated methods, including declining balance (38), sum of the years' digits (11), and unspecified accelerated (69), are used less frequently (some firms use more than one method). Over the four-year period shown, these methods, which tend to reduce reported earnings, have declined in use.

Even companies using the same method of depreciation may not be comparable due to other factors that can affect reported depreciation. The useful life (the period over which the asset is depreciated) can vary from firm to firm, and excessively long lives will understate periodic depreciation expense. While companies are required to disclose depreciation lives, in practice such disclosures are often vague, providing ranges rather

---

[39]See Chapter 12 for an extensive discussion of goodwill.

than precise data. In such cases, the analyst must use the available data to compute approximate depreciation lives (see analysis of fixed asset disclosures later in the chapter).

While usually a less significant factor, salvage values are also subject to management estimates. High estimates will reduce the depreciation base (cost less salvage value) and, therefore, reduce depreciation expense. (Note that salvage values are not employed in declining-balance depreciation methods.) In practice, companies rarely disclose data regarding salvage values, except when estimates are changed.

Impact of Depreciation Methods on Financial Statements

The choice of depreciation method impacts both the income statement and balance sheet; for capital-intensive companies the impact can be highly significant. As depreciation is an allocation of past cash flows, the method chosen for financial reporting purposes has no impact[40] on the statement of cash flows.

Accelerated depreciation methods, with higher depreciation expense in the early years of asset life, tend to depress both net income and stockholders' equity when compared with the straight-line method. As the effect on net income is usually greater than the effect on net assets (in percentage terms), return ratios tend to be lower when accelerated depreciation methods are used. Consequently, these methods are considered more conservative.

Toward the end of an asset's life, however, the effect on net income reverses. In Exhibit 6-8A–C, notice that depreciation expense in years 4 and 5 is lower using accelerated methods than using the straight-line method. For companies with stable or rising capital expenditures, the early year impact of new assets acquired will dominate, and depreciation expense on a total firm basis will be higher under an accelerated method. When capital expenditures decline, however, accelerated depreciation will result in lower depreciation expense because the later year effect on older assets will dominate. This effect is illustrated using the example of General Motors later in the chapter.

Depreciation lives and salvage values also impact both depreciation expense and stated asset values. Shorter lives and lower salvage values are considered conservative in that they lead to higher computed depreciation expense. These factors interact with the depreciation method to determine the expense; for example, use of the straight-line method with short depreciation lives may result in depreciation expense similar to that obtained from use of an accelerated method with longer lives. Conservative depreciation practices will clearly increase asset turnover ratios by decreasing the denominator.

Accelerated Depreciation and Taxes

Notwithstanding the theoretical arguments and the financial statement effects discussed, the primary reason for the existence of accelerated depreciation methods lies in their beneficial effect on the firm's tax burden. At the onset of an asset's life, the total amount of depreciation expense available is fixed. Depreciation acts as a tax shelter insofar as it

---

[40]This assumes that the method chosen for tax purposes is independent of the method chosen for financial statement purposes.

reduces the amount of taxes to be paid in a given year. Thus, for any positive interest rate, firms are better off using accelerated depreciation methods to obtain the benefit of increased cash flows (from reduced taxes) in the earlier years.

The tax code has long been used by governments to encourage investment, and this was the intent of the U.S. government when it first allowed accelerated depreciation methods for tax purposes in 1954. Many foreign governments also permit the use of accelerated depreciation methods. Since 1954, the U.S. government has frequently changed tax depreciation regulations to increase or decrease investment incentives in certain types of fixed assets or simply to raise revenues. The present system is known as MACRS—modified accelerated cost recovery system—which consists of specified depreciation patterns and depreciable lives (generally shorter than actual useful service lives). Different MACRS schedules exist for different property classes, as Exhibit 6-13 indicates.

MACRS schedules use double declining balance and 150% declining balance, methods few companies use for financial reporting purposes. However, depreciation accounting is one area where the accounting method used for financial statements often differs from that used for tax purposes. The implications of this difference will be discussed in Chapter 7.

Inflation and Its Impact on Depreciation

The argument made previously that income can be measured using depreciation expense based on the original cost of the asset holds as long as the amount deducted for depreciation is enough to replace the asset after it has been fully utilized. If, however, the replacement cost of the asset is increasing, then depreciation expense based upon the original cost will be insufficient.

Returning to the example in Exhibit 6-5, assume that after three years, the firm will require $300 to replace the asset. Then the total economic income earned by the firm is $0. Using the historical cost basis, however, the amount of depreciation taken is limited to the original $240 cost. Reported income is overstated as all revenue is needed to replace productive capacity. In addition, because firms are only allowed to use historical cost basis depreciation for tax purposes, the resultant taxes are too high. Income taxes become, in effect, a tax on capital rather than a tax on income. The resulting disincentives for investment are illustrated in the context of a simple capital budgeting model in Box 6-5.

To some extent, accelerated depreciation methods partially compensate for this inflation effect. Depreciating the asset over a shorter life serves a similar purpose. A number of studies have examined whether accelerated methods compensate for inflation and/or are reflective of economic depreciation (however defined). Generalizing research results to time periods other than those examined requires a great deal of caution, as the economic environment is forever changing, particularly for studies that examined whether depreciation practices (whether for tax or book purposes) reflected or compensated for the actual economic or physical depreciation of assets. These comparisons are a function of the provisions of the tax code, the inflation rate, and varying degrees of technological obsolescence across industries during the comparison period. During the 1980s, the provisions of the tax code with respect to depreciation were changed three

EXHIBIT 6-13
MACRS Depreciation Rates by Class of Property

Year	3 Year	5 Year	7 Year	10 Year	15 Year	20 Year
1	33.33%	20.00%	14.29%	10.00%	5.00%	3.75%
2	44.44	32.00	24.49	18.00	9.50	7.22
3	14.81	19.20	17.49	14.40	8.55	6.68
4	7.41	11.52	12.49	11.52	7.70	6.18
5		11.52	8.93	9.22	6.93	5.71
6		5.76	8.92	7.37	6.23	5.28
7			8.93	6.55	5.90	4.89
8			4.46	6.55	5.90	4.52
9				6.55	5.91	4.46
10				6.55	5.90	4.46
11				3.29	5.91	4.46
12					5.90	4.46
13					5.91	4.46
14					5.90	4.46
15					5.91	4.46
16					2.96	4.46
17						4.46
18						4.46
19						4.46
20						4.46
21						2.25
	100.00%	100.00%	100.00%	100.00%	100.00%	100.00%

Description of Property

3-year property	Special tools and assets used in R&D
5-year property	Machinery and equipment not classified elsewhere, automobiles and light trucks
7-year property	Office furniture, agriculture equipment, oil exploration equipment, railroad track
10-year property	Certain public utility property, railroad tank cars, mobile homes, coal conversion boilers
15-year property	Public utility property and certain low-income housing
20-year property	Other personal property

Method of Calculation

For 3-year, 5-year, 7-year, and 10-year property, double declining balance.

For 15-year and 20-year property, 150% declining balance.

For all property, for first and final years, only half year depreciation taken; switch to straight line when change results in depreciation greater than under declining-balance method.

BOX 6-5
Disincentives for Investment Arising from Historical Cost Depreciation

We begin by assuming that the inflation rate p is equal to zero. A project is profitable if the net present value (NPV) of the cash flows of the invesment,

$$\text{NPV}_{(p=0)} = -I + (1 - t) \Sigma \frac{C_i}{(1 + r)^i} + t \Sigma \frac{d_i I}{(1 + r)^i}$$

is greater than zero (i.e., NPV > 0), where C_i is the pretax (real) cash flow in period i, t is the marginal tax rate, d_i is the rate of depreciation in period i, I is the cost of the original investment, and r is the appropriate real discount rate.* The summation on the right reflects the depreciation tax shelter, and the NPV can be disaggregated into

NPV = −Investment + Present value (after-tax cash flows)
+ Present value (depreciation tax shelter)

If we introduce an annual inflation rate of $p > 0$, then the expected (nominal) cash flows in any period will increase. In addition the discount rate will change to reflect inflation. The depreciation deduction based on historical costs will not change. The expression for net present value now becomes

$$\text{NPV}_{(p>0)} = -I + (1 - t) \Sigma \frac{(1 + p)^i C_i}{(1 + p)^i (1 + r)^i} + t \Sigma \frac{d_i I}{(1 + p)^i (1 + r)^i}$$

As the $(1 + p)^i$ terms in the first summation cancel, inflation (when it is expected) will not affect the after-tax cash flows. However, the depreciation tax shelter will now be worth less as

$$t \Sigma \frac{d_i I}{(1 + r)^i} > t \Sigma \frac{d_i I}{(1 + p)^i (1 + r)^i}$$

The decline in the depreciation tax shelter will reduce the profitability of the project,

$$\text{NPV}_{(p>0)} < \text{NPV}_{(p=0)}$$

and *ceteris paribus,* there is less likelihood that the project will be undertaken.

---

*Generally, the depreciation tax shelter would be discounted at a rate lower than the cash flows themselves as the tax deduction is "riskless." We do not make the distinction here for the sake of simplification. Alternatively, one can view this problem in the context of certainty, and r is the risk-free rate.

times, inflation declined from double digit rates to approximately 4%, and technological change was rapid in many industries. In addition, practices vary from country to country.

Kim and Moore (1988), for example, report that, for the Canadian trucking industry, economic depreciation tended to be less than the amount of depreciation taken for tax purposes, resulting in a tax subsidy. Focusing on reported income, Most (1984) found that in the United States the useful life (used for financial statement depreciation) is generally longer than the economic life of the asset. This serves to understate reported depreciation and overstate reported income. Skinner (1982), on the other hand, reported the opposite phenomenon in the United Kingdom.

Beaver and Dukes (1973) examined firms' price/earnings ratios and found that market prices, on average, "assign a more accelerated form of depreciation than is implied by reported earnings."[41] Their study did not attempt to discern the reasons for this result but recognized that it was consistent with either a constant rate of return depreciation model (with declining cash flows) or depreciation based upon current costs rather than a historical cost system.

An important question that emerges from these studies concerns the benchmark to be used: How does one determine the "correct" useful life and economic depreciation rate? This, of course, is important for analytic purposes as well. Estimates of economic lives on an aggregate industry basis can be derived from data made available by the Department of Commerce.

On a more micro level, in 1982 the FASB issued SFAS 33 (Changing Prices), which required very large firms[42] to disclose supplementary, unaudited data on the effects of changing prices. Among the required disclosures were

1. The current cost of fixed assets.

2. Depreciation expense on a current cost basis.

These disclosures were intended to help financial statement users adjust for the shortcomings of historical cost depreciation discussed earlier. However, studies that examined the informational content of the replacement cost data found that although historical cost earnings had informational content above and beyond that of replacement cost data provided by SFAS 33,[43] the reverse did not hold. Inflation-adjusted data did not appear to have any marginal information content above that provided by historical cost data. The reasons offered for this surprising result were that

1. The information was too difficult to comprehend and the market had as yet not learned how to do so.

---

[41]William H. Beaver and Roland E. Dukes, "Interperiod Tax Allocation and δ-Depreciation Methods: Some Empirical Results," *The Accounting Review* (July 1973), pp. 549–559.

[42]SFAS 33 applied to firms with inventories and gross (before deducting depreciation) property exceeding $125 million (in the aggregate) or with total assets exceeding $1 billion.

[43]Some of the studies (e.g., Beaver, Christie, and Griffin (1980) and Beaver, Griffin, and, Landsman (1982)) found little information content, focusing on ASR 190 disclosures. Others (Beaver and Landsman (1983)) examined the SFAS 33 data with similar results. It should be noted that although the consensus was that the data did not have information content, the conclusions (see, for example, Easman, Falkenstein, and Weil (1979) and Murdoch (1986)) were by no means unanimous.

2. The information was not new as the market knew[44] how to adjust historical cost information for inflation without the newly required SFAS 33 disclosures.

3. The information was irrelevant either from a conceptual point of view or in the manner in which it was prepared and reported.

Whatever the reason, in practice the data were difficult to prepare and use. Facing intense complaints regarding the cost of preparing the data, and empirical research that seemed to belie the usefulness of the data, the FASB subsequently modified SFAS 33, making the disclosures voluntary. A detailed discussion of the effects of inflation on fixed assets and depreciation appears in Appendix 6-C.

Changes in Depreciation Method

Companies may change the reported depreciation of fixed assets in different ways:

1. Change in method *applicable only to newly acquired assets*
2. Change in method *applicable to all assets*
3. Changes in asset lives or salvage value

A company can change its depreciation method only for newly acquired assets and continue to depreciate previously acquired similar assets using the same method(s) as in the past. The impact of the new method will be gradual, increasing as fixed assets acquired after the change grow in relative importance. Such a change is not considered a change in accounting principle, and no special disclosures are required.

Snap-on Tools, for example, switched from the accelerated method to straight-line for all property acquired after December 30, 1989. The footnote disclosure (Exhibit 6-14) states that the change had no material impact on 1990 financial results; no additional disclosures were required.

Alternatively, the new method can be applied retroactively so that all fixed assets are depreciated using the new method. In this case the effect will be greater and can be significant in the year of the switch as well as in future years. For a sample of 38 companies that switched to straight-line depreciation, Healy et al. (1987) estimated that the median increase in income was 8% to 10% in the 10-year period following the change. In addition to the effect on current and future depreciation expense (and net income), there will be a cumulative effect given the retroactive nature of the change, that is, the difference between originally reported depreciation and the cumulative restated depreciation for all past periods. When the new method is applied retroactively, companies must also disclose the pro forma impact of the new method on prior periods.

A change in depreciation method for all assets is considered as a change in accounting principle under Accounting Principles Board (APB) 20, Accounting

---

[44]An example of such an effort can be found in the work of Angela Falkenstein and Roman L. Weil, "Replacement Cost Accounting: What Will Income Statements Based on the SEC Disclosures Show?—Part I," *Financial Analysts Journal* (January–February 1977), pp. 46–57 and "Replacement Cost Accounting: What Will Income Statements Based on the SEC Disclosures Show?—Part II," *Financial Analysts Journal* (March–April 1977), pp. 48–57.

EXHIBIT 6-14. SNAP-ON TOOLS CORPORATION
Notes to Financial Statements

Note 1 (in Part): Summary of Accounting Policies
G. Property and equipment

Land, buildings, machinery and equipment are carried at original cost. Depreciation and amortization are provided for primarily by using accelerated depreciation methods on all property acquired prior to December 31, 1989. For financial statement purposes, the Company adopted the straight-line depreciation method for all property acquired after December 30, 1989. The Company believes the new method will more accurately reflect its financial results by better matching costs of new property over the useful lives of these assets. In addition, the new method more closely conforms with that prevalent in the industry. The effect of the change was not material to the 1990 financial results.

The estimated service lives of property and equipment are as follows:

Buildings and improvements	5 to 45 years
Machinery and equipment	3 to 15 years
Furniture and fixtures	3 to 15 years
Transportation vehicles	2 to 5 years

The costs and related accumulated depreciation of the Company's property and equipment values were as follows for fiscal years ended:

(Amounts in thousands)	1990	1989
Land	$ 21,075	$ 20,120
Buildings and improvements	112,194	103,974
Machinery and equipment	213,911	193,713
	347,180	317,807
Less accumulated depreciation	(136,766)	(122,787)
Property and equipment—net	$ 210,414	$ 195,020

Source: Accounting Trends and Techniques, 1991 Edition, p. 49. Copyright, 1991, American Institute of Certified Public Accountants. Reprinted with permission.

Changes. The cumulative effect of the change must be reported separately and net of taxes. Despite the similarity in reporting and its location on the income statement, a change in accounting method is not an extraordinary item.

Changes in asset lives and salvage values are changes in accounting estimates and are not considered changes in accounting principles. Their impact is only reported prospectively; that is, only the impact on the current and future periods is considered, and no retroactive or cumulative effects are recognized. Estimate changes attract much less notice than do changes in depreciation methods. They are not, for example, referred to in the auditor's opinion. Thus it is important to read financial statement footnotes carefully to be sure that no changes in accounting estimates have been made.

EXHIBIT 6-15. FORD MOTOR COMPANY
Notes to Financial Statements, Note 1

Note 1 (in Part): Accounting Policies
Depreciation and Amortization—Automotive

Depreciation is computed using an accelerated method that results in accumulated depreciation of approximately two-thirds of asset cost during the first half of the asset's estimated useful life. On average, buildings and land improvements are depreciated based on a 30-year life; automotive machinery and equipment are depreciated based on a 14½-year life.

It is the company's policy to review periodically fixed asset lives. A study completed during 1990 indicated that actual lives for certain asset categories generally were longer than the useful lives used for depreciation purposes in the company's financial statements. Therefore, during the third quarter of 1990, the company revised the estimated useful lives of certain categories of property retroactive to January 1, 1990. The effect of this change in estimate was to reduce 1990 depreciation expense by $211 million and increase 1990 net income principally in the U.S., by $135 million or $0.29 per share.

When plant and equipment are retired, the general policy is to charge the cost of such assets, reduced by net salvage proceeds, to accumulated depreciation. All maintenance, repairs and rearrangement expenses are expensed as incurred. Expenditures that increase the value or productive capacity of assets are capitalized. The cost of special tools is amortized over periods of time representing the productive use of such tools. Preproduction costs incurred in connection with new facilities are expensed as incurred.

Source: Accounting Trends and Techniques, 1991 Edition, p. 48. Copyright, 1991, American Institute of Certified Public Accountants. Reprinted with permission.

Exhibit 6-15 contains an excerpt from Ford Motor's *1990 Annual Report* disclosing that in 1990 it revised the estimated useful lives used to depreciate certain assets. The impact of this change is not shown on the income statement, and no reference is made to the change in the auditor's opinion, but the footnote reports a decrease of $211 million in depreciation expense and an increase of $135 million in net income ($0.29 per share).

Motivation for and reaction to depreciation changes is examined in Box 6-6. Whenever a change in depreciation method or lives is reported, the impact of the change on operating performance should be analyzed; that is, what is the contribution of the change to current year earnings? General Motors provides a comprehensive example of how changes in depreciation lives impact reported income.

Analysis of Depreciation Disclosures: General Motors

General Motors' *1990 Annual Report* provides, among the disclosures of "Significant Accounting Policies" in its footnotes, a description of the accounting method for fixed assets, as shown in Exhibit 6-16.

The footnote is vague; it does not indicate *which* accelerated method the company uses, and no information regarding assets lives or salvage values is provided. This is a

BOX 6-6
Changes in Depreciation Methods: Motivation and Reaction

When the Internal Revenue Code of 1954 permitted the use of accelerated depreciation for tax purposes, many firms also adopted these methods for financial statement purposes. Subsequently, many of these firms "switched back" to straight-line depreciation for financial reporting purposes. The effect of the switch-back was to increase the firm's reported net income, (tangible) assets, and retained earnings.

Unlike the FIFO-LIFO switch discussed in Chapter 5, the depreciation switchback was a "pure accounting" change without any direct cash flow consequences as accelerated depreciation was retained for tax purposes. The phenomenon was originally studied by Archibald (1972) and Kaplan and Roll (1972) as a test of whether the efficient market hypothesis (EMH) or the functional fixation hypothesis prevailed with respect to financial statements; that is, was the market "fooled" by the numbers, or did it see through the accounting change, realizing that it had no economic consequence? As detailed in Chapter 4, the results of these studies (using weekly and monthly data) were consistent with the EMH, finding no market reaction to the switch.

With the advent of positive accounting research, the assumption of no economic consequences to a "pure accounting" change was reexamined. Management compensation contracts as well as debt covenants based on accounting numbers are affected by accounting changes. Holthausen (1981) examined the accounting switchbacks in this framework. He argued that an accounting change that increases reported income, given earnings-based management contracts, should result in negative market reaction, as there would be a wealth transfer from the owners of the firm to the managers. Conversely, the presence of debt covenants should result in a positive market reaction, as the increase in reported earnings and assets would generally increase the slack associated with any leverage constraints. Empirical results did not confirm these hypotheses.

As noted in Chapter 4, studies of market reaction to voluntary accounting changes have generally not found results consistent with the positive accounting framework, as (it is argued that) by the time the change is made, it has been generally anticipated that the firm (or its managers) will make the change to improve reported performance. Thus, although the motivation for the change (compensation, debt covenants) is as specified, the market has already taken it into account.

Evidence consistent with the compensation motivation for depreciation switchbacks is reported by Dhaliwal et al. (1982), who found that management-controlled firms are more likely to adopt straight-line depreciation methods. Furthermore, Healy et al. (1987) found that when firms changed reporting methods to straight-line depreciation,

> the CEO's bonus and salary awards are based on reported earnings both before and after the accounting changes. We find no evidence that subsequent to either the inventory change or the depreciation change, reported earnings are transformed to earnings under the original accounting method for computing compensation awards.*

Generally, however they note that the percentage of the CEO's compensation attributable to the accounting change is small relative to their overall compensation package. On average, these results do not find a debt covenant or (significant) management compensation motivation for the change in depreciation method. For a given company, however, an analyst would be wise to check these factors whenever an income-increasing accounting change is implemented.

*Paul M. Healy, Sok-Hyon Kang and Krishna Palepu, "The Effect of Accounting Procedure Changes on CEO's Cash Salary and Bonus Compensation," *Journal of Accounting and Economics* (1987), pp. 7–34

EXHIBIT 6-16. GENERAL MOTORS
Fixed Assets

Significant Accounting Policies

Depreciation is provided based on estimated useful lives of groups of property generally using accelerated methods, which accumulate depreciation of approximately two-thirds of the depreciable cost during the first half of the estimated useful lives.

Expenditures for special tools are amortized over their estimated useful lives. Amortization is applied directly to the asset account. Replacement of special tools for reasons other than changes in products is charged directly to cost of sales.

General Motors Acceptance Corporation provides for depreciation of automobiles and other equipment on operating leases or in company use generally on a straight-line basis.

Real Estate, Plants, and Equipment and Accumulated Depreciation (in $ millions)

	1990	1989
Real estate, plants, and equipment		
Land	$ 688.4	$ 673.2
Land improvements	1,814.0	1,711.5
Leasehold improvements less amortization	326.9	185.6
Buidings	13,060.7	12,445.3
Machinery and equipment	43,601.0	41,125.6
Furniture/office equipment	3,257.0	2,843.2
Satellites and related facilities	863.0	504.6
Capitalized leases	1,237.7	1,170.2
Construction in progress	2,370.7	2,731.5
Total	$67,219.4	$63,390.7
Accumulated depreciation		
Land improvements	1,041.6	968.7
Buildings	6,354.4	5,731.0
Machinery and equipment	27,747.2	25,468.1
Furniture/office equipment	2,176.6	1,849.0
Satellites and related facilities	231.4	192.1
Capitalized leases	729.6	640.8
Total	$38,280.8	$34,849.7

Source: General Motors, *1990 Annual Report.*

typical problem with such disclosures. No reference is made to the capitalization of interest. However, the company discloses, in a footnote not shown here, that interest cost of $98.3 million was capitalized in 1990. Another footnote, included in Exhibit 6-16, contains a breakdown of gross real estate, plants, and equipment and accumulated depreciation.

These data facilitate the analysis of depreciation policy. The trends of depreciation of and expenditures for real estate, plants, and equipment by General Motors can be compared as follows (in $ millions):

Year	Depreciation Expense	Capital Expenditures
1986	$ 3529.9	$ 8159.5
1987	3454.4	4804.4
1988	3561.0	3432.1
1989	3680.3	4577.3
1990	3699.2	4432.5

The trend of depreciation expense is surprising, at first glance, since for most companies it tends to rise, reflecting both increasing real investments and higher prices. The trend of capital expenditures, combined with knowledge of GM's depreciation policy, helps explain the lack of growth in depreciation expense.

GM's capital expenditures have not grown in dollar terms (and have probably declined in real terms) over the 1987–1990 period. They remain well below the figure for 1986. Given GM's use of accelerated depreciation, the depreciation expense associated with the high capital expenditures in 1986 is declining. The high early year depreciation associated with the newer capital expenditures barely compensates for that decline.

There is, however, another factor that affects the trend of depreciation expense. In its *1987 Annual Report,* GM disclosed that

> In the third quarter of 1987, the Corporation revised the estimated service lives of its plants and equipment and special tools retroactive to January 1, 1987. These revisions, which were based on 1987 studies of actual useful lives and periods of use, recognized current estimates of service lives of the assets and had the effect of reducing 1987 depreciation and amortization charges by $1,236.6 million or $2.55 per share of $1-2/3 par value common stock.

While a portion of the $1.237 billion impact of the change applied to special tools (short-lived tooling, capitalized and amortized separately), most of it applied to the depreciation of real estate, plant, and equipment. As this change applied only to assets acquired in 1987 and later years, older assets continue to be depreciated at a faster rate. Over time, this change gradually reduces depreciation expense. The reduction in depreciation expense in 1987 presumably reflects the impact of the use of longer lives on capital assets acquired in that year.

The change in asset lives increased the pretax income of General Motors by $1237 million in 1987, accounting for 28% of consolidated pretax income of $4408 million for that year. The change contributed to an increase in pretax earnings of 24%; without the accounting change, pretax earnings would have declined by 8%.

In the same year General Motors Acceptance Corp. (GMAC) extended the depreciable lives of autos leased to retail customers, decreasing depreciation expense by nearly $255 million. *Together these two changes accounted for fully one-third of GM's earnings for 1987.*

These changes have continued to affect the earnings trend of the company. *Because they were changes in accounting estimates rather than changes in principles, subsequent year disclosure is not required.* This illustrates the need for analysts to maintain their own records of accounting data.

Change to Units-of-Production Depreciation: Ratliff Drilling

The decline in oil prices in the early 1980s resulted in a sharp drop in the demand for oil drilling services in the United States. Companies such as Ratliff, which had expanded their capacity based on optimism regarding the demand for drilling, had their earnings significantly reduced by the drop in demand. The utilization rate for the company's oil drilling rigs dropped sharply as can be seen in the following table from the company's annual report for the year ended September 30, 1983:

Rig Utilization Rates, 1981–1983

	1st Qtr	2nd Qtr	3rd Qtr	4th Qtr	Total
1981	97%	98%	99%	95%	97%
1982	92	84	72	63	78
1983	45	57	40	32	44

In the fourth quarter of fiscal 1983, but effective at the beginning of the fiscal year, Ratliff changed its depreciation method for drilling rigs from the straight-line method to the units-of-production method. This change was explained in the first footnote included in Exhibit 6-17.

The new depreciation method was explained in the second footnote in Exhibit 6-17, entitled Property and Equipment.

The impact of this change in accounting method on previously reported operating results can be seen from the exhibits that follow.

The data in Exhibit 6-18 depict the company's operating results and the effect of the change in depreciation method. A comparison of the rig utilization rate with the impact of the accounting change is shown in Exhibit 6-19.

While the relationship between rig utilization rate and effect of the change in depreciation method is not precise, it is clear that the effect increases dramatically as the utilization rate falls. Notice that the effect in the fourth quarter of fiscal 1983 is about the same as that in the third quarter despite the drop in rig utilization; the use of a 40% minimum provision (see second footnote in Exhibit 6-17) means that the maximum effect of the change in method is realized at that level. Any further decline in utilization has no impact on reported depreciation.

Ratliff recorded the impact of the accounting change using the cumulative effect method. Thus the entire impact of the change on prior years was shown as a line item ($460,074) in the 1983 income statement. The company did provide pro forma data for 1982 and 1981, showing that the new method would have increased net income by $257,563 and $7,858, respectively. The remaining effect ($460,074 − $257,563 − $7858 = $194,653) must apply to years of low rig utilization prior to 1981.

The effect of the change on net income is derived completely from the effect on depreciation expense. Depreciation expense relating to drilling equipment can be obtained from Schedule VI of Ratliff's 10-K:

EXHIBIT 6-17. RATLIFF DRILLING & EXPLORATION COMPANY
Depreciation of Rigs

During the fourth quarter of 1983 (effective October 1, 1982), the Company changed from straight-line to a units-of-production method for depreciating drilling rigs. The straight-line method accurately estimated depreciation during periods of high rig utilization; however, during periods of low rig utilization, as occurred during fiscal 1983, this method was no longer appropriate. The Company anticipates that future utilization will be more volatile and that the units-of-production method will more accurately measure physical depreciation of the Company's rigs. The new method will result in a better matching of cost and revenue and, because of the growing industry movement to adopt the method, will provide more comparability of the Company's financials with other drilling companies.

The effect of the accounting change was to decrease the Company's 1983 consolidated net loss by $1,422,407, or $0.48 per share, of which $460,074 (after reduction for income taxes of $425,000), or $0.16 per share, related to the cumulative effect of the change on prior years. The pro forma amounts shown on the income statement have been adjusted for the effect of the accounting change had it been applied retroactively.

Property and Equipment

Drilling Equipment

Drilling rigs are depreciated on a units-of-production method, based on operational days. During periods of inactivity, a 40 percent minimum provision is recorded (see Note 3). Drill pipe and collars are depreciated on the straight-line method. The Company uses the following useful lives for drilling equipment:

	Years
Drilling rigs	7 to 12
Drill pipe and collars	5

Source: Ratliff Drilling & Exploration Company, *1983 Annual Report.*

Year Ended	Depreciation Expense (Drilling Only)
9-30-81	$ 3,842,932
9-30-82	5,160,239
9-30-83	3,833,529

Depreciation expense for fiscal 1983 showed a decline of 26% from the fiscal 1982 figure. While the decline is less than the 56% drop in drilling revenues, the units-of-production method does make depreciation a somewhat variable expense rather than one that is fixed. *If the accounting change had not been made, depreciation expense for fiscal 1983 would have been approximately 9% higher[45] than the fiscal 1982 level.*

The change to the units-of-production method has the additional effect of increasing the assumed life of the drilling rigs (in years) by stretching out depreciation. There is an

[45]The 1983 effect on net income of the accounting change was $962 million. Given the prevailing tax rate of 46%, depreciation expense would have been ($962 million/0.54) $1780 million higher or $3834 million + $1780 million = $5614 million. This is approximately 9% higher than 1982 depreciation of $5160 million.

EXHIBIT 6-18. RATLIFF DRILLING & EXPLORATION COMPANY
Summarized Quarterly Financial Information (Unaudited)

	Revenues	Operating Income	Net Income (Loss)	Earnings Per Share
1983	(In thousands, except per share data)			
First Quarter				
As previously reported	$ 5,928	$ (649)	$ (741)	$(.25)
Depreciation restatement(a)............	—	425	221	.07
Cumulative effect on prior years (b) (c)	—	—	460	.16
	$ 5,928	$ (224)	$ (60)	$(.02)
Second Quarter				
As previously reported	$ 6,171	$(1,812)	$(1,367)	$(.46)
Depreciation restatement (a)...........	—	371	193	.06
	$ 6,171	$(1,441)	$(1,174)	$(.40)
Third Quarter				
As previously reported	$ 4,927	$(1,106)	$ (941)	$(.32)
Depreciation restatement (a)...........	—	529	275	.09
	$ 4,927	$ (577)	$ (666)	$(.23)
Fourth Quarter	$ 4,055	$ (811)	$ (782)	$(.25)
Year..	$21,081	$(3,053)	$(2,682)	$(.90)
1982				
First Quarter	$11,139	$ 2,805	$ 1,600	$ .54
Second Quarter	9,561	1,870	1,035	.35
Third Quarter................................	8,650	909	649	.22
Fourth Quarter	8,016	(863)	(670)	(.23)
Year..	$37,366	$ 4,721	$ 2,614	$ .88
1982 Pro Forma Accounts Assuming Retroactive Application of Accounting Change				
First Quarter	$11,139	$ 2,871	$ 1,634	$ .55
Second Quarter	9,561	1,892	1,046	.36
Third Quarter................................	8,650	1,034	715	.24
Fourth Quarter	8,016	(581)	(523)	(.18)
Year..	$37,366	$ 5,216	$ 2,872	$ .97

(a) Effect on current year of change to units-of-production method of depreciation. (See Note 3 to the financial statements.)

(b) Cumulative effect on prior years of the change in depreciation method.

(c) On a pro forma basis assuming the change was made retroactively, this amount would be eliminated and all other 1983 amounts would remain the same.

Source: Ratliff Drilling & Exploration Company, *1983 Annual Report.*

EXHIBIT 6-19. RATLIFF DRILLING & EXPLORATION COMPANY

Quarter Ended	Utilization Rate (Percent)	Impact of Change* on Net Income ($ thousands)
December 1981	92%	$ 34
March 1982	84	11
June 1982	72	66
September 1982	63	147
Fiscal 1982	78%	$258
December 1982	45	221
March 1983	57	193
June 1983	40	275
September 1983	32	273†
Fiscal 1983	44%	962†

*The changes for 1982 are derived by subtracting the "as reported" numbers from the pro forma numbers. Thus, the first quarter 1982 calculation is ($1,634 − $1,600) = $34.

†Derived as follows:

Total impact of change	$1,422
Less: Cumulative effect	(460)
Equals: Fiscal 1983 effect	$ 962
Less: Total prior quarters (221 + 193 + 275)	(689)
Equals: Fourth quarter	$ 273

Derived from Ratliff Drilling & Exploration Company, *1983 Annual Report*.

increased risk, therefore, that technical obsolescence or other factors such as a permanent decline in the demand for rigs could lead to impairment write-offs in future years. The reduced depreciation taken as the "impairment" begins can lead to a larger write-off amount later.

Adoption of the units-of-production method of depreciation by Ratliff had no cash flow effect. Tax depreciation, we can assume, remained the same. The only impact of the accounting change was to soften the impact of adverse business conditions on reported earnings.

ANALYSIS OF FIXED ASSET DISCLOSURES

In practice, firms use varying accounting methods, lives, and residual value assumptions for fixed assets, hampering comparisons between firms. It is frequently possible, however, to use financial statement disclosures to gain insight into a company's depreciation accounting. The raw material for the analysis of fixed assets is most readily

EXHIBIT 6-20. A.M. CASTLE & CO.
Property, Plant, and Equipment

FOR THE YEARS ENDED DECEMBER 31, 1990, 1989, and 1988
(Dollars in thousands)

CLASSIFICATION	BALANCE AT BEGININING OF PERIOD	ADDITIONS AT COST	RETIREMENTS AND SALES	BALANCE AT END OF PERIOD
1990				
Land	$ 4,162	$ —	$ 47	$ 4,115
Buildings	30,319	3,798	224	33,893
Machinery and Equipment	48,634	11,055	349	59,340
	$83,115	$14,853	$ 620	$97,348
1989				
Land	$ 3,687	$ 475	$ —	$ 4,162
Buildings	26,642	3,677	—	30,319
Machinery and Equipment	42,932	6,229	527	48,634
	$73,261	$10,381	$ 527	$83,115
1988				
Land	$ 3,241	$ 446	$ —	$ 3,687
Buildings	25,111	1,531	—	26,642
Machinery and Equipment	38,696	5,839	1,603	42,932
	$67,048	$ 7,816	$1,603	$73,261

Source: A. M. Castle & Co., 1990 10-K Report Schedule V.

obtained from Schedules V and VI from the SEC 10-K filings, which cover property, plant, and equipment and accumulated depreciation respectively.[46]

Exhibits 6-20 and 6-21 show Schedules V and VI for A. M. Castle, a steel wholesaler that operates throughout the United States.

Exhibit 6-20 (Schedule V) shows a breakdown of the original cost of property, plant, and equipment (before depreciation) for the three years ended December 31, 1990. Fixed assets include land, buildings, and machinery and equipment. Other companies may report different classifications, depending on their mix of assets. For each year the schedule shows capital spending (additions at cost) and the carrying cost (not the proceeds received, which is sometimes available from the cash flow statement) of assets retired or sold.

[46]These schedules are required for all companies whose fixed assets (net of depreciation) exceed 25% of net assets.

EXHIBIT 6-21. A.M. CASTLE & CO.
Accumulated Depreciation

FOR THE YEARS ENDED DECEMBER 31, 1990, 1989, and 1988
(Dollars in thousands)

CLASSIFICATION	BALANCE AT BEGINNING OF PERIOD	PROVISION CHARGED TO INCOME	RETIREMENTS AND SALES	BALANCE AT END OF PERIOD
1990				
Buildings	$11,344	$ 962	$ 140	$12,166
Machinery and Equipment	26,495	4,254	332	30,417
	$37,839	$5,216	$ 472	$42,583
1989				
Buildings	$10,416	$ 928	$ —	$11,344
Machinery and Equipment	23,449	3,450	404	26,495
	$33,865	$4,378	$ 404	$37,839
1988				
Buildings	$ 9,523	$ 893	$ —	$10,416
Machinery and Equipment	21,824	3,021	1,396	23,449
	$31,347	$3,914	$1,396	$33,865

Source: A. M. Castle & Co., 1990 10-K Report Schedule VI.

Exhibit 6-21 (Schedule VI) shows data for the accumulated depreciation account, using the same classifications as in Schedule V. Note that because land is not a depreciable asset, there is no land classification in Schedule VI.

Changes in the cost of fixed assets (Schedule V) can result from four types of events:

1. Capital spending (acquisition of fixed assets)

2. Sale or retirement (no longer in use) of fixed assets

3. Increases in fixed assets due to acquisitions

4. Changes due to the effects of foreign currency translation

The effect of exchange rate changes is not important for A. M. Castle, which has insignificant foreign operations.[47]

To analyze the fixed asset accounts of Castle, several portions of the company's cash flow statement are needed. Cash flow from investing activities for the three years ended December 31, 1990 is as follows (in $ thousands):

[47]This issue is discussed in Chapter 13.

	Years Ended December 31		
	1988	1989	1990
Cash flows from investing activities			
Acquisition of Norton Steel Co., Ltd.	—	—	$ (2,529)
Proceeds from sale of facilities/equipment	$ 503	$ 196	34
Capital expenditures	(7816)	(10,381)	(13,390)
Net cash used by investing activities	$(7313)	$(10,185)	$(15,885)

Cash flow from operating activities contains the following adjustment:

Gain on sale of facilities/equipment	$ (296)	$ (72)	$ (17)

Source: A.M. Castle & Co. 1990 Annual Report.

Notice, first, that the additions at cost for 1988 and 1989 in Schedule V are exactly equal to the capital expenditures shown in the cash flow statement.

For 1990, additions at cost are $14,853,000, while capital expenditures are $13,390,000. The difference must reflect fixed assets acquired as part of the acquisition of Norton Steel. Purchase method acquisitions (see Chapter 12), which include fixed assets, will always affect the data in Schedule V.[48] Sometimes the fixed assets acquired in the acquisition will be shown separately. In the case of Castle, we can deduce the figure of $1,463,000 ($14,853,000 − $13,390,000).

The retirements and sales shown in Schedule V are the gross cost (before depreciation) of fixed assets sold or removed from service during the year. The cash received from the sale of fixed assets is shown in the extract from the cash flow statement. What is the relationship between the two?

The net (after depreciation) cost of assets sold or retired can be determined by combining the data from Schedules V and VI. A comparison of the proceeds of sale with the net cost yields the gain or loss, if any. These computations follow (in $ thousands):

Year	(1) Cost	(2) Accumulated Depreciation	(3) Net Cost (1) − (2)	(4) Proceeds	(5) Gain/(Loss) (4) − (3)
1988	$ 1603	$ 1396	$ 207	$ 503	$ 296
1989	527	404	123	196	73
1990	620	472	148	34	(114)

The gain computed for 1988 and 1989 conforms precisely to the gain on asset sales shown by Castle. The computed loss for 1990 differs from the $17,000 gain reported for the year. The difference is probably due to the acquisition; some of the assets acquired

[48]Pooling transactions simply add together assets of both entities and mandate restatement of all prior years presented, reflecting no additions from the acquisition in the year of the transaction. See Chapter 12.

with Norton may have been sold during 1990 and the proceeds received netted against the cost of the acquisition rather than shown separately in the cash flow statement.

Under normal circumstances, the data in Schedules V and VI can be used to determine the gain or loss on asset sales, whether or not disclosed by the company. Examining asset sales can be important for several reasons. First, a pattern of gains suggests that the company's depreciation method is conservative, resulting in net carrying amounts for fixed assets below market values. A pattern of losses would suggest that depreciation expense is understated and that fixed assets are overvalued on the balance sheet.

Second, gains and losses resulting from asset sales are considered by many analysts to be "nonrecurring" in nature and the inclusion of such gains in reported income lowers the "quality of earnings." Of course, if such gains occur in most years, it is difficult to consider them "nonrecurring." Nonetheless, variations from year to year in gains or losses from asset sales can distort operating trends.[49]

A third reason for looking at asset sales is more fundamental. Sale of a significant portion of fixed assets is an indicator of change—in product line or production location. The examination of trends in capital spending and fixed asset sales can help the analyst ask perceptive questions regarding changes in operations.

Estimating Relative Age and Useful Lives

The data in Schedules V and VI can also be used directly to estimate the relative age of companies' asset mixes. This analysis can be performed when straight-line depreciation is used; the use of accelerated methods of depreciation invalidates the methodology shown. The relative age as a percentage of depreciable ("useful") life of each asset category can be calculated as

$$\text{Average age \%} = \frac{\text{Accumulated depreciation}}{\text{Ending gross investment}}$$

For Castle, Exhibits 6-20 and 6-21 can be used to prepare the following table:

Average Age as Percentage of Depreciable Life

Classification	1988	1989	1990
Buildings	39%	37%	36%
Machinery and equipment	55	54	51

[49]Gains and losses from sales of assets are pervasive. The 1991 *Accounting Trends and Techniques* survey of 600 companies reported the following:

Number of Companies

	1987	1988	1989	1990
Gains on sales of assets	151	141	160	131
Losses on sales	28	25	29	36

Source: Accounting Trends and Techniques, 1991 Edition, p. 48. Copyright, 1991, American Institute of Certified Public Accountants. Reprinted with permission.

As long as straight-line depreciation is used, these percentages are accurate estimates of the age of the assets as a percentage of depreciable life. Neither changes in asset mix (additions with longer or shorter lives than existing assets) nor the timing of purchases will affect the calculation. The average age is declining, indicating that either Castle is increasing its net stock of assets or that the new assets being acquired to replace older ones have longer depreciable lives.[50]

Some insight can be gained by calculating the average depreciable life of each asset category:

$$\text{Average depreciable life} = \frac{\textbf{Ending gross investment}}{\textbf{Depreciation expense}}$$

For Castle the corresponding table would be

Average Depreciable Life (Years)

Classification	1988	1989	1990
Buildings	29.8	32.7	35.2
Machinery and equipment	14.2	14.1	13.9

This latter calculation is only a rough approximation as it can be affected by the change in asset mix. During periods of rapid growth in fixed assets, the timing (within the year) of when assets are placed into service can also affect the ratio. Over longer time periods, however, this ratio can be useful in evaluating a firm's depreciation policy and comparing it with competitors.

In the case of Castle, the data alone are inconclusive, comparisons with competitors would be worthwhile. The average depreciable life of buildings seems to be increasing while that of machinery and equipment is declining. Management would have to be questioned to learn the significance of these trends.

Estimating the Age of Assets

Finally, an approximation of the age (in years) of a firm's fixed assets can also be calculated. The average age of a firm's fixed assets is estimated by comparing accumulated depreciation with depreciation expense:

$$\text{Average age} = \textbf{Average age as percentage of depreciable life} \\ \times \textbf{Depreciable life}$$

$$= \frac{\textbf{Accumulated depreciation}}{\textbf{Depreciation expense}}$$

---

[50]As noted earlier depreciable lives and economic lives for reporting purposes are not equivalent. See earlier reference to Most (1984).

For Castle, the results of the calculations are contained in the following table:

Average Age of Fixed Assets (Years)

Classification	1988	1989	1990
Buildings	11.7	12.2	12.6
Machinery and equipment	7.8	7.7	7.2

As in the case of depreciable life calculations, the average age calculations can be distorted by changes in asset mix and by acquisitions. Nonetheless, these data are useful for comparison purposes and can suggest a useful line of questioning when meeting with management.

The data as to average age, either as a percentage of gross cost or in absolute terms, are useful for two reasons. First, older assets tend to be less efficient; inefficient or obsolete fixed assets may make the firm uncompetitive. Second, knowing past patterns of capital replacement helps the analyst estimate when major capital expenditures will be required. The financing implications of capital expenditure requirements may be significant. Furthermore, in forecasting the capital expenditure requirements, the data should be compared with benchmark data on the useful (economic) life of fixed assets for that industry.

III. IMPAIRMENT OF LONG-LIVED ASSETS

INTRODUCTION

Accounting principles require that fixed assets be carried at acquisition cost less accumulated depreciation. While there is no provision (under U.S. GAAP) for recognizing increases in value, there is a requirement that carrying amounts be reduced when there is no longer the expectation that those amounts can be recovered from future operations. Assets carried at more than the recoverable amount are considered "impaired," although current rules contain no specific definition of recoverable amount or when a firm should measure such impairment.

Significant changes in markets (demand for the product or supply of raw materials) and technology (end use or production process) may suggest the need for an evaluation of long-lived assets. Reassessments of their carrying amounts, estimated salvage values, depreciation methods, and service lives may be required.

Reporting requirements (both measurement and disclosure) for changes in depreciation methods and estimates for assets that continue in use have been discussed in preceding sections of this chapter. Although the timing of these changes is discretionary and management has considerable flexibility in reporting depreciation changes, they can be valuable signals of enterprise health.

However, economic conditions often result in reduced use of facilities and market demand, or technology changes may temporarily idle some assets. Other assets may be permanently impaired in that a portion or all of their carrying cost cannot be recovered through current or expected levels of operations.

Firms may dispose of or continue to operate impaired assets. Dispositions may involve outright sale or abandonment of assets, whereas the impaired assets retained may be temporarily idled or operated at a significantly reduced level.

There is an important distinction between assets the firm has decided to dispose of and those it intends to keep. The disposition decision severs the link between those assets and continuing operations, as those assets are no longer expected to contribute to the ongoing operations of the firm. Impaired assets retained by the firm are expected to contribute to operations and cash flows, but at reduced levels, and their level of contribution may be highly uncertain.

The second important difference between these asset categories involves reporting requirements. APB 30, Reporting Results of Operations (1973), governs the timing, quantification, and reporting of the disposal or sale of a segment of a business. A related American Institute of Certified Public Accountants (AICPA) interpretation delineates reporting requirements for disposition or sale of portions of a segment. (See Chapter 2 for a discussion of these reporting requirements.)

For impaired assets to be retained by the firm, the primary issue is how to report the firm's inability to recover fully their carrying amount. The reporting problem involves the timing, quantification (measurement), and disclosure of the impaired assets expected to continue in operation or be temporarily idled. Current accounting rules are not well specified and inadequate at best. Given the increasing frequency of impairment announcements, the absence of reporting guidelines has resulted in diverse accounting practices that are not comparable across companies and inconsistently applied within firms over time. Timely recognition of impairment could correct understated past depreciation or permit recognition of changes in markets or technology.

FASB standards for leases, capitalization of interest, and oil and gas activities all contain references to the recognition of nontemporary declines in value. SFAS 33, Financial Reporting and Changing Prices (1979), in a significant departure from historical cost, required a write-down to "recoverable amount" when the asset's value in business or use declined below its carrying cost. However, SFAS 89, Financial Reporting and Changing Prices (1986), made these supplementary disclosures voluntary. Both the acceptability (because of the departure from historical cost principles) and the availability (because of the voluntary nature of SFAS 89) of these write-downs is uncertain.

Impairment of Oil and Gas Properties: Pennzoil

Reporting for oil and gas activities requires the periodic assessment of unproved properties[51] to determine whether they have been impaired. The full cost method of accounting for oil and gas activities also limits the capitalization of exploration costs. Companies must compare the carrying amount of their oil and gas reserves with the present value of the future cash flows associated with those reserves. If the carrying amount exceeds the present value, impairment has taken place, and a write-down is required.

[51]This term, and other technical terms used in the discussion of Pennzoil, are defined in the glossary.

The sharp decline in oil and gas prices during the 1980s subjected many full cost companies to this process. In some cases, companies retroactively adopted the successful efforts method, reducing the carrying value of their reserves, and making impairment provisions unnecessary.[52]

Exhibit 6-22 contains footnote 9, Unusual Items, from Pennzoil's 1988 financial statements and provides a comprehensive example of disclosures of impairments of and losses on disposal of oil and gas properties. Pennzoil reviewed both proved and unproved properties and recognized impairments of $225 million ($141 million or $3.63 per share after tax) on unproved properties because of "lease expiration dates and anticipated future oil and gas prices"—among the criteria cited in SFAS 19 as examples of factors suggesting impairment.

Pennzoil also recognized impairments and abandonments of proved properties of $162 million ($101 million or $2.60 per share after taxes). Note that the firm had

---

[52]Changing to the successful efforts method resulted, in effect, in writing down the carrying amount of reserves retroactively. The "advantage" to the company is that current year earnings were not impacted.

EXHIBIT 6-22. PENNZOIL CO.
Notes to Consolidated Financial Statements, Note 9

Unusual Items—

Provisions for Losses and Gains On Disposition and Write-Down of Assets

During the quarter ended June 30, 1988, Pennzoil's management and board of directors completed a strategic review of Pennzoil. As a result of this review, write-downs of certain assets and other charges were provided for, which Pennzoil considered appropriate to reflect permanent impairment of recorded values and other identified liabilities. The following is a summary of the write-downs and other charges provided in 1988 (in millions):

Impairments and Abandonments	$387
Write-down of Refinery Assets	115
Gain on Disposition of Oil and Gas Properties	(59)
Other Write-downs and Charges	46
	$489

(a) Impairments and Abandonments—

Pennzoil's review included an evaluation of current and anticipated future industry market conditions together with an evaluation of the impact of those conditions on the recoverability of its investments in unproved and proved oil and gas properties. Based on the results of the review, Pennzoil concluded that a substantial portion of its domestic and foreign lease acreage could not be economically drilled and developed given applicable lease expiration dates and anticipated future oil and gas prices. As a result, impairments of approximately $225 million ($141 million after tax, or $3.63 per share) were incurred. In addition, the carrying amounts of proven properties were evaluated pursuant to the company's policy of periodically assessing recoverability of proven properties, resulting in impairments and abandonments of approximately $162 million ($101 million after tax, or $2.60 per share).

EXHIBIT 6-22. *(Continued)*

(b) Write-down of Refinery Assets—

A substantial portion of Pennzoil's investment in the refinery assets of Atlas Processing Company, a wholly owned subsidiary, was permanently impaired as a result of continuing operating losses and increasing difficulty in maintaining access to economical supplies of high-quality crude oil. Accordingly, a write-down of approximately $115 million ($72 million after tax, or $1.85 per share) was recorded to reflect the portion of the refinery investment which will not be recoverable from future operations.

(c) Gain On Disposition of Oil and Gas Properties—

Pennzoil sold its interests in its Dutch North Sea oil and gas properties, resulting in a gain of approximately $59 million ($39 million after tax, or $1.00 per share).

(d) Other Write-downs and Charges—

Charges totaling $33 million ($20 million after tax, or $.51 per share) were recorded to reflect the liability for certain employee benefits earned in prior periods. The annual charge to earnings for such benefits was not previously considered to be significant.

Write-downs of other individually non-significant assets of approximately $13 million were provided in the second quarter representing the company's estimate of the realizability of those investments.

Capitalized Oil and Gas Properties—

Pennzoil's net income for 1986 reflected a non-cash charge of approximately $58 million, or $1.42 per share, as a result of a first quarter write-down of the capitalized oil and gas property costs of its affiliate, PPI. The write-down resulted from PPI's assessment of the recoverability of its investment in oil and gas properties. The charge by Pennzoil is reflected in the Consolidated Statement of Income as "Equity (loss) in net income of Proven Properties Inc." and is based on Pennzoil's 48.7% voting interest in PPI.

Gain on Pension Asset Reversion—

For the year ended December 31, 1986, other income included a fourth quarter after-tax gain of $32.1 million realized by Pennzoil on the recovery of excess assets from its salaried retirement plan (See Note 4 herein). This gain increased earnings per share by $.77.

Source: Pennzoil Co., *1988 Annual Report.*

reported a write-down of $58 million ($1.42 per share) in 1986 to reflect the impairment of oil and gas properties held by an equity affiliate, PPI.

The firm's 1988 net income was thus reduced by a total of $387 million ($225 million + $162 million) or $245 million ($6.23 per share) after tax due to impairments. These adjustments were recognized in the same year that the firm announced a change from the full cost to the successful efforts method of accounting for its oil and gas properties, as previously discussed, a change that resulted in a retroactive adjustment to retained earnings of $301.6 million. Pennzoil's provision for impairments reduced net income by $245 million in 1988, but the larger amount, $301 million, was taken directly to retained earning and never affected reported income. As stated in the discussion of the accounting change, the switch allowed the firm to report a smaller reduction in current income and may have allowed it to avoid or delay future write-downs.

Recognition of impairments in the oil and gas industry has been common, in part, because of GAAP and SEC reporting requirements (specifically, the SFAS 69 supplementary disclosures) previously discussed and, in part, because of the availability of reasonably reliable prices in secondary markets. However, the absence of both reporting guidelines and reliable market prices has long limited the disclosure of impairments of other long-lived assets.

FINANCIAL STATEMENT IMPACT OF IMPAIRMENTS

Write-downs and impairments of long-lived assets have pervasive and significant effects on financial statements and financial ratios. These effects are often hard to discern due to the inherently subjective nature of the impairment decision and the absence of standardized reporting requirements.

The lack of reporting guidelines for impairments has resulted in widely divergent timing, measurement, and reporting practices. Fried, Schiff, and Sondhi (FSS) (1989) and two Financial Executives Institute surveys[53] found that a majority of companies used net realizable values (NRV) to measure impairments. However, significant evidence suggests that NRV means different things to different firms, and the definition used is rarely disclosed. The problem is compounded by SFAC 5, where NRV is defined as a short-term, gross, *undiscounted cash flow*. The use of undiscounted cash flows results in an overstatement of asset values because of the failure to recognize the time value of money.

The lack of reporting guidelines also affects the level of aggregation (single assets; plant, business unit, or segment; etc.) used by different companies in measuring impairments. Combined with the discretionary nature of the timing of announcements, these problems suggest that it is difficult to compare the impact and the resulting ratios over time and across companies.

Impairments or write-offs fall into two general categories: write-downs and restructurings. Although treated similarly for accounting purposes, the two reflect distinct events. The former has no future economic consequences and is a result of changed market conditions. The latter term is more encompassing and often subsumes the first. Restructurings are indicative of a major reorganization of a company's affairs. To a great extent, the charges taken reflect future costs recorded in the current year in addition to write-downs of assets.

Because managements have a great deal of discretion as to timing, anticipation can be only general in nature. Substandard profitability, especially when persistent, is probably the surest sign of impaired assets. Segment data (see Chapter 11) can help the analyst to spot underperforming operations.

---

[53]Financial Executives Institute, Committee on Corporate Reporting, "Survey on Unusual Charges", (1986 and 1991).

Interpretation, as it depends on disclosure, is often difficult. "Restructuring" provisions often include impairment provisions. It is important, when a company makes such a provision, to separate impairment (noncash write-downs of past cash outflows) from severance costs and other items requiring current and future cash outflows. Only the latter will affect cash flow directly.

The cash flow and tax implications of write-offs are also unclear in some cases. Generally, impairments recognized for financial reporting are not deductible for tax purposes until the affected assets are disposed of. Recognition of the impairment, therefore, leads to a deferred tax asset (a probable future tax benefit) not a current refund. Beneficial cash flow impacts may occur only in the future, when tax deductions are realized.[54] It is important to understand the income tax consequences of impairment or restructuring provisions. Close attention to the income tax footnote (see Chapter 7) should be helpful, but a complete understanding may require posing questions to management.

In November 1988, the FASB began work on a project to establish standards for the recognition and measurement of impairments. The following summary is based on decisions taken through November 1992. The proposed standards would apply to long-lived assets, identifiable intangibles, and goodwill. The project's scope was expanded to include assets the firm intends to dispose of but the Board has not yet established measurement rules for those assets.

The proposed standard would require recognition of impairment when there is evidence of a lack of recoverability of the carrying amount of an asset or a group of assets. Lack of recoverability may be signaled by the presence of one or more of indicators such as:

- a significant decrease in the market value or use of the assets
- adverse changes in the legal or business climate
- significant cost overruns
- forecast of a significant decline in the long-term profitability of the asset.

Impairment would be recognized when the carrying value of the assets exceeds the *undiscounted* future cash flows from their use and disposal. The loss would be measured as the excess of the carrying amount over the fair value of the assets. When fair value cannot be determined, the *discounted* present value of future cash flows (discounted at the firm's incremental borrowing rate) would be used. The loss would be reported before tax as a component of income from continuing operations.

The recoverability test and loss measurement are based on assets grouped at the lowest level for which cash flows can be identified independently of cash flows of other asset groups. The standard would prohibit restoration of previous impairments. It would require disclosure of the amount of the loss, segments affected, events and circum-

---

[54]Important exceptions include settlements or curtailments of pension plans, severance payments for early retirement, and the purchase of annuities to satisfy these claims. These events require current outlays but may decrease future outflows for these benefits. Such events may also have current cash flow consequences due to immediate tax impacts.

stances surrounding the impairment, and whether fair value or present value was used to measure the loss; when the latter was used, the discount rate would have to be disclosed.

A final standard is expected to be issued in 1993.

The impact of write-offs is confounded by the existence of an unusually strong set of beliefs about the nature and effects of announcements of impairments. Articles in the financial and popular press often talk about the "big bath"—a tendency to take large write-offs during adverse times and of "house cleaning"—large write-offs assumed to accompany changes in senior management. Consequently, write-off announcements often are viewed as a signal that the worst is over to be followed by an upturn in the firm's fortunes.

Various studies have examined the write-off phenomenon, including Elliott and Shaw (1988), Fried, Schiff and Sondhi. (FSS, 1989, 1990), Lindhal and Ricks (1990), and Strong and Meyer (1987). These studies have documented a number of recurring characteristics of write-offs. Many of these findings are not consistent with the big bath hypothesis.

1. The studies have found an increasing frequency in the number and dollar amount of write-downs. FSS reported that write-offs had increased from $1 billion (average write-off of $28 million per company) in 1980 to $24 billion ($117 million per company) before taxes in 1986.[55]

2. The majority of write-offs (approximately 60%) are announced in the fourth quarter. Given the detailed review undertaken in preparation of the annual report, it is likely that the fourth quarter will always contain the largest number of write-offs. However, this finding also reflects fundamental problems with the financial reporting for impairments; it is subjective as to the timing of announcements and uncertain as to measurement.

3. Write-offs are usually preceded by poor financial as well as stock market performance. Exhibit 6-23A and B from Elliott and Shaw shows that, when compared to industry medians, firms that experienced write-offs had lower earnings, ROA, and ROE and had higher debt/equity ratios. These results hold for the year of the write-off[56] as well as in the three-year period preceding the write-off. FSS (1987), using a control group of firms matched by industry and size, found similar results. Strong and Meyer, however, report that, although the write-off firms are not the best performers in their industry, they are not in the bottom quintile either, but tend to cluster in the middle quintiles.

4. Consistent with the foregoing, the stock market performance of write-off firms tends to be poorer than the control group. Exhibit 6-23C indicates that for three years prior to the write-off, the sample companies had significantly worse returns than the industry. Similar results occur around the time of the write-off itself and for up to 18 months following the write-off. Elliott and Shaw report that the size of the write-off is

---

[55]The most recent survey of impairments was undertaken by the Financial Executives Institute (FEI). In 1991, questionnaires were sent to 523 firms that had recently announced write-offs. The FEI was updating its 1986 survey of 110 announcers. In 1991 (1986), 109 (55) firms responded with information on various write-downs. Unfortunately, it is not possible to determine the numbers or dollar amounts of write-downs announced either by all firms in the sample or by those responding.

[56]These conditions hold even without taking the write-off into consideration (see the "AS-IF" results in Exhibit 6-23A).

EXHIBIT 6-23
Characteristics of Writeoff Firms

A. *Accounting Measures During the Write-Off Year: 240 Sample Firms Versus Industry Medians*

Characteristic	Sample Firms' Median Value	Difference = Firm − Industry			
		Mean[a]	Median[a]	%>0[b]	Wilcoxon Significance[c]
Revenues	860.882	1460.60	246.229	63.3	0.001
Assets..........................	867.734	1454.99	293.999	62.1	0.001
Debt/equity	.502	0.491	0.120	62.9	0.001
Net earnings	−9.526	−58.848	−27.615	23.3	−0.001
Net earnings/assets..........	−.020	−0.091	−0.052	13.3	−0.001
Net earnings/equity	−.051	−0.399	−0.096	15.4	−0.001
"AS-IF"					
Net earnings	9.653	40.202	−2.208	45.4	−0.879
Net earnings/assets..........	0.023	−0.027	−0.016	32.5	−0.001
Net earnings/equity	0.050	−0.011	−0.016	40.4	−0.001

[a]Mean or median difference between the sample firm and the median of all other non-write-off firms with December year-ends in the same four-digit SIC code. Dollars are in millions.

[b]The percentage of differences greater than zero. Values less than .43 (greater than .57) are statistically significant at $a \leq .05$ for sample sizes of about 200.

[c]Two-tailed significance levels are shown for a Wilcoxon signed-ranks test. A negative sign indicates the industry control values are larger.

B. *Accounting and Market Measures Three Years Prior to the Write-Off: 240 Sample Firms Versus Industry Medians*

Characteristic[a]	Financial/Accounting Measures (Dollars in millions)				
	Write-Off Firms' Median Value	Difference = Firm − Industry			
		Mean	Median	%>0[b]	Wilcoxon Significance[c]
Average net earnings	21.781	58.483	7.422	57.5	0.001
Net earnings growth[d].......	−.095	0.065	−0.057	41.3	−0.025
Average return	889.598	1512.010	273.247	65.8	0.001
Revenue growth[d]	.026	0.108	−0.006	46.3	0.958
Average net earnings/assets.............	.038	−0.010	−0.006	39.6	−0.001
Average net earnings/equity............	.076	−0.024	−0.000	49.6	−0.103

EXHIBIT 6-23. *(Continued)*

| | Market-Based Measures | | | | |
| | | Difference = Firm − Industry | | | |
	Write-Off Median	Mean	Median	% > 0[b]	Wilcoxon Significance
Market return[e]................	0.218	−0.121	−0.219	25.5	−0.001

[a]All measured as three-year averages ending in the year prior to the write-off.

[b]The percentage of differences greater than zero. Values less than 43 (greater than 57) are statistically significant at a ≤ .05 for sample sizes of about 200.

[c]Two-tailed significance levels are shown for a Wilcoxon signed-ranks test. A negative sign indicates the industry control value is larger.

[d]Geometric growth rates and rates of return.

[e]All return data were obtained from *CRSP* monthly data. Return data were available for 196 firms.

C. Regression Results for the Write-Off Announcement: Cross-Sectional Variation in Two-Day Industry-Adjusted Returns (214 Observations, 1982–85)

Independent Variable	Predicted Sign	Coefficient	t-statistic	Two-Tailed Significance Level
Intercept	+	−0.006	−0.984	0.327
Write-off/market value (negative values).................................	+	0.022	2.435	0.016
Earnings forecast error[a]	+	0.248	3.331	0.001
Bad news (0, 1)[b] (1 = neutral or unfavorable)	−	−0.043	−4.036	0.001
Stock repurchase (0, 1) (0 = no announcement)	+	0.051	2.498	0.013
Write-off type (0, 1) (0 = write-down)	?	−0.001	−0.088	0.930
Management change (0, 1) (0 = no change)	+	0.004	0.531	0.596
Successive write-off (0, 1) (0 = initial write-off)...............	?	0.015	1.617	0.107
Adjusted R^2			.158	

[a]Earnings forecast error is defined as:

$$\frac{\text{Reported } EPS + \text{After-Tax Effect of Write-Off} - \text{Last Analyst Forecast}}{\text{Share Price}}$$

where the analyst forecast is the median analyst forecast before earnings are announced. This variable is nonzero only for cases where the write-off is disclosed concurrently with annual earnings.

[b]The dichotomous bad news variable reflects the characterization of the write-off in the *Wall Street Journal* announcement (for example, the simultaneous disclosure of a dividend reduction).

Source: J. A. Elliott and W. H. Shaw, "Writeoffs as Accounting Procedures to Manage Perceptions", *Journal of Accounting Research*, Vol. 26, Supp. 1988, A: p. 99 (table 3), B: p. 101 (table 4), C: p. 107 (table 7).

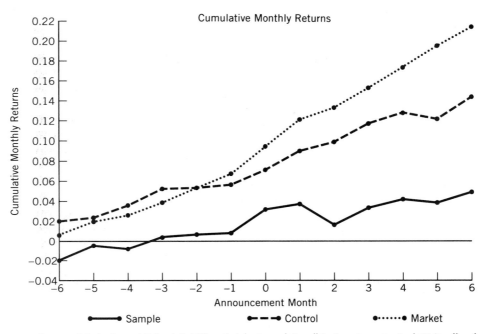

Source: Fried, Dov, Michael Schiff and Ashwinpaul Sondhi, *Impairments And Writeoffs of Long-Lived Assets,* Figure 6-9, pp. 101. (Montvale, New Jersey, National Association of Accountants 1989)

FIGURE 6-7

directly related to the degree of negative return experienced around the time of the write-off; the larger the write-off, the more negative the reaction.

In general, these results contradict the popular belief that write-offs result in positive market reaction. Figure 6-7 from FSS provides some insight into this. The write-offs occurred during a general "bull market." Thus the firms that took write-offs had positive returns. However, relative to the control group, they did worse. Relative to the market as a whole, both they and the control group did poorly.

On the other hand, Lindhal and Ricks indicated that although, in general, market reaction is negative, the results depend on whether the event is a write-down or a restructuring. For the latter type of event, they report positive market reaction.

5. Economy- and industrywide factors seem to dominate firm-specific factors as signals of problems. FSS reported that the highest proportion of write-offs are taken in the oil and gas, chemicals, electronics, iron and steel, and machinery industries. These industries went through difficult times in the early 1980s. Similarly, as Figure 6-7 notes, FSS's control group (which was matched by industry) consistently did poorer than the market as a whole.

6. Problems leading to write-offs are rarely short lived and generally persist after the write-off. This is confirmed by the poor market reaction persisting up to 18 months following the write-off. In addition, write-offs tend not to be one-time affairs. FSS reported that firms generally take multiple write-offs. They find that

45% of the companies who take a writeoff experience a subsequent one the next year, over 61% do so within two years, and 73% announce another writeoff within three years.[57]

In effect they "warehouse" bad news and report it through multiple write-offs. Furthermore, they found that the size of subsequent write-offs tended to be larger than previous ones.[58]

The prevalence of multiple write-offs and their increasing size is inconsistent with big bath behavior, usually associated with a "once and for all" write-off. Once a firm has taken a write-off, there exists a strong potential for a second, larger write-off. Given the significance and frequency of write-offs, it is unfortunate that indicators of initial write-offs are hard to come by. FSS found that LIFO liquidations and poor financial condition were the most reliable indicators of potential write-offs. Similar results appear in other studies. Better disclosure in financial statements (or the Management Discussion and Analysis section of the SEC 10-K) of problems with particular segments would make it easier to predict write-offs.

INTERNATIONAL ACCOUNTING DIFFERENCES AFFECTING LONG-LIVED ASSETS

This section describes significant international differences in the financial reporting practices discussed in this chapter.

Long-lived assets are generally reported at historical acquisition costs adjusted for accumulated depreciation. However, replacement cost is commonly used in the Netherlands, and net realizable value can be used under certain circumstances. Periodic revaluations of fixed assets are common practice in the United Kingdom and Australia and are permitted in Canada and France, but they are not allowed in Germany or Japan. Since current standards in most countries do not specify either the method(s) to be used for revaluations or the intervals at which they must be made, the resulting balance sheet accounts are not comparable and, in many cases, may be misleading. When subsequent depreciation charges are based on revalued amounts, the result is lower earnings per share. In some countries, depreciation based on revalued amounts can be used for tax purposes.

The negative impact on earnings per share reduces the incentive for revaluations, and many U.K. companies have discontinued the practice. A recent proposal from the U.K. Accounting Standards Board is designed to remedy the situation by reverting to historical cost in the financial statements with current values in the footnotes. Long-lived assets, marketable securities, and certain inventories would have to be regularly revalued. The IASC, in ED 43, has proposed similar rules. ED 43 would, however, result in some revaluation changes being included in reported earnings.

---

[57]Dov Fried, Michael Schiff and Ashwinpaul Sondhi, "Big Bath or Intermittent Showers? Another Look at Write-offs," Working paper (1990), P.12

[58]This result could also explain why FSS found that market reaction to second write-offs tended to be worse than for the original write-offs.

Multinational corporations translate the fixed assets of some of their subsidiaries using the current rate at the end of each period. This translation process adds volatility to the reported balances and affects the analysis of these companies. (See Chapter 13 for a detailed discussion of this problem and applicable analytical techniques). Disclosure of the impact of translation on asset balances would assist the financial analysis of such companies and comparisons of firms across countries.

International comparisons require adjustments to earnings (for depreciation based on other than historical costs) and to net worth (for revaluations). These comparisons may be difficult for the reasons mentioned earlier, the different tax status of revaluations in different countries, and the varying treatment of the revaluation surplus (often added to a reserve account, changes in which are not always fully disclosed).

Capitalization of Borrowing Costs

No specific standards on the capitalization of interest costs exist in the United Kingdom or Canada. As capitalization is not prohibited, practice is diverse. In October 1992, the IASC reviewed comments on ED 39 and revised IAS 23, Capitalization of Borrowing Costs. The benchmark treatment requires the expensing of all borrowing costs; the allowed alternative permits capitalization of borrowing costs in certain circumstances. The treatment under the allowed alternative is substantially similar to U.S. GAAP.

Research and Development Expenditures

Research outlays are expensed in the period incurred in most countries. Qualifying development costs must be capitalized in Canada and may be so treated in the Netherlands, the United Kingdom, and France when recovery criteria are satisfied. In Japan these costs are generally expensed as incurred but may also be capitalized and amortized over five years.

In October 1992, the IASC revised IAS 9, Accounting for Research and Development Activities. Development costs must be capitalized when certain criteria are met but expensed otherwise. Capitalization of development costs represents a major departure from U.S. GAAP and will require adjustments of net income and net worth in international comparisons.

Goodwill

With few exceptions, the primary difference in accounting for goodwill is the amortization period used in different countries. In France, it ranges from 10 to 20 years and, in Germany, from 5 years to expected useful life. In the United Kingdom and the Netherlands, it is generally written off immediately to retained earnings[59] or to reserve accounts that may be specially created for this purpose. Only Japan and Germany allow partial tax benefits for goodwill deductions. The IASC's ED 45 on Business Combinations prohibits the writeoff of goodwill to reserves in the equity account and calls for amortization of goodwill over its useful life (not exceeding five years unless a period of

---

[59]The analysis of Smithkline Beecham in Chapter 12 includes a discussion of the treatment of acquisition goodwill in the United Kingdom.

up to twenty years can be justified). This treatment differs from U.S. GAAP and will create a significant difference between U.S. and foreign reporting.

Oil and Gas Accounting

The successful efforts method is used in the United Kingdom and Canada, although the latter has no accounting standard covering this issue.[60] Canada does have detailed recommendations governing the impairment of oil and gas properties; these are similar to U.S. standards.

Depreciation Methods

Straight-line depreciation is the dominant international practice. However, in Germany and France tax rules determine the depreciation methods and rates used for financial reporting. In Germany and Japan, depreciable lives used are frequently shorter than economic lives, and both countries allow immediate expensing of some fixed assets. In most European countries, excess depreciation (additional depreciation to reflect obsolescence) is also allowed. As noted in Part I of the chapter, Canada permits real estate and utility firms to use increasing charge depreciation methods.

The IASC's ED 43 would permit any of the commonly used depreciation methods, including increasing charge methods, to be used in IASC GAAP. Thus, firms may use multiple methods without disclosing different methods used across geographic regions, business segments, and classes of fixed assets. Also, firms may disclose only the ranges of useful lives used for various categories of assets; disclosure of weighted average useful life for each category would improve analysis and comparability.

CONCLUDING COMMENTS

The IASC's ED 43 states that

> Property, plant and equipment is often a major portion of the total assets of an enterprise, and therefore is significant in the presentation of financial position. Furthermore, the determination of whether an expenditure represents an asset or an expense can have a significant effect on an enterprise's reported results of operations.[61]

As a result, differences in depreciation methods and lives are frequently the most important single cause of noncomparability between firms, within the United States as well as internationally. Yet neither any American standard setter nor the IASC appears willing to narrow the range of acceptable methods. Perhaps because accounting depreciation has so little to do with economic depreciation, standards setters seem unwilling to choose arbitrarily one of the methods of allocating asset cost to periodic income.

---

[60]It should be noted that, historically, the Canadian oil industry was dominated by subsidiaries of large U.S. companies, which, as already noted, use successful efforts accounting. However the full cost method is widely used by Canadian oil and gas firms.

[61]IASC ED 43, Property, Plant and Equipment, Para. 9 (1992).

Analysis of firms with large fixed assets, therefore, requires close attention to depreciation methods as well as estimates of useful lives and salvage values. Changes in method or estimate are common, but disclosure is often minimal. Yet these changes can have major impacts on reported income even though cash flow is rarely affected.

These problems are compounded by the lack of standards regarding impaired assets. While an FASB project is underway, it is not clear that any standard can reduce the subjectivity inherent in the measurement of fixed assets, especially operating assets with limited marketability.

Intangible assets present their own difficulties. The value of a research project, computer program, patent, or brand name may bear little relationship to its cost, regardless of the accounting standard followed. Given the rapidity with which market prices incorporate information regarding the business outlook for a firm, it seems that the accountants will remain hopelessly behind in recording the economic impact of such assets.

The financial analyst must, therefore, use financial and other data to anticipate events. Accounting changes and impairments, for example, often signal significant changes in firm operations. Some changes have cash flow implications, while others do not. One goal of this chapter was to point out the difference.

Another goal was to examine the accounting for long-lived assets and show how variations in accounting methods affect reported income, cash flows, and stockholders' equity. In many cases, intercompany comparisons will require adjustments for differences in accounting method if the analyst is to distinguish real from cosmetic differences between the firms.

Chapter 6

Problems

1. [Capitalization of interest; 1988 CFA adapted] Rogan Development, a real estate developer, is developing an office building in Charlottesville, Virginia. The average balance for 19X7 of the "building under construction" account was $10 million. Rogan had the following debt outstanding during 19X7 (in millions of dollars):

	Average Balance	Interest Rate
Development loan	$ 6	11%
Mortgage debt	10	9
Senior debentures	40	10

A. Calculate each of the following for 19X7, assuming that the development loan applied solely to the Charlottesville building:

(i) Interest payable for 19X7

(ii) Capitalized interest for 19X7

(iii) Interest expense for 19X7

B. As a bond analyst, you use the interest coverage ratio to assess Rogan's ability to meet interest payments. Discuss how you would calculate that ratio for 19X7.

C. Discuss the impact of the capitalization of interest on the comparison of the following for different firms:

    (i) Interest coverage ratios

    (ii) Cash flow from operations

    (iii) Profitability ratios

(Your answer should consider the effects of (1) the availability of internally generated funds for construction, (2) the cost of capital, and (3) amortization periods and methods.)

2. [Brand names] "Buildings age and become dilapidated. Machines wear out. Cars rust. But what lives on are brands," argues Sir Hector Laing of Britain's United Biscuits (*The Economist,* December 24, 1988, p. 100).

A. Using this quotation as a point of departure, discuss the advantages and disadvantages (from the point of view of financial analysis) of the balance sheet recognition of brand names.

B. Discuss the advantages and disadvantages (also from the point of view of financial analysis) of the amortization of brand name intangible assets through charges to income.

3. [Capitalization versus expense] The following footnote appeared in the *1991 Annual Report* of Morrison Knudsen Corp.:

> **Development Costs:** Effective April 1, 1991 the Corporation adopted a new accounting policy to defer certain costs related to the design, engineering, construction, and ongoing operation and maintenance of certain major projects in which the Corporation for the first time intends to retain an ownership interest. Such costs include licenses, fees, permits, outside professional consulting costs and engineering and technical labor costs which are expected to benefit future operations. Such costs will be capitalized as part of the project when the project becomes operational. When the commercial success of a particular project becomes doubtful, deferred development costs are written off immediately. Development costs of $4,710 have been deferred during 1991 and are included in the balance sheet caption "Other Investments and Assets."

A. Discuss the impact of this accounting change on:

    (i) Reported income in 1991.

    (ii) Reported cash flows in 1991.

    (iii) Reported income in future years.

    (iv) Reported cash flows in future years.

B. Discuss the effect of this accounting change on the level and trend of the following ratios:

    (i) Debt to equity

    (ii) Return on assets

4. [Capitalization versus expense] Exhibit 6P-1 contains a footnote from the *1991 Annual Report* of Grant Tensor Geophysical, which gathers, processes, and markets seismic data used by oil and gas exploration companies.

The company reported income for years ended December 31, 1990–1991 (in thousands of dollars):

	1990	1991
Income before extraordinary item and cumulative effect of change in accounting principle	$(8640)	$ 2770
Extraordinary item (debt extinguishment)	—	(504)
Cumulative effect of accounting change	—	983
Dividends on preferred shares	(640)	(2263)
Net income (loss) applicable to common stock	$(9280)	$ 986
Pro forma amounts assuming the change in accounting principle is applied retroactively:		
Net income (loss) applicable to common stock	$(8499)	$ 3

EXHIBIT 6P-1. GRANT TENSOR GEOPHYSICAL CORP.

Proprietary Geophysical Data

Effective January 1, 1991, the Company changed its method of amortizing proprietary geophysical data from the cost recovery method to a method whereby costs are amortized over sales the Company anticipates receiving from the licensing of its proprietary geophysical data. The Company believes the new method of accounting results in a better matching of costs and revenues and more properly reflects the carrying value of the asset.

Under the cost recovery method, equal amounts of revenue and expense were recognized as sales were made until all costs were recovered, postponing any recognition of profit until that time. Costs not recovered through sales were amortized over 36 months. Under the new method of accounting, costs are amortized based on the sales that the Company expects to realize from the licensing of its proprietary geophysical data. Management has established guidelines requiring that a minimum of 40% of the cost be amortized within 12 months from the completion date of a geophysical data program and the remainder, except for a residual of 10%, be amortized ratably over the next 24 months.

The $983,000 cumulative effect of the change on prior years (to December 31, 1990) is included in income for the year ended December 31, 1991. The cumulative effect of the change is shown without a tax effect as the Company has net operating losses available for U.S. Federal tax purposes. The effect of the change for the year ended December 31, 1991 is an increase in income before the cumulative effect of the change in accounting principle of $1,720,500 ($0.14 per share - assuming no and full dilution) and an increase in net income applicable to common stock of $737,500 ($0.06 per share - assuming no and full dilution). The pro forma amounts on the statement of operations reflect the effect of retroactive application of the change in accounting principle that would have been made for the eleven months ended December 31, 1989 and the year ended December 31, 1990 had the new method been in effect.

Source: Grant Tensor Geophysical Corp., *1991 Annual Report.*

A. Compute income before extraordinary item and cumulative effect of change in accounting principle and net income for 1991, assuming that the accounting change had not been made.

B. Compare pro forma net income for 1990 with that originally reported. Explain why that difference does not equal the cumulative effect reported in 1991.

C. The accounting change increased 1991 income (before cumulative effect) by $1,720,000. Discuss the two effects of the accounting change that resulted in that increase.

D. Grant Tensor reports changes in capitalized geophysical costs as part of cash from operations. Given this, explain why the accounting change had no effect on reported cash flows.

E. The balance sheet reports proprietary geophysical data at year end of $1,739,000 (1990) and $4,092,000 (1991). The cash flow statement shows an increase for 1991 of $2,943,000. Explain the difference and interpret the meaning of the $2,943,000 figure.

F. The third paragraph of the footnote contains an apparent error. Explain.

5. [Capitalization versus expense: computer software and R&D] Digital Equipment first began to capitalize computer software development costs in 1987. Its footnote at that time stated:

> During the year, the Company capitalized $35,115,000 of computer software development costs which are included in other assets, net on the balance sheet. These costs are amortized over three years from the date the products are available for general release. Costs amortized during the year were $1,431,000.

Exhibit 6P-2 presents the amount of computer software development costs amortized each year for 1987–1992, and the balance of the unamortized computer software development costs; other selected financial information for Digital is presented for the years 1984–1992 in millions of dollars).

A. Compute Digital's expenditure for computer software development for each year during the period 1987–1992.

B. Based on the data provided in the exhibit and your answer to A, estimate the lag between the time software is developed and the time it is "available for general release."

C. Digital's other research and engineering costs are expensed as they are incurred.

    (i) Discuss the rationale for expensing these costs while capitalizing computer software development costs.

    (ii) Discuss how the different accounting treatment of these costs will affect trends in profitability and solvency ratios, assuming that software becomes a more significant factor in Digital's products.

D. Assuming that Digital expensed computer software development costs as incurred, compare the (adjusted) operating income, return on assets, and return in equity with the amounts reported for 1987–1992. (Ignore income tax effects.)

EXHIBIT 6P-2. DIGITAL EQUIPMENT
Computer Software Development Costs, for Years Ended June 30, 1984–1992
(in $ millions)

	1984	1985	1986	1987	1988	1989	1990	1991	1992
Capitalized Software Costs									
Amortization expense	$ 0	$ 0	$ 0	$ 1	$ 12	$ 27	$ 37	$ 44	$ 64
Unamortized cost									
(year end)	0	0	0	34	66	90	110	112	134
Selected Financial Data									
Research and engineering									
costs*	$ 631	$ 717	$ 814	$1010	$ 1,306	$ 1,525	$ 1,614	$ 1,649	$ 1,754
Operating income†	395	450	829	1612	1,635	1,336	563	511	(636)
Total assets (year end)	5593	6369	7173	8407	10,112	10,668	11,655	11,875	11,284
Stockholders' equity									
(year end)	3979	4555	5728	6294	7,510	8,036	8,182	7,624	4,931

*Assume that research and engineering costs include amortized portion of software costs.
†Operating income calculated prior to restructuring charges taken in 1990–1992.
Source: Digital Equipment annual reports, 1987–1992.

E. Repeat part D assuming that Digital capitalized all research and engineering costs (as well as software costs) and amortized them over three years beginning the following year.

F. Digital Equipment's cash from operations was $1434 million, $1041 million, and $446 million in the years 1990–1992, respectively. How would the accounting assumptions made in parts D and E affect these reported numbers?

6. [Change in accounting methods: successful efforts versus full costing] In 1991 Sonat, Inc., switched its accounting method for oil and gas properties from full cost to successful efforts. As a result of the switch, the company (in its *1991 Annual Report*) restated its 1990 results to conform with the new accounting method. Selected data from the original and restated reports are reported in columns X and Y below. However, some of the originally reported (full-cost) numbers have been placed in column X and some in column Y. The same is true for the restated (successful efforts) data. Additionally, some of the data are missing.

	X	Y
Cash flow from operations	$361	$382
Cash flow from investing	(325)	?
Cash flow from financing	?	(30)
Net change in cash	?	6
Net income	94	110
Depreciation, depletion, and amortization	200	193

Using your knowledge of the difference between the two accounting methods:

A. Determine the "missing" data and, for each of the data provided, identify which are the original (full-cost) numbers and which are the restated (successful efforts) numbers.

B. Given your answer to A, can you explain why Sonat made the switch?

7. [Depreciation methods and cash flows (courtesy of Professor Stephen Ryan)] The Capital Company is considering investing in either of two assets. Cash flows of each asset are listed as follows:

Year	Asset A	Asset B
1	36	26
2	23	24
3	11	22

A. At an interest rate of 10%, how much should Capital be willing to pay for each of the assets?

B. Assuming that the amount calculated in A is paid for each asset, calculate the depreciation schedule for each asset that results in a constant rate of return.

C. What type of historical cost depreciation is equal to present value depreciation for asset A? asset B?

8. [Effect of depreciation methods; 1992 CFA adapted] Compare the straight-line method of depreciation with accelerated methods with respect to their impact on:

(i) Reported cash flows.

(ii) Reported return on equity and return on assets.

(iii) Trend of depreciation expense.

9. [Effect of depreciation methods] The Jonathan Corp. acquires a machine with an original cost of $9000 on January 1, 19X3. The machine has a five-year life and estimated salvage value of $1000. Compute depreciation for 19X3 and 19X4 under each of the following methods:

(i) Sum of years' digits

(ii) Double declining balance

(iii) Straight line

(iv) Modified accelerated cost recovery system

10. [Effect of assumptions on depreciation] The Juliet Company acquires a machine with an original cost of $9000 on January 1, 19X3. Juliet uses the straight-line method of computing depreciation. Compute depreciation expense for 19X3 under the following assumptions:

(i) Eight-year life, $1800 salvage value

(ii) Nine-year life; $1800 salvage value

(iii) Eight-year life, $1080 salvage value

(iv) Nine-year life, $1080 salvage value

11. [Accounting change: depreciation method] Exhibit 6P-3 contains the property, plant, and equipment footnote from the *1991 Annual Report* of Cummins Engine.

The following data are taken from the income statements of Cummins Engine for years ended December 31, 1989–1991 (in millions of dollars):

	1989	1990	1991
Net sales	$3520	$3462	$3406
Earnings (loss) before extraordinary credit and cumulative effect of accounting change	(6)	(165)	(66)
Extraordinary credit (debt repurchase)	—	27	—
Cumulative effect of accounting changes*	—	—	52
Net earnings (loss)	$ (6)	$(138)	$ (14)
Pro forma net earnings (loss) assuming the accounting changes had been applied retroactively	$ 3	$(124)	$ (66)

*Effect of capitalization of overhead in inventory	$25
Effect of change in method of depreciation	27
Total cumulative effect of accounting changes	$52

A. Compute Cummins' net earnings for 1991 assuming that the change in depreciation method had not taken place.

B. The change in depreciation method increased Cummins' net income for all three years. What can you infer from these increases about the level of production over the period 1989–1991?

EXHIBIT 6P-3. CUMMINS ENGINE

Property, Plant and Equipment: Property, plant and equipment are recorded at cost. Effective January 1, 1991, the company changed its method of depreciation for substantially all engine production equipment from straight-line to a modified units-of-production method, which is based upon units produced subject to a minimum level. The company believes that modified units-of-production is preferable to the method previously used because the new method recognizes that depreciation of this equipment is related substantially to both physical wear and the passage of time. This method, therefore, more accurately matches costs and revenues. The change in accounting increased results of operations $18.6 million ($1.26 per share) in 1991, exclusive of the cumulative effect of $26.5 million. Depreciation of all other equipment is computed using the straight-line method for financial reporting purposes. The estimated service lives to compute depreciation range from 20 to 40 years for buildings and 3 to 20 years for machinery, equipment and fixtures. Maintenance and repair costs are charged to earnings as incurred.

Source: Cummins Engine, *1991 Annual Report.*

C. Discuss the effect of the change in depreciation method on the components of Cummins' cash flow in 1991.

D. Discuss the likely effect of the change in depreciation method on the variability of Cummins' net income in future years.

12. [Change in depreciation method: capitalization of interest] The *1989 Annual Report* of Rohm and Haas, a chemical company, contains the following footnotes:

> Land, buildings and equipment are carried at cost. Assets are depreciated over their estimated useful lives. Effective January 1, 1989, the company changed its method of depreciation for newly acquired buildings and equipment to the straight-line method. Buildings and equipment acquired before that date continue to be depreciated principally by accelerated methods. Maintenance and repairs are charged to earnings; replacements and betterments are capitalized.
>
> Effective January 1, 1989, the company changed its method of depreciation for newly acquired buildings and equipment to the straight-line method. The change had no cumulative effect on prior years' earnings but did increase net earnings by $9 million, or $.14 per share in 1989.
>
> At December 31, 1989, the gross book values of assets depreciated by accelerated methods totaled $1,449 million and assets depreciated by the straight-line method totaled $682 million.
>
> In 1989, 1988 and 1987, respectively, interest costs of $20 million, $16 million and $11 million were capitalized and added to the gross book value of land, buildings and equipment. Amortization of such capitalized costs included in depreciation expense was $8 million in 1989, $7 million in 1988 and $5 million in 1987.

A. Explain why there was no cumulative effect for the change in depreciation method.

B. Discuss the effect of the change in depreciation method on the trend of future depreciation expense and net income.

C. Compute the effect of capitalization of interest on net income for the period 1987–1989.

D. Compute the effect of capitalization of interest on the components of cash flow for the period 1987–1989.

E. For the year ended December 31, 1989 Rohm and Haas reported interest expense of $39 million and pretax income of $251 million. Calculate the company's times interest earned ratio as reported and after adjustment for capitalized interest.

13. [Analysis of fixed assets: 10-K Schedules V and VI] Exhibit 6P-4 reproduces Schedules V and VI from the fiscal 1992 10-K filing of Daniel Industries, a manufacturer of equipment used to measure and control the flow of fluids, primarily oil and gas.

A. The firm's statement of cash flows reported $1,203,000 and $133,000 as proceeds from sales of assets for the years ended September 30, 1992, and 1991, respectively. Estimate the gain or loss on sales of assets in each year.

B. According to Schedule V, the firm acquired a facility in Germany in 1992. Explain why this transaction is not included in "additions at cost."

EXHIBIT 6P-4. DANIEL INDUSTRIES, INC. AND SUBSIDIARIES
Property, Plant and Equipment (in thousands)

Classification	Balance at beginning of period	Additions at cost	Retirements	Other	Balance at end of period
For the year ended September 30, 1992:					
Land	$ 4,387	$ 1,285		$ 2,490	$ 8,162
Buildings.	26,301	2,328	$ 39	660	29,250
Machinery and equipment.	41,763	3,162	1,019	1,477	45,383
Computer and peripheral equipment. . .	6,830	1,401	408	(8)	7,815
Office furniture and equipment	4,759	770	111	(63)	5,355
Automotive equipment	1,862	284	137	86	2,095
Other transportation equipment	8,663		4,480		4,183
Other.	7,454	398	187	6	7,671
Construction in progress	1,798	(870)		(249)	679
	$103,817	$ 8,758	$6,381	$ 4,399 (a)	$110,593
For the year ended September 30, 1991:					
Land	$ 4,259	$ 280		$ (152)	$ 4,387
Buildings.	25,166	2,101	$ 11	(955)	26,301
Machinery and equipment.	40,731	4,265	1,544	(1,689)	41,763
Computer and peripheral equipment. . .	8,140	745	1,944	(111)	6,830
Office furniture and equipment	5,200	289	584	(146)	4,759
Automotive equipment	1,795	314	123	(124)	1,862
Other transportation equipment	4,485	4,211	13	(20)	8,663
Other.	7,244	462	87	(165)	7,454
Construction in progress	2,978	(1,129)		(51)	1,798
	$99,998	$11,538	$4,306	$(3,413) (b)	$103,817
For the year ended September 30, 1990:					
Land	$ 4,239			$ 20	$ 4,259
Buildings.	23,143	$1,958	$ 310	375	25,166
Machinery and equipment.	40,422	2,169	2,072	212	40,731
Computer and peripheral equipment. . .	7,297	863	183	163	8,140
Office furniture and equipment	4,923	1,004	850	123	5,200
Automotive equipment	1,618	374	271	74	1,795
Other transportation equipment	4,485				4,485
Other.	6,870	516	194	52	7,244
Construction in progress	505	2,595	70	(52)	2,978
	$93,502	$9,479	$3,950	$ 967	$ 99,998

(a)   Includes acquisition of a facility in Germany.

(b)   Includes reclassification on disposal of gas lift equipment assets.

EXHIBIT 6P-4. *(Continued)*

ACCUMULATED DEPRECIATION OF PROPERTY, PLANT AND EQUIPMENT
(in thousands)

Classification	Balance at beginning of period	Additions charged to costs and expenses	Retirements	Other	Balance at end of period
For the year ended September 30, 1992:					
Buildings.	$ 6,309	$ 761	$ 4	$ (32)	$ 7,034
Machinery and equipment.	26,150	2,759	776	68	28,201
Computer and peripheral equipment. . .	3,851	907	253	(35)	4,470
Office furniture and equipment	2,794	471	87	(97)	3,081
Automotive equipment	1,207	273	123	(29)	1,328
Other transportation equipment	2,968	545	3,013		500
Other.	4,604	535	167	(58)	4,914
	$47,883	$6,251	$4,423	$ (183)	$49,528
For the year ended September 30, 1991:					
Buildings.	$ 5,788	$ 734	$ 9	$ (204)	$ 6,309
Machinery and equipment.	25,935	2,671	1,154	(1,302)	26,150
Computer and peripheral equipment. . .	4,877	945	1,910	(61)	3,851
Office furniture and equipment	2,997	434	548	(89)	2,794
Automotive equipment	1,194	209	102	(94)	1,207
Other transportation equipment	2,707	292	13	(18)	2,968
Other.	4,258	520	86	(88)	4,604
	$47,756	$5,805	$3,822	$(1,856)(a)	$47,883
For the year ended September 30, 1990:					
Buildings.	$ 5,168	$ 577	$ 45	$ 88	$ 5,788
Machinery and equipment.	24,549	2,596	1,336	126	25,935
Computer and peripheral equipment. . .	3,910	1,061	159	65	4,877
Office furniture and equipment	3,306	400	765	56	2,997
Automotive equipment	1,215	154	238	63	1,194
Other transportation equipment	2,521	186			2,707
Other.	3,941	477	193	33	4,258
	$44,610	$5,451	$2,736	$ 431	$47,756

(a)   Includes reclassification on disposal of gas lift equipment assets.

Source: Daniel Industries, Inc., *1992 Annual Report.*

C. Use the data provided in Schedules V and VI to estimate:

(i) Average depreciable life.

(ii) Average age of the major categories of property, plant, and equipment used by Daniel.

Briefly discuss how you would use this information when analyzing the company.

14. [Impairment] Digital Equipment's financial statements show the following (in millions of dollars):

	June 30, 1990	June 29, 1991	June 27, 1992
Operating revenues	$ 12,953	$ 13,911	$ 13,931
Operating expenses	(12,391)	(13,399)	(14,566)
Restructuring charges	(550)	(1,100)	(1,500)
Operating income (loss)	$ 12	$ (588)	$ (2,135)
Increase in restructuring reserve*	444	593	510
Restructuring reserve at year end	444	1,037	1,547

*From statement of cash flows.

A. Discuss the cash flow consequences of the restructuring charges for fiscal 1991 and 1992.

B. Discuss whether Digital's restructuring charges conform to the "big bath" theory.

C. Discuss the impact of these restructuring charges on Digital's future reported earnings and cash flows from operations.

15. [Impairment] Comsat reported a provision for restructuring of $97,576,000 in 1990; the footnote is shown in Exhibit 6P-5.

A. Discuss the cash flow consequences of the provision for 1990 and future years.

B. Discuss the impact of the provision on Comsat's:

(i) Future return on assets.

(ii) Future asset turnover ratio.

(iii) Future net income.

16. [Revaluation of assets] Exhibit 6P-6 contains excerpts from the fiscal 1992 financial statements issued by News Corporation, an Australian media company.

A. Discuss the impact of revaluation on the trend of the firm's reported income, return on equity, and cash flow from operations:

(i) At the time of revaluation

(ii) As the revalued assets are used in operations

(iii) At the time they are sold.

EXHIBIT 6P-5. COMSAT

PROVISION FOR RESTRUCTURING

In the fourth quarter of 1990, the Corporation recorded a $97,576,000 provision for restructuring its Video Entertainment business. This action was taken when it became apparent that the operations, as structured, would not generate sufficient margins to recover the Corporation's fixed investment.

The restructuring provision includes a write-down of property, $57,504,000, a write-off of goodwill, $24,235,000, and a write-down of other assets, $4,000,000. In addition, the provision included $11,837,000 for costs to reduce the work force, improve the delivery system and restructure other aspects of the operations.

Source: Comsat, *1990 Annual Report.*

EXHIBIT 6P-6. NEWS CORPORATION

Notes to and Forming Part of the Accounts

For the year ended 30 June, 1992

SIGNIFICANT
ACCOUNTING
POLICIES

(c) Valuation of non-current assets
Certain non-current assets are revalued from time to time. Revalued assets are shown at their latest valuation. All non-current assets which have not been revalued are shown at cost. Increments in the value of a class of assets are taken to the asset revaluation reserve. Decrements are offset against previous increments relating to the same class of assets, or charged against profit.

Non-current assets are written down to the recoverable amount where the carrying value of the non-current asset exceeds the recoverable amount.

The recoverable amount of property, plant and equipment, publishing rights, titles, television licences and goodwill has been determined by discounting the expected net inflow of cash, arising from their continued use.

(e) Publishing rights, titles and television licences
These assets are stated at cost or valuation. No amortisation is provided on publishing rights and titles since, in the opinion of the Directors, they do not have a finite useful economic life. Although television licences in the United States are renewable every five years, the Directors have no reason to believe that they will not be renewed and, accordingly, no amortisation has been provided.

	Equity Consolidated	
	1992 $'000	1991 $'000
PUBLISHING RIGHTS, TITLES AND TELEVISION LICENCES		
At cost	1,609,334	1,479,238
At valuation June 1990		
Original cost	6,601,954	6,504,875
Revaluation increment	4,702,037	4,411,577
	11,303,991	10,916,452
	12,913,325	12,395,690

On 30 June, 1990 in accordance with the group's accounting policy, the Directors in office at that time revalued the group's publishing rights, titles and television licences, with the exception of those rights, titles, and licences acquired during the year. The film library, distribution rights and trade names of the Twentieth Century Fox Film group were not revalued.

The Directors' valuation at June 1990 was based on advice from Hambros Securities Limited (Australia and United Kingdom) and R. Gary Gomm and Associates (United States of America). The publishing rights, titles and television licences at valuation June 1990 include the original cost and the revaluation increment. When valuations have resulted in incremental values being attributed to those rights, titles and licences the Directors adopted valuations that resulted in the incremental revaluation being 70% of the net difference between the original cost and the advised total valuation. Where book values of the publishing rights, titles and television licences were greater than the valuation, the decrement was treated in accordance with the group's accounting policies.

The primary valuation technique used was a methodology based on the maintainable revenues of the publishing rights, titles and television licences. This incorporates multiples which take account of the market factors particular to the rights, titles and licences and which reflect the composition of the revenues and profitability, the loyalty of readership, the risk attaching to the advertising revenue and the potential for future growth. The results derived using the primary methodology have been supported by an extensive review of market transactions in the United States of America, the United Kingdom, Australia and Hong Kong.

Source: News Corporation, *1992 Annual Report.*

B. Provide arguments for and against the use of these revalued amounts in the company's financial statements.

C. Evaluate the company's policy of not amortizing these assets.

D. If the company did amortize these assets, how would the revaluation affect News Corporation's reported:

    (i) Net income.

    (ii) Cash from operations.

Appendix 6-A

Analysis of Oil and Gas Disclosures

SFAS 69, Disclosures About Oil and Gas Activities, requires detailed information about the results of operations for oil and gas activities and disclosure of a standardized measure of proved oil and gas reserves. Additional summary disclosures of these activities by equity method investees and minority interests are also required. This appendix describes and analyzes the data provided by these disclosures. Various analytical techniques and their implications for financial statement ratios are discussed.

Disclosure of Physical Reserve Quantities

Exhibit 6A-1 provides data on the physical quantities of Pennzoil's proved oil and gas reserves, including

- Separate disclosure of oil and gas reserves.
- Separate disclosure by geographic area.
- Separate disclosure of the reserves of PPI, an affiliate accounted for using the equity method (see Chapter 11).
- Reconciliation of the year-to-year change in proved reserves.
- Disclosure of proved developed[1] reserves.

These data describe the company's physical reserves at each balance sheet date. The first two features listed help the user understand the nature of the reserves. For example, oil reserves in the United States have different economic characteristics from gas reserves in Nigeria. Separate disclosure of the reserves of equity method affiliates aids the evaluation of the investment in such companies.

The reconciliation is one of the most significant features as it enables us to understand how reserves change from year to year as a result of

- Production, which reduces reserves.
- Discoveries, which increase reserves.
- Purchases and sales of reserves.
- Revisions of estimates.

[1] This term, and other technical terms used in this appendix, are defined in the glossary.

• Price changes, which can make reserves economically feasible to produce, or not.[2]

Each of these disclosures provides useful data because physical quantities can be related to cash flows. For example, the cost of finding reserves can be derived by comparing exploration expenditures with reserves discovered. This is considered an important measure of management ability.

[2]For example, in 1985, Atlantic Richfield removed 8.3 trillion cubic feet (trillion = billion MCF) of natural gas reserves located in northern Alaska from its estimate of proved reserves, reducing its domestic gas reserves by more than 50%. The company explained that this change was prompted by a review of economic factors, especially the significant drop in oil and gas prices in that year.

EXHIBIT 6A-1. PENNZOIL CO.
Disclosures of Oil and Gas Reserves (unaudited)

Estimated Quantities of Proved Oil and Gas Reserves

Presented below are Pennzoil's estimated net proved oil and gas reserves as of December 31, 1988, 1987 and 1986. Reserves in the United States are located onshore in all the main producing states (except Alaska and California) and in offshore California, Louisiana and Texas. Foreign reserves are located in Canada. Pennzoil sold its interests in its Dutch North Sea properties in 1988.

The estimates of proved oil and gas reserves have been prepared by Ryder Scott Company Petroleum Engineers, and are based on data supplied by Pennzoil. The reports of Ryder Scott Company, which include a description of the basis used in preparing the estimated reserves, are included in or as exhibits to Pennzoil's Annual reports on Form 10-K for the respective years. Oil includes crude oil, condensate and natural gas liquids.

Proved Oil Reserves (millions of barrels)	1988 United States	1988 Foreign	1988 Total	1987 United States	1987 Foreign	1987 Total	1986 United States	1986 Foreign	1986 Total
Proved developed and undeveloped reserves									
Beginning of year	135	2	137	138	2	140	156	2	158
Revisions of previous estimates	7	1	8	7	—	7	(10)	—	(10)
Extensions and discoveries	2	—	2	1	—	1	2	—	2
Estimated production	(11)	—	(11)	(11)	—	(11)	(12)	—	(12)
Purchases of minerals in place, net	1	—	1	—	—	—	2	—	2
End of year	134	3	137	135	2	137	138	2	140
Proved developed reserves									
Beginning of year	78	2	80	81	2	83	93	2	95
End of year	95	3	98	78	2	80	81	2	83
Equity in proved reserves of PPI	13	—	13	15	—	15	15	—	15

EXHIBIT 6A-1. *(Continued)*

Proved Natural Gas Reserves (billions of cubic feet)	1988 United States	1988 Foreign	1988 Total	1987 United States	1987 Foreign	1987 Total	1986 United States	1986 Foreign	1986 Total
Proved developed and undeveloped reserves[1]									
Beginning of year	821	82	903	883	81	964	932	78	1,010
Revisions of previous estimates	126	1	127	14	1	15	39	6	45
Extensions and discoveries	56	—	56	21	5	26	31	3	34
Estimated production	(124)	(3)	(127)	(103)	(5)	(108)	(121)	(6)	(127)
Purchases of minerals in place	14	—	14	6	—	6	2	—	2
Sales of minerals in place	(2)	(27)	(29)	—	—	—	—	—	—
End of year	891	53	944	821	82	903	883	81	964
Proved developed reserves[1]									
Beginning of year	773	66	839	809	64	873	865	67	932
End of year	763	52	815	773	66	839	809	64	873
Equity in proved reserves of PPI	23	—	23	25	—	25	27	—	27

[1]United States natural gas reserves for 1988, 1987, 1986 and 1985 exclude 126 Bcf, 130 Bcf, 134 Bcf and 137 Bcf, respectively, of carbon dioxide gas for sale or use in company operations.
Source: Pennzoil Co., *1988 Annual Report.*

  The revisions, as noted by Clinch and Magliolo (1992) (see footnote 27), are important indicators of the "quality" of management's estimates. Companies reporting predominantly downward revisions are viewed with some skepticism, reflecting the apparent overoptimism of past estimates. Investors prefer positive surprises, that is, upward revisions of estimated reserves.

Disclosure of Capitalized Costs

  Exhibit 6A-2 contains two sets of disclosures: the balance sheet "carrying cost" of the reserves disclosed in Exhibit 6A-1 and the current year costs incurred.

Analysis of Finding Costs

  The bottom portion of Exhibit 6A-2 contains data regarding the firm's exploration costs. *This table includes all costs, regardless of whether they are capitalized or expensed, making the data comparable among companies with different accounting methods.*

EXHIBIT 6A-2. PENNZOIL CO.
Disclosure of Exploration Costs

Capitalized Costs and Costs Incurred Relating to Oil and Gas Producing Activities

The following table shows the aggregate capitalized costs related to oil and gas producing activities and related accumulated depreciation, depletion and amortization and valuation allowances.

	December 31	
	1988	1987
	(Expressed in millions)	
Capitalized costs		
Proved properties	**$ 2,997**	$ 2,986
Unproved properties	**293**	354
	3,290	3,340
Accumulated depreciation, depletion, amortization and valuation allowances	**(2,399)**	(1,988)
	$ 891	$ 1,352
Equity in net capitalized costs of PPI	**$ 58**	$ 61

The following table shows costs incurred in oil and gas producing activities (whether charged to expense or capitalized).

	Year Ended December 31								
	1988			1987			1986		
	United States	**Foreign**	**Total**	United States	Foreign	Total	United States	Foreign	Total
	(Expressed in millions)								
Costs incurred in oil and gas producing activities									
Property acquisition									
Unproved	**$ 20**	**$ 1**	**$ 21**	$ 30	$ 4	$ 34	$ 34	$ 3	$ 37
Proved	**26**	**—**	**26**	13	—	13	8	—	8
Exploration	**62**	**9**	**71**	31	12	43	22	14	36
Development	**63**	**1**	**64**	76	8	84	82	2	84
	$171	**$11**	**$182**	$150	$24	$174	$146	$19	$165
Equity in costs incurred by PPI	**$ 5**	**$—**	**$ 5**	$ 4	$—	$ 4	$ 1	$—	$ 1

Source: Pennzoil Co., *1988 Annual Report.*

These expenditures can be compared with reserves found to compute the actual "finding cost" on a per unit basis. While periodic finding costs are volatile, over longer time periods they provide evidence as to management's proficiency at the discovery of reserves.

Turning to the capitalized costs at the top of Exhibit 6A-2, note that the

- *Capitalized costs depend on the accounting method followed:* companies using the full cost method will capitalize more of the cost of finding oil and gas reserves than will companies employing the successful efforts method. Notice that the capitalized costs of PPI are disclosed separately, just as its reserve quantities are disclosed separately.
- Costs are net of accumulated depreciation, amortization, and valuation allowances; *different accounting choices in these areas will affect the carrying cost.*
- Costs of unproved properties are separately disclosed.
- Capitalized costs are aggregated for oil and gas and for all geographical areas, unlike reserve quantities.

These data give analysts a balance sheet cost to match against the physical reserves with all oil and gas reserves combined into one measure, usually termed *barrel of oil equivalent (BOE)*. Quantities can be combined into units of BOE based either on energy equivalence (1 barrel of oil = 6 MCF of gas)[3] or on the basis of relative price.[4]

Once this has been done, the balance sheet cost per BOE can be computed. For Pennzoil, at December 31, 1988, the calculation would be

$$\text{\# BOE} = \text{\# Barrels of oil} + \text{BOE equivalent of gas reserves}$$
$$= 137 \text{ million} + \frac{944 \text{ BCF (billion cubic feet}^5)}{6}$$
$$= 137 + 157$$
$$= 294$$

The capitalized cost per BOE is

$$\frac{\$}{\text{BOE}} = \frac{\$891}{294} = \$3.03$$

Since part of the capitalized cost is for unproved properties, for which no reserves have yet been calculated, there is a strong argument for excluding those costs from the calculation. To do so would require knowing the net (after depletion, etc.) cost of such properties; those data are often not provided. In the case of Pennzoil, it appears that the "net" carrying value of unproved properties is small and their exclusion from the capitalized cost/BOE calculation would make little difference. When the investment in unproved properties is large, however, this factor cannot be ignored.

The capitalized cost per BOE is a crude means of comparing the cost of reserves for different companies. *It reflects both the accounting method used and the "efficiency" in finding oil (the finding cost per BOE).* Companies that use the successful efforts method

---

[3]Natural gas is measured in MCF (thousand cubic feet).

[4]In recent years, in the United States, gas has sold at a lower relative price than its energy equivalent would suggest. Thus many analysts use a ratio of 1:10 to combine oil and gas reserves.

[5]1 billion cubic feet = 1 million MCF.

and that have low finding costs will have a low capitalized cost per BOE. Companies using the full cost method or recording higher finding costs will have higher capitalized cost per BOE.

The capitalized cost per BOE can also be compared with the market value of oil and gas reserves, as revealed by market transactions. If the capitalized cost is higher than transaction prices, that indicates that the balance sheet amount is overstated; if transaction prices are higher, the reverse is true.

However, using the capitalized cost per BOE is, at best, only an approximation of the value of reserves. It is deficient because it fails to recognize the following factors:

- Reserves in different markets vary in value.
- Oil reserves have different values from natural gas reserves of equivalent energy content.
- The cost of producing reserves (bringing them to the surface) may vary depending on location.
- A barrel of oil produced today is more valuable (assuming constant pricing) than one produced in five years because of the time value of money.
- Tax rates vary by jurisdiction and, within jurisdictions, may vary by location and type of resource.

For these reasons, aggregation of all reserves by physical quantities does not capture the value of reserves. Fortunately, better data are available.

Disclosure of Present Value Data

Exhibit 6A-3 contains data with the cumbersome title, Standardized Measure of Discounted Future Net Cash Flows Relating to Proved Oil and Gas Reserves. This disclosure provides data regarding the estimated future cash flows of the specific reserves owned by the firm.

The following elements are presented:

1. *Future cash inflows:* based on a year-by-year schedule of planned unit production, multiplied by *current price levels,* that is, future gross revenues based on current prices. Companies are not permitted to forecast price changes, unless a firm contract provides for future price changes, which may then be incorporated into the computation.
2. *Future production costs:* also based on current prices. Production costs include all expenditures required to bring the oil or gas to market.
3. *Development costs:* include the cost at current price levels of additional wells and other production facilities that may be required to produce the reserves.

Future net cash flows, which are inflows net of production and development costs, are a forecast of net cash flows from existing oil and gas reserves. The data take into

EXHIBIT 6A-3. PENNZOIL CO.
Disclosures of Present Values of Oil and Gas Reserves

Standardized Measure of Discounted Future Net Cash Flows Relating to Proved Oil and Gas Reserves (Standardized Measure)

The Standardized Measure is determined on a basis which presumes that year-end economic and operating conditions will continue over the periods during which year-end proved reserves would be produced. Neither the effects of future inflation nor expected future changes in technology and operating practices have been considered.

The Standardized Measure is determined as the excess of future cash inflows from proved reserves less future costs of producing and developing the reserves, future income taxes and a discount factor. Future cash inflows represent the revenues that would be received from production of year-end proved reserve quantities assuming the future production would be sold at year-end prices plus any fixed and determinable future escalations (but not escalations based on inflation) of natural gas prices provided by existing contracts. Because of continued volatility in oil and natural gas markets, future prices received from oil, condensate and gas sales may be higher or lower than current levels.

Future production costs include the estimated expenditures related to production of the proved reserves plus any production taxes without consideration of inflation. Future development costs include the estimated costs of drilling development wells and installation of production facilities, plus the net costs associated with dismantlement and abandonment of wells and production platforms, assuming year-end costs continue without inflation. Future income taxes were determined by applying legislated statutory rates to the excess of (a) future cash inflows, less future production and development costs, over (b) the tax basis in the properties involved. Existing and future permanent differences and tax credits are considered in the computation of future income tax expenses. The discount was determined by applying a discount rate of 10% per year to the annual future net cash flows.

The Standardized Measure does not purport to be an estimate of the fair market value of Pennzoil's proved reserves. An estimate of fair value would also take into account, among other things, the expected recovery of reserves in excess of proved reserves, anticipated changes in future prices and costs and a discount factor more representative of the time value of money and the risks inherent in producing oil and gas. In the opinion of Pennzoil's management, the estimated fair value of Pennzoil's oil and gas properties is in excess of the amounts set forth below.

		Year Ended December 31				
	1988			1987		
	United States	Foreign	Total	United States	Foreign	Total
	(Expressed in millions)					
Future cash inflows	$ 3,848	$106	$ 3,954	$ 3,526	$180	$ 3,706
Future production costs	(1,121)	(9)	(1,130)	(1,106)	(29)	(1,135)
Future development costs[1]	(314)	(7)	(321)	(304)	(35)	(339)
Future net cash flows before income taxes	2,413	90	2,503	2,116	116	2,232
10% annual discount for estimated timing of net cash flows before income taxes	(889)	(44)	(933)	(777)	(48)	(825)
Present value of future net cash flows before income taxes	1,524	46	1,570	1,339	68	1,407
Future income tax expense discounted at 10%[2]	(362)	(15)	(377)	(302)	(24)	(326)

EXHIBIT 6A-3. *(Continued)*

| | Year Ended December 31 | | | | | |
| | 1988 | | | 1987 | | |
	United States	Foreign	Total	United States	Foreign	Total
	(Expressed in millions)					
Standardized measure of discounted future net cash flows relating to proved oil and gas reserves	$ 1,162	$ 31	$ 1,193	$ 1,037	$ 44	$ 1,081
Equity in discounted future net cash flows of PPI	$ 78	$ —	$ 78	$ 81	$ —	$ 81

[1]Includes future dismantlement and abandonment costs, net of salvage values.

[2]Future income taxes before discount were $653 million (U.S.) and $36 million (foreign) and $560 million (U.S.) and $54 million (foreign) for 1988 and 1987, respectively.

Changes in the Standardized Measure

The following table sets forth the principal elements of the changes in the Standardized Measure for the years presented. All amounts are reflected on a discounted basis.

| | Year Ended December 31 | | |
	1988	1987	1986
	(Expressed in millions)		
Standardized measure—beginning of period	$1,081	$1,359	$1,840
Revisions—			
Net changes in prices, net of production costs	107	(305)	(905)
Revisions of quantity estimates	188	65	(15)
Changes in estimated future development costs	(30)	(4)	47
Accretion of discount	141	175	266
Changes in production rates (timing) and other	(78)	(75)	(101)
Net Revisions	328	(144)	(708)
Extensions, discoveries and improved recovery, net of future production and development costs	74	32	57
Sales and transfers, net of production costs	(286)	(304)	(332)
Development costs incurred during the period that reduced future development costs	50	67	66
Net change in estimated future income taxes	(51)	66	427
Purchases of reserves in place	20	5	9
Sales of reserves in place	(23)	—	—
Standardized measure-end of period	$1,193	$1,081	$1,359

Source: Pennzoil Co., *1988 Annual Report.*

account all the variables mentioned except one, the time value of money. The data must, therefore, be discounted to obtain a present value. SFAS 69 requires that all firms use a discount rate of 10%. The objective is comparability; the "correct" discount rate will vary over time and, perhaps, from firm to firm.

The result is a net present value of the cash flows expected to be derived from the firm's reserves, before income taxes. Deducting the present value of income taxes[6] gives a "standardized measure" of net present value. Note that these data are provided separately for U.S. and foreign reserves.

Companies providing these data routinely state that the standardized measure is not market value and suggest that the data have limited usefulness. Nonetheless, the data are widely used in the analysis of companies with oil and gas reserves and, in practice, are a useful approximation of market values. Despite some limitations, the data are far more representative of market values than the cost shown on the balance sheet, regardless of the accounting method used.

Using Present Value Disclosures

How can the data be used? One simple adjustment is to replace the capitalized cost of reserves with the net present value (standardized measure). This would be one step in preparing a current value balance sheet (see Chapter 14) or computing an adjusted net worth. Before making this adjustment, the following issues should be considered:

1. Have prices or costs changed since the balance sheet date? If so, the present value data must be adjusted to current prices, for example, a 10% increase in oil prices increases future cash flows by 10%. (Because oil and gas prices do not always move together, use a weighted average based on the composition of reserves.)

Costs may also be adjusted. While hard data are difficult to come by, industry sources can provide a rough guide as to changes in production and development costs.

2. Do economic or other factors suggest a need for assumptions of future price changes? Some analysts construct their own price scenarios and make their own computations of future cash flows.

3. Is 10% the right discount rate? The discount rate is a function of the general level of interest rates and the relative riskiness of the firm's reserves. Adjustments may be required.

A higher discount rate, of course, reduces the net present value calculation; a lower rate increases the present value.

---

[6]Pennzoil deducts the present value of tax payments from the net present value of pretax cash flows. Other firms deduct tax payments from net cash flows (both undiscounted) and then discount the after-tax cash flows. The result is the same, but the method varies. In the latter case we can compute the discounted income taxes by using the ratio of the discounted pretax cash flows to the undiscounted cash flows. (This assumes a constant tax rate.)

4. Should pretax or after-tax net present values be used? The answer will depend on the tax status of the firm and the purpose of the analysis.[7] In a liquidation analysis, for example, when all cash flows are evaluated on a pretax basis, pretax present values would be used for consistency.

In the case of Pennzoil, the data are provided by the firm and the following assumptions are used:

1. No change in prices or costs
2. A 10% discount rate
3. Pretax net present values for U.S. reserves but after-tax present values for foreign reserves (see footnote 7)

The data in the exhibits can be used to adjust Pennzoil's equity at December 31, 1988, for the difference between the present value of its oil and gas reserves and the carrying amount. The present values are obtained from Exhibit 6A-3 (in $ millions):

United States (pretax)	$1524
Foreign (after tax)	31
Total	$1555
The carrying value is shown in Exhibit 6A-2	891
The difference is	$664
Stated equity at 12/31/88	1291
Adjusted equity at 12/31/88	$1955

This adjustment increases the equity of Pennzoil at December 31, 1988, by 51%. The use of after-tax present value for all reserves would generate an increase of $302 million ($1193 million − $891 million), or 23%. Varying the discount rate or making assumptions about changes in prices or costs would also lead to different adjustments.

Chapter 14 provides a discussion of the significance of equity adjustments in greater detail, but a brief comment is required here. The adjustment of net worth is not an end in itself, but one step in the analysis of a firm. While equity after adjustment is not a precise measure of the market value of Pennzoil's net assets, it is a better measure than the historical cost of those assets.

---

[7]Disclosures for firms with significant reserves outside of North American will frequently show very high income tax rates for these reserves. These high rates reflect the fact that royalties in many countries are a percentage of the gross value of the oil or gas produced. Calling these royalties "income taxes" results in better income tax treatment in the United States. This suggests that net present value data for such reserves should always be used on an after-tax basis.

Changes in Present Values

The second part of Exhibit 6A-3 is a reconciliation of *changes* in the standardized measure, akin to the reconciliation of reserve quantities. But these data are richer as they include the impact of such factors as

- Changes in prices and costs.
- Accretion of discount (the passage of time reduces the discount period)
- Expenditures that reduce future required cash flows.
- Changes in estimates.
- Purchases and sales of reserves.
- Effect of production.

Pennzoil's reconciliation provides the following insights:

1. Declining prices were the single largest factor in reducing the net present value over the 1986–1988 time period.
2. Pennzoil has stretched out its production plans (reducing the present value by increasing the discount period), possibly because of lower prices.
3. Revisions are mostly positive, suggesting that the company's estimates have been conservative.

Appendix 6-B

Research and Development Partnerships

Introduction

A research and development partnership allows a company to defer the recognition of R&D costs. The partnership raises funds from investors. Those funds are then used to pay the company for research. Any patents or products resulting from that research belong to the partnership, but the company can either purchase the partnership or license the product. Thus the company controls the technology without reporting the expenses resulting from research costs, as the "revenue" from the partnership offsets the research expense (see the Centocor example that follows). Exhibit 6B-1 describes a typical arrangement.

This arrangement has many of the attributes of an option; the firm has a call option on the patents or products developed by the partnership, with the purchase price being equivalent to the exercise or strike price. Shevlin (1991) treats such limited partnerships (LPs) as an option and uses option pricing theory to value the LP:

EXHIBIT 6B-1
Biotech Partners, L.P.

On January 1, 1993, the Biotech Corporation establishes a partnership to conduct biotechnology research with the goal of creating new drugs. The firm raises $10 million by selling partnership units in Biotech Partners, L.P. (BTP).

Biotech Corp. assigns its patents to the partnership and signs a contract to provide research services. BTP agrees to pay 100% of the research costs in return for the right to any drugs developed. Biotech may license any drugs developed by paying BTP a royalty of 10% of the wholesale selling price of drugs sold.

Biotech has the right to purchase the partnership interests during various time periods at a total price (payable in cash or in Biotech Corp. shares) of

$20 million (January 1–March 31, 1995)
$30 million (January 1–March 31, 1996)
$45 million (January 1–March 31, 1997)

BTP disburses funds to Biotech Corp. at the rate of $5 million per year. Biotech Corp. treats these receipts as revenue and the associated research costs as contract research expenses. The revenue offsets the R&D costs, so that Biotech's reported earnings are not affected.

On February 1, 1995, Biotech Corp. exercises its right to acquire the entire partnership interest for a price of $20 million. That payment is shown as an expense for the quarter ended March 31, 1995.

The value of the LP call option to the R&D firm may be decomposed into the present value of the underlying project financed by the LP (an asset) less the present value of the payments to the limited partners if the firm exercises its option (liablity). [1]

Statement of Financial Accounting Standards (SFAS) 68 (1982), Research and Development Arrangements, created criteria to distinguish true transfers of risk from disguised borrowings. The following are indicators that there has not been a true transfer of risk:

1. The company has an obligation to the partnership (or investors) regardless of the outcome of the research. Such obligation may exist in the form of a guarantee of partnership debt or granting of a "put" option to the investors.

2. Conditions make it probable that the company will repay the funds raised by the partnership. Possible conditions include the company's need to control the technology owned by the partnership or the existence of relationships between the company and the investors (e.g., top management invests in the partnership).

If there has not been a true transfer of risk, then the company is required to expense the actual research costs and treat funds received from the partnership as borrowings.

When the requirements of SFAS 68 are met, however, the company can recognize revenue from the partnership to offset research and development costs. The result is, in effect, a deferral of research cost until products are sold (and license fees paid) or the partnership is purchased. Such arrangements are disclosed in financial statement footnotes (see Centocor), and analysts should be alert to their effects on reported income.

In recent years, the R&D partnership has been largely superseded by a new vehicle: a separate company that sells "callable common" shares to the public. The shares are usually packaged with warrants of the (parent) company to make the resulting "units" more attractive to investors. The new common shares are callable at prices that promise a high rate of return to investors if the venture is successful.

Centocor: R&D Arrangements in Practice

Centocor, a biotechnology firm, is a good example of how these arrangements are structured. Exhibit 6B-2 contains footnotes from the company's *1989 Annual Report,* discussing its limited partnerships and its affiliate Tocor.

Note 8 discloses the revenues and expenses resulting from the agreements with the three R&D partnerships. Notice that the revenues from these agreements equal or exceed the research expenses. Not only do the partnerships pay the direct cost of the research, but they make a contribution to overhead as well.

Note 9 discloses the agreement with Tocor. Tocor is to reimburse Centocor for 110% of its research costs; $6.127 million was paid during 1989. Centocor has the right to purchase ("call") all the shares of Tocor for amounts ranging from $69 million to $126 million, depending on the date of purchase.

---

[1]Shevlin, Terry, 'The Valuation of R&D Firms with R&D Limited Partnerships," *The Accounting Review* (January 1991), pp. 1–21

EXHIBIT 6B-2. CENTOCOR, INC.

Research and Development Revenues (Note 8)

Limited Partnership Arrangements

The Company has organized three limited partnerships: CCIP, CPII and Centocor Partners III, L.P. ("CPIII"). The general partners of CCIP, CPII and CPIII are each wholly owned subsidiaries of the Company. The Company and each of these partnerships sold units consisting of limited partnership interests and warrants to purchase Common Stock of the Company.

The net proceeds from the sale of the limited partnership interests have been used by CCIP, CPII and CPIII to fund research and development under agreements with the Company ("the Development Agreements"). The CCIP, CPII and CPIII Development Agreements provide that the Company is reimbursed for 110 percent, 114.5 percent and 102.5 percent, respectively, of its related direct and indirect expenses incurred in its research efforts. For both CCIP and CPII, the initial available funding was exhausted and, as further described in *Note 5*, in 1989 the Company obtained $18,250,000 of funding for these research programs, and the use of $11,981,000 of such funding is included in 1989 revenues in the table below.

In connection with these research programs, the Company recorded revenues and expenses as follows:

Year ended December 31,		1989	1988	1987
Revenues	CCIP	$ 6,367,000	$ 648,000	$ 8,050,000
	CPII	12,261,000	20,784,000	15,822,000
	CPIII	16,126,000	8,955,000	5,000
		$34,754,000	$30,387,000	$23,877,000
Expenses	CCIP	$ 7,015,000	$ 679,000	$ 8,978,000
	CPII	12,029,000	19,530,000	13,817,000
	CPIII	15,733,000	8,736,000	6,000
		$34,777,000	$28,945,000	$22,801,000

Not included in the above table are revenues in 1988 and 1987 of $500,000 and $5,000,000, respectively, from the receipt of nonrefundable fees from CPIII for the Company's prior research and development efforts, and expenses of approximately $7,970,000 and $4,800,000 in 1989 and 1988, respectively, representing CCIP and CPII's research costs funded by the Company. Included in related party receivables at December 31, 1989, is approximately $6,000,000 due from the partnerships.

The Company has formed Centocor Cardiovascular Ventures ("CCV"), Centocor Ventures II ("CVII") and Centocor Ventures III ("CVIII"), joint ventures with CCIP, CPII and CPIII, respectively, for the purpose of commercializing any products developed by these partnerships. Profit and losses are to be allocated 20 percent to CCIP and 80 percent to the Company for CCV; 25 percent to CPII and 75 percent to the Company for CVII; and 23 percent to CPIII and 77 percent to the Company for CVIII. The joint ventures will terminate upon the occurrence of certain events, principally related to the exercise or expiration of the partnership purchase options granted to the Company.

Commercialization and Other Agreements

The Company has entered into various commercialization agreements under which it has recognized revenues from nonrefundable fees or milestone payments in support of its research and development efforts from companies which have received marketing rights or

EXHIBIT 6B-2. *(Continued)*

will receive such rights to certain products. Revenues recorded from these agreements amounted to approximately $2,602,000, $2,229,000 and $7,257,000 for the years ended December 31, 1989, 1988 and 1987, respectively.

Tocor, Inc. (Note 9)

In August 1989, the Company and Tocor, Inc. ("Tocor") completed a public offering of 2,875,000 units, each unit consisting of one share of callable common stock of Tocor and one warrant to purchase one share of the Company's Common Stock (see *Note 6*). Tocor received all of the approximately $31,000,000 net proceeds of the offering.

The Company and Tocor have entered into a technology license agreement under which the Company has granted to Tocor a perpetual worldwide exclusive license to proprietary rights owned or controlled by the Company during the term of the research and development agreement described below, which are necessary or useful for the research, development, manufacture, or sale of products being developed by Tocor. The Company has the option to license certain products or classes of products developed by Tocor. Additionally, the Company has an option to purchase all of the callable common stock of Tocor (see *Note 13*). The Company and Tocor have entered into agreements under which the Company will conduct the initial phases of research and development on products being developed by Tocor and provide Tocor with certain administrative services. The Company is reimbursed by Tocor for 110 percent of costs incurred. Tocor is obligated to pay to the Company substantially all of the net proceeds of the offering pursuant to these agreements.

In connection with the Company's agreements with Tocor, approximately $6,127,000 of research and development revenues, net of warrant amortization, were recorded by the Company in the year ended December 31, 1989, including a $2,500,000 nonrefundable payment for the Company's prior research and development efforts.

Certain officers and directors of the Company are also officers and directors of Tocor.

Commitments and Contingencies (Note 13)

The Company has guaranteed a bank loan to CPIII which requires principal repayments of $2,111,000 in September 30, 1990, and $7,389,000 on September 30, 1991. In connection with this guarantee, the Company has agreed, until the loan is repaid, to comply with certain financial covenants and to maintain securities in amounts and maturities equal to the outstanding loan balance at the lending bank.

The Company's option to purchase the limited partnership interests in CCIP expires in December 1990. To exercise such option, the Company would be required to make an advance payment of $3,465,000 in cash or, at the Company's election, $3,765,000 in the Company's Common Stock and cash. The Company's individual options to purchase the limited partnership interests in CPII and CPIII would require advance payments in the aggregate of approximately $24,556,000 in cash or, at the Company's election, approximately $27,283,000 in the Company's Common Stock and cash. Each option, if exercised, generally requires future payments ranging from approximately 3 to 8 percent of sales of products developed by the related partnership. The advance payment may be recouped by the Company as a credit against such future payments. As more fully described in *Note 5,* the Company has issued Convertible Subordinated Debentures the repayment terms of which are adjusted, and which are convertible into the Company's Common Stock, in the event that the Company acquires the limited partnership interests in, or assets of, either CCIP or CPII. If CPIII is unsuccessful in obtaining additional funding either from the Company or others, the Company has the option (the "Capiscint Purchase Option") to purchase CPIII's rights to the

EXHIBIT 6B-2. *(Continued)*

Capiscint technology. The purchase price under the Capiscint Purchase Option would be determined by independent appraisal of CPIII's economic interest in the technology.

The Company has entered into indemnity agreements with the Partnerships pursuant to which the Company would be obligated, under certain circumstances, to compensate the Partnerships for the fair market value of their respective interests under any license agreements with the Company relating to their respective products which are lost through the exercise by the United States Government of any of its rights relating to the licensed technology. The amount of such loss would be determined annually by independent appraisal.

The Company also has the option to license any of the various products or class of products being developed under the Tocor research and development agreement described in *Note 9*. For each product or class of products, if any, so licensed, the Company and Tocor would enter into a license agreement requiring an initial payment to Tocor of $15,000,000. To maintain the exclusivity of each license, the Company would be obligated to pay to Tocor an additional $15,000,000 upon United States Food and Drug Administration approval, for each approved indication for each product or product class licensed. Additionally, the Company will be obligated to pay to Tocor royalties of 5 percent of net sales by the Company for the product or product class licensed or 25 percent of sublicensing fees. Any of the $15,000,000 payments may be made in cash, in shares of the Company's Common Stock or in such combination thereof as the Company determines.

Further, the Company also has an option to purchase all of the callable common stock of Tocor at aggregate exercise prices ranging from $69,000,000 to $92,000,000 during the period July 1, 1991, through June 30, 1993, payable in cash or Common Stock. The option period may be extended by the Company to December 31, 1994, upon the payment by the Company of an additional $34,000,000. The exercise price during the extended option period would be $92,000,000.

Source: Centocor, Inc., *1989 Annual Report.*

The impact of the three partnerships on Centocor's reported financial results can be analyzed beginning with 1989 when "revenues" from these affiliates accounted for $41 million, or 53%, of Centocor's $77 million of revenues. Had these revenues been considered borrowing (or just the firm's own funds), reported pretax income of $235,000 would have been replaced by a pretax loss of approximately $41 million, as all research costs would have been expensed but no revenue recognized.

Further, obtaining those funds would have required additional debt or equity capital. The R&D financing arrangements permitted the company to conduct research without incurring debt or equity dilution, in addition to avoiding the effects of reporting the research costs as an expense.

There is a cost to this capital, however. For example, we can look at the promised return to Tocor shareholders. An investment of $31 million in August 1989, if called in July 1991, would more than double in value to $69 million (see Note 13). If Centocor calls the Tocor shares in December 1994, it will pay $126 million ($92 million + $34 million), or four times the funds raised, a high cost of capital.

The second cost factor is the impact when the partnerships or Tocor shares are purchased. At that time the entire amount must be written off as research costs. For example, the company wrote off $99 million in the fourth quarter of 1990 in connection with the purchase of CCIP and CCII.

As a result, the use of these arrangements results in the write-off of a larger amount than the funds originally raised. But that write-off is delayed until the partnerships are purchased. In effect, these arrangements permit the deferral of research costs, but with the penalty of a high interest factor (cost of capital).

Appendix 6-C

Analysis of Changing Prices Information

Introduction

Statement of Financial Accounting Standards (SFAS) 33 (1979), *Financial Reporting and Changing Prices*, was the first attempt to establish accounting standards in the United States regarding the impact of changing prices. Before discussing its provisions, it is important to distinguish between two types of price changes: general inflation and specific price changes.

General inflation refers to price changes for an economy as a whole. Indices such as the consumer price index in the United States attempt to measure the impact of price changes on the broad population. Specific price changes refer to the prices of specific goods and services that are the inputs and outputs of firms in a given industry.

The goal of this appendix is to show how price changes impact financial statements and suggest analytical tools that can help the analyst adjust for that impact. We start with general inflation.

Analysis of General Inflation

From the financial analysis point of view, general inflation does have an impact: the purchasing power of capital is continuously eroded. Analytically, there is a well-developed method of dealing with this phenomenon, constant dollar accounting.

Constant dollar is the name the Financial Accounting Standards Board (FASB) gave to a method previously known as *general price level accounting* or *purchasing power accounting*.[1] Its goal is to measure the impact of changes in purchasing power (general inflation) on the financial capital of the firm. A simple example is contained in Exhibit 6C-1.

In this simple model, the firm invests its starting capital in inventory at the start of each year and sells that inventory at the end of the year. At the beginning of the next year, it again invests its capital (obtained from the sale of inventory one day earlier) in inventory. For simplicity we assume that there are no markups and no expenses other than cost of goods sold.

The historical cost model recognizes as income the difference between the proceeds of sale and the cost of inventory for each year. The total income over the three-year

---

[1] Accounting Principles Board (APB) Statement 4 (1969), Financial Statements Restated for General Price-Level Changes.

EXHIBIT 6C-1
Accounting for Changing Prices

Assumptions: Capital at January 1, 1991, is $1000.
Each January 1, the firm will invest entire capital in inventory.
Each December 31, the firm will sell entire inventory.
Price of inventory is $100 per unit at January 1, 1991, and rises at 10% per annum.
The general price level (CPI-U) rises at 25% per annum. Base period is January 1,
1991 = 100.

Historical Cost Model

Year	Sales	Cost of Goods Sold	Income
1991	$1100	$1000	$ 100
1992	1210	1100	110
1993	1331	1210	121
Total			$ 331

Constant Dollar Model

(January 1, 1991 dollars)

1991	$ 880	$1000	$(120)
1992	774	880	(106)
1993	681	774	(93)
Total			$(319)

Current Cost Model

1991	$1100	$1100	$ 0
1992	1210	1210	0
1993	1331	1331	0
Total			$ 0

CPI-U:	January 1, 1991	100	December 31, 1991	125
	January 1, 1992	125	December 31, 1992	156.25
	January 1, 1993	156.25	December 31, 1993	195.31

period is $331, representing the difference between beginning capital ($1000) and ending capital ($1331).

The historical cost (or nominal dollar) model, however, gives no recognition to the real value of money. Given a rate of inflation of 25%, financial capital depreciates at that rate. The purchasing power of $1000 declines to $800 ($1000/1.25) in one year due to inflation.

Constant Dollar Method

The constant dollar method recognizes this effect by restating all monetary amounts into *units of constant purchasing power*. This method requires designating a base period, which can be any period of time or point in time. For example, the base period could have been all of 1991 or January 1, 1994. The base fixes the purchasing power yardstick being used.

In our example we have chosen January 1, 1991, as the base so that all cash flows will be restated into units of January 1, 1991 purchasing power. Let us apply this method to 1991 sales:

$$\text{1991 Sales (\$1/1/91)} = \frac{\$1100}{1.25} = \$880$$

The nominal dollar cash flow was $1100 but was received at December 31, 1991. Because of inflation, the purchasing power of those dollars was only 80% (1/1.25) of the purchasing power of dollars at the base date of January 1, 1991. Thus we must divide the cash flow by the relevant index to obtain revenues in January 1, 1991, dollars.

Cost of goods sold (COGS) resulted from a cash flow at January 1, 1991, and, therefore, requires no restatement. In constant dollar terms, therefore, net income for 1991 is

$$\text{1991 Income} = \$880 - \$1000 = \$(120)$$

In purchasing power terms, the firm's capital has declined. This results from the fact that the inventory rose in price by less than the rate of inflation.

For 1992, we compute income in the same manner:

$$\text{1992 Sales (\$1/1/91)} = \frac{\$1210}{1.5625} = \$774$$

The cash flow received on December 31, 1992, has lost purchasing power over a two-year period. Similarly,

$$\text{1992 COGS (\$1/1/91)} = \frac{\$1100}{1.25} = \$880$$

The cash paid on January 1, 1992, must be adjusted for one year's inflation. Subtracting COGS from sales results in

$$\text{1992 Income (\$1/1/91)} = \$774 - \$880 = \$(106)$$

The calculations for 1993 are similar, resulting in

$$\text{1993 Income (\$1/1/91)} = \$681 - \$774 = \$(93)$$

Over the three-year period, the constant dollar method produces a loss of $319. What does this mean? At the end of 1992 the firm has $1331, representing the proceeds of inventory sold at December 31, 1992. But in units of 1/1/91 purchasing power, the firm's capital is only $681 ($1331/1.9531). Its opening capital was $1000. The constant dollar method has measured the loss of purchasing power of the firm's capital over the three-year period.

Note that these computations use the company's actual cash flow but the price index is for the economy as a whole. The calculations do not take into account the specific price changes faced by the firm. This feature of the constant dollar method is both its strength and its weakness.

Advantages of Contant Dollar Method

The constant dollar method of accounting offers the following advantages:

1. Simplicity of calculation.
2. Objectivity: No judgment is involved except, perhaps, in the choice of inflation index.
3. Verifiability: Given the same data, the calculated result will always be the same.
4. Understandability: The erosion of purchasing power is a simple economic concept.
5. Ease of preparation and ease of audit (see points 1–4).

For these reasons corporate financial statement preparers and auditors have generally supported use of the constant dollar method to disclose the impact of inflation.

Disadvantage of Constant Dollar Method

From the standpoint of financial analysis, however, the constant dollar method has a significant drawback: constant dollar data do not have any apparent usefulness. While loss of purchasing power is a useful economic concept, it has limited application in the financial world. Stock prices, interest rates, and other financial data are stated in nominal currency units, not real (purchasing power) units.

Contributing to the lack of utility of constant dollar data is their lack of specificity; they treat all companies identically regardless of the composition of their assets and liabilities. For data that relate to specific companies, analysts prefer the current cost method.

Current Cost Method

The current cost[2] method takes an entirely different approach to measuring the impact of changing prices: it ignores general inflation in favor of the specific price and cost changes faced by the individual firm. It starts with the idea that income, when properly measured, must include a provision for the replacement of capacity used during the

---

[2]Current cost is the term used in SFAS 33 and other FASB standards. Previous accounting literature has used such terms as replacement cost, current value, and fair value. The distinction among these terms is more theoretic than real and varies with the user. We will treat them as equivalents.

period.[3] Otherwise, income will be overstated in that it includes an amount representing the consumption of capacity.[4]

It follows that the provision for the cost of replacing capacity must be made at current prices. While application of this principle is difficult in practice, it is essential in theory. If a firm has used up a machine, and must replace it to remain in business, it is the cost of buying a new machine that is relevant, not the cost of the worn-out machine.

The current cost method, therefore, measures income by matching revenues with operating costs, including the cost of replacing inventory sold and fixed assets used up during the period.

Exhibit 6C-1 applies this principle to our model company. At the end of 1991, the firm has $1100 representing the proceeds of sales. To remain in business the firm must purchase new inventory on January 1, 1992. The cost of that new inventory will be $110 per unit, as prices have risen by 10% since January 1, 1991. The cost of new inventory will be $1100 (10 @ $110). Under the current cost method, therefore, there was no earned income in 1991, as income is

$$\$1100 - \$1100 = 0$$

In other words, the firm has simply maintained its ability to do business. It can purchase 10 units of inventory, the same as its "capacity" one year earlier. From this point of view, the firm has neither a profit nor a loss for 1991 but has simply maintained its *physical capital* (capacity to do business). This contrasts with the constant dollar method, which is concerned with maintaining *financial capital*.

In 1992 and 1993, the same results are obtained. There is no income in current cost terms because the firm has simply maintained its physical capital.

Disadvantages of Current Cost

As compared with the constant dollar method, the current cost method has the following disadvantages:

1. *Complexity:* For each type of inventory and for each category of fixed assets, the firm must estimate the cost of replacing that asset. We discuss the difficulty of estimating current costs shortly.

2. *Subjectivity:* Current cost estimates require judgments about how the firm will replace used up capacity (discussed shortly).

3. *Lack of reliability:* Different assumptions lead to different computations.

4. *Difficulty of preparation and audit:* Because of the foregoing factors, current cost data are more expensive and time consuming to prepare and to audit than are constant dollar data.

For all these reasons, financial statement preparers and auditors have mostly opposed the presentation of current cost data in financial statements. In some cases,

---

[3]J.R. Hicks, *Value and Capital,* 2nd ed. (Oxford: Chaundon Press, 1946), p. 176.
[4]This concept was more fully developed in Chapter 2.

however, corporations have stated that they find such data useful when managing their business.[5]

From the financial analysis point of view, however, current cost data are greatly preferred to constant dollar data. The main reason is the relevance of such data to the operations of specific firms.

Accounting Series Release 190

The high rate of inflation in the 1970s and large specific price changes in some industries resulted in action by the Securities and Exchange Commission to require the supplementary disclosure of current cost data. Accounting Series Release (ASR) 190 (1976) required that large firms disclose the replacement cost of inventory and fixed assets as well as cost of goods sold and depreciation expense computed on a replacement cost basis. Disclosures were first required in 1976.

At about the same time, the FASB placed inflation accounting on its agenda and issued SFAS 33 in 1979. The provisions of the new standard were effective in 1979, at which time the SEC withdrew ASR 190.

SFAS 33 Requirements

SFAS 33 was a hybrid; it attempted to combine both the current cost and constant dollar methods into one standard. In theory, the two approaches can be combined. Data adjusted for specific price changes can then be further adjusted for changes in purchasing power. The resulting complexity, however, made it difficult for analysts and other financial statement users to use the data properly. Preparers and auditors also objected to the cost and complexity of the data.

The standard was issued with a provision that it would be reviewed after five years. In SFAS 89 (1989), which superseded SFAS 33, the disclosure requirements were made voluntary. The change resulted from three factors. First, the rate of inflation subsided greatly in the 1980s, making the issue of general inflation effects less important. Second, firms complained that the costs of compliance were too high. Finally, little or no benefit could be traced to the disclosures due to limited usage. As a result of the voluntary nature of SFAS 89, the disclosures are rarely provided.

Problems with SFAS 33 Disclosures

The data disclosed under the provisions of SFAS 33 received little use, we believe, for the following reasons:

1. Uncertainty exists regarding the measurement of current cost. It is unclear whether companies should attempt to measure the *market value* of their fixed assets, the *reproduction cost* of those assets, or the *replacement cost* of existing capacity. Each of these choices results in a different measure of cost and a different set of problems.

---

[5]See, for example, Kenneth R. Todd, Jr., "How One Financial Officer Uses Inflation-Adjusted Accounting Data," *Financial Executive* (October 1982). Todd was vice president and controller of American Standard, Inc.

Market value is often difficult to estimate because many productive assets are customized or unique. While market values can be estimated for office buildings, for example, there is no readily available market information for steel mills. Curiously, the FASB did not permit the disclosure of market values in lieu of "current cost" for such assets as oil and gas properties, timberland, and real estate, for which active markets do exist.[6]

2. Reproduction cost is an estimate of what it would cost to build existing facilities at current prices. However, it is hard to price machines that are no longer being manufactured (having been replaced by newer models or machines using different production processes). Use of reproduction cost also assumes that the firm would replace its existing capacity with exactly the same mix of factory sizes and locations.

3. Replacement cost is, in theory, the cost of replacing existing productive capacity. Such an estimate must, first, define whether capacity should be measured in physical units (tons of steel or pairs of shoes) or financial units (dollars of revenue). Second, the firm must decide what mix of geographic locations, plant capacities, and product mixes it would construct if it were to replace its facilities today. Finally, the firm must estimate what production processes, raw and intermediate materials, and markets it would pursue if it could "start from scratch."

As can be seen from the preceding comments, the computations become increasingly speculative as one moves from market value to reproduction cost to replacement cost. In many cases, companies complied with SFAS 33 by simply applying construction and machinery cost indices to the historical cost of fixed assets.

Problems with Current Cost Depreciation

SFAS 33 also required that companies providing current cost data disclose their depreciation expense on a current cost basis. At first glance, this is a simple exercise; companies would simply apply their existing depreciation methods and lives to their estimated current cost of fixed assets.

The difficulties in defining current cost apply equally to current cost depreciation expense derived from those data. In addition, however, the interpretation of current cost depreciation expense is subject to another problem. If we simply replace historical cost depreciation with current cost depreciation, we are assuming that the operating costs of the firm would be unaffected by the "replacement" process. We would be assuming that more expensive new machines and processes are no more cost efficient than the original machines and processes.

That assumption is, of course, absurd in most cases. In theory, therefore, we should also adjust the operating costs of the firm to reflect the greater efficiency of the new equipment. Such an adjustment would be very subjective if made by the firm; a financial analyst outside the firm cannot possibly make such an estimate.

Because of the subjectivity of the data, lack of comparability of disclosures by competing firms, difficulty of interpreting the data, and lack of a well-defined way of

---

[6]SFAS 39, Mining and Oil and Gas, SFAS 40, Timberlands, and SFAS 41 Income Producing Real Estate, were all issued in 1980.

incorporating the data into investment decision models, use of the current cost data provided by SFAS 33 was limited. Perhaps for that reason there was little evidence that current cost data impacted financial markets.

Adjusting Financial Statements for Changing Prices

Given the voluntary nature of changing prices disclosures under SFAS 89, the analysis of the impact of changing prices must be done by each analyst. As we believe that constant dollar calculations are of use only under limited circumstances (see the following section), we will devote our attention to adjustments for specific price changes. As the effects of changing prices on inventories have been dealt with in Chapter 5, we will concern ourselves here only with the effects on fixed assets.

Changing prices for fixed assets have two primary effects on financial statements:

1. Since fixed assets are carried at cost (net of accumulated depreciation), the carrying amount does not reflect the current cost of those assets. The result is that the assets and, as a consequence, the net worth are understated if prices have risen (the normal case).

2. As depreciation expense is based on the carrying amount of the fixed assets, understatement of assets results in understatement of depreciation expense. Depreciation expense, which should be a measure of the capacity used up during the period, is instead just an arbitrary allocation of past cash flows. Understatement of depreciation expense results in overstatement of reported earnings.

Adjustments to Fixed Assets

In the absence of company-provided data, the analyst must make adjustments using other sources of information. In some cases, data on the cost of capacity are available from industry sources; this is more likely to be true for relatively homogeneous industries such as paper, oil refining, chemicals, and so forth. Cost per ton of capacity data for such industries is frequently mentioned in trade publications or can be gleaned from company contacts.

Another possible source of data is actual construction. Companies frequently report the cost of new plants as well as their capacity. Such data from the company or its competitors can be used to estimate the "current cost" of facilities.

Acquisitions also provide possible data sources. As discussed more fully in Chapter 12, acquisitions accounted for under the purchase method result in restatement of acquired fixed assets to their fair value. Such restatement can indicate the "current cost" of fixed assets.

Another approach is the use of construction cost statistics. If the year of construction of a plant is available, the historical cost can be indexed to estimate the current construction cost.

For real estate assets, current land and construction cost data are frequently included in industry publications. By knowing the nature of the assets, one can use the current cost of construction for factories, warehouses, and so forth. For some categories of real estate, especially income-producing properties (office buildings, shopping centers, hotels), market value estimates may also be available. When market value estimates are available, they should be used as the measure of current costs as market values are generally more relevant.

In some cases, industry-specific disclosures are available. For example, see the discussion of the disclosures of the net present value of oil and gas reserves discussed in Appendix 6-A to this chapter.

All these approaches involve estimates. Just because an exact result is not possible does not mean that the exercise is not worthwhile. Remember that estimates are present in the reported financial statements as well.

Using Current Cost Asset Values

The main use for current cost data is for preparation of a current cost balance sheet. The historical cost of all assets and liabilities should be replaced with the current cost (market value) of those assets. As compared with the historic cost balance sheet, a current cost balance sheet provides a better measurement of the net assets available to management. These data can be used to make a better evaluation of

1. Management's use of available resources.
2. The borrowing ability of the company.
3. Security for creditors.
4. Liquidating value of the company.

These issues will be discussed more fully in Chapter 14.

Estimating and Using Current Cost Depreciation

Once the current cost of fixed assets is estimated, the next step is to estimate depreciation on a current cost basis. The current cost of fixed assets must be amortized over the estimated economic life of the assets, allowing for salvage values.

The depreciation lives used for financial reporting purposes may not be adequate for this purpose. As discussed in the section on impairment, write-offs sometimes reflect inadequate past depreciation of fixed assets. For analysis purposes, the choice of depreciation method, lives, and salvage value should be carefully considered.

Some companies provide approximate data regarding the purpose of current capital expenditures. The portion allocated to "maintenance of existing capacity" may be a good proxy for current cost depreciation.[7] Remember that the goal is to estimate the cost to replace capacity used up during the accounting period.

In some cases, companies disclose the cost of major capital projects, allowing the analyst to "back into" an estimate of "maintenance" expenditures.

---

[7]In its standard on cash flows, the IASC has recommended that companies disclose the portion of capital expenditures required to maintain capacity.

Finally, it is important to look at overall corporate trends. If real output is static, then one can argue that *all* capital expenditures have been made to replace used up capacity. As SFAS 14[8] requires disclosure of capital expenditures and depreciation expense for each reportable segment, this analysis can be done for each segment of a multi-industry company.

Estimates of current cost depreciation should be used to adjust reported income to a current cost basis. Along with the adjustment to last-in, first-out (LIFO) where applicable (see Chapter 5), the replacement of historic cost depreciation by current cost will produce a better measure of sustainable income.[9]

The use of current cost data also results in ratios that are more representative of management performance. When prices are increasing, the use of current cost data will reduce the return on equity (ROE) as income is reduced (higher depreciation) and equity is increased (higher asset values). If the current cost ROE is very low, for example, it tells us that the company might be better off selling assets and investing the proceeds in other assets providing higher returns.

Using Constant Dollar Data

While we have stated that constant dollar data are generally not useful for financial analysis, there are some applications. Constant dollar data are most useful when we wish to look at investment returns from the investor point of view.

An investor is generally concerned with the performance of an investment, not in absolute terms, but relative to inflation. Investors defer current consumption to obtain a higher level of future consumption. In highly inflationary societies, the instinct to save is stifled because nominal rates of return are below the inflation rate. Under those conditions, consumption deferred is consumption reduced.

The way to measure the impact of changing prices on the investor is quite simple: deflate returns by a measure of purchasing power such as the consumer price index. The index for the investor, not the investment, should be used. For example, an investment in General Motors shares by a Canadian investor must be evaluated by deflating the returns (translated into Canadian dollars) by the Canadian consumer price index. This is quite easy to do (refer back to Exhibit 6C-1 for an illustration of the constant dollar method).

The constant dollar method is also widely used in highly inflationary economies, especially when their financial systems are indexed. In many cases, the constant dollar method (sometimes in modified form) is used to produce the primary financial statements for financial reporting and tax purposes.

While the analysis of such statements is beyond the scope of this text, we will provide one caveat. Unless the input and output prices of the firm subjected to analysis are fully indexed, the constant dollar method will not provide a satisfactory basis for analysis. To make sound investment decisions it is important to understand the effects of the specific price changes faced by the firm.

[8]Financial Reporting for Segments of a Business Enterprise (1976), Para. 27. (Segment reporting is discussed in Chapter 11.)

[9]Sustainable income is defined and discussed in Chapter 2.

Concluding Remarks

With the adoption of SFAS 89, changing prices disappeared as an accounting issue. Yet prices continue to change. While general inflation has remained at low levels in virtually all industrialized countries, the prices of specific commodities continue to fluctuate.

Thus financial analysis requires that the effects of significant price changes be isolated. Some of these effects can be dealt with summarily. For example, it is relatively easy to use an index of retail prices to understand the extent to which a department store's sales are affected by inflation. It is more complex (and more difficult) to discern the effect of a change in oil prices on an oil refiner's profit margins, turnover ratios, and return on equity. The objective of this appendix, and the material on the effect of price changes in Chapters 5 and 6, was to provide some tools to permit such analysis.

7

ANALYSIS OF INCOME TAXES

INTRODUCTION

ACCOUNTING FOR INCOME TAXES: BASIC ISSUES

DEFERRED TAXES: ALTERNATIVE APPROACHES
APB 11: The Deferred Tax Method
  Deferred Tax Liabilities
  Deferred Tax Assets
  Effect of Tax Rate and Tax Law Changes
  Behavior of Deferred Tax Liabilities Over Time
  Need for Changes in Accounting for Income Taxes
SFAS 96: The Liability Method
  Effect of Tax Rate and Tax Law Changes
  Deferred Tax Assets and Liabilities
  Limitations on Deferred Tax Assets
  Adoption Dates and Methods
SFAS 109: Modified Liability Method
  Deferred Tax Assets and the Valuation Allowance
  Effective Date and Transition Method

DEFERRED TAXES: ANALYTICAL ISSUES
Liability or Unrecognized Income?
Effective Tax Rates

ACCOUNTING FOR TAXES: SPECIALIZED ISSUES
Temporary Versus Permanent Differences
Treatment of Operating Losses
Indefinite Reversals
Accounting for Acquisitions

FINANCIAL STATEMENT PRESENTATION AND DISCLOSURE REQUIREMENTS

USEFULNESS OF ANALYSIS OF INCOME TAXES

ACCOUNTING OUTSIDE THE UNITED STATES

CONCLUSION

INTRODUCTION

Income taxes have always been an extremely contentious issue in financial reporting. Probably the most important reason for this controversy is the difference in objectives and methods of financial and tax reporting. The former uses accrual accounting in reporting the results of periodic events and transactions to provide users with information needed to evaluate a firm's financial performance and cash flows. In addition, management may select revenue and expense recognition methods that allow them to smooth or maximize reported net income.

Tax reporting, on the other hand, is a function of diverse and changing political and social objectives. A modified cash basis is used to determine the periodic liability from currently taxable events. The tax liability is determined by revenue and expense recognition methods that may not coincide with those used for financial reporting since the firm has strong incentives to use methods allowing it to minimize taxable income and thereby taxes paid. U.S. generally accepted accounting principles (GAAP) are not tax based or tax driven, unlike those of most major countries.[1]

The differences between the periodic tax obligation and the tax expense recognized in the financial statements are a result of the difference between accrual and modified cash bases compounded by the differences in reporting methods used. These differences, defined as deferred tax liabilities (credits) or deferred tax assets (debits or prepaid taxes), are difficult to interpret. There is a lack of agreement as to whether they are true assets or liabilities and their attributes as indicators of future cash flows. Moreover, the growing balances of deferred tax liabilities for some companies and prepaid taxes for others served as an impetus to changes in standards of accounting for income taxes.

Accounting Principles Board (APB) Opinion 11 (December 1967) provided tax-reporting rules based on the matching concept. Significant drawbacks in this method led to the promulgation of two liability-based approaches: first, the short-lived Statement of Financial Accounting Standards (SFAS) 96 (December 1987) and, more recently, SFAS 109 (February 1992). Due to repeated delays in the effective date of SFAS 96 and its negative impact on certain types of firms, many continued to use APB 11, but others adopted SFAS 96. Since all firms must use SFAS 109 in 1993, this chapter provides an analysis of all three reporting standards.

A review of the basic approaches to income tax accounting in general and deferred taxes in particular in standards in effect and/or in transition is provided in the following sections. Their impact on financial reporting and effective tax rates is evaluated along with a discussion of their implications for financial analysis. We also discuss the potential impact of the adoption of SFAS 109 by firms using APB 11 and SFAS 96.

---

[1]In some countries, notably, Japan, Germany, and Switzerland, financial reporting is required to conform to tax reporting. In these countries, the problems discussed in this chapter do not occur. However, financial statements prepared in conformity with tax reporting may not provide useful information for investment and credit decisions. In the United States, conformity between tax and financial reporting is rare. In Chapter 5 we discussed the most common case, last-in, first-out (LIFO) inventory accounting, where such conformity is required.

ACCOUNTING FOR INCOME TAXES: BASIC ISSUES

The central issue in accounting for income taxes is whether the tax and cash flow effects of revenues, expenses, and other transactions should be recognized in the period(s) in which they affect taxable income or in the period(s) in which they are recognized in the financial statements. Because these alternatives produce different measures of operating and financial performance, the reporting decision is also relevant to analysts who need information that facilitates the evaluation of a firm's operating performance and earning power.

Exhibit 7-1 provides an illustration of the issues faced when tax accounting differs from accounting for financial statements. Part A depicts the income tax reporting choice. The company depreciates a $6000 asset over two years giving rise to current tax expense or tax payable of $800, $800, and $2000 over the next three years. For financial reporting purposes (part B), the firm depreciates the asset over three years. Pretax income is higher than taxable income in the first two years and lower in year 3. What should the company report as its tax expense on the financial statements?

Tax expense may be defined as the amount recognized for tax purposes. Part B1 shows that tax expense would equal tax payable for the period in which revenues and expenses are reported for tax purposes (since tax liabilities are based on taxable income and prevailing tax laws, not pretax income).

This approach is not allowed under U.S. GAAP for two reasons: one is income statement oriented; the other is based on balance sheet considerations. The income statement argument relies on the matching principle: the relationship between tax expense and pretax income would not be consistent either across years or with the prevailing tax rate. Pretax income is the same in all three years, but tax expense differs as the tax deferred in earlier years is paid in year 3. For example, although the actual tax rate is 40%, the tax rate reported in part B1 is 26.7% for the first two years and 66.7% for year 3.

Part B2 bases tax expense on pretax income, not taxable income. Income tax under this approach is treated as a cost of operations and is accounted for accordingly under the matching principle.

The balance sheet argument focuses on the fact that tax deferred in the early years by the use of accelerated depreciation methods will have to be paid in later years.[2] The expected future cash flow consequences are recognized as a liability.[3] Part B2 illustrates GAAP as in APB 11. Tax expense is calculated as the tax rate times pretax income. The matching principle is satisfied as the relationship between revenues and expenses (40% tax rate) is maintained. Alternatively, from the balance sheet perspective, a liability ("credit") is recorded equal to the amount of tax that will have to be paid in year 3 when the difference in accounting methods reverses.

Specifically, the depreciation timing difference generates deferred tax expense of $400 (40% of the $1000 difference in depreciation expense) in years 1 and 2. The

---

[2]Had the company depreciated the asset over three years, depreciation would have been $1000 lower in years 1 and 2 and $2000 higher in year 3. This would have resulted in higher taxes of $400 in the first two years and $800 less in year 3.

[3]For the moment we defer any discussion of the merits of these arguments and their analytic implications.

EXHIBIT 7-1
Alternative Approaches to Tax Expense and Tax Payable

Assumptions

- A firm purchases a machine costing $6000 with a three-year estimated service life and no salvage value.
- For financial reporting purposes, the firm uses straight-line depreciation with a three-year life.
- For income tax reporting the machine is depreciated over two years.
- The machine is used to manufacture a product that will generate annual revenue of $5000 for three years.
- The tax rate is 40% in all three years.

A. Income Tax Reporting: Straight-Line Depreciation over Two Years

	Year 1	Year 2	Year 3	Total
Revenue	$5000	$5000	$5000	$15,000
Depreciation	3000	3000	0	6,000
Taxable income	$2000	$2000	$5000	$ 9,000
Tax payable @40%	800	800	2000	3,600
Net income	$1200	$1200	$3000	$ 5,400

B. Financial Statement Reporting: Straight-Line Depreciation over Three Years

B1. Method rejected by APB and FASB

- No recognition of deferred taxes
- Tax expense defined as tax payable

	Year 1	Year 2	Year 3	Total
Revenue	$5000	$5000	$5000	$15,000
Depreciation	2000	2000	2000	6,000
Pretax income	$3000	$3000	$3000	$ 9,000
Tax expense = payable	800	800	2000	3,600
Net income	$2200	$2200	$1000	$ 5,400

B2. Required Presentation Under GAAP (APB 11)

- Recognition of deferred taxes
- Tax expense differs from tax payable

	Year 1	Year 2	Year 3	Total
Revenue	$5000	$5000	$5000	$15,000
Depreciation	2000	2000	2000	6,000
Pretax income	$3000	$3000	$3000	$ 9,000
Tax expense @40%	1200	1200	1200	3,600
Net income	$1800	$1800	$1800	$ 5,400
Tax payable (part A)	800	800	2000	3,600
Deferred tax expense	400	400	(800)	0
Deferred tax credit (on balance sheet)	400	800	0	0

EXHIBIT 7-1. *(Continued)*

Journal Entries

Years 1 and 2

Tax expense	$1200	
Deferred tax liability		$ 400
Tax payable		800

Year 3

Tax expense	$1200	
Deferred tax liability	800	
Tax payable		$2000

cumulative timing difference is $2000 and the aggregate deferred tax liability is $800 at the end of year 2. No tax depreciation remains to be recorded in year 3, but book depreciation expense of $2000 must be reported. Pretax income will be lower than taxable income, resulting in the elimination of the deferred tax liability accumulated during the first two years.

The income-based approach of APB 11 was heavily criticized, leading to the balance sheet– and liability[4]-based methods of SFAS 96 and 109: reported tax expense is derived from the computed tax liability and related deferred taxes.

In this example, the income and liability approaches yield the same result. In more complex situations, the two approaches often produce different results, and these are discussed in later sections of this chapter. The primary differences between the methods stem from

1. Accounting for changes in tax rates.

2. The recognition and treatment of deferred tax assets.

The following sections provide detailed discussions of the different reporting rules used in the United States and their implications.

DEFERRED TAXES: ALTERNATIVE APPROACHES

APB 11: The Deferred Tax Method

The comprehensive, interperiod tax allocation mandated by APB 11 allocates tax effects to the periods in which the underlying revenues and expenses are recognized in the financial statements. The method is designed to match periodic tax expense to the operating results and pretax financial statement income in each period.

---

[4]These methods are "liability" approaches in that they focus on the computation of current and future cash consequences. SFAS 96 severely limited the recognition of deferred tax assets (reductions in future cash outflows), whereas SFAS 109 allows their recognition subject to a valuation allowance.

Exhibit 7-2 illustrates the computation of tax expense, current tax expense, and deferred taxes over a three-year period. It extends our example of Exhibit 7-1 by introducing another timing difference that gives rise to a deferred tax asset in years 1 and 2; the amount charged to warranty expense for financial statement purposes is larger than that allowed for tax purposes.

Tax expense is based on pretax income, and the reported net income reflects the use of machinery (depreciation) and estimated warranty expense for products sold. The tax liability measures the effects of tax depreciation and allowable warranty deductions on the tax return. Total revenues are $15,000, total depreciation expense is $6000, and total warranty expense is $1500[5] on both the financial statements and the tax return. The timing of expense recognition differs, but the total amount is the same.[6]

Deferred Tax Liabilities

The calculation of the deferred tax liability or credit is identical to that of Exhibit 7-1.

Deferred Tax Assets

Warranty expenses of $500 are recognized each year. Since no expenditures are incurred in years 1 and 2, no deductions can be taken on the tax return for those years. The higher taxable income results in a prepayment of taxes; tax expense in the financial statements reflects lower pretax income. The timing difference of $500 during the first two years generates a deferred tax asset of $200 ($500 × 0.4) each year.

In year 3; tax-deductible expenditures of $1500 are incurred for repairs, reducing taxable income and tax payments. This reversal of timing differences (expenditures now exceed expenses by $1000, offsetting the same amount of expense recognized in years 1 and 2) also eliminates the deferred tax asset generated during the first two years.

Do the deferred tax liabilities at the end of years 1 and 2 actually represent a liability[7] for tax payments due in year 3? Similarly, does the deferred tax asset qualify as an asset?

These are important issues from an analytical perspective to which we will return after discussing various pronouncements dealing with deferred taxes. Conceptually, the income statement focus of APB 11 gives rise to deferred assets (debits) and liabilities (credits) due to the application of the matching principle. The interpretation of the liability (asset) was never of prime concern to the APB. One result of the switch to the balance sheet approach (SFAS 96 and 109) from the income statement approach (APB 11) is reflected in the different treatment of changes in tax rates.

---

[5]Warranty expense and repair costs are assumed to be identical for illustration only; it is unlikely that firms could predict expected repair costs perfectly. Bad debt expenses and estimated litigation losses are other examples of timing differences where predictions may be similarly uncertain.

[6]The timing of revenue recognition may also differ; for example, subscriptions are recognized when received for tax purposes but as revenues for financial reporting purposes as the subscriptions are filled. However, the total revenue recognized must be the same.

[7]Paragraph 184 in SFAS 96 allows that deferred tax assets and liabilities as measured and reported under APB 11 do not meet the definitions of assets and liabilities in SFAC 6. However, our concern is whether deferred tax assets and liabilities are useful indicators of future cash flows, not whether they fit the theoretical definition of an asset or liability.

EXHIBIT 7-2
Basic Example: Accounting for Income Taxes

Assumptions

Identical to Exhibit 7-1
- A firm purchases a machine costing $6000 with a three-year estimated service life and no salvage value.
- For financial reporting purposes, the firm uses straight-line depreciation with a three-year life.
- For income tax reporting the machine is depreciated over two years.
- The machine is used to manufacture a product that will generate annual revenue of $5000 for three years.
- The tax rate is 40% in all three years.

Additional for Exhibit 7-2
- Warranty expenses are estimated at 10% of revenues each year; all repairs are provided in year 3.

A. Financial Statements

Year	Gross Revenues	Total Expense	Pretax Income	Tax Expense*	Net Income
1	$ 5,000	$2500†	$2500	$1000	$1500
2	5,000	2500†	2500	1000	1500
3	5,000	2500†	2500	1000	1500
	$15,000	$7500	$7500	$3000	$4500

*Tax expense is 40% (tax rate) × pretax income.
†Depreciation expense is $2000 ($6000/3); warranty expense is $500 ($5000 × 10%).

B. Tax Return

Year	Gross Revenues	Total Expense	Taxable Income	Taxes Payable*	Posttax Income
1	$ 5,000	$3000†	$2000	$ 800	$1200
2	5,000	3000†	2000	800	1200
3	5,000	1500‡	3500	1400	2100
	$15,000	$7500	$7500	$3000	$4500

*Taxes payable are 40% (tax rate) × taxable income.
†Annual depreciation expense is $6000/2 = $3000; no expenditures are incurred for warranties during the first two years.
‡There is no depreciation expense, as equipment is fully depreciated at end of year 2; repair expenditures of $1500 are incurred.

EXHIBIT 7-2. *(Continued)*

C. Deferred Tax Assets and Liabilities

In years 1 and 2, the difference in depreciation lives generates a timing difference of $1000 (pretax income *exceeds* taxable income), resulting in a deferred tax liability of $400 ($1000 × 0.40) each year. At the end of the second year, the cumulative timing difference is $2000, and the cumulative deferred tax liability is $800.

No tax depreciation remains to be recorded in year 3, but book depreciation of $2000 is recognized. Pretax income is *less than* taxable income, resulting in a timing difference in the opposite direction and the elimination of the deferred tax liability accumulated during the first two years.

Warranty expense of $500 is recognized each year. Since no expenditures are incurred in years 1 and 2, no expense can be recognized on the tax return for those years. The timing difference (pretax income is *less than* taxable income) results in a deferred tax asset of $200 for each year. In year 3, an expense of $500 is recognized in the financial statements, but tax-deductible expenditures of $1500 are made for repairs; pretax income *exceeds* taxable income by $1000, and the cumulative deferred tax assets are eliminated.

Journal Entries

Years 1 and 2

Tax expense	$1000	
Deferred tax asset	200	
Deferred tax liability		$ 400
Taxes payable		800

Year 3

Tax expense	$1000	
Deferred tax liability	800	
Deferred tax asset		$ 400
Taxes payable		1400

Each year, the deferred tax assets and liabilities have been shown separately to highlight their different sources and expected cash consequences. Note that over the entire three-year period, tax expense and taxes payable are identical. By the end of the third year, all timing differences have reversed so that all deferred tax assets and liabilities have been offset.

Effect of Tax Rate and Tax Law Changes

Under APB 11, deferred taxes are computed at the tax rates in effect in the period of origination, and these are not adjusted to reflect subsequent changes in tax rates or laws. Reversals in deferred taxes are often recorded at tax rates different from those in effect when the timing differences originated. The result is a higher (or lower) tax expense relative to that expected at origination. The future cash consequences of significant and growing deferred tax asset and liability balances are unclear, and inadequate (and often irreconcilable) disclosures do not facilitate analysis.

Exhibit 7-3 depicts the impact of a change in tax rates on the deferred tax balances reported under APB 11. Tax rates are assumed to change at the beginning of year 2. All computations for year 1 are unchanged from the example in Exhibit 7-2. That is, even though the actual reversal will occur at a lower rate, no adjustment is made to the liability or asset. Only timing differences originating in year 2 affect deferred tax assets and credits, computed at the new tax rate of 35%. Reversals in year 3 (of year 1 differences) are, however, effected at the same 40% rate at which they were originated, assuming use of the *gross change method*.

If, however, the *net change method* were used, the timing differences would reverse at the current lower rate of 35%. The differences originated in year 1 at 40% would reverse at the lower rate, leaving a balance in both the deferred tax asset and credit accounts. This difference would remain in the financial statements until partially or fully eliminated by the impact of future tax rate changes[8] on tax expense.

Generally, a firm's deferred tax liability[9] grows over time, indicating nonreversal of timing differences. One of the factors contributing to this phenomenon was the lack of adjustment for changes in tax rates. When corporate tax rates were reduced from 46% to 34% by the Tax Reform Act of 1986, this lack of adjustment resulted in "overstated" deferred tax credits. The second factor contributing to the large nonreversing deferred tax accounts on the balance sheet was the impact of growth (for example, increased or higher-cost investments in fixed assets).

Behavior of Deferred Tax Liabilities over Time

In principle, timing differences originated by specific events and transactions will reverse and generate future taxable income and tax obligations. However, these reversals may be offset by similar or other events, for example, other originating timing differences. Cash consequences of deferred tax liabilities depend on the aggregate of future taxable income, tax rates, tax laws, and price levels, as well as the firm's growth rate.

---

[8]APB 11 allows firms to use the rate prevailing at origination for reversing differences (gross change method) or apply the current rate to the net of originating and reversing differences (net change method). However, since the choice is not disclosed, the impact on deferred tax balances and any cash consequences are obscured.

[9]A similar analysis can be made with respect to tax assets. We focus our discussion on the liability because that is generally the more prevalent and larger of the two.

In the example, the firm realizes a tax benefit due to the reversal in year 3. The amount and timing of realization depends on taxable income, tax rates, and tax laws in year 3. It also depends on other originating and reversing differences, trends in repair costs, and manufacturing efficiency and price level changes.

Generally, warranty expenses are recognized on the financial statements prior to their deduction on the tax return. The timing difference is the result of an estimate, and the amount and timing of its reversal is reasonably predictable. In general, management has substantially more discretion with respect to the amount and timing of deferred tax assets originated since it controls the recognition of warranty expense, bad debt reserves, and provisions for litigation losses, all of which generate such assets.

The amount and timing of their reversal may not be as discretionary or as predictable as other timing differences, for example, depreciation differences, that generate deferred tax liabilities. Recurring differences such as warranty and bad debt expense may produce a constant deferred tax asset over time in some cases, but the pattern of reversal is unlikely to be as predictable as that due to depreciation differences.

EXHIBIT 7-3

Impact of Tax Rate Change Under APB 11 (Basic assumptions as in Exhibit 7-2)

Year 1: Tax rate is 40%

Journal Entries			Selected T-Accounts			

			Deferred Tax Asset		Deferred Tax Liability	
Tax Expense	$1000					
Deferred tax asset	200		$200			
Deferred tax liability		$ 400				$400
Taxes payable		800				
			$200			$400

Year 2: Tax rate changes to 35%

			Deferred Tax Asset		Deferred Tax Liability	
Tax expense	$ 875*		$200		$400	
Deferred tax asset	175†		$175			
Deferred tax credit		$ 350‡			$350	
Taxes payable		700§	$375		$750	

*$2500 × 0.35 = $875 (pretax income × tax rate).
†$ 500 × 0.35 = $175 (deferral due to warranty expense).
‡$1000 × 0.35 = $350 (deferral due to depreciation).
§$2000 × 0.35 = $700 (tax return).

Year 3: Tax rate remains at 35%

			Deferred Tax Asset		Deferred Tax Liability	
Tax expense	$ 850*					$750
Deferred tax asset	750†		$375			
Deferred tax liability		$ 375‡			750	
Taxes payable		1225§		375		
			$ 0			$ 0

*$2500 × 0.35 = $875 − $25 (benefit of rate change, see text).
†$2000 × 0.375 = $750 (reversals at average origination rates).
‡$1000 × 0.375 = $375 (reversals at average origination rates).
§$3500 × 0.35 = $1225 (tax return).

    The computations for year 3 are made under the gross change method, which assumes that each timing difference is treated separately. Under the net change method, the year 3 effect on the deferred tax asset would be $350 ($1000 × 0.35), where $1000 is the net effect of the two timing differences (depreciation and warranty). Under this method, a deferred tax asset of $25 and a deferred tax liability of $50 would remain on the balance sheet at the end of year 3 even though both timing differences have reversed! While the gross change method is considered preferable, the net change method is frequently used in practice.

Insight as to the effects of a firm's growth rate is presented in Exhibit 7-4.

Exhibit 7-4 extends the illustration depicted in Exhibit 7-1. It focuses on the deferred tax consequences of depreciation differences. Assume that the firm acquires one machine each year and that it continues to use the depreciation lives given in Exhibit 7-1. The depreciation timing differences will produce a deferred tax expense of $400 in each year during the first two years of each machine's operation, with a reversal of $800 in its third year to eliminate the deferred tax liability generated over the first two years.

The $400 deferred tax liability at the end of the first year represents the effect of the timing difference from the single machine in use. In year 2, machine 1 adds an additional deferred tax liability of $400. The acquisition of the second machine in year 2 adds another timing difference of $400; there is now an accumulated deferred tax liability of $1200 at the end of the year.

In year 3, the firm acquires and uses the third machine that generates its first year timing difference, and the asset acquired in year 2 originates its second year timing difference. However, the machine acquired in year 1 now generates a reversal of timing difference because it has completed the final year of operation; while depreciated in the financial statements, no depreciation remains to be recorded for the asset on the tax

EXHIBIT 7-4
Impact of Growth on Deferred Tax Liability

Assumptions

A firm purchases one machine during each year of operation. All other assumptions are identical to those used in Exhibit 7-1. Most important, timing differences are originated and reversed as in Exhibit 7-1 and at the same tax rate, which is assumed to remain constant over time.

Deferred Tax Liability

Year 1	$ 400	Machine 1 (origination)
Year 2	400	Beginning balance
	400	Machine 1 (origination)
	400	Machine 2 (origination)
Year 3	$1200	Beginning balance
	(800)	Machine 1 (reversal)
	400	Machine 2 (origination)
	400	Machine 3 (origination)
Year 4	$1200	Beginning balance
	(800)	Machine 2 (reversal)
	400	Machine 3 (origination)
	400	Machine 4 (origination)
Year 5	$1200	Beginning balance

Note: The balance stabilizes at $1200 in this example at the end of year 3, with the originations exactly offset by the reversals. This result assumes constant levels of asset acquisitions, price levels, tax rates, and regulations. Increases in either price levels or acquisitions would result in rising balances of deferred tax liabilities.

return. The originating timing differences from the second and third machine have offset the reversal due to the first machine; there will be no change in the net deferred tax liability.

Note that the deferred tax consequences of one asset have reversed, generating taxable income that is offset by other originating differences. The deferred tax liability has stabilized at $1200 and will remain at that level if asset acquisitions, depreciation methods, and tax rates and tax laws remain constant. Increased asset purchases above present levels (either in physical quantity or due to higher prices) will result in a growing deferred tax liability as originations exceed reversals. Thus, as a result of growth, either in real or nominal terms, the deferred tax credit rarely is reversed. For reversals to exceed originations, the firm must begin to decline or suffer a significant loss. The deferred tax liability, in that case, may decline, but the cash consequences remain a function of future taxable income. Declining demand may lead to a decrease in asset acquisitions, but these conditions may also reduce taxable income to a point where the deferred taxes are never paid.

Need for Changes in Accounting for Income Taxes

APB 11's focus on the income statement effects of income taxes generated deferred tax assets and liabilities not meeting Financial Accounting Standards Board (FASB) criteria for asset and liability classification. Also, the cash consequences of the reported deferred tax balances were difficult, if not impossible, to determine since (1) changes in tax rates and tax laws were not always recognized and (2) while individual timing differences reverse, in the aggregate the reversals may not result in cash effects.

Numerous amendments and technical interpretations added to the complexity and the lack of relevance of the output of these rules. Also, APB 11 did not deal effectively with the impact of other differences[10] between tax bases of assets and liabilities and their carrying amounts in financial statements. These concerns resulted in the FASB's decision to reconsider accounting for income taxes in 1982 and culminated in the issuance of SFAS 96 in December 1987.

SFAS 96: The Liability Method

The objective of the new standard was to recognize the current and deferred taxes payable or refundable on all events recognized in the financial statements with the measurement based on prevailing tax laws.

This objective was met by radically shifting the focus of accounting for income taxes. Under APB 11, the focus is on the income statement; the balance sheet deferred tax assets and liabilities are the result of the calculation of deferred tax expense in connection with the determination of income tax expense. Under SFAS 96, the focus shifts to the balance sheet as deferred tax assets and liabilities are calculated directly; deferred tax expense used to determine reported net income is a consequence of the balance sheet calculations. The effects of SFAS 96 can best be highlighted by contrasting its treatment of tax rate changes with those of APB 11.

---

[10]These other differences are discussed in the next section. See footnote 11.

Effect of Tax Rate and Tax Law Changes

SFAS 96 remedied a significant drawback of APB 11. The balance sheet orientation of SFAS 96 requires adjustments to deferred tax assets and liabilities to reflect the impact of a change in tax rates or tax laws. The effect is reported as a component of earnings from continuing operations in the year the changes are effective.

Exhibit 7-5 depicts the effect of tax rate changes under SFAS 96 on the example in Exhibit 7-2. We assume that the decrease in tax rates is enacted at the beginning of year 2. The balance of deferred taxes at the end of year 1 is adjusted to reflect the lower rate. Year 2 income is increased since the lower rate results in a lower expected tax liability when the depreciation timing difference reverses, partially offset by a lower expected benefit when the warranty expense is tax deductible. Note that under this approach the net tax expense ($850) is a function of changes in the deferred tax liability and asset accounts and there is no attempt to match the relationship of tax expense directly to pretax income.

Thus an important consequence of the liability method of SFAS 96 is that changes in tax rates (or other tax regulations) that affect the estimated future tax liability are recognized in reported income in the year of the change. Under APB 11 such changes would be recognized, if at all, only when the timing differences reverse.

Deferred Tax Assets and Liabilities

The balance sheet focus in SFAS 96 led to a redefinition of deferred tax accounts in terms of traditional concepts of assets and liabilities. This resulted in an asymmetric approach to the treatment of deferred tax assets and liabilities with a narrowing of the recognition of assets.

SFAS 96 recognizes the deferred tax consequences of *temporary differences,* a concept broader than that of timing differences used in APB 11, as it includes consideration of other events[11] that result in differences between the tax bases of assets and liabilities and the carrying amounts in financial statements. The new standard mandates the recognition of deferred tax liabilities for temporary differences expected to generate net taxable amounts in future years.

In SFAS 96 (and again in SFAS 109), the FASB argues that deferred tax consequences of temporary differences that will result in net taxable amounts in future years meet the SFAC 6 definition of liabilities.[12, 13] The Board contends that deferred

---

[11]These temporary differences arise when (1) the tax basis of an asset is reduced by tax credits, (2) investment tax credits are accounted for under the deferred method, (3) the tax basis of a foreign subsidiary's assets is increased as a result of indexing, and (4) carrying amounts and tax bases of assets differ in purchase method acquisitions.

[12]The temporary difference in Exhibit 7-1 derives from the firm's use of depreciation lives for financial reporting different from those for tax return reporting, creating a difference between the carrying amount of the asset and its tax basis. Use of the asset in operations will result in taxable income in year 3, when no depreciation can be recorded on the tax return. The board acknowledges that certain events may offset the net taxable amounts that would be generated as temporary differences reversed, but because those events have not yet occurred and they are not assumed in the financial statements, their tax consequences should not be recognized.

[13]See Paras. 83–89, SFAS 96, and Paras. 75–79, SFAS 109.

EXHIBIT 7-5
Impact of Tax Rate Change: SFAS 96 (Basic assumptions as in Exhibit 7-2)

Year 1: Tax rate is 40%

Journal Entries		Selected T-Accounts	

Tax expense	$1000
Deferred tax asset	200
Deferred tax liability	$400
Taxes payable	800

Deferred Tax Asset		Deferred Tax Liability	
$200			$400
$200			$400

Year 2: Tax rate changes to 35%

Deferred Tax Asset		Deferred Tax Liability	
$200			$400
	25	50	
$175			$350

Deferred tax liability	$ 50*
Deferred tax asset	$ 25†
Tax expense	$ 25‡

*Year 1 depreciation timing difference is $1000 × 0.05 (change in rate).
†Year 1 warranty timing difference is $500 × 0.05.
‡Net effect.

Deferred Tax Asset		Deferred Tax Liability	
$175			$350
175			
		350	
$350			$700

Tax expense	$ 875*
Deferred tax asset	175†
Deferred tax liability	$350‡
Taxes payable	700§

*Pretax income × tax rate is $2500 × 0.35 = $875.
†$ 500 × 0.35 = $175.
‡$1000 × 0.35 = $350.
§$2000 × 0.35 = $700.

Year 3: Tax rate remains at 35%

Deferred Tax Asset		Deferred Tax Liability	
$350			$700
		700	
	350		
$0			$0

Tax expense	$ 875*
Deferred tax liability	700†
Deferred tax asset	$ 350‡
Taxes payable	1225§

*$2500 × 0.35 = $875.
†$2000 × 0.35 = $700.
‡$1000 × 0.35 = $350.
§$3500 × 0.35 = $1225.

taxes are legal obligations imposed by tax laws and that temporary differences will generate taxable income in future years as they reverse. The reported depreciation in the example in Exhibit 7-1 is regarded as the past event generating the tax liability.

The expected reversal of the temporary difference is confirmed by the firm's decision to report the asset on its balance sheet; use of the asset in operations suggests continued depreciation on the financial statements and therefore a reversal of the timing difference. These considerations are the basis of the FASB's contention that the only question is when, not whether, the use of the asset will generate taxable income in future periods.

Limitations on Deferred Tax Assets

The recognition of deferred tax assets (tax benefits of temporary differences that are expected to reduce taxable income in future years) is constrained by SFAS 96 to amounts that can offset the tax consequences of other temporary differences and amounts recoverable as refunds of taxes paid in current or prior years. The remaining tax benefits of temporary differences cannot be recognized under SFAS 96 and are treated as tax loss carryforwards.[14]

SFAS 96 does not change the measurement and recognition of deferred taxes in year 1 for the example in Exhibit 7-2. The tax benefit due to that year's warranty expense can be recognized since its reversal is forecast to occur in year 3 when the firm expects to report taxable income due to the reversal of the depreciation timing difference. The deferred tax asset generated by the warranty expense in year 1 would also be recognized under SFAS 96 if it could be used to obtain tax refunds for amounts paid within the three-year carryback period.

However, if we assume that the repairs are to be provided in year 7, the tax benefit could not be recognized since it cannot be offset against a reversing taxable difference (occurs in year 3) or carried back to obtain a refund for taxes paid in previous three years. The firm would measure and recognize income taxes for year 1 as

Tax expense	$1200	
Taxes payable		$800*
Deferred tax liability		400†

*Taxable income of $2000 times tax rate of 40%.
†Timing difference of $1000 times tax rate of 40%.

The reported tax expense is determined by the current tax expense (that is, taxes payable) and the deferred tax liability. No deferred tax asset is reported since none qualifies under SFAS 96 rules. The resulting tax expense ($1200/$2500 = 48% of pretax income) no longer fully reflects accrual accounting and bears no relationship to current statutory tax rates. This is a consequence of the shift in emphasis to the liability method and the balance sheet.

The FASB defended the resulting asymmetric recognition of deferred tax liabilities and assets by recourse to U.S. tax law, which limits the period over which losses can be carried forward. Further, it argued that recognition of additional tax benefits would require the assumption of future pretax income, in effect, involving events neither recognized nor assumed in financial statements. Notwithstanding the foregoing, the

---

[14]The distinction between deferred tax assets requiring future taxable income for realization and deferrals of taxes paid currently was eliminated by these limitations on recognition.

constraint of zero future pretax income reflects a rather conservative view of the going concern assumption that is used in the preparation of financial statements.

SFAS 96 does permit firms to incorporate the effect of expected, qualifying tax-planning strategies in the measurement and recognition of deferred tax consequences of temporary differences. It encourages tax-planning strategies designed to manage reported deferred tax amounts that need not be used if future taxable income allows realization of the expected tax benefits. However, these efforts would be wasteful and costly since the impact on earnings, reported operating performance, and the cash flow consequences, if any, of resulting deferred tax amounts were unclear at best.

Adoption Dates and Methods

The standard allowed significant flexibility with respect to adoption methods and effective dates. Firms adopting SFAS 96 could do so by one of two methods: either retroactively or prospectively. The effective date was extended repeatedly,[15] further confounding both year-to-year comparisons of effective tax rates for companies and in a given year, across companies. SFAS 109 has created other problems for analysts because the majority of firms continued to use APB 11 although a significant number did adopt SFAS 96. The 1991 survey by the American Institute of Certified Public Accountants (AICPA) in *Accounting Trends and Techniques* indicates that 174 of its sample of 600 companies had adopted SFAS 96 by year-end 1990.[16]

The two methods of adoption can be illustrated with reference to Amerada Hess, which adopted SFAS 96 in 1987. Exhibit 7-6 contains excerpts of financial statements and footnotes from 1986 and 1987 annual reports of the Amerada Hess Corporation that will be used to contrast accounting for income taxes under SFAS 96 with that under APB 11. The change was applied retroactively by restating financial statements of prior years. The original and the restated 1986 balance sheets and income statements have been shown together to facilitate comparison and analysis.

Notice, first, the difference between the originally reported balance sheet at December 31, 1986 (right-hand column), and the restated balance sheet (left-hand column). On the asset side, only one account has changed: prepaid expenses. This restatement tells us that Amerada included deferred tax assets (or prepaid taxes) in that account; that fact was not previously disclosed.

On the liability side of the balance sheet, there are a number of restated accounts: taxes payable, deferred income taxes, retained earnings, and the foreign currency translation adjustment included in stockholders' equity. Restatement of the first two accounts is not surprising; deferred taxes computed under SFAS 96 are quite different from those computed under APB 11. See Chapter 13 for a discussion of the foreign currency translation account, but note that this account is reported net of deferred tax effects (which depend on the accounting method used in translation).

Amerada restated December 31, 1986 retained earnings because it applied SFAS 96 *retroactively*. When the new method was adopted in December 1987, Amerada restated

---

[15]These extensions were the result of FASB reconsideration of some of the provisions of the standard, notably, the conditions under which deferred tax assets could be recognized. The outcome of this process was a new standard, SFAS 109, as discussed shortly.

[16]No breakdown of adoption methods was available.

EXHIBIT 7-6. AMERADA HESS CORPORATION
Condensed Consolidated Balance Sheet
(thousands of dollars)

At December 31	1986*	1986†
Assets		
Current Assets		
Cash and cash equivalents	$ 92,681	$ 92,681
Accounts receivable and inventories	1,111,629	1,111,629
Prepaid expenses	62,394	71,738
Total current assets	1,266,704	1,276,048
Property, Plant and Equipment (Net)	3,529,183	3,529,183
Other Assets	108,823	108,823
Total Assets	$4,904,710	$4,914,054
Liabilities and Stockholders' Equity		
Current Liabilities		
Notes payable	$ 90,525	$ 90,525
Accounts payable—trade	282,777	282,777
Accrued liabilities	333,999	333,999
Taxes payable	237,807	173,443
Current maturities of long-term debt	89,994	89,994
Total current liabilities	1,035,102	970,738
Long-Term Debt	1,347,848	1,347,848
Deferred Liabilities and Credits		
Accrued excess shipping costs	217,598	217,598
Deferred income taxes	293,492	255,511
Other	71,877	71,877
Total deferred liabilities and credits	582,967	544,986
Stockholders' Equity		
Preferred stock	304	304
Common stock	305,222	305,222
Retained earnings	1,758,445	1,885,092
Equity adjustment from foreign currency translation	(125,178)	(140,136)
Total stockholders' equity	1,938,793	2,050,482
Total Liabilities and Stockholders' Equity	$4,904,710	$4,914,054

*Restated. As reported in the 1987 financial statements.
†As originally reported in the 1986 financial statements.

EXHIBIT 7-6. *(Continued)*

Condensed Statement of Consolidated Income
(thousands of dollars, except per share data)

For the Years Ended December 31	1986*	1986†
Revenues	$4,062,255	$4,062,255
Costs and Expenses		
Operating costs	4,252,092	4,252,092
Provision for income taxes	(7,267)	29,606
Total costs and expenses	4,244,825	4,281,698
Net Income (Loss)	$ (182,570)	$ (219,443)
Net Income (Loss) Per Share	$(2.16)	$(2.60)

From 1987 Financial Statements

Condensed Statement of Consolidated Retained Earnings
(thousands of dollars, except per share data)

For the Years Ended December 31	1987	1986*	1985*
Balance at Beginning of Year			
As previously reported			$2,458,196
Adjustment to reflect change in method of accounting for income taxes			(201,818)
As restated	$1,758,445	$1,941,938	2,256,378
Net income (loss)	229,860	(182,570)	(222,111)
Dividends	(38,227)	(923)	(92,329)
Redemption of preferred and common stock	(53,865)	—	—
Balance at End of Year	$1,896,213	$1,758,445	$1,941,938

*Restated.

Income Taxes: Deferred income taxes are determined on the liability method in accordance with Statement of Financial Accounting Standards (FAS) No. 96, Accounting for Income Taxes (see Note 2).

No provision is made for U.S. income taxes applicable to undistributed earnings of foreign subsidiaries that are indefinitely reinvested in foreign operations.

Change in Accounting for Income Taxes
In December 1987, the Corporation changed its method of accounting for income taxes to comply with the provisions of FAS No. 96, Accounting for Income taxes. The accounting change was applied retroactively by

EXHIBIT 7-6. *(Continued)*

restating the financial statements of prior years, resulting in a decrease in retained earnings at January 1, 1985 of $201,818,000. The effect in 1987, 1986 and 1985 was to increase net income as follows:

Thousands of dollars	Amount	Per share
1987	$47,421	$.56
1986	36,873	.44
1985	38,298	.45

The effect of the accounting change in 1987 resulted principally from a revision in the estimated liability for deferred Petroleum Revenue Tax in the United Kingdom in the fourth quarter of the year. There was no material effect on the earlier quarters of 1987. Net income for each of the 1986 quarters increased as follows: first quarter—$8,208,000 ($.10 per share), second quarter—$2,492,000 ($.02 per share); third quarter—$6,450,000 ($.08 per share) and fourth quarter—$19,723,000 ($.24 per share).

Provision for Income Taxes
The provision for income taxes consists of the following:

Thousands of dollars	1987	1986*	1985*
United States			
Federal**			
Current	$ 17,660	$ —	$ 12,972
Deferred	—	(10,881)	(93,352)
State	2,899	3,272	4,489
	20,559	(7,609)	(75,891)
Foreign			
Current	110,002	40,358	435,449
Deferred	(67,812)	(25,998)	44,368
	42,190	14,360	479,817
Benefit of net operating loss carryforwards			
United States			
Current	(5,022)	—	—
Foreign			
Current	(39,005)	—	—
Deferred	—	(6,715)	(23,888)
	(44,027)	(6,715)	(23,888)
Adjustment of deferred tax liability for rate changes	4,268	(7,303)	(4,761)
Total	$ 22,990	$(7,267)	$375,277

*Restated to reflect adoption of FAS No. 96.
**Income tax benefits on 1986 operating losses of U.S. operations (and certain foreign subsidiaries) have not been recorded, except to the extent of deferred tax credits arising from revision of prior year income tax estimates. No investment tax credits were recorded in 1987 and 1986. Investment tax credits amounted to $11,465,000 in 1985.

EXHIBIT 7-6. *(Continued)*

The provision for income taxes is based on income (loss) before income taxes as follows:

Thousands of dollars	1987	1986	1985
United States	$ (11,391)	$(271,830)	$ 76,507
Foreign*	264,241	81,993	613,351
Special charge			
United States	—	—	(513,032)
Foreign*	—	—	(23,660)
Total	$252,850	$(189,837)	$ 153,166

*Foreign income includes the Corporation's Virgin Islands, shipping and other operations located outside of the United States.

The difference between the Corporation's effective income tax rate and the United States statutory rate is reconciled below:

	1987	1986	1985
United States statutory rate	40.0%	(46.0)%	46.0%
Income from foreign operations subject to varying income tax levies	(7.5)	(16.7)	29.2
Losses for which no U.S. tax benefit was recorded	—	60.7	—
Investment tax credit and government grants	(9.4)	—	(1.7)
Net operating loss carryforwards	(17.4)	(3.5)	(3.4)
Taxes related to prior years	4.7	—	—
Other items	(1.3)	1.7	(0.6)
Total	9.1%	(3.8)%	69.5%*

*Excluding effect of 1985 special charge. Inclusion of such special charge and related income tax benefit described in Note 3 would result in a 1985 effective income tax rate of 245%.

The Corporation has not recorded deferred income taxes applicable to undistributed earnings of foreign subsidiaries that are indefinitely reinvested in foreign operations. Undistributed earnings amounted to approximately $625 million at December 31, 1987, excluding amounts which, if remitted, generally would not result in any additional U.S. income taxes because of available foreign tax credits. If the earnings of such foreign subsidiaries were not indefinitely reinvested, a deferred tax liability of approximately $148 million would have been required.

At December 31, 1987, the Corporation has a net operating loss carryforward for United States income tax purposes of approximately $380 million, expiring in the year 2001. Because of temporary differences, the operating loss carryforward for financial reporting purposes is approximately $450 million. The future benefit to be realized on utilization of net operating loss carryforwards may be affected by limitations on foreign tax credits and other factors.

The Corporation also has an investment tax credit carryforward of approximately $38 million, expiring in years through 2001.

Net operating loss carryforwards (expiring in years 1996 to 2001) applicable to certain foreign subsidiaries for income tax and financial reporting purposes at December 31, 1987 amount to approximately $270 million and $150 million, respectively.

EXHIBIT 7-6. *(Continued)*

From Original 1986 Financial Statements

Provision for Income Taxes

The provision for income taxes consists of the following:

Thousands of dollars	1986	1985	1984
United States			
Federal*			
Current	$ —	$ 12,972	$ (14,188)
Deferred...	(10,881)	(87,853)	(24,801)
State..	3,272	4,489	4,255
	(7,609)	(70,392)	(34,734)
Foreign			
Current	40,358	435,449	629,431
Deferred...	(3,143)	48,518	(4,935)
	37,215	483,967	624,496
Total	$ 29,606	$413,575	$589,762

*Income tax benefits on 1986 operating losses of U.S. operations (and certain foreign subsidiaries) have not been recorded, except to the extent of deferred tax credits arising from revision of prior year income tax estimates. No investment tax credits were recorded in 1986. Investment tax credits amounted to $11,465,000 in 1985 and $33,286,000 in 1984.

The difference between the Corporation's effective income tax rate and the United States statutory rate is reconciled below:

	1986	1985	1984
United States statutory rate...............................	(46.0)%	46.0%	46.0%
Income from foreign operations subject to varying income tax levies...	(8.2)	30.5	36.7
Losses for which no U.S. tax benefit was recorded..............	60.7	—	—
Adjustment resulting from Tax Reform Act of 1986..............	7.4	—	—
Investment tax credit......................................	—	(1.7)	(4.4)
Other items..	1.7	.2	(.7)
Total	15.6%	75.0%*	77.6%

*Excluding effect of 1985 special charge. Inclusion of such special charge and related income tax benefit described in Note 2 would result in a 1985 effective income tax rate of 270%.

For financial reporting purposes, the Corporation has a net operating loss carryforward applicable to United States operations of approximately $525 million at December 31, 1986. Because of timing differences, the Corporation's net operating loss carryforward for income tax purposes is approximately $400 million expiring in the year 2001. The future benefit to be realized on utilization of net operating loss carryforwards for financial reporting and income tax purposes may be affected by limitations on foreign tax credits.

For income tax purposes, the Corporation also has an investment tax credit carryforward of approximately $39 million (net of adjustments required by the Tax Reform Act of 1986) expiring in years through 2001.

Source: Amerada Hess 1986 and 1987 Annual Reports (condensed)

reported net income for 1985, 1986, and the first three quarters of 1987. As permitted by SFAS 96, the effect of the new standard on years prior to 1985 was shown as an adjustment to retained earnings at January 1, 1985.

The details of the change are shown in the "Change in Accounting for Income Taxes" footnote in Exhibit 7-6. Extracting the data, we can compute the net effect of the new standard as follows:

	($ thousands)
Effect on January 1, 1985, retained earnings	$(201,818)
Effect on 1985 net income	38,298
Effect on 1986 net income	36,873
Effect on 1987 net income	47,421
Net effect of change	$ (79,226)

Had Amerada adopted SFAS 96 using the cumulative effect method (prospective adoption), the change would have *reduced* reported 1987 net income by $79 million (approximately $0.94 per share). By adopting the new standard retroactively, 1987 net income was *increased* by $47 million ($0.56 per share). As either method was permitted by SFAS 96, the company could choose the adoption method with the best impact on reported income. The difference between the two methods was $1.50 per share. Amerada reported earnings per share for 1987 of $2.73 under the retroactive method; use of the prospective method would have resulted in reported earnings per share (EPS) of $1.23, a reduction of 55%!

Amerada's tax footnote does not explain the large negative impact of SFAS 96. That standard's limitation on deferred tax assets is a likely reason.

Deere, on the other hand, adopted SFAS 96 in the first quarter of fiscal 1988, using the prospective method of adoption. The cumulative effect of the change was a gain of $28.7 million ($0.42 per share), shown separately in the income statement[17] for that year. The income tax footnote indicates that the gain related entirely to Deere's financial subsidiaries as the manufacturing subsidiaries had no (net) deferred tax liabilities. The gain from the adoption of SFAS 96 must be due to the effect of the lowering of the statutory tax rate in the United States.

The method of adoption of SFAS 96, as we have seen, can significantly affect reported net income. Because SFAS 109 also allows firms to use either adoption method (retroactive or prospective), analysts need to examine the method chosen to separate ongoing operating income from the effect of the accounting change.

The immediate recognition of tax rate changes under SFAS 96 provided significant benefits to firms reporting large deferred tax liability balances, primarily capital-intensive firms with timing differences due to depreciation. The reduction in tax rates from 46% to 34% (over the period 1986–1988) allowed firms to report higher income due to a reduction in deferred tax liabilities originated at the higher rate.

---

[17]See Exhibit 1B-1, Appendix 1-B (tax footnote not shown).

The new standard did not, however, benefit all firms. The limitations on the recognition of deferred tax assets meant that some firms (e.g. Amerada) could no longer recognize such assets.[18] In addition, the effect of SFAS 96 on purchase method acquisitions (discussed shortly) resulted in adverse effects for some firms.

Because of the limitations on the recognition of deferred tax assets:

1. Some firms reported higher deferred tax liabilities (as compared with APB 11) albeit at lower statutory tax rates.

2. Some financial institutions and other firms showing operating losses reported higher tax expense and lower net income under SFAS 96 as they were unable to recognize all deferred tax assets generated under APB 11.

In many cases the most pernicious impact of SFAS 96 was on reported income and tax rates, as reported tax expense bore little or no relationship to pretax income as a result of its focus on the liability method. Distortions resulted from the revaluation of deferred tax liabilities requiring hypothetical tax-planning strategies and the restrictive legal interpretation of deferred tax assets. These drawbacks led to the issuance of a new standard, SFAS 109.

SFAS 109: Modified Liability Method

The newest reporting standard maintains the balance sheet focus of SFAS 96 when accounting for income taxes, but with several significant changes, which are discussed in the paragraphs that follow. SFAS 109 has two objectives:

1. To recognize taxes payable or refundable for the current year.

2. To recognize the deferred tax liabilities and assets measured as the future tax consequences of events that have been recognized in financial statements or tax returns.

Deferred tax expense is, as under SFAS 96, measured as the change during the year in the firm's deferred tax assets and liabilities. The reported tax expense or benefit for the year represents the sum of the taxes currently payable or refundable (current tax expense or benefit) and the deferred tax expense. The standard retains the SFAS 96 requirement to adjust deferred tax assets and liabilities for the effects of tax rate and tax law changes. Also, as before, the effect must be reported as a component of income from continuing operations.

Deferred Tax Assets and the Valuation Allowance

The most significant change involves the recognition of deferred tax assets; the FASB now allows that, in many cases, the event that generates a deductible temporary

---

[18]The restrictions on deferred tax assets also presented a major roadblock to the early adoption of SFAS 106 (other postemployment benefits). Adoption of this standard creates significant deferred tax assets that, under SFAS 96, could be recognized only by firms with deferred tax liabilities extending far into the future. General Electric is a good example, given its deferred tax liabilities due to the leasing operations of its financial units. For further discussion of this issue, see Chapter 9, especially the simultaneous adoption of SFAS 106 and SFAS 109 by Westinghouse in 1992.

difference and operating loss or tax credit carryforward is a sufficient past event to permit recognition of the deferred tax asset.[19]

However, it requires an evaluation of the realizability of future taxable income; that is, management has to defend the recognition of deferred tax assets. A valuation allowance reducing the deferred tax asset is required if an analysis of the sources of future taxable income suggests that it is *more likely than not* that some portion or all of the deferred tax asset will not be realized.[20]

Tax-planning strategies can be used to reduce required valuation allowances, but they have to be disclosed. SFAS 109 provides examples of positive and negative evidence[21] that must be weighed to determine the need for a valuation allowance and to measure the amount of the allowance. Changes in the valuation account must be reflected in income from continuing operations.

Effective Date and Transition Method

SFAS 109 is effective for fiscal years beginning after December 15, 1992. Few companies adopted the new standard for 1991, as SFAS 109 was not formally issued until February 1992.

Exhibit 7-7 provides an excerpt from the *1991 Annual Report* of Sears, Roebuck and Co., one of the early adopters of SFAS 109. The footnote shows that adoption resulted in a decrease of $134 million in tax expense due to recognition of deferred tax assets not reported under SFAS 96. It also shows the cumulative amount of unremitted income of its international affiliates and the taxes that would be paid in the event of remittance.

Exhibit 7-8 contains portions of the financial statement footnotes from Kenwin Shops' *1991 Annual Report*. The company, which had previously adopted SFAS 96 in 1988, adopted SFAS 109 in the fourth quarter of 1991. The new method was adopted retroactively, and previously reported net income for 1989 and 1990 was restated. As in the case of Amerada, opening retained earnings (January 1, 1989, for Kenwin) were reduced by the cumulative effect of the new standard for years prior to the first year restated.

The restatements for 1989 and 1990 had a minimal impact on those years as profitability was low. The major impact of the new standard was on 1991, with a reduced loss of $187,000 ($0.46 per share). Had the new standard not been adopted, the reported loss of $565,743 ($1.39 per share) would have been one-third higher.

The reduced loss, it appears, was due to the ability under SFAS 109 to recognize deferred tax assets. However, that ability was not unlimited. As shown in Note D, Kenwin provided a valuation allowance of $66,000, reducing the deferred tax assets recognized. The valuation allowance reduced the beneficial impact of SFAS 109.

---

[19]Thus, SFAS 109 permits recognition of deferred tax assets due to temporary differences as under APB 11.

[20]Sources of future taxable income include existing taxable temporary differences, future taxable income net of reversing temporary differences, taxable income recognized during qualifying carryback periods, and applicable tax-planning strategies.

[21]Existing contracts or backlogs expected to be profitable, appreciated assets, earnings over the past few years, and the nature (nonrecurring) of the loss would suggest that a valuation allowance is not needed. Examples of negative evidence include cumulative losses in recent years, past inability to use loss or tax credit carryforwards, and other indications of the inability to use the tax benefits.

EXHIBIT 7-7. SEARS, ROEBUCK AND CO.
Year Ended December 31, 1991

Except from Summary of Significant Accounting Policies

Income taxes

Effective Jan. 1, 1991 the Company adopted SFAS No. 109, "Accounting for Income Taxes." Adoption of this statement reduced income tax expense by $134.0 million in 1991, primarily due to the recognition of deferred tax assets previously not recorded under SFAS No. 96. No cumulative effect adjustment was required for the adoption of SFAS No. 109 due to the Company's previous use of the liability method.

The consolidated federal income tax return of Sears, Roebuck and Co. includes results of the domestic operations of the business groups. Tax liabilities and benefits are allocated as generated by the respective business groups, whether or not such benefits would be currently available on a separate return basis. U.S. income and foreign withholding taxes are not provided on unremitted earnings of international affiliates which the Company considers to be permanent investments. The cumulative amount of unremitted income and the taxes which would be paid upon remittance of those earnings totaled $534.9 and $216.8 million, respectively, at Dec. 31, 1991.

Source: 1991 Annual Report, Sears, Roebuck and Co.

EXHIBIT 7-8. KENWIN SHOPS, INC. AND SUBSIDIARIES
Statements of Consolidated Operations and Retained Earnings

	FOR THE YEARS ENDED		
	DECEMBER 29, 1991	DECEMBER 30, 1990*	DECEMBER 31, 1989*
NET SALES (Note A(e))	$28,146,436	$31,012,886	$27,023,976
COST AND EXPENSES:	28,897,179	31,000,920	26,972,425
INCOME (LOSS) BEFORE PROVISION (CREDIT) FOR INCOME TAXES	(750,743)	11,966	51,551
Provision (credit) for income taxes (Notes A(d) and D)	(185,000)	10,000	14,000
NET INCOME (LOSS)	(565,743)	1,966	37,551
RETAINED EARNINGS AT BEGINNING OF YEAR	6,319,073	6,317,107	6,279,556
RETAINED EARNINGS AT END OF YEAR	$ 5,753,330	$ 6,319,073	$ 6,317,107
NET INCOME (LOSS) PER SHARE (Note G)	$ (1.39)	$ .01	$ .09
WEIGHTED AVERAGE NUMBER OF SHARES USED IN COMPUTING EARNINGS PER SHARE	406,390	406,404	406,410

*Restated (Note A(d))
The accompanying notes are an integral part of these statements.

EXHIBIT 7-8. *(Continued)*

Notes to Consolidated Financial Statements

NOTE A - *SUMMARY OF SIGNIFICANT ACCOUNTING POLICIES*

(d) Change in Accounting Method for Income Taxes

The Company adopted Statement of Financial Accounting Standards (SFAS) No. 109, "Accounting for Income Taxes", for the recording of deferred income taxes, in the fourth quarter of the year ended December 29, 1991. As a result of the change, the net loss for the year ended December 29, 1991 has been reduced by $187,000 ($.46 per share). The Company has elected to apply the provisions retroactively to its years ended December 30, 1990 and December 31, 1989. It was not practical to restate years prior to 1989. Accordingly, retained earnings at January 1, 1989 have been reduced by $22,000, the cumulative effect of the change in the method of accounting for income taxes.

The consolidated financial statements for the years ended December 30, 1990 and December 31, 1989 have been restated for the effect of adopting the statement as follows:

	December 30, 1990	December 31, 1989
Net income as previously reported	$ 6,966	$36,551
Adjustment for the effect of adoption of Statement No. 109	(5,000)	1,000
Net income as restated	$ 1,966	$37,551
Earnings per share:		
Net income per share as previously reported	$ .02	$ .09
Adjustment for effect of adoption of Statement No. 109	(.01)	—
Net income per share	$ .01	$ .09

A requirement of SFAS No. 109 is that deferred tax assets and liabilities be adjusted in the period of enactment for the effect of an enacted change in tax laws or rates. The statement establishes procedures to assess whether a valuation allowance should be established for deferred tax assets.

NOTE D - *INCOME TAXES*

(a) The provision (credit) for income taxes is comprised of the following:

	For the Years Ended		
	December 29, 1991	December 30, 1990*	December 31, 1989*
Federal	$(205,000)	$ 89,000	$ 116,000
State	(3,000)	28,000	23,000
Deferred	23,000	(107,000)	(125,000)
Total	$(185,000)	$ 10,000	$ 14,000

*Restated (Note A(d))

EXHIBIT 7-8. *(Continued)*

(b) Deferred income taxes, resulting from timing differences in the recognition of income and expense for tax and financial statement purposes, are as follows:

	For the Years Ended		
	December 29, 1991	December 30, 1990*	December 31, 1989*
Difference between tax and book depreciation and amortization	$(18,000)	$ (21,000)	$ (14,000)
Difference between tax and book allowance for doubtful accounts	9,000	(56,000)	(50,000)
Difference between the tax and book basis of merchandise inventories	24,000	(30,000)	(61,000)
Net operating loss carryforward	(58,000)	—	—
	(43,000)	(107,000)	(125,000)
Valuation allowance	66,000	—	—
Net deferred tax expense (income)	$ 23,000	$(107,000)	$(125,000)

*Restated (Note A(d))

(c) The following is a summary of the components of the net deferred tax asset and liability accounts recognized in the accompanying consolidated balance sheets:

	1991	1990
Deferred tax assets:		
Difference between tax and book amortization	$164,000	$134,000
Difference between tax and book allowance for doubtful accounts	154,000	163,000
Difference between the tax and book basis of merchandise inventories	97,000	121,000
Net operating loss carryforward	58,000	—
Total	473,000	418,000
Valuation allowance	66,000	—
	407,000	418,000
Deferred tax liability:		
Difference between tax and book depreciation	246,000	234,000
Net deferred taxes	$161,000	$184,000

EXHIBIT 7-8. *(Continued)*

(d) The accompanying financial statements are subject to final determination of federal and state taxes.

(e) As a result of losses incurred in 1991, the Company has a net operating loss carryforward of approximately $156,000, which will expire in December 2006.

(f) The effective tax rate for the Company is reconcilable to the federal statutory tax rate as follows:

	1991	1990*	1989*
Statutory rate	(34.0)%	34.0%	34.0%
State income taxes—net of federal income tax benefit	(.3)	154.4	29.5
Federal tax benefit of contribution carryover	—	—	(14.5)
Expenses producing no current tax benefit	.3	21.5	3.5
Deferred taxes—re valuation allowance—SFAS 109	8.8	—	—
Deferred taxes—re changes in tax laws and rates and lower tax rates applicable to income tax brackets	.1	(80.3)	(26.2)
Lower tax rates applicable to income tax brackets	.4	(46.0)	—
Sundry	.1	—	.9
	(24.6)%	83.6%	27.2%

*Restated (Note A(d))
Source: Kenwin 1991 Annual Report (condensed).

DEFERRED TAXES: ANALYTICAL ISSUES

Current and deferred tax expense affect the assessment of the firm's liability position as well as estimates of its future cash flows or earning power. The key analytic issue is whether the deferred tax liability (or asset) will be reversed in the future. If the underlying timing differences are not expected to reverse,

1. The deferred tax liability should not be considered debt; a strong case exists for adding it to equity.
2. In assessing a firm's future cash flows for valuation purposes, analysts should ignore those deferred taxes. They are based on the firm's statutory rate under the assumption of eventual reversal. If that assumption is invalid, then the rate of actual taxes paid relative to forecast income would be more appropriate.

Liability or Unrecognized Income?

Financial analysts need to establish whether deferred tax liabilities represent debt. How should they be treated in the analysis of a firm's leverage position? Two arguments are presented:

1. As indicated earlier, a firm's growth pattern may continually generate deferred tax liabilities. Alternatively, losses in the future may result in the nonpayment of taxes even if timing differences reverse. Both these factors suggest that deferred taxes are unlikely to be paid.

2. Even assuming payment of the deferred taxes, the present value of the eventual payment is considerably lower than the stated amount. Thus, as with other liabilities that are recorded on the basis of the present value of the future payments (see Chapter 8), the deferred tax amount should be discounted at an appropriate interest rate.[22]

These two arguments suggest that the components of the deferred tax liability should be analyzed to evaluate the likelihood of reversal or continued growth. A liability should be recorded[23] only for those components that are likely to reverse rather than the full amount of the liability. In addition, an estimate of the timing of reversal would facilitate discounting the liability to its present value and analysis of future cash flows.

The income tax footnote discloses the components of the deferred tax liability for each year. Examining these components over a number of years will indicate which tend to reverse and which do not. For example, the effect of different depreciation methods tends not to reverse. In addition, if reversal occurs, the time horizon is usually longer than for other differences, suggesting a large discount to present value. Similar analysis can be applied to other major differences, keeping in mind any changes in the tax law.

To the extent that deferred taxes are not a liability, then they are unrecognized income. Had they never been recorded, previous tax expense would have been lower and stockholders' equity higher. Thus equity should be increased. The effect of this argument on the debt/equity ratio can be substantial: debt is decreased and equity is increased by the same amount, reducing the ratio considerably.

Alternatively, in some cases deferred taxes are neither liability nor equity. For example, when tax depreciation is a better measure of economic depreciation (see Chapter 6) than financial statement depreciation, adding the deferred tax liability to equity would overstate the value of the firm. Yet, if the deferred tax liability is unlikely to result in a cash outflow, it is not a liability either. Ultimately, the financial analyst must decide on the appropriate treatment of deferred taxes on a case by case basis.

In practice, the analytic treatment of deferred taxes varies. Some creditors, notably, banks, do not consider them to be liabilities (but neither do they include them as part of equity). In calculating solvency and other ratios, most analysts ignore deferred taxes altogether. Box 7-1 contains a discussion of evidence provided by research regarding the relevance of deferred taxes to securities valuation.

Deferred taxes influence both the evaluation of liability and equity and the forecasting of income and future cash flows. One input in this process is the firm's effective tax rate. The next section discusses a number of alternative measures of assessing a firm's effective tax rate.

---

[22]Discounting of deferred taxes is currently allowed *only* in the Netherlands. However, only a minority of firms use it.

[23]The U.K. standard follows a partial allocation method, and deferred taxes are recognized only when reversal is expected within three years.

```
┌────────────────────────────────────────────────────────────────────────────┐
│  BOX 7-1                                                                     │
│  Market Valuation of Deferred Taxes                                         │
├────────────────────────────────────────────────────────────────────────────┤
```

Surprisingly, there have not been many empirical studies that examined whether the market as a whole treats deferred tax liabilities as debt. Earlier discussion noted that the extent to which deferred tax liabilities should be treated as debt is a function of the probability that the deferrals will be reversed and the debt (if considered) should be discounted to its present value.

Givoly and Hayn (1992) examined these issues in the context of the Tax Reform Act (TRA) of 1986. The TRA cut the statutory tax rate for U.S. corporations from 46% fo 34%. This affected a firm's current tax position as well as the amount that would have to be repaid if and when future reversals of timing differences occurred.

The TRA was debated for over two years in Congress. Givoly and Hayn examined the effects on stock prices of events that indicated an improved chance of the measure passing as well as events that indicated a decreased chance of the measure passing. After controlling for the effects on current tax payments,* they argued that if the market treated the deferred tax as a liability,

1. The larger the deferred taxes, the more positive the impact of the TRA on the firm's market price.
2. No matter how large the firm's deferred tax account is, if timing differences will not be reversed or future tax losses will result in nonpayment of the tax at reversal, the effects of the TRA should be minimal. Thus they argued that the larger the growth rate in the deferred tax account and the greater the probability of tax losses,† the less likely there would be a positive impact on stock prices.

If the market ignored the deferred tax liability, there would be no impact of any of these factors. Overall, their results confirmed that the market incorporated the deferred tax liability into valuation.

When chances of the TRA being adopted increased (decreased), then

1. The larger the deferred tax account, the more positive (negative) the market reaction.
2. A large growth rate and increased probability of losses decreased (increased) the abnormal return.

A by-product of their study was the indication that the market incorporated a discount factor in valuing the deferred tax liability. The deferred tax accounts of high-risk‡ firms tended to affect market valuation less than low-risk firms. This result is consistent with a higher discount rate being applied to the higher-risk firms.

The Givoly and Hayn study focused on the deferred tax account in the balance sheet. It found that deferred tax accounting is incorporated in balance sheet valuation. Focusing on earnings, an earlier study by Beaver and Dukes (1972) also found that the market "favors" the deferral process. They found market reaction tended to be more closely associated with income that incorporated deferrals than with income that ignored deferrals and calculated taxes on the basis of current tax expense.§ Rayburn (1986), however, found that the association between deferred tax accruals and security returns was dependent on the expectations model assumed.

---

*Givoly and Hayn also controlled for other factors such as the present stock and age of machinery and equipment.

†The probability of losses was estimated using the frequency of losses that occurred in the previous five years.

‡High-risk was determined on the basis of the firm's market beta.

§The authors found this result surprising as they expected the number closer to cash flows (earnings without deferral) to be more closely associated with security prices. In a subsequent paper (Beaver and Dukes, 1973), the authors offered a different explanation. They demonstrated (see discussion in Chapter 6) that the market generally imputes a more accelerated form of depreciation than straight-line depreciation. As deferred taxes increase expense shown for firms using straight-line depreciation, they argued that the observed results with respect to deferred taxes may be a function of deferred taxes masking as a form of accelerated depreciation.

Effective Tax Rates

Changing methods of accounting for income taxes have a significant impact on reported effective tax rates. The trend in effective tax rates over time for a firm and the trends in relative effective tax rates for comparable firms within an industry can provide information useful in assessing operating performance and the income available for stockholders.

The reported effective tax rate is measured as

$$\frac{\textbf{Income tax expense}}{\textbf{Pretax income}}$$

Effective tax rates based on reported tax expense and pretax income may not reflect true economic differences between firms. Both reported tax expense and pretax income are affected by management choices as to revenue and expense recognition methods.

Revenue and expense recognition methods used on the tax return reflect the *cash consequences* of management choices and provide a different measure of the effective tax rate,[24] computed as the reported periodic tax liability divided by the taxable income:

$$\frac{\textbf{Current tax expense}}{\textbf{Taxable income}}$$

The denominator, taxable income, is not a required disclosure and has to be estimated. The difference between (financial reporting) pretax and (tax return) taxable income is due to temporary differences that create deferred tax assets and liabilities. This relationship can be used to estimate taxable income as follows:

$$\textbf{Estimated taxable income} = \textbf{Pretax income} \pm \frac{\textbf{Deferred tax expense}}{\textbf{Statutory tax rate}}$$

This computation estimates taxable income by assuming that all components of deferred tax credits and debits were computed at the same tax rate.[25]

---

[24]Some empirical evidence (see Zimmermann, 1983) indicates that effective tax rates calculated on the basis of actual taxes paid and/or current tax expense tend to be larger for large firms. This result is cited as evidence of the political cost hypothesis as large-sized firms, being more politically sensitive, are required to make larger wealth transfers than smaller-sized firms. Given that, in large part, these results are driven by the oil and gas industry, it is difficult to tell whether the political costs are a result of size or industry classification. Wang (1991) notes that smaller firms are more likely to have net operating losses than are larger firms, at which time their effective tax rate is zero. Ignoring these losses in the analyses may tend to bias the results.

[25]Stickney (1979) describes the use of footnote disclosures of the major categories of deferred taxes to develop more precise estimates of taxable income; note that the footnotes used are all based on APB 11 accounting. Because SFAS 96 limits the recognition of deferred tax assets, this method will not generate acceptable estimates of taxable income. The valuation allowance in SFAS 109 may also affect this analysis, but disclosure may allow the development of usable estimates of taxable income.

EXHIBIT 7-9. AMERADA HESS
Effective Income Tax Rates, 1986

	APB 11		SFAS 96	
$\dfrac{\text{Tax expense}}{\text{Pretax income}}$ $=$	$\dfrac{\$29,606}{\$(189,837)}$	$= -15.6\%$	$\dfrac{(\$7,267)}{\$(189,837)}$	$= 3.8\%$
$\dfrac{\text{Current tax expense}}{\text{Taxable income}}$ $=$	$\dfrac{\$43,630^*}{\$(220,324)\dagger}$	$= -19.8\%$	$\dfrac{\$43,630^*}{\$(300,483)\dagger}$	$= -16.9\%$
$\dfrac{\text{Current tax expense}}{\text{Pretax income}}$ $=$	$\dfrac{\$43,630}{\$(189,837)}$	$= -23.0\%$	$\dfrac{\$43,630}{\$(189,837)}$	$= -23.0\%$

*Income tax footnote in Exhibit 7-6 shows that taxes payable in 1986 included state taxes of $3,272,000 and foreign taxes of $40,358,000 for a total of $43,630,000.

†Deferred tax expense was $(14,024,000) under APB 11 and $(50,897,000) under SFAS 96. Assuming that these deferred taxes were computed at the 1986 statutory tax rate of 46%, we added $(30,487,000), and $(110,646,000) to pretax income under APB 11 and SFAS 96, respectively, to obtain estimated taxable income.

To forecast earnings and cash flows, a third ratio may be useful:

$$\frac{\textbf{Current tax expense}}{\textbf{Pretax income}}$$

This ratio may also be used with cash taxes paid instead of current tax expense. The amount of cash taxes paid can be easily obtained as SFAS 95, Statement of Cash Flows, requires separate disclosure of this amount. Due to interim tax payments and refunds, cash taxes paid may be quite different from current tax expense.

Exhibit 7-9 calculates these differing measures of effective tax rate for Amerada Hess. Because the firm restated previously reported net income, the impact of SFAS 96 on reported effective tax rates can be seen. Exhibit 7-9 calculates effective tax rates under both APB 11 and SFAS 96.

The first calculation is the reported effective tax rate. Under APB 11 (see the original 1986 footnote on income taxes), the rate was −15.6% (reported tax expense despite negative pretax income). An effective tax rate of 3.8% is reported under SFAS 96 (see the restated 1986 footnote on income taxes) as both tax expense and pretax income are negative. This swing accounts for the positive impact of the new standard on Amerada's reported income for 1986 ($29,606,000 + $7,267,000 = $36,873,000).

The second effective tax rate calculated in Exhibit 7-9 compares the current tax expense (excluding deferred tax expense) with estimated (tax return) taxable income. We would expect this calculation to be unchanged, as the tax return is unaffected by any change in financial reporting methods.

Current tax expense is, as expected, unchanged. However, the calculation of estimated taxable income changes significantly, resulting in a different (but still negative) tax rate. Information in the footnote does not enable us to explain this phenomenon.[26]

What is important is that current tax expense was positive: the company incurred a tax liability for 1986 despite its losses. The analyst would want to understand why this is the case and what implication it has for future income and tax flows.

The third measure of effective tax rate compares current tax expense with pretax income. As neither ratio component is affected by the choice of tax standard, the ratio is identical under both methods. As cash taxes paid were not reported for 1986, that variant of the ratio is not shown.

The preceding discussion has focused on differences among accounting treatments of deferred taxes. The next section provides a discussion of some specialized issues and highlights other differences among the reporting standards.

ACCOUNTING FOR TAXES: SPECIALIZED ISSUES

Temporary Versus Permanent Differences

The diverse objectives of financial and tax reporting generate *temporary (timing) differences* between pretax financial income and taxable income. Some differences, however, are permanent because they involve revenues and expenses that are reportable on either tax returns or in financial statements but not on both. For example, interest income on tax-exempt bonds, premiums paid on officers' life insurance, and amortization of goodwill are included in financial statements but will never be reported on the tax return. Similarly, certain dividends are not fully taxed, and tax or statutory depletion may exceed cost-based depletion reported in the financial statements.

No deferred tax consequences are recognized for *permanent differences;* however, they result in a difference between the effective tax rate and the statutory tax rate that should be considered in the analysis of effective tax rates.

Treatment of Operating Losses

Operating losses are due to an excess of deductions for tax purposes over taxable revenues. These tax losses may be carried back and applied to prior years to obtain refunds of taxes paid, and the tax impact of the carryback is recognized as a component of net income in the loss period because it can be measured and is currently realizable.

Tax losses may also be carried forward if insufficient taxes were paid during the carryback period or if the firm would lose valuable tax credits if losses were carried back to that period. Because the realization of tax loss carryforwards depends on future taxable income, the expected benefits could not be recognized, under APB 11, unless their realization was assured beyond reasonable doubt.[27] If recognized in subsequent periods, the tax benefits were reported as extraordinary items. As discussed previously,

---

[26]The explanation is probably that some of Amerada's foreign oil producing subsidiaries have extremely high tax rates; this problem was discussed in Appendix 6-A.

[27]Realization could be assumed if two conditions were met: (1) the loss was an isolated and nonrecurring event for a profitable firm, and (2) timely, sufficient future taxable income is virtually assured.

SFAS 96 and 109 changed both the recognition and classification criteria for loss carry forwards.

Indefinite Reversals

APB 11 identifies several cases with shared characteristics, particularly tax consequences, where comprehensive allocation and the recognition of deferred taxes are not required. The amount and timing of the reversal of timing differences in some of these cases are at the discretion of management, and others may never reverse at all. The accounting for these "special" timing differences was governed by the provisions of APB 23 and 24, issued in April 1972.

The undistributed earnings of unconsolidated subsidiaries and joint ventures are the most common example of these exceptions. The U.S. tax code requires 80% ownership to consolidate for tax purposes, ruling out joint ventures and many subsidiaries that are consolidated for accounting purposes. In addition, foreign subsidiaries are not consolidated in the U.S. tax return.[28]

As a result, the income of these affiliates is taxable on the parent's (U.S.) tax return only when dividends are received or the affiliate is sold, not when earnings are recognized. Thus, a timing difference is created between (tax return) taxable income and (financial reporting) pretax income. If the affiliate earnings are permanently reinvested, then affiliate earnings may *never* be taxable on the parent company tax return. This is the "indefinite reversal" criterion of APB 23. In such cases firms are required to disclose their intention of permanent reinvestment and report the cumulative undistributed earnings on which taxes have not been recognized.

APB 23 states that deferred tax effects for unconsolidated subsidiaries are not recognized when earnings are expected to be permanently reinvested or distributed in a tax-free liquidation.[29] If the parent expects to receive the undistributed earnings as dividends or capital gains, however, it must recognize the appropriate tax effects of the timing differences.[30] Any changes to or from "indefinite reversal" status generates tax effects that are recognized as adjustments to tax expense but not reported as extraordinary items.

APB 24 provides different reporting rules for equity method investments other than controlled subsidiaries and joint ventures because the assumption of permanent reinvestment of undistributed earnings can be justified only when the parent controls the investee. The deferred tax effects of undistributed earnings are computed based on whether they are expected to be received as dividends or as capital gains.[31]

---

[28]In some cases even wholly owned U.S. subsidiaries may not be consolidated for tax purposes. Insurance subsidiaries, which are governed by special tax regulations, are one example.

[29]Criteria for "indefinite reversal" include history of reinvestment (lack of dividend payments) and operational budgets (intent to reinvest).

[30]Since dividends from qualifying investments (45-day holding period and at-risk rules for intercorporate investments) are eligible for an 80% dividends received exclusion, the effective tax rate is much lower than the rate applicable to income received as capital gains even though the statutory rate on dividends and capital gains is currently equal.

[31]See Chapter 11 for a discussion of the effect of this issue on the analysis of investments accounted for under the equity method.

In the income taxes footnote to Deere's 1991 financial statements (see Appendix 1-B), we can see that the firm has not recorded deferred taxes on undistributed earnings of foreign affiliates in the amount of $364 million at October 31, 1991. If the indefinite reversal assumption had not been applicable, the firm would have reported an additional unspecified deferred tax liability.

APB 23 also describes reporting requirements for other timing differences meeting the indefinite reversal criteria. It discusses timing differences due to (1) estimated bad debt reserves of savings and loan associations versus the reserves allowed by the tax authorities and (2) policyholders' surplus of stock life insurance companies. Since the associations and the insurance companies control the amount and timing of reversals, no deferred taxes need be recognized. Required disclosures are similar to those in the case of undistributed earnings of controlled subsidiaries.

SFAS 96 did not amend APB 23 and left the "indefinite reversal" criteria unchanged. SFAS 109, however, has superseded APB 23 by requiring recognition of a deferred tax liability for temporary differences[32] due to the undistributed earnings of essentially permanent domestic subsidiaries and joint ventures[33] that arise in fiscal years beginning on or after December 15, 1992. This provision adversely impacts the reported earnings of firms with such affiliates that have not been providing deferred taxes.

However, SFAS 109 maintains the APB 23 exemption from the provision of deferred taxes in the following cases:

1. Undistributed earnings of a *foreign* subsidiary or joint venture that are considered to be permanently reinvested.

2. Undistributed earnings of a *domestic* subsidiary or joint venture arising in fiscal years *prior* to December 15, 1992.

Accounting for Acquisitions

SFAS 96 introduced substantial changes in the accounting for acquisitions reported under the purchase method.[34] It requires recognition of deferred tax assets or liabilities for any differences between the allocated fair market values and the tax bases of acquired assets and liabilities. APB 16 required firms to record acquired assets and liabilities net of related deferred taxes. Tax planning strategies (economic and reporting driven) could be used by acquiring firms to purchase targets with deferred tax positions that would complement theirs and allow higher reported earnings.

SFAS 109 continues the requirements of SFAS 96 for recognition of the deferred tax effects of any differences between the financial statement carrying amounts and tax bases of assets and liabilities recognized in purchase method acquisitions. The account-

---

[32]SFAS 109 also amended APB 23 as follows: deferred taxes must be provided on bad debt reserves of U.S. thrift lenders originating after 1987, on deposits in statutory reserve funds of U.S. steamship enterprises, and on post-1992 policyholders' surplus of stock life insurance companies; these issues are beyond the scope of this book.

[33]But if the parent has the statutory ability to realize those earnings tax free, no deferred tax provision is required (see Para. 33, SFAS 109).

[34]The purchase method of accounting for an acquisition is discussed in Chapter 12.

ing for acquired APB 23 differences (indefinite reversal category) changes because of the amendments noted in the previous section.

The most significant difference stems from any valuation allowance recorded for deferred tax assets due to the acquired firm's temporary differences or to its operating loss or tax credit carryforwards. The tax benefits of subsequent reversals of the valuation allowance must be used, first, to reduce all related goodwill, second, to eliminate all other related noncurrent intangible assets, and third, to reduce reported income tax expense.

FINANCIAL STATEMENT PRESENTATION AND DISCLOSURE REQUIREMENTS

Deferred tax assets and liabilities must be separated into current and noncurrent components based on the classification of the assets and liabilities generating the deferral. However, deferred tax assets due to carryforwards are classified by reference to expected reversal dates. SFAS 109 permits offsets of deferred tax effects only within tax-paying components of the firm and within tax jurisdictions.

While the disclosure requirements of the new standard are quite similar to those of SFAS 96 (which incorporated Securities and Exchange Commission disclosure requirements that had been in effect for many years), there are several changes. SFAS 109 specifically requires, among others:

1. Separate disclosure of all deferred tax assets and liabilities, any valuation allowance, and the net change in that allowance for the period.

2. Disclosure of the amounts of any unrecognized deferred tax liability for the undistributed earnings of domestic or foreign subsidiaries and joint ventures. These disclosures should facilitate the comparison of the operating results of firms that have different policies with respect to deferred tax recognition or the remission of income from such affiliates.

3. Disclosure of the current year tax effect of each type of temporary difference.

4. Disclosure of the components of income tax expense.

5. Reconciliation of reported income tax expense with the amount based on the statutory income tax rate (the reconciliation can be either in amounts or percentages).

6. Disclosure of tax loss carryforwards and credits.

Kenwin's footnotes (Exhibit 7-8) provide an excellent example of the disclosure provisions of SFAS 109. Note the disclosure of the different temporary differences (the footnote still uses the APB 11 term "timing differences") for each year and on a cumulative basis. The impact of the valuation allowance on both reported income tax expense and recognized tax assets can be clearly seen as well.

These disclosures provide some insight into the company's financial reporting practices. Footnote D(c) indicates that

1. The company has amortized unspecified assets faster for book (financial reporting) purposes than for tax purposes.

2. The company has a larger allowance for doubtful accounts for book than for tax purposes. (Bad debts are generally not deductible for tax purposes until the account is written off.)

3. Inventories have a lower cost basis for book than for tax purposes. (Kenwin has probably taken write-offs for book purposes that do not affect taxable income until the merchandise is sold.)

4. Depreciation has been higher for tax than for book purposes. (This is normally the case; see Chapter 6 for discussion.)

These insights can be used to question management regarding past operating results and to gain a better understanding of the factors affecting future operating results.

USEFULNESS OF ANALYSIS OF INCOME TAXES

Accounting for income taxes is complex; for a large company there will be many permanent and temporary differences between financial statement income and taxable income reported to tax authorities. A large multinational pays taxes in a number of jurisdictions, further complicating the process. From an analyst's perspective, unraveling these layers can seem daunting indeed. Box 7-2, however, shows how insights regarding a firm (can be derived from its income tax disclosures.)

Some analysts respond to this complexity by ignoring the issues. They analyze corporate performance on a pretax basis and simply accept that variations in the reported tax rate occur. We agree that analysis on a pretax basis is sound, but we believe that a firm's income tax accounting is too important to ignore. Summing up this chapter, an analysis of income tax is useful in the following ways:

1. Examine the firm's tax rate, the trend in that rate, and the rate relative to similar companies.
   a. Such analysis can offer important clues as to the sources of income (foreign versus domestic). Different tax jurisdictions have different tax rates, which will affect the composite rate for the firm.
   b. Some firms have operations in countries offering "tax holidays"; such earnings usually cannot be remitted without payment of tax. Be alert to possible changes in the operations in such countries or the need to remit the accumulated earnings.
   c. Permanent differences between financial and taxable income, if significant, indicate tax-exempt income, tax credits, or the impact of tax loss carryforwards. Under SFAS 96 and 109, the effect of tax rate changes also affect the tax rate; separate disclosure of this effect is required. Careful attention to footnotes may be required to understand the impact of these factors on past and future net income and cash flows.

BOX 7-2
Analysis of the 1991 Income Tax Footnote of Ashland Oil, Inc.

ASHLAND OIL, INC., AND SUBSIDIARIES
Note E—Income Taxes, 1989–1991 (in $ thousands)
A summary of the provision for income taxes follows.

	1991	1990	1989
Current*			
Federal	$32,885	$ 78,660	$24,280
State	7,105	17,410	9,650
Foreign	5,824	7,200	7,890
	$45,814	$103,270	$41,820
Deferred			
Federal and state	2,018	(22,410)	14,040
Foreign	2	230	170
	$ 2,020	$ (22,180)	$14,210
	$47,834	$ 81,090	$56,030

*Income tax payments amounted to $61,925,000 in 1991, $88,512,000 in 1990 and $92,427,000 in 1989.

Deferred income taxes and benefits are provided for significant income and expense items recognized in different years for tax and financial reporting purposes. Deferred income taxes result principally from the use of accelerated depreciation for tax purposes, prepaid contributions to the LESOP, intangible drilling costs expensed for tax purposes, and undistributed equity income. Deferred income tax benefits result principally from reserves not being deductible until paid, including insurance claims and reserves, accrued pension costs, and environmental reserves. Major components of the deferred income tax provision follow.

	1991	1990	1989
Accelerated depreciation	$ 2,675	$ (6,853)	$ (3,366)
NIOC settlement	—	—	19,688
Insurance claims and reserves	4,948	(10,995)	(6,059)
Construction contract reserves	(927)	7,610	1,489
Performance compensation reserves	1,612	(1,488)	5,245
Intangible drilling costs	5,817	2,923	4,075
Depletion	(195)	(277)	(2,952)
Other property related items	2,445	(9,612)	11,159
Environmental reserves	(565)	441	(6,993)
LESOP costs	(6,235)	(5,800)	(5,889)
Pension costs	(6,681)	1,433	417
Other items	(874)	438	(2,604)
	$ 2,020	$(22,180)	$14,210

The U.S. and foreign components of income before income taxes and a reconciliation of the normal statutory federal income tax with the provision for income taxes follow.

	1991	1990	1989
Income before income taxes			
United States	$129,479	$206,535	$ 98,243
Foreign	63,353	56,614	43,992
	$192,832	$263,149	$142,235
Income taxes computed at			
U.S. statutory rates	$ 65,563	$ 89,471	$ 48,360
Increase (decrease) in amount computed resulting from			
Equity income	(4,011)	(13,639)	(11,044)
State income taxes	4,168	6,412	6,615
Net impact of foreign results	(10,736)	4,403	11,708
Nonconventional fuel credit	(4,500)	(2,700)	(1,900)
Amortization of goodwill	1,219	1,689	6,911
Other items	(3,869)	(4,546)	(4,620)
	$ 47,834	$ 81,090	$ 56,030

The Internal Revenue Service (IRS) has examined Ashland's consolidated U.S. income tax returns through 1987. As a result of its examinations, the IRS has proposed adjustments, certain of which are being contested by Ashland. Ashland believes it has adequately provided for any income taxes that may ultimately be assessed on contested issues.

Source: Ashland Oil, 1991 Annual Report.

This analysis of the Ashland Oil income tax footnote is intended to highlight information provided by the firm. As required, the tax footnote contains a breakdown of the sources of taxable income and current taxes payable. Ashland discloses that the major portion ($129,479 thousand or 67% of total 1991 pretax income of $192,832 thousand) of pretax income was derived from domestic operations; these operations accounted for an even greater percentage ($39,990 thousand or 87% of total $45,814 thousand) of current taxes payable for fiscal 1991.

Ashland provides a reconciliation of the statutory federal tax (34% rate) to its reported tax expense reflecting the impact of different foreign tax rates and other permanent differences. If we apply the 34% statutory (U.S.) tax rate to foreign pretax income of $63,353 thousand, foreign tax would be expected to be $21,540 thousand rather than the $5,826 thousand reported. Of this $15,714 thousand difference, only two thirds ($10,736 thousand) is specifically identified in the footnote. The remaining difference must be due to factors included in "other items."

The tax rate reconciliation also reflects the tax impact of other permanent differences including:

(1) equity income reported in financial statement income whereas only dividends received must be reported on the tax return (decreases tax expense by $4,011 thousand)*

(2) amortization of goodwill, which is not deductible for tax purposes (increases tax expense by $1,219 thousand).

Another important component of the tax footnote is Ashland's disclosure of temporary differences generating deferred taxes. The list contains few surprises given the nature of the firm's operations. One important source is the use of accelerated depreciation for tax purposes: in 1991, it generated $2,675 thousand in deferred tax provisions. This disclosure allows us to determine the depreciation reported for tax purposes: using the 34% statutory rate,† excess depreciation for tax purposes must be $7,868 thousand ($2,675/.34). The deferred tax effect of accelerated depreciation reduced taxes payable in 1991 but increased taxes payable for 1990 and 1989. The analyst should examine trends in capital spending and the age of fixed assets to determine the probable causes of the 1989 and 1990 reversals.

Ashland also reports the impact (deferred tax benefits) of prepaid contributions to the leveraged employee stock ownership plan (LESOP) and the impact of pension contributions. The deferred tax consequences of these transactions can be used to determine the difference between amounts recorded as expense and actual cash contributions made during the year.

Other significant sources of deferred taxes for the 1989–1991 period include:

1. (1989 only) the tax settlement related to Ashland's dispute with the National Iranian Oil Company (NIOC). As the liability had been accrued in prior years (generating a deferred tax asset), payment resulted in a reversal of that temporary difference as an expense was recorded in 1989 for tax purposes only.

2. Insurance claims and reserves: as tax deductions are based on payments, differences between accruals and payments generate temporary differences.

3. Intangible drilling costs: this difference results from the capitalization and subsequent amortization for financial reporting purposes of costs which are expensed for tax purposes.

The footnote data can also be used to compute effective tax rates as discussed in the section on Amerada Hess. Cash taxes paid, current taxes payable, and reported tax expense in 1991 are reported for each year. The firm discloses the cash taxes paid as required by SFAS 95; this disclosure is not always provided in this footnote, but may be located elsewhere in the financial statements.

---

*Ashland's Note D, "Unconsolidated Affiliates" (not shown here, but see Exhibit 10-9), reports that its retained earnings include $202 million of undistributed earnings from equity method unconsolidated affiliates. Under SFAS 109, deferred taxes may be required on some of these earnings and tax expense and payments may be required if any affiliate is sold.

†The use of a 34% rate understates the excess depreciation since income is taxed at the state level as well.

d. Look at the accounting for foreign affiliates and unconsolidated domestic affiliates. Some companies provide deferred taxes on such earnings; others do not. Note that, under SFAS 109, companies must provide deferred taxes for some affiliates that previously were exempt under the indefinite reversal criteria.

e. Watch for changes in tax laws, especially tax rates, and anticipate the impact on reported income.

2. Examine the source of deferred taxes (see Box 7-2 for an example). Companies are required to provide details of temporary differences, although formats vary.

    a. Temporary differences are generally the result of the use of different accounting policies or estimates for tax purposes than for financial reporting differences. Frequent examples include

(1) Depreciation: different methods and/or lives (see Chapter 6).

(2) Restructuring costs: usually tax deductible when paid rather than when accrued.

(3) Inventories: companies using last-in, first-out (LIFO) accounting for tax purposes in the United States must also use LIFO for reporting purposes, but when other methods are used, differences may occur (see Kenwin example).

(4) Postretirement benefits: SFAS 87 (pensions) and SFAS 106 (other postemployment benefits) are discussed in Chapter 9. Tax treatment of these costs is generally different from the financial reporting treatment, generating deferred tax effects.

b. Watch for companies that report substantial income for financial reporting purposes but little or no income for tax purposes. This situation often indicates important differences in revenue and expense recognition methods. In such cases, caution is indicated as the methods used for financial reporting purposes may be based on optimistic assumptions.

c. Look for current or pending reversals of past temporary differences. For example, a decline in capital spending may result in a greater proportion of depreciation coming from old assets that have already been heavily depreciated for tax purposes. Thus financial reporting depreciation may exceed tax depreciation, generating a tax liability. Remember that deferred tax assets and liabilities may have near-term cash consequences.

Tax law changes may also result in the reversal of past temporary differences. In the United States, tax law changes in recent years have curtailed the use of the completed contract and installment methods for tax purposes, generating substantial tax liabilities for affected companies.

3. Compare cash taxes paid with income tax expense. While cash taxes paid is affected by refunds and estimated payments, over longer periods it should track current tax expense. Differentiate deferred tax assets and liabilities that will generate near-term tax refunds or payments from those whose cash impact is indefinite as to timing.

4. Until the end of 1993, when the transition to SFAS 109 is complete, some firms will remain under APB 11 or SFAS 96. Comparison of companies using different tax reporting methods is complicated by the differences between the methods. Be alert to the effect on reported income and net worth of the different methods.

Even more important, however, is the need to look at the transition method used to change methods. As we have seen, retroactive restatement and the cumulative change method have quite different impacts on reported income in the year of the change and on prior periods. It is important to isolate the effect of the accounting changes to discern operating performance.

ACCOUNTING OUTSIDE THE UNITED STATES

As already noted, many foreign jurisdictions require conformity between financial reporting and tax reporting in separate (parent company) financial statements. In such cases, the issues discussed in this chapter do not occur. This statement is no longer true, however, once consolidated statements include (foreign) subsidiaries that are not consolidated for tax purposes. Given the worldwide tendency toward consolidated reporting,[35] even tax conformity countries will be grappling with the question of deferred tax accounting. Many countries require the recognition of deferred taxes on timing differences. Germany and the United Kingdom use the liability method whereas France and Japan allow either the deferred or the liability method. Most countries limit recognition of deferred tax liabilities and few address the issue of deferred tax assets.

The International Accounting Standards Committee (IASC) issued an exposure draft (ED 33) in 1989 to replace International Accounting Standard (IAS) 12, which is more than 10 years old. The exposure draft would require use of the liability method but would permit companies to use "indefinite reversal" criteria to avoid recognizing deferred taxes on the reinvested earnings of affiliates. However, the IASC has stated that it plans to reexamine the issue of income tax accounting, with a new exposure draft planned for 1993.

CONCLUSION

In this chapter we have seen how income tax expense and balance sheet assets and liabilities are affected by the accounting method used and by management choices and assumptions. As all business enterprises are subject to income tax, no financial analysis is complete until the issues raised in this chapter have been examined.

---

[35]See Chapter 11 for discussion.

Chapter 7

Problems

1. [Deferred tax classification; 1990 CFA adapted] In which of the following categories can deferred taxes be found?

    (i) Current liabilities

    (ii) Long-term liabilities

    (iii) Stockholders' equity

    (iv) Current assets

    (v) Long-term assets

Provide an example for each category in your answer.

2. [Deferred taxes—changes in tax law; 1990 CFA adapted] Under SFAS 109, which of the following statements are correct? Explain why.

    (i) The deferred tax liability account must be adjusted for the effect of enacted changes in tax laws or rates in the period of the enactment.

    (ii) The deferred tax asset account must be adjusted for the effect of enacted changes in tax laws or rates in the period of the enactment

    (iii) The tax consequences of an event must not be recognized until that event is recognized in the financial statements.

    (iv) Both deferred tax liabilities and deferred tax assets must be accounted for based on the tax laws and rates in effect at their origin.

3. [Permanent versus temporary differences; 1991 CFA adapted] Define "permanent differences" and describe two events or transactions that generate such differences. What is the impact of permanent differences on a firm's effective tax rate?

4. [Treatment of deferred tax liability] In calculating a firm's debt-to-equity position, many analysts exclude the deferred tax liability from both the numerator and the denominator.

    A. Describe the arguments for including it as equity

    B. Describe the arguments for including it as debt.

    C. Describe the arguments for including a portion of the deferred taxes as equity and a portion as debt.

5. [Depreciation methods and deferred taxes] The Incurious George Company acquires assets K, L, and M at the beginning of year 1. Each asset has the same cost, a five-year life, and an expected salvage value of $3000. For financial reporting, the firm uses the straight-line, sum-of-the-years'-digits, and double-declining-balance depreciation methods for asset K, L, and M, respectively. It uses the double-declining-balance method for all assets on its tax return; its tax rate is 34%. Depreciation expense of $12,000 was reported for asset L for financial reporting purposes in year 2. Using this information:

    A. Calculate the *tax return* depreciation expense for each asset in year 2.

B. Calculate the *financial statement* depreciation expense for assets K and M in year 2.

C. Calculate the deferred tax credit (liability) or debit (asset) for each asset at the end of:

    (i) year 2

    (ii) year 5

6. [Deferred tax; 1988 CFA adapted] On December 29, 1992, Mother Prewitt's Handmade Cookies Corp. acquired a numerically controlled chocolate chip milling machine. Due to differences in tax and financial accounting, depreciation for tax purposes was $150,000 more than indicated in the financial statements, adding $51,000 to deferred taxes. At the same time, Mother Prewitt's sold $200,000 worth of cookies on an installment contract, but recognized the resulting $100,000 profit immediately. For tax purposes, however, $80,000 of the profit will be recognized in 1993, requiring $27,200 of deferred taxes.

A. Discuss any differences in the expected cash consequences of the two deferred tax items just described. When calculating Mother Prewitt's solvency and leverage ratios, how would you treat the deferred tax liability?

B. In 1993, Mother Prewitt's tax rate will be 40%. Briefly discuss what adjustments will be made to *each* of the two deferred tax items in 1993 because of the change in the tax rate, assuming use of:

    (i) APB 11.

    (ii) SFAS 96.

    (iii) SFAS 109.

C. Assume that Mother Prewitt will adopt SFAS 109 in 1993. Under what conditions will it need to recognize a valuation allowance for any deferred tax assets?

Problems 7–9 are based on information from Exxon's 1989 Annual Report contained in Exhibit 7P-1.

7. [Tax expense, taxes paid, effective tax rates]

A. In 1989, Exxon's cash payment for income taxes was $2881 million. Using transactional analysis, and the tax liability balances that follow, reconcile this amount (to the extent possible) with income tax expense. What additional information is needed?

December 31, 1988–1989 (in $ millions)

	1988	1989
Income taxes payable	$ 1,995	$ 1,646
Deferred income taxes	11,849	12,353

EXHIBIT 7P-1. EXXON CORPORATION

21. Income, excise and other taxes	1987			1988			1989		
	United States	Foreign	Total	United States	Foreign	Total	United States	Foreign	Total
Income taxes			*(millions of dollars)*						
Federal or foreign – current	$ 514	$ 1,983	$ 2,497	$ 780	$ 2,084	$ 2,864	$ 313	$ 1,817	$ 2,130
–deferred–net	337	(97)	240	26	138	164	(192)	35	(157)
U.S. tax on foreign operations	(75)	—	(75)	12	—	12	5	—	5
	776	1,886	2,662	818	2,222	3,040	126	1,852	1,978
State	41	—	41	84	—	84	50	—	50
Total income tax expense	817	1,886	2,703	902	2,222	3,124	176	1,852	2,028
Excise taxes	1,368	4,299	5,667	1,770	5,925	7,695	1,827	6,690	8,517
Other taxes and duties	861	14,223	15,084	881	15,270	16,151	993	15,624	16,617
Total	$3,046	$20,408	$23,454	$3,553	$23,417	$26,970	$2,996	$24,166	**$27,162**

Reconciliation between income tax expense and a theoretical U.S. tax computed by applying a rate of 40 percent to earnings before income taxes in 1987 and 34 percent in 1988 and 1989:

	1987	1988	1989
		(millions of dollars)	
Earnings before Federal and foreign income taxes			
United States	$2,159	$2,653	$ 213
Foreign	5,343	5,647	4,740
Total	$7,502	$8,300	$4,953
Theoretical tax	$3,001	$2,822	$1,684
Adjustments for foreign taxes in excess of/(less than) theoretical U.S. tax	(251)	302	240
U.S. tax on foreign operations			
—current	55	12	5
—deferred	(130)	—	—
U.S. investment tax credit	(20)	(7)	—
Other U.S.	7	(89)	49
Federal and foreign income tax expense	$2,662	$3,040	$1,978
Total effective tax rate	40.7%	41.3%	44.3%

The effective income tax rate includes state income taxes and Exxon's share of income taxes of equity companies. Equity company taxes totaled $622 million in 1987, $582 million in 1988 and $337 million in 1989, essentially all in the foreign area.

Income taxes do not include $21 million, $35 million and $35 million in 1987, 1988 and 1989, respectively, of state franchise taxes which are based on income.

Deferred income taxes reflect the impact of temporary differences between the amount of assets and liabilities rec-

ognized for financial reporting purposes and such amounts recognized for tax purposes. The net deferred tax expense shown above relates to the following temporary differences:

Tax effects of temporary differences for:	1987	1988	1989
		(millions of dollars)	
Depreciation	$ 235	$ 277	$ 41
Inventories	(45)	161	(234)
Intangible development costs	(102)	(314)	41
Valdez provision	—	—	(382)
Interest expense	(21)	(14)	134
Other	173	54	243
Net deferred income taxes	$ 240	$ 164	$(157)

	1989		
	(millions of dollars)		
Tax effects of temporary differences for:	United States	Foreign	Total
Depreciation	$ 64	$ (23)	$ 41
Inventories	(7)	(227)	(234)
Intangible development costs	(49)	90	41
Valdez provision	(382)	—	(382)
Interest expense	134	—	134
Other	48	195	243
Net deferred income taxes	$(192)	$ 35	$(157)

About $4.3 billion of undistributed earnings of foreign subsidiaries are considered to be indefinitely reinvested, but could be subject to additional taxes, beyond those provided, if they were remitted. These earnings are hypothetically subject to about $0.4 billion of withholding taxes, but it is not practicable to estimate the actual amount of tax which might be due.

Source: Exxon Corporation, *1989 Annual Report.*

B. Exxon's 1989 pretax income is provided in footnote 21. Determine Exxon's taxable income for 1989?

C. Compute Exxon's effective tax rates for 1989 based on:

(i) Income tax expense.

(ii) Taxes payable.

(iii) Cash taxes paid.

Compare the utility of these effective tax rates as predictors of future effective tax rates. [Hint: Consider the impact of the Valdez provision.]

8. [Temporary differences in cost of goods sold] Footnote 21 (Exhibit 7P-1) reflects the tax effects of temporary differences of $(234) million due to inventories, including $(7) million in the United States and $(227) million from foreign operations.

A. State whether the cost of goods sold reported for financial statement purposes or for tax purposes is higher. Explain your reasoning.

B. Explain what may cause a difference between cost of goods sold reported on the tax return and that reflected on the income statement.

9. [Determining expenses used for tax purpose] Exxon's 1989 income statement reports interest expense of $1265 million. Cash interest paid was $1702 million for 1991.

A. Which of these two interest amounts did Exxon use for tax purposes?

B. Describe *two* possible causes for the difference between interest paid and interest expense.

10. [Tax expense, tax payable, taxes paid, effective tax rates] Exhibit 7P-2 contains extracts from the *1992 Annual Report* of Catalina Marketing Corporation (CMC), which provides promotional services to packaged goods manufacturers and retailers. In 1992, CMC adopted SFAS 109; the firm used SFAS 96 in 1990 and 1991. Footnote 5 states that the adoption had no effect on 1992 and prior years' net income. The company has not restated 1990 and 1991 results and has not adjusted 1992 net income or retained earnings for the change in method.

A. Discuss one reason that would explain why the adoption of SFAS 109 had no effect on reported net income.

B. The statement of cash flows reports that CMC paid income taxes of $3,254,000 in 1992.

(i) Compute income taxes paid by CMC for the year ended March 31, 1992, by using the following balances of income tax-related accounts as of March 31:

	1991	1992
Deferred tax benefits, current	$363,000	$2,254,000
Deferred tax benefits, long term	0	945,000
Taxes payable, current	818,000	1,896,000

(ii) Explain the discrepancy between your calculation and the amount shown in the statement of cash flows.

EXHIBIT 7P-2. CATALINA MARKETING CORPORATION

5. INCOME TAXES

In 1992, the Company adopted SFAS 109. The adoption had no effect on 1992 and prior years' net income. Therefore, the Company has not restated 1990 and 1991 results, and no adjustments to 1992 net income or retained earnings are required to reflect the change.

Net deferred tax assets at year-end consist of the following:

Dollars in thousands		*March 31,*	
	1992	1991	1990
Components of deferred taxes:			
Depreciation	$ 811	$149	$–
Deferred revenue	1,101	163	–
Provision for doubtful accounts	540	–	–
Computer equipment upgrades	463	–	–
Other	994	51	–
Total	$3,909	$363	$0
Components of net deferred tax asset:			
Total deferred liability	$ (292)	$ –	$–
Total deferred asset	4,201	363	–
Sub-total	3,909	363	–
Valuation allowance	(710)	–	–
Net deferred tax asset	$3,199	$363	$0

Temporary differences for financial statement and income tax purposes result primarily from charges to operations for financial statement reporting purposes which are not currently tax deductible. These amounts and the provision for income taxes consist of the following:

Dollars in thousands	*For the Year Ended March 31,*		
	1992	1991	1990
Components of deferred tax provision:			
Depreciation	$ 514	$ 149	$ –
Deferred revenue	737	163	–
Provision for doubtful accounts	422	19	–
Computer equipment upgrades	379	–	–
Other	784	32	–
	$ 2,836	$ 363	$ –
Current taxes:			
Federal	$ 3,947	$ 510	$ 75
State	788	200	25
Foreign	12	9	–
	4,747	719	100
Deferred taxes:			
Federal	(2,540)	(261)	–
State	(296)	(102)	–
	(2,836)	(363)	–
Provision for Income Taxes	$ 1,911	$ 356	$ 100

The reconciliation of a provision for income taxes based on the U.S. statutory federal income tax rate (34%) to the Company's provision for income taxes is as follows:

Dollars in thousands	*For the Year Ended March 31,*		
	1992	1991	1990
Expected federal statutory tax (34%)	$2,264	$ 604	$ 227
State and foreign income taxes, net of federal benefit	529	176	21
Amortization of option-related compensation	8	2	17
Tax benefit of credits	(93)	(109)	–
Tax benefit of net operating losses	(627)	(325)	(177)
Other	(170)	8	12
Provision for Income Taxes	$1,911	$ 356	$ 100

Source: Catalina Marketing Corp., *1992 Annual Report.*

C. CMC reported net income of $4,760,000 for 1992. Compute the effective tax rate based on:

    (i) Income tax expense.

    (ii) Taxes payable.

    (iii) Cash taxes paid.

Discuss which, if any, of these rates is a good indicator of expected future tax payments? [Hint: Use the reconciliation of reported tax expense to the statutory rate provided by the firm in footnote 5].

D. The two major components of deferred tax assets on March 31, 1992, were temporary differences due to depreciation ($811,000) and deferred revenue ($1,101,000). Using an effective tax rate of 34%, compute the amounts of the temporary differences, determine whether book or tax expense (income) was higher (in each case), and briefly explain why.

E.   **(i)** Explain the impact of the valuation account on your assessment of future effective tax rates and expected profitability.

    (ii) Which component(s) of deferred tax assets is (are) most likely to have required recognition of a valuation allowance?

11. [Analysis of deferred tax liability, effective tax rates] In fiscal 1992, The Clorox Company adopted SFAS 106, "Employers' Accounting for Postretirement Benefits Other than Pensions," and SFAS 109, "Accounting for Income Taxes." Exhibit 7P-3 contains footnotes on the accounting changes, income taxes, and postretirement benefits other than pensions.

A. Determine the amount of deferred taxes recognized in *fiscal 1992* applicable to postretirement health benefits (including the cumulative effect of adopting SFAS 106). Compute the effective tax rate used by the firm to determine this amount.

B. The firm recorded a *pretax* restructuring charge of $125,250,000 in the fourth quarter of 1991.

    (i) Explain why deferred tax liabilities of $31,348,000 and $42,493,000 were reported at June 30, 1992, and 1991, respectively.

    (ii) What information does the deferred tax liability convey about the cash flows in fiscal 1991 and 1992 resulting from the restructuring charge?

    (iii) What does the deferred tax liability at June 30, 1992 tell you about the *future* cash flows associated with the restructuring charge?

C. Clorox reported net income (before cumulative effect of accounting changes of $117,765,000 for fiscal 1992. Calculate the firm's effective tax rate using:

    (i) Income tax expense.

    (ii) Taxes payable.

    (iii) Cash taxes paid of $73,709,000.

D. Explain how the deferred tax effects of postretirement health benefits and restructuring charges affect the computations in part C.

EXHIBIT 7P-3. CLOROX COMPANY

ACCOUNTING CHANGES

In Fiscal 1992, the Company adopted SFAS No. 106, "Employers' Accounting for Postretirement Benefits Other Than Pensions," and No. 109, "Accounting for Income Taxes."

SFAS No. 106 requires accrual of the expected cost of providing postretirement health care benefits during the years that employees provide service. Previously, retiree health care benefits were expensed as incurred. In adopting this standard, the Company elected to fully recognize the accumulated postretirement benefit obligation as of July 1, 1991 (see Note 12) and, accordingly, restated the results for the first three quarters of Fiscal 1992. The cumulative effect of adoption resulted in a charge to earnings of $19,061,000 ($.35 per share), net of $11,832,000 tax benefit. Earnings before the cumulative effect of accounting change decreased $2,912,000 during 1992 as a result of applying SFAS No. 106. Operating results for years preceding 1992 were not restated for the adoption of this new standard.

The Company elected to apply the provisions of SFAS No. 109 retroactive to July 1, 1990. The effect of adopting SFAS No. 109 at July 1, 1990 was not material; nor was it material to either 1991 or 1992 earnings. SFAS No. 109 changes the method of accounting for income taxes from the deferred to the liability method. Under the liability method, deferred income taxes are determined based upon enacted tax laws and rates applied to the differences between the financial statement and tax bases of assets and liabilities. Under the deferred method, deferred income taxes were recognized using the rates in effect when the tax was first recorded, without adjustment for subsequent rate changes.

NOTE 11. INCOME TAXES

Income tax expenses are (in thousands):

	1992	1991	1990
Current			
Federal	**$61,055**	$ 54,938	$58,285
State	**12,397**	10,387	12,027
Foreign	**6,325**	3,602	3,341
Total current	**79,777**	68,927	73,653
Deferred			
Federal	**10,261**	(30,094)	13,059
State	**1,769**	(5,355)	2,172
Foreign	**1,300**	(65)	1,107
Total deferred	**13,330**	(35,514)	16,338
Total expense	**$93,107**	$ 33,413	$89,991
Effective income tax rate	**44.2%**	38.8%	36.9%

The reconciliation between the Company's effective income tax rate and the statutory federal income tax rate is as follows:

	1992	1991	1990
Federal statutory rate	**34.0%**	34.0%	34.0%
State income taxes, net of federal tax benefit	**4.1**	3.4	3.7
Taxes on foreign earnings	**2.4**	3.0	0.1
Nondeductible asset writedowns	**2.7**	–	–
Other	**1.0**	(1.6)	(0.9)
Effective income tax rate	**44.2%**	38.8%	36.9%

The net deferred income tax liabilities (assets), both current and non-current, at June 30, result from the following temporary difference between financial statement and tax return amounts (in thousands):

	1992	1991
Amortization/depreciation	**$88,385**	$ 84,917
Safe harbor lease agreements	**34,617**	36,707
Unremitted foreign earnings	**24,243**	14,958
Restructuring expenses	**(31,348)**	(42,493)
Postretirement health benefits	**(13,636)**	–
Other	**(7,063)**	(953)
Total	**$95,198**	$ 93,136

Source: Clorox Company, *1992 Annual Report.*

E. Clorox's deferred tax liability is approximately $95 million. In assessing Clorox's liability position and net worth, how would you treat this amount?

12. [Deferred tax liability] Deere's income tax footnote for 1991 (Exhibit 1B-2) provides a detailed breakdown of the elements of the deferred tax liability.

A. Focusing only on installment sales and depreciation, how would you treat these components in assessing Deere's leverage ratios and net worth?

B. Compare the amount of depreciation taken for tax purposes with the amount reported in the financial statements.

13. [Analysis of income tax footnote] Exhibit 7P-4 contains a portion of the income tax footnote from the fiscal 1992 annual report of Dresser Industries.

A. Describe *three* of the accounting differences that generated the deferred tax assets listed. For each, discuss the factors that will determine whether (and when) those differences will generate cash inflows to Dresser.

B. Discuss the significance of the valuation allowance as an indicator of Dresser's expectations regarding the realization (cash inflow) of the deferred tax assets.

EXHIBIT 7P-4. DRESSER INDUSTRIES

NOTE G – INCOME TAXES *(continued)*

The components of the net deferred tax asset as of October 31, 1992, were as follows (in millions):

	1992
Deferred tax assets:	
Post retirement benefits	$201.2
Warranty reserves	14.1
Restructuring costs	17.3
Insurance reserves	21.0
Bad debt	19.4
Pension	9.0
Deferred compensation	12.8
Net operating loss carryforwards	17.6
Other items	32.7
Valuation allowance	(30.5)
Total deferred tax asset	314.6
Deferred tax liability - Depreciation	(13.0)
Net deferred tax asset	$301.6

Since the Company plans to continue to finance foreign operations and expansion through reinvestment of undistributed earnings of its foreign subsidiaries (approximately $515 million at October 31, 1992), no provisions are generally made for U.S. or additional foreign taxes on such earnings. When the Company identifies exceptions to the general reinvestment policy, additional taxes are provided.

Source: Dresser Industries, Inc., *1992 Annual Report.*

C. Which deferred tax asset appears most likely to have required the valuation allowance? Why?

D. Discuss the significance of Dresser's disclosure regarding the undistributed earnings of its foreign subsidiaries.

14. [Deferred taxes and interim reports] State Auto Financial reported the following operating results for the first three quarters of 1991 and 1992 (in $ thousands):

	1991			1992		
	Q1	Q2	Q3	Q1	Q2	Q3
Pretax income	$ 4797	$2600	$3244	$1123	$3723	$ 98
Income tax expense	(1224)	(624)	(848)	(232)	(934)	583
Net Income	$ 3573	$1976	$2396	$ 891	$2789	$681

The 1992 third quarter 10-Q reported that:

> The estimated annual effective tax rate was revised during the third quarter of 1992 from 25% to 17% to reflect the estimated tax impact of a decrease in taxable earnings, as prescribed by generally accepted accounting principles. The effect of this adjustment in the current quarter was a benefit of approximately $600,000.

A. Compute the tax rate used to compute net income for each quarter.

B. Using the data given, show how the change in estimated tax rate increased third quarter 1992 income by approximately $600,000.

C. Explain how the changed tax rate assumption distorted the comparison of third quarter net income for 1991 and 1992.

D. Suggest *two* ways by which the distortion discussed in part C can be offset.

E. Assume that State Auto had assumed a tax rate of 17% for the first two quarters of 1992. Compute the effect of that assumption on reported net income for those quarters.

8

ANALYSIS OF FINANCING LIABILITIES

INTRODUCTION

BALANCE SHEET DEBT
Current Liabilities
Long-Term Debt
  Income Statement, Balance Sheet, and Cash
  Flow Statement Effects
  Zero-Coupon Bonds
  Variable Rate Debt
Debt with Equity Features
  Perpetual Debt
  Preferred Stock
Effects of Changes in Interest Rates
  Accounting for Restructured Debt
  Loan Impairment
  Estimating Market Value of Debt
  Calculating the Market Value of Deere's
  Long-Term Debt
  Debt: Market or Book Value?
Retirement of Debt Prior to Maturity
  Callable Bonds

BOND COVENANTS
Nature of Covenants
Calculating Accounting-Based Constraints
Analysis of Deere's Covenants

LEASES
Incentives for Leasing
Lease Classification: Lessees
Lease Classification: Lessors
Financial Reporting by Lessees: Illustration
  Comparative Analysis of Capitalized and
  Operating Leases
  Financial Reporting by Lessees: An Example
Financial Reporting by Lessors:
  Sales-type Leases
  Direct Financing Leases
  Financial Reporting by Lessors: An Example
  Financial Reporting for Sales with Leasebacks
Lease Accounting Outside the United States

CONCLUSION

INTRODUCTION

The burden of a firm's liabilities is crucial to the assessment of its long-run viability and growth. A firm can incur liabilities in myraid ways. Some obligations are a consequence of the firm's operating activities, whereas others result from its financing decisions. The former are characterized by exchanges of goods and services for later payment of cash (or vice versa), whereas debt arising from financing decisions is generally characterized by current receipts of cash in exchange for later payments of cash. These forms of debt are generally reported "on balance sheet," and our focus is on their measurement, interpretation, and analysis.

More complex arrangements and exchanges, however, are also possible. These complex transactions are often contractual in nature and thus, under GAAP, might not appear on the firm's balance sheet. Before such "off-balance-sheet" debt can be measured, interpreted, and analyzed, it must first be identified. A thorough analysis of the firm's financial structure requires recognition of these liabilities.

An additional impact that must be recognized is that creditors, to protect themselves, often impose restrictions on the firm's operations, its distributions to shareholders, and the amount of additional debt or leverage the firm can assume. These restrictions, in the form of bond covenants, can induce firms to alter their operations and modes of financing and also to change their accounting policies in an effort to operate within the confines of these covenants. The analysis of the direct impact of debt on the firm must also consider incentives for management decisions regarding the ratio of on-versus off-balance-sheet debt.

This chapter is the first of a series of chapters that deal with these issues. The first part of the chapter examines primarily liabilities resulting from financing activities. The second part deals with leases: a combined financing and investment activity. Chapter 9 covers liabilities that arise from dealings between a firm and its employees in the area of pensions and other postretirement benefits. Chapter 10 deals with various "modes" of "off-balance-sheet" debt, contingencies, and debt carried by a firm's subsidiaries and affiliates.[1]

Recognition of these various forms of debt and financing activities are important aspects of the analysis of a firm's short-term liquidity and long-term solvency position. Debt-to-equity and interest coverage ratios, for example, are affected by which transactions are recognized and how they are accounted for.

The subtleties of the financing equation can be overwhelming and obscure the sight of the forest for the trees.

We suggest that the reader keep two basic principles in mind when reading this chapter:

1. Debt is equal to the present value of the future stream of (interest and principal) payments. For book value, the discount rate is the rate in effect when the debt was incurred. For market value measurements, it is the current rate.

---

[1]This last topic is also covered extensively in Chapter 11.

2. Interest expense can be defined simply as the amount paid by the debtor to the creditor in excess of the amount received. Thus the total amount of interest to be paid over time is known; its allocation to individual time periods may vary.

These points may seem simplistic at first but referring back to them from time to time may help put some of the discussions to follow in focus.

BALANCE SHEET DEBT

Current Liabilities

Current liabilities are defined as those due within one year. For liabilities, in general, the amount shown is not the total amount the firm will have to pay but only the principal portion, that is, the present value of the payment due. For example, if the firm owes $100 on which it will pay interest of 10%, the actual amount payable within the year is $110, whereas the current liability is the present value of the future payment or $100.

Current liabilities include four categories of debt, and it is important to distinguish among the types for analytic purposes.

Consequences of Operating Activities

1. *Operating and trade liabilities,* the most frequent type, are the result of credit granted to the company by its suppliers and employees.

2. *Advances from customers* arise when customers pay in advance for services to be rendered by the company. The firm is obligated to render the service and/or deliver a product to the customer in the near future.

Consequences of Financing Activities

3. *Short-term debt* is the short-term credit the firm has received from banks or the credit markets.

4. *Current portion of long-term debt* constitutes the portion of long-term debt that is payable within the next year; it has been transferred from the long term to the current liability section of the balance sheet.

Operating and trade debt is carried at the expected (undiscounted) cash flow and is the exception to the rule that liabilities are recorded at present value. A credit purchase of $100 paid within the normal operating cycle of the firm is recorded at $100 even though its present value is less. This treatment is justified by the short period between the incurrence of the debt and its payment, rendering the adjustment to present value immaterial.

When analyzing a firm's liquidity, advances from customers should be distinguished from other payables. Payables require a future outlay of cash. Advances from customers, on the other hand, are satisfied by delivery of goods or services,[2] requiring a

---

[2]Only if these goods and services are not delivered does the firm have a cash obligation. Thus the primary liability does not require cash.

lower cash outlay (otherwise the firm would be selling below cost) than the advances recorded. *Advances are a prediction of future revenues rather than a prediction of cash outflows.*

Short-term debt and the current portion of long-term debt are the result of prior financing cash inflows. They indicate the firm's need for either cash or a means of refinancing the debt. The inability to repay short-term credit is a sign of financial distress.

It is important to monitor the relative levels of debt from operating as compared to financing activities. The former arise from the normal course of business activities: a shift from operating to financing sources may indicate the beginning of a liquidity crisis.

Long-Term Debt

Firms obtain long-term financing from the public issuance of bonds; from private placements of debt with insurance companies, pension plans, and other institutional investors; or from long-term bank credit agreements. Creditors may receive a claim on specific assets pledged as security for the debt (e.g., mortgages), or they may have only general claims on the assets of the firm. Some creditors' claims may be *subordinated* in that their claims rank below those of *senior* creditors whose claims have priority.

Long-term liabilities are interest bearing in nature, but the structure of interest and principal payments varies widely. The different payment terms are, however, conceptually identical, and we will use a bond example as a framework for illustration.

A bond is a "contract" or written agreement that obligates the borrower (bond issuer) to make certain payments to the lender (bondholder) over the life of the bond. A typical bond promises two types of payments: periodic interest payments (usually semiannual in the United States) and a lump-sum payment when the bond matures.

The *face value* of the bond is the lump-sum payment made at maturity. The *coupon rate* is the stated cash interest rate (but not necessarily the actual rate of return). The

$$\text{Periodic payment} = \text{``Coupon rate''} \times \text{face value}$$

The coupon rate is in quotation marks because it is stated on an annual basis, whereas payments are made semiannually. The "coupon rate" (CR) used for the payment calculation is therefore equal to one-half the stated coupon rate.

The example in Exhibit 8-1 is based on a three-year bond[3] with the following terms:

$$\text{Face value (FV)} = \$100,000$$

$$\text{Coupon} = 10\%$$

$$\text{Interest payment: Semiannual}$$

The purchaser of the bond expects six payments of interest (each payment $5000) and a final principal payment of $100,000 for a total of $130,000. Note that this stream

---

[3]Bonds issued for periods of 10 years or less are usually called "notes." There is no analytic distinction, and we will call all debt issues bonds for convenience.

of payments does not uniquely determine the principal amount borrowed by the bond issuer. The bond terms simply define the obligation of the issuer; the *allocation of these amounts between interest and principal depends on the current market interest rate*.

The amount borrowed depends on both the payments and the market rate of interest for bonds of a similar maturity and risk. Bondholders lend the firm an amount equal to the present value of the stream of promised payments discounted at the current market rate. The market rate may be less than, equal to, or greater than the coupon rate.

As Exhibit 8-1A–C indicates, the economics of the bond and the treatment of the stream of payments are affected by the relationship of the market and coupon rates. To analyze the transactions over the life of the bond, we must take note of the following points:

1. The initial liability is the amount of money paid to the issuer by the creditor (present value of the stream of payments discounted at the market rate), not necessarily the bond's face value.

2. The *effective interest rate* on the bond is the market (not the coupon) rate, and interest expense is the market rate times the bond liability.

EXHIBIT 8-1
Comparison of Bond Issued at Par, Premium, and Discount

Bond: Face value (FV) = $100,000
     Coupon (CR) = 5% (Semiannual payment; 10% Annual Rate)
     Maturity: 3 years
     Semiannual payments of $5000 (0.5 × 10% × $100,000)

A. Bond Issued at Par: Market Rate = 10% (MR = 5%)

	(1)	(2) (1) × MR	(3) FV × CR	(4) (2) − (3)	(5) (1) + (4)	(6) FV
Period Ending	Liability Opening	Interest Expense	Coupon Payment	Change in Liability	Liability Closing	Face Value of Bond
1/1/91	Proceeds	(see below)			$100,000	$100,000
6/30/91	100,000	$ 5,000	$ 5,000	$0	100,000	100,000
12/31/91	100,000	5,000	5,000	0	100,000	100,000
6/30/92	100,000	5,000	5,000	0	100,000	100,000
12/31/92	100,000	5,000	5,000	0	100,000	100,000
6/30/93	100,000	5,000	5,000	0	100,000	100,000
12/31/93	100,000	5,000	5,000	0	100,000	100,000
Totals		$30,000	$30,000			

Calculation of Proceeds

Present value of annuity of $5000
    for 6 periods discounted at 5%: $5000 × 5.0756 = $ 25,378
Present value of $100,000
    in 6 periods discounted at 5%: $100,000 × 0.74622 =   74,622
                                             $100,000

EXHIBIT 8-1. *(Continued)*

B. Bond Issued at Premium: Market Rate = 8% (MR = 4%)

	(1)	(2) (1) × MR	(3) FV × CR	(4) (2) − (3)	(5) (1) + (4)	(6) FV	(7) (5) − (6)
Period Ending	Liability Opening	Interest Expense	Coupon Payment	Change in Liability	Liability Closing	Face Value of Bond	Premium
1/1/91	Proceeds (see below)				$105,242	$100,000	$5242
6/30/91	$105,242	$ 4,210	$ 5,000	$ (790)	104,452	100,000	4452
12/31/91	104,452	4,178	5,000	(822)	103,630	100,000	3630
6/30/92	103,630	4,145	5,000	(855)	102,775	100,000	2775
12/31/92	102,775	4,111	5,000	(889)	101,886	100,000	1886
6/30/93	101,886	4,075	5,000	(925)	100,961	100,000	961
12/31/93	100,961	4,039	5,000	(961)	100,000	100,000	0
Totals		$24,758	$30,000	$(5,242)			

Calculation of Proceeds

The amount that will be paid is calculated by finding the present value* of the stream of payments discounted at the market rate of 8% compounded semiannually or 4% per semiannual period:

Present value of annuity of $5000
  for 6 periods discounted at 4%: $5000 × 5.2421 = $ 26,211
Present value of $100,000
  in 6 periods discounted at 4%: $100,000 × 0.79031 =   79,031
                                                 $105,242

C. Bond Issued at Discount: Market Rate = 12% (MR = 6%)

	(1)	(2) (1) × MR	(3) FV × CR	(4) (2) − (3)	(5) (1) + (4)	(6) FV	(7) (5) − (6)
Period Ending	Liability Opening	Interest Expense	Coupon Payment	Change in Liability	Liability Closing	Face Value of Bond	Discount
1/1/91	Proceeds (see below)				$ 95,083	$100,000	$(4917)
6/30/91	$95,083	$ 5,705	$ 5,000	$ 705	95,788	100,000	(4212)
12/31/91	95,788	5,747	5,000	747	96,535	100,000	(3465)
6/30/92	96,535	5,792	5,000	792	97,327	100,000	(2673)
12/31/92	97,327	5,840	5,000	840	98,167	100,000	(1833)
6/30/93	98,167	5,890	5,000	890	99,057	100,000	(943)
12/31/93	99,057	5,943	5,000	943	100,000	100,000	0
Totals		$34,917	$30,000	$4,917			

Calculation of Proceeds

The amount that will be paid is equal to the present value of the stream of payments discounted at the market rate of 12% compounded semiannually.

Present value of annuity of $5000
  for 6 periods discounted at 6%: $5000 × 4.9173 = $24,587
Present value of $100,000
  in 6 periods discounted at 6%: $100,000 × 0.70496 =   70,496
                                                $95,083

*The calculations in the table are not generally required. Bond tables and computer programs that yield the premium or discount for various combinations of market rates, coupon rates, and time to maturity are readily available.

3. The coupon rate and face value are used only to calculate the actual cash flows (stream of payments from the issuer).

4. The liability over time is a function of (a) the initial liability and the relationship of (b) interest expense to (c) the actual cash payments.

5. Total interest expense is equal to the amounts paid by the issuer to the creditor in excess of the amount received. (Thus, total interest expense = $130,000 − initial liability.)

Market Rate = Coupon Rate (Exhibit 8-1A). If the market rate equals the coupon rate of 10% (compounded semiannually), the bond will be issued at par; that is, the proceeds will equal the face value.[4] The creditor is willing to pay $100,000, the present value of the stream of payments and the face value of the bond. In this case, the initial liability will equal the face value.

Since the loan has been made at the market rate of 10%, periodic interest expense (Exhibit 8-1A, column 2) will equal periodic payments (column 3). There are no adjustments made to the liability that stays at (column 5) $100,000 throughout the life of the bond. This situation is straightforward and needs no further elaboration.

Market Rate < Coupon Rate (Exhibit 8-1B). If the market rate is less than the coupon rate, the creditor is willing to pay (and the bond issuer will demand) a *premium* above the face value of $100,000.[5] Assuming a market rate of 8%, the proceeds and initial liability (Exhibit 8-1B) are $105,242 (face value of $100,000 plus premium of $5,242).

After six months, the bondholder earns interest of $4210 (4% × $105,242) but receives a payment of $5000 (coupon rate times face value). The $5000 payment includes interest expense of $4210 and a $790 payment of principal, reducing the liability to $104,452. In the second period, interest expense is $4178 (4% × $104,452), lower than in the first period since the liability has been reduced. After the second payment of $5000, the liability is further reduced. This process is continued until the bond matures. By that time, as Exhibit 8-1B indicates, the liability will be reduced to $100,000, the face value of the bond, which is repaid at maturity.

The process by which a bond premium (or discount) is amortized over the life of the bond is known as the *interest method*. This process, which results in a constant rate of interest over the life of the obligation, is widely used in financial reporting.

Market Rate > Coupon Rate (Exhibit 8-1C). If the market rate exceeds the coupon rate, the bondholder would not be willing to pay the full face value of the bond.[6]

---

[4]We ignore, for simplicity, the underwriting costs and expenses associated with the bond issuance. These costs are generally capitalized and amortized over the life of the bond issue.

[5]Assuming a market interest rate of 8%, the bond issuer could find someone willing to lend $100,000 in exchange for a semiannual annuity stream of (4% × $100,000) or $4000 (in addition to the lump-sum payment at maturity). For the borrower to obligate itself to pay the higher annuity of $5000, additional proceeds above the face value would be required.

[6]Were the bondholder to purchase a 12% bond, she would receive periodic payments of $6000. By buying this bond, the periodic payments would only be $5000. Thus, she would only purchase the bonds at a *discount*.

Assuming a market rate of 12%, the bond would be issued at a *discount* of $4917, and the proceeds and initial liability would be $95,083.

At a semiannual rate of 6%, interest expense for the first six months will be $5705 (6% × $95,083). However, the cash interest paid is only $5000; the shortfall of $705 is added to principal. As a result, the liability used to calculate interest expense for the second period is higher, increasing interest expense, increasing the shortfall, and further increasing the liability. This cycle repeats for the full six periods until the bond matures. At that point, the initial principal of $95,083 plus the accumulated unpaid interest of $4917 equals $100,000 — the face value payment that retires the debt.

Income Statement, Balance Sheet, and Cash Flow Statement Effects

The interest expense shown on the income statement (column 2 of Exhibit 8-1) is the effective interest on the loan based on the market rate in effect at issuance times the opening balance sheet liability. The actual cash payments (column 3) may not equal interest expense, but do equal the reduction in cash from operations (CFO). The balance sheet liability is shown in column 5. The initial cash received and the final face value payment of $100,000 are both treated as cash from financing (CFF). The financial statement effects on an annual basis (assuming a December fiscal year end) are summarized in Exhibit 8-2.

Note that for bonds issued at a premium (discount), the interest expense goes down (up) over time. This is a direct function of the decreasing (increasing) balance sheet liability; for each period, interest expense is the product of the beginning liability and the effective (market) interest rate. At any point in time, the liability on the balance sheet will equal the present value of the remaining payments discounted at the effective interest rate.[7]

The reported cash flows are identical across all three scenarios; the $100,000 face value payment is treated as cash from financing, and the periodic cash payments of $5000 are reported as reductions in CFO.[8] For bonds issued at a premium or discount, however, the reported cash flows (Exhibit 8-2) *incorrectly* describe the economics of the bond transaction.

The misclassification of cash flows results from reducing CFO by the total coupon payments over the life of the bond. For bonds sold at a premium, cash flow from operations is understated as part of the coupon payment is a reduction of principal;

---

[7]To illustrate this property, note the balance sheet liability of $96,535 at December 31, 1991, for the bond issued at a discount. Taking the present value of the remaining four periodic payments and the lump-sum payment yields

> Present value of annuity of $5000
>   for 4 periods discounted at 6%: $5000 × 3.46511 = $17,326
> Present value of $100,000
>   for 4 periods discounted at 6%: $100,000 × 0.79209 =   79,209
> $96,535

[8]Under the indirect method, this is accomplished by adding to or deducting from income the change in bond discount/premium (the periodic amortization of the bond/discount premium) to derive CFO. Thus for the first year the cash flow statement will show an addback of $1612 in the premium case and a deduction of $1452 in the discount case.

EXHIBIT 8-2
Comparison of Financial Statement Effects of Bonds Issued at Par, Premium, and Discount

Bond: Face value = $100,000
      Maturity = 3 years

      Coupon rate = 10% (semiannual payments)
      Premium: Market rate = 8%
      Discount: Market rate = 12%

| | Interest Expense | | | Balance Sheet Liability | | | Cash Flow from | |
| | Bond Issued at | | | Bond Issued at | | | Operations | Financing |
Year	Par	Premium	Discount	Par	Premium	Discount	(for all cases)	
1991*	$10,000	$ 8,388	$11,452	$100,000	$103,630	$ 96,535	$10,000	
1992*	10,000	8,256	11,632	100,000	101,886	98,167	10,000	
1993*	10,000	8,114	11,833	100,000	100,000	100,000	10,000	$100,000
Totals	$30,000	$24,758	$34,917				$30,000	$100,000

*Interest expense and cash flow: summation of June 30 and December 31 for each year (Exhibit 8-1); balance sheet liability (Exhibit 8-1).

financing cash flow is overstated by an equal amount. When bonds are issued at a discount, CFO is overstated as part of the amortization of the discount represents additional interest expense; financing cash flow is understated by that amount.[9]

Consequently, the cash flow classification of debt payments depends on the coupon rate, not the effective interest rate.

Exhibit 8-3 presents a reclassification of the components of cash flows. As bonds are generally issued at or close to par, the cash flow classification issue is not significant in most cases. On the other hand, when bonds are issued at a large discount to face value, the classification issue may become significant. Firms taking on the same level of debt at the same interest rate will report different CFO and solvency ratios by selecting differing coupon rates. Thus, in comparison to a firm that issues debt at a coupon rate close to market, a firm issuing debt at a discount will report a CFO and (for example) an interest coverage ratio (calculated on a cash basis) that will be distorted during the life of the bond. CFO will be high as will the interest coverage ratio given the low level of cash interest payments. The result may be a misleading representation of the firm's relative solvency positions. The issuer of the discounted bond has just deferred payments to a later date; when they become due they may prove to be onerous. Zero-coupon bonds, a financing technique that has gained popularity in recent years, is a case in point.

[9]In Chapter 2 we suggest that interest paid should be classified as a financing cash flow rather than as an operating cash flow as mandated by SFAS 95. If interest were reclassified to financing cash flow, this problem would disappear.

EXHIBIT 8-3
Reclassification of Cash Flows For bonds Illustrated in Exhibit 8-1 and 8-2

Year	Current Cash Flow Classification			More Appropriate Cash Flow Classification			
	For All Bonds			Premium Bond		Discount Bond	
	Actual Cash Flow	Operations	Financing	Operations	Financing	Operations	Financing
1991	$ 10,000	$10,000		$ 8,388	$ 1,612	$11,452	$(1,452)
1992	10,000	10,000		8,256	1,744	11,632	(1,632)
1993	110,000	10,000	$100,000	8,114	101,886	11,833	$98,167
Totals	$130,000	$30,000	$100,000	$24,758	$105,242	$34,917	$95,083

This reclassification allocates the cash interest paid between its operating and financing components. In 1991, for the premium case, $8388 (the interest expense) is shown as operating cash flow and the difference of $1612 ($10000 − $8388) as financing. The interest expense reported for the discount issue, $11452, is shown as operating cash flow and the excess over interest paid $1452 ($11452 − $10000) is reported as a financing cash inflow. The 1993 financing cash flow for the discount issue, therefore, reflects an outflow of $100,000 to repay the debt and an inflow of $1833 to adjust for the interest payment. The reclassified cash flows now reflect the effective interest rate rather than the coupon rate, analogous to the interest expense reported in the income statement.

Zero-Coupon Bonds

A zero-coupon bond has no periodic payments (coupon = 0).[10] As such, it is issued at a deep discount to face value and the lump-sum payment at maturity includes all the unpaid interest (equal to the face value minus the proceeds) from the time of issuance.

The proceeds from the issue will equal the present value of the face amount, discounted at the market interest rate. Thus, in a market requiring a rate of 10%, a $100,000 face value zero-coupon bond payable in three years will be issued at $74,622.

Exhibit 8-4 shows the income statement, cash flow, and balance sheet effects for this bond. Note that the repayment of $100,000 includes (approximately) $25,000 of interest *that will not be reported as CFO;* the full $100,000 payment will be treated as cash from financing. The contrast with the bond issued at par (Exhibit 8-1A) is striking.

The interest on a zero-coupon bond never reduces operating cash flow. This surprising result has two important analytic consequences. One is that CFO is systematically "overstated" when a zero-coupon (or deep discount) bond is issued. The second is that the cash eventually required to repay the obligation may be a significant burden.[11]

---

[10]The following discussion also applies to bonds sold at deep discounts, that is, with coupons that are far below market rates.

[11]In fact, additional interest expense will increase cash flow by generating income tax deductions. (Zero-coupon bond interest is tax deductible even though it is not paid.) This result can have real-world consequences. When valuing a company for leveraged buyout (LBO) purposes, the use of zero-coupon or low-coupon debt (both issued at a discount) can result in the following anomaly: the higher the interest rate, the higher the cash flow, mistakenly resulting in a higher price for the company. An investment banker recently commented to one of the authors that this factor contributed to overbidding in the late 1980s. Of course when the zero-coupon bond comes due, the cash must be found to repay the (much higher) face amount.

EXHIBIT 8-4
Zero-Coupon Bond Analysis

Bond: Face value (FV) = $100,000
      Coupon = 0%
      Maturity = 3 years
      Market Rate = 10% (MR = 5%)

	(1) Liability Opening	(2) (1) × MR Interest Expense	(3) FV × CR Coupon Payment	(4) (2) − (3) Change in Liability	(5) (1) + (4) Liability Closing	(6) FV Face Value of Bond	(7) (5) − (6) Discount
1/1/91	Proceeds (see below)				$ 74,622	$100,000	$(25,378)
6/30/91	$74,622	$ 3,731	$0	$ 3,731	78,353	100,000	(21,647)
12/31/91	78,353	3,917	0	3,917	82,270	100,000	(17,730)
6/30/92	82,270	4,114	0	4,114	86,384	100,000	(13,616)
12/31/92	86,384	4,319	0	4,319	90,703	100,000	(9,297)
6/30/93	90,703	4,535	0	4,535	95,238	100,000	(4,762)
12/31/93	95,238	4,762	0	4,762	100,000	100,000	0
Totals		$25,378	$0	$25,378			

Calculation of Proceeds

Present value of $100,000
  in 6 periods discounted at 5%: $100,000 × 0.74622 = $74,622

Cash flow from operations: Zero in all periods

Cash flow from financing: $74,622 inflow at 1/1/91; $100,000 outflow at 12/31/93

EQK Realty Investors I, a real estate investment trust, issued zero-coupon mortgage notes in 1985 and 1988, as disclosed in Exhibit 8-5. While the company accrued interest cost (amortization of discount) on these notes, that amortization is added back when CFO is computed. When CFO is reduced by the noncash interest expense, the impact is significant:

EQK Realty Investors I
Adjustment of Operating Cash Flow (CFO),
for Years Ending December 31, 1989–1991
(in $ thousands)

	1989	1990	1991
CFO as reported	$10458	$ 9795	$ 5728
Interest on zero-coupon debt	(7486)	(8318)	(9229)
Adjusted CFO	$ 2972	$ 1477	$(3501)

Reported CFO declined by approximately 50% over the 1989–1991 period but remained positive. After adjustment, the deterioration is striking, with 1991 CFO

EXHIBIT 8-5. EQK REALTY
Zero-Coupon Financing

Zero Coupon Mortgage Notes

On December 18, 1985, the Company issued a zero coupon mortgage note which matures on December 18, 1992 at a face amount of $94,720,000. At issuance, the Company received $45,000,000 representing an effective interest rate of 10.92% compounded semi-annually.

On February 4, 1988, the Company issued a zero coupon mortgage note which matures on December 18, 1992. The original maturity value of the note was $7,772,500; however, in December 1991 the Company prepaid a portion of the note with proceeds from the sale of buildings at Castleton reducing the maturity value to $4,264,000 (see Note 3). At issuance, the Company received $5,000,000 representing an effective interest rate of 9.255% compounded semi-annually. The proceeds of this note were used to reduce the bank note balance outstanding on that date.

The zero coupon mortgage notes are collateralized by first liens on the Peachtree and Castleton real estate and a subordinate lien on the Harrisburg real estate.

As discussed in Note 2, the Company is currently in negotiations to refinance the existing zero coupon mortgage notes.

Source: EQK Realty Investors I Annual Report. 1991

---

turning negative. Note the increasing trend of interest on the zero-coupon debt, similar to the trend in Exhibit 8-4. With the maturity of the debt approaching, EQK faced a possible liquidity crisis.[12]

Variable Rate Debt

Some debt does not have a fixed coupon payment; the periodic interest payment varies with the level of interest rates. These debt instruments are generally designed to trade at their face value. To achieve this objective, the interest rate "floats" above the rate on a specified maturity U.S. Treasury obligation or some other benchmark rate. The "spread" above the benchmark is related to the credit rating of the issuer.

Such variable or "floating rate" debt issues do not pose any analytical problem. Given the variable rate, there should be no impact on market price from interest rate changes, and the only market fluctuation should be the result of perceived changes in credit quality.

The analyst should note, however, that the use of variable rate debt exposes the firm's interest expense to the effects of rate changes. The impact of interest rate changes can, of course, be either positive or negative.[13]

Debt with Equity Features

To reduce the cost of issuing debt, many companies make their bond issues convertible into their common shares or issue a combination of bonds and warrants to purchase

---

[12]EQK's auditors referred to the impending maturity in its 1991 auditors' report.
[13]We return to this issue in the analysis of Deere's long-term debt in Chapter 14.

common shares. While conceptually these two types of "equity linked" debt are identical,[14] their accounting consequences differ.

Under APB 14 (1969), the convertibility feature of a bond is completely ignored when the bond is issued. Thus the entire proceeds of the bond are recorded as a liability, and interest expense is recorded as if the bond were nonconvertible. However, the conversion feature results in a lower interest rate.

From an analytic perspective, however, recognition should be given to the equity feature. When the stock price is (significantly) greater than the conversion price and one can readily assume that the debt will not have to be repaid, then the convertible bond should be treated as equity rather than debt in calculation of solvency ratios such as debt to equity. When the stock price is significantly below the conversion price, the bond should be treated as debt. At levels close to the conversion price, the instrument has both debt and equity features, and its treatment becomes a more difficult issue.

One possibility would be to attempt to price the debt and equity features of the convertible bond by the use of option pricing models. Discussion of this analysis is, however, beyond the scope of this book.[15] In its absence, the analyst must examine the sensitivity of the ratios on a "what if" basis, first treating the bond as debt and then as equity to see whether the differences are significant. If the differences prove to be significant, the comparative ratios serve to point out that a complete analysis of the company may hinge on the question of whether the debt will be ultimately converted. Again the ratios point out what to look for rather than providing all the answers.

When warrants are issued with bonds, the accounting treatment differs. The proceeds must be allocated between the two financial instruments. The portion relating to the bond is the recorded liability. As a result, the bond will be issued at a discount, and interest expense will include amortization of that discount. The portion of proceeds related to the warrants will be included in equity and will have no income statement impact.

As a result, reported interest expense will be higher when the bond plus warrant is issued than that for convertible bonds. However, the reported liability will be lower (but will increase as the discount is amortized). Reported cash flow from operations will be the same, as only the coupon interest is included.

When the convertible bond is converted into common stock by the bondholder, the entire proceeds will be reclassified from debt to equity. When a warrant is exercised, the additional cash will increase equity capital.

Because of the accounting difference, American companies rarely issue debt/warrant combinations. However, such issues are common outside of the United States where convertible debt is less frequently issued.

---

[14]A convertible bond can be disaggregated into a bond plus an option to convert the bond into common shares. The only difference between a convertible and a debt-plus-warrant issue is that, in the former case, the bond must be surrendered to exercise the option, whereas in the latter case, the bond and warrant are not linked. Thus the issuer can use the proceeds of exercised warrants for purposes other than the retirement of the associated debt. (In the 1960s some U.S. companies permitted warrantholders to use the associated bond to exercise the warrant; this provision protected bondholders as the bond was valued at face value regardless of its market value.)

[15]For a further discussion of the option features of convertible bonds (and warrants) and the difficulty in pricing them, see Zvi Bodie, Alex Kane, and Alan J. Marcus, *Investments,* Homewood, Ill.: Richard D. Irwin, (1989) Chap.20.

From an analyst's perspective, be aware of the systematic understatement of interest expense when convertible debt is issued. For both cases, remember to consider the impact of equity linked bonds on earnings per share. (See Appendix 3-C.)

Perpetual Debt

Some debt issues have no stated maturity; an example is the issue of perpetual "consols" by the British government. In recent years some companies (mainly in Europe) have issued perpetual debt. When debt does not have a maturity date, it may be considered preferred equity rather than a liability for analytic purposes.

Preferred Stock

Many companies issue more than one class of shares. Preferred (or preference) shares have priority over common shares with respect to dividends and entitlement to proceeds of sale or liquidation. In exchange for this privileged position, preferred shareholders usually give up their right to participate fully in the success of the company.

Preferred shares generally have a fixed dividend payment and a fixed preference on liquidation. Dividend payments are almost always *cumulative*; if they are not paid when due, they remain a liability (but one that is not recorded). Dividend arrears must be paid before any dividend can be paid to common shareholders. When calculating the net worth of a company with preferred shares outstanding, two cautions are necessary:

1. Subtract the liquidating value of the preferred, not the stated value, which may be lower.
2. Subtract any cumulative dividends that are in arrears.

Preferred shares may have a variable interest rate. Some issues ("auction rate" preferreds) have interest rates that change frequently, making them attractive to buyers seeking "money market"–type investments.[16] From an analytic perspective, these preferred shares function as short-term liabilities and should be treated as such, They are often called when market conditions change, making them a less permanent source of funds.

Preferred shares are almost always callable by the issuer. Many issues are, however, redeemable by the preferred shareholder, normally over a period of years.[17] Because of these "sinking fund" provisions, redeemable preferreds should be treated as debt[18] for purposes of analysis. *They should be included as debt in solvency ratios, and dividend payments should be treated as interest.*

The line between debt and equity has become increasingly blurred in recent years. Corporate issuers have looked for instruments that minimize the after-tax cost of financing yet provide maximum flexibility. Some issues are designated preferreds but

---

[16]For U.S. corporate buyers, preferred dividends are 80% tax free, making these issues more attractive on an after-tax basis than many other short-term investments.

[17]These provisions provide preferred shareholders with a guaranteed future value for the shares.

[18]Consistent with this view, the SEC requires that redeemable preferred shares not be included as part of stockholders' equity.

are really debt; others are called debt but are functionally equity. While help from accounting standards setters may eventually arrive,[19] it is up to the analyst to look at such instruments and decide whether to treat them as debt or as equity.

Effects of Changes in Interest Rates

The bond liability reported on the balance sheet is equal to the present value of future cash payments at issuance when the discount rate used is equal to the market rate. Increases (decreases) in this market rate will affect the present value of the future bond payments, decreasing (increasing) the market value of the debt. A company that issued debt prior to an increase (decrease) in market rates experiences an economic gain (loss) when the rates change. This economic gain or loss is not reflected in the company's financial statements. Market value changes will not appear on the income statement or the balance sheet, and the book value of the debt will therefore not be equal to its market value.

For analytic purposes, however, the market value of a company's debt may be more relevant than its book value. It better reflects the firm's economic position and is as important as the current market values of a firm's assets. Analysis of a firm's absolute and relative level of debt and borrowing capacity should be based on current market conditions. Consider two firms carrying the same book value of debt. One firm issued the debt when interest rates were low; the other at current interest rates, which are higher. Debt-to-equity ratios based on book values may be the same. However, the firm that issued the bonds at the lower interest rate has a stronger solvency position. Its borrowing capacity is higher as the economic value of its debt is lower.[20] Calculating the ratios using the market value of debt will reflect the stronger solvency position.

Furthermore, in valuation models[21] that deduct the value of debt from the value of the firm (or of its assets) the relevant measure is the market value rather than the book value of debt. Firms that issued debt at lower rates are relatively better off when interest rates increase, and this increase should be reflected in a higher equity value of the firm.

An important exception may be the debt of troubled companies. When the credit quality changes significantly (in either direction), the market price of debt will follow. When credit quality and debt prices decline, there will appear to be a large gain to the firm.[22] Yet, it is difficult to argue that shareholders are better off. The solution for this apparent paradox is that, when credit quality changes, the value of assets has probably changed as well. It is reasonable to assume that some assets of such troubled companies are impaired (see the discussion in Chapter 6).

---

[19]The FASB issued a discussion memorandum entitled Distinguishing Between Liability and Equity Instruments and Accounting for Instruments with Characteristics of Both in August 1990

[20]Theoretically, it could refinance its current debt at the same interest rate as the other firm with a resultant lower book and market value of debt.

[21]Similarly (as discussed in Chapter 15), in discounted cash flow valuation analysis, the calculation of a firm's (weighted average) cost of capital is based on market rather than book values of debt (and equity).

[22]The treatment of this "gain" is one of the issues concerning the FASB in its consideration of "mark-to-market" accounting for debt.

Accounting for Restructured Debt

When a debtor is in financial difficulty, an arrangement may be made with creditors to "restructure" the obligation by modifying its terms (for example, reducing the interest rate or deferring principal payments). Both debtor and creditor accounting for restructured debt is governed by SFAS 15 (1977).

When debt is extinguished, both the debtor and creditor will recognize gain or loss measured as the difference between the fair value of the assets (cash or other assets) used to repay the debt and its carrying amount. This accounting treatment raises neither accounting nor analysis issues.

When the obligation is restructured, however, there may be no recognized gain or loss. SFAS 15 provides that the carrying amount of the debt be compared with the *undiscounted* gross cash flows (principal and interest) to be received after restructuring. As long as the gross cash flows exceed the carrying amount, no loss is recognized by the creditor or gain by the debtor. For example, even if the interest rate on a loan is reduced to zero, there is no accounting effect as long as the expected principal payments exceed the carrying amount of the loan.

Yet in economic terms the present value of the cash flows has been reduced; the debtor has gained at the expense of the creditor. The accounting mandated by SFAS 15 recognizes this transfer only over the life of the loan as payments are made; the creditor will earn less interest income while the debtor will show lower interest expense.

For purposes of analysis, therefore, restructured debt should be restated to fair market value using a market rate of interest to discount the cash flows required by the restructured obligation.

Loan Impairment

This issue resurfaced in 1992 when the FASB considered the proper accounting by financial institutions for loans which are considered "impaired." Once again, the issue was whether to recognize the time value of money and require the use of present value to account for debt obligations; but now the context was valuation without any change in debt terms, as well as restructuring.

The FASB exposure draft, issued in June 1992, would require that both impaired and restructured loans be accounted for at fair value. Thus, SFAS 15 would be amended and lenders would be required to account for restructured loans at the present value of cash flows expected after modification of the loan terms. The FASB has not yet decided whether to require use of the historical rate or the current rate to compute present value. Similarly, impaired loans (where the debtor is in financial difficulty but no modification of terms has been effected) would also be accounted for at present value. The proposed standard would not affect banks' accounting for loan loss reserves, however.

In the next section we demonstrate, using the Deere Company, how the conversion of debt to market values can be carried out. The analysis will suggest when such a conversion is worthwhile.

Estimating Market Value of Debt

In many cases, the conversion of book value to market value is straightforward. For publicly traded debt, market values are readily available. If the debt is not publicly traded, its present value can be calculated by applying the current market rate to the original debt terms. The maturity, coupon rate, and other terms of long-term debt are generally disclosed for each debt security issued by the company. (See, for example, Deere's debt footnotes in Exhibit 1B-2.)

The relevant current market rate can be obtained from a number of sources:

1. Use other publicly traded debt of the company having approximately the same maturity, and estimate the rate used by the market to discount that debt.

2. Use publicly traded debt of equivalent companies in the same industry, and estimate the rate being used to discount that debt.

3. Add a risk premium to the current rate on U.S. government notes/bonds of that maturity. The amount of the risk premium to be added would depend on the bond rating "risk" class of the company's bonds. (See Chapter 14.)

Calculating the Market Value of Deere's Long-Term Debt

Exhibit 8-6A–C provides details of the conversion of Deere's book value of long-term debt to market values at 10-31-91. Included in the calculation is the current portion of the long-term debt, which is classified on Deere's balance sheet as part of short-term borrowings. In many cases we have used approximations; in our discussion we will point out where more elaborate analyses may be appropriate. The objective is to demonstrate the general method rather than get bogged down in detail.

Part A deals with the debt of the equipment operations, Part B with financial services debt, and Part C with the subordinated debt. These parts parallel the partitioning of the debt in Deere's long-term borrowings footnote (Appendix 1-B).

The first set of conversions for the publicly traded debt is straightforward. Market prices[23] that are expressed as a percentage of face value were obtained from the *Bond Guide*, issued monthly by Standard & Poor's Corporation. The face values were multiplied by market prices to get market values. The yield-to-maturity (YTM), the implicit market rate of interest used to discount the bonds to market value, is also provided.

The bonds have been arranged in order of maturity. Note that YTM increases for longer maturities, implying a (conventional) upward-sloping yield curve. The only exception occurs for the debentures maturing in 2000 and 2002, which have a lower YTM. These bonds are both callable, which can affect market prices (the call provisions affect both the yield and the maturity).

For the notes without publicly available market prices, market values were calculated by discounting the cash flows at an assumed YTM of 8.25%. This estimate was based on the YTM's (7.57% - 8.80%) of Deere's debt of similar maturities (1996-2019) with available market prices. For the medium term notes, the midpoint maturity of 2000 was assumed for discounting purposes.

Deere has a minimal amount of convertible debt ($2 million) that we included as part of the miscellaneous debt at face value. Were convertible debt significant, then the

---

[23]We have calculated the market value at October 31, 1991.

EXHIBIT 8-6. DEERE
Market Valuation of Long-Term Debt at 10-31-91

A. Equipment Operations

Description	Maturity	Book Value	Market Price	Market Value	Market YTM
Debt for Which Market Prices Are Available					
5.40% debentures*	1992	$ 17	99.75%	$ 17.0	6.21%
8.60% notes*	1992	100	102.00	102.0	6.31
8.25% notes	1996	150	102.63	153.9	7.56
9.125% notes	1996	100	106.00	106.0	7.57
8.45% debentures	2000	60	99.50	59.7	8.53
8% debentures	2002	126	98.75	124.4	8.17
8.95% debentures	2019	199	101.50	202.0	8.80
Subtotal		$ 752		$ 765.0	
Debt for Which Market Prices Are Not Available					
Medium-term notes, average rate 8.9%	1993– 2006	$ 272	104.10%	$ 283.2	Assumed 8.25%
Adjustable rate senior notes, 8.7%	2002	100	104.60	104.6	8.25
Miscellaneous†		16	100.00	16.0	
Totals		$1140		$1168.8	

*Included in current portion of long-term debt.
†Includes current portion of 5, foreign borrowings of 9, and convertible debentures of 2.

B. Financial Services

Description	Maturity	Book Value	Market Price	Market Value	Market YTM
Debt for Which Market Prices Are Available					
9.00% notes	1993	$ 124	103.50	$ 128.3	7.01%
7.5% debentures	1998	50	96.13	48.1	8.28
Subtotal		$ 174		$ 176.4	
Debt for Which Market Prices Are Unavailable or Inappropriate					
Medium-term notes average rate 7.4%	1992– 1995	$ 253	100.70%	$ 254.8	Assumed 7.00%
Variable rate notes	1993	150	100.00	150.0	
Floating rate	1993	9	100.00	9.0	
11 5/8%	1995	150	100.00	150.0	
Swiss franc	1999	97	100.00	97.0	
Miscellaneous, current portion		220	100.00	220.0	
Totals		$1053		$1057.2	

EXHIBIT 8-6. *(Continued)*

C. Subordinated Debt

Description	Maturity	Book Value	Market Price	Market Value	Market YTM
Debt for Which Market Prices Are Available					
9.35%	2003	$ 55	102.75%	$ 56.5	8.97%
Debt for Which Market Prices Are Unavailable or Inappropriate					
Swapped debt					
9 5/8%	1998	$ 150	100.00%	150.0	
8 5/8%	2019	150	100.00	150.0	
Totals		$ 355		$ 356.5	

adjustment to market value would be more complicated. (Convertible debt was discussed in a preceding section.)

Similar procedures are used in parts B and C to estimate the market value of financial services debt and subordinated debt with one important exception. Deere uses interest rate swaps on a substantial portion of its debt. For example, Deere has swapped its obligation to pay interest on the 7.4% notes (due 1993) for an obligation to pay a variable interest rate on the same principal amount. Thus while Deere has benefitted from the trend to lower interest rates, it assumed the additional risk of variable rates.

As a result of the swap, Deere effectively faces payments that are different from the stated payments on its outstanding debt. The market price of this outstanding debt is therefore not relevant. So how does one arrive at a market value for the swapped debt?

Presumably, when the swap was made, it was based on market values at the time (many swaps are entered into concurrently with the debt issuance). As variable rate debt normally shows little market fluctuation, we have assumed that the principal (face) and market values of this debt are the same. Given the short maturities of this debt, any adjustment would be small in any case.

The adjustments to market value in Exhibit 8-6 are summarized here:

Adjustment of Deere Debt to Market Value (in $ millions)

	Historical Cost			Market Value
	Long Term	Current Portion	Total	
Equipment operations	1018	122	1140	1169
Financial services	833	220	1053	1057
Subordinated debt	355	—	355	357
Totals	2206	342	2548	2583

The total effect of the adjustment of debt to market value was only $35 million, 1.4% of total debt of $2.5 billion. Is this relatively insignificant adjustment the norm or is the Deere case unique?

What factors need to be considered when deciding whether it is worthwhile to adjust debt from book value to market value?

Debt: Market or Book Value?

Given the absence of market prices in many cases and the assumptions required to estimate market values, book values are often used for analytic purposes. The small change in Deere's value of debt is a result of three factors: the short maturity of much of Deere's debt, the large amount of variable rate debt, and the modest change in long-term interest rates in recent years. These factors (confirmed by empirical results discussed in Box 8-1) provide us with some of the conditions that make it unnecessary to carry out conversion to market value.

Debt of Short Maturity

The effect of a change in interest rate on the market value of debt increases with the maturity of the debt. Thus, if a firm's debt is mostly short-term in nature, changes in interest rates will not appreciably affect its market value.[24] When the analysis includes trade debt, whose maturity is in terms of months rather than years, no adjustment may be required.

Variable Interest Rate Debt

Many firms today borrow through the use of adjustable rate debt whose interest rate varies with the market rate of debt. For this form of debt, book value is always equal to market value and no adjustment is required.

Changes in Market Rate of Interest

If the market rate of interest has not changed dramatically over time, the change in market values will also not be large.

When considering whether an adjustment is worthwhile, the percentage of debt that is short-term, variable rate, and issued at rates close to market should be considered. If this percentage is high, then even if the adjustments are significant for some debt, the overall adjustment will be small.

Finally, the focus of analysis must also be considered. If the focus is how a firm's debt position (e.g., debt-to-equity ratio) compares to that of other firms on a *relative* basis, then the adjustment may not be as relevant even for dramatic shifts in interest rates. Such changes affect all firms in a similar fashion, raising or lowering the market

---

[24]Thus, even if its long-term debt is adjusted by 10%, total debt will only be affected by 10% times the percentage of long-term debt. The smaller the percentage of long-term debt, the smaller the overall adjustment.

BOX 8-1
Empirical Evidence: Market or Book Values?

Bowman (1980) examined the relationship between firms' market betas and the debt/equity ratio. Finance theory predicts (see Chapter 14) that the higher a firm's debt/equity ratio (using market values), the higher the firm's beta.

Letting the superscripts "M" and "B" refer to market and book value, respectively, Bowman examined which of the following four measures of the debt/equity ratio, D^M/E^M, D^M/E^B, D^B/E^M, and D^B/E^B, were more closely associated with the firm's beta.

Bowman obtained the best results when he used the market value of equity in the denominator. *Whether debt was measured on a market basis or debt basis made little difference* as the ratios D^B/E^M and D^M/E^M yielded similar results. The pure book value ratio D^B/E^B did not perform as well; the measure of market value of debt to book value of equity (D^M/E^B) performed the poorest.

These results can be partly attributable to the fact that for close to 60% of the debt in Bowman's sample, book and market value were equivalent.* Furthermore, the correlation between the market value of debt and book value of debt was close to 100%. As the study was based on the ranking of debtors by relative debt rather than absolute levels of debt, changes in market rates of interest shifted debt valuations without changing ranks.

Mulford (1986) replicated Bowman's study using a later time period. Bowman's analysis was based on 1973 data, predating the dramatic rise in market interest rates of the late 1970s. Mulford, referring to Bowman's study, noted that:

> His failure to find evidence of superior performance for a debt-to-equity ratio based on market values of debt may have been due to small differences between the book and market values of debt which accompanied the general level of interest rates at that time.†

To remedy this, Mulford focused on 1980 when market rates of interest were historically high. In addition, to alleviate potential measurement problems arising from the conversion of book to market values, Mulford examined the performance of portfolios of firms in addition to individual firms. Mulford's results were more in line with theory but only on a portfolio basis. No matter which of the variations were used to measure the relationship between beta and debt/equity, the market-based debt/equity ratio was always the most closely associated with beta on a portfolio basis. On an individual basis, D^M/E^M did not always perform as well, but the differences between it and the best performing ratio were minimal.

These results confirm the intuition that, when the difference between stated and market rates of interest is not very large, the book value of debt may perform as well as market value of debt. The additional cost of obtaining market values of debt may not be worthwhile.‡ It is only when the gap between historic and market rates of interest is large that adjustment may be necessary. Even then, potential measurement problems§ in estimating market values may offset any benefits from the adjustment process.

---

*This proportion is similar to the amount we derived for Deere.

†Mulford, Charles W., "The Importance of a Market Value Measurement of Debt in Leverage Ratios: Replications and Extensions", *Journal of Accounting Research* (Autumn 1985), pp. 897–906.

‡Given the high correlation between the two levels of debt, this is especially true for analyses that focus on relative rather than absolute debt burdens.

§The issue of measurement problem also calls into question Bowman and Mulford's results from a different perspective. They adjusted only on-balance-sheet debt. Any debt that was "off-balance-sheet" was ignored by them. As Chapter 10 will make clear, these amounts can be significant.

value of debt. Thus, even though absolute levels of debt may change, relative rankings may not.

Retirement of Debt Prior to Maturity

When firms retire bonds prior to maturity, the difference between the book value of the liability and the amount paid to buy back the bonds is treated as an extraordinary gain or loss in the income statement.

Using the par bond example in Exhibit 8-1A, assume that on December 31, 1991, the market interest rate for the firm is 12%. As a result, the market price of the bonds should be 96,535.[25] The firm could pay $96,535 to retire the bond, resulting in a gain of $3465 on the bond retirement since the book value is $100,000.[26] The gain must be recognized as an *extraordinary item* under SFAS 4. The reasons for this treatment are

1. In reality, the firm is no better off as a result of the refinancing. To finance the retirement of the bond, it would issue new debt[27] bearing the same or higher current effective interest rate. Effectively, over the remaining life of the original bond, the net borrowing cost would be identical; the company has simply replaced 10% coupon debt with 12% coupon debt. In economic terms, the gain took place when interest rates rose, not when the refinancing took place, Because of the use of historic cost as a measure of the bond liability, however, only refinancing results in a recognized gain.

2. The decision to refinance has nothing to do with the firm's operating activities. It is a function only of the change in market interest rates.[28] Thus, segregating the gain/loss as extraordinary is appropriate.

In the early 1970's, interest rates hit double digits at the same time the U.S. economy entered a recession. Firms found their outstanding low-coupon bonds selling at deep discounts. Many of these firms had poor operating profitability, but were able to increase reported income by retiring bonds. The issuance of SFAS 4 in 1975 was partially a response to this income manipulation activity.

In recent years, however, refinancing has more often involved the retirement of high-coupon debt issued when interest rates were higher or as part of a leveraged buyout (LBO) or similar transaction. Such refinancing results in a recognized loss. It should be viewed, however, as a signal of lower future interest expense, as high-coupon debt is replaced by lower-coupon debt.

---

[25]This can be seen from Exhibit 8-1C as the carrying amount of the discount bond is the present value at the (original) 12% interest rate.

[26]We have ignored unamortized debt issuance costs. When bonds are retired, the firm must write off these costs that were capitalized when the bonds were issued. This write-off becomes a component of the gain or loss on retirement.

[27]Even if it did not issue new debt to retire the bond but rather used internal funds, the firm would experience an opportunity cost of the forgone interest revenue.

[28]If the gain or loss is recognized at all, it should be in the period in which interest rates change, not in the year in which the refinancing takes place. In our example, the year is the same, but that coincidence is rare in practice.

Bond retirements are normally accomplished by paying cash, although new debt issues may take place at the same time. In the past, new debt securities or equity (or some combination thereof) were sometimes offered in exchange for outstanding debt. Prior to 1980, the capital gain on exchange transactions could be treated, for tax purposes, in a manner that made them essentially tax free. After 1980, however, only debt equity swaps, carried out in a certain fashion, were tax exempt.[29] The Deficit Reduction Act of 1984 eliminated this last loophole.

The change in tax status has all but closed the door on these transactions. According to one estimate (Hand, 1989), only two debt equity swaps were completed after July 1984 as compared to 291 between August 1981 and July 1984.

Our discussion of debt retirement indicates that amount and timing of the accounting gain and the economic gain from debt retirement are quite different. This problem also applies to callable bonds, whose retirement may give rise to economic profit (even in nominal terms) but that generates a loss for accounting purposes.

Callable Bonds

A callable bond contains a provision allowing the issuer to buy back (call) the bond from the bondholders at predetermined dates and prices. This situation differs from the case in which the issuer retires the old bond at a market price equal to the present value of the future payment stream. The call price is usually set at a premium over the face value of the bond and is independent of the present value of the payment stream at the time the call is made. However, the actual exercise will depend on the relationship of the call price to that present value.

Exhibit 8-7 contains an analysis of a callable bond. The decline in interest rates constitutes an economic loss at the time of the rate change. A decision to refinance, as noted, would, in the absence of the call provision, have no impact on the firm. To refinance the debt at market rates, Cole would have to raise $106,624. However the call provision permits the firm to retire the bonds for only $102,000; the economic gain is the difference.[30]

Economically, it is beneficial to refinance the debt, but the income statement reports a loss. One can only speculate as to how many firms have not refinanced under such conditions because of the financial statement impact. This is yet another reason why analysts typically ignore gains and losses from the retirement of debt.

BOND COVENANTS

Creditors use bond covenants in lending agreements to protect their interests by restricting certain activities of the debtor that could jeopardize the creditor's position. Auditors and management must certify that the firm has not violated the convenants. If

---

[29]See Hand (1989) for a discussion of the tax status of these transactions in the pre-1980, 1981–1984, and post-1984 periods.

[30]When bonds are issued, the call provisions are often an important ingredient in the market reception. As call provisions benefit only the issuer, bond buyers will bargain against them. Many shorter-term issues are noncallable.

EXHIBIT 8-7
Analysis of Callable Bond

On January 1, 1991, Cole issues the following bond:

Face value = $100,000
Coupon = 10% (annual payments assumed for simplicity)
Maturity = 5 years
Call provision: Callable at any time after one year at 102

If the market interest rate applicable to Cole is 10%, then the bonds will be issued at par. They will be shown as a liability of $100,000.

Annual interest expense will be $10,000 (10% × $100,000).

Assume that, on December 31, 1991, the interest rate applicable to Cole has declined to 8%. This change will have no accounting impact on the company.

However, the present value of the cash flows associated with the debt will be $106,624 (discounted at 8%). Absent the call provision, the market price of the bonds would be expected to be 106.624.

By calling the bonds at a price of 102, Cole realizes an economic gain of $4624 [(106.624 − 102)($100,000)]. However, for accounting purposes, there is a loss of $2000 [(100 − 102)($100,000)].

---

any covenant is violated, the firm is in technical default of its lending agreement, and the creditor can demand immediate repayment of the debt.

This section presents a review of the most common forms of debt covenants. Any analysis of a firm's debt position must take into consideration the nature of these covenants and the risk that the firm may violate them.

Information on bond covenants is important both to evaluate the firm's credit risk as well as to obtain an understanding of the implication of such restrictions for the firm's dividend and growth (investment) prospects. In addition, to the extent these covenants are accounting based, the effects and choice of accounting policies on the ratios must also be examined.

Nature of Covenants

Smith and Warner (1979) characterize debt covenants as placing limits on one or more of the following activities:

1. Payment of dividends (includes share repurchases by the firm)
2. Production and investment (includes mergers and acquisitions, sale and lease-back, or outright disposal of certain assets)
3. Issuance of new debt (or incurrence of other liabilities)
4. Payoff patterns (includes sinking fund requirements and the priorities of claims on assets).

In addition to direct restrictions on activities, covenants are also expressed in terms of the maintenance of certain levels of accounting-based financial variables such as retained earnings, working capital, net assets, and debt-to equity ratios. These levels are often related to the four types of activities by restricting a certain activity if the accounting variable falls below a certain level. In some cases, falling below the level itself may signal the breach of a covenant even without any subsequent firm activity. A summary of the nature of these accounting-based debt covenant restrictions, adapted from Duke and Hunt (1990), is presented in Exhibit 8-8.

Exhibit 8-8 refers to *restricted retained earnings* as a constraint on dividend payments. This constraint is one of the most common forms used. Its definition is outlined in Exhibit 8-9.

Information as to the nature of these covenants was obtained by Smith and Warner (1979) and Duke and Hunt (1990) among others from the American Bar Foundation's *Commentaries on Debentures*, which provides a summary of typical covenants found in lending agreements. A cursory examination of the nature of these restrictions makes it clear that creditors are interested in limiting the firm's level of risk (investment and debt restrictions) and preserving the assets of the firm to ensure that debts are repaid (payment restrictions). Thus covenants attempt to limit shareholders' ability to transfer assets to themselves (dividend restrictions), to new shareholders (mergers and acquisition restrictions), or to new creditors (debt restrictions).

The information provided in the *Commentaries* is of a general nature. The best source of information on specific bond covenants (and other terms of the bond issue) for publicly issued bonds is the bond indenture, the legal document created when the bond is issued. The trustee (normally a bank) will have a copy of the indenture and is responsible

EXHIBIT 8-8
Common Accounting-Based Debt Covenant Restrictions

Attribute:	Retained earnings
Measured as:	Restricted retained earnings
Limits:	Payments of dividends or stock repurchase below minimum level of restricted retained earnings
Attribute:	Net assets
Measured as:	Net tangible assets or net assets
Limits:	Investments, dividend payments, and new debt issues if net assets fall below a certain level
Attribute:	Working capital
Measured as:	Minimum working capital or current ratio
Limits:	Mergers and acquisitions, dividend payments, and new debt issues if the working capital or the current ratio fall below a certain level
Attribute:	Debt-to-equity
Measured as:	Debt divided by net tangible assets or debt divided by net assets
Limits:	Issuance of additional debt

Source: Joanne C. Duke and Herbert G. Hunt III, "An Empirical Examination of Debt Covenant Restrictions and Accounting-related Debt Proxies" *Journal of Accounting and Economics,* (January 1990), Adapted from Table 1 (Page 52).

EXHIBIT 8-9
Unrestricted Retained Earnings: Inventory of Payable Funds

The most frequent accounting-based restriction specified is the dividend constraint. Dividends cannot be paid out of restricted retained earnings. Only unrestricted retained earnings, often referred to as the inventory of payable funds (IPF), is available for dividends. The general formulation of IPF is defined (see Smith and Warner, 1978) as the sum of

1. A specified percentage (k) of earnings (E) from the date of the debt issuance to the present period, plus
2. Proceeds from the sale of common shares (CS) from the date of the debt issuance to the present period, plus
3. A prespecified constant (F), less
4. The sum of dividends (DV) and stock repurchases from the date of the debt issuance to the present period.

Algebraically, this is equal to

$$IPF_t = k \sum_{i=0}^{t} E_i + \sum_{i=0}^{t} CS_i + F - \sum_{i=0}^{t} DV_i$$

where period 0 represents the date of the debt issuance and period t refers to the current date. The prespecified constant F is usually set at approximately one year's earnings.* This builds some slack into the system in the event the firm has a loss.

*See Smith and Warner (1979), note 36.

for the enforcement of its terms. The bond prospectus will contain a good summary of these terms.

For all debt issues, summarized data can be found in

- Services such as *Moody's Industrial Manual*.
- Annual reports.
- SEC filings by debtors.

Press and Weintrop (1990) contend that information obtained from annual reports and Moody's is not comprehensive, especially with respect to covenants relating to privately placed debt, and that in these cases, it is necessary to access the original SEC filings.

Calculating Accounting-Based Constraints

Each type of constraint is defined in the covenants. In addition, the convenants specify

- Whether GAAP definitions are to be used or whether GAAP is to be modified. (For example, see Exhibit 8-10.) Leftwich (1983) notes that, generally, such modifications are most often associated with private rather than public debt indentures.

- Whether GAAP in effect at the time of the debt issuance is maintained throughout the life of the bond ("frozen" GAAP) or whether calculations in subsequent years are to be based upon GAAP in effect at the date of the calculation ("rolling" GAAP). This is important when important new accounting standards are adopted. (See, for example, footnote 33 in Ch. 9, referring to the effect of SFAS 106 on the debt covenants of Westinghouse.)

Leftwich (1983) examined a number of private lending agreements to see the extent to which they "followed" GAAP. Exhibit 8-10 summarizes those situations where GAAP is totally or partially modified.

These modifications are interesting for two reasons. Most important they suggest how one set of financial statement users, creditors, modify GAAP for their own purposes. The second reason is that they suggest adjustments that can be made when financial statements are used for other purposes. Some of these modifications have been discussed earlier, and some will be discussed in later chapters. We highlight them now for reference purposes:

1. Deferred tax credits not included as liability (see Chapter 7)
2. Inclusion of "off-balance"-sheet debt (see Chapter 10) and capitalization of all leases (this chapter)
3. Ignoring the equity method of accounting by including only dividends from unconsolidated subsidiaries (see Chapter 11)
4. Restrictions on income effects of pooling and balance sheet effects of purchase accounting (see Chapter 12)
5. Ignoring income from foreign subsidiaries unless received (see Chapter 11)

Analysis of Deere's Covenants

Exhibit 8-11 contains information relating to Deere's covenants found in Deere's short-term borrowings and long-term borrowings footnote (Appendix 1-B).

The most significant covenants pertain to John Deere Capital, a U.S. credit subsidiary. The fixed charge coverage ratio and modified debt/equity ratio are typical of covenants for finance companies. The import of the first covenant is that it indirectly requires Deere to sell receivables to John Deere Capital at a price that produces the required earnings. The second covenant limits the ability of John Deere Credit to borrow, given its capital base. Note that subordinated debt is considered equity; this is a common definition used by banks and other senior lenders.

Other footnotes also show that Deere's credit agreements require maintenance of a minimum tangible net worth. At this point in time, those requirements appears to be benign.[31]

While the footnote information is suggestive, it is incomplete. It does not tell us how earnings and fixed charges are defined (are restructuring provisions included?) or exactly

---

[31]In Chapter 14 we discuss the effect on Deere of SFAS 106 (postretirement benefits). If Deere adopts the standard by recognizing the obligation immediately, its tangible net worth will decline sharply. This may place the company in danger of violating its net worth covenants.

EXHIBIT 8-10
Summary of Negotiated Accounting Rules That Are Entirely Outside GAAP (Group 1)

Category	Negotiated Accounting Rule
(i) Business combinations	Retained earnings of an acquired firm do not relax the negotiated restrictions on funds available for dividends even if pooling is used. Some upward revaluation of the acquired assets is allowed but only if the assets are independently appraised. If upward asset revaluation is allowed, the amount of any revaluation, even if classed as goodwill, can be included in tangible assets.
(ii) Contingencies	All charges for contingencies must be made against income, not against reserve accounts. Specific contingent liabilities, particularly guarantees of third-party indebtedness, are included in balance sheet liabilities.
(iii) Equity investments	Investments, especially short-term investments, are valued primarily at the lower of cost or market. Investments are frequently excluded from the asset base against which firms may borrow. Income from unconsolidated investments is not recognized until it is received; i.e., the equity method is not used.
(iv) Foreign Subsidiaries	Foreign subsidiaries are seldom consolidated. Income from foreign investments is recognized only when it is actually received.
(v) Goodwill and intangibles	Goodwill and intangibles are frequently excluded from the asset base against which firms may borrow. The accounting double entry is not preserved—goodwill is eliminated from balance sheet numbers but amortization is required in the income statement.
(vi) Income tax	Deferred tax credits are not always classified as a liability. Deferred tax debits are excluded from the firm's asset base.
(vii) Stock dividends and stock splits	No distinction is made between stock dividends and stock splits.

Summary of Negotiated Accounting Rules That Are Consistent with GAAP but Exclude One or More of the Generally Accepted Alternatives (Group 2)

Category	Negotiated Accounting Rule
(i) All-inclusive income statements	Specific income-increasing items (e.g., transfers to income from contingency reserves) are excluded from income, and specific income-decreasing items (e.g., depreciation of lease-hold improvements) are charged against income.
(ii) Convertible bonds	An issue of stock for debt conversion is valued at the face value of the converted debt.
(iii) Gain or loss on debt redemption	There is no attempt to classify the gain or loss as an ordinary or extraordinary item.
(iv) Leases	Capitalization of most leases is required.
(v) Ratio of earnings to fixed charges	All fixed charges (e.g., sinking fund and lease payments) are included, not just the imputed interest component.
(vi) Treasury stock	Stock repurchases are treated as cash dividends and treasury stock sales are treated as new issues of common.
(vii) Valuation of fixed assets	Fixed assets are valued at depreciated historical cost. Upward revaluations are prohibited, except in some business combinations. Current-cost data are ignored.

Source: Richard Leftwich, "Accounting Information in Private Markets: Evidence from Private Lending Agreements," *The Accounting Review,* (January 1983) pp. 23–42. Table 2 (P. 39).

EXHIBIT 8-11. DEERE & CO.
Debt Covenants

Certain of these credit agreements have various requirements of John Deere Capital Corporation, including the maintenance of its consolidated ratio of earnings before fixed charges to fixed charges at not less than 1.05 to 1 for each fiscal quarter. In addition, the Capital Corporation's ratio of senior debt to total stockholder's equity plus subordinated debt may not be more than 8 to 1 at the end of any fiscal quarter. The credit agreements also contain provisions requiring Deere & Company to maintain a consolidated tangible net worth of $1,600 million.

Certain of the company's current credit agreements contain provisions requiring the maintenance of a minimum consolidated tangible net worth. Under these provisions, $864 million of the consolidated retained earnings balance of $2,119 million at October 31, 1991 was free of restrictions as to payment of dividends or acquisition of the company's common stock.

Source: Deere & Co., Annual Report 1991.

how tangible net worth is computed. Thus footnote disclosures are a starting point for analysis, but are not the whole answer.

LEASES

Incentives for Leasing

Firms generally acquire the rights to use property, plant, and equipment (land and depreciable assets) by outright purchases, partially or fully funded by internal resources or externally borrowed funds. In a purchase transaction, the buyer acquires (and the seller surrenders) ownership, which includes all the benefits and risks embodied in the property. A firm may also acquire the use of property, including some or all of the benefits and risks of ownership, for specific periods of time and stipulated rental payments through contractual arrangements called leases.

Short-term leases allow the lessee to use leased property for only a portion of its economic life. Such leases are referred to as *operating leases* and are accounted for as contracts. The lessee reports only the required rental payments as they are made. Because the lessor retains substantially all the risks of ownership of leased property, the leased assets remain on its balance sheet and are depreciated over their estimated economic lives; rental payments are recognized as income over time according to the terms of the lease.

Alternatively, certain long-term leases may effectively transfer all (or substantially all) the risks and rewards of the leased property to the lessee. Such leases are the economic equivalent of sales with financing arrangements designed to effect the purchase (by the lessee) or sale (by the lessor) of the leased property. Such leases, referred to as *capital leases*, are treated for accounting purposes as sales. The asset and associated debt are carried on the books of the lessee, and the lessor records a gain on "sale" at the inception of the lease. The lessee depreciates the asset over its life, and lease payments are treated as payments of principal and interest. The financial reporting differences between accounting for a lease as an operating or capital lease are far reaching and affect the balance sheet, income statement, cash flow statement, and associated ratios.

The choice between treating (structuring) a lease as an operating or capital lease may not be independent of the original motivation for leasing as opposed to buying the asset. These interrelationships are explored in Box 8-2.

One motivation for leasing rather than borrowing and buying an asset directly is to avoid recognition of the debt on the lessee's financial statements. Having to report the lease as a capital lease removes this advantage. Whether a lease is reported as operating or capital depends, as we shall see, on the terms of the lease and their relationship to criteria specified by SFAS 13.

From the point of view of financial analysis, however, it is most important to note that leases may be structured as operating leases to achieve desired financial reporting effects and capital structure benefits. That is, lessees may use them to avoid financial statement recognition of the asset and related liability for contractual payments. This has the effect of improving profitability ratios and, more important, reducing reported leverage. The analyst must be able to adjust for (long-term) leases that are structured in a manner that allows avoidance of balance sheet recognition.

BOX 8-2
Incentives for Leasing and Their Effect on the Capital Versus Operating Lease Choice

Management choice between purchase and leasing may be a function of strategic investment and capital structure objectives, the comparative costs of leasing versus costs of internal resources or externally generated funds, the availability of and ability to use tax benefits, and perceived financial reporting advantages. Other benefits or risks related to the leased property, such as residual values and obsolescence, also affect the comparison of leasing and ownership costs.

Tax Incentives

The tax benefits of owning assets can be exploited best by transferring them to the party in the higher marginal tax bracket. Firms with lower effective tax rates more readily engage in leasing than firms in higher tax brackets as the tax benefits can be passed on to the lessor. El-Gazzar, Lilien, and Pastena (1986) provide evidence consistent with this hypothesis; firms with lower effective tax rates had a higher proportion of lease debt to total assets than did firms with higher effective tax rates. Moreover, El-Gazzar et al. argue that tax effects also influence the choice of accounting method as the lessee attempts to influence the tax interpretation (by the IRS) of lease contracts. That is, it is more difficult to argue for capital lease treatment for tax purposes if the lease is treated as an operating lease for book purposes. Citing evidence by Mellman and Bernstein (1966) of substantial conformity (pre-SFAS 13)* between tax and book accounting for lessees, they note that

> Apparently, a high-tax-rate lessee's claim of material equity on the tax return could be enhanced by showing ownership for reporting purposes.†

Their sample of firms confirmed this finding as firms with high effective tax rates tended to capitalize their leases.

Nontax Incentives

Smith and Wakeman (1985) analyzed nontax incentives related to the lease versus purchase decision. Their list of eight nontax factors that make leasing more likely than purchase is presented here. Some of these reasons are not directly related to the lessee's choice but are motivated by the manufacturer or lessor and/or the type of asset involved. We have arranged these conditions in terms of their potential impact on the operating versus capitalization accounting choice.

Nontax Incentives for Leasing Versus Purchase

Incentives Arranged in Terms of Impact
on Operating Versus Capital Lease Choice

Favors Operating Lease as per SFAS 13

1. Period of use is short relative to overall life of asset.
2. Lessor has comparative advantage in reselling the asset.

Favors Structuring Lease as Operating Lease

3. Corporate bond covenants contain specific covenants relating to financial policies that the firm must follow.
4. Management compensation contracts contain provisions expressing compensation as a function of returns on invested capital.

Not Relevant to Operating Versus Capital Lease Decision

5. Lessee ownership is closely held so that risk reduction is important.
6. Lessor (manufacturor) has market power and can thus generate higher profits by leasing the asset (and controlling the terms of the lease) than selling it.
7. Asset is not specialized to the firm.
8. Asset's value is not sensitive to use or abuse (owner takes better care of asset than lessee).

Based on Smith and Wakeman (1985).

Short periods of use and the resale factor favor the use of operating leases, and under GAAP, these conditions would lead to lease agreements consistent with operating leases. The bond covenant and the management compensation incentives also favor the *negotiated structuring* of the agreement as an operating lease.

Consistent with the foregoing, Abdel-Khalik (1981) and Nakayama, Lilien, and Benis (1981) both note that the expected covenant violations resulting from SFAS 13 influenced firms to lobby against its adoption. Furthermore, Abdel-Khalik noted that firms renegotiated terms of their leases during SFAS 13's transition period to make them eligible for treatment as operating leases. Imhoff and Thomas (1988) found that subsequent to SFAS 13, there was a general decline in leases as a form of financing. Further evidence with respect to the choice of accounting method is provided by El-Gazzar et al., who note that in the pre-SFAS 13 period, firms that had high debt/equity ratios and/or had incentive-based contracts based on income after interest expense were more likely to have leases classified as operating leases. Taken together, these results confirm that debt covenant and compensation factors affect both the choice of leasing as a form of financing as well as the choice of accounting treatment of the lease.

---

*Prior to SFAS 13, GAAP also required that certain leases be treated as capital leases. The effect of SFAS 13 was to tighten the requirements, making more leases qualify as capital leases.

†El-Gazzar, Samir, Steven Lilien and Victor Pastena, "Accounting for Leases by Lessees", *Journal of Accounting and Economics* (1986), pp. 217–237.

Additionally, short-term operating leases, even though they do not present any substantial accounting issues, transfer some property rights and involve *contractually fixed payments*. Extensive use of operating leases should be evaluated carefully to see if debt measurements and coverage ratios require adjustment.

Lessors, on the other hand, seek to structure leases as capital leases to allow earlier recognition of revenue and reported income by reporting as completed sales transactions that are in substance installment sales or financing arrangements. The resulting higher profitability and turnover ratios are powerful incentives for lessors.

The analyst's objective is to determine whether the accounting treatment of a lease adequately portrays the transfer of economic risks and benefits of the leased property and (when evaluating the lessor) whether the earnings process is complete. Analytical adjustments may be needed to reflect the economic impact of leases on current and future income statements, profitability relationships, and firms' debt and solvency position. Balance sheets and related ratios often must be adjusted to include leased assets and obligations.

Lease arrangements also impact the operating, investing, and financing components of cash flow statements. The analysis of cash flow, including the evaluation of the fixed versus discretionary nature of cash flow commitments, may also require adjustment for leases.

Lease Classification: Lessees

Financial reporting standards for leases are based on an evaluation of economic characteristics of lease agreements at the *inception of the lease* to determine whether they should be capitalized or reported as operating leases. Classification is a function of the transfer of risks and rewards specified by contractual provisions of the lease agreement. It depends on the following factors:

1. Whether the lessee or lessor has ownership at the end of the *lease term*
2. Who bears the risk of changes in property values over the lease term
3. The rights to the *estimated residual value of leased property* at the end of the lease term
4. Guarantees, if any, of these residual values by the lessee

Lease classifications are not intended to be alternative reporting methods. However, since management actively negotiates and controls the provisions of lease agreements, terms are often designed to achieve specific reporting objectives. A lease that, in economic substance, transfers substantially all the risks and rewards inherent in the leased property is a financing or capital lease and should be capitalized by the lessee and the lessor.

SFAS 13 attempted to promulgate "objective" and "reliable" criteria that facilitate the evaluation of the economic substance of lease agreements. [One objective was to ensure that either lessee or lessor but not both (or neither) recognize leased assets on their books. Standards discourage off-balance-sheet financing by lessees and front-end loading of income by lessors.]

A lease meeting *any one* of the following criteria at the inception of the lease must be classified as a capital lease by lessees:

1. The lease transfers ownership of the property to the lessee at the end of the lease term.
2. The lease contains a *bargain purchase option*.
3. The lease term is equal to 75% or more of the *estmated economic life* of the leased property (not applicable when the lease term begins within the final 25% of the economic life of the asset).
4. The present value of the *minimum lease payments* (MLPs) equals or exceeds 90% of the *fair value of leased property* to the lessor. The discount rate used to compute the present values should be the lessee's *incremental borrowing rate* or the *implicit interest rate* of the lessor, whichever is lower.

Leases not meeting any of these criteria are classified as operating leases.

The ownership and bargain purchase criteria imply a transfer of all the risks and benefits of the leased property to the lessee; in economic substance such leases are financing arrangements. Lease terms extending to at least 75% of the economic life of the leased asset are also considered to achieve such a transfer; there is an implicit assumption that most of the value of an asset accrues to the user within that period. (The use of accelerated depreciation is conceptually similar.)

Finally, a lease must be capitalized when the present value of the minimum lease payments is equal to or exceeds 90 percent of the fair value of the leased property at the inception of the lease. The use of the lower of the lessee's incremental borrowing rate or the interest rate implicit in the lease generates the higher of two present values, increasing the probability that this criterion will be met and the lease capitalized, In effect, the lessee has contractually agreed to payments ensuring that the lessor will recover its investment along with a reasonable return. The transaction is, therefore, an installment purchase for the lessee financed by the lessor, and capitalization reflects this economic interpretation of the leasing transaction.[32]

Lease Classification: Lessors

Lease capitalization by lessors is required when the lease meets *any one* of the four criteria specified for capitalization by lessees and *both* of the following revenue recognition criteria:

1. Collectibility of the MLPs is reasonably predictable.
2. There are no significant uncertainties regarding the amount of unreimbursable costs yet to be incurred by the lessor under the provisions of the lease agreement.

---

[32]Leases are classified at the inception of the lease; the classification is not changed when the lessee or lessor is acquired unless the provisions of the lease agreement are changed. See FASB Interpretation 21 (1978).

Leases not meeting these criteria must be reported as operating leases since either the risks and benefits of leased assets have not been transferred or the earnings process is not complete.

The lessor's assumptions regarding the economic life of leased property should be compared to those used by competitors for similar property as they may be tailored to ensure that the lease term is at least 75% of the economic life, allowing capitalization. The probability of exercise of renewal options (especially when lease capitalization depends on the assumption that renewal options will be exercised), impact of renewal payments, adequacy of residual value guarantees, and other assumptions regarding residual values also impact the transfer of risk to lessees.

Many manufacturers and dealers use sales-type leases to market their products. Sales-type leases include both a manufacturing or merchandising profit (the difference between the fair value at the inception of the lease and the cost or carrying value of the leased property) and interest income due to the financing nature of the transaction. Financial institutions and leasing intermediaries engage in direct financing lease agreements that contain only interest income. Operating leases may be created by either class of lessors.

Financial Reporting by Lessees: Illustration

Financial reporting by lessees will be illustrated using a noncancellable lease of equipment beginning on January 1, 1990, with the following terms:

1. Annual payments are $100,000 for 10 years. Annual *executory costs* (maintenance, taxes, and insurance) are $5000 and are paid by the lessee.

2. At the end of the lease term, the equipment is expected to have a residual value of $22,500.

3. The fair market value of the equipment is $651,270.

4. The estimated economic life of the equipment is 15 years.

5. The lessor's implicit interest rate is 9%, and the lessee's incremental borrowing rate is 10%.

In addition, it is assumed that the lessee's income before lease-related expenses is $200,000 each year during the lease term. Finally, we assume that the lease is an operating lease for tax purposes so that $100,000 is the annual tax deductible expense.

Comparative Analysis of Capitalized and Operating Leases

Classification of the Lease. Since the agreement contains neither a bargain purchase option nor the transfer of ownership to the lessee at the end of the lease term, neither of the first two criteria for lease capitalization is met. The lease term of 10 years is also less than 75% of the 15-year expected economic life of the leased equipment. (However, lessees may use liberal assumptions of economic lives of leased assets to ensure that this criterion is not met.)

The lease must, however, be capitalized because it meets the fourth test: the present value of the MLPs,[33] discounted at the lessor's interest rate of 9%, is $641,766, more than 90% of the fair market value of $651,720.

Lease Capitalization. The present value of the MLPs is the amount at which the leased asset and obligations are initially reported on the lessee's balance sheet. The capitalized amount cannot exceed the fair value of the leased property. Generally, depreciation methods used for similar purchased property are applied to leased assets over their estimated economic lives when one of the transfer of ownership criteria (1 and 2) is met and over the lease term when one of the other capitalization criteria (3 and 4) is satisfied.

Exhibit 8-12A illustrates the lessee's lease amortization schedule. At the inception of the lease, January 1, 1990, the lessee capitalizes the MLPs at the lessor's implicit rate of 9%. The effective interest method is used, as required by SFAS 13, to amortize the lease obligation over the lease term, allocating the periodic payments between interest expense and reduction of the lease liability. This schedule is the basis of the comparison with operating leases.

Operating Leases. Leases not meeting any of the four criteria detailed in SFAS 13 are not capitalized since no purchase is deemed to have occurred and no asset or obligation is reported in the financial statements. Such leases are classified as operating leases, and payments are reported as rental expense. SFAS 13 mandates the use of the straight-line method of recognizing periodic rental payments unless another, systematic basis provides a better representation of the use of leased property. As a result, for leases with rising rental payments, lease expense and cash flow will not be identical.

Balance Sheet Effects (Exhibit 8-12B). When leases are capitalized, the gross and net (of accumulated depreciation) amounts are reported at each balance sheet date. Capitalization increases asset balances, resulting in lower asset turnover and return-on asset ratios as compared with the operating lease method, which does not record leased assets.

The current and noncurrent components of the lease obligation are reported as liabilities under capitalization. The current component is the principal portion of the lease payment to be made in the following year. Note that, at the inception of the lease, the leased asset and liability are equal at $641,766. Since the asset and liability are amortized using different methods, this equality is not again observed until the end of the lease term when both asset and liability are equal to zero.

The most important effect of lease capitalization is its impact on leverage ratios. As lease obligations are not recognized for operating leases, leverage ratios are understated. Part B shows that capitalization adds a current liability of $50,187 ($46,043) and a noncurrent liability of $503,295 ($553,482) to debt as of December 31, 1991 (1990), resulting in a corresponding increase in the debt-to-equity and other leverage ratios.

---

[33]MLPs include residual values guaranteed by lessees since the guarantee results in a contractually fixed residual value and effectively transfers the risk of changes in residual values to the lessee.

EXHIBIT 8-12
Lessee Financial Reporting

A. Lease Amortization Schedule for Capital Lease

Year Ending	Annual Lease Payment (A)	Interest Expense* (B)	Reduction in Lease Obligation (C) = (A) − (B)	Balance of Lease Obligation† (D)
January 1, 1990				$641,766
December 31, 1990	$ 100,000	$ 57,759	$ 42,241	599,525
December 31, 1991	100,000	53,957	46,043	553,482
December 31, 1992	100,000	49,813	50,187	503,295
December 31, 1993	100,000	45,297	54,703	448,592
December 31, 1994	100,000	40,373	59,627	388,965
December 31, 1995	100,000	35,007	64,993	323,972
December 31, 1996	100,000	29,157	70,843	253,129
December 31, 1997	100,000	22,782	77,218	175,911
December 31, 1998	100,000	15,832	84,168	91,743
December 31, 1999	100,000	8,257	91,743	0
Totals	$1,000,000	$358,234	$641,766	

*9% of lease obligation at previous year end.

†Equals the beginning-of-year present value reduced by that year's amortization of the lease obligation. Also equal to the present value of remaining payments (MLPs) of $100,000 each, discounted at 9% over the remaining lease term.

*B. Balance Sheet Impact of Lease Capitalization**

	January 1, 1990	December 31 1990	December 31 1991
Property, plant, and equipment			
Leased assets	$641,766	$641,766	$ 641,766
Accumulated depreciation	(0)	(64,177)	(128,353)
Leased assets, net	$641,766	$577,589	$ 513,413
Current liabilities:			
Current portion of lease obligation	42,241	$ 46,043	$ 50,187
Long-term debt: Lease obligation	599,525	553,482	503,295
Total liabilities	$641,766	$599,525	$ 553,482

*Operating leases are not recognized as assets or liabilities.

EXHIBIT 8-12. *(Continued)*

C(1). Income Statement Effects of Capital Lease

Year Ended December 31	Income Before Lease Expense (A)	Depreciation Expense (B)	Interest Expense (C)	Total Expense (D) = (B) + (C)	Pretax Income (E) = (A) − (D)	Tax Expense @ 35%* (F)	Net Income (G) = (E) − (F)
1990	$ 200,000	$ 64,177	$ 57,759	$ 121,936	$ 78,064	$ 27,322	$ 50,742
1991	200,000	64,177	53,957	118,134	81,866	28,653	53,213
1992	200,000	64,177	49,813	113,990	86,010	30,104	55,906
1993	200,000	64,177	45,297	109,474	90,526	31,684	58,842
1994	200,000	64,177	40,373	104,550	95,450	33,408	62,042
1995	200,000	64,177	35,007	99,184	100,816	35,286	65,530
1996	200,000	64,177	29,157	93,334	106,666	37,333	69,333
1997	200,000	64,177	22,782	86,959	113,041	39,564	73,477
1998	200,000	64,177	15,832	80,009	119,991	41,997	77,994
1999	200,000	64,173	8,257	72,430	127,570	44,649	82,921
Totals	$2,000,000	$641,766	$358,234	$1,000,000	$1,000,000	$350,000	$650,000

*Assuming that the lease is considered an operating lease for tax purposes, only the rental expense of $100,000 each year is deductible. Thus firms using the capital lease method will realize the same annual tax reduction of $35,000 as reported by firms using the operating lease method. For financial reporting, rental expense is replaced by depreciation and interest expense. In the initial years of the lease term, this temporary difference will result in deferred tax debits (prepaid income taxes), which will be eliminated by the end of the lease term.

C(2). Income Statement Effects of Operating Lease

Year Ended December 31	Income Before Lease Expenses (A)	Rental Expense (B)	Pretax Income (C) = (A) − (B)	Tax Expense @ 35%* (D)	Net Income (E) = (C) − (D)
1990	$ 200,000	$ 100,000	$ 100,000	$ 35,000	$ 65,000
1991	200,000	100,000	100,000	35,000	65,000
1992	200,000	100,000	100,000	35,000	65,000
1993	200,000	100,000	100,000	35,000	65,000
1994	200,000	100,000	100,000	35,000	65,000
1995	200,000	100,000	100,000	35,000	65,000
1996	200,000	100,000	100,000	35,000	65,000
1997	200,000	100,000	100,000	35,000	65,000
1998	200,000	100,000	100,000	35,000	65,000
1999	200,000	100,000	100,000	35,000	65,000
Totals	$2,000,000	$1,000,000	$1,000,000	$350,000	$650,000

*Since financial statement and tax reporting are identical under the operating lease method, the tax expense reported is equal to taxes payable, and no deferred taxes are required.

EXHIBIT 8-12. *(Continued)*

C(3). Income Differences Between Lease Methods
Capital Lease Less Operating Lease

Year	Operating Income*	Pretax Income	Net Income
1990	$ 35,823	$(21,936)	$(14,258)
1991	35,823	(18,134)	(11,787)
1992	35,823	(13,990)	(9,094)
1993	35,823	(9,474)	(6,158)
1994	35,823	(4,550)	(2,958)
1995	35,823	816	530
1996	35,823	6,666	4,333
1997	35,823	13,041	8,477
1998	35,823	19,991	12,994
1999	35,827	27,570	17,921
Totals	$358,234	$ 0	$ 0

*Operating income under the capital lease method equals income before lease expense less depreciation (column (A) less column (B) in Exhibit 8-12C(1) or $135,823 each year). Under the operating lease method, operating income is income before lease expense less rental expense (column (A) less column (B) in Exhibit 8-12C(2) or $100,000 each year).

D. Footnote Disclosures

Capitalized Leases (Future MLPs)				Operating Leases (Future MLPs)			
December 31, 1991		December 31, 1990		December 31, 1991		December 31, 1990	
1992	$ 100,000	1991	$ 100,000	1992	$100,000	1991	$100,000
1993	100,000	1992	100,000	1993	100,000	1992	100,000
1994	100,000	1993	100,000	1994	100,000	1993	100,000
1995	100,000	1994	100,000	1995	100,000	1994	100,000
1996	100,000	1995	100,000	1996	100,000	1995	100,000
Thereafter	300,000	Thereafter	400,000	Thereafter	300,000	Thereafter	400,000
				Total		Total	
Total	$ 800,000	Total	$ 900,000	MLPs	$800,000	MLPs	$900,000
Less: Interest component	(246,518)	Less: Interest component	(300,475)				
Equals: Present value of net MLPs, including current portion of $50,187	$ 553,482	Equals: Present value of net MLPs, including current portion of $46,043	$ 599,525				

EXHIBIT 8-12. *(Continued)*

E(1). Cash Flow Effects of Lease Methods
Direct Method, Years Ended December 31, 1990–1991

	Capital Lease		Operating Lease	Difference
1990				
CFO				
Interest	$(57,759)	Rental Expense	$(100,000)	$ 42,241
Tax benefit	35,000	Tax benefit	35,000	0
	$(22,759)		$ (65,000)	$ 42,241
Financing cash flow	$(42,241)	Financing cash flow	$ 0	$(42,241)
1991				
CFO				
Interest	$(53,957)	Rental Expense	$(100,000)	$ 46,043
Tax benefit	35,000	Tax benefit	35,000	0
	$(18,957)		$ (65,000)	$ 46,043
Financing cash flow	$(46,043)	Financing cash flow	$ 0	$(46,043)

E(2). Difference in CFO
Indirect Method, Year Ended December 31, 1990–1991

	Capital Lease Less Operating Lease	
	1990	1991
Lower net income	$(14,259)	$(11,787)
Depreciation expense	64,177	64,177
Deferred income tax expense	(7,677)	(6,347)
Net Difference in CFO	$ 42,241	$ 46,043

Analytical methods for evaluating operating leases are described in a following section on analysis of lease disclosures. The analyst should capitalize operating leases where appropriate to develop more inclusive leverage ratios and to facilitate both the evaluation of firm risk and capital structure over time and the analysis of comparable investments across industries and markets.

Income Statement Effects (Exhibit 8-12C). The income statement effects of lease reporting are also significant. The operating lease method charges the periodic rental payments to expense as accrued, whereas capitalization results in the recognition of depreciation and interest expense over the lease term. Part C provides a comparison of the income reported under the two methods.

Operating Income. Capitalization results in higher operating income (earnings before interest and taxes, or EBIT) since annual straight-line depreciation expense of $64,177 will be lower than annual rental expense of $100,000 reported under the operating lease method. For an individual lease, this difference is never reversed and remains constant over the lease term given use of the straight-line depreciation method. Use of accelerated depreciation will result in a smaller difference in early years, with an increasing difference as depreciation declines, increasing both the level and trend of EBIT.

Total Expense and Net Income Under capitalization, lease expense includes interest expense and depreciation of the leased asset. Interest expense falls over time since it is computed at a constant rate applied to a declining lease obligation. Depreciation expense will be constant (straight-line method) or declining (accelerated depreciation method).

Total lease expense will, therefore, decline over the lease term. Initially, total expense for a capital lease will exceed rental expense reported for an operating lease, but it declines over the lease term. In later years, total lease expense will be less than rental expense reported for an operating lease.

In our example, total lease expense for 1991 is $121,936, including depreciation expense of $64,177 and interest expense of $57,759. Pretax income is $78,064 in 1991, and, using a tax rate of 35%, tax expense is $27,322; net income is $50,742 in the first year under capitalization. Assuming that the lease is an operating lease for tax purposes, only the annual rental payment of $100,000 is deductible, and the tax payable is $35,000 regardless of the financial reporting method used.

Because the capital lease method reports tax expense of $27,322, it also reports a deferred tax asset of $7678 at the end of the first year. The balance in the deferred tax account accumulates until the total expense falls below the $100,000 deductible for taxes, at which point it starts to decline and is eliminated at the end of the lease term.

Part C(2) shows income under the operating lease method: rental expense of $100,000, pretax income of $100,000, and net income is $65,000 each year over the lease term. No deferred taxes are reported since the amount deductible for taxes and the reported rental expense in the financial statements are always identical.

Note that total expense (interest plus depreciation) for a capital lease must equal total rental expense for an operating lease over the life of the lease. Consequently, while net income over the lease term is not affected by capitalization, the timing of income recognition is changed; lower net income is reported in the early years followed by higher income in later years.

This relationship must hold for individual leases, but the effect on a firm depends on any additional leases entered into in subsequent periods. The effect of inflation on asset prices (and lease rentals) means that the impact of old leases nearing expiration may be swamped by the impact of new leases. In general, firms with operating leases report higher profitability, interest coverage, and return-on-asset ratios relative to firms with capital leases. Higher ROA results from both higher profitability (numerator effect) and lower assets (denominator effect) as assets under operating leases are not reported on the balance sheet.

Lease Disclosure Requirements SFAS 13 requires disclosure of gross amounts of capitalized lease assets as of each balance sheet date, by major classes or grouped by their nature or function; they may be combined with owned assets. Information regarding renewal terms, purchase options, contingent rentals, any escalation clauses, and restrictions on dividends, additional debt, and leasing is also required; such disclosure is usually general in nature.

Lessees must also disclose future MLPs for each of the five succeeding fiscal years and the aggregate thereafter. The net present value of the capitalized leases, as shown in part D, is reported net of executory costs and interest. Separate disclosure of minimum sublease rentals receivable from noncancellable subleases is also required. (See reporting requirements for lessors on page 606.)

Lessees under operating leases must disclose rental expense (classified as to minimum, contingent, and sublease rentals) for each period for which an income statement is presented. Future minimum lease payments (MLPs) (for operating leases with inital or remaining noncancellable lease terms exceeding one year) for each of the five succeeding fiscal years, and in the aggregate thereafter, must be disclosed as of the latest balance sheet. Lessees must also disclose aggregate minimum rentals receivable under noncancellable subleases and provide a general statement of operating lease arrangements similar to that required for capital leases.

As noncancellable leases in effect constitute (off-balance-sheet) debt, this information is useful. It allows analysts to calculate the implicit debt borne by lessees and adjust the statements accordingly (see Ashland Oil example).

Exhibit 8-12D also shows the required footnote disclosure if the lease is accounted for as an operating lease. Unlike the case of capital leases, disclosure of the interest component of MLPs and their present value is not required.

Cash Flow Effect of Lease Classification (Exhibit 8-12E(1)) Lease classification provides another example where accounting methods affect the classification of cash flows. Under the operating lease method, all cash flows are operating and there is an operating cash outflow of $65,000 per year. The required annual payments of $100,000 generate a tax benefit of $35,000 per year; that amount is deductible regardless of the accounting method used for financial reporting purposes. However, *lease capitalization results in both operating and financing cash flows*.

The 1990 rental payment of $100,000 is allocated between interest expense ($57,759) and amortization of the lease obligation ($42,241). CFO under capitalization is $(22,759), which reflects the interest payment and the tax benefit. Thus CFO differs between the two methods by $42,241, the amortization of the lease obligation (classified as a financing cash flow for the capital lease). Because interest expense declines over the lease term and an increasing proportion of the annual payment is allocated to the lease obligation, the difference in CFO increases over the lease term. Thus lease capitalization systematically decreases the operating cash outflow[34] while increasing the financing cash outflow.

---

[34]Exhibit 8-12E(2) shows the difference in operating cash flows computed using the indirect method.

Therefore, while the capitalized lease method adversely affects some financial statement ratios, it allows firms to report higher operating cash flows compared to those reported using the operating lease method.

Financial Reporting by Lessees: An Example

Exhibit 8-13 provides an example of lessee financial statement reporting. The 1991 balance sheet of Ashland Oil includes capitalized lease assets under the caption "Properties, Plant and Equipment," and the related "Capital Lease Obligations" are reported after long-term debt. The current portion of the lease obligations is included in current debt on the balance sheet but is disclosed in the footnotes.

Exhibit 8-14 contains Ashland's lease disclosures (Note G) and an excerpt from the "Summary of Significant Accounting Policies" (Note A), which states that the firm uses straight-line depreciation for leases over the shorter of the lease terms or useful lives, as appropriate. Capital lease obligations and operating leases are shown separately in Note G, which contains other required disclosures for operating leases, including data on past minimum rentals, contingent rentals, and sublease rental income.

Future MLPs for the next five years, and the aggregate thereafter, are disclosed for both capital and operating leases. For capital leases, interest has been deducted to report their present value. The present value of MLPs for operating leases is not disclosed. Present value data, while not mandated by SFAS 13, are occasionally provided. Investors can use the disclosures for capital and operating leases to determine whether the firm's operating leases should be capitalized and, if so, to compare their estimate of the present value of operating leases to that provided by the firm.

Analysis of Lessee Disclosures. Ashland depreciates all property and equipment on a straight-line basis. The depreciation method(s) and lives should be compared to those used by similar firms. (See Chapter 6, which discusses various analytical techniques applicable to fixed assets. In particular, analysts can adjust reported depreciation expense and property values for comparative purposes.)

Future MLPs under capitalized leases have a present value of $55.3 million, of which $7.8 million[35] represents the current portion included in current debt maturities. Aggregate MLPs for the next five years are $43.7 million or about 53% of total future MLPs; the annual amounts decline from $12.3 million (1992) to $6.6 million (1996), about 46%. Total MLPs for the remaining years are $38.3 million or 47% of the total MLPs of $82 million over the lease terms. Capitalized MLPs, generally, decline slowly over time, and a substantial proportion of the payments occurs after the initial five years, suggesting long-term leases.

The average lease term of the capitalized leases can be estimated by computing the number of payments included in the "later years" amount of $38.3 million—5.8 ($38.31 million/$6.58 million) if we assume that annual payments remain at the 1996 level. This suggests a lease term of approximately 11 (initial 5 plus the estimated 5.8) years.

---

[35]That is, $7.774 million, deduced by subtracting the balance sheet obligation of $47.552 million from the total obligation of $55.326 million.

EXHIBIT 8-13. ASHLAND OIL
Condensed Consolidated Balance Sheets
September 30

(In thousands)	1991	1990
Assets		
Current assets		
Cash and cash equivalents—Note A	$ 70,700	$ 80,579
Accounts receivable (less allowances for doubtful accounts of $17,711 in 1991 and $15,007 in 1990)	1,205,478	1,147,444
Construction completed and in progress—at contract prices	51,846	57,641
Inventories—Note A	660,057	716,541
Deferred income tax benefits	62,716	70,953
Other current assets	67,827	70,296
	2,118,624	2,143,454
Investments and other assets		
Investments in and advances to unconsolidated affiliates	310,007	343,816
Investments of captive insurance companies—Note A	150,363	128,746
Cost in excess of net assets of companies acquired (less accumulated amortization of $21,072 in 1991 and $15,990 in 1990)—Notes A and B	64,356	69,426
Other noncurrent assets	241,348	167,632
	766,074	709,620
Property, plant and equipment—Notes A and G		
Cost	5,166,058	4,696,649
Accumulated depreciation, depletion and amortization	(2,601,658)	(2,431,823)
	2,564,400	2,264,826
	$ 5,449,098	$ 5,117,900
Liabilities and Stockholders' Equity		
Current liabilities		
Debt due within one year		
Notes payable to banks	$ 79,000	$ 84,768
Commercial paper	59,081	42,967
Current portion of long-term debt and capitalized lease obligations	57,425	42,085
Trade and other payables	1,579,533	1,538,357
Income taxes	47,862	97,369
	1,822,901	1,805,546
Noncurrent liabilities		
Long-term debt (less current portion)	1,289,010	1,179,776
Capitalized lease obligations (less current portion)—Note G	47,552	55,379
Deferred income taxes	312,062	323,811
Claims and reserves of captive insurance companies	141,101	117,632
Accrued pension costs	105,292	87,571
Other long-term liabilities and deferred credits	287,673	268,172
	2,182,690	2,032,341
Preferred stock		
Common stockholders' equity	1,443,507	1,280,013
	$ 5,449,098	$ 5,117,900

Source: Ashland Oil, Annual Report, 1991

EXHIBIT 8-14. ASHLAND OIL

Note A—Significant Accounting Policies

Property, plant and equipment

Oil and gas exploration and development costs are accounted for using the successful efforts method. Capitalized exploration and development costs are depreciated by the units-of-production method over the estimated recoverable reserves.

The cost of plant and equipment (other than assets under capital leases and capitalized exploration and development costs) is depreciated principally by the straight-line method over the estimated useful lives of the assets. Assets under capital leases are depreciated by the straight-line method over the shorter of the lease terms or the useful lives of the assets. Costs in excess of net assets of companies acquired are amortized by the straight-line method over periods generally ranging from ten to forty years (with an average remaining life of 15 years).

Note G—Leases and Other Commitments

Leases

Ashland and its subsidiaries are lessees in noncancelable leasing agreements for office buildings and warehouses, pipelines, transportation and marine equipment, service stations, manufacturing facilities and other equipment and properties which expire at various dates. Future minimum lease payments at September 30, 1991 and assets (included in property, plant and equipment) under capital leases follow.

(In thousands)

Future minimum lease payments		Assets under capital leases	1991	1990
1992	$ 12,347	Cost		
1993	10,266	Ashland Petroleum	$120,700	$121,581
1994	7,964	SuperAmerica Group	104	—
1995	6,586	Valvoline	1,060	1,060
1996	6,579	Chemical	7,297	7,297
Later years	38,311	Corporate	7,600	7,600
	82,053		136,761	137,538
Imputed interest	(26,727)	Accumulated depreciation	(98,136)	(95,624)
Capitalized lease obligations	$ 55,326	Net assets	$ 38,625	$ 41,914

Future minimum rental payments at September 30, 1991 and rental expense under operating leases follow.

(In thousands)

Future minimum rental payments		Rental expense	1991	1990	1989
1992	$ 59,538				
1993	52,880	Minimum rentals			
1994	43,268	(including rentals under			
1995	38,699	short-term leases)	$ 88,459	$ 86,146	$105,610
1996	34,060	Contingent rentals	11,999	10,795	12,341
Later years	176,096	Sublease rental income	(16,412)	(13,636)	(11,938)
	$404,541		$ 84,046	$ 83,305	$106,013

Source: Ashland Oil, Annual Report, 1991.

Alternatively, the rate of decline implicit in the MLPs reported for the next 5 years may be used to estimate the number of payments included in the $38.3 million in MLPs reported for periods after the initial five years.

The 1992 payment is $12.35 million, of which $7.78 million represents the current portion of the lease obligation, resulting in estimated interest of $4.57 million on a reported present value of $55.3 million. We can now estimate the interest rate on the capitalized leases as 8.3% ($4.57 million/$55.3 million). This rate should be compared to the firm's cost of capital and other long-term debt of similar maturity.

The interest rate can also be estimated by solving for the implicit interest rate (internal rate of return), which equates the MLPs and their present value. Both estimates should be the same in theory; in practice they may differ because of the imprecision of the disclosed data. In Ashland's case, the internal rate of return, which equates with the following stream of payments

Year	Payments
1992	$12.35 million
1993	10.27
1994	7.96
1995	6.59
1996	6.58
1997–2001*	6.58
2002*	5.40
	$82.05 million

*Assumes a level payment estimate (equal to that of year 5–1996) for the later year payments of $38.3 million: (5 × $6.58 million + $5.40 million).

with the present value of $55.3 million, is also[36] 8.3%.

Future MLPs under operating leases decline by 43% from 1992 to 1996; the first five years account for about 57% of total MLPs of $404.5 million. The remaining payments of $176 million thus represent 43% of the total MLPs. The rate of decline over the initial five years is only slightly below that of capitalized leases (46%). Moreover, a substantial portion (43%) of the MLPs will be paid after the first five years (as for capitalized leases), indicating substantial long-term commitments.

These characteristics suggest that Ashland's operating leases are substantially similar to its capitalized leases, and at the very least for comparative purposes, they

[36]Using another estimate (declining rate over seven years) for the stream of payments in the later years yields an implicit interest rate of 7.9%, which is relatively close to the 8.3% calculated under the other two methods. These estimation methods yield similar results as long as the initial principal payment is not a significant portion of the overall liability. This is the case when the remaining lease term is relatively long. For shorter periods, the timing of the payments can have a significant impact on the estimate. If (a portion of) the principal payment is made at the beginning of the year, the first year's expense will be a function more of the closing than the opening liability balance and estimates of the interest rate will diverge. In such cases, the use of the average liability balance will yield a better estimate. This method provides an estimate of interest rates in effect at the inception of the leases.

should be capitalized. *However, even if these characterisitcs did not mirror those of a capital lease, adjustment would also be appropriate to give liability recognition to the noncancellable minimum payments.*

The average lease term may be estimated at 10 years with the initial 5 years augmented by an additional 5 years ($176 million future payments/$34 million 1996 payment). Using the interest rate of 8.3% estimated for capitalized leases, the lease term of 10 years, and the estimated payment schedule, we can derive a present value of $275 million.

Ashland's Oil's stated leverage (financing debt-to-equity) ratio at September 30, 1991, is 106% (debt is $1532 million and equity is $1444 million). Since the right to use leased assets contributes to the cash generating ability of the firm, assets under operating leases contribute to a firm's leverage. Therefore, the present value of operating lease payments should be added to the reported debt, increasing it to $1807 million, resulting in an adjusted leverage ratio of 125%. The estimated present value of $275 million should also be added to the total assets to compute adjusted asset turnover and return-on-assets ratios.

Financial Reporting by Lessors

This section discusses sales-type and direct financing leases. Some capital leases may qualify as leveraged leases; such leases are beyond the scope of this text. Lessor financial reporting will be illustrated using the lessee example with the additional assumption that the leased equipment costs $500,000 to manufacture. Once again we assume that the lease is an operating lease for income tax purposes.

Sales-type Leases

Exhibit 8-15 presents financial reporting by a lessor for a sales-type lease using the lessee example. Part A illustrates the accounting recognition at inception and the determination of gross and net investment in the lease; part B provides the lessor's amortization schedule for the sales-type lease.

The lessor recognizes sales revenues of $641,766, the present value of the MLPs (net of executory costs). The cost of goods sold is the cost or carrying amount of the leased property. The *initial direct costs* may be treated as period costs and expensed as incurred for sales-type leases. The present value of the unguaranteed residual value of the leased property constitutes continuing investment by the lessor and is not included in costs charged against income.

The lessor's gross investment in the lease is $1,022,500, the sum of the MLPs and the unguaranteed residual value. Net investment in the lease is $651,270, determined by discounting the MLPs and the unguaranteed residual value at the interest rate implicit in the lease (9%), as shown in Part A.

The difference between the gross and net investment represents unearned income, the interest component of the transaction. Unearned income is systematically amortized to income over the lease term, using the interest method that reports a rate of return of 9% on the net investment in the lease. The lessor reports the current and noncurrent components of the net investment in the lease on the balance sheet. Contingent rentals, if any, are reported as they are earned. SFAS 13 requires an annual review of the

EXHIBIT 8-15
Lessor Financial Reporting

A. Sales-Type Lease

Lessor's Gross Investment in Leased Equipment

MLPs: $100,000 × 10	$1,000,000
Unguaranteed residual value	22,500
	$1,022,500

Lessor's Net Investment in Leased Equipment

Present value at 9% of an annuity of 10 payments of $100,000	$ 641,766
Present value at 9% of $22,500, 10 periods hence	9,504
	$ 651,270

Unearned Income

Gross investment in lease	$1,022,500
Less: Net investment	(651,270)
	$ 371,230

Accounting Recognition at Lease Inception

Sales revenue*	$ 641,766	
Cost of goods sold†	(490,496)	
Gross profit on sale		$151,270
Gross investment in lease	1,022,500	
Unearned income	(371,230)	
Net investment in lease		$651,270
Initial direct costs	(10,000)	
(may be treated as a period cost)		

*Present value of lease payments, excluding residual value.
†Cost to manufacture less PV of residual value.

B. Lessor Amortization Schedule: Sales-Type Lease, Years Ended December 31, 1990–1999

Year	Annual Payment Received (A)	Interest Income (B)	Reduction in Investment (C) = (A) − (B)	Net Investment (D)
January 1, 1990				$651,270
December 31, 1990	$ 100,000	$ 58,614	$ 41,386	609,884
December 31, 1991	100,000	54,890	45,110	564,774
December 31, 1992	100,000	50,830	49,170	515,604
December 31, 1993	100,000	46,404	53,596	462,008
December 31, 1994	100,000	41,581	58,419	403,589
December 31, 1995	100,000	36,323	63,677	339,912
December 31, 1996	100,000	30,592	69,408	270,504
December 31, 1997	100,000	24,345	75,655	194,849
December 31, 1998	100,000	17,536	82,464	112,385
December 31, 1999	100,000	10,115	89,885	22,500
Totals	$1,000,000	$371,230	$628,770	

EXHIBIT 8-15. *(Continued)*

C. Balance Sheet, Years Ended December 31, 1990–1991

| | Capital Lease | | | Operating Lease | |
	1990	1991		1990	1991
Current assets: Net investment in leases	$ 45,110	$ 49,170	Assets under lease	$500,000	$500,000
Long-term assets: Net investment in leases	564,774	515,604	Accumulated depreciation	(47,750)	(95,500)
			Net	$452,250	$404,500
Totals	$609,884	$564,774			

D(1). Income Statement Effect: Sales-Type Lease, Years Ended December 31, 1990–1999

Year	Sales Profit (A)	Interest Income (B)	Pretax Income (C) = (A) + (B)	Tax Expense (D) = (C) (35%)	Net Income (E) = (C) − (D)
1990	$ 151,270	$ 58,614	$209,884	$ 73,459	$136,425
1991		54,890	54,890	19,212	35,678
1992		50,830	50,830	17,790	33,039
1993		46,404	46,404	16,242	30,163
1994		41,581	41,581	14,553	27,027
1995		36,323	36,323	12,713	23,610
1996		30,592	30,592	10,707	19,885
1997		24,345	24,345	8,521	15,824
1998		17,536	17,536	6,138	11,399
1999		10,115	10,115	3,540	6,575
Totals	$ 151,270	$371,230	$522,500	$182,875	$339,625

D(2). Income Statement Effect: Operating Lease, Years Ended December 31, 1990–1999

Year	Rental Income (F)	Depreciation Expense (G)	Pretax Income (H) = (F) − (G)	Tax Expense (I) = 0.35(H)	Net Income (J) = (H) − (I)
1990	$ 100,000	$ 47,750	$ 52,250	$ 18,287	$ 33,963
1991	100,000	47,750	52,250	18,287	33,963
1992	100,000	47,750	52,250	18,287	33,963
1993	100,000	47,750	52,250	18,287	33,963
1994	100,000	47,750	52,250	18,287	33,963
1995	100,000	47,750	52,250	18,287	33,963
1996	100,000	47,750	52,250	18,287	33,963
1997	100,000	47,750	52,250	18,287	33,963
1998	100,000	47,750	52,250	18,287	33,963
1999	100,000	47,750	52,250	18,287	33,963
Totals	$1,000,000	$477,500	$522,500	$182,875	$339,625

*Totals affected by rounding.

EXHIBIT 8-15. *(Continued)*

D(3). *Income Effects of Lessor Accounting Methods,*
Years Ended December 31, 1990–1999

Sales-Type Lease Less Operating Lease

Year	Pretax Income	Net Income
1990	$157,634	$102,462
1991	2,640	1,716
1992	(1,420)	(923)
1993	(5,846)	(3,800)
1994	(10,669)	(6,935)
1995	(15,927)	(10,353)
1996	(21,658)	(14,078)
1997	(27,905)	(18,138)
1998	(34,714)	(22,564)
1999	(42,135)	(27,388)
Totals	$ 0	$ 0

E. *Disclosures Required For Lessor*

Sales-Type Lease, December 31				Operating Lease, December 31			
1990		**1991**		**1990**		**1991**	
1991	$ 100,000	1992	$ 100,000	1991	$100,000	1992	$100,000
1992	100,000	1993	100,000	1992	100,000	1993	100,000
1993	100,000	1994	100,000	1993	100,000	1994	100,000
1994	100,000	1995	100,000	1994	100,000	1995	100,000
1995	100,000	1996	100,000	1995	100,000	1996	100,000
Thereafter	400,000	Thereafter	300,000	Thereafter	400,000	Thereafter	300,000
Total MLPs	$ 900,000		$ 800,000	Total MLPs	$900,000		$800,000
Unearned income	(312,616)		(257,726)				
Net investment	$ 587,384*		$ 542,274*				
Current portion	45,110		49,170				
Noncurrent	542,274		493,104				
Net investment	$ 587,384*		$ 542,274*				

*These amounts do not include the unguaranteed residual value, $22,500.

F(1). *Cash Flow Effects of Lessor Accounting Methods: Direct Method,*
Years Ended December 31, 1990–1991

	Sales-Type Lease		Operating Lease	Difference
1990				
CFO				
Gross profit on sale	$ 151,270	Rental	$100,000	
Interest income	58,614			
Income tax paid	(18,287)		(18,287)	
	$ 191,597		$ 81,713	$ 109,884

EXHIBIT 8-15. *(Continued)*

	Sales-Type Lease		Operating Lease	Difference
Investment cash flows				
Net investment in lease	(151,270)			
Less: Reduction in net investment	41,386			
	$(109,884)		$ 0	$(109,884)
1991				
CFO				
Interest income	$ 54,890	Rental	$100,000	(45,110)
Income tax paid	(18,287)		(18,287)	
	$ 36,603		$ 81,713	$ (45,110)
Investment cash flows				
Reduction in net investment	$ 45,110		$ 0	$ 45,110

F(2). Effect of Lessor Accounting Method on CFO: Indirect Method,
Years Ended December 31, 1990–1991

	Sales-Type Lease	Operating Lease	Difference
1990			
Net income	$ 136,425	$ 33,963	
Addback: Depreciation	0	47,750	
Deferred tax credit	55,172	0	
CFO	$ 191,597	$ 81,713	$ 109,884
1991			
Net income	$ 35,678	$ 33,963	
Addback: Depreciation	0	47,750	
Deferred tax credit	925	0	
CFO	$ 36,603	$ 81,713	$ 45,110

estimated residual value. Nontemporary declines must be recognized; however, increases in value or subsequent reversals of declines cannot be reported.

Balance Sheet Effects (Exhibit 8-15C). The lessor reports the current and non-current components of net investment in sales-types leases, which total $564,774 ($609,884) as of December 31, 1991 (1990). Lessors using the operating lease method do not report any investment in leases, but they continue to report the assets on the balance sheet as long-term assets, net of accumulated depreciation.

In Part C, the lessor reports net assets under operating leases of $404,500 ($452,250) as of December 31, 1991 (1990). These figures assume straight-line depreciation over 10 years of the original cost of the asset less estimated residual value ($500,000–$22,500). The operating lease method reports lower net assets and, ignoring income effects, tends to increase return on assets relative to the sales-type lease method.

Income Statement Effects (Exhibit 8-15D). For sales-type leases, the lessor records profit at inception of $151,270. The annual rental of $100,000 is partly allocated to interest income to reflect a constant 9% return on the declining net investment in the lease. The balance of the rental payment is applied to amortize the net investment systematically over the lease term.

The operating lease method reports constant income over the lease term as straight-line depreciation is charged against the constant annual rental. The use of accelerated depreciation would result in a pattern of increasing income over the lease term as depreciation declines.

Thus the sales-type lease reports substantially higher income in the first year of the lease due to recognition of manufacturing profit at the inception of the lease. However, reported income declines thereafter due to declining interest income over the remainder of the lease term, relative to constant or increasing income under the operating lease method. As shown in part D(3), reported net income is higher under the operating lease method starting in the third year of the lease. Over the lease term, the total net income is, once again, the same under both methods.

Footnote Disclosures (Exhibit 8-15E). The sales-type lease method requires the disclosure of gross MLPs receivable, unearned income, and the current and noncurrent components of the net investment in leases. Lessors must also provide information on lease terms, future MLPs receivable over the next five years, and the aggregate thereafter. Disclosure for operating leases is limited to MLPs receivable over the next five years and the aggregate thereafter.

Cash Flow Effects (Exhibit 8-15F(1)). For the sales-type lease, the lessor reports 1990 operating cash flow of $191,597: sales profit of $151,270 at the inception of the lease, interest income of $58,614 at the end of the first year of the lease, less income tax paid[37] of $18,287. The operating lease method reports CFO of $81,713 ($100,000 less taxes of $18,287), a difference of $109,884.[38]

The sales-type lease method also results in a net investment of $651,270 and a reduction of $500,000 in the carrying amount of the leased property, an increased "investment" of $151,270 at inception. In addition, it reports an inflow of $41,386, reflecting the first year reduction in the net investment. Thus a net cash outflow for investment of $109,884 is reported using the sales-type lease method. No investment cash flows can be reported under the operating lease method.

During the remainder of the lease term, the sale-type lease method results in CFO equal to interest income less income tax paid; the operating lease method reports a larger

---

[37]Since tax regulations generally recognize only operating leases, the tax effect for sale-type leases is identical to that reported for operating leases. Annual rental income of $100,000, less depreciation of $47,750, (on the carrying amount of $500,000 less the residual value of $22,500, using the straight-line method), results in a tax payment of $18,287 [0.35 ($100,000 − $47,750)].

[38]Exhibit 8-15F(2) show the computation of operating cash flow under the indirect method.

CFO equal to the after-tax rental (constant over the lease term). Since interest income declines over the lease term, this difference in CFO increases. Simultaneously, a correspondingly higher reduction in net investment is recognized and reported as an increasing investment cash flow.

Note that total cash flow (operating plus investing) is unaffected by the method of lease accounting. The actual cash flow in each year is the lease payment received less income tax paid. Only under the operating lease method does CFO record faithfully the cash flows associated with the lease. Capitalization of the lease by the lessor reclassifies reported cash flows between operating and investing activities.

The use of sales-type lease accounting allows firms to recognize income earlier than the operating lease method. Lease capitalization also allows forms to report higher CFO at inception of the lease. This aggressive recognition of income and cash flows ("front end loading") improves financial ratios; it accurately reflects the firm's operations only if the risks and benefits of leased property have been fully transferred to the lessee and the lessor has no further performance obligation.

Direct Financing Leases

Financial reporting for direct financing leases reflects the fact that the leases are pure financing transactions. No sale is recognized at the inception of the lease, and there is no manufacturing or dealer profit. Only financing income is reported. Unlike sales-type leases, initial direct costs are not charged to income but instead are capitalized and amortized to income over the lease term.

Unearned income is the difference between the gross investment in the lease and the cost or carrying amount of the leased property. Both unearned income and initial direct costs are amortized to report a constant periodic return (effective interest method) on the net investment in the lease (gross investment plus initial direct costs less unearned income).

Lessors must disclose MLPs receivable over the next five fiscal years and the aggregate thereafter. Any allowance for uncollectibles, executory costs, unguaranteed residual value, and unearned income must be also be reported. The initial direct costs for direct financing leases should be disclosed separately.

Lessor Accounting for Operating Leases. Lessors must report property under operating leases along with similar property and depreciate it using methods applied to comparable property. No revenue can be recognized at the inception of the lease, and rental income must be reported as it is realized. Initial direct costs may be amortized over the lease term in proportion to periodic rental income or may be expensed as incurred. Minimum future rentals on noncancellable leases for the next five years must be disclosed.

Financial Reporting by Lessors: An Example

Exhibit 8-16 contains Pillsbury's footnote on its investments as a lessor. The company finances restaurant expansion through leases of land and buildings to Burger King franchisees. Building leases are direct financing leases; land leases are operating leases.

EXHIBIT 8-16. THE PILLSBURY COMPANY
Disclosures of Direct Financing Leases by Lessor

Notes to Consolidated Financial Statements

Investments as Lessor

Restaurant subsidiaries lease buildings and land to franchisees. The building portions of the leases are direct financing leases, while the land portions are operating leases. Substantially all leases are for 15 to 20 years, provide for minimum and contingent rentals, and require the franchisee to pay executory costs.

Minimum Future Lease Receipts During Fiscal Years Ending May 31

	Direct Financing Leases	Operating Leases
	(in millions)	
1989	$ 32.2	$ 30.0
1990	32.5	29.5
1991	32.4	29.4
1992	31.7	29.0
1993	31.2	28.4
Thereafter	282.2	$261.1
	$442.2	$407.4

Net Investment in Direct Financing Leases at May 31, 1987–1988

	1988	1987
	(millions)	
Minimum future lease receipts	$ 442.2	$ 475.5
Allowance for uncollectibles	(4.2)	(4.4)
Estimated unguaranteed residual value	8.7	5.0
Unearned amount representing interest	(247.7)	(271.0)
Net investment	$ 199.0	$ 205.1
Current portion included in receivables	(6.6)	(5.1)
Net investment in direct financing leases	$ 192.4	$ 200.0

	Year Ended May 31		
	(in millions)		
Rental Income	1986	1987	1988
Minimum rental income	$31.7	$31.8	$34.7
Contingent rental income	32.3	30.1	28.8
Totals	$64.0	$61.9	$63.5

Source: The Pillsbury Company, Annual Report, 1988.

Pillsbury discloses MLPs receivable in each of the next five years and in the aggregate thereafter. Note the long term of these leases; the average lease term for both direct financing and operating leases is about 14 years. Both sets of leases have similar characteristics (rate of decline, for example). We can assume that the operating leases do not meet the capitalization requirements of SFAS 13.

There are additional disclosures for the capitalized direct financing leases: current and noncurrent components, allowance for uncollectibles, estimated unguaranteed residual values, and unearned interest. We can see that most of the 1989 payments will be for interest (total MLP less current portion), and we can compute the interest rate inherent in these leases:

$$\frac{\$32.2 - \$6.6}{\$199.0} = 12.86\%$$

Contingent rentals are also reported. Such rentals probably depend on restaurant sales. The negative trend from 1986 to 1988 may suggest weakness in franchisee sales.

Financial Reporting for Sales with Leasebacks

Sale-leaseback transactions are sales of property by the owner which then leases it back from the buyer-lessor. Financial reporting for these transactions is governed by SFAS 28, Accounting for Sales with Leasebacks (1979), as amended by SFAS 66, Accounting for Sales of Real Estate (1982).

The amount and timing of profit (or loss) recognized on a sale-leaseback transaction are determined by the proportion of the rights to use the leased property retained by the owner-lessee after the sale. If all or substantially all the use rights are retained by the owner-lessee, it is a financing transaction, and no profit or loss on the transaction should be recognized.

The extent of continuing use is determined by the proportion of the present value of *reasonable rentals* relative to the fair value of assets sold and leased back. This proportion is used to assign sale-leaseback transactions to the following financial reporting categories:

Minor Leasebacks: Present value of reasonable rentals is less than 10% of the fair value of the leased property; the buyer-lessor obtains substantially all the rights to use the leased property. Any gain (or loss) on the transaction is recognized in full at the inception of the lease.

More than Minor but Less than "Substantially All" Leasebacks: Present value of reasonable rentals exceeds 10% but is less than 90% of the fair value of the asset sold; depending on specific criteria, some or all of the gain or loss must be deferred and amortized over the lease term.

"Substantially All" Leasebacks: Present value of MLPs equals or exceeds 90% of the fair value of property sold; the total gain (loss) must be deferred and amortized over the lease term. The leaseback is a financing transaction, and the gain (loss) is recognized as the leased property is used.

Lease Accounting Outside the United States

U.S. financial reporting standards for leases are the most detailed and comprehensive in the world. Lessee and lessor reporting standards in Canada, the Netherlands, and the United Kingdom are similar to those in the United States, but they are more general, and disclosure requirements are substantially poorer.

International Accounting Standards are representative; they require capitalization when substantially all the risks and rewards of ownership are transferred, based on four criteria similar to those used in the United States. However, capitalization is required,

1. When the lease term is for a major portion of the asset's life; it does not specify 75% as in the United States
2. The present value of the MLPs is equal to or greater than the fair value of the asset, unlike the 90% test specified in the United States.

Capitalization is less likely under these two criteria than under U.S. standards. In Germany and Japan, lease capitalization is uncommon since lease accounting follows tax rules. In Germany, capitalization is required when the lease term exceeds 90% of the economic life; the present value of minimum lease payments criterion is not used. Few countries provide detailed criteria for lessor capitalization or financial reporting standards for sale-leasebacks, real estate, and leveraged leases. Sale-leasebacks result in higher profits than allowed in the United States and should be analyzed with care.

As discussed earlier, U.S. GAAP footnote disclosures of lease payments can be used to capitalize operating leases and develop adjusted ratios. Footnote disclosures provided by foreign firms are rarely adequate to permit capitalization adjustments.

For example, in its Form 20-F for 1990, Beazer discloses that profit on a sale-leaseback was £6.6 million, accounting for nearly 10% of net income before extraordinary items under U.K. GAAP. A footnote states that, under U.S. GAAP, this gain would be deferred and recognized only over the life of the lease. No further disclosures are made regarding leases.

As non-U.S. financial statements generally lack detailed lease data, the analyst must look for indirect disclosures or must question management regarding lessee or lessor activities.

CONCLUSION

Financial liabilities can take many forms, from simple, full-coupon debt to off-balance-sheet operating leases. The analyst must be alert to the need to adjust financial statements for market values of debt, for financial instruments with equity characteristics, and for operating leases that should be capitalized. The effects of financing choices on reported income and cash flows must also be recognized.

Chapter 9 contains an analysis of employee benefit plans, an important form of "off-balance-sheet" financing. Other methods of obtaining the use of assets without showing related debt are discussed in Chapter 10. Chapter 14 will bring together many strands to provide a detailed analysis of the effects of debt financing.

Chapter 8

Problems

1. [Current liabilities, customer advances] The working capital accounts and net revenues of American Airlines for 1987 and 1988 are presented in Exhibit 8P-1.

A. Calculate the company's reported working capital and current, quick, and cash ratios for each year.

B. The air traffic liability primarily reflects tickets sold in advance. Discuss the treatment of this item when calculating an airline's short-term liabilities. Your answer should include a discussion of any differences between the air traffic liability and other liabilities.

C. Eliminate the air traffic liability and recompute the ratios in part A. Discuss the differences from your previous calculation.

D. Exhibit 8P-1 also presents data for Eastern Airlines. At December 31, 1988, Eastern was just months away from declaring bankcuptcy. Compare Eastern's short-term liquidity position with that of American Airlines at December 31, 1988.

E. The chapter states that accounts such as the air traffic liability may be better viewed as an indicator of future profitability rather than a liability. Evaluate this statement using the data in Exhibit 8P-1.

EXHIBIT 8P-1
Partial Balance Sheets, at December 31, 1987–1988 (in $ millions)

	American Airlines		Eastern Airlines	
	1987	1988	1987	1988
Cash and short-term investments	$1012.4	$1286.6	$ 332.9	$ 402.3
Net receivables	729.2	833.6	463.1	396.5
Inventories	299.4	375.1	182.1	163.7
Other current assets	105.3	119.7	44.3	37.4
Current assets	$2146.3	$2615.0	$1022.4	$ 999.9
Accounts payable	560.4	710.4	267.2	242.7
Accrued liabilities	728.5	1072.0	344.9	455.7
Air traffic liability*	577.0	800.0	390.5	302.4
Notes payable and current portion long-term debt	205.1	213.2	190.1	153.0
Current liabilities	$2071.0	$2795.6	$1192.7	$1153.8
Net revenues	$7198.0	$8824.3	$4447.5	$3806.1

*For Eastern Air Lines includes $7.8 million and 19.2 million in frequent flier miles for 1987 and 1988, respectively.

Source: 1988 annual reports.

2. [Understanding bond relationships, coupon versus effective interest] The Walk & Field Co. has outstanding bonds that were originally issued at a discount. During the year 19X2, the bond discount account decreased from $8652 to $7290. Interest paid on an annual basis is $7200. The market rate of interest was 12% when the bond was issued. Using the data given calculate:

    (i) Interest expense for 19X2.

    (ii) The face value of the bond.

    (iii) The coupon rate of the bond.

Note: You do not need present value calculations or tables to solve this problem.

3. [Bonds—book value versus market value] The long-term debt footnote for Sonat, Inc., at December 31, 1991, is presented in Exhibit 8P-2. The exhibit also presents the market price of some of the company's debt on the same date, taken from the Standard & Poor's *Bond Guide*. Using these data, estimate the market value of the company's long-term debt at December 31, 1991.

4. [Zero-coupon bonds] The Null Company issued a zero-coupon bond on January 1, 1991. The face value of the bond, due December 31, 1995 was $100,000. The bond was issued at an effective rate of 12% (compounded annually).

    A. Calculate the proceeds of the bond issue.

    B. Complete the following table on a pretax basis, assuming that all interest is paid in the year it is due.

	1991	1992	1993	1994	1995
Earnings before interest and taxes	$50,000	$50,000	$50,000	$50,000	$50,000
Cash flow from operations before interest and taxes	60,000	60,000	60,000	60,000	60,000
Interest expense					
Cash flow from operations					
Times interest earned					
Times interest earned (cash basis)					

    C. Assume that Null had raised the same amount of capital with a conventional bond issued at par paying interest annually and the principal at maturity. Complete the following table, under the same assumptions used in part B.

	1991	1992	1993	1994	1995
Earnings before interest and taxes	$50,000	$50,000	$50,000	$50,000	$50,000
Cash flow from operations before interest and taxes	60,000	60,000	60,000	60,000	60,000
Interest expense					
Cash flow from operations					
Times interest earned					
Times interest earned (cash basis)					

7. Long-Term Debt and Lines of Credit

<u>Long-Term Debt</u> – Long-term debt consisted of:

December 31,	1991	1990
	(In Thousands)	
Sonat Inc.		
Revolving Credit Agreement at rates based on prime, international, certificate of deposit or money-market lending rates (an effective rate of 5.32% at December 31, 1991) due December 31, 1994	$ 240,000	$ 112,000
9⅞% Notes due June 1, 1996	200,000	200,000
9½% Notes due August 15, 1999	100,000	100,000
7¼% Zero Coupon, Subordinated Convertible Notes due September 6, 2005 (face value $661,250,000)	249,580	232,424
9% Term Loan due through December 1993	8,000	12,000
8.65% Notes due through July 29, 1997	55,714	—
9.41% Notes due July 29, 1997	35,000	—
9% Notes due May 1, 2001	100,000	—
Southern Natural Gas Company		
7.7% Sinking Fund Debentures due through April 1991	—	2,000
11⅜% Sinking Fund Debentures due 1992 to 1994	—	100,000
9⅝% Notes due June 15, 1994	100,000	100,000
10% Notes due December 1995	100,000	100,000
8⅞% Notes due February 15, 2001	100,000	—
South Georgia Natural Gas Company		
9.85% Term Loan due December 31, 1997	4,400	—
Southern Energy Company		
Promissory Note (an effective rate of 6.75% at December 31, 1991) due through April 1999	40,000	45,000
Sonat Finance Inc.		
11⅛% Guaranteed Notes due June 1992	—	100,000
Other Notes and Capital Leases	1,832	2,704
Total Outstanding	1,334,526	1,106,128
Less Long-Term Debt Due within One Year	19,435	12,102
	$1,315,091	$1,094,026

Source: Sonat, *1991 Annual Report.*

EXHIBIT 8P-2. *(Continued)*

Market Values of Publicly Traded Debt at December 31, 1991

Issuer	Coupon	Maturity	Price	YTM*
Sonat, Inc. (rating BBB+)				
Notes	9⅞%	July 1, 1996	110.125	7.16%
Notes	9%	May 1, 2001	107.750	7.81%
Southern Natural Gas (rating A−)				
Notes	9⅝%	June 15, 1994	107	6.49%
Notes	8⅞%	February 15, 2001	108.500	7.57%

*Yield to maturity.
Source: Standard & Poor's Corporation, *Bond Guide*, January 1992.

D. Using the results of parts B and C, discuss the impact on reported cash flow from operations and interest coverage of Null's choice of bond.

E. How would your answers to parts B–D change if income taxes were considered?

5. [Issue and repurchase of debt] On January 1, 1994, Derek Corporation issues $20 million (face value) coupon bonds due on January 1, 2014. Interest is payable semiannually on January 1 and July 1 at a coupon rate of 10%. The market (effective interest) rate on the date of issuance is 8%.

A. Compute the impact of the bond issuance on Derek's balance sheet, income statement, and statement of cash flows for 1994 and 1995.

Assume that Derek repurchases the entire bond issue on July 1, 1997 at an effective interest rate of 10%.

B. Calculate the gain or loss recorded by Derek as a result of the repurchase.

C. Discuss whether this gain (loss) should be considered a component of continuing operating income.

D. Discuss at least two reasons that would explain why Derek would replace 8% coupon debt when current interest rates are higher.

6. [Zero-coupon bonds] Sonat, Inc., issued 7¼% zero-coupon notes due September 6, 2005, with a face value of $661,250,000. The liability shown on Sonat's balance sheet on December 31, 1991 was $249,580,000.

A. Calculate interest expense for the notes for 1992.

B. Calculate the liability for the notes shown on Sonat's balance sheet on December 31, 1992.

C. Compare the impact of these notes with that of conventional notes with the same interest rate on cash flow from operations in 1992 and over the life of the notes.

D. Compare the impact of these notes with that of conventional notes with the same interest rate on other components of cash flow over the life of the notes.

7. [Preferred shares, debt ratios, book value; 1989 CFA adapted] The balance sheet of Mother Prewitt's Handmade Cookie Corporation (MPH) follows:

	December 31, 19X1

Assets

Cash	$15,000,000
Plant and equipment (net)	17,000,000
Total	$32,000,000

Liabilities

Long-term debt	$ 4,000,000

Stockholders' Equity

Preferred stock—issued 100,000, par value $150, 5% cumulative, liquidation value $160, callable at $165	15,000,000
Common stock—issued 200,000 shares, par value $75	15,000,000
Capital contributed in excess of par value	100,000
Retained earnings (deficit)	(2,100,000)
	$28,000,000
Total liabilities and equity	$32,000,000

Note: Preferred dividends are two years in arrears.

A. Calculate the company's debt-to-equity ratio assuming the company's preferred shares are:

(i) Nonredeemable.

(ii) Redeemable by stockholders at $160 per share.

B. Due to several years of losses, the company is being offered for sale. Calculate the book value per share of MPH *common stock* assuming the company's preferred shares are:

(i) Nonredeemable.

(ii) Redeemable by stockholders at $160 per share.

C. Discuss whether the preferred shares should be considered as debt or equity, making reference to your answers to parts A and B.

8. [Analysis of lessee; 1992 CFA adapted] If a lease is capitalized, as compared to being treated as an operating lease, describe the first year impact on:

(i) The current ratio.

(ii) The debt-to-equity ratio.

(iii) Operating income.

(iv) Net income.

(v) Cash flow from operations.

9. [Leases, effect of interest rate] For assets under capital leases, lease expense has two components: interest and amortization (depreciation). Assume that a lease can be capitalized at either 9% or 10%. Compare the effects of this choice *in the first year and over the life of the lease on:*

(i) Interest expense.

(ii) Amortization expense.

(iii) Total lease expense

(iv) Cash flow from operations.

(v) Average assets.

(vi) Average liabilities.

Problems 10–11 are based on data from the financial statements of the DQE Company presented in Exhibit 8P-3. The questions touch on various aspects of debt and solvency analysis. The questions may be assigned separately or together.

10. [Bonds, preferred shares, debt ratios]

A. Prepare a capitalization table for DQE listing its financing debt and equity. Using that table, calculate the company's debt-to-equity ratio.

B. Calculate the company's times interest earned and fixed charges coverage ratio.

11. [Analysis of lessee] Note E of DQE's *1991 Annual Report* discloses future minimum lease payments for its capital and operating leases.

A. Estimate the interest rate implicit in the capital leases:

(i) Based on 1992 lease interest expense.

(ii) Based on minimum lease payments over the life of the leases.

B. The rates calculated by the two methods are not similar. Suggest why, based on the pattern of capital lease payments.

C. Discuss whether DQE's operating leases should be capitalized for purposes of analysis. Justify your answer.

D. Compute the present value of the minimum lease payments for DQE's operating leases. Use the higher of the interest rates calculated in part A.

E. Describe the impact of capitalizing the operating leases on DQE's statement of cash flows.

EXHIBIT 8P-3. DQE
Selected Financial Information

A. Condensed Capitalization and Liabilities
December 31, 1991 (in $ thousands)

Trade payables and accruals	$ 229,518
Dividends payable	25,545
Sinking fund and purchase requirements	28,665
Current portion of long-term debt and capital leases	119,428
Current liabilities	$ 403,156
Long-term debt	1,420,726
Obligations under capital leases	87,861
Other long-term liabilities	774,502
Long-term liabilities	$2,283,089
Nonredeemable preferred and preference stock	121,906
Redeemable preferred and preference stock	45,437
Deferred employee stock ownership plan benefit	(30,000)
Subtotal	$ 137,343
Common stock	674,437
Retained earnings	436,684
Total common equity	$1,111,121
Total liabilities and equity	$3,934,709

B. Condensed Statement of Consolidated Income,
for Year Ended December 31, 1991 (in $ thousands)

Revenues	$1,199,468
Operating expenses	(932,562)
Operating income	$ 266,906
Other income	14,738
Income before interest and taxes	$ 281,644
Interest expense	(131,397)
Preferred stock dividends	(10,801)
Income tax expense	(5,881)
Net income	$ 133,565

C. Supplemental Cash Flow Information (in $ thousands)

Cash paid during the year for interest	$ 136,147
Noncash investing and financing activities: Capital lease obligations recorded	$ 22,208

EXHIBIT 8P-3. *(Continued)*

D. Note E—Leases

Leased nuclear fuel is amortized as the fuel is burned. The amortization of all other leased property is based on the rental payments made. Such payments for capital and operating leases are charged to operating expenses on the Statement of Consolidated Income. The following summarizes those rental payments reported in the Statement of Consolidated Income for the three years ended December 31, 1991.

Amounts in Thousands of Dollars for Year Ended December 31,	1991	1990	1989
Operating leases	$ 65,414	$ 65,989	$ 65,292
Amortization of capital leases	39,323	43,368	29,287
Interest on capital leases	10,057	10,334	8,555
Total Rental Payments	**$114,794**	$119,691	$103,134

Future minimum lease payments for capital leases are related principally to building leases and the estimated usage of nuclear fuel financed through leasing arrangements. Minimum payments for operating leases are related principally to Beaver Valley Unit 2 and the corporate headquarters. Future minimum lease payments at December 31, 1991 were as follows:

Amounts in Thousands of Dollars for Year Ending December 31,	Operating Leases	Capital Leases
1992	$ 66,507	$ 52,998
1993	65,187	35,134
1994	62,468	31,000
1995	61,236	14,589
1996	61,221	8,395
1997 and thereafter	1,302,161	36,000
Total Minimum Lease Payments	**$1,618,780**	178,116
Less amount representing interest		(45,387)
Present value of minimum lease payments for capital leases		$132,729

Source: DQE, *1991 Annual Report.*

F. Describe the impact of capitalizing the operating leases on DQE's leverage and interest coverage ratios.

12. [Analysis of lessee] The Tolrem Company has decided to lease an airplane on January 1, 1993. The firm and its lessor have not yet decided the terms of the lease. Assume that the terms can be adjusted to permit Tolrem to either capitalize the lease or record it as an operating lease.

A. State the effect (higher, lower, or equal) of the choice of capitalizing the lease on the following for 1993 (the initial year of the lease):

   (i) Cash flow from operations

   (ii) Financing cash flow

   (iii) Investing cash flow

   (iv) Net cash flow

   (v) Debt-to-equity ratio

   (vi) Interest coverage ratio

   (vii) Operating income

   (viii) Net income

   (ix) Deferred tax asset or liability

   (x) Taxes paid

   (xi) Pre- and post tax return on assets

   (xii) Pre- and post tax return on equity

B. You recall that the difference between net income under the two methods changes direction at some point during the lease term. State which answers to part A will change in the year after the switch occurs and describe the change.

C. Assume that Tolrem enters into new aircraft leases at a constant annual rate. Describe the effect of the choice of accounting method on the items in part A.

13. [Analysis of lessee; 1992 CFA adapted] Dale Mail leases a computer from Gray Computing Services for 10 years at an annual rental of $2400. Dale guarantees that the residual value will be $4000 at the end of the lease. Dale uses the straight-line method of depreciation. Assume that the lease is accounted for by Dale as a capital lease.

A. Calculate the present value of the lease using a 9% interest rate.

B. Calculate total lease expense in the first year of the lease.

C. Describe the trend of total lease expense over the lease term.

Problems 14 and 15 are based on information taken from Vicorp Restaurants, Inc.'s 1991 Annual Report and presented in Exhibit 8P-4.

14. [Convertible bonds] The company's 13½% convertible bonds are due in the year 2009 with interest payable semiannually. The bonds are convertible into common stock any time prior to maturity at $25.20 per share. Few bonds were converted in 1990–1991. The reduction in bonds outstanding was due primarily to a partial call of $20 million of the bonds by the company in 1991.

A. Discuss the factors that must be considered when deciding whether these bonds should be treated as debt or equity. Compare the firm's leverage ratios under these two alternatives.

B. Discuss why few bondholders exercised the conversion right, even after the bonds were called.

EXHIBIT 8P-4. VICORP RESTAURANTS
Extracts from Financial Statements, Fiscal 1990–1991 (in $ thousands)

	1990	1991
Short-term debt and capital leases	$ 3,087	$ 2,569
Long-term debt	40,186	32,563
Capital lease obligations	23,691	20,696
Stockholders' equity	102,622	110,715
Earnings before interest and tax	23,560	16,526
Interest expense	9,428	8,027
Capitalized interest	205	533
Long-Term Debt		
13½% convertible subordinated bonds	$ 38,517	$ 18,394
Other	1,815	14,293
	$ 40,332	$ 32,687
Less: Current maturities	146	124
	$ 40,186	$ 32,563

Trading range for Vicorp's common stock during fiscal 1991:

	Quarter			
	1	2	3	4
High	21⅞	27¾	31⅜	28½
Low	6¾	21½	25	20¾

Minimum Payments for Operating and Capital Leases, End of Fiscal 1991
(in $ thousands)

	Capital leases	Operating leases	Lease and sublease rentals
1992	$ 5,154	$ 17,936	$ (2,632)
1993	4,217	17,195	(2,320)
1994	3,951	16,695	(2,140)
1995	3,859	15,498	(1,879)
1996	3,695	14,173	(1,772)
Later years	19,136	94,220	(8,286)
Total minimum lease payments	40,012	$ 175,717	$(19,029)
Less amount representing interest	16,871		
Present value of minimum lease payments	23,141		
Current maturities of capitalized lease obligations	2,445		
Capitalized lease obligations	$ 20,696		

Source: Vicorp Restaurants, Inc., *1991 Annual Report.*

15. [Analysis of lessee]

A. Estimate the interest rate used to compute the present value of $20,696,000 for Vicorp's capital leases.

B. The footnote reflects expected (1992) minimum lease payments of $5,154,000 for capital leases and $17,936,000 for operating leases. Assuming that these are the actual lease payments made in 1992, discuss their impact on 1992 operating and financing cash flows.

C. State whether the operating leases should be capitalized for analytic purposes. Justify your conclusion.

D. Estimate the present value of Vicorp's operating leases.

E. (i) Calculate Vicorp's reported leverage and interest coverage ratios based on reported data.

   (ii) Adjust these ratios for the effect of capitalizing the operating leases from part D.

F. Assume that at December 31, 1991, the "market" rate for leases similar to the ones undertaken by Vicorp was 7%.

   (i) What would be the current value of Vicorp's lease obligations?

   (ii) How would these values alter the ratios calculated in part E?

   (iii) Discuss whether the effect of the interest rate change is solely to increase Vicorp's liabilities and, therefore, reduce its net worth.

16. [Leases, tax effects, cash flows and deferred taxes] On January 1, 1993, two identical companies, Caramino Corp. and Aglianico, Inc., lease similar assets with the following characteristics:

1. Economic life is 8 years.

2. Lease term is 5 years.

3. Lease payments of $10,000 per year are payable at the *beginning* of each year with the first payment due on January 1, 1993.

4. Fair market value is $48,000.

5. Each firm has an incremental borrowing rate of 8% and a tax rate of 40%.

Caramino capitalizes the lease while Aglianico uses the operating lease method. Both firms use straight-line depreciation for all assets on their financial statements. Assume that both firms treat the lease as an operating lease on their tax returns.

Assume that each firm generates income before lease-related expense and income taxes of $20,000 in 1993.

A. Compute earnings before interest and taxes and earnings before taxes for 1993 for each firm. Identify the sources of the difference.

B. Compute the deferred taxes resulting from the lease for each firm in the first year of the lease.

C. Compute the effect of the lease on the 1993 reported cash flow from operations for both firms. Explain the difference.

D. Compute the impact of the lease on the 1993 reported financing cash flows of both firms. Explain the difference.

E. Compute the impact of the lease on the 1993 reported cash flow for investing of both firms. Explain the difference.

F. Using your answers to parts C–E, compute the effect of the lease on the 1993 reported net cash flow of both firms. Explain why they are identical.

G. Using your answers to parts A–F, discuss the reasons why Caramino and Aglianico may have wished to use different accounting methods for the same transaction.

17. [Analysis of lessee] The Pallavi Company leases equipment (fair market value of $125,000) from Priyanka Corp. The lease contains a bargain purchase option and requires 15 annual minimum lease payments of $15,000 payable at the end of each year. The economic life of the equipment is 20 years. The lessee's borrowing rate is 10%, and the lessor's implicit rate is 8%.

A. Compute the amount at which Pallavi should capitalize the lease.

B. Select the number of years over which Pallavi should depreciate the leased equipment.

C. Discuss whether the absence of a bargain purchase option would change your answer to part B.

18. [Analysis of lessor] Carignane Corp., a manufacturer/lessor, enters into a sales-type lease agreement with Mourvedre, Inc., as lessee. The lessor capitalizes the lease rather than reporting it as an operating lease.

Describe the effect (lower, higher, or none) of this choice on the following accounts and ratios of Carignane (the lessor) in the 1st and 9th years of a 10-year lease:

    (i) Total assets

   (ii) Revenues

  (iii) Expenses

  (vi) Asset turnover ratio

   (v) Interest income

  (vi) Cost of goods sold

 (vii) Net income

(viii) Retained earnings

  (ix) Income taxes paid

   (x) Posttax return on assets

  (xi) Cash flow from operations

 (xii) Investment cash flow

19. [Analysis of lessor and lessee] On January 1, 1994, The Malbec Company leases a Willmess winepress to the Baldes Group under the following conditions:

1. Annual lease payments are $20,000 for 20 years.

2. At the end of the lease term, the press is expected to have a value of $5500.

3. The fair market value of the press is $185,250.

4. The estimated economic life of the press is 30 years.

5. Malbec's implicit interest rate is 12%; Baldes' incremental borrowing rate is 10%.

6. Malbec reports similar presses at $150,000 in finished goods inventory.

A. Based on the data given, state whether Baldes should treat this lease as an operating or a capital lease. Justify your answer. What additional information would help to answer the question?

B. Assume that Baldes capitalizes the lease. List the financial statement accounts affected (at January 1, 1994) by that decision and calculate each effect.

C. Assume that Baldes uses straight-line depreciation for financial reporting purposes. Compute the income statement, balance sheet, and statement of cash flows effects of the lease for 1994 and 1995 under each lease accounting method.

D. Based on the data given, state whether Malbec should treat this lease as an operating or a sales-type lease. Justify your answer. What additional information would help to answer the question?

E. Assume that Malbec treats the lease as an operating lease. List the financial statement accounts affected (at January 1, 1994) by that decision and calculate each effect.

F. Assume that Malbec treats the lease as a sales-type lease and that the residual value of the winepress is *not* guaranteed by the lessee. List the financial statement accounts affected (at January 1, 1994) by that decision and calculate each effect.

G. Assume that Malbec uses straight-line depreciation for financial reporting purposes. Compute the income statement, balance sheet, and statement of cash flows effects of the lease for 1994 and 1995 under each lease accounting method.

20. [Adjusting lessor financial statements] The Knogo Corporation engages in the manufacturing and marketing of security devices, that are sold or leased to customers. Information from Knogo's financial statements is presented in Exhibit 8P-5.

A. Convert Knogo's operating leases to sales-type leases. Estimate the effect of this conversion on Knogo's assets, liabilities, and stockholders' equity.

B. Discuss how the choice of accounting method has affected Knogo's reported balance sheet, income statement, statement of cash flow, and financial ratios.

21. [Bond covenants and financing options] As manager of the Sleepman company you are facing the following problem. You have to acquire $1 million in plant and equipment. You can acquire these assets by outright purchase and/or leasing. If you purchase the assets, the funds can be raised from any combination of preferred shares or bonds (including zero coupon). If you lease, the lease can be structured as either an operating or capital lease. Your only constraint is that you cannot violate any of the following bond convenants:

EXHIBIT 8P-5. KNOGO CORPORATION
Selected Financial Information

A. Balance Sheet

	February 29, 1992
Cash and marketable securities	$ 8,276,900
Accounts receivable (net)	35,867,300
Net investment, sales-type leases	17,853,900
Security investments (net)	25,655,600
Property, plant, and equipment	21,221,800
Intangibles and other assets	4,496,700
Total assets	$113,372,200
Notes payable	$ 32,447,900
Accounts payable and accrued liabilities	16,879,800
Income taxes, deferred and payable	1,436,700
Deferred lease rentals	3,182,300
Total liabilities	$ 53,946,700
Common stock	34,969,800
Retained earnings	9,889,400
Cumulative translation adjustment	14,566,300
Total equity	$ 59,425,500
Total liabilities and equity	$113,372,200

B. 1992 Income Statement

Revenues	$ 80,695,000
Cost of security devices	(30,611,000)
Gross profit	$ 50,084,000

C. NET INVESTMENT IN SALES-TYPE LEASES
AND OPERATING LEASE DATA

The Company is the lessor of security devices under agreements expiring in various years through 1999. The net investment in sales-type leases consist of:

	February 29, 1992	February 28, 1991
Minimum lease payments receivable	$ 23,982,700	$ 22,088,000
Allowance for uncollectable minimum lease payments	(934,600)	(662,600)
Unearned income	(5,298,300)	(5,156,500)
Portion of lease payments representing executory costs	(717,700)	(588,800)
Unguaranteed residual value	821,800	594,800
	$ 17,853,900	$ 16,274,900

EXHIBIT 8P-5. *(Continued)*

At February 29, 1992, future minimum lease payments receivable under sales-type leases and noncancellable operating leases are as follows:

	Sales-type Leases	Operating Leases
1993	$ 7,704,700	$ 10,165,900
1994	6,943,100	8,097,200
1995	5,207,400	6,177,000
1996	3,021,000	3,920,500
1997 and thereafter	1,106,500	2,283,400
	$ 23,982,700	$ 30,644,000

Source: Knogo Corporation, *1992 Annual Report.*

1. Times interest earned (cash basis) calculated as

$$\frac{\text{Cash from operations before interest}}{\text{Interest payments + Preferred dividends}}$$

   must be at least 1.8.

2. Fixed charge coverage ratio (cash basis) calculated as

$$\frac{\text{Cash from operations before interest and rent payments}}{\text{Interest payments + Rent payments + Preferred dividends}}$$

   must be at least 1.4.

3. Debt to gross tangible assets calculated as

$$\frac{\text{Long-term debt + Capital lease liability}}{\text{Gross tangible fixed assets}}$$

   must not exceed 0.50.

The company has made the following financial projections for the coming year:

Interest expense (= interest paid)	$ 200,000
Preferred dividends	0
Cash flow from operations before interest	390,000
Lease payments	0
Long-term debt	2,000,000
Capital lease liability	0
Tangible fixed assets (gross)	5,000,000

These amounts include the operating results generated by the new plant and equipment. They exclude, however, the accounting impacts of the new plant and equipment (i.e., depreciation, interest expense, lease payments) as well as the asset or liability that may arise from acquisition of the asset. These depend on the mode of financing and on any accounting choices associated with the financing method.

For simplicity, assume that all financing is available at an interest rate of 10% with a maturity of 10 years. Similarly, any required depreciation or amortization should assume a life of 10 years using the straight-line method and zero residual value. Ignore income taxes.

A. Assume that there are five alternative financing methods:

1. Issue preferred shares and buy the assets.
2. Issue conventional (full-coupon) bonds and buy the assets.
3. Issue zero-coupon bonds and buy the assets.
4. Lease the assets; account for the lease as a capital lease.
5. Lease the assets; account for the lease as an operating lease.

Calculate the three ratios in the bond covenants for each of these five alternatives for the first year. Discuss which of the alternatives would permit Sleepman to acquire the assets without violating at least one of the covenants.

B. Assume that the assets are divisible (you can acquire any amount using any of the modes of financing). Calculate a combination of financing techniques that will enable Sleepman to acquire the assets without violating any of the covenants.

9

PENSIONS AND OTHER POSTEMPLOYMENT BENEFITS

INTRODUCTION

PENSION PLANS
Defined Contribution Pension Plans
Defined Benefit Pension Plans

DEFINED BENEFIT PENSION PLANS
Estimating Benefit Obligations
Factors Affecting Benefit Obligations
Service Cost
Interest Cost
Actuarial Gains and Losses
Prior Service Costs
Benefits
Pension Plan Assets
Pension Funding—Contributions
Return on Assets
Benefits

ACCOUNTING FOR PENSIONS UNDER SFAS 87
Computing Pension Cost
Service Cost and Interest Cost
Expected Return on Assets
Net Amortization and Deferral

Amortization of Prior Service Cost
Amortization of Transition Asset or Liability
Disclosure of Plan Status

ANALYSIS OF PENSION COSTS AND LIABILITY
Importance of Assumptions
Impact of Assumptions on Obligations
Impact of Assumptions on Pension Cost
Pension Analysis: Plan Status and Plan Costs
Motivation for Adjustments to Liability and Cost

ANALYZING PENSION PLAN DISCLOSURES
The General Motors Plan
Estimating GM's Pension Status
Minimum Liability Provision
Implications for General Motors
GM's Pension Costs
Analysis of GM Pension Trends
Pension Obligation Trends
Trends in Pension Cost
Investment Performance Trends
Cash Flow Trends
Estimating Future Pension Cost
The Importance of Pension Plans to GM

IMPACT OF DISCONTINUITIES
Acquisitions and Divestitures
Curtailments and Settlements

NON-U.S. REPORTING REQUIREMENTS

OTHER POSTEMPLOYMENT BENEFITS
Estimating Health Care Benefits
Computing Postretirement Benefit Cost
Disclosure of Plan Status
Importance of Assumptions
Effect of Assumptions

Transition Methods
Effects of Transition Method
Transition in Practice
Analysis of General Electric
Forecasting Postretirement Benefit Cost
Using SFAS 106 Disclosures
Non-U.S. GAAP Treatment

PRERETIREMENT BENEFITS

SUMMARY

INTRODUCTION

This chapter discusses the analysis of pension and other postemployment benefit plans. Such plans include pension or profit-sharing plans as well as life and health insurance benefits after retirement. As the cost of such plans has grown significantly, especially for large (often unionized) companies with generous benefits, the accounting for these benefits has become a significant issue. The FASB has issued several important new standards on accounting for postemployment benefits in recent years.

PENSION PLANS

A pension plan is an agreement, usually in writing, under which an employer agrees to pay monetary benefits to employees once their period of active service has come to an end. The payment of benefits is normally dependent on meeting certain requirements such as age and number of years of service. The deferred compensation nature of pension plans may motivate employees to stay with a firm for a longer period of time, at least until vesting. Some labor economists therefore consider pensions as "implicit contracts" between the firm and its employees.[1]

[1]The "implicit contract" argument suggesting that pensions "tie" employees to a firm is further supported by evidence (as our example in Exhibit 9–1 will show) that given an equal level of deferred compensation, the *present value* of that compensation will tend to be much less for younger workers as compared to older workers. Thus, defined benefit plans generally undercompensate employees far away from retirement and overcompensate them in the later years. On average, the over and under compensation should even out. However, for young employees to obtain the average fair wage they must work the "full" term to make up for the early period of undercompensation.

The "implicit contract" argument has further implications (discussed in later sections) in terms of measuring the pension liability and in explaining motivations for plan terminations. It should be noted that the implicit contract view of pensions is by no means unanimous (see Bulow (1982)).

The pension fund, where one exists, is an intermediary used to satisfy the employer's pension obligations. The employer makes payments to the fund. The fund is invested, and the original payments plus the earnings on those payments are used to make pension payments to employees. In the United States, pension plans are virtually always funded because of the requirements of the Employee Retirement Income Security Act of 1974 (ERISA) and tax advantages, including tax deductibility of the employer's contribution and tax-exempt status of earnings on fund investments. Outside the United States, pension obligations are often unfunded.

Box 9-1 discusses in greater detail incentives for the creation and funding of pension plans. The discussion contained therein can serve as a useful background in understanding the implications of the analytical procedures discussed in the chapter.

The relationship among employer, employees, and fund can be seen from the following diagram:

Employer
(makes contribution to)
↓
Pension Fund
(invests employer contributions
and makes benefit payments to)
↓
Employees

Two types of pension plan exist; the defined contribution plan and the defined benefit plan. Accounting for the former is straightforward. Major accounting and analytical issues discussed in this chapter are related to defined benefit plans.

BOX 9-1
Incentives for Overfunding and Underfunding of Pension Plans

Tax incentives are a powerful motivation for both the existence of pension plans and for firms to overfund their pension plans. Contributions to a pension plan are tax deductible (subject to IRS limits), and the income earned by the pension fund is tax exempt. Because employees pay taxes on pensions only when the benefits are actually received,* money in a pension plan is able to grow at a faster (compounded tax-free) rate than if it were held by either the firm or its employees. *Ceteris paribus*, firms with higher tax rates should have a greater incentive to fund pension plans compared to those with lower tax rates or tax loss carryforwards.

Firms facing a temporary downturn in cash flows must reduce capital spending, cut dividends, or obtain external financing. Myers and Majluf (1984) argued that management would prefer to use internal funds to fund investments as opposed to either cutting dividends or obtaining costly (due to administrative and underwriting fees) external financing. When management has superior information relative to potential investors/creditors as to the desirability of certain projects, any new securities issued would be underpriced. Therefore, to have internal funds available, managers build up "financial slack." Pension plans (with their added benefits in the form of favorable tax treatment) can be used to store this slack. When needed, the firm can draw on it by reducing future contributions (by changing actuarial methods or assumptions) or by terminating the pension plan.

In addition to the bonding mechanism implied by the "implicit contract" view of pensions, firms in effect turn their employees into creditors of the firm by underfunding pension plans. This can act as an effective "control mechanism" with respect to management (who are also the beneficiaries of the pension plan) and the rank and file employees. Management has an incentive not to take any actions that might hurt the firm in the long run. Moreover, the fact that managers are also creditors means that other bondholders will be less fearful of any actions that would benefit shareholders at the expense of creditors. This would reduce the monitoring costs of creditors and hence the cost of debt to the firm. With respect to employees, underfunding can act as a control mechanism on unions who might otherwise make demands on the firm that could hurt the economic well-being of the shareholders.

Francis and Reiter (1987) examined the pension plan status of a sample of 255 firms over the years 1980 and 1981. They found (consistent with the arguments presented here) that a firm's funding status was related in a direct fashion to its tax status (discussed shortly) and capital availability; i.e., the higher the tax rate and the more financial slack available, the higher the funding status. Conversely, separate pension plans for unions and higher benefits per employee were found to be significantly related to the underfunding of plans. This result is consistent with firms using the underfunding of plans as a control mechanism.

> The support found for labor underfunding incentives suggests that for some firms a long-term or implicit contract is evidenced. Other firms may choose, as a policy matter, to adopt the view that pension plans could be terminated at any time and overfund them. Tax and financial slack motivations are consistent with this point of view. Therefore it is not possible to reach an unambiguous conclusion as to which view of the pension contract is 'correct.' Both views of pension promises appear to co-exist in our sample and this is one of the choices or tradeoffs firms can make.[†]

Thus, the role of a pension plan and its funding status is highly dependent on the specific situation of the firm and its relationship with its employees.

With respect to the tax status, results were highly dependent on how tax status was measured. Firms were divided on a zero–one basis: "zero" firms had tax loss carryforwards, and "one" firms did not. A "zero" tax status was consistent with underfunding and a "one" tax status with overfunding. However, when tax status was based on the firm's actual average tax rate, the results were also significant but in the opposite directions! Higher tax rates were associated with underfunding. Francis and Reiter's explanation for these results was

> One reason for this apparent anomaly is a connection between profitability and average tax rate. Highly profitable firms in the sample have higher average tax rates (correlation of $r = 0.36$). *If highly profitable firms are able to earn higher after-tax returns on internal investments than on tax-free pension fund investments, then the incentive is to minimize rather than maximize pension funding.*[‡]

In addition to the pension-specific variables examined, they also found that firms with higher debt/equity ratios tended to underfund their plans, consistent with the debt covenant hypothesis that holds that firms would be reluctant to lower income and net worth if it could affect the status of their debt covenants.[§]

---

*For many employees, the marginal tax rate at retirement will be lower than the rate during their peak working years, thus providing further tax-induced incentives for the existence of pension plans.

†Francis, Jere R and Sara Ann Rieter "Determinants of Corporate Pension Funding Strategy" Journal of Accounting and Economics (1987), p. 35.

‡Ibid., p. 54 (emphasis added).

§Prior to SFAS 87 a firm's funding policy and its method of recognizing pension expense were equivalent.

Defined Contribution Pension Plans

The accounting is quite simple for a *defined contribution plan*. The employer is obligated to make only a specified contribution that may be fixed or variable (e.g., profit-sharing plans). There is no promise of any specific level of future benefit. The pension cost is exactly the same as the contribution made. In this case it is the employees who bear the risk of investment performance. If the contributions are invested well, benefits will be high; poor investments result in lower benefits. In the case of defined contribution plans, the employer's balance sheet asset or liability for pensions reflects the excess or shortfall in payments relative to the specified contributions. Shifting the investment risk to employees simplifies the accounting considerably. The remaining discussion of pension plan accounting will deal solely with defined benefit plans.

Defined Benefit Pension Plans

The more difficult accounting issues pertain to *defined benefit pension plans*. Under a defined benefit plan an employer promises a specified monetary benefit upon retirement. In a "flat benefit" plan, it will be fixed (e.g., $50 per month for each year worked). More commonly, in a "pay-related" plan, it will be a function of employee earnings, that is, final salary (e.g., final year compensation or highest three of last five years compensation) or "career average" earnings. The accounting for pay-related plans is necessarily more complicated than is that for "flat benefit" plans because of the difficulty of incorporating predictions of future employee earnings in the former case.

All defined benefit plans share one essential characteristic—the plan sponsor (employer) bears the investment risk. By promising a specific benefit, the employer has agreed to make whatever contributions are necessary to provide the promised benefits. As discussed shortly, the employer must first estimate future benefit payments and then work backward to estimate the contributions necessary to make those payments.

Prior to SFAS 87, adopted in 1985, employer accounting for pension plans was governed by APB 8, adopted in 1966. Under APB 8, employers had a great deal of latitude in accounting for their pension plans. They were able to choose among different actuarial methods and make a variety of assumptions. None of the choices, moreover, required disclosure in the financial statements. As a result financial statement users had neither comparability nor the disclosure necessary to understand the differences among companies.

SFAS 87 remedies both these shortcomings. It provides that all companies use the same actuarial cost method, and it requires disclosure of the key assumptions used to compute the pension obligation and pension cost. These assumptions, combined with the detailed disclosure requirements of SFAS 87, permit users of financial statements to obtain a great deal of insight into the status of the pension plan and the performance of the pension fund.

The adoption of SFAS 87 had one drawback. Previously, most firms made contributions using the same actuarial methods and assumptions used to determine pension cost. Under SFAS 87, the contribution ("funding") method and the method used for financial reporting purposes are often different. We will discuss this difference further in the remainder of the chapter.

DEFINED BENEFIT PENSION PLANS

Understanding the mechanics of pension plans themselves is the first step toward understanding pension plan accounting and the insights that can be derived therefrom. Two important elements of pension plans are

- The benefit obligation to be paid to retirees;
- The plan assets that are invested to meet the obligation.

The factors that affect the benefit obligation and the plan assets are illustrated in Figure 9-1. The link between the two is the use of plan assets to pay the plan benefits.

Exhibit 9-1 presents a simple example of a defined benefit plan for a hypothetical company: the DBP Co. The example is extended over four years with additional complexities added each year. Throughout the section that follows, as we introduce new terms we will indicate in square brackets [] where in the exhibit the concept is first illustrated.

Estimating Benefit Obligations

[Exhibit 9-1, Year 1]

The first step in pension accounting is for the employer to forecast the cash outflows required by the plan by estimating future benefits. These estimates, made by actuaries, are complex. They require estimates of such employee variables as turnover, mortality, quit rates, and retirement dates. For pay-related plans future salary increases must also

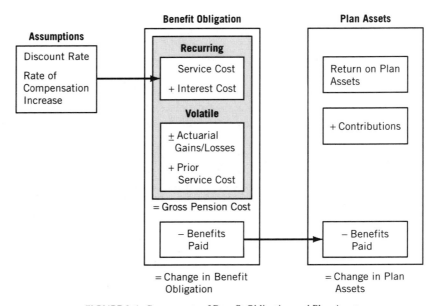

FIGURE 9-1 Components of Benefit Obligation and Plan Assets

EXHIBIT 9-1. DBP CO.
Pension Plan

The DBP Co. has adopted a pension plan covering its two employees, JR and SR, effective at the beginning of year 1. The plan provides for pension payments calculated as follows:

Retirement age: 65

Annual pension: one m. ath's salary × number of years of service

Benefits based on salary at retirement

Pension benefits vest immediately

Currently each employee earns $1000 per month under a contract with five years remaining.

SR is expected to retire at the end of year 3, at age 65.

JR is expected to retire at the end of year 26, at age 65. At that time JR's monthly salary is expected to be $1500.

Each employee has a life expectancy of 15 years following retirement, collecting pension benefits until age 80.

Year 1

The employees work one year. As a result, based on current salary scales, each will receive a pension of $1000 per year for 15 years (age 66–80). At an assumed discount rate of 10%, the present value of the accumulated and projected pension liability for each employee is computed as follows:

Accumulated Benefit Obligation (ABO)

Present value (at retirement) of a 15-year annuity of $1000 per year = $7606. For JR, we must discount this amount to find the present value at the end of year 1 (25 years prior to retirement): $7606 $\times$ $(1.1)^{-25}$ = $702.

For SR, we must discount this amount to find the present value at the end of year 1 (two years prior to retirement): $7606 $\times$ $(1.1)^{-2}$ = $6286.

The accumulated benefit obligation is equal to $702 + $6286 = $6988.

Projected Benefit Obligation (PBO)

Based on the projected salary at the time of retirement, JR will receive a pension of $1500 per year, and SR will receive a pension of $1000 per year. JR's PBO will be 1.5 times ($1500/$1000) as large (1.5 $\times$ $702 = $1053) as the ABO, while SR's PBO will be the same as the ABO (because salary at retirement is the same as current salary).

The projected benefit obligation is equal to $1053 + $6286 = $7339.

Summarizing

	ABO			PBO		
	JR	SR	Total	JR	SR	Total
Retirement annuity	$1000	$1000		$ 1,500	$1000	
Years paid out	15	15		15	15	
Present value at retirement	$7606	$7606		$11,409	$7606	
Years to retirement	25	2		25	2	
Present value today	$ 702	$6286	$6988	$ 1,053	$6286	$7339

Reconciliation of Change in ABO/PBO

Service cost

The changes in the ABO/PBO include the service cost incurred, which is calculated using both the current salary scale (ABO) and the expected salary scale (PBO) at retirement. Since it is the first year of the plan, the service cost is equal to the benefit obligation at the end of the year. *For financial reporting purposes the service cost of $7339 based on projected salary (PBO) is used.*

EXHIBIT 9-1. *(Continued)*

	ABO			PBO		
	JR	SR	Total	JR	SR	Total
Closing balance	$ 702	$6286	$6988	$ 1,053	$6286	$7339
Opening balance	0	0	0	0	0	0
Change	**702**	**6286**	**6988**	**1,053**	**6286**	**7339**
Service cost						
Retirement annuity	$1000	$1000		$ 1,500	$1000	
Years paid out	15	15		15	15	
Present value at retirement	$7606	$7606		$11,409	$7606	
Years to retirement	25	2		25	2	
Present value today	**$ 702**	**$6286**	**$6988**	**$ 1,053**	**$6286**	**$7339**

Year 2

In year 2, both employees work another year. Each has expected benefits at retirement of $2000 (2 × $1000) annually based on current salary scales; based on projected salaries, the expected benefit is $3000 ($1500 × 2) for JR and $2000 for SR. The ABO and PBO are calculated as follows:

	ABO			PBO		
	JR	SR	Total	JR	SR	Total
Retirement annuity	$ 2,000	$ 2,000		$ 3,000	$ 2,000	
Years paid out	15	15		15	15	
Present value at retirement	$15,212	$15,212		$22,818	$15,212	
Years to retirement	24	1		24	1	
Present value today	$ 1,544	$13,829	$15,373	$ 2,317	$13,829	$16,146

Reconciliation of Change in ABO/PBO

Service cost

Interest cost

The change in the ABO/PBO now has two elements. The service cost component is calculated as in year 1. It represents the (present value of) increase in benefits earned this year. In addition, the amounts earned in previous years are one year closer to realization, requiring the accretion of interest on outstanding obligations. The resulting interest cost component is based on the opening PBO and ABO. Again, for financial reporting, the PBO numbers are used.

Notice that service cost for year 2 is higher than for year 1 even though salary and all assumptions are unchanged. Service cost increases with age (that is proximity to retirement) under the actuarial method required by SFAS 87.

	ABO			PBO		
	JR	SR	Total	JR	SR	Total
Closing balance	$1544	$13,829	$15,373	$ 2,317	$13,829	$16,146
Opening balance	702	6,286	6,988	1,053	6,286	7,339
Change	**842**	**7,543**	**8,385**	**1,264**	**7,543**	**8,807**
Service cost						
Retirement annuity	$1000	$ 1,000		$ 1,500	$ 1,000	
Years paid out	15	15		15	15	

EXHIBIT 9-1. *(Continued)*

	ABO			PBO		
	JR	SR	Total	JR	SR	Total
Present value at retirement	7606	7,606		11,409	7,606	
Years to retirement	24	1		24	1	
Present value today	**772**	**6,914**	**$ 7,686**	**1,159**	**6,914**	**$ 8,073**
Interest cost						
Opening liability balance	$ 702	$ 6,286		$ 1,053	$ 6,286	
Interest at 10%	**70**	**629**	**$ 699**	**105**	**629**	**$ 734**
Total change	**842**	**7,543**	**8,385**	**1,264**	**7,543**	**8,807**

Year 3

At the end of year 3, SR retires and she will start collecting her pension benefits of $3000 per year ($1000 × 3 years of service) next year. Also, the actuaries have revised their estimate of JR's life expectancy and now estimate that he will live to age 85. The calculations are now:

	ABO			PBO		
	JR	SR	Total	JR	SR	Total
Retirement annuity	$ 3,000	$ 3,000		$ 4,500	$ 3,000	
Years paid out	20	15		20	15	
Present value at retirement	$25,541	$22,818		$38,311	$22,818	
Years to retirement	23	0		23	0	
Present value today	$ 2,852	$22,818	$25,670	$ 4,279	$22,818	$27,097

Reconciliation of Change in ABO/PBO

Service cost

Interest cost

Actuarial gains and losses

The change in ABO and PBO now has three elements. Service cost and interest cost are calculated as before. In addition, because of the revised actuarial assumption, we assume that JR will receive the $2000 ($3000 using projected salary) annual pension for an additional five years. The increase in present value resulting from this change in assumption is the actuarial loss.

	ABO			PBO		
	JR	SR	Total	JR	SR	Total
Closing balance	$2852	$22,818	$25,670	$ 4,279	$22,818	$27,097
Opening balance	1544	13,829	15,373	2,317	13,829	16,146
Change	**$1308**	**$ 8,989**	**$10,297**	**$ 1,962**	**$ 8,989**	**$10,951**
Service cost						
Retirement annuity	$1000	$ 1,000		$ 1,500	$ 1,000	
Years paid out	20	15		20	15	
Present value at retirement	$8514	$ 7,606		$12,770	$ 7,606	
Years to retirement	23	0		23	0	
Present value today	**$ 951**	**$ 7,606**	**$ 8,557**	**$ 1,426**	**$ 7,606**	**$ 9,032**

EXHIBIT 9-1. *(Continued)*

	ABO			PBO		
	JR	SR	Total	JR	SR	Total
Interest cost						
Opening liability balance	$1544	$13,829		$ 2,317	$13,829	
Interest at 10%	**154**	**1,383**	**$ 1,537**	**232**	**1,383**	**1,615**
Actuarial gains/losses						
Retirement annuity	$2000	$ 0		$ 3,000	$ 0	
Additional years paid	5	0		5	0	
Present value of annuity	$7582	0		$11,372	0	
Years from now	38*	0		38	0	
Present value today	**$ 203**	**0**	**$ 203**	**$ 304**	**0**	**$ 304**
Total change	**$1308**	**$ 8,989**	**$10,297**	**$ 1,962**	**$ 8,989**	**$10,951**

*Retirement in 23 years; additional pension after 15 years.

Year 4

The plan is amended to make the pension benefit 1.1 times the monthly salary for each year worked retroactive to the beginning of the plan for all workers still in the company's employ (JR). JR works one more year so that his estimated annual benefit is $4400 ($1000 × 4.4). Included are $1100 (1.1 × salary) for this year's service, $3000 (3.0 × salary) previously earned, and $300 (0.3 × salary) as prior service cost. SR receives the first year benefits of $3000. The ABO and PBO calculations are now

	ABO			PBO		
	JR	SR	Total	JR	SR	Total
Retirement annuity	$ 4,400	$ 3,000		$ 6,600	$ 3,000	
Years paid out	20	14		20	14	
Present value at retirement	$37,459	$22,100		$56,189	$22,100	
Years to retirement	22	0		22	0	
Present value today	$ 4,601	$22,100	$26,701	$ 6,902	$22,100	$29,002

Reconciliation of Change in ABO/PBO

Service cost

Interest cost

Actuarial gains and losses

Prior service cost

Benefits paid

Note that in calculating the ABO/PBO, SR has only 14 more years of benefits expected since the first year of benefits were paid this year. This reduces the ABO and PBO.

EXHIBIT 9-1. *(Continued)*

	ABO			PBO		
	JR	SR	Total	JR	SR	Total
Closing balance	$4601	$22,100	$26,701	$ 6902	$22,100	$29,002
Opening balance	2852	22,818	25,670	4279	22,818	27,097
Change	**$1749**	**$ (718)**	**$ 1,031**	**$ 2623**	**$ (718)**	**$ 1,905**
Service cost						
Retirement annuity	$1100	$ 0		$ 1,650	$ 0	
Years paid out	20	0		20	0	
Present value at retirement	$9365	0		$14,054	0	
Years to retirement	22	0		22	0	
Present value today	**$1150**	**0**	**$ 1,150**	**$ 1,725**	**0**	**$ 1,725**
Interest cost						
Opening liability balance	$2852	$22,818		$4,279	$22,818	
Interest at 10%	**285**	**2,282**	**$ 2,567**	**428**	**2,282**	**$ 2,710**
Actuarial gains/losses	0	0	0	0	0	0
Prior service cost						
Increase in annuity	$ 300	$ 0		$ 450	$ 0	$ 0
Years paid out	20	0		20	0	
Present value at retirement	$2553	0		$3,829	0	
Years to retirement	22	0		22	0	
Present value today	**$ 314**	**0**	**$ 314**	**$ 470**	**0**	**470**
Benefits paid	**0**	**(3,000)**	**(3,000)**	**0**	**(3,000)**	**(3,000)**
Total change (net)	**$1749**	**$ (718)**	**$ 1,031**	**$2,623**	**$ (718)**	**$ 1,905**

be estimated. These estimates, combined with the terms of the plan, produce a forecast of benefits to be paid stretching decades into the future. The present value of these forecasted benefits is the pension obligation.

Under SFAS 87 three different measures of the pension obligation must be disclosed. The *accumulated benefit oblication* (ABO) is the present value of pension benefits earned as of the balance sheet date based on current salaries. The *projected benefit obligation* (PBO) includes projected salary increases for career average or final pay plans. The ABO and the PBO are based on the same assumptions and are discounted using the same discount rate; they differ only with respect to the exclusion or inclusion of future compensation growth. For a flat benefit (non pay-related) plan, therefore, the ABO and PBO will be identical. These measures of the pension obligation include some benefits that require further employee service to be earned. The *vested benefit obligation* (VBO) includes only that part of the obligation that is not contingent upon future service.

All three benefit obligation measures are highly sensitive to the assumptions (see Figure 9-1) used in estimating future benefits. The most significant assumption is the *discount rate* used to compute the present value of the benefit obligation. It is intended to be a current interest rate (such as the rate at which the pension obligation could be settled).[2] Companies are free to change the discount rate, and financial statement users must be alert to such changes as they may significantly affect the computed benefit obligation and pension cost, as discussed shortly. The *rate of compensation increase* is another key assumption under SFAS 87. Firms are expected to choose a rate of compensation increase that is economically consistent with other assumptions made. For example, a high inflation scenario is not compatible with a very low compensation growth rate.

Except for the general guidance indicated, SFAS 87 does not limit an employer's choice of compensation growth rate and discount rate. An AICPA survey[3] as of December 31, 1990, of 483 firms with defined benefit pension plans showed discount rates ranging from 6.5% to 11.5%, with 60% using a discount rate of 8.5% or 9%. The same survey group showed a median rate of compensation growth of 6%.

Factors Affecting Benefit Obligations

There are five factors that can change the benefit obligations (ABO and PBO) from year to year. The discussion will refer primarily to the PBO, as SFAS 87 requires that projected salaries be used to compute pension cost[4] in the financial statements.

(1) Service Cost

[DBP—Year 1]. The first element in pension cost is the *service cost*, the present value of benefits earned during the current period. This cost is sensitive to all the assumptions used to compute the pension obligation, most particularly the discount rate. Service cost trends should generally track employee age and compensation trends, except when assumptions are changed.

(2) Interest Cost

[DBP—Year 2]. The second element of pension cost is interest on the projected benefit obligation. As the passage of time brings all future pension payments one year closer, there must be explicit recognition of the increase in the obligation, that is, accretion of discount. This component is obtained by multiplying the beginning projected benefit obligation by the discount rate. Note that the discount rate used to compute the PBO as of the previous year end is used to compute this element of pension cost for the entire current year.

---

[2]Settlement means transfer of the obligation to another entity (such as insurance company) in return for a cash payment from the employer (or plan).

[3]American Institute of Certified Public Accountants, *Accounting Trends and Techniques* (New York, NY: AICPA, 1991), p. 287.

[4]SFAS 87 governs the determination of *pension cost*. For most companies, that cost will be *pension expense* as well. In some cases, however, part of the cost will be capitalized. For example, Philadelphia Electric disclosed in its *1990 Annual Report* that 86% of pension cost was charged to operations; the remainder was capitalized as part of utility plant.

(3) Actuarial Gains and Losses

[DBP—Year 3]. Gains or *Losses* originate when the PBO is recomputed each year due to changes in one or more actuarial assumptions, such as quit rates, retirement dates, or mortality.

(4) Prior Service Cost

[DBP—Year 4]. Pension plan amendments may increase (or decrease) previously computed pension benefit obligations. The changes relating to periods of employment prior to the amendment are known as prior service cost.

(5) Benefits

[DBP—Year 4]. Benefits paid to retired employees reduce the PBO as a portion of the obligation has been met.

A four-year summary of the changes in the ABO and PBO of the DBP Co. follows.

Four-Year Summary: ABO and PBO

The reconciliation of the ABO and PBO for all four years of the DBP Co. is presented here. Notice the five elements that reconcile the opening and closing balances of the ABO and PBO.

Year	1	2	3	4
ABO				
Opening balance	$ 0	$ 6,988	$15,373	$25,670
(1) Service cost	6988	7,686	8,557	1,150
(2) Interest cost	0	699	1,537	2,567
(3) Actuarial loss	0	0	203	0
(4) Prior service cost	0	0	0	314
(5) Benefits paid	0	0	0	(3,000)
Closing balance	$6988	$15,373	$25,670	$26,701
PBO				
Opening balance	$ 0	$ 7,339	$16,146	$27,097
(1) Service cost	7339	8,073	9,032	1,725
(2) Interest cost	0	734	1,615	2,710
(3) Actuarial loss	0	0	304	0
(4) Prior service cost	0	0	0	470
(5) Benefits paid	0	0	0	(3,000)
Closing balance	$7339	$16,146	$27,097	$29,002

Pension Plan Assets

The assets of the pension fund (see Figure 9-1 and Exhibit 9-2) are affected by three factors:

- Employer contributions
- The investment return actually earned by the assets
- The benefits paid out

(1) Pension Funding—Contributions

To provide cash to meet the benefit obligations, employers make periodic contributions to the pension fund. When funding a pension plan, firms can choose from a number of actuarial cost methods. Prior to SFAS 87, the actuarial cost method used determined both the amount of pension cost accrued and the amount contributed to the pension plan.

EXHIBIT 9-2. DBP CO.
Plan Assets

To fund the plan, the company contributes $6500 each year for the first three years and $1500 in the fourth year to a pension fund. All funding is done at the beginning of the year. The pension fund manager promises a long-term rate of return on plan assets of 12%.

In the first year, plan assets (year 1 contribution of $6500) actually return 12%, yielding $780 (12% × $6500). The fair value of plan assets is therefore $7280 ($6500 + $780) at the end of year 1.

In the second year, plan assets actually return 10%, yielding $1378—10% × ($7280 + $6500). The fair value of plan assets is now $15,158 ($7280 + $6500 + $1378) .

In the third year, plan assets actually return 14%, yielding $3032—14% × ($15,158 + $6500). The fair value of plan assets is $24,690 ($15,158 + $6500 + $3032).

In the fourth year, plan assets actually return 12% yielding $3143—12% × ($24,690 + $1500). Benefits of $3000 to SR are paid from the plan assets, at the end of the year. The fair value of plan assets is $26,333 ($24,690 + $1500 + $3143 − $3000) at the end of year 4.

Reconciliation of Fair Value of Plan Assets

Contributions

Actual return on plan assets

Benefits paid

		Year		
Plan Assets	1	2	3	4
Opening balance	$ 0	$ 7,280	$15,158	$24,690
(1) Contribution	6500	6,500	6,500	1,500
(2) Actual return	780	1,378	3,032	3,143
(3) Benefits paid	0	0	0	(3,000)
Closing balance	$7280	$15,158	$24,690	$26,333

Employer contributions need not follow the same pattern as pension cost computed under the provisions of SFAS 87. Funding may be governed by income tax and ERISA rules, as well as employer cash flow considerations.

(2) Return on Assets

The pension fund is (usually) managed by a trustee or investment advisor. The return on assets (ROA) represents the actual return (capital gains plus dividends and interest) earned during the year. The return on assets can fluctuate[5] from year to year.

(3) Benefits

The benefits paid from plan assets are, of course, those discussed in the section on the pension obligation. This linkage permits reconciliation of the PBO and plan assets. The four-year summary position of DBP Co.'s pension fund assets is shown in Exhibit 9-2.

ACCOUNTING FOR PENSIONS UNDER SFAS 87

The discussion so far has focused primarily on the mechanics of pension funds themselves with only tangential reference to financial reporting. This section will now address these issues directly. Exhibit 9-3 presents the relevant income statement, balance sheet, and footnote disclosures[6] for year 4 (and comparative year 3) under the assumption that SFAS 87 was adopted at the beginning of year 3.

Computing Pension Cost

[Exhibit 9-3]

The elements of pension cost under SFAS 87 are as follows:

- Service cost (increase in PBO from current year service)
- Interest cost (increase in PBO due to interest factor)
- Expected return on assets
- Net amortization and deferral
- Amortization of prior service cost
- Amortization of transition asset or liability

Figure 9-2 illustrates the relationship of these elements to the factors that make up the mechanics of pension plans discussed earlier. Note that some components are reported for accounting purposes as they happen. For others, only a "smoothed" number is reported. In addition, some items are aggregated with others.

---

[5]Because of this fluctuation, the *expected long-term rate of return on plan assets* (the forecasted rate of return) is used for accounting purposes.

[6]The exhibit also explains (in its notes) how these numbers were derived. These data are generally not available in the statements themselves.

EXHIBIT 9-3. DBP CO.
Footnote Disclosures

Assume that DBP adopts the provisions of SFAS 87 at the beginning of year 3. The fair value of plan assets (Exhibit 9-2) is $15,158, and the PBO (Exhibit 9-1) is $16,146. The difference is the transition liability of $988, which is to be amortized over 23 years (JR's remaining service life) assuming that for years 1 and 2, DBP had expensed the exact amount it contributed each year to the pension plan, leaving no balance sheet accrual. The income statement will show the following pension cost for years 3 and 4:

Year		3		4
Net pension cost		$ 8091		$ 1350

Footnote disclosure:

Year		3		4
(1) Service cost[1]		$ 9032		$ 1725
(2) Interest cost[1]		1615		2710
Actual return[2]	$(3032)		$(3143)	
Less: deferred	433		0	
(3) Expected return[3]		(2599)		(3143)
(4) Amortization losses (gains)[4]		0		(6)
(5) Amortization prior service[5]		0		21
(6) Amortization transition liability[6]		43		43
Net pension cost		$ 8091		$ 1350

The balance sheet will show a pension liability of

Year		3		4
Pension liability		$ 1591		$ 1441

Footnote disclosure of plan status:

Year		3		4
Plan assets[2]		$24,690		$26,333
ABO[1]		25,670		26,701
Excess (deficit)[8]		$ (980)		$ (368)
PBO[1]		27,097		29,002
Excess (deficit)		$(2,407)		$(2,669)
Less: Unamortized portion				
Actuarial loss[4]		$ 304		$ 290
Excess returns[4]		(433)		(413)
Prior service costs[5]		0		449
Transition liability[6]		945		902
Pension liability[7]		$(1,591)		$(1,441)

The unamortized portion represents amounts that have impacted the calculation of net assets and the PBO but have not yet been recognized in the financial statements of DBP.

EXHIBIT 9-3. *(Continued)*

Explanations*

1 Exhibit 9-1.
2 Exhibit 9-2.
3 Expected return calculated by multiplying (plan assets + contribution) by 12%, the expected long-run rate of return. (See Exhibit 9-2). The difference between the actual return and expected return is deferred. The deferral is frequently included in the "amortization and deferral" line, with only the actual return shown as a component of pension cost.
4 Deferred gain of $433 at end of year 3 is *amortized in year 4* over 22 years ($433/22 = $20), leaving $413 balance; actuarial loss of $304 (Exhibit 9-1) is *amortized in year 4*, over 22 years ($304/22 = $14), leaving $290 balance.
5 Prior service cost (Exhibit 9-1) in year 4 of $470 is amortized over 22 years, assuming it originated at beginning of year: $470/22 = $21.
6 Amortization of transition liability of $988/$23 = $43.
7 This is equivalent to opening balance + pension cost − contributions. For year 3, 0 + $8091 − $6500 = $1591; for year 4, $1591 + $1350 − $1500 = $1441.
8 Note that the ABO exceeds plan assets. We must therefore be alert to the SFAS 87 requirement to recognize a "minimum liability." However, in this case, the accrued pension liability exceeds the shortfall (ABO less plan assets); no minimum liability is therefore required. For a contrasting example, see the analysis of General Motors later in the chapter.

*Not provided in financial statements.

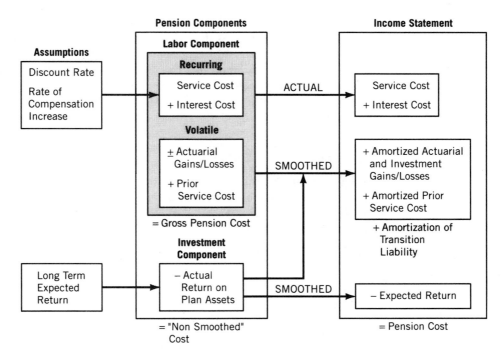

FIGURE 9-2 Relationship Between Actual Pension Components and Income Statement Presentation

The computation of pension cost is complicated, partly due to the complexity inherent in pension plans themselves. Much of the complexity is, however, the result of the accounting requirements intended to dampen possible volatility in pension cost. These smoothing techniques are, however, clearly revealed in most cases. An important objective of the analysis is to unravel the smoothing and aggregating process to see the underlying events.

Service Cost and Interest Cost

These two elements of pension cost have been defined. Remember that pension cost is calculated using projected benefits rather than accumulated benefits.

Expected Return on Assets

The third component of pension cost is the return on assets. The investment return on pension fund assets is an offset to other elements of pension cost. Because of concern about the short-term volatility of investment returns, pension cost does not reflect the actual investment returns for the period.

The company must estimate an expected long-term rate of return on plan assets. In contrast to the discount rate, this is intended to be a stable assumption. Companies do have the freedom, however, to change this assumption at will. The AICPA survey for 1990[7] shows a median return assumption of 9% and a range of 6% to $11\frac{1}{2}\%$ or above.

The expected return on assets is obtained by multiplying the expected long-term rate of return by the opening fair value of plan assets. Alternatively, the *market-related value of plan assets* can be used as the base for this calculation. The difference between the expected return on assets and the actual return on assets is deferred, sometimes shown as a separate line item and sometimes included in the "net amortization and deferral" line item. *As a result, pension cost reflects the expected return on assets rather than the actual return.* The difference is deferred on the assumption that the unexpected returns will balance out over time.

Net Amortization and Deferral

Actuarial gains and losses and the difference between expected return on assets and actual return on assets are deferred and accumulated. Total deferrals in excess of 10% of the larger of the PBO and the fair value of plan assets[8] must be amortized over the average remaining employee service life. Any amortization of these combined deferrals will be an additional element of pension cost. Amortization of deferred amounts starts, when required, in the year following the year in which the deferrals originate.

---

[7]AICPA, *Accounting Trends and Techniques,* 1991, p. 287.

[8]This is the "corridor method" permitted by SFAS 87. The rationale is that there is no need to amortize gains and losses (which are expected to equalize over time) unless they become so large that there is reason to question their eventual reversal. The corridor method is an arbitrary means of deferring recognition of "temporary" gains and losses until these unrecognized items become too large to ignore. Note that the amount to be amortized is recomputed each year.

Amortization of Prior Service Cost

Any *prior service cost* arising from plan amendments must be amortized as an additional component of pension cost over the average remaining service life of the employee population.

Amortization of Transition Asset or Liability

Under SFAS 87, the initial adoption of the new standard gives rise to either a transition asset or a liability that represents the difference between the projected benefit obligation and the sum of the fair value of plan assets plus employer accruals as of the adoption date. This transition asset or liability, which remains "off balance sheet" (except when a "minimum liability" must be recognized), must be amortized over the average remaining service life of employees.[9] This amortization is yet another component of pension cost.

Companies are required to disclose these components of pension cost. This disclosure enables analysts to determine which changes in pension cost are due to operational factors as opposed to changes in assumptions or the effects of misestimation in the past.

Disclosure of Plan Status

[Exhibit 9-3].

SFAS 87 requires a detailed reconciliation of the funded status of defined benefit pension plans. Companies must disclose

- The projected benefit obligation
- The accumulated benefit obligation
- The vested benefit obligation
- The fair value of plan assets.

As a result the analyst can see the status of the plan at a glance. However, the benefit obligation measures are dependent on the assumptions made, especially the discount rate, and a plan may appear to be overfunded (assets exceeding benefit obligation) if an unrealistically high discount rate is used (reducing the present values of pension obligations) or appear underfunded (assets less than benefit obligation) if a very low discount rate is employed.

SFAS 87 requires that all pension plan assets (other than operating assets such as office furniture) be carried at fair value. For assets without market quotations (real estate, venture capital, etc.), current appraisals should be made. In practice, we believe that some employers smooth the recognition of value changes for assets with no clearly defined market value. As already noted, a smoothed asset valuation method can be used to compute the expected return-on-assets component of pension cost.

In addition, employers must reconcile their balance sheet accruals related to the plan with the plan status. Balance sheet accruals reflect the difference between pension cost

---

[9]If the average is less than 15 years, then 15 years can be used as the period of amortization.

and contributions. *For plans where the sum of balance sheet accruals and the fair value of assets is less than the accumulated benefit obligation, the shortfall must also be recognized on the balance sheet as a "minimum liability"* (see the General Motors example later in this chapter). The reconciliation reveals, among other things, unamortized transition amounts as well as deferred actuarial and investment gains or losses. The next section shows how these data can be used to delve into the details of a pension plan.

ANALYSIS OF PENSION COSTS AND LIABILITY

The accounting process masks the underlying cost and status of the pension plan. Analysis of reported pension costs and liabilities requires the analyst to focus on the following issues:

1. The effect of the assumptions used.
2. The underlying status of the pension plan and pension costs:
   a. What is the firm's actual economic liability?
   b. What are the trends in the elements of pension cost? How are they affected by "smoothing"? Is the smoothing justified? What are the costs (or gains) not recognized for accounting purposes? Included in the foregoing is the need to separate the "labor"-related components of pension cost from those related to the investment performance of the plan assets.

Importance of Assumptions

Under the provisions of SFAS 87, all companies are required to use the same actuarial method when calculating pension cost and the status of the pension plan. This enhances comparability across companies. However, companies are free to choose actuarial assumptions within a wide range.

The importance of the company's assumptions must never be forgotten. Assumptions about the employee population are unknown; we must assume that the company's estimates of such factors as mortality, quit rates, and retirement ages are realistic. Three key assumptions—discount rate, rate of compensation increase, and expected long-term rate of return on plan assets—are, however, disclosed. A comparison can be made between the company's choices and those of its competitors. One should expect that companies in the same industry, dealing with the same unions or the same market conditions, will have the same assumed rate of compensation increase. In practice, of course, companies do use different rates, just as they use different depreciation methods and lives for similar assets.

The discount rate assumption, which drives the fund obligations and hence the fund status (assets versus obligations), should also, in theory, be identical for all U.S. companies.[10] Yet, in practice, discount rates also vary from company to company. The

---

[10]Different discount rates for plans in foreign jurisdictions, however, would be expected.

differences are sometimes a function of corporate personality (some companies are more conservative than others) and sometimes a function of the plan status itself (a company with an underfunded plan may be tempted to use a higher discount rate to minimize the reported underfunding).

The third key assumption, the expected long-term rate of return on plan assets, impacts only pension cost. The higher the expected rate, the lower pension cost. Once again, theory says that all companies should have the same expected rate available to them in the marketplace. Here again, in practice, the choice of rate varies. Companies have an incentive to choose a high assumed rate, to report lower pension cost, but an unrealistically high rate will create deferred losses that will, eventually, have to be amortized as a component of future pension cost. The choice of assumptions affects the reported status of the pension plan and pension cost in a number of ways.

Impact of Assumptions on Obligations

Pension obligations and most related data are "off balance sheet." As a result, variations in pension assumptions usually have no direct impact on conventionally calculated balance sheet ratios. Exceptions would be companies subject to the "minimum liability" provisions of SFAS 87 and those with pension assets or liabilities resulting from purchase method acquisitions (see the discussion that follows). Because they eventually impact both pension cost and contributions, however, assumptions do have an indirect impact on the balance sheet. The most immediate impact of assumptions, however, is on the reported pension plan status.

The discount rate assumption has the greatest impact on the reported pension plan status, as it is used to compute the present value of the various benefit obligation measures. A higher (lower) discount rate will result in a lower (higher) calculated PBO. As companies are required to disclose the choice of discount rate, the effect of that choice can be examined, and choices of different employers can be compared. Because of the mathematics of present value, adjustments for different rates are difficult to make. Increasing the discount rate from 10% to 11% will *not*, for example, change the calculated PBO by exactly one-tenth.

The rate of compensation growth also has an impact on the calculated PBO, but one that is smaller than that of the discount rate. A higher rate (assuming that employee compensation increases more rapidly) will increase the calculated PBO, while a lower rate will decrease the PBO. (Note that the assumed rate is zero for a plan that is not pay related). The reported ABO is *not* impacted by this choice since it *excludes* the impact of future pay increases; an increase in the assumed rate of compensation growth will therefore increase the difference between the ABO and the PBO.

When comparing the PBO and ABO with the market value of plan assets, therefore, it is important to recognize the impact of the choice of discount rate and rate of compensation growth. Aggressive assumptions (high discount rate, low rate of compensation increase) will improve the reported status of the plan, while conservative assumptions (low discount rate, high rate of compensation increase) will make the plan appear less well funded.

Impact of Assumptions on Pension Cost

Income statement ratios and those using income data (such as return on assets) are more directly affected by pension accounting assumptions. The effects of the choice of assumptions on pension cost are more complex, however.

The discount rate directly affects the calculation of service cost as it is used to compute the present value of benefits earned in the current year. The impact is similar to the effect on the pension obligation: a higher rate reduces the cost, a lower rate increases the cost.

Calculation of the interest component of pension cost (the product of the PBO and the discount rate) is also affected by the discount rate because both elements of the computation change. Although the effects are opposite (higher discount rate reduces the PBO), the net result of increasing the discount rate is an increase in interest cost.[11] While the interest cost effect offsets part of the service cost effect, the effect on service cost is normally much greater. Thus, in most cases,[12] a higher discount rate will reduce reported pension cost.

The effect of a change in the rate of compensation increase is easier to predict. A higher rate will increase both the service cost and the interest component of pension cost (by increasing the PBO). Conversely, a lower rate of compensation increase will decrease all present value calculations that employ it and will reduce pension cost. Finally, higher assumed rates of return on assets also lower pension cost,[13] since the expected return on assets is an offset to other components of pension cost.

Summing up, a low rate of compensation increase and high assumed rate of return on assets serve to decrease pension cost and, therefore, increase reported earnings. Higher discount rates will lower the obligation and pension cost. From a quality of earnings viewpoint, these choices would be considered aggressive and they would result in earnings of lower quality. Ultimately, however, overly aggressive choices are likely to result in experience (actuarial) losses that will have to be amortized and that will increase pension cost in the future.

Pension Analysis: Plan Status and Plan Costs

[Exhibit 9-3 and 9-4]

It is essential to go beyond the amounts recognized in the financial statements to obtain a better understanding of the impact of the pension plan on the firm. The FASB, in adopting SFAS 87, reasoned that ultimately the obligations of the pension plan are the firm's; the assets in the pension fund are simply a means of satisfying the firm's obligation. The FASB project director for pensions suggested that a firm's pension plan be viewed as an "unconsolidated subsidiary" of the firm and that the effect of SFAS 87 would be, ultimately, to consolidate the subsidiary. Given that the pension cost under

---

[11]This is not obvious, but an analogy may help. When interest rates rise, bond prices fall. The interest cost of subsequent borrowings, however, is higher.

[12]In a very mature plan, with very high interest cost relative to service cost, the effect of the discount rate on interest cost may dominate the analysis.

[13]When a company uses the market-related value of plan assets rather than actual asset value, the return on assets calculation will be slower to reflect changes in market value. When asset values are rising, therefore, this choice will result in higher pension cost.

SFAS 87 is a result of a host of arbitrary accounting accruals and that the liability shown on the balance sheet reflects nothing more than the interaction of this calculated cost with pension contributions, there is a need for other measures of a firm's pension cost and liability. We shall first examine these different measures and then turn to a brief discussion of the method of calculation with reference to the DBP example.

Adjustments that can be made include

1. Replacing the balance sheet liability with measures reflecting the actual plan status. The DBP Co., for example, shows a liability of $1441 in year 4. This number is not the actual pension obligation facing the firm. Possible measures of the obligation and the relevant amounts for DBP include

   - PBO less market value of plan assets—$2669 liability.
   - ABO less market value of plan assets—$368 liability.
   - PBO—$29,002.
   - ABO—$26,701
   - VBO[14]—$26,701

   Depending on the purpose of the analysis and on the firm's tax status, the measurements might be made on a pretax or after-tax basis.

2. Analyzing the components of pension cost, which include elements of labor cost (benefits earned), investment returns, and the impact of past events (amortization). Trends in each of these elements can be examined separately. In addition, alternative measures of pension "cost" can be computed and analyzed.

   These alternative measures of pension cost are not used for accounting purposes but, as in the case of the alternative liability measures, may be more relevant for analysis.

   (1) *Service cost:* A narrow measure of the "labor" cost portion of pension cost earned in the current period. It ignores interest cost and other adjustments (actuarial) on previously earned benefits. The trend in service cost indicates the trend in payroll cost and employee age. Sharp drops (or increases) in this item (e.g., Exhibit 9-4, year 4) indicate significant changes in payroll.[15]

   (2) *Recurring cost:* Service cost plus interest cost, excluding actuarial gains or losses and adjustments for prior service.

   (3) *Gross pension cost:* The change in PBO exclusive of benefits paid, but encompassing all *labor-related cost factors* (including the gross actuarial gains and losses and prior service cost). It can also be calculated on an ABO basis as the change in ABO plus the benefits paid.

   (4) *Nonsmoothed pension cost:* The gross pension cost less the *actual* investment returns; this measures pension cost without the smoothing effects of SFAS 87.

---

[14]As, in the DBP plan, all benefits vest immediately, the VBO is identical to the ABO.

[15]Trends in service cost should be evaluated carefully following the firm's announcement of significant layoffs.

EXHIBIT 9-4. DBP CO.
Analyzing Footnote Disclosures

Using only the data presented in Exhibit 9-3, the exhibit illustrates how the information given in Exhibits 9-1 and 9-2 can be reconstructed enabling analysts to understand what actually transpired in the pension plan. This enables us to arrive at the actual trends of the components that make up pension costs.

	Year			
	1	2	3	4
(1) Service cost	$7339	$ 8073	$ 9,032	$ 1725
Interest cost	—	734	1,615	2710
(2) Recurring cost	7339	8807	10,647	4435
Actuarial loss	—	—	304	—
Prior service cost	—	—	—	470
(3) Gross pension cost	$7339	$ 8807	$10,951	$ 4905
Actual investment return	(780)	(1378)	(3,032)	(3143)
(4) Nonsmoothed pension cost	$6559	$ 7429	$ 7819	$ 1762
(5) Contribution to plan	6500	6500	6500	1500
(6) Benefits paid	0	0	0	3000
Net pension cost (SFAS 87)	N/A	N/A	8,091	1350

N/A – Not applicable.

Explanation of Calculations for Year 4

Begin by estimating the cash flow components. The contribution made by the firm to the pension plan is

Contribution = Change in balance sheet liability + Pension cost
$1500   = [$(1441) − $(1591)]   + $1350

As the actual return on plan assets is provided directly, the elements of the plan assets can now be used to estimate the benefits paid.

Benefits paid = Change in plan assets − Contributions − Actual return
$(3000)   = [$26,333 − $24,690] − $1500   − $3143

(Changes in plan assets must reflect contributions, investment returns, and benefits paid.)

To estimate pension cost components, service cost and interest cost are provided directly in the footnotes (see Exhibit 9-3). The gross pension cost can now be calculated as

Gross pension cost = Change in PBO   + Benefits paid
$4905   = [$29,002 − $27,097] + $3000

Alternatively, the components (in addition to service cost and interest cost) that make up the gross pension cost, that is, the actuarial gains/losses as well as the prior service cost incurred during the year, can be estimated directly.

Prior service cost = Change in unamortized amount + Amortization
$470   = $449   + $21

(The amortization of the prior service cost and its unamortized portion are taken from the footnote in Exhibit 9-3). Note this equals the prior service cost created by the plan amendment in year 4. It was derived indirectly without reference to Exhibit 9-1.

EXHIBIT 9-4. *(Continued)*

The actuarial gains/losses are a little more difficult to calculate as the disclosure bundles the amortization of actuarial gains/losses with deferred investment gains/losses. This just requires an extra step:

Amortization of deferred investment gain/losses =

Change in amortized amount	$(20)	(Exhibit 9-3: $413 − $433)
Less: Year 4 excess return	0	(Exhibit 9-3)
	$(20)	

Since total amortized losses are $(6), the amortization of actuarial gains/losses must have been $14. We can now calculate the actuarial losses incurred in year 4.

Actuarial losses = Change in unamortized amount + Amortization
0   = $(14)   + $14

There were no actuarial gains or losses in year 4.

We can now confirm our calculation of gross pension cost (5) as

Service cost	$ 1725
+ Interest cost	2710
+ Actuarial gains/losses	0
+ Prior service cost	470
Gross pension cost	$ 4905

These figures can also be used to check the calculation made earlier for benefits paid (6):

Change in PBO	$ 1905	($29,002 − $27,097)
− Service cost	(1725)	
− Interest cost	(2710)	
− Actuarial gains/losses	0	
− Prior service cost	(470)	
Benefits paid	$(3000)	

(These are the elements of the change in the PBO; if we subtract out all other changes, the remainder must be benefits paid. This computation "proves" our calculations.)

This cost would tend to be more volatile because it includes *actual* investment performance rather than *expected* returns and the total amounts of actuarial gains or losses and prior service cost rather than only the net amortization of these amounts.

None of these measures the actual cash flows related to the plan. The analysis of the plan is, however, incomplete without examining contributions and benefits paid (items (5) and (6)).

(5) *Contribution to plan:* The actual cash flow from the company to the plan. We are also interested in estimates of future cash flows. The plan status can help develop these: a growing plan deficit (PBO less plan assets) would suggest that higher contributions will be required in the future; a surplus would suggest that future contributions can be reduced.

(6) *Benefits paid:* The actual payments made by the plan to retirees.

The different measures and the detailed calculations[16] are illustrated for year 4 of the DBP Co. in Exhibit 9-4.

The first step is to estimate the cash flows relating to the pension plan. The contributions are calculated as the change in the pension liability plus the pension expense recognized in the income statement. The contributions together with the actual return on plant assets allow reconciliation of the plan assets and calculation of the benefits paid by the pension plan to the beneficiaries.

The nonsmoothed components of pension cost, service cost, and interest cost are provided directly in the footnote. For the smoothed components, actuarial gains/losses and prior service cost, the new additions can be calculated as the difference in the unamortized balance plus the amounts amortized.

Computation of the individual components of plan assets and pension costs in this manner allows examination of the actual trends affecting pension cost and obligations. As we will see in the GM example, the "nonrecurring" items may actually recur in a predictable fashion.

Motivation for Adjustments to Liability and Cost

Box 9-2 provides evidence that the market incorporates the "off-balance-sheet" liability in its assessment of a firm's debt position. Furthermore, the market tends to ignore the smoothed elements of cost and, instead, focuses on actual results.

The precise adjustments that should be made depend on the interpretation of two issues defining the relationship of a firm to its pension plan. The finance and labor economics literature discuss these issues in great detail. This section provides a general discussion of the issues.

The first issue deals with measurement of the firm's liability (and hence expense) to its employees. Is the appropriate measure of the liability the PBO, the ABO, or the VBO? In theory, firms can terminate the plan or individual employees at any time. Upon termination, the firm's obligation would be measured by either the ABO or the VBO, depending on the circumstances. SFAS 87 requires that pension cost be measured using the PBO, making the following implicit assumptions:

1. The firm will not terminate employees prior to their reaching vested status (other than "normal" employee turnover that is one of the actuarial assumptions);

2. The firm will not terminate employees in their intermediate or later work years (excluding "normal" turnover) when the projections upon which the PBO are based come to fruition;

---

[16]The calculations are based on projected benefits. They could, however, also be presented on the basis of accumulated benefits for some of the components (i.e., Gross Pension and Non-smoothed Cost). For recurring costs, the interest cost component can be estimated by multiplying the ABO by the discount rate. Estimation of service cost is more problematic. One possibility is to multiply the reported service cost by the ratio of the ABO to the PBO.

BOX 9-2
Market Valuation of Pension Liability and Costs

Research on the market's view of corporate pension liabilities has focused on three issues:

1. Does the market value a dollar of pension liability in the same manner as it values a dollar of other liabilities of a firm?
2. What is the most appropriate basis for measurement of the liability: the PBO, the ABO, or the VBO?
3. Does the market evaluate the pension liability (however measured) on a gross basis or net of the pension fund's assets?

The first issue is complicated by the argument that the pension liability *should differ* from other liabilities by virtue of its tax deductibility. Unlike other debt where the payment of principal is not tax deductible, reductions in the liability due to firm contributions are usually tax deductible. Thus, if the market reduces its valuation of a firm by $1 for each dollar of debt, $1 of pension liability should reduce valuation by only $(1 − t)$, where t represents the firm's marginal tax rate.

The second question relates to the going concern assumption underlying pension measurements. This assumption is consistent with the view that pensions are a form of implicit contract between the firm and its employees. Use of the PBO measure recognizes that an implicit contract exists whereby the firm will continue to adjust salaries upward with inflation. Moreover, the firm will not terminate the plan early, thereby ultimately redressing the undercompensation of younger workers relative to older ones.

The third issue implicitly addresses the ownership of the underlying property rights of the pension assets. Landsman (1986) studied pension assets separately from the pension liabilities, and

disaggregated corporate assets into pension and non-pension assets and corporate liabilities into pension and non-pension liabilities. This procedure does two things. First, it allows for the possibility that pension assets represent assets to which the firm has claim, and that pension liabilities represent a debt obligation of the firm. Second, if in fact pension assets are corporate assets and pension liabilities are corporate obligations, it also permits the pension and non-pension components of corporate assets and liabilities to be differentially priced by the securities markets.*

Prior to SFAS 87, pension accounting was based on APB 8, under which the only disclosure required was the *unfunded portion of the VBO*. SFAS 36, issued in 1980, required disclosure of the entire ABO but not the PBO. Hence, many researchers were constrained by the lack of data as to the total ABO, PBO, and value of pension assets.

Beta and the Pension Liability

One of the determinants of a firm's risk is its financial leverage, with a leveraged firm being riskier than an unleveraged one. Using beta (β) to measure the systematic risk of the firm, this relationship is expressed as

$$\beta_L = \beta_U \left(1 + \frac{D}{E}\right)$$

where β_L and β_U are the betas of the unleveraged and leveraged firms, respectively, and D/E is the firm's debt-to-equity ratio.

Using a sample of 55 firms, Dhaliwal (1986) found that adjusting the debt/equity ratio by including unfunded (vested) pension liabilities improved the explanatory power of his predictive model and that market participants view unfunded (vested) pension liabilities in much the same way as they view other debt in assessing a firm's systematic risk. This conclusion reinforces our view that financial statements adjusted for pension plan status are more useful for financial analysis.

Market Valuation of Liability

Feldstein and Morck (1983) examined the market's valuation of a firm's pension liability. Using 1979 data for 132 companies, they were limited insofar as only the unfunded ABO and unfunded vested ABO information was available. They hypothesized that these liabilities should reduce the value of the firm on a dollar-for-dollar basis. Thus a market valuation equation that includes pension liabilities as one of its explanatory variables should yield a coefficient of -1 for the pension liabilities. Depending on how they measured the other variables in their valuation equation, they found that the coefficient on pension liabilities ranged from -0.7 to -1.50 (one could not reject the hypothesis that these coefficients were equal to -1). Results for the vested and total ABO were similar. Additionally, they found that interest rate assumptions varied widely among firms. When an average rate† was used, they found a better fit for their equations, suggesting that the market adjusts the rates used by firms to some overall average.

Daley (1984) argued that the pension liability should not be valued on a dollar-for-dollar basis but rather on an after-tax basis. Thus the appropriate coefficient for an unadjusted pension liability would be $-(1 - t)$, where t is the firm's tax rate. Only for an adjusted liability, that is, the liability multiplied by $(1 - t)$ would the expected coefficient be -1. Daley, however, found that for his sample, the unfunded vested pension benefit (UVB), adjusted for taxes, had coefficients ranging from -1.5 to -3 and that these variables were significantly different than -1. He does however note that

> This result is consistent with prior research, once an adjustment for the average marginal tax rate is imposed. In Oldfield (1976) and Feldstein and Seligman (1981), no tax adjustment was used and the coefficients associated with UVB measure are approximately -1.0 to -1.5. Impounding the tax rate of $(1 - t)$ tax adjusted values of these coefficients would be -1.92 to -2.88 (assuming a .48 marginal tax rate) Thus, the results here are at least partially supported by earlier research.‡

Daley also examined the effects of using pension expense rather than UVB in the valuation model and found that the pension expense had more explanatory power than the UVB.

An explanation for the finding that the absolute value of the coefficient is greater than -1 might be that these studies were limited to the use of liabilities based on the ABO. The PBO is greater than the ABO. Thus it is possible that the market based its valuation of the PBO by adjusting each ABO dollar by an amount greater than 1. Alternatively, misspecified coefficients may result if there are missing variables that are systematically related to those variables used in the equation. This raises the intriguing possibility that pension liabilities were acting as a surrogate for postretirement health benefits not contained in these equations. They are off balance sheet and would be expected to be systematically related to pension obligations.

Market Valuation of Pension Cost Components

Barth, Beaver, and Landsman (1992) using SFAS 87–based data compared the market valuation of various components of pension expense with nonpension expense items. Market valuation of a revenue or expense item reflects the extent to which the market discounts the future stream of this component. Therefore, a higher valuation means that the market uses a lower discount rate for that item. They found that pension expense was more heavily valued than other nonpension items. The reason for this higher valuation may be that the market views nonpension expense as less risky; hence a lower discount rate is appropriate. The fact that pension expense includes the return on plan assets, which are usually invested in less risky assets such as bonds, is consistent with this result. Moreover, the interest component of pension expense is also relatively predictable and hence less "risky."

With respect to the components of pension expense, they found the interest component as well as the expected and actual return on plan assets to have the highest valuation. The actual return had a slightly greater valuation measure than the expected return, but the difference between the two was not significant. A "zero" valuation for the three amortization components was found. This is to be expected as these items reflect no new information. The most surprising result was that the service cost component seemed to be valued "incorrectly" by the market (i.e., the higher the component, the higher the firm's value). The authors attributed this result to correlations among the various components.

Notwithstanding this anomalous finding, the study also found that the income components as well as the balance sheet elements of the pension costs were incrementally informative when included in a firm's valuation model. Again, this suggests that detailed analysis of a firm's pension plan contributes to better investment and credit decisions.

*Landsman, Wayne "An Empirical Investigation of Pension and Property Rights," The Accounting Review, (October 1986) p. 664

†They used the average rate calculated over all firms in the sample. The adjustment procedure was approximate; they multiplied the ABO by the ratio of the firm's assumed interest rate to the average rate.

‡Daley, Lane A. "The Valuation of Reported Pension Measures For Firms Sponsoring Defined Benefit Plans," The Accounting Review, (April 1984) p. 194

3. The firm will continue to grant pay raises;

4. The firm will not terminate the plan and pay off the obligations early.

These assumptions, in total, constitute the *going concern assumption* that underlies the preparation of financial statements. That is why we suggest that, in most cases, projected benefits data be used to analyze a company's pension plan. If we want to assume termination of the plan (perhaps in takeover analysis), then the ABO would be the appropriate measure of the pension obligation. Assuming termination of the plan, however, also requires analysis of the impact of such termination on the work force of the company.

If the going concern assumption is not valid (bankruptcy, for example), then the ABO or VBO should be used to measure the pension obligation.[17] Under these circumstances, however, *all* assets and liabilities of the firm need to be evaluated for the impact of this event.

The second issue is whether the pension plan should be viewed as an integral part of the firm or whether the plan is an independent entity. Under a defined benefit plan it is the employer who bears the risk of investment performance. If the pension fund is

[17]However, in case of bankruptcy, regulations of the Pension Benefit Guaranty Corp. (PBGC) may limit the firm's obligation to 40% of shareholders' equity.

insufficient to meet the obligations of the pension plan, the firm must cover the shortfall. Conversely, however, the firm can capture any excess assets either by lowering its future contributions or by terminating the plan directly. There are some restrictions (mainly ERISA) affecting the level of contributions and the ability of the firm to utilize the assets of the plan.[18]

If one views the pension plan as an integral part of the firm, then its balance sheet should be adjusted by adding pension plan assets to the firm's assets and the PBO to the firm's liabilities. The difference between plan assets and the liability (PBO) would be added to stockholders' equity. Pension cost would be the "gross pension cost" defined earlier. The return on plan assets would be included in the income statement as investment income. The only cash flow effect of the pension plan would be the benefits paid; contributions to the plan would be transfers of cash from one "subsidiary" of the firm to another.

If one views the pension plan as independent of the firm, then only the *net* difference between the plan assets and the PBO should be added to the firm's liabilities (or assets, if pension assets exceed PBO). The offset to this adjustment would again be stockholders' equity. This approach recognizes that retirees have first claim against pension assets; only the residual is an asset or liability of the employer. In this case pension cost would be net of the actual returns on the pension plan; that is, the nonsmoothed amount shown earlier and the cash flow effect would be the contributions from the firm to the pension plan.

SFAS 87 treats the pension plan as a separate entity. Only the *net* asset or liability and the *net* pension cost (to the extent there is recognition) are reflected in the financial statements. Generally speaking, we concur with this view. In addition, based on the going concern view, we believe that under most circumstances, the PBO should be used to measure the liability.

ANALYZING PENSION PLAN DISCLOSURES

The General Motors Plan

Exhibit 9-5 contains the pension footnote from the *1990 Annual Report* of General Motors[19] (GM). As required by SFAS 87, it provides separate disclosure of the status of U.S. and non-U.S. plans and of the overfunded and underfunded (as measured by the difference between the fair market value of assets and the ABO) plans.

Note that plans can migrate between categories from year to year. While it is useful to know that some plans are underfunded (see discussion later), we cannot analyze these

---

[18]For companies in regulated industries, such as public utilities, any surplus may belong to the ratepayers rather than the employer. Similarly, there is some question as to the "ownership" of surplus pension assets of defense contractors, whose profits are regulated by the U.S. government. For example, the pension footnote from the *1990 Annual Report* of McDonnell Douglas states that the U.S. government indicates that it is "entitled to its equitable share [of pension fund reversions] to the extent that the Government participated in pension costs through their contracts." Yet McDonnell Douglas was able to recognize a substantial settlement gain in 1990 (see discussion later in the chapter).

[19]GM presents the plans for years ending (measurement dates) October 1 and December 1 for various plans; up to a three-month lag behind the balance sheet date is permitted by SFAS 87.

EXHIBIT 9-5. GENERAL MOTORS
Pension Footnote from *1990 Annual Report*

NOTE 6. Pension Program and Postemployment Benefits

The Corporation and its subsidiaries have a number of defined benefit pension plans covering substantially all employes. Plans covering U.S. and Canadian represented employes generally provide benefits of negotiated stated amounts for each year of service as well as significant supplemental benefits for employes who retire with 30 years of service before normal retirement age. The benefits provided by the plans covering its U.S. and Canadian salaried employes, and employes in certain foreign locations, are generally based on years of service and the employe's salary history. The Corporation and its subsidiaries also have certain nonqualified pension plans covering executives which are based on targeted wage replacement percentages and are unfunded.

Plan assets are primarily invested in United States Government obligations, equity and fixed income securities, commingled pension trust funds, GM preference stock valued at approximately $690.8 million as of the measurement date in 1990, and insurance contracts. The Corporation's funding policy with respect to its qualified plans is to contribute annually not less than the minimum required by applicable law and regulation nor more than the maximum amount which can be deducted for Federal income tax purposes.

Certain changes in actuarial assumptions had the effect of reducing the 1990 consolidated net loss by $289.8 million or $0.48 per share of $1-2/3 par value common stock.

Total pension expense of the Corporation and its subsidiaries amounted to $368.9 million in 1990, $810.8 million in 1989, and $544.4 million in 1988. Net periodic pension cost (credit) for 1990, 1989, and 1988 of U.S. plans and plans of subsidiaries outside the United States included the components shown in the table.

1990		U.S. Plans		Non-U.S. Plans
		(Dollars in Millions)		
Benefits earned during the year		$ 713.6		$ 105.5
Interest accrued on benefits earned in prior years		3389.4		373.0
Return on assets				
—Actual loss	$ 2,117.1		$ 159.9	
—Plus deferred loss	(6,153.9)	(4,036.8)	(517.0)	(357.1)
Net amortization		93.2		7.9
Net periodic pension cost		$ 159.4		$ 129.3
1989				
Benefits earned during the year		$ 661.2		$ 90.7
Interest accrued on benefits earned in prior years		3,331.6		335.4
Return on assets				
—Actual gain	($ 6,443.9)		($ 532.2)	
—Less deferred gain	3,025.6	(3,418.3)	204.5	(327.7)
Net amortization		87.0		(7.9)
Net periodic pension cost		$ 661.5		$ 90.5

EXHIBIT 9-5. *(Continued)*

1988				
Benefits earned during the year		$ 616.6		$ 83.1
Interest accrued on benefits earned in prior years		3,190.3		301.4
Return on assets				
—Actual loss	$ 56.1		$ 25.7	
—Plus deferred loss	(3,420.2)	(3,364.1)	(394.2)	(368.5)
Net amortization		74.9		(47.0)
Net periodic pension cost (credit)		$ 517.7		$ (31.0)

The table on the next page reconciles the funded status of the Corporation's U.S. and non-U.S. plans with amounts recognized in the Corporation's Consolidated Balance Sheet at December 31, 1990 and 1989.

The unfunded liability in excess of the unamortized prior service cost and net transition obligation was recorded as a reduction of $1,004.7 million in Stockholders' Equity during 1990 in accordance with Statement of Financial Accounting Standards No. 87, Employers' Accounting for Pensions. The remaining portion of the unfunded liability of $5,874.9 million and $2,101.0 million was primarily recorded as an intangible asset at December 31, 1990 and 1989, respectively.

Measurement dates used for the Corporation's principal U.S. plans are October 1 for GM's plans (including Delco Electronics Corporation) and EDS, and December 1 for Hughes plans. For non-U.S. plans, the measurement dates used are October 1 for certain foreign plans and December 1 for Canadian plans.

The weighted averaged discount rate used in determining the actuarial present values of the projected benefit obligation shown in the table on the next page for U.S. plans was 10.0% at December 31, 1990 and 9.5% at December 31, 1989 and for non-U.S. plans was 10.5% at December 31, 1990 and 9.8% at December 31, 1989. The rate of increase in future compensation levels of applicable U.S. employes was 5.4% at both December 31, 1990 and December 31, 1989 and of applicable non-U.S. employes was 5.9% at December 31, 1990 and 5.5% at December 31, 1989. Benefits under the hourly plans are generally not based on wages and therefore no benefit escalation beyond existing negotiated increases was included. The expected long-term rate of return on assets used in determining pension expense for U.S. plans was 11.0% for 1990 and 10.1% for 1989, and for non-U.S. plans was 10.9% for 1990 and 10.5% for 1989. The assumptions for non-U.S. plans were developed on a basis consistent with that for U.S. plans, adjusted to reflect prevailing economic conditions and interest rate environments.

In addition to providing pension benefits, the Corporation and certain of its subsidiaries provide certain health care and life insurance benefits for active and retired employes. The Corporation recognizes the cost of providing those benefits as incurred. The cost of such benefits amounted to $3,782.1 million in 1990, $3,450.4 million in 1989, and $3,507.7 million in 1988, of which $1,198.7 million in 1990. $1,067.4 million in 1989, and $1,130.6 million in 1988 related to retired employes.

	U.S. Plans				Non–U.S. Plans			
	1990		1989		1990		1989	
Actuarial present value of benefits based on service to date and present pay levels	Assets Exceed Accum. Benefits	Accum. Benefits Exceed Assets	Assets Exceed Accum. Benefits	Accum. Benefits Exceed Assets	Assets Exceed Accum. Benefits	Accum. Benefits Exceed Assets	Assets Exceed Accum. Benefits	Accum. Benefits Exceed Assets
Vested	$15,236.9	$18,901.1	$14,300.3	$16,948.5	$2,037.4	$1,638.1	$1,969.9	$1,261.0
Nonvested	493.3	4,466.4	614.9	3,731.4	137.7	40.2	161.1	38.1

EXHIBIT 9-5. *(Continued)*

Accumulated benefit obligation	15,730.2	23,367.5	14,915.2	20,679.9	2,175.1	1,678.3	2,131.0	1,299.1
Additional amounts related to projected pay increases	1,517.7	111.4	1,553.6	78.5	165.8	312.1	154.7	225.9
Total projected benefit obligation based on service to date	17,247.9	23,478.9	16,468.8	20,758.4	2,340.9	1,990.4	2,285.7	1,525.0
Plan assets at fair value	18,678.8	16,209.7	21,166.0	18,885.9	3,080.9	49.8	3,174.2	8.6
Projected benefit obligation (in excess of) less than plan assets	1,430.9	(7,269.2)	4,697.2	(1,872.5)	740.0	(1,940.6)	888.5	(1,516.4)
Unamortized net amount resulting from changes in plan experience and actuarial assumptions	1,886.2	1,086.8	(915.0)	(1,093.7)	448.0	(99.3)	120.3	(221.0)
Unamortized prior service cost	818.6	4,306.3	16.5	1,612.8	323.5	212.5	334.0	203.3
Unamortized net obligation (asset) at date of adoption	(1,751.9)	1,345.4	(1,946.1)	1,480.0	(691.5)	437.2	(696.1)	417.6
Adjustment for unfunded pension liabilities	—	(6,627.1)	—	(1,920.6)	—	(252.5)	—	(180.4)
Net prepaid pension cost (accrued liability) recognized in the consolidated balance sheet	$ 2,383.8	$ (7,157.8)	$ 1,852.6	$ (1,794.0)	$ 820.0	$(1,642.7)	$ 646.7	$(1,296.9)

Source: General Motors *1990 Annual Report.*

plans separately because the pension cost components are disclosed on a combined basis. Therefore, we must combine the plan status data for underfunded and overfunded plans, and the result, shown in Exhibit 9-6, is the basis for our analysis.

Estimating GM's Pension Status

Exhibit 9-6 shows us that the PBO exceeds plan assets by $5.8 billion at December 31, 1990. This shortfall is nearly 20% of the company's net worth of $30 billion. In GM's case, most of this difference ($4.8 billion) is not off balance sheet but is reflected[20] on GM's balance sheet because of the "minimum liability" provision.

Minimum Liability Provision

SFAS 87 requires that, for pension plans whose assets are below the accumulated benefit obligation, the difference *must* be immediately recognized on the balance sheet. In

---

[20]As will be discussed, only the liability section fully reflects the minimum liability. Only a portion of the minimum liability is generally charged to equity; the rest is offset by an intangible asset.

EXHIBIT 9-6. GENERAL MOTORS
Status of U.S. Pension Plans, at December 31, 1989–1990 (in $ millions)

	1989	1990
Projected benefit obligation	$(37,227.2)	$(40,726.8)
Plan assets at fair value	40,051.9	34,888.5
PBO (exceeding) less than assets	$ 2,824.7	$ (5,838.3)
Less: Unamortized net amount of (gains)/losses	(2,008.7)	2,973.0
Prior service cost	1,629.3	5,124.9
Transition (asset)	(466.1)	(406.5)
Subtotal	$ (845.5)	$ 7,691.4
Prepaid cost (liability) before adjustment for minimum liability	1,979.2	1,853.1
Minimum liability recognized	(1,920.6)	(6,627.1)
Net prepaid cost (liability) recognized on balance sheet	$ 58.6	$ (4,774.0)

Exhibit 9-5 (the footnote from GM's *1990 Annual Report*), the "underfunded" plans are disclosed separately from those with assets exceeding accumulated benefits. We can compute the degree of underfunding for these plans:

Accumulated benefit obligation	$ 23,367.5 million
Plan assets	(16,209.7)
ABO excess over assets	$ 7,157.8 million

Because of the delayed recognition of actuarial losses, prior service cost, and the transition liability related to these plans, GM's accrued (balance sheet) liability for these plans is only $530.7 million (PBO excess less the three unamortized elements just listed). To bring the accrued liability up to the level of the ABO excess, GM is required under SFAS 87 to recognize this "minimum liability" of $6,627.1 million ($7,157.8 million − $530.7 million).

The minimum liability adjusts for most of the PBO-based obligation. This is true for GM because, as Exhibit 9-5 indicates, the difference between the PBO and the ABO for the underfunded plans is very small (less than 0.5%). The footnote tells us that

> Benefits under the hourly plans are generally not based on wages and therefore no benefit escalation beyond existing negotiated increases was included.

That is, the hourly plans have essentially "flat" provisions, which would make the difference between the PBO and ABO close to zero, as we discussed earlier in the chapter. For firms whose PBO differs from the ABO, the minimum liability will not "cover" the PBO-based liability.

Implications for General Motors

The minimum liability has *not* been included in pension cost or net income. In the short run, therefore, the minimum liability is a "cosmetic" accounting entry with no cash flow or income consequence. Approximately $1 billion (the minimum liability less unamortized prior service cost and unamortized transition liability) was directly charged to stockholders' equity;[21] the remainder is offset by an intangible asset on GM's balance sheet. If the "pension intangible," which is really just a means of deferring recognition, was fully charged to equity, the effect would be to lower equity by nearly $5 billion (or approximately 17%).

This treatment does not, however, mean that the liability will never affect reported income. Amortization of prior service cost, in particular, will affect pension cost (and net income) quite rapidly, as we will see when we project GM's 1991 pension cost. In addition, underfunding of the pension plan will eventually have to be made up by higher contributions or by investment performance.

GM's footnote shows separately those plans that are significantly underfunded; the minimum liability provision is most likely related to the plans covering (unionized) hourly workers. Presumably, the union leaders also know the plan status, as they receive financial statements of the plan itself (with the same information regarding the benefit obligation and plan assets). This situation may not bode well for future labor negotiations.

These plans have a very substantial amount of unrecognized prior service cost (over $5 billion). As we shall see (in Exhibit 9-7), prior service cost (resulting from plan amendments) was created in 1987 as well as 1990. This suggests a pattern of periodically increasing benefits to recognize the effects of inflation. The increased benefits do not affect GM's pension plan accounting until they are granted. However, the analysis does suggest that the obligation to provide pensions is understated in GM's financial statements. This issue is not discussed by GM in its annual report.

Finally, GM's discount rate at 10% is higher than average for American firms (see AICPA survey). Using a lower discount rate would increase the pension obligation and make the company's plans appear even more underfunded.

GM's Pension Costs

The analysis used for the DBP plan can be applied to the GM plans. The methodology is shown in Exhibits 9-7 and 9-8 for the U.S. plans on a combined basis.

Let us start with Exhibit 9-7. First we can calculate the contribution by adding the change in the balance sheet asset or liability to pension cost. This change is calculated on the basis of the balance sheet asset/liability prior to the inclusion of the "minimum liability" provision; that provision has no direct cash flow or income statement consequences.

Second, we can determine benefits paid by subtracting the actual return on assets (shown in the calculation of pension cost in Exhibit 9-5) and GM contributions to the plan from the change in pension assets. Third, we confirm our estimate of benefits paid

---

[21]The adjustment to shareholders' equity is made after an allowance for deferred taxes. For the portion reported as an intangible asset no adjustment for deferred taxes is made.

EXHIBIT 9-7. GENERAL MOTORS
Analysis of U.S. Pension Plans, 1986–1990 (in $ millions)

	1986	1987	1988	1989	1990
Pension cost	$ 734.9	$ 810.5	$ 517.7	$ 661.5	$ 159.4
Change in liability	871.3	644.5	337.9	(720.3)	(126.1)
Contribution*	$ 1606.2	$ 1455.0	$ 855.6	$ (58.8)	$ 33.3
Pension plan assets					
Closing balance	$32,084.8	$38,521.5	$36,410.3	$40,051.9	$34,888.5
Opening balance	25,810.0	32,084.8	38,521.5	36,410.3	40,051.9
Change	$ 6,274.8	$ 6,436.7	$(2,111.2)	$ 3,641.6	$(5,163.4)
Less: Actual return	6,711.2	7,436.6	(56.1)	6,443.9	(2,117.1)
Contribution	1,606.2	1,455.0	855.6	(58.8)	33.3
Equals: Benefits paid	$ (2,042.6)	$ (2,454.9)	$ (2,910.7)	$ (2,743.5)	$ (3,079.6)
Projected benefit obligation					
Closing balance	$32,916.7	$31,822.1	$34,785.9	$37,227.2	$40,726.8
Opening balance	24,259.7	32,916.7	31,822.1	34,785.9	37,227.2
Change	$ 8,657.0	$(1,094.6)	$ 2,963.8	$ 2,441.3	$ 3,499.6
Less: Service cost	622.3	798.2	616.6	661.2	713.6
Interest cost	2,517.7	2,718.0	3,190.3	3,331.6	3,389.4
Actuarial adjustments	7,559.5	(4,241.7)	2,070.0	1,183.2	(1,172.2)
Prior service cost	0	2,085.9	(2.4)	8.8	3,648.4
Equals: Benefits paid	$ (2,042.5)	$ (2,455.0)	$ (2,910.7)	$ (2,743.5)	$ (3,079.6)
Deferred gains (losses)					
Opening balance	$ 0	$ (3193.7)	$ 5656.5	$ 166.3	$ 2008.7
Less: Amortization	0	0	0	0	0
Plus: Deferred investment					
gains (losses)	4365.8	4608.4	(3420.2)	3025.6	(6153.9)
Deferred actuarial gains					
losses	(7559.5)	4241.7	(2070.0)	(1183.2)	1172.2
Ending balance	$ (3193.7)	$ 5656.5	$ 166.3	$ 2008.7	$ (2973.0)
Transition asset					
Closing balance	$ 644.7	$ 585.2	$ 525.4	$ 466.1	$ 406.5
Opening balance	704.5	644.7	585.2	525.4	466.1
Amortization	$ 59.8	$ 59.5	$ 59.8	$ 59.3	$ 59.6
Prior service cost					
Closing balance	$ 0	$ 1903.9	$ 1766.8	$ 1629.3	$ 5124.9
Opening balance	0	0	1903.9	1766.8	1629.3
Change	$ 0	$ 1903.9	$ (137.1)	$ (137.5)	$ 3495.6
Less: Amortization	0	(182.0)	(134.7)	(146.3)	(152.8)
Equals: New prior service cost	$ 0	$ 2085.9	$ (2.4)	$ 8.8	3648.4

EXHIBIT 9-7. *(Continued)*

	1986	1987	1988	1989	1990
Actuarial assumptions (year end)					
Discount rate (%)	8.5	10.4	10.0	9.5	10.0
Compensation growth rate (%)	5.6	5.5	5.6	5.4	5.4

*The computation of periodic contributions uses the change in the balance sheet liability *excluding* the minimum liability recognized. Unlike other components of the balance sheet liability (prior service cost, transition asset or liability, etc.), the minimum liability does not have a direct impact on pension cost or cash flows.

by subtracting the following elements from the change in the projected benefit obligation:

- Service cost
- Interest cost
- Actuarial gains or losses
- Prior service cost

The first two of these elements are shown among the components of pension cost (Exhibit 9-5). The last two must be calculated using the data in the footnote. The calculations for 1990 follow:

First, we must disentangle the "net amortization" element of pension cost, which contains the amortization of the transition asset, prior service cost, and unamortized deferred gains and losses. (All these appear in the plan reconciliation in Exhibit 9-6.) We start with the transition asset, which GM calls "unamortized net obligation (asset) at the date of adoption":

$$\text{Amortization} = \text{Change in unamortized asset}$$
$$= \$466.1 \text{ million} - \$406.5 \text{ million} = \$59.6 \text{ million}$$

As the total "net amortization" is $(93.2) million, this leaves $152.8 million ($93.2 million + $59.6 million) as the amortization of prior service costs and/or deferred gains and losses.

We turn now to the unamortized gains and losses, which are the result of deferred investment gains and losses and the impact of actuarial adjustments. The net change is from a gain of $2008.7 million at the end of 1989 to a loss of $2973.0 million at the end of 1990. This change must encompass any amortization of the 1989 balance *and* newly originating gains and losses. We also know (from the calculation of pension cost in Exhibit 9-5) that GM deferred investment losses of $6153.9 million.

As it appears that GM uses the corridor method[22] (total amortization for 1988 was low despite the large deferred losses at the end of 1987), we can make the simplifying

[22]See Page 650 and Footnote 8 for a definition of the corridor method.

assumption that amortization of gains and losses has been zero. The actuarial gains and losses can now be deduced as follows:

Change in unamortized amounts ($2973.0 million) − $2008.7 million =	$(4981.7) million
Amortization of 1989 balance assumed to be	0
Less: Deferred investment loss in 1990	(6153.9)
Equals: Deferred actuarial gain in 1990	$1172.2 million

We can now complete our disaggregation of the "net amortization" element of 1990 pension cost:

Net amortization	$(93.2) million
Less: Amortization of	
Transition asset	59.6
Gains and losses	0
Equals: Amortization of prior service	$(152.8) million

This result can be used to calculate the amount of prior service cost that was created in 1990:

$$\text{Prior service cost} = \text{Change for year} + \text{Amortization}$$
$$= (\$5124.9 \text{ million} - \$1629.3 \text{ million}) + \$152.8 \text{ million}$$
$$= \$3648.4$$

Finally, we are able to reconcile the PBO and reach the same benefits paid figure we obtained by reconciling plan assets. These calculations are shown in Exhibit 9-7.

While GM is an extreme example, the analysis of a company's pension plan footnotes can be complex. The order of steps is not always the same but depends on the presentation of data, which varies from company to company. The best approach is to write out the identities shown in Exhibit 9-7 and then start to "fill in the blanks" until all the data are derived. Assumptions (such as the one we made about the amortization of gains and losses) may be required. The payoff is a detailed picture of the pension plan similar to Exhibits 9-7 and 9-8. These data can be used to understand better the impact of the plan on past, present, and future net income and cash flows.

Analysis of GM Pension Trends

The data in Exhibits 9-6, 9-7, and 9-8 can now be used to gain insights into the impact of the U.S. pension plans on GM.

Pension Obligation Trends

Looking at all of GM's U.S. plans together, the PBO has grown by more than $16 billion or two-thirds over the five-year period ending December 31, 1990. By looking at the elements of the change in PBO in Exhibit 9-7, we can better understand the reasons for this growth. Current employee service has contributed little to the growth; service cost (discussed under pension cost trends shortly) has shown little growth. Large benefit payments (benefit payments in 1990 were four times service cost) have reduced the PBO. This is typical of a mature work force. Interest cost has been a major factor in the increase in the PBO as employees move closer to retirement.

Two other factors are worthy of mention. Prior service cost, resulting from benefit increases in 1987 and 1990, accounted for fully one-third of the increase in the PBO over the five-year period. The fact that the hourly plans provide "flat" benefits leaving pensioners exposed to inflation makes benefit improvements an important objective when labor contracts are renegotiated. *Analysts should be wary of "flat benefit" plans that show periodic amendments accounted for as "prior service" cost since the PBO may significantly understate the pension obligation by excluding benefit increases that are likely to occur.*

Actuarial losses, when summed over the five-year period, also account for about one-third of the net increase in the PBO. Part of the actuarial loss reflects changes in assumptions. The January 1, 1986, PBO was based on a discount rate of 10.9%. The large "loss" in 1986 was primarily due to the change in discount rate to 8.5%. The change to 10.4% in 1987 recovered much of the 1986 "loss." GM has changed its discount rate in every year, resulting in gains and losses in subsequent years as well.

GM has changed the assumed compensation growth rate in amost every year as well. This affects those plans that do take salaries into account. In Exhibit 9-5, note that the "overfunded" plans at December 31, 1990, have a PBO nearly 10% above the ABO, indicating that some plans are pay related. The gradual decrease in the assumed compensation growth rate from 5.8% at January 1, 1986, to 5.4% at December 31, 1990, has helped reduce the growth of the PBO for these plans.

Over the five-year period, the effects of changing assumptions do not explain the aggregate actuarial loss of more than $5 billion.[23] It appears likely, although we do not have the data to be certain, that GM's employee-related assumptions (mortality, quit rates, etc.) proved to be optimistic as well.

Trends in Pension Cost

At the beginning of 1986, when GM adopted SFAS 87, assets exceeded the PBO by $1.55 billion (see opening balances for 1986 in Exhibit 9-7). Pension cost for 1986 was $735 million. After peaking at $810 million in 1987, pension cost has declined steadily, reaching $159 million in 1990. How is this possible, given the deteriorating plan status?

Exhibit 9-8 provides some answers. Service cost has shown little change. It appears that the effects of higher wages and salaries (and of the advancing age of the work force) have been offset by declining employment levels. The continued use of an aggressive (high) discount rate assumption has helped keep service cost low.

Interest cost has grown by only 35% as compared with a 68% increase in the projected benefit obligation from January 1, 1986, to December 31, 1990. That is because the big increase in the PBO in 1990 does not affect interest cost until 1991 (see the forecast that follows).

---

[23]This amount is not shown directly but can be deduced by calculating the individual additions to actuarial gains/losses from 1986 through 1990.

Expected return on assets has grown even faster, 72% from 1986 to 1990. The 60% increase in plan assets from January 1, 1986, to December 31, 1989, accounted for most of the growth; the increase in the return-on-assets assumption to 11% in 1990 accounted for the rest (see the upcoming discussion of investment performance). As the expected return has grown faster than service cost and interest cost, the net of these three components has gone from a cost of $795 million in 1986 to $66 million in 1990! Amortization components have only partly offset this trend.

The alternative pension cost measures for the General Motors plan look quite different from reported net pension cost. Nonsmoothed pension cost varies from $8.7 billion to a credit of more than $6 billion. Net pension cost, on the other hand, varied only from a high of $811 million to a low of $159 million, and some of that variation was caused by changes in the return-on-assets assumption. The amortization provisions were intended to smooth the pattern of pension costs, and they certainly have achieved that objective in GM's case. However, the justification for smoothing is that the fluctuations will tend to even out; the cumulative cost calculations cause us to question that assumption in this case.

Cumulative net pension cost over the 1986–1990 period was $2.9 billion, while cumulative "nonsmoothed" cost was $11.3 billion, a difference of $8.4 billion. The deferral of actuarial losses and prior service cost account for most of the difference. SFAS 87 does reduce pension cost volatility. However, it also postpones the recognition of that cost and asset and liability changes.

Investment Performance Trends

The analysis of the data in Exhibit 9-7 also allows us to examine the actual investment performance of GM's pension plans. Exhibit 9-8 shows the computation of actual investment returns for each year; 1988 and 1990 were poor,[24] but the other three years were excellent. While we cannot compute performance exactly (because we lack data on the timing of contributions), the mean return for the five-year period was just under 12%; the time weighted return would be slightly lower.

Over the past five years, therefore, the investment performance of GM's plan assets has exceeded its assumed rates (also shown in Exhibit 9-8). However, the use of a high assumed rate has meant that relatively little deferral is left to absorb future shortfalls. If we sum the deferred return elements of pension cost, we find that the cushion is $2,426 million or less than 7% of December 31, 1990, pension plan assets. If GM had used a lower assumed rate, the cushion would be greater.

While the footnote disclosure regarding the asset allocation of GM's plans is virtually nonexistent, some companies do make the data available. Thus it may be possible to make rough judgments regarding plan performance. Even when asset allocation data are absent, the analyst can examine investment performance over market cycles and draw some conclusions. In the case of GM, the negative returns for fiscal 1988 and 1990 and the large returns for the other three years suggest significant equity

---

[24]As most of GM's plans use an October 1 measurement date, the October 1987 market crash did not impact actual returns reported for 1987, but was reflected in the 1988 performance.

EXHIBIT 9-8. GENERAL MOTORS
U.S. Pension Plans, Computation of Pension Cost, 1986–1990 (in $ millions)

	1986	1987	1988	1989	1990
Service cost	$ 622.3	$ 798.2	$ 616.6	$ 661.2	$ 713.6
Interest cost	2517.7	2718.0	3190.3	3331.6	3389.4
Actual return	(6711.2)	(7436.6)	56.1	(6443.9)	2117.1
Deferred return	4365.8	4608.4	(3420.2)	3025.6	(6153.9)
Expected return	$(2345.4)	$(2828.2)	$(3364.1)	$(3418.3)	$(4036.8)
Amortization of losses (gains)	0	0	0	0	0
Amortization of prior service	0	182.0	134.7	146.3	152.8
Amortization of transition asset	(59.9)	(59.5)	(59.8)	(59.3)	(59.6)
Net pension cost	**$ 734.9**	**$ 810.5**	**$ 517.7**	**$ 661.5**	**$ 159.4**
Cumulative	$ 734.9	$ 1545.4	$ 2063.1	$ 2724.6	$ 2884.0
% Discount rate*	10.9	8.5	10.4	10.0	9.5
% Assumed ROA	10.0	10.0	10.0	10.1	11.0
% Actual ROA	24.3	23.2	(0.1)	17.7	(5.3)

*Rate used to discount PBO at prior year end.

Alternative Measures of Pension Cost

	1986	1987	1988	1989	1990
(1) Service cost	**$ 622.3**	**$ 798.2**	**$ 616.6**	**$ 661.2**	**$ 713.6**
Interest cost	2517.7	2718.0	3190.3	3331.6	3389.4
(2) Recurring cost	**$ 3140.0**	**$ 3516.2**	**$ 3806.9**	**$ 3992.8**	**$ 4103.0**
Prior service cost	0	2085.6	(2.4)	8.8	3648.4
Actuarial (gains)/losses	7559.5	(4241.7)	2070.0	1183.2	(1172.2)
(3) Gross pension cost	**$10699.5**	**$ 1360.1**	**$ 5874.5**	**$ 5184.8**	**$ 6579.2**
Actual ROA	(6711.2)	(7436.6)	56.1	(6443.9)	2117.1
(4) Nonsmoothed pension cost	**$ 3988.3**	**$(6076.5)**	**$ 5930.6**	**$(1259.1)**	**$ 8696.3**
Cumulative	3988.3	(2088.2)	3842.4	2583.3	11279.6
(5) Contributions	**1606.2**	**1455.0**	**855.6**	**(58.8)**	**33.3**
(6) Benefits paid	**(2042.6)**	**(2454.9)**	**(2910.7)**	**(2743.5)**	**(3079.6)**

holdings in the plans. While not a major issue in the GM case,[25] pension plans sometimes invest in securities of the employer (which must be disclosed). Such investments can result in plan performance that differs sharply from that of a diversified portfolio.

Cash Flow Trends

Exhibit 9-8 also tells us about the cash flows of the plan. GM's contributions have dropped from $1.6 billion for 1986 (twice pension cost) to a nominal amount for 1990. (In 1989, it appears that GM received a refund, possibly from a plan termination.)

[25]GM's pension note (Exhibit 9-5) states that the pension plans hold GM preference stock worth $690.8 million, approximately 2% of total plan assets.

At the same time, benefit payments have grown by 50% over the 1986–1990 period to more than $3 billion per year. While net cash outflows are characteristic of mature pension plans, this trend does give some concern. It appears that company contributions will have to rise again in the future.

Estimating Future Pension Cost

We have examined the trends of GM's pension costs in the period 1986–1990. Box 9-3, based on a Kidder, Peabody research study, provides some interesting insights into pension trends in the United States in the 1980s.

The analysis made there depends on the forecast of future pension costs. Fortunately, the provisions of SFAS 87 make it possible to forecast future pension cost. Exhibit 9-10 contains a forecast of 1991 pension cost for GM.

The first element, service cost, is difficult to forecast. We know that, all other things being equal, service cost should decline in 1991 because GM increased the discount rate in 1990. Under SFAS 87 the discount rate used to compute the PBO at year end 1990 must be used to compute pension cost for 1991. Notice, for example, the decline in service cost in 1988, reflecting the increase in the discount rate used at year-end 1987.

BOX 9-3
Trends in Pension Expense and Income in the 1980s

Exhibit 9-9, from a study by E. K. Easton Ragsdale and George H. Boyd III of Kidder, Peabody's Quantitative Research Group, compares trends in pension expense and earnings of the S&P 500 companies. In the period 1982–1988, pretax profits grew from $148 billion to $260 billion. Pension expense at the same time dropped from $26 billion to $13 billion, the decline accounting for 12% of the increase in pretax profits.* The decline in pension expense was due to the following factors:

- The spate of restructurings and layoffs in traditional manufacturing industries. Firms in these industries tend to be unionized, employ large labor forces, and have high pension expense. These firms experienced the greatest declines in pension costs as they reduced their work force.†
- The adoption of SFAS 87. Early adopters of SFAS 87 tended to be firms with transition assets. The amortization of these transition assets reduced pension expense.
- The strong stock market performance in the 1980s, which increased the return on pension plan assets, thus reducing pension expense.

These factors cannot be expected to continue indefinitely. Thus declining pension expense will no longer serve as a "source" of increases in net income. Indeed in 1989, the trend did reverse, and thus the possibility exists that pension expense may begin to be a drag on profits. However, as pension expense has declined relative to overall earnings (in 1988 pension expense was less than 5% of pretax profits compared to 18% in 1982), changes in pension expense in the near future will have a lesser bottom-line impact.

---

*In terms of growth rates, this represented over 20% of the compound annual growth rate in profits.
†The severance costs associated with the layoffs are reported as part of restructuring costs (see Chapter 6), not as part of pension cost.

EXHIBIT 9-9
Impact of Declining Pension Expenses on S&P 500 Profits, 1980–1989
(in $ billions, except per share data and percentages)

	Pretax Prepension Profits	Pension Expense	Pretax Profits	Net Income	Pension Expense as a % of Pretax Prepension Profits	Pretax Profits	Earnings per Share ($)
1980	$189.3	$ 25.2	$164.1	$ 93.9	13.3%	15.3%	$14.82
1981	193.6	25.9	167.7	100.5	13.4	15.4	15.36
1982	174.5	26.7	147.8	85.5	15.3	18.1	12.64
1983	203.1	26.1	177.0	96.5	12.8	14.7	14.03
1984	230.2	24.2	206.0	121.9	10.5	11.8	16.64
1985	216.1	22.5	193.6	105.9	10.4	11.6	14.61
1986	201.5	15.3	186.2	111.7	7.6	8.2	14.48
1987	226.5	13.9	212.6	129.6	6.2	6.6	17.50
1988	273.2	13.2	260.1	177.7	4.8	5.1	23.75
1989	264.4	14.4	250.0	163.8	5.4	5.8	22.87
			Compound Annual Growth Rates				
1980–89	3.8%	−6.0%	4.8%	6.4%	—	—	4.9%
1982–89	6.1	−8.4	7.8	9.7	—	—	8.8

Source: Kidder, Peabody & Co., Quantitative Analysis: Pension Expense, August 6, 1990, Table 1, p. 3.

But service cost also depends on changes in payroll and employee ages, so we must estimate the change in these factors for the coming year.

A naive estimate would assume no change in service cost from the 1990 level, on the grounds that wage increases are balanced out by the effect of the higher discount rate. We also keep in mind that older employees have higher service costs because of the actuarial method required by SFAS 87. As we proceed through the year, this estimate can be

EXHIBIT 9-10. GENERAL MOTORS
U.S. Pension Plans, Forecast of 1991 Pension Cost (in $ millions)

Service cost	$ 642	(See text)
Interest cost	4073	(0.10 × $40,727 million)
Estimated ROA	(3838)	(0.11 × $34,888 million)
Amortization of gains/losses	0	(See text)
Amortization of prior service	304	($3648 million/12)
Amortization of transition asset	(60)	(See text)
Net pension cost	$1,121	

refined based on known employment and wage trends. As this estimate was made late in 1991, when it was known that employment had declined, we assumed a 10% decline in service cost.

The second component, interest on the PBO, is easier to forecast. It is simply the product of the discount rate (10%) and the December 31, 1990, PBO of $40,727 million. To compute the estimated return-on-assets component of pension cost, we assume that the company will continue to use the same 11% return-on-assets assumption it used for 1990. Bear in mind, however, that the company is free to change that rate. Multiplying 11% by the year-end 1990 asset value of $34,388 million produces an estimated return-on-assets component of $3838 million. Remember that the ROA component *reduces* net pension cost.

Changes in the ROA assumption have an immediate impact on pension cost and, therefore, net income. The increase in GM's assumed ROA in 1990 increased pretax income (decreased pension cost) by approximately $400 million (1% of $40 billion) in that year. As GM reported a pretax loss of $2217 million in 1990, this change in estimate decreased that loss by more than 15%. Note that changes in pension *assumptions* are not considered changes in accounting principles and are *not* highlighted in the auditor's report. The after tax impact of this change is disclosed in GM's pension note (third paragraph, Exhibit 9-5) but is *not* included in its discussion of operating results. It is up to the analyst to discern the significance of such estimate changes.

As previously discussed, we have assumed no amortization of gains and losses. Under the corridor method, GM need not amortize gains or losses unless they exceed $4 billion (10% of PBO, which is larger than plan assets). Deferred losses at December 31, 1990 are well below this level.

The amortization of prior service cost is affected by the large increase in prior service cost in 1990. Prior service cost must be amortized over the remaining service life of the employee group. Using amortization of the transition asset and previously incurred prior service cost as a guide, we will use 12 years, resulting in amortization of $304 million. The final component, amortization of the transition asset, has been constant over the 1986–1990 period, so we can use $60 million.

Putting all the components together would indicate that 1991 pension cost for General Motors' U.S. plans should be approximately $1121 million as compared with $159 million for 1990, an increase of about seven times! The main factors in this increase are

- Higher interest cost, due to higher PBO.
- Lower return on assets due to lower asset levels resulting from the combination of poor actual investment returns in 1990 and high benefit payments.
- Higher amortization of prior service cost resulting from benefit increases granted in 1990.

While the forecast is based on a number of assumptions, there is not too much room for error. The main risks in the forecast are that service cost varies from that estimated or that GM changes the expected return on assets. The second is, in general, the greater risk due to the large effect on pension cost of changes in that assumption. Given GM's

---

BOX 9-4
Review of 1991 Forecast of General Motors' Pension Cost

GM's pension cost components are listed here, along with the forecast of those components (from Exhibit 9-10) that was made* on the basis of 1990 pension data and the actual components of 1990 pension cost (all data in $ millions):

	1990 Actual	1991 Forecast	1991 Actual
Service cost	$ 714	$ 642	$ 772
Interest cost	3389	4073	3907
Estimated ROA	(4037)	(3838)	(3828)
Amortization	93	244	390
Net pension cost	$ 159	$ 1121	$ 1241

We refrained from a retroactive "revision" of this forecast to illustrate both the risks and benefits of forecasting. The risk is obvious: only one of the four components was forecast correctly. The causes of error are instructive:

Service Cost. GM's 1991 annual report explains that, while employees were laid off during the year, the company's union contract required that they be paid. As service cost is a function of employee salaries, our forecast was too low.

Interest Cost. The error was small on a percentage basis. The forecast did capture the large increase in interest cost.†

Expected ROA. As GM did not change its assumed ROA rate, our forecast was almost precisely correct.

Amortization. It appears that GM amortized the prior service cost, which arose from benefit increases granted in 1990, over a shorter period (about eight years) than we assumed.

Despite the errors in forecasting individual components, the forecast of pension cost was approximately correct; it predicted the large percentage increase in GM's pension cost for 1991. This illustrates the benefit of using SFAS 87 disclosures to forecast pension cost. Curiously, the increase in pension cost of more than $1 billion was not mentioned in GM's Management Discussion and Analysis!

We have not updated Exhibits 9-7 and 9-8; the 1991 data would not change the analysis. The 1991 contribution to the pension plan was nominal, despite the much higher pension cost. GM's pension plan remained significantly underfunded.

---

*This forecast was made using only 1990 data and was not revised after 1991 data were available.

†GM lowered its discount rate to 9.3% at December 31, 1991. It appears that it applied the new rate during 1991 instead of following the normal practice of using the discount rate from the prior year end. If so, that would account for the forecast error.

---

already high assumption, a further increase can be considered unlikely, although not impossible.

Box 9-4 contains an evaluation of the 1991 forecast, using the actual GM pension cost reported in its 1991 Annual Report.

The Importance of Pension Plans to GM

In conclusion, we can draw a number of inferences from our analysis of GM's U.S. pension plans:

1. The obligation has grown substantially in recent years, fueled by higher wages, plan improvements, and the effects of an aging work force. Frequent plan amendments and use of a high discount rate suggest that the obligation may be understated. GM has apparently substituted future benefits for current wages; the latter must be recognized immediately while the cost of benefits can be deferred to future periods.

2. Investment performance has been good, but use of an aggressive return assumption has left little cushion for future disappointments.

3. Favorable investment performance and the use of aggressive assumptions have resulted in declining pension cost despite the deterioration of the plan status. Contributions have also been reduced, possibly reflecting the difficult operating environment faced by the company.

4. Pension cost for 1991 is expected to rise sharply and will remain at higher levels unless asset growth accelerates. These same factors suggest that GM will have to increase its contributions to its pension plans. The fact that the underfunded plans are for unionized employees may result in union pressure on the company to accelerate funding sooner rather than later.

IMPACT OF DISCONTINUITIES

Acquisitions and Divestitures

Acquisitions and divestitures often create discontinuities in financial data that hamper financial analysis (see Chapter 12). This is true in the postemployment benefit area as well when the acquired firm or divested unit has such benefits.

Under the pooling of interests method, the financial statements of the newly acquired entity are simply added to those of the acquiring company, and past statements are restated. Thus the pension and other postretirement benefit footnote will now contain a plan that was previously not included. If the plan data for the previous year are restated, then the analysis discussed in this paper will be possible for the latest year. However, the data will no longer be consistent with that of earlier years.

If data for previous years have not been restated, or if the purchase method of accounting is used, lack of separate data on the postemployment benefit plan obligations and assets for the divested unit or acquired firm makes meaningful analysis impossible. These data are necessary to reconcile the data in the footnotes.

Under SFAS 87, the funded status of an acquired firm's plan must be explicitly recognized as part of accounting for an acquisition using the purchase method. The excess of plan assets over the projected benefit obligation at the date of acquisition is treated as a purchased asset; if the pension benefit obligation exceeds the value of plan assets, a liability in that amount must be recognized. The acquisition of a firm with a defined benefit pension plan impacts the balance sheet as well as the related footnotes. The resulting discontinuity makes analysis of the plans for that year difficult or impossible.

Divestitures of subsidiaries with postemployment benefit plans create a similar problem. The assets and obligation of the divested plan may be removed from those of the divesting firm, complicating the analysis of the footnotes for that year.

Curtailments and Settlements

SFAS 88 created new standards of accounting for curtailments and settlements.[26] A *plan curtailment* is a change in the pension obligation itself due to plan termination in total or as a result of closing down a division, effectively freezing the benefits of the affected employees. Any gain or loss due to a plan curtailment must be recognized in the current period's income.

A *plan settlement* shifts the obligation to an outside entity; for example, an employer may pay an insurance company to assume the pension obligation for a group of employees. Any difference between the amount paid and the PBO "sold" is recognized as a gain or loss from settlement of the plan.

Settlements and curtailments hamper the analysis of retirement plan disclosures, unless the gross amounts are provided. Analyses of pension data would misstate benefits paid, as these transactions reduce both the benefit obligation and the plan assets by the amount (generally unknown) paid; the benefit obligation is further reduced by the amount of the recognized gain.

For example, in 1990, McDonnell Douglas transferred its benefit obligation for approximately 37,000 retirees to two insurance companies. The settlement generated an after-tax gain of $376 million, or $9.82 per share, which exceeded the company's 1990 earnings from continuing operations of $7.18 per share; there would have been a reported loss if not for the settlement. There was no immediate cash flow consequence to McDonnell from this transaction; the company simply recognized a portion of the excess of pension plan assets over the PBO. Both plan assets and the PBO declined sharply during 1990, reflecting the transfer of pension plan assets to the insurance companies that assumed the pension liability.[27] Because the firm did not disclose the gross amounts involved and it divested a subsidiary during 1990, the disclosures mandated by SFAS 87 are insufficient to analyze fully the pension plan.

When a plan curtailment or settlement occurs as part of a plan to dispose of a segment or line of business, the effect must be included in the gain or loss from discontinued operations. For example, Vulcan Materials discontinued its Metals segment in 1987. In 1989, the company recognized additional environmental costs of $13 million relating to the discontinued operations and a gain of $6.5 million from the "curtailment and settlement in 1988 and 1989 of certain pension obligations referable to former Metals employees." The net of these two amounts, less income tax benefit, was shown as a loss from discontinued operations in 1989.

The potential for settlements and/or curtailments of pension plans are important considerations for analysts. "Capturing" the excess assets in the plan can greatly increase

---

[26]Similar principles apply to settlements or curtailments of other postemployment benefits accounted for under SFAS 106.

[27]The only cash consequences are the effects of the curtailment or settlement on future contributions. Only when a plan is terminated does the firm get the immediate use of excess assets.

a firm's liquidity. The excess can be obtained immediately by termination[28] or gradually by reducing future contributions. Settlements, which are transactions between the plan and an outside party, generally have no immediate cash flow consequences for the firm, despite the gain recognized in reported income. Box 9-5 reviews some of the research on the termination of pension plans.

[28]Note that recent tax law changes have made it less attractive for firms to withdraw "excess" assets from pension plans.

BOX 9-5
The Termination of Overfunded Plans

As our example in Exhibit 9-1 showed, for the same year of work, the cost of the pension plan to the firm was much smaller for the younger worker (JR) as compared to the older one (SR). In other words, the deferred compensation earned by the younger worker was much less than the amount earned by the older one.* Thus defined benefit plans generally undercompensate employees in the initial stages of employment and overcompensate them in the later years. On average, the over- and undercompensation even out.

However, young employees must work the "full" term to make up for the early period of undercompensation to obtain the average fair wage. A termination would amount to a breach of the "implicit contract" as young, undercompensated employees would never have the chance to "get even." The resultant transfer of wealth from employees to shareholders would be greatest at an intermediate stage of their careers as the cumulative undercompensation would be greatest at that point.

Thomas (1989) examined two methods used by firms to extract funds from overfunded pension plans. The first is a slow withdrawal using changes in actuarial assumptions to lower contributions. The second type involves termination of the pension plan. The excess funds revert to the sponsoring firm, and the liabilities are rolled over into a new defined benefit or defined contribution plan. Thomas hypothesized that the motivation for terminations depends on (1) whether there was a change in control of the firm and (2) whether the change in control was a result of a friendly or hostile takeover.

Thomas made a cross-sectional comparison of firms that terminated their pension plans with firms that did not and also examined time series data for firms that terminated their plans to see if there was anything significant (or "optimal") about the timing of the termination decision.

Three competing hypotheses were offered:

1. *Liquidation of financial slack.* This motivation has been explained previously in our discussion of incentives for over/underfunding pensions (see Box 9-1).
2. *Wealth transfer from bondholder to shareholders.* If a firm were to become insolvent, the excess pension assets could be used to pay the firm's bondholders. Terminations would funnel money out of such a firm to its shareholders.
3. *Breach of implicit contracts.* The motivation here is seen as not honoring previous implicit agreements between employees and the owners. The bondholders/shareholders gain at the expense of the employees.

Exhibit 9-11, reproduced from the study, lists the predicted financial and behavior patterns that might be expected with each of the competing hypotheses.

In addition, Thomas examined whether a decline in tax status was associated with terminations or withdrawal behavior. He found that on the whole

EXHIBIT 9-11
Predictions of Competing Explanations

Nature of Predictions	Competing Hypotheses		
	Liquidation of Financial Slack	Wealth Transfers from Bondholders and PBGC	Breach of Implicit Contracts
Cross-sectional (relative to benchmark overfunded firms)	Low cash flows relative to investment opportunities Low stock of internal slack	Low equity values, in financial distress	High proportion of workers of intermediate tenure (with highest pension bonds)
Time series	Decline in operating cash flows and/or increases in investments Depletion of lower cost sources of financial slack	Substantial decline in profitability and equity value Alter portfolio of firm assets to increase risk Increase payouts to equityholders No equity issues/debt repurchases	Reversion preceded by control change
Relation between terminations and slow withdrawals	Terminations represent an extreme case, and are used if slow withdrawals are insufficient	No systematic relation	Slow withdrawals are not breaches of implicit contracts
Type of replacement plan	Defined benefit	Defined benefit	Defined contribution

Source: J.K. Thomas, "Why Do Firms Terminate Their Overfunded Pension Plans?" Journal of Accounting and Economics (1989) Table 1, p. 362.

both slow withdrawal and terminating groups are associated with unusually high proportions of low tax status firms (currently not paying taxes or carrying forward NOLs and ITCs), relative to the benchmark group. Similarly, time series analyses indicated that tax status declined for both groups.†

However, the tax status argument did not explain why some firms chose to terminate and others used the slow-withdrawal route.

Exhibit 9-12 presents the median attributes of selected financial and pension variables of firms in the study. Note that there is little difference between the terminating group with control changes and the benchmark no-withdrawal group. On the other hand, the terminating group without control changes "is significantly less profitable, is more highly levered, and has lower amounts of funds from operations than the no-withdrawal benchmark group." The slow-withdrawal group is positioned in between the benchmark no-withdrawal group and the terminating/no-control-change group.

Further examination of the terminating/no-control-change group indicated that in the years immediately preceding the termination, the firms suffered declines in funds flows, cut back on new investment, and reduced contributions to pension plans. The firms did not raise new equity or debt to make up for the shortfalls in working capital. These patterns are consistent with the

EXHIBIT 9-12

Median Attributes of Samples with Overfunded Pension Plans Taken One Year Prior to Termination 1980–1985[a]

Financial and pension variables[b]	Terminating Firms		Nonterminating Firms	
	No Control Changes (T-NC) (88 firms)	With Control Changes (T-C) (31 firms)	Slow Withdrawal (SW) (199 firms)	No Withdrawal Benchmark (NW) (688 firms)
Book debt / Book equity	0.63 (0.01)	0.43 (0.41)	0.34 (0.00)	0.46
Book debt / Market equity	0.67 (0.02)	0.38 (0.08)	0.28 (0.00)	0.44
Operating income / Total assets	0.06 (0.00)	0.10 (0.31)	0.11 (0.84)	0.11
Net income / Market equity	0.05 (0.00)	0.10 (0.02)	0.15 (0.00)	0.17
Working capital flows / Market equity	0.14 (0.00)	0.20 (0.46)	0.17 (0.26)	0.18
Cash flows / Market equity	0.16 (0.01)	0.22 (0.30)	0.19 (0.43)	0.18
# Vested / Total benefits	0.30 (0.43)	0.29 (0.52)	0.34 (0.19)	0.30
% taxpayers[c]	51% (0.00)	70% (0.11)	74% (0.02)	82%
% NOL Cfwd.[c]	35% (0.00)	11% (0.82)	9% (0.89)	9%

[a] Values reported in parentheses below the medians are p-values from two-tailed rank sum tests of the null hypothesis that the median for that sample equals the median for the benchmark (NW) sample. For the last two variables (% taxpayers and % NOL cfwd.) the p-values are based on chi-squared tests of equal proportions.

[b] Additional details regarding variable definitions are provided in the appendix to the paper. All variables are based on beginning-of-year values for the year of termination for the (T-C) terminating sample, the first year of slow withdrawal for the SW sample, and a randomly assigned year (designed to maintain a distribution similar to the SW sample) for the benchmark (NW) sample. For the T-NC terminating sample, the most recent year prior to termination with available data is used.

[c] Taxpayers and NOL cfwd. refer to firms with positive current federal tax payments (data item #63), and positive NOL carryforwards (data item #52) reported on Compustat, respectively.

Source: Thomas, Jacob K., "Why Do Firms Terminate Their Overfunded Pension Plans," *Journal of Accounting and Economics* (1989), Table 4, p. 382.

financial slack hypothesis and also suggest that slow withdrawals take place prior to terminations.‡

Thomas could not find convincing support for the wealth transfer from debtholders hypothesis. Although the low-profitability results (see Exhibit 9-12) for the terminating/no-control-change firms are consistent with firms facing financial distress, Thomas found that this group of firms repaid some long-term debt as well as cut dividends in the years leading up to the termination. This behavior is inconsistent with wealth transfers from bondholders to shareholders.

Vested employees tend to be in the intermediate stage of their employment lives and hence are significantly affected by a plan termination; they lose the additional benefits that depend on salary increases prior to retirement. On the other hand, employees whose benefits are not vested (or partially vested) lose some or all of the benefits already earned. As it is unclear which conditions result in the maximum wealth transfer from employees to bondholders/shareholders, the vesting argument cannot be used to support the breach of contract hypothesis. Not surprisingly, Exhibit 9-12 shows that the proportion of vested employees does not differ among the categories of firms.

An examination of 63 of the 88 terminating/no-control-change firms indicated that 62% of the firms (by number) replaced their defined benefit plans with a defined contribution plan. This lends some support to the breach of contract hypothesis, as by switching to a defined contribution plan, the later promised payments will not materialize. However, it was found that 61% of the plans (in dollar terms) were replaced by another defined benefit plan.

An examination of the 29 terminating/control-change firms indicate that 11 were the result of friendly takeovers. These terminations were motivated by the wish to consolidate the various plans of the merging firms into one overall plan. The remaining control-change firms were unfriendly takeovers. Thomas suggests that such takeovers are often characterized by financial restructuring, leaving the firms highly leveraged and suffering stringent financial conditions. The terminations could therefore be motivated by a desire to obtain additional funds to finance the takeover and alleviate the financial constraints much the same way firms engage in asset sales following costly takeovers.

---

*This point can perhaps be better understood if one considers what happens if the firm terminated the plan after one year. Each employee would be paid the present value of his or her future benefits. The amount that would be paid the younger worker is much less than the amount paid to the older worker.

†Thomas (1989), p. 374

‡These results are consistent with those of Ghicas (1990), who also found that firms reduced their funding on a step-by-step basis: "The reduction in pension funding is accomplished first by the use of higher interest rates that decrease pension liabilities, and then by the switch into a benefit-allocation method. It is suggested that the last change is adopted if firms have limited freedom to make further changes in actuarial assumptions. To this extent, the study provides preliminary evidence on the *pecking order* of actuarial choices by firms attempting to reduce pension funding." Ghicas, Dimitrios C. "Determinants of Actuarial Cost Method Changes For Pension Accounting and Funding," *The Accounting Review* (April 1990), p. 401.

NON-U.S. REPORTING REQUIREMENTS

U.S. GAAP financial reporting requirements for pension plans are probably the most comprehensive of all international standards. Reporting standards in Canada and the United Kingdom are the closest, with rules in France, Germany, the Netherlands, and Japan considerably less well specified and plans are rarely funded. In France, there are no specific standards, and most firms use the cash basis to recognize pension payments. Plans are normally unfunded, with no liability reported on or off the balance sheet.

Lump-sum or severance payments on retirement are the norm in Japan, and these are recognized systematically in income and on the balance sheet. However, the liability recognized rarely exceeds 40% of the obligation to date. This amount approximates the accumulated benefit obligation as defined under U.S. GAAP, although it may not be discounted at a "settlement" (current) rate as in the United States. The obligations are generally not funded as contributions are not deductible for taxes.

Pension plans in Germany and the Netherlands are also generally unfunded. Pension expense is based on the benefits as of the balance sheet date, discounted at the rate allowed for taxes. Prior service costs are expensed immediately or over the three-year period allowed for taxes. Japanese, French, German, and Dutch firms are thus likely to report higher pension expense but lower pension liabilities compared to those of similar U.S. firms. The understatement of obligations by these firms is compounded by higher risk, since the plans are normally unfunded.

The Canadian, International Accounting Standards Committee (IASC),[29] and U.K. standards are the closest to SFAS 87. There are, however, several important differences. The interest rate used in these standards is a more stable, long-term rate, adjusted for actual experience, compared with a more volatile, short-term, settlement rate used in the United States. Actuarial methods are not limited to the projected unit credit method as in the United States, and there are no requirements to recognize liabilities due to a plan's underfunded status (minimum liability under SFAS 87).

The computation of periodic pension cost is probably the most significant difference among these standards. In the United Kingdom and Canada, pension cost is the sum of the *regular cost* (service cost in SFAS 87, although may be computed using different actuarial methods) and *variations to regular costs*, including experience gains and losses. However, since no corridor method is specified, the amortization of experience and actuarial gains and losses is more conservative in these countries.

Most foreign standards mandate significantly less disclosure than SFAS 87; in particular, foreign rules either mandate immediate recognition of prior service costs or permit amortization without specifying a method and provide limited or no disclosure of the ABO and little, if any, information on plan assets. This difference may be the most critical given the nature of these liabilities and the uncertainties in their measurement.

Exhibit 9-13 contains the pension footnote of SmithKline Beecham, a U.K. drug company. This footnote details pension plans in the United Kingdom, United States, and Germany, covering some 65% of the firm's labor force. The German plan is unfunded and carries the lowest salary growth rate assumption reflecting the low expected inflation rate. Recent higher inflation suggests that the salary growth rate assumption may have to be increased. Note also that the U.S. plan is better funded and pension cost is greatly reduced by "variations from regular cost."

In sum, accounting standards for pension plans outside the United States permit more choice of methods with less disclosure. Careful attention to disclosures provided,

---

[29]The IASC plans to issue a new standard late in 1993. It appears that the standard will be roughly similar to SFAS 87, with the following differences:

Companies will have a choice of actuarial methods.

Plan amendments affecting retirees would be recognized immediately rather than being recognized over the average life expectancy.

Disclosures will be more limited.

EXHIBIT 9-13. SMITHKLINE BEECHAM
Pensions

The Group operates pension plans throughout the world covering the majority of employees. These plans are devised in accordance with local conditions and practices in the country concerned. The assets of the Group's plans are generally held in separately administered trusts or are insured, although in Germany the Group's pension funds are not externally funded. The contributions to the plans are assessed in accordance with independent actuarial advice mainly using the projected unit credit method.

The total pension cost for the Group was £31 million (1989—£45 million), of which £22 million (1989—£31 million) relates to plans in the U.K., U.S.A., and Germany which cover some 65 percent of total employees, and for which further disclosures are set out below.

	United Kingdom	United States	Germany
Main assumptions:			
Investment return	10.0%	10.25%	N/A
Salary increases p.a.	7.0%	6.00%	4.0%
Pension increases p.a.	5.0%	—	2.0%
Last valuation date	1.5.90	1.1.90	1.4.90
Market valuation of investments at last valuation date (£m):	283	400	N/A
Level of funding, being the actuarial value of assets expressed as a percentage of the accrued service liabilities:	119%	134%	N/A
Regular Pension Cost (£m):	15	17	4
Variations from regular cost (£m):	(5)	(9)	—
Total pension cost for 1990 (£m):	10	8	4

Variations from regular costs are spread over the remaining service lives of current employees in the plans.

A provision of £40 million (1989—£47 million) is included in creditors, representing the excess of the accumulated pension cost over the amount funded (see Note 18), including £30 million (1989—£28 million) relating to Germany.

In addition to pension benefits, substantially all employees in the U.S.A. become eligible for certain healthcare and life insurance benefits upon retirement. The cost of providing these benefits is recognised as an expense in the year in which payments are made. The amounts charged to the profit and loss account in the year were £7 million (1989—£4 million).

Source: SmithKline Beecham, *1990 Annual Report.*

supplemented by discussions with management, may permit the analyst to obtain a rough understanding of the extent to which the balance sheet reflects the true plan status.

OTHER POSTEMPLOYMENT BENEFITS

Many employers, especially large companies with unionized work forces, have historically provided other benefits to retirees in addition to pension benefits. Most significant are life insurance and health care, often provided for dependents as well as for retirees. In the past, almost all companies accounted for such benefits on a "pay-as-you-go" basis. That is, they expensed the actual payments when made. As the cost of medical care grew, there was increasing concern that employers that provide these benefits were systematically overstating reported earnings and net worth by not accruing the cost of these benefits during employees' periods of active service, when the right to benefits is being earned.

Another factor driving the FASB to develop new accounting standards was the growing cost of providing health care benefits to employees. Decades ago, the cost of such benefits was insignificant. Advances in medical technology, increased utilization of health care, and general inflation have driven benefit cost to increasingly high levels. According to a survey[30] by A. Foster Higgins & Co., total health benefit costs per employee exceeded $3200 in 1990 and have doubled since 1985. For GM, for example, the cost of providing such benefits to retirees was more than $4 billion in 1991!

Postemployment benefits other than pensions were, with rare exceptions, unfunded as well. The lack of funding reflected the fact that (in contrast to pension plans) contributions to other plans are generally not tax deductible for U.S. income tax purposes. Only payments for actual benefits are deductible. In addition, earnings of such plans are not tax exempt. As a result employers have had no incentive to fund these plans.

In 1990, the FASB issued SFAS 106 mandating new accounting for postemployment benefits other than pensions. While the provisions of this standard follow the format of SFAS 87, there are some significant differences, reflecting the different nature of these other benefits. Because postretirement health care is generally the most significant of these benefits, we will discuss the provisions of SFAS 106 mainly with reference to health care benefits.

Health care benefits are different from pension benefits in one important respect. Pensions are stated in terms of monetary amounts; medical benefits entitle retirees (and, in many cases, their dependents) to "coverage" under which the cost may range from zero to a very large sum. "Entitlement" benefits are, therefore, much harder to estimate. As a result, the cash flow consequences (to employers) of these plans are much more difficult to predict.

Estimating Health Care Benefits

Some of the estimation process is identical to that for pensions: the employer must forecast how many employees will become eligible for benefits and over what time period retirees (and, in many cases, dependents) will be eligible to receive them. Such variables as employee turnover, mortality, and retirement ages must also be predicted.

Estimation of the *expected postretirement benefit obligation*, however, requires additional assumptions not needed to forecast pension benefits. Among the most significant of these are the *health care cost trend rate*, the *assumed per capita claims cost* (by age), and *Medicare reimbursement rates*. Also required are estimates of any required

---

[30] As reported by Ron Winslow, "Medical Cost Soar, Defying Firms' Cures," *The Wall Street Journal*, January 29, 1991.

employee contributions (or cost sharing) and the effect of any cost limitations ("caps") that are part of the benefit plan.

Forecasting health care cost is the most difficult aspect of estimating postretirement health care benefits. Due to increases in health care use and technological advances, health care costs (both direct reimbursement and insurance) have grown rapidly in recent years, outstripping the rate of inflation. Under the provisions of SFAS 106, employers have some latitude in making these estimates. Companies whose plans have cost-sharing provisions (employee contributions, coinsurance provisions, deductibles, etc.) are permitted to take such provisions into account when forecasting benefits.

The expected postretirement benefit obligation is computed by taking the present value of expected postretirement benefits. As in the case of pension benefits, the choice of discount rate has an important effect on the present value; it is intended to be a current rate and may be changed by the employer from time to time. In contrast to SFAS 87, the discount rate is not described as a settlement rate, as it is not possible (because there have been no buyers) to "settle" (sell to another entity such as an insurance company) obligations to provide health care benefits.

Computing Postretirement Benefit Cost

The elements of net postretirement benefit cost are identical to the components of net pension cost previously discussed. They are as follows:

- Service cost
- Interest cost
- Return on plan assets
- Amortization and deferral
- Amortization of unrecognized prior service cost
- Amortization of transition asset or liability

The computation of these elements is, for the most part, the same as the corresponding elements of net pension cost. Service cost is the portion of the expected postretirement benefit obligation resulting from employee service during the period, in other words the present value of benefits earned during the period. Interest cost reflects the passage of time. The discount rate used to compute both service cost and interest cost is, as in SFAS 87, the same rate used to compute the benefit obligation at the previous year end.

The other elements are also analogous to the elements of net pension cost. Once again, the difference between the actual return on assets and the expected return is deferred. When a postretirement health care plan is unfunded, however, the return-on-assets component will not be present, and the net cost will no longer be sensitive to the assumed rate of return on assets.[31]

---

[31]When a postretirement benefit plan is funded, and if the earnings of the fund are taxable, then fund earnings must be recognized on an after-tax basis.

Because of the absence of plan funding, the transition liability is large for most employers. As a result, the amortization of this liability (for those companies that adopt the standard prospectively) is usually more significant for postretirement health care plans than for pension plans. SFAS 106 permits amortization of the transition liability over 20 years rather than the average remaining service period of active employees. This extended amortization period softens the impact of this element on reported earnings. On the other hand, companies adopting the standard using the cumulative adjustment method report a large one-time reduction of net income.

Disclosure of Plan Status

Employers with nonpension postretirement benefit plans are required to disclose the plan status in a manner similar to the disclosures required for pension plans by SFAS 87. The *accumulated postretirement benefit obligation* (APBO), that portion of the expected postretirement obligation that reflects service to date, must be disclosed, broken down among retirees, eligible nonretirees, and other active plan participants. Eligible nonretirees are those who have met all the age and service requirements to receive benefits but are not yet receiving them (generally because they have not reached retirement age or have not retired).

If the plan is funded, the fair value of plan assets must be disclosed. In addition any accrual on the employer's balance sheet must be shown. The difference between the plan status (accumulated benefit obligation less plan assets) and the accrual will consist of the following:

- Unrecognized prior service cost
- Unrecognized net gain or loss
- Unrecognized transition obligation (if standard adopted prospectively)

These unrecognized amounts have the same origin and meaning as those arising for pension plans, which we have previously discussed. The General Electric example that follows discusses the first two of these differences.

Importance of Assumptions

As in the case of pensions, the assumptions (which must be disclosed) used to compute the postretirement benefit obligation can significantly affect the stated obligation as well as the net postretirement benefit cost.

The effect of the discount rate on health care and other nonpension plans is similar to the impact on pension plans. A higher discount rate reduces the present value of the benefit obligation and results in an improvement in the reported plan status (benefit obligation compared with plan assets). A higher discount rate reduces the service cost but increases the interest cost.

The health care cost trend rate also directly affects the measured obligation. A lower cost trend rate will lower the estimated benefit obligation and improve the reported plan status. A lower cost trend rate will also reduce benefit cost by reducing both service and interest cost.

Because of the importance of the assumed health care cost trend rate, companies with postretirement health care plans are required to disclose the rate used for the next year as well as the pattern of rates assumed thereafter. This disclosure is intended to help financial statement users to understand the assumptions made by the employer in measuring its benefit obligation. For example, Commercial Intertech discloses (see Exhibit 9-14) that

> The weighted-average annual assumed rate of increase in the per capita cost of covered benefits in the medical plans, or health care trend rate, is 14% for both 1991 and 1992. The trend rate is assumed to decrease gradually to 6% in the year 2008 and remain at that level thereafter.

Employers are also required to disclose the impact of a one-percentage-point increase in the assumed health care trend rate for each future year on

- The accumulated postretirement benefit obligation.
- The combined service and interest cost components of the net postretirement health care benefit cost.

EXHIBIT 9-14. COMMERCIAL INTERTECH
Company-Sponsored Defined Postretirement Plans, 1991

In addition to pension benefits, the company sponsors other defined benefit postretirement plans in the United States that provide medical and life insurance benefits for certain hourly and salaried employees. Benefits are provided on a noncontributory basis for those salaried retirees who have attained the age of 55 with 15 years of service and those hourly retirees who have attained the age of 60 with 15 years of service or 30 years of service with no age restriction, up to 65 years of age. Coverage is also provided for surviving spouses of hourly retirees. Medical plans for both employee groups incorporate deductibles and coinsurance features. New cost-saving measures regarding medical coverages were adopted during the year for salaried employees retiring after July 1, 1991. The plans are unfunded, and postretirement benefit claims and premiums are paid as incurred. Company-sponsored postretirement benefits are not available to employees of foreign subsidiaries.

In 1991, the company adopted FASB 106, Employers' Accounting for Postretirement Benefits Other Than Pensions. The effect of adopting the new rules increased 1991 net periodic post-retirement benefit cost by $644,000 and reduced income before cumulative effect of the accounting change by $396,000 or $0.04 per share. Postretirement benefit costs for 1990 and 1989, which were recorded on a cash basis, have not been restated.

In adopting the new accounting standard, the Company elected to immediately recognize in net income the initial unfunded liability, or transition obligation, as the effect of a change in accounting principle. The after-tax cumulative effect of the accounting change to November 1, 1990 amounted to a charge to net income of $9,015,000 or $0.91 per share ($0.83 per share on a fully diluted basis). As required, previously reported earnings for the first quarter of 1991 have been restated as if the change had occurred as of November 1, 1990. Restated quarterly amounts can be found in Note G. Restatement of prior-year financial statements is not permitted under this pronouncement, and the pro forma effects on income in 1990 and 1989 of retroactive application of this accounting change are immaterial.

EXHIBIT 9-14. *(Continued)*

Components of net periodic postretirement benefit cost are shown below. Net periodic cost associated with retiree life insurance benefits amounted to $276,000 in 1991.

	1991	1990	1989
	(in $ thousands)		
Service cost	$ 258		
Interest cost	1361		
Actual return on plan assets	0		
Amortization of transition obligation	0		
Net amortization and deferral	0		
Net periodic postretirement benefit cost	$1619	$1114	$1028

The following table shows the aggregated funded status of the benefit plans reconciled with amounts recognized in the Company's statement of financial position. The accrued postretirement cost associated with retiree life insurance benefits amounted to $2,785,000 as of October 31, 1991.

October 31,	1991	1990
	(in $ thousands)	
Accumulated postretirement benefit obligations		
Retirees	$ (8,452)	$ (8,087)
Fully eligible active plan participants	(2,125)	(1,802)
Other active plan participants	(5,943)	(4,652)
	$(16,520)	$(14,541)
Plan assets at fair value	0	0
Accumulated postretirement benefit obligation (in excess of) plan assets	(16,520)	(14,541)
Unrecognized net loss	1,335	0
Unrecognized prior service cost	0	0
Unrecognized transition obligation	0	14,541
(Accrued) postretirement benefit cost	$(15,185)	$ 0

The weighted average annual assumed rate of increase in the per capita cost of covered benefits in the medical plans, or health care cost trend rate, is 14% for both 1991 and 1992. The trend rate is assumed to decrease gradually to 6% in the year 2008 and remain at that level thereafter. Increasing the assumed health care cost trend rate by one percentage point in each year would increase the accumulated postretirement benefit obligation as of October 31, 1991 by $1,520,200 and the aggregate of service and interest cost components of net periodic postretirement benefit cost for 1991 by $278,000. The weighted-average discount rate used in determining the accumulated postretirement benefit obligation was 8.5% and 9.5% at October 31, 1991, and 1990, respectively. The annual assumed rate of salary increase for retiree life insurance is 5% at October 31, 1991, and 1990.

Source: Commercial Intertech, 1991 Annual Report

These disclosures are intended to improve the comparability of the computed cost and benefit obligations of different employers when they are computed under different assumptions. They also reveal the sensitivity of the measured benefit obligation to the trend rate assumption. Plans with a high degree of cost sharing can be expected to have a lower degree of sensitivity to the trend rate of health care costs. In other words, the plan will pass on some of the cost if it exceeds expectations.

Effect of Assumptions

Commercial Intertech, for example, discloses (Exhibit 9-14) that the effect of a one-percentage-point increase in trend rates for each future year would increase the APBO by approximately $1.520 million (9.2%) and the combined service and interest cost by approximately $0.278 million (17.2%). General Electric (GE), however, states (Exhibit 9-15) that a 1% increase in trend rates would increase its APBO by $50 million (1.4%) and the combined service and interest cost by $5 million (1.2%).

The different degree of sensitivity to changes in the trend rate is dramatic. The very low sensitivity of GE suggests that it has substantial cost-sharing provisions in its plan that limit the impact of unexpected inflation in health care costs. These provisions may include employee contributions and plan limits (caps). Commercial Intertech appears to be much more at risk should the trend rates exceed those assumed.

Assumptions about the effectiveness of the cost-sharing provisions of the employer plan thus have an important impact on the benefit obligation and benefit cost. Some employers will be tempted to be overly optimistic about the effect of such provisions on their benefit costs. Overoptimism with respect to any assumptions will, however, result in actuarial losses that will eventually require amortization and increase the benefit cost.

Transition Methods

SFAS 106 contains the longest transition period of any new accounting standard ever issued. As a result, the standard will not be fully implemented by all companies until the year 2005. Until that time financial analysts will need to make adjustments to compare the financial statements of companies that have taken different roads to adopting the standard.

Because so few postretirement health care plans have been funded, and because of the size of the unrecognized benefit obligation for many companies, the FASB came under strong pressure from the business community to build flexibility into the standard, as well as to delay its implementation.

The provisions of the standard are not required accounting until calendar 1993; for non–U.S. plans and the plans of nonpublic companies with no more than 500 plan participants, there is an additional two-year delay.

Companies adopting the new standard may take either of two paths. They may recognize the transition obligation (cumulative effect of the standard) immediately, as a charge against net income in the year of adoption.

The alternative is to delay recognition of the transition obligation, which requires amortization of that obligation over the greater of the average remaining service life of active plan participants or 20 years (prospective adoption).

Effects of Transition Method

Giving employers a choice of transition methods permits them to pick the lesser of the evils. The choice between immediate recognition and delayed recognition may, however, be more complex than meets the eye. The characteristics of the employee population, for example, affect the impact of the new standard on both net postretirement benefit cost and the transition liability.

Consider, for example, a slow-growth company with a mature (older average age) work force and a low ratio of active employees to retirees. Such a company is already paying a substantial sum in postretirement health care benefits. While adoption of SFAS 106 will increase the reported cost (because of the need to accrue benefits for active employees), cost computed under the new standard may be only three or four times the "pay-as-you go" cost.

In contrast, a rapidly growing company with a relatively young work force, and a very high ratio of active employees to retirees, may find that SFAS 106 increases net postretirement benefit cost by a factor of 10. Most of its employees have not fully earned the right to postemployment health care benefits; even fewer are already collecting benefits. Thus pay-as-you-go cost (benefits currently being paid) is quite small, and adoption of the accrual method of SFAS 106 has a large impact on cost.

Turning to the transition liability under the new standard, the effects are likely to be similar. The slow-growth, mature company is likely to have a transition liability that is a small multiple of the pay-as-you-go cost. But because so many of its employees are either near or past retirement age, the transition liability may be large relative to the company's net worth. This is especially true of companies whose profitability has been low.

The rapid-growth, younger company will find that its transition liability, while a larger multiple of the pay-as-you-go cost, is relatively small relative to net worth. Younger companies may also find that, having few retirees, it is easier to reduce these benefits and, therefore, the transition liability.

Transition in Practice

Few companies adopted the new standard in 1990 and 1991. Reasons for delay included

- Lack of data to implement the new standard; many companies had not accumulated detailed data on retiree medical costs because there was no need to do so.
- Inability to tax effect the transition liability under SFAS 96. For this reason, some companies delayed adoption of SFAS 106 until the new tax standard (SFAS 109) was adopted.[32]

---

[32]For example, Westinghouse Electric adopted both standards in the first quarter of 1992. It recorded an after-tax charge (cumulative adjustment) of $742 million for postretirement benefits and a $404 million credit (deferred tax asset) under SFAS 109. The net effect of the simultaneous adoption of both standards was $338 million. If SFAS 109 had not been adopted (and assuming that Westinghouse would not have been able to tax effect the cumulative effect of SFAS 106 otherwise), the cumulative effect would have been recorded pretax and would have been more than $1 billion.

- Need to amend debt agreements.[33]
- Management desire to take actions to reduce the size of the liability prior to adoption of the standard.
- Unwillingness to be the first company in an industry to reduce reported earnings by adopting the standard early.

Many more companies adopted SFAS 106 in 1992. Companies with small transition liabilities (relative to net worth), low debt/equity ratios, and nonrestrictive debt covenants adopted the new standard by charging the transition liability against earnings in the year of adoption. This method has the benefit of getting the charge behind the company and reducing the impact on future earnings (because there will be no transition liability requiring amortization).

International Business Machines, one of those companies that did adopt the new standard in 1991, announced in late March of that year that it was adopting the provisions of SFAS 106 in the first quarter, resulting in a charge against first quarter earnings of $2263 million after tax effects of $350 million. This charge reduced stockholders' equity by approximately 5%. IBM had previously been accruing such benefits at retirement. Cost under this method was $96 million in 1990; cost under SFAS 106 was $394 million in 1991.

If IBM had chosen to amortize the transition liability over 20 years, earnings would have been reduced by $130 million pretax ($2263 million/20) in each future year. Charging off the liability immediately therefore increases the computed return on equity of IBM as future earnings are higher (without amortization) and equity is lower.

General Electric also adopted the new standard effective with the first quarter of 1991, but it did not make the decision to do so until the third quarter of that year. Like IBM, GE charged its transition liability ($1.8 billion after tax, or $2.07 per share) against first quarter 1991 earnings. The effect of this method of adoption on GE is discussed shortly.

Companies with relatively large transition liabilities, on the other hand, often delayed implementation of the new standard as long as possible. For the large auto companies, for example, the transition liability is a significant percentage of net worth.[34] Charging a liability of this size against current earnings has a major effect on debt/equity and other financial statement ratios. For some companies, the effect on bond or loan covenants will also play a role in the choice of transition method. Finally, the trend of reported earnings may be a factor; it may be convenient to charge off the liability in a year when operating results are poor anyway.

Some companies will adopt the standard prospectively, meaning that the transition liability will be amortized over the next 20 years. For that entire time period, financial analysts will need to remember that a (perhaps significant) element of cost is completely unrelated to current operations but is a result of the past failure to accrue postretirement benefit cost.

---

[33]In September 1991, Westinghouse Electric announced that it was asking bank lenders to change terms of its loan agreement in anticipation of adopting SFAS 106.

[34]In February 1993, General Motors announced that its adoption of SFAS 106 for 1992 resulted in an after-tax charge of $20.8 billion. Book value per share at December 31, 1992 was $1.98 after that charge (and small other charges) as compared with $37.18 per share one year earlier.

EXHIBIT 9-15. GENERAL ELECTRIC
Note 6 Pension and Retiree Insurance Benefits

GE and its affiliates sponsor a number of pension and retiree health and life insurance plans. Principal plans are discussed below; other plans are not significant individually or in the aggregate.

1991 accounting change. Statement of Financial Accounting Standards (SFAS) no. 106, Employers' Accounting for Postretirement Benefits Other than Pensions, was implemented using the immediate recognition transition option, effective as of January 1, 1991.

SFAS no. 106 required recognition, during employees' service with the Company, of the cost of their retiree health and life insurance benefits. At January 1, 1991, the accumulated postretirement benefit obligation was $4287 million; however, $1577 million of this obligation had been provided through the fair market value of related trust assets ($1037 million) and recorded liabilities ($540 million), thus resulting in a pretax adjustment (i.e., transition obligation) of $2,710 million. The effect on net earnings and share owners' equity was $1799 million ($2.07 per share) after deferred tax benefit of $911 million. Aside from the one-time effect of the adjustment, adoption of SFAS no. 106 was not material to 1991 financial results. Prior to 1991, GE health benefits for eligible retirees under age 65 and eligible dependents were generally included in costs as covered expenses were actually incurred. For eligible retirees and spouses over age 65, the present value of future health benefits was included in costs in the year the retiree became eligible for benefits. The present value of future life insurance benefits for each eligible retiree was included in costs in the year of retirement.

Principal pension plans are the GE Pension Plan and the GE Supplementary Pension Plan.

The GE Pension Plan covers substantially all GE employees in the United States and approximately 50% of GEFS employees. Generally, benefits are based on the greater of a formula recognizing career earnings or a formula recognizing length of service and final average earnings. Benefit provisions are subject to collective bargaining. At the end of 1991, the GE Pension Plan covered approximately 485,000 participants, including 195,000 employees, 125,000 former employees with vested rights for future benefits and 165,000 retirees or beneficiaries receiving benefits.

The GE Supplementary Pension Plan is an unfunded plan providing supplementary retirement benefits primarily to higher-level, longer-service professional and managerial employees in the United States.

Principal retiree insurance plans generally provide health and life insurance benefits to employees who retire under the GE pension plan with 10 or more years of service. Benefit provisions are subject to collective bargaining. At the end of 1991, the plans covered approximately 237,000 retirees and dependents.

Employer costs for principal pension and retiree insurance plans follow.

Cost (Income) for Pension Plans, 1989–1991
(in $ millions)

	1989	1990	1991
Benefit cost for service during the year—net of employee contributions	$ 413	$ 425	$ 446
Interest cost on benefit obligation	1259	1315	1400
Actual return on plan assets	(4026)	260	(4331)
Unrecognized portion of return	2452	(1988)	2272
Amortization	(339)	(392)	(483)
Pension cost (income)	$ (241)	$ (380)	$ (696)

Cost (Income) for Retiree Insurance Plans, 1991
(in $ millions)

	Total	Health	Life
Benefit cost for service during the year—net of retiree contributions	$ 88	$ 65	$ 23
Interest cost on benefit obligation	318	214	104
Actual return on plan assets	(138)	(9)	(129)
Unrecognized portion of return	44	5	39
Amortization	(33)	(33)	—
Retiree insurance cost	$ 279*	$242	$ 37

*Retiree insurance cost was $249 million in 1990 and $283 million in 1989.

EXHIBIT 9-15. *(Continued)*

Actuarial assumptions used to determine 1991 costs and benefit obligations for principal plans include a discount rate of 9.0% (8.5% in 1990 and 1989) and an average rate of future increases in benefit compensation of 6.0% (6.5% in 1990 and 1989). Recognized return on plan assets for 1991 was determined by applying the expected long-term rate of return of 9.5% (8.5% in 1990 and 1989) to the market-related value of assets. The assumed rate of future increases in per capita cost of health care benefits (the health care cost trend rate) was 13.0% for 1991, decreasing gradually to 6.6% by the year 2050. These trend rates reflect GE's prior experience and management's expectation that future rates will decline. Increasing the health care cost trend rates by one percentage point would increase the accumulated postretirement benefit obligation by $50 million and would increase annual aggregate service and interest costs by $5 million. In connection with its 1992 annual funding review, GE may revise certain actuarial assumptions effective January 1, 1992; however, it is anticipated that any such revision would increase benefit obligations by no more than 5%.

Pension gains and losses that occur because actual experience differs from that assumed are amortized over the average future service period of employees. Amounts allocable to prior service for amendments to pension and retiree insurance plans are amortized in a similar manner.

Funding policy for the GE Pension Plan is to contribute amounts sufficient to meet minimum funding requirements set forth in U.S. employee benefit and tax laws plus such additional amounts as GE may determine to be appropriate from time to time. GE has not made contributions since 1987 because the fully funded status of the GE Pension Plan precludes current tax deduction and any Company contribution would generate annual excise taxes. The present value of future life insurance benefits for each eligible retiree is funded in the year of retirement. In general, retiree health benefits are paid as covered expenses are incurred.

The following table compares the market-related value of assets with the value of benefit obligations, recognizing the effects of future compensation and service. The market-related value of assets is based on cost plus recognition of market appreciation and depreciation in the portfolio over five years, a method that reduces the impact of short-term market fluctuations.

Funded Status for Principal Plans, December 31, 1990–1991
(in $ millions)

	1990	1991
Pension plans		
Market-related value of assets	$22,237	$23,192
Projected benefit obligation	16,751	17,355
Retiree insurance plans		
Market-related value of assets	1,037	1,124
Accumulated postretirement benefit obligation	4,110	3,675

Reconciliation of Benefit Obligation with Recorded Liability
December 31, 1990–1991 (in $ millions)

	Total Principal Plans		Pension Plans		1991 Retiree Insurance Plans		
	1990*	1991	1990	1991	Total	Health	Life
Benefit obligation	$ 20,861	$ 21,030	$ 16,751	$ 17,355	$ 3,675	$2,414	$ 1,261
Fair value of trust assets	(23,970)	(27,304)	(22,933)	(26,133)	(1,171)	(50)	(1,121)
Unamortized balances							
SFAS no. 87 transition gain	1,539	1,385	1,539	1,385	—	—	—
Experience gains (losses)	3,091	5,433	3,091	5,784	(351)	(364)	13
Plan amendments	101	252	101	(577)	829	829	—
Recorded prepaid asset	1,905	2,657	1,905	2,657	—	—	—
Recorded liability	$ 3,527	$ 3,453	$ 454	$ 471	$ 2,982	$2,829	$ 153

*1990 amounts include the pro forma effects of adopting SFAS no. 106 as of January 1, 1991.

EXHIBIT 9-15. *(Continued)*

The portion of the projected benefit obligation representing the accumulated benefit obligation for pension plans was $16,362 million and $15,589 million at the end of 1991 and 1990, respectively. The vested benefit obligation for pension plans was $16,214 million and $15,433 million at the end of 1991 and 1990, respectively.

For retiree insurance plans, the portion of the accumulated postretirement benefit obligation attributable to current retirees was $1,756 million for health insurance and $849 million for life insurance; the portion attributable to active plan participants eligible to retire was $152 million for health insurance and $91 million for life insurance; and the portion attributable to other active plan participants was $506 million for health insurance and $321 million for life insurance.

Unamortized balances for amendments include the effects of changes in pension and retiree insurance plan provisions during 1991.

Assets in trust consist mainly of common stock and fixed income investments. GE common stock represents less than 1% of trust assets and is held mainly in an indexed portfolio.

Source: General Electric, 1991 Annual Report

Analysis of General Electric

The General Electric footnote (Exhibit 9-15) indicates a complex set of circumstances. In contrast to Commercial Intertech and most health benefit plans, the GE plan is significantly funded. In addition, a plan amendment in 1991 significantly reduced the APBO. Finally, the calculation of postretirement benefit cost is complicated. Nonetheless, we can use the footnote data to analyze the plan.

Exhibit 9-15 contains the pension and retiree insurance benefit footnote (Note 6) from General Electric's 1991 annual report. GE's disclosure of postretirement benefits is closely integrated with, and follows the same format as, the pension plan disclosures.

GE used the cumulative effect method of adopting SFAS 106, as already discussed. The transition liability ($2710 million) was reduced by a deferred income tax effect ($911 million) to arrive at the cumulative adjustment ($1799 million, or $2.07 per share). GE does not disclose the "not material" impact of the standard on postretirement benefit cost; we shall calculate it shortly. Notice that GE uses a health care trend rate assumption of 13% for 1991 trending down to 6.6% by 2050. Given these limited data, we cannot compare GE's trend assumptions with those of other companies.

Exhibit 9-16 uses the footnote data to analyze GE's postretirement benefit plans. While more complex, the calculations follow the format used previously for pension plans.

First, we calculate the contribution to the plan. Using this result, we reconcile plan assets to calculate benefits paid. By then reconciling the APBO, we confirm our calculation of benefits paid. To reconcile the APBO, we must deal with two problems. One is the matter of gains and losses. In the case of GE, they arise from two sources: investments and actuarial gains and losses. The investment gain (deferral of return in excess of the assumed ROA) is easy to find in GE's benefit cost disclosure. The balance must be an actuarial loss.

Where does this loss come from? The APBO at December 31, 1991, was discounted using a 9% rate, as opposed to an 8.5% rate used at December 31, 1990. The higher rate, however, should *reduce* the APBO, resulting in an actuarial gain. We can conclude only that other revisions more than offset that gain, resulting in an overall actuarial loss.

The footnote disclosures also indicate that there was a plan amendment during 1991. The amendment *reduced* the APBO; apparently GE reduced benefit levels. It appears that the amendment took effect during 1991 and that there was some amortization of its effect, as shown in the calculation of net benefit cost.

We can now calculate the effect of SFAS 106 on GE's postretirement benefit cost. As benefits paid were $374 million (which would have been the cost if the new standard had not been adopted), benefit cost under SFAS 106 of $279 million was actually *lower*. Excluding the cumulative effect, SFAS 106 increased GE's reported earnings.

Forecasting Postretirement Benefit Cost

We can also use the data from the GE footnotes to forecast benefit cost for 1992. In Exhibit 9-16, we make an estimate for General Electric. To forecast benefit cost we must estimate each component.

Service cost, the present value of benefits earned in 1991, can be estimated by using 1990 as a starting point. Service cost in 1991 will be higher if the number of active employees increases, if benefits increase, or if assumptions change. Assuming that employee count will increase by 3% and that health care costs will increase by 10%, we would increase 1991 service cost by 13%. In addition, it appears that we need to adjust

EXHIBIT 9-16. GENERAL ELECTRIC
Analysis of Postretirement Benefits

Calculation of Contribution to Plan

1991 Benefit cost	$ 279	
Change in liability	91	($3073 − $2982)
Contribution	$ 370	(Paid to fund by company)

Postretirement Plan Assets

Closing balance	$ 1171	(12/31/91)
Opening balance	(1037)	(1/1/91)
Change	$ 134	
Less: Actual return	(138)	(Component of 1991 benefit cost)
Contribution	(370)	(Calculated above)
Equals: Benefits paid	$ (374)	(Outflow)

Accumulated Postretirement Benefit Obligation

Closing balance	$ 3675	(12/31/91)
Opening balance	(4110)	(1/1/91)
Change	$ (435)	
Less: Service cost	88	(Component of 1991 benefit cost)
Interest cost	318	(Component of 1991 benefit cost)
Actuarial loss	395	(Calculated below)
Plan amendment	(862)	(Calculated below)
Equals: Benefits paid	$ (374)	

EXHIBIT 9-16. *(Continued)*

Deferred Gains (Losses)

Closing balance	$ (351)	(12/31/91)
Opening balance	–0–	(1/1/91)
Change	$ (351)	
Deferred investment gain	44	(Component of 1991 benefit cost)
Deferred actuarial loss	$ (395)	

Plan Amendment (Prior Service Cost)

Closing balance	$ 829	(12/31/91)
Opening balance	–0–	(1/1/91)
Change	$ 829	
1991 Amortization	33	(Component of 1991 benefit cost)
Equals: Effect of amendment	$ 862	

Forecast of Postretirement Benefit Cost

	1991A	1992E	Calculation
Service cost	88	$ 99	(See text)
Interest cost	318	331	(0.09 × $3675)
Return on assets	(94)	(107)	(0.095 × $1124)
Amortization	(33)	(64)	($829/13)
Net benefit cost	$279	$ 259	

for the change in discount rate as well. However, GE applied the new discount rate to 1991 cost.[35] Thus, assuming no 1992 rate change, we will assume a 13% increase in service cost.

Interest cost for 1992 is calculated in Exhibit 9-16, based on the year-end 1991 APBO and the discount rate. The forecast of the return-on-assets component is complicated by GE's use of the market-related value of assets. Fortunately, that amount is disclosed in the footnote. Assuming that GE continues to use a 9.5% ROA assumption results in an estimated ROA of $107 million, an offset to benefit cost.

We will assume that GE uses the corridor method and does not amortize its deferred loss. However, we must assume continued amortization of the effect of the 1991 plan amendment. Using a 13-year amortization period[36] produces amortization (another offset) of $66 million. The net result of these calculations is a forecast of net postretirement benefit cost in 1992 of $259 million, an 8% decrease from the 1991 level.

---

[35]This conclusion cannot be clearly derived from the vague footnote disclosure but was confirmed by GE management.

[36]Estimated from the period over which GE amortizes its pension transition asset. The result "fits" if we assume that 1991 amortization was for six months; the 1992 figure is exactly double the 1991 amount.

Using SFAS 106 Disclosures

As the accounting for postretirement benefits other than pensions parallels the accounting for pension benefits, the analytical adjustments are the same. On the balance sheet, the accrued amount should be replaced by the excess of the APBO over plan assets (if any). For Commercial Intertech and General Electric, the adjustment would be immaterial. For companies adopting SFAS 106 on a prospective basis, however, the unamortized transition liability (amortized over 20 years) will be significant in most cases.

Companies with postretirement benefits have argued that they can reduce or eliminate benefits, although this argument is more difficult to accept when benefits are mandated under union contracts. The result of recent litigation suggests that benefits for retirees cannot be summarily discontinued, even in cases of severe financial distress. In recent years, however, companies have made considerable efforts to limit their exposure to health care costs.[37] Note the GE plan amendment discussed earlier.

Nonetheless, on a "going concern" basis, these benefits must be considered, as are pension benefits, a corporate liability. Thus, unless there is evidence that benefits will be curtailed or eliminated, financial analysis must take any unrecognized liability into account. While SFAS 106 does not change cash flow, the APBO does represent a forecast of future cash outflows that will require the use of firm resources.[38]

Adjustment of the income statement may also be necessary. Exhibit 9-4 can be used as a guide to the alternatives available. For companies adopting SFAS 106 prospectively, however, additional discussion is required. For 20 years after adoption, such firms will be amortizing the transition liability, yet this liability reflects cost for prior periods. Current period earnings, one can argue, should not be burdened with the impact of these costs. The matching principle suggests that amortization of the transition liability should, therefore, be removed from postretirement benefit cost when evaluating a firm's earning power.

Non–U.S. GAAP Treatment

Health care and life insurance benefits are rarely provided in other countries, accounting for the absence of related reporting standards. SSAP 24 in the United Kingdom, for example, does not contain any specific disclosure requirements. However, a technical release by the U.K. standard-setting group has recently ruled that the cash basis remains an acceptable method.[39] To the extent that a foreign firm provides these benefits, its income and net worth will be overstated.

---

[37]In May 1992, IBM announced a plan to cut medical benefit costs for active employees and retirees in the United States. Elements of the plan include cost sharing, greater deductibles, and limits on spousal coverage. An IBM spokesperson was quoted: "our goal is to keep the growth in health care costs at below 10%, compared with a U.S. corporate average of 14%."

[38]Thus satisfying the FASB definition of a liability (see Chapter 1).

[39]Another problem in the United Kingdom stems from its tax standard that would disallow recognition of a deferred tax asset for these liabilities because no net reversal can be assumed in the absence of funding.

PRERETIREMENT BENEFITS

Some employee benefits apply to periods of active service or to periods following active service but prior to retirement. Such benefits include:

1. Insurance benefits (mainly health and life)
2. Vacations, holidays, and sick days
3. Severance benefits (including salary and benefit continuation costs)
4. Supplemental unemployment, disability, and similar benefits

The first class of benefits listed is accounted for on a pay-as-you-go basis; life and health insurance benefits are period costs. The second category is covered by SFAS 43 (1980), Accounting for Compensated Absences. That standard requires employers to accrue the cost of these benefits when that cost can be reasonably estimated and employees have earned the right to receive them.

SFAS 112 (1992) extends the reasoning behind SFAS 43 to the third and fourth benefit groupings listed above. Previous practice was varied, with some firms using the pay-as-you-go method, some recognizing benefit cost only under certain conditions (e.g. disability of worker), and others accruing benefit cost over the period of active service. SFAS 112 was intended to unify practice.

The new standard is effective for fiscal years beginning after December 15, 1993 and must be adopted using the cumulative effect method. Merck, for example, adopted the new standard effective January 1, 1992; the cumulative effect was $29.6 million (net of $20.4 million of income tax benefit). The effect of the new standard on 1992 income (before cumulative effect) was "not material." Depending on the benefits provided and the prior method of accounting, the effect of SFAS 112 on other companies may be more significant.

SUMMARY

Current accounting practices for pensions and other postemployment benefits result in an amalgam of smoothed and unsmoothed costs appearing on the income statement. The actual obligations are disguised and partly or wholly off balance sheet. In this chapter we have shown how to use footnote disclosures to unravel the underlying events that occurred during the period. This permits calculation of the actual components of benefit costs, cash flows, and benefit obligations, and the examination of trends in these components. The chapter suggests alternative measures of benefit cost and obligations. In addition, motivation for firms to over- or underfund their pension plans and the potential for terminating these plans is discussed.

Chapter 9

Problems

Problems 1–4 concern the analysis of the pension plans of Alcoa. Note N, "Pension Plans" from the 1990 Annual Report of Alcoa is reproduced here; all amounts are in millions of dollars

1.

A. The note states that "The projected benefit obligation at December 31 was determined using a settlement discount rate of 8% for 1990 and 1989, and 8.75% for 1988." What was the impact of the 1989 change in the discount rate on the trends of service cost, interest cost and total pension cost?

B. Alcoa used an assumed rate or return on assets of 9% for each year. How would an *increase* in the assumed rate affect:

    (i) Pension cost in the year of the change?

    (ii) The actual plan status in the year of the change?

    (iii) The balance sheet pension asset/liability?

2. On December 31, 1989, close to 100% of Alcoa's pension plans were in the overfunded category. On December 31, 1990, however, approximately 50% (measured by dollars of ABO, PBO, or plan assets) of the plans were underfunded. Describe the specific factor(s) that contributed to this shift. Would you expect this trend to continue in the future?

3.

A. What is meant by minimum liability? Compute the minimum liability of $63.6 million and $11.4 million recorded by Alcoa for its underfunded plans at December 31, 1990, and 1989, respectively.

B. What is the impact of the minimum liability on the balance sheet?

C. What is the impact of the minimum liability on the income and cash flow statements?

D. Identify and compute the four alternative measurements of Alcoa's pension liability (see Exhibits 9-4 and 9-8) and state the circumstances under which each would be most appropriate for analytic purposes.

4.

A. Reconcile Alcoa's PBO (total for all plans) without disaggregating prior service costs and actuarial gains and losses.

B. Compute three alternative measures of Alcoa's pension cost and compare each with the amount actually reported.

C. Using only the data in the footnote, forecast the components of Alcoa's pension cost for 1991.

EXHIBIT 9P-1

N. Pension Plans

Alcoa and certain subsidiaries maintain pension plans covering substantially all U.S. employees and certain other employees. Pension benefits generally depend upon length of service, job grade and remuneration. Substantially all benefits are paid through pension trusts that are funded in amounts sufficient to ensure that all plans have adequate funds to pay benefits to retirees as they become due.

Pension costs include the following components which were calculated as of January 1 of each year:

	1990	1989	1988
Benefits earned	$ 76.2	$ 66.2	$ 50.5
Interest accrued on projected benefit obligation	229.6	220.1	211.0
Net amortization	16.8	15.0	2.2
	322.6	301.3	263.7
Less: expected return on plan assets*	236.7	211.1	195.4
	$ 85.9	$ 90.2	$ 68.3

*The actual returns were higher (lower) than the expected returns by $(183.7) in 1990, $185.4 in 1989 and $32.6 in 1989 and were deferred as actuarial gains (losses).

The following table describes the funded status of the pension plans. The funded status of a plan is defined as the difference between the accumulated benefit obligation (actuarial present value of benefits earned to date based on present pay levels) and the amount provided for future benefits.

	December 31, 1990		December 31, 1989	
	Over-funded plans	Under-funded plans	Over-funded plans	Under-funded plans
Accumulated benefit obligation:				
Vested	$1,239.7	$1,363.5	$2,517.1	$27.4
Non-vested	114.3	118.5	196.5	3.0
Additional obligation for projected compensation increases	64.5	139.1	160.2	8.5
Projected benefit obligation	1,418.5	1,621.1	2,873.8	38.9
Plan assets, primarily stocks and bonds, at market	1,441.6	1,353.8	2,890.8	.5
(Prepaid) accrued pension costs	(48.8)	64.6	(48.6)	18.5
Amount provided for future benefits	1,392.8	1,418.4	2,842.2	19.0
Projected benefit obligation in excess of amount provided for future benefits	$ 25.7	$ 202.7	$ 31.6	$19.9
Consists of:				
Unamortized initial obligations of plans	$ (62.0)	$ 78.8	$ 6.7	$12.9
Unamortized prior service costs	45.3	103.8	63.1	(1.5)
Unrecognized net actuarial (gains) losses	42.4	20.1	(38.2)	8.5
	$ 25.7	$ 202.7	$ 31.6	$19.9

Source: Alcoa, 1990 annual report.

For the underfunded plans at December 31, 1990 and 1989, Alcoa recorded a deferred charge and an additional liability of $63.6 and $11.4, respectively. These amounts are the difference between the accumulated benefit obligation and the amount provided for future benefits.

The projected benefit obligation at December 31 was determined using a settlement discount rate of 8% for 1990 and 1989, and 8.75% for 1988. The assumed long-term rate for compensation increases was 5.5% for all three years. Assumed earnings on plan assets used for determining pension expense was 9% for all three years.

D. Repeat part A, but now disaggregate the prior service cost and the actuarial gains and losses.

E. Your answer to part D should indicate an increase in prior service cost offset by an actuarial gain. Would you expect this pattern to persist in the future for Alcoa?

Problems 5–10 relate to the pension plans of Deere. The "Pension and Other Retirement Benefits" note from Deere's 1991 Annual Report is located in Exhibit 1B-2. Unless otherwise specified, the questions refer to the U.S. plans for fiscal 1991; all amounts are in millions of dollars.

5.

A. Deere does not explicitly disclose its expected return on assets. The difference between the expected return and actual return is included as part of "net amortization and deferral." Estimate the expected return and the amount deferred.

B. Compute Deere's 1991 contribution to its U.S. plans.

C. Compute the benefits paid by Deere's U.S. pension plans by reconciling the opening and closing balances of plan assets.

6.

A. What was the pension cost recorded by Deere in 1991 for its U.S. plans?

B. Estimate recurring, gross, and nonsmoothed pension cost (on a projected benefits basis) for fiscal 1991. Compare each of these to the actual pension cost recorded by Deere.

C. Explain the two items that constitute the difference between gross and recurring pension cost? What do these items represent? What events have caused these items?

D. Reconcile the fiscal 1991 change in Deere's U.S. projected benefit obligation.

E. Calculate gross and nonsmoothed pension cost on an accumulated benefits basis. Estimate recurring pension cost on an ABO basis.

7.

A. Deere recorded a minimum liability of $359 million (1991) and $277 (1990) for its underfunded U.S. plans. How were these amounts calculated?

B. Explain why recognition of the minimum liability better reflects the status of the underfunded plans on Deere's balance sheet.

C. The minimum pension liability recognized by Deere did not affect pension expense in either 1990 or 1991. However, Deere's adjustment to stockholders' equity of $86 ($88) million was net of deferred income taxes of $45 ($46) million in 1991 (1990). Explain why the firm could recognize these deferred taxes when there was no impact on Deere's pension cost in either year.

D. Discuss and calculate the adjustments required for Deere's pension plans to compute a more "realistic" debt-to-equity ratio at October 31, 1991.

8.

DEERE
Combined Status of U.S. Pension Plans,
October 31, 1987 ($ millions)

Accumulated benefit obligation	$(1789)
Excess of projected benefit obligation over accumulated benefit obligation	(272)
Projected benefit obligation	$(2061)
Plan assets	2043
Projected benefit obligation in excess of plan assets	$ (18)
Unrecognized net gain	(48)
Prior service cost not yet recognized in net periodic pension cost	115
Remaining unrecognized transition net asset from November 1, 1985	(213)
Unfunded accrued pension cost recognized in the consolidated balance sheet	$ (164)

Source: Deere, 1988 Annual Report (Exhibit 1B-1).

A. Compare the October 31, 1987, plan status to the status at October 31, 1991, and answer the following questions:

B. How has the funded status of Deere's U.S. plans changed over the four-year period? Discuss the elements of this change.

C. To what extent has this change been reflected in Deere's:

(i) Assets and liabilities?

(ii) Stockholders' equity?

(iii) Reported pension cost?

D. What are the implications of this change for Deere's future pension cost and contributions?

9. Estimate 1992 pension cost for Deere's U.S. plans, using only the data in the 1991 footnote. [Hint: Treat each component of the "net amortization and deferral" separately.]

10. [This question relates to Deere's foreign plans.]

A. Explain why Deere shows a range of actuarial assumptions for its foreign plans, as opposed to the single set of assumptions used for its U.S. plans?

B. Explain why there is no amount shown for "Nonvested benefit obligation" for the overfunded plans.

C. Explain why there is no amount shown for "Plan assets" for the under-funded plans.

EXHIBIT 9P-2

Retirement Plans The company and its subsidiaries have retirement plans covering substantially all employees. The total cost of all plans for 1990, 1989 and 1988 was $94 million, $328 million and $460 million, respectively.

Pension cost in 1990 was lower than in 1989 principally due to the growth in the expected return on plan assets exceeding the growth in annual interest and service cost. Pension cost in 1989 was lower than in 1988 principally due to changes in actuarial assumptions in the U.S. and several non-U.S. plans, partially offset by amendments to the U.S. plan.

Annual cost is determined using the Projected Unit Credit actuarial method. Prior service cost is amortized on a straight-line basis over the average remaining service period of employees expected to receive benefits. An assumption is made for modified career average plans that the average earnings base period will be updated to the years prior to retirement.

It is the company's practice to fund amounts for pensions sufficient to meet the minimum requirements set forth in applicable employee benefit and tax laws, and such additional amounts the company may determine to be appropriate from time to time. The assets of the various plans include corporate equities, government securities, corporate debt securities and income-producing real estate.

The tables on page 54 provide information on the status of the U.S. retirement plan, and selected non-U.S. plans which represent approximately 98% of the total non-U.S. accumulated benefit obligations.

U.S. Plan: U.S. regular and part-time employees are covered by a noncontributory plan which is funded by company contributions to an irrevocable trust fund, which is held for the sole benefit of employees. Monthly retirement benefits generally represent the greater of a fixed amount per year of service, or a percent of career compensation. For plan purposes, annual compensation before January 1, 1991, is defined as the average annual compensation paid for the years 1981 through 1990. Effective January 1, 1989, benefits become vested upon the completion of five years of service. Prior to January 1, 1989, benefits became vested upon completion of 10 years of service. The number of individuals receiving benefits at December 31, 1990, and December 31, 1989, was 52,895 and 44,701, respectively.

The expected long-term rate of return on plan assets used in the calculation of net periodic pension cost was 9% for 1990, 1989 and 1988. Measurement of the 1990 and 1989 projected benefit obligation was based on an 8½% discount rate and a 5% long-term rate of compensation increase.

Non-U.S. Plans: Most subsidiaries and branches outside the U.S. have retirement plans covering substantially all employees, under which funds are deposited under various fiduciary-type arrangements, annuities are purchased under group contracts, or reserves are provided. Retirement benefits are based on years of service and the employee's compensation, generally during a fixed number of years immediately prior to retirement.

Problems 11–13 relate to the U.S. pension plans of the International Business Machines Corporation (IBM). The "Retirement Plans" footnote from IBM's 1990 annual report is reproduced in Exhibit 9P-2; all amounts are in millions of dollars.

11.

    A. Estimate the elements of the net amortization component of IBM's 1990 pension cost of $253.

    B. Using footnote data and the answer to Part A, compute the 1990 actuarial gain or loss by reconciling the 1990 change in IBM's unrecognized net gain.

EXHIBIT 9P-2. *(Continued)*

Notes to Consolidated Financial Statements

The ranges of assumptions used for the non-U.S. plans reflect the different economic environments within the various countries. The expected long-term rates of return on plan assets used in the calculation of net periodic pension cost ranged from 5% to 12% in both 1990 and 1989 and from 5% to 11% in 1988. Measurement of the 1990 and 1989 projected benefit obligation was based on discount rates ranging from 4½% to 10% and long-term rates of compensation increase ranging from 3% to 8½%.

The funded status at December 31 was as follows:	U.S. Plan		Non-U.S. Plans	
	1990	1989	1990	1989
(Dollars in millions)				
Actuarial present value of benefit obligations:				
Vested benefit obligation	$(13,112)	$(11,642)	$ (9,022)	$ (6,892)
Accumulated benefit obligation	$(13,146)	$(11,708)	$(10,347)	$ (8,056)
Projected benefit obligation	$(17,091)	$(15,451)	$(14,338)	$(11,582)
Plan assets at fair value	22,225	22,867	12,382	11,231
Projected benefit obligation less than (in excess of) plan assets	5,134	7,416	(1,956)	(351)
Unrecognized net (gain) loss	(2,665)	(4,902)	459	(1,108)
Unrecognized prior service cost	1,323	1,092	332	241
Unrecognized net asset established at January 1, 1986	(2,747)	(2,951)	(152)	(163)
Prepaid (accrued) pension cost recognized in the statement of financial position	$ 1,045	$ 655	$ (1,317)	$ (1,381)

Net periodic pension cost for the years ended December 31 included the following components:	U.S. Plan			Non-U.S. Plans		
	1990	1989	1988	1990	1989	1988
(Dollars in millions)						
Service cost—						
benefits earned during the period	$ 573	$ 562	$ 579	$ 575	$ 501	$ 482
Interest cost on the						
projected benefit obligation	1,309	1,194	1,120	837	679	648
Return on plan assets—						
Actual	(160)	(3,950)	(2,058)	665	(1,315)	(1,003)
Deferred	(1,859)	2,214	456	(1,644)	564	340
Net amortizations	(253)	(174)	(152)	(5)	2	5
Net periodic pension cost	$ (390)	$ (154)	$ (55)	$ 428	$ 431	$ 472
Total net periodic pension cost for all non-U.S. plans				$ 484	$ 482	$ 515

Source: IBM, 1990 annual report.

C. Using footnote data and the answer to part A, compute new prior service cost for 1990 by reconciling the unrecognized prior service cost of $1323.

12.

A. Compute IBM's contribution to its pension plans for 1990.

B. Compute benefits paid by the pension plans for 1990 by reconciling the change in plan assets.

Notes to Consolidated Financial Statements

International Business Machines Corporation and Subsidiary Companies

Nonpension Postretirement Benefits

The company and its U.S. subsidiaries have defined benefit postretirement plans that provide medical, dental, and life insurance for retirees and eligible dependents. In August 1990, the company announced several changes to its retiree medical plans. Among these changes was the establishment of plan cost maximums in order to more effectively account for and control future medical costs.

Effective January 1, 1991, the company and its subsidiaries implemented on the immediate recognition basis Statement of Financial Accounting Standards (SFAS) 106, "Employers' Accounting for Postretirement Benefits Other Than Pensions." This statement requires that the cost of these benefits, which are primarily for health care, be recognized in the financial statements during the employee's active working career. The company's previous practice was to accrue these costs, principally at retirement.

The transition effect of adopting SFAS 106 on the immediate recognition basis, as of January 1, 1991, resulted in a charge of $2,263 million to 1991 earnings, net of approximately $350 million of income tax effects.

This charge includes a previously unrecognized accumulated postretirement benefit obligation of approximately $4.8 billion, offset by $2.2 billion related to plan assets and accruals under the company's previous accounting practice. This obligation was determined by application of the terms of medical, dental, and life insurance plans, including the effects of established maximums on covered costs, together with relevant actuarial assumptions and health-care cost trend rates projected at annual rates ranging ratably from 14 percent in 1991 to 6 percent through the year 2007. The effect of a 1 percent annual increase in these assumed cost trend rates would increase the accumulated postretirement benefit obligation by approximately $300 million; the annual service costs would not be materially affected.

Certain of the company's non-U.S. subsidiaries have similar plans for retirees. However, most retirees outside the United States are covered by government sponsored and administered programs, and the cost of these programs is not significant to the company.

The total cost for all plans amounted to $394 million, $96 million, and $303 million in 1991, 1990, and 1989, respectively.

Cost in 1991 was higher than in 1990 principally due to the adoption of SFAS 106. Cost in 1990 was lower than in 1989 primarily because of amounts recorded in the 1989 restructuring charge.

It is the company's practice to fund amounts for postretirement benefits with an independent trustee, as deemed appropriate from time to time. The plan assets include corporate equities and government securities. The accounting for the plan is based on the written plan.

The following tables provide information on the status of the plans.

(Dollars in millions)

The funded status at December 31, 1991, was as follows:

Accumulated postretirement benefit obligation:	
Retirees	$ (3,277)
Fully eligible active plan participants . .	(303)
Other active plan participants	(1,869)
Total	(5,449)
Plan assets at fair value	1,632
Accumulated postretirement benefit obligation in excess of plan assets.	(3,817)
Unrecognized net loss	117
Accrued postretirement benefit cost recognized in the statement of financial position.	$ (3,700)

(Dollars in millions)

Net periodic postretirement benefit cost for 1991 included the following:

Service cost—benefits attributed to service during the period	$ 132
Interest cost on the accumulated postretirement benefit obligation	389
Return on plan assets—	
Actual	(325)
Deferred	198
Net periodic postretirement benefit cost . . .	$ 394

The assumed rate of return on the plan assets was 9 percent. Measurement of the accumulated postretirement benefit obligation was based on an 8.5 percent assumed discount rate.

Source: IBM 1991 annual report.

C. Confirm your answer to part B by reconciling the 1990 change in IBM's projected benefit obligation.

13.

A. Explain why IBM's prepaid pension cost asset rose during 1990 despite the fact that the excess of the PBO over plan assets declined.

B. Explain why IBM's pension cost has been negative and why the negative amounts have been increasing.

Problems 14–16 are related to IBM's nonpension postretirement benefits. The Nonpension Postretirement Benefits footnote from IBM's 1991 Annual Report is shown on pages 707–708; all amounts are in millions of dollars.

14.

A. IBM has partially funded its nonpension postretirement benefits. Most companies, however, have not provided such funding. Other than any legal requirement to do so, suggest why firms may be motivated to fund their pension benefits but not their nonpension benefits.

B. Discuss the possible motivations for IBM to fund its nonpension postretirement plans.

C. Prior to SFAS 106, most companies accounted for nonpension post-retirement benefits on a pay-as-you-go basis. How does the method now used by IBM differ from the pay-as-you-go basis?

D. What is the major difference between the method previously used by IBM (to calculate its nonpension liability and cost) and that specified by SFAS 106? On a cumulative basis, quantify the difference between the two methods.

E. Explain why IBM's plan status shows no transition asset/liability.

15. The plan status at the transition date of 1-1-91 follows (in $ millions):

Accumulated postretirement benefit obligation*	$(4800)
Plan assets	?
Excess of APBO over plan assets	$(?)
Accrued liability prior to adoption of SFAS 106	?
Transition liability†	$(2613)

*Given in footnote.
†On a pretax basis from footnote: $2263 + $350 = $2613.

A. Estimate the fair value of IBM's plan assets at January 1, 1991. [Hint: Calculate the expected return on plan assets for 1991 first.]

B. What was the accrued liability prior to the adoption of SFAS 106?

C. Explain the significance of the unrecognized net loss component of the funded status at December 31, 1991.

    D. Using the above table and the footnote data:

        (i) Compute the contribution made to the plan during 1991.

        (ii) Compute benefits paid during 1991.

    E. What was the effect on IBM's 1991 earnings of adopting SFAS 106 (excluding recognition of the transition liability) as compared with use of the pay-as-you-go method?

    16. Using the footnote data, forecast IBM's postretirement benefit cost for 1992.

7. Non-Pension Post Retirement Benefits

Fibreboard currently provides post employment benefits to employees who meet certain requirements until they reach age 65. The benefits provided are mainly health care and dental. In addition, post employment benefits are available to certain collective bargaining units of facilities which have been sold.

On January 1, 1991 Fibreboard adopted Financial Accounting Standards No. 106, Employers Accounting for Post Retirement Benefits Other than Pensions, and recorded the full transition obligation. Fibreboard does not hold any assets to fund the obligation.

The status of Fibreboard's non-pension post retirement benefits at December 31, 1991 is as follows:

Net Periodic Post Retirement Benefit Cost	Year ended December 31, 1991
Service cost	$ 68
Interest cost	178
Return on plan assets	—
Transition obligations	3,102
Net total of other components	—
Total	$3,348

Accrued Benefit Cost	
Accumulated post retirement benefit obligation (APBO)	
Retirees	$ 2,513
Fully eligible plan participants	43
Other active plan participants	597
Total	3,153
Plan assets	—
Unrecognized net (gain) loss	3
Unrecognized transition obligation	—
Total	$3,150

A 17% annual rate of increase in the per capita cost of covered health care benefits was assumed for 1992. The cost trend rate was assumed to decrease slightly until 2003 at which time the rate was assumed to stabilize at 7%. Increasing the assumed health care cost trend rates by 1% in each year would increase the accumulated post retirement benefit obligation as of December 31, 1991 by $138 and the aggregate of the service and interest cost components of net periodic post retirement cost for the year then ended by $138. The weighted average discount rate used in determining the accumulated post retirement benefits was 8%.

Source: Fibreboard 1991 annual report.

Problems 17–23 relate to the nonpension postretirement plans of Fibreboard (FBD). Footnote 7, from FBD's 1991 annual report, is shown on page 710; all amounts are in thousands of dollars.

17. Why does the accrued benefit cost (plan status) table show no unrecognized transition obligation at December 31, 1991?

18. Why does Fibreboard's computation of postretirement benefit cost show no return on plan assets?

19. Compute Fibreboard's nonpension benefits paid during 1991.

20. What was the effect on 1991 benefit cost of adopting SFAS 106, as compared to the pay-as-you-go method, excluding the transition obligation?

21. Forecast Fibreboard's nonpension benefit cost for 1992. State your assumptions.

22. What changes in assumptions could Fibreboard have made during 1991 to reduce:

  (i) The reported APBO at December 31, 1991?

  (ii) 1992 benefit cost?

23. FBD's footnote on income tax policies indicates the sources of deferred income taxes due to timing differences. One major component listed is postretirement benefits (includes pensions) that contributed $(1175) for the year ended December 31, 1991. [1991 net pension cost was $608; the 1991 contribution was $398.]

  A. Compute the implied timing difference and determine the amounts recorded on the firm's 1991 tax return for postretirement benefits. [The statutory tax rate was 34%.]

  B. Discuss how these amounts differ from the tax-deductible amounts the firm would have recorded had it not adopted SFAS 106.

  C. FBD had not yet adopted SFAS 109. Given the limits placed by SFAS 96 on the recognition of deferred tax assets, explain how FBD was able to recognize the deferred tax assets generated by its adoption of SFAS 106.

24. [Analysis of pension plan; 1988 CFA adapted] Anheuser-Busch has a defined benefit plan for its employees. Effective January 1, 1986, the company adopted the provisions of SFAS 87, "Employer's Accounting for Pensions," which had the effect of reducing 1986 pension expense by $45.2 million.

The funded status of the plan on December 31, 1986, was summarized in the *1986 Annual Report* of Anheuser-Busch as shown; all amounts are in millions of dollars.

Plan assets at fair market value	$666.1
Actuarial present value of	
Vested benefit obligation	287.1
Accumulated benefit obligation	319.3
Projected benefit obligation	398.7

Other information included the following:

Excess of plan assets over projected benefit obligation on January 1, 1986	$215.1
Service cost (benefits earned during 1986)	21.1
Actual return on plan assets in 1986 (return of 15.1% on beginning plan assets of $581.1 million)	87.7
Assumptions:	
Discount rate	9.0%
Rate of increase in future compensation	6.5%
Expected long-term rate of return on plan assets	9.0%

In 1987, service cost rose to $23.0 million. To assess the impact of a sharp fall-off in plan assets due to the stock market crash, assume that the actual return on plan assets was −5% in 1987. In addition, assume that the company suffered small actuarial losses related to the projected benefit obligation of $4.0 million in 1986 and $10.0 million in 1987. The closing balance of unrecognized investment and actuarial losses as of December 31, 1986, amounted to $31.4 million, which is being amortized over a 10-year period. The excess of plan assets over projected benefit obligation on January 1, 1986, is being amortized over a 15-year period.

A. Using the data provided, calculate estimated net pension cost for 1987. Note that annual pension cost is based on assumptions as of the beginning of the year. Show calculations for all components.

B. Discuss the likely impact of the adverse investment and actuarial experience in 1987 on pension expense and on the plan status for both 1987 and future years.

10

THE ANALYSIS OF OFF-BALANCE-SHEET ACTIVITIES AND HEDGING TRANSACTIONS

INTRODUCTION

I. OFF-BALANCE-SHEET FINANCING ACTIVITIES

EXAMPLES OF OFF-BALANCE-SHEET FINANCING TRANSACTIONS

Accounts Receivable

Inventories

Commodity-Linked Bonds

Fixed Assets

Joint Ventures

Investments

ANALYSIS OF OBS ACTIVITIES: ASHLAND OIL

II. HEDGING ACTIVITIES

FOREIGN CURRENCY TRANSACTIONS

INTEREST RATE SWAPS

OPTIONS

COMPARISON OF ACCOUNTING FOR HEDGES, OPTIONS AND SWAPS

EXAMPLES OF HEDGE DISCLOSURES

DISCLOSURE STANDARDS FOR FINANCIAL INSTRUMENTS

SUMMARY

INTRODUCTION

Rapid changes in manufacturing and information technology and expanding international trade and capital markets have resulted in the growth of multinational corporations that must cope with increasingly mobile capital, labor, and product markets. These changes have been accompanied by a substantial increase in the volatility of commodity and other factor price levels, fluctuating interest and foreign currency exchange rates, and a frenzy of domestic and international tax and regulatory changes. In addition, general inflation and industry-specific price changes have raised most asset prices and have increased the risks of operations and investments.

This economic climate has required increasing amounts of capital as firms have had to acquire operating capacity (both for expansion and replacement purposes) at ever higher prices. Because of increased volatility, the risks of owning operating assets have also increased. These trends have driven firms to seek methods of (i) acquiring assets other than the traditional direct purchases, financed by debt and (ii) controlling the risks of operations through hedging transactions.

The trend toward "off balance sheet" financing activities and hedging transactions has been encouraged by drawbacks in the historical cost-based financial reporting system, in which recognition and measurement depend primarily on actual transactions and changes in market values are ignored. In addition, financial reporting standards have not been developed for many hedging transactions. The emphasis on accounting assets and liabilities rather than the recognition of economic resources and obligations has two effects:

1. It limits the usefulness of financial statements as indicators of future earnings and cash flows, and
2. It encourages firms to keep resources and obligations off balance sheet.

The first of these effects has been dealt with elsewhere in this book.[1] The second effect stems from "off-balance sheet" (OBS) activities that are the subject of this chapter. As increases in market value (the norm in recent years) are not recognized unless the asset is sold, historical cost balance sheets often understate the true net equity of the firm. Obligations incurred to acquire these assets must be recognized, along with the higher interest rates required to obtain financing under conditions of inflation[2] and higher risk. As balance sheets recognize the "pain" but not the gain, there is little incentive for "on balance sheet" financing when an alternative exists.

The alternative is transactions that circumvent current reporting and disclosure rules. Long-term "executory contracts" are the primary form of OBS transactions. Contracts are entered into to ensure supplies of raw materials, manufacturing or distribution capacity, or other inputs. As contracts are considered legal promises, and

---

[1]See discussion in Appendix 6-C, Analysis of Changing Prices Information, and Chapter 11, Analysis of Intercorporate Investments.

[2]We would argue that a portion of the interest expense (the inflation premium) on debt used to acquire assets should be "matched" against the appreciation of those assets over time.

neither cash nor goods has changed hands, no accounting recognition is required in most cases.

Hedging is designed to protect the firm against adverse movements in prices, interest rates, and foreign currency exchange rates. Hedging transactions include, but are not limited to, futures contracts, options, forward commitments, interest rate swaps, and combined interest rate and currency swaps. Firms may hedge existing assets and liabilities, *firm commitments,* and eligible, *anticipated transactions.* The primary financial reporting and analysis issue is the timing of the recognition of gains and losses on the hedge transaction as compared with gains and losses on the assets or liabilities, firm commitments, or anticipated transactions being hedged.

The growth in hedging activities has paralleled the increased volatility of prices, interest rates, and foreign currency exchange rates. As financial markets have developed, and instruments suitable for hedging have become more available, firms have increasingly used hedging techniques to control their exposure to these risks.

Hedges have been employed to control or reduce price, interest rate, or currency exchange rate risks associated with

1. Physical or tangible assets such as inventories of commodities
2. Assets with interest rate or currency exposure
3. Liabilities with interest rate or currency exposure
4. Firm commitments to purchase or sell raw materials or financial instruments, borrow funds, or repay debt
5. Anticipated transactions such as acquisitions and repatriation of funds, in addition to items included in (4).

This chapter addresses the financial statement effects of off-balance-sheet activities and hedging transactions that require the development of analytical techniques. These techniques allow financial statement users to assess management's use of such transactions and improve their ability to compare firms. The following section provides examples of off-balance-sheet financing transactions, a discussion of applicable analytical techniques, and a comprehensive illustration. The accounting for specific hedge transactions, examples of hedge disclosures, and a discussion of disclosure standards for financial instruments close out the chapter.

I. OFF-BALANCE-SHEET FINANCING ACTIVITIES

Many economic transactions and events are not recognized in the financial statements because they do not qualify as accounting assets or liabilities under current financial reporting standards (or because of measurement problems). Yet these OBS activities generate economic assets and obligations with real current or future cash consequences; their exclusion has a significant impact on the usefulness of reported capital structure and leverage ratios.

Firms may engage in these transactions precisely to avoid reporting high debt levels and leverage ratios and to reduce the probability of technical default under restrictive covenants in debt indentures. OBS transactions may also serve to keep assets and potential gains out of the financial statements but under the control of management, which can orchestrate the timing of the recognition of the gains to offset periods of poor operating performance. Most important, however, the assets excluded from the financial statements do contribute to the operations of the firm.

Footnote disclosures constitute the best source of information about off-balance-sheet activities. Additional information may be available from disclosures in 10-K filings and from other company publications. In some cases, the economic meaning behind the disclosures requires explanation from management.

Thus a complete analysis of the firm must include a review of all financial statement disclosures to obtain data on off-balance-sheet activities. In many cases, straightforward analytic techniques can be used to bring OBS assets and liabilities back on the balance sheet. Such adjustments result in a balance sheet that presents a more complete portrait of the firm's resources and obligations and financial ratios that are more comparable to those of competitors whose use of OBS techniques is different.

EXAMPLES OF OFF-BALANCE-SHEET FINANCING TRANSACTIONS

The most common examples of OBS activities are discussed in the paragraphs that follow. The list is not complete; new forms (and variations of old ones) continue to emerge. The examples presented are representative of techniques commonly used.

Accounts Receivable

Legally separate, wholly owned finance subsidiaries have long been used to purchase receivables from the parent firm that uses the proceeds to retire debt or reduce borrowing. Until 1987, most firms used the equity method to account for finance subsidiaries; the consolidated balance sheet reported only the parent's net investment, suppressing the debt used to finance the receivables. (See Chapter 11 for a comparison of the equity method and consolidation.) As shown by Livnat and Sondhi (1986), exclusion of subsidiary debt allowed firms to report higher coverage and lower leverage ratios, stabilized reported debt and debt ratios over time, and reduced the probability of a technical violation of bond covenants.

Heian and Thies (1989) identified 182 companies (in 35 industry groups) reporting unconsolidated finance subsidiaries in 1985. Supplementary disclosures provided by 140 of these companies indicated a total of $205 billion in subsidiary debt that had not been reported on the parent's balance sheet. The authors also computed debt-to-capital ratios on the basis of a pro forma consolidation and compared them to the preconsolidation ratios; the average increase for the sample was 34%, but nearly 90% for the firms with the 21 largest finance units.

The FASB eliminated the nonconsolidation option (SFAS 94)—and all financial statements must now consolidate the assets and liabilities of controlled financial subsidiaries. In some cases, parent firms have reduced their ownership of finance subsidiaries below 50% and continue to report these units using the equity method. In

---

EXHIBIT 10-1. THE CONTINENTAL CORPORATION
Sale of Receivables

In December 1991, Continental sold $473.6 million in premiums receivable balances due within the next twelve months ($458.7 million were sold in December 1990). These sales accelerated the cash flow associated with the premiums receivable, increasing cash in the year of the sale and reducing it during the following year, when such receivables would otherwise have been collected. These receivables are sold on a nonrecourse basis by Continental. In the event of nonpayment, Continental's credit risk is limited to the amount that the purchaser of the receivables holds as a deposit ($13.6 million in 1991 and $13.5 million in 1990).

Source: 1991 Annual Report.

Sale of Premiums Receivable

In December 1991, Continental sold $474 million of premiums receivable balances. This accelerated the cash flow from the sold receivables, increasing cash provided by operations in 1991, but reducing it by $195 million for the first quarter of 1992, when this portion of the receivables would have been collected. As a result, the balance sheet caption "Premiums Receivable" at March 31, 1992, is lower by $279 million than it otherwise would have been.

Source: 1992 First Quarter Report.

these cases, the analyst should compute (proportionately) consolidated debt/equity ratios because the parent firm generally supports finance subsidiary borrowings through extensive income maintenance agreements and direct or indirect guarantees of debt.[3]

Receivables may also be financed by sale (or securitization) to unrelated parties with the proceeds used to reduce debt. Most sales of receivables provide that the buyer (normally a financial institution) has "limited recourse" to the seller. However, the recourse provision is generally well above the expected loss ratio on the receivables; thus the seller retains all the expected loss experience. These transactions are effectively collateralized borrowings[4] but are accounted for as sales. Thus a firm may recognize a gain or loss on the sale that is, however, rarely disclosed.

Regardless of the merits of the accounting treatment of the sale of receivables, the analysis required is clear. The sale of receivables distorts the pattern of cash flow from operations (CFO) as the firm receives cash earlier than if the receivables had been collected in due course. Exhibit 10-1 provides an example. The sale of receivables in December 1991 increased Continental's cash flow (from operations) by $474 million. From the first quarter 1992 footnote, we can see that CFO was reduced by $195 million (the receivables that would have been collected in that quarter) and CFO over the balance of the year will be reduced by $279 million ($474 million − $195 million). If the same

---

[3]Where subsidiary financial statements are available, separate analysis is required to assess the operating efficiency and leverage of the subsidiary.

[4]SFAS 77, Reporting by Transferors for Transfers of Receivables with Recourse (FASB, 1983), governs the accounting for sales of receivables. This standard allows sales treatment when the risks and rewards have been substantially transferred to the buyer, even though the buyer has "limited recourse' to the seller for nonpayment. The primary requirement is that the recourse obligation (probability of nonpayment) can be estimated, permitting the seller to provide an adequate reserve for bad debts.

amount of receivables is sold each year, there is no distortion. Any variation in the amount sold, however, affects the year-to-year comparison of cash flows. (See the analysis of Deere in Chapter 14 for an example.)

Exhibit 10-2 contains a simplified illustration of a sale of receivables and its impact on selected ratios. Note the beneficial impact on reported liquidity, turnover, leverage, and return ratios.

The analytic solution is to reverse the sale, reinstate the receivables, and treat the proceeds of sale as debt in computing the debt/equity ratio as well as the current ratio, receivables turnover, fixed charge coverage, and the return on average total capital. The adjustment process can be illustrated using Georgia-Pacific as an example.

At December 31, 1990, Georgia Pacific (GP) had outstanding $850 million of receivables that had been sold under a three-year agreement. Note 5 (Exhibit 10-3) states that

> The full amount of the allowance for doubtful accounts has been retained because the Corporation has retained substantially the same risk of credit loss as if the receivables had not been sold.

This language suggests that GP sold the receivables under limited resource provisions where the recourse exceeds the expected loss; the company has not really transferred the risk associated with the receivables, although the transfer met the conditions required by SFAS 77 to record a sale.

For analysis purposes, therefore, we should treat the transfer as a borrowing. Using the balance sheet at December 31, 1990 (Exhibit 12-16, Chapter 12), we increase both receivables and short-term debt by $850 million. The effect on GP's debt/equity ratio is:

GEORGIA PACIFIC
Capitalization at December 31, 1990 ($ millions)

	As Reported	Adjusted
Short-term debt	$1444	$2294
Long-term debt	5218	5218
Total debt	$6662	$7512
Stockholders' equity	2975	2975
Debt/equity ratio	2.24×	2.52×

A second adjustment would be to the income statement, adding interest on the receivables sold to *both* income and expense. Using a rate of 8.8%[5] (and assuming, for simplicity, that the interest rate at which the receivables were sold is equal to that on the receivables themselves), the amount of interest added is $75 million (8.8% × $850 million).

---

[5]The average rate on Georgia Pacific's commercial paper.

EXHIBIT 10-2
Basic Illustration: Sale of Receivables

Balance Sheet Prior to Sale, December 31, 1992

Receivables	$200		Notes payable (15%)	$100
Other current assets	200		Other current liabilities	100
Total		$400	Total	$200
			Long-term debt (12.5%)	200
Fixed assets		400	Equity	400
Total assets		$800	Total	$800

Transaction: $100 of receivables are sold for $100 on January 1, 1993, proceeds are used to retire $100 of notes payable.*

Balance Sheet, December 31, 1993

Receivables	$100		Notes payable (15%)	$ 0
Other current assets	200		Other current liabilities	100
Total		$300	Total	$100
			Long-term debt (12.5%)	200
Fixed assets		400	Equity	400
Total assets		$700	Total	$700

Income Statement

	1992	1993
Sales	500	500
Operating income	$110	$110
Interest income†	30	15
Earnings before interest and tax	140	125
Interest expense		
Notes	(15)	0
Debt	(25)	(25)
Pretax income	$100	$100

Ratios

Current ratio	2.00×	3.00×
Debt/equity	0.75×	0.50×
Interest coverage	3.5×	5.0×
Receivable turnover	2.50×	5.00×
Return on average total capital	20.0%	20.8%

*The illustration assumes no gain or loss on the sale of receivables; any gain would alter the liquidity, leverage, and return ratios.

†For simplicity, we assume that the interest rate on the receivables is 15%, equal to the rate on notes payable. Thus the sale has no impact on income as the reduction of interest income equals the reduction of interest expense.

EXHIBIT 10-3. GEORGIA PACIFIC
Disclosure of Sale of Receivables

Note 5. Receivables

The Corporation has a large, diversified customer base.

As of December 31, 1990, the Corporation had sold fractional ownership interests in a defined pool of trade accounts receivable for $850 million. The net cash proceeds are reported as operating cash flow in the accompanying statement of cash flows. The sold accounts receivable are reflected as a reduction of receivables in the accompanying balance sheet. Under a three-year agreement, the purchasers have agreed to use the collections of receivables to purchase new receivables up to $1 billion. The purchasers' level of investment is subject to change based on the level of eligible receivables and restrictions on concentrations of receivables. Receivables of a certain age and uncollectible receivables are not eligible to be included in the pool. The full amount of the allowance for doubtful accounts has been retained because the Corporation has retained substantially the same risk of credit loss as if the receivables had not been sold. The Corporation pays fees based on its senior debt ratings and the purchasers' level of investment and borrowing costs. The fees, which were $48 million for 1990, are included in selling, general and administrative expense in the accompanying statement of income.

Source: 1990 Annual Report.

GEORGIA PACIFIC
Income Statement, for Year Ended December 31, 1990
(in $ millions)

	As Reported	Adjusted
Earnings before interest	$1325	$1400
Interest expense	606	681
Coverage ratio	2.19×	2.06×

The third required adjustment is to CFO. As stated in Note 5, the proceeds of sale are reported as CFO. Assuming that receivables had not been sold in prior years, the entire $850 million should be deducted from CFO[6] to eliminate the distorting effect of the sale:

GEORGIA PACIFIC
Cash Flow from Operations, for Years Ended December 31, 1989
and December 31, 1990 (in $ millions)

	As Reported	Adjusted
1989	$1358	$1358
1990	2073	1223
% Change	+53%	−10%

[6]Cash flow from financing activities should be increased by $850 million. See Exhibit 12-17, Chapter 12.

As these adjustments show, the sale of receivables had a significant effect on GP's financial statements. To restore consistency with years prior to the sale, and with competitors who do not sell receivables, the adjustments shown are required.

In recent years, the securitization of receivables has increasingly replaced the sale of receivables to financial subsidiaries. The major auto companies, retailers, and credit card issuers have become major sources of securitized receivables. The seller retains the effective recourse obligation, sometimes through a direct obligation and sometimes through "subordination" agreements. Bank letters of credit are sometimes used to enhance the securities.

The impact of the sale or securitization of receivables also depends on cash flow classification. Some firms treat the acquisition, collection, and sale of receivables as investment cash flows, while others treat them as operating.

Inventories

Firms use *take-or-pay contracts* to ensure the long-term availability of raw materials and other inputs necessary for operation. These arrangements are common in the natural gas, chemical, paper, and metal industries. Natural resource companies use *throughput arrangements* with pipelines or processors (such as refiners) to ensure required distribution or processing needs.

Both types of contracts have the effect of acquiring the use of operating capacity without showing the associated assets and liabilities on the balance sheet. These contracts are often used by the supplier to obtain bank or other financing. SFAS 47 requires that, when a long-term commitment is used to obtain financing, the purchaser must disclose the nature of the commitment and the minimum required payments in its financial statement footnotes. An example is Reynolds Metals, whose footnote appears in Exhibit 10-4.

Note B shows Reynolds' investment in unincorporated joint ventures and associated companies. Some of these ventures produce bauxite and alumina (both aluminum bearing ores). The footnote discloses that Reynolds has minimum commitments of $48 million per year for 1991–1996 plus additional amounts that equate to a present value of $257 million. (Note that disclosure of the present value is not required by SFAS 47.)

As take-or-pay contracts and throughput agreements effectively keep some operating assets and liabilities off the balance sheet, the analyst should add the present value of minimum future commitments to both property and debt. This adjustment includes the proportional amount of supplier debt that is, in effect, guaranteed by the purchaser. (Also see the discussion of joint ventures that follows.)

In the case of Reynolds, debt is affected as follows:

REYNOLDS METALS
Balance Sheet, at December 31, 1991 (in $ millions)

	Reported	Adjusted
Total debt	$2096	$2353
Stockholders' equity	2960	2960
Debt/equity ratio	0.71×	0.79×

EXHIBIT 10-4. REYNOLDS METALS
Off-Balance-Sheet Obligations

Note B—Unincorporated Joint Ventures and Associated Companies

The Company has interests in unincorporated joint ventures which produce alumina and gold (Note A). It also has interests in foreign based associated companies which provide the Company with bauxite, alumina, primary aluminum, fabricated aluminum products and hydro-electric power. At December 31 the Company's investment in these activities consisted of the following:

	1991	1990	1989
Unincorporated Joint Ventures			
Current assets..	**$ 30.2**	$ 24.8	$ 23.8
Current liabilities	**(22.7)**	(24.3)	(15.6)
Property, plant and equipment and			
other assets...	**622.7**	623.4	614.9
Net investment..	**$630.2**	$623.9	$623.1
Associated Companies			
Investments	**$189.4**	$171.2	$142.9
Advances	**13.0**	8.3	20.9
Net investment..	**$202.4**	$179.5	$163.8

The Company has committed to pay its proportionate share of annual production charges (including debt service) relating to its interests in certain of these entities. These arrangements include minimum commitments of approximately $48 million annually through 1996 and additional amounts thereafter which together, at present value, aggregate $257 million at December 31, 1991, after excluding interest of $92 million and variable operating costs of the facilities. During 1991 the Company purchased approximately $230 million (1990— $170 million. 1989—$150 million) of raw materials under these arrangements.

Source: 1991 Annual Report.

Exhibit 10-5 contains the commitments and contingencies footnote from Alcan's *1990 Annual Report,* disclosing take-or-pay and similar obligations. As Alcan does not disclose present values, the techniques used to analyze operating leases must be employed. The impact of the $923 million adjustment (calculated in exhibit) is

ALCAN
Balance Sheet, at December 31, 1990 (in $ millions)

	Reported	Adjusted
Total debt	$2616	$3539
Stockholders' equity	4942	4942
Debt/equity ratio	0.53×	0.72×

EXHIBIT 10-5. ALCAN
Analysis of Off-Balance-Sheet Financing Techniques

Footnote: Commitments and Contingencies

To ensure long-term supplies of bauxite and access to alumina and fabricating facilities, Alcan participates in several long-term cost sharing arrangements with related companies. Alcan's fixed and determinable commitments, which comprise long-term debt service and "take-or-pay" obligations, are estimated at $129 in 1991, $128 in 1992, $119 in 1993, $117 in 1994, $117 in 1995 and $219 thereafter. Total charges from these related companies were $322 in 1990, $308 in 1989 and $267 in 1988. In addition, there are guarantees for the repayment of approximately $21 of indebtedness by related companies. Alcan believes that none of these guarantees is likely to be called. Commitments with third parties for supplies of other inputs are estimated at $52 in 1991, $52 in 1992, $51 in 1993, $45 in 1994, $45 in 1995 and $292 thereafter. Total fixed charges from these third parties were $47 in 1990, $51 in 1989 and $33 in 1988.

Minimum rental obligations are estimated at $72 in 1991, $62 in 1992, $49 in 1993, $32 in 1994, $26 in 1995 and lesser annual amounts thereafter. Total rental expenses amounted to $113 in 1990, $102 in 1989 and $102 in 1988.

Source: 1990 Annual Report.

Analysis: Fixed and Determinable Payments, 1991–1995 and Beyond (in $ millions)

	Long-Term Debt Service and Take-or-Pay Obligations	To Third Parties
1991	$129	$ 52
1992	128	52
1993	119	51
1994	117	45
1995	117	45
Thereafter	219	292

Using the technique for capitalizing operating leases (see Chapter 8), these payment streams can be discounted to their present value. Estimated payments after 1995 are

$$\frac{\$219 \text{ million}}{\$117 \text{ million}} = 1.87 \text{ years} \qquad \frac{\$292 \text{ million}}{\$45 \text{ million}} = 6.48 \text{ years}$$

Given these payment streams, the present values can be estimated using an estimated cost of debt (based on capitalized lease disclosures or other long-term debt). For Alcan, we estimate an interest rate of 9.29%. When applied to the minimum payments shown above, the resulting present value equals $596 million for long-term debt service and take-or-pay obligations and $327 million for the obligations to third parties. The total of $923 million is used to adjust Alcan's total debt, as shown in the text.

Inventories can also be financed through product financing arrangements under which inventories are sold and later repurchased. SFAS 49 (1981) requires that such arrangements that do not effectively transfer the risk of ownership to the buyer must be accounted for as debt financing rather than sale of inventory.[7]

Commodity-Linked Bonds

Natural resource firms may also finance inventory purchases through commodity-indexed debt where interest and/or principal repayments are a function of the price of underlying commodities. Changing commodity prices should be monitored to determine their impact on the related debt and debt/equity ratios. Exhibit 10-6 contains one such disclosure.

The LAC bonds are denominated in Swiss francs and are exchangeable for a specified amount of gold. As LAC is a gold producer, these bonds can be viewed as a hedge. If the price of gold were to rise, the bondholders would exchange them for gold (which would have a higher value than the bonds). This loss (to Lac) would offset a portion of its earnings gain from the higher gold price. If the price of gold remains low, Lac will benefit from the low stated interest rate on the bonds (which investors accept because of the option to convert to gold). The sale of these bonds, therefore, reduces the sensitivity of LAC's earnings to the price of gold.

When the issuer can force conversion or redemption, or when economic conditions suggest that the holder would benefit from conversion or redemption, the analyst should compute the potential gain or loss to the issuer assuming conversion. Leverage, interest coverage, turnover, and profitability ratios should also be recomputed. Because the lower stated interest rate affects the calculation of the weighted average interest rate or cost of capital, those computations also require adjustment.

---

[7]In such cases the cost of holding inventories (storage, insurance) and interest cost on the imputed debt must be recognized as incurred. Prior to SFAS 49, companies sometimes used these arrangements to defer these costs and accelerate the recognition of profit. Product financing arrangements are still used outside of the United States.

EXHIBIT 10-6. LAC MINERALS
Commodity-Linked Bond

Swiss franc 14,505,000 (1990 − 92,035,000) gold equivalent convertible bonds, due November 1995, bearing interest at 4 per cent. Each Swiss franc 5,000 bond entitles the holder to exchange it at any time for the cash equivalent in U.S. dollars of 6.835 troy ounces of gold, based on the market price of gold on the day of the investor election. During the year, the Company made an offer to the bond holders to acquire all bonds outstanding at a discount to the par value of the bonds. Pursuant to this offer, the Company retired Swiss franc 77,530,000 bonds for cash consideration totalling $44,685,000 and recorded a gain on retirement of $2.8 million.

Source: 1991 Annual Report.

Fixed Assets

Firms acquire rights to use plant and equipment through contractual arrangements, including

- Operating leases (see Chapter 8)
- Take-or-pay contracts and throughput agreements
- Joint ventures

The first two of these issues have already been discussed. Joint ventures are discussed in the next section. Use of any of these financing techniques understates reported fixed assets, depreciation expense, debt, and interest expense as well as related ratios.

Joint Ventures

Firms may acquire manufacturing and distribution capacity through investments in affiliated firms, including suppliers and end users. Joint ventures with other firms may offer economies of scale and provide opportunities to share operating, technological, and financial risks. To obtain financing for the venture, the investors often enter into take-or-pay or throughput contracts with minimum payments designed to meet the venture's debt service requirements. Direct or indirect guarantees of the joint venture debt may also be present.

Generally, firms account for their investments in joint ventures using the *equity method* (discussed in Chapter 11), since no single firm holds a controlling interest. The balance sheet reports only the net investment in the venture. Footnotes may disclose the assets, liabilities, and results of operations of the venture in a summarized format. These disclosures should be used to develop a proportionate consolidation of the joint venture with the firm (see Chapter 11 for examples). Any guarantees of joint venture debt should also be evaluated for adjustments to reported debt, interest coverage, and the debt/equity ratio.

Exhibit 10-7 contains a portion of Georgia Pacific's commitments and contingencies footnote from its *1990 Annual Report,* disclosing a joint venture with Metropolitan Life. GP is clearly liable for one-half of this off-balance-sheet debt, and $85 million should be added to both property and debt.

Investments

Some firms issue long-term debt exchangeable (at the option of the bondholder) for the common stock of another publicly traded firm held as an investment. Motives for these transactions include lower borrowing costs, the deferral of capital gains tax liability, tax benefits related to the low corporate tax rates on dividends to corporations in the United States, and the desire to maintain an investment while having the use of cash. Exhibit 10-8 describes an exchangeable bond issued by Panhandle Eastern.

When the bonds were originally issued by Panhandle, it obtained $105 million of

EXHIBIT 10-7. GEORGIA PACIFIC
Joint Venture Financing

The Corporation is a 50% partner in a joint venture (GA-MET) with Metropolitan Life Insurance Company (Metropolitan). GA-MET owns and operates the Corporation's office headquarters complex in Atlanta, Georgia. The Corporation accounts for its investment in GA-MET under the equity method.

During 1986, GA-MET borrowed $170 million from Metropolitan for the primary purpose of retiring debt incurred from the acquisition and construction of the Atlanta headquarters complex. The note bears interest at 9½% and requires monthly payments of principal and interest with a final installment due in 2011. The note is secured by the land and building of the Atlanta headquarters complex. In the event of foreclosure, each partner has severally guaranteed payment of one-half of any shortfall of collateral value to the outstanding secured indebtedness. Based on the present market conditions and building occupancy, the likelihood of any obligation to the Corporation with respect to this guarantee is considered remote.

Source: 1990 Annual Report.

EXHIBIT 10-8. PANHANDLE EASTERN
Exchangeable Bonds

In May 1985, Panhandle issued $105,750,000 of 12% subordinated debentures due 2010 which were exchangeable for 3,000,000 shares of common stock of Quantum Chemical Corporation owned by Panhandle. At December 31, 1987, $104,623,000 principal amount of the debentures were outstanding and were exchangeable for 2,968,036 shares of the Quantum stock. Beginning May 1, 1988, these debentures are callable by Panhandle upon not less than thirty days' notice at 108.4% of face amount unless exchanged prior to the redemption date.

Source: 1987 Annual Report.

cash while maintaining its strategic investment in Quantum Chemical.[8] Because of the low cost of the stock investment ($7.42 million), the bond sale allowed Panhandle to defer the capital gains tax on the unrealized gain of $98.33 million ($105.75 million − $7.42 million). In 1988, at the time of Panhandle's choosing, the bonds were called, and an exchange of the bonds for the Quantum Chemical shares was forced. Possible reasons for the call were the desire to recognize the capital gain for both tax purposes (corporate capital gains taxes had been reduced) and financial reporting purposes. The decline in corporate tax rates had also made the tax deduction for interest expense less valuable.

As in the case of commodity linked bonds, conversion should be assumed when it can be forced by the issuer or when it is advantageous to holders. The assumption of exchange should be a function of the terms of the issue, as disclosed in the issuer's footnotes. Adjusted leverage, interest coverage, and profitability ratios, as well as the adjusted cost of capital should then be computed.

---

[8]The two firms had a joint venture and common board members. Thus Panhandle may have seen an advantage in maintaining a large (10%) stock interest.

ANALYSIS OF OBS ACTIVITIES: ASHLAND OIL

Exhibit 10-9 contains an analysis of the off-balance-sheet financing techniques used by Ashland Oil, a major oil refiner with other interests, including coal and natural gas. Ashland's reported debt has been adjusted for its off-balance-sheet obligations for operating leases and affiliate companies. Adjusted debt is approximately 50% above reported debt for each year; both reported and adjusted debt rose in 1991.

After adjustment, Ashland's debt ratios are considerably higher, whether viewed in relation to stated equity or to the market value of equity. In this case, the adjustment does not affect the year-to-year trend. When new commitments are entered into, however, only the adjusted ratios will capture the increase in leverage.

This analysis is incomplete, however. We have not marked Ashland's debt to market and have ignored other off-balance-sheet liabilities relating to Ashland's employee benefit plans (see Chapter 9). Finally, we have not considered whether any adjustment should be made to Ashland's deferred income tax liability. In Chapter 14 a complete balance sheet adjustment is illustrated for Deere.

EXHIBIT 10-9. ASHLAND OIL
Adjustments to Capitalization, at September 30, 1990–1991 (in thousands)

	Reported Debt	
	September 30, 1991	September 30, 1990
Short-term debt	$ 195,506	$ 169,820
Long-term debt	1,289,010	1,179,776
Capitalized leases	47,552	55,379
Insurance reserves	141,101	117,632
Total debt	$1,673,169	$1,522,607
Stockholders' equity	1,515,314	1,363,594
Total capital	$3,188,483	$2,886,201
Market value of equity	1,818,825	1,777,442
Total capital (MV)	$3,491,994	$3,300,049
Debt/equity	1.10	1.12
Debt/equity (MV)	0.92	0.86
Debt/total capital	0.52	0.53
Debt/total capital (MV)	0.48	0.46

Note: This table depicts the capital structure of Ashland Oil as reported on its balance sheet without any adjustment for off-balance-sheet financing techniques discussed in the chapter. Adjustments are shown below along with their impact on leverage ratios.

EXHIBIT 10-9. *(Continued)*

	Adjustments to Reported Debt	
	September 30, 1991	September 30, 1990
As reported	$1,673,169	$1,522,607
50% of Arch Mineral's noncurrent liabilities	206,384	216,921
46% of Ashland Coal's liability and redeemable preferred	132,159	123,620
20% of LOOP and LOCAP's debt*	124,083	122,999
Contingent liability for Ashland Coal's debt and lease obligations (Footnote G)	9,660	9,200
Contingent liability for AECOM Technology	1,617	4,538
Operating leases	275,000	260,000
Adjusted debt	2,422,072	2,259,885
Adjusted total capital	$3,937,386	$3,623,479
Adjusted total capital (MV)	$4,240,897	$4,037,327
Adjusted debt/equity	1.60	1.66
Adjusted debt/equity (MV)	1.33	1.27
Adjusted debt/capital	0.62	0.62
Adjusted debt/capital (MV)	0.57	0.56

Note: MV refers to the market value of equity. Debt (adjusted or not) is based on book value.

*Alternatively, use Ashland's contingent liability for LOOP and LOCAP debt secured by throughput and deficiency agreements; Footnote G reports $118,000,000 in 1991 and $119,000,000 in 1990.

EXHIBIT 10-9. *(Continued)*

CONSOLIDATED BALANCE SHEETS
September 30

(In thousands)	1991	1990
Assets		
Current assets		
Cash and cash equivalents – Note A	$ '70,700	$ 80,579
Accounts receivable (less allowances for doubtful accounts of		
$17,711 in 1991 and $15,007 in 1990)	1,205,478	1,147,444
Construction completed and in progress – at contract prices	51,846	57,641
Inventories – Note A	660,057	716,541
Deferred income tax benefits – Note E	62,716	70,953
Other current assets	67,827	70,296
	2,118,624	2,143,454
Investments and other assets		
Investments in and advances to unconsolidated affiliates – Note D	310,007	343,816
Investments of captive insurance companies – Note A	150,363	128,746
Cost in excess of net assets of companies acquired (less accumulated		
amortization of $21,072 in 1991 and $15,990 in 1990) – Notes A and B	64,356	69,426
Other noncurrent assets	241,348	167,632
	766,074	709,620
Property, plant and equipment – Notes A and G		
Cost		
Ashland Petroleum	2,389,396	1,970,683
SuperAmerica Group	528,836	519,862
Valvoline	221,969	211,690
Chemical	488,106	465,344
Construction	544,594	560,505
Exploration	835,124	794,198
Corporate	158,033	174,367
	5,166,058	4,696,649
Accumulated depreciation, depletion and amortization	(2,601,658)	(2,431,823)
	2,564,400	2,264,826
	$5,449,098	$5,117,900

EXHIBIT 10-9. *(Continued)*

(In thousands)	1991	1990
Liabilities and Stockholders' Equity		
Current liabilities		
Debt due within one year		
Notes payable to banks	$ 79,000	$ 84,768
Commercial paper	59,081	42,967
Current portion of long-term debt and capitalized lease obligations	57,425	42,085
Trade and other payables	1,579,533	1,538,357
Income taxes	47,862	97,369
	1,822,901	1,805,546
Noncurrent liabilities		
Long-term debt (less current portion) – Note F	1,289,010	1,179,776
Capitalized lease obligations (less current portion) – Note G	47,552	55,379
Deferred income taxes – Note E	312,062	323,811
Claims and reserves of captive insurance companies	141,101	117,632
Accrued pension costs – Note J	105,292	87,571
Other long-term liabilities and deferred credits	287,673	268,172
	2,182,690	2,032,341
Preferred stock – Note H		
Common stockholders' equity – Notes F, H and K		
Common stock, par value $1.00 per share		
Authorized–150,000 shares		
Issued–59,879 shares in 1991 and 57,803 shares in 1990	59,879	57,803
Paid-in capital	130,314	69,507
Retained earnings	1,325,121	1,236,284
Deferred translation adjustments	2,754	7,411
Loan to leveraged employee stock ownership plan (LESOP)	(34,519)	(34,519)
Prepaid contribution to LESOP	(40,042)	(56,473)
	1,443,507	1,280,013
Commitments and contingencies – Notes G and I		
	$5,449,098	$5,117,900

EXHIBIT 10-9. *(Continued)*

Note D – Unconsolidated Affiliates

Investments accounted for on the equity method include: Arch Mineral Corporation (a 50% owned coal company); Ashland Coal, Inc. (a 46% owned publicly traded coal company); LOOP INC. and LOCAP INC. (18.6% and 21.4% owned joint ventures operating a deepwater offshore port and related pipeline facilities in the Gulf of Mexico); and various petroleum, chemical and engineering companies. Summarized financial information reported by these investments and a summary of the amounts recorded in Ashland's consolidated financial statements follow.

(In thousands)	Arch Mineral Corporation	Ashland Coal, Inc.	LOOP INC. and LOCAP INC.	Other	Total
September 30, 1991					
Financial position					
Current assets	$ 150,002	$ 90,769	$ 49,380	$ 175,843	
Current liabilities	(146,668)	(54,232)	(119,025)	(111,721)	
Working capital	3,334	36,537	(69,645)	64,122	
Noncurrent assets	663,514	441,054	721,192	197,100	
Noncurrent liabilities	(412,767)	(254,873)	(620,415)	(113,208)	
Redeemable preferred stock	–	(32,429)	–	–	
Stockholders' equity	$ 254,081	$ 190,289	$ 31,132	$ 148,014	
Results of operations					
Sales and operating revenues	$ 582,025	$ 438,739	$ 154,177	$ 540,397	
Gross profit	7,741	71,847	43,250	132,745	
Net income (loss)	(13,575)[1]	32,238	(5,096)	6,591	
Amounts recorded by Ashland					
Investments and advances	134,618	96,513[2]	5,252	73,624	$ 310,007
Equity income (loss)	(5,433)	15,020	(776)	5,041	13,852
Dividends received	5,000[3]	2,769	–	3,188	10,957
September 30, 1990					
Financial position					
Current assets	$ 227,611	$ 74,212	$ 37,055	$ 177,923	
Current liabilities	(140,450)	(40,536)	(141,895)	(122,594)	
Working capital	87,161	33,676	(104,840)	55,329	
Noncurrent assets	684,366	400,980	756,062	200,543	
Noncurrent liabilities	(433,842)	(237,530)	(614,994)	(111,720)	
Redeemable preferred stock	–	(31,209)	–	–	
Stockholders' equity	$ 337,685	$ 165,917	$ 36,228	$ 144,152	
Results of operations					
Sales and operating revenues	$ 664,248	$ 386,914	$ 144,268	$ 373,007	
Gross profit	93,787	62,514	50,899	101,723	
Net income (loss)	44,716	29,544	(1,427)	20,644	
Amounts recorded by Ashland					
Investments and advances	177,190	84,262	6,028	76,336	$ 343,816
Equity income (loss)	27,978	13,652	(113)	8,085	49,602
Dividends received	4,000	2,354	–	2,521	8,875

(1) Includes an after-tax charge of $22,010,000 for the write-down of the investment in the Oven Fork mine which was closed due to geological problems encountered.

(2) The market value of Ashland's investment is $209,421,000 based on the closing market price of Ashland Coal's common stock at September 30, 1991.

(3) Excludes a special dividend of $20,000,000 to reduce excess liquidity and a reduction of $10,016,000 representing the excess of proceeds over the carrying value of Ashland's interest in a land trust sold to Arch Mineral (see Note B).

Ashland's retained earnings include $202,417,000 of undistributed earnings from unconsolidated affiliates accounted for on the equity method.

EXHIBIT 10-9. *(Continued)*

Note G – Leases and Other Commitments

Leases

Ashland and its subsidiaries are lessees in noncancelable leasing agreements for office buildings and warehouses, pipelines, transportation and marine equipment, service stations, manufacturing facilities and other equipment and properties which expire at various dates. Future minimum lease payments at September 30, 1991 and assets (included in property, plant and equipment) under capital leases follow.

(In thousands)

Future minimum lease payments		Assets under capital leases	1991	1990
1992	$ 12,347	Cost		
1993	10,266	Ashland Petroleum	$120,700	$121,581
1994	7,964	SuperAmerica Group	104	–
1995	6,586	Valvoline	1,060	1,060
1996	6,579	Chemical	7,297	7,297
Later years	38,311	Corporate	7,600	7,600
	82,053		136,761	137,538
Imputed interest	(26,727)	Accumulated depreciation	(98,136)	(95,624)
Capitalized lease obligations	$ 55,326	Net assets	$ 38,625	$ 41,914

Future minimum rental payments at September 30, 1991 and rental expense under operating leases follow.

(In thousands)

Future minimum rental payments		Rental expense	1991	1990	1989
1992	$ 59,538				
1993	52,880	Minimum rentals			
1994	43,268	(including rentals under			
1995	38,699	short-term leases)	$88,459	$ 86,146	$105,610
1996	34,060	Contingent rentals	11,999	10,795	12,341
Later years	176,096	Sublease rental income	(16,412)	(13,636)	(11,938)
	$404,541		$84,046	$ 83,305	$106,013

Other commitments

Under agreements with LOOP and LOCAP (see Note D), Ashland is committed to advance funds against future transportation charges if these joint ventures are unable to meet their cash requirements. Such advances are limited to Ashland's share, based on its equity interests, of the total debt service and defined operating and administrative costs of these companies. Such advances, however, are reduced by (1) transportation charges Ashland paid, (2) a pro rata portion of transportation charges paid by other equity participants in excess of their required amounts and (3) a pro rata portion of transportation charges paid by third parties who are not equity participants. Advances made to LOOP and LOCAP by Ashland which had not yet been applied to subsequent transportation charges amounted to $5,946,000 at September 30,1991 and $10,106,000 at September 30, 1990. Transportation charges incurred amounted to $24,866,000 in 1991, $22,076,000 in 1990 and $22,155,000 in 1989. At September 30, 1991, Ashland's contingent liability for its share of the indebtedness of LOOP and LOCAP secured by throughput and deficiency agreements amounted to approximately $118,000,000.

Ashland is contingently liable under guarantees of certain debt and lease obligations of Ashland Coal, Inc., an unconsolidated affiliate. At September 30, 1991, such obligations have a present value of approximately $21,000,000. Ashland is also contingently liable for up to $20,000,000 of borrowings under a revolving credit agreement of AECOM Technology Corporation, an unconsolidated affiliate. At September 30, 1991, borrowings of $1,617,000 were outstanding under this agreement.

II. HEDGING ACTIVITIES

The FASB has provided guidance on accounting for foreign exchange forward contracts, currency futures, and currency swaps in SFAS 52, Foreign Currency Translation. Accounting for all other futures is delineated in SFAS 80, Accounting for Futures Contracts. However, as Stewart (1989) points out:

1. There are no reporting standards for interest rate forwards, nearly all categories of options, and interest rate swaps, and
2. Existing standards are inconsistent.

The primary accounting issue in hedging activities concerns the timing of recognition of the gains or losses on the hedge and those on the underlying assets or liabilities, firm commitments, or anticipated transactions being hedged. Some general guidelines can be inferred from SFAS 52 and SFAS 80. The latter defines two criteria that must be met for an instrument to qualify as a hedge: (i) the hedged item exposes the firm to interest rate or price risk, and (ii) the hedging insturment reduces that exposure and is designated as a hedge.

Realized and unrealized gains and losses are recognized in current income

1. For hedging instruments that do not meet *hedge criteria.*
2. When the gains and losses on the hedged items are also reported in income in the period of occurrence; that is, when the hedged items are carried at market value.

In effect, these two types of hedges are "marked to market" on each financial statement date.

In some cases, gains or losses on the hedged item are reported in a valuation allowance in the stockholders' equity section, for example, net investment in foreign subsidiaries and long-term investments in securities. Gains or losses on hedges of such items must also be reported the same way. *In the case of anticipated transactions and hedged items reported at historical cost or lower of cost or market, gains and losses on hedges should be deferred and recognized when changes in value in the hedged item are recognized.*

FOREIGN CURRENCY TRANSACTIONS

Firms with foreign operations face *economic exposure* due to their net investment and the impact of changing currency rates on operating activities. Subsidiaries and parent companies are also affected by *transaction exposure* because exchange rate changes affect the contractual cash flow streams.

SFAS 52 specifies the accounting rules for foreign currency transactions not denominated in the functional currency of the foreign subsidiary (see Chapter 13 for a discussion of functional currencies). The asset, liability, revenue, or expense generated by the foreign currency transaction must be translated into the functional currency using the current exchange rate on the transaction date. These balances must be adjusted to recognize the impact of changes in exchange rates on all subsequent balance sheet dates and on settlement.

Resulting gains or losses must be recognized in current income unless the transaction is a hedge of a net investment in a foreign entity or it involves a long-term intercompany foreign currency transaction. In these cases, the gains or losses are reported in the equity section as components of the *cumulative translation adjustment*. Forward exchange contracts may be used as hedges of identifiable foreign currency commitments, and the required accounting is the same as for hedges. The difference between the current or spot rate and the forward rate reflects the premium or discount on the forward contract and is accounted for separately over the life of the contract.

INTEREST RATE SWAPS

Interest rate swaps are used to manage interest rate risk, decrease borrowing costs, and in some cases, avoid restrictive bond covenants. For example, firms may swap fixed for variable interest[9] (or vice versa), exchange one variable rate index for another, or use their credit standing in one marketplace to borrow funds at favorable terms and swap them for preferred terms in another market. Some swaps may involve combined transfers of interest rate and specific currency-denominated payment streams. For example, a bond issue may be payable in fixed rate Australian dollars and the proceeds swapped for variable rate debt payable in Swiss francs.

Interest rate swaps may qualify as hedges of existing or proposed debt, and recognition of the gain or loss on the swap transaction follows the reporting method used on the underlying debt. Swaps may be used primarily to affect interest rate risk, but they may change the credit and enterprise risk. The former changes because swaps entail an exchange of creditworthiness and the parties to the swap may have different probabilities of default. As Rue, Tosh, and Francis (1988) note, swaps are considered integral components of related debt; since changes in the market value of debt are not recognized, changes in the market value of swaps are also not recognized when they occur.

Generally, cash payments on swaps are reported as a component of interest expense as they are incurred. Unmatched swaps are treated as speculative transactions, and changes in their market value are reported in current income. However, firms are not required to provide separate disclosure of unmatched swaps. Current disclosures are not very informative as they are limited to the principal (notional) amounts involved, whether the swaps are matched or not, and the effective interest rate on both total and variable debt after the swap. Firms are not required to disclose the duration of the swap, net present value of the swap, or the probability and amount of loss on default by a counterparty or intermediary.[10]

---

[9]For an example, see the long-term borrowings footnote of Deere's 1991 annual report (Appendix 1–B). The impact of the swap was discussed in Chapter 8.

[10]In late 1990, the British House of Lords ruled that local governmental authorities did not have the authority to enter into interest rate swaps. This decision left financial intermediaries with losses estimated at more than £750 million (*Financial Times*, November 5, 1990).

OPTIONS

Options, like foreign exchange forwards and futures contracts, can be used as hedges against volatility in prices, interest rates and foreign currency exchange rates because they give the holder the right (but not the obligation) to purchase or sell a security or commodity at a specific price for a specific period. The similarity suggests that hedge accounting rules discussed above may be used for options.[11]

COMPARISON OF ACCOUNTING FOR HEDGES, OPTIONS AND SWAPS

Exhibit 10-10 reproduces an exhibit from Stewart (1989) in which he compares hedge accounting criteria in SFAS 52 and SFAS 80 with those used in accounting practice for interest rate swaps and the AICPA recommendations for accounting for options. Some of the differences and inconsistencies warrant brief comment.

First, both standards allow hedge accounting when risk is reduced, except that SFAS 80 uses an *enterprise approach* in contrast to SFAS 52, which is based on a *transaction approach*. Gains and losses on economically similar transactions may, therefore, receive different accounting treatment.

Under SFAS 80, futures contracts may be treated as hedges of anticipated transactions but SFAS 52 does not allow firms to use forwards or futures as hedges of anticipated foreign currency transactions. Movements in different foreign currencies may be highly correlated, and firms may use them as hedges,[12] but SFAS 52 does not allow cross-hedging. Again, similar transactions may produce different results.

The absence of accounting standards and inconsistencies in the disclosure requirements for OBS transactions, executory contracts, and hedging techniques indicate critical limitations of the existing financial reporting system in its treatment of changes in market values and the volatility in operating performance. These limitations would be eased by a reporting system that used market values rather than historical costs. The use of market values would permit companies to recognize gains in asset value, removing one incentive for OBS transactions. If hedged items were reported at market value, there would be no reason to delay recognition of gains and losses on hedges.

EXAMPLES OF HEDGE DISCLOSURES

Despite the difficulties with hedge accounting rules, disclosures sometimes provide useful information regarding a firm's hedging activities. One example is LAC Minerals,

---

[11]See the AICPA Issues Paper, Accounting for Options, and Hauworth and Moody (1987) for a discussion of differences between options and other hedging instruments and an analysis of the application of hedge criteria to purchased and written options.

[12]For example, the Austrian schilling tends to move with the German mark. As financial markets in Germany are much more liquid than are those in Austria, firms may use mark financial instruments to hedge schilling exposures. Under SFAS 52, such transactions would not be considered hedges.

EXHIBIT 10-10
Comparison of Hedge Accounting Requirements

	FASB 52*	FASB 80†	AICPA issues paper on options‡	Interest rate swaps in practice§
Hedge Accounting Criteria				
Designation as a hedge	Yes	Yes	Yes	Frequently but not always
Risk reduction basis	Transaction	Enterprise	Transaction	Sometimes
Degree of correlation	Not explicit	High	High	Matching
Ongoing assessment	Not explicit	Yes	Yes	Usually
Hedge of anticipated transaction (not firm commitment)	No	Yes	Yes	Yes
Cross hedges	Usually not	Yes	Yes	Yes
Hedge of an asset carried at cost	NA	Yes	No	Yes
Application of Accounting				
Split accounting for inherent elements (premium or discountl)	Yes	Usually not	Yes	Frequently not necessary
Amortization of premium on hedge of net investment in a foreign entity	Income or equity	NA	Income	NA
Cap on deferred losses to fair value	No	No	Yes	No
Accounting if hedge criteria not met	Formula value	Market	Market	Market or lower of cost or market

NA – Not applicable.

*Statement 52 covers foreign exchange forwards, futures, and swaps, but not options explicitly.

†Statement 80 covers all (and only) exchange-traded futures except foreign currency futures, which are covered by Statement 52.

‡The recommendations included in the AICPA issues paper cover all options (whether or not exchange traded). These recommendations do *not* constitute authoritative generally accepted accounting principles. The chart covers only purchased options.

§There's no authoritative GAAP for interest rate swaps, although the emerging issues task force has dealt with several swap issues. Existing practice for interest rate swaps is not uniform. Summarized here is the author's perception of practice. The federal banking regulators are working on a release that would provide guidance for regulatory accounting.

Source: Stewart, John E., "The Challenges of Hedge Accounting," *Journal of Accountancy,* November 1989, Exhibit 2, p. 54.

a Canadian gold producer, whose hedging activities footnote is contained in Exhibit 10-11.

The footnote indicates that LAC has sold both gold and copper for future delivery. These sales have the effect of locking in the price at which future output will be sold.

As the price of gold and copper is denominated in U.S. dollars, and LAC's costs are in Canadian dollars, the company's profit margins are affected by changes in the exchange rate between those two currencies. LAC has used hedging techniques to limit that risk for 1992 and 1993.

Reynolds Metals also engages in hedging techniques to hedge output prices, as

EXHIBIT 10-11. LAC MINERALS
Disclosure of Hedging Activities

The Company engages in forward sales and other hedging transactions to reduce the impact of fluctuations in metal prices, foreign currency and interest rates on its profitability and cash flow. Commitments to deliver gold and other metals arise from forward sales contracts, gold loans and other similar arrangements. The credit risk exposure associated with these activities would be limited to all unrealized gains on contracts based on current market prices. The Company believes that this credit risk has been minimized by dealing with highly rated international institutions.

At December 31, 1991, the Company had future delivery commitments for a total of 1,543,000 ounces of gold at an average selling price of $398 per ounce which are considered as hedges of future production as follows:

	Forward Sales		Gold Loans	
	Ounces	Average Price	Ounces	Average Price
1992	840,000	$395	52,500	$414
1993	488,000	396	70,000	414
1994			70,000	414
1995			22,500	414
	1,328,000	$395	215,000	$414

In addition, at December 31, 1991, the Company had future delivery commitments in 1992 for a total of 15,000 tonnes of copper at an average selling price of $1.03 per pound and 8,000 tonnes of zinc at $0.51 per pound.

Through a combination of foreign exchange forward contracts and put and call options, the Company has hedged Canadian dollar proceeds to be received on U.S. dollar gold sales sufficient to fund certain of its Canadian dollar operating costs. In 1992, the Company has effectively established a fixed exchange rate of $1.18 for US$52 million of revenues and a minimum exchange rate of $1.16 for US$107 million and a maximum exchange rate of $1.19 for US$53 million. In 1993, the Company has established a fixed exchange rate of $1.20 for US$44 million of revenues and a minimum exchange rate of $1.16 for US$8 million and a maximum exchange rate of $1.21 for US$4 million. Based on the exchange rate at January 28, 1992, the unrealized loss on the outstanding foreign currency contracts is estimated to be $1 million.

Source: 1991 Annual Report.

shown in Exhibit 10-12. Reynolds' footnote also indicates that it has hedged input prices (natural gas and raw materials) and interest rate risks (through swaps). These disclosures, while less informative than those of LAC, can be used to question management regarding their use of hedges.

Monsanto, a major chemical producer, has significant foreign operations and is, therefore, exposed to the effect of changing exchange rates. The footnote in Exhibit 10-13, while vague, does indicate the major currencies to which the company is exposed. The footnote discloses Monsanto's use of hedging for anticipated transactions as well as current exposures. Finally, the footnote discloses the accounting principles it

EXHIBIT 10-12. REYNOLDS METALS
Disclosure of Hedging Activities

The Company utilizes forward contracts, futures contracts, option contracts and swap agreements related to certain of its business activities. Gains and losses on these contracts are recognized or accrued as a component of the related transactions. The contractual amounts stated below are outstanding as of the end of 1991 and are indicative of the levels of involvement by the Company and are not indicative of gains or losses. The Company is exposed to certain losses in the event of non-performance by the other parties to these agreements, but the Company does not anticipate non-performance by the counterparties.

The Company manages a portion of its exposures to fluctuations in aluminum, gold and raw material prices and production costs with short- and long-term strategies after giving consideration to market conditions, contractual agreements, anticipated sale and purchase transactions and other factors affecting the Company's risk profile. To hedge prices on a short-term basis, the Company had $194 million of aluminum contracts and $49 million of gold contracts that fix the price for a small portion of anticipated sales in 1992. Certain of the aluminum contracts are protected from significant upward movements in aluminum prices with option contracts. To hedge cost on a long-term basis, the Company had $200 million of aluminum contracts that fix a portion of the variable costs of certain fixed-price aluminum sales commitments which run from 1992 to 1995 and $75 million of natural gas contracts that fix the variable price of natural gas supply agreements which run from 1992 to 1994. Certain aluminum sales and raw material acquisitions in foreign markets are hedged with foreign currency contracts ($116 million, maturing in 1992 to 1994).

The Company manages its exposure to interest rate fluctuations after giving consideration to market conditions and levels of variable-rate and fixed-rate debt outstanding. The Company had $225 million of long-term agreements (1 to 3 years) and $365 million of short-term agreements (principally 1 to 6 months) which fix the interest rate on certain variable-rate debt. Due to the significant issuances of fixed-rate debt and repayments of variable-rate debt in 1991, the Company entered into $300 million of three-year interest rate agreements in early 1992 which convert a portion of fixed-rate debt to variable rate.

Source: 1991 Annual Report.

follows for hedging activities. These disclosures can be used, in conjunction with the financial statements and discussions with management, to obtain some insight into the firm's risk strategy.

DISCLOSURE STANDARDS FOR FINANCIAL INSTRUMENTS

In May 1986, the FASB added a project on financial instruments and OBS financing activities to its agenda with the objectives of developing comprehensive financial reporting standards in response to the problems discussed in the preceding sections and providing guidelines for recognition, measurement, and disclosure issues concerning financial instruments, OBS transactions, and hedging activities.

FASB deliberations on recognition and measurement issues are in progress. In the interim, the FASB has issued several disclosure standards to permit financial statement users to obtain additional information about these activities.

EXHIBIT 10-13. MONSANTO
Disclosure of Foreign Currency Exposures

Currency Translation

Most of Monsanto's ex-U.S. entities' financial statements are translated into U.S. dollars using current exchange rates. Unrealized currency adjustments in the Statement of Consolidated Financial Position are accumulated in shareowners' equity. The financial statements of ex-U.S. entities that operate in hyperinflationary economies, principally Brazil, are translated at either current or historical exchange rates, as appropriate. These currency adjustments are included in net income.

Major currencies are the U.S. dollar, British pound sterling and Belgian franc. Other important currencies include the Brazilian cruzeiro, Canadian dollar, French franc, German mark, Italian lira and Japanese yen. Currency restrictions are not expected to have a significant effect on Monsanto's cash flow, liquidity or capital resources.

Currency option contracts are utilized to manage currency exposure for anticipated transactions (e.g., export sales for the following year). Currency option and forward contracts are utilized to manage other currency exposures. At December 31, 1991 and 1990, Monsanto had currency forward and option contracts to purchase $240 million and $136 million, respectively, and sell $714 million and $372 million, respectively, of other currencies, principally the British pound sterling, Japanese yen and German mark. *Gains and losses on contracts that are designated and effective as hedges are deferred and recognized in the period of the exposure being hedged. Gains and losses on other currency forward and option contracts are included in net income immediately.* Monsanto is subject to loss in the event of non-performance by the counterparties to these contracts.

Source: 1991 Annual Report.

SFAS 105 (1990) requires disclosures about financial instruments with off-balance-sheet risk of accounting loss and those with concentrations of credit risk. For all financial instruments with off-balance-sheet credit or market value risk, SFAS 105 requires disclosure of the contractual or notional principal amount, nature and terms of the instruments, and a discussion of their credit and market risk, accounting loss in the event of complete default by the counterparty, collateral policy, and a description of collateral held by the firm. The disclosures in Exhibits 10-12 and 10-13 are a product of those requirements.

SFAS 105 also requires firms to disclose concentrations of credit risk from individual or groups of counterparties. Exhibit 10-14 contains Monsanto's disclosure of concentrations in its trade accounts receivable. While these data reflect vulnerability that could be inferred from the company's segment disclosures, there is some additional information. Note, for example, the doubling of receivables from European agricultural product distributors.

SFAS 107 requires the disclosure of market values for all financial instruments (on and off balance sheet). It exempts insurance contracts, leases, equity investments, and trade receivables and payables. Firms must disclose assumptions and methods used to develop estimates of fair values. Additional narrative disclosures are required if it is not practicable to estimate fair values. In keeping with the exploratory nature of these

EXHIBIT 10-14. MONSANTO COMPANY
Disclosure of Concentrations

Footnote: Commitments and Contingencies, 1990–1991 (in $ millions)

The more significant concentrations in Monsanto's trade receivables at year-end were

	1991	1990
U.S. agricultural product distributors	$141	$150
European agricultural product distributors	176	90
Pharmaceutical distributors worldwide	332	283

Management does not anticipate incurring losses on its trade receivables in excess of established allowances.

Source: 1991 Annual Report.

standards, the Board has not specified or limited estimation methods but instead asked for qualitative information. SFAS 107 disclosures are required[13] in financial statements issued for fiscal years ended after December 15, 1992.

The International Accounting Standards Committee (IASC) issued an Exposure Draft (ED) on Financial Instruments in September 1991. The scope was broader than that of the two U.S. disclosure standards discussed earlier. Many of the issues included in the ED are still being considered by the FASB.

Some important differences between the IASC ED and SFAS 105 and 107 are that the ED

- Does not exclude leases and insurance contracts
- Has fewer specific disclosure requirements
- Would eliminate lower of cost or market for investments

The ED would permit the hedging of anticipated transactions when it is "highly probable" that they will materialize; their accounting treatment in the United States remains inconsistent and the subject of much debate.

SUMMARY

Off-balance-sheet financing and hedging techniques have been management responses to rising and more volatile asset prices, increased operating, investing and financing risks, and the limited ability of a historical cost-based financial reporting system to cope with these trends. OBS transactions are designed to obtain the use of assets without financial statement recognition of assets and related liabilities. Hedging techniques allow managers to control the impact of uncertainty on reported income.

[13]For firms with total assets of less than $150 million, the effective date is December 15, 1995.

OBS techniques generate economic resources and obligations with real cash flow consequences that affect capital structure, leverage and operating results. Hedging transactions can similarly affect the level and trend of reported firm performance. The analyst's ability to evaluate these effects is constrained by lack of financial statement recognition, divergent and incomplete disclosure and, in the case of hedging transactions, the absence of a coherent set of reporting requirements.

The chapter provides a discussion of the accounting for and analysis of OBS activities and hedging transactions. Analytic adjustments which bring OBS transactions back into the financial statements are suggested, using examples. While hedge accounting can be complex, disclosures often provide information on these activities. The trend toward increased market value reporting and disclosure may mitigate some of the analytic difficulties.

Chapter 10

Problems

1. [Off-balance-sheet obligations; 1990 CFA adapted] Extracts from The Bowie Company's December 31, 1993, balance sheet and income statement are presented in the following schedule, along with its interest coverage ratio:

Debt	$12 million
Equity	20
Interest expense	1
Times interest earned	5.0X

The Bowie Corporation's financial statement footnotes include the following:

1. At the beginning of 1993, Bowie entered into an operating lease with total future payments of $40 million ($5 million/year) with a discounted present value of $20 million.

2. Bowie has guaranteed a $5 million, 10% bond issue, due in 1999, issued by Crockett, a nonconsolidated 30%-owned affiliate.

3. Bowie has committed itself (starting in 1994) to purchase a total of $12 million of phosphorous from PEPE, Inc., its major supplier, over the next five years. The estimated present value of these payments is $7 million.

A. Adjust Bowie's debt and equity, and recompute the debt-to-equity ratio, using the information in footnotes 1–3.

B. Adjust the times interest earned ratio for 1993 for these commitments.

C. Discuss the reasons (both financial and operating) why Bowie may have entered into these arrangements.

D. Describe the additional information required to evaluate fully the impact of these commitments on Bowie's current financial condition and future operating trends.

Problems 2 and 3 are based on the information contained in Exhibit 10P-1.

2. [Off-balance-sheet obligations] Exhibit 10P-1A contains extracts from Texaco's 1991 financial statements.

A. Using Texaco's reported balance sheet and income statement (without any adjustments), prepare a capitalization table for Texaco for the years ended December 31, 1990, and December 31, 1991. Compute the company's debt-to-equity, return-on-assets, and times interest earned ratios.

B. Using footnote data from Exhibit 10P-1A, compute the appropriate adjustments to Texaco's debt for its off-balance-sheet obligations.

C. Using the result of part B, recompute the ratios in part A.

D. Discuss the significance of your results.

3. [Extension of Problem 2] Exhibit 10P-1B contains information from the 1991 financial statements of Caltex, one of Texaco's affiliates.

A. Discuss how the information on off-balance-sheet obligations contained in the notes to Caltex's financial statements should be used to adjust Caltex's financial statements.

B. Use the results of part A to further adjust Texaco's debt, equity, and ratios calculated in Problem 2.

C. Describe the information *not* contained in the Caltex financial data that would help you evaluate the impact of its off-balance-sheet obligations on Caltex and Texaco. (Your discussion should include both financial and operational factors.)

4. [Sales of receivables: conceptual issues] Chapters 1 and 2 include discussions of the definition of assets and revenue recognition. The benefits of owning receivables (the right to expected cash flows) are accompanied by risks (collectibility and interest rate changes). The following table considers sales of receivables across these two dimensions, that is, whether the risks and benefits are retained by the "seller."

		Benefits	
R		Yes	No
i	Yes	(1)	(2)
s			
k	No	(3)	(4)
s			

A. For *each* of the four cells (1)–(4), determine whether a sale has taken place (e.g., cell 3 includes sales where the seller transfers all the benefits of owning the assets but retains the risk of collectibility and interest rate changes.)

B. Under what conditions does your answer *differ* from the GAAP accounting treatment?

C. Discuss the impact on liquidity, turnover, leverage, and profitability ratios when the conditions in part B exist.

EXHIBIT 10P-1A. TEXACO, INC., AND SUBSIDIARY COMPANIES

Statements of Consolidated Income and Retained Earnings

Texaco Inc. and Subsidiary Companies

Millions of dollars

	For the years ended December 31	1991	1990	1989
Revenues	Sales and services (includes transactions with significant affiliates of $4,210 million in 1991, $4,701 million in 1990 and $3,431 million in 1989).	$37,271	$40,899	$32,416
	Equity in income of affiliates, income from dividends, interest, asset sales and other (includes gains on asset sales related to restructuring of $2,112 million in 1989).	1,051	923	3,240
		38,322	41,822	35,656
Deductions	Purchases and other costs (includes transactions with significant affiliates of $2,165 million in 1991, $2,803 million in 1990 and $2,174 million in 1989)	27,612	30,246	23,036
	Operating expenses.	3,720	3,799	3,908
	Selling, general and administrative expenses.	1,847	1,656	1,407
	Maintenance and repairs.	564	566	573
	Exploratory expenses.	436	499	361
	Depreciation, depletion and amortization.	1,560	1,658	1,662
	Interest expense.	558	568	687
	Taxes other than income taxes	589	643	558
	Restructuring and associated charges	—	—	378
	Minority interest.	16	12	2
		36,902	39,647	32,572
	Income before income taxes.	1,420	2,175	3,084
	Provision for income taxes.	126	725	671
Net Income		$ 1,294	$ 1,450	$ 2,413
Net Income Per Common Share (dollars)	Primary.	$ 4.61	$ 5.18	$ 9.12
	Fully diluted	$ 4.55	$ 5.08	$ 8.74
Average Number of Common Shares Outstanding (thousands)	Primary.	258,410	259,933	257,722
	Fully diluted	270,071	282,354	282,643
Retained Earnings	Balance at beginning of year	$ 7,150	$ 6,595	$ 7,172
	Add: Net income	1,294	1,450	2,413
	Deduct:			
	Cash dividends on preferred stock	103	102	64
	Dividends on common stock—			
	Quarterly cash ($3.20 per share in 1991, $3.05 per share in 1990 and $3.00 per share in 1989).	827	793	773
	Special cash ($7.00 per share).	—	—	1,862
	Special Series C Variable Rate Cumulative Preferred Stock issuance ($1.00 per share).	—	—	267
	Preferred stock rights redemption	—	—	24
	Balance at end of year.	$ 7,514	$ 7,150	$ 6,595

EXHIBIT 10P-1A. *(Continued)*

Consolidated Balance Sheet

Texaco Inc. and Subsidiary Companies

	Millions of dollars	
As of December 31	**1991**	1990
Assets		
Current Assets		
Cash and cash equivalents	**$ 843**	$ 693
Short-term investments—at cost, which approximates market	**40**	136
Accounts and notes receivable (includes receivables from significant affiliates of $200 million in 1991 and $221 million in 1990), less allowance for doubtful accounts of $28 million in 1991 and 1990	**4,041**	4,907
Inventories	**1,503**	1,378
Other current assets	**154**	142
Total current assets	**6,581**	7,256
Investments and Advances	**4,112**	3,842
Properties, Plant and Equipment		
At cost	**34,103**	32,591
Less—Accumulated depreciation, depletion and amortization	**19,159**	18,314
Net properties, plant and equipment	**14,944**	14,277
Deferred Charges	**545**	600
Total	**$26,182**	$25,975
Liabilities and Stockholders' Equity		
Current Liabilities		
Notes payable, commercial paper and current portion of long-term debt	**$ 1,331**	$ 1,516
Accounts payable and accrued liabilities (includes payables to significant affiliates of $92 million in 1991 and $152 million in 1990)	**3,553**	4,329
Estimated income and other taxes	**1,406**	1,123
Total current liabilities	**6,290**	6,968
Long-Term Debt	**4,861**	4,122
Capital Lease Obligations	**312**	363
Deferred Income Taxes	**1,682**	1,669
Deferred Credits and Other Noncurrent Liabilities	**3,044**	3,307
Minority Interest in Subsidiary Companies	**165**	161
Total	**16,354**	16,590
Stockholders' Equity		
Series C Variable Rate Cumulative Preferred Stock	**267**	267
Series E Variable Rate Cumulative Preferred Stock	**381**	381
Series B ESOP Convertible Preferred Stock	**497**	499
Series F ESOP Convertible Preferred Stock	**50**	50
Unearned employee compensation (related to ESOP Series B and F)	**(435)**	(479)
Common stock—274,293,417 shares issued	**1,714**	1,714
Paid-in capital in excess of par value	**658**	656
Retained earnings	**7,514**	7,150
Currency translation adjustment	**(19)**	(40)
	10,627	10,198
Less—Common stock held in treasury, at cost—15,799,603 shares in 1991 and 16,132,322 shares in 1990	**799**	813
Total stockholders' equity	**9,828**	9,385
Total	**$26,182**	$25,975

EXHIBIT 10P-1A. *(Continued)*

Notes to Consolidated Financial Statements (continued)

Note 3. Investments and Advances

As of December 31 (Millions of dollars)	1991	1990
Affiliates accounted for on the equity method		
Caltex group of companies................	$1,742	$1,502
Star Enterprise.........................	907	855
Other affiliates	680	653
	3,329	3,010
Miscellaneous investments (at cost), long-term receivables, etc., less reserve	783	832
Total.................................	$4,112	$3,842

Texaco's equity in the net income of affiliates accounted for on the equity method, adjusted to reflect income taxes for partnerships whose income is directly taxable to Texaco, is as follows:

Millions of dollars	1991	1990	1989
Equity in net income			
Caltex group of companies.......	$ 421	$ 298	$ 304
Star Enterprise..................	85	123	77
Other affiliates	103	88	69
Total.......................	$ 609	$ 509	$ 450
Dividends received from these companies	$ 389	$ 390	$ 255
Undistributed earnings of these companies included in Texaco's year-end retained earnings...............	$2,239	$1,954	$1,610

Caltex Group

Texaco has investments in the Caltex group of companies, owned 50% by Texaco and 50% by Chevron Corporation. The Caltex group consists of Caltex Petroleum Corporation and subsidiaries, P.T. Caltex Pacific Indonesia and American

Overseas Petroleum Limited and subsidiaries. This group of companies is engaged in the exploration for and production, transportation, refining and marketing of crude oil and products in Africa, Asia, the Middle East, New Zealand and Australia.

Star Enterprise

Star Enterprise is a joint-venture partnership owned 50% by Texaco and 50% by the Saudi Arabian Oil Company. The partnership refines, distributes and markets Texaco-branded petroleum products in 26 East and Gulf Coast states and the District of Columbia.

The table below provides summarized financial information on a 100 percent basis for the Caltex group, Star Enterprise and all other affiliates accounted for on the equity method, as well as Texaco's share. The net income of all partnerships, including Star Enterprise, is net of estimated income taxes. The actual income tax liability is reflected in the accounts of the respective partners and not shown in the table below.

Star's assets at the respective balance sheet dates include the remaining portion of the assets which were originally transferred from Texaco to Star at the fair market value on the date of formation. Texaco's investment and equity in the income of Star, as reported in the consolidated financial statements, reflect the remaining unamortized historical carrying cost of the assets transferred to Star at formation. Additionally, Texaco's investment includes adjustments necessary to reflect contractual arrangements on the formation of this partnership, principally involving contributed inventories.

Millions of dollars	Caltex group			Star Enterprise			Other equity affiliates			Texaco's share		
	1991	1990	1989	1991	1990	1989	1991	1990	1989	1991	1990	1989
For the years ended December 31:												
Gross revenues	$15,921	$15,297	$11,782	$7,165	$8,067	$6,522	$2,387	$2,407	$2,225	$12,377	$12,511	$9,891
Income before income taxes........	1,526	1,264	1,142	265	377	205	563	535	504	1,059	965	785
Net income	839	601	609	175	249	135	346	311	329	609	509	450
As of December 31:												
Current assets	$ 2,494	$ 2,861	$ 2,522	$1,089	$1,219	$1,235	$ 572	$ 538	$ 418	$ 1,829	$ 2,077	$1,848
Noncurrent assets.................	4,869	4,244	3,823	2,813	2,438	2,113	3,433	3,264	3,240	4,989	4,394	3,851
Current liabilities	(2,398)	(2,839)	(2,472)	(665)	(687)	(607)	(784)	(840)	(623)	(1,850)	(2,067)	(1,727)
Noncurrent liabilities and deferred credits	(1,354)	(1,136)	(1,010)	(762)	(608)	(572)	(1,915)	(1,732)	(1,795)	(1,576)	(1,332)	(1,265)
Minority interest in subsidiary companies............	(126)	(123)	(115)	—	—	—	—	—	—	(63)	(62)	(58)
Net assets (or partners' equity)	$ 3,485	$ 3,007	$ 2,748	$2,475	$2,362	$2,169	$1,306	$1,230	$1,240	$ 3,329	$ 3,010	$2,649

EXHIBIT 10P-1A. *(Continued)*

Note 9. Foreign Currency

Currency translations resulted in pre-tax gains of $27 million in 1991, $129 million in 1990 and $17 million in 1989. After applicable income taxes, gains were $48 million in 1991, $136 million in 1990 and $43 million in 1989. These amounts include Texaco's equity in such gains and losses of affiliates accounted for on the equity method. The currency translation results for 1991 also included amounts for hyperinflationary economies that were recorded to accounts other than currency. The currency gains in 1990 were primarily related

to operations in developing countries which experienced high inflation and currency fluctuations throughout the year.

Not included in the foregoing amounts were currency translation effects included in the Statement of Consolidated Income as deferred income taxes, amounting to gains of $93 million in 1991, $90 million in 1990 and $126 million in 1989.

Currency translation adjustments reflected in the separate stockholders' equity account result from translation items pertaining to certain affiliates of Caltex.

Note 10. Lease Commitments and Rental Expense

The company has leasing arrangements involving service stations, tanker charters and other facilities. Amounts due under capital leases are reflected in the company's balance sheet as obligations, while Texaco's interest in the related assets is principally reflected as properties, plant and equipment. The remaining lease obligations are operating leases, and are reflected in the company's income statement as rental expense.

As of December 31, 1991, Texaco Inc. and its subsidiary companies had estimated minimum commitments for payment of rentals (net of noncancelable sublease rentals) under leases which, at inception, had a noncancelable term of more than one year, as follows:

Millions of dollars	Operating leases	Capital leases
1992	$ 122	$110
1993	105	101
1994	86	82
1995	79	68
1996	76	53
After 1996	588	178
Total lease commitments	$1,056	592
Less amounts representing		
Executory costs		79
Interest		196
Add noncancelable sublease rentals netted in capital lease commitments above		57
Present value of total capital lease obligations		374
Less current portion of capital lease obligations		62
Present value of long-term portion of capital lease obligations		$312

Rental expense relative to operating leases, including contingent rentals based on factors such as gallons sold, is provided in the table below. Such payments do not include rentals on leases covering oil and gas mineral rights.

Millions of dollars	1991	1990	1989
Rental expense			
Minimum lease rentals	$258	$254	$205
Contingent rentals	19	24	11
Total	277	278	216
Less rental income on properties subleased to others	32	35	28
Net rental expense	$245	$243	$188

EXHIBIT 10P-1A. *(Continued)*

Note 14: Other Financial Information

Environmental Reserves

Texaco's financial reserves relating to environmental restoration and remediation programs represent the company's efforts to remain in full compliance with existing governmental regulations. It is likely that changes in governmental regulations and/or a re-evaluation of Texaco's programs will result in additional future charges. However, it is not anticipated that such future charges will be material to the financial position of the company.

Sale of Receivables

In September 1988, a wholly owned subsidiary of Texaco Inc. entered into an accounts receivable agreement with a syndicate of major domestic and international banks, under which it had the right to sell up to $300 million of accounts receivable on a continuing basis with recourse for uncollectible amounts. In September 1991, this agreement was terminated and replaced with a new third-party accounts receivable agreement in the amount of $400 million.

Receivables sold under these facilities totaled approximately $1 billion during 1991. No receivables remained uncollected at December 31, 1991.

Note 15: Contingent Liabilities and Commitments

Other Litigation

As of December 31, 1991, several states had Federal antitrust suits pending against Texaco Inc. and a number of other petroleum companies alleging a conspiracy regarding the sale and distribution of petroleum products. Plaintiffs seek treble damages against defendants in unspecified amounts. Trial is expected to commence in the fall of 1992.

Commitments

Texaco Inc. and certain of its subsidiary companies have entered into certain long-term agreements wherein they have committed either to ship through associated pipeline companies and an offshore oil port, or to refine at associated refining companies a sufficient volume of crude oil or products to enable these associated companies to meet a specified portion of their individual debt obligations, or, in lieu thereof, to advance sufficient funds to enable these associated companies to meet these obligations. The company's maximum exposure to loss was $367 million and $518 million at December 31, 1991 and 1990, respectively. However, based on Texaco's right of counterclaim against other third parties in the event of nonperformance, Texaco's net exposure was approximately $328 million and $341 million at December 31, 1991 and 1990, respectively. No loss is anticipated by reason of such obligations.

In the normal course of its business, the company enters into financial instrument transactions with off-balance-sheet risk in order to hedge its exposure to market risk regarding petroleum prices, currency translations and interest rates.

Contracts to hedge petroleum prices which are required to be settled in cash were immaterial in amount at December 31, 1991.

At December 31, 1991 the company had outstanding $767 million of forward exchange contracts to purchase foreign currency. The exposure to credit risk is minimal since the counterparties are major financial institutions. The company does not anticipate nonperformance by any of the multiple counterparties. The risk exposure is essentially limited to market risk related to currency rate movements. The gains or losses arising from these contracts are applied to offset exchange gains or losses on related hedged assets, liabilities or future commitments.

Also, the company has outstanding interest rate swaps of various maturities with multiple major financial institutions. At December 31, 1991, the aggregate notional principal amount was $726 million. Notional amounts do not represent cash flow and are not subject to credit risk. Credit and market risk exposures are limited to the net interest differentials. The interest differentials are reflected in interest expense as a hedge of interest on outstanding debt.

In the company's opinion, while it is impossible to ascertain the ultimate legal and financial liability with respect to the above-mentioned and other contingent liabilities and commitments, including lawsuits, claims, guarantees, Federal taxes, Federal regulations, etc., the aggregate amount of such liability in excess of financial reserves, together with deposits and prepayments made against disputed tax claims, is not anticipated to be materially important in relation to the consolidated financial position of Texaco Inc. and its subsidiaries.

Source: Texaco, Inc., *1991 Annual Report.*

EXHIBIT 10P-1B. CALTEX GROUP OF COMPANIES
Combined Balance Sheet—December 31, 1991 and 1990 (millions of dollars)

ASSETS

	1991	1990
CURRENT ASSETS:		
Cash and cash equivalents (including time deposits of $238 in 1991 and $194 in 1990)	$ 370	$ 362
Notes and accounts receivable, less allowance for doubtful accounts of $30 in 1991 and $26 in 1990:		
Trade	1,047	1,389
Other	320	196
Nonsubsidiary companies	61	154
	1,428	1,739
Inventories:		
Crude oil	125	231
Refined products	510	477
Materials and supplies	61	52
	696	760
Total current assets	2,494	2,861
INVESTMENTS AND ADVANCES:		
Nonsubsidiary companies at equity	1,294	1,094
Nonsubsidiary companies at cost	17	14
Miscellaneous investments and long-term receivables, less allowance of $9 in 1991 and $8 in 1990	132	111
	1,443	1,219
PROPERTY, PLANT AND EQUIPMENT, AT COST:		
Producing	2,462	2,179
Refining	1,111	1,008
Marketing	1,915	1,689
Marine	55	54
Capitalized leases	113	111
	5,656	5,041
Less: Accumulated depreciation, depletion and amortization	2,433	2,201
	3,223	2,840
PREPAID AND DEFERRED CHARGES	203	185
Total assets	$7,363	$7,105

See accompanying Notes to Combined Financial Statements.

EXHIBIT 10P-1B. *(Continued)*

LIABILITIES AND STOCKHOLDERS' EQUITY

	1991	1990
CURRENT LIABILITIES:		
Notes payable and long-term debt due within one year:		
Notes payable to banks and other financial institutions	$ 684	$ 893
Note payable to nonsubsidiary company	150	-
Other notes payable	73	84
Long-term debt due within one year	15	8
	922	985
Accounts payable:		
Trade and other	921	1,281
Stockholder companies	168	172
Nonsubsidiary companies	94	83
	1,183	1,536
Accrued liabilities	114	116
Estimated income taxes	179	202
Total current liabilities	2,398	2,839
LONG-TERM DEBT	427	313
ACCRUED LIABILITY FOR EMPLOYEE BENEFITS	56	50
DEFERRED CREDITS	563	501
DEFERRED INCOME TAXES	308	272
MINORITY INTEREST IN SUBSIDIARY COMPANIES	126	123
STOCKHOLDERS' EQUITY:		
Common stock	355	355
Additional paid-in capital	2	2
Retained earnings	2,955	2,518
Currency translation adjustment	173	132
Total stockholders' equity	3,485	3,007
COMMITMENTS AND CONTINGENT LIABILITIES	——	——
Total liabilities and stockholders' equity	$7,363	$7,105

See accompanying Notes to Combined Financial Statements.

EXHIBIT 10P-1B. *(Continued)*

CALTEX GROUP OF COMPANIES
COMBINED STATEMENT OF INCOME
FOR THE YEARS ENDED DECEMBER 31, 1991, 1990 AND 1989
(MILLIONS OF DOLLARS)

	1991	1990	1989
SALES AND OTHER OPERATING REVENUES[1]	$15,445	$15,147	$11,507
OPERATING CHARGES:			
Cost of sales and operating expenses[2]	13,394	13,168	9,868
Selling, general and administrative expenses	408	324	293
Depreciation, depletion and amortization	257	224	205
Maintenance and repairs	156	146	128
Taxes other than income taxes	29	29	26
Provision for doubtful accounts	7	7	4
	14,251	13,898	10,524
Operating income	1,194	1,249	983
OTHER INCOME (DEDUCTIONS):			
Equity in net income of nonsubsidiary companies	188	34	96
Dividends, interest and other income	288	116	179
Foreign exchange, net	(5)	29	36
Interest expense	(131)	(151)	(136)
Minority interest in subsidiary companies	(8)	(13)	(16)
	332	15	159
Income before provision for income taxes	1,526	1,264	1,142
PROVISION FOR INCOME TAXES:			
Current	649	684	520
Deferred	38	(21)	13
Total provision for income taxes	687	663	533
Net income	$ 839	$ 601	$ 609
(1) Includes sales to:			
Stockholder companies	$ 1,124	$ 1,685	$ 1,175
Nonsubsidiary companies	$ 2,610	$ 2,812	$ 1,945
(2) Includes purchases from:			
Stockholder companies	$ 3,181	$ 3,409	$ 1,908
Nonsubsidiary companies	$ 2,217	$ 2,212	$ 1,777

See accompanying Notes to Combined Financial Statements.

EXHIBIT 10P-1B. *(Continued)*

CALTEX GROUP OF COMPANIES

NOTES TO COMBINED FINANCIAL STATEMENTS

(3) Nonsubsidiary Companies at Equity

Investments in and advances to nonsubsidiary companies at equity at December 31 include the following (in millions):

	Equity Share	1991	1990
Nippon Petroleum Refining Company, Ltd.	50%	$ 667	$ 539
Koa Oil Company, Ltd.	50%	249	199
Honam Oil Refinery Company, Ltd.	50%	324	308
All other	Various	54	48
		$1,294	$1,094

Shown below is summarized combined financial information for these nonsubsidiary companies (in millions):

	100%		Equity Share	
	1991	1990	1991	1990
Current assets	$4,960	$5,403	$2,466	$2,692
Other assets	4,128	3,473	2,040	1,724
Current liabilities	4,648	5,574	2,310	2,781
Other liabilities	1,826	1,097	903	542
Net worth	2,614	2,205	1,293	1,093

	100%			Equity Share		
	1991	1990	1989	1991	1990	1989
Operating revenues	$10,267	$9,433	$7,506	$5,102	$4,701	$3,748
Operating income	839	139	399	416	69	200
Net income	380	67	190	188	34	96

Retained earnings at December 31, 1991 includes $965 million representing the Group's share of undistributed earnings of nonsubsidiary companies at equity.

Cash dividends received from these nonsubsidiary companies were $26 million, $23 million and $28 million in 1991, 1990 and 1989, respectively.

Sales to the other 50 percent owner of Nippon Petroleum Refining Company, Ltd. of products refined by Nippon Petroleum Refining Company, Ltd. and Koa Oil Company, Ltd. were approximately $2.1 billion in 1991 and 1990 and $1.7 billion in 1989.

(7) Operating Leases

The Group has various operating leases involving service stations, equipment and other facilities for which net rental expense was $53 million, $44 million and $67 million in 1991, 1990 and 1989, respectively.

Future net minimum rental commitments under operating leases having noncancelable terms in excess of one year are as follows (in millions): 1992 - $36; 1993 - $32; 1994 - $29; 1995 - $27; 1996 - $25; and after 1996 - $55.

(8) Commitments and Contingent Liabilities

Certain Group companies were contingently liable at December 31, 1991 for $15 million as guarantors. The Group also had commitments of $54 million in the form of letters of credit which have been issued on behalf of Group companies to facilitate either the Group's or other parties' ability to trade in the normal course of business.

On January 25, 1990, Caltex Petroleum Corporation and certain of its subsidiaries were named as defendants, along with privately held Philippine ferry and shipping companies and the shipping company's insurer, in a lawsuit filed in a Houston, Texas State Court. The case was subsequently removed to Federal District Court in Houston. The plaintiffs' petition purports to be a class action on behalf of at least 3,350 parties, who are either survivors of, or next of kin of persons deceased in a collision in Philippine waters on December 20, 1987. One vessel involved in the collision was carrying Group products in connection with a freight contract. Although the Group had no direct or indirect ownership or operational responsibility for either vessel, various theories of liability are alleged against the Group. No specific monetary recovery is sought although the petition contains a variety of demands for various categories of compensatory as well as punitive damages. A motion to dismiss the case was granted by the Federal District Court and affirmed on appeal whereupon the plaintiffs filed an application for a writ of certiorari from the U.S. Supreme Court. That application was denied and the case has been remanded to the Federal District Court for further consideration of a motion to dismiss for forum non conveniens. That court is also expected to rule, at the same time, on the Group's motion to dismiss a more recently filed second case which is a virtual mirror image of the first case. Management is contesting these cases vigorously.

The Group is also involved in certain other lawsuits, arbitration proceedings and Internal Revenue Service tax claims that could involve significant payments if such cases are all ultimately resolved adversely to the Group.

While it is impossible to ascertain the ultimate legal and financial liability with respect to the above mentioned and other contingent liabilities, including lawsuits, arbitration proceedings, taxes, claims, guarantees and the like, the aggregate amount that may arise from such liabilities is not anticipated to be material in relation to the Group's combined financial position.

(9) Financial Instruments

Certain Group companies are parties to financial instruments with off-balance sheet credit and market risk, principally interest rate risk. As of December 31, the Group had commitments outstanding for interest rate swaps and foreign currency transactions for which the notional or contractual amounts, respectively, at December 31 are as follows (in millions):

	1991	1990
Interest rate swaps	$216	$211
Commitments to purchase foreign currencies	$217	$284
Commitments to sell foreign currencies	$182	$173

The interest rate swaps are intended to hedge against fluctuations in interest rates on debt. Interest rate movements applicable to these contracts are recognized as they occur.

Commitments to purchase and sell foreign currencies are made to provide exchange rate protection for specific transactions and to maximize economic benefit based on expected currency movements. The above purchase and sale commitments are at year end exchange rates and mature during the following year. These commitments are marked to market and the resulting gains and losses are recognized in current year income unless the contract is a specific hedge of an identifiable transaction.

Financial instruments exposed to credit risk consist primarily of trade receivables. These receivables are dispersed among the countries in which the Group operates thus limiting concentrations of such risk.

The Group performs ongoing credit evaluations of its customers and generally does not require collateral. Letters of credit are the principal security obtained to support lines of credit when the financial strength of a customer or country is not considered sufficient. Reserves for potential credit losses have been historically within management's expectations.

Source: Texaco, Inc., 1991 10-K

EXHIBIT 10P-2. MORRISON KNUDSEN

Accounts Receivable

In December 1991, the Corporation entered into a three year agreement with banks to sell, with limited recourse, up to $60,000 of undivided interests in a designated pool of accounts receivables. As collections reduce previously sold undivided interests, new receivables can be sold up to the $60,000 level. In addition, receivables were sold to a bank under an agreement which ends February 1992. At December 31, 1991, accounts receivable in the accompanying balance sheet are net of the $66,796 sold under the agreements.

Source: Morrison Knudsen, *1991 Annual Report.*

D. Discuss the impact of sales of receivables on reported cash flows from operations.

5. [Sale of Receivables] Exhibit 10P-2 contains the accounts receivable footnote from the 1991 annual report of Morrison Knudsen. Selected reported financial data follow:

Years ended December 31 ($thousands)

	1991	1990
Sales	$1,979,986	$1,706,535
Earnings before interest and taxes	73,932	72,935
Interest expense	16,020	11,172
Accounts receivable	129,823	182,283
Current assets	642,641	645,440
Current liabilities	374,272	404,795
Short-term debt	88	3,143
Long-term debt	193,484	194,215
Stockholders' equity	385,725	281,940
Cash flow from operations	98,949	72,272

A. Compute the impact of the sale of receivables on the current ratio, cash cycle, and receivable turnover ratio for 1991.

B. Compute the reported and adjusted (for the sale of receivables) debt–to–equity, times interest earned and return on assets ratios for 1991.

C. Discuss the impact of the sale on the trend of the firm's cash flow from operations over the period 1990–1992.

EXHIBIT 10P-3. HONEYWELL

In 1990 Honeywell entered into a five-year agreement whereby it can sell an undivided interest in a designated pool of trade accounts receivable up to a maximum of $100.0 million on an ongoing basis. At December 31, 1990 $100.0 million of receivables has been sold for cash under this agreement. The discount on sales of receivables amounted to $2.8 million in 1990 and is included in selling, general and administrative expenses in the income statement. Honeywell retains collection and administrative responsibilities as agent for the purchaser of the receivables sold.

Source: Honeywell, *1990 Annual Report.*

6. [Sale of receivables] Exhibit 10P-3 provides a footnote from the *1990 Annual Report* of Honeywell. Selected reported financial data follow for the years ended December 31, 1989–1990 (in millions of dollars):

	1989	1990
Sales	$6058.6	$6309.1
Earnings before interest and taxes	811.1	622.4
Interest expense	135.2	106.0
Accounts receivable	1255.3	1083.5
Current assets	2280.9	2582.2
Current liabilities	2415.8	2175.1
Short-term debt	146.6	109.0
Long-term debt	692.5	616.3
Stockholders' equity	1858.4	1566.1
Cash flow from operations	486.0	721.3

A. Evaluate Honeywell's income statement classification of the discount on sale of receivables. Suggest an alternative reporting method that would provide better information regarding the effect of the transaction.

B. Determine the impact of the sale of receivables on the current and receivable turnover ratios for 1990. How does the sale affect the comparison of those ratios with 1989 ratios?

C. Compute the effect of the sale of receivables on the reported debt-to-equity, times interest earned, and return-on-assets ratios.

D. Discuss the impact of the sale on the trend of Honeywell's reported cash flow from operations over the 1989–1991 period.

7. [Off-balance-sheet obligations] Portions of footnotes 5, 10, and 16 from the *1991 Annual Report* of Panhandle Eastern Corp. are reproduced in Exhibit 10P-4. Selected

EXHIBIT 10P-4. PANHANDLE EASTERN CORP.

5. Leases and Other Commitments

The Company utilizes assets under operating leases in several areas of its operations. The consolidated rental expense for continuing operations amounted to $24.8 million, $26.8 million and $20.4 million for the years 1991, 1990 and 1989, respectively. The minimum rental payments under the Company's various operating leases for the years 1992 through 1996 are $24.2 million, $18.5 million, $16.6 million, $11.7 million and $8.8 million, respectively. Thereafter, payments aggregate $40.3 million through 2011.

In connection with the sale of Petrolane Incorporated (Petrolane) in 1989, TEC has agreed to indemnify the purchaser against certain guaranteed lease obligations. Certain of these obligations relate to Petrolane's divestiture of supermarket operations prior to its acquisition by TEC and total approximately $118.6 million over the remaining terms of the leases, which expire in 2006. In the opinion of management, the probability that TEC will be required to perform under this indemnity provision is remote.

Pursuant to a transportation agreement, PEPL is required to pay a portion of Northern Border Pipeline Company's (Northern Border) cost of service for transportation over the life of the agreement. Such agreement expires in 2001, subject to cancellation on a year-to-year basis thereafter. Northern Border's cost of service to be shared by its U.S. shippers will be reduced by the revenues received for volumes transported for others.

On an estimated basis, assuming no transportation for others, PEPL will be required to pay Northern Border a minimum of $223.9 million over the remaining term of the agreement. Payments for 1991, 1990 and 1989 amounted to $26.6 million, $28.6 million and $34.4 million, respectively. The estimated annual payments range from $19.1 million to $24.4 million in the years from 1992 to 2001.

Trunkline has contracts with other companies which provide for a minimum monthly charge determined by those companies' effective rates as approved by FERC. Trunkline's payments for such transportation services in 1991, 1990 and 1989 were $16.3 million, $17.2 million and $15.1 million, respectively. These amounts include payments to a former affiliate for 1991, 1990 and 1989 of $5.3 million, $10.6 million and $11.2 million, respectively. This former affiliate was sold in mid-1991. Minimum annual payments under the above agreements are $12.7 million for 1992 and 1993, $11.9 million in 1994, and $2.7 million in 1995 and 1996. Thereafter, payments aggregate $4.0 million through 1998.

10. Customers/Accounts Receivable Sales

Accounts Receivable Sales and Financings

The Company has implemented agreements to sell with limited recourse, on a continuing basis, current accounts receivable at a discount and to obtain financing, from time to time on a short-term basis, secured by PEPL and Trunkline future demand charges. Approximately $281.3 million remained outstanding at December 31, 1991 on the current accounts receivable sold. At December 31, 1991, 34% and 66% of such accounts receivable sold under this program originated in the Midwest and Northeast markets, respectively. See above discussion of customer concentrations and overall credit risk.

At December 31, 1991 and 1990, there were no amounts outstanding secured by future demand charges. This financing remains available to the Company and will continue to be utilized in 1992.

16. Redeemable Preferred Stock

Redeemable preferred stock of TETCO, PEPL and Trunkline has a $100 par value and is cumulative.

	TETCO	PEPL		Trunkline	
Series	5.00-5.07%	4.64%	8.60%	4.75%	9.12%
Shares outstanding, December 31					
1991	63,500[1]	10,000[2]	30,000[2]	24,273[3]	40,000[3]
1990	97,750	20,000	40,000	34,440	40,000

[1] Includes three Series which are callable at par.

[2] 4.64% Series are callable at par, and the 8.60% Series are callable at $100.96 until September 30, 1992 and at reducing amounts thereafter.

[3] 4.75% Series are callable at par, and the 9.12% Series are callable at $101.53 until April 14, 1992 and at reducing amounts thereafter.

At December 31, 1991, TETCO, PEPL and Trunkline had $100 par value cumulative preferred shares authorized totaling 97,750, 500,000 and 382,149, respectively. These totals include the shares authorized under the series identified above.

The cumulative preferred stock is not convertible and is scheduled to be redeemable at par through operation of sinking funds. Redemptions in the periods shown were as follows:

Millions	TETCO	PEPL		Trunkline	
Series	5.00-5.07%	4.64%	8.60%	4.75%	9.12%
Beginning balance, 1989	$17.3[1]	$4.0	$6.0	$4.9	$5.9
Redemptions					
1989	4.1[2]	1.0	1.0	0.7	—
1990	3.4	1.0	1.0	0.8	1.9
1991	3.4[2]	1.0	1.0	1.0	—
Ending balance, 1991	$ 6.4	$1.0	$3.0	$2.4	$4.0

[1] Balance at April 27, 1989.

[2] The 5.60% Series was fully redeemed during 1989 and the 5.52% Series was fully redeemed in 1991.

Source: Panhandle Eastern Corp., *1991 Annual Report.*

reported financial data follow for years ended December 31, 1990–1991 (in millions of dollars):

	1990	1991
Sales	$2988.3	$2454.2
Earnings before interest and taxes	63.3	504.9
Interest expense	352.8	331.3
Accounts receivable	182.3	147.8
Current assets	986.6	813.8
Current liabilities	1370.6	1277.9
Short-term debt	258.0	224.7
Long-term debt	2483.8	2267.1
Stockholders' equity	1137.8	1333.1
Cash flow from operations	(5.1)	322.0

A. Determine the impact of the sale of receivables on the current ratio and receivable turnover ratio for 1991.

B. Compute reported and adjusted debt-to-equity, times interest earned, and return-on-total-assets ratios for 1991. Your adjustments should reflect the impact of the off-balance-sheet techniques disclosed in the footnotes.

C. Discuss the impact of Panhandle's use of these techniques on reported cash flow from operations. Describe the additional information required to compute an accurate adjusted cash flow from operations.

D. Discuss what the footnote data tell you about the riskiness of Panhandle's operations.

8. [Exchangeable debt] The long-term data of Alleghany Corp. at December 31, 1990, included $59,600,000 debentures (6.50%, due 2014) exchangeable for common shares of American Express (at a rate of 22.8833 shares for each $1000 bond). Exhibit 10P-5 contains a portion of Schedule I (Marketable Securities) from the firm's 10-K filing.

EXHIBIT 10P-5. ALLEGHANY CORPORATION AND SUBSIDIARIES
Schedule I Marketable Securities, December 31, 1990 (in $ thousands)

	Face Value or Shares	Cost	Market Value	Carrying Value
American Express Company	1366	$22,033	$28,182	$28,182
Armco, Inc.	3000	21,137	15,375	15,375
Other	1677	17,490	10,330	10,330
Total Alleghany equity securities	6043	$60,660	$53,887	$53,887
Total equity securities	8082	$91,525	$78,107	$78,107

Source: Alleghany Corporation, *1990 10-K*.

EXHIBIT 10P-6. MORRISON KNUDSEN

December 31,	1991	1990
Long-Term Debt		
Zero coupon, convertible notes, yield 7.25%,		
due 2005	$193,484	$180,184
Other	88	17,174
Total	193,572	197,358
Less current portion	(88)	(3,143)
Long-term portion	$193,484	$194,215

On May 1, 1990, the Corporation received proceeds of $166,235, net of expenses of issuance and distribution of $5,570, from the sale of $500,000 (principal amount at maturity) of convertible Liquid Yield Option Notes ("LYONs"). The LYONs are zero coupon notes due in 2005 and are unsecured general obligations of the Corporation priced to yield 7.25% if held to maturity. The issuance and distribution expenses are being amortized on a straight-line basis over 15 years. The LYONs are convertible at the option of the holder on or prior to maturity into the Corporation's common stock at the rate of 6.245 shares per LYON, subject to adjustment under certain circumstances. After May 1, 1992, the LYONs are redeemable for cash at any time at the option of the Corporation at redemption prices equal to the issue price plus accrued original issue discount to the date of redemption. The LYONs are redeemable at the option of the holder as of May 1, 1995 and the Corporation, at its option, may elect to pay the redemption price in cash (equal to the issue price plus accrued original issue discount to the date of redemption), shares of common stock or subordinated extension notes due 2005. In addition, the LYONs may be redeemable earlier, at the option of the holder, upon the occurrence of certain events at a price equal to the issue price plus accrued original issue discount to the date of redemption.

Source: Morrison Knudsen, *1991 Annual Report.*

A. Determine the gain or loss that would be recorded by Alleghany if the debenture holders exchange their bonds for American Express stock.

B. Compute the effective interest cost of this debt (net of dividend income on the American Express shares) for 1991. (American Express common stock paid 1991 dividends of $0.94 per share; assume a tax rate of 36%.)

C. Discuss why Alleghany may have chosen to issue the exchangeable bonds rather than simply to sell its shares of American Express.

9. [Convertible zero-coupon debt] Exhibit 10P-6 contains the long-term debt footnote from the *1991 Annual Report* of Morrison Knudsen Corp. Selected reported financial data follow for the years ended December 31, 1990–1991 (in millions of dollars, except per share data):

	1990	1991
Earnings before interest and taxes	$ 72,935	$ 73,932
Interest expense	11,172	16,020
Amortization of discount on LYONs	8,379	13,300
Short-term debt	3,143	88
Long-term debt	194,215	193,484
Stockholders' equity	281,940	385,141
Cash flow from operations	72,272	98,949
Net income	36,481	35,145
Primary earnings per share	$ 2.93	$ 2.60

A. Given the terms of the notes, derive the reported liability balances of $180,184 and $193,484 as of December 31, 1990, and 1991, respectively.

B. Compute the firm's debt-to-equity and times interest earned ratios and primary earnings per share at December 31, 1990, and 1991, assuming conversion of the bonds.

C. Discuss the advantages to the firm of issuing convertible, zero-coupon LYONs compared to issuing:

   (i) nonconvertible zero-coupon bonds.

   (ii) full-coupon convertible bonds.

10. [Exchange rate and interest rate swaps] Exhibit 10P-7 reproduces the footnote on long-term debt from the *1992 Annual Report* of Syntex Corporation.

A. Explain why the company is exposed to credit risk equal to the difference between the current value of the debt and its carrying amount of $100.0 million.

B. Under what circumstances would Syntex be subject to loss and how would that loss be measured?

C. Explain why the company took on this risk.

D. How would you determine whether the currency exchange agreement and interest rate swap were cost effective?

E. How did the swaps affect the debt-to-equity and interest coverage ratios of Syntex in fiscal 1992 (as opposed simply to maintaining the original debt obligation)?

11. [Take-or-pay agreements] Exhibit 10P-8 contains an extract from the Other Contingencies footnote of Amoco Corporation's 1986 financial statements.

A. Discuss the adjustments to Amoco's debt and equity that should be considered as a result of these disclosures.

B. Discuss reasons both why and why not these adjustments should be made.

C. Describe the information required to evaluate fully the impact of these arrangements on Amoco's financial condition and operations.

EXHIBIT 10P-7. SYNTEX CORPORATION

Note 6: Long-Term Debt

In fiscal 1986, Syntex (U.S.A.) Inc., a wholly owned subsidiary of the company, issued 6.625 percent fixed-rate Euroyen notes due in fiscal 1993 in the amount of 20 billion yen. Principal and interest payments due in yen are covered by currency exchange agreements that fix the exchange rate over the term of the notes and effectively result in a $100.0 million liability. At July 31, 1992, the company was exposed to credit risk to the extent of the difference between the current value of 20 billion yen ($157.1 million) and $100.0 million. However, the company does not anticipate nonperformance by the counterparties. In addition, related interest rate swap agreements effectively result in a variable rate of interest for the term of the notes.

Certain commercial paper borrowings are classified as long-term because the company intends to maintain such indebtedness on a long-term basis. At July 31, 1992, the company had unused long-term bank lines of credit of $104.8 million, expiring in fiscal 1994, of which $100.0 million is available for the support of long-term commercial paper borrowings.

Long-term debt consists of the following:

($ in Millions)	1992	1991	1990
Euroyen notes, variable rates based on LIBOR (3.3% at July 31, 1992, 6.0% at July 31, 1991, and 7.8% at July 31, 1990), maturing in 1993	$ 100.0	$100.0	$100.0
Commercial paper borrowings (3.4% at July 31, 1992, 5.9% at July 31, 1991, and 8.0% at July 31, 1990)	100.0	100.0	100.0
Other	131.2	73.1	26.4
Total long-term debt	331.2	273.1	226.4
Less current portion	(100.0)	—	(1.4)
Noncurrent portion	$ 231.2	$273.1	$225.0

Source: Syntex Corporation, *1992 Annual Report.*

EXHIBIT 10P-8. AMOCO CORPORATION

21. Other Contingencies

At December 31, 1989, contingent liabilities of the corporation included guarantees of $177 million on outstanding loans of others. The corporation also has entered into various working capital maintenance agreements and pipeline throughput and deficiency contracts with affiliated companies. These agreements supported an estimated $166 million of affiliated company borrowings at December 31, 1989. The corporation has contracted on a take-or-pay basis to purchase certain quantities of materials used in oil and gas producing activities. The present value of the future payments at December 31, 1989, was $37 million.

Amoco is subject to federal, state, and local environmental laws and regulations. Amoco is currently participating in the clean-up of numerous sites pursuant to such laws and regulations. The estimated future costs of known environmental obligations have been provided for in the company's results of operations. As the scope of the obligations become more defined, there may be changes in the estimated future costs, which could result in charges against the company's future operations. The amount of any such future costs is uncertain and, although the costs could be significant, they are not expected to have a material effect on Amoco's consolidated financial position.

Source: Amoco Corporation, *1986 Annual Report.*

12. [Take-or-pay agreements] The following paragraphs were extracted from an article in the *Financial Times* on March 4, 1993:

Brazilians Cannot Afford to Cut Aluminum Losses

Any hopes that Brazil will this year relieve the pressure of oversupply on the languishing aluminum market by cutting its output seem destined to be disappointed. Despite a combination of low international prices and what local industry considers high domestic energy costs, the country registered record production of aluminum in 1992, and output is expected to remain at a similar level this year.

Many energy contracts are "take-or-pay" agreements. . . . Some bauxite supply contracts run on a "take-or-pay" basis, meaning that [aluminum] producers must withdraw their share of raw material whether or not they intend to use it.

Explain the relationship between these two paragraphs. (Note: Aluminum is refined from bauxite using large amounts of energy.)

11

ANALYSIS OF INTERCORPORATE INVESTMENTS

OVERVIEW

COST METHODS
Marketable Equity Securities
Lower of Cost or Market: Portfolio versus Individual Basis
Current and Noncurrent MES
Unrealized Gains and Losses
MES: Special Industry Provisions
Analysis of Marketable Securities
Effects of Classification of MES
Separation of Operating from Investment Results
Analysis of Investment Performance
Mark to Market Accounting
Comparison of Mark to Market Return with Cost Methods
Mark to Market: Insurance Company Example
Summary of Analytical Considerations
U.S. Practice Compared to the Practices of Major Foreign Countries

EQUITY METHOD OF ACCOUNTING
Conditions for Use
Illustration
Comparison of Equity Method and Cost Method

The Equity Method and Deferred Taxes
Equity Accounting and Analysis: Concluding Comments

CONSOLIDATION
Illustration
Applicability of Consolidation
Nonhomogeneous Subsidiaries
Consolidation Practices Outside the United States
Comparison of Consolidation with Equity Method
Consolidated Versus Equity Method: The Case of Deere
Balance Sheet Eliminations
Income Statement Consolidation
Consolidated Cash Flows
Impact of Consolidation on Ratios
Significance of Consolidation
Analysis of Minority Interest

ANALYSIS OF JOINT VENTURES
Jointly Controlled Entities
Alternatives to the Equity Method
Proportionate Consolidation
Effects of Proportionate Consolidation

761

Use of the Alternatives to the Equity Method in Practice

ANALYSIS OF SEGMENT DATA

Geographic Segment Reporting

Analysis of Segment Data: Dow Chemical

Uses of Segment Data

Segment Reporting in Practice

Using Segment Data to Estimate Consolidated Earnings and Risk

U.S. GAAP COMPARED TO MAJOR FOREIGN COUNTRIES

Proportionate Consolidation

Segment Reporting

APPENDIX 11–A: EXPANDED EQUITY METHOD

EXPANDED EQUITY VERSUS PROPORTIONATE CONSOLIDATION

OVERVIEW

The modern corporation rarely consists of a single corporate entity. The larger the enterprise, the more likely that it will contain more than one unit: the largest multinational may have hundreds of subsidiaries in dozens of jurisdictions. In addition, large enterprises frequently invest in other entities, including joint ventures and partnerships. The goals of this chapter are to examine the accounting principles applicable to intercorporate investments, evaluate the impact of the choice of principles on the financial statements and discuss applicable analytical techniques.

Enterprises invest in the securities of other companies for various reasons. The investment may involve a temporary purchase of equity or debt securities to capture dividend or interest income or capital gains.[1] Intercorporate investments may also involve strategies aimed at developing technological alliances, risk sharing, or initial investments in new markets and technologies. Finally, the investment may be a precursor to an acquisition.

The appropriate accounting method used to report intercorporate investments depends primarily on the amount or percentage of ownership (generally defined in terms of direct or indirect ownership or control of investee common stock) in the investee firm as indicated by the following:

Accounting Method	Degree of Ownership	Criterion
Cost	<20%	No significant influence
Equity	20 – 50%	Significant influence
Consolidation	>50%	Control

---

[1]See Chapter 7 for a discussion of the tax consequences of intercorporate investments.

The ownership percentages are practical guidelines designed to make operational the relevant criterion of significant influence or control; if significant influence exists at a percentage below 20%, the equity method is used. Similarly, if control does not exist even with ownership exceeding 50%, consolidation is not appropriate.

The primary conceptual distinction among the different reporting requirements lies in the extent to which the investee is viewed as an integral part of the parent company. Under the cost method, the two companies are treated as separate entities, and the parent's income from its investment is based on actual dividends paid and/or changes in the investee's market price over the period the investment is held. Under the equity method, the affiliate is considered a part of the parent to the extent that its income (in an amount corresponding to the parent's ownership percentage) is deemed to be income earned by the parent irrespective of actual dividends paid. Changes in market prices do not affect income under the equity method, unless the investment is sold or price decline is considered permanent. Finally, consolidated reporting views the two companies as a single, unified, economic entity even if they are legally separate entities. All revenues and expenses of the subsidiary, net of intercompany transactions, are added to those of the parent.

COST METHODS

Enterprises often invest in the common and preferred shares, bonds, or other securities of another entity. Generally, when such investments are small relative to the capital of the investee, the investor is unable to influence the activities of the investee. Such investments must be accounted for under the cost method, which reflects this characteristic.

For example, assume that Company P purchases 1 share (out of 100 shares outstanding) of Company S for $100. Company P would report the purchased asset on its balance sheet at the acquisition cost as follows:[2]

Investment in Company S $100

The income statement of Company P would reflect any dividends received from Company S. If Company S declared a dividend of $10 per share on its common stock, then Company P's income statement would include (as other income) the following:

Dividend received $10

When the security is sold, a realized gain or loss would be recognized and quantified as the difference between the proceeds of the sale and the original cost.

[2]The account name actually employed would normally not be identified with a specific company, but rather a more general name such as "Investment in affiliate(s)" would be used.

In the absence of a dividend, sale, or write-down of the investment as described shortly, the operating, financing, and investing activities of Company S would have no impact on the financial statements of Company P. The carrying value of the investment would remain at $100 until the investment is sold, unless

1. Company P determined that the investment in Company S was permanently impaired (due to the latter's financial problems, for example). The investment would have to be written down to its estimated value and a loss recognized equal to the amount of the write-down. The estimated value would be the new carrying amount until sale, at which time the gain or loss would be determined by comparing the proceeds of sale with the written-down value of the investment. Under no circumstances could the investment be written up in value.

2. The security purchased was a marketable equity security. For marketable equity securities (MES), the carrying amount may change with changes in market prices.

Marketable Equity Securities

When equity securities (common shares, warrants, and nonredeemable preferreds)[3] have a public market, then under the provisions of Statement of Financial Accounting Standards (SFAS) 12 (1975), the accounting takes into consideration changes in market prices. *The accounting method used is the lower of cost or market on a portfolio basis*. If the market value of the portfolio of marketable equity securities is below original cost, then the portfolio must be written down to market value giving rise to an unrealized loss. Any subsequent recovery of accumulated unrealized losses (up to original cost, but not higher) will also be recognized as an unrealized gain.[4]

The provisions of SFAS 12 do not apply to investments in bonds or redeemable preferred shares. These investments (along with such nonmarketable investments as mortgages) are carried at amortized cost, that is, acquisition costs adjusted for premia or discounts on purchase.

Lower of Cost or Market: Portfolio versus Individual Basis

SFAS 12 requires that MES be carried at the lower of cost or market (LCM) on a portfolio rather than on an individual basis. The latter method, used in certain countries, is a more conservative method. The example that follows illustrates the difference between the two approaches.

---

[3]Preferreds with required redemption (by sinking fund, for example) or which are redeemable at the option of the investor are not treated as equity securities under SFAS 12 but as the equivalent of bonds.

[4]Since the carrying value of the MES can never exceed original cost, the unrealized gains never exceed previously accumulated unrealized losses and are generally reported as "Recovery of Unrealized Losses."

Security	Original Cost	Market	Lower of Cost or Market on Individual Basis
A	$500	$400	$400
B	50	25	25
C	300	325	300
Portfolio	$850	$750	$725

On a portfolio basis (SFAS 12) the lower of cost or market is $750; all securities are carried at market value. The lower of cost of market on an individual basis would be $725 rather than $750; some securities are at cost, whereas others are carried at market value. The difference of $25 is due to security C, which is carried at market value under the portfolio method and at (lower) cost on the individual basis.

Current and Noncurrent MES

Under the provisions of SFAS 12, the accounting treatment of unrealized gains and losses on investments in MES depends on whether the securities have been classified as current or noncurrent assets. The classification is determined by management intent; if the securities are to be sold within one year or the operating cycle, whichever is longer, they are current assets. A longer expected holding period requires classification as noncurrent assets.[5]

If MES are reported as current assets, the unrealized gains (losses) are included in current period operating results on the income statement. If the portfolio is classified as a "noncurrent" asset, any write-down (and any subsequent recovery) is excluded from operating results. Instead, a securities valuation account, which is a component of stockholders' equity, is used to accumulate these adjustments.

In the event of reclassification of MES from current to noncurrent (or vice versa), SFAS 12 states that transfers must take place at current market prices if below cost; that is, unrealized losses have to be recognized immediately. This provision is designed to ensure that firms cannot avoid reporting unrealized losses on the income statement by reclassifying the current portfolio as noncurrent.[6]

Notwithstanding that provision, it is still possible for managers to manipulate earnings and eliminate losses from the income statement by shifting between noncurrent and current. Consider a case where the current MES portfolio has a loss but the noncurrent MES is showing a gain. By reclassifying the noncurrent MES as current, all or part of the current MES loss could be eliminated.

The lower of cost and market provision is the only difference in accounting for MES as opposed to other (nonmarketable) securities carried at cost. Regardless of the

---

[5]The intended holding period determines classification at both the initial and the subsequent reporting dates.

[6]Consider the amount of reclassification that might have gone on otherwise after the stock market crash of October 1987.

classification of the portfolio, dividends received from holdings of marketable equity securities are included as part of reported income. In addition, realized holding gains (losses) are calculated by comparing original cost with the proceeds of sale of individual securities. Previous write-downs (resulting from the application of LCM to the portfolio of MES) are ignored when calculating realized gains/losses on individual securities.

A comparison of the accounting for MES to that for other securities carried at cost is presented in Exhibit 11-1.[7] Note that market values are relevant only for MES and then only when they are below cost. In neither case is the operating performance of the investee (earnings or cash flow) relevant. Finally, for both current and noncurrent MES, the carrying amount is the acquisition cost less any write-down to market value.

The impact of the difference in classification lies primarily in the income statement. For MES carried as current assets, write-downs or valuation adjustments are recognized

[7]This example is extended in Exhibit 11-6.

EXHIBIT 11-1
Comparison of Cost Methods

Number of Shares Purchased (Sold) @ Price/Share

1991	100	shares @ $80/share
1992	(30)	shares @ $60/share
1993	40	shares @ $70/share

Note: All sales and purchases are assumed to occur on January 1. These prices can vary from the previous day's (December 31) prices.

Investee	1991	1992	1993
Earnings per share	$7	$8	$7
Dividend per share	2	2	2

Year-End Holdings Valued at Cost and Market

Year	No. of Shares	Cost/ Share	Total Cost	Price/ Share	Market Value
1991	100	$80	$8000	$70	$7000
1992	70	80	5600	80	5600
1993	70	80	5600	90	6300
	40	70	2800	90	3600
	110		$8400		$9900

Investment Account (Balance Sheet)

Classification	1991	1992	1993	Carried at
Not MES	$8000	$5600	$8400	Cost
MES current	7000	5600	8400	Lower of cost or market
MES noncurrent	7000	5600	8400	Lower of cost or market

EXHIBIT 11-1. (Continued)

Total Investment Income (Income Statement)
Dividends + Recognized Gains (Realized and Unrealized)

Classification	1991	1992	1993
Not MES	$ 200	$(460)	$220
MES current	(800)	540	220
MES noncurrent	200	(460)	220

Components of Investment Income

Dividend Income

	1991	1992	1993
All cost methods	$200	$140	$220

Recognized Gains
(Realized and Unrealized)

Classification	1991	1992	1993
Not MES	$ 0	$(600)	$ 0
MES current	(1000)	400*	0
MES noncurrent	0	(600)	0

*$(600) realized + $1000 unrealized.

as components of income; for noncurrent assets, there is no income statement effect since the write-downs are reflected in the stockholders' equity account. Note that the income statement impact of the cost method is identical to the treatment when MES are classified as noncurrent assets (although the balance sheet amounts are different).

Unrealized Gains and Losses

When recording MES as a current asset, the interpretation and interrelationship of realized and unrealized losses/gains can be quite confusing as the next example illustrates.

Company P carries its MES portfolio as a current asset. The portfolio consists of three securities purchased in year 1, one of which is sold in year 2. In year 2, there are no changes in market prices. The original cost, the closing market values, and the sales price are as follows:

Security	Year 1 Cost	Year 1 Market	Year 2 Cost	Year 2 Market
A	$500	$400	(Sold for $400)	
B	50	25	$ 50	$ 25
C	300	325	300	325
Portfolio	$850	$750	$350	$350

In year 1, on a portfolio basis, the market value is below cost, and Company P will write down its MES portfolio to the market value of $750 and recognize the unrealized loss of $100 in its income statement. The write-down, it should be noted, is not charged directly to the marketable securities account but rather to a valuation allowance account, a contra-asset account. This valuation allowance represents the difference between the cost and market value of the MES.

The accounting entries in year 1 will be

At Acquisition		Year-End Valuation	
Investment in MES	$850	Unrealized loss	$100
Cash	$850	Investment in MES	$100
		(valuation allowance)	

In year 2 there will be a realized loss of $100 on the sale of security A giving rise to the following accounting entry:

Cash	$400	
Realized loss	$100	
Investment in MES		$500

The "Investment in MES" (net of the valuation allowance) account will now be $250 (investment in MES $350 − valuation allowance $100). At year end, however, the cost and market values of the portfolio will now be identical. A write-up to original cost (by eliminating the valuation allowance) will now be required, giving rise to an unrealized gain or recovery of the previously recognized unrealized loss.

Investment in MES (valuation allowance)	$100	
Recovery of unrealized loss		$100

Thus the income statement will show the following for year 2:

Realized loss	$(100)
Recovery of unrealized loss	100
	$ 0

Because the previously unrealized loss was realized in year 2, the balance of unrealized losses must be adjusted. To avoid double counting the loss on security A, the previous adjustment to market must be reversed this year. The income statement thus reflects the fact that there was no change in market prices during year 2.

MES: Special Industry Provisions

For some industries, the provisions of SFAS 12 are modified by other accounting standards:

1. SFAS 60 (1982) provides that insurance companies carry all common stocks and nonredeemable preferreds at market value (even if higher than cost). Bonds that are held in trading accounts or are otherwise held for sale must also be carried at market value. Changes in market value are reflected in stockholders' equity (see the later example of Continental Corp.).

2. The American Institute of Certified Public Accountants (AICPA) audit guide for banks provides that trading securities be carried either at market value or at the lower of cost or market.

3. Brokers and dealers are required to carry all trading and investment accounts at market value. Investment companies are required to carry all investments at market value.

In addition, the Securities and Exchange Commission (SEC) requires that all industrial companies, insurance companies, and banks disclose the market value of all marketable securities (whether carried at cost or at market value) either parenthetically in the balance sheet or elsewhere in the financial statements. Detailed information is also available in Schedule I, Investments in Marketable Securities and Other Securities, in the firm's SEC 10-K filings.

Analysis of Marketable Securities

To illustrate some of the issues discussed in this section, relevant information from the financial statements and 10-Ks of Dawson Geophysical (Dawson) and Helmerich & Payne (HP) is presented in Exhibits 11-2 and 11-3 and 11-4 and 11-5, respectively. Both companies are in the oil and gas industry and have extensive holdings of marketable securities. Dawson carries MES as current assets, whereas HP carries MES as noncurrent assets.

In analyzing these holdings of MES, the following issues are relevant:

- The differential effects of the current or noncurrent classification
- The need to segregate the operating results of the firm from the investment results[8]
- The assessment of investment results

Effects of Classification of MES

Dawson. Dawson maintained a relatively large portfolio of marketable securities among its current assets. The condensed income statements in Exhibit 11-2 show that the investment had a mixed impact on reported earnings. Over the three-year period, recognized losses more than offset the portfolio's dividend and interest income (as interest and dividend income includes interest on cash equivalents, the impact of capital losses is worse than it appears).

---

[8]See the footnote 39 reference to Foster (1975).

EXHIBIT 11-2. DAWSON GEOPHYSICAL
Marketable Securities as Current Assets

Balance Sheet, at September 30, 1989–1990 (in $ thousands)

	1989	1990
Cash and equivalents	$ 1,935	$ 1,678
Marketable securities	6,155	5,732
Other current assets	635	1,284
Total current assets	8,725	$ 8,694
Property—net	3,211	2,942
Total assets	$11,936	$11,636
Current liabilities	$ 164	$ 521
Stockholders' equity	11,772	11,115
Total equities	$11,936	$11,636

Income Statement, for Years Ended September 30, 1988–1990
(in $ thousands)

	1988	1989	1990
Revenues	$ 7417	$ 5242	$ 7734
Operating costs	(7617)	(6846)	(8818)
Loss from operations	$ (200)	$(1604)	$(1084)
Other income	199	38	183
Interest and dividend income	804	776	646
Realized loss on marketable securities	(2202)	—	(940)
Unrealized gain (loss) on marketable securities	(888)	189	538
Total recognized gain (loss)	$(3090)	189	$ (402)
Loss before income tax	$(2287)	$ (601)	$ (657)

Footnote and Supplementary Information

| | Marketable Securities, September 30, 1989–1990 (in $ thousands) ||
	1989	1990
Marketable securities at original cost	$ 7482	$6521
Marketable securities at market value	6155	5732
Valuation adjustment	$(1327)	$ (789)

Source: Dawson Geophysical, 1990 Annual Report (condensed).

EXHIBIT 11-3. DAWSON GEOPHYSICAL
Marketable Securities and Other Security Investments, September 30, 1990

Description	Number of Shares or Principal Balance	Cost	Market Value	Amount at Which Carried in Balance Sheet
Preferred stocks				
Cleveland Electric Pr M	18,300	$1,844,000	$1,775,000	$1,775,000
Enserch Corp. Pr E	21,000	2,215,000	1,596,000	1,596,000
Texas Utilities Elec Pr B	9,500	707,000	712,000	712,000
Torchmark Corp. Pr	12,000	1,006,000	902,000	902,000
		$5,772,000	$4,985,000	$4,985,000
U.S. Treasury notes	$750,000	749,000	747,000	747,000
		$6,521,000	$5,732,000	$5,732,000

Source: Dawson Geophysical, 1990 10-K, Schedule I

Had Dawson carried its investments as noncurrent assets, only the recognized losses would have been reported as part of income. We can recompute pretax income for these years as follows:

	Years Ended September 30 (in $ thousands)		
	1988	1989	1990
Pretax loss as reported	$(2287)	$(601)	$ (657)
Less: Unrealized gain (loss)	(888)	189	538
Adjusted pretax loss	$(1399)	$(790)	$(1195)

The adjusted pretax loss is what Dawson would have reported if it had been carrying its marketable securities as noncurrent assets. The 1988 pretax loss would have been reduced by $888, and the 1989 and 1990 pretax losses increased by $189 and $538, respectively. Management's decision to carry its portfolio as a current asset hurt reported earnings in fiscal 1988 but helped in fiscal 1989 and 1990.

The current ratio, on the other hand, was greatly improved by management's classification decision. A comparison of the current ratio (current assets/current liabilities) with and without the marketable securities follows:

	Current Ratio, September 30	
	1989	1990
As reported	53.20	16.69
Adjusted	15.67	5.69

The decision to carry marketable securities as current assets had the effect of improving the reported current ratio, which may have helped Dawson convince its customers and/or creditors that it was financially strong.

Helmerich & Payne (HP). HP has a large portfolio of MES that is reported as a component of noncurrent assets as shown in Exhibit 11-4. The details of HP's portfolio from Schedule I of the company's 10-K are shown here as Exhibit 11-5.

The market value of the portfolio[9] exceeds the carrying amount (historical costs) by more than $77 million. This unrealized gain has not been recognized in Helmerich's financial statements. If there were an unrealized loss, however, that would have to be reflected in a separate account included in stockholders' equity (but bypassing the income statement).

Under SFAS 12, MES must be reported on the basis of the total portfolio. Since there is an unrealized gain on a total portfolio basis, no recognition is required for the unrealized losses on some individual holdings.

The total carrying amount of the portfolio ($111.2 million) exceeds the amount shown under investments ($99.6 million) on the balance sheet. That is because some shares are to be issued in exchange for outstanding exchangeable debt (see discussion in Chapter 8) during the first quarter of fiscal 1991. The investment (of $11.6 million) in these shares has been transferred to current assets. The gain from the exchange has not been reflected in income, pending realization. If there were an unrealized loss, however, that loss would have to be recognized immediately under the provisions of SFAS 12 governing transfers between portfolios.

The fact that changes in market values above cost are not recognized in the financial statements does not mean that the analyst should not use them. Recognizing market values fully affects both the balance sheet and income statement. Adjustments to income will be presented in a subsequent section.

On the balance sheet, the current value of an investment indicates the resources available to the owner. Schedule I (Exhibit 11-5) indicates that the market value of HP's portfolio exceeds cost by $77.6 million. After estimated income taxes of 34%, the adjustment would be $51.1 million, or $2.08 per share (on 24.5 million HP shares outstanding). Along with other valuation adjustments, this can be used to compute a current value net worth per share. If there were reason to believe that capital gains taxes would not be payable on the gain (if, for example, the company had a large capital loss carryforward), then the posttax adjustment would be equal to the pretax adjustment.

Separation of Operating from Investment Results

Income from investments should be separated from operating results to avoid the distortion of operating trends. While the success of corporate investments does impact the well-being of the enterprise, investment results and operating results must be clearly segregated and analyzed separately.

---

[9]Note that two of the investments shown are accounted for under the equity method, discussed later in this chapter. Therefore the carrying amount for Atwood and Baruch-Foster is the cost plus equity in reinvested earnings rather than original cost. That the market values exceed the carrying amount provides some comfort regarding the carrying amounts.

EXHIBIT 11-4. HELMERICH & PAYNE
Marketable Securities as Noncurrent Assets

Balance Sheet, at September 30, 1989–1990
(in $ millions)

	1989	1990
Current assets	$ 168.3	$ 200.6
(includes investment of		
$11.6 million in 1990)		
Investments—historical cost	130.4	99.6
Property—net	292.5	282.7
Total assets	$ 591.2	$ 582.9
Current liabilities	$ 53.9	$ 53.9
Noncurrent liabilities	93.9	49.5
Stockholders' equity	443.4	479.5
Total equities	$ 591.2	$ 582.9

Income Statement, for Years Ended September 30, 1989–1990
(in $ millions)

	1989	1990
Revenues	$ 150.6	$ 199.2
Operating costs	(138.8)	(168.2)
Operating income	$ 11.8	$ 31.0
Investment income	18.5	15.6
Realized gains on marketable		
securities	2.2	23.2
Income before income tax	$ 32.5	$ 69.8

Footnote and Supplementary Information,
September 30, 1989–1990
(in $ millions)

	Marketable Securities	
	1989	1990
Marketable securities at original cost	$ 138.9	$ 111.2
Marketable securities at market value	245.4	188.8
Unrealized gain	$ 106.5	$ 77.6

Source: Helmerich & Payne, 1990 Annual Report.

EXHIBIT 11-5. HELMERICH & PAYNE
Schedule I—Marketable Securities as of September 30, 1990

Column A	Column B	Column C	Column D
			Value Based on Current Market Quotations at Balance Sheet Date
		Amount at Which Carried in Balance Sheet*	
Name of Issuer and Title of Issue	Number of Shares	Sheet* ($ thousands)	Date ($ thousands)
Atwood Oceanics, Inc., common stock	1,600,000	$ 26,341	$ 29,800
Schlumberger, Ltd., common stock	740,000	23,511	45,048
Sun Company, Inc., common stock	1,226,932	14,717	34,930
Oryx Energy Company, common stock	1,130,892	11,466	47,295
Banks of Midamerica, common stock	903,037	13,130	7,789
Weyerhaeuser, Inc. common stock	220,000	4,893	4,400
Phillips Petroleum, common stock	200,000	4,809	5,150
Baruch-Foster Corporation, common stock	765,677	3,701	4,977
Other—common stock, debentures, and other		8,654	9,392
Total consolidated		$111,222	$188,781

*Investments are carried in the balance sheet at cost, except the investments in Atwood and Baruch-Foster, which are carried on the equity method. Equity income (loss) for 1990 from Atwood was $(612) and from Baruch-Foster was $(64). No dividends were received from Atwood or Baruch-Foster.
Source: Helmerich & Payne, 1990 10-K

Failure to segregate the impact of marketable securities can also confuse the interpretation of cash flow statements. Valuation adjustments are noncash accounting entries and are excluded from cash flow from operations. Likewise gains or losses on the sale of marketable securities (net of income taxes) are classified as investing cash flows. This is an extension of arguments made in Chapter 2 that dividends or interest from investments should be segregated from the normal operating results of a firm.[10] Management should be evaluated on the performance of its investments by analyzing the total return on the portfolio over an appropriate time span.

[10]SFAS 95 requires firms to report dividends and interest income from investments as operating cash flows.

Analysis of Investment Performance

Dawson's portfolio has performed poorly, and an investor or creditor would want to question management on this subject. Dawson's revenues and earnings depend on the demand for its services from oil and gas companies. Such demand has been weak in recent years. The best way to analyze Dawson's income statement is by segregating the impact of the marketable securities entirely. Examining the loss from operations over the three-year period gives the best perspective on the operating performance of the company.

Dawson has maintained a relatively large (given its size) portfolio of marketable securities, which has helped it to survive its difficult operating environment. That portfolio, carried in current assets, accounts for approximately half of the company's total assets, as can be seen from the condensed balance sheet, and clearly strengthens the balance sheet. But surprisingly, the impact on the company's reported earnings has been mixed, as the condensed income statement shows. Over the three-year period, recognized losses have more than offset the dividend and interest income from Dawson's investment portfolio. We can get some insight into the problem by looking at Dawson's 10-K report (filed with the Securities and Exchange Commission) for these years. Exhibit 11-3 contains Dawson's Schedule I listing the individual investments.

Most of Dawson's investments consist of preferred stocks. In prior years, Dawson invested heavily in the preferred shares of a Texas bank holding company that had financial difficulties. A large loss resulted.

More meaningful analysis is, however, possible if the analyst looks beyond the requirements of SFAS 12. From an analytic standpoint, the distinction between current and noncurrent portfolios is meaningless. In addition there is no reason to record market values only when they are lower than cost. For purposes of analysis, all marketable securities should be shown at current market value even if such value is above cost. Gains and losses should be attributed to the period they were earned[11] rather than when they are recognized. It is important to remember that the periods in which gains/losses took place and those in which they are recognized (by sale) may be completely different. Essentially, the analyst should track investment performance on a mark to market basis.

Mark to Market Accounting

The required disclosure of market values in addition to cost makes the calculation of actual portfolio returns a relatively straightforward one. Define the market valuation adjustment (MVA)[12] to be equal to the difference between market value and cost. Then, the actual portfolio performance (excluding dividends) in any year is equal to the sum of

Change in the market valuation adjustment
+ Realized gains/losses
= Actual return

[11]Provision should be made, however, for the income tax that would have to be paid upon sale of the securities, unless it is expected that no tax will be payable.

[12]Note that this definition is similar to the valuation allowance defined earlier. The latter term, however, has a specific meaning in the context of SFAS 12 when market is below cost. The market valuation adjustment is a broader term, including those situations where market is above cost as well.

This holds true whether or not new securities are added to the portfolio during the year. Whether or not this mark to market return differs from the return reported on the income statement depends on

1. Whether the company carries the MES as a noncurrent asset.
2. For MES carried as a current asset, whether the market valuation adjustment shows an unrealized gain in either the opening or closing MES balances.

For noncurrent MES, the mark to market return will always differ from the amount reported as in this case no unrealized gains/losses are reported on the income statement. Helmerich & Payne (Exhibit 11-4) is a case in point.

The actual return on HP's MES earned in 1990 is equal to

Change in MVA [$77.6 million − $106.5 million] = $(28.9) million
Realized gains   23.2
Mark to market return $ (5.7) million

Because HP carries its MES as noncurrent assets, avoiding any income statement recognition of (unrealized) holding gains or losses, the calculated mark to market return will obviously differ from that reported on the income statement under SFAS 12.

For firms whose MES is carried as a current asset, the direction of the valuation adjustment is important in determining whether mark to market returns will differ from reported returns. The actual return on Dawson's MES earned in 1990 is equal to

Change in MVA [($789,000) − ($1,327,000)] = $ 538,000
Realized loss   (940,000)
Mark to market return $(402,000)

The mark to market return calculated for Dawson is identical to the amount recognized on its income statement because Dawson experienced holding losses. That is, when marketable securities are carried as current assets, losses are recognized in the income statement whether realized or unrealized; that is, the total portfolio return is recognized in income. If there were unrealized gains (above original cost), however, those gains would not be recognized, and the mark to market amount would differ from the amount reported in the financial statements.

Comparison of Mark to Market Return with Cost Methods

Exhibit 11-6 extends the example of Exhibit 11-1 and compares the mark to market return to the recognized (realized and unrealized) gains recorded under the various cost methods.[13] Note that for the first two years, when the market value is below cost, the recognized gain (loss) for the MES carried as a current asset is identical to the mark to

---

[13]The exhibit also compares the equity method with the other methods. The equity method will be covered in a subsequent section.

EXHIBIT 11-6
Comparison of Cost Methods with Mark to Market and Equity

Number of Shares Purchased (Sold) @ Price/Share

1991	100	shares @ $80/share
1992	(30)	shares @ $60/share
1993	40	shares @ $70/share

Note: All sales and purchases are assumed to occur on January 1.

Investee	1991	1992	1993
Earnings per share	$7	$8	$7
Dividend per share	2	2	2

Year-End Holdings Valued at Cost and Market

	No. of Shares	Cost/ Share	Total Cost	Price/ Share	Market Value
1991	100	$80	$8000	$70	$7000
1992	70	80	5600	80	5600
1993	70	80	5600	90	6300
	40	70	2800	90	3600
	110		$8400		$9900

Investment Account (Balance Sheet)

Classification	1991	1992	1993	Carried at
Not MES	$8000	$5600	$8400	Cost
MES current	7000	5600	8400	Lower of cost or market
MES noncurrent	7000	5600	8400	Lower of cost or market
Mark to market	7000	5600	9900	Market
Equity method	8500	6370	9720	Cost + equity in reinvested earnings

Total Investment Income (Income Statement)

Dividends + Recognized Gains
(Realized and Unrealized)

Classification	1991	1992	1993
Not MES	$ 200	$(460)	$ 220
MES current	(800)	540	220
MES noncurrent	200	(460)	220
Mark to market	(800)	540	1720
Equity method	700	(190)	770

EXHIBIT 11-6. *(Continued)*

	Components of Investment Income			
	Dividend Income			
Classification	1991	1992	1993	
All cost methods	$200	$140	$220	Actual dividends
Mark to market	200	140	220	received (DPS ×
Equity method		Not relevant		no. shares held)

	Equity in Earnings of Investee			
	(Only relevant under equity method)			
	1991	1992	1993	
Equity method	$700	$560	$770	EPS × no. shares held

	Recognized Gains (Realized and Unrealized)		
Classification	1991	1992	1993
Not MES	$ 0	$(600)	$ 0
MES current	(1000)	400*	0
MES noncurrent	0	(600)	0
Mark to market	(1000)	400	1500
Equity method	0	(750)†	0

*$(600) realized + $1000 unrealized.
†Loss on shares sold: 30 × ($80 + $5 − $60).

market return. In year 3, however, the mark to market return and the recognized amounts differ significantly even for the case of MES carried as current assets.

The ability to obtain detailed portfolio listings from the 10-K also permits analytical adjustments during the year, assuming that the portfolio is unchanged. The analyst can take current market prices and recompute the market value of the portfolio. This exercise may be particularly useful after significant market changes (such as the October 1987 market crash).

Mark to Market: Insurance Company Example

SFAS 60 (1982) governs insurance company accounting generally, including the accounting for securities portfolios. As do other financial companies, insurance companies provide unclassified balance sheets, with no distinction between current and noncurrent assets.

Under the provisions of SFAS 60, fixed income investments (including redeemable preferreds) are carried at amortized cost with market value disclosed. This accounting (Para. 45) is based on management's intent to hold the investments to maturity, and its ability to do so. Fixed income trading portfolios and the entire portfolio of equities (common and nonredeemable preferred) are carried at market value with historical cost disclosed. Unrealized gains and losses on portfolios valued at market are shown as a separate component of stockholders' equity. Income statement recognition is given only to dividend and interest income, to realized gains and losses, and to unrealized losses when the decline is considered to be permanent.

The principles of mark to market accounting, however, can be readily applied to insurance companies in much the same fashion as discussed earlier.

Analysis of Insurance Company Portfolio. Continental Corporation, a property/casualty insurance company with annual revenues of more than $5 billion, provides a good example of insurance company accounting for marketable securities as it maintains a large equity portfolio. Its condensed balance sheet and relevant footnotes are included in Exhibit 11-7.

The footnote describing the unrealized appreciation of investments tells us that this account is calculated after a deduction for deferred income taxes and provides the breakdown between the portfolios.

The net realized gain of $69 million accounted for 49% of Continental's 1990 net income. In 1989 realized capital gains accounted for fully 82% of net income.

As can be seen, insurance company accounting for investments is a mixed bag of amortized cost and market values. Fortunately, adequate disclosure enables the analyst to separate reality from accounting convention.

The following table summarizes the data obtained from Continental's financial statements, putting all investment accounts on the same basis and calculating the actual 1990 mark to market return.

Investment Portfolios ($ millions)

1990	Fixed Maturity Portfolios		Equity Securities	Total
	Investment	Trading		
Market	$5818	$1376	$ 933	
Cost	5781	1369	865	
Market valuation adjustment	$ 37	$ 7	$ 68	
1989				
Market	$5887	$1024	$1350	
Cost	5812	1024	989	
Market valuation adjustment	$ 75	$ 0	$ 361	

Calculation of 1990 Mark to Market Return

Change in MVA	$ (38)	$ 7	$ (293)	$(324)
Realized gains (losses)	(39)	(9)	167	119
Mark to market return	$ (77)	$ (2)	$ (126)	$(205)

EXHIBIT 11-7. CONTINENTAL CORP.
Investment Portfolio, for Years Ended December 31, 1989–1990 (in $ millions)

	1989	1990
Fixed maturity investment portfolio—cost*	$ 5,812	$ 5,781
Fixed maturity trading portfolio—market†	1,024	1,376
Equity securities—market‡	1,350	933
Other investments	1,513	1,232
Total investments	$ 9,689	$ 9,322
Other assets	4,570	4,605
Total assets	$14,259	$13,927
Total liabilities	$11,972	$11,866
Unrealized appreciation of investments	294	50
Other stockholders' equity	1,993	2,011
Total equities	$14,259	$13,927

*Market $5,887 million and $5,818 million, respectively.
†Cost $1,024 million and $1,369 million, respectively.
‡Cost $989 million and $865 million, respectively.

The following additional data were obtained from the footnotes:

Unrealized Appreciation of Investments

	1989	1990
	($ millions)	
Fixed maturity trading portfolio	$ 0	$ 7
Equity portfolio	361	68
Total	$361	$ 75
Less: Deferred taxes	(67)	(25)
Unrealized appreciation net of tax	$294	$ 50

Schedule of Realized Capital Gains for 1990

Fixed maturity investment	$ (39) million
Fixed maturity trading	(9)
Equity portfolio	167
	$119
Other investments	(13)
Total realized gain	$106
Less: Income tax	(37)
Net realized gain	$ 69 million

Source: Continental Corp. 1990 Annual Report.

We can now put all three portfolios together on the same basis and see which components of the actual return earned during the year are recognized in income, which in the balance sheet, and which are completely unrecognized.

Change in Market Value, for Year Ended December 31, 1990 (in $ millions)

	Actual Change	Recognized in Income	Balance Sheet	Not Recognized
Fixed maturity investment	$ (77)	$ (39)	—	$(38)
Fixed maturity trading	(2)	(9)	$ 7	—
Equity portfolio	(126)	167	(293)	—
Total	$(205)	$119	$(286)	$(38)

Finally, we can see the confusing impact of the mixed system of accounting for marketable securities of insurance companies. The actual investment performance (excluding dividends and interest) was a decline of $205 million before tax rather than the $119 million gain reported by Continental. Had Continental been required to recognize the actual change in market values (the actual investment performance), it would have reported a loss of $154 million before taxes instead of pretax income of $170 million. This is computed a follows:

Reported 1990 income before taxes	$170 million
Less: Recognized gains (net)	(119)
Less: Actual change in market values	(205)
Adjusted income before taxes	$(154) million

This loss is a much better indicator of Continental's performance than reported income before taxes. The loss reflects all changes in market value during 1990 rather than an arbitrary mixture of realized and unrealized gains and losses. (Remember that many of the gains realized in 1990 had occurred in previous years.)

Looking again at the table of market values, notice that the actual change in market value is recognized in asset valuation for both the fixed maturity trading and the equity portfolios. The change of $286 million, however, is not reflected in the income statement but goes directly to stockholders' equity.[14] As the fixed maturity investment portfolio is carried at amortized cost, the actual change is not recognized. This hybrid system means that balance sheet values are current in some cases but not in others. As "management intent" governs the distinction between investment and trading, the potential for abuse is evident.

More important, reported earnings include only realized gains and losses. As long as the portfolio contains some unrealized gains, management has the ability to determine

---

[14]Before adjustment for deferred taxes, the "Unrealized appreciation of investment" account was reduced by $286 million from $361 million to $75 million.

the amount and timing of capital gains recognized in income regardless of the performance of the total portfolio. This ability can be used to smooth reported income by realizing some gains each year regardless of market performance. That appears to be Continental's strategy.

This selective recognition process can be abused by "cherry picking" gains for recognition while allowing losses to remain in the portfolio unrecognized. The abuse of selective recognition by troubled financial institutions was one factor contributing to the pressure from regulators and politicians for the use of market value accounting for all investments.

Because of those pressures, the FASB put the subject of accounting for investments on its agenda in June, 1991. A summary of the Exposure Draft issued on September 9, 1992 appears in Box 11-1. In June 1993, as this text went to press, the FASB issued SFAS 115. The new standard, which becomes effective for calendar 1994, is virtually unchanged from the Exposure Draft.

BOX 11-1
FASB Exposure Draft: Accounting for Debt and Equity Investments

On September 9, 1992, the FASB issued an exposure draft (proposed SFAS) which would replace SFAS 12 and amend many other current accounting standards. The proposed standard would require firms to categorize investments in debt and equity securities* as follows:

1. *Debt securities classified as held to maturity:* such investments would be measured at amortized cost. Any realized gains or losses would be included in reported income. This classification would require that the firm have both the intent and the ability to hold the securities until maturity.

2. *Trading securities (debt and equity):* these investments would be measured at fair (market) value as current assets. Unrealized (as well as realized) gains and losses would be included in reported income.

3. *Securities available for sale (debt and equity):* these securities, which could be carried either as current or non-current assets, would also be measured at fair value. However, unrealized gains and losses would be reported as a separate component of stockholders' equity and excluded from reported earnings until sold.

The proposed standard would differ from SFAS 12 in the following respects:

1. The accounting followed would depend entirely on intent, an inherently subjective standard.

2. The SFAS 12 link between accounting and balance sheet classification would be eliminated. For securities held for sale, balance sheet classification (current or non-current) would be completely discretionary.

3. Securities not carried at amortized cost would be measured at fair (market) value rather than at the lower of cost or market required by SFAS 12. The conservative bias of SFAS 12 would be eliminated, as investments could be carried at values higher than cost.

The following provisions of SFAS 12 would remain the same (except that they would be extended to debt securities):

- Dividend and interest income would be included in reported income regardless of asset classification.
- Transfers between categories would be made at fair value with the unrealized gain or loss recognized in income.

The ED also provides for expanded disclosures regarding the types of investments held, the realized and unrealized gains and losses for each type, and contractual maturities for investments in debt securities.

The new standard would continue to permit "gains trading", the selective recognition of gains and deferral of losses. As portfolio transfers would be made at market value, a firm could recognize gains simply by transferring a security from the "available for sale" to the "trading securities" portfolio.

From the analysis point of view, the ED in its current form would make little difference. We would continue to have a mixed cost/market value system with some market value changes recognized in income, others reported within equity, and some ignored entirely. Thus the analytic procedures described in this chapter would continue to be necessary to obtain a complete view of the investment performance of the firm's total portfolio.

*The new standard would maintain the current practice of considering preferred shares with fixed redemption provisions (or which are redeemable at the option of the investor) as debt securities while non-redeemable preferreds are considered equity.

Summary of Analytical Considerations

The following procedures should be followed to

- Segregate operating and investment results.
- Eliminate the effects of selective recognition and inconsistent accounting rules from the measurement of investment results.

1. Identify the existence of a portfolio of marketable securities from footnote disclosures and data in the financial statements. Using Schedule I in 10-K filings or equivalent disclosures, obtain information regarding the risk and income characteristics of the company's portfolio.

2. Identify the method of valuation used in the financial statements. When investments are not valued at market, obtain actual or estimated market values. When looking at net worth, and such equity-based ratios as debt-to-equity, and turnover ratios, substitute market value for cost or other carrying value whenever possible. Provision for capital gains tax should be made where applicable.

3. Remove realized gains and losses and all valuation adjustments from reported earnings. The result should be an earnings trend that represents the actual results of operations and that is unaffected by selective recognition decisions by management.

4. If dividends are significant, you may wish to remove them (on an after-tax basis) from reported earnings and operating cash flows as well. These adjustments will leave only the results of operating activities. Removing all investment returns from income and all marketable securities from equity would result in a computation of return on equity that excludes the impact of investments entirely.

5. Examine the actual returns on the investment portfolio over an appropriate time period—at least one market cycle. Compare the results with the risk level of the portfolio and with benchmark returns for portfolios of the same type.

6. When using earnings to value a company, normalize investment returns by including in earnings the average return over the cycle rather than capital gains realized in that time period.

7. For companies with large investment portfolios, management should be held accountable, as would any investment manager, for returns on the portfolio.

U.S. Practice Compared to the Practices of Major Foreign Countries

The requirement of SFAS 12 to apply lower of cost or market on a portfolio basis differs from International Accounting Standard (IAS) 25 and practices in other countries.[15] In addition, the basic accounting requirements for MES also vary.

IAS 25 allows firms to report current investments at market value or use the lower of cost or market calculation on a security by security basis. IAS 25 requires firms to carry noncurrent investments at cost; nontemporary declines are reported as a component of equity. In exposure draft ED 32, Comparability of Financial Statements, the International Accounting Standards Committee (IASC) proposed prohibition of the portfolio basis in applying LCM. In its revision of ED 32, the IASC has deferred reconsideration of the valuation of MES pending completion of its Financial Instruments project.

France, Japan, Canada, and the United Kingdom use LCM on an individual security basis. Germany allows revaluation after write-downs, and firms must report the write-down in the financial statements if it is required for taxes. However, financial statement treatment is discretionary if write-downs are not required for tax purposes. In the United Kingdom as in the United States, nontemporary declines are treated as realized losses, and the excess of market value over cost may be taken to a revaluation reserve.

EQUITY METHOD OF ACCOUNTING

Conditions for Use

An investor may acquire less than a majority of the shares of an investee but own enough of an interest to have significant influence on its management, operations, and investing and financing decisions. Under the equity method, this ability to influence investee operations and strategic decisions is reflected by the investor's recognition of a

---

[15]Current MES held in trading accounts by financial institutions are, however, generally marked to market in most countries.

proportionate share of the income of the investee, regardless of whether that portion is actually received in the form of a dividend or is reinvested. The investor also reports its proportionate share of the investee's net assets.

Accounting Principles Board (APB) Opinion 18 (1971), which governs the use of the equity method, requires the assumption that the investor has significant influence over the operations of the investee when ownership reaches the 20% level. Financial Accounting Standards Board (FASB) Interpretation 35 (1981) of APB 18 refines the application of the "significant influence" test. It states that an investor may not use the equity method, despite ownership of 20% or more, if any of the following conditions is present:

- Litigation between the investor and investee prevents the investor from exercising its "influence."
- A "standstill agreement" or similar restriction precludes the investor from voting its shares or influencing management of the investee.
- The investee has a majority holder that controls its operations.
- There are other indicators of a lack of ability to influence the investee such as lack of seats on the Board of Directors or lack of ability to obtain financial and operating data.

In practice, the equity method has been applied to holdings of as low as 10% when "significant influence" has been demonstrated. On the other hand, holdings of well over 20% may be insufficient. The user of financial statements cannot take for granted that the equity method will be used if and only if the voting interest is in the range of 20–50%.

Harnischfeger Industries, for example, owned 18.83% of Measurex on October 31, 1990. An agreement limits Harnischfeger to a 20% interest, but gives the company one seat on the Board of Directors. The equity method is used to account for the investment in Measurex, allowing Harnischfeger to include in its earnings its proportionate share of Measurex's earnings rather than only dividends received.

Illustration

To illustrate the application of the equity method, examine the following events:

1. On December 31, 1990, Company P invests $300 in Company S and receives 30% of the shares of Company S in return.
2. During the year ended December 31, 1991, assume that Company S earns $100 and pays common stock dividends of $20.

The accounting for the stock purchase by Company P is quite simple. On its balance sheet at December 31, 1990, Company P will report the purchased asset at its acquisition cost as follows:

Investment in Company S $300

To account for the investment in Company S for the year ended December 31, 1991, consider first the effect of the income earned and the dividends paid by Company S. Its equity (or, equivalently, its net assets) will increase by $100 as a result of the income earned during the year. Company P's share of that income (alternatively, its share in the increased equity of Company S) is $30 (30% of $100).

Using the equity method of accounting, Company P will therefore include the $30 in its income statement as well as increase its "Investment in Company S" account by $30, thereby reflecting its 30% share of the earnings (and increase in the net assets) of Company S:

Investment in Company S	$30	
Equity in net income of Company S		$30

Company P has also received $6 in cash dividends (30% of $20). In contrast to the cost method, these dividends are not included directly as part of its income. Company P's income from Company S under the equity method is a function of the earnings of Company S and is independent of dividends received. Any dividends received are recorded as a reduction in the "Investment in Company S" account.

Cash	$6	
Investment in Company S		$6

The rationale for this reporting method flows from the decline in Company S's equity (and net assets) due to the declaration of dividends. The dividend of $20 reduces Company S's equity by $20. Thus, Company P's share of that decrease in equity is $6.

The net effect is that Company P's share of the undistributed (reinvested) earnings of Company S ($80 = $100 − $20) is, under the equity method, simply added to the "Investment in Company S" account on Company P's balance sheet. That is, the account is increased by $24 ($30 − $6, or 30% of $80). Company P will report the following asset on December 31, 1991:

Investment in Company S $324

The investment account consists of the original cost of the investment plus the equity in the undistributed earnings of the investee. If the investment were sold, any realized gain/loss (for financial reporting only, the tax basis is unaffected by the accounting method applied) would be based on a comparison of the proceeds with the cost basis of $324 and not the original cost of $300.

For the second year, assume that Company S earns $150 and pays cash dividends of $60. Company P will receive cash of $18 (30% of $60) but recognize earnings of $45 (30% of $150). The excess of income recognized over dividends received ($45 − $18 = $27) will be added to the investment account that, at December 31, 1992, will be reported as

Investment in Company S $351

The investment account now consists of the following:

Original investment in Company S	$300
Equity in reinvested 1991 income	24
Equity in reinvested 1992 income	27
Investment in Company S	$351

Comparison of Equity Method and Cost Method

The following table shows the differences between the cost and equity methods for the previous example.

Year	Investment in Company S		Income Reported		Cash Received	
	Cost	Equity	Cost	Equity	Cost	Equity
1991	$300	$324	$6	$30	$6	$6
1992	300	351	18	45	18	18

Under the cost method, Company P will include in income only dividends received. Use of the equity method results in higher earnings for Company P as it reports its proportionate share of the reinvested earnings of Company S. Whenever the investee has earnings and a dividend payout ratio of less than 100%, use of the equity method will increase the earnings of the investor relative to the cost method.

Cash flows, however, will not differ. While under the cost method, income and cash flow are identical (assuming no write-down of the investment), under the equity method they are no longer the same.

The additional income recognition under the equity method results in improved interest coverage and return on investment ratios for Company P. Its total assets and stockholders' equity will rise as a result of recognition of its share of the reinvested earnings of Company S. This higher base may, in time, reduce the return-on-investment and return-on-equity ratios if the profitability of Company S declines. The increase in stockholders' equity will also increase its book value per share. Moreover, as only assets and equity are affected, without any recognition of the subsidiary's debt the debt-to-equity and debt-to-total capital ratios will be decreased.

The preceding discussion assumes that the investee is profitable. When it reports losses, the investor must write down the carrying value of the investment. However, the carrying value cannot be written down below zero, unless the investor has economic exposure in addition to its investment (such as a loan guarantee). Subsequent profits cannot be recognized until any unrecognized losses have been made up.

Returning to Exhibit 11-6, we extend our previous example of Exhibit 11-1 and compare the equity method with the cost method(s) and mark to market accounting. Note that only under the equity method do the actual earnings of the investee directly affect the performance of the parent. On the other hand, market values are ignored. When the equity method is applied to an investee whose shares are publicly traded, changes in market price do not affect the application of the equity method unless there is a permanent impairment. In our example, the difference in results for the various methods is striking. For financial analysis, however, the value placed by the securities markets on the investee can be compared with the carrying amount under the equity method. Generally, the public market value should be considered a better indicator of value than the carrying amount in the financial statements of the investor.

The Equity Method and Deferred Taxes

The equity method is a financial reporting requirement. Because it cannot be used on corporate tax returns, it creates timing differences between financial income and taxable income.[16] In the United States, dividends received by corporations from qualifying domestic corporations are taxed at an effective tax rate of less than 7% (due to an 80% dividends received exclusion available to eligible corporate investors). Thus the income tax expense related to the dividend component of equity method income can be computed quite precisely. However, estimates of tax expense related to undistributed income (income recognized under the equity method less that portion received as dividends) are difficult because they depend on future events.

Two different assumptions can be made. One assumption is that the reinvested income will be received in the future in the form of dividends in excess of future earnings; the deferred component of tax expense is computed using the effective tax rate on dividends (currently about 7%). The alternative assumption is that the reinvested income will be realized via sale of the investment, requiring the use of the corporate capital gains rate (currently 34%) to compute deferred taxes.

If the proportion of reinvested (undistributed) income is significant, then the choice of tax rate applied to reinvested income can materially affect reported income. Unfortunately, explicit disclosure of the choice is almost never made. In some cases, analysis of the income tax footnote (see Chapter 7) will provide the information needed to evaluate the impact of the choice made on reported income.[17]

For example, Corning's income tax footnote for 1990 discloses deferred taxes of $8.7 million on $107.5 million of equity in earnings of associated companies. This disclosure suggests that Corning is assuming that reinvested earnings will be paid in the form of dividends ($8.7 million/$107.5 million = 8.1%).

A second issue arises upon sale of the investment. As the equity method is not applied for income tax purposes, the cost basis of the investment (for tax purposes) remains unchanged. In the financial statements, however, cost is augmented by reinvested income recognized under the equity method (net of deferred tax expense).

---

[16]See Chapter 7 for a detailed discussion of timing differences and deferred taxes.

[17]SFAS 109 continues the APB 23 indefinite reversal criteria and does not require deferred tax liabilities for the undistributed earnings of a domestic subsidiary or corporate joint venture that arose in fiscal years beginning prior to December 15, 1992. Tax effects must be recognized when these temporary differences are expected to reverse in the foreseeable future.

However, SFAS 109 requires that deferred taxes must be provided on such undistributed earnings effective in 1993.

When the investment is sold, the capital gain for income tax purposes will, in all likelihood, be far greater than the capital gain for financial accounting purposes. In some cases there will be a loss for accounting purposes despite the gain for income tax reporting purposes.

If the corporate investor has accrued deferred taxes based on the dividend assumption, and later sells the investment, the deferred tax provision will be inadequate. Thus, even if there is a pretax capital gain (sales price exceeds the sum of original cost and the recorded reinvested earnings), there may be an after-tax loss.

If the investee is a foreign corporation, the issues and analysis are slightly different. For foreign investees, the preferential tax treatment for dividends is not available. On the other hand, credits for foreign income taxes paid may be available to offset the U.S. tax liability when reinvested income is paid out in the form of dividends. More significantly, no deferred tax provision is required for reinvested foreign earnings because of the "permanent reinvestment" option. Thus, in the case of foreign investees, it may be that no deferred tax provision has been made.

Summing up, if there is reason to believe that a major investment accounted for under the equity method is to be sold, the tax issue must be considered. Try to determine the tax basis (cost for income tax purposes) of the investment; footnotes sometimes disclose the original cost. Look for information regarding the company's tax rate and the existence of any capital loss carryforwards that might shelter the gain from being taxed. Most important, be aware that the accounting gain and the taxable gain might be quite different.

Equity Accounting and Analysis: Concluding Comments

The issue of reinvested earnings goes beyond the implication for deferred taxes to the heart of the justification for the equity method. That method relies on the underlying principle of accrual accounting, the assumption that the accrual measure is a better indicator of the earning power or cash generating ability of the firm.

Ricks and Hughes (1985) offer evidence that is consistent with the assumption that the equity method provides data used for valuation purposes by the market. The equity method was mandated by APB 18 (1971) as an alternative to the cost method. Ricks and Hughes found positive market reaction at the time the first financial statements using the equity method were issued. The positive reaction was positively correlated to both the size of the equity earnings as well as the degree to which analysts underestimated earnings in their forecasts. This led them to surmise that the market found the information useful, as "the equity method provided information concerning affiliate earnings not previously available from other sources."[18]

The usefulness of this information is predicated on the assumption that the parent has or will have access to the earnings. If the undistributed earnings are going to remain permanently reinvested and the parent does not really have access to those earnings (or cash flows), then it is questionable whether they should be considered income at all for purposes of analysis. In some cases, therefore, analysts adjust equity earnings to the cost basis for analytic purposes. That is, they include only actual dividends received from the

---

[18]Ricks, William E. and John S. Hughes, "Market Reactions to a Non-Discretionary Accounting Change: The Case of Long-Term Investments", *The Accounting Review* (January 1985), p. 50.

investee as income of the parent. This adjustment is independent of the use of market value instead of carrying value for the investment.

Conversely, in certain cases, for firms using the cost method, it may be appropriate to adjust reported earnings to the equity basis. Information regarding investments is available in Schedule I in the firm's SEC 10-K filing. For publicly traded affiliates, earnings information will be easily available; that will not be the case for privately held affiliates and joint ventures.

This adjustment should be made when companies, although they have "significant influence" over their affiliates, have chosen to use the cost method. The criterion of "significant influence" is subject to some discretion, and although 20% is usually the cutoff point, that level itself is arbitrary. A firm wishing to use the cost method can purchase less than 20% of a subsidiary; if it desires to use the equity method, it can purchase just over 20%. As Box 11-2 indicates, there is some evidence that firms straddle the 20% line to get the desired accounting treatment.

CONSOLIDATION

When we see the financial statements of Exxon, General Motors, Royal Dutch, or any other huge enterprise, we are viewing a consolidated set of statements that includes a large number of individual corporate entities. Each statement (and each account therein) in a set of consolidated financial statements consists of the sum (less any intercompany eliminations) of the corresponding statements of each included entity.[19] The inventories shown, for example, are the inventories of each corporate entity, added together, and adjusted for any intercompany transactions.

The "parent-only" statement carries its investment in the subsidiary on the equity basis, as the assets and liabilities of the subsidiary are included in a single investment account. When the firms are consolidated, it is implicitly assumed that the assets and liabilities of the subsidiary belong to the parent company. As we shall see, there are times when that assumption must be questioned.

Illustration

Exhibit 11-8 provides an illustration of a firm's (Company P, the parent) purchase of an 80% interest in Company S (the subsidiary). To simplify matters, it is assumed that the amount paid ($2000) equals the proportionate share of the book value of the subsidiary (80% of $2500) being purchased. When this is not the case, the subsidiary accounts will be written up to their fair market values, and a goodwill account may be recorded. A discussion of goodwill is contained in Chapter 12, Business Combinations. The exhibit shows both the equity method and full consolidation, allowing for a comparison of the two methods.

The first part of Exhibit 11-8 shows the equity method as well as the consolidated statements immediately following the acquisition. The second part shows the income statement, cash flows, and balance sheets after one year. Note that only the assets and

---

[19]See Chapter 13 for an analysis of financial statements when some of those entities keep their records in a currency other than that of the parent.

BOX 11-2
Equity Accounting and Its Impact on Ownership Position

Comiskey and Mulford (1986) tested whether "the inclusion in APB 18 of the 20 percent ownership criterion for application of the equity method (hereafter the 20 percent standard) influences the ownership position taken by investing firms."* Figure 11-1, from their study, shows the distribution of ownership positions taken by investing firms in 1982. The solid line indicates the actual percentage positions taken, and the dashed line depicts the predicted "fitted" distribution.†

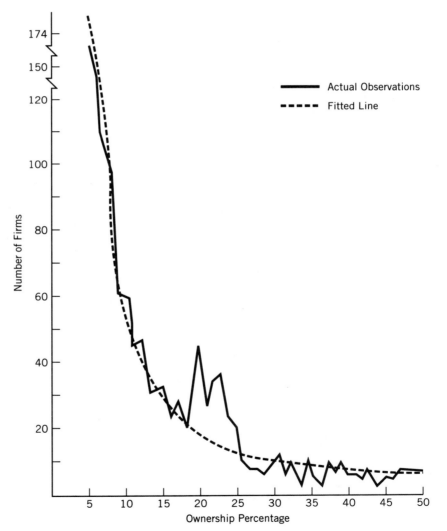

FIGURE 11-1 Ownership Percentage Distribution, 1982 Data.
Source: Comiskey, Eugene and Charles W. Mulford, "Investment Decisions and the Equity Accounting Standard", *The Accounting Review* (July 1986), pp. 519–525, Figure 1, P. 521

As indicated in Figure 11-1, the actual concentration of firms in the 16–24% range is significantly greater than expected. Comiskey and Mulford argue that the 20% standard mandated by APB 18 may be responsible for the abnormal concentration. Different firms may have different motivations with respect to whether they want to report on the cost or equity basis and stake out positions accordingly.

In further support of this contention, they found that affiliates in the 19–19.99% ownership range had reported (on average) a net loss 30.4% of the time in the previous four years. Firms in the 20–20.99% range reported losses only 16.1% of the time. As the equity method is increasingly preferable as the subsidiary's income (or more precisely, the undistributed income) increases, these results make sense. Owners of affiliates that are less likely to report losses are more likely to choose an ownership interest permitting use of the equity method. Alternatively, firms facing losses and holding over 20% may decide to sell some of their holdings to bring them below the 20% level.‡

---

*Comiskey, Eugene and Charles W. Mulford, "Investment Decisions and the Equity Accounting Standard", *The Accounting Review* (July 1986), p. 519.

†The "fitted" line was determined on the basis of extrapolation of the patterns existing below 16% and above 24%.

‡As discussed later, similar possibilities exist for firms that want to avoid consolidation (i.e., they acquire only 49% of the subsidiary).

EXHIBIT 11-8
Comparison of Equity Method and Consolidation

Balance Sheet at Acquisition Date

	Preacquisition		After Acquisition of 80% of Company S for $2000 Company P	
	Company P	Company S	Equity Method	Consolidated
Current assets	$12,000	$4000	$10,000	$14,000
Investment in Company S	—	—	2,000	—
Other assets	8,000	2000	8,000	10,000
	$20,000	$6000	$20,000	$24,000
Current liabilities	$10,000	$3500	$10,000	$13,500
Minority interest	—	—	—	500
Common stock	7,000	1500	7,000	7,000
Retained earnings	3,000	1000	3,000	3,000
	$20,000	$6000	$20,000	$24,000

EXHIBIT 11-8. *(Continued)*

Results of First Year After Acquisition

Additional information:
  Dividends paid by S equal $250.
  There are no changes in noncash working capital.
  There are no noncash expenses.
  Company P loaned Company S $350.

		Company P	
	Company S	Equity Method	Consolidated
Revenue	$5000	$15,000	$20,000
Expense	4000	10,000	14,000
Operating income	$1000	$ 5,000	$ 6,000
Equity in income			
of Company S	—	800	—
Minority interest	—	—	(200)
Net income	$1000	$ 5,800	$ 5,800
Noncash adjustment		(600)*	200‡
Cash from operations	$1000	$ 5,200	$ 6,000
Cash from affiliates	350	(350)	—
Dividends paid/received	(250)		(50)†
Change in cash	$1100	$ 4,850	$ 5,950

*Reinvested earnings of Company S ($800 earned − $200 dividends received).
†Paid to minority investors.
‡Minority interest

Balance Sheet, End of First Year

		Company P	
	Company S	Equity Method	Consolidated
Current assets	$5100	$14,850	$19,950
Investment in Company S	—	2,600	—
Receivable from Company S	—	350	
Other assets	$2000	8,000	10,000
	$7100	$25,800	$29,950
Current liabilities	$3500	$10,000	$13,500
Payable to Company P	350	—	
Minority interest	—	—	650
Common stock	1500	7,000	7,000
Retained earnings	1750	8,800	8,800
	$7100	$25,800	$29,950

liabilities are changed by consolidation, the common equity of the consolidated firm is the equity of the parent firm.

Similarly, while consolidation results in inclusion of the revenues and expenses of Company S in the income statement of Company P, net income is unchanged. But reported cash flows are affected by the consolidation. The consolidated operating cash flows are higher by $800, which is equal to the cash flows of Company S less the dividends received by Company P (which were already included in cash flow under the equity method). Thus consolidation means that all the subsidiary's cash flows are included, not just those paid to the parent.

Clearly the addition of a subsidiary to (or subtraction from) the consolidated group will also change financial statement ratios. Less obviously, it also means that data in the financial statement footnotes will include (or exclude) the data of the subsidiary.

Although the parent owns only 80% of the subsidiary, when the subsidiary's statements are consolidated with the parent, its total accounts are included, reflecting the control perspective in consolidated financial reporting.[20] As the parent owns less than 100% of the subsidiary, however, it does not derive benefits from all the subsidiary's assets and earnings (and it may not be at risk for all subsidiary liabilities).

Consolidated financial statements reflect this fact through accounts known as *minority interest*. On the consolidated balance sheet, the share of the subsidiary's net worth (assets less liabilities) that does not accrue to the parent is shown as a liability (strictly speaking, it is a credit balance rather than a liability), normally just above shareholders' equity. In Exhibit 11-8, minority interest is $500 (20% of $2500) at acquisition. After one year, it is $650 (20% of $3250). On the income statement, minority interest of $200 (20% of $1000) is shown as a deduction.[21] We will provide a discussion of minority interest later.

Applicability of Consolidation

Consolidated financial statements include all entities in which the parent controls (directly or indirectly) more than 50% of the voting shares of the subsidiary. There are two exceptions to this rule. Consolidation is not appropriate when control is temporary. The second exception concerns subsidiaries that are not considered controlled, despite majority ownership, due to governmental action, a nonconvertible currency, or civil disorder. The legal status of the subsidiary, such as bankruptcy or reorganization, may also preclude consolidation. These exceptions are made because under the circumstances, the parent company does not have unrestricted use of the subsidiary's assets or cannot be considered to exercise control. An example of the second type of exception is presented in Exhibit 11-9.

Control may also be present at ownership levels below a majority. The ownership of warrants or convertible securities, control of management, or other factors may indicate that the parent company does exercise control. Such subsidiaries would have to be consolidated.

---

[20]In some cases, however, proportionate consolidation may be more appropriate; that methodology is discussed in a separate section of this chapter.

[21]Generally, minority interest is shown as a separate line item in both balance sheet and income statement; some firms include it in other accounts.

EXHIBIT 11-9
Exception to Consolidation Rule: The Acquisition of Avdel plc by Textron

An exception to the requirement to consolidate subsidiaries occurred with the acquisition by Textron of Avdel plc, a British manufacturer, in 1989. The acquisition was challenged by the Federal Trade Commission, and Textron was enjoined by a court order from exercising control over Avdel. As a result, Textron's 1990 annual report included the following footnote:

> While Textron's results of operations for 1990 and 1989 do not include the results of Avdel, (a) they do include interest expense of $21 million and $22 million, respectively, on the borrowings related to the purchase of Avdel and (b) they include in 1990 $7 million of cash dividends received from Avdel. Avdel's sales and earnings before taxes (unaudited) were $163 million and $22 million, respectively. Avdel's sales were $149 million in 1989 and its earnings before income taxes were $23 million. Such results do not reflect any purchase adjustments which would be required as a result of Textron's acquisition of Avdel, principally amortization of goodwill.

As Textron reported earnings before income taxes of approximately $410 million and $459 million for 1989 and 1990, respectively, the inclusion of Avdel would have increased such earnings by more than 5% in 1989 and by more than 3% in 1990 ($22 million less the $7 million received as a dividend), ignoring any goodwill amortization.

Source: Textron, 1990 Annual Report.

For example, in its *1990 Annual Report,* Volkswagen disclosed that it would take over 31% of the capital of Skoda, a Czechoslovak auto company, in 1991, with the intention of increasing its holding to 70% by 1995. Volkswagen further states that

> Volkswagen will assume management responsibility from the outset and will therefore be including this company in the consolidated financial statements from 1991 onwards.

Nonhomogeneous Subsidiaries

Prior to the adoption of SFAS 94, which became effective in 1988, credit, insurance, leasing, and other "nonhomogeneous" subsidiaries were excluded from the consolidated financial statements. This issue has been the subject of much debate. Proponents of exclusion argued that these financial subsidiaries have capital structures that differ significantly from those of their manufacturing or retailing parents. Even the form of financial statements is different: financial companies, for example, have unclassified balance sheets with no distinction between "current" and "noncurrent" assets or liabilities. The degree of control over and claims on assets and cash flows may also differ. Consolidation of such dissimilar entities would, it was argued, confuse financial statement users.

On the other hand, proponents of full consolidation argued that it is illogical to segregate some subsidiaries from the consolidated group, especially when the operations of the subsidiary are integral to the business of the parent. For example, when a finance subsidiary provides credit to the dealers and customers of the parent, its assets are, in effect, the parent's accounts receivable. Financing those receivables through a separate subsidiary may facilitate the parent's borrowing activities, but it does not justify exclusion of the subsidiary from the consolidated financial statements.

As in the case of many theoretical arguments on accounting alternatives, there is truth on both sides. We believe that consolidation, by providing information about the enterprise on a comprehensive scale, generally serves the needs of financial statement users best; in particular, it serves the needs of the parent's stockholders.

In many cases, fully disaggregated information is useful (or necessary) for analysis. This is true when the subsidiary is in an unrelated line of business whose financial characteristics differ from those of the remaining lines, for example, an oil company owned by a chemical or steel company as well as an insurance company owned by a manufacturer or retailer. We believe that the relevant factor is the degree of integration rather than the "homogeneity" of the financial structure (see discussion of "captive" finance subsidiaries later in this chapter). In addition, existence of subsidiary debt or other restrictions (e.g., regulatory) on the ability of the enterprise to draw on the assets of the subsidiary further strengthen the case for separate disclosure.

Information about different lines of business is usually provided in the form of segment data (see page 820). Data are often available to permit the financial analyst to restate financial statements to a form better suited to the analysis at hand. At times it will be necessary to consolidate an unconsolidated subsidiary; at other times deconsolidation will be required. In the balance of this chapter, we will provide several examples of "do-it-yourself" restatement.

Consolidation Practices Outside the United States

While consolidation of majority-owned subsidiaries has been the general rule in the United States for several decades, that has not been the case for other nations. In Japan, and in parts of Western Europe, parent company reporting has been the norm until quite recently. In Japan, for example, "parent-only" financial statements are still considered to be the primary set of statements. This may be due to the fact that financial reporting in Japan is based on tax reporting. In Germany, consolidated financial statements normally include only domestic subsidiaries; investments in foreign subsidiaries and affiliates are carried at acquisition cost. In the United Kingdom and Canada, firms may exclude nonhomogeneous subsidiaries from consolidated financial statements. However, current trends indicate that excluded affiliates are limited to those operating in the banking and insurance industries.

IAS 27 requires that all controlled subsidiaries be consolidated. As this standard became effective in 1990, all financial statements prepared in accordance with IASC standards should now be comparable in this respect. In time, assuming increasing conformity with IASC standards, full consolidation should become the norm worldwide.

Comparison of Consolidation with Equity Method

Consolidation and the equity method produce the same "bottom line" in that net income and net worth are identical under the two methods. In most other respects, however, these methods impact financial statements quite differently.

Under consolidation, all the assets, liabilities, revenues, expenses, and cash flows of the subsidiary are included in the corresponding accounts of the investor. When ownership is less than 100%, the "minority interest" is subtracted out. In contrast, the equity method incorporates the parent's share of the net income and net assets of the investee in parent company results, reporting them as equity in the earnings of the subsidiary and investment in the subsidiary, respectively.

Under the equity method, only the investment account and the net income are affected by investee results. Virtually every account in consolidated financial statements and the accompanying footnotes will be affected by the subsidiary's operating, investing, and financing activities.

Reported cash flows will also differ. Under the equity method, parent company cash flow will include *only* capital flows between parent and investee (dividends, additional investments, and redemptions). When the investee is consolidated, parent company cash flow will include all cash flows of the investee *except* those between parent and investee. Inclusion of the cash flows of an investee may give misleading indications of the resources available to the parent.

Depending on the financial characteristics of the subsidiary, consolidation may result in financial statements that look either better or worse than those resulting from use of the equity method. Parent ownership levels just below 50% may signal a desire to avoid consolidation;[22,23] ownership of 50% or more may indicate a preference for consolidation.

Consolidation versus Equity Method: The Case of Deere

In this section, we examine Deere and Company, a major manufacturer of agricultural equipment, to illustrate the differences between consolidation and use of the equity method. Deere has credit subsidiaries that primarily provide financing for Deere customers and insurance subsidiaries whose customers include Deere. The credit and insurance operations of Deere, collectively referred to as "financial services" in the company's financial statements, were accounted for using the equity method prior to the effective date of SFAS 94.

To provide detailed information on its different operating segments while complying with the requirements of SFAS 94, Deere provides disaggregated financial statements in addition to the consolidated ones. An extensive analysis is provided here for three reasons.

First, this section serves as an introduction to consolidated financial statements; as these statements become the norm in international reporting, the analyst needs to develop tools to analyze them.

Second, whereas disaggregated data on previously unconsolidated subsidiaries are required under SFAS 94, while the FASB continues work on various related issues, that requirement may not be continued in the future. If these data are not available, analysts will have to do their own deconsolidation, using available financial statements.

---

[22]In Chapter 10, we noted that after SFAS 94, which required the use of consolidation for finance subsidiaries, many companies sold off parts of their finance subsidiaries, leaving themselves with 49% ownership.

[23]For these cases, the analyst may want to use proportionate consolidation. This approach is discussed later in the chapter.

Finally, the analysis also illustrates the separate evaluation of the debt structure, bond covenants (which govern transfers of resources between the investor and investee), and risk of subsidiaries. (Required data are often available since such affiliates must file separate financial statements with the SEC if they have issued publicly held debt.)

Exhibit 1B-2 contains the disaggregated balance sheets for Deere's equipment operations (with financial services on the equity basis) and financial services units for the two years ended October 31, 1991.[24] These statements are the basis for the discussion of Deere that follows.

Balance Sheet Eliminations

As already stated, the consolidated amounts do not simply equal the sum of the two individual statements. Intercompany accounts have been eliminated, as required by consolidation. Deere did not directly provide data on eliminations, but they can be deduced by comparing the consolidated total with the sum of the segment accounts. For example, October 31, 1991, receivables from unconsolidated subsidiaries and affiliates are $200.5 million for equipment operations, zero for financial services, and $17.8 million fully consolidated. The difference of $182.7 million, apparently owed by the financial services segment to the equipment segment, has been eliminated in consolidation.

When making (or deriving) elimination entries, it is important to remember that all eliminations have two components. An intercompany balance shown as an asset of one entity must be included among the liabilities of the other. Both the asset and the corresponding liability must be removed. Removal of only one will result in an "unbalanced" set of financial statements. Sometimes an intercompany account will be clearly identified on only one set of financial statements. In such cases we must assume that the "other side" is included somewhere in the statements of the other and must determine the most likely (and appropriate) location.

In the case of the $182.7 million receivable already identified, we can find the "other side" on the financial services balance sheet. "Payables to unconsolidated subsidiaries and affiliates" of $192.8 million is partly offset by "receivables from unconsolidated subsidiaries and affiliates" of $10.0 million; the net is (after rounding) the $182.7 million eliminated in consolidation.[25] What remains is $5.5 million owed by the equipment operations, presumably to other affiliates still not consolidated.

Note that stockholders' equity is unchanged by the consolidation of financial services. Deere's net investment in unconsolidated subsidiaries at October 31, 1991, has been reduced from $1221.7 million for the equipment operations to $106 million for the consolidated group. This elimination of $1115.7 million represents the equity of Deere's financial services operations ($1143.6 million) less an investment by the financial

---

[24]Note that the balance sheets for Deere are unclassified—there is no separation of current from noncurrent assets and liabilities, reflecting the inclusion of financial services operations. While many believe this distinction to be of limited usefulness, the inability to compute the current ratio may be bothersome to some.

[25]At October 31, 1990, the elimination is simpler: $71.5 million has been eliminated in the consolidated balance sheet, representing the balance owed by the financial services companies to the parent company.

services unit ($28.0 million).[26] The offset to this elimination is the inclusion of the gross assets and liabilities of the financial services group (whose equity is $1143.6 million) less the investment of $28 million, also eliminated in consolidation. The "bottom-line" equity is, therefore, unchanged.

Some accounts—inventories, for example—have not changed at all from those of the equipment operations. Others show considerable change. Most significantly, the receivables and debt of the financial services segment are now included in the consolidated balance sheet. While "Credit receivables" are shown separately from "Dealer accounts and notes receivables—net," both represent amounts due to Deere from past sales.

Because of the importance of credit receivables to finance subsidiaries of manufacturers and retailers, a few words of explanation may be helpful. Some of these receivables originate at the parent company level from credit sales (such as department store charge cards). These receivables are then sold to a finance subsidiary. In some cases (notably, auto financing), the receivable is originated directly by the subsidiary. In some cases, finance subsidiaries also provide credit to dealers.

The terms of credit are, of course, critical to the profitability of the finance subsidiary. Lenders to these subsidiaries frequently require the parent to guarantee a minimum interest coverage ratio for the subsidiary. If the manufacturer wishes to offer low-cost financing, a subsidy from the parent is necessary, an arrangement that affects the reported profitability of the different parts of the consolidated entity.[27] Such indirect guarantees strengthen the case for requiring consolidation of finance subsidiaries.

In the case of Deere, inclusion of the additional receivables has a major impact on the computation of accounts receivable turnover, as well as calculation of the length of the operating cycle.

Similarly, nearly $3.8 billion of debt has been added as a result of the consolidation of the financial services segment. As the equity base is unchanged, reported leverage ratios are sharply increased.

Income Statement Consolidation

Exhibit 1B-2 also contains consolidating income statements for Deere, again on a separate basis as well as fully consolidated. Once again we can deduce the eliminating entries.

The eliminating entries, which reflect intercompany transactions, are often illuminating. For example, the reduction of fiscal 1991 insurance and health care premiums from $568.4 million to $444.1 million tells us that more than 20% of Deere's insurance

---

[26]Again, October 31, 1990, is simpler. The reduction in Deere's investment in unconsolidated subsidiaries and affiliates account of $1102.7 million is exactly equal to the stockholders' equity of the financial services segment being consolidated.

[27]For example, in recent years auto manufacturers have offered low-cost financing to customers. The cost of such "sales incentives" is not separately identified in the income statement. Depending on the classification of these costs, and the extent to which the manufacturing segment absorbs the discount from normal financing terms, the relative profitability of the finance unit may be affected. Support agreements and minimum coverage ratios may limit the ability to shift these costs to the finance unit. Because of these factors, separate financial statements or disclosures are essential to the analysis of the profitability of the different segments of the company.

business is self-generated. (It also indicates that Deere "self-insures" its employee insurance benefits.) Not surprisingly, about 20% ($105.7 million out of $511.2 million in 1991) of claims and benefits paid by the insurance affiliates also disappear in consolidation. The flow of premiums from equipment to insurance companies is balanced by the flow of claims payments in the opposite direction.

As in the case of the balance sheet, consolidation does not change the bottom line. Deere's $111.8 million equity in the earnings of its credit and insurance subsidiaries for 1991 is eliminated in consolidation, but it is replaced by the individual revenue and expense lines (net income is the same $111.8 million). Consolidated net income remains unchanged for all three years.

Consolidated Cash Flows

Exhibit 1B-2 also contains cash flow statements, again separately as well as consolidated. Once again, these can be used to deduce the elimination entries. For example, dividends paid for the consolidated entity are identical to dividends paid by the equipment operations; the dividends paid by financial services to the parent company are eliminated in consolidation.

On the other hand, consolidation appears to result in higher cash flow from operating activities for 1991 as the operating cash flows of the financial services segment are now included. However that conclusion depends on accepting the classification of changes in credit receivables as investing transactions. When we analyze Deere's cash flows in Chapter 14, we will question that classification.

At this point, however, we simply compare Deere's cash flows on a fully consolidated basis with the amounts reported with the financial services units reported using the equity method. The analysis of 1991 cash flows will suffice:

DEERE
Summarized Cash Flows, for Year Ended October 31, 1991
(in $ millions)

	Consolidated	Equity Method
Operating activities	$ 613.0	$ 468.1
Investing activities	(1379.0)	(388.2)
Excess	$ (766.0)	$ 79.9
Financing cash flows	860.6	(5.0)
Effect of exchange rates	(1.5)	(1.5)
Net increase in cash	$ 93.1	$ 73.4

The contrast is striking. With the financial services shown using the equity method, operating cash flows exceed investing cash flows by $79.9 million. If we add back the amount spent for acquisitions ($71.1 million), the excess grows to $151 million. This amount approximates dividend payments of $152.3 million in 1991. These data show a company with sufficient operating cash flows to cover both normal investment needs and cash dividends.

On a fully consolidated basis, however, Deere's operating cash flows are far below the firm's investment needs. As a result, consolidated debt increased by approximately $1 billion during 1991. Cash flows for 1990 and 1989 show a similar pattern: the consolidated data show financing requirements well beyond those indicated by the equity method statements. These data suggest a significant cash shortage; a full analysis of the company would require consideration of its borrowing capacity.

There are several insights in this analysis. First, consolidation impacts reported cash flows because of the inclusion of the cash flows of the newly consolidated entity. Depending on the subsidiary cash flows, inclusion can make the consolidated entity look better or worse.

Second, manufacturers and retailers have historically used their unconsolidated financial subsidiaries to provide financing "off balance sheet." When these subsidiaries are consolidated, the cash requirements of financing affiliates are reflected in the consolidated cash flow statement. The ability of these affiliates to obtain financing sufficient to support parent operations must be considered when evaluating the long-run solvency of the parent.

Impact of Consolidation on Ratios

The addition of a new entity to the consolidated group changes, as we have seen, all three basic financial statements. As a result, financial statement ratios will change as well. For subsidiaries that were previously accounted for using the equity method, consolidation will leave both net income and stockholders' equity unchanged. However, other asset, liability, revenue, and expense categories will increase. Therefore leverage ratios will tend to increase, and "return on" ratios will decrease.

The consolidation of Deere's financial subsidiaries provides an excellent example of these effects. Using the consolidating financial statements in Exhibit 1B-2, we can compute a few of the more widely used ratios. Let us start with leverage.

DEERE
Capital Structure, for Years Ended October 31, 1990–1991
(in $ millions)

	Equity Method		Consolidated	
	1990	1991	1990	1991
Short-term debt	$ 850	$ 880	$ 2892	$ 3471
Long-term debt	804	1018	1786	2206
Total funded debt	$ 1654	$ 1898	$ 4678	$ 5677
Stockholders equity	3008	2836	3008	2836
Total capital	$ 4662	$ 4734	$ 7686	$ 8513
Average total capital	$4698		$8100	
Funded debt as a % of total capital	35.5%	40.1%	60.9%	66.7%

The consolidation of Deere's debt-heavy finance subsidiaries has, not surprisingly, significantly increased the reported debt ratio. The trend is unchanged, but the debt ratio is significantly higher. Adding back the "off-balance-sheet" debt resulting from the sale of receivables would increase the consolidated debt ratios further (see Chapter 14).

Now look at the interest coverage ratio (times interest earned), one of the most significant measures of debt safety.

DEERE
Interest Coverage Ratio, for Years Ended October 31, 1990–1991
(in $ millions)

	Equity Method		Consolidated	
	1990	1991	1990	1991
Income before income taxes*	$413.3	$(189.1)	$ 587.5	$(26.2)
Interest expense†	190.6	192.7	435.2	450.0
Earnings before interest and tax (EBIT)	603.9	3.6	1022.7	423.8
Interest coverage ratio‡	3.17	0.02	2.35	0.94

*Excludes equity in income of unconsolidated subsidiaries, which does not provide cash flow to the parent except to the extent of dividends.

†We have not adjusted for interest capitalized (see Chapter 6).

‡EBIT/interest expense.

Interest coverage is significantly different after consolidation of Deere's financial subsidiaries. Finance subsidiaries typically have higher debt ratios and lower interest coverage ratios than do manufacturing companies. In years of normal profitability (such as 1990), consolidation will reduce interest coverage.[28] For 1991, a year of poor operating results in Deere's equipment operations, the better profitability of the financial services businesses results in an improved coverage ratio after consolidation. As a general rule, however, whenever a previously unconsolidated finance company is consolidated, interest coverage will decline.

[28]Our calculation of EBIT excluded the earnings of Deere's financial services entities when accounted for under the equity method. But Deere did receive dividends of $86.5 million in 1991; including dividends received in EBIT increases the equity method interest coverage ratio as follows:

	1990	1991
Dividends received ($ millions)	79.7	86.5
Adjusted EBIT ($ millions)	683.6	90.1
Adjusted coverage ratio	3.58	0.47

For 1990 (normal profitability) this adjustment increases the disparity between the consolidated ratio and the ratio based on use of the equity method.

It should be noted that the interest coverage ratio as calculated for Deere on a consolidated basis raises an interesting question. An objective of the interest coverage (or fixed charge) ratio is to measure the degree to which operating flows "cover" the fixed interest charges. The ratio provides a measure of the margin of safety in the event that the firm's operations enter a downturn. For a finance subsidiary (or for that matter any financial institution), interest expense is an operating item and not fixed. If operating levels drop, so will interest charges. The interpretation of the preceding calculation ratio is thus not clear cut as reduced profitability and demand can potentially generate an improvement in the ratio.[29]

One more ratio, turnover of accounts receivable, is worthy of discussion. If we aggregate dealer accounts and notes receivable with credit receivables (which we have already agreed are also a form of accounts receivable), we obtain the following:

DEERE
Accounts Receivable, for Years Ended October 31, 1990–1991
(in $ millions)

	Equity Method		Consolidated	
	1990	1991	1990	1991
Dealer accounts/notes receivable	$3100	$2967	$3100	$2967
Credit receivables	65	75	3896	4746
Balance of receivables sold	—	—	534	247
Total receivables	$3165	$3042	$7530	$7960
Average receivables	$3104		$7745	

Notice that we have not added in receivables from subsidiaries and affiliates or "other" receivables. Only receivables from customers should be included in this calculation. However, we have added back the outstanding balance of receivables sold during the period. If we leave out these receivables, we will overstate the turnover ratio, as discussed in Chapter 10.

To calculate the turnover ratio, we use 1991 revenues of $5848 million for both the equity method calculation and the consolidated calculation. The financial affiliates revenues consist of interest, investment income, and insurance premiums that do not generate receivables. (Note that the affiliates have no "dealer accounts and notes

[29]A possible alternative would be to only consider the interest on Deere's equipment operations as fixed interest but compare that to Deere's consolidated income, that is,

	1990	1991	
Income before income taxes	587.5	(26.2)	(Consolidated)
Interest expense	190.6	192.7	(Equipment operations)
Earnings before interest and tax	778.1	166.5	
Interest coverage ratio	4.09	0.87	

receivable.") To include these revenues in our turnover calculation would distort the result. We can now calculate accounts receivable turnover:

Calculation of Receivable Turnover Ratio for 1991

	Equity	Consolidated
Ratio: Sales to average receivables	1.88	0.76
No. Days sales (365/turnover ratio)	194	480

These calculations show that inclusion of the financial subsidiaries, which provide extended credit to Deere's customers, results in significantly lower turnover of accounts receivable. (See Chapter 10 for further discussion of the impact of receivables sales on turnover ratios.) Again, this result is not surprising given the nature of Deere's operations.

Significance of Consolidation

The preceding sections have discussed various types of intercorporate investments, different methods of accounting for them, and the analysis of the resulting (significantly different) reported cash flows, ratios, and other financial statement data. We now summarize the process and the most significant insights for the financial analyst.

First, when examining a set of financial statements, it is essential to determine the accounting methods used for investments in affiliates. This is especially true of non–U.S. companies, as consolidation practices vary widely.

The second step should be to ask what form of presentation will make the financial data most useful given the objectives of the analysis. If you are evaluating several different companies, the most overriding concern is likely to be comparability of basic data. You cannot compare, for example, General Motors, Toyota, Volkswagen, and Hyundai unless they present financial data in a comparable way.

An important aspect of this second step is to ask what form of presentation accords most closely with the objectives of the analysis. Current and prospective lenders to Deere's financial subsidiaries need separate financial statements for those entities; consolidated statements that include the manufacturing operations of the parent company will be less useful.

As we have seen, accounting conventions do not always reflect economic reality. The analyst should determine, for example, which unconsolidated affiliates are integral to the enterprise and should, therefore, be consolidated. Analysts should also be aware of the potential use of "off-balance-sheet" unconsolidated affiliates to obtain financing.

The third step should be to adjust the reported financial statements to the basis that best reflects the operations of the enterprise for the relevant analytic purpose. For U.S. companies relevant data are often available in 10-K reports or in supplemental data (such as "fact books") that many companies prepare for financial analysts. Even condensed statements may be useful; it is better to be approximately right than precisely wrong!

Adjustments should not be made mechanically. They should be appropriate in the context of the company's operations and the objectives of the analysis. Finally, and most important, adjusted financial statements and ratios should be examined carefully for insights regarding the company's past results, current operations, and future performance. Analysts should concentrate on the differences between adjusted statements and the financial statements before adjustment.

Analysis of Minority Interest

The balance in the minority interest account shown on the balance sheet and the minority interest in net income are necessarily related. If the subsidiary pays no cash dividends, then the entire minority interest in net income will show up as a change in the balance sheet account. If a dividend is paid, then the balance sheet accrual will be equal to the minority interest in net income less the dividends paid to minority owners; that is, the accrual will reflect their share of the undistributed earnings. Capital contributions or withdrawals will also affect the minority interest shown on the parent company balance sheet.

For example, in 1990 the Aydin Corporation set up a 51%-owned subsidiary Aydin-Aymet in connection with a major contract with the government of Turkey. This subsidiary generated the following entries in Aydin's 1990 financial statements:

AYDIN CORP.
Analysis of Minority Interest

Income statement: Minority interest	$(108,000)
Liability: Minority interest	511,000
Adjustment to operating cash flow*	108,000
Financing cash flow (minority investment in consolidated subsidiary)	403,000

*Under the indirect method, noncash deductions from income are added back to net income to calculate operating cash flow.

From these entries we can deduce the following transactions:

1. The minority partner invested $403,000 in the subsidiary.
2. The subsidiary earned $220,000 in 1990 ($108,000/0.49), of which 49% (or $108,000) accrued to the minority investor.
3. The subsidiary paid no dividends. Thus the minority interest at the end of the year was

Original investment	$403,000
Minority share of 1990 net income	108,000
Total	$511,000

Notice that the accounting for minority interest is the mirror image of the equity method. Assuming that the Turkish owner of the 49% interest in Aydin-Aymet used the equity method, it would show its investment as $511,000 and its 1990 earnings from the venture as $108,000.

The Aydin *1990 Annual Report* also contains the following footnote:

> Short-term investments . . . include $20.3 million held by the Company's 51% owned Turkish subsidiary.[30]

The significance of this footnote is to remind the reader that the assets of a less than wholly owned subsidiary are not as freely available to the parent as those of a 100%-owned subsidiary because of the minority investor.

Minority interest can be quite significant. In the case of Aydin, it constituted less than 1% of equity. In the case of Alcoa, which has large majority-owned subsidiaries, the numbers are far more significant. At December 31, 1990, Alcoa's minority interest was $1.58 billion or more than 30% of shareholders' equity of $5.16 billion. Minority interest in earnings was $358 million and reduced net income for 1990 by 55%. Finally, dividends to the minority shareholders of the majority-owned subsidiaries was $300 million, exceeding the $267 million paid to Alcoa's own stockholders.

In some respects, minority interest can be considered equity for purposes of analysis. Minority shareholders do have only a residual claim on the assets of the subsidiary. From the point of view of both creditors and stockholders of the parent, however, minority interest has the characteristics of a preferred shareholder. Generally, the creditors and shareholders of the parent cannot benefit from the assets of the subsidiary without respecting the claims of its creditors and minority holders. Thus, minority interest occupies a special position and cannot be aggregated with either liabilities or equity in all cases.

ANALYSIS OF JOINT VENTURES

Joint ventures are frequently found in the business world. They offer such advantages as economies of scale, risk sharing, and technology sharing. They may also allow access to previously restricted markets such as Eastern Europe or newly privatized state-owned enterprises. These ventures take various legal forms due to tax, legal, and operational requirements. As a result, accounting sometimes follows form rather than substance, and the financial statements may need adjustment to reflect the economic nature of the joint venture and its impact on the venturers more appropriately.

Some joint ventures are merely contractual arrangements whereby the venturers agree to cooperate toward a common goal but no new entity is created. Each venturer maintains its own assets and liabilities and recognizes revenues and expenses separately. This type of joint venture creates neither accounting nor analysis difficulties as each venturer already reflects the results of the venture in its financial statements. However,

---

[30]Aydin Corp. 1990 Annual Report.

disclosure of the impact of the venture is highly variable across firms given the absence of specific reporting requirements.

Other joint ventures result in common ownership of assets, but without a separate legal entity being formed. Each venturer recognizes its proportionate share of common assets, liabilities, revenues, and expenses. Here, again, because each venturer already reflects its share of the operations in its financial statements, neither accounting nor analysis is required to go further. (Guarantees, if any, of the debt of co-venturers must be disclosed separately in the footnotes.) Pipelines (oil and gas) and electric utility plants are common applications of this form of joint venture.

For example, Wisconsin Public Service had partial ownership of three different electric generating facilities on December 31, 1989. A proportionate share of the depreciated cost of each facility was included in Wisconsin's Utility Plant account shown on its balance sheet. The total investment was $248 million gross, or $73 million net of accumulated depreciation. The investment in the jointly owned facilities represented 18% of Wisconsin's gross plant, and 12% of net plant.[31]

Because public utilities are regulated, and because their allowed rates are based on invested assets (the "rate base"), they have an incentive to include their share of jointly owned facilities in their financial statements.[32] Unregulated companies may have an incentive to keep assets (and related liabilities) out of their financial statements (see the discussion of off-balance-sheet financing in Chapter 10).

Jointly Controlled Entities

In many cases, however, the joint venture is a separate entity, either a corporation or partnership. The entity is created by capital contributions (cash and/or operating assets) from two or more venturers and is governed by a contract. The contract will generally specify how operating, investing, and financing decisions are to be made by the venturers.

Because the joint venture is a separate legal entity, it will prepare its own financial statements that may be publicly available if it has issued debt. However, if the venture is financed with bank debt, the statements will not be public documents. The venturers will, in most cases, account for their interests in such jointly controlled entities using the equity method of accounting, reporting their proportionate share of both net income and net investment in the venture.

Use of the equity method means that the gross assets and liabilities, as well as revenues and expenses, are excluded from the financial statements of the venturers. Footnotes of the venturers will also exclude data relating to the joint venture in such areas as leases, retirement plans, and contingent obligations (including off-balance-sheet financing). (As was pointed out earlier, a specific requirement for disclosure of guarantees of indebtedness of others exists under GAAP.)

Yet the operations of the joint venture may be as much a part of the integrated operations of the parent companies as their wholly owned subsidiaries. Mead, a major

---

[31]Data obtained from 1989 Annual Report of Wisconsin Public Service.

[32]The incentive of public utilities to show larger assets is discussed in Chapter 6.

paper and paperboard manufacturer, included most of the earnings of its joint venture affiliates (primarily suppliers of raw materials and intermediate products for Mead's manufacturing process) as adjustments to cost of goods sold, in recognition of the integrated nature of these operations. In such cases, the "one-line consolidation" resulting from use of the equity method clearly understates the importance of the joint venture to the parent company. This method effectively offsets equity in income of the joint venture against the cost of goods purchased from the venture; when such offsets occur, analysts must evaluate the appropriateness of the equity method.

As the equity method includes only the net assets of the investee in the investor's balance sheet, the venture's often significant debt is excluded. In the case of Mead, proportionate consolidation depicts a significantly riskier firm; the existence of this debt may have been an important incentive to use the equity method in annual reports. Mead provided detailed information on the joint ventures in a supplementary "Financial Fact Book," which included condensed financial statements, assets, earnings history, financial structure, and contractual arrangements governing transactions between Mead and these ventures.

Alternatives to the Equity Method

Because of the inadequacies of the equity method as a means of conveying the risks associated with unconsolidated affiliates, alternative accounting methods have been developed for such ventures. These alternatives can provide better information to financial statement users whether they are used by the reporting entity or are created by the financial analyst. Two alternatives to the equity method are

- Proportionate consolidation (sometimes called pro rata consolidation).
- The expanded equity method.

These alternatives have recently gained support from the IASC. IAS 31, adopted in 1990, states that proportionate consolidation is the preferred method of accounting for jointly controlled entities. Paragraph 24 states that

> proportionate consolidation better reflects the substance and economic reality of a venturer's interest in a jointly controlled entity, that is control over the venturer's share of the future economic benefits.[33]

IAS 31, which became effective in 1992, considers the expanded equity method to be a reporting variant of proportionate consolidation, and either one is acceptable under the standard.

While use of the equity method is an allowed alternative under IASC 31, the strong endorsement of proportionate consolidation is likely to lead to greater use of the method.[34] We illustrate this method in the next section and discuss the expanded equity method and its relationship to proportionate consolidation in Appendix 11-A.

---

[33]IAS 31, Financial Reporting of Interests in Joint Ventures (1990).

[34]The Financial Accounting Standards Board has the subject of joint venture accounting on its agenda.

Proportionate Consolidation

Under proportionate consolidation, the parent company includes its share of each asset and liability account of the affiliate in the corresponding account of the parent. For example (assuming 40% ownership of the joint venture), the parent includes 40% of the cash, inventories, receivables, and so forth of the joint venture in the parent's cash, inventories, and receivables. Only stockholders' equity is unaffected as the investment in the affiliate account is eliminated against the parent's share of the affiliate's equity.

Similarly, the parent includes 40% of the revenues and of each expense category in its income statement. There would be no impact on parent company net income, as the parent's share of affiliate income is eliminated in consolidation. However, most financial statement ratios would be affected. To illustrate the proportionate consolidation method, consider the example shown in Exhibit 11-10.

Effects of Proportionate Consolidation

While both net income and equity of Petroleum Corp. are the same under proportionate consolidation as under the equity method, virtually all other numbers in the financial statements are different. As a result, most financial ratios are changed. The following are examples:

PETROLEUM CORP.
Comparison of Ratios, 1991

	Proportionate Consolidation (After eliminations)	Equity Method
Current ratio	2.87	3.00
Long-term debt to equity	0.54	0.40
Interest coverage*	4.96	6.20
Return on total capital†	0.174	0.177

*EBIT (earnings before interest and taxes)/interest expense.
†EBIT/(long-term debt + equity).

However, notice that return on equity is the same ($64/$500 = 12.8%) under both methods, as both net income and equity are unchanged.

Use of Alternatives to the Equity Method in Practice

Neither proportionate consolidation nor the expanded equity method has been widely used. In the United States it is unclear whether these methods are permitted under GAAP. Within the construction industry, however, where joint ventures are the dominant form of doing business, proportionate consolidation is frequently used.

EXHIBIT 11-10
Illustration of Proportionate Consolidation

Assume that Petroleum Corp. owns 40% of a joint venture (Supply Corp.). The investment in Supply Corp., exactly equal to 40% of Supply Corp.'s net worth, is $16 on December 31, 1990. Let us look at the operations for 1991 and the year-end 1991 balance sheets:

Income Statements, for Year Ended December 31, 1991

	Petroleum Corp.	Supply Corp.
Revenues	$1000	$ 200
Equity in earnings of Supply Corp.	4	—
Cost of goods sold	(800)	(140)
Selling, general, and administrative expenses	(80)	(26)
Interest expense	(20)	(17)
Pretax earnings	$ 104	$ 17
Income tax expense	(40)	(7)
Net income	$ 64	$ 10

Note that since Petroleum owns 40% of Supply, its equity in the 1991 earnings of Supply will be $4 (40% of $10).

Balance Sheets, at December 31, 1991

Petroleum Corp.				Supply Corp.			
Assets		**Liabilities**		**Assets**		**Liabilities**	
Cash	$100	Accounts payable	$200	Cash	$ 20	Accounts payable	$ 80
Inventory	200			Inventory	50		
Accounts receivable	300			Accounts receivable	50		
PPE	280	Long-term debt	200	PPE	180	Long-term debt	170
Investment	20	Equity	500			Equity	50
Totals	$900		$900	Totals	$300		$300

If we change Petroleum's accounting method to proportionate consolidation, the result is the following:

Petroleum Corp. Income Statements, for Year Ended December 31, 1991

	Proportionate Consolidation	Equity Method
Revenues	$1080	$1000
Equity in earnings of Supply Corp.	—	4
Cost of goods sold	(856)	(800)
Selling, general, and administrative expenses	(90)	(80)
Interest expense	(27)	(20)
Pretax earnings	$ 107	$ 104
Income tax expense	(43)	(40)
Net income	$ 64	$ 64

EXHIBIT 11-10. *(Continued)*

Petroleum Corp. Balance Sheets, at December 31, 1991

Proportionate Consolidation				Equity Method			
Cash	$ 108	Accounts payable	$ 232	Cash	$100	Accounts payable	$200
Inventory	220			Inventory	200		
Accounts receivable	320			Accounts receivable	300		
PPE	352	Long-term debt	268	PPE	280	Long-term debt	200
		Equity	500	Investment	20	Equity	500
Totals	$1000		$1000	Totals	$900		$900

Under the proportionate consolidation method, 40% of the assets and liabilities of Supply Corp. have been added to the corresponding assets and liabilities of Petroleum Corp. For example, consolidated cash equals $100 + (0.40 × $20).

Notice that the investment in Supply Corp. has been replaced by Petroleum Corp.'s proportionate share of each asset and liability account of the affiliate. In the income statement, the equity in earnings of Supply has been replaced by a proportionate share of each revenue and expense line of Supply. These changes are identical to those made for a full consolidation except that only 40% of the accounts of the affiliate have been included.

This example assumes, thus far, that there are no intercompany transactions. To the extent that a joint venture is either a supplier to or a customer of the investor company, there will be intercompany payables/receivables and intercompany sales. To complete the proportionate consolidation, we must eliminate these items from the consolidated statements. To make these eliminations, assume that

1. Petroleum Corp. purchases 30% of Supply Corp.'s output.

2. Supply Corp. has accounts receivable from Petroleum Corp. of $10 at December 31, 1991.

The consolidated revenues are, therefore, $1000 + (0.4 × $200) − (0.3 × $200) = $1020. The third item is the subtraction of the intercompany sales.

Consolidated cost of goods sold can now be computed to be $800 + (0.4 × $140) − (0.3 × $200) = $796. The third item, which represents sales from Supply to Petroleum, must also have been included in Petroleum's cost of goods sold. Whenever there are intercompany sales, we must eliminate them from the sales of the seller and the COGS of the buyer.

The second elimination, of intercompany payables, is simpler. We simply reduce the accounts receivable of Supply by $10 and, at the same time, reduce the accounts payable of Petroleum by the same amount. Consolidated accounts receivable are $300 + (0.4 × $50) − $10 = $310; accounts payable are $200 + (0.4 × $80) − $10 = $222.

The result is the following comparison of Petroleum Corp.'s income statement and balance sheet under the proportionate consolidation method with the statements prepared using the equity method.

EXHIBIT 11-10. *(Continued)*

Petroleum Corp. Income Statements, for Year Ended December 31, 1991

	Proportionate Consolidation (After eliminations)	Equity Method
Revenues	$1020	$1000
Equity in earnings of Supply Corp.	—	4
Cost of goods sold	(796)	(800)
Selling, general, and administrative expenses	(90)	(80)
Interest expense	(27)	(20)
Pretax earnings	$ 107	$ 104
Income tax expense	(43)	(40)
Net income	$ 64	$ 64

Petroleum Corp. Balance Sheet, at December 31, 1991

Proportionate Consolidation (After eliminations)				Equity Method			
Cash	$108	Accounts payable	$222	Cash	$100	Accounts payable	$200
Inventory	220			Inventory	200		
Accounts receivable	310			Accounts receivable	300		
PPE	352	Long-term debt	268	PPE	280	Long-term debt	200
		Equity	500	Investment	20	Equity	500
Totals	$990		$990	Totals	$900		$900

Morrison Knudsen, for example, uses proportionate consolidation for its construction joint ventures with respect to the income statement. As a result revenues of $157 million (nearly 10% of total corporate revenues) and costs of $136 million were included in its 1990 income statement rather than the net operating income of $21 million. On its balance sheet, however, Morrison Knudsen shows its net equity in construction joint ventures of $62 million, using the equity method rather than its share of gross assets and liabilities.

Brascan is a large Canadian conglomerate. One of its basic business principles is to own approximately half of the shares of its major affiliates. In actuality, Brascan owns less than 50% of its principal operating companies and accounts for them using the equity method of accounting. Its consolidated financial statements are shown in Exhibits 11-11, 11-12, and 11-13. Note that all Brascan's financial statements are presented in Canadian dollars.

These financial statements consolidate only a few of Brascan's affiliates. Most operations are accounted for using the equity method, and we shall refer to these as the

EXHIBIT 11-11. BRASCAN BALANCE SHEET

Consolidated Balance Sheet
Audited

December 31

millions	1990	1989
Assets		
Cash and short-term investments	$ 456.5	$ 375.1
Loans and accounts receivable	383.9	756.0
Corporate investments	4,637.3	4,526.6
Property and equipment	210.8	321.7
Other assets	29.7	17.2
	$5,718.2	$5,996.6
Liabilities		
Bank indebtedness	$ 18.1	$ 14.5
Accounts payable	47.3	56.6
Dividends and interest payable	52.7	41.1
Term debt	1,384.3	1,052.5
Deferred credits	80.7	195.5
	1,583.1	1,360.2
Shareholders' equity and minority interests		
Minority interests	1,724.2	2,169.1
Shareholders' equity	2,410.9	2,467.3
	$5,718.2	$5,996.6

Source: Brascan 1990 Annual Report.

equity method statements. The company states in its *1990 Annual Report* that proportionate consolidation financial statements:

> provide a greater awareness of the composition of Brascan's underlying assets, earnings base and overall financial strength.[35]

As a result Brascan provides a supplementary (unaudited) set of financial statements prepared using the proportionate consolidation method of accounting for its less than

[35]Brascan 1990 Annual Report.

EXHIBIT 11-12. BRASCAN STATEMENT OF INCOME

Consolidated Statement of Income
Audited

Years ended December 31

millions	1990	1989
Income before unallocated expenses		
Natural resources	$ 89.9	$ 252.0
Consumer and industrial products	87.0	80.4
Financial services	31.3	86.7
Other operations	37.9	34.5
Investment and other	122.6	164.3
	368.7	617.9
Unallocated expenses		
Interest	119.5	87.7
Corporate expenses	5.1	4.9
Depreciation and depletion	46.7	74.1
Income and resource taxes	1.7	1.4
Minority interests	115.4	169.0
	288.4	337.1
Net income for year	$ 80.3	$ 280.8
Earnings per class A common share	$ 0.40	$ 2.90

Source: Brascan 1990 Annual Report.

50%-owned affiliates, principally Noranda (minerals, energy, and forest products), John Labatt (brewing and foods), and Trilon (financial services). These statements are shown in Exhibits 11-14, 11-15, and 11-16.

Start by comparing the balance sheets (Exhibits 11-11 and 11-14). The equity method balance sheet is relatively uninformative as investments constitute 81% of total assets. This balance sheet is similar to parent company–only statements sometimes presented as supplementary data by companies whose primary statements are fully

EXHIBIT 11-13. BRASCAN STATEMENT OF CHANGES
IN FINANCIAL POSITION

Consolidated Statement of Changes in Financial Position
Audited

Years ended December 31

millions	1990	1989
Provided from operations	$ 225.2	$ 238.8
Provided from financing		
Borrowings	329.9	599.0
Proceeds on disposal of Scott Paper warrants	—	238.1
Minority interests	(375.7)	408.4
Shares redeemed	(11.5)	(9.3)
	(57.3)	1,236.2
Used for investing		
Loans and accounts receivable	(361.1)	653.5
Corporate investments	143.1	881.3
Proceeds on disposal of petroleum assets	—	(402.2)
Plant and equipment	9.3	46.9
Other	10.5	(13.6)
	(198.2)	1,165.9
Dividends		
Corporate	132.6	129.4
Minority interests	152.1	142.5
	284.7	271.9
Cash and short-term investments		
Increase	81.4	37.2
Balance		
Beginning of year	375.1	337.9
End of year	$ 456.5	$ 375.1

Consolidated Statement of Retained Earnings
Audited

Years ended December 31

millions	1990	1989
Balance, beginning of year	$1,169.9	$1,018.5
Net income for year	80.3	280.8
	1,250.2	1,299.3
Dividends declared		
Preferred	48.2	46.9
Class A common	84.4	82.5
	132.6	129.4
Balance, end of year	$1,117.6	$1,169.9

Source: Brascan 1990 Annual Report.

EXHIBIT 11-14. BRASCAN PROPORTIONAL CONSOLIDATED BALANCE SHEET (UNAUDITED)

Proportional Consolidated Balance Sheet
Unaudited

December 31

millions	1990	1989
Assets		
Cash and securities	$ 7,072	$ 7,702
Loans and other receivables	16,760	16,359
Inventories	1,043	1,106
	24,875	25,167
Corporate investments	1,804	1,709
Property and equipment	5,924	5,445
Other assets	930	832
	$33,533	$33,153
Liabilities		
Savings deposits	$18,564	$18,179
Accounts payable	1,686	1,619
Term debt	5,507	4,741
	25,757	24,539
Deferred credits	848	1,054
Shareholders' equity and minority interests		
Minority shareholders' interests	4,517	5,093
Brascan shareholders' equity	2,411	2,467
	$33,533	$33,153

Source: Brascan 1990 Annual Report.

EXHIBIT 11-15. BRASCAN PROPORTIONAL CONSOLIDATED STATEMENT OF INCOME (UNAUDITED)

Proportional Consolidated Statement of Income
Unaudited

Years ended December 31

millions	1990	1989
Gross revenues	$10,275	$ 9,622
Cost of products sold	5,020	4,829
Operating income	5,255	4,793
Selling and other expenses	1,656	1,491
Interest expense	2,490	1,812
Depreciation and depletion	513	422
Income and other taxes	296	359
Minority interests	220	428
	5,175	4,512
Net income for year	$ 80	$ 281
Earnings per class A common share	$ 0.40	$ 2.90

Source: Brascan 1990 Annual Report.

consolidated. The equity method balance sheet for Brascan does, however, provide some insight into the company's financial structure:

1. The large minority interest indicates that those subsidiaries that are consolidated are not wholly owned.
2. Brascan has a substantial debt burden, but also has significant cash and short-tern investments.

These circumstances suggest that Brascan's ability to service debt and pay dividends to shareholders may depend on its ability to obtain dividends from its affiliates or sell investments. As it generally owns less than half of the shares of its investees, dividend payments flow largely to outside shareholders. We will return to this issue later.

The proportionate consolidation balance sheet is, in some respects, more informative. We can see the importance of Brascan's financial affiliates whose large asset categories (cash and securities, and loans and other receivables) and liability for savings

EXHIBIT 11-16. BRASCAN PROPORTIONAL CONSOLIDATED STATEMENT OF CHANGES IN FINANCIAL POSITION (UNAUDITED)

Proportional Consolidated Statement of Changes in Financial Position
Unaudited

Years ended December 31

millions	1990	1989
Operations	$ 650	$ 1,061
Financing		
Savings deposits	385	6,263
Minority interest	(372)	1,071
Term debt	766	2,151
Shares redeemed	(4)	(9)
	775	9,476
Investing		
Loans and other receivables	401	6,038
Property and equipment	1,235	1,262
Corporate investments	15	262
Inventories	(56)	160
Other	(100)	154
	1,495	7,876
Dividends		
Corporate	136	129
Minority interest	424	407
	560	536
Cash and securities		
Increase (decrease)	(630)	2,125
Beginning of year	7,702	5,577
End of year	$ 7,072	$ 7,702

Source: Brascan 1990 Annual Report.

deposits dominate the balance sheet. We also get a different view of Brascan's financial structure, with debt and minority interest relatively larger:

BRASCAN
Capital Structure, December 31, 1990
(in $CAN millions)

	Equity Method		Proportionate	
	Amount	As a % Total	Amount	As a % Total
Debt	$1402	25%	$ 5507	44%
Minority interest	1724	31	4517	36
Brascan common equity	2411	44	2411	20
Total capital	$5537	100%	$12435	100%

This analysis indicates that the leverage of the group is somewhat greater than indicated by the equity method statements. Brascan shareholders have $CAN 4 of outside capital for each dollar of shareholders' equity. While this leverage can result in above-average returns, it also increases risk. Most if not all of that capital ranks prior to Brascan shareholders in claims against both income and assets. Returns must "trickle up" the chain of holding companies before they can be paid out to Brascan shareholders.

Turn now to the income statements, shown in Exhibits 11-12 and 11-15. Here again the equity method statement has limited utility. Income is shown on a one-line basis, after all expenses except for those of the small consolidated entities. The proportional income statement, with gross revenues exceeding $CAN 10 billion, indicates the size of the group. Remember that revenues shown include only Brascan's proportionate share of group revenues. Gross revenues (disclosed elsewhere in the annual report) exceed $CAN 21 billion.

The proportionate income statement also provides some data regarding the composition of expenses. It also, once again, indicates the leverage inherent in Brascan's corporate structure:

BRASCAN
Net Income, For Year Ended December 31, 1990
(in $CAN millions)

	Equity Method	Proportionate
Earnings before interest, income taxes, and minority interests	$ 317	$ 3086
Less: Interest	(120)	(2490)
Income tax	(2)	(296)
Minority interest	(115)	(220)
Equals: Net income	$ 80	80

This analysis indicates that only 2.5% ($Can 80 Million/$Can 3086 Million) of the more than $Can 3 billion of earnings before interest, income taxes, and minority interest generated by the group in 1990 accrued to the benefit of Brascan stockholders. Again this indicates the high degree of leverage inherent in Brascan's financial structure.

Turning to the statements of cash flow (Exhibits 11-13 and 11-16), we again see a contrast. The equity method statement shows operating cash flow of $CAN 225.2 million in 1990, a slight reduction from the 1989 level. New borrowings of $CAN 329.9 million were more than offset by funds used to reduce minority interests ($CAN 375.7 million) resulting in a financing outflow of $CAN 57.3 million. A net investing inflow of $CAN 198.2 million (largely due to collection of receivables) was more than offset by dividends paid. The net result was an increase in cash of $CAN 81.4 million.

The proportionate cash flow statement shows an entirely different picture. While operating cash flow was much higher ($CAN 650 million) than the equity method figure, there was a decline of 39% from the 1989 level. Financing provided $CAN 775 million (increase in debt and savings deposits less the reduction in minority interest). $CAN 1495 million was needed for new investment (mainly property) and $CAN 560 million was paid in dividends. The net result was a cash decrease of $CAN 630 million.

Brascan's presentation of supplementary financial statements using the proportionate consolidation method does, in fact, provide data that are useful for financial analysis. By providing a broader set of data regarding the company's activities, it helps us to understand better the risks and opportunities. However, it is worth noting that there would be some loss of information if the proportionate consolidation statements were provided in place of the consolidated statements. Having both sets allows us to view the company from two different perspectives and results in a richer set of financial data.

ANALYSIS OF SEGMENT DATA

The analysis of companies with more than one line of business has inherent difficulties as compared with the analysis of companies engaged in a single business. The aggregation of financial data for businesses with differing financial structures, risk attributes, and indicators of performance must necessarily obscure the characteristics of each segment. The rise of the conglomerate corporation in the 1960s aggravated the problem as multidivisional corporations proliferated.

With strong encouragement from the financial analyst community, the Financial Accounting Standards Board placed segment reporting on its agenda soon after it was established in 1973. The result was SFAS 14, Financial Reporting for Segments of a Business Enterprise. The stated goal of the standard is to

> assist financial statements users in analyzing and understanding the enterprise's financial statements by permitting better assessment of the enterprise's past performance and future prospects.[36]

---

[36]SFAS 14, Financial Reporting for Segments of a Business Enterprise (1974), Para. 5.

The key to segment disclosure is defining the segments of the enterprise. The FASB realized that a precise definition could not be written into a standard so SFAS 14 provides for management judgment. Profit centers established for internal management and control purposes are the logical starting point for determining reportable segments. The FASB also suggested that the following factors be considered:

- Product similarity
- Similarity of production process
- Similarity of markets or marketing methods

For a segment to be reportable, it must account for at least 10% of *any one* of the following:

- Total revenues (before elimination of intersegment sales)
- Combined operating profit (of profitable segments), or its operating loss must exceed 10% of the combined operating loss of segments with losses
- Combined identifiable assets of all segments

For each reportable segment, the following must be disclosed:

- Sales to unaffiliated customers and intersegment sales
- Operating profit or some other measure of profitability; any unusual income component or any impact of an accounting change must be disclosed as well
- Identifiable assets
- Depreciation, depletion, and amortization expense
- Capital expenditures

Geographic Segment Reporting

For companies operating in more than one country, data on foreign operations must also be disclosed, when significant. For geographic segment reporting, the significance test is slightly different. A reportable geographic segment must exceed 10% of *either*

- Sales to unaffiliated customers as compared to consolidated revenues.
- Identifiable assets as compared to consolidated total assets.

             hic areas can be grouped into segments using management judgment. As in   s of business, precise definition proved to be impossible. For each   hic segment, the company must report

           gment sales shown separately.
         r some other measure of profitability.

In addition, SFAS 14 requires disclosure of

- Export sales from domestic operations, if greater than 10% of consolidated sales.
- Sales to major customers, for any customer accounting for more than 10% of sales. Disclosure is also required if 10% of sales comes from domestic government agencies as a group or foreign governments as a group. Note that the name of the major customer need not be disclosed, only the amount of the sales.

Analysis of Segment Data: Dow Chemical

Exhibit 11-17 contains the segment disclosures of Dow Chemical from its *1990 Annual Report*. Dow breaks its operations into four segments:

1. Chemicals and Performance Products (mainly raw materials)
2. Plastic Products
3. Hydrocarbons and Energy (petroleum-based raw materials)
4. Consumer Specialties (includes agricultural and health care)

For simplicity we will refer to these segments as chemicals, plastics, hydrocarbon, and consumer, respectively.

In compliance with SFAS 14, Dow discloses sales to unaffiliated customers, intersegment sales, operating income, identifiable assets, depreciation, and capital expenditures for each segment for each year.

Dow's segments are highly integrated, as suggested by the large intersegment transfers, especially from the hydrocarbon segment, which supplies the chemicals segment, which, in turn, supplies the plastics segment. Integration tends to protect Dow against shortages. On the other hand, the pricing of intersegment transfers affects the profitability of each segment, which might be different if all inputs were purchased externally.

Second, there are major differences in the sales trends among the four segments. Sales growth has been fastest for the consumer segment (67% growth, 1988–1990); chemicals sales have declined by 2% over the same time period. However, it is not cle that the consumer segment has performed better than the others; that comparis more analysis.

Sales growth is the result of four factors:

1. Unit growth
2. Price changes
3. Exchange rate changes
4. Acquisitions and divestitures

Disclosures in Dow's Management some information that can be used to analyz 7% in the chemicals segment.

EXHIBIT 11-17. DOW CHEMICAL COMPANY AND SUBSIDIARIES
Segment Data, 1990 (in $ millions, except per share data)

In millions, except for share amounts

R Industry Segments and Geographic Areas

The Company conducts its worldwide operations through separate geographic area organizations which represent major markets or combinations of related markets. Transfers between areas are valued at cost plus a markup.

Aggregation of products is generally made on the basis of process technology, end-use markets and channels of distribution. The Chemicals and Performance Products and Hydrocarbon and Energy segments are described in the Corporate Profile section on page 22. The Plastic Products segment, also described in the same section, is comprised of thermoplastics, thermosets and fabricated products. Consumer Specialties include agricultural chemicals, pharmaceuticals, and food protection, cleaning and personal care products.

The Unallocated segment includes activities of the insurance companies, the finance operations, and unallocated overhead cost variances.

Transfers between industry segments are generally valued at standard cost.

	Chemicals & Perform.	Plastic Prods.	H&E	Consumer Specialties	Unallocated	Corporate and Elim.	Consolidated
Industry Segment Results							
1990							
Sales to unaffiliated customers	$5,088	$7,392	$2,210	$5,053	$ 30		$19,773
Intersegment transfers	816	274	2,440	1	5	$(3,536)	—
Operating income	779	990	156	832	61		2,818
Identifiable assets	4,597	5,970	3,037	6,556	860	2,933	23,953
Depreciation	434	350	212	159	15		1,170
Capital expenditures	637	746	516	220			2,119
1989							
Sales to unaffiliated customers	$5,407	$6,994	$1,778	$3,407	$ 14		$17,600
Intersegment transfers	729	224	2,020	2	8	$(2,983)	—
Operating income	1,718	1,586	239	462	5		4,010
Identifiable assets	3,918	5,105	3,021	6,602	729	2,633	22,008
Depreciation	337	302	231	108	12		990
Capital expenditures	458	707	416	175			1,756
1988							
Sales to unaffiliated customers	$5,190	$6,938	$1,502	$3,029	$ 23		$16,682
Intersegment transfers	469	258	1,886	27	10	$(2,650)	—
Operating income (loss)	1,529	1,886	220	540	(126)		4,049
Identifiable assets	3,822	4,478	2,326	2,759	679	2,009	16,073
Depreciation	327	254	240	109	3		933
Capital expenditures	349	471	265	179			1,264

Geographic Area Results							
1990							
Sales to unaffiliated customers		$ 9,494		$6,278	$4,001		$19,773
Transfers between areas		1,344		418	361	$(2,123)	—
Operating income		1,622		692	504		2,818
Identifiable assets		13,074		6,654	4,225		23,953
Gross plant properties		10,037		6,108	3,004		19,149
Capital expenditures		1,063		817	239		2,119

EXHIBIT 11-17. *(Continued)*

In millions, except for share amounts	United States	Europe	Rest of World	Corporate Elimination	Consoli- dated
1989					
Sales to unaffiliated customers	$8,084	$5,523	$3,993		$17,600
Transfers between areas	1,157	331	194	$(1,682)	—
Operating income	1,876	1,160	974		4,010
Identifiable assets	12,223	5,467	4,318		22,008
Gross plant properties	9,162	4,733	2,805		16,700
Capital expenditures	955	562	239		1,756
1988					
Sales to unaffiliated customers	$7,497	$5,147	$4,038		$16,682
Transfers between areas	1,109	323	381	$(1,813)	—
Operating income	1,651	1,283	1,115		4,049
Identifiable assets	7,557	4,229	4,287		16,073
Gross plant properties	8,083	3,970	2,645		14,698
Capital expenditures	724	345	195		1,264

Source: Dow Chemical 1990 Annual Report

The large sales gain in the consumer segment is due to the merger of Dow's pharmaceutical operations with Marion Labs, which became effective in December 1989. As Dow's ownership exceeds 50%, the sales are fully consolidated, increasing segment sales as compared with those prior to the acquisition.

Dow's operating income fell sharply in 1990 as operating income declined in every segment except consumer. Again the MD&A provides further explanation. Having the operating results of each segment is, however, helpful in breaking down corporate performance into more easily understandable components.

The trend in identifiable assets also varies from segment to segment. As the disclosure relates to assets only (without any data on liabilities), the usefulness is limited to information about trends in the allocation of corporate resources to different segments.

Once again, the consumer segment shows the largest growth in assets, with most of the increase taking place in 1989. The merger with Marion became effective in December 1989, so that the asset growth occurs in 1989 even though the revenue growth did not take place until 1990. Assets grew in the other segments as well. Some of the growth apparently reflects heavy capital spending in 1989 and 1990. Asset growth can also be affected by changes in foreign currency exchange rates (see Chapter 13).

The last two disclosures are of depreciation and capital spending. Capital spending exceeds depreciation expense for each segment in each year even though Dow uses declining-balance depreciation, an accelerated method (see Chapter 6). This suggests that Dow is expanding its operations rather than just replacing outdated capacity. Given the effects of inflation, the low level of capital spending relative to depreciation in the chemicals segment suggests that real capital spending may be very low. In the case of plastics, capital spending is twice depreciation, suggesting large increases in capacity.

Segment data can also be used to develop inferences about segment profitability. The following ratios have been computed from the segment data:

DOW CHEMICAL
Segment Profitability, 1990

Ratio	Chemicals	Plastics	Hydrocarbon	Consumer
Operating income/Sales	0.153	0.134	0.070	0.165
Operating income/Total sales	0.132	0.129	0.034	0.165
Return on assets	0.183	0.179	0.052	0.126

The first ratio is computed by dividing operating income by sales to unaffiliated customers, a measure of profit margin. The second ratio uses total sales, including intersegment sales, in the denominator. The latter ratio is a better indicator, especially for the hydrocarbon segment with its large intersegment sales. Presumably the intersegment sales are profitable; excluding them would overstate the segment profitability.

The third ratio is return on average assets, computed by dividing operating income by average identifiable assets. This is the only available return-on-investment ratio by segment.

The hydrocarbon segment has the lowest profitability by any of these measures. However, limitations in segment data make it difficult to draw firm conclusions about segment performance.

One limitation is the lack of information on liabilities. Funded debt is, however, not the issue. As operating income is before interest expense, return on total capital by segment would be comparable. The issue is noninterest-bearing liabilities such as payables and accruals. These liabilities reduce the net investment and increase the percentage return.

A second limitation is the computation of segment profit. As already noted, profitability may be affected by intersegment pricing. There may also have been allocation of corporate overhead, affecting segment profitability.

There is a third, nonquantitative issue that relates to intersegment sales. The ability to provide the inputs for one segment from the output of another has operational advantages that may not show up in operating profit in any particular year.

Uses of Segment Data

These limitations do not mean that segment data are useless, far from it. They do mean that segment data must be used with some care rather than in a simplistic manner.

The best use of segment data is for examination of trends. Presumably, the method of computing segment profitability is consistent from year to year, as is the ratio of liabilities to assets. Therefore, disclosed levels of profitability may not be useful,[37] but the information about trends in profitability is useful and may be more reliable. This is especially true when segment data are presented on a quarterly basis.

Segment trends can, and should, be compared to trends in the sales and operating income of companies in similar businesses and similar segments of multidivisional companies. Again, differences in levels are less reliable indicators than trends. It is also

---

[37]Empirical results discussed later in the chapter indicate that segment data are most beneficial in forecasting sales. The aggregated sales forecast can then be used to forecast consolidated earnings.

important to adjust for any differences in accounting methods (especially for inventories) and for any unusual items included in reported earnings. Many companies report the allocation of unusual items to individual segments. For example, see Deere's segment disclosures in Exhibit 1B-2.

Perhaps most important, segment data enable the analyst to obtain a better understanding of a company's operations. Segment disclosures can be used to ask questions that will illuminate better the determinants of sales growth and profitability. This understanding can then be applied to expected future trends, resulting in better estimates of sales and earnings.

The second part of Dow's segment disclosures concerns geographic areas. Dow breaks its operations into three segments: United States, Europe, and rest of world (ROW), with non–U.S. operations accounting for more than half of corporate sales. Because geographic data include operations from many segments, its usefulness may be more limited. There are two principal ways in which geographic results can aid the analyst.

One use of geographic data is to look for trends. As in the case of industry segments, trends that are submerged in the consolidated results may surface from segment breakouts. For example, the decline in Dow's operating income in 1990 occurred primarily outside the United States. Understanding why that occurred should, when combined with economic projections regarding different economies, improve projections of future operating results.

Second, geographic segment data can be used to highlight the effects of changes in exchange rates. While this is more difficult when geographic segments are broadly defined as in the case of Dow, it may still be possible. Chapter 13 contains a detailed discussion of how exchange rates affect reported income statement and balance sheet accounts; we defer to that chapter further analysis of geographic segment data.

Segment Reporting in Practice

In practice, the segment reporting mandated by SFAS 14 has worked reasonably well. Management judgment, auditor involvement, and oversight from the SEC have produced disclosures that generally serve the desired objective.

From an analytic perspective, each segment should contain operations with similar economic risk characteristics. For example, the production of crude oil differs from the refining and marketing of the oil into consumer and industrial products, even though the two activities are frequently integrated within one enterprise. Similarly, life insurance has different economic characteristics from auto insurance, even though the customer base may be identical.

Most companies provide segment disclosures that meet the spirit as well as the letter of SFAS 14. This is especially true of larger companies that devote considerable management time and resources to the "care and feeding of analysts." Such companies are generally responsive to analyst concerns regarding the usefulness of segment data.

Using Segment Data to Estimate Consolidated Earnings and Risk

Segment data can be useful in assessing both the expected return (profitability) and risk characteristics of a consolidated firm. After elimination of intercompany transactions, the expected earnings of a consolidated firm is a summation of the expected earnings of the individual segments. Similarly, the overall risk of the consolidated entity is a weighted average of the risk of the individual segments.

A number of studies have compared the forecasting accuracy of models that predict consolidated earnings directly with those that predict the individual segment earnings first and then combine the individual segments to get a consolidated forecast. The earliest of these studies, Kinney (1971), found that such segment-based forecasts did improve forecasting ability relative to consolidated-based forecasts.

Although intuitively one would expect to be able to improve forecasting accuracy by using segment data to forecast consolidated earnings, in practice the results depend on the interrelationships among the various segments and on the forecasting models used. Hopwood, Newbold, and Silhan (1982) note that no gains in forecasting ability will be realized from the use of segment data if

1. The time series models of the component segments are identical.
2. None of the component series leads or lags the consolidated series.

If the various industries that make up the segments are influenced by similar factors (e.g., they tend to move together during the business cycle), then a forecast based on consolidated data should be just as good as a forecast based on segment data. The more dissimilar the series or the greater the lag effects between the various segments, the greater the benefits of forecasting with segment data. Thus the degree of improvement in forecasting ability will depend on the nature of the segments in the consolidated firm.

However, even under the best of conditions (disparate segments), knowledge of the parameters of the forecasting model is needed. As segment-based models require the estimation of more parameters (a set for each segment) than consolidated-based models do, measurement error may affect the results. To the extent that there is measurement error in estimating the parameters, the benefits of segment data are diluted.

Chapter 15 discusses time series models used to forecast accounting earnings. Many are based (extrapolative models) on the previous time series history of the variables being predicted. Thus future earnings are forecast as a function of past earnings. As will be seen, there has been very little success in distinguishing firm-specific models for this class of models. That is, a firm-specific model does not forecast any better than does a general *uniform* model applied to all firms. Measurement error has been given as one of the reasons for this finding. Thus, given the first condition specified by Hopwood and coworkers, for extrapolative models, it is unlikely that forecasting ability would be improved using segment data.[38]

Improvement would be more likely for models that exploit the differences between segments. The Collins (1976) study is noteworthy in this respect as it combined firm-specific and industrywide data in generating sales and earnings forecasts. The following procedure was used:

---

[38]This is consistent with Silhan (1982). Silhan simulated "mergers" of existing companies and tested (using extrapolative models) whether the individual series or the aggregated series better forecast the aggregated series. His results indicated no difference between the two approaches.

1. The *U.S. Industrial Outlook* provides estimates of the increases in shipments (sales) expected for the following year on an industrial sector basis. The percentage increase was obtained for each industrial sector corresponding to the individual segments of the consolidated firm.

2. Current year sales for each segment were multiplied by the appropriate expected percentage increase obtained in step 1. The segment sales forecasts were then aggregated to obtain a segment-based consolidated sales forecast (SBCSF).

3. A segment-based consolidated earnings forecast (SBCEF) was obtained by applying the current year's profit margin to the sales forecast obtained in step 2.

These segment-based forecasts were then compared to seven consolidated-based earnings and sales forecasts (CBCEF and CBCSF) generated purely on the basis of consolidated sales and earnings. These latter forecasts were generated by the use of six extrapolative models and by the use of a consolidated-based model that mirrored the procedure used for the segment-based data. The previous year's consolidated sales (earnings) was forecast by multiplying the current year's sales (earnings) by the expected increase in overall GNP.

The segment-based earnings forecasts had the lowest prediction errors. Two variations were followed in generating the segment-based earnings. The first applied the individual segment profit margin to the individual sales forecasts and then summed the earnings forecasts. The second aggregated the individual segment sales forecasts and then applied the consolidated profit margin to the aggregated sales forecast to obtain the consolidated earnings forecast. Both variations yielded similar results. This suggests that although segment-based data improved earnings predictability, the improvement was due mainly to the "better" sales forecast, and there was little marginal benefit in segment data beyond that of sales.

For sales forecasts the six extrapolative models had the highest prediction errors. The gross national product (GNP)–based consolidated sales forecast did as well as the sales forecasts using segment data. Given this result for sales, one wonders how an earnings forecast using the consolidated profit margin times the consolidated-based sales forecast would have fared. Unfortunately, Collins did not provide this information. This calls into question the conclusion that time series forecasts using segment-based data can aid in the prediction of earnings or sales.

Other evidence that segment data can be used to improve forecasting ability is provided implicitly by Baldwin (1984). Baldwin compared analyst forecast accuracy before and after the disclosure of segment-based data that was first required in 1971. Three groups were compared:

1. Multisegment firms that had previously not provided segment data

2. Multisegment firms that had previously (voluntarily) provided segment data

3. Single-segment firms that continued to report only on a consolidated basis

Forecast accuracy improved for all three groups. However, the most significant improvement was for those firms that had previously not provided segment data and were now providing it. The results indicate that analysts were able to use the segment data to improve their forecasting ability. Similarly, Swaminathan (1991) noted a reduction in the dispersion of analysts' forecasts.

In addition to earnings forecasts, segment information should also be used in assessing a firm's risk. A firm's overall market beta is the weighted average of the beta of the individual segments. These, in turn, are a function of the industries in which they operate. Knowledge of the degree of concentration in each segment should provide information as to the relative risk class or beta of the overall firm.[39]

Collins and Simonds (1979) show that when segment data were first provided in 1971, there was a significant downward shift in betas of firms[40] reporting segment data for the first time. These results should be viewed in the context of Swaminathan's finding of a reduction in the dispersion of analysts' forecasts, and Cragg and Malkiel's (1982) study showing that firms' overall risk levels are highly correlated with the dispersion of analysts' forecasts.

While empirical evidence on the usefulness of segment data for forecasting purposes is mixed, analyst forecasts in practice are made on a segmented basis. Particularly in the case of firms operating in different industries, sales and earnings forecasts are based on a segment-by-segment analysis. Segment data provide information regarding the source of revenue and earnings growth and indications of the future direction of the firm.

U.S. GAAP COMPARED TO MAJOR FOREIGN COUNTRIES

Proportionate Consolidation

This method may be used for unincorporated joint ventures in the United Kingdom and is also allowed in Canada. German rules specify that it may be used for jointly managed enterprises, whereas it *must* be used for jointly controlled enterprises in France.

Segment Reporting

France, Germany, and the Netherlands require segment data by sector and market. Firms in the United Kingdom provide sales and pretax profit by location (geographic segment) and by industry. Better disclosure has been available in the United Kingdom primarily due to listing requirements of the International Stock Exchange in London. A recent Accounting Standards Board (U.K.) exposure draft has proposed disclosures of sales, pretax profits, and capital employed.

An important difference between SFAS 14 requirements in the United States and the IASC and U.K. requirements stems from the U.S. focus on aggregate assets in contrast to the IASC and U.K. rules based on net operating assets. However, rules defining segments are vague and inconsistently applied in all jurisdictions.

---

[39]In a related study of insurance companies, Foster (1975) found that the market discriminated between them on the basis of the performance of their three primary subearnings series: underwriting results, investment results, and capital gains results.

[40]Horwitz and Kolodny (1977) did not find any beta shifts. However, Collins and Simonds (1979) note a number of problems with their methodology.

Chapter 11

Problems

1. [Comparison of cost and equity methods; 1988 CFA adapted] The Burry Corporation acquired 19% of the Bowman Company for $10 million on January 1, 1990. The Bowman Company's securities are not publicly traded. On January 1, 1991 the Burry Corporation purchased an additional 1% share in the Bowman Company for $500,000.

For the years ended December 31, 1990, and December 31, 1991, Bowman reported earnings and paid dividends as follows:

	Net Income (Loss)	Dividends Paid
1990	$ (600,000)	$ 800,000
1991	2,000,000	1,000,000

A. Under a strict reading of U.S. GAAP, what method of accounting should Burry use for Bowman in 1990? 1991?

B. Based on the accounting choices made in part A, how would the Burry Company's financial statements be affected by the Bowman Company's operations in 1990 and 1991?

C. Repeat part B assuming that Burry used the cost method in both 1990 and 1991.

D. Repeat part B assuming that Burry used the equity method in both 1990 and 1991.

E. Which of the three answers (parts B, C, or D) provides the most useful information in Burry's financial statements regarding the investment in Bowman?

2. [Marketable securities: realized gains/losses and mark to market returns] During 1991, Korbi Corporation sold all its shares of Nachum, Inc., reporting a realized capital gain of $900. The Nachum shares had been carried as part of current marketable securities. The other marketable securities in the company's portfolio did not experience any price changes during the year. There were no other purchases or sales of marketable securities during the year.

A. Assuming that the company sold the stock for $4000, determine the purchase price of the Nachum stock if:

(i) The valuation allowance had *increased* by $700 during 1991.

(ii) The valuation allowance had *decreased* by $700 during 1991.

B. Calculate the mark to market returns for 1991 under each of the scenarios in part A. State any assumptions required to calculate these returns.

3. [Marketable securities: current versus noncurrent, equity and mark to market returns; 1992 CFA adapted] Bart Company owns the following marketable securities on December 31, 1991:

Firm	No. Shares Owned by Bart	Ownership Held by Bart	Bart's Original Cost per Share	Market Value 12/31/91	Market Value 12/31/90	Annual Dividend	Total 1991 Earnings
W	200,000	25%	$10.00	$ 9.00	$12.00	$0.085	$200,000
X	100,000	15	50.00	49.00	46.00	0.10	100,000
Y	800,000	40	35.00	32.00	30.00	0.09	900,000
Z	150,000	10	25.00	30.00	27.00	0.00	100,000

Investee Data (per share except total 1991 earnings)

The investment in firm Z is classified by management as current, while the investments in firms W, X, and Y are noncurrent.

A. Compute the following income statement effects of Bart's investment in marketable securities for 1991:

(i) Realized gains/losses

(ii) Unrealized gains/losses

(iii) Dividend income

(iv) Equity in income of affiliates

B. Calculate any valuation allowances required in Bart's stockholders' equity at December 31, 1990, and 1991.

C. Calculate Bart's total investment return (mark to market basis) on each investment for 1991.

4. [Marketable securities: comparison of cost, equity method, and consolidation; 1989 CFA adapted]

The following data are derived from the annual report of San Francisco Company, a manufacturer of cardboard boxes:

	19X6	19X7	19X8
Sales	$25,000	$30,000	$35,000
Net income	2,000	2,200	2,500
Dividends paid	1,000	1,200	1,500
Book value per share (year end)	$ 11.00	$ 12.00	$ 13.00

San Francisco had 1000 common shares outstanding during the entire period.
There is no public market for San Francisco shares.

Potter Company, a manufacturer of glassware, made the following acquisitions of San Francisco common shares:

January 1, 19X6	10 shares at $10 per share
January 1, 19X7	290 shares at $11 per share, increasing ownership to 300 shares
January 1, 19X8	700 shares at $15 per share, resulting in 100% ownership of San Francisco

In answering the following questions, ignore income tax effects and the effect of lost income on funds used to make these investments.

A. Calculate the effect of these investments on Potter's reported sales, net income and cash flow for *each* of the years 19X6 and 19X7.

B. Calculate the carrying value of Potter's investment in San Francisco as of December 31, 19X6, and December 31, 19X7.

C. Briefly discuss how Potter would account for its investment in San Francisco during 19X8. State the additional information needed to calculate the impact of the acquisition on Potter's financial statements for 19X8.

Problems 5, 6, and 7 are extensions of the Helmerich & Payne (HP) example presented in the chapter. Exhibit 11-P1 contains information about HP's marketable securities investments taken from its 10-K Schedule I. The company's 1991 and 1992 income statements and information from relevant footnotes are also provided.

5. [Marketable securities: assessing investment performance]

A. HP carries its investments in marketable securities as noncurrent assets. For 1991 and 1992, compute HP's reported income, assuming that it had classified these marketable securities as current assets.

B. HP's short-term investments are primarily debt instruments. Would you expect the cost and market values of these investments to differ considerably?

C. Disaggregate HP's reported income for 1991 and 1992 into the following components:

    (i) Income from operations

    (ii) Income from affiliates carried on equity basis

    (iii) Income from short-term investments and other marketable securities

D. Calculate the reported return on assets (ROA) for each component of income calculated in part C (for each year) as well as HP's overall ROA.

E. Discuss the usefulness of the results of parts C and D in explaining HP's operating results for the two years.

F. For the investments HP carries at cost or lower of cost or market (LOCM), calculate each of the following for 1991 and 1992:

    (i) Dividends and interest earned

    (ii) Realized gains and losses

    (iii) Unrealized gains and losses

EXHIBIT 11P-1. HELMERICH & PAYNE
Financial Statements, Years ended September 30, 1990–1992 (in $ thousands)

Condensed Balance Sheet

	1990	1991	1992
Short-term investments*	$ 33,798	$ 28,527	$ 13,128
Other current assets	155,215	113,648	120,000
Current assets	$189,013	$142,175	$133,128
Marketable securities	111,222	96,471	87,780
Property, plant, and equipment (net)	282,692	336,522	364,596
Total assets	$582,927	$575,168	$585,504
Current liabilities	$ 53,920	$ 33,963	$ 35,881
Noncurrent liabilities	49,522	50,072	56,337
Stockholders' equity	479,485	491,133	493,286
Total liabilities and stockholders' equity	$582,927	$575,168	$585,504

*Based on notes to financial statements, short-term investments consist of various interest-bearing instruments as well as marketable securities. For 1990, we have reclassified marketable securities that were transferred from current to noncurrent as noncurrent for purposes of comparability.

Condensed Income Statement

	1991	1992
Sales and other operating revenues	$190,425	$230,498
Income from investments	23,521	9,202
	$213,946	$239,700
Operating costs	178,505	214,993
Interest expense	380	632
	$178,885	$215,625
Income before taxes and equity in loss of affiliates	35,061	24,075
Income tax	12,280	8,641
	$ 22,781	$ 15,434
Equity in loss of affiliates (net of taxes)	1,540	4,585
Net income	$ 21,241	$ 10,849

EXHIBIT 11P-1. *(Continued)*

Schedule of Marketable Securities

	1990			1991			1992		
	No. of Shares	Carrying Cost	Market Value	No. of Shares	Carrying Cost	Market Value	No. of Shares	Carrying Cost	Market Value
Equity Basis									
Atwood Oceanic	1,600,000	$26,341	$ 29,800	1,600,000	$24,677	$ 14,400	1,600,000	$19,720	$ 15,200
Baruch-Foster	765,677	3,701	4,977	—	—	—	—	—	—
		$30,042	$ 34,777		$24,677	$ 14,400		$19,720	$ 15,200
LOCM Portfolio									
Banks of Midamerica	903,037	13,130	7,789	903,037	13,130	11,288	—	—	—
Liberty Bancorp	—	—	—	—	—	—	700,000	10,178	18,725
Oneok	—	—	—	293,200	3,585	4,105	230,000	2,812	3,996
Oryx Energy	1,130,892	11,466	47,295	811,124	7,848	26,970	756,124	7,271	18,525
Phillips Petroleum	200,000	4,809	5,150	300,000	7,470	7,875	300,000	7,470	8,250
Schlumberger	740,000	23,511	45,048	740,000	23,511	49,950	740,000	23,511	50,043
Sun Company	1,226,932	14,717	34,930	907,164	10,637	28,689	907,164	10,637	22,112
Weyerhauser	220,000	4,893	4,400	—	—	—	—	—	—
Other		8,654	9,392		5,613	6,157		6,181	6,412
		$81,180	$154,004		$71,794	$135,034		$68,060	$128,063
Total		$111,222	$188,781		$96,471	$149,434		$87,780	$143,263

Note 5 Investments

Short-term and long-term investments consist mainly of marketable equity securities, commercial paper, treasury notes, investments in money market preferred funds and certificates of deposits. The aggregate quoted market value of the marketable equity securities was approximately $143,000,000 and $149,000,000 at September 30, 1992 and 1991, respectively.

At September 30, 1992, unrealized gains and losses applicable to the marketable equity securities were approximately $60,800,000 and $5,300,000, respectively. In 1992, 1991 and 1990, the Company realized gains from the sale of marketable equity securities of approximately $1,920,000, $1,570,000 and $864,000, respectively, in addition to the $10,771,000 and 22,376,000 realized in 1991 and 1990, respectively, as a result of the conversion of the 7.5% debentures for Sun and Oryx common stock.

Source: Helmerich & Payne, 1992 annual report.

G. For the investments HP carries at cost or LOCM, calculate HP's mark to market return and ROA for 1991 and 1992.

H. HP did not receive any dividends from those affiliates accounted for by the equity method. Calculate the mark to market return and ROA for those investments for 1991 and 1992.

I. Compare HP's overall mark to market returns (capital gains plus dividends/interest) and ROA on its investments with those actually reported for 1991 and 1992.

J. Discuss the benefits and drawbacks (from the analyst point of view) of the cost, equity, and mark to market methods of accounting, using the results of parts A–I.

6. [Comparison of lower of cost or market methods] Many non-U.S. companies use the lower of cost or market *on an individual basis* for marketable securities. How would HP's reported investment income have differed on that basis in 1991 and 1992? How would its mark to market return have differed?

7. [Equity basis, tax rate assumptions] HP reports its equity from loss in affiliates on a net of tax basis in the income statement. HP did not receive any dividends from these affiliates.

A. Calculate the loss on a pretax basis for 1991 and 1992. (Hint: Reconcile the change in the investment account for the equity affiliates.)

B. What assumption is HP using as to how it will eventually receive any income earned by its equity method affiliates? Discuss a different assumption and compute the reported after-tax loss from these affiliates for 1991 and 1992 under that assumption.

C. Suggest why HP reports the loss (income) from these affiliates separately net of taxes.

Problems 8 and 9 are based on Moore Motors Company and Exhibit 11P-2.

Exhibit 11-P2 presents the consolidated financial statements of Moore Motors Company (Moore). Its 100%-owned finance subsidiary, MM Finance (MMF), provides financing for the dealers and customers of Moore. MMF's balance sheet and income statement are also included.

8. [Finance subsidiaries] Moore's consolidated statements aggregate Moore's manufacturing as well as financing operations. For some purposes the combination may be advantageous; for other modes of analysis it has drawbacks, and it may be more useful to treat the subsidiary on an equity basis.

A. Prepare a balance sheet for Moore Motors at December 31, 1988–1989 using the equity method of accounting for MMF.

B. Prepare an income statement for Moore Motors for 1989 using the equity method of accounting.

EXHIBIT 11P-2. MOORE MOTORS
Balance Sheets, at December 31, 1988–1989 (in $ thousands)

	Moore Motors Consolidated Balance Sheet		MM Finance	
	1988	1989	1988	1989
Cash and equivalents	$ 10,181	$ 10,213	$ 3,272	$ 3,143
Accounts receivable				
Trade	4,541	5,447		
Parent			14,840	14,460
Finance receivables	87,477	92,355	74,231	79,120
Inventories	10,020	10,065		
Fixed assets (net)	36,936	39,125	6,698	6,839
Miscellaneous assets	14,908	16,092		
Total assets	$164,063	$173,297	$99,041	$103,562
Accounts payable				
Trade	$ 7,897	$ 7,708		
Parent			$ 3,515	$ 2,898
Bank debt	88,130	93,425	81,875	86,868
Accrued liabilities	27,434	29,861	6,380	6,014
Accrued income tax	4,930	5,671		
Total liabilities	$128,391	$136,665	$91,770	$ 95,780
Common stock	6,702	5,401	500	500
Retained earnings	28,970	31,231	6,771	7,282
Total equity	$ 35,672	$ 36,632	$ 7,271	$ 7,782
Total liabilities and equity	$164,063	$173,297	$99,041	$103,562

Income Statements, for Year Ended December 31, 1989 (in $ thousands)

	Moore Motors Consolidated	MM Finance
Sales	$110,448	—
Finance revenues	14,504	$14,504
Interest income	1,980	—
Total revenues	$126,932	$14,504
Cost of goods sold	94,683	—
Selling and administrative expense	9,926	3,540
Interest	8,757	7,908
Depreciation and amortization	7,168	1,504
Total expenses	$120,534	$12,952
Pretax income	6,398	1,552
Income tax expense	(2,174)	(441)
Net income	$ 4,224	$ 1,111

EXHIBIT 11P-2. *(Continued)*

Statement of Cash Flows, for Year Ended December 31, 1989 (in $ thousands)

	Moore Motors Consolidated
Net income	$ 4,224
Depreciation and amortization	7,168
Change in accounts receivable	(906)
Change in inventory	(45)
Change in accrued liabilities	2,427
Change in accrued income tax	741
Change in accounts payable	(189)
Other	(414)
Operating cash flow	$ 13,006
Investment in fixed assets	(9,938)
Sale of fixed assets	228
Investment in finance receivables	(100,689)
Liquidation of finance receivables	95,394
Investing cash flow	$ (15,005)
Increase in bank debt	15,267
Decrease in bank debt	(9,972)
Repurchase of shares	(1,474)
New shares issued	173
Dividends paid	(1,963)
Financing cash flow	$ 2,031
Net change in cash and equivalents	$ 32

C. Compute *each* of the following ratios for Moore on a fully consolidated basis, for MMF alone, and for Moore (with MMF on an equity basis):

    (i) Gross profit margin

    (ii) Return on assets

    (iii) Return on equity

    (iv) Receivables turnover

    (v) Times interest earned

    (vi) Debt-to-equity

D. For each of the six ratio classifications in part C, discuss which of the three reporting methods results in ratios that are most relevant for analytic purposes.

9. [Finance subsidiaries, cash flow analysis] MMF's finance or credit receivables arise from long-term financing provided by MMF for Moore's customers. MMF "pays" Moore, and the customer repays the loan plus interest to MMF.

A. How does Moore classify the cash "received" from such transactions in its cash flow statement? Do you agree with this treatment? If not, how would you adjust Moore's cash flow statement?

B. In Chapter 2 we argued that interest payments should be included in financing cash flows rather than operating cash flows. Evaluate this argument as applied to Moore's (consolidated) interest payments.

C. Moore's consolidated cash flow statement combines cash flows from Moore's manufacturing as well as MMF's financing activities. Using the data in Exhibit 11P-2 and your answers to parts A and B, prepare 1989 statements of cash flows (using the direct method) for:

> **(i)** MMF.

> **(ii)** Moore's manufacturing operations.

D. Using the cash flow statements prepared in part C, compute the cash flow from MMF to Moore's manufacturing operations (from all sources) during 1991.

E. Discuss how the segmentation of Moore's financial statements aids your understanding of the company's financial condition.

Problems 10–12 are based on the Coca-Cola Company and Exhibit 11P-3.

[Comparison of equity method, consolidation, and proportionate consolidation] Exhibit 11P-3 contains the balance sheets and income statements of The Coca-Cola Company (Coke) and its affiliate, Coca-Cola Enterprises, Inc. (Enterprises), for 1989 and 1990, as well as additional information culled from the footnotes of the companies. Enterprises is the largest bottler of Coca-Cola in the world. It manufactures and markets Coca-Cola products in areas serving 40% of the population of the United States. Coke owns approximately 49% of Enterprises and uses the equity method of accounting to report on its investment.

The relationship between Coke and Enterprises is complex. Enterprises produces virtually all its products under license from Coke and buys soft drink syrup, concentrates, and sweeteners from Coke as well. In effect, Coke controls the products and a substantial portion of the input costs of Enterprises. Enterprises' board of directors includes three current and one retired senior officer of Coke.

10. Given the relationship between Coke and Enterprises, discuss the appropriateness of Coke's use of the equity method to account for its investment in Enterprises. Discuss the conditions under which full consolidation and/or proportionate consolidation would provide a more useful set of financial statements. Discuss the drawbacks of each alternative from an analyst's perspective.

11. A. Prepare proportionate consolidated balance sheets at December 31, 1989–1990 and 1990 income statement for Coke and Enterprises.

B. Compute the following ratios for Coke and Enterprises on an individual and proportionately consolidated basis.

> **(i)** Debt to equity
>
> **(ii)** Times interest earned
>
> **(iii)** Inventory turnover
>
> **(iv)** Receivable turnover
>
> **(v)** Gross profit margin
>
> **(vi)** Return on sales
>
> **(vii)** Return on assets
>
> **(viii)** Return on equity

EXHIBIT 11P-3. COCA-COLA AND COCA-COLA ENTERPRISES
Comparative Balance Sheets, at December 31, 1989–1990 (in $ millions)

	1989		1990	
	Coca-Cola (Coke)	Coca-Cola Enterprises	Coca-Cola (Coke)	Coca-Cola Enterprises
Cash and marketable securities	$1182	$ 10	$1492	$ 1
Accounts receivable				
Trade	768	297	914	297
Finance subsidiaries	52		38	
Inventories	789	128	982	128
Prepaids	812	59	717	69
Current assets	$3603	$ 494	$4143	$ 495
Investment				
Enterprises	695		667	
Other bottlers	1731	73	1358	
Finance receivables, other			450	106
Property, plant, and equipment	2021	1286	2385	1373
Intangible assets	232	2879	275	3047
Total assets	$8282	$4732	$9278	$5021
Accounts payable	$1387	$ 395	$1576	$ 457
Accounts payable, Coke		52		21
Current debt	1432	549	2001	577
Accrued taxes	839		719	
Current liabilities	$3658	$ 996	$4296	$1055
Long-term debt	549	1756	536	1960
Deferred taxes	296	266	265	335
Other liabilities	294	34	332	44
Preferred equity		250		250
Common equity	3485	1430	3849	1377
Total liabilities and equity	$8282	$4732	$9278	$5021

EXHIBIT 11P-3. *(Continued)*

Income Statement, for Year Ended December 31, 1990 (in $ millions)

	Coca-Cola (Coke)	Coca-Cola Enterprises
Revenues*	$10,236	$ 4034
Cost of goods sold	(4,209)	(2359)
Gross profit	$ 6,027	$ 1675
Selling and general expense	(4,076)	(1349)
Operating income	$ 1,951	$ 326
Interest income	170	6
Interest expense	(231)	(207)
Equity in income of affiliates	110	
Other income	14	59
Pretax income	$ 2,014	$ 184
Income tax expense	(632)	(91)
Net income	$ 1,382	$ 93
Preferred dividends	(18)	(16)
Net available for common	$ 1,364	$ 77

*1990 intercompany revenues and expenses (from the footnotes of Enterprises):

Purchases from Coke	$920 million
Sales to Coke	132
Marketing payments from Coke	191

Source: Coca-Cola and Coca-Cola Enterprises, 1990 annual reports.

C. Discuss the differences in the ratios in part B between proportionate consolidation and the equity method.

12. Repeat Problem 11, but on a fully consolidated basis. Justify your treatment of minority interest in the calculation of the ratios in part B.

13. [Interpretation of ratios for companies with finance subsidiaries] The Deere Company consolidates its equipment operations and finance subsidiary in its financial statements. This makes it difficult to calculate and interpret (some of) the ratios discussed in the book for two reasons:

1. Finance companies do not classify their balance sheets in the same manner as industrial companies.

2. The nature of the operations of the two segments differs considerably.

A. Discuss how these factors affect the calculation and interpretation of activity and short-term liquidity ratios.

B. Using the Deere financial statements in Appendix 1–B, calculate Deere's times interest earned ratio for 1990 and 1991 on a consolidated basis as well as for the equipment operations alone.

C. Discuss the appropriateness of the calculation of the times interest earned ratio on a consolidated basis. Your discussion should consider the purpose of this ratio. Suggest another way of calculating the times interest earned ratio for Deere that would provide more useful information.

14. [Minority interest] The following data were obtained from the *1991 Annual Report* of Nucor Corporation, which has a 51%-owned consolidated subsidiary:

Minority interest at December 31, 1990:	$105,441,000
Minority interest at December 31, 1991:	$124,048,000
Distribution to minority interest:	$ (7,507,000)
(1991 financing cash flow)	

A. Nucor's operating cash flow reported minority interest for 1991. From the data given, compute that number and explain its significance.

B. Using the data provided and the result of part A, compute the net profit and return on equity of the subsidiary for 1991.

C. Discuss the conditions under which the proportionate consolidation method would be more appropriate for this subsidiary.

D. Discuss the advantages and disadvantages of the proportionate consolidation method in this case from the point of view of:

    (i) Nucor's management.

    (ii) A financial analyst.

15. [Analysis of segment data] Exhibit 11P-4 contains industry segment data reported by Hercules, a worldwide producer of chemicals and related products and solid fuel systems. Use the exhibit data to answer the following questions.

A. Compute the following ratio for each of Hercules' four segments for the years 1990–1992:

    (i) Operating profit margin

    (ii) Return on assets

    (iii) Asset turnover

    (iv) Ratio of capital expenditures to depreciation

B. For each ratio calculated in A, discuss what the level and trend of the ratio conveys about the business segment.

C. Discuss the limitations of segment data, both in terms of trends within the company over time and comparisons with similar segments of other companies.

D. Discuss what additional information you would require to improve your analysis of segment operations.

EXHIBIT 11P-4. HERCULES, INC.

Notes to Financial Statements

Operations by Industry Segment and Geographic Area *(Dollars in millions) continued*

Industry Segments 1992	Chemical Specialties	Food & Functional Products	Aerospace	Materials	Other	Total
Net Sales	$835	$813	$745	$463	$9	$2,865
Profit (Loss) from Operations	122	105	62	22	(67)[1]	244
Identifiable Assets	513	694	730	512	14	2,463
Capital Expenditures	40	71	15	23	1	150
Depreciation	37	54	43	37	1	172
1991						
Net Sales	794	894	748	484	9	2,929
Profit (Loss) from Operations	90	107	(3)	4	(11)[2]	187[2]
Identifiable Assets	528	833	718	552	7	2,638
Capital Expenditures	50	95	30	39	—	214
Depreciation	35	59	49	37	—	180
1990						
Net Sales	773	874	996	546	11	3,200
Profit (Loss) from Operations	67	87	60	(24)	0[2]	190[2]
Identifiable Assets	606	699	721	555	5	2,586
Capital Expenditures	69	54	74	76	—	273
Depreciation	43	43	64	41	—	191

*Includes environmental and rationalization charges of $65 million.
Source: Hercules, Inc., *1992 Annual Report.*

Appendix 11−A

Expanded Equity Method

The second alternative to the equity method is the expanded equity method. Like the proportionate consolidation method, it replaces the "one-line consolidation" of the equity method with the proportionate share of the assets, liabilities, revenues, and expenses of the affiliate. The display of these numbers is, however, somewhat different.

Under the expanded equity method, the proportionate shares of assets, liabilities, revenues, and expenses are segregated from those of the consolidated group. For Petroleum Corp., the results are shown in Exhibit 11A−1.

EXPANDED EQUITY VERSUS PROPORTIONATE CONSOLIDATION

Because neither of these methods has been in widespread use (but see discussion of IAS 31 on page 808), the two methods must be discussed in the abstract rather than by reference to experience. The expanded equity method has the advantage of disclosing the investor's proportionate share of operating results and exposures but without commingling the investee operations with those of the investor. As the investor may not truly control (even its share of) the cash flows of the affiliate, total aggregation may lead to misleading inferences about the financial condition of the consolidated group.

On the other hand, use of the proportionate consolidation method implicitly assumes that the investor does control its share of the cash flows of the investee. Given that assumption, it does make sense for the financial statements of the investor to include its

EXHIBIT 11A−1. PETROLEUM CORP.
Illustration of Expanded Equity Method*

Income Statement, for Year Ended December 31, 1991

	Expanded Equity (After eliminations)	Equity Method
Revenues	$1000	$1000
Equity in earnings of Supply Corp.	—	4
Share of revenues of Supply Corp.	20	—
Cost of goods sold	(800)	(800)
Selling, general, and administrative expenses	(80)	(80)
Interest expense	(20)	(20)
Share of expenses of Supply Corp.	(13)	—
Pretax earnings	$ 107	$ 104
Income tax expense	(43)	(40)
Net income	$ 64	$ 64

EXHIBIT 11A.1. *(Continued)*

Petroleum Corp. Balance Sheet, at December 31, 1991

Expanded Equity (After eliminations)				Equity Method			
Cash	$100	Accounts payable	$200	Cash	$100	Accounts payable	$200
Inventory	200			Inventory	200		
Accounts receivable	300			Accounts receivable	300		
PPE	280	Long-term debt	200	PPE	280	Long-term debt	200
				Investments	20	Equity	500
Share of Supply Corp.							
Current assets	38	Current liabilities	22				
PPE	72	Long-term debt	68				
		Equity	500				
Totals	$990		$990	Totals	$900		$900

*See Exhibit 11-10 for underlying data.

proportionate share of the assets, liabilities, revenues, and expenses of the affiliate. Under the proportionate consolidation method, one can be surer that accounts are included in the appropriate place in the investor statements.

However, we may not know what amounts relate to the venture because of the paucity of disclosure; this may result in misleading ratios depending on the degree of control over the assets, liabilities, and cash flows of the venture. But the expanded equity method may result in the loss of information. For example, in the Petroleum Corp. example, the expanded equity method reports total current assets of Supply Corp. rather than each current asset account.

Thus neither of these two alternative methods has a clear-cut advantage for analytic purposes. As in the case of consolidation versus the equity method, the analyst must evaluate each situation and decide on the appropriate adjustments.

12

BUSINESS COMBINATIONS

INTRODUCTION

THE PURCHASE METHOD
Illustration

THE POOLING OF INTERESTS METHOD
Conditions Necessary for Use
Illustration

EFFECTS OF ACCOUNTING METHOD
Comparison of Balance Sheets
Comparison of Income Statements
Effects on the Cash Flow Statement
Impact of Accounting Method on Ratios

INCOME TAX EFFECTS OF BUSINESS COMBINATIONS

ANALYSIS OF A POOLING METHOD ACQUISITION: THE CONAGRA-GOLDEN VALLEY MERGER
Balance Sheet Under Pooling Method
Balance Sheet Under Purchase Method
Income Statement Under Pooling Method
Income Statement Under Purchase Method
Comparison of Financial Ratios
Summary

ANALYSIS OF A PURCHASE METHOD ACQUISITION: GEORGIA PACIFIC'S PURCHASE OF GREAT NORTHERN NEKOOSA
Balance Sheet Under Purchase Method
Restating the GP-GNN Transaction to Pooling
Income Statement Under Pooling Method
Effects on Balance Sheet
Effects on Cash Flow Statement
Comparison of Financial Ratios
Using Pro Forma Information
Summary

ANALYSIS OF INTERNATIONAL DIFFERENCES: THE SMITHKLINE BEECHAM MERGER
The Merged Balance Sheet
Differences in Accounting Methods
Comparison of Stockholders' Equity
Restatement of the Balance Sheet
Income Statement Effects
Restatement of the Income Statement
Comparison of Financial Ratios
Summary

INTERNATIONAL DIFFERENCES IN ACCOUNTING FOR BUSINESS COMBINATIONS

CHOOSING THE ACQUISITION METHOD
Income Maximization as Motivation for the
Pooling/Purchase Choice
Market Reaction and the Pooling/Purchase
Choice
Interpreting the Research Results
Other Factors Influencing Mergers, Bid Premia,
and the Pooling/Purchase Choice
  Characteristics of Transaction
  Characteristics of Acquirer
  Characteristics of Target
Summary

THE ANALYSIS OF GOODWILL
Goodwill and the Income Statement

PUSH-DOWN ACCOUNTING
Push-Down in Practice: The GM-Hughes
Transaction
Impact on the Balance Sheet
Impact on the Income Statement

Effect on Cash Flows
Effect on Financial Ratios
Push–Down Summed Up

**LEVERAGED BUYOUTS: DURACELL
INTERNATIONAL**
Balance Sheet Effects
Income Statement Effects
Comparing Buyout Firms with Others

SPINOFFS
Analysis of Spinoffs
Reasons for Investment in Spinoffs
The Spinoff of ESCO Electronics

**CORPORATE REORGANIZATION AND
REVALUATION**
Quasi-Reorganizations
Miscellaneous Restructuring Methods

SUMMARY

INTRODUCTION

Corporate reorganizations have become an important aspect of the financial landscape in recent years, both within and outside the United States. Acquisitions of other companies as well as divestitures of business segments have been used to restructure and to change the scale of operations. These transactions are generally accompanied by changes in ownership and control of the acquired (or divested) company or business segment. These reorganizations are undertaken for many reasons, including vertical integration, diversification and growth designed to obtain higher market share, improvement of operating efficiency, and plans to increase the market value of the firm.

Another category involves financial restructuring through leveraged buyouts (LBOs) to change the capital structure of a firm, increasing the use of debt and adding substantial goodwill to the balance sheet. Again these transactions change the ownership or control of the restructured unit. The capital structure, ownership, or control of voting rights may also be changed through reorganizations in bankruptcy, quasi-reorganizations, recapitalizations, and initial public offerings or secondary issues of stock in subsidiaries.

Corporate reorganizations raise important accounting and financial analysis issues. In the case of mergers or acquisitions, the primary accounting issues involve the required reporting at transaction date and the preparation of subsequent financial statements for the combined operations of the two entities. Put differently, the question is whether the transaction establishes a new accounting basis for the assets and liabilities of the acquired company, requiring the recognition of the market values used in the transaction. The answer leads to different reporting methods with diverse impacts on resulting financial statements.

The relevant issues for financial analysts involve the analysis and comparability of reported results before and after acquisitions, given different reporting methods. Since sales (and expenses) of the combined entity following the combination will clearly be greater than those of the acquirer alone, the question is whether to restate premerger results to facilitate comparisons of pre- and postmerger operations.

Many economic and financial reporting considerations affect the accounting method chosen to report acquisitions; comprehensive analysis is required to understand management incentives for these choices. Much has been written in recent years regarding the comparative merits of the different methods of accounting for business combinations, their differential ability to obscure "true" operating results, and their impact on international competition because of international tax and reporting differences. While this chapter shows how each of these methods may have these effects, its objectives are to enable the financial analyst to interpret postmerger financial statements prepared using either method and to provide some insights into management decisions.

Financial restructurings, particularly leveraged buyouts, often imply a fair value, which is quite different from the reported book value of the restructured firm. Again the critical accounting issue is whether a new basis (fair value) should be recognized for the assets and liabilities of these firms. The same question may be raised when less than 100% of a firm's common stock is acquired and the investee has to continue providing separate financial statements. Should the new basis be "pushed down" into those separate statements? The accounting problems are compounded because these transactions generate substantial goodwill and the implications for equity and liability valuation can be quite complex.[1]

Quasi-reorganizations enable firms to eliminate deficits in retained earnings and use a new basis for the assets and liabilities, although existing Securities and Exchange Commission (SEC) accounting rules prohibit write-ups of assets and liabilities. The impact is similar to that of reorganizations in bankruptcy. Recapitalizations and sales of stock in subsidiaries may also imply a new basis.

The large numbers of LBOs and other types of financial restructuring in recent years have created relatively new accounting problems. Given sometimes inconsistent accounting practices in these areas, the development of analytical techniques to restate

---

[1]Similar accounting problems arise when firms repurchase substantial amounts of their stock, issue stock in existing subsidiaries, make secondary stock offerings, and restructure their interests in joint ventures, other subsidiaries, and unincorporated entities.

similar transactions on a comparable basis is required. Several recent Financial Accounting Standards Board (FASB) projects tackle these accounting issues, and analysts need to evaluate them for potential changes in reporting and disclosure methods.[2]

The chapter begins with illustrations of the purchase and pooling methods of accounting for mergers and acquisitions, followed by a comparison of their impact on financial statements and ratios. The next section analyzes the ConAgra-Golden Valley merger, which was reported using the pooling method and which we restate to the purchase method. Then, using the acquisition of Great Northern Nekoosa by Georgia Pacific, we reverse the analysis, restating a purchase method acquisition to the pooling method. These restatements facilitate a comparison of financial statements and ratios resulting from use of these two methods.

These illustrations and analytical techniques are then applied to international differences. The SmithKline Beecham merger is used to illustrate how differences in accounting methods hamper the comparison of firms in different countries. Next, a review of empirical research into market reaction and management incentives to engage in acquisition activities is followed by a discussion of the issue of acquisition goodwill.

Push-down accounting, leveraged buyouts, and spinoffs are discussed next with analyses of actual transactions. The chapter ends with a brief discussion of reorganizations.

THE PURCHASE METHOD

The purchase method of accounting treats an acquisition as a purchase of the assets and assumption of the liabilities of one company, the acquired or target firm, by another. The transaction changes control (the ownership interest of one group of stockholders has been bought by another), requiring a new accounting basis for the acquired assets and liabilities.[3] Generally, the purchase price paid for the acquired company must be equated to the fair market value of the tangible and intangible assets acquired less the fair market value of the liabilities assumed.

The purchase method requires the allocation of the purchase price to all identifiable assets and liabilities regardless of whether they were recognized in the financial statements of the acquired company. *As a result, the assets and liabilities of the acquired company (and the acquired company only) are received into the financial statements of the acquirer at their fair market values.*

The income statement includes the operating results of the acquired company effective with the date of acquisition. Operating results prior to the merger are not restated, although pro forma data on a combined basis may be disclosed. As a result, pre- and postmerger income (and cash flow) statements are not comparable.

---

[2]See FASB Discussion Memoranda on New Basis Accounting (December 18, 1991) and Consolidation Policy and Procedures (September 10, 1991).

[3]Note that nontaxable purchase method transactions involve the exchange of 51% or more of voting common stock with the remainder acquired for cash and/or debt.

Illustration

As an illustration of the application of the purchase method of accounting, consider Acquire Company's June 30, 1991, acquisition of the Target Company for $490 million. Assume that Acquire raises the funds by selling new common stock.

Exhibit 12-1 shows the balance sheets of both companies and the fair market values of Target's assets and liabilities on the merger date. Note that Target's net assets prior to acquisition are given by its common equity of $250 million ($500 million assets less $250 million liabilities). The assumed fair market values of Target's assets and liabilities are based on adjustments typical of those found in real companies.

Inventories reported at the lower of cost or market value are frequently carried at amounts below fair value, especially if the last-in, first-out (LIFO) inventory method is employed. Property is another common area of adjustment; in an inflationary world, fair value usually exceeds historical cost.

The adjustment to long-term debt depends on the current level of interest rates as compared to the interest rate imbedded in the company's long-term debt. In the case of Target, it is assumed that the company's long-term debt carries an interest rate that is below current rates. The fair market value of this debt is the present value, at the current interest rate, of the cash flows (both principal and interest) required by the company's debt or $130 million in this case, which is below the face amount ($150 million) of the debt. If the current interest rate were lower than the historic rate, then the present value would be higher than the face amount.

EXHIBIT 12-1. ACQUIRE AND TARGET
Comparative Balance Sheets, at June 30, 1991 (in $ millions)

	Historical Cost				Fair Value	
	Acquire		Target		Target	
Inventories	$250		$150		$200	
Receivables	250		100		100	
Current assets		$ 500		$250		$300
Property		500		250		350
Purchase method intangibles*		0		0		70
Total assets		$1000		$500		$720
Payables	150		50		50	
Accrued liabilities	100		50		50	
Current liabilities		250		100		100
Long-term debt		250		150		130
Common stock	400		225		490†	
Retained earnings	100		25		—	
Common equity		500		250		490
Total equities		$1000		$500		$720

*See discussion in the text of the purchase method for allocation rules.
†Acquire has agreed to pay $490 million for Target's net assets; the $490 million presented for common stock reflects that purchase price.

Application of the purchase method requires that all assets and liabilities be revalued to fair market value. In addition, previously unrecognized contingencies and "off-balance-sheet" items may also have to be recognized. Examples include lawsuits and environmental contingencies as well as employee benefit plans.

Having determined the fair values of assets and liabilities, we must compare the net amount with the purchase price. The net assets of Target at fair market value are

Assets at fair market value	$650 million
Liabilities at fair market value	(230)
Net assets at fair market value	$420 million

But the purchase price is $490 million, or $70 million higher than the fair value of net assets. Once all tangible assets and liabilities are restated at fair market value, any excess purchase price must be allocated to intangible assets. Identifiable intangibles may include

Patents

Customer lists

Licenses

Brand names

Any excess purchase price that cannot be attributed to identifiable intangibles must be accounted for as a general intangible, usually called goodwill.[4] In Target's case, if we cannot attribute any of the purchase price to identifiable intangibles, we must account for the $70 million excess purchase price as goodwill. This is the normal case; in most acquisitions all of the excess purchase price is allocated to goodwill rather than to identifiable intangibles.

In some cases the fair value of the net assets acquired exceeds the purchase price of the entire company.[5] Purchase method reporting requires the fair value of property to be reduced to the extent necessary to equate the net fair value of assets to the purchase price. In such cases the new carrying amount of property may be less than its fair market value.

Exhibit 12-2 (column 5) shows how the consolidated balance sheet is affected by use of the purchase method to account for the acquisition of Target. Note that Target's common equity has not been carried forward; it has been eliminated as a result of the merger. The combined common equity reflects instead Acquire's preacquisition and newly issued equity.

The balance sheet of the combined firm carries forward the assets and liabilities of Acquire without any change; adjustments are made only to the assets and liabilities of Target. If Target had purchased Acquire, the results would be quite different. Acquire's

[4]Goodwill is one of the most controversial subjects in the accounting literature. As it is a residual and it is not measured directly, many believe it to be a nonasset; we will discuss this question shortly. For the moment, let us accept the concept of goodwill as the residual of purchase price over the fair market value of all specific assets, net of specific liabilities.

[5]This may be due to unrecognized obligations or a low rate of return on assets.

EXHIBIT 12-2
Comparison of Purchase and Pooling Methods Consolidated Balance Sheets,
at June 30, 1991 (in $ millions)

	(1) Historical Cost Acquire	(2) Historical Cost Target	(3) Pooling Consolidated	(4) Adjustments	(5) Purchase Consolidated
Inventories	$ 250	$150	$ 400	$ 50	$ 450
Receivables	250	100	350	0	350
Current assets	$ 500	$250	$ 750	$ 50	$ 800
Property	500	250	750	100	850
Goodwill	—	—	—	70	70
Total assets	$1000	$500	$1500	$220	$1720
Payables	150	50	200	—	200
Accrued liabilities	100	50	150	—	150
Current liabilities	$ 250	$100	$ 350	—	$ 350
Long-term debt	250	150	400	(20)	380
Common stock	$400	$225	$625	$265	$890
Retained earnings	100	25	125	(25)	100
Common equity	500	250	750	240*	990
Total equities	$1000	$500	$1500	$220	$1720
Current ratio	2.00×	2.50×	2.14×	NA	2.29×
Debt/equity ratio	50.0%	60.0%	53.3%	NA	38.4%

NA – Not applicable.
*The net adjustment of $240 million reflects the purchase and retirement of all Target's equity ($225 million common stock + $25 million retained earnings) and the issuance of Acquire common stock with value of $490 million. $490 million − $250 million = $240 million.

assets and liabilities would have been restated, and Target's would have remained unchanged.

The application of the purchase method of accounting to the balance sheet can be summarized as follows:

1. The purchase price is allocated to the assets and liabilities of the acquired firm; all assets and liabilities are restated to their fair market value.

2. The restated net fair value is compared to the purchase price; any excess purchase price over net fair value is attributed to identifiable intangible assets when possible, otherwise to goodwill.

3. If the restated net fair value exceeds the purchase price, then the writeup of property is reduced until equality is achieved.

4. The common equity of the acquired firm is eliminated.

THE POOLING OF INTERESTS METHOD

The other method of accounting for a business combination is known as the pooling of interests method (or merger accounting). This method differs from the purchase method in the following respects:

1. The two parties are treated identically; there is no acquirer or acquired firm.

2. The financial statements are consolidated without adjustment; fair market values are not recognized for either company.

3. Operating results for the combined firm are restated for periods prior to the merger date.

The nature of the pooling of interests method is clearly defined in Paragraph 12 of Accounting Principles Board (APB) 16:

> The pooling of interests method accounts for a business combination as the uniting of the ownership interests of two or more companies by exchange of equity securities. No acquisition is recognized because the combination is accomplished without disbursing resources of the constituents. Ownership interests continue and the former bases of accounting are retained.

Conditions Necessary for Use

APB 16 sets the conditions under which the pooling method can be used to account for an acquisition. The major requirements are the following:

1. Each of the combining companies is independent; pooling is precluded when either has been a subsidiary or division of another company within two years prior to the merger. Significant intercompany stockholdings also preclude pooling.

2. Only voting common shares can be issued; the use of multiple classes of common or other securities (e.g., nonvoting preferred) violates the "risk sharing" that lies behind the pooling concept.

3. Stock reacquisitions (other than "normal" purchases, such as for use in employee benefit plans) are prohibited as are special distributions or other changes in capital structure prior to the merger. These provisions are also intended to preserve the "uniting of equity interests." (The special distributions to stockholders prior to the merger discussed in the analysis of SmithKline Beecham are examples of transactions that preclude pooling in the U.S.)

4. Absence of planned transactions that have the effect of benefiting some shareholders. For example, the combined company could not agree to tender for shares to guarantee some stockholders a fixed price for their shares.

5. The combined company must not intend to dispose of a significant portion of the existing businesses of the combining companies, other than duplicate facilities or excess capacity.

If all these conditions are met, then the pooling of interests method of accounting must be used. if any one of the conditions is violated, then the purchase method is required. Thus, strictly speaking, the methods are not alternatives for any given transaction.

In practice, however, transaction terms can usually be set to meet (or violate) the conditions specified in APB 16. Companies planning an acquisition develop pro forma financial statements[6] to estimate the impact of a proposed transaction and evaluate different terms and their different accounting consequences. Even in the case of "unfriendly" acquisitions, for example, American Telephone's acquisition of NCR in 1991, pooling treatment can be obtained by restructuring the terms after the surrender.

Illustration

The pooling method is illustrated using the assumptions developed for the purchase method example. However, to meet the pooling method's reporting requirement of an exchange of common stock, we must restructure the transaction. We now assume that Acquire exchanges its shares directly for those of Target. The consolidated balance sheet is also shown in Exhibit 12-2 (column 3) and is simply the summation of Target and Acquire's balance sheets.

Notice that the pooling method is similar to consolidation of a previously unconsolidated subsidiary, as discussed in Chapter 11. All assets and liabilities of the two firms are combined (and intercompany accounts eliminated), without any adjustment for fair values. When the pooling method is used, fair market values are irrelevant to recording the combination. The actual market price and premium paid for the acquired firm are suppressed from both the balance sheet and income statement.

Unlike the purchase method, the pooling method is symmetrical. It doesn't matter whether Target is being acquired or is the firm making the acquisition; the accounting result is identical.

Finally, note that the common equity of the two firms is simply combined. Neither company's share price has any bearing on the accounting result.[7]

EFFECTS OF ACCOUNTING METHOD

Comparison of Balance Sheets

Exhibit 12-2 shows that the two methods produce very different consolidated balance sheets. Yet the economic reality resulting from the transaction is identical (ignoring, for the moment, income tax effects) regardless of the method used to account for it in the financial statements.

The differences reflect the application of the purchase method: recognition of the market value of the transaction and the fair values of Target's assets and liabilities. As a

---

[6]See, for example, Michael S. Devine, "Using Pro Forma Allocations to Evaluate Business Purchases," *Financial Executive,* June 1981.

[7]The relative prices have no bearing on the accounting result once the terms of the deal have been entered into. They will, however, affect the basic terms of the transaction and the exchange ratio and may affect, as will be discussed, the choice of accounting method.

result, a number of financial ratios are changed; we show two examples within the exhibit. The purchase method current ratio benefits from the adjustment of the acquired firm's current assets to their fair market value. The impact on the current ratio depends on the relative size of the two firms' current assets and liabilities, the amount of cash used in the purchase, and the restatement of the acquired current assets.

The purchase method debt-to-equity ratio benefits in this example because the transaction involves sale (or exchange) of common stock. Generally, purchase transactions involve the use of cash and/or debt, which would be reflected in a higher debt/equity ratio.

Comparison of Income Statements

To complete our analysis of accounting for business combinations, we must evaluate the income statements resulting from application of the two methods. Exhibit 12-3 contains condensed income statements for Target and Acquire for 1990, 1991, and 1992 as well as for the second half of 1991.

EXHIBIT 12-3. ACQUIRE AND TARGET
Income Statements, for Years Ended December 31, 1990–1992 (in $ millions)

	1990	1991	1991*	1992
Target				
Sales	$ 600	$ 660	$ 340	$ 726
Cost of goods sold	(300)	(330)	(170)	(363)
Gross margin	$ 300	$ 330	$ 170	$ 363
Selling expense	(115)	(125)	(65)	(135)
Depreciation expense	(25)	(28)	(14)	(32)
Interest expense	(10)	(10)	(5)	(10)
Pretax income	$ 150	$ 167	$ 86	$ 186
Income tax expense	(50)	(56)	(29)	(62)
Net income	$ 100	$ 111	$ 57	$ 124
Gross margin as a % of sales	50.0	50.0	50.0	50.0
Acquire				
Sales	$1000	$1000	$ 500	$1000
Cost of goods sold	(600)	(600)	(300)	(600)
Gross margin	$ 400	$ 400	$ 200	$ 400
Selling expense	(130)	(130)	(65)	(130)
Depreciation expense	(50)	(50)	(25)	(50)
Interest expense	(20)	(20)	(10)	(20)
Pretax income	$ 200	$ 200	$ 100	$ 200
Income tax expense	(68)	(68)	(34)	(68)
Net income	$ 132	$ 132	$ 66	$ 132
Gross margin as a % of sales	40.0	40.0	40.0	40.0

*Six months ended December 31.

Under the purchase method, results of Target's operations are included only after the effective date of the merger. Thus the combined income statement will include the operations of Acquire for the entire year but the operations of Target only for the six months following the merger on June 30, 1991. The restatement of Target's assets and liabilities to their fair market values affects certain categories of expense as well. These include

- Cost of goods sold (COGS), which may be increased as inventory that has been written up in value is sold
- Depreciation expense, which is increased as a result of the higher value of property recognized
- Goodwill recognized, which must be amortized
- Debt discount created by revaluing long-term debt, which must be amortized over the remaining life of the debt

Each of these adjustments and the application to Target's acquisition is discussed shortly.

When inventory is accounted for by using either first- in, first-out (FIFO) or average cost, written-up inventory values will flow into cost of goods sold fairly quickly, depressing gross margins (Exhibit 12-4). While reported income is reduced, some of the cost of the acquisition is recovered quickly as the higher costs reduce taxable income in a taxable purchase transaction. When last-in, first-out inventory accounting is used, the higher costs will remain in inventory indefinitely unless a LIFO invasion (reduction of inventory quantities) takes place.

For the acquisition of Target, we assume use of the average cost method and that $30 million of the inventory write-up flows through COGS prior to the end of 1991. The remainder would flow through COGS in 1992.

Additional depreciation expense is a consequence of the higher depreciable base of property assets. The same depreciation methods and lives applied to a higher cost will result in higher depreciation expense and lower reported income, but will also generate income tax savings in taxable purchases.

Comparing depreciation expense with property, and assuming use of the straight-line method, it appears that Target's fixed assets have an average life of 10 years. Applying this factor[8] to the property write-up of $100 million results in an increased depreciation expense of $10 million per year, or an increase of $5 million (one-half) for the six months ended December 31, 1991.

Amortization of goodwill is not deductible for tax purposes in the United States. For that reason companies prefer to allocate the cost of an acquisition to depreciable property, even though this results in faster amortization in the financial statements. Under APB 17 (1970), goodwill may be amortized over any period from 10 to 40 years.

For Target, we assume a write-off over 35 years; this is within the normal range in

---

[8]Note that this assumes that Target's property was all written up by the same factor. If the write-up is disproportionately high in a class of property with an average life significantly different from the company average, this assumption will not hold.

EXHIBIT 12-4
Purchase Method Consolidated Income Statement, for Years Ended December 31, 1991–1992 (in $ millions)

A. Year Ended December 31, 1991

	Acquire	Target	Adjustments	Consolidated
Sales	$1000	$ 340	—	$1340
Cost of goods sold	(600)	(170)	$(30)	(800)
Gross margin	$ 400	$ 170	$(30)	$ 540
Selling expense	(130)	(65)	(1)*	(196)
Depreciation expense	(50)	(14)	(5)	(69)
Interest expense	(20)	(5)	(1)	(26)
Pretax income	$ 200	$ 86	$(37)	$ 249
Income tax expense	(68)	(29)	12	(85)
Net income	$ 132	$ 57	$(25)	$ 164
Gross margin as a % of sales	40.0	50.0	NA	40.3

NA – Not applicable.

B. Year Ended December 31, 1992

	Acquire	Target	Adjustments	Consolidated
Sales	$1000	$ 726	—	$1726
Cost of goods sold	(600)	(363)	$(20)	(983)
Gross margin	$ 400	$ 363	$(20)	$ 743
Selling expense	(130)	(135)	(2)*	(267)
Depreciation expense	(50)	(32)	(10)	(92)
Interest expense	(20)	(10)	(3)	(33)
Pretax income	$ 200	$ 186	$(35)	$ 351
Income tax expense	(68)	(62)	11	(119)
Net income	$ 132	$ 124	$(24)	$ 232
Gross margin as a % of sales	40.0	50.0	NA	43.0

NA – Not applicable.
*Goodwill amortization.

the United States. This assumption results in goodwill amortization expense of $2 million for 1992 and $1 million (one-half) for the last six months of 1991.

The treatment of debt discount follows the method used when a bond is issued at a discount. The effective interest rate reflects the stated (coupon) interest rate as well as amortization of the discount. This principle, when applied to discounted debt in a purchase method acquisition, requires that additional interest expense be recognized. Otherwise, the reported debt liability would be insufficient at maturity, resulting in a loss. (See Chapter 8.) We assume an increase in interest expense of $1 million for the second half of 1991 and $3 million for 1992.

Part A of Exhibit 12-4 contains the purchase method income statement for the year ended December 31, 1991. It reflects Acquire's operations for the full year, Target's operations for the six months following the merger, and the effects of the purchase method adjustments (net of tax savings, if any). Part B shows the income statement for 1992 for the combined firm.

We can now analyze purchase accounting's impact on the income statement. Acquire's income statement for the three years ended December 31, 1992, is presented in Exhibit 12-5. The 1990 data in the exhibit are the actual results for Acquire only; the 1991 and 1992 data are obtained from parts A and B, respectively, of Exhibit 12-4 and include Target for the period following the merger on June 30, 1991.

First, note the distortion of sales growth. From 1990 to 1992, Acquire reports a sales increase of 72.6%, none of which is due to its own internal growth. All the growth is due to the inclusion of Target's sales starting with the second half of 1991; part is due to the sales growth of Target following its acquisition.

The second problem is the distortion of profitability ratios. Acquire alone (see Exhibit 12-3) has a constant gross margin (sales less COGS) of 40% of sales; Target has a constant gross margin of 50% of sales. The combined gross margin percentage (see Exhibit 12-5) shows a rising trend, reflecting Target's growing influence.

Without the underlying data it would be impossible to determine whether the rising profitability of Acquire was due to improvement in its own operations, the higher profitability of Target, efficiencies from the merger, or the impact of purchase method adjustments. In some cases we can keep track of an acquired company through the use of segment data (see Chapter 11). However, as the frequency of acquisition rises, the ability to discern the impact of any single acquisition diminishes. Companies that make many small acquisitions or acquisitions within existing segments become impossible to analyze.

For comparison purposes, we now examine the income statements for the years 1990, 1991, and 1992 that result from accounting for the merger as a pooling of interests.

EXHIBIT 12-5. ACQUIRE CORP.
Purchase Method Income Statement, for Years Ended December 31, 1990–1992
(in $ millions)

	1990	1991	1992
Sales	$1000	$1340	$1726
Cost of goods sold	(600)	(800)	(983)
Gross margin	$ 400	$ 540	$ 743
Selling expense	(130)	(196)	(267)
Depreciation expense	(50)	(69)	(92)
Interest expense	(20)	(26)	(33)
Pretax income	$ 200	$ 249	$ 351
Income tax expense	(68)	(85)	(119)
Net income	$ 132	$ 164	$ 232
Gross margin as a % of sales	40.0	40.3	43.0

EXHIBIT 12-6. ACQUIRE CORP.
Pooling Method Income Statement, for Years Ended December 31, 1990–1992
(in $ millions)

	1990	1991	1992
Sales	$1600	$1660	$1726
Cost of goods sold	(900)	(930)	(963)
Gross margin	$ 700	$ 730	$ 763
Selling expense	(245)	(255)	(265)
Depreciation expense	(75)	(78)	(82)
Interest expense	(30)	(30)	(30)
Pretax income	$ 350	$ 367	$ 386
Income tax expense	(118)	(124)	(130)
Net income	$ 232	$ 243	$ 256
Gross margin as a % of sales	43.8	44.0	44.2

These income statements, presented in Exhibit 12-6, are obtained by simply adding together (without any adjustment) the income statements of Acquire and Target for the respective years.

Exhibits 12-5 and 12-6 show considerable differences. *When the pooling method is used, the operating results of Target are included for all three years, including the periods prior to the merger*. The restatement of prior period results is one of the salient features of the pooling of interests method of accounting, and it facilitates comparability.

Because the operating results of all three years include both Acquire and Target, the purchase method's "illusion" of growth is absent. Sales growth over the period 1990 to 1992 is 7.9%, reflecting only the internal sales growth of Target. All categories of expense are comparable as well. The gross margin percentage shows a small year-to-year increase, reflecting the growing influence of Target's higher-margin operations.

However, the pooling of interests method can also distort reality. The first problem is that it creates a fictitious history. Results for 1990 have been restated as if the two companies were combined in that year. The reality is that they were separate enterprises, with different managements. The pooling method permits the management of Acquire to take credit for the operating results of Target for the period prior to its acquisition.

The pooling method allows companies whose shares sell at high price/earning ratios to improve earnings per share via acquisition. If a company uses its highly valued shares (that is, high price/earnings multiple) to acquire a company whose shares sell at a low multiple of earnings under the pooling method, then earnings per share will increase. This technique is sometimes known as "bootstrapping," as the acquired company can raise earnings per share through financial engineering rather than operating improvement (see ConAgra example later in this chapter). In theory,[9] this technique should fail as the market assigns a lower price/earnings ratio to the postmerger firm to reflect the

---

[9]The efficient markets hypothesis suggests that the market price of the acquirer should adjust instantaneously.

inclusion of "lower-quality" earnings. In practice the technique can be effective for many years.

In the extreme case, an acquisition can be made after the close of the fiscal year to meet sales and earnings objectives. Because of the restatement feature of the pooling method, a company can include in its reported results the operations of firms acquired after the end of the year but before release of the annual report.[10]

Another serious problem with the pooling method of accounting is the suppression of the true cost of the acquisition. Since the pooling method carries forward historical costs, no recognition is given to the true value of the assets acquired or any securities used to pay for the acquired company. (See Exhibit 12-2, column 3.)

There are several consequences of this failure to recognize the fair values acquired and paid for. One is that the acquiring company may obtain assets whose carrying cost is well below fair or market value. Some of those assets can be sold (and in the case of operating assets, such as inventory, *will* be sold). As a result, fictitious "gains" will be reported as part of income since the acquirer presumably paid the full value of the assets acquired but the pooling method does not require the recognition of the true price paid. Similarly, depreciation and amortization will reflect the historical cost of assets acquired rather than their market value. As a result, income is overstated.[11]

Effects on the Cash Flow Statement

Use of the pooling method to account for a merger has no special implications for the cash flow statement. The consolidated cash flow statement reported will just be the sum of the individual cash flow statements. As in the case of the income statement, previously issued cash flow statements will be restated on a combined basis.

Under purchase method accounting, however, the acquisition itself must be recognized. To illustrate this recognition in a simplified setting, we assume that Acquire prepares a cash flow statement for June 30, 1991, reflecting only the acquisition (during that short time period, no income is earned by the combined entity). The cash flow statement and balance sheet changes are presented in Exhibit 12-7.

Note that although current assets and liabilities have increased, the change is not reflected in cash from operations (CFO). The cash flow change in operating accounts does not equal the actual change on the balance sheet.[12] Because the additional inventories and receivables are acquired as part of an acquisition, the cash paid for their acquisition is treated as cash for investment.

---

[10]National Student Marketing, a "high flyer" in the late 1960s and early 1970s before its collapse, was reported to have made acquisitions *after the end of each fiscal year* to bring reported earnings up to the forecasted level.

[11]Abraham J. Briloff has written extensively over the years on the problems associated with use of the pooling method. For example, see Briloff, "Distortions Arising from Pooling-of-Interests Accounting," *Financial Analysts Journal*, March–April 1968. Despite the age of this article, it remains a superb illustration of how the pooling method suppresses the fair value of acquisitions, permitting the reporting of "gains" on assets acquired.

[12]Acquisitions (or divestitures) are one of the two cases under which changes in operating accounts shown in the cash flow statement differ from the actual change reflected on the balance sheet. The other case (to be discussed in Chapter 13) relates to changes in foreign currency exchange rates.

EXHIBIT 12-7
Cash Flow Effects of Purchase Method Acquisition, as of June 30, 1991
(in $ millions)

A. Acquire Company Balance Sheet, Pre- and Postacquisition

	Pre*	Post†	Change	
	Acquisition		Change	
Inventories	$ 250	$ 450	$ 200	⎫
Receivables	250	350	100	⎬ Changes ignored in CFO
Current assets	$ 500	$ 800	$ 300	⎭
Property	500	850	350	
Goodwill	—	70	70	
Total assets	$1000	$1720	$ 720	
Payables	150	200	50	⎫
Accrued liabilities	100	150	50	⎬ Changes ignored in CFO
Current liabilities	$ 250	$ 350	$ 100	⎭
Long-term debt	250	380	130	
Common stock	$400	$890	$490	
Retained earnings	100	100	—	
Common equity	500	990	490	
Total equities	$1000	$1720	$ 720	

B. Statement of Cash Flows

Cash from operations			
Net income		$ 0	
Changes in operating accounts		0	$ 0
Cash for investment			(490)	Net assets acquired
Cash from financing			490	Common equity issued
Net change in cash			$ 0	

*Exhibit 12-2, column 1.
†Exhibit 12-2, column 5.

However, reported cash from operations in the year of the acquisition (and in subsequent years) may still be distorted. The degree of distortion depends on whether the level of working capital immediately after the acquisition is maintained over time.

The potential distortion can be illustrated by considering the inventory acquired. Although the cash paid for the acquisition of the inventory does not flow through cash from operations, the cash received when the inventory is sold does. Thus, CFO is inflated as the proceeds of sale are included while the cost of acquiring the inventory is not.

This distortion will be somewhat mitigated if inventory is continually replaced, as the cash outflows for new inventory will offset cash inflows from sales. However, if there is a reduction in the acquired firm's working capital, CFO may be distorted, and careful analysis is required to understand the impact. An example appears in the analysis of Georgia Pacific's acquisition of Great Northern Nekoosa later in the chapter.

Impact of Accounting Method on Ratios

The common shares issued by the buyer, Acquire, are accounted for on the basis of the acquired company's shareholders' equity at book value of $250 million under the pooling method. In contrast, the market value of $490 million is recognized under the purchase method. As a result, financial statement ratios are quite different under the two methods.

Exhibit 12-2 shows that the purchase method reports higher asset values and higher common equity[13] (albeit lower retained earnings) than the pooling of interests method when the purchase price exceeds the stated net worth of the acquired company. As a result, the base for activity and return ratios will be higher. In addition, adjustments required by the purchase method usually reduce reported earnings. (Acquire's 1992 earnings are $256 million under the pooling method but only $232 million under the purchase method.) The result is that profitability ratios will generally be lower when the purchase method has been used.

The purchase method also makes financial ratios difficult to interpret in other ways. Under this method, Acquire's assets and liabilities are carried forward at historical cost. Target's are accounted for at fair market value, generating a mixture of historical costs and market values in the combined accounts. As a result, activity ratios are difficult to compare with those of other companies.

In addition, postmerger ratios will not be comparable with premerger ratios, because

1. Target may have had a different turnover ratio than Acquire, reflecting the nature of its business; the postmerger ratio is a blend of the ratios of the two companies.

2. In addition, turnover will be reduced solely because of the accounting adjustments required by the purchase method.

Comparison of a company that has made a purchase method acquisition with one that has made a pooling acquisition (or none at all) is also affected by these same problems.

The reader is cautioned, however, that ratio effects are generally firm specific. Depending on the purchase price relative to book value, the fair values of assets and liabilities acquired, the means of financing, and the earnings of the target firm, the effect on ratios of use of the purchase method or pooling method will vary in practice. *We can, however, make the general statement that the choice of method will affect the ratios of the combined enterprise, often significantly.*

In addition, a purchase method acquisition creates a discontinuity throughout the financial statements of the acquiring company. Comparison with premerger data for the same company and comparison with other companies is hampered by the inclusion of the

---

[13]This is a consequence of the assumptions used in this illustration; if the firm had used debt in the acquisition, it would report higher debt and leverage ratios.

acquired entity at the acquisition date (balance sheet effects), and it is also affected subsequently by the purchase method adjustments (balance sheet and income statement effects). Use of trend data for such companies can easily lead to misleading conclusions.

INCOME TAX EFFECTS OF BUSINESS COMBINATIONS

The income tax aspects of accounting for business combinations have always been complex. Changes in U.S. tax laws in recent years have only served to increase the complexity. A thorough discussion of this subject is well beyond the scope of this book. However, a few general comments may be helpful.

In general, pooling of interests acquisitions are nontaxable events under the Internal Revenue Code (the Code) of the United States. Nontaxability has two consequences. First, shareholders of the acquired company do not recognize gain or loss as a result of the merger. They transfer the cost basis of their shares in the acquired company to the shares of the acquirer that they receive in exchange.

The second consequence is that the cost basis of the assets and liabilities of the acquired company are not affected by the merger. There is no income tax recognition of the fair value of assets and liabilities and no change in tax benefits or deductibility as these assets are used or liabilities paid.

A purchase method acquisition, in contrast, is generally a taxable event under the Code. Selling shareholders do recognize gain or loss on the sale of their shares, even if they receive securities of the acquiring company in a taxable exchange. In addition, for tax purposes the basis of assets and liabilities of the acquired firm is changed from original cost to fair value, reflecting the price paid for the company.

In most cases, the accounting treatment and the income tax treatment are identical. In these circumstances, the accounting basis and the tax basis of assets and liabilities are the same, and no analytical adjustment is required.

However, the accounting and tax rules do differ in some respects, and there are times when the tax treatment of an acquisition is different from the accounting treatment. In such cases care must be taken to discern the impact of the difference on future earnings and cash flows. Careful reading of the income tax footnote (see Chapter 7) will usually make it possible to discover that there is a difference between the tax basis and the accounting basis for some assets and liabilities. Differential merger treatment is usually the cause of such differences.

When a merger is tax free, but accounted for as a purchase, the tax basis of the assets will be below the accounting basis (assuming that purchase price exceeds historical net worth). As a result, the additional depreciation and other expenses resulting from purchase method adjustments will not be tax deductible. This will increase the effective tax rate.

Another effect is that recognized gains on the sale of assets will be higher for tax purposes than for accounting purposes, reducing after-tax cash proceeds and adversely affecting the after-tax gain or loss from the sale. In addition, the carrying amount of assets and liabilities will reflect, for companies not yet adopting Statement of Financial Accounting Standards (SFAS) 109, the tax accounting differences. Companies adopting Statement 109 must provide deferred taxes on these differences.

ANALYSIS OF A POOLING METHOD ACQUISITION: THE CONAGRA–GOLDEN VALLEY MERGER

This section provides an analysis of the ConAgra-Golden Valley merger to illustrate the differences between the two accounting methods just discussed and to evaluate the impact of the pooling method on the combined firm. In July 1991, Golden Valley Microwave Foods, a manufacturer of popcorn and other microwave foods, was merged into ConAgra, a diversified food company. The merger was accounted for using the pooling of interests method of accounting.

Balance Sheet Under Pooling Method

The proxy statement (dated June 10, 1991) that was sent to shareholders of Golden Valley contains a pro forma combined condensed balance sheet, shown here as Exhibit 12-8.

ConAgra and Golden Valley had a joint venture (Lamb-Weston, a manufacturer of frozen potato products) that each firm accounted for using the equity method of accounting. As a result of the merger, Lamb-Weston is 100% owned and must be consolidated, with its total equity of $104,863,000 (common stock plus retained earnings) eliminated and replaced by the asset and liability accounts. (See the section on consolidation in Chapter 11.) This is the major adjustment shown in the pro forma balance sheet.

The elimination from the investment account is $104,847,000 which is slightly different from the equity of Lamb-Weston, apparently due to other, but related, balance sheet accounts. Footnote 2 lists all the adjustments related to the elimination of the intercompany investment in Lamb-Weston required to convert the equity method treatment to consolidation. As expected, consolidation does not change the net investment, but it reflects all the assets and liabilities of the joint venture. The accounting entries (debits and credits each total $110,090) are as follows (in $ thousands):

Brands, etc.	$4,560	
Other current liabilities	667	
Common stock	53,255	
Retained earnings	51,608	
Investment account		$104,847
Other noncurrent liabilities		5,243

Footnote 1 shows the exchange of ConAgra shares for Golden Valley shares. The common equity of Golden Valley is carried forward unchanged in total amount. Because Golden Valley's shares had a par value of $0.01 per share while ConAgra shares have a par value of $5.00 each, the sum of $49,619,000 (the increase in par value) must be transferred from additional paid-in capital to common stock. This sum is computed as follows:

Par value of 9,958,731 ConAgra shares @ $5.00	$49.794 million
Par value of 17,545,333 Golden Valley shares @ $0.01	(0.175)
Net increase in par value	$49.619 million

EXHIBIT 12-8. CONAGRA, INC. AND SUBSIDIARIES
Pro Forma Combined Condensed Balance Sheet—Unaudited (in Thousands)

The following unaudited pro forma combined condensed balance sheet for ConAgra, Golden Valley and Lamb-Weston has been prepared based upon the historical consolidated balance sheets for ConAgra, Golden Valley and Lamb-Weston as of February 24, 1991, March 30, 1991, and February 24, 1991, respectively. The pro forma combined condensed balance sheet gives effect to the Merger as if it had occurred as of February 24, 1991 and as if it had been accounted for as a pooling of interests.

	ConAgra, Inc. and Subsidiaries	Golden Valley Microwave Foods, Inc. and Subsidiaries	Pro Forma Adjustments Lamb-Weston, Inc.	Other	Pro Forma Combined
ASSETS					
Current Assets:					
Cash and Cash Equivalents	$ 115,386	$ 275	$ 22,792	$ 8,308 (5)	
				(31,100)(6)	$ 115,661
Receivables, Net	1,396,592	22,927	30,298	—	1,449,817
Inventories	2,387,066	34,869	76,833	—	2,498,768
Other Current Assets	382,844	150	12,970	—	395,964
Total Current Assets	4,281,888	58,221	142,893	(22,792)	4,460,210
Property, Plant and Equipment	1,853,294	65,185	171,602	2,842 (3)	2,092,923
Brands, Trademarks and Goodwill, Net	2,707,742	—	23,319	4,560 (2)	
				4,763 (3)	2,740,384
Investments in Unconsolidated Subsidiaries	166,754	54,843	—	(104,847)(2)	116,750
Other Assets	272,132	2,591	14,496	(22,328)(4)	266,891
	$9,281,810	$180,840	$352,310	$(137,802)	$9,677,158
LIABILITIES AND STOCKHOLDERS' EQUITY					
Current Liabilities:					
Notes Payable	$915,274	$ —	$ —	$ —	$ 915,274
Current Installments of Long-Term Debt	422,867	413	9,428	—	432,708
Accounts Payable, Accrued Expenses and Other Current Liabilities	2,661,160	17,972	46,806	(667)(2)	
				8,308 (5)	2,733,579
Total Current Liabilities	3,999,301	18,385	56,234	7,641	4,081,561
Long-Term Debt	1,947,660	52,649	172,593	(31,100)(6)	2,141,802
Deferred Income Taxes	—	1,843	17,595	2,890 (3)	
				(22,328)(4)	—
Other Noncurrent Liabilities	1,230,842 (7)	—	1,025	5,243 (2)	1,237,110
Preferred Shares Subject to Mandatory Redemption	356,162	—	—	—	356,162
Common Stockholders' Equity					
Common Stock	697,392	175	53,255	(53,255)(2)	
				49,619 (1)	747,186
Additional Paid-in Capital	435,837	27,768	—	(49,619)(1)	413,986
Retained Earnings	623,184	80,020	51,608	(51,608)(2)	
				4,715 (3)	707,919
Foreign Currency Translation Adjustment	4,204	—	—	—	4,204
Less Cost of Treasury Shares	(3,160)	—	—	—	(3,160)
Less Unearned Restricted Stock	(9,612)	—	—	—	(9,612)
Total Common Stockholders' Equity	1,747,845	107,963	104,863	(100,148)	1,860,523
	$9,281,810	$180,840	$352,310	$(137,802)	$9,677,158

EXHIBIT 12-8. *(Continued)*

(1) Reflects the assumed conversion of 17,545,333 shares of Golden Valley Common Stock into 9,958,731 shares of ConAgra Common Stock (assuming an Exchange Ratio of .5676 of a share of ConAgra Common Stock for each share of Golden Valley Common Stock and assuming no fractional shares of ConAgra Common Stock are created upon the conversion of Golden Valley Common Stock).

(2) Reflects elimination of equity of Lamb-Weston upon consolidation—previously carried at equity.

(3) Reflects adjustment to conform Golden Valley accounting practices to those followed by ConAgra, including capitalization of certain acquired intangible assets and depreciation policies.

(4) Reclassification of deferred income taxes.

(5) Reclassification of Lamb-Weston cash overdraft.

(6) Reflects an assumed prepayment of a portion of Lamb-Weston long-term debt from Lamb-Weston excess cash.

(7) Other noncurrent liabilities of ConAgra consist principally of estimated liabilities of Beatrice Company for post-retirement health care, pensions, income taxes and various litigation, environmental and other matters. See ConAgra's Quarterly Report on Form 10-Q for the quarter ended February 24, 1991.

This table should be read in conjunction with the other pro forma financial information contained in this Proxy Statement/Prospectus and the consolidated financial statements of the companies and the notes thereto incorporated herein by reference.

Source: Golden Valley Microwave Foods, Inc. Proxy Statement, June 10, 1991.

This adjustment has no analytic significance, but it serves to clarify the application of the pooling of interests method.

Note 3 indicates that there were some differences in accounting methods between the two companies. Apparently, Golden Valley was more conservative in its accounting methods. Pulling out all these adjustments, we find that conversion to ConAgra's methodology has the following impact:

Increase in property	$2.842 million
Increase in brands, etc.	4.763
Deferred tax effect	(2.890)
Net effect on retained earnings	$4.715 million

In other words, if Golden Valley had been using ConAgra's accounting methods, its total accumulated (retained) earnings would have been higher by $7.60 million ($2.84 million plus $4.76 million) less additional income tax expense of $2.89 million. This information may have some use when evaluating the quality of earnings (see Chapter 15) of ConAgra.

Notes 4 and 5 are essentially reclassifications to bring uniformity to the combined statement. They remind us that different companies classify the same financial items differently, creating problems in comparability. Note 5 suggests that ConAgra may have a cash overdraft (negative cash balance) classified as a liability. Note 6 offsets

Lamb-Weston's cash balance and debt, reducing each by $31.1 million and affecting such debt-related ratios as debt to total capital.

Because of ConAgra's size, the pro forma combined balance sheet looks little different from that of ConAgra alone. Even with the consolidation of Lamb-Weston, total assets increase by less than $400 million or 4.26%. Common equity increases by $113 million or 6% as a result of the merger.

Balance Sheet Under Purchase Method

What would the merged company look like if the purchase method of accounting were employed? We must start by computing the value of the transaction. ConAgra issued 9,958,731 issues of common stock. On the date of the merger (July 11, 1991), ConAgra shares closed at a price of $40.875 per share, giving the shares a total value of $407 million.

Under the pooling of interests method, the historical equity of Golden Valley was carried forward to the equity account of ConAgra. Under the purchase method, the actual market value of the shares issued must be reflected, increasing ConAgra's equity by $407 million rather than the $108 million added under the pooling method.

The actual purchase price must be allocated to Golden Valley's assets and liabilities, using fair market values. While we are not provided with these data, we can make some inferences from data provided by Golden Valley in its *1990 Annual Report*.[14]

Golden Valley uses the first-in, first-out method of accounting for its inventories. This suggests that the fair value of its inventories is not greatly above historical cost of $35 million. For purposes of this analysis, we assume that fair value exceeds cost by 20%, or $7 million. For a LIFO company, we would add back the LIFO reserve to approximate fair value.

Golden Valley's property (net of depreciation) is $65 million at March 30, 1991. Schedule V in Golden Valley's 1990 10-K report shows that most of the company's property (mostly machinery and equipment rather than real estate) has been acquired within the past three years. This suggests that fair value does not greatly exceed historical cost. For purposes of analysis, we assume the fair value to be $75 million or 15% higher than historical cost.

Golden Valley's debt is mainly a revolving line of credit at floating interest rates. Therefore, there is no scope to revalue debt to fair value using current interest rates. As the company does not appear to have any postretirement benefits, there is no requirement to recognize their funded status. Finally, as Golden Valley's deferred tax liability is small (even after the recognition of the additional deferred tax liability due to conformity with ConAgra's accounting methods), the elimination of deferred taxes resulting from application of the purchase method would have little impact.

Golden Valley's 50% share of Lamb-Weston must also be reflected at fair value. Lamb-Weston was established by a purchase of assets in June 1988, generating a large allocation of the purchase price to goodwill as part of the purchase method's recognition of the fair market value of acquired assets and liabilities. Purchase method accounting

---

[14]One of the purposes of this allocation procedure is to arrive at an estimate of the premium ConAgra paid for Golden Valley's "goodwill." Our write-ups of the other assets will be "liberal," thus providing a conservative assessment of the goodwill that will turn out to be close to 70% of the total purchase price.

for the ConAgra–Golden Valley merger would require a recognition of changes in fair value since June 1988. We assume that fair values of the individual assets of Lamb-Weston are unchanged.

Lamb-Weston does, however, have a defined benefit pension plan with an underfunding (projected benefit obligation less assets and accruals) of $2.67 million on July 31, 1990 (the latest figure available). Under purchase accounting a liability of this amount must be recognized (see Chapter 9 for a full discussion). Further Lamb-Weston has a substantial liability for deferred income taxes ($17.6 million before any adjustments) that must be eliminated under the purchase method. Because purchase method adjustments apply only to the target's assets and liabilities, these adjustments are made only to the 50% of Lamb-Weston owned by Golden Valley; ConAgra's 50% share is not adjusted.

Available information and the assumptions just made can be used to allocate the purchase price under the purchase method:

Purchase price	$407 million
Less: Equity of Golden Valley	(108)
Equals: Excess to be allocated	$299 million
Adjustments to Golden Valley	
Inventories	$7 million
Property	10
Deferred tax (liability reduced)	5
Adjustment to Lamb-Weston	
Pension plan (50% only)	$(1) million
Deferred tax (50% of liability)	9
Total adjustments	$30 million
Remaining excess purchase price	$269 million

This remaining excess purchase price would have to be allocated to intangible assets. Some could be allocated to Golden Valley's brand names; the remainder would be classified as goodwill. Exhibit 12-9 shows a pro forma balance sheet for the merger using the purchase method of accounting.

The major differences between the pro forma balance sheet under the pooling method and that under the purchase method are the increases in intangible assets and common equity.

Income Statement Under Pooling Method

Exhibit 12-10, taken from the proxy statement, shows a combined income statement for the year ended February 24, 1991.[15] As in the case of the balance sheet, the combined income statement reflects the sales and expenses of Golden Valley. Use of the pooling

[15]ConAgra acquired the Beatrice Company on August 14, 1980. The column in Exhibit 12-11 headed "ConAgra-Golden Valley, Pro Forma Combined" includes the results of Beatrice (acquired using the purchase method of accounting) for the period March 1–August 14, 1990. For the sake of simplicity, we have omitted the details of this combination.

EXHIBIT 12-9. CONAGRA–GOLDEN VALLEY
Pro Forma Combined Condensed Balance Sheet—Purchase Method, February 24, 1991
(in $ millions)

	Pooling	Adjustments		Purchase
Current assets	$4460	$ 7	(1)	$4467
Property	2093	10	(2)	2103
Intangible assets	2740	269	(3)	3009
Investments and other	384	—		384
Total assets	$9677	$286		$9963
Current liabilities	4082	—		4082
Long-term debt	2142	—		2142
Deferred income tax	—	(14)	(4)	(14)
Other liabilities	1237	1	(5)	1238
Preferred equity	356	—		356
Common equity	1860	299	(6)	2159
Total equities	$9677	$286		$9963

Adjustments

   (1) Write-up of Golden Valley inventories to fair value.
   (2) Write-up of Golden Valley property to fair value.
   (3) Residual excess purchase price allocated to intangibles.
   (4) Reduction of deferred income taxes of Golden Valley and Lamb-Weston (50% only).
   (5) Pension liability of Lamb-Weston (50% only).
   (6) Excess of fair value of ConAgra shares issued over common equity of Golden Valley.

method means that past results will be restated when presented in future financial statements. The sales and expenses of Lamb-Weston are also included, reflecting its consolidation because of the merger. Once again there are some adjustments.

   Note 2 shows the elimination of the earnings of Lamb-Weston, which had been accounted for using the equity method; the full sales and expenses of Lamb-Weston are now included in the consolidated income statement. In addition, selling expense is increased by $2,822,000 presumably reflecting intercompany payments that are now eliminated in consolidation. These numbers can be reconciled as follows (in $ thousands):

Increase in net income due to consolidation of income statement of Lamb-Weston	$28,912
Reduction of net income due to elimination of equity in net income of Lamb-Weston	(26,090)
Increase in selling expense	(2,822)
Net impact	$0

would result in income statement adjustments as well. The impact of these adjustments is shown in Exhibit 12-11:

1. Adjustment of inventories to fair value would flow into cost of goods sold, reducing income by $7 million.

2. Write-up of property to fair value would result in additional depreciation expense. From Schedules V and VI of Golden Valley's 10-K, we compute an average life of approximately 10 years for its property. The increase in carrying value of property of $10 million would result, therefore, in $1 million per year of additional depreciation.

3. The $269 million of intangibles must also be amortized. Goodwill can be amortized over a period of up to 40 years; other intangibles might have shorter lives. If we arbitrarily assume a 30-year amortization period, annual amortization expense would be $9 million per year.

The effect of use of the purchase method on the combined income statement is somewhat greater than its impact on the balance sheet. Net income for common (after preferred dividends) is reduced by more than 6%. The effect on earnings per share is a reduction of $0.10 to $1.42 per share.

EXHIBIT 12-11. CONAGRA–GOLDEN VALLEY
Pro Forma Combined Condensed Income Statement—Purchase Method,
Twelve Months Ended February 24, 1991 (in $ millions)

	Pooling	Adjustments	Purchase
Net sales	$ 21,249	—	$ 21,249
Cost of goods sold	(18,334)	(8) (1)	(18,342)
Selling expense	(2,113)	(9) (2)	(2,122)
Interest expense	(374)	—	(374)
Income before equity	$ 428	$(17)	$ 411
Equity income	9	—	9
Pretax income	$ 437	$(17)	$ 420
Income tax expense	(189)	3 (3)	(186)
Net income	$ 248	$(14)	$ 234
Preferred dividends	(24)	—	(24)
Net income for common	$ 224	$(14)	$ 210
Earnings per share	$ 1.52		$ 1.42

Adjustments

(1) Additional cost of goods sold resulting from inventory write-up and additional depreciation expense ($7 million + $1 million = $8 million).

(2) Amortization of goodwill and other intangibles.

(3) Income tax saved because of additional expenses; note that goodwill amortization is not tax deductible.

Comparison of Financial Ratios

The pro forma balance sheets and income statements can also be used to compute financial ratios resulting from each method of accounting, and these are presented in Exhibit 12-12.

Debt to total capital (where debt includes both short- and long-term debt as well as redeemable preferred) decreases when the purchase method is used because the newly issued stock is recorded at market value rather than the equity of Golden Valley. Alternatively, we may wish to look at debt relative to tangible equity (common equity less intangible assets). But ConAgra already had negative tangible equity; use of the purchase method results in a small improvement because the write-up of other assets increases tangible equity.

As we only have end-of-year data, we have used ending equity and capital (rather than averages) to compute return ratios. These ratios are clearly lower under the purchase method. Equity (and, therefore, capital) is increased while earnings are reduced. Because of the high leverage of ConAgra, the effect on return on ending common equity (net income for common/ending common equity) is more dramatic than is the impact on return on ending total capital (earnings before interest and taxes/ending total capital).

Because of the large relative size of ConAgra, activity ratios are virtually identical under the two methods, and we have not shown them in Exhibit 12-12. However, the higher net profit margins (net income/sales) of Golden Valley are diluted when the purchase method is used and the impact is noticeable.

But the most telling difference between the two methods emerges when we look at the marginal impact of Golden Valley on ConAgra. Under the pooling method, the results are as follows:

Additional net income for common*	$22.21 million
Additional ConAgra shares issued*	10.23 million
Marginal earnings per share	$2.16

*Data derived from Exhibit 12-10; number of shares includes common equivalents and is, therefore, higher than shares shown in the balance sheet in Exhibit 12-8.

As Exhibit 12-10 clearly shows, the acquisition of Golden Valley is antidilutive for the year ended February 24, 1991. Earnings per share increased from $1.47 before the acquisition to $1.52 after. ConAgra used its highly valued (its price/earnings ratio was

EXHIBIT 12-12. CONAGRA–GOLDEN VALLEY
Comparison of Ratios: Pooling Versus Purchase, for Year Ended February 24, 1991

	Pooling	Purchase
Debt to total capital	67.4%	64.0%
Return on ending total capital	14.1	13.1
Return on ending common equity	12.0	9.7
Net profit margin	1.17	1.10

27.8 on the acquisition date) shares to purchase a company at a lower multiple of earnings and enhance earnings per share.

The calculation under the purchase method shows

Additional net income for common*	$8.21 million
Additional ConAgra shares issued	10.23 million
Marginal earnings per share	$0.80

*Net income of $22.21 million under pooling method less $14 million of purchase method adjustments.

The acquisition is now dilutive and reduces ConAgra's earnings per share from $1.47 to $1.42. The economics of the acquisition do not change, but the immediate effect is to reduce earnings per share.

Summary

The comparison of the two methods of accounting for acquisitions on the ConAgra–Golden Valley transaction can be summarized as follows:

1. The purchase method increases equity and assets, particularly intangibles.
2. The purchase method reduces reported earnings because the asset increases must be amortized, resulting in higher expenses.
3. Profitability ratios decrease; the debt–to–total capital ratio declines under the purchase method.
4. Reduced profitability under the purchase method makes the acquisition dilutive rather than increasing earnings per share.

ANALYSIS OF A PURCHASE METHOD ACQUISITION: GEORGIA PACIFIC'S PURCHASE OF GREAT NORTHERN NEKOOSA

This section provides an analysis of a purchase method transaction to illustrate both the effects of that accounting method and the differences between the purchase and pooling methods.

In March 1990 Georgia Pacific (GP), a major forest products firm, purchased a controlling interest in Great Northern Nekoosa (GNN), a pulp and paper company, pursuant to a tender offer for shares of that company. The merger was accounted for as a purchase. The sales of GNN were approximately 40% of those of GP.

Balance Sheet Under Purchase Method

The net purchase price of nearly $3.7 billion was allocated to the acquired assets and liabilities using their fair values. Using the GNN balance sheet as of December 31, 1989, the company's 10-Q report for the quarter ended March 31, 1990, and disclosures regarding GNN in GP's *1990 Annual Report,* we have developed the data shown in Exhibit 12-13.

The first column in Exhibit 12-13 is the estimated balance sheet of GNN at March 8, 1990, just prior to the merger. The last column is the postmerger balance sheet. The middle column shows the adjustments necessary to get from the first column to the last. The total adjustments equal the excess of the purchase price over the stated equity of GNN. The major adjustments are

(1) Inventories were written up to fair market value. GNN used the LIFO method and had a LIFO reserve of approximately $94 million at December 31, 1989. The estimated write-up is slightly greater than this reserve.

EXHIBIT 12-13
Acquisition of Great Northern Nekoosa, Purchase Method Adjustments, March 8, 1990 (in $ millions)

	GNN (Historical)	Adjustments		GNN (Fair Value)
Cash	$ 96	—		$ 96
Accounts receivable	484	—		484
Inventories	271	117	(1)	388
Other current assets	44	—		44
Current assets	$ 895	$ 117		$1012
Timber and timberlands	338	98	(2)	436
Property	2460	20	(2)	2480
Goodwill	482	(482)	(5)	—
		2001	(5)	2001
Other assets	109	(45)		64
Total assets	$4284	$1709		$5993
Short-term debt	146	—		146
Payables and accruals	400	—		400
Current liabilities	$ 546	—		$ 546
Long-term debt	1513	3		1516
Deferred income taxes	460	(421)	(3)	39
Other liabilities	31	162	(4)	193
Total liabilities	$2550	$ (256)		$2294
Equity (net worth)	$1734			
Total adjustments		$1965		
Net assets acquired				$3699

Note: See text for discussion of adjustments (1)–(5). The GNN data and adjustments are approximations. The data available do not permit precise allocations in some cases. For simplicity it is assumed that such accounts as accounts receivable and payables and accruals are already stated at fair value, requiring no further adjustment.

(2) Timber and property are written up by $98 million and $20 million, respectively, surprisingly little. A partial explanation is that GNN itself made a major acquisition in 1987, and property acquired at that time was written up to fair market value. Thus approximately 30% of GNN's property was already written up.[16]

(3) Deferred income taxes are reduced by $421 million. As the merger was taxable, the difference between the tax basis and accounting basis for most assets disappeared. The small remaining difference appears to relate to GNN's 1987 acquisition.

(4) Other long-term liabilities increased by $162 million. While no explanation is provided, two possible reasons are

    (a) provision for postemployment benefits (see Chapter 9),

    (b) provision for environmental obligations.

(5) Goodwill is the residual and can be computed as follows:

Fair value of tangible assets acquired	$ 3,992 million
Fair value of liabilities assumed	(2,294)
Fair value of net assets acquired	$ 1,698 million
Purchase price	$ 3,699
Fair value of net assets acquired	(1,698)
Goodwill	$ 2,001 million

Restating the GP–GNN Transaction to Pooling

To see the impact of the purchase method of acquisition accounting, we have recast the acquisition as a pooling of interests assuming that Georgia Pacific issued common stock to acquire Great Northern Nekoosa. To obtain the same capital structure and cash position, however, we must also assume that GP repurchased $3699 million of common stock. Such repurchase would preclude use of the pooling method under U.S. Generally Accepted Accounting Principles (GAAP); the assumption is made here for educational purposes only.

Under these revised assumptions, the assets and liabilities of GNN would be included in the financial statements of Georgia Pacific without any adjustment. Exhibit 12-14 provides the results of subtracting (reversing) the adjustments shown in Exhibit 12-13 from the December 31, 1990, balance sheet of Georgia Pacific.

Note that the total of the adjustments column is zero; we have not changed the cash effect of the acquisition. We have merely assumed two steps (acquisition for stock, then repurchase of stock) in place of one (acquisition for cash).

[16]GNN's March 1990 10-Q shows timber and property being written up by an additional $700 million based on a preliminary evaluation. Apparently, GP later decided to allocate more of the purchase price to goodwill and less to timber and property. While it is fruitless to speculate on why this change took place, we can note two results.

First, as GP amortizes goodwill over 40 years, that amortization may be lower than depreciation expense resulting from the write-up of fixed assets. Second, GP recognized gains in 1990 and 1991 from the sale of portions of the GNN assets acquired; if those assets had been written up at the time of acquisition, the gains would be smaller or nonexistent.

Thus the allocation of purchase price to goodwill rather than to fixed assets apparently increased the reported earnings of GP subsequent to the acquisition.

EXHIBIT 12-14. GEORGIA PACIFIC
Postacquisition Balance Sheet, Purchase Method Versus Pooling, as of December 31, 1990 (in $ millions)

	Purchase	Adjustments	Pooling
Cash	$ 58	—	$ 58
Accounts receivable	409	—	409
Inventories	1,209	$ (117)	1,092
Other current assets	90	—	90
Current assets	$ 1,766	$ (117)	$ 1,649
Timber and timberlands	1,630	(98)	1,532
Property	6,341	(20)	6,321
Goodwill	2,042	482	
		(2001)	523
Other assets	281	45	326
Total assets	$12,060	$(1709)	$10,351
Short-term debt	1,444	—	1,444
Payables and accruals	1,091	—	1,091
Current liabilities	$ 2,535	—	$ 2,535
Long-term debt	5,218	(3)	5,215
Deferred income taxes	928	421	1,349
Other liabilities	404	(162)	242
Total liabilities	$ 9,085	$ 256	$ 9,341
Equity of GP	2,975		
Equity of GNN		1734	
Stock repurchase		(3699)	
Equity after adjustments			1,010
Total equities	$12,060	($ 1709)	$10,351

The effect of this assumption and the use of the pooling method of accounting is considerable. Total debt is unchanged, but equity is much lower. While the stated equity of Great Northern Nekoosa has been added in, recall that pooling does not recognize the actual purchase price.[17] The excess of the purchase price of GNN over its stockholders' equity has effectively reduced equity rather than being capitalized in the form of goodwill and other assets. We can see this by computing tangible equity (equity less goodwill) for both cases, using data from Exhibit 12-14:

Purchase method: $2975 million − $2042 million = $933 million

Pooling method: $1010 million − $523 million = $487 million

---

[17]Also note that the cash outflow for stock repurchase reduces equity but that effect is a result of our recasting assumptions and should be considered separately from the impact of the differences between the accounting methods.

More than three quarters of the difference in equity under the two methods is caused by the creation of goodwill under the purchase method. The remaining difference is caused by the other adjustments, notably deferred taxes.

Income Statement Under Pooling Method

Changing the accounting method also has a major impact on the income statement. While we do not have the detail necessary to construct an income statement under the pooling method, we can discuss the impact of the change on reported sales and net income:

1. Sales of Great Northern Nekoosa would be included for all of 1990, not just the period following the merger. In addition, 1989, 1988 (and all previous periods) would be restated. The sales trend would be quite different from that under the purchase method as shown in part A of Exhibit 12-15.

Reported sales, which include GNN only after the acquisition date of March 8, 1990, give the impression of substantial sales growth. Restatement to include GNN for all periods gives a more correct view of the sales trend; 1990 was a year of lower sales.

2. Earnings would also be affected by use of the pooling method. First, the earnings of GP must be restated to include the results of GNN prior to the acquisition date. Second, earnings must be adjusted for the interest expense associated with the debt used

EXHIBIT 12-15. GEORGIA PACIFIC
Sales and Income Trend, Purchase Versus Pooling, 1988–1990 (in $ millions)

	1988	1989	1990
A. Sales			
Sales as reported (purchase)	$ 9,509	$10,171	$12,665
GNN sales prior to acquisition	3,566	3,853	710
Sales as restated (pooling)*	$13,075	$14,024	$13,375

*Pro forma sales disclosed by GP in its *1990 Annual Report* are slightly lower, perhaps reflecting some intercompany sales, which must be eliminated in consolidation.

B. Net Income

	1988	1989	1990
Income as reported (purchase)	$ 467	$ 661	$365
GNN income prior to acquisition*	342	321	(57)
Interest expense†	(259)	(259)	(49)
Purchase adjustments‡	—	—	40
Income as adjusted (pooling)	$ 550	$ 723	$299

*Reported earnings of GNN for 1988, 1989, and 1990 through March 8th.
†Assumed 7% after taxes on $3.699 billion.
‡Estimated effect of purchase method adjustments for period March 9–December 31, 1990.

to acquire Great Northern. Third, the effects of the purchase method adjustments must be removed from 1990 earnings. Note that the first two adjustments for 1990 are only for the period prior to the merger; postmerger, we must only reverse the purchase method effects. These calculations are shown in part B of Exhibit 12-15.

The exhibit shows that the acquisition of GNN would have augmented the reported earnings of GP in 1988 and 1989 as the income contribution exceeded the interest expense resulting from the purchase. Even with use of the pooling method, which increases net income because the effects of the purchase accounting adjustments are removed, the acquisition was dilutive for the portion of 1990 prior to the merger.[18]

Effects on Balance Sheet

The purchase method creates a discontinuity in the financial statements as the assets and liabilities acquired are consolidated effective with the acquisition date. This impact can be seen in Exhibit 12-16, which contains the Georgia Pacific balance sheets at December 31, 1989 and 1990.

Exhibit 12-13 shows that the acquisition of GNN increased the assets of Georgia Pacific by roughly $6 billion. As a result, the year-to-year balance sheet changes are dominated by the impact of the acquisition, which increased the assets of GP by 85%.

Effects on Cash Flow Statement

SFAS 95 requires that the statement of cash flows exclude the initial impact of acquisitions. Exhibit 12-17, GP's Statement of Cash Flows for 1990, allows a comparison of the cash flows with the year-to-year changes in balance sheet accounts. We also need to refer to Exhibit 12-13, which shows the fair values of the assets and liabilities of GNN on the acquisition date.

For example, let us analyze the change in inventories during 1990. The cash flow statement indicates a decrease of $34 million in the inventory balance, whereas the balance sheet shows an increase of $333 million ($1209 million − $876 million). As discussed previously, the inventory acquired by means of the acquisition is "ignored" in the CFO calculation. From Exhibit 12-13 we know that the amount of inventory acquired was $388 million, leaving us with the following reconciliation:

Balance at December 31, 1989	$876 million
Inventories of GNN acquired	388
Operating change (cash flow)	(34)
Expected balance, December 31, 1990	$1230 million
Actual balance, December 31, 1990	$1209 million

---

[18]Note that the "income as adjusted (pooling)" data in Exhibit 12-15 would not be the same as the "pro forma" data that companies making purchase method acquisitions disclose. Those "pro forma" calculations assume retroactive use of the purchase method of accounting.

EXHIBIT 12-16. GEORGIA PACIFIC CORPORATION AND SUBSIDIARIES
Balance Sheets, as of December 31, 1989–1990

Balance Sheets

(Millions, except shares and per share amounts)	December 31 1990	December 31 1989
Assets		
Current assets		
Cash.	$ 58	$ 23
Receivables, less allowances of $39 and $30	409	890
Inventories		
Raw materials.	379	299
Finished goods.	760	644
Supplies	238	102
LIFO reserve.	(168)	(169)
Total inventories	1,209	876
Other current assets	90	40
Total current assets	1,766	1,829
Timber and timberlands, net	1,630	1,246
Property, plant and equipment		
Land and improvements	195	151
Buildings	871	688
Machinery and equipment	8,489	6,016
Construction in progress.	493	140
Total property, plant and equipment, at cost	10,048	6,995
Accumulated depreciation	(3,707)	(3,304)
Property, plant and equipment, net	6,341	3,691
Goodwill	2,042	91
Other assets	281	199
Total assets	$12,060	$ 7,056

Georgia-Pacific Corporation and Subsidiaries

	December 31 1990	December 31 1989
Liabilities and shareholders' equity		
Current liabilities		
Bank overdrafts, net.	$ 136	$ 100
Commercial paper and other short-term notes	984	79
Current portion of long-term debt	324	31
Accounts payable	550	394
Accrued compensation.	160	111
Accrued interest	140	58
Other current liabilities	241	151
Total current liabilities	2,535	924
Long-term debt, excluding current portion.	5,218	2,336
Deferred income taxes.	928	841
Other long-term liabilities.	404	238

EXHIBIT 12-16. *(Continued)*

Shareholders' equity		
Common stock, par value **$**.80; authorized 150,000,000 shares; 86,704,000 and		
86,664,000 shares issued	69	69
Additional paid-in capital	995	1,009
Retained earnings	1,939	1,713
Long-term incentive plan deferred compensation	(30)	(56)
Other	2	(18)
Total shareholders' equity	2,975	2,717
Total liabilities and shareholders' equity	**$12,060**	**$7,056**

The accompanying notes are an integral part of these financial statements.

Source: Georgia Pacific, 1990 Annual Report.

The expected ending balance of inventories of $1230 million reflects the GNN acquisition and operations during 1990 (including the operations of GNN following the merger). But the balance sheet shows an actual ending balance of $1209 million. The difference is most likely the inventories of operations sold (divestitures) during 1990. Note the proceeds from sale of assets ($204 million) shown under cash flow from investment activities and the gain on sale reported in cash from operations.

Inventories of subsidiaries sold, like those of acquisitions, must be excluded from the operating change shown in the cash flow statement. We can deduce their amount ($1230 million − $1209 million = $21 million) if we assume that no inventories are denominated in foreign currencies.[19]

Property can be analyzed in the same way:

Balance at December 31, 1989	$3691 million
Property of GNN acquired	2480
Capital expenditures	833
Depreciation expense	(622)
Expected balance, December 31, 1990	$6382 million
Actual balance, December 31, 1990	$6341 million

Once again the difference is probably due to asset sales. For goodwill, the analysis works perfectly:

Balance at December 31, 1989	$91 million
Goodwill of GNN acquired	2001
Amortization of goodwill	(50)
Expected balance, December 31, 1990	$2042 million
Actual balance, December 31, 1990	$2042 million

[19]See Chapter 13 for a discussion of those effects.

EXHIBIT 12-17. GEORGIA PACIFIC CORPORATION AND SUBSIDIARIES
Statement of Cash Flows, for Years Ended December 31, 1988–1990

Statements of Cash Flows Georgia-Pacific Corporation and Subsidiaries

(Millions)	Year ended December 31		
	1990	1989	1988
Cash provided by (used for) operations			
Net income	$ 365	$ 661	$ 467
Items in net income not affecting cash			
Depreciation	622	445	392
Depletion	77	69	58
Gain on sales of assets	(64)	(27)	(17)
Amortization of goodwill	50	10	9
Deferred income taxes	48	53	44
Common stock compensation	4	32	6
Other	20	72	15
	1,122	1,315	974
Cash provided by (used for) working capital			
Receivables	929	15	(102)
Inventories	34	16	(38)
Other current assets	(6)	(7)	20
Accounts payable and accrued liabilities	(6)	19	11
	951	43	(109)
Cash provided by operations	2,073	1,358	865
Cash provided by (used for) investment activities			
Capital expenditures			
Property, plant and equipment	(833)	(447)	(697)
Timber and timberlands	(33)	(46)	(14)
Total capital expenditures	(866)	(493)	(711)
Acquisition of Great Northern Nekoosa Corporation	(3,565)	(23)	—
Other acquisitions	(8)	(6)	(468)
Proceeds from sales of assets	204	66	74
Other	6	(44)	10
Cash (used for) investment activities	(4,229)	(500)	(1,095)
Cash provided by (used for) financing activities			
Additions to long-term debt	7,111	133	1,534
Repayments of long-term debt	(5,543)	(305)	(884)
Fees paid to issue debt	(114)	(20)	(10)
Net increase (decrease) in bank overdrafts	(29)	(38)	37
Net increase (decrease) in commercial paper and other short-term notes	905	(69)	63
Common stock repurchased	—	(468)	(395)
Cash dividends paid	(139)	(130)	(123)
Cash provided by (used for) financing activities	2,191	(897)	222
Increase (decrease) in cash	35	(39)	(8)
Balance at beginning of year	23	62	70
Balance at end of year	$ 58	$ 23	$ 62

The accompanying notes are an integral part of these financial statements.

Source: Georgia Pacific, 1990 Annual Report.

Comparison of balance sheet changes with cash flows can be useful in several different circumstances:

1. When the breakdown of assets and liabilities acquired in a purchase method acquisition is not given, this analysis can provide rough estimates of the data through the separation of balance sheet changes due to acquisitions and divestitures from those resulting from operations.

2. Discrepancies between the expected and actual balance can suggest undisclosed transactions (purchases or sales) or valuation adjustments (such as those due to foreign currency changes).

3. Finally, it also highlights distortions in CFO that can follow an acquisition. Analysis of the receivables account will illustrate this point:

Although income declined by 45% from 1989 to 1990, CFO increased by approximately 53% from $1358 million to $2073 million. Analysis of the components of CFO indicates that the increase was all due to a decrease in accounts receivable. Fully 45% of the CFO of $2074 million and over 100% of the increase of $715 million results from the reported decline in accounts receivable of $929 million. The balance sheet shows a reduction of only $481 million. *Both* these reductions are large considering that

1. GP acquired $484 million of GNN's receivables (Exhibit 12-13);

2. The reduction was large by historical standards (see previous two years); and

3. Based on the reconciliation that follows, the amount of receivables included in divestitures of other subsidiaries was a mere $36 million.

Balance at December 31, 1989	$890 million
Receivables of GNN acquired	484
Operating change (cash flow)	(929)
Expected balance, December 31, 1990	$445 million
Actual balance, December 31, 1990	$409 million
Receivables sold by divestiture	$36 million

The answer to this mystery is provided by GP's financial statement footnotes, which state that the firm sold $850 million of trade accounts receivable (see Chapter 10 for discussion). To the extent that receivables sold include GNN receivables acquired as part of the acquisition, this is an example of the distortion in CFO discussed earlier. GNN's receivables did not arise from GP's operations but rather from the acquisition. Cash collected from these receivables is not properly cash from operations but is included there, thus overstating GP's CFO.

Comparison of Financial Ratios

Financial statement ratios under the two methods of accounting for the merger can be computed using data from Exhibit 12-14. The total debt-to-total capital ratio is 0.69

($6662 million/$9637 million) based on Georgia Pacific's actual December 31, 1990 balance sheet. Under pooling, the ratio is 0.87 ($6662 million/$7672 million) reflecting the lower level of stockholders' equity. Much of the difference is due to goodwill created under the purchase method. Debt to tangible capital (capital less goodwill) is 0.88 ($6662 million/$7595 million) under the purchase method and 0.93 ($6662 million/ $7149 million) when pooling is used. On the other hand, the current ratio is higher (0.93 versus 0.88) when the purchase method is used because of the write-up of inventory under purchase accounting.

The return on equity (we use ending equity for simplicity) is also greatly affected by the method of accounting for the merger:

Georgia Pacific
Return on Ending Equity

	1989*	1990
As reported (purchase)	24.3%	$365million/$2975million=12.3%
Adjusted (pooling)	88.1%	$299million/$1010million=29.6%

*Computations require data not provided

Under both methods, return on ending equity dropped sharply in 1990. However, the levels are quite different. The higher return under the pooling method reflects the lower level of equity and, for 1989, higher earnings (see part B in Exhibit 12-15) as well.

Using Pro Forma Information

Firms making purchase method acquisitions are required to report pro forma operating results. Exhibit 12-18 contains the portion of note 3 from GP's *1990 Annual Report* dealing with the acquisition of GNN.

The footnote contains several important categories of information:

1. A description of the acquisition, including the amount paid and the form of payment (in this case cash)

2. An allocation of the purchase price to the assets acquired and liabilities assumed

3. Pro forma sales, net income, and EPS assuming that the acquisition was consummated on January 1, 1989

The first two categories of information were used in the preceding analysis of the acquisition. Note that the breakdown of purchase price by GP is more detailed than the breakdown provided in many cases. This breakdown facilitated the preparation of Exhibit 12-13.

The third category of data permits analysts to understand how the acquisition affected the trend of sales and earnings reported by the acquiring firm. In Exhibit 12-15 we approximated the sales and net income for GP assuming that the pooling method had been used.

EXHIBIT 12-18
Footnote Disclosure of GNN Acquisition

. . . .

Georgia-Pacific Corporation and Subsidiaries

N*ote 3. Acquisitions*

Great Northern Nekoosa Corporation   In March 1990, the Corporation acquired a controlling stock interest in Great Northern Nekoosa Corporation (GNN). GNN was a producer of pulp, communication papers, newsprint and containerboard, a converter of corrugated boxes and envelopes, and a distributor of communication and other papers. In addition, GNN owned three wood products operations, hydroelectric plants and 3,436,000 acres of fee timberland and controlled 233,000 acres of leased timberland.

The amount required to purchase the stock and pay related fees and expenses was approximately $3.7 billion. The results of GNN's operations have been included in the accompanying statements of income and cash flows beginning on March 9, 1990. The following unaudited pro forma information shows the results of the Corporation's operations, as though the acquisition of GNN had been completed on January 1, 1989.

| (Millions, except per share amounts) | Year ended December 31 | |
	1990	1989
Net sales	$13,359	$13,944
Net income	331	627
Earnings per share	3.88	7.04

Source: Georgia Pacific, 1990 Annual Report.

The acquisition was recorded using the purchase method. The preliminary values assigned to GNN's assets and liabilities are shown in the following table. The purchase price exceeded the fair value of net assets acquired by approximately $2.0 billion. This amount is included in goodwill and is being amortized over 40 years.

(Millions)	March 8, 1990
Cash	$ 96
Receivables	484
Inventories	388
Other current assets	44
Timber and timberlands	436
Property, plant and equipment	2,480
Goodwill	2,001
Other assets	64
Total assets	5,993
Bank overdrafts	65
Current portion of long-term debt	81
Accounts payable and accrued liabilities	400
Long-term debt	1,516
Deferred income taxes	39
Other long-term liabilities	193
Total liabilities	2,294
Net assets acquired	$3,699

The pro forma data are similar to those in Exhibit 12-15 in that previously reported income statements are restated for the acquisition. Thus we see that the reported sales gain for 1990 was caused by the acquisition; when GNN is included for the entire period, 1990 sales declined.

The difference between the pooling data in Exhibit 12-15 and the pro forma data in Exhibit 12-18 is that the latter applies all the purchase method adjustments to the restated data. (In Exhibit 12-15 we made an adjustment only for interest expense on the purchase price.) The two sets of data are quite similar; both show that net income declined more sharply on a combined basis than on an "as reported" basis.

These data are also helpful when assessing 1991 operating results. As the acquisition took place during 1990, the comparison of reported 1990 and 1991 operations is affected by the "illusion of growth" already discussed. Using the pro forma data gives us a better comparison:

Georgia Pacific
Sales Comparison, 1990–1991
(in $ millions)

	1990	1991	% Change
Reported data for both years	12,665	11,524	−9.0%
Pro forma data for 1990	13,359	11,524	−13.7

Because reported 1990 sales excluded GNN until the acquisition date (March 8), the sales comparison looks better on an "as reported" basis. On an "apples to apples" basis, using pro forma sales for 1990, we obtain a truer picture of the sales trend.

Note that such pro forma data are provided only for the current and prior years. Unless previously reported data are restated, the long-term operating trends remain distorted by purchase method acquisitions.

Summary

The reported financial statements of Georgia Pacific following the acquisition of GNN are highly dependent on the accounting method used. The purchase method recognizes the fair values of the assets and liabilities acquired, including substantial goodwill. The income statement, which includes GNN only following the merger, is distorted by the acquisition, making comparisons difficult. Disclosures allow at least rough adjustments to facilitate comparison of financial statements under the different accounting methods and to discern the impact of the acquisition on the acquirer.

ANALYSIS OF INTERNATIONAL DIFFERENCES: THE SMITHKLINE BEECHAM MERGER

In July 1989 SmithKline Beckman, an American health care company, merged with Beecham Group, a similar U.K. company. The acquisition was accounted for under U.K. GAAP as a pooling of interests (merger accounting in U.K. terminology) but would have been reported as a purchase acquisition under U.S. GAAP because of differences in the accounting standards of the two countries.

The merger provides an unusual opportunity to compare the effects of both methods on the same transaction, without recourse to estimates or assumptions. It also allows an analysis of accounting differences across countries. The merged company reconciles its stockholders' equity and net income on Form 20-F[20] to show the effects of the different accounting principles of the two jurisdictions.

[20]Annual report filed by non-U.S. companies with the Securities and Exchange Commission (see Chapter 1 for discussion).

The Merged Balance Sheet

Exhibit 12-19 reproduces the merged company's (SKB) consolidated balance sheets from the Form 20-F report. Those familiar with U.K. financial statements will notice that these statements are not in the usual U.K. format. The accounting principles used are those of the United Kingdom, the currency is pounds sterling, and the numbers are the same as in the U.K. statements. However, the 20-F version (which uses the U.S. format) should be more comfortable for most readers. The 1989 balance sheet has also been translated (for convenience) into U.S. dollars.

Because the pooling method has been used, the December 31, 1988, balance sheet has been restated to include both companies. As a result, the year-to-year changes in assets and liabilities are not large, except for debt and stockholders' equity.

Total assets have decreased slightly; cash is down sharply, all other assets are higher. On the liability side, the major changes are a large increase in debt and reduction in equity. Stockholders of both SmithKline and Beecham received special cash dividends in connection with the merger. These special dividends (which preclude use of the pooling method under U.S. GAAP) resulted in a shift in capital structure from equity to debt. Notice that equity is shown net of a reserve for goodwill. This practice is one of the key differences between American and British merger accounting standards.

Differences in Accounting Methods

Before looking at financial statements prepared under U.S. accounting standards, it would be useful to list some of the principal differences between U.S. and U.K. standards. These differences include the following:

1. Under U.S. GAAP, acquisition goodwill must be capitalized and amortized over no more than 40 years. Under U.K. GAAP, goodwill can be amortized over its expected economic life (generally ranging from 5 to 20 years) or charged immediately to stockholders' equity, or a reserve can be created.

2. Capitalization of interest is required in the United States (SFAS 33, discussed in Chapter 6). It is not required in the United Kingdom.

3. Deferred taxes are required in the United States for all timing differences (see Chapter 7); in the U.K. provision of deferred taxes is predicated on the probability of reversal.

4. U.S. GAAP is restrictive regarding extraordinary items (Chapter 2) while U.K. GAAP is more permissive. While this difference does not affect net income, it does affect income before extraordinary items, which most analysts prefer as a measure of recurring income.

5. Revaluation of property is not permitted under U.S. GAAP; it is common practice in the United Kingdom to replace historical cost with revalued amounts, with the difference credited to equity.

6. Under U.S. GAAP, dividends must be declared before they can be reflected in the financial statements. In the United Kingdom, they are an appropriation of earnings for the year.

EXHIBIT 12-19. SMITHKLINE BEECHAM PLC AND SUBSIDIARIES
Consolidated Balance Sheets

		December 31	
	1988	1989	1989 [1]
	£m	£m	$m
Assets			
Current assets			
Cash and cash equivalents	879.9	233.2	376.5
Trade receivables, less allowances of £37.8 million in 1988 and £43.0 million in 1989	704.8	857.1	1,383.8
Inventories	479.8	509.4	822.4
Prepaid expenses and other current assets	293.2	409.0	660.3
Assets held for disposal	168.0	182.7	295.0
Total current assets	2,525.7	2,191.4	3,538.0
Investments	84.5	90.6	146.3
Property, plant and equipment, less accumulated depreciation of £756.3 million in 1988 and £812.5 million in 1989	1,283.9	1,464.6	2,364.6
Total assets	3,894.1	3,746.6	6,048.9
Liabilities and shareholders' equity			
Current liabilities			
Accounts payable	241.2	266.9	430.9
Short-term borrowings	492.6	966.5	1,560.4
Accrued liabilities	829.9	1,283.5	2,072.2
Current portion of long-term debt	9.1	17.6	28.4
Total current liabilities	1,572.8	2,534.5	4,091.9
Long-term debt	550.9	999.5	1,613.7
Accrued pension obligations	60.4	64.3	103.8
Restructuring costs	109.2	300.1	484.5
Other liabilities	218.2	123.2	198.9
Minority interests	22.6	21.5	34.8
Total liabilities	2,534.1	4,043.1	6,527.6
Shareholders' equity			
A and B Ordinary shares of £0.25 each, 1,250,000,000 and 750,000,000 shares authorized respectively; 666,754,000 and 621,175,000 issued in 1988 and 670,410,000 and 654,752,000 in 1989 respectively	322.0	331.3	534.9
Subsidiary preferred stock at stated value of U.S. $0.25 each, 200,000,000 shares authorized; 131,001,000 issued in 1989.	—	19.6	31.6
Revaluation reserve	107.7	156.2	252.2
Other reserves	88.9	(1,040.9)	(1,680.5)
Related companies reserves	11.4	12.5	20.1
Retained earnings	1,798.6	1,220.3	1,970.2
Total shareholders' equity before elimination of goodwill	2,328.6	699.0	1,128.5
Goodwill reserve	(968.6)	(995.5)	(1,607.2)
Total shareholders' equity after elimination of goodwill	1,360.0	(296.5)	(478.7)
	3,894.1	3,746.6	6,048.9

[1] The translation of pounds sterling into U.S. dollars has been made at $1.6145 to £1 solely for the convenience of the reader and does not form part of the financial statements as such.

See Notes to Consolidated Financial Statements

Source: SmithKline Beecham, Form 20-F, 1989.

Comparison of Stockholders' Equity

With these differences in mind, we can now examine Exhibit 12-20, which is a reconciliation of SKB's shareholders' equity under U.K. GAAP to that under U.S. accounting methods.

At December 31, 1988, prior to the merger date, equity under U.S. GAAP is approximately 21% higher than it is under U.K. GAAP (£1647 million versus £1360 million). The major difference is Beecham's practice of writing off goodwill immediately following an acquisition. A partial offset is the elimination of the increase in equity resulting from the revaluation of fixed assets. Another offset is the inclusion (under U.K. GAAP) of SmithKline's retained earnings through 1988, as required by the pooling method. Under U.S. GAAP (purchase method), SmithKline is not included in the consolidated group at December 31, 1988, resulting in the elimination of SmithKline's

EXHIBIT 12-20. SMITHKLINE BEECHAM PLC AND SUBSIDIARIES
Effect on Shareholders' Equity of Differences Between U.K. and U.S. Generally Accepted Accounting Principles

Note 3   Summary of differences between U.K. and U.S. Generally Accepted Accounting Principles and Other U.S. Information (continued)

Approximate effect on shareholders' equity of differences between U.K. GAAP and U.S. GAAP

	Year ended December 31		
	1988	1989	1989 [1]
	(in millions, except per share data)		
	£	£	$
Shareholders' equity under U.K. GAAP	1,360	(297)	(480)
U.S. GAAP adjustments:			
Elimination of SmithKline equity prior to Combination	(98)	—	—
Goodwill — Beecham	441	461	744
Capitalization of interest	7	37	60
Dividends	74	50	81
Deferred taxation			
— due to timing differences	(61)	(66)	(107)
— due to ACT	32	5	8
Revaluation reserve	(108)	(156)	(252)
Other, net	—	(12)	(19)
Purchase accounting:			
Property, plant and equipment	—	69	111
Intangible assets	—	754	1,217
Goodwill	—	2,665	4,303
Other, net	—	35	57
Shareholders' equity under U.S. GAAP	1,647	3,545	5,723

[1] The translation of pounds sterling into U.S. dollars has been made at $1.6145 to £1 solely for the convenience of the reader and does not form part of the financial statements as such.

Source: SmithKline Beecham, Form 20-F, 1989.

tangible equity of £98 million. The other adjustments reflect the accounting differences listed.

At December 31, 1989, following the merger, the preexisting goodwill and revaluation differences persist. However, they are dwarfed by new ones arising from the differential treatment of the merger under the accounting principles of the two countries.

Under U.K. GAAP (pooling) the assets and liabilities of SmithKline were consolidated without change, and Beecham's equity was added to the tangible equity of SmithKline (goodwill already on SmithKline's books was written off against equity at the time of the acquisition, conforming the accounts of the acquired company to U.K. GAAP). Stockholders' equity fell from £1360 million at December 31, 1988, to a negative £297 million at December 31, 1989. The additional earnings resulting from the inclusion of SmithKline were not large compared with the special dividends to the shareholders of Beecham and SmithKline prior to the merger, which reduced equity by more than £1800 million.

The numbers change dramatically under U.S. GAAP (purchase). The value of the acquisition (based on stock prices at the acquisition date of July 27, 1989) was £3205 million. Compare this with the tangible equity of £98 million used to measure the transaction under the pooling method! SmithKline's assets and liabilities were restated to fair market value. Almost all the purchase price was allocated to intangible assets (partly, we can assume, patents and brand names), with goodwill alone accounting for three quarters of the total. These allocations (less amortization between the date of the acquisition and year end) account for the large purchase accounting adjustments in Exhibit 12-20. Equity rises £1.9 billion, from £1647 million to £3545 million, in sharp contrast to the decrease in equity of nearly £1.7 billion under U.K. accounting principles.

Tangible equity (equity less intangible assets) under U.S. GAAP is quite close to equity computed under U.K. GAAP, and the year-to-year change is similar, as shown by the following computations:

Computation of Tangible Equity (U.S. GAAP), December 31, 1988–1989 (in £ millions)

	1988	1989
Stated equity (Exhibit 12-20)	£1647	£3545
Less: Beecham goodwill	(441)	(461)
Acquisition intangibles	—	(754)
Acquisition goodwill	—	(2665)
Equals: Tangible equity (U.S. GAAP)	£1,206	£(335)
Equity under U.K. GAAP	£1,360	£(297)

The difference between the two accounting methods, it can be seen, comes down mainly to a matter of goodwill. We will examine this issue shortly.

Restatement of the Balance Sheet

The data provided in Exhibit 12-20 are sufficient to enable us to restate the balance sheets (Exhibit 12-19) to a U.S. GAAP basis. The restatement for December 31, 1989, is shown as Exhibit 12-21.

The adjustment entries come directly from the GAAP reconciliation and descriptions provided in Exhibit 12-20. (Note that each adjustment appears twice: once in the equity account and once in the appropriate asset or liability account. The increase in assets plus the decrease in liabilities must, necessarily, be equal to the change in stockholders' equity).

The following three items require some explanation:

1. Current assets are decreased by the (net) increase in deferred tax (£66 million − £5 million) because of footnote disclosure that current assets include deferred taxes.

EXHIBIT 12-21. SMITHKLINE BEECHAM BALANCE SHEET
Conversion to U.S. GAAP, at December 31, 1989 (in £ millions)

	U.K. GAAP	Adjustments	U.S. GAAP
Cash	£ 233.2		£ 233.2
Other current assets	1958.2	£ (61.0)	1897.2
Current assets	£2191.4	£ (61.0)	£2130.4
Investments	90.6	69.0	90.6
Property (net)	1464.6	(156.0)	1414.6
		37.0	
Intangible assets	—	754.0	754.0
Goodwill	—	461.0	3126.0
		2665.0	
Total assets	£3746.6	£3769.0	£7515.6
Short-term debt	984.1		984.1
Other current liabilities	1550.4	(50.0)	1500.4
Current liabilities	£2534.5	£ (50.0)	£2484.5
Long-term debt	999.5		999.5
Accrued pensions	64.3		64.3
Restructuring	300.1		300.1
Other liabilities	123.2	(23.0)	100.2
Minority interest	21.5		21.5
Total liabilities	£4043.1	£ (73.0)	£3970.1
Stockholders' equity	(296.5)	3842.0	3545.5
Total equities	£3746.6	£3769.0	£7515.6
Current ratio	0.86		0.86
Debt-to-total assets	0.53		0.26
Debt-to-equity	NMF*		0.56

*Not meaningful

2. Another footnote indicates that dividends payable are included in current liabilities. This adjustment is made because, under U.S. GAAP, dividends are not accounted for until actually declared.

3. The "other" adjustments (−£12 million + £35 million = £23 million) are nowhere described; we have arbitrarily reduced other liabilities by this amount.

The effect of the restatement is to double the assets of the company. The allocation of the purchase price of SmithKline combined with the reinstatement of goodwill (which was written off under U.K. GAAP) result in the addition of £3769 million to consolidated assets. Because most of the purchase price of SmithKline was allocated to intangible assets (including goodwill), few other accounts are materially affected by this restatement.

However, financial ratios based on the restated balance sheet reflect some major changes. The debt-to-equity ratio (including short- and long-term debt) is a moderate 0.56. Using the U.K. GAAP data, the negative equity makes this ratio meaningless. Of course using the U.S. GAAP data, debt to tangible equity would also be meaningless. Debt-to-total assets falls from 0.53 to 0.26 under U.S. GAAP. The current ratio, however, is unchanged at 0.86 as current assets and liabilities are both reduced only slightly.

In Exhibit 12-22, we compare the U.S. GAAP balance sheet (December 31, 1989) just derived with the U.S. GAAP balance sheet for December 31, 1988. The 1988 balance sheet cannot be derived from the 1988 balance sheet shown in Exhibit 12-19 because the latter has been restated to include SmithKline.

Under the purchase method, the December 31, 1988, balance sheet would be unaffected by the merger but would be the actual 1988 balance sheet of Beecham. We have taken that balance sheet (from the Form 20-F filing) and, using the data in Exhibit 12-20, adjusted it to U.S. GAAP (mainly by restoring written off goodwill). The result is included in Exhibit 12-22, which shows the two balance sheets as they would have been reported under U.S. GAAP.

Total assets appear to have multiplied nearly three times over the course of the year, while total liabilities have increased to four times their previous level. Stockholders' equity has more than doubled. This comparison illustrates how the purchase method creates discontinuity in the pattern of asset and liability growth. Users of databases must be especially careful of the effect of purchase method acquisitions.

Income Statement Effects

The two methods of accounting for the merger also result in considerable differences in reported income. The income statement of the company under U.K. GAAP (pooling method) is shown in Exhibit 12-23.

While the income statement is, like the balance sheet, in the normal U.S. format, there are some features requiring comment. First, note that sales of discontinued operations are shown (but separately); under U.S. GAAP such sales would be excluded, and the income statement would reflect only the income components of discontinued operations.

Second, notice the large extraordinary items. As we have already mentioned, U.S. standards are much more restrictive, and these items are not extraordinary under U.S.

EXHIBIT 12-22. SMITHKLINE BEECHAM
Comparative Balance Sheets on U.S. GAAP Basis, at December 31, 1988–1989
(£ millions)

	1988	1989
Cash	£ 735.5	£ 233.2
Other current assets	899.0	1897.2
Current assets	£1634.5	£2130.4
Investments	11.5	90.6
Property (net)	505.5	1414.6
Intangible assets		754.0
Goodwill	441.4	3126.0
Total assets	£2592.9	£7515.6
Short-term debt	238.2	984.1
Other current liabilities	434.8	1500.4
Current liabilities	£ 673.0	£2484.5
Long-term debt	127.3	999.5
Accrued pensions	38.9	64.3
Restructuring	27.1	300.1
Other liabilities	64.4	100.2
Minority interest	15.3	21.5
Total liabilities	£ 946.0	£3970.1
Shareholders' equity	1646.9	3545.5
Total equities	£2592.9	£7515.6
Current ratio	2.43	0.86
Debt-to-total assets	0.14	0.26
Debt-to-equity	0.22	0.56

GAAP. As in the case of the balance sheet, SKB provides a reconciliation of net income under both sets of accounting standards, as shown in Exhibit 12-24.

The difference in net income for 1988 reflects two main factors. First is the impact of differences in accounting methods, with goodwill amortization the most important. These differences were discussed in reference to the balance sheet (Exhibit 12-20). If Beecham had capitalized goodwill, amortization would have reduced 1988 earnings by 10%.

The second main difference is the elimination, under U.S. GAAP, of the 1988 net income of SmithKline. Remember that under the pooling method, 1988 was restated to include SmithKline. Under the purchase method, the results of SmithKline are included only following the date of the merger. In 1989, both these factors are still at work. *U.S. GAAP net income reflects the different accounting methods and excludes the earnings of SmithKline for the portion of 1989 prior to the effective date of the merger.*

But the more important differences in 1989 net income stem from the differential accounting treatment of the merger itself. Under the purchase method (U.S. GAAP), the write-up of property and intangible assets requires amortization of £130 million (£60 million + £28 million + £42 million) over the last five months of 1989. For a full year the amortization would be much higher.

EXHIBIT 12-23. SMITHKLINE BEECHAM PLC AND SUBSIDIARIES
Consolidated Income Statements

	Year ended December 31		
	1988	1989	1989 [1]
	£	£	$
	(in millions, except per share data)		
Net sales			
Continuing operations	3,682.0	4,276.4	6,904.2
Operations discontinued and held for sale	619.8	620.6	1,002.0
	4,301.8	4,897.0	7,906.2
Cost of goods sold	(1,722.5)	(1,983.2)	(3,201.9)
Gross profit	2,579.3	2,913.8	4,704.3
Selling, general and administrative expenses	(1,520.4)	(1,705.9)	(2,754.2)
Research and development expenses	(331.1)	(390.1)	(629.8)
Trading income of continuing operations	646.1	738.0	1,191.5
Trading income of operations discontinued and held for sale	81.7	79.8	128.8
Interest (net)	(31.1)	(102.0)	(164.7)
Equity in earnings of related companies	6.4	7.9	12.8
Income before taxes, minority interests and extraordinary items	703.1	723.7	1,168.4
Taxes on income	(227.7)	(243.6)	(393.3)
Income before minority interests and extraordinary items	475.4	480.1	775.1
Minority interests	(5.8)	(3.7)	(6.0)
Income before extraordinary items	469.6	476.4	769.1
Extraordinary items (net)	(102.3)	(346.3)	(559.1)
Net income	367.3	130.1	210.0
Per Ordinary Share			
Income before extraordinary items	36.5p	36.5p	58.9 cents
Net income	28.6p	10.0p	16.1 cents
Per Equity Unit			
Income before extraordinary items	182.5p	182.5p	294.6 cents
Net income	143.0p	50.0p	80.7 cents
Dividends post Combination			
A Ordinary Shares (paid by the Company)	—	5.2p	
Equity Units (paid by SmithKline)	—	55.25cents	
Weighted average number of shares in issue	1,286.4m	1,305.9m	

[1] The translation of pounds sterling into U.S. dollars has been made at $1.6145 to £1 solely for the convenience of the reader and does not form part of the financial statements as such.

The Group prepares its consolidated financial statements in accordance with accounting principles generally accepted in the U.K. ("U.K. GAAP") which differ in certain significant respects from accounting principles generally accepted in the U.S. ("U.S. GAAP"). A reconciliation to U.S. GAAP of certain amounts at December 31, 1989 and 1988 and for the two years ended December 31, 1989 is set forth in Note 3 of the Notes to Consolidated Financial Statements.

See Notes to Consolidated Financial Statements.

Source: SmithKline Beecham, Form 20-F, 1989.

EXHIBIT 12-24. SMITHKLINE BEECHAM PLC AND SUBSIDIARIES
Effect on Net Income of Differences Between U.K. and U.S. GAAP

Note 3 Summary of differences between U.K. and U.S. Generally Accepted Accounting Principles and Other U.S. Information (continued)

Approximate effect on net income of differences between U.K. GAAP and U.S. GAAP

	Year ended December 31		
	1988	1989	1989 [1]
	(in millions, except per share data)		
	£	£	$
Net income after extraordinary items per U.K. GAAP	367	130	210
U.S. GAAP adjustments (net of taxation):			
Elimination of SmithKline results prior to Combination	(62)	(144)	(232)
Combination transaction and SmithKline restructuring costs	—	281	454
Goodwill — Beecham	(36)	(26)	(42)
Deferred taxation			
— due to timing differences	(6)	(3)	(5)
— due to ACT	(5)	(27)	(44)
Other, net	(1)	6	10
Purchase accounting:			
Amortization of intangible assets	—	(60)	(97)
Amortization of goodwill	—	(28)	(45)
Depreciation and other	—	(42)	(68)
Net Income per U.S. GAAP	257	87	141
Represented by:			
Income before non-recurring charges and taxation	412	349	564
Non-recurring charges	—	(115)	(186)
Taxation	(181)	(162)	(262)
Income from continuing operations	231	72	116
Income from discontinued operations (net of tax)	26	15	25
Net Income per U.S. GAAP	257	87	141
Average number of A and B Ordinary Shares in issue	665.2m	951.5m	
Per Ordinary Share per U.S. GAAP:			
Income from continuing operations	34.7p	7.5p	12.1 cents
Net income	38.6p	9.1p	14.7 cents
Per Equity Unit per U.S. GAAP:			
Income from continuing operations	173.5p	37.5p	60.5 cents
Net income	193.0p	45.5p	73.5 cents

[1] The translation of pounds sterling into U.S. dollars has been made at $1.6145 to £1 solely for the convenience of the reader and does not form part of the financial statements as such.

Source: SmithKline Beecham, Form 20-F, 1989.

As a result of these differences, net income according to U.S. accounting standards fell by two-thirds in 1989 to £87 million. Income from continuing operations fell by nearly 70% to £72 million. While net income under U.K. GAAP (Exhibit 12-23) also shows a steep decline, much of the 1989 decline is deemed to be extraordinary; income before extraordinary items shows a slight increase for 1989. The reported earnings per share data reflect this disparity:

Reported Earnings per Share (in pence)

	1988	1989
U.K. GAAP before extraordinary charges	36.5	36.5
U.S. GAAP from continuing operations	34.7	7.5

Note that the number of shares is not the same for the computations under U.S. and U.K. GAAP. Under U.S. GAAP, the additional shares issued to acquire SmithKline are considered outstanding only following the merger; under U.K. GAAP, they are considered to be outstanding for the entire period, as 1988 results have been restated to include SmithKline. For 1990, however, the number of shares outstanding are the same under both GAAPs.

Which earnings per share figure is more appropriate? The major factors are the extraordinary items, shown in Exhibit 12-25. The largest one relates to the merger, but it is vaguely described, providing little information.

Presumably, the "restructuring" charge will have a positive impact on future earnings. Such charges often include severance pay for discharged employees and write-downs of assets (reducing future amortization). The size of this charge suggests that both companies had overvalued assets, but in the case of SmithKline, this does not square with the huge price paid for the company relative to stated book value.

From an earnings point of view, the extraordinary items do appear to be mostly nonrecurring. Thus we can add them back to net income under U.S. GAAP, resulting in adjusted 1989:

	Earnings (£ millions)	Per Share (pence)
Continuing operations (U.S. GAAP)	72.0	7.5
Extraordinary charges	346.3	36.4
Continuing operations (adjusted)	418.3	43.9

We can make the same adjustment for 1988:

	Earnings (£ millions)	Per Share (pence)
Continuing operations (U.S. GAAP)	231.0	34.7
Extraordinary charges	102.3	15.4
Continuing operations (adjusted)	333.3	50.1

Note: All the data used for the computations are derived from Exhibits 12-24 and 12-25.

EXHIBIT 12-25. SMITHKLINE BEECHAM
Extraordinary Items

	Year ended December 31	
	1988	1989
	£m	£m
Group restructuring and rationalization costs, including transaction expenses of £77.3 million arising from the Combination	—	(577.7)
Other restructuring costs	(159.8)	—
Profits on disposal of businesses	20.2	143.5
	(139.6)	(434.2)
Taxation	37.3	87.9
	(102.3)	(346.3)
Company	—	(4.5)
Beecham	20.2	(100.4)
SmithKline	(122.5)	(241.4)
	(102.3)	(346.3)

The tax relating to extraordinary items includes deferred tax relief of £81.3m.

Source: SmithKline Beecham, Firm 20-F, 1989.

Using these definitions of earnings, SKB's 1989 earnings from continuing operations rose (under U.S. GAAP), but earnings per share fell. In other words, the higher earnings from the inclusion of SmithKline were more than offset by the additional shares outstanding; the merger was dilutive.

Restatement of the Income Statement

We have already looked at the U.K. GAAP income statements for 1988 and 1989 in Exhibit 12-23. To convert them to U.S. GAAP income statements, we need to make two sets of adjustments:

1. Apply the purchase method of accounting by including the results of SmithKline only following the date the company was acquired (July 26, 1989) and by including the purchase method adjustments to income.

2. Adjust for other differences in accounting methods between U.S. GAAP and U.K. GAAP.

Exhibit 12-24 contains the adjustments to net income but does not show the necessary adjustments to sales, cost of goods sold, and so forth. The inclusion of the results of discontinued operations in the U.K. statements is especially difficult to deal with analytically. Thus we would have to make many assumptions and approximations to recast the entire income statement to a U.S. GAAP basis. We can, however, easily restate sales.

Under U.S. GAAP, the 1988 sales of SKB would be only those of Beecham (since the acquisition of SmithKline took place in 1989). Further we must exclude sales of discontinued operations. From the Beecham 1988 income statement (not shown here), we obtain the desired data, in Exhibit 12-26.

Sales in 1989, under U.S. GAAP, include the full-year sales of Beecham (excluding discontinued operations) plus the sales of SmithKline for the period July 27–December 31. We use five-twelfths of SmithKline's actual 1989 sales ($3591 million) as estimated sales for the first five months of 1989. We multiply this figure ($1496 million) by the average exchange rate for the pound sterling versus the dollar for the same five-month period (0.604) to obtain estimated sales in pounds (£903 million). Subtracting this number from reported consolidated sales for 1989 yields estimated sales on a purchase basis, which would include SmithKline only for the period following the merger.

For 1990, however, the results of SmithKline are included for the full year under either method. The actual sales from continuing operations for 1990 are also shown in Exhibit 12-26 and are identical to sales reported under U.K. GAAP.

As we can see from part A, Sales Comparisons, in Exhibit 12-26, the difference between the pooling and purchase method is not just the variation in reported income already discussed. Because, under the purchase method, the sales of the acquired company (SmithKline) are included only following the merger date, the sales trend is quite different as well. The sales trend reported under U.K. GAAP reflects the combination of the two firms for periods prior to the merger as well. Comparability is preserved. Under the purchase method, the "phase-in" of SmithKline's sales results in the illusion of growth, which we observed in the Acquire-Target example.

EXHIBIT 12-26. SMITHKLINE BEECHAM
U.S. Versus U.K. GAAP, for Years Ended December 31, 1988–1990 (in £ millions)

	1988	1989	1990
A. Sales Comparisons			
U.S. GAAP—Purchase	£1939	£3373	£4501
U.K. GAAP—Pooling (from continuing operations)	3672	4276	4501
B. Return on Total Capital			
Earnings Before Interest and Taxes (from continuing operations, before nonrecurring items)			
U.S. GAAP		451	790
U.K. GAAP		826	970
Average total capital (total debt plus total equity)			
U.S. GAAP		3771	5417
U.K. GAAP		2050	1963
Return on total capital (EBIT/average total capital)			
U.S. GAAP		12.0%	14.6%
U.K. GAAP		40.3%	49.4%

Comparison of Financial Ratios

Not surprisingly, the financial ratios reported by SKB also depend on the accounting method followed. Exhibit 12-26, part B, shows the computation of return on total capital, a commonly used performance measure, under both methods for the year of the merger (1989) and the following year (1990).

The difference in earnings before interest and taxes (EBIT) mainly reflects the absence, under U.K. GAAP, of the amortization of goodwill and the other asset write-ups resulting from use of the purchase method. The difference in average total capital reflects the absence of the purchase method adjustments as well as the U.K. practice of immediate write-off of goodwill against equity. The U.K. total capital is (as we have already noted) very close to tangible capital.

The return ratios computed under each method are totally different. The U.S. ratio is much lower as a result of the lower income and higher capital base. The 1989–1990 trend is, however, quite similar. Neither set of ratios is inherently more correct than the other; each reflects the data from which it was computed. The point we wish to make is that analysis of SKB and, even more important, comparisons with other drug companies should not be mechanical. Analysis requires an understanding of financial reporting differences and their impact on financial statements.

Summary

This section provided an illustration of the hazards of making company comparisons without adjusting for the impact of acquisition accounting on reported data. When the companies to be compared are subject to different national accounting systems, the acquisition problem is compounded by differences in presentation and in accounting methods. With attention to these differences, and with adequate disclosure, adjustments can be made to achieve some semblance of comparability. But analysis of noncomparable data is unlikely to result in sound investment conclusions.

INTERNATIONAL DIFFERENCES IN ACCOUNTING FOR BUSINESS COMBINATIONS

The purchase method must be used to account for acquisitions under International Accounting Standard (IAS) 22, and pooling (merger) accounting is allowed in rare cases. Requirements for pooling are similar to those in APB 16, but the rules are not as detailed, permitting a wider range of interpretations. Purchased goodwill may be amortized over a 5-year period or its expected economic life (not to exceed 20 years). Although IAS 22 allows firms to charge goodwill to equity, the International Accounting Standards Committee (IASC) proposed elimination of this alternative in the revised Exposure Draft (ED) 32.

The IASC has proposed the virtual elimination of pooling by imposing very strict requirements for its use.

U.K. standards effectively make pooling or merger accounting optional, as they do not contain the detailed conditions spelled out in APB 16 for pooling. Generally, application of the purchase method in the U.K. results in the allocation of a higher proportion of the purchase price to goodwill for two reasons. First, the U.K. standard contains only a broad description of the process of allocating the purchase price to the acquired assets and liabilities; second, goodwill may be charged directly to equity through any type of reserve account or one created specifically for goodwill. A significant portion of the purchase price may never be reflected in the income statement; as a result, future results will not be impacted by amortization charges. Finally, the accounting standard permits firms to recognize future costs of the merged firm, further augmenting income reported in subsequent years.

In France, only the purchase method is used, but the price is rarely allocated to tangible assets to avoid tax penalties; the resulting, comparatively higher goodwill amounts can be immediately charged to equity. Pooling has been the norm in Germany, but new rules akin to APB 16 have been adopted.

Proposed changes in U.K. accounting, the IASC's proposal to eliminate direct charge-offs of goodwill to equity, and the capitalization of goodwill in the United States will most likely make capitalization the norm. However, the maximum 40-year amortization period allowed in the United states is at odds with international practice, which ranges from a minimum of 5 years to a ceiling of 20 years under IAS standards and in Germany and the Netherlands. We expect practice to move closer to the IAS and European models.

The information on acquisitions provided by cash flow statements in the United States is generally lacking, although the recently issued IASC cash flow standard will alleviate this problem. Footnote disclosures outside the United States rarely provide detailed information regarding acquisitions. This absence of data is compounded by the lack of adequate segment disclosures.

As a result, it may be difficult to analyze acquisitions made by foreign companies. Look for evidence as to which method is used, the treatment of goodwill, and the restatement of previously issued financial statements (this is forbidden in some countries) as these are the key issues in acquisition accounting. Applying the principles discussed in this chapter should permit the analyst to draw some inferences regarding the impact of acquisitions and, if management can be questioned, indicate the questions that should be asked. As the SmithKline Beecham example shows, the choice of acquisition method can radically affect the reported results of operations and financial condition of the combined entity.

CHOOSING THE ACQUISITION METHOD

The analyses of Acquire-Target, ConAgra–Golden Valley, Georgia Pacific–Great Northern Nekoosa, and SmithKline Beecham may suggest that the purchase and pooling methods of acquisition accounting are optional alternatives. Strictly speaking, that is not the case; the conditions mandating the use of the purchase or pooling method in the United States are delineated in APB 16. However, it would be naive to believe that acquirers ignore the accounting consequences of planned acquisitions when deciding on their terms and form.

The accounting for acquisitions under U.S. GAAP has remained unchanged since APB 16 was promulgated in 1970. Opinion 16 was intended to eliminate abuses of the pooling method during the acquisition binge of the 1960s and the optional nature of acquisition accounting by defining the conditions under which each method would be applicable. For example, to be eligible for pooling treatment, 12 separate criteria must be satisfied. Many of these criteria are related to the structure of the transaction itself, its tax effect, and the mode of payment. Thus the accounting method used is intertwined with the characteristics of the transaction itself.

From the corporate viewpoint, use of the pooling method is usually preferred under the following conditions:

1. Purchase price greatly exceeds stated equity or book value of target.
2. Target does not have significant depreciable assets that can be written up substantially for tax purposes, creating higher tax deductions.
3. Acquiring company does not wish to increase its leverage or has limited borrowing power.
4. Target has securities or other assets with market values above historic cost. Under pooling the cost is unchanged; after the acquisition these assets can be sold, increasing reported income.

The first two conditions would result in a large amount of goodwill under the purchase method. Amortization reduces reported earnings without any cash flow (tax reduction) benefit. The SmithKline-Beecham merger is a good example of the adverse impact of purchase accounting on acquisitions meeting the first two conditions.

The third condition needs little elaboration. Georgia Pacific's acquisition of GNN greatly increased its debt load (see Exhibit 12-16) as compared with the result under a stock transaction (without stock repurchase). Apparently, GP felt that the large cash flow of GNN, combined with asset sales, would make the debt load manageable.

In general, the acquisition of service companies, and others with low asset intensity will "look better" when pooling is used. Such companies have few assets to write up. Targets with high returns on equity (implying purchase prices well above stated equity) also lend themselves to pooling.

On the other hand, purchase accounting can be advantageous under some conditions:

1. Target is "asset rich" with ample scope for write-ups and consequent tax reduction. Tax reduction recovers the cost of an acquisition quickly, especially if some of the purchase price can be allocated to inventory. (See the Duracell example later in this chapter.)
2. Purchase price is below stated book value. In this case there is potential for writing down assets, reducing depreciation and amortization and increasing reported earnings.
3. Target has "off-balance-sheet" obligations that would reduce reported income following the acquisition. Purchase accounting includes these liabilities (e.g., underfunded postretirement plans) in the allocation of purchase price, reducing future charges to earnings.
4. Shareholders of acquirer do not wish to dilute their voting control or equity

interest by issuing additional shares. They may prefer to use cash or securities with little or no voting power to effect the acquisition.

It should be clear that the accounting method is a consequence of the acquisition terms and that the terms reflect the specific circumstances of the acquirer, target company, and shareholders. The accounting method, while not truly "optional" is subject to management control, and the terms of the merger can be fashioned to achieve the desired accounting alternative. In fact, anecdotal evidence suggests that certain mergers would not have gone through had they not been able to be accounted for as a pooling or that the accounting treatment significantly affected the negotiated terms.[21]

In any case, the choice of accounting method must, therefore, be understood in the context of the overall motivation for mergers. Similarly, differing market reactions to mergers accounted for as pooling or purchases must also be understood within this overall framework. These issues can be illustrated by examining the "income maximization" hypothesis often used to explain the choice of pooling over purchase.

Income Maximization as Motivation for the Pooling/Purchase Choice

Many researchers have explored the "income maximization" hypothesis and the price (P) to book value (BV) ratio as motivations for the pooling/purchase choice. Under this hypothesis, when the price paid exceeds the target's book value ($P > BV$), pooling is preferred as subsequent reported income, return on equity (ROE) and return on assets (ROA) will be higher. On the other hand, when $P < BV$, purchase accounting is preferred.

Exhibit 12-27, adapted from Robinson and Shane (1990), summarizes the results of a number of studies of this hypothesis. When $P > BV$ there is a strong preference for the pooling method (84% overall). For $P < BV$, although the purchase method does not dominate, there is clearly less of a preference for the pooling method. Thus the results are generally consistent with the overall hypothesis albeit in an asymmetric fashion.

Consistent with the foregoing, Davis (1990) (see Exhibit 12-28A) documents that the price to book value differential is considerably larger for mergers accounted for as poolings. The price to book value differential is, of course, related to the bid premium (the price paid for the target relative to the premerger price of the target) that Robinson and Shane show (see Exhibit 12-28B) to be larger for poolings.

Thus the evidence indicates that for mergers where

1. $P > BV$ and
2. Relatively higher prices are paid for targets.
   Pooling is the preferred method of accounting, consistent with the income maximization hypothesis.

---

[21]The AT&T–NCR merger is an example. Moreover, the FASB Discussion Memorandum, An Analysis of Issues Relating to Accounting for Business Combinations and Purchased Intangibles (August 19, 1976) reports that two-thirds of its respondents concurred with the statement that many of the mergers that used the pooling of interests method would not have been consummated had they been required to use the purchase method. Only 14% disagreed with the statement.

EXHIBIT 12-27
Summary of Previous Studies of Income Maximization Hypothesis

	P > BV Firms Choosing			BV > P Firms Choosing		
	POOLING	PURCHASE	IM%	POOLING	PURCHASE	IM%
Gagnon (1967)	94	90	51.1%	18	17	48.6%
Copeland and Wojdak (1969)	101	8	92.7	4	5	55.6
Anderson and Louderback (1975)	153	16	90.5	3	6	66.7
Crawford (1987)	81	67	54.7	8	27	77.1
Nathan (1988)	226	12	95.0	41	22	34.9
"Summary"*	561	103	84.5	56	60	51.7

Note: IM% represents the percentage consistent with the income maximization hypothesis.

*Summary may be biased as merging firms may have appeared in more than one study.

Source: Robinson, John R. and Philip B. Shane, "Acquisition Accounting Method and Bid Premia for Target Firms," *The Accounting Review,* (January 1990), pp 25–48. Adapted from Table 1 (p. 27).

EXHIBIT 12-28
Comparison of Price to Book Differentials and Bid Premia for Pooling and Purchase Firms

A. Price to Book Value Differentials (Mean Values)

	Pooling	Purchase
(1) $P - BV$	$61 million	$22 million
(2) $(P - BV)/BV$	206%	81%
(3) $(P - BV)/Income$	202%	77%

Source: Davis, Michael L., "Differential Market Reaction to Pooling and Purchase Methods," *The Accounting Review* (July 1990) pp. 696–709. Table 5 (P. 706).

B. Bid Premia (Mean Values)

	Pooling	Purchase
(1) $(P_a - P_{t-40})/P_{t-40}$	64%	42%
(2) Target's total return in period starting 40 days prior to merger announcement until Target is delisted	57%	44%
(3) Target's total abnormal return over the same period as in (2)	28%	17%

P_a = Price paid in acquirer's shares (price of acquirer's shares times exchange ratio)
P_{t-40} = Price of target's shares 40 days prior to merger announcement

Source: Robinson, John R. and Philip B. Shane, "Acquisition Accounting Method and Bid Premia for Target Firms," *The Accounting Review,* (January 1990), pp 25–48. Adapted from Table 3 (p. 38).

Market Reaction and the Pooling/Purchase Choice

For mergers in general, Morck et al. (1990) report that "average returns to bidding shareholders are at best slightly positive and significantly negative in some studies."[22] Focusing on whether the choice of accounting method makes a difference, Hong, Kaplan, and Mandelker (1978) compared the abnormal returns of acquiring firms using the pooling method with those using the purchase method. They were testing whether the market reacts positively to the increased income generated when the pooling method is used.

Their results indicated little or no market reaction for firms that chose the pooling method, either around the time of the first earnings announcement after the merger or in the period leading up to the merger. However, for a smaller sample of firms that opted for the purchase method, they found significant positive reaction in the 12-month period leading up to the effective date of the merger.

Davis (1990), using weekly data and an expanded sample of firms, found similar results. His results are presented in Figure 12-1. Unlike firms using pooling, purchase method acquirers show abnormal positive returns over a 26-week period leading up to the announcement of the merger.

What is interesting about these results is that Hong et al. and Davis studied two separate time periods (1954–1964 and 1971–1982, respectively) but both found positive returns to bidder firms using the purchase method. Bradley, Desai, and Kim (1988), after noting that target firms almost always earn abnormal positive returns, point out that returns to bidder[23] firms are time specific:

> Acquiring firms, on the other hand, realized a significant positive reaction only during the unregulated period 1963–1968 and in fact suffered a significant loss during the most recent sub-period 1981–1984.[24]

Interpreting the Research Results

The difficulty with drawing conclusions from the foregoing findings is twofold. First, as cash or debt (taxable) transactions cannot be accounted for by use of the pooling method, comparable purchase method firms are confined to nontaxable acquisitions using shares of the acquirer. In many cases, however, factors that preclude the use of pooling are characteristic of higher bid premia. Evidence exists that when the method of payment is cash, the bid premium tends to be higher.[25] Moreover, when the transaction is taxable to the target shareholders, a higher bid premium may be required to compensate them for the tax consequences.

Thus, from the set of mergers accounted for by the purchase method, these studies

---

[22]Randall Morck, Andrei Shleifer, and Robert W. Vishny, "Do Managerial Objectives Drive Bad Acquisitions?," *Journal of Finance* (1990) pp. 31–48. These results contrast to those of target shareholders, who generally fare well as a result of the merger.

[23]Bradley, Desai, and Kim (1988) did not differentiate between purchase and pooling firms.

[24]J. Bradley, A. Desai, and E.H. Kim, "Synergistic Gains from Corporate Acquisitions and Their Division Between the Stockholders of Target and Acquiring Firms", *Journal of Financial Economics* (May 1988), pp. 3–40.

[25]See Robinson and Shane (1990), p. 81.

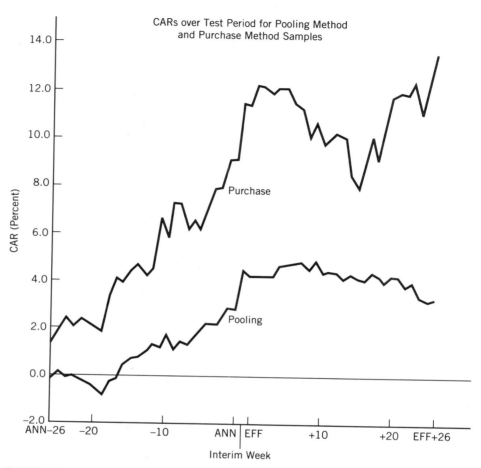

FIGURE 12-1 CARs over test period for pooling method and purchase method samples. Legend: CAR—Cumulative Abnormal Return; ANN—Announcement week per Wall Street Journal; EFF—Effective week of merger. *Source:* Davis, Michael L., "Differential Market Reaction to Pooling and Purchase Methods," *The Accounting Review* (July 1990), pp. 696–709. Figure 1 (P. 703).

have confined themselves to those where the bid premia are a priori smaller. This *self-selection bias* may explain findings of smaller price to book value differentials associated with the purchase accounting choice. This may limit generalizations drawn from these studies.

Similarly, the positive market reaction to the purchase acquisitions may be associated with the low bid premia paid. The market reacted positively to the "bargain purchase." On the other hand, relatively higher payments for the pooling transactions may indicate overpayment (or at least no bargain) and hence the muted market reaction. Thus the market reaction may be related to the level of payment rather than the choice of accounting method.

This explanation assumes that the market reacted to merger news that had been anticipated because of leaks in the weeks leading up to the merger announcement.[26] An alternative explanation offered by Hong et al. was that the firms that instigated purchase transactions were better performing firms and that

> firms who choose the purchase method can "afford" to report the lower earnings caused by the use of this method.[27]

We will return to this explanation later.

The second issue in interpreting research results is related to the question of *cause and effect*. Let us first explore reasons why firms may be interested in income maximization. One possibility is that managers with compensation plans based on earnings, ROA, or ROE are motivated to choose pooling over purchase to enhance their compensation.

This line of reasoning is consistent with theories of merger activity that argue that managers initiate mergers for their own self-interest. They enter into mergers to "buy" growth or to diversify their own risk even if this growth or diversification is not (necessarily) in the best interests of their shareholders.[28] As a result of pursuing their own interests, they may overpay for the target.

If this is the case, then the underlying motivation may explain (1) the merger, (2) the accounting choice, and (3) the degree of overpayment. If the accounting choice is deemed desirable, then it may be that the accounting choice itself was one of the terms of the negotiation. The acquirer may have paid more for the target to obtain a deal structure permitting it to use the pooling method.

Thus, the choice of accounting method cannot be viewed separately from the acquisition itself. In many ways it is endogenous to the overall terms of the merger and must be seen in that light. This is true not only for the effects implied by the income maximization theory and the differential market reactions discussed above. Similar patterns can be shown in the context of other merger characteristics. These are discussed in the next section.

Other Factors Influencing Mergers, Bid Premia, and the Pooling/Purchase Choice

Exhibit 12-29 lists a number of factors that can impact the pooling/purchase choice either directly or indirectly (through its influence on the bid premium). In addition, (some of) these factors have been found in other studies to be associated with positive market reaction to mergers. The discussion of these categories should serve to illustrate the complexities involved in analyzing the relationship of accounting choice and economic characteristics of mergers.

[26]As most of the reaction was in the 11-week period leading up to the merger announcement (see Figure 12-1), this explanation is plausible.

[27]Hai Hong, Robert S. Kaplan, and Gershon Mandelker, "Pooling vs. Purchase: The Effects of Accounting for Mergers on Stock Prices," *The Accounting Review*, (January 1978), pp. 31–47.

[28]See Morck, Shleifer, and Vishny (1990), pp. 31–36. Roll (1986) goes so far as to suggest that managers suffer from hubris and are convinced that they can do a better job with the target than its current management.

EXHIBIT 12-29
Merger Characteristics, Bid Premia, and Choice of Accounting Method

	"+" Indicates Preference for Pooling	"+" Indicates Larger Bid Premia
Characteristics of Transaction		
1. Cash Payment	−	+
2. Tax status	−	+
3. Small percentage acquired	−	−
Characteristics of Acquirer		
4. $P > BV$ and Management compensation contract	+	
5. $P > BV$ and Bond covenant, debt constraint	−	
6. $P > BV$ and Bond covenant, dividend constraint	+	
7. "Good" managers Owner versus manager control	−	−
Characteristics of Target		
8. Low leverage High liquidity		+
9. Relative size of target to acquirer	−	−
10. "Poor" managers Low market to book ratio Low Q ratio		−
11. Low price-earnings multiple	+	

The three categories are characteristics of

1. The transaction

2. The acquirer firm

3. The target firm

Characteristics of Transaction

(1) Cash Transaction and (2) Tax Status. These were discussed earlier. Under APB 16, pooling is permissible only if the merger is a noncash transaction. Moreover, pooling transactions tend to be nontaxable acquisitions. Generally, higher bid premia are associated with mergers that involve cash payments and are taxable to the target shareholders. These factors tend to result in higher bid premia for purchase rather than pooling transactions and also preclude the choice of pooling.

(3) Percentage Acquired. The larger the percentage of the target acquired, the larger the bid premium. Under APB 16, unless the transaction is for over 90% of the

shares of the target, the transaction must be accounted for as a purchase. Thus a higher bid premia is implied for a pooling rather than purchase transaction.

Characteristics of Acquirer

The first three aspects of the acquirer firms are tied to the nature of the price to book value differential.

(4) Compensation Plans. When $P > BV$, then compensation plans can induce managers to attempt to increase their compensation by choosing the pooling method (Dunne, 1990).

(5) and (6) Effects of Bond Covenants. Depending on the nature of a firm's debt covenants, different preferences for the purchase or pooling method may result. When $P > BV$ the purchase method shows higher assets and equity. This would tend to improve current ratios and the debt-to-equity ratio. Thus firms whose debt covenants are binding in terms of liquidity and leverage ratios would prefer the purchase method.[29] Consistent with this discussion, Davis, for example, found that firms that chose the purchase method had significantly higher leverage ratios than did those that chose pooling accounting.[30]

On the other hand, if the constraint is in terms of restrictions on dividends that are related to levels of retained earnings, then the pooling method may be preferred. The pooling method, although it gives lower total equity, yields higher retained earnings, as the retained earnings of both the acquirer and target are combined. Under purchase accounting, only the acquirer's retained earnings are carried forward. However, firms generally exhibit covenants based on liquidity, leverage, and dividend restrictions. Both the terms of the merger and preferences for accounting methods may be affected by the most limiting set of covenants.

(7) Type of Management. Empirical evidence (e.g., Servaes, 1991) indicates that better managers make better acquisitions. One of the signs of better managers is superior market performance of their firms. Thus the evidence with respect to acquisitions using the purchase method may be indicative of a combination of:

1. Firms with better managers (making better acquisitions) explaining the abnormal positive reaction prior to the merger;
2. Since better managers make better acquisitions, they do not tend to overpay and hence the lower bid premia; and
3. Since they are better managers they do not need or use artificial income

---

[29]Leftwich (1981), on the other hand, argues that firms with high leverage ratios would prefer pooling as it shows higher income. His argument, it seems to us, ignores the increased equity reported at the time of the purchase and focuses on the income increases realized over time.

[30]Davis did not provide any information as to whether the firms had bond covenants expressed in terms of leverage ratios. This does not allow us to speculate whether the positive market reaction associated with the choice of the purchase method was in any way related to wealth transfers from bondholders to equityholders.

increasing methods. This argument was put forward earlier by Hong et al. (1978).

Dunne (1990) found evidence consistent with these propositions. In her sample, she found that owner-controlled firms were more likely to choose the purchase method over pooling. Actions taken by owner-controlled firms would be more likely to be beneficial to the welfare of the firm as opposed to manager-controlled firms that may attempt to maximize their own welfare at the expense of the firm.

Characteristics of Target

(8) High Liquidity/Low Leverage. Firms that have excess cash are often acquisition targets as the acquiring firm wants to capture and use the firm's liquid assets. Such firms would likely receive higher bid premia. Firms that have excess cash may be characteristic of strong performers in the past in industries whose growth potential has declined.

(9) Relative Size of Target. Robinson and Shane note that the larger the size of the target relative to the acquirer the less likely the acquirer would be willing to give the target's shareholders common shares with full voting rights. The acquirer's shareholders would be fearful of losing control of the firm. Under APB 16, lack of voting rights precludes use of the pooling method. Empirical evidence, referenced by Robinson and Shane, indicates that bid premia tend to be lower when the target is relatively large. Again, we have a situation when lower bid premia are consistent with the accounting choice of purchase independent of any income/asset "manipulation" motivation.

(10) Type of Management. Firms run by poor managers are often viewed as prime takeover targets. The new managers feel they can do a better job of running the firm. The relationship of the firm's price to its book value is often viewed as an indicator of poor management as the firm is not valued favorably by the market.

Tobin's Q ratio, the ratio of a firm's market value to the replacement value of its assets is also used as an indicator of poor managerial performance. Low Q ratios (below 1, for example) indicate that any dollar invested internally in the firm will not generate a return whose present value is equal to $1.

It should be noted that alternative explanations (to poor management) exist for low market price to book value ratios and low Q's. Such firms may be in industries where growth opportunities have stagnated as it is too expensive to grow by investing internally. The efficient way to expand is to acquire another company in the same industry. It is cheaper to buy a firm with existing assets than to replace the assets directly. In any event, target firms with low market to book value and/or low Q ratios can typically be obtained as bargains with low bid premia.

(11) Low P/E Ratios. A low P/E ratio may be another manifestation of the poor performance noted earlier. However, we discuss it separately as it is often given another dimension relating to the "bootstrapping" phenomenon noted earlier. It is hypothesized that a firm with a high P/E ratio can increase its own market price by acquiring companies with low P/E ratios. The newly acquired earnings will be valued by the market at the

acquirer's higher P/E ratio. For this to work, the market has to be incredibly naive. When companies using this technique make many small "nonsignificant" mergers (with little disclosure), however, it may be hard for analysts to "see through" the technique.

Summary

The discussion indicates that the relationship between choice of accounting method and the underlying motivation for mergers is quite complex. One should, therefore, not draw immediate conclusions as to managers' motivations and/or potential market reaction. The effects and implications of the accounting method cannot be understood without a thorough examination of the merger's economic characteristics.

THE ANALYSIS OF GOODWILL

Goodwill is one of the most controversial subjects in all of accounting and has been so for at least three decades. In most cases, goodwill and other intangible assets arise as residuals in purchase method acquisitions, and they represent the portion of the purchase price that cannot be allocated to other, tangible assets. Goodwill reflects the premium paid for the target's reputation, brand names, or other attributes that enable it to earn an excess return on investment, justifying the premium price paid. Hence the name goodwill.

Since goodwill arises as a residual, it cannot be measured directly. It can be independently appraised only by measuring the "excess" return earned by the enterprise; such measurements require many assumptions, making such appraisals controversial.

Proponents of goodwill recognition argue that some companies are able to earn "excess" returns and that goodwill is simply the capitalized present value of those returns. As such it is no more or less subjective than the present value of future cash flows connected with tangible assets.

Opponents of the goodwill concept dislike the subjective nature and indirect measurement of this "asset." They argue that it often turns out to be ephemeral; write-offs of goodwill are common (see discussion of impairment in Chapter 6). Prices paid for acquisitions often turn out to be excessive, based on unrealistic expectations rather than true earnings prospects.

Both arguments, in our view, have merit both when stated in the abstract and when applied to specific companies. We believe that goodwill can, and should, be examined only with respect to a specific enterprise. There are many companies that are able to earn above-average returns over long periods of time. The common shares of such companies usually sell at prices well above tangible book value, even after tangible assets are revalued to current cost.

In such cases investors are saying that the company does have intangible assets, such as reputation, brand names, patents, management expertise, or other factors. The allocation of the excess purchase price to these factors can only be arbitrary, and accounting cannot measure every attribute of an enterprise.

In other cases, companies earn below-average returns despite the existence on their balance sheet of intangible assets. These assets may be overstated; share prices of such companies are often below stated book value. The fact that an intangible asset originated in an acquisition does not guarantee that it will have continuing value any more than if the intangible asset were self-generated.

Summing up, the existence of economic goodwill is largely independent of the existence of accounting goodwill. The former is a function of economic performance; the latter is a function of accounting standards. Investors and financial analysts are primarily interested in economic goodwill, yet accounting goodwill exists in abundant quantity in the financial statements of many companies. The analyst should, therefore, adjust financial statements in many cases to better reflect economic reality. Where a company clearly earns excess returns, goodwill can be left on the balance sheet (or even imputed); where such returns are absent, it should be removed for purposes of analysis.

Goodwill and the Income Statement

For companies whose statements are subject to U.S. GAAP, and for some others, the creation of acquisition goodwill necessarily leads to amortization. Standards are flexible, and goodwill can be amortized over a period as long as 40 years under APB 17. As companies are free to choose the period of amortization, and in practice make different choices, comparability is poor.[31]

Further, amortization of goodwill is a noncash charge; it represents merely the amortization of a past expenditure. In the United States, goodwill is not a deductible expense under the Internal Revenue Code so that there is no income tax benefit. In short, the amortization of goodwill is a nonevent, with no real consequences. For purposes of analysis, therefore, the amortization of goodwill is added back to net income by some analysts. Others believe that goodwill amortization should remain a deduction from net income in the same way that depreciation expense (also an allocation of a past expenditure) is deducted.

We believe that goodwill amortization should be restored to net income. By comparing income before amortization to the total cost of the acquisition (including goodwill), the analyst can evaluate the return on the acquisition in the same manner as the return on other investments.

PUSH-DOWN ACCOUNTING

Acquired firms (in effect subsidiaries of new parents) often continue to issue their own financial statements, due to such factors as

- Statutory or regulatory reporting requirements
- Minority equity interest, including preferred shareholders
- Need to provide information to creditors

---

[31]Goodwill can be immediately charged to equity in certain foreign countries. This practice avoids periodic charges to the income statement but is difficult to justify as it writes off an often significant portion of the price paid. The effect is to reduce the carrying amount of newly acquired operations.

The issuance of such financial statements raises an interesting accounting issue. Should they reflect the operations of the firm, assuming that it had not been acquired, or should the financial statements be adjusted to reflect the purchase method adjustments shown on its (new) parent company statements? In other words, should the parent company's purchase method adjustments be "pushed down" into the financial statements of the subsidiary?

Push-down accounting has a controversial history. The SEC requires its use when all the equity of a company is sold to the public, thus marking a complete change in ownership.[32] This issue is one case of a broader accounting question: When should a new basis of accounting be required? The Financial Accounting Standards Board has the subject on its current agenda; new standards are expected by 1995. The large-scale use of the leveraged buyout (LBO) technique has raised the importance of this issue as in many cases a substantial portion of an LBO's assets is goodwill. The discussion that follows focuses on the impact of the use of push-down accounting rather than the theoretical concerns.

Push-Down in Practice: The GM-Hughes Transaction

Effective December 31, 1985, General Motors (GM) acquired the Hughes Aircraft Company (Hughes) in a purchase transaction for $2.7 billion in cash and 50 million shares of GM Class H stock, with a stated value of $2,561 million, making the total cost $5,261 million. The purchase price was allocated as follows:

Allocation of Purchase Price of Hughes

Net assets of Hughes at historical cost	$1016 million
Patents and technology	500
Future benefit of Hughes incentive plan	125
Intangible assets (goodwill)	3620
Total	$5261 million

Because Hughes was a defense contractor, and there was substantial uncertainty whether asset values exceeding historical cost would be recoverable under the company's contracts with the U.S. government, there was no revaluation of Hughes' tangible assets; the entire excess of purchase price over stated equity was, therefore, assigned to intangible assets, mostly goodwill.

The Class H shares of General Motors are entitled to dividends based on the earnings of Hughes. As a result, Hughes has continued to publish its own separate financial statements, although it is a subsidiary of GM. The Securities and Exchange Commission required that the purchase method adjustments shown be "pushed down" into the separate financial statements of Hughes.

---

[32]One of the earliest uses of push-down accounting occurred when Hughes Tool was formed in 1972 to acquire the oil tool division of Summa Corporation. All the shares of the newly formed company were sold in a public offering. At the insistence of the SEC, the value of the shares sold was used to establish a new basis for the assets and liabilities acquired.

EXHIBIT 12-30. GM HUGHES
Effect of Push-Down Adjustments on Balance Sheet (Condensed), at December 31, 1985 (in $ millions)

	Historical*	Adjustments†	Fair Value
Current assets	$3062	—	$3062
Property	2578	—	2578
Intangible assets	—	$4245	4245
Total assets	$5640	$4245	$9885
Current liabilities	3070	—	3070
Long-term liabilities	449	—	449
Stockholders' equity	2121	4245	6366
Total equities	$5640	$4245	$9885

*The historical data shown include the assets and liabilities of Delco Electronics, a GM subsidiary merged into Hughes as part of the merger transaction.

†Excess of purchase price of Hughes over net assets at historical cost ($5261 million − $1016 million).
Source: Data from GM Hughes Annual Report.

Impact on the Balance Sheet

If Hughes had not been required to reflect the purchase method adjustments in its financial statements, those statements would have been unchanged except for the merger-related expenses and a requirement to fund the Incentive Plan. The impact of push-down accounting can be seen in the condensed balance sheet at December 31, 1985, shown in Exhibit 12-30. Push-down accounting nearly doubles the assets (because of goodwill) of Hughes and triples its stockholders' equity.

Impact on the Income Statement

The large intangible assets on the balance sheet of GM Hughes (Hughes following the merger) as a result of "push-down" accounting also affect the income statement. General Motors decided to amortize the acquired patents over 15 years, the incentive plan benefit over 5 years, and the remaining intangibles over 40 years. This amortization sharply reduced the reported earnings of GM Hughes, shown in Exhibit 12-31.

Because the amortization of the purchase method adjustments is constant, its percentage effect should diminish as income grows. But as income declined during the period 1988–1990, the percentage reduction grew. The annual amortization in dollars was unchanged, however, until 1991 when amortization decreased by $25 million as the incentive plan benefit was fully amortized. In 2001, it will decrease by a further $33 million as the acquired patents are fully amortized. The goodwill amortization of $90.5 million will continue, however, through the year 2015 unless written off earlier. Over time, therefore, the effect of the purchase method adjustments decreases, more rapidly if net income grows.

EXHIBIT 12-31. GM HUGHES
Effect of Push-Down Accounting on Net Income, for Years Ended December 31, 1988–1990 (for $ millions)

	1988	1989	1990
Net income before push-down	$ 802	$ 781	$ 726
Purchase method adjustments*	(149)	(149)	(149)
Reported net income	$ 653	$ 632	$ 577
Percentage reduction	18.6%	19.1%	20.5%

*Amortization of		
Incentive plan, over 5 years	$125/5 =	$ 25.0
Patents, over 15 years	$500/15 =	33.3
Goodwill, over 40 years	$3620/40 =	90.5
Total		$148.8

Effect on Cash Flows

As the amortizations of the purchase method adjustments that have been pushed down into the financial statements of GM Hughes are noncash charges, they have no impact on the company's cash flow. There would be an indirect impact if dividend policy and capital spending decisions were based on reported earnings, but that is unlikely. In the case of GM Hughes, the purchase method adjustments are explicitly ignored when computing income available for dividends. In other words, dividend decisions are based on net income prior to those adjustments.

Effect on Financial Ratios

The effects of push-down accounting on financial ratios are similar to those of the purchase method from whence it derives. Activity ratios decline. Return ratios are affected by the change in both numerator (income) and denominator (total capital). Exhibit 12-32 reflects the impact of push-down accounting based on data from GM Hughes annual reports.

Exhibits 12-31 and 12-32 provide the data required to compute the debt to total capital ratio and the return on average equity ratios.

Financial Ratios of GM Hughes, 1989–1990

	As Reported		Adjusted	
	1989	1990	1989	1990
Debt to total capital	10.4	12.1	19.6	18.9
Return on average equity	8.2	7.2	21.6	18.2

The debt–to–total capital ratio is higher when the push-down adjustments are removed because equity is lower. (Of course, if the "as reported" data were used to

EXHIBIT 12-32. GM HUGHES
Effect of Push-Down Accounting on Balance Sheet, at December 31, 1988–1990
(in $ millions)

	1988	1989	1990
As reported (push-down)			
Total debt	$1019	$ 918	$ 983
Equity	7550	7898	8098
Total capital	$8569	$8816	$9081
Adjusted* (excluding intangibles)			
Total debt	$1019	$ 918	$ 983
Equity	3469	3768	4212
Total capital	$4488	$4686	$5195

   *Assumes that purchase method adjustments had not been "pushed down" to the financial statements of GM Hughes.

compute debt to tangible capital, the result would also be a higher ratio.) The trend is also changed. Tangible equity grew faster than total debt in 1990. As a result, the debt ratio declined. Using the "as reported" data, debt grew faster, increasing the debt ratio.

   For return on average equity, the trend is the same, but the levels are very different. Removing the goodwill pushed down into GM Hughes results in higher earnings, lower equity, and thus a higher return on equity.

Push-Down Summed Up

Push-down accounting remains a controversial topic, and the FASB is likely to find it difficult to establish new standards in this area. Push-down accounting replaces historical cost with current values, which may be more useful for making investment decisions.

   It is important to understand the effects of push-down because it radically changes the financial statements (and ratios) of affected companies. Consistency over time and comparability with other companies are destroyed by push-down; if the impact of "push-down" adjustments is not understood, financial data may be misinterpreted.

   As noted, push-down accounting is no more than an application of the purchase method to the separate statements of the acquired firm. Financial statements with purchase method adjustments are seen, with increasing frequency, as "recycled" LBO firms issue stock to the public. The analysis of Duracell, which follows, is an example of how purchase method adjustments transform the financial statements of such firms.

LEVERAGED BUYOUTS: DURACELL INTERNATIONAL

Duracell, a worldwide manufacturer of alkaline batteries, was a subsidiary of Kraft, Inc., until June 1988. At that time a group led by Kohlberg Kravis Roberts & Co. (KKR) formed a holding company to acquire Duracell in a purchase method transaction for $1861.1 million, mostly financed by debt. A portion of the excess of the purchase price over stated equity was allocated to inventory and property, with most of the excess reflected as intangible assets.

Balance Sheet Effects

In May 1991, approximately 20% of Duracell shares were sold to the public in an underwritten public offering. The financial data that follow were derived from the prospectus for that offering.

Because of the intervening buyout, the recent financial history of Duracell is divided into two segments: the predecessor company and the (new) company. The buyout date of June 23, 1988, is the dividing line. As can be seen from the selected financial data in Exhibit 12-33, the company changed its financial characteristics radically on that date.

The purchase method balance sheet shows total assets on June 24, 1988, of $2394 million, or more than twice the level ($935 million) six months earlier. Yet during the first half of 1988, net property purchased was $18 million, and current assets decreased sharply. The acquisition required the following accounting entries:

1. Kraft's investment (the equity of "old" Duracell) of $561.4 million (on the acquisition date) was eliminated.

2. KKR's equity investment of $356.3 million and debt financing of more than $1.5 billion were used to purchase the company from Kraft.

3. The excess purchase price over the stated equity of "old" Duracell, which we estimate exceeded $1.3 billion, was allocated to the assets of Duracell, including

   Inventory write-up of $52.3 million.

   Property write-up, believed to be small. (See the upcoming discussion of depreciation expense.)

   Goodwill and other intangibles of approximately $1.4 billion; the preexisting goodwill of Duracell was eliminated.

The consequences of these accounting entries can be seen in the balance sheet data in Exhibit 12-33. The increase in total assets reflects the increase in goodwill in particular. The large increase in debt results from the debt taken on to finance the acquisition. Kraft's equity in Duracell is replaced by the stockholders' equity of the new investors.

Income Statement Effects

The buyout of Duracell also had a major impact on its income statement, as can be seen from the pro forma income statement (Exhibit 12-34) for the year ended June 23, 1988 (the last year under Kraft's ownership). Pro forma adjustments are explained in the accompanying notes; some additional insights are based on analyses of other data in the prospectus.

EXHIBIT 12-33. DURACELL INTERNATIONAL, INC.

	Predecessor Company			26 Weeks Ended June 23, 1988	Company			
	Fiscal Year Ended				Fiscal Year Ended June 30,		Six Months Ended	
	Dec. 28, 1985	Dec. 27, 1986	Dec. 26, 1987		1989 (4)	1990 (4)	Dec. 30, 1989	Dec. 29, 1990
	(In millions, except per share amounts)							
Operating Data								
Net sales	$854.3	$962.6	$1,134.9	$ 432.5	$1,249.0	$1,334.6	$ 807.1	$ 921.9
Operating income	66.7	27.4	125.2	16.4	126.0	225.6	171.8	193.8
Adjusted operating income (1)	66.7	64.4	125.2	16.4	214.0	265.6	191.8	215.8
Interest expense (income)—net (2)	2.2	.8	(.6)	.9	217.4	201.7	103.1	108.4
Net income (loss)	34.9	4.6	63.8	6.6	(105.9)	5.8	52.8	61.3
Depreciation and amortization (3)	28.2	38.2	41.9	20.7	81.8	80.3	39.8	41.8
Net income (loss) per share					(1.46)	.08	.73	.83
Weighted average number of shares and share equivalents outstanding					72.8	72.8	72.8	73.8
Pro Forma Operating Data(5)								
Operating income						$ 225.6	$ 171.8	$ 193.8
Interest expense—net						166.2	85.5	90.8
Income before extraordinary loss						37.5	68.6	77.1
Income before extraordinary loss per share						.40	.74	.82
Weighted average number of shares and share equivalents outstanding						92.8	92.8	93.8

	Predecessor Company			Company				
	Dec. 28, 1985	Dec. 27, 1986	Dec. 26, 1987	June 24, 1988	June 30, 1989	June 30, 1990	Dec. 29, 1990	Dec. 29, 1990
	(In millions)						(actual)	(pro forma)(6)
Balance Sheet Data								
Total assets	$783.6	$917.4	$935.6	$2,394.1	$2,133.6	$2,111.3	$2,249.6	$2,244.1
Working capital (deficiency)	253.6	256.2	272.6	(55.3)	129.9	141.4	198.6	198.6
Long-term debt	2.3	3.0	2.9	1,281.1	1,469.4	1,430.7	1,409.6	1,162.6
Parent company investment	587.0	620.8	630.7	—	—	—	—	—
Stockholders' equity	—	—	—	356.3	231.1	263.9	342.3	584.2

(1) Adjusted operating income excludes purchase accounting adjustments so as to make operating income data comparable between the Company and the Predecessor Company. These excluded amounts were $88 million and $40 million for the fiscal years ended June 30, 1989 and 1990, respectively, and $20 million and $22 million for the six months ended December 30, 1989 and December 29, 1990, respectively. See Note 2 to the Consolidated Financial Statements. Adjusted operating income for the fiscal year ended December 27, 1986 excludes a nonrecurring $37 million restructuring charge.

(2) Includes noncash interest expense from accretion of debt discount and amortization of deferred financing costs of $64 million and $62 million in the fiscal years ended June 30, 1989 and 1990, respectively, and $30 million and $42 million for the six months ended December 30, 1989 and December 29, 1990, respectively. See Note 9 to the Consolidated Financial Statements.

(3) Includes amortization of $46.2 million and $47.3 million for the fiscal years ended June 30, 1989 and 1990, respectively, and $23.6 million and $24.3 million for the six months ended December 30, 1989 and December 29, 1990, respectively.

(4) Fiscal year 1989 included 53 weeks and fiscal year 1990 included 52 weeks.

Source: Duracell, preliminary prospectus, March 26, 1991.

EXHIBIT 12-34. DURACELL INTERNATIONAL, INC.

NOTES TO CONSOLIDATED FINANCIAL STATEMENTS
(unaudited as of December 29, 1990 and for the six months ended December 30, 1989 and December 29, 1990)
(dollar amounts in millions except per share amounts)

16. Pro Forma Financial Statements (Unaudited)

	Predecessor Company Historical	Pro Forma Adjustments	Company Pro Forma
Net sales	$1,170.7	$ —	$1,170.7
Cost of products sold	549.3	(4.2)(a) 52.3 (b)	597.4
Selling, general and administrative expense	484.2	49.9 (a)	534.1
Total operating expenses	1,033.5	98.0	1,131.5
Operating income	137.2	(98.0)	39.2
Interest expense	6.6	202.2 (c)	208.8
Other income (expense)	2.4	(5.9)(d)	(3.5)
Income (loss) before income taxes	133.0	(306.1)	(173.1)
Provision for income taxes	64.4	(59.8)(e)	4.6
Net income (loss)	$ 68.6	$(246.3)	$ (177.7)

(a) Reflects depreciation adjustment and additional amortization from the allocation of the excess of the purchase price over the historical cost of the net assets acquired and $11.0 representing management's estimate of the incremental pension, insurance and other costs to be incurred as a stand-alone company.

(b) Reflects a charge for the impact on cost of products sold of the fair value adjustment to opening inventories.

(c) Assumes interest expense based upon the pro forma debt capitalization after refinancing of the Company, as if such financing and refinancing had been consummated as of the beginning of the period presented, as follows:

Revolving credit loans averaging $121.2 at an annual rate of 12.3%	$ 14.9
Term loans of $537.0 at an annual rate of 11%	59.1
Senior subordinated discount notes of $350.3 at an annual rate of 13.3%	46.6
Subordinated debentures of $400.0 at an annual rate of 13.5%	54.0
Foreign borrowings of $155.0 at a blended annual rate of 11%	17.1
Amortization of financing costs on above debt	10.5
	$202.2

(d) Reflects the elimination of interest income as all excess cash is assumed to be used to reduce debt.

(e) Reflects the elimination of U.S. federal and local income taxes from the provision for income taxes, the reduction of the provision for certain foreign income taxes and reversal of deferred taxes related to the excess of purchase accounting cost over manufacturing cost. Tax benefits have not been recognized on the pro forma loss of the Company due to the uncertainties of the realization of such benefits.

Source: Duracell, preliminary prospectus, March 20, 1991.

Footnote (a) is in two parts. The cost reduction of $4.2 million represents the elimination of amortization of the preexisting goodwill that has been eliminated.

The second portion of footnote (a) shows incremental cost of $49.9 million. Amortization of newly created intangibles is more than $46 million. Note (a) refers to $11 million of incremental pension, insurance, and other costs. This suggests that pro forma depreciation expense declines following the merger, perhaps due to use of longer lives. Reported depreciation expense declined from $37.7 million in calendar 1987 to $35.6 million in fiscal 1989, which suggests that the property of Duracell was written up very little or not at all.

Footnote (b) refers to the write-up of inventory already mentioned. As Duracell uses the first-in, first-out method of inventory accounting, the written-up inventory amounts passed through cost of goods sold in the first year following the buyout.

Footnote (e) discusses the income tax expense consequences of the purchase method adjustments. The offset is largely limited to the actual provision for income taxes due to the uncertainty of future realization of the tax benefit of losses carried forward (see discussion of this issue in Chapter 7). As goodwill amortization, which constitutes some portion of the additional expense, is not tax deductible, the tax effect of the additional expenses would be limited in any case.

Note that the additional interest expense resulting from the leveraged buyout is a principal factor in the pro forma loss, but not the only one. Nearly one-third of the swing in pretax income is the result of purchase method adjustments.

Referring back to Exhibit 12-33, we can now comprehend the trend in operating data. The swing from profit to loss over the calendar 1987–fiscal 1989 period is the result of the additional interest expense and the purchase method adjustments. The total depreciation and amortization reflects, as we have already seen, the increased amortization of intangible assets. The adjusted operating income, provided for comparative purposes, excludes the impact of the purchase method adjustments.

Comparing Buyout Firms with Others

As the "recycling" of LBOs continues, more companies are "going public" with balance sheets and income statements that reflect purchase method adjustments. When comparing these companies with others that have maintained their accounting systems on the original cost basis, it is important to be aware of the following problems:

- Post-LBO companies will generally have lower asset turnover ratios because of the write-ups of property and other long-term assets.

- The write-up of inventory will distort the turnover ratio in the period following a buyout, generally when the FIFO or average cost inventory methods are used. For firms on LIFO, there will be no LIFO reserve except for time periods following the buyout.

- Firms using historical cost may have undervalued assets such as properties and investments. The existence of goodwill after a purchase method acquisition almost always indicates that all other assets have been written up to fair value (and sometimes overstated). Postbuyout companies are, as a result, more vulnerable to impairments of asset value (see Chapter 6).

- Post-LBO companies will generally have large intangible assets as a result of purchase accounting. Use of cash flow analysis is one way to compare such companies with historic cost firms.

- Return ratios are greatly affected by purchase method acquisitions as income is reduced and the capital structure is transformed. Return on assets is the best way to compare companies with differing capital structures.

SPINOFFS

A spinoff occurs when a company separates a portion of its business into a newly created subsidiary and distributes shares of that subsidiary to its shareholders pro rata. The accounting for such spinoffs is quite simple and can be characterized as a "reverse pooling." The assets and liabilities of the subsidiary to be spun off are removed from the balance sheet of the parent company at their historical amounts, that is, without adjustment. The spinoff's balance sheet "inherits" the historical cost of the assets and liabilities transferred. The stockholders' equity of the parent company will be reduced by the stockholders' equity (net assets) of the spinoff. The only adjustment will be for any capital transactions (debt repayment, equity infusion, or dividend) with the parent that are part of the spinoff transaction.

The income statement of the spinoff will be little changed from what it would have been if it had remained part of its former parent. The only differences will be the impact of any capital transactions (for example, reduced interest expense on debt forgiven by the parent) and the additional administrative expenses borne by the subsidiary as a public company. The pro forma income statements issued in connection with the spinoff disclose these impacts.

From the parent company perspective, spinoffs offer some advantages. First, a spinoff can be an easy way to dispose of a "problem" subsidiary without recognizing any gain or loss. Sometimes the spinoff will have a higher market value as a public company than could have been realized via sale, for reasons that are discussed in the paragraphs that follow. Thus stockholders are better off receiving the spinoff shares than if the subsidiary had been sold.

Second, spinoffs often pay special dividends to their parent as part of the spinoff transaction. In addition, the debt of the spinoff is removed from the parent company's balance sheet. The result will be lower parent company debt and, possibly, reduced financial leverage.

Third, if the spinoff was losing money (or had very low profitability), the income statement of the parent company will show either higher net income or, at least, higher profit margins. Fixed income coverage may also be improved.

Analysis of Spinoffs

When analyzing a spinoff, it is important to look for the following information, usually found in the financial statement footnotes:

1. Has the spinoff company paid a special dividend to the parent or, alternatively, has the parent forgiven debt or contributed capital? Such transactions alter the financial structure of the spinoff and its profitability going forward.

2. How have postretirement benefits been dealt with? If the parent company retains responsibility for all benefits for retirees, for example, the spinoff company will have a lesser burden. Also evaluate the allocation of pension plan assets and liabilities.

3. Examine income tax sharing agreements, which detail the impact of additional tax assessment or refunds covering periods prior to the spinoff. Also keep in mind that the spinoff company inherits the *tax basis* as well as the accounting basis of assets and liabilities. If tax depreciation of fixed assets has exceeded depreciation expense, then future tax deductions will be below depreciation expense. While the deferred tax liability in the balance sheet should provide for the reversal of this and other timing differences, there may still be a cash flow consequence as income taxes paid exceed income tax expense in the future.

4. Look for other transactions between parent and spinoff that may affect future profitability or cash flow. Possible problem areas include

   a. Contingent liability for debt or other obligations of the parent company.

   b. Guarantees of spinoff obligations by the parent, but with the spinoff company paying a fee for the guarantee.

   c. Parent company charges for administrative or other services.

   d. Higher rental costs due to spinoff company occupancy of parent company office space or operating facilities.

   d. Intercompany supply agreements, which can be either positive or negative for the spinoff depending on their terms. Such agreements often have "sunset" provisions providing for termination or diminishment over time.

5. Read the footnotes of the spinoff subsidiary carefully, even if you are familiar with the operations of the parent. Some data (off-balance-sheet financing, for example) may not have been significant for the parent but are significant to the spinoff company because of its smaller size.

Reasons for Investment in Spinoffs

While some investors immediately sell the shares of spinoffs they receive, others find spinoffs to be attractive investment opportunities. The following factors may make spinoffs profitable investments:

1. Operations that are "lost" as part of a large corporation may benefit from the focus of a management undistracted by other activities. Spinoff firms frequently provide stock options and other incentives for managers to improve profitability.

2. The smaller size of a spinoff may increase the flexibility of managers no longer bound by the bureaucracy of the former parent.

3. The spinoff may attract investors who wish to invest in its industry but were deterred by the other operations of the former parent.

4. Even if the spinoff company has poor current profitability, investors may be attracted by high book value, cash flow, or other attributes.

As a result, a spinoff may increase shareholder wealth as the combined market value of the spinoff and parent company shares exceeds the prespinoff market value of the parent. While financial theory says that shouldn't happen, in practice it often does.[33] Operations that contributed little or nothing to the parent company's market value (because of low profitability, or lack of visibility) may have substantial market value as a stand-alone company.

The Spinoff of ESCO Electronics

In September 1990, the Emerson Electric Company spun off to its stockholders shares of Esco Electronics, a wholly owned subsidiary. The effect on Emerson was not significant; Esco accounted for 7% of consolidated sales and 15% of stockholders' equity prior to the spinoff. Esco showed a small loss for the year ended September 30, 1990.

Emerson accounted for the spinoff by reducing its stockholders' equity by $523 million. The assets and liabilities of Esco were removed from the balance sheet of Emerson, but that company did not restate its previously issued financial statements for the spinoff.

Because Esco's sales had been stagnant over the period 1986–1990, and its profitability had declined, the restatement of Emerson's income statement to exclude the result of Esco results in higher growth rates for both sales and net income of Emerson. We can see this from the data provided in Exhibit 12-35.

The spinoff clearly enhanced Emerson's reported growth rate. The reduction of stockholders' equity probably had little effect; the price of Emerson's shares already sold

[33]For example, see Schipper and Smith (1983).

EXHIBIT 12-35. EMERSON ELECTRIC
Effect of Spinoff of Esco, for Years Ended September 30, 1986–1990 (in $ millions)

	1986	1987	1988	1989	1990
Sales (as reported)	$5242	$6170	$6652	$7071	$7573
Sales of Esco	(511)	(599)	(607)	(599)	(538)
Pro forma sales	$4731	$5571	$6045	$6472	$7035
Net income (as reported)	$ 427	$ 467	$ 529	$ 588	$ 613
Net income of Esco	(30)	(24)	(2)	(12)	2
Pro forma net income	$ 397	$ 443	$ 527	$ 576	$ 615

Growth rate, 1986–1990 (%)	As Reported	Pro Forma
Sales	9.63%	10.43%
Net income	9.46	11.56

Source: Data from 1990 Annual Reports.

at a high multiple of book value because of the high return on equity. Moreover the spinoff, by reducing profitability only slightly (actually increasing net income for 1990) while reducing equity by 15%, increased return on equity.

Thus the spinoff of the poorly performing Esco subsidiary may have enhanced the value (assuming a constant price/earnings ratio) of Emerson shares. If the higher growth rate ex-Esco increased their price/earnings multiple, then the positive effect would be greater. In addition Emerson stockholders received shares of Esco.

From June 30, 1990 (three months prior to the spinoff) to June 30, 1991 (nine months after), the price of Emerson common shares (excluding the value of the spinoff shares) rose by 13.7% as compared with a 3.7% increase in the Standard & Poor's 500 stock index for the same time period. When the value of the Esco shares are included, the gain in Emerson was 14.5%. While comparisons of this type are imprecise (there may have been other factors at work), the superior performance of Emerson does suggest that the company may have increased the value of its shares by "giving away" part of its operations.

While spinoffs have become increasingly common in recent years, most companies still dispose of unwanted operations by selling them. The accounting for such discontinued operations was discussed in Chapter 2.

CORPORATION REORGANIZATION AND REVALUATION

Purchase method acquisitions, buyouts, and transactions requiring push-down accounting generate a new basis of accounting. However, some of these accounting rules are a result of standards developed many decades ago, and others represent ad hoc responses to newly developed corporate financing techniques. Chapter 6 contained discussions of international reporting methods with regard to revaluations of fixed assets and intangibles. As the FASB Discussion Memorandum (DM) on new basis accounting points out, these are generally responses to the impact of price level changes rather than systematic rules designed to reflect the changes in ownership or control. Most foreign countries do not provide reporting rules for buyouts or for "push-down" cases.

The new basis DM presents a detailed discussion of accounting problems in this area, but those discussions are beyond the scope of this text. However, we urge analysts to follow these developments as they will certainly impact financial statements and their analysis as the financial markets continue to develop different responses to business problems. The next section provides a brief discussion of certain transactions wherein a new basis is established.

Quasi-Reorganizations

Current accounting standards permit a partial change to a new basis of accounting in the process of a corporate reorganization or through a quasi-reorganization in which retained earnings deficits are eliminated against additional paid-in capital (and common stock if needed) and the firm may use a new basis for assets and liabilities.[34] However, the SEC

---

[34]Firms are also allowed to change their accounting policies in a quasi-reorganization.

does not allow firms to write up their net assets. Regardless of the form used, both actions require formal approval of stockholders.

Assets and liabilities may be restated to fair values, and the firm may also recognize provisions for losses or charges incurred through the restatement date. Subsequent adjustments must be made directly to equity accounts. Generally, quasi-reorganizations are undertaken when a firm has a deficit in retained earnings, book value of net assets exceeds their fair value, and the firm expects to be profitable in the future. The most important benefit involves the elimination of the retained earnings deficit, which enables the firm to pay dividends and issue equity or debt in the future. However, the write-down may trigger or increase the probability of technical violations of debt covenants.

Quasi-reorganizations do not involve changes in ownership or control, unlike reorganizations in bankruptcy, which entail transfers of ownership (and, in some cases, control) from equityholders to creditors. Bankruptcy reorganizations may require a write-up of assets, reduction in liabilities, and the recognition of a deficit in equity. They produce the same result as quasi-reorganizations but at a higher cost of legal proceedings.

Miscellaneous Restructuring Methods

Firms may recapitalize or change their capital structure through a large dividend distribution to stockholders financed by debt or the sale of assets. Leveraged recapitalizations are sometimes deemed to allow a new basis, but opinion and practice are split with respect to unleveraged recapitalizations. The difference may be due to the absence of external evidence of fair values in this case, whereas the leveraged recapitalization includes a substantial investment by lenders.

Spinoffs may also raise questions as to the need for a new basis. Ownership changes, but there may be no change in control. However, market prices after the spinoff may suggest fair value of assets at odds with book value. This discussion of transactions and events that raise questions regarding the need for a new basis of accounting is merely representative; the new basis DM lists several other possibilities. As we have noted, reorganization methods abound, and reporting appears to react in an ad hoc fashion; attention to proxy statements and footnote disclosures is essential to proper analysis of these investments.

SUMMARY

This chapter provides a detailed analysis of the accounting and financial analysis issues posed by the growing numbers of and types of corporate reorganizations. It begins with a discussion and analysis of mergers and acquisitions, the most common restructuring methods used. The two allowed reporting methods—purchase and pooling—are not alternatives, but their financial statement and ratio effects are so significantly different that they are clearly important variables in any acquisition decision.

The differences across methods are illustrated using stylized and actual examples. Two recent pooling and purchase method transactions are analyzed, and each case is restated to the other method to highlight the impact on financial statements and ratios.

These analyses are followed by an evaluation of a United Kingdom firm's acquisition of a U.S. firm. This transaction was reported as a merger (pooling) in the U.K. and as a purchase transaction in the U.S., providing the opportunity to analyze the difference between purchase and pooling as well as the difference caused by varying international accounting standards.

The analyses show that the purchase method recognizes the change in ownership and control of the acquired firm by recording the price paid, allocating it to the assets and liabilities acquired with any excess reported as an intangible or goodwill. Pooling does not recognize the price paid since it assumes a merger or uniting of interests rather than a change in ownership or control.

The acquisition date and subsequent purchase method financial statements report higher assets and liabilities (relative to comparable pooled statements), lower income (because of higher depreciation, amortization and allocation of recorded purchase price), and profit margin and return ratios. Some acquisitions generate significant amounts of goodwill and other, tangible assets may provide little collateral for the increased debt that often accompanies these transactions. The impact on income is normally dilutive.

The U.K.-U.S. example is also instructive in its depiction of the impact of different accounting and presentation methods. Another important issue is the relevance of disclosure to the analysis of acquisitions, particularly critical in the case of the international transaction. These analyses and the review of empirical research in this area highlight the complex relationship between reporting methods and the acquisition decision.

The chapter also provides a discussion and analysis of other reorganization techniques, including leveraged buyouts, spinoffs, and quasi-reorganizations. These transactions reflect important changes in financial markets and managerial methods creating new reporting and analytical challenges. Financial analysts and other users need to evaluate the FASB's proposals and emerging practice to develop effective analytical techniques.

Chapter 12

Problems

1. [Purchase versus pooling; 1990 CFA adapted] You have been asked to analyze the merger of two firms, Drew and Pierson, using the data in Exhibit 12P-1.

A. Prepare a pro forma combined balance sheet for the merger under the pooling of interests method of accounting.

B. Prepare a pro forma combined balance sheet for the merger under the purchase method, assuming that Pierson is considered to have acquired Drew.

C. Prepare a pro forma combined balance sheet for the merger under the purchase method, assuming that Drew is considered to have acquired Pierson. [For part C, assume that Drew (prior to the merger) does a reverse stock split, reducing its shares outstanding

EXHIBIT 12P-1. PIERSON AND DREW
Selected Financial Data, 1991–1993 ($ millions)

A. Balance Sheet Data, at June 30, 1992

	Pierson		Drew	
	Historical Cost	Fair Value	Historical Cost	Fair Value
Current assets	$ 70	$ 75	$ 60	$65
Land	60	65	10	10
Buildings	80	90	40	40
Equipment	90	100	20	60
Total assets	$300		$130	
Current liabilities	$120	$120	$ 20	20
Long-term debt	80	90	10	15
Stockholders' equity	100		100	
Total liabilities and stockholders' equity	$300		$130	

B. Income Statements, for Years Ended December 31

	Pierson			Drew		
	1991	1992	1993	1991	1992	1993
Sales	$ 300	$ 315	$ 331	$ 150	$ 165	$ 181
Operating expenses	(240)	(252)	(265)	(135)	(148)	(162)
Interest expense	(8)	(8)	(8)	(1)	(1)	(1)
Pretax income	$ 52	$ 55	$ 58	$ 14	$ 16	$ 18
Income tax expense	(20)	(22)	(23)	(6)	(6)	(7)
Net income	$ 32	$ 33	$ 35	$ 8	$ 10	$ 11
Earnings per share	$1.28	$1.32	$1.40	$0.80	$1.00	$1.10

During the entire period, Pierson had 25 million shares outstanding while Drew had 10 million shares outstanding (excluding merger effects).

The proposed merger would be effected on June 30, 1992, by Pierson issuing 0.6 share for each share of Drew. On that date, the market price of Pierson shares was $20; the market price of Drew shares was $12.

to 6 million (each share should now sell at $20); Drew then issues 1 new share for each share of Pierson.]

D. Prepare pro forma combined condensed income statements (including earnings per share) for 1991–1993 under *each* of the assumptions in parts A–C. State any other assumptions made.

E. Compute the following ratios for 1991–1993 under *each* of the assumptions in parts A–C:

      (i) Debt–to–equity

      (ii) Book value per share (postmerger)

      (iii) Interest coverage

      (iv) Return on total capital

      (v) Return on equity

    F. Using your answers to parts A–E, compare the effects of *each* of the three accounting assumptions in parts A–C on the levels and trend of the following:

      (i) Reported sales and earnings per share

      (ii) Financial condition

    G. Describe the effects on reported cash flow of *each* of the accounting assumptions in parts A–C:

      (i) At the merger date

      (ii) For the period following the merger

2. [Effects of purchase acquisition; 1989 CFA adapted] After the market closed on October 17, 1988, Philip Morris announced a $90-per-share cash offer for all outstanding Kraft shares. At the time of the announcement, your supervisor handed you Exhibit 12P-2 and asked you to complete the "merged company pro forma" column. You

EXHIBIT 12P-2. PHILIP MORRIS AND KRAFT
Selected Financial Data (in $ millions, except per share data)

	Current		Merged Company
	Philip Morris	Kraft	(Pro Forma)
Common shares outstanding	234	120	
Long-term debt	$ 4700	$ 800	
Stockholders' equity	7394	1920	
Earnings before interest and tax	4340	796	
Interest expense	(475)	(81)	
Pretax income	$ 3865	$ 715	
Income tax expense	(1623)	(279)	
Net income	$ 2242	$ 436	
Cash flow from operations	$ 2974	$ 607	
Capital expenditures	850	260	
Dividends paid	892	251	
Earnings per share	$ 9.58	$ 3.63	
Debt–to–equity	0.64	0.42	
Times interest earned	9.14	9.82	

assumed that Philip Morris would raise the funds required for the takeover by issuing 11% notes and that the excess purchase price over the equity of Kraft was allocated entirely to goodwill, amortized over a period of 40 years.

Discuss the effect of the purchase on Philip Morris' financial quality. Your answer should include discussion of ratios from *each* of the following categories:

- **(i)** Profitability
- **(ii)** Solvency
- **(iii)** Activity
- **(iv)** Liquidity

3. [Comparison of pooling and purchase methods] Exhibit 12P-3 contains excerpts from the proxy statement for shareholders in connection with the merger of Contel Corporation into GTE Corporation. The merger was effected March 14, 1991, on the following terms:

EXHIBIT 12P-3. GTE AND CONTEL CORPORATION

UNAUDITED COMBINED PRO FORMA CONDENSED CONSOLIDATED FINANCIAL STATEMENTS

The following Unaudited Combined Pro Forma Condensed Consolidated Balance Sheet at June 30, 1990, and Unaudited Combined Pro Forma Condensed Consolidated Statements of Income for the six month periods ended June 30, 1990 and 1989 and for the years ended December 31, 1989, 1988 and 1987, give effect to the proposed Merger as if it had occurred at the beginning of the earliest period presented. The pro forma combinations give effect to the Merger as a "pooling of interests" for accounting purposes. These statements should be read in conjunction with the historical consolidated financial statements and the related notes contained in the respective companies' Annual Reports on Form 10-K for the year ended December 31, 1989 and subsequent filings with the SEC, which have been incorporated by reference into this Joint Proxy Statement and Prospectus. See "INCORPORATION BY REFERENCE."

The pro forma data are presented for informational purposes only and are not necessarily indicative of the operating results or financial position that would have occurred had the Merger been consummated at the dates indicated, nor are they necessarily indicative of future operating results or financial position.

GTE CORPORATION AND CONTEL CORPORATION

UNAUDITED COMBINED PRO FORMA CONDENSED CONSOLIDATED BALANCE SHEET
(In millions)

	June 30, 1990			
	GTE	CONTEL	Pro Forma Adjustments	Pro Forma Combined
ASSETS				
CURRENT ASSETS	$ 5,554	$ 847		$ 6,401
PROPERTY, PLANT and EQUIPMENT, at cost	37,734	7,283		45,017
Accumulated depreciation	(13,852)	(2,464)		(16,316)
Property, Plant and Equipment, net	23,882	4,819		28,701
INVESTMENTS and OTHER ASSETS	2,600	256		2,856
GOODWILL	131	1,399		1,530
Total Assets	$ 32,167	$ 7,321		$ 39,488

EXHIBIT 12P-3. *(Continued)*

LIABILITIES AND SHAREHOLDERS' EQUITY

CURRENT LIABILITIES

Short-term debt, including current maturities	$ 1,164	$ 566		$ 1,730
Other current liabilities	4,283	866		5,149
Total Current Liabilities	5,447	1,432		6,879
LONG-TERM DEBT and REDEEMABLE PREFERRED STOCK	11,369	3,240		14,609
DEFERRED INCOME TAXES.	3,860	607		4,467
OTHER NONCURRENT LIABILITIES	2,800	366		3,166

SHAREHOLDERS' EQUITY

Preferred stock	464	—		464
Common stock	35	159	$(149)	45
Amounts paid in, in excess of par value	5,414	551	131	6,096
Reinvested earnings.	4,650	984		5,634
Foreign currency translation adjustment.	(46)	—		(46)
Guaranteed ESOP obligation	(700)	—		(700)
Common stock held in treasury	(1,126)	(18)	18	(1,126)
Total Shareholders' Equity	8,691	1,676	—	10,367
Total Liabilities and Shareholders' Equity.	$ 32,167	$ 7,321	$ —	$ 39,488

GTE CORPORATION AND CONTEL CORPORATION

UNAUDITED COMBINED PRO FORMA CONDENSED CONSOLIDATED STATEMENTS OF INCOME
(In millions, except per share data)

	Year Ended December 31, 1989		
	GTE	Pro Forma Contel(1)	Pro Forma Combined
REVENUES AND SALES	$17,424	$3,173	$20,597
COSTS AND EXPENSES	14,235	2,595	16,830
Operating Income	3,189	578	3,767
OTHER DEDUCTIONS:			
Interest expense.	1,016	343	1,359
Other—net.	109	(40)	69
	1,125	303	1,428
Income before income taxes	2,064	275	2,339
INCOME TAX PROVISION.	647	96	743
Income from continuing operations	1,417	179	1,596
PREFERRED STOCK DIVIDENDS OF PARENT	47	—	47
Income from continuing operations applicable to common stock	$ 1,370	$ 179	$ 1,549
INCOME FROM CONTINUING OPERATIONS PER COMMON SHARE.	$ 2.08	$ 1.13	$ 1.80
AVERAGE COMMON SHARES OUTSTANDING	659	159	861

Source: GTE Corporation Proxy Statement, November 2, 1990

Each share of Contel was exchanged for 1.27 shares of GTE. The price of GTE at the time of the merger was approximately $33 per share. Assume that GTE had 666 million shares and Contel 159 million shares outstanding just prior to the merger.

The merger was accounted for using the pooling of interest method. The exhibit shows combined pro forma balance sheets as of June 30, 1990, and pro forma income statements for the two years ended December 31, 1989.

Use the following assumptions as to the "fair value" of Contel's assets and liabilities on the date of the merger:

1. Current assets equal $900 million (increase of $53 million for inventory).

2. Fixed assets exceed historical cost by 50% (note that fixed assets are approximately one-third depreciated, making them relatively new).

3. The transaction is treated as a purchase for tax purposes.

4. No other adjustments are made for tangible assets or liabilities.

Based on these assumptions and the data provided:

A. Prepare a combined pro forma balance sheet at June 30, 1990, using the purchase method.

B. Prepare a combined pro forma income statement for 1989 using the purchase method.

C. Compute the following (postmerger) statistics under *each* of the two methods.

   (i) Book value per share at June 30, 1990

   (ii) Tangible book value per share at June 30, 1990

   (iii) Debt-to-equity ratio at June 30, 1990

   (iv) Debt–to–tangible equity ratio at June 30, 1990

   (v) Earnings per share for 1989

   (vi) Interest coverage ratio for 1989

   (vii) Return on assets

   (viii) Return on tangible assets

   (ix) Return on equity

   (x) Return on tangible equity

[Hint: Ratios vii–x must be computed using 1989 income statement data but June 30, 1990 balance sheet data.]

D. Discuss the factors that are most responsible for the financial statement differences between the two methods you found in parts A–C.

E. Comment briefly on how your answers to parts A and B would differ if GTE's shares had been trading at a price $1 higher at the time of the merger.

4. [Analysis of series of pooling of interest acquisitions; adapted from an article by Abraham Briloff in *Barron's* October 8, 1990, p. 14. (courtesy of Professor Ashiq Ali)] Exhibit 12P-4 contains excerpts from the 1988 and 1989 annual reports of Allwaste, Inc., a firm that has grown rapidly through acquisitions. Generally, it uses the pooling of

EXHIBIT 12P-4. ALLWASTE, INC., AND SUBSIDIARIES

During fiscal 1989 the company acquired nine companies in transactions accounted for as poolings of interest. Aggregate consideration consisted of 8,615,960 shares of common stock. As an integral part of each acquisition, all former shareholders signed noncompete agreements, and key management entered into agreements with the company to continue managing these businesses.

Net revenues, net income, and stockholders' equity of the company are shown below, both at August 31, 1988 and (after restatement) at August 31, 1989. Operations of the pooled companies are included for their fiscal year ending closest to that of the company's.

Financial Data, for Years Ended August 31, 1987–1989
(thousands, except per share data)

Report Date	1987			1988			1989		
	Net Revenues	Net Income	Earnings Per Share	Net Revenues	Net Income	Earnings Per Share	Net Revenues	Net Income	Earnings Per Share
8-31-88	$45,894	$2,667	$.16	$ 67,804	$5,329	$.27	—	—	—
8-31-89	$86,771	$5,205	$.22	$125,258	$9,877	$.35	$165,689	$11,797	$.40

Report Date	Stockholders' Equity	Shares Outstanding	Stockholders' Equity	Shares Outstanding	Stockholders' Equity	Shares Outstanding
8-31-88	$14,562	17,242	$33,814	20,154	—	—
8-31-89	$17,820	25,858	$38,077	28,770	$52,359	29,594

Source: Allwaste, Inc., 1988 and 1989 annual reports.

interests method for these acquisitions. During fiscal 1989, Allwaste issued 8.6 million shares with an estimated market value of $70 million to acquire nine companies.

A. Discuss how the pooling method acquisitions changed the level and trend of the following for the 1987–1989 period:

(i) Revenues

(ii) Net income

(iii) Return on equity

B. Recast Allwaste's 1989 acquisitions using the purchase method assuming that:

(i) Allwaste sold common stock and used the proceeds to acquire these firms.

(ii) The excess of the purchase price over book value of the acquired firms was goodwill, amortized over a 40-year life.

(iii) The acquisitions were made at the close of the fiscal year.

C. Using the recast data from part B, repeat part A. Comment on your results.

D. Discuss the impact on your answer to part C of each of the following changes in assumptions:

(i) Goodwill amortization over a 10-year life

(ii) Acquisitions made halfway through the fiscal year

E. **(i)** Using the exhibit data (pooling method), compute the impact of the acquisitions on earnings per share for 1987 and 1988.

(ii) Repeat part (i) using the results of part C (purchase method).

(iii) Discuss how the choice of accounting method affected the impact of the acquisitions on Allwaste's earnings per share.

F. **(i)** Describe the impact of the acquisitions (pooling method) on Allwaste's statement of cash flows in the acquisition years.

(ii) Using the results of part B, estimate the reported cash from financing in the acquisition years under the purchase method, and compare them to the amounts reported under the pooling method.

(iii) Discuss any other differences in reported cash flows between the pooling and purchase methods in the acquisition years.

(iv) Discuss how reported cash flows in the years following the acquisitions vary with the accounting method used.

5. [Derivation of acquisition data from cash flow statement] On June 24, 1992, Roadway Services, a large U.S. motor carrier, acquired Cole Enterprises, a regional carrier. Exhibit 12P-5 contains the financial statement footnote describing the transaction. Elsewhere, Roadway states that 1991 revenues of Cole were approximately $19 million.

Exhibit 12P-5 also contains Roadway's statement of cash flows (1992) and balance sheets (1991–1992).

A. Using the data in Exhibit 12P-5, derive the balance sheet of Cole at the date of its acquisition. (Hint: You must compare each balance sheet change with the corresponding cash flow; some aggregation is required. Remember that noncash transactions are excluded from the cash flow statement.)

B. Using the data in Exhibit 12P-5 and the results of part A, compute the following ratios for Cole (postacquisition) and Roadway (at December 31, 1991):

(i) Fixed asset turnover

(ii) Accounts receivable turnover

(iii) Equity to assets

C. Discuss the possible reasons for the ratio differences in part B. Describe the possible implications of the ratio differences for future cash flows.

EXHIBIT 12P-5. ROADWAY SERVICES, INC., AND SUBSIDIARIES

Note B — Acquisitions

On June 24, 1992, the company acquired Cole Enterprises, Inc., the parent company of Coles Express, Inc., a New England regional motor common carrier based in Bangor, Maine, for $4,617,000 in cash and 235,892 shares of the company's common stock valued at $15,127,000. The acquisition was accounted for as a purchase and the cost in excess of net assets acquired was $3,441,000. Earnings of Coles since its acquisition are included in the accompanying statement of consolidated income, and are not material in relation to consolidated operations.

EXHIBIT 12P-5. *(Continued)*

A. Statement of Consolidated Cash Flows

	Year Ended December 31 1992
CASH FLOWS FROM OPERATING ACTIVITIES	
Net Income	$ 147,407
Adjustments to reconcile net income to net cash provided by operating activities:	
Depreciation and amortization	172,695
(Gain) loss on sale of carrier operating property	23
Issuance of treasury shares for stock plans	18,507
Changes in assets and liabilities, net of effects from the purchase of Cole Enterprises, Inc.:	
(Increase) in accounts receivable	(39,999)
(Increase) decrease in prepaid expenses and supplies	7,925
Increase in accounts payable and accrued items	34,269
Increase (decrease) in current income taxes payable	3,022
Increase (decrease) in other liabilities	(4,984)
Total adjustments	191,458
NET CASH PROVIDED BY OPERATING ACTIVITIES	338,865
CASH FLOWS FROM INVESTING ACTIVITIES	
Purchases of carrier operating property	(211,073)
Sales of carrier operating property	10,062
Purchases of marketable securities	(197,263)
Sales of marketable securities	124,787
Purchase of Cole Enterprises, Inc., net of cash acquired	(866)
NET CASH USED IN INVESTING ACTIVITIES	(274,353)
CASH FLOWS FROM FINANCING ACTIVITIES	
Dividends paid	(48,984)
Purchases of common stock for treasury	—
Proceeds from exercise of stock options	186
NET CASH USED IN FINANCING ACTIVITIES	(48,798)
NET INCREASE (DECREASE) IN CASH	15,714
CASH AT BEGINNING OF YEAR	25,322
CASH AT END OF YEAR	$ 41,036

EXHIBIT 12P-5. *(Continued)*

B. Consolidated Balance Sheet

ASSETS

	December 31	
	1992	**1991**
	(dollars in thousands)	
CURRENT ASSETS		
Cash	$ 41,036	$ 25,322
Marketable securities	274,898	201,917
Accounts receivable, net of allowance for uncollectible accounts	304,645	261,252
Prepaid expenses and supplies	55,954	61,650
TOTAL CURRENT ASSETS	676,533	550,141
CARRIER OPERATING PROPERTY — at cost		
Land	130,605	120,280
Structures	476,102	430,862
Revenue equipment	971,621	901,110
Other operating equipment	466,123	398,159
	2,044,451	1,850,411
Less allowances for depreciation	1,148,791	998,217
TOTAL CARRIER OPERATING PROPERTY	895,660	852,194
COST IN EXCESS OF NET ASSETS OF BUSINESSES ACQUIRED — net of amortization — Note B	87,330	86,297
	$ 1,659,523	$1,488,632

EXHIBIT 12P-5. *(Continued)*

LIABILITIES AND SHAREHOLDERS' EQUITY

	December 31	
	1992	**1991**
	(dollars in thousands)	
CURRENT LIABILITIES		
Accounts payable — Note C	$ 225,361	$ 186,496
Salaries and wages	149,501	154,514
Income taxes payable	25,792	22,712
Freight and casualty claims payable within one year	81,395	78,747
Dividend payable	12,803	11,664
TOTAL CURRENT LIABILITIES	494,852	454,133
OTHER LIABILITIES		
Deferred federal income taxes — Note D	41,096	49,507
Future equipment repairs	21,321	18,572
Casualty claims payable after one year	80,894	76,164
TOTAL OTHER LIABILITIES	143,311	144,243
SHAREHOLDERS' EQUITY — Note F		
Serial preferred stock — without par value:		
Authorized — 40,000,000 shares		
Issued — none		
Common stock — without par value:		
Authorized — 200,000,000 shares		
Issued — 40,896,414 shares	39,898	39,898
Additional capital	50,392	31,271
Earnings reinvested in the business	966,061	868,777
	1,056,351	939,946
Less cost of common stock in treasury		
(1992 — 1,163,000 shares, 1991 — 1,704,000 shares)	34,991	49,690
TOTAL SHAREHOLDERS' EQUITY	1,021,360	890,256
	$ 1,659,523	$ 1,488,632

Source: Roadway Services, Inc., *1992 annual report.*

D. Roadway has insignificant non-U.S. operations. Discuss how this impacts the accuracy of your answer to part A.

E. Discuss how you would measure the future return on Roadway's acquisition of Cole.

6. [Analysis of spinoffs] Exhibit 12P-6A contains reported segment data from the *1991 Annual Report* of Adolph Coors Company. In December 1992, Coors spun off ACX Technologies, consisting of virtually all the nonbeer operations of Coors, including aluminum and packaging operations that supply the beer operations. Exhibit 12P-6B contains selected data from the *1991 Annual Report* of Coors and from an information statement on the spinoff of ACX.

A. Using the data in Exhibit 12P-6A, prepare an estimated pro forma income statement for Coors (excluding ACX) for the period 1989–1991. Discuss the additional

EXHIBIT 12P-6. ADOLPH COORS AND ACX TECHNOLOGIES
Selected Financial Data, for Years Ended December 31, 1989–1991 (in $ thousands)

A. Segment Data, Adolph Coors Company

Segment Information

The Company's operations include four reportable segments: beer business, ceramics business, aluminum business and packaging business. The beer segment is composed of those operations principally involved in the manufacture, sale and distribution of malt beverage products. The ceramics segment is made up of those operations which manufacture ceramic products. The aluminum segment is involved in the manufacture of aluminum rigid container sheet products and reclamation and recycling of used beverage containers and other secondary metals. The packaging segment produces high-performance folding cartons and flexible packaging.

Developmental businesses include those subsidiaries that produce corn syrup, vitamin products and other food ingredients; manufacture and assemble standard electronic modules (SEM) and multilayer interconnect boards (MIB); develop innovative technologies based on expertise in engineering and technology; and develop oil and gas proper-

ties. In 1991, the nature of operations changed for the subsidiary that manufactures and assembles SEMs and MIBs. This subsidiary was reclassified to developmental businesses from the ceramics business segment. All segment data for prior years have been restated to reflect this change. The operating loss for developmental businesses in 1991 included asset write-downs in the oil and gas operations (Note 7).

The operating results for the beer business in 1990 included a special charge for remediation costs associated with the Lowry Landfill Superfund site (Note 7).

The operating loss for developmental businesses in 1989 includes asset write-downs in oil and gas, coal and snack foods operations (Note 7).

Intersegment activity is composed of sales, accounts receivable and profit on the transfer of inventory between segments. Operating income (loss) for reportable segments is exclusive of certain corporate expenses.

Corporate assets primarily include cash, short-term interest bearing investments, and certain fixed assets.

	Net sales	Operating income (loss)	Assets	Depreciation, depletion and amortization	Additions to properties
1991			*(In thousands)*		
Beer business	$1,530,347	$ 59,126	$1,285,311	$100,992	$235,044
Ceramics business	180,146	1,983	167,330	10,969	25,589
Aluminum business	95,996	6,346	252,691	8,061	67,552
Packaging business	188,141	17,185	109,831	9,291	11,217
Developmental businesses	111,309	(44,158)	111,970	13,684	10,266
Intersegment activity	(188,517)	(819)	(28,546)	—	—
Corporate	—	(17,979)	87,722	892	4,861
	$1,917,422	$ 21,684	$1,986,309	$143,889	$354,529

EXHIBIT 12P-6. *(Continued)*

1990					
Beer business - continuing	$1,477,271	$100,662	$1,114,962	$ 90,757	$175,199
- Special charge	—	(30,000)	—	—	—
Ceramics business	179,796	2,214	147,848	9,858	14,356
Aluminum business	113,445	16,322	194,152	7,620	83,236
Packaging business	155,809	9,804	102,800	9,141	4,187
Developmental businesses	105,547	(9,684)	142,749	12,181	20,550
Intersegment activity	(193,302)	1,531	(31,666)	—	—
Corporate	—	(16,465)	90,819	819	4,493
	$1,838,566	$ 74,384	$1,761,664	$130,376	$302,021
1989					
Beer business	$1,366,108	$ 71,081	$ 967,486	$ 85,249	$ 81,499
Ceramics business	166,215	14,802	150,908	8,051	32,957
Aluminum business	94,173	9,110	93,572	6,822	15,826
Packaging business	136,848	772	110,961	8,281	3,108
Developmental businesses	104,069	(48,290)	130,570	12,761	14,407
Intersegment activity	(176,710)	(2,300)	(18,574)	—	—
Corporate	—	(11,429)	95,860	1,275	1,819
	$1,690,703	$ 33,746	$1,530,783	$122,439	$149,616

B. Selected Financial Data

	1989	1990	1991
Adolph Coors Company			
Net sales	$1,690,703	$1,838,566	$1,917,422
Operating income	33,746	74,384	21,684
Interest expense	(1,699)	(371)	(589)
Other income (expense), net	(6,415)	(9,813)	2,122
Income tax expense (benefit)	12,500	25,300	(700)
Net income	13,132	38,900	23,917
Total assets	1,530,783	1,761,664	1,986,309
Working capital	193,590	201,043	110,443
Long-term debt	—	110,000	220,000
Stockholders' equity	1,060,900	1,091,547	1,099,420
Number of shares	36,900	37,484	37,482
ACX Technologies, Inc.			
Net sales	$ 466,818	$ 521,229	$ 543,503
Operating income	14,881	15,948	8,897
Interest expense	(2,997)	(4,681)	(8,653)
Other income (expense), net	(3,951)	(4,708)	3,301
Income tax expense	2,900	3,000	2,200
Net income	5,033	3,559	1,345
Total assets	422,757	576,435	640,951
Working capital	78,850	124,356	100,999
Debt to parent (Coors)	19,676	131,737	185,782
Stockholders' equity	286,827	294,657	294,709

Source: Coors 1991 Annual Report; ACX Technologies information statement, December 9, 1992

information required to prepare a more accurate pro forma income statement for the period.

B. Compute the following reported and pro forma (excluding ACX) statistics for Coors for the 1989–1991 period:

> **(i)** Debt–to–equity
>
> **(ii)** Times interest earned
>
> **(iii)** Return on sales
>
> **(iv)** Return on equity
>
> **(v)** Book value per share
>
> **(vi)** Asset turnover
>
> **(vii)** Working capital
>
> **(viii)** Growth rate of sales, operating income, and net income, for 1989–1991

C. Discuss the limitations of your pro forma results (parts A and B) as indicators of the future results of Coors.

D. Assume that ACX consists entirely of the nonbeer segments of Coors, as shown in Exhibit 12P-6B.

> **(i)** Under that assumption, describe how the Coors segment data could have been used to estimate the pro forma balance sheet and income statement data for ACX.
>
> **(ii)** Describe the missing data required to complete the estimate.
>
> **(iii)** Discuss the usefulness of the historic segment data as predictors of the future operating results of ACX.

E. ACX shares more than doubled in price after trading commenced in December 1992. The total share value (Coors after the spinoff plus ACX) rose by 25% from November 30, 1992, to January 29, 1993.

> **(i)** Using data in Exhibit 12P-6 and your answers to earlier parts, discuss why investors may have been attracted to ACX.
>
> **(ii)** Discuss the implications of the behavior of stock prices described here for the efficient market hypothesis.

F. Using your answers to parts A–E, discuss why Coors may have chosen to spin off ACX rather than sell it to another company or through an initial public offering.

7. [Comparison of LBO with another company; 1992 CFA adapted] In 1988, NECCO borrowed $700 million at an interest rate of 14% to complete a leveraged buyout (LBO) transaction initiated by its management. Management states that the poor profitability since the buyout is due to high interest costs. NECCO now plans to double the number of its shares outstanding by selling 20 million new shares to investors through an initial public offering (IPO), using the entire proceeds to retire a major portion of the 14% debt, which is callable at par without penalty to NECCO.

You have decided to use CONCO, a company that competes directly with NECCO and has a very similar product line, as the basis for comparison in your evaluation of the

NECCO offering. Exhibit 12P-7 contains highlights of both CONCO's and NECCO's financial data as reported for 1981 and 1991.

Compare the trends in return on equity of CONCO and NECCO by identifying and commenting upon the changes in *both* firms':

(i) Operating profitability

(ii) Asset utilization

(iii) Financial leverage

In your comments on NECCO, include specific reference to the impact of the LBO on *each* of these three factors.

8. [Goodwill amortization] Hanson Industries is a U.K. conglomerate with operations in the United Kingdom and the United States. In July 1989, it acquired Consolidated Gold Fields, PLC, for £3.3 billion of which £2.1 billion was allocated to goodwill. Hanson charged this goodwill to reserves, in keeping with its normal practice and U.K. GAAP. Exhibit 12P-8 contains data derived from the "Reconciliation to U.S. Accounting Principles" provided by the firm in its 1989–1991 annual reports.

EXHIBIT 12P-7. CONCO AND NECCO
Selected Financial Data, for Years Ended December 31, 1981 and 1991 (in $ millions)

| | A. CONCO | | | |
| | 1981 | | 1991 | |
	Amount	% of Sales	Amount	% of Sales
Operating Highlights				
Net revenues	$1243	100.0%	$ 3044	100.0%
Cost of goods sold	(778)	(62.6)	(1918)	(63.0)
Gross profit	$ 465	37.4%	$ 1126	37.0%
Selling and general expense	(250)	(20.1)	(612)	(20.1)
Pretax operating income	$ 215	17.3%	$ 514	16.9%
Interest expense	(5)	(0.4)	(7)	(0.2)
Pretax income	$ 210	16.9%	$ 507	16.7%
Income tax expense	(95)	(7.6)	(201)	(6.6)
Net income	$ 115	9.3%	$ 306	10.1%
Balance Sheet Highlights, at Year End				
Total assets	$1075		$ 2950	
Current liabilities	$ 300		$ 1070	
Long-term debt	60		80	
Total liabilities	$ 360		$ 1150	
Stockholders' equity	715		1800	
Total liabilities and stockholders' equity	$1075		$ 2950	

EXHIBIT 12P-7. *(Continued)*

	B. NECCO			
	1981		1991	
	Amount	% of Sales	Amount	% of Sales
Operating Highlights				
Net revenues	$165	100.0%	$ 710	100.0%
Cost of goods sold	(82)	(49.7)	(410)	(57.7)
Gross profit	$ 83	50.3%	$ 300	42.3%
Selling and general expense	(41)	(24.8)	(190)	(26.8)
Pretax operating income	$ 42	25.5%	$ 110	15.5%
Interest expense	0	(0.0)	100	(14.1)
Pretax income	$ 42	25.5%	$ 10	1.4%
Income tax expense	(21)	(12.8)	(4)	(0.6)
Net income	$ 21	12.7%	$ 6	0.8%
Balance Sheet Highlights, at Year End				
Total assets	$140		$1170	
Current liabilities	$ 45		$ 250	
Long-term debt	0		720	
Total liabilities	$ 45		$ 970	
Stockholders' equity	95		200	
Total liabilities and stockholders' equity	$140		$1170	

A. Recompute reported income and return on equity for 1988–1991, assuming use of a 10-year life for *all* goodwill.

B. Compare and discuss the differences in the levels and trends of reported income and return on equity for 1988–1991 under the three methods: U.K. GAAP, U.S. GAAP (from the exhibit), and your answer to part A.

C. The U.K. Financial Reporting Standard (FRS) 3 (effective for fiscal year ends after June 22, 1992) requires that all remaining goodwill relating to a unit sold or disposed of must be written off at the time of sale or discontinuation. Recalculate profits on the sale of businesses in 1988–1991 on this basis.

D. Discuss the impact of your results in part C on reported earnings and return on equity for 1988–1991.

9. [Push-down accounting, extension of Problem 2] Exhibit 12P-2 contains data regarding the merger of Philip Morris and Kraft. Assume that Kraft continued to issue separate financial statements following the merger with Philip Morris. Using the data in Problem 2 and Exhibit 12P-2, and assuming that Kraft applies "push-down" accounting to its financial statements, answer the following questions *from the point of view of a Kraft bondholder.*

EXHIBIT 12P-8. HANSON INDUSTRIES
Data Derived from "Reconciliation to U.S. Accounting Principles," for Years Ended September 30, 1988–1991 (in £ millions)

	1988	1989	1990	1991
U.K. GAAP income				
Continuing operations	£676	£813	£971	£1035
Extraordinary income	445	288	29	71
Total	£1121	£1101	£1000	£1106
Estimated adjustments				
Goodwill on disposals	(180)	(92)	(171)	(46)
Goodwill amortization	(50)	(56)	(97)	(95)
Other adjustments[1]	(11)	(26)	218	(9)
U.S. GAAP, net income	£880	£927	£950	£956
Continuing operations	523	759	955	972
Extraordinary income	357	168	(5)	(16)
Total	£880	£927	£950	£956
Profit on sales of business units (included above)	445	288	168	115
U.K. GAAP				
Stockholders' equity	£2192	£1046	£2834	£3325
Estimated adjustments				
Goodwill	1811	3724	3550	3438
Other[1]	(42)	55	248	330
U.S. GAAP				
Stockholders' equity	£3961	£4825	£6632	£7093

[1]Other adjustments include foreign currency translation, pensions, revaluation of land, buildings and timberlands, and taxes.

Source: Hanson Industries annual reports, 1989–1991.

A. Compute the following ratios immediately prior to and immediately following the merger (state any assumptions made):

    (i) Debt-to-equity

    (ii) Return on total capital

    (iii) Interest coverage ratio

    (iv) Net profit margin

B. Discuss the comparability of Kraft financial data before and after the merger.

C. Discuss the comparability of Kraft financial data (postmerger) with that of companies that have not been acquired.

D. Discuss any insights regarding Kraft that you might draw from the push-down adjustments themselves.

E. Discuss the pros and cons of Kraft's use of push-down accounting following the merger.

13

ANALYSIS OF MULTINATIONAL OPERATIONS

INTRODUCTION

BASIC ACCOUNTING ISSUES

FASB'S FIRST ATTEMPT: SFAS 8

FOREIGN CURRENCY TRANSLATION UNDER SFAS 52
Treatment of Exchange Gains and Losses
Role of the Functional Currency
Remeasurement Versus Translation

ILLUSTRATION OF TRANSLATION AND REMEASUREMENT
Translation
Cumulative Translation Adjustment
Remeasurement

COMPARISON OF TRANSLATION AND REMEASUREMENT
Income Statement Effects
  Effect on Gross Profit Margin
  Effect on Net Income
Balance Sheet Effects
Impact on Financial Ratios

Comparison of Ratios Under Translation and Remeasurement
Comparison of Translated and Local Currency Ratios
Impact on Reported Cash Flows

ACCOUNTING PRINCIPLES USED OUTSIDE OF THE UNITED STATES
Foreign Currency Translation
Foreign Currency Transactions
IASC Exposure Draft

CASE STUDIES OF MNC ANALYSIS
IBM Corp.
  Balance Sheet Effects
  Income Statement Effects
  Ratio Effects
  Concluding Comments on IBM
Alcoa
  Alcoa of Australia (Change in Functional Currency)
  Alcoa Aluminio (Hyperinflationary Economies)
Analysis of Hyperinflationary Operations

ANALYTIC DIFFICULTIES RELATED TO FOREIGN OPERATIONS

Relationship Among Interest Rates, Inflation, and Exchange Rates

Nonmonetary Assets

Monetary Assets

Consistency in Reporting

Economic Interpretation of Results

Impact of SFAS 8 and SFAS 52 on Management and Investor Behavior

CONCLUDING COMMENTS

INTRODUCTION

International capital markets and trade have expanded significantly in recent years. The entry of the Eastern European bloc into world markets, the growth of the Pacific Rim countries, increased integration of the European Economic Community, and the industrialized countries' continuing search for markets are among the factors contributing to the escalating growth and internationalization of trade and capital markets.

In addition to their traditional merchandising operations, multinational companies (MNCs) are increasingly adding manufacturing capacity in foreign countries. Trade frictions and political considerations have joined economic factors such as access to low-cost labor or raw materials as incentives for such international expansion. Expanding international capital markets have also facilitated this growth by allowing MNCs to borrow and lend in foreign currencies and markets and to hedge foreign operations with an array of complex instruments, including options, forward contracts (futures), and combined interest rate and currency swaps.

MNCs often conduct their foreign operations in countries where they are subject to local financial reporting regulations that are quite different from those providing the basis for the parent company's financial statements. Foreign operations are carried out under varied economic conditions and in different currencies whose relative prices (i.e., exchange rates) fluctuate widely with significant effects on both actual and reported operating performance, financial position, and cash flows. Hedging operations often involve innovative instruments for which the financial reporting requirements are still under development, making it difficult to evaluate the risk/return trade-offs.

MNCs must consolidate financial statements for their domestic and foreign operations that are based on different sets of accounting principles (with varying methods and estimates) and in different measurement units (currencies) with fluctuating exchange rates. The foreign currency–denominated financial statements of foreign subsidiaries must be translated into their parent's reporting currency to permit consolidation.

This chapter discusses the impact of the translation of operations denominated in foreign currencies and accounting for foreign currency transactions in the consolidated financial statements of U.S. MNCs with foreign operations. International Accounting Standards Committee (IASC) requirements and the standards of selected countries for foreign currency transactions and translation are also examined.

BASIC ACCOUNTING ISSUES

When operations are conducted in foreign currencies, and when exchange rates fluctuate, the accounting for such operations presents difficulties beyond those of single-currency statements. The differing currencies are an additional dimension: operations must be measured using multiple units (currencies). Accounting for foreign operations raises three basic issues.

The first issue is the choice of exchange rate used to translate foreign currency transactions and financial statements into the parent company currency, often referred to as the "reporting currency". For convenience we will use the U.S. dollar as the parent currency in the examples that follow. However, the principles apply equally whether the reporting currency is U.S. dollars, Swiss francs, or Japanese yen.

All transactions that are denominated in currencies other than the parent currency must be translated into that currency as part of the process of preparing consolidated financial statements. But at what exchange rate? There are two obvious choices: the historical rate and the current rate. The historical rate is the exchange rate at the time the transaction (sale of output, purchase of inventory, borrowing, etc.) took place. The current rate is the exchange rate as of the balance sheet date. Moreover, the rate chosen may be used for *all* transactions not denominated in the reporting currency, or different rates may be used for different types of transactions. We shall discuss the implications of these choices shortly.

The other two issues are the definition of exposure to exchange rate changes and the treatment of translation gains and losses. Both are a consequence of fluctuating exchange rates. *When exchange rates change, financial data recorded in the parent currency (after translation) will change, even if the local currency data have not.* These translated financial statements commingle the effects of exchange rate changes with the results of operating, investment, and financing activities. Further, these exchange rate effects, often referred to as translation gains and losses, must be accounted for. They can be recognized immediately as a component of net income in the period of change, deferred (and possibly amortized), or accounted for as adjustments to stockholders' equity.

Ideally, the translation gain or loss should capture the impact of changing exchange rates on the parent's investment in the foreign operations, that is, the parent's "economic exposure" to exchange rate changes. In practice, however, the reported translation gain or loss depends on two characteristics of the reporting method: (1) the exchanges rate(s) chosen for translation, and (2) the transactions selected for translation. In other words, it reflects the impact of changing exchange rates on the parent's "accounting" rather than its "economic" exposure.

The interaction of the choice of exchange rate, the definition of exposure, and the disposition of the resulting translation adjustments can significantly affect the reported earnings and financial condition of MNCs.

FASB'S FIRST ATTEMPT: SFAS 8

In 1975, the Financial Accounting Standards Board (FASB) issued Statement of Financial Accounting Standards (SFAS) 8, Accounting for the Translation of Foreign

Currency Transactions and Foreign Currency Financial Statements, to bring uniformity to accounting practice in the United States. SFAS 8 deals with the three basic accounting issues as follows:

1. The *temporal method* is used to translate foreign currency balance sheets into the reporting currency prior to consolidation. Under this method (described more fully in the paragraphs that follow), nonmonetary assets (mainly inventories and fixed assets) are translated using the historical rate while almost all other assets are translated using the current rate.

2. The standard defines the accounting exposure as the net monetary asset or liability position since nonmonetary assets (inventories and fixed assets) are translated at historical rates and therefore are not affected by changing exchange rates.[1]

3. The resulting translation gains and losses are recognized as a component of net income. Thus the effects of volatile exchange rates are transmitted directly to reported earnings on a quarterly basis.[2]

Because of this earnings volatility, SFAS 8 was one of the most unpopular standards issued by the FASB. Because the accounting exposure and the economic exposure to a currency are frequently quite different, companies wishing to hedge were forced to choose between hedging their accounting exposure and hedging their "real" exposure. Within a few years, the FASB reexamined the accounting for foreign operations and issued a new standard. These criticisms also led Canadian regulators to suspend the issuance of their equivalent of SFAS 8.

FOREIGN CURRENCY TRANSLATION UNDER SFAS 52

SFAS 52, Foreign Currency Translation (1981), prescribes reporting requirements for translation of the financial statements of foreign operations. The primary objectives of the new standard are set out in Para. 4:

---

[1]As noted in the next section, this is true only for unrealized gains and losses on nonmonetary assets. Realized gains and losses on nonmonetary assets are recognized and commingled with operating income.

[2]These concepts can be illustrated with a simple example. Assume that a U.S. parent acquires a foreign subsidiary for $500 on December 31, 1990, when the exchange rate between the local currency (LC) and the U.S. dollar is LC 1 = $US 1. The subsidiary has cash = LC 400 and inventory = LC 100. The inventory is sold, during 1991, when the exchange rate is LC 1 = $US 1.50, for LC 200 ($US 300). At year-end 1991, the exchange rate is LC 1 = $US 2. The subsidiary now has cash of LC 600 ($US 1200) and the parent reports total profit of $US 700 ($US 1200 − $US 500) during the year, which includes both operating and translation gains.

Under the temporal method only the cash has any accounting exposure to exchange rate changes. The actual translation gain on the cash is $US 500. (The original LC 400 increased in dollar terms from $US 400 to $US 800 for a gain of $US 400. The LC 200 received from the sale of inventory increased from $US 300 to $US 400 for an additional translation gain of $US 100). The remaining $US 200 profit is from operations. (Revenues from the sale were $US 300 and COGS were $US 100, the original cost of the inventory, since under the temporal method inventories (and fixed assets) are not adjusted for exchange rate changes).

a. Provide information that is generally compatible with the expected economic effects of a rate change on an enterprise's cash flows and equity.
b. Reflect in consolidated statements the financial results and relationships of the individual consolidated entities as measured in their functional currencies in conformity with U.S. GAAP.[3]

We will discuss both these objectives later in the chapter.

SFAS 52 introduced the *all current rate method,* which answered the basic accounting issues quite differently. SFAS 52 did not, it must be emphasized, replace the temporal method (SFAS 8) with the all current method for all situations. Rather, it delineated the conditions under which each method would be appropriate. When the temporal method is not deemed to be appropriate, SFAS 52 requires that

- The all current rate method is used to translate foreign currency financial data into the parent currency. That is, the exchange rate as of the balance sheet date is employed for all assets and liabilities.

- The accounting exposure is defined as the parent's net investment in the foreign operations, since all assets and liabilities are translated at the current rate.

- Gains and losses arising from the translation process are reported separately as a component of stockholders' equity and are excluded from reported net income.[4]

As we shall see shortly, the differences between the two methods have significant implications for the financial statements of MNCs. Before proceeding, however, it is important to note where the two methods differ (and where they do not) in the recognition of the effects of changes in exchange rates.

Treatment of Exchange Rate Gains/Losses

One component of exchange rate gains/losses is a result of the net asset or liability position (the exposure) of the foreign subsidiary. The financial reporting treatment of this component is the primary difference between the temporal method (SFAS 8) and the all current method (added by SFAS 52). However, even if the foreign subsidiary liquidated its asset and liability positions each day, the parent would still be affected by changes in exchange rates.

For example, assume a parent company in the United States has a subsidiary in Canada that generates revenues of $CAN 10,000 per day and the exchange rate on day 1

---

[3]Statement of Financial Accounting Standards No. 52, Foreign Currency Translation, Financial Accounting Standards Board, December, 1981.

[4]Under SFAS 52, the example in footnote 2 would be reported as follows. Under the all current method, *both cash and inventory face accounting exposure to exchange rate changes.* The total *translation gain* would be $US 550. (Translation gain on cash is $US 500 as calculated in footnote 2. The *translation gain* on the inventory is $US 50 as its value in dollars increased from $US 100 to $US 150 between the time it was bought and the time it was sold.) Operating profit would be $US 150. (Revenues from the sale were $US 300, and *COGS* were $US 150, the *cost of the inventory in dollars at the time of sale, since under the all current method, all assets and liabilities are adjusted for exchange rate changes*). Only the operating profit of $US 150 will appear on the income statement; the $US 550 translation gain will appear as the cumulative translation adjustment in the stockholders' equity section.

EXHIBIT 13-1
Summary of Differences Between Temporal and All Current Methods in Treatment of Exchange Rate Holding Gains and Losses

Asset/ Liability	Nature of Gain/Loss	Treatment	
		Temporal Method	All Current Method
Monetary	Realized and unrealized	Income statement, explicit disclosure of translation gain/loss	Equity, cumulative translation adjustment
Nonmonetary	Realized	Income statement, implicit within operating income	Equity, cumulative translation adjustment
	Unrealized	Ignored	Equity, cumulative translation adjustment
Summary		All gains and losses except unrealized nonmonetary in income statement	All gains and losses in cumulative translation adjustment

is $US 0.85 per $CAN 1.00. Assume that daily Canadian dollar receipts are immediately converted to U.S. dollars, yielding $US 8500. On day 2, the exchange rate changes to $US 0.86 per $CAN 1.00 (the Canadian dollar rises). *Then the parent would be better off, as the identical revenues of $CAN 10,000 earned on day 2 would translate into more U.S. dollars ($US 8600 rather than $US 8500).* The analytic issue in this case is to disaggregate the increase in operating results into the portion due to effects of changes in exchange rates (in this case $US 100) and the portion due to the change in actual operating performance (in this case $US 0) of the Canadian subsidiary.[5] While this issue is important, it is not the explicit focus of either accounting standard.

Alternatively, if the parent retains the day 1 Canadian dollar receipts, then its financial position improves on day 2 as the Canadian dollars held from the previous day's revenues can be converted into an additional $US 100. *The treatment of this effect of exchange rate changes on assets held ("currency holding gain") is the crux of the difference between the temporal and all current method.*

Exhibit 13-1 summarizes these differences in accounting treatment. Under the all current method, all exchange rate holding gains and losses, whether realized or not, are recognized. However, they are not reported in the income statement but flow into the *cumulative translation adjustment* account in shareholders' equity.

Under the temporal method only some exchange rate holding gains and losses are recognized. *Unrealized gains and losses on nonmonetary assets are ignored. Realized gains and losses on nonmonetary assets are recognized but are "buried" within reported*

---

[5]See the IBM illustration that follows for an expanded discussion of this issue.

operating profits.[6] This important distinction is often overlooked, and it is incorrectly assumed that only gains and losses derived from monetary assets are explicitly recognized in the income statement under the temporal method.[7] The gains and losses on monetary assets are, however, given separate disclosure.

Notice that the gains and losses on monetary items and the realized gains and losses on nonmonetary items are identical under both methods. Thus the difference between the two methods is the treatment of unrealized gains and losses on nonmonetary assets and liabilities. As these include inventories and fixed assets, the difference may be highly significant; we return to this subject later.

SFAS 52 requires the use of the temporal method, originally introduced by SFAS 8, in certain cases and mandates the all current method to be used in other cases. *For ease of exposition, from time to time, the terms "temporal method" and "SFAS 8" will be used interchangeably.*

Generally, the choice as to which method is to be used follows from the choice of *functional currency* for each subsidiary. The choice of the functional currency depends on the operating characteristics of that subsidiary and (in some cases) the economy in which it operates.

Role of the Functional Currency

A foreign subsidiary's functional currency is the primary currency of its operating environment. Management must determine the functional currency of each foreign subsidiary based on an evaluation of the unit's operating environment. Factors to be considered in the choice of functional currency include sales markets, input sources, and financing sources.[8] Ultimately, however, the choice of functional currency is based on management judgment and may not be completely objective.[9]

The results of operations, financial position, and cash flows of all foreign operations must be measured in their designated functional currencies. The functional

---

[6]Returning to our previous example of footnotes 2 and 4, under the temporal method, the amount of operating profit is $US 200. Under the all current method, operating profit is $US 150. The difference of $US 50 is the realized exchange rate gain on the inventory held from the beginning of the year to the time of sale. Under the temporal method, this $US 50 is reported as a component of operating income; under the current rate method, it is calculated separately and "moved" from operating income to the cumulative translation adjustment.

[7]The situation is analogous to LIFO and FIFO. FIFO includes holding gains due to inflation as part of operating income, whereas LIFO removes them.

[8]Appendix A of SFAS 52 lists the following indicators to be used when choosing the functional currency: cash flows, output markets and prices, inputs, financing, and intercompany transactions. The general principle is that functional currency should be the primary currency for most of these indicators.

The functional currency designated for a foreign operation must be used consistently unless changing economic circumstances require change to a different functional currency. No restatement of prior financial statements is required, since a change in functional currency reflects new economic circumstances and as such does not qualify as a change in accounting principle. However, the change should be disclosed in the financial statement footnotes. See the discussion of Alcoa of Australia later in this chapter.

[9]At times, management may be able to justify the choice of either one of two functional currencies. In such cases, the functional currency that produces the better reported operating result is likely to be chosen. For example, in the early 1980s, companies with operations in Mexico could justify either the Mexican peso or the U.S. dollar as the functional currency for those operations. Employees of major drug companies told one of the authors that "we looked at the numbers both ways and chose the better result."

currency may be the foreign subsidiary's local currency, the parent's reporting currency, or a third currency. If the functional currency is not the parent's reporting currency, then the functional currency financial statements must be translated into the parent's reporting currency.

SFAS 52 defines three categories of foreign operations:

1. Relatively self-contained, independent entities operating primarily in local markets. Operating, financing, and investing activities are primarily local, although there may be reliance on the parent's patents and managerial or technological expertise and there may be some exports. *The functional currency for such an "autonomous" affiliate is generally the local currency.*

2. Foreign subsidiaries may be significantly integrated operations serving as sales outlets for the parent's products and services with substantially all the operating, financing, and investing decisions based on the parent's reporting currency. *In such cases the functional currency would be the parent's reporting currency.*

3. Finally, *SFAS 52 mandates the use of the parent (reporting) currency as the functional currency for foreign operations in highly inflationary economies* (an economy with cumulative inflation of 100% or more over three years).

Some foreign operations may not maintain records in their functional currency. This is likely to be the case with the second and third categories just described, or when a third currency is the designated functional currency. Financial statements of these foreign operations must first be *remeasured* into the functional currency and then translated into the reporting currency.

Thus the choice of functional currency is a key element in accounting for the operations of foreign subsidiaries. Management's choice of functional currency determines whether the temporal method or the current rate method will be used.

Remeasurement Versus Translation

Much of the confusion that surrounds the accounting for foreign operations under SFAS 52 concerns the two terms, *remeasurement* and *translation*. Before going any further, it is important to clarify the distinction.

As Figure 13-1 implies, accounting for foreign operations is a two-step process. The first step is the remeasurement of the subsidiary's financial data into its functional currency. For example, a subsidiary located in Germany, whose functional currency is the deutsche mark (DM), may have transactions denominated in other currencies. If it sells its output in other European countries, it will have cash and accounts receivable in the currency of each market. If it purchases inputs outside Germany, it will have accounts payable in other currencies. Alternatively, SFAS 52 criteria may suggest French francs as the functional currency, but the unit's records may be kept in deutsche marks given its location.

At year end, a balance sheet in the functional currency (deutsche marks or French francs) must be prepared, and each nonfunctional currency asset and liability must be converted into the functional currency. *This is the process that is called remeasurement under SFAS 52, and it is carried out using the temporal method (essentially SFAS 8),*

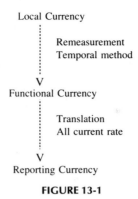

Local Currency

Remeasurement
Temporal method

V
Functional Currency

Translation
All current rate

V
Reporting Currency

FIGURE 13-1

with all gains and losses recognized in reported income. The second step is the translation of all functional currency statements into the parent (reporting) currency. Translation gains and losses occurring at the translation stage do not appear in the income statement but flow directly to the stockholders' equity section. However, translation gains or losses that arose during remeasurement remain in the income statement even after the translation stage.

Figure 13-1 is an overall representation of the process. In many cases only one step will be needed. If the foreign subsidiary conducted business only in deutsche marks, then the local currency would be the functional currency and the remeasurement step would not be needed. (See Figure 13-1A).

Alternatively, if the functional currency for a subsidiary is the parent currency (for example, a subsidiary operating in a highly inflationary economy), then it is only necessary to remeasure its accounts into the parent's reporting currency and no further translation is required. (See Figure 13-1B).

Otherwise, all financial data denominated in functional currencies other than the parent's reporting currency must be translated into the parent currency, using the principles of SFAS 52, as part of the consolidation process.

There is an important consequence of this two-step process of remeasurement and translation. The accounting for a particular transaction may depend on geography—its location within the consolidated group. For example, if the German subsidiary (whose functional currency is the deutsche mark) has DM-denominated debt, changes in the exchange rate between the deutsche mark and the dollar will not impact reported

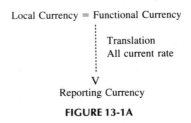

Local Currency = Functional Currency

Translation
All current rate

V
Reporting Currency

FIGURE 13-1A

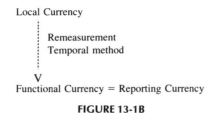

Local Currency

    Remeasurement
    Temporal method

V
Functional Currency = Reporting Currency

FIGURE 13-1B

earnings. The gains or losses arising from translation of the DM debt into dollars will flow directly into stockholders' equity.

If the DM-denominated debt is incurred by the parent company, or by another subsidiary whose functional currency is the dollar or another currency, then fluctuations in the exchange rate between the dollar and the deutsche mark will affect reported earnings. Gains and losses arising from remeasurement of the DM debt into the functional currency will be reported as part of net income.

Thus consolidated financial statements may incorporate various types of foreign operations with different functional currencies remeasured and/or translated into the reporting currency. The processes and effects of remeasurement and translation on consolidated financial statements are described next.

ILLUSTRATION OF TRANSLATION AND REMEASUREMENT

Exhibit 13-2 provides balance sheets and exchange rates for the three years ended December 31, 1992, for a hypothetical foreign subsidiary of a U.S. multinational. It is assumed that the subsidiary was acquired on December 31, 1990. Exhibit 13-3 contains the subsidiary's income statements for 1991 and 1992. These statements will provide the basis for our discussion of the process of and the differences between the effects of remeasurement and translation. These differences are presented in Exhibits 13-4 through 13-7 under the heading of SFAS 52 for translation and SFAS 8 for remeasurement.

Note that throughout the exhibits, we have used SFAS 8 and SFAS 52 as shorthand expressions. SFAS 8 means the temporal method, used for remeasurement under SFAS 52. SFAS 52 means the all current rate method, used for translation of functional currency statements into the reporting (parent) currency.

Translation

If management designates the local currency (LC) as the functional currency of Foreign Subsidiary, Inc., then the all current rate method (SFAS 52) is used to translate the LC-based financial statements into U.S. dollars (the reporting currency). All assets and liabilities are translated using the exchange rate in effect at the balance sheet date. This process is illustrated in Exhibit 13-4 in the columns headed SFAS 52. All assets and liabilities are translated at LC 0.95 = $US 1.00 (LC 0.85 = $US 1.00) at December 31, 1991 (1992). For example,

EXHIBIT 13-2. FOREIGN SUBSIDIARY, INC.
Comparative Balance Sheets, at December 31, 1990–1992 (in LC millions)

	1990		1991		1992	
Cash	LC 34		LC 170		LC 333	
Accounts receivable	300		410		475	
Inventory	175		220		310	
Current assets		509		800		1118
Fixed assets	860		1260		1690	
Accumulated depreciation	(150)		(360)		(610)	
Fixed Assets—net		710		900		1080
Total assets		LC 1219		LC 1700		LC 2198
Operating payables	LC 255		LC 290		LC 240	
Current debt	110		130		180	
Long-term debt	140		440		790	
Total liabilities		505		860		1210
Common stock		230		230		230
Retained earnings		484		610		758
Total equities		LC 1219		LC 1700		LC 2198

Exchange Rates

Fixed assets and stockholders'			
equity	LC 1.06 = $US 1.00		
Inventory	LC 1.06 = $US 1.00		
Year end	LC 1.06 = $US 1.00	LC 0.95 = $US 1.00	LC 0.85 = $US 1.00
Average	N/A	LC 1.02 = $US 1.00	LC 0.90 = $US 1.00

N/A – not applicable.

EXHIBIT 13-3. FOREIGN SUBSIDIARY, INC.
Income Statements, for Years Ended December 31, 1991–1992
(in LC millions)

	1991	1992	Percent Change
Revenues	LC 1290	LC 1430	10.9%
Less: Cost of goods sold	(540)	(611)	
Gross margin	750	819	
Other expenses	(414)	(421)	
Depreciation expense	(210)	(250)	
Net income	LC 126	LC 148	17.5%

EXHIBIT 13-4. FOREIGN SUBSIDIARY INC.
Translated Balance Sheets, at December 31, 1990–1992 (in $US millions)

	1990		1991		1992	
	SFAS 8	SFAS 52	SFAS 8	SFAS 52	SFAS 8	SFAS 52
Cash	$US 32	$US 32	$US 179	$US 179	$US 392	$US 392
Accounts receivable	283	283	431	431	559	559
Inventory	165	165	216	232	344	364
Current assets	480	480	826	842	1295	1315
Fixed assets	811	811	1203	1327	1680	1988
Accumulated depreciation	(141)	(141)	(341)	(379)	(590)	(717)
Fixed assets—net	670	670	862	948	1090	1271
Total assets	$US 1150	$US 1150	$US 1688	$US 1790	$US 2385	$US 2586
Operating liabilities	$US 241	$US 241	$US 305	$US 305	$US 282	$US 282
Current debt	103	103	137	137	212	212
Long-term debt	132	132	463	463	929	929
Total liabilities	476	476	905	905	1423	1423
Common stock	217	217	217	217	217	217
Retained earnings	457	457	566	581	745	745
Cumulative Transaction Adjustment	—	—	—	87	—	201
Total equities	$US 1150	$US 1150	$US 1688	$US 1790	$US 2385	$US 2586

Computation of Translation Adjustment Under SFAS 8

	1990	1991	1992
Net monetary liability (year end)	LC 171	LC 280	LC 402
Increase during year	—	109	122

1991:	Loss on December 31, 1990, liability		1992:	Loss on December 31, 1991, liability	
	LC 171 $[(1/1.06) - (1/0.95)] =$	19		LC 280 $[(1/0.95) - (1/0.85)] =$	35
	Loss on 1991 increase in liability			Loss on 1991 increase in liability	
	LC 109 $[(1/1.02) - (1/0.95)] =$	8		LC 122 $[(1/0.90) - (1/0.85)] =$	8
	Total translation loss	27		Total translation loss	43

Note: The translation loss appears in the income statement. See Exhibit 13-5.

Computation of Translation Adjustment Under SFAS 52

Net assets	December 31, 1991	LC 840	December 31, 1992	LC 988
	December 31, 1990	714	December 31, 1991	840
Increase for the year		LC 126		LC 148

EXHIBIT 13-4. *(Continued)*

1991:	Gain on December 31, 1990, net assets		1992:	Gain on December 31, 1991, net assets	
	LC 714 [(1/1.06) − (1/0.95)] =	78		LC 840 [(1/0.95) − (1/0.85)] =	104
	Gain on 1991 increase in net assets			Gain on 1992 increase in net assets	
	LC 126 [(1/1.02) − (1/0.95)] =	9		LC 148 [(1/0.90) − (1/0.85)] =	10
	Total translation gain	87		Total translation gain	114

In 1991, the subsidiary begins operations with net assets (stockholders' equity) of LC 714 and ends the year with net assets of LC 840. The beginning balance of net assets translates to $US 674, as the exchange rate is LC 1.06 = $US 1.00 on December 31, 1990. These assets are held for the year, at the end of which they translate to $US 752 (LC 0.95 = $US 1.00), for a gain of $US 78.

However, net assets have increased during the year by LC 126, the net income for the year (assuming no dividend payout). We assume this income is generated evenly throughout the year, at the average exchange rate of LC 1.02 = $US 1.00, or $US 124. At the end of the year, the net income translates to $US 133 (LC 126/0.95), an increase of $US 9. Thus, the change in the local currency/dollar exchange rate has increased the net assets expressed in dollars by a total of $US 87 ($US 78 + $US 9); this amount is reported as the translation gain in the equity section of the translated balance sheet.

The 1992 translation gain of $US 114 is computed using the procedures just described. This translation gain is added to the 1991 gain of $US 87, and the aggregate translation gain of $US 201 ($US 87 + $US 114) is reported as the cumulative translation adjustment (CTA) in the equity section of the 1992 balance sheet.

- Accounts receivable at December 31, 1991, is LC 410 (Exhibit 13-2). With the exchange rate on that date of LC 0.95 = $US 1.00, the dollar equivalent is $US 410/0.95 = $US 431. This result is shown as accounts receivable in dollars on December 31, 1991, in the SFAS 52 column in Exhibit 13-4.

- Inventory at December 31, 1992, is LC 310 (Exhibit 13-2). Using the exchange rate on that date of LC 0.85 = $US 1.00, the dollar equivalent is LC 310/0.85 = $US 364. This result is shown in Exhibit 13-4 in the SFAS 52 column as of December 31, 1992.

Components of the income statement (Exhibit 13-3) must be translated at the exchange rates in effect at the dates of the underlying transactions. However, the weighted average exchange rate for the period may be more practical and has been used instead in our example as it is in practice. All revenues and expenses have been translated at the average rate for each year, as listed in Exhibit 13-2. For example,

- Revenue for 1991 is LC 1290 (Exhibit 13-3). Using the *average* exchange rate for 1991 of LC 1.02 = $US 1.00 (Exhibit 13-2), we compute the U.S. dollar revenue for that year as LC 1290/1.02 = $US 1265. The result is shown in Exhibit 13-5.

- Other expenses for 1992 equal LC 421 (Exhibit 13-3). Using the *average* exchange rate of LC 0.90 = $1.00 (Exhibit 13-2) we compute the U.S. dollar equivalent to be LC 421/0.90 = $US 468, which is shown in Exhibit 13-5.

EXHIBIT 13-5. FOREIGN SUBSIDIARY INC.
Translated Income Statements, for Years Ended December 31, 1991–1992
(in $US millions)

	1991		1992	
	SFAS 8	SFAS 52	SFAS 8	SFAS 52
Revenues	$US 1265	$US 1265	$US 1589	$US 1589
COGS	(523)	(529)	(650)	(679)
	742	736	939	910
Depreciation expense	(200)	(206)	(249)	(278)
	542	530	690	632
Other expenses	(406)	(406)	(468)	(468)
Net income before translation	136	124	222	164
Translation loss	(27)	—	(43)	—
Net income	$ US 109	$ US 124	$ US 179	$ US 164

Rate of Increase, 1991–1992

Sales	= 25.6%
Net income	
SFAS 8	= 64.0
SFAS 52	= 32.3

Note that for these two items, the results are identical in Exhibit 13-5 under both the SFAS 8 and SFAS 52 columns.

For the columns headed SFAS 52 in Exhibit 13-5, all the U.S. dollar equivalents can be easily computed by dividing the LC amounts by the appropriate exchange rate. Note that some of the numbers in the SFAS 8 columns are different; we will see why shortly.

The translation process generates gains or losses since assets and liabilities are translated at different exchange rates at the beginning and the end of the period. In addition, income statement components are translated at average rates, but their contribution to equity (change in retained earnings) is translated at the year-end rate.

Cumulative Translation Adjustment

The cumulative translation adjustment (CTA) is not included in periodic net income but, instead, is reported as a separate component of stockholders' equity. Thus, volatility due to fluctuating exchange rates is not reported as part of income, but is indefinitely accumulated in the equity section of the balance sheet. When the foreign operation is sold, liquidated, or considered impaired, the translation adjustment is recognized as a component of the resulting gain or loss.

In theory, accumulated gains and losses should balance out over time. If the CTA account consistently reports significant translation losses, this may signal a failure to manage currency exposure. As accumulated losses must be recognized in income if the foreign operations are sold or liquidated, a negative CTA also represents a potential loss.

Computation of the translation gain or loss under SFAS 52 is shown in Exhibit 13-4. Note that under the current rate method, the accounting exposure is defined as the net asset position (the financial statement–based measure of the parent's reported net investment in the subsidiary). However, this accounting definition of exposure may not reflect the economic exposure. We will discuss the effects of this lack of congruence later in this chapter.

The more immediate question is what analysts should do with the CTA. The prevailing practice is simply to accept it, to use the financial statement data without any adjustment. Similarly, few analysts argue that the change in the CTA should be added to net income.

We concur in the latter practice, for two different reasons. First, the change in the CTA does not represent economic gain or loss (as is discussed later in this chapter). Neither theory nor evidence suggests that adding the change to reported earnings produces a better measure of corporate performance.

Second, analysis that considers the CTA alone is incomplete. The CTA is nothing more than an accounting "plug," accumulating the effect of exchange rate changes on assets and liabilities denominated in foreign currencies. It is the effect of rate changes on those assets and liabilities (and on reported sales and net income) that distorts financial statements. Our emphasis, therefore, is on understanding how that distortion occurs, and on how adjustments can be made to offset it. It is these issues, not the issue of "what do I do with the CTA," to which this chapter is devoted.

Remeasurement

The principles of remeasurement apply under each of the following conditions:

- The reporting currency (the U.S. dollar in our examples) is the functional currency of Foreign Subsidiary, Inc.
- The unit operates in a hyperinflationary economy.
- The foreign operation's records are kept in a currency other than its functional currency.

SFAS 52 mandates remeasurement into the reporting currency (also the functional currency in the first two cases) or the designated functional currency (in the third case) using the temporal method, essentially the translation method used in SFAS 8.[10]

Unlike the current rate method, the temporal method applies the current rate only to monetary assets and liabilities, such as accounts receivable, marketable securities carried at market, current liabilities, and long-term debt. Exhibit 13-4 depicts this translation process for the Foreign Subsidiary, Inc., balance sheet, assuming that the U.S. dollar is the functional currency and that remeasurement is therefore required.

Note that the process for monetary assets and liabilities is the same as under SFAS 52. However, nonmonetary accounts are translated at the rates in effect when the transaction occurred. As a result inventories and fixed assets have been translated at their

---

[10]See Appendix B to SFAS 52 for additional information on remeasurement and for changes in the temporal method relative to SFAS 8 requirements.

historical rates. The derivation of U.S. dollar inventories and fixed assets is shown in Exhibit 13-6.

Similarly, cost of goods sold and depreciation expense are translated at historical rates (also shown in Exhibit 13-6), whereas all other revenues and expenses are translated at the weighted average exchange rate for the period.

The translation adjustment resulting from remeasurement is based on the net monetary assets or liabilities (the accounting exposure under the temporal method) rather than the net assets of the foreign operation. The reported translation adjustment, therefore, ignores the impact of changing exchange rates on inventories and fixed assets even though they may be effective hedges for major components of the net monetary position, that is, accounts payable and long-term liabilities.[11]

Remeasured income statements will also differ from translated income statements because the temporal method reflects the translation gain or loss as a component of periodic income (as well as the realized gains/losses on the nonmonetary assets), thereby adding significant volatility to the income statement. Moreover, where the translation gain or loss does not reflect the economic exposure, the accounting-induced volatility reduces the utility of financial statements.

These calculations for Foreign Subsidiary, Inc., are shown in Exhibit 13-4. *As the local currency has appreciated against the dollar during the period, the net monetary liability has increased in U.S. dollar terms, resulting in a translation loss.* Like the SFAS 52 calculation, the adjustment is in two parts. There is a loss as a result of the increase in the beginning balance of the net monetary liability (due to the appreciating local currency). There is an additional loss resulting from the impact of the rising local currency on the *increase* in the net monetary liability during the year. The first portion of the loss is based on the change in the local currency/dollar exchange rate during the year. The second part results from the difference between the *average rate* during the year (the rate at which the incremental liability is assumed to have been incurred) and the year-end rate.

The resulting translation losses are reported as a component of net income rather than as part of equity under translation. *Notice that under the current rate method there is a translation gain while under the temporal method there is a translation loss. The choice of the functional currency defines the accounting exposure, thereby determining the amount of the reported translation gain or loss and its accounting treatment (income versus equity).*

The differences in the exchange gains and losses reported and their treatment are summarized[12] in Exhibit 13-1.

Fluctuating exchange rates can therefore generate substantial volatility in reported income for MNCs with foreign operations whose functional currency is the reporting currency or that have substantial transactions in currencies other than the functional currency. *The choice of functional currency matters!*

---

[11]As inventories are sold for cash, it can be argued that a change in the exchange rate changes the expected amount of cash to be received when inventories are sold. In that sense, inventories can be considered monetary assets, hedging accounts payable, which will be repaid from the proceeds of the sale of inventories. A similar argument can be made for fixed assets, which are used to produce inventories.

[12]In the problem section we ask for the computation of the different components of the gains and losses.

EXHIBIT 13-6. FOREIGN SUBSIDIARY, INC.
Analysis of Inventory and Fixed Assets: Temporal Method

	LC	Rate	$US		LC	Rate	$US
Analysis of Inventory							
December 31, 1990	175	1.06	165	COGS (FIFO):	175	1.06 =	165
1991 purchases	585	1.02	574		365	1.02 =	358
1991 COGS (at right)	(540)		(523)	Total	540		523
December 31, 1991	220	1.02	216				
1992 purchases	701	0.90	779	COGS (FIFO):	220	1.02 =	216
1992 COGS (at right)	(611)		(650)		391	0.90 =	434
December 31, 1992	310		345	Total	611		650
Analysis of Fixed Assets							
December 31, 1990	860	1.06	811				
1991 investment	400	1.02	392				
December 31, 1991	1260		1203				
1992 investment	430	0.90	477				
December 31, 1992	1690		1680				
Analysis of Accumulated Depreciation							
December 31, 1990	150	1.06	141				
1991 expense	210	1.047*	200				
December 31, 1991	360		341				
1992 expense	250	1.005†	249				
December 31, 1992	610		590				

*December 31, 1991, blended rate for fixed assets.

†December 31, 1992, blended rate.

Note: The exchange rate used to translate depreciation expense is a blend of the historical rates at the time fixed assets were acquired. Under the temporal method, depreciation expense is determined in U.S. dollars; the blended rate is derived by dividing $US depreciation expense by LC depreciation expense.

COMPARISON OF TRANSLATION AND REMEASUREMENT

Income Statement Effects

As shown in Exhibit 13-5, the current rate method (SFAS 52) translates all revenues, expenses, gains, and losses at the weighted average rate. The temporal method (SFAS 8) also uses the weighted average for all the elements of the income statement *except* cost of goods sold and depreciation expense. Thus these two expense lines are different, reflecting the choice of functional currency.

Effect on Gross Profit Margin

The temporal method, when combined with the use of first-in, first-out (FIFO) inventory accounting (the method generally used outside of the United States), can distort reported earnings. Use of the historical rate for inventories results in a lag in the recognition of the effects of rate changes, just as FIFO delays the recognition of price level changes. In the case of Foreign Subsidiary,Inc., with an appreciating local currency, historical-cost-basis cost of goods sold is lower than the cost of goods sold translated at the average rate. If the local currency were declining in value, cost of goods sold would be higher under the temporal method.

In either case, for the temporal method, gross profit margins are distorted. We can see the effect by comparing the gross profit margin under each method (shown in Exhibit 13-7) with the actual gross profit margin in local currency units.

The gross margin resulting from remeasurement is higher than the actual gross margin in local currency (59.1% compared to 57.3% in 1992). Equally important, it appears that the gross margin percentage in 1992 increased slightly from that in 1991, 58.7% to 59.1%; in local currency units the gross margin percentage declined to 57.3% in 1992 from 58.1% in 1991. The gross margin percentage resulting from translation, however, preserves the trends and relationships from the functional currency of the subsidiary. This preservation of local currency trends and relationships is an advantage of the all current rate method.

Effect on Net Income

Depreciation expense is also significantly altered when the temporal method is used. Again, an appreciating currency results in depreciation expense that is lower as compared with that resulting from the current rate method (see Exhibit 13-5). Net income before the effect of translation is again inflated by this effect.

Once again, the all current rate method faithfully reproduces the net profit margin (as shown in Exhibit 13-7) from the original local currency statements, whereas the temporal method results in higher profit margins and a larger increase in the net profit margin in 1992.

The inclusion of translation gains and losses in net income under the temporal method results in further distortion. As there are translation losses in both 1991 and 1992, the effect is to reduce the positive impact of the temporal method. If the local currency were declining, both cost of goods sold and depreciation expense would be higher under the temporal method. The resulting lower reported income would be offset by the inclusion of translation gains in income. The fact that the operating effects and translation effects are opposite, it must be noted, is a function of the asset and liability composition of the particular company and the direction of change in exchange rates. While the situation described here is not unusual, some companies will have operating effects and translation effects in the same direction.

While the remeasurement net profit margin for 1991 (Exhibit 13-7) falls below the original local currency results, the exaggerated profit margin improvement in 1992 remains. Translation still does the better job of reflecting the local currency operating results in U.S. dollars.

The use of weighted average rates to translate the income statement does not,

EXHIBIT 13-7. FOREIGN SUBSIDIARY, INC.
Financial Ratios*, 1991–1992

	Year	LC Units	SFAS 52	SFAS 8
Gross margin percentage	1991	58.1%	58.1%	58.7%
	1992	57.3%	57.3%	59.1%
Net income as a % of sales	1991	9.8%	9.8%	10.8%
(Before translation loss)	1992	10.3%	10.3%	14.0%
Net income as a % of sales:	1991	9.8%	9.8%	8.6%
	1992	10.3%	10.3%	11.3%
Debt as a % of equity	1991	67.9%	67.9%	76.6%
	1992	98.2%	98.2%	118.6%
Inventory turnover	1991	2.73×	2.66×	2.75×
	1992	2.31×	2.27×	2.43×
Receivable turnover	1991	3.63×	3.54×	3.54×
	1992	3.23×	3.21×	3.21×
Fixed asset turnover	1991	1.60×	1.56×	1.65×
	1992	1.44×	1.43×	1.63×
Total asset turnover	1991	0.88×	0.86×	0.89×
	1992	0.73×	0.72×	0.78
Return on average equity	1991	16.2%	15.9%	18.7%
(Before translation loss)	1992	16.2%	16.0%	25.4%
Return on average equity	1991	16.2%	15.9%	15.0%
	1992	16.2%	16.0%	20.5%
Return on average assets	1991	8.8%	8.4%	9.5%
(Before translation loss)	1992	7.6%	7.5%	10.5%
Return on average assets	1991	8.8%	8.4%	7.7%
	1992	7.6%	7.5%	8.8%

*See Chapter 3 for definitions of ratios.

however, eliminate the effects of fluctuating exchange rates from reported sales and net income.[13] A strengthening (declining) local currency creates the illusion of higher (lower) sales and earnings of foreign operations. Foreign Subsidiary, Inc.'s sales increased by 10.9% in 1992 in local currency units but by 25.6% in U.S. dollars. Net

[13]These effects are separate from translation gains and losses.

income increased by 17.5% in local currency units but by 32.3% in U.S. dollars (SFAS 52).[14] The better than 13% appreciation of the local currency against the dollar inflated both the sales and earnings comparisons. For companies with significant foreign operations, the effect of changing exchange rates can make it difficult to discern true operating trends.

Balance Sheet Effects

The choice of functional currency also affects the balance sheet of the foreign operation and, after consolidation, that of the parent company. Exhibit 13-4 shows the balance sheets of Foreign Subsidiary, Inc., for 1990, 1991, and 1992 under both methods.

Since the subsidiary was acquired on December 31, 1990, the balance sheets as of December 31, 1990, are identical under both methods. For 1991 and 1992 many of the asset and liability accounts are still identical as both methods translate monetary assets and liabilities at the current (balance sheet date) exchange rate. There are, however, some significant differences.

When the reporting currency (here the U.S. dollar) is the functional currency, the temporal method requires that inventories, fixed assets, and other nonmonetary accounts be translated at historic rates. Exhibit 13-6 provides detail for both the inventory and fixed asset accounts.

Because the local currency has appreciated against the dollar, the historic costs of both inventories and fixed assets are lower than their stated amounts under the current rate method. If the local currency had declined in value, the opposite would be true. As a result, total assets are lower under the temporal method. Asset turnover ratios will be affected as a result.

Turning to the right side of the balance sheet, stockholders' equity is also lower under the temporal method. Under the current rate method, equity includes the cumulative translation adjustment gains for 1991 and 1992. Retained earnings at December 31, 1991 are lower under the temporal method as earnings have been reduced by translation losses resulting from the impact of the appreciation of the local currency on the net monetary liability. However, retained earnings are, by coincidence, the same under both methods at December 31, 1992.

Impact on Financial Ratios

We have already seen how the choice of functional currency affects income statement ratios. Because the balance sheet and income statement are both affected, many financial ratios vary with the choice of the functional currency. Exhibit 13-7 includes a number of financial ratios.

Reviewing this exhibit leads to two conclusions: first, that the ratios are quite different under translation and remeasurement, and second, that the ratios under translation are often different from those in the local currency. While the first conclusion should not surprise us, the second is not so obvious. Let us examine each conclusion in detail.

[14]Note that under SFAS 8 the growth in net income (even after translation losses) was 64%: twice the growth shown under SFAS 52 and close to four times the growth experienced in local currency terms! This is partly due to the computation of cost of goods sold and depreciation expense at historical exchange rates.

Comparison of Ratios Under Translation and Remeasurement

As can be seen by comparing the translation ratios with the remeasurement ratios, they give quite different indications of the performance of Foreign Subsidiary, Inc. We have already discussed the differences in the gross margin and net margin ratios.

The debt/equity ratio (current and long-term debt) is significantly higher under remeasurement. While the debt is the same, the lower level of equity results in a higher debt ratio.

The asset turnover ratios are also different, with one exception. The receivable turnover ratio is identical under both translation and remeasurement because the same rates are used to translate receivables and sales under both methods.

For inventory turnover, however, that is not true. Under remeasurement, both cost of goods sold and average inventories are lower, reflecting the lagged effect of the higher value of the local currency against the dollar. The result is a higher turnover ratio for both years. This result, however, reflects the assumed turnover rate and exchange rate changes in this example. You may not assume that this result holds in all cases.

The fixed asset turnover ratio is significantly higher under remeasurement, reflecting the lower historic cost of fixed assets under the temporal method (given the appreciating local currency). This is a universal result; a rising local currency will always result in higher fixed asset turnover for remeasurement as compared with translation. A depreciating local currency would result in higher fixed assets under remeasurement and a lower turnover ratio.

Total asset turnover is also higher under remeasurement, reflecting the lower historic costs of inventory and fixed assets. As in the case of all turnover ratios *except inventory*, the numerator (sales) is the same under both methods. Thus the difference in the turnover ratio is driven by the denominator. Given a rising local currency, assets are higher under translation, resulting in lower turnover ratios.

Return ratios are also different under the two methods, as *both* numerator and denominator are different. Under translation, return on equity is virtually unchanged; under remeasurement, return on equity shows a sharp increase in 1992. Both the levels and the trend are therefore dependent on the choice of functional currency.

This is also true of the return-on-assets ratio. This ratio (before translation losses) is higher under remeasurement than under translation for both years. The trend is also different: return on assets (ROA) rises in 1992 under translation but declines under remeasurement.

Comparison of Translated and Local Currency Ratios

Turning to our second (perhaps surprising) conclusion, compare the U.S. dollar ratios with the local currency ratios. In most cases, even the translation ratios are different from the local currency ratios. The exceptions are the pure income statement (e.g., gross margin) and pure balance sheet (e.g., debt/equity) ratios. As all income statement components are translated at the average rate and all balance sheet components are translated at the ending rate, it is mathematically true that the LC ratios and the U.S. dollar ratios will be the same.

When ratios combine income statement and balance sheet components, however, the equality is disturbed. That is because the numerator and denominator do not rise or fall by the same percentage. Thus turnover and return ratios are changed even by translation. The differences between the ratios under translation and the local currency ratios are not large, and the 1991–1992 trends are similar, but the ratios are different.

One more effect of changing exchange rates on ratios deserves comment. When foreign operations have different trends and ratio characteristics than domestic operations, then exchange rate changes can distort consolidated ratios by changing the weight of foreign data. For example, if the local currency appreciates, foreign data will constitute a larger percentage of the consolidated group, and consolidated ratios will be affected. We can see this from the following example.

Let us assume that a foreign subsidiary has the following debt and equity levels:

	Foreign Subsidiary	
	1991	1992
Debt	LC 570	LC 570
Equity	840	840
Ratio	0.679	0.679

Also assume that the parent company has domestic (U.S.) operations with the following debt and equity levels:

	U.S. Parent	
	1991	1992
Debt	$US 200	$US 200
Equity	1000	1000
Ratio	0.20	0.20

As there has been no financing cash flow, there has been no real change in debt, equity, or the debt/equity ratio. However, let us assume that the exchange rate has changed from LC 0.95 = $US 1.00 at the end of 1991 to LC 0.85 = $US 1.00 at the end of 1992. The appreciation of the local currency will increase the foreign subsidiary's debt and equity. After consolidation (and translation) the total debt and equity will be as follows:

	Consolidated	
	1991	1992
Debt	$US 800	$US 871
Equity	1884	1988
Ratio	0.425	0.438

In consolidation, the debt/equity ratio has increased only because of the change in exchange rates. *Whenever a financial ratio differs between the foreign subsidiary and the remainder of the consolidated group, a change in exchange rate will affect the consolidated ratio even if there has been no change in the underlying ratios.*

We conclude our discussion of ratios therefore with the following observations:

- For pure income statement and pure balance sheet ratios, SFAS 52 translation maintains the local currency relationships.

- For ratios using both income statement and balance sheet components, SFAS 52 ratios do not exactly maintain the local currency relationships, but usually do not differ greatly.

- Ratios computed under SFAS 8 remeasurement, in most cases, differ markedly from both the local currency ratios and those computed from translated data.

- Changes in exchange rates can affect consolidated ratios, even when there is no real change, by increasing or decreasing the "weighting" of the foreign subsidiary.

Impact on Reported Cash Flows

Exhibit 13-8 contains cash flow statements for Foreign Subsidiary, Inc., for 1991 and 1992, both in local currency units and in U.S. dollars. Before discussing the specific cash flows, some general comments are in order.

Subsequent to SFAS 52, the FASB issued SFAS 95, Statement of Cash Flows (1987), which affects the reporting of cash flows for foreign operations. SFAS 95 provides that cash flows in the parent (reporting) currency must replicate the cash flows in the local currency. To accomplish this objective, *cash flows in the reporting currency must exclude the effects of exchange rate changes.* The requirement means that the cash flow statement should be unaffected by whether the temporal or the all current rate method is used.

To understand the consequences of this requirement, we must compare the statement of cash flows with the balance sheet and income statement. First, let us look at the local currency statements.

The local currency cash flow statements in Exhibit 13-8 were prepared from the balance sheet data (Exhibit 13-2) and income statement (Exhibit 13-3) for Foreign Subsidiary, Inc. The cash flows in Exhibit 13-8 consist of a mixture of income statement data and changes in balance sheet accounts. For example, the change in receivables for 1992 is the difference between the balance of accounts receivable at December 31, 1991 and the balance at December 31, 1991 (LC 475 − LC 410 = LC 65).

Investing cash flow consists of capital spending, or the change in fixed assets (before depreciation). Financing cash flow is equal to the increase in current and long-term debt. The net cash flow is necessarily equal to the change in cash for the year.

When local currency cash flows are expressed in U.S. dollars, these relationships break down because of the impact of exchange rate changes. For example, the U.S. dollar cash flow statement for 1992 shows an increase of $US 72 in accounts receivable, whereas the year-to-year increase in accounts receivable on the U.S. dollar balance sheet (Exhibit 13-4) is $US 128 under either method of translation. How can we reconcile this difference?

EXHIBIT 13-8. FOREIGN SUBSIDIARY, INC.
Cash Flow Statements, 1991–1992 (in millions)

	LC		$US	
	1991	1992	1991	1992
Revenues	LC 1290	LC 1430	$US 1265	$US 1589
Change in receivables	(110)	(65)	(108)	(72)
Collections	LC 1180	LC 1365	$US 1157	$US 1517
Cost of goods sold	(540)	(611)	(529)	(679)
Change in inventories	(45)	(90)	(44)	(100)
Change in payables	35	(50)	34	(56)
Inputs	LC (550)	LC (751)	$ US (539)	$ US (834)
Expenses	(414)	(421)	(406)	(468)
Operating cash flow	LC 216	LC 193	$ US 212	$ US 214
Investing cash flow	(400)	(430)	(392)	(478)
Financing cash flow	320	400	313	445
Effect of translation on cash*	—	—	14	32
Net cash flow	LC 136	LC 163	$ US 147	$ US 213

*1991:	Opening cash balance	LC 34/1.06 = $ US 32	
	1991 increase in cash	136/1.02 =	133
	Total	170	165
	Actual cash balance	170/0.95 =	179
	Effect of translation	—	14

*1992:	Opening cash balance	LC 170/0.95 = $US 179	
	1992 increase in cash	163/0.90 =	181
	Total	333	360
	Actual cash balance	333/0.85 =	392
	Effect of translation	—	32

1992: Alternative Computation

Beginning cash balance   LC 170

Effect of change in exchange rate* $\dfrac{170}{0.95} - \dfrac{170}{0.85} = \$US\ 21$

Effect on operating activities

Cash Flow from Operations (CFO)   LC 193

Effect of change in exchange rate† $\dfrac{193}{0.90} - \dfrac{193}{0.85} = 13$

Effect on investing activities

Cash flow from investing activities   LC (430)

Effect of change in exchange rate† $\dfrac{(430)}{0.90} - \dfrac{(430)}{0.85} = (28)$

EXHIBIT 13-8.   *(Continued)*

Effect on financing activities		
Cash flow from financing activities	LC 400	
Effect of change in exchange rate†	$\dfrac{400}{0.90} - \dfrac{400}{0.85} =$	$\dfrac{26}{}$
Total effect of exchange rate changes on cash		$US 32

*The revaluation of the LC cash balance to reflect the change in exchange rate during the year.
†The difference between the amount shown on the cash flow statement (translated at the average rate for the year) and the U.S. dollar equivalent of that cash flow at the year-end rate.

While the $US 56 difference between $US 72 and $US 128 can easily be reconciled,[15] the important point is to understand why the two numbers are different. The year-to-year increase in accounts receivable in U.S. dollars is the result of two changes. First is the change in accounts receivable in LC units. Second is the impact of changing exchange rates on the balance.

Given the change in the value of the local currency against the dollar, this difference exists for every balance sheet account. In each case the U.S. dollar cash flow *excludes* the impact of exchange rate changes; the cash flow in U.S. dollars is simply the cash flow in the local currency, translated at the *average rate* for the year (LC 0.90 = $US 1.00 for 1992). For accounts receivable the computation is

$$\frac{LC\ 65}{0.90} = \$US\ 72$$

As a result of this methodology, the U.S. dollar cash flow statement replicates the local currency statement, consistent with the objectives of SFAS 95. Prior to the implementation of SFAS 95, cash flow statements were distorted by the inclusion of exchange rate effects. Cash flow statements not prepared in accordance with standards containing rules similar to SFAS 95 (non–U.S. GAAP) retain the distortion resulting from exchange rate changes.[16]

According to the provisions of SFAS 95, the consolidated cash flows of MNCs should present the reporting currency equivalent of local currency cash flows of foreign operations that are therefore *unaffected by the choice of functional currency*.[17]

[15]Effect of exchange rate change on December 31, 1991, balance = LC 410 (1/0.95 − 1/0.85) = $US 51. Effect on 1992 increase = LC 65 (1/0.90 − 1/0.85) = $US 4. Total effect is $US 51 + $US 4 = $US 55. Difference from $US 56 is rounding error. This computation is analogous to the translation adjustments computed in Exhibit 13-4.

[16]The IASC has adopted (1992) a cash flow standard largely consistent with SFAS 95. Adoption of that standard outside the United States would make cash flow statements similar to those prepared in the United States under SFAS 95.

[17]Discussions with some preparers and a review of reported cash flow statements convince us that this is *not* true in all cases. We believe that, in some cases, consolidated cash flow statements are prepared from translated *functional currency* cash flow statements rather than from local currency statements. We conclude that, in these cases, the choice of functional currency does affect reported cash flows!

The U.S. dollar cash flows all exclude the impact of exchange rate changes. The net cash flow, however, would not be equal to the year-to-year change in cash unless the effect of rate changes on cash were recognized. This effect is computed in Exhibit 13-8.[18]

This effect ($US 32 for 1991) of exchange rate changes may also be reflected in terms of its components, the cash flow effects of operating, investing, and financing activities. This breakdown is also detailed in Exhibit 13-8.

While we have stated that SFAS 95 mandates the removal of the effects of exchange rate changes on cash flows, that statement is not entirely true. *Reported cash flows exclude only the impact of changing exchange rates on changes in assets and liabilities.*

However, as local currency cash flows are translated at the average exchange rate for the year, changes in currency rates do affect the reporting currency cash flows. This effect is similar to the impact on reported sales and earnings that we previously discussed. When a foreign currency rises in value, the parent company equivalent of cash flows in that currency will also rise; when a currency falls, the translated cash flows will be lower. So while the provisions of SFAS 95 do provide us with a cash flow statement that replicates the local currency cash flow statement, the parent company cash flow statement is still affected by changes in currency rates.

ACCOUNTING PRINCIPLES USED OUTSIDE OF THE UNITED STATES

Foreign Currency Translation

Translation practices outside of the United States are often quite different from the requirements of SFAS 52. Major areas of variation are

1. In some countries (the United Kingdom, France, and the Netherlands), the balance sheet rate ("closing rate") is used to translate the income statement as well. During periods of significant change in exchange rates, use of the closing rate rather than the average rate will exaggerate the effects of rate changes on reported sales and earnings.

2. The "functional currency" concept is not explicitly used outside of the United States. However, many countries differentiate between foreign operations that are "autonomous" and those that are "integral" (branches). The all current rate method is used for autonomous operations (local currency is functional currency under U.S. GAAP), while the temporal method is used for branches (parent

---

[18]A simplified way to view the issue is to assume that all LC cash flows are received in the middle of the year. That is what the cash flow statement represents. However, between the middle of the year and the year end, there was an exchange gain on the cash received as the LC became stronger. In addition, the opening balance of LC currency increased in dollar terms. The $US 32 represents these exchange gains. We can use the methodology of Exhibit 13-4 to obtain the same answer. For example, the effect on December 31, 1991 cash is LC 170 (1/0.95 − 1/0.85) = $US 21. The effect on 1992 increase in cash is LC 163 (1/0.90 − 1/0.85) = $US 11. The total effect for 1992 is $US 21 + $US 11 = $US 32.

currency is functional currency under U.S. GAAP). However, few countries have standards defining "autonomous," leaving much to management judgment.

3. Translation gains and losses may be deferred regardless of the translation method. Deferrals are usually contained in reserves and are not separately disclosed. In some countries (Germany), gains are deferred, but losses are immediately charged against earnings. Lack of disclosure may make it difficult to discern the impact of translation gains and losses from published financial statements alone.

4. Definitions of "hyperinflationary" economies are vague, even where the concept is specifically used (Canada, the United Kingdom). The designation is consequently more discretionary.

As a result of these differences from U.S. practice, the financial statements of foreign firms will frequently reflect changes in exchange rates differently. While disclosures are generally poor in this area, careful reading of footnotes may provide clues to the financial statement impacts of these changes. When management can be questioned, additional information can be obtained, especially if the analyst understands the issues well enough to ask the right questions.

Foreign Currency Transactions

Extensive use of foreign currency debt is a relatively recent phenomenon in the United States given its well-developed capital market. However, firms in most other countries often use foreign markets; for example, Canadian companies often raise funds in the United States.

U.S. GAAP requires remeasurement at the current rate for assets and liabilities denominated in foreign currencies with gains or losses reported as components of current income. In Canada, unrealized gains and losses on long-term foreign currency assets and liabilities are deferred and amortized over their lives. In Germany and France, unrealized gains may be deferred until realized, and unrealized losses are recognized immediately.

In Japan, these transactions are translated at historical rates. In Sweden, foreign currency transactions are translated at year-end rates. Unrealized gains and losses are offset, and any remaining unrealized losses are recognized currently. However, unrealized losses are defined net of foreign exchange contracts that are expected to be covered by foreign currency flows generated by operations. Excess unrealized gains, if any, are not recognized. Some companies recognize the difference between unrealized gains and losses currently.

These differences result in vastly different reported income for similar transactions in different countries, and analysts should use reported income numbers with care in their decision models. Another difference arises when a portion of unrealized gains or losses is designated as extraordinary: the definition of extraordinary items is highly variable across countries, and the use of reported income before extraordinary items can be misleading. The latter problem is particularly acute when price/earnings (P/E) ratios are compared using computerized databases.

IASC Exposure Draft

The International Accounting Standards Committee expects to issue a new standard on accounting for the effects of changes in foreign exchange rates during 1993. Based on Exposure Draft ED 44 (May 1992), it appears that the final standard will be similar to SFAS 52. While the IASC does not use the term "functional currency," it does classify subsidiaries into operations that are "integral" and those that are "foreign entities." The clear implication of this distinction is that parent companies would use the temporal method to account for "integral" operations but the all current method for "foreign entities." For the latter, exchange gains and losses would go directly to stockholders' equity, bypassing the income statement as in SFAS 52.

For foreign currency transactions, and for "integral" operations, the temporal method would be required, with gains and losses on monetary items included in income (except for those arising from hedges and from some long-term intercompany items). Recognizing that, in some countries, revaluations are permitted, the IASC would require that such revalued assets and liabilities be translated at the exchange rate at the date of revaluation.

The IASC proposal would require that the average exchange rate be used to translate all income statement accounts. If adopted, this provision would mark a strong contrast to current practice in some countries (notably, the United Kingdom), where the closing rate is used. The proposed IAS also appears to be more flexible than U.S. standards on hedging (see discussion in Chapter 10).

CASE STUDIES OF MNC ANALYSIS

IBM Corp.

International Business Machines (IBM) is one of the world's largest multinational corporations. In 1990 foreign operations provided more than 60% of revenues and 76% of net income. As IBM's financial statements provide supplementary data regarding its foreign operations, we shall use the company to illustrate the analysis of multinational corporations.

Balance Sheet Effects

Exhibit 13-9 is IBM's balance sheet at December 31, 1989, and 1990. Within the stockholders' equity section, we see "translation adjustments" of $1698 billion and $3266 billion (4.4% and 7.6% of net assets), respectively. *These entries tell us that the company has significant non-U.S. operations and that it uses foreign functional currencies. If the company used the U.S. dollar as the functional currency for all foreign operations, all gains and losses would have been included in income.*

Exhibit 13-10 is IBM's income statement for the three years ended December 31, 1990, and Exhibit 13-11 provides the consolidated statement of cash flows for the same three years. Notice that the only reference to translation in the cash flow statement is the "effect of exchange rate changes on cash and cash equivalents" near the bottom. (See the preceding discussion on cash flow statements and Exhibit 13-8.)

EXHIBIT 13-9. IBM
Balance Sheet

At December 31:	1990	1989
(Dollars in millions)		
Assets		
Current Assets:		
Cash	$ 1,189	$ 741
Cash equivalents	2,664	2,959
Marketable securities, at cost, which approximates market	698	1,261
Notes and accounts receivable—trade, net of allowances	20,988	18,866
Other accounts receivable	1,656	1,298
Inventories	10,108	9,463
Prepaid expenses and other current assets	1,617	1,287
	38,920	35,875
Plant, Rental Machines and Other Property	53,659	48,410
Less: Accumulated depreciation	26,418	23,467
	27,241	24,943
Investments and Other Assets:		
Software, less accumulated amortization (1990, $5,873; 1989, $4,824)	4,099	3,293
Investments and sundry assets	17,308	13,623
	21,407	16,916
	$87,568	$77,734
Liabilities and Stockholders' Equity		
Current Liabilities:		
Taxes	$ 3,159	$ 2,699
Short-term debt	7,602	5,892
Accounts payable	3,367	3,167
Compensation and benefits	3,014	2,797
Deferred income	2,506	1,365
Other accrued expenses and liabilities	5,628	5,780
	25,276	21,700
Long-Term Debt	11,943	10,825
Other Liabilities	3,656	3,420
Deferred Income Taxes	3,861	3,280
Stockholders' Equity:		
Capital stock, par value $1.25 per share	6,357	6,341
Shares authorized: 750,000,000		
Issued: 1990—571,618,795; 1989—574,775,560		
Retained earnings	33,234	30,477
Translation adjustments	3,266	1,698
	42,857	38,516
Less: Treasury stock, at cost (Shares: 1990—227,604; 1989—75,723)	25	7
	42,832	38,509
	$87,568	$77,734

Source: IBM Corporation, 1990 Annual Report.

EXHIBIT 13-10. IBM
Income Statement

For the year ended December 31:	1990	1989	1988
(Dollars in millions except per share amounts)			
Revenue:			
Sales	$43,959	$41,586	$39,959
Support services	11,322	9,858	9,285
Software	9,952	8,424	7,927
Rentals and financing	3,785	2,842	2,510
	69,018	62,710	59,681
Cost:			
Sales	19,401	18,001	17,499
Support services	6,617	5,701	4,971
Software	3,126	2,694	2,110
Rentals and financing	1,579	1,305	1,068
	30,723	27,701	25,648
Gross Profit	38,295	35,009	34,033
Operating Expenses:			
Selling, general and administrative	20,709	21,289	19,362
Research, development and engineering	6,554	6,827	5,925
	27,263	28,116	25,287
Operating Income	11,032	6,893	8,746
Other Income, principally interest	495	728	996
Interest Expense	1,324	976	709
Earnings before Income Taxes	10,203	6,645	9,033
Provision for Income Taxes	4,183	2,887	3,542
Net Earnings before Cumulative Effect of Accounting Change	6,020	3,758	5,491
Cumulative Effect of Change in Accounting for Income Taxes	—	—	315
Net Earnings	$ 6,020	$ 3,758	$ 5,806
Per share amounts:			
Before cumulative effect of accounting change	$10.51	$6.47	$9.27
Cumulative effect of change in accounting for income taxes	—	—	.53
Net earnings	$10.51	$6.47	$9.80
Average number of shares outstanding:			
1990—572,647,906			
1989—581,102,404			
1988—592,444,409			

Source: IBM Corporation, 1990 Annual Report.

EXHIBIT 13-11. IBM
Statement of Cash Flows

For the year ended December 31:	1990	1989	1988
(Dollars in millions)			
Cash Flow from Operating Activities:			
Net earnings	$ 6,020	$ 3,758	$ 5,806
Adjustments to reconcile net earnings to cash provided from operating activities:			
Depreciation	4,217	4,240	3,871
Amortization of software	1,086	1,185	893
Loss (gain) on disposition of investment assets	32	(74)	(133)
(Increase) in accounts receivable	(2,077)	(2,647)	(2,322)
Decrease (increase) in inventory	17	(29)	(1,232)
(Increase) in other assets	(3,136)	(1,674)	(1,587)
Increase in accounts payable	293	870	265
Increase in other liabilities	1,020	1,743	519
Net cash provided from operating activities	7,472	7,372	6,080
Cash Flow from Investing Activities:			
Payments for plant, rental machines and other property	(6,509)	(6,414)	(5,390)
Proceeds from disposition of plant, rental machines and other property	804	544	409
Investment in software	(1,892)	(1,679)	(1,318)
Purchases of marketable securities and other investments	(1,234)	(1,391)	(2,555)
Proceeds from marketable securities and other investments	1,687	1,860	4,734
Net cash used in investing activities	(7,144)	(7,080)	(4,120)
Cash Flow from Financing Activities:			
Proceeds from new debt	4,676	6,471	4,540
Payments to settle debt	(3,683)	(2,768)	(3,007)
Short-term borrowings less than 90 days—net	1,966	228	1,028
Payments to employee stock plans—net	(76)	(29)	(11)
Payments to purchase and retire capital stock	(415)	(1,759)	(992)
Cash dividends paid	(2,774)	(2,752)	(2,609)
Net cash used in financing activities	(306)	(609)	(1,051)
Effect of Exchange Rate Changes on Cash and Cash Equivalents	131	(158)	(201)
Net Change in Cash and Cash Equivalents	153	(475)	708
Cash and Cash Equivalents at January 1	3,700	4,175	3,467
Cash and Cash Equivalents at December 31	$ 3,853	$ 3,700	$ 4,175
Supplemental Data:			
Cash paid during the year for:			
Income taxes	$ 3,315	$ 3,071	$ 3,405
Interest	$ 2,165	$ 1,605	$ 1,440

Source: IBM Corporation, 1990 Annual Report.

Exhibit 13-12, which provides the primary raw material for our analysis, is supplementary data on IBM's non–U.S. operations. While much of this disclosure is unfortunately not required (and rarely provided), it will enable us to obtain some understanding of the effect of changing exchange rates on the company's financial condition and operating performance.

The first part of Exhibit 13-12 contains summarized balance sheets and income statements for IBM's non–U.S. operations. These data suggest steady growth in foreign revenue, net earnings, and net assets over the period 1988–1990. Comparison of these data with IBM's consolidated balance sheet and income statement indicates that foreign operations accounted for 60% of revenue for 1990. We will return to the analysis of these data shortly.

The second portion of Exhibit 13-12 contains the geographic segment data required by SFAS 14.[19] The total non–U.S. data are subdivided into three geographic segments. While the data are fragmentary, and the segments highly aggregated, some analysis is possible. The following observations can be made:

1. Revenue growth has been fastest in the Americas, with a gain of more than 29% over the 1988–1990 time span.

2. The "interarea transfers" data suggest that IBM is exporting more from the United States and the Americas, less from Europe and Asia Pacific.

3. Profit margins are generally higher outside of the United States, except for the Americas where they remain low despite rapid sales growth. Segment profit data, however, are unreliable as they may reflect transfer prices and cost allocations designed to minimize taxes.[20] In addition, financing costs, research and development, and management overhead may not be spread proportionately across all segments. Thus the trend in segment profits may be a more useful indicator than the level of profits, assuming that none of these factors changes significantly from year to year.

4. Asset growth[21] in the Europe and Asia Pacific segments has outpaced revenue growth over the 1988–1990 period. The disparity could suggest investments for the future or disappointing revenues.

Geographic segment disclosures, used in conjunction with the Management Discussion and Analysis (MD&A) and other annual report data, provide significant clues regarding the role of foreign operations. Unfortunately, these data are significantly impacted by changes in exchange rates. To understand that impact requires further analysis. The objective of this analysis is to separate the effects of exchange rate changes from real operating trends.

[19]See Chapter 11 for a discussion of segment data by line of business.

[20]However, tax authorities do examine transfer prices carefully, limiting the ability of firms to manipulate profits by country.

[21]IBM does not disclose capital expenditures and depreciation by geographic segment, which is not required by SFAS 14. Many companies do provide such data (see Exhibit 1B-2 for example). These data indicate which geographic segments are receiving capital expenditures, suggesting where revenue growth is expected. The balance between capital expenditures and depreciation is suggestive of whether or not capacity is being expanded.

EXHIBIT 13-12. IBM
Data on Non-U.S. Operations

Non-U.S. Operations	1990	1989	1988
(Dollars in millions)			
At end of year:			
Net assets employed:			
Current assets	$24,337	$20,361	$20,005
Current liabilities	15,917	12,124	11,481
Working capital	8,420	8,237	8,524
Plant, rental machines and other property, net	11,628	9,879	9,354
Investments and other assets	9,077	6,822	5,251
	29,125	24,938	23,129
Long-term debt	5,060	3,358	2,340
Other liabilities	2,699	2,607	2,505
Deferred income taxes	2,381	1,814	1,580
	10,140	7,779	6,425
Net assets employed	$18,985	$17,159	$16,704
Number of employees	168,283	167,291	163,904
For the year:			
Revenue	$41,886	$36,965	$34,361
Earnings before income taxes	$ 7,844	$ 7,496	$ 7,088
Provision for income taxes	3,270	3,388	3,009
Net earnings	$ 4,574	$ 4,108	$ 4,079†
Investment in plant, rental machines and other property	$ 3,020	$ 2,514	$ 2,389

† 1988 net earnings before cumulative effect of accounting change for income taxes.

Non-U.S. subsidiaries which operate in a local currency environment account for approximately 90% of the company's non-U.S. revenue. The remaining 10% of the company's non-U.S. revenue is from subsidiaries and branches which operate in U.S. dollars or whose economic environment is highly inflationary.

As the value of the dollar weakens, net assets recorded in local currencies translate into more U.S. dollars than they would have at the previous year's rates. Conversely, as the dollar becomes stronger, net assets recorded in local currencies translate into fewer U.S. dollars than they would have at the previous year's rates. The translation adjustments, resulting from the translation of net assets, amounted to $3,266 million at December 31, 1990, $1,698 million at December 31, 1989, and $1,917 million at December 31, 1988. The changes in translation adjustments since the end of 1988 are a reflection of the strengthening of the dollar in 1989 and the weakening of the dollar in 1990.

EXHIBIT 13-12   *(Continued)*

Geographic Areas	1990	1989	1988†
(Dollars in millions)			
United States			
Revenue—Customers	$ 27,132	$25,745	$25,320
Interarea transfers	6,195	5,476	4,951
Total	$ 33,327	$31,221	$30,271
Net earnings	1,459	(325)	1,408
Assets at December 31	43,542	41,635	39,245
Europe/Middle East/Africa			
Revenue—Customers	$ 27,234	$23,170	$21,600
Interarea transfers	976	1,101	955
Total	$ 28,210	$24,271	$22,555
Net earnings	2,977	2,676	2,349
Assets at December 31	30,689	24,732	22,745
Asia Pacific			
Revenue—Customers	$ 9,564	$ 9,202	$ 8,824
Interarea transfers	1,496	1,673	1,837
Total	$ 11,060	$10,875	$10,661
Net earnings	1,151	1,296	1,394
Assets at December 31	8,646	7,666	7,633
Americas			
Revenue—Customers	$ 5,088	$ 4,593	$ 3,937
Interarea transfers	1,615	1,461	1,290
Total	$ 6,703	$ 6,054	$ 5,227
Net earnings	420	173	328
Assets at December 31	6,357	5,395	4,915
Eliminations			
Revenue	$ (10,282)	$ (9,711)	$ (9,033)
Net earnings	13	(62)	12
Assets	(1,666)	(1,694)	(1,501)
Consolidated			
Revenue	$ 69,018	$62,710	$59,681
Net earnings	$ 6,020	$ 3,758	$ 5,491
Assets at December 31	$ 87,568	$77,734	$73,037

Source: IBM Corporation, 1990 Annual Report.

975

EXHIBIT 13-13
Dollar's Trade-Weighted Exchange
Index, 1988–1990 (1973 = 100)

December 31	Index
1988	92.8
1989	93.7
1990	83.7

Average Rates for Year, 1980–1990

Year	Index
1980	87.4
1981	103.4
1982	116.6
1983	125.3
1984	138.2
1985	143.0
1986	112.2
1987	96.9
1988	92.7
1989	98.6
1990	89.1

Sources: Economic Report of the President, February 1991 (annual data) and Federal Reserve Bank of St. Louis (December 31 data).

Before starting our analysis, we need data on exchange rates. For a company operating in a single currency (such as Foreign Subsidiary, Inc.), we would obtain year-end and average exchange rates covering the period being analyzed. For a multinational such as IBM, we would need data on many currencies and a breakdown of IBM's operations by functional currency. The latter is unavailable[22] (at least to an external user), and the analysis of many currencies would be very time consuming. We need a shortcut.

Fortunately, there exist indices showing the value of the U.S. dollar against a basket of foreign currencies, normally computed on a trade-weighted basis. Using such a series for IBM requires us to make the assumption that IBM's business has the same currency mix (distribution over various currencies) as U.S. trade flows. While that assumption might be untenable for a smaller company with more limited foreign operations, it appears reasonable for a giant multinational such as IBM. Exhibit 13-13 shows average and year-end exchange rates for the period covered by our analysis.

---

[22]In some cases, annual reports for foreign subsidiaries of multinational companies are available, either because of local filing requirements or because of subsidiary financing. These reports can shed light on significant foreign operations. However, these reports are generally prepared in local currencies according to local accounting standards, not in U.S. dollars under U.S. GAAP. In some cases reports will be available only in the local language, further hampering use. Nonetheless, when a company has one or a few highly significant foreign subsidiaries, the subsidiary annual report may provide insights not available from the parent's consolidated financial statements.

Exhibit 13-12 tells us that IBM had non-U.S. revenue of nearly $42 billion in 1990 and non-U.S. net assets of approximately $19 billion. What functional currencies does the company use for these operations? The exhibit tells us that

> Non–U.S. subsidiaries which operate in a local currency environment account for approximately 90% of the company's non–U.S. revenue. The remaining 10% . . . is from subsidiaries and branches which operate in U.S. dollars or whose economic environment is highly inflationary.

In other words, the local currency is the functional currency for 90% of IBM's foreign operations. The dollar is the functional currency for the remainder, including subsidiaries operating in hyperinflationary economies.

Assuming that the 90% figure applies equally to the balance sheet, we conclude that IBM had net assets in nondollar functional currencies of $17.086 billion (90% of total nondollar net assets of $18.985) at December 31, 1990. The corresponding figures for year-end 1989 and 1988 are $15.443 billion (0.90 × $17.159 billion) and $15.034 billion (0.90 × $16.704 billion), respectively. *These amounts represent IBM's exposure to changes in exchange rates under SFAS 52.*

Translation gains and losses resulting from exchange rate fluctuation have been accumulated as a component of stockholders' equity, in accordance with SFAS 52. The text of Exhibit 13-12 gives us the cumulative translation adjustments at each year end:

December 31	Cumulative Translation Adjustments
1988	$ 1.917 billion
1989	1.698
1990	3.266

These calculations enable us to compute the actual increase in IBM's foreign net assets. By taking the reported change, and subtracting the effects of translation (change in accumulated adjustment), we get the real change ($ in millions):

Year	Reported	−	Translation	=	Real
1989	$ 455		$(219)		$674
1990	1826		1568		258

From the reported change, it appears that IBM's foreign net assets rose significantly more in 1990 than in 1989. The reality is that the large increase in 1990 was mostly due to the appreciation of foreign currencies against the dollar; before translation (in real terms) there was a larger increase in 1989.

The year-to-year change in the cumulative translation adjustment account is the effect of translation for each year. Let us compare those changes with IBM's exposure:

$$1989: \quad \frac{1.698 \text{ billion} - \$1.917 \text{ billion}}{\$15.034 \text{ billion}} = -1.46\%$$

$$1990: \quad \frac{\$3.266 \text{ billion} - \$1.698 \text{ billion}}{\$15.443 \text{ billion}} = +10.15\%$$

These figures tell us that the IBM-weighted functional currency composite declined by 1.46% against the dollar in 1989 and rose by 10.15% against the dollar in 1990.[23]

Turning to our trade-weighted index in Exhibit 13-13, the percentage changes are

$$1989: \quad -1.0\%$$
$$1990: \quad +11.9\%$$

The closeness of these changes to the IBM-weighted changes reassures us that our index is a good proxy. But where possible, we will use the IBM-weighted index that we have now derived.

Let us apply this methodology to the company's inventories. Exhibit 13-12 does not break out non–U.S. inventory, so we must assume that inventories are a constant percentage of current assets.[24] At December 31, 1989, consolidated inventories were 26.4% of consolidated current assets (Exhibit 13-9). We will assume that non–U.S. inventories also were 26.4% of non–U.S. current assets of $20.361 billion or $5.375 billion, of which $4.838 billion (90%) were in nondollar functional currencies.

Applying the IBM-weighted exchange rate change of 10.15% results in an estimated increase in non–U.S. inventories of $491 million due to changing exchange rates. This accounts for most of the $645 million ($10.108 billion − $9.463 billion) increase in IBM's consolidated inventories during 1990 (data from Exhibit 13-9). Thus it appears that most of the company's inventory increase in 1990 was not real, but was due to the impact of changing exchange rates.

Can we confirm this result? We can—from the company's cash flow statement. In Exhibit 13-11 we find that IBM's inventory change, excluding the effect of translation, was a decrease of $17 million, suggesting that the true effect of exchange rate changes was $662 million—$645 million actual change less (−$17 million) real change.[25]

While our estimated effect of $491 million is not equal to the true effect of $662 million for 1990, they are not far apart. Clearly our assumptions did not precisely hold. But even if we did not have the true figure, our estimate would still have told us that IBM's inventory increase in 1990 was due primarily to currency effects rather than operating causes. It is this conclusion that makes the analysis worthwhile. This technique, while superfluous when the cash flow statement excludes the impact of

[23]Perceptive readers will note that we have left out the effect of changing exchange rates on the increase in IBM's net assets in functional currencies. Given the small change in those assets (in functional currency terms) over the period 1988–1990, we have opted for simplification.

[24]IBM uses the FIFO inventory method worldwide. For companies with significant LIFO inventories, this calculation should be made on a FIFO basis by adding back the LIFO reserve (see Chapter 5).

[25]This computation, and similar computations in this section of the chapter, is possible only because IBM made no purchase method acquisition during 1990. See Chapter 12 for discussion of the impact of purchase method acquisitions on the statement of cash flows.

exchange rate changes, is useful when cash flow statements (such as those for non-U.S. firms) are not adjusted to exclude that impact.

We can perform this same analysis for IBM's fixed assets. Exhibit 13-12 shows that non-U.S. fixed assets were $9.879 billion; we estimate that $8.891 billion (90% of $9.879 billion) was in nondollar functional currencies. The estimated effect of currency changes is $902 million (10.15% of $8.891 billion).

The actual impact of currency changes on fixed assets is disclosed in IBM's 10-K report, in Schedules V and VI. These reconciliations of fixed assets (gross) and accumulated depreciation reveal that translation increased fixed assets by $963 million ($2,143 million for gross fixed assets less $1,180 million for accumulated depreciation).

Again our estimate is approximately correct, despite the crude assumptions made. Consolidated net fixed assets rose by $2.298 billion in 1990 (Exhibit 13-9), or 9.2%. Nearly half the gain resulted from exchange rate changes rather than new investment. Even if the 10-K data had not been available (because the foreign exchange effects were not shown or because the schedules were not required), we would have the same knowledge.

Income Statement Effects

Turning to the income statement (Exhibit 13-10), IBM had revenues of $41.886 billion in currencies other than the dollar, an increase of 13.3% from the 1989 level of $36.965 billion. On the surface it appears that there was a much larger gain in foreign sales than in 1989 (up 7.6% from the 1988 level of $34.361 billion). Using our knowledge of accounting for foreign operations, we can question that conclusion.

Applying the 90% factor to 1990 non–U.S. sales, $37.697 billion was in operations with nondollar functional currencies (FC) (the remainder is in operations with nondollar local currencies but with the dollar as the functional currency). These revenues (and all expenses) were translated into dollars at the *average* rate for 1990. Using the data in Exhibits 13-12 and 13-13, we can make this computation for each year and then examine the impact of currency changes:

	1990	1989	1988
	(in $ millions)		
Non-U.S. revenues ($, Exhibit 13-12)	$41,886	$36,965	$34,361
Non-$ FC revenues ($, 90%)	$37,697	33,268	$30,925
% increase	+13.3%	+7.6%	—
Dollar index (Exhibit 13-13)	89.1	98.6	92.7
FC revenues	FC 33,588	FC 32,802	FC 28,667
% increase	+2.4%	+14.4%	—

The last entry, "FC revenues," is an artificial index, derived by multiplying the estimated "Non–$ FC revenues" by the "Dollar index."[26] The result is a measure of

---

[26]We must use the index because we do not have average "IBM weights," only year-end to year-end data. As we have shown that the index seems to track the "IBM weights" well, we can be comfortable using it to examine the trend of revenues and pretax income.

revenue from which the impact of changes in the value of the dollar has been removed. As a result, we can estimate the "real" change in foreign revenues.

We find that the decline in the value of the dollar accounted for most of the gain in foreign revenues in 1990; the gain is only 2.4% when the factor is removed. Conversely (since the dollar rose in value in 1989), the real (FC) gain is 14.4% as compared with a gain in dollars of 7.6%. The rise in the dollar in 1989 resulted in a smaller percentage sales gain in dollars than in local currencies. (These calculations assume that local currency prices were unaffected by exchange rate changes.)

Thus by this simple exercise we can approximate the impact of changing exchange rates on IBM's nondollar revenues. A similar calculation will approximate the effect on net income. IBM's annual report to shareholders provides virtually no disclosure of this impact.

In Exhibit 13-14, we have performed this analysis for the 11-year period 1980–1990.[27] The comparison of the "as-reported" data with the "adjusted" data reveals differences that are quite significant.

The year-to-year percentage changes in both revenues and pretax earnings are, for most years, quite different after adjustment for changes in the value of the dollar. We have already discussed the impact on the period 1988–1990. For a broader perspective, we have summarized the data for the entire period:

Percentage Changes in IBM Foreign Results, 1980–1990

Period	Revenues		Pretax Income	
	Reported	Adjusted	Reported	Adjusted
1980–85	+56.3%	+155.7%	+100.1%	+227.3%
1985–90	+94.4	+21.1	+41.4	−11.9
1980–90	+203.8	+209.7	+183.0	+188.4

Source: Data in Exhibit 13-14.

Over the entire period, the reported and adjusted trends are quite similar. As the dollar showed a very small increase in value over the period, we can conclude that "real" revenue growth was slightly greater than that reported in dollars.

---

[27]The analysis in Exhibit 13-14 uses total non-U.S. sales rather than the proportion for which IBM uses non-dollar functional currencies. This proportion has declined over the 1980–1990 period but the disclosure on this point is vague. For simplicity, and because we believe the analysis would not be significantly affected, we omit that step in our analysis.

In principle, it would be preferable to use only sales in non-dollar functional currencies, as in the 1988–1990 computations above. While other foreign sales are also affected by exchange rate changes, there is an important difference. foreign sales for which the dollar is the functional currency are likely to be in hyperinflationary countries or where local selling prices are the local currency equivalent of dollar prices. In these cases changes in exchange rates may affect volume but do not affect dollar prices; they do not create income statement distortion as discussed in this section. In addition, the "index" derived from changes in the cumulative translation adjustment will not be applicable to these situations.

In practice, however, the proportion of sales for which the dollar is the functional currency is rarely available and, therefore, the analyst will have to use total foreign sales for analytic purposes.

EXHIBIT 13-14
Analysis of IBM's Foreign Operations, 1980–1990

Year	Revenues	% Change	Pretax Income	% Change
	Reported Data (in $US millions)			
1980	$US 13,787		$US 2772	
1981	13,982	+1.4%	2664	−3.9%
1982	15,336	+9.7	3226	+21.1
1983	17,053	+11.2	3841	+19.1
1984	18,566	+8.9	4640	+20.8
1985	21,545	+16.0	5546	+19.5
1986	25,888	+20.2	5871	+5.9
1987	29,280	+13.1	5683	−3.2
1988	34,361	+17.4	7088	+24.7
1989	36,965	+7.6	7496	+5.8
1990	41,886	+13.3	7844	+4.6
	Adjusted Data (in millions of FC units)			
1980	FC 12,050		FC 2423	
1981	14,457	+20.0%	2755	+13.7%
1982	17,882	+23.7	3762	+36.6
1983	21,367	+19.5	4813	+27.9
1984	25,658	+20.1	6412	+33.2
1985	30,809	+20.1	7931	+23.7
1986	29,046	−5.7	6587	−16.9
1987	28,372	−2.3	5507	−16.4
1988	31,853	+12.3	6571	+19.3
1989	36,447	+14.4	7391	+12.5
1990	37,320	+2.4	6989	−5.4

But when we look at the two subperiods, the adjusted data tell us a completely different story from the reported data. During the period 1980–1985, the value of the dollar rose sharply; the data in Exhibit 13-13 tell us that the average value of the dollar in 1985 was 63.6% higher in 1985 than in 1980 (143.0/87.4 = 1.636). Thus revenues and earnings in foreign currencies were continuously devalued when translated into dollars. The growth in revenues during this period was 155.7% in local currencies but only 56.3% when translated into dollars. Pretax earnings were similarly devalued; the local currency growth was 227.3%, while the dollar growth was only 100.1%.

The year-to-year changes also reflect the impact of the strengthening dollar. In 1981, for example, reported pretax earnings declined by 3.9%; after adjustment there was a gain of 13.7%. *In every year during the period 1980–1985, the performance of IBM's foreign operations was better in local currencies than in dollars.*

During the second half of the decade, 1985–1990, the impact of exchange rates reversed. The value of the dollar declined in most years, and by 1990 it had returned to a level very close to 1980. The declining value of the dollar inflated foreign currency revenues and earnings when translated into dollars.

Over the entire five-year period, 1985–1990, IBM's foreign revenues (in dollars) increased by 94.4%, suggesting that growth was higher than in the 1980–1985 period. The adjusted data tell us that the reverse was true; in local currencies, IBM's revenues grew by only 21.1% over the second half of the decade, a marked slowing from the 155.7% growth during the first half.

While the decline of the dollar was not consistent, some of the individual year data echo this conclusion. In both 1986 and 1987, foreign revenues (in dollars) rose sharply, suggesting favorable performance trends. The adjusted data tell us that, for both years, foreign currency revenues declined.

The pretax data also look significantly different after adjustment for changes in the value of the dollar. Over the period 1985–1990, foreign pretax earnings rose by 41.4% in dollars, but *declined* by 11.9% in local currencies. The years 1986 and 1990 are the clearest examples of this effect in individual years: in both cases pretax earnings rose in dollars but declined in local currencies.

We must not forget that this analysis makes a crucial assumption—that IBM's foreign operations were unaffected by exchange rate changes. In reality, selling prices (and, therefore, revenues and earnings) may be affected by variations in exchange rates, which impact the cost of imported components, and the prices of competitive products. We cannot assume in all cases that local currency results are independent of exchange rates.

Nonetheless, it is apparent that the rising value of the dollar during the 1980–1985 period disguised the excellent performance of IBM's foreign operations. It is equally clear that the declining dollar during the second half of the decade masked the deterioration of the operating performance of the company's foreign subsidiaries.

It should be clear, at this point, that analysis of a multinational enterprise is seriously deficient unless the impact of changing exchange rates is taken into account. Despite the approximations and assumptions required, the analyst gains important insights into operating trends and can use these insights to question management more perceptively about its real operating performance.

Ratio Effects

The impact of foreign currency changes on IBM's financial ratios is hard to determine, because of inadequate data. Since IBM uses functional currencies other than the U.S. dollar for 90% of its non–U.S. operations, we can conclude that income statement ratios in dollars largely replicate the local currency data. This would also be true of ratios using only balance sheet data, such as the current or debt/equity ratios.

The increased importance of foreign operations in 1990, resulting from the weakness of the dollar, tells us that foreign operations have more weight in the consolidated total in 1990 than in 1989. Without details of the income statement and balance sheet for foreign operations, we cannot easily tell which ratios are improved (or worsened) by this effect.[28]

---

[28]By using cash flow data and the technique previously employed to estimate the effect of exchange rate changes on various balance sheet and income accounts, we could approximate various ratios for IBM's foreign operations.

Concluding Comments on IBM

As we stated at the outset, the analysis of IBM is made possible by the voluntary disclosures (the first part of Exhibit 13-12) regarding its non–U.S. operations. Few companies provide similar data. Why, then, have we devoted so many pages to this analysis?

Our major objective was to illustrate how changing currency rates distort financial statements in the context of a real company. The analysis issues exist for all companies with significant foreign operations. Our hope is that analysts and other readers of this text can apply portions of the analysis of IBM to other companies.

For example, the change in the CTA for any firm can be used to estimate the year-end to year-end change in foreign currency rates weighted by the operations of the firm itself. The firm-specific "index" generated by this exercise can be used to discern the distortion of assets and liabilities by exchange rate changes.

The application of our analysis to the income and cash flow statements requires an "average for the period" index. In some cases (as for IBM), a trade-weighted index will serve the purpose. For companies whose operations are concentrated in a few countries, it may be possible to construct a firm-specific index.

What is most important, however, is not the precise measurement of the distortions resulting from exchange rate changes, but the recognition that they exist. Once you recognize the issues, you can usually obtain at least a "ball park" estimate of the effects. Given the imprecision of financial statements to begin with, even a general understanding of the effects of changing exchange rates should improve your investment decisions.

Alcoa

Aluminum Company of America (Alcoa), the world's largest aluminum company, has significant affiliates in both Brazil and Australia. Both are consolidated as required by SFAS 94 (see Chapter 11), although neither is wholly owned. Each can be used to illustrate the principles of accounting for foreign operations. First, we analyze the Australian affiliate for the impact of a change in the functional currency.

Alcoa of Australia (Change in Functional Currency)

Alcoa of Australia (AA) is a 51% owned-consolidated subsidiary of Alcoa. Through the end of 1990, the U.S. dollar was the functional currency for AA. As a result the temporal method was used to remeasure the results of Alcoa of Australia into U.S. dollars, generating significant translation gains and losses and adding to the volatility of reported earnings.

Effective January 1, 1991, Alcoa adopted the Australian dollar as the functional currency for its Australian operations (AA). The press release announcing the change stated that

> Based on significant changes in the economic facts and circumstances related to Alcoa of Australia's financial operations, among them substantially eliminating its exposure to currencies other than the Australian dollar, the change in the functional currency is

required under the guidelines in Financial Accounting Standard No. 52 regarding Foreign Currency Translation.

Alcoa expects the change will reduce the effect that wide exchange rate fluctuations have on Alcoa of Australia's earnings. Gains or losses from translating Alcoa of Australia's financial statements to U.S. dollars now will be reflected in a separate stockholders' equity account on the balance sheet rather than in the income statement.

Alcoa indicated that Alcoa of Australia's earnings in 1990 would have totaled $624.7 million with the change, compared to the reported $614.0 million.

The change also had the effect of reducing Alcoa's consolidated shareholders' equity by $133 million, effective January 1, 1991.[29]

The immediate effect of the change was the reduction in equity of $US 133 million alluded to. More detail is provided in the company's 10-Q report:

As of January 1, 1991 Alcoa adopted the Australian dollar as the functional currency for translating financial statements of Alcoa of Australia. The change reduced Alcoa's consolidated shareholders' equity at January 1 by $133 million and minority interests by $128 million. These amounts were offset principally by a reduction in properties, plants, and equipment.[30]

What does all this mean? The Australian dollar has generally declined against the U.S. dollar in recent years. With the U.S. dollar as the functional currency, this decline had no impact on the nonmonetary assets of AA, which were remeasured into U.S. dollars at the historical rate as required by the temporal method. With the adoption of the Australian dollar as the functional currency for these operations, the nonmonetary assets must now be translated at the (lower) current exchange rate, reducing their U.S. dollar equivalent. As fixed assets account for more than half of the assets of AA, these assets accounted for most of the effect.

The total impact of the change in functional currency was to reduce the U.S. dollar equivalent of AA's net assets by $US 261 million. The minority interest (49% of AA is owned by outside shareholders) was reduced by $128 million (49% of $261 million), with the remainder being accounted for as an adjustment to Alcoa's equity as of January 1, 1991.

The change in functional currency has several implications for Alcoa. First, by reducing assets and equity, the return-on-assets and return-on-equity ratios are enhanced. Second, the quarterly volatility resulting from changes in the exchange rate between the U.S. and Australian dollars is largely removed from Alcoa's income statement. Further declines in the value of the Australian dollar impact stockholders' equity but not reported income.

Remember, as well, that the accounting exposure to rate changes is also different. With the U.S. dollar as the functional currency, the exposure (temporal method) was net monetary assets. With the Australian dollar as functional currency, the exposure is defined as net assets. We can see the difference by looking at the balance sheet of AA:

[29]Alcoa press release, April 3, 1991.
[30]Alcoa 10-Q, Quarter Ended March 31, 1991.

ALCOA OF AUSTRALIA LIMITED (AA)
Summarized Balance Sheets, at December 31, 1989–1990
(in \$US millions)

	1989	1990
Cash and equivalents	\$ 297	\$ 394
Other current assets	525	671
Fixed assets	1585	1559
Other assets	165	173
Total assets	\$ 2572	\$ 2797
Current liabilities	588	696
Long-term debt	228	179
Other liabilities	351	367
Total liabilities	\$ 1167	\$ 1242
Net assets	\$ 1405	\$ 1555

Source: Alcoa 1990 Annual Report (amounts rounded).

The net assets are the accounting exposure under the all current rate method.

Assuming that all monetary assets and liabilities are denominated in Australian dollars, and assuming that inventories account for half of other current assets, we can compute the accounting exposure under each method for both years:

	1989	1990
Temporal method		
Cash and equivalents	\$ 297	\$ 384
Other current assets	262	235
Other assets (monetary)	165	173
Total liabilities	(1167)	(1242)
Accounting exposure (net monetary assets)	\$ (143)	\$ (450)
Current rate method (net assets)	\$ 1405	\$ 1555

With the U.S. dollar as the functional currency, use of the temporal method creates a negative exposure to the Australian dollar; depreciation of the Australian dollar would result in a translation gain (included in reported income). With the Australian dollar as the functional currency, there is a positive exposure measured by the net assets: depreciation of the Australian dollar would result in a translation loss (included in the currency translation adjustment).

We can, therefore, see that the choice of functional currency affects both the amount of the exposure and the disposition of the translation gain or loss. By changing the functional currency of AA to the U.S. dollar, Alcoa may have increased its accounting exposure, but it removed the translation effects from reported earnings.

Prior to 1991, translation gains and losses were included in reported earnings. In 1988 and 1987, for example, AA (using the temporal method) reported foreign currency losses of $US 105.6 million and $US 89.9 million, respectively due to strength in the Australian dollar. Had the Australian dollar been the functional currency, there would have been translation gains based on the net asset position.

However, there is one major complication that affects the analysis: our assumption that all monetary items are in Australian dollars is not correct. In the 1980s, AA's long-term debt was primarily denominated in U.S. dollars. As AA exported much of its output, and pricing was in U.S. dollars, the company presumably decided to hedge its revenue exposure by borrowing in the same currency. This decision complicated its accounting.

Had the Australian dollar been the functional currency in the past, AA would have recognized translation gains or losses on its $US dollar–denominated debt based on changes in the exchange rate. If, for example, the U.S. dollar rose against the Australian dollar (as it did during most of the 1980s), the company's debt would have risen in Australian dollars, reflecting the exchange rate changes. This increase would have been a translation loss (under the temporal method). Upon translation of AA's results into U.S. dollars, the translation loss would have remained a component of income. Thus the parent company (Alcoa) would have gains or losses on liabilities denominated in the parent company's currency (U.S. dollars). *This anomalous result occurs whenever the parent company uses the local currency as the functional currency for a subsidiary with net assets or liabilities in the parent currency.*

Over the period 1985–1990, AA sharply reduced its U.S. dollar–denominated debt, reducing Alcoa's exposure to translation gains or losses from this source. Changing the functional currency to the Australian dollar therefore no longer exposes the company to this source of phantom translation adjustments. (Because the source of financing is one factor in the choice of functional currency, the decline in the importance of U.S. dollar debt helped to justify the change.)

Note that the change in functional currency is not a change in accounting principle. The change therefore may not always receive the prominence it may deserve. While changes in functional currency are unusual, they do take place. Careful reading of financial statement footnotes is required.

Alcoa Aluminio (Hyperinflationary Economies)

Aluminio is Alcoa's Brazilian affiliate, 59% owned at December 31, 1990. As Brazil's inflation rate is very high, the hyperinflationary economy rule applies, and the U.S. dollar is the functional currency. Application of the temporal method results in translation losses in most years.

In 1990, however, there was a small translation gain. How was this possible given the continual decline in the Brazilian cruzeiro during this period? Presumably, the gain was due to a net monetary liability; the declining exchange rate would then result in a gain. Use of short-term local currency borrowing may have been one factor in obtaining this result: local currency borrowing can hedge monetary assets (receivables) required for operating purposes.

Approximately three quarters of Aluminio's assets consist of fixed assets and inventories, which are translated at the historic rate. Since only the net monetary assets or liabilities are exposed to changes in the exchange rate under the temporal method, companies operating in hyperinflationary economies seek to minimize their monetary asset position.

Analysis of Hyperinflationary Operations

Countries experiencing very high rates of inflation present difficult problems for both accountants and financial analysts. Because the currencies of high-inflation countries normally depreciate at a rapid rate (reflecting the diminishing purchasing power of the currency), translation into "strong" currencies of the financial statements of companies operating in such countries compounds the difficulties.

If the current exchange rate were used to translate the assets and liabilities of subsidiaries located in high-inflation countries, their translated amounts would quickly become insignificant. Such accounting would also misrepresent the financial condition of the subsidiary.

In most cases, the "real" value of nonmonetary assets is not destroyed by the high rate of inflation. Inventories and fixed assets generally rise in value (in local currency) enough to offset the rate of inflation. This is to be expected as, otherwise, such assets could be transported to other countries where their value would be higher. This effect is usually explicitly recognized in the accounting system of such countries by indexing the carrying value of nonmonetary assets by the rate of inflation. (See discussion of constant dollar accounting in Appendix 6-C.)

One solution to the accounting problem would be to translate the indexed value of nonmonetary assets, using the current exchange rate. This would have the effect of approximately maintaining the carrying amount of the asset in the reporting currency. SFAS 52 obtains this effect by requiring that the parent currency be used as the functional currency for all operations in highly inflationary economies. (SFAS 52 defines hyperinflationary as cumulative three-year inflation exceeding 100%.)

With the parent (reporting) currency as the functional currency, use of the temporal method results in the historical cost of nonmonetary assets and liabilities (most significantly, inventory and fixed assets) being maintained in the parent currency. Neither changes in exchange rates nor inflation affects that carrying value. Cost of goods sold and depreciation expense are also accounted for in the parent currency.

The temporal method also has the result of including gains and losses resulting from the remeasurement process in reported earnings. Companies operating in high-inflation countries generally try to balance their exposure (net monetary position) to the local currency by borrowing locally if necessary. Because they are frequently unable to do so, it is common for companies with large operations in hyperinflationary economies to frequently report translation losses.

Borrowing in a high-inflation currency creates another analysis problem. Such currencies normally have extremely high nominal interest rates, as the lender must be compensated for the loss of purchasing power (due to high inflation). The high interest rate is acceptable because the borrower invests in comparatively inflationproof assets and reduces its net monetary asset exposure. The high interest expense, in reality, is mostly offset by the purchasing power gain from the diminishing real value of the debt.

An example of this appears in the footnotes to the *1990 Annual Report* of Caterpillar, Inc., which has large operations in Brazil:

> During 1990, net foreign exchange gains of $176 [million] arising from operations in Brazil's highly inflationary economy were removed from "other income" . . . and included on the operating statement lines where the related inflationary effects were reported. Consequently, exchange gains and losses on local currency denominated debt and cash deposits, where the interest rates reflect the rate of inflation, were offset against interest expense, $138 [million], and interest income, $5 [million], respectively.

If Caterpillar had not made this adjustment, the company's income statement would have shown larger translation gains balanced by larger net interest expense. The adjustment effectively replaces nominal interest expense with real interest expense, much closer to the measure of interest in countries with lower inflation rates (and therefore low inflation premia in nominal rates). Where companies have not made this adjustment, the analyst should do so to obtain more useful income statement data.

ANALYTIC DIFFICULTIES RELATED TO FOREIGN OPERATIONS

The provisions of SFAS 52 lower the volatility of reported earnings and produce ratios similar to those under the local currency. However, they also generate two types of problems. The first relates to the lack of consistency or symmetry in the accounting for equivalent transactions. The second concerns the economic interpretation of the financial reports generated by SFAS 52.

These problems are illustrated using the highly stylized environment of perfect markets. The following exposition summarizes work by Beaver and Wolfson (1982, 1984). The analysis is used to demonstrate the relationships among inflation, interest rates, and exchange rates that form the basis for much of the discussion that follows.

Relationships Among Interest Rates, Inflation, and Exchange Rates

Consider two countries, A and B, where the ratio of exchange rates between their currencies is 1:1 (i.e., $1 \, LC_A = 1 \, LC_B$). Let $i_A = 1\%$ and $i_B = 6.8\%$ reflect the inflation rates of countries A and B, respectively. Assuming a real interest rate of r (equal in both countries) of 3%, inflation will result in a higher nominal interest rate, R. The relationship among inflation and real and nominal interest rates in equation form is

$$R = [(1 + i)(1 + r)] - 1$$

The (nominal) interest rates in countries A and B, respectively, are $R_A = [(1 + 0.01)(1 + 0.03)] - 1 = 4\%$ and $R_B = [(1 + 0.068)(1.03)] - 1 = 10\%$. Given these conditions, *ceteris paribus,* the exchange rate at the end of the year should be $1 \, LC_A = 1.058 \, LC_B$. This can be demonstrated by examining the effects on either nonmonetary or monetary assets.

Nonmonetary Assets

A nonmonetary asset with a cost of $P(0)$ at the beginning of a year will cost $P(1) = P(0)$ $(1 + i)$ at the end of the year. An asset that cost 1 LC in each country's respective currencies at the beginning of the year (when the exchange rate is 1 LC_A = 1 LC_B) will cost 1.01 LC_A in Country A and 1.068 LC_B in Country B. Since in real terms the assets are identical, they should carry an equivalent real price. That is, 1.01 LC_A = 1.068 LC_B or, equivalently, 1 LC_A = 1.058 LC_B, which of course is the year-end exchange rate.

Monetary Assets

Under perfect markets investors are indifferent as to where to invest money. At the year-end exchange rate of 1 LC_A = 1.058 LC_B, as the following table indicates, investors would be indifferent[31] as to investing in country A or B.

Comparison of Return on $100 Investment

	Country A	Country B
Interest rate	4%	10%
Return on LC 100 after 1 year		
In local currencies	104 LC_A	110 LC_B
Converted to common currency at exchange rate 1 LC_A = 1.058 LC_B		
To currency A	104 LC_A	110/1.058 = 104 LC_A
To currency B	104 × 1.058 = 110 LC_B	110 LC_B

This illustration can now be used to discuss the two analytic issues referred to earlier.

Consistency in Reporting

When the local currency is the functional currency, local currency–denominated assets and liabilities are translated at the current exchange rate as of each balance sheet date. For monetary assets and liabilities, the result is reasonable: the parent company balance sheet includes the assets and liabilities in the parent currency at amounts reasonably similar to their fair value. For nonmonetary assets and liabilities, that is not the case.

Consider the case of the nonmonetary asset mentioned earlier. If it is purchased at the beginning of year 1 by a subsidiary located in Country B, it will be carried at the end of the year on the subsidiary's books at either (1) the historical cost of 1 LC_B or (2) the current cost (if permitted) of 1.068 LC_B.

Similarly, if the parent (located in Country A) had purchased the asset, it would carry it at either (1) the historical cost of 1 LC_A or (2) the current cost (if permitted) of 1.01 LC_A.

---

[31]Otherwise, arbitrage opportunities would exist with money flowing into one currency from the other until the equilibrium of 1:1.058 was reached.

However, SFAS 52 requires the assets of the foreign subsidiary to be reported on the parent's books at *the historical cost divided by the current exchange rate* or ($1 \text{ LC}_B/1.058 = 0.95 \text{ LC}_A$), which is neither the historical cost nor the current cost.

Assume that a company builds two identical factories, one in the United States and one in Country G with identical initial costs and the currency of Country G appreciates relative to the dollar, rising by 50% over the next five years. If the currency of Country G is the functional currency for that operation, the "cost" of the factory in that country will be 50% higher than the "cost" of the U.S. plant.

Presumably the rise in Country G's currency is due to a lower rate of inflation. But the rate of inflation does not change the historical cost of an asset. The higher carrying amount for the factory in Country G (and higher depreciation expense as well) is not logical. It would be equally absurd for a factory in a country whose currency depreciates against the dollar to decline steadily in carrying amount. Yet this is the consequence of the application of SFAS 52 translation. Financial ratios would also be impacted, giving improper signals regarding the performance of operations in different countries.

Selling and Sorter make this argument as follows:

> The balance sheet (and income) numbers provided under Statement No. 52 may be difficult to interpret. Under Statement No. 8, a historical cost . . . would be multiplied by the exchange rate prevailing at the time of the transaction to yield a dollar-denominated amount that is easy to interpret: it is simply a description of the actual cash flow that occurred in order to acquire an asset, translated at the dollar equivalent of that time period. The same local-currency-denominated historical cost multiplied by the current exchange rate (per Statement No. 52) yields a number that defies description: It is not a meaningful description of past cash flows, nor is it a description of future flows.
>
> Statement No. 52 further confounds interpretation . . . by requiring that these meaningless balances be consolidated with the accounts of the parent company. The result is an aggregation of parent company figures representing a history of the cash flows with a number that is neither fish nor fowl.[32]

In extreme cases, when a factory is located in a hyperinflationary economy, the parent currency must be used as the functional currency, and the problem is solved. Both factories would be accounted for at historical cost in the parent currency and would retain identical historical costs and depreciation expense.

The problem can be traced to the use of historical cost for nonmonetary assets. If current cost were used, and if assets and liabilities were translated at current exchange rates, then balance sheet carrying amounts would have more meaning. Until current cost accounting is adopted, analysts must simply be aware that the carrying amounts of nonmonetary assets in nondollar functional currencies (and the original or reporting currency) are not representative of fair value and are distorted by changes in price levels and exchange rates.

These issues are compounded by generally inadequate disclosure in the financial statements of companies with significant foreign operations. We have already noted that IBM's disclosures, while far greater than those required, still require approximations to draw analytical conclusions.

---

[32]Selling, Thomas and George Sorter, "FASB Statement No. 52 and Its Implications for Financial Statement Analysis," *Financial Analysts Journal* (May/June 1983) pp. 66–67.

Deere (see Appendix 1-B) has limited disclosure of its accounting for foreign operations. The MD&A does contain some general discussion of the impact of exchange rates on the company's foreign affiliates. The segment data (required by SFAS 14) disclose overseas sales, operating profit, total assets, capital additions, and depreciation expense. A footnote analyzes the changes in the CTA over the three years ending in 1991 and briefly discusses Deere's accounting for foreign exchange contracts and options.

However, there is no disclosure of Deere's choice of functional currency for its foreign operations. Because of the existence of the CTA, we know that Deere has some operations using functional currencies other than the U.S. dollar. But there are no data available to begin to do the type of analysis performed for IBM. Unfortunately, as the disclosure requirements of SFAS 52 are minimal, Deere is the norm and IBM the exception.

This brings us to the second and more serious problem with the use of SFAS 52: the accounting data may provide false signals regarding the economic impact of currency changes on foreign operations.

Economic Interpretation of Results

We noted earlier that one of the stated objectives of SFAS 52 was to provide information "compatible with the expected economic effects of a rate change." Current accounting standards do not meet that objective in most cases.

Using our previous example of an investment of 100 LC in monetary assets, assume a parent firm in Country A has a subsidiary in Country B whose functional currency is LC_B. Then, under the provisions of SFAS 8, the investment would be reported as follows on the parent and subsidiary income statements:

	Subsidiary	Parent
Interest income	$LC_B 10$	$10/1.058 = LC_A\ 9.5$
Translation loss		$100 \times [(1/1.058) - 1] =$ (5.5)
Net gain		$LC_A\ 4.0$

This would reflect the actual economics of the transaction as the parent has earned $LC_A\ 4$ during the year and that is the amount reported. Under SFAS 52, however, the translation loss would not be reported in the income statement. Income would reflect the interest income of $9.5\ LC_A$. Since the (monetary) asset would also be restated to $95\ LC_A$, the 10% nominal return relationship would be maintained. However, the economic reality would be misstated and distorted.

Although this example is constructed in the realm of perfect markets, Exhibit 13-15 from Beaver and Wolfson (1984) confirms the association of high interest rates in one country with a weakening of that country's currency relative to currencies of other countries. An examination of spot and forward exchange rates as well as prime rates indicates that markets anticipate the weakening of the currency and thus compensate for it by requiring higher *nominal* interest rates.

EXHIBIT 13-15
The Relationship of Interest Rates and Exchange Rates

	Percent					Foreign Units per U.S. Dollar (top)/U.S. Dollars (bottom)						
	U.S. Treasury Bills	Certificates of Deposit			Euro-market Time Deposits*	German Mark	Swiss Franc	Japanese Yen	Canadian Dollar	French Franc	British Pound	Italian Lire
		U.S.	Euro-market	Singapore								
Spot	X	X	X	X	X	2.61	2.10	233	1.23	7.96	0.6764	1582
						0.3836	0.4756	0.004296	0.8117	0.1257	1.4784	0.000632
Three month	8.67%	9.20%	9.37%	9.49%	9.63%	2.58	2.07	231	1.23	8.05	0.6762	1614
						0.3872	0.4824	0.004328	0.8123	0.1242	1.4790	0.000619
Six month	8.87	9.40	9.52	9.63	9.75	2.56	2.05	230	1.23	8.19	0.6758	1648
						0.3907	0.4886	0.004358	0.8124	0.1220	1.4797	0.000607
One year	8.99	9.80	9.95	10.07	10.06	2.52	1.99	226	1.23	8.42	0.6752	1710
						0.3972	0.5019	0.004429	0.8129	0.1188	1.4811	0.000585
Bank prime	11.00	X	X	X	X	6.00%	5.50%	5.75%	11.00%	12.25%	10.00%	18.75%

Data: from Boston Corp. and Irving Trust Co. as of Oct. 4, 1983.

*At London interbank offered rates.

Source: *Business Week*, October 17, 1983.

Source: Beaver, William H. and Mark Wolfson, "Foreign Currency Translation Gains and Losses: What Effect Do They Have and What Do They Mean?" *Financial Analysts Journal* (March–April 1984) pp. 28–36, Table 2, P. 30

First, note that the Germany mark, Swiss franc and Japanese yen are all expected to strengthen against the dollar throughout the year; the French franc and Italian lire are expected to weaken; and the Canadian dollar and British pound are expected to remain approximately stable. Second, note that the currencies that are expected to strengthen all have prime rates below the United States rate of 11 per cent (6.0, 5.5 and 5.75 per cent); the currencies expected to weaken both have prime rates above the U.S. rate (12.25 and 18.75 per cent); and the stable currencies have approximately the same prime rates (11 and 10 per cent).[33]

Other plausible scenarios can also lead to distortion of economic realities. First, consider a foreign subsidiary operating within the local environment, with no exports and no import competition. Such an operation is well served by SFAS 52. The parent company data will largely replicate in dollars the performance of the subsidiary in its local currency. The net investment in the subsidiary, the measure of exposure under SFAS 52, will rise or fall depending on the exchange rate. When the local currency rises, the net investment will increase in dollars. The net investment seems to be a fair proxy for the value of the investment to the parent.

However, consider a Canadian manufacturing subsidiary, which exports all its output to the United States. All its revenues are in U.S. dollars, while its costs are entirely in Canadian dollars.

If the Canadian dollar rises against the U.S. dollar, the subsidiary's profit margins will be squeezed. Its Canadian dollar revenues decline (assuming that U.S. dollar prices remain the same), while costs remain unchanged. To the extent that the subsidiary can maintain revenues in Canadian dollars, by raising U.S. dollar prices, it may lose volume. Either way, sales and earnings are likely to fall.

Yet with the Canadian dollar as the functional currency, the accounting consequences will be identical to the first case. The U.S. parent will translate assets and liabilities at the higher exchange rate, and the U.S. dollar net worth will increase (despite lower earnings). Yet the economic impact of the rising Canadian dollar is to reduce the subsidiary's revenues, net income, and cash flows (in either currency) and therefore its value to the parent company.

Consider a third case, a British manufacturing subsidiary whose output is sold entirely within Great Britain and whose costs are incurred entirely in pounds sterling. If the value of the pound sterling rises, imports will enter, taking market share from the British subsidiary. The result is likely to be lower sales, lower earnings (price cutting may be necessary to keep market share), and lower cash flows. Once again, with sterling as the functional currency, the U.S. dollar net assets will increase. Yet the value of the British subsidiary has almost certainly declined, despite the higher currency exchange rate.

A partial answer to these contradictions is that accounting net worth is not meant to represent the value of a business. The role of accounting is to provide data that help users to make better investment decisions. Analysis of that data, and conclusions regarding the value of investments, are not part of that role. Analysts must not fall into the trap of believing that preparers and auditors have done their job for them. While the

---

[33]Beaver, William and Mark Wolfson, "Foreign Currency Translation Gains and Losses: What Effect Do They Have and What Do They Mean?" *Financial Analysts Journal* (March/April 1984) p. 29.

examples given are superficial, they should suggest the need for a thorough analysis of the economic impact of exchange rate changes.

Impact of SFAS 8 and SFAS 52 on Management and Investor Behavior

SFAS 8 was, as noted, one of the most unpopular standards issued by the FASB. Much of the criticism was due to the volatility introduced into net income. Ziebart and Kim (1987) note that a number of studies reported that, as a result of SFAS 8, MNCs increased their hedging activities in the currency markets to *hedge against the volatility of the accounting "paper" gains/losses rather than their actual underlying economic exposure*. Such speculative activities are, of course, costly and can actually add to the economic exposure facing such firms. One can only speculate as to the motivations underlying this "irrational" behavior in terms of the various theories concerning investor and management behavior discussed throughout this book.

1. Management believed (rightly or wrongly) that its investors or creditors were "taken in" by volatile reported income.

2. The added volatility adversely affected contractual arrangements such as management compensation and debt covenants that the firm had entered into. At the very least the volatility adversely affected the monitoring role played by financial statements.

3. The volatility lowered the predictability of the firm's income and future cash flows as the reported exchange gains/losses masked the underlying economic events. This added to the firm's uncertainty and risk.

Empirical studies[34] did not address these motivational issues. Rather they examined market reaction hypothesizing that SFAS 8 was viewed adversely by the market and the introduction of SFAS 52, with its dampening of earnings volatility, would result in positive market reaction.

Early studies (e.g., Dukes, 1978) could not document a negative market reaction to the introduction of SFAS 8. Ziebart and Kim[35] carried out an extensive analysis of the major events surrounding the inception of SFAS 8 in 1974 and its eventual replacement by SFAS 52 in 1980. In addition to the actual introduction of exposure drafts and pronouncements, they hypothesized that other events that eventually led to the introduction of SFAS 52 would also have positive market reaction. Exhibit 13-16 presents a chronology of these events. For the first three events, which deal with the introduction of SFAS 8, its implementation, and the FASB's initial refusal to reconsider the pronounce-

---

[34]Some of these studies were commissioned by the FASB at that time in response to the criticism of SFAS 8. (See Exhibit 13-16, April and July 1977.)

[35]Their methodology differed from the previous studies in the manner in which they calculated abnormal returns. In addition, and perhaps more important, they focused on a shorter test period. The previous studies used time periods ranging from five months to two years, whereas in their study they used (for any of the event dates) a two-month test period. Use of a shorter test period increases the possibility of picking up abnormal returns as, if they exist, they are not "swamped" by other events.

EXHIBIT 13-16
Events Leading Up to SFAS 52: Expected and Actual Market Reaction of MNCs

Test Period	Date	Event	Sign of Expected Market Reaction of MNC	Actual Sign and Significance
1	December 31, 1974	Exposure draft of SFAS 8	−	+
2	October 6, 1975	SFAS 8 issued	−	−*
3	April 29, 1976	FASB votes not to reconsider SFAS 8	−	−**
4	April 19, 1977	FASB announces its interest in research regarding foreign currency translation	+	+
5	July 8, 1977	FASB announces it will sponsor research regarding foreign currency translation	+	−**
6	November 10, 1977	FASB proposes a technical change in SFAS 8	+	+*
7	June 2, 1978	FASB solicits comments regarding a change in SFAS 8	+	+**
8	January 18, 1979 / January 31, 1979	FASB announces results of its sponsored research / FASB votes to reconsider SFAS 8	+	+
9	April 1, 1980	The Wall Street Journal reports the tentative changes	+	−*
10	August 28, 1980	FASB releases an exposure draft of SFAS 52	+	+**

*Significant at least at .01 level.
**Significant at least at .001 level.
Source: Ziebart, David A. and David H. Kim, "An Examination of the Market Reactions Associated With SFAS No. 8 and SFAS No. 52," *The Accounting Review* (April 1987), pp. 343–357, Tables 1, P. 347 and 3, P. 349 (Adapted)

ment, they expect negative market reaction to MNC firms. For the next seven events leading to the eventual introduction of SFAS 52, they expect positive reaction.

The results (presented in the last column of Exhibit 13-16) confirm that, with respect to the actual pronouncements, market reaction is as expected. For two of the three events associated with SFAS 8, there is significant negative market reaction. The lack of any significant reaction at the time of the initial SFAS 8 exposure draft (test period 1) may be due, the authors argue, to the market not fully understanding the implications of SFAS 8 until later, as the details of SFAS 8 were not known prior to the release.[36]

With respect to the introduction of SFAS 52, the market reaction is significantly positive (as expected) at the time of the SFAS 52 exposure draft (test period 10). For the other events the results are mixed and inconclusive. Two show no significant reaction (test periods 4 and 8), whereas others (test periods 5 and 9) show significant results but in a negative direction. The authors explain these results by arguing that, although in retrospect we now know that these events eventually lead to SFAS 52, at the time of their occurrence it was not yet clear what the outcome would be. They may have been viewed as delaying tactics by the FASB or as events that would result in the maintenance of the

[36]Prior to SFAS 8, companies were free to use a variety of accounting methods, and disclosure was minimal. Thus it is possible that the market could not discern the impact of SFAS 8 on companies with foreign operations prior to its adoption.

status quo. These results would seem to be generally consistent with adverse effects associated with SFAS 8 and positive effects with SFAS 52.

Bartov and Bodnar (1992) demonstrated that the market seems to experience difficulty in understanding the implications of the effects of changes in foreign currencies. They examined a sample of MNCs for which weakness (strength) in the dollar should translate into higher (lower) income.[37] As changes in the exchange rate are known, one would expect the market to react in the quarter when the changes in the exchange rate occurred. *They found no significant reaction during the quarter when changes in the exchange rate occurred but rather in the following quarter when the previous quarter's reports were issued.* The degree of lagged reaction, although still in existence, was mitigated after the issuance of SFAS 52. They hypothesized that this might result from the lessened volatility in the income statement, perhaps enabling investors to assess more accurately the impact of exchange rate changes on a firm's income.

Financial analysts also did not seem to appreciate fully the effect of the exchange rate changes. Examining whether analysts incorporated these effects in their forecasts, the authors note that analysts

> could have improved the accuracy of their estimates by using information contained in the past movements of the U.S. dollar. These results also give further credence to the view that investors fail to correctly characterize the contemporaneous relation between dollar fluctuations and firm value when they form future expectations of the value of the firm.[38]

Understanding the effects of changes in exchange rates is obviously no easy task.

CONCLUDING COMMENTS

Changing exchange rates introduce an additional layer of complication to the analysis of financial statements. The most significant insights in this chapter are

- The choice of functional currency is an important determinant of the accounting for foreign operations.
- Translation and remeasurement are fundamentally different accounting processes—both the definition of exposure and the disposition of exchange adjustments differ.
- Exchange rate changes distort all financial data for nonparent currency operations.
- The goal is to separate the effects of currency changes from actual operating changes; analysis can often approximate the currency effects.
- Accounting effects of currency changes are frequently different from the economic effects; analysis of the business is required to discern the impact of exchange rate changes on the value of a business.

---

[37]This higher income effect, as noted earlier, is not necessarily a function of the accounting method used.

[38]Bartov, Eli and Gordon M. Bodnar, "Firm Valuation, Earnings Expectations and the Exchange-Rate Exposure Effect", Working Paper (June 1992), p. 33.

Chapter 13

Problems

1. [Effects of functional currency choice; 1991 CFA adapted] Bethel Company uses the U.S. dollar as its functional currency worldwide. Star Company uses the local currency for each country in which it operates as its functional currencies. Explain how the choice of functional currency affects each of the following:

   (i) Reported sales

   (ii) Cash flow from operations

   (iii) Computation of translation gains and losses

   (iv) Reporting of translation gains and loss

2. [Disaggregating operating and exchange rate effects] Consolidated income statements for the E&O Corporation follow (in millions of dollars):

	19X0	19X1	19X2
Revenues	$100.0	$110.0	$120.0
Operating expenses	70.0	72.0	74.0
Income taxes	9.0	11.4	13.8
Net income	$ 21.0	$ 26.6	$ 32.2

These statements include the operations of E&O's foreign subsidiary, Erzi Limited, which operates in a country whose currency is the LC. Erzi has no inventory and no fixed assets. Excluding the effects of Erzi, E&O's income statement was constant for years 19X0 to 19X2 at:

Revenues	$50.0 million
Operating expenses	45.0
Income tax	2.0
Net income	$ 3.0 million

Average and year-end exchange rates for the years 19X0 through 19X2 were as follows:

	19X0	19X1	19X2
Average	LC1 = $1.00	LC1 = $1.50	LC1 = $0.75
Year end	LC1 = $1.50	LC1 = $2.00	LC1 = $0.50

As E&O's revenues and income are constant over the three-year period, all variations must result from the operations of Erzi.

A. Calculate how much of the observed growth in revenues and income over the 19X0–19X2 period resulted from Erzi's operations and how much was due to changes in exchange rates.

B. Discuss how the choice of functional currency affected the $U.S. income statement.

EXHIBIT 13P-1. FUNIMUNI, INC.
Balance Sheet, at December 31, 1989

	Ponts (millions)	Exchange Rate (ponts/U.S.$)	U.S.$ (millions)
Cash	82	4.0	20.5
Accounts receivable	700	4.0	175.0
Inventory	455	3.5	130.0
Fixed assets (net)	360	3.0	120.0
Total assets	1597		445.5
Accounts payable	532	4.0	133.0
Capital stock	600	3.0	200.0
Retained earnings	465		112.5
Total liabilities and shareholders' equity	1597		445.5

Income Statement, for Year Ended December 31, 1989

	Ponts (millions)	Exchange Rate (ponts/U.S.$)	U.S.$ (millions)
Sales	3500	3.5	1000.0
Cost of sales	(2345)	3.5	(670.0)
Depreciation expense	(60)	3.0	(20.0)
Selling expense	(630)	3.5	(180.0)
Translation gain (loss)	—		(17.5)
Net income	465		112.5

3. [Effects of functional currency choice; 1990 CFA adapted] On December 31, 1988, U.S. Dental Supplies (USDS) created a wholly owned foreign subsidiary, Funimuni, Inc. (FI), located in the country of Lumbaria. The balance sheet of FI as of December 31, 1988, stated in local currency (the pont), follows:

FUNIMUNI, INC.
Balance Sheet, at December 31, 1988
(in millions of ponts)

Cash	180
Fixed assets	420
Total assets	600
Capital stock	600

FI initially adopted the U.S. dollar as its functional currency and translated its 1989 balance sheet and income statement in accordance with SFAS 52 (shown in Exhibit 13P-1). USDS subsequently instructed FI to change its functional currency to the pont. Assume the following exchange rates:

January 1, 1989	3.0 ponts/U.S.dollar
1989 average	3.5
December 31, 1989	4.0

A. Prepare a balance sheet as of December 31, 1989, *and* a 1989 income statement for FI, both in U.S. dollars, using the pont as the functional currency for FI.

B. Describe the impact of the change in FI's functional currency to the pont on FI's:

(i) U.S. dollar balance sheet as of December 31, 1990.

(ii) U.S. dollar 1990 income statement.

(iii) U.S. dollar financial ratios for 1990.

4. Exhibit 13P-2 presents extracts from the 1991 financial statements of International Paper (IP).

A. Describe the functional currency (currencies) that IP uses for its foreign operations. How does this choice affect IP's reported income, cash flow from operations, and stockholders' equity?

EXHIBIT 13P-2. INTERNATIONAL PAPER

Translation of International Currencies

Balance sheets of the Company's international operations are translated into U.S. dollars at year-end exchange rates while income statements are translated at average rates. Adjustments resulting from financial statement translations are included as cumulative translation adjustments in Paid-In Capital. Gains and losses resulting from foreign currency transactions are included in income.

	Net Sales		
In millions	1991	1990	1989
United States	$ 9,811	$10,119	$ 9,937
Europe	2,833	2,730	1,355
Other	318	314	235
Less: Intergeographic Sales	(259)	(203)	(149)
Net Sales	$12,703	$12,960	$11,378

Source: International Paper, *1991 Annual Report.*

B. Compare the trend in sales of the company's European segment from 1989 to 1991 with those of the U.S. segment. Discuss the *four* factors that may have accounted for the difference in sales growth.

C. Discuss how IP's choice of functional currency affected the observed trend in sales growth?

Problems 5–8 are based on the foreign subsidiary example and on Exhibit 13-1 in the chapter.

Exhibit 13-1 summarizes the differences between the temporal and all current methods in their treatment of exchange rate holding gains and losses. The following table shows those gains and losses in 1991 for the foreign subsidiary example:

Asset/ Liability	Nature of Gain/Loss	Treatment Temporal	Treatment All Current
Monetary	Realized and unrealized	$(27)	$ (27)
Nonmonetary	Realized	12	12
Nonmonetary	Unrealized	Ignored	102
Total		$(15)	$ 87

5. Using Exhibits 13-4 and 13-5 determine what each of the following amounts for 1991 corresponds to:

   (i) The monetary loss of $27.

   (ii) The nonmonetary realized gain of $12.

   (iii) The nonmonetary unrealized gain of $102.

   (iv) All gains and losses of $87.

   (v) All gains and losses (except unrealized nonmonetary) of $(15).

6. The monetary loss of 27 can be calculated as:

Loss on December 31, 1990, liability: LC 171 $\left[\dfrac{1}{1.06} - \dfrac{1}{0.95}\right] = \$19$

Loss on 1991 increase in liability: LC 109 $\left[\dfrac{1}{1.02} - \dfrac{1}{0.95}\right] = \quad 8$

   Total $\underline{\underline{\$27}}$

Using this calculation as a guide, calculate the other four amounts listed in Problem 5.

7. The following table shows exchange rate holding gains and losses in 1992 for the foreign subsidiary example:

| | | Treatment | |
| Asset/ | Nature of | | All |
Liability	Gain/Loss	Temporal	Current
Monetary	Realized and unrealized	$(43)	$(43)
Nonmonetary	Realized	58	58
Nonmonetary	Unrealized	Ignored	99
Total		$ 15	$114

Using Exhibits 13-4 and 13-5, determine what each of the following amounts correspond to:

(i) The monetary loss of $43.

(ii) The nonmonetary realized gain of $58.

(iii) The nonmonetary unrealized gain of $99.

(iv) All gains and losses of $114.

(v) All gains and losses (except unrealized nonmonetary) of $15.

8. The 1992 monetary loss of $43 can be calculated as:

Loss on December 31, 1991, net monetary liability: LC 280 $\left[\dfrac{1}{0.95} - \dfrac{1}{0.85}\right] = \mathbf{\$35}$

Loss on 1992 increase in this liability: LC 122 $\left[\dfrac{1}{0.90} - \dfrac{1}{0.85}\right] = \quad \mathbf{8}$

   Total $\underline{\underline{\mathbf{\$43}}}$

Using this calculation as a guide, calculate the other four amounts listed in Problem 7.

9. Exhibit 13-8 contains a breakdown of the 1992 effect of exchange rate changes on cash (for foreign subsidiary) into its operating, investing, and financing components. Replicate this computation for 1991.

Problem 10 is based on the IBM example in the chapter. The questions focus on Exhibit 13-12. For exchange rate information use the data provided in Exhibit 13-13. When solving this problem, make the simplifying assumption that IBM uses local currencies as the functional currency for all foreign subsidiaries.

10. Exhibit 13-12 contains the balance sheet and income statement for IBM's non-U.S. operations after translation to U.S. dollars.

A. Convert the 1989 and 1990 balance sheets to LC units.

B. Convert the 1990 income statement to LC units.

C. Using *only* LC net income, try to reconcile the change in LC equity (net assets) during 1990. Provide one possible reason for the discrepancy.

D. Exhibit 13-12 indicates that IBM invested $3020 million in plant, rental machine, and other properties during 1990. Calculate the amount in LC units. Using this information estimate the depreciation expense (in LC units) for IBM's non-U.S. operations.

E. Assume that cash is 5% of the current assets shown in Exhibit 13-12. Prepare a 1990 cash flow statement in LC units for IBM's non-U.S. operations.

F. Convert the LC unit cash flow statement prepared in part E to a U.S. dollar cash flow statement.

G. **(i)** Compute the percentage of IBM's 1990 consolidated cash from operations that came from its non-U.S. operations.

    (ii) Compute the percentage of IBM's 1990 consolidated borrowings made by its non-U.S. operations.

    (iii) Compute the percentage of IBM's 1990 investment in fixed assets that took place in its non-U.S. operations.

    (iv) Discuss how your answers to parts (i)—(iii) contribute to your understanding of the importance of IBM's non-U.S. operations to the company.

    (v) Discuss the limitations of your answers to parts (i)–(iii).

H. Using the cash flow data calculated in part F compute the "Effect of exchange rate changes on cash and cash equivalents." Compare your result to the amount shown in IBM's statement of cash flows (Exhibit 13-11) and explain any discrepancy.

11. [Analysis of foreign operations] Exhibit 13P-3 contains the balance sheet and statement of cash flows from the *1990 Annual Report* of Bristol-Myers (BMY) as well as additional excerpts from that report.

A. What can you infer about BMY's choice of functional currencies for its foreign operations?

B. Estimate the effect of currency changes on the sales trend of BMY's foreign operations over the period 1988–1990 (show your computations).

C. **(i)** Explain why the inventory change in the cash flow statement differs from the change in balance sheet amounts.

    (ii) Using the CTA, try to approximate the discrepancy for 1990.

D. BMY's *net* foreign assets declined in 1989, although *total* foreign assets (from geographic segment data) rose.

    (i) How is this possible?

    (ii) Suggest a motivation for the decline.

    (iii) Using the data for 1990, suggest whether the decline benefited the company.

E. How is the information in Note 11 relevant to an analysis of BMY's exposure to currency gains and losses?

EXHIBIT 13P-3. BRISTOL-MYERS

Consolidated Balance Sheet

		December 31,		
(in millions of dollars)		**1990**	1989	1988
Assets	**Current Assets:**			
	Cash and cash equivalents	$ 596	$ 510	$1,966
	Time deposits	282	175	149
	Marketable securities.	1,080	1,597	397
	Receivables, net of allowances.	1,776	1,578	1,467
	Inventories.	1,366	1,139	1,044
	Prepaid expenses.	570	553	399
	Total Current Assets.	5,670	5,552	5,422
	Property, Plant and Equipment—net.	2,631	2,350	2,188
	Other Assets.	722	371	435
	Excess of cost over net tangible assets received in business acquisitions.	192	224	228
		$9,215	$8,497	$8,273
Liabilities	**Current Liabilities:**			
	Short-term borrowings	$ 397	$ 281	$ 679
	Accounts payable.	530	475	476
	Accrued expenses	1,354	1,414	974
	U.S. and foreign income taxes payable	540	489	484
	Total Current Liabilities	2,821	2,659	2,613
	Other Liabilities	745	517	428
	Long-Term Debt	231	237	284
	Total Liabilities	3,797	3,413	3,325
Stockholders' Equity	Preferred stock, $2 convertible series: Authorized 10 million shares; issued and outstanding 37,871 in 1990, 65,938 in 1989 and 81,730 in 1988, liquidation value of $50 per share.	—	—	—
	Common stock, par value of $.10 per share: Authorized 1.5 billion shares; issued 532,603,203 in 1990, 525,775,524 in 1989 and 546,877,104 in 1988	53	53	55
	Capital in excess of par value of stock.	504	396	487
	Cumulative translation adjustments	(61)	(149)	(114)
	Retained earnings.	5,428	4,796	5,207
		5,924	5,096	5,635
	Less cost of treasury stock—8,784,350 common shares in 1990, 437,118 in 1989 and 26,086,073 in 1988.	506	12	687
	Total Stockholders' Equity.	5,418	5,084	4,948
		$9,215	$8,497	$8,273

EXHIBIT 13P-3. *(Continued)*

Consolidated Statement of Cash Flows

	Year Ended December 31,		
(in millions of dollars)	**1990**	1989	1988
Cash Flows From Operating Activities:			
Net earnings	**$1,748**	$ 747	$1,254
Depreciation and amortization	**244**	196	185
Provision for integrating businesses	**—**	855	—
Other operating items	**38**	16	18
Receivables	**(219)**	(211)	(159)
Inventories	**(168)**	(123)	(114)
Prepaid expenses	**(8)**	(162)	(22)
Accounts payable	**72**	38	109
Accrued expenses and income taxes	**(44)**	51	148
Deferred income taxes	**85**	(103)	25
Other assets and liabilities	**4**	(114)	45
Net Cash Provided by Operating Activities	**1,752**	1,190	1,489
Cash Flows From Investing Activities:			
Proceeds from sales of time deposits and marketable securities	**1,733**	7,639	5,083
Purchases of time deposits and marketable securities	**(1,330)**	(8,679)	(4,413)
Additions to fixed assets	**(513)**	(555)	(468)
Other, net	**(54)**	(35)	(29)
Net Cash (Used in) Provided by Investing Activities	**(164)**	(1,630)	173
Cash Flows From Financing Activities:			
Short-term borrowings	**88**	(409)	269
Long-term debt	**(49)**	(23)	(3)
Issuances of common stock under stock plans	**145**	197	63
Purchases of treasury stock	**(562)**	(51)	(487)
Dividends paid	**(1,116)**	(722)	(641)
Net Cash Used in Financing Activities	**(1,494)**	(1,008)	(799)
Effect of Exchange Rates on Cash	**(8)**	(8)	2
Increase (Decrease) in Cash and Cash Equivalents	**86**	(1,456)	865
Cash and Cash Equivalents at Beginning of Year	**510**	1,966	1,101
Cash and Cash Equivalents at End of Year	**$ 596**	$ 510	$1,966

EXHIBIT 13P-3. *(Continued)*

Net Sales and Earnings

Worldwide sales increased 12% in 1990 to $10.3 billion compared to increases of 7% and 13% in 1989 and 1988, respectively. The 1990 consolidated sales growth resulted from volume increases of 6%, price increases of 4% and an increase of 2% due to favorable foreign currency translation. In 1989, the increase in sales was attributable to approximately 6% of volume growth and 3% of price increases, partially offset by a 2% decline due to unfavorable foreign currency translation. Domestic operations reported sales growth of 7% in 1989 versus 8% in 1988, while international operations reported sales growth of 8% and 24% in 1989 and 1988, respectively.

Note 4   Foreign Currency Translation

Cumulative translation adjustments which represent the effect of translating assets and liabilities of the company's non-U.S. entities, except those in highly inflationary economies, were:

(in millions of dollars)	1990	1989	1988
Balance, January 1	**$149**	$114	$116
Effect of balance sheet translations:			
Amount	**(81)**	33	(2)
Tax effect	**(7)**	2	—
Balance, December 31	**$ 61**	$149	$114

Losses resulting from foreign currency transactions and translation adjustments, primarily related to non-U.S. entities operating in highly inflationary economies, principally Brazil, of $74 million, $40 million and $34 million, net of applicable income taxes, are reflected in net earnings for 1990, 1989 and 1988, respectively.

Unallocated expenses consist principally of general administrative expenses and net interest income, and in 1989 include a portion of the charge for integrating operations. Other assets are principally cash and cash equivalents, time deposits and marketable securities. Inter-area sales by geographic area for each of the three years ended December 31, 1990, 1989 and 1988, respectively, were: United States—$741 million, $638 million and $558 million; Europe, Mid-East and Africa—$360 million, $302 million and $306 million; Other Western Hemisphere—$34 million, $30 million and $31 million; and Pacific—$3 million, $4 million and $8 million. These sales are usually billed at or above manufacturing costs.

Net assets relating to operations outside the United States amounted to approximately $1,186 million, $957 million and $1,563 million at December 31, 1990, 1989 and 1988, respectively.

Note 11   Financial Instruments

The company is party to certain financial instruments to reduce its exposure to fluctuations in interest rates and foreign currencies. These financial instruments include interest rate protection agreements on investments and foreign exchange contracts. The contract amounts of these instruments were:

December 31, (in millions of dollars)	1990	1989	1988
Interest rate protection agreements	**$900**	$850	$700
Foreign exchange contracts	**824**	876	337

At December 31, 1990, the company was party to interest rate protection agreements and foreign exchange contracts maturing from 1991 to 1993.

Geographic Areas (in millions of dollars)	Net Sales			Profit[b]			Year-End Assets		
	1990	1989	1988	**1990**	1989	1988	**1990**	1989	1988
United States	**$ 7,017**	$6,478	$6,013	**$1,747**	$1,259	$1,462	**$4,251**	$3,943	$3,484
Europe, Mid-East and Africa	**2,682**	2,127	1,992	**633**	228	372	**1,590**	1,272	1,172
Other Western Hemisphere	**906**	769	672	**198**	119	130	**382**	336	330
Pacific	**833**	789	784	**80**	40	71	**550**	496	505
Inter-area eliminations	**(1,138)**	(974)	(903)	**(48)**	(97)	(94)	**(482)**	(395)	(288)
Net sales, operating profit and assets	**$10,300**	$9,189	$8,558	**2,610**	1,549	1,941	**6,291**	5,652	5,203
Unallocated expenses and other assets				**(86)**	(272)	(52)	**2,924**	2,845	3,070
Earnings before income taxes and total assets				**$2,524**	$1,277	$1,889	**$9,215**	$8,497	$8,273

Source: Bristol-Myers, *1990 Annual Report.*

F. Discuss the insights that are provided by the geographic segment data of BMY regarding:

(i) Relative operating performance during 1988–1990.

(ii) Future growth prospects.

G. Discuss the factors other than actual operating performance (in local currencies) that may have affected the reported segment data.

12. [Analysis of foreign operations] Exhibit 13P-4 contains extracts from the *1991 Annual Report* of Commercial Intertech regarding its foreign operations.
The "foreign currency translation" footnote discusses a subsidiary in Switzerland.

A. What was the functional currency used to account for that subsidiary? Explain.

B. What economic events caused the $3,213,000 amount to appear in the company's financial statements?

C. Discuss whether the gain resulting from the liquidation of the subsidiary:

(i) Should be considered operating income.

(ii) Should be considered 1992 income.

EXHIBIT 13P-4. COMMERCIAL INTERTECH

Foreign Currency Translation

The cumulative effects of foreign currency translation gains and losses are reflected in the translation adjustment account of the balance sheet. Translation adjustments decreased shareholders' equity by $6,405,000 and $3,607,000 in 1991 and 1989, respectively, and increased equity in 1990 by $13,246,000. The translation adjustment account was further reduced by $3,213,000 in the current year due to the liquidation of an inactive subsidiary located in Switzerland. The liquidation, which was completed during the first quarter, increased income from continuing operations by $3,213,000 ($.31 per share after related taxes) as a result of recognizing deferred translation gains in income. The gain is recorded as nonoperating income in the income statement.

Foreign currency transaction gains and losses, as well as U.S. dollar translation gains and losses in Brazil, are reflected in income. For the three-year period reported herein, foreign currency losses have decreased income from continuing operations before income taxes as follows:

(in thousands)

1991—$1,790
1990—   95
1989— 2,154

Net assets of foreign subsidiaries at October 31, 1991 and 1990 were $94,709,000 and $100,146,000, respectively, of which net current assets were $47,320,000 and $56,795,000, also respectively.

In the following table, data in the column labeled "Europe" pertains to subsidiaries operating within the European Economic Community. Data for all remaining overseas subsidiaries is shown in the column marked "Other."

EXHIBIT 13P-4. *(Continued)*

GEOGRAPHIC AREA

(in thousands)

1991	United States	Europe	Other	Elimination	Consolidated
Sales to customers	$207,860	$174,967	$54,134		$436,961
Inter-area sales	20,602	2,888	533	$24,023	
Total sales	228,462	177,855	54,667	24,023	436,961
Operating income	15,796	18,868	3,628		38,292
Identifiable assets	178,857	99,982	42,805		321,644
1990					
Sales to customers	$219,522	$169,820	$63,733		$453,075
Inter-area sales	20,953	2,983	622	$24,558	0
Total sales	240,475	172,803	64,355	24,558	453,075
Operating income	25,748	23,199	8,336		57,283
Identifiable assets	190,570	112,209	41,493		344,272
1989					
Sales to customers	$230,664	$139,005	$65,106		$434,775
Inter-area sales	19,384	1,476	482	$21,342	0
Total sales	250,048	140,481	65,588	21,342	434,775
Operating income	16,831	19,191	11,873		47,895
Identifiable assets	185,185	82,507	36,292		303,984

Source: Commercial Intertech, *1991 Annual Report.*

D. Using the change in the cumulative translation adjustment, compute the composite effect of exchange rate changes on the company's foreign assets with nondollar functional currencies. [Hint: Don't forget about the Swiss subsidiary.]

E. Using the result of part D, estimate Commercial Intertech's cash balances in nondollar functional currencies.

F. Using the result of part D, estimate the effect of exchange rate changes on the company's inventories during fiscal 1991. Compare your result with the estimate derived from cash flow data and explain any discrepancy.

G. Do you agree with the statement that Commercial Intertech reduced its investment in its foreign subsidiaries? Why or why not?

H. The company's foreign sales declined from $233.5 million (fiscal 1991) to $229.1 million (fiscal 1992).

(i) Considering only exchange rates, does this result surprise you? Why or why not?

(ii) What additional information would be required to determine exchange rate effects on the trend of sales?

(iii) Briefly discuss the other factors that affect the sales trend.

13. [Interaction of inflation, inventory valuation, and foreign exchange effects; 1989 CFA adapted] The Emerald Company has a wholly owned subsidiary in Hibernia, whose currency is the hib. Emerald reports its financial results in U.S. dollars. The exchange rate between the dollar and the hib has been as follows:

December 31, 1987	$1 = 4 hib
December 31, 1988	$1 = 6 hib
1988 average	$1 = 5 hib

On December 31, 1987, the subsidiary acquired 100 units of inventory at a cost of 60 hib per unit. During 1988, 100 additional units were purchased at a cost of 75 hib per unit. On December 31, 1988, 100 units were sold at a price of 150 hib per unit.

A. Assume that the hib is the functional currency for the subsidiary. Calculate the cost of goods sold and closing inventory in U.S. dollars using *both* the first-in, first-out (FIFO) and the last-in, first-out (LIFO) inventory methods.

B. Assume that the U.S. dollar is the functional currency for the subsidiary. Calculate the cost of goods sold and closing inventory in U.S. dollars using *both* the FIFO and LIFO methods.

C. During periods of rising prices, the choice of inventory method and the choice of functional currency impact both reported income and inventory valuation. Briefly discuss how *both* choices impact reported income *and* inventory valuation during periods of rising prices.

14. Exhibit 13P-5 contains the reconciliation of the net income and shareholders' equity of Volvo based on Swedish accounting principles to net income and shareholders' equity based on U.S. GAAP for the years 1988–1991.

A. Suggest differences between U.S. and Swedish accounting principles that could have accounted for *three* of the reconciling items in equity. [Hint: Pay attention to the direction of the difference.]

B. While the adjustment for income taxes decreases equity in each year, the effect on net income varies. Explain why.

C. Compare the trend of net income reported by the firm using Swedish accounting principles with that reported by U.S. GAAP.

D. Which set of accounting principles provides more useful information? Explain why.

EXHIBIT 13P-5.

Application of U.S. GAAP would have the following approximate effect on Consolidated net income and Shareholders' equity of the Group:

Net Income (Loss)

	1991	1990
Net income (loss) in accordance with Swedish accounting principles	682	(1,020)
Items increasing (decreasing) reported net income:		
Shares and participations	(572)	—
Tooling costs	333	425
Income taxes	268	484
Business combinations	(85)	(50)
Foreign currency translation	(70)	(31)
Interest costs	54	84
Leasing	41	41
Other	165	44
Net increase in net income	134	997
Approximate net income (loss) in accordance with U.S. GAAP	816	(23)
Approximate net income (loss) per share in accordance with U.S. GAAP, SEK	10.90	(0.30)
Weighted average number of shares outstanding (in thousands)	75,184	77,605

Shareholders' Equity

	1991	1990
Shareholders' equity in accordance with Swedish accounting principles	33,864	35,291
Items increasing (decreasing) reported shareholders' equity:		
Shares and participations	112	—
Tooling costs	1,397	1,385
Income taxes	(5,156)	(5,450)
Business combinations	111	196
Interest costs	210	210
Leasing	(310)	(322)
Other	(734)	120
Net decrease in shareholders' equity	(4,370)	(3,861)
Approximate shareholders' equity in accordance with U.S. GAAP	29,494	31,430

Source: Volvo, 1991 annual report.

Generally Accepted Accounting Principles in the United States (U.S. GAAP)

The consolidated financial statements of AB Volvo and its subsidiaries have been prepared in accordance with accounting principles generally accepted in Sweden. These accounting principles differ in certain significant respects from accounting principles generally accepted in the United States (U.S. GAAP). Approximate net income in accordance with U.S. GAAP for 1989 amounted to 5,400 (4,953) compared with net income in accordance with Swedish accounting principles of

EXHIBIT 13P-5. *(Continued)*

5,128 (3,329). Estimated net income per share in accordance with U.S. GAAP amounted to 69.60 (63.80), while income per share in accordance with Swedish accounting principles was 45.20 (52.80). The difference in 1989 amounted to 24.40 and was due primarily to differences in accounting for income taxes.

Application of U.S. GAAP would have the following approximate effect on Consolidated net income and Shareholders' equity of the Group:

Net Income

	1989	1988
Net income in accordance with Swedish accounting principles	5,128	3,329
Items increasing (decreasing) reported income:		
Adjustments to untaxed reserves	(365)	2,311
Income taxes	(350)	(1,489)
Tooling costs	492	123
Equity method investments	96	326
Business combinations	512	105
Foreign currency translation	57	165
Leasing	(361)	—
Other	191	83
Net increase in net income	272	1,624
Approximate net income in accordance with U.S. GAAP	5,400	4,953
Approximate net income per share in accordance with U.S. GAAP	69.60	63.80
Weighted average number of shares outstanding (in thousands)	77,605	77,605

Shareholders' Equity

	1989	1988
Shareholders' equity in accordance with Swedish accounting principles	19,581	14,834
Items increasing (decreasing) reported shareholders' equity:		
Untaxed reserves	26,044	26,528
Income taxes	(15,304)	(15,128)
Tooling costs	1,990	1,500
Equity method investments	(49)	339
Business combinations	246	(266)
Leasing	(294)	66
Other	366	174
Net increase in shareholders' equity	12,999	13,213
Approximate shareholders' equity in accordance with U.S. GAAP	32,580	28,047

Source: Volvo, *1989 Annual Report.*

15. Exhibit 13P-6 provides a reconcilation from Australian GAAP to U.S. GAAP of net income and stockholders' equity for The News Corporation Limited and its subsidiaries, a South Australian corporation.

A. Briefly discuss the major differences between Australian and U.S. GAAP.

B. Compare the trends in net income reported by the firm using:

(i) Australian GAAP.

(ii) U.S. GAAP.

(iii) Your estimate of operating earnings.

EXHIBIT 13P-6

	Year Ended June 30,		
	1990	1991	1992
	(in millions of Australian dollars)		
As reported in the consolidated statements of operations	A$343	A$(393)	A$502
Items increasing (decreasing) reported income before extraordinary items:			
Amortization of publishing rights, titles and television licenses	(184)	(216)	(190)
Deferred taxes related to the amortization of publishing rights, titles and television licenses	—	—	(54)
Amortization of excess of cost over net assets acquired	12	12	12
Equity in earnings of associated companies	(53)	(38)	19
Interest on convertible notes	39	39	11
Gain on sale of revalued assets	76	139	41
Revaluation of non current assets	(98)	—	—
New business start up costs	134	—	—
Refinancing costs	—	152	(100)
Benefit from the utilization of tax loss carryforwards netted against income tax expense	(64)	(46)	(22)
Net increase (decrease) in reported income before extraordinary items	(138)	42	(283)
Approximate income (loss) before extraordinary items in accordance with accounting principles generally accepted in the United States	205	(351)	219
Approximate extraordinary items in accordance with accounting principles generally accepted in the United States	65	46	22
Approximate net income (loss) in accordance with accounting principles generally accepted in the United States	A$270	A$(305)	A$241

EXHIBIT 13P-6. *(Continued)*

	June 30,	
	1991	1992
	(in millions of Australian dollars)	
Stockholders' equity as reported in the consolidated balance sheets	A$9,707	A$11,699
Items increasing (decreasing) reported equity:		
Amortization of publishing rights, titles and television licenses	(674)	(869)
Amortization of excess of cost over net assets acquired	87	100
Revaluation of assets	(4,441)	(4,777)
Associated companies reserve	(1,050)	(1,079)
Reclassification of redeemable preference shares	(377)	(418)
Reclassification of minority interest in subsidiaries	(350)	(391)
Refinancing costs	152	68
Other	(102)	(101)
Net decrease in reported stockholders' equity	(6,755)	(7,467)
Approximate stockholders' equity in accordance with accounting principles generally accepted in the United States	A$2,952	A$ 4,232

Source: News Corporation Prospectus, October 1992.

14

CREDIT AND RISK ANALYSIS

INTRODUCTION

I. CREDIT ANALYSIS: OBJECTIVES, METHODOLOGY, AND USE

OBJECTIVES

ANALYSIS OF AND ADJUSTMENTS TO BOOK VALUE

Adjustments to Assets

Adjustments to Liabilities

CREDIT ANALYSIS OF DEERE

Adjustments to Deere's Assets

Cash, Cash Equivalents, and Marketable Securities

Credit Receivables

Sales of Receivables

Inventory

Intangible Assets and Deferred Charges

Property, Plant, and Equipment

Adjustments to Deere's Liabilities

Short-Term Borrowing, Payables, and Accruals

Income Taxes

Long-Term Borrowings

Pension and Other Postemployment Benefits

Off-Balance-Sheet Financing

Adjustments to Stockholders' Equity

Adjusted Book Value

Analysis of Deere's Capital Structure

Analysis of Cash Flow

Analysis of Cash Flow from Operations

Analysis of Investing Cash Flow

Analysis of Financing Cash Flow

Free Cash Flow

II. ACCOUNTING- AND FINANCE-BASED MEASURES OF RISK

OVERVIEW

Earnings Variability and Its Components

Operating and Financial Risk

Measures of Financial and Operating Leverage

Accounting Beta

THE PREDICTION OF BANKRUPTCY

Usefulness of Bankruptcy Prediction

Model Results

Bankruptcy Prediction and Cash Flows

Concluding Comments

THE PREDICTION OF DEBT RISK

The Prediction of Bond Ratings

Bond Rating Classifications

The Bond Ratings Process

Impact of Ratings

Usefulness of Bond Ratings Predictions

Choice of Explanatory Variables

Model Results

The Significance of Ratings—Another Look

Measurement of Financial Variables

THE PREDICTION OF EQUITY RISK

Importance and Usefulness of Beta (β_e)

Review of Theoretical and Empirical Findings

Theoretical Framework

Empirical Studies

Summary of Research

CONCLUDING COMMENTS

INTRODUCTION

This chapter and the next address debt and equity analysis and provide a bridge between financial statement and security analysis. These chapters are, in substance, both a review and synthesis of concepts and techniques discussed in prior chapters. The current chapter deals primarily with the analysis of credit and equity risk, whereas the next examines valuation of the firm and forecasting.

This chapter is divided into two parts. The first focuses on credit analysis through a detailed examination of issues pertaining to a company's credit and risk position. The analysis may be incomplete due to lack of information since our primary focus is on information contained in financial statements and how it may be used in conjunction with other modes of analysis, some of which are beyond the scope of this book. It is important for the reader to keep in mind that financial statements and their analysis are only a subset of overall security analysis. The concepts and techniques discussed in this chapter are illustrated with reference to Deere and Company.

Part II of the chapter introduces new material extending risk analysis by examining the use of accounting-based measures in the prediction of credit and equity risk.

I. CREDIT ANALYSIS: OBJECTIVES, METHODOLOGY, AND USE

OBJECTIVES

The primary objective of credit analysis is an evaluation of the firm's ability to service and repay its debt. Creditors use this information to evaluate the profitability and safety of their loans to the firm. Equity investors are concerned with the firm's credit risk since defaults and bankruptcy may cost them some or all of their investment. The first step in the analysis is to ascertain the scope of a firm's existing obligations and the assets available as protection for creditors. The amounts reported in the financial statements, which are based on historical costs, accrual accounting methods, and management discretion, must be adjusted to provide a better estimate of the firm's tangible net worth. The adjustment process serves two purposes. First, the adjusted figures are more relevant for analytic purposes and ratio analyses. Second, and perhaps more important, the adjustments involve a comprehensive examination of a firm's assets and liabilities, fostering an improved understanding of the firm's operations and its creditworthiness in particular.

The analysis of adjusted book value must be extended by recourse to an evaluation of the firm's capital structure, including the modifications to assets, liabilities, and equity developed in the first step. The analysis of capital structure provides insights into trends in the firm's liquidity and its borrowing needs. The final step in this process involves a comprehensive analysis of the firm's cash flows to evaluate its ability to meet its cash flow needs through operations, external borrowing, or equity financing. Finally, these analyses are augmented by recourse to various other measures of debt, equity, and bankruptcy risk of the firm.

ANALYSIS OF AND ADJUSTMENTS TO BOOK VALUE

Book value[1] is the reported net worth of the company. When the liquidating value of any preferred shares is subtracted, the residual is the book value of the common shares. While book value per common share is often displayed in corporate reports, it is frequently misunderstood. Except by coincidence, book value equals neither the market value of the firm nor the fair value of its net assets. It is primarily the accumulation of accounting entries and adjustments over the lifetime of the company and contains the following elements:

1. Original capital used to start the firm and any additional issuances less shares repurchased.
2. Retained earnings accumulated over the firm's life.
3. Accounting adjustments. Certain accounting standards result in entries and adjustments to the equity section without flowing through the income statement.

[1]In prior chapters we have used the term "stockholders' equity" to describe the net worth of a firm. Book value is widely used in practice to describe the net worth of the common shares and is frequently computed on a per share basis. Because of this usage, we will use the term "book value" throughout Chapters 14 and 15.

Examples include unrealized gains and losses resulting from changes in the market value of long-term marketable securities (Chapter 11) and foreign exchange rates (Chapter 13). In addition, adjustments relating to the minimum liability provision for pensions (Chapter 9) flow through the equity section.

Firms do not distinguish between original capital and subsequent additional investments. They often report a "treasury stock" account, accumulating the cost of shares repurchased, and may, from time to time, "retire" treasury shares, eliminating this account. Such retirement is legalistic in nature and has no analytic significance. The accounting adjustments must be evaluated with reference to their distinctive characteristics; the timing of their realization is uncertain and at management's discretion. For example, the cumulative foreign currency translation gain or loss account is eliminated and gains or losses are realized in the income statement (and thereby in the equity section) in the event of a sale of the foreign operation; the timing of the sale is discretionary.

Reported book value has several shortcomings because of the accounting choices available and the selective recognition inherent in GAAP. However, book value after adjustment provides a better basis for decision making than does stated book value, and it can be of considerable use to financial analysts. Adjustments to book value involve analyses of assets and liabilities, each of which is discussed in the following sections.

Adjustments to Assets

Given the objective of credit analysis, reported book values of assets should be adjusted to their current market value to approximate their value as collateral for creditors and protection available to equityholders. The current market value also facilitates an assessment of the earning power and cash generating potential of the assets. The assets also must be adjusted for the impact of accounting choices, for example, adjustment of last-in, first-out (LIFO) inventories to first-in, first-out (FIFO) (i.e., current cost) (see Chapter 5).

Certain gains and losses accrued or deferred by GAAP impact reported asset amounts and must be evaluated for their relevance to value. Examples include the reserve for bad debts, possible impairment of assets (see Chapter 6), impact of changes in exchange rates (Chapter 13), and the valuation reserve for deferred tax assets (Chapter 7).

Chapter 11 addressed the use of market value versus original cost for marketable securities. *In principle, market values should be used for all assets and liabilities that have a determinable market:* bank loans, mortgages, private placement debt, and so forth. Nonfinancial assets including real estate, timberland, and mineral properties should also be "marked to market." Over the next few years we expect financial reporting standards to increasingly require the disclosure or use of market value for such assets.

However, it is less useful to replace the original cost of a steel mill with its estimated current value. Valuation of an operating facility is far more subjective than is that of a company's home office building or warehouse. The latter have alternate uses whereas operating facilities may not. Even if precision of measurement is not a problem, it is not clear which measure of "current value" should be used (see Appendix 6–C, for discussion of this issue).

For other assets, notably such intangible assets as brand names, customer relationships, and technology, reliable valuation is virtually impossible. The value of the intangible can be derived only by valuing the firm and working backward (subtracting all tangible assets and liabilities). That exercise serves no useful purpose in this context.

Thus somewhere a line must be drawn between those assets and liabilities that are revalued and those that are not. This line is easier to draw in practice than in theory. The right decision depends on the purpose of the analysis and a judgment of the reliability of the "market value" data.

Adjustments to Liabilities

The market value adjustment and recognition of the effect of accounting choices are equally applicable to liabilities for the same reasons given earlier for assets. An important adjustment to liabilities involves the recognition of "off-balance-sheet" activities, including all the adjustments for off-balance-sheet debt discussed in Chapters 8 and 10, consolidation of unconsolidated affiliates deemed to be integral to the firm's operations (see Chapter 11), and replacement of the balance sheet accrual for pensions and other postemployment benefits with the actual status of the plan (see Chapter 9). The goal is to ascertain the total liability of the firm by recognizing obligations that do not meet the accounting definition of debt or whose recognition is not required under current GAAP. Note that some of these adjustments affect both assets and liabilities; for example, operating leases that the analyst concludes should be capitalized, will increase both assets and liabilities.

Finally, reported liability balances must be adjusted through the elimination or reclassification of certain balance sheet activities. Since the matching principle is pervasive, underlying many accounting standards, deferred revenues and income are not reflected in the equity section of the balance sheet. Rather, they are included in the liability section of the balance sheet until they can be recognized. These "liability balances" are not debt, as they will not require cash repayment (they will be satisfied through the delivery of goods or services). They may be thought of as indicators of a firm's future profitability. Examples of items that may be excluded from debt are the following:

Advances from Customers. Examples of activities not requiring additional outlays by the firm are the sale of syndication rights of books, movies, or videos when the cost of creating the product has already been incurred. Income from the sale of rights is recognized over the term of the contract. The deferred amount is unearned income, not debt.

Investment tax credits recognized under the deferral method are another example; they are purely unrecognized income, not debt.

Deferred Income Taxes. These outlays are estimates of future taxes that would be paid when the tax basis of income measurement "catches up" to the accounting basis. As discussed in Chapter 7, the balance in the deferred tax account may continually grow. In many cases, especially for those arising from depreciation, the net difference between accounting and book depreciation will not reverse in the near future. For this reason some analysts treat deferred taxes as part of equity. Others believe that approach to be incorrect. Deferred taxes result from the use of different accounting methods and estimates for financial reporting than for tax purposes. The deferred tax liability is an offset to the different amounts of income recognized for financial reporting and tax purposes. To the extent that income recognized in the financial statements may be overstated (for example, by using depreciation lives that are too long), retained earnings are overstated. To add the deferred tax liability to equity would increase the degree of overstatement. When the deferred tax asset or liability is significant, the analyst should examine its source and the likelihood of its reversal. Components that are likely to reverse should be included, but restated to present value.

Box 14-1 contains a listing of the most common balance sheet adjustments. Such adjustments generate measures of book value and debt that can be used for analytical purposes. The adjusted measures, and ratios derived from them, should be better indicators of shareholder wealth and risk than measures based on unadjusted data. The next section illustrates adjustment techniques by applying them to Deere.

BOX 14-1
Checklist of Balance Sheet Adjustments

Account Area of Analysis or Adjustment Required*	Adjustment Effects		
	Asset	Liability	Equity
Marketable securities			
Mark to market (11)	x		x
Accounts receivable			
Revenue recognition methods (2)	x		x
Analysis of bad debts (14)	x		x
Interest rate effects (14)	x		x
Sale of receivables (10)	x	x	x
Inventories			
Capitalization policy (5)	x		x
Addback of LIFO reserve (5)	x		x
Foreign currency effects (13)	x		x
Property, plant, and equipment			
Capitalization policy (6)	x		x
Capitalization of interest (6)	x		x
Foreign currency effects (13)	x		x
Effects of inflation (6)	x		x
Computer software (6)	x		x
Natural resource assets (6)	x		x
Depreciation methods and lives (6)	x		x
Impairment (6)	x		x

Long term investments			
Proportionate consolidation (11)	x	x	
Mark to market (11)	x		x
Intangible assets			
Treatment of goodwill (12)	x		x
Brand names (6)	x		x
Research and development (6)	x		x
Deferred charges			
Expense recognition policy (2)	x		x
Advances from customers			
Deferred revenue (8)		x	x
Long term debt			
Capitalization of leases (8)	x	x	x
Guarantees (10)	x	x	x
Take-or-pay contracts (10)	x	x	
Convertible debt (8)		x	x
Redeemable preferred stock (8)		x	x
Employee benefits			
Pension plans (9)	x	x	x
Health and life insurance (9)	x	x	x
Stock option plans (9)			x
Deferred income taxes			
Probability of reversal (7)	x	x	x
Valuation allowance (7)	x		x
Tax loss carryforwards (7)	x		x
Discount to present value (7)	x	x	x

*In many cases the adjustment may be either pretax or aftertax.
Note: The chapter where the issue is discussed is shown in parentheses after each item.

CREDIT ANALYSIS OF DEERE

Exhibit 14-1 contains the consolidated balance sheet for Deere at October 31, 1991, and applies a number of adjustments to derive a current cost "adjusted" balance sheet.[2]

Adjustments to Deere's Assets

Each asset account is evaluated for relevant adjustments ranging from recognition of market value to adjustments for the effects of accrual accounting and management choices.

Cash, Cash Equivalents, and Marketable Securities

Cash and cash equivalents (line 1) require no adjustment as they represent current cash balances (with foreign currency amounts translated at current exchange rates). Market-

[2]Exhibit 1B-2 contains the financial statements of Deere for the year ended October 31, 1991.

EXHIBIT 14-1. DEERE
Adjustment of Balance Sheet to Current Cost, October 31, 1991 (in $ millions)

	As Reported (Historical)	Adjusted (Current Cost)	Adjustments (See Text)
Assets			
1. Cash and cash equivalents	$ 278.5	$ 278.5	
2. Marketable securities	856.6	916.0	+59.4
3. Receivables, affiliates	17.8	17.8	
4. Receivables, dealers	2,966.6	2,966.6	
5. Credit receivables, net	4,745.6	4,877.6	+247.0, −115.0
6. Other receivables	108.9	108.9	
7. Equipment on lease	184.8	184.8	
8. Inventories	538.1	1,655.0	+1,116.9
9. Property and equipment, net	1,235.2	1,235.2	
10. Investment in affiliates	106.0	106.0	
11. Intangible assets	371.5	—	−371.5
12. Other assets	133.2	133.2	
13. Deferred income taxes	17.0	—	−17.0
14. Deferred charges	89.6	—	−89.6
15. Total assets	$11,649.4	$12,479.6	+830.2
Liabilities and Equity			
16. Short-term borrowings	3,471.1	3,718.1	+247.0
17. Payables, affiliates	5.5	5.5	
18. Accounts payable/accrued expenses	1,803.6	1,688.6	−115.0
19. Insurance reserves	491.1	491.1	
20. Accrued taxes	84.8	84.8	
21. Deferred income taxes	75.4	32.4	−88.0, +45.0
22. Long-term borrowings	2,206.3	2,241.3	+35.0
23. Pension and other liabilities	675.8	692.8	+17.0
24. Estimated SFAS 106 transition liability		1,450.0	+1,450.0
25. Total liabilities	$ 8,813.6	$10,404.6	+1,591.0
26. Common stock	838.7	838.7	
27. Retained earnings	2,119.0	2,119.0	
28. Minimum pension liability	(86.4)	—	+86.4
29. Cumulative translation adjustment	(16.4)	—	+16.4
30. Unamortized stock compensation	(6.5)	—	+6.5
31. Treasury stock	(12.6)	(12.6)	
32. Adjustment to assets and liabilities, net after deferred tax		(870.1)	−870.1
33. Stockholders' equity	$ 2,835.8	$ 2,075.0	−760.8
34. Book value per common share*	$ 37.20	$ 27.22	−$9.98

*Based on 76.231 million shares outstanding.

able securities (line 2) are carried at historical cost. Deere's "marketable securities" footnote tells us that the market value of these securities is $916 million. The market value is the more relevant measure, and replaces historical cost in the adjusted balance sheet.

Credit Receivables

The next four categories represent receivables from the sale of Deere products to dealers and final customers. Restating the historical cost of these amounts to current cost requires consideration of two issues: credit risk and interest rates.

In the Management Discussion and Analysis (MD&A) section, Deere provides data regarding its credit operations, augmenting the "credit receivables" footnote in the financial statements. These data, while highly summarized, provide some insight into the nature of these receivables.

Approximately 80% of the total credit receivables resulted from the sale of Deere products; only $924 million (net of unearned finance income) out of nearly $5 billion resulted from the sale of non-Deere products. It is also reasonable to assume that the total $2966 million due from dealers relates to Deere products. Since nearly 90% of Deere's credit receivables stem from the sale of its own products, its credit subsidiaries can be considered "captives"; that is, their primary operating relationships are with the parent firm.[3]

The underlying credit risk (the probability that receivables will not be collected on time, or at all) is thereby related to Deere's manufacturing businesses. The "credit receivables" footnote indicates that 60% of Deere's credit receivables are derived from its agricultural equipment business. *If, for example, farm income declines, not only will Deere not sell new tractors, but it may have difficulty collecting receivables.* Dealers, suffering from a low level of sales, may face financial distress. Farmers, who have borrowed funds from Deere's finance units to purchase tractors or other farm equipment from the firm, may be unable to continue to make payments if crops fail or if prices are low.

The relationship between Deere's manufacturing operations and its credit receivables can be seen from the "allowance for doubtful credit receivables" described in the receivables footnote. Amounts written off in fiscal 1991 were $58 million, nearly three times the amounts written off two years earlier. The increase in bad debts paralleled the poor 1991 results of operations. The provision for loss did not increase as much as Deere allowed the year-end balance to decline as a percentage of gross receivables (from 1.80% at October 31, 1990 to 1.68% at October 31, 1991). Although the discussion of credit operations in the MD&A indicates that delinquency rates have risen, Deere appears to assume that actual write-offs will not increase further.

In addition to the $81 million allowance for doubtful credit receivables, Deere notes that it has withheld $115 million from dealers as additional protection[4] against losses.

---

[3]A noncaptive or independent credit subsidiary does most or all of its lending to noncustomers of the manufacturing business. General Electric Financial Services is a prominent noncaptive; it does little business with the manufacturing operations of General Electric.

[4]Credit subsidiaries use such "holdback reserves" to discourage dealers from extending credit unwisely; if the customer doesn't pay, the dealer will lose as well.

The $115 million is now carried in Deere's accounts payable and accrued liabilities. As it is really a reserve against bad debts, it should be removed from liabilities, and Deere's allowance for doubtful receivables can be considered to be $196 million ($81 million + $115 million), or approximately 4% of net (after finance charges) receivables.[5]

Sales of Receivables

Deere has also sold receivables and, at October 31, 1991, the unpaid balance of such receivables was $247 million. The (partial) recourse obligation (shown in the "commitments and contingent liabilities" footnote) was $26 million. In Chapter 10, we noted that sales with recourse are really a form of secured borrowing against receivables. In Exhibit 14-1, $247 million has been added back to both receivables (line 5) and short-term borrowings (line 16).

The market value of Deere's credit receivables depends not only on credit risk but on current interest rates as well. Given the information available, any adjustment must be of the "ball park" variety. We use the book value for our analysis. However, as receivables account for two-thirds of total assets (too big to ignore), we will point out the considerations that must be evaluated when adjusting the credit receivables to market value.

With respect to interest rates, almost no data are available. Deere's credit affiliates appear to have mostly floating rate debt, but no information is provided regarding the rates charged by Deere. If the rates charged are fixed, profitability is affected by changes in the spread between the rate charged and the rate paid. More important, fixed rate receivables may have a market value that differs significantly from historic cost. In the case of floating rate receivables, the market value (absent credit risk) would be equal to historical cost, and the spreads will show little change.

Fiscal 1991 results for Deere's credit operations show that interest income grew faster than interest expense (9% versus 5%), suggesting that the average interest rate received fell more slowly than the rate paid. Either some portion of receivables are based on fixed rates or Deere was able to widen the spread between interest rates received and its cost of funds.

There is one additional issue to consider: whether Deere has matched the duration and interest rate characteristics of its credit assets and liabilities. If so, we can assume that changes in interest rates will affect the market values of receivables and debt identically, so that historical cost is "equally wrong" in both cases, with the errors netting out. We will return to this argument when we discuss Deere's long-term debt.

Given the decline in interest rates during fiscal 1991 and subsequently, the market value of receivables may, on the one hand, be higher than historical cost, reflecting fixed rates that are higher than current rates.[6] On the other hand, given economic conditions, a higher allowance for doubtful receivables may be indicated. These effects may cancel out, justifying the use of book value.[7]

---

[5]In addition, it has a reserve of $19 million for doubtful dealer receivables (about 0.6%).

[6]As of July 1992.

[7]An additional argument for no adjustment is the assumption that Deere's credit receivables and debt have similar interest rate characteristics.

When Statement of Financial Accounting Standards (SFAS) 107 becomes effective (see Chapter 11), Deere will be required to disclose the estimated market value of its credit receivables. These disclosures will facilitate the analysis carried out in this section.

Inventory

The adjustment for inventories (line 8) is straightforward. Deere uses LIFO accounting for 80% of its inventories (see footnote), and the "LIFO reserve" is $1117 million. In our current cost balance sheet, we simply replace the historic (LIFO) cost with the current cost amount shown in the footnote. This adjustment increases the net worth of the firm considerably.

The question arises as to whether the adjustment should be made on a pre- or posttax basis, as for tax purposes the LIFO cost is still relevant. If all LIFO inventories were liquidated, the company would be forced to pay increased taxes. (This issue is, of course, similar to the general treatment of deferred taxes.) While Deere did have a LIFO invasion in fiscal 1991, we cannot assume that its inventories will be completely liquidated without violating the going concern assumption. Thus complete tax recognition of the LIFO reserve is an unrealistic assumption, and we will not make any adjustment for taxes.[8]

Intangible Assets and Deferred Charges

The adjustment for intangible assets is also quite simple, total elimination. As stated in the "intangible assets" footnote, most of this asset is the result of pension accounting, which we will deal with separately. The remainder appears to be goodwill resulting from acquisitions. Since goodwill has no value separate from the business, we eliminate it from our current cost balance sheet.

Deferred charges reflect unrecognized expenses. For many firms they represent the deferral of financing fees, start-up expenses, or major maintenance expenditures. Where cash outlays have occurred but have yet to be recognized as expenses, they should not be considered assets for purposes of analysis and should be removed from the adjusted balance sheet.

Property, Plant, and Equipment

Fixed assets have been left unchanged, primarily because there is no information available to justify any adjustment. Deere's gross property (before accumulated depreciation, see "property and depreciation" footnote) of nearly $3.6 billion appears to consist mostly of manufacturing facilities.[9] With no indication of market values, no adjustment can be made.

The carrying amount of several other asset categories, including equipment on lease

---

[8]Recall that, even if we would make a partial adjustment, it would be more appropriate to do it on a present value basis. Thus the magnitude of the adjustment would be smaller, depending on the date of expected liquidation.

[9]As noted earlier, such facilities may not have a market value based on alternative use. An obsolete steel mill, for example, has no real value even though its replacement cost is substantial.

and investment in affiliates, has not been adjusted since no information is available on which to base any adjustment. It should be noted, however, that Deere has an investment in Re Capital (see "cash flow information" footnote), which is a publicly traded company, accounted for by Deere using the equity method. By obtaining the number of shares held, and Deere's cost, we would replace the carrying cost with the market value of the Re Capital shares.

The net effect of these adjustments to Deere's assets has been to increase them by $830 million from $11,649 million to $12,479 million. We now turn to the adjustments applicable to the firm's liabilities.

Adjustments to Deere's Liabilities

Short-Term Borrowings, Payables, and Accruals

Most of these accounts are unchanged. Short-term borrowings, payables, and accruals can be assumed to be at current interest rates; given their short-term nature, any present value adjustments would be insignificant. For short-term borrowings the only adjustment is the addition of $247 million, corresponding to the credit receivable adjustment discussed previously. For accounts payable and accruals, we need to remove the $115 million in dealer deposits. The adjustment of insurance reserves and unearned premiums, which might be material, is beyond the scope of this book.

Income Taxes

Deere adopted SFAS 96 in fiscal 1988 (see discussion of fiscal 1988 financial statements in Appendix 1–B). The adoption of SFAS 109 in fiscal 1992 had little impact. Deere's "income taxes" footnote does not quantify its unrecognized tax loss carryforward; small amounts of loss carryforwards have been recognized in each of the past three years. SFAS 109 may allow the firm to recognize larger amounts of loss carryforwards, and its more liberal attitude toward deferred tax assets will be important if Deere adopts SFAS 106 (other postemployment benefits) using the cumulative adjustment method.

However, Deere also indicates that $363 million of overseas earnings would be subject to both withholding tax ($33 million) and U.S. income tax if remitted; the "indefinitely reinvested" provisions of Accounting Principles Board (APB) 18 and SFAS 96 have been used to avoid any U.S. tax provision. Under SFAS 109, future foreign earnings will have to be reduced by deferred U.S. income tax.

Deere's footnote analyzes the components of the deferred tax liability of $75 million shown on the balance sheet. The $75 million liability can be reduced by $33 million, reflecting the net effect of two adjustments:

1. The elimination of the $88 million deferred tax liability related to the excess of tax depreciation over book depreciation. Given the trend of Deere's capital spending (see Exhibit 14-9), reversal appears unlikely.
2. The elimination of the $45 million deferred tax asset related to the minimum pension liability, as the minimum liability will be subsumed in the overall pension liability.

These adjustments reduce the deferred tax liability to $42 million. That amount could be further reduced by discounting to its present value. Given the insignificant magnitude of the liability and the uncertain timing of reversal, we have made no further adjustment.

On the asset side, however, we have eliminated the $17 million deferred tax asset. While Deere's footnotes provide no explanation regarding this item, it appears to be related to Deere's financial services segment. Lacking further information, we assume that this asset will not reverse in the foreseeable future.

Long-Term Borrowings

The adjustment of long-term debt (including the current portion of long-term debt) to market value was computed in Chapter 8 (see Exhibit 8-6). The adjustment was approximately $35 million. Deere's "long-term borrowings" footnote tells us that the long-term debt of the financial services segment is relatively short in duration, mostly due within five years. Thus most of the long-term debt adjustment relates to debt of the equipment operations.

As a result we do not need to deal with one of the major issues in the dispute over marking financial instruments to market, the linkage between financial assets and liabilities. By implicitly assuming that Deere's credit receivables and credit borrowings are "matched," we can leave both at historic cost.[10]

Pensions and Other Postemployment Benefits

To adjust for Deere's postemployment benefits, we draw on the analysis in Chapter 9. For Deere's pension plans (see Exhibit 14-2), replace the amount recognized on the balance sheet with the *unfunded projected benefit obligation*. To do so, add together U.S. and foreign plans, each of which has been segregated by plan status:

EXHIBIT 14-2. DEERE
Pension Plans, October 31, 1991 (in $ millions)

	Balance Sheet	PBO Funded Status
U.S. plans: Assets exceed ABO	$(225)	$(214)
ABO exceeds assets	(388)	(415)
Foreign: Assets exceed ABO	14	53
ABO exceeds assets	(187)	(227)
Net pension liability	$(786)*	$(803)

*Differs from the amount shown on line 23 in Exhibit 14-1 due to the allocation of pension obligations to other accounts.

[10]This assumption should not be made lightly. Financial institutions that do not match assets and liabilities, for example, by using short-term floating rate obligations to invest in long-term fixed rate securities, are assuming substantial risks. If interest rates rise (short and long), the consequences may be dire. For this reason, banks and thrift institutions provide substantial data in their annual reports regarding the maturities and rate characteristics of loans, investments, and financial liabilities.

Due to Deere's recognition of a minimum pension liability, most of the unfunded status has already been recorded as a liability. The net adjustment to the liability is only $17 million ($803 million − $786 million). The minimum liability adjustment is eliminated from the equity account and, in effect, is replaced with the recognition of the unfunded projected benefit obligation. However, the most significant effect of the pension adjustment on book value stems from the elimination of the pension intangible asset of approximately $250 million, which effectively reduces net worth by a corresponding amount.

Turning to other postemployment benefits, the footnote discloses that Deere estimates its transition obligation under SFAS 106 at $1.2–$1.7 billion. Taking the midpoint of that estimate results in an obligation of $1.45 billion, shown (line 24) as an additional liability. A careful reading of the footnote indicates that this adjustment is on an after-tax basis. To recognize the tax benefits associated with these future deductions, Deere must return to profitability.

Off-Balance-Sheet Financing

Deere's footnotes disclose several examples of off-balance-sheet financing:

Summary of Significant Accounting Policies. Deere has unconsolidated affiliates in Brazil, Mexico, and the United States. The investment in these affiliates is $106 million (line 10). Due to the lack of further information, no adjustment will be made. If data were available, we would consider pro rata consolidation, as illustrated in Chapter 11.

Credit Receivables. As already discussed, Deere has sold credit receivables with partial recourse. We have already made the appropriate adjustment by adding the unpaid balance of $247 million to both credit receivables and short-term borrowings.

Leases. Deere has operating leases with total future payments of $68 million. Given the small size and short duration, the present value would be insignificant to Deere's financial position. In other cases, procedures discussed in Chapter 8 should be used to compute the present value of operating leases, adding the result to both property and debt.

Commitments and Contingent Liabilities. We have already accounted for Deere's recourse obligation for receivables sold. There seem to be no other significant items for Deere. In other cases, adjustments need to be made for guarantees and similar obligations (see Chapter 10).

Stock Options. At October 31, 1991, Deere has outstanding employee stock options on 1,676,628 shares (2% of outstanding shares) at an average price of $45.57 per share. Under current GAAP option shares are not accounted for, except in their impact on earnings per share (Appendix 3–C). However, such options have value and do represent a form of employee compensation. Until new accounting standards are developed, analysts must develop their own valuations. Option valuation is beyond the scope of this book. In this case the amount would be immaterial.[11]

Adjustments to Stockholders' Equity

The stockholders' equity section of Deere is typical[12] and includes a treasury stock account. The retained earnings figure reflects a reinvestment of more than $2 billion of earnings over its lifetime. Deere has three other equity accounts. The cumulative translation account was discussed in Chapter 13; the pension liability was discussed in Chapter 9. The unamortized stock compensation account represents cost of such compensation that has not yet been charged against earnings.[13] For reasons discussed earlier in this chapter and in other related chapters, these three equity accounts have been eliminated from the balance sheet shown in Exhibit 14-1.

Adjusted Book Value

The difference between stockholders' equity at historical cost of $2.8 billion and at current cost of $2.1 billion is $760 million, a decrease of 27%. Similarly, current cost book value per share is equal to

$$\frac{\$2075 \text{ million}}{76.231 \text{ million shares}} = \$27.22 \text{ per share}$$

which is 27% below reported historical cost book value of $37.20 per share.

Adjusted book value is more useful than historical book value for purposes of analysis. It is not an end in itself but, rather, represents a better estimate of the net assets available to the firm. This is important for current and potential creditors interested in the firm's solvency (see next section) and for purposes of valuation (see Chapter 15). Additionally, it provides a measure on which an adequate return must be earned. The next section turns to the analysis of Deere's capital structure to further our understanding of its obligations, liquidity, short- and long-term borrowing needs, and credit risk.

Analysis of Deere's Capital Structure

Exhibit 14-3 compares Deere's capitalization at October 31, 1991, as reported with the amounts after our adjustment procedures.

The reported debt-to-equity ratio is incomplete and can be misleading if used for

---

[11]Even if we arbitrarily assign a value of one-third of the strike price to the stock option, Deere's outstanding options would represent a value of approximately $25 million ($1/3 \times \$45.57 \times 1,676,628$), about 1% of equity. When option shares are significant, the value of options granted should be considered an annual expense; a liability should be recognized for the accumulated value of options granted. Details of stock option plans can be found in footnotes and in proxy statements. Several widely used option valuation techniques are available.

[12]Notice that, in contrast to most firms, Deere does not separate "additional paid-in capital" from the par or other value of common stock. That distinction is almost never relevant to analysis.

[13]Employee stock ownership plans (ESOPs), which are often funded over a period of years, are another circumstance where this type of account is found.

EXHIBIT 14-3. DEERE
Capital Structure, October 31, 1991 (in $ millions, except ratios)

	As Reported		Adjusted	
	Amount	% of Total	Amount	% of Total
Short-term debt	$3471	41%	$ 3,718	46%
Long-term debt	2206	26	2,241	28
Total debt*	$5677	67	5,959	74
Stockholders' equity	2836	33	2,075	26
Total capital	$8513	100%	$ 8,034	100%
Total liabilities	$8813		$10,405	
Ratios				
Long-term debt to equity		0.78		1.08
Total debt to equity		2.00		2.87
Total liabilities to equity		3.11		5.01

*Operating liabilities, payables to affiliates, and postemployment liabilities are not included here since the focus is on obligations to external creditors. The total liabilities–to–equity ratio captures the effect of including all liabilities. Alternatively, leverage can be computed using debt to external creditors plus pension obligations in the numerator.

comparative analysis since it does not include the impact of off-balance-sheet financing techniques and is a product of management's reporting choices. The adjustments discussed in the preceding sections allow the development of a more comprehensive analysis of the firm's capital structure and ratios facilitating comparisons. The adjustment process yields a tangible net worth of $2.07 billion, a reduction of approximately 27% from the reported figure of $2.84 billion. Although this reduction is significant, it still leaves Deere with a substantial net worth. The effect of these adjustments on Deere's debt ratios, however, raises important questions.

Exhibit 14-3 shows that Deere's capital structure is extremely debt heavy, even prior to the adjustments in Exhibit 14-1. For example, recorded (total) debt to equity is 2.00; inclusion of trade liabilities increases this ratio to 3.11. The adjustment process (by reducing equity as well as including off-balance-sheet obligations such as for health benefits) increases these ratios significantly: debt to equity rises to 2.87 and total liabilities to equity to 5.01. In light of these ratios, Deere's credit status needs further exploration.

The first issue that needs to be examined is Deere's liquidity versus short-term borrowing needs. Deere does not classify its balance sheet according to current and noncurrent categories,[14] making it harder to distinguish short-term from long-term needs. However, certain insights are possible.

Over 50% of Deere's liabilities are short term in nature: short-term borrowings of $3.5 billion plus accounts payable of $1.8 billion. Dealer and credit receivables

---

[14]Financial companies (including banks and insurance companies as well as finance companies) do not provide classified balance sheets.

approximate $5 billion. Adding these receivables to the firm's cash and marketable securities yields a quick ratio of about 1.2. This level, by itself, does not raise any flags.

However, the key to Deere's ability to service its short-term debt is the collectibility of its receivables. As discussed earlier, there are questions as to the "riskiness" of these receivables. Deere's finance subsidiary is "captive"; most of the credit receivables as well as dealer receivables are tied to Deere's primary manufacturing lines. Significant problems in either of Deere's cyclical lines of business would create doubt about the collectibility of receivables.

In addition to the credit quality issue, there is also the question of the timing of these payments. The $5 billion figure for receivables assumes that dealer accounts and net receivables are collected within one year. A careful reading of the footnotes indicates that only $1.96 billion (including interest) is due within one year. On this basis, the quick ratio is 0.58.

Deere's receivable turnover ratios confirm the "slowness" of collections. Sales of Deere's Equipment Division were $5.8 billion in 1991, and average receivables of equipment operations were $6.4 billion at the end of the year. This results in a receivables turnover ratio of 0.90 and an average of 402 days outstanding. At the same time as sales declined from $6.8 billion (1990) to $5.8 billion (1991), receivables grew from $6.0 billion to $6.8 billion. Thus not only is the collection period long, the trend is unfavorable.

The slowness in collections requires Deere to not only maintain existing credit facilities but also expand them if current trends continue. Further complicating Deere's short-term credit needs is the fact that a substantial portion of its long-term debt is intermediate in nature, due within the next five years. While Deere's "short-term borrowings" footnote indicates ample bank credit lines currently, the company's expanding credit needs and poor 1991 operating results suggest some concern for the future. This concern increases when we analyze Deere's cash flow position for additional insights into the firm's ability to generate cash flows in the future to meet its needs.

Analysis of Cash Flow

The adjustments to book value indicated the current or market value of the resources of the firm that are available for operations and generation of cash flows. The credit analysis provided evidence of the firm's liquidity needs. We now turn to an analysis of cash flows to evaluate Deere's ability to meet these cash flow needs to service and repay debt and to generate cash flows for investment or return of capital to the equityholders.

The analysis is based on our discussion in Chapter 2, where we cover the use of cash flow analysis to develop insights into a firm's financial position and performance. It also uses analyses from other chapters where we discussed the cash flow implications of different reporting methods. We focus on the components of cash flows and trends in these components. Our primary objective is to determine a firm's ability to generate cash flows to meet operating needs and to evaluate the role of different sources of financing for current operations and growth.

Another goal of our analysis is to illustrate the extent to which cash flow classifications can be affected by reporting choices. This issue has been discussed numerous times throughout the book. Examples include:

EXHIBIT 14-4. DEERE
Condensed Statement of Cash Flows, for Years Ended October 31, 1989–1991
(in $ millions)

	1989	1990	1991
Operating activities	$ 419	$ 397	$ 613
Investing activities	(732)	(968)	(1379)
Deficit	$(313)	$(571)	$ (766)
Financing activities	252	552	861
Effect of exchange rate changes	(1)	1	(2)
Net change in cash	$ (62)	$ (18)	$ 93

Source: 1991 Annual Report (Exhibit 1B-2).

- Capitalization of fixed assets, such as the cost of finding natural resources or developing new products (Chapter 6)
- Exclusion of "off-balance-sheet" obligations from the firm's financial statements (Chapter 10)
- Accounting methods applied to affiliates (Chapter 11)
- Accounting method used for acquisitions (Chapter 12)
- Choice of functional currency for foreign operations (Chapter 13)

Adjustment for these effects is seldom easy. The most important step is to recognize that distortion is present. In many cases the analyst may judge that the degree of distortion is too small to warrant adjustment. In other cases (accounting for affiliates, for example), analytical techniques have been presented (proportionate consolidation) that permit approximate adjustment.

As discussed in Chapter 2, the classification of cash flows among operating, investing, and financing activities is the starting point for cash flow analysis. For Deere, these categories are easily obtained from the cash flow statement (Exhibit 14-4).

The cash flows shown are for Deere on a consolidated basis.[15] The net change in cash is essentially meaningless: a firm can sell assets or incur liabilities to improve its cash position at the end of an accounting period (often called "window dressing"). What is important is the trend in the components of cash flow and the relationship among them.

Analysis of Cash Flow from Operations

Cash Flow from Operations (CFO) reports the cash flows generated by the firm's operating activities. Deere reports a positive and increasing CFO over the last three years. Even in 1991, when income was its lowest in three years, CFO was highest. However, in our analysis we will show that our intuition with respect to the collectibility

---

[15]In Chapter 11 we compared consolidated cash flows with cash flows reported with Deere's financial services subsidiaries accounted for using the equity method.

of receivables is justified and that Deere's operations are a constant cash drain requiring ever-increasing debt to maintain them.

Deere's reported CFO includes interest and dividend income as well as interest expense, as required by SFAS 95. For many firms, this inclusion distorts the "core" business CFO; the reported amount is not a pure "operating" cash flow but is affected by the firm's investment policies and by its financing decisions. In Deere's case, because most interest income and expense are related to the company's finance subsidiaries (which are operating in nature), no adjustment for these items is necessary.

What is questionable, however is the classification of the credit receivables as "investments." These receivables are a major portion of Deere's consolidated assets. They originate from the sale of Deere products to customers and dealers. They should be viewed, therefore, as identical to accounts receivable, and changes should be included in the computation of operating cash flow. Complicating the analysis is the year-to-year differences in the sale of receivables (discussed in Chapter 10).

For fiscal 1991, the net increase in consolidated credit receivables was $907.4 million ($3537.3 million acquired, less $2623.9 million collected and $6.0 million proceeds from sales). Similarly, in 1990 and 1989, credit receivables increased by $560 million and $339 million, respectively. If we remove the "investment" in credit receivables from investing cash flow (ICF) and include it in operating cash flow, the effect is significant (see Exhibit 14-5).

This adjustment for the increase in credit receivables changes positive operating cash flows into negative flows for both 1990 and 1991, *and* it changes the trend: the increase reported in 1991 becomes an additional year of declining CFO. The "flat" performance in 1990 becomes a sharp decline. The analysis, however, is incomplete because the trend is also affected by Deere's policy of selling credit receivables and by collections of these receivables.

As we have noted, these sales are really borrowings. Therefore, the true operating cash flow occurs when the sold receivables are collected. According to Deere's "credit receivables" footnote (and as reported in the cash flow statement), the company sold only $6 million of credit receivables in 1991 as compared with $590 million in 1990. This policy change inflated 1990 cash flow as compared with 1991. To adjust for this change, we must use the net unpaid balances of credit receivables previously sold. These amounts are

October 31, 1991	$247 million
October 31, 1990	534 million
October 31, 1989	276 million (not shown in 1991 footnote)
October 31, 1988	23 million (shown in 1988 footnote)

Using these data, we can make a further adjustment to CFO in Exhibit 14-6.

The second adjustment changes the trend again: Deere's consolidated CFO improved in fiscal 1991 after adjusting for both the credit receivables acquired and the change in policy regarding sales. Thus, while CFO remained negative in 1991, it improved sharply from the 1990 level.

This argument can be taken a step farther. Since leases of equipment are another

EXHIBIT 14-5. DEERE
Cash Flow from Operations, for Years Ending October 31, 1989–1991 (in $ millions)

	1989	1990	1991
CFO as reported	$ 419	$ 397	$ 613
Less: Net increase in credit receivables	(339)	(560)	(907)
Equals: Adjusted CFO	$ 80	$(163)	$(294)

EXHIBIT 14-6. DEERE
Cash Flow from Operations for Years Ending October 31, 1989–1991 (in $ millions)

	1989	1990	1991
Adjusted CFO (from Exhibit 14-5)	$ 80	$(163)	$(294)
Less: Increase in unpaid balance	(253)	(258)	287
Equals: 2nd Adjusted CFO	$(173)	$(421)	$ (7)

form of providing financing, changes in the investment in operating leases should also be factored into the computation of cash flow from operations. While the impact is not large, the inclusion of leases results in a further reduction of adjusted CFO (see Exhibit 14-7).

In summary, when credit receivables are treated as operating cash flows, inclusion depresses reported CFO. In other words, the provision of financing to customers ties up working capital (from the perspective of the consolidated economic entity). Similarly, when receivables are "sold," current (operating) cash flows are increased at the expense of future cash flows. While Deere's fully adjusted CFO improved sharply in fiscal 1991, it remained negative. The analysis clearly shows that the need to provide credit to customers and dealers is a significant cash drain for Deere.

EXHIBIT 14-7. DEERE
Cash Flow from Operations for Years Ending October 31, 1989–1991 (in $ millions)

	1989	1990	1991
2nd adjusted CFO (Exhibit 14-6)	$(173)	$(421)	$ (7)
Less: Change in operating leases*	(64)	(47)	(22)
Equals: 3rd adjusted CFO	$(237)	$(468)	$(29)

*Cost of leases acquired less proceeds from sales.

EXHIBIT 14-8. DEERE
Investing Cash Flow, for Years Ended October 31, 1989–1991 (in $ millions)

	1989	1990	1991
Investing cash flow as reported	$(732)	$(968)	$(1379)
Increase in credit receivables	339	560	907
Increase in operating leases	64	47	22
Adjusted ICF	$(329)	$(361)	$ (450)

Analysis of Investing Cash Flow

Investing cash flow must be adjusted for the cash flows that have been "transferred" to CFO as shown in Exhibit 14-8. Note that there is no adjustment for the change in the unpaid balance of receivables sold; the sale and collection of these receivables are "off-balance-sheet" *financing* transactions and do not affect ICF.[16]

The remaining balance of ICF, however, consists of three different components that deserve separate analysis (see Exhibit 14-9). Marketable securities are investments that do not meet the "cash equivalent" test of SFAS 95. While for some firms such investments also serve as a form of liquidity, for Deere they probably represent investments made by Deere's insurance affiliates and are, therefore, unavailable to meet short-term liquidity needs.

Purchases of property and equipment represent the capital expenditures of Deere's equipment affiliates. The 1990 and 1991 amounts are well above the 1989 level and also exceed depreciation expense. Deere's MD&A states only that such expenditures "will be primarily for new product and operations improvement programs."[17] To allocate capital spending between "replacement" and "growth" more information is required.[18]

Deere's acquisition activity has been modest. Segregating these expenditures, which are presumably optional, will be useful when we reassemble Deere's cash flow data shortly.

[16]They do, however, affect financing cash flow (FCF), and we will adjust FCF accordingly.
[17]Chapter 1, Appendix 1–B.
[18]See discussion in Chapter 6.

EXHIBIT 14-9. DEERE
Components of Investing Cash Flow, for Years Ended October 31, 1989–1991
(in $ millions)

	1989	1990	1991
Net change in marketable securities	$ (60)	$ (74)	$ (64)
Purchases of property and equipment	(181)	(292)	(298)
Acquisitions of businesses	(87)	—	(87)
Total*	$(328)	$(366)	$(449)

*These totals differ from adjusted ICF (in Exhibit 14-8) due to insignificant "other" cash flows.

EXHIBIT 14-10. DEERE
Adjustment of Financing Cash Flows for Receivables Sold for Years Ended October 31, 1989–1991 (in $ millions)

	1989	1990	1991
Reported financing cash flow	$252	$552	$ 861
Change in unpaid balance (Exhibit 14-6)	253	258	(287)
Adjusted financing cash flow	$505	$810	$ 574

Analysis of Financing Cash Flow

To compute financing cash flow properly, the reported financing cash flows (FCFs) must be adjusted for the sale of receivables (see Exhibit 14-10). The change in the unpaid balance of credit receivables is a form of financing and should be added to net debt. Exhibit 14-11 combines the adjusted change in net debt with dividends paid to produce an adjusted measure of financing cash flow.

The two components of FCF should be treated separately. They represent different sources of financing. Additionally, dividends paid are, to some extent, discretionary and can be reduced or eliminated.

Exhibit 14-12 compares the operating, investing, and financing activities as reported by Deere with the adjusted figures at which we have derived. Notice the shifts in the overall components. Deere's operations as well as its investments are a "drain" on the firm's cash flow.

Free Cash Flow

The nature of Deere's financing requirements can be illustrated by examining Deere's free cash flows. Exhibit 14-13 takes all the components of cash flow and assembles them in a format that facilitates analysis.

EXHIBIT 14-11. DEERE
Components of Financing Cash Flow, for Years Ended October 31, 1989–1990 (in $ millions)

	1989	1990	1991
Net change in debt as reported	$332	$ 690	$1025
Change in unpaid balance	253	258	(287)
Adjusted change in debt	$585	$ 948	$ 738
Dividends paid	(86)	(140)	(152)
Total*	$499	$ 808	$ 586

*The total differs from the amount derived in the previous table because of insignificant "other" cash flows.

EXHIBIT 14-12
Comparison of Reported and Adjusted Cash Flow Components, 1989–1991

	1989	1990	1991	
Cash Flow from Operations				
Adjusted	$(237)	$(468)	$ (29)	(Exhibit 14-7)
Reported	419	397	613	
Investment cash flows				
Adjusted	(329)	(361)	(450)	(Exhibit 14-8)
Reported	(732)	(968)	(1379)	
Financing cash flows				
Adjusted	499	808	586	(Exhibit 14-11)
Reported	252	552	861	

Free cash flow can be defined as the cash flows from operating activities that are subject to management discretion. Management may choose to use those cash flows for

- Payments to owners (dividends or repurchase of shares)
- Expansion (acquisitions or investments)
- Risk reduction (debt repayment)

Under some circumstances a portion of these expenditures may be considered nondiscretionary. For example, some debt may have scheduled repayments. Deere's

EXHIBIT 14-13. DEERE
Cash Flow, for Years Ended October 31, 1989–1990 (in $ millions)

	1989	1990	1991
Operating cash flow*	$(237)	$(468)	$ (29)
Increase in marketable securities†	(60)	(74)	(64)
Capital expenditures†	(181)	(292)	(298)
Free cash flow	$(478)	$(834)	$(391)
Dividends paid‡	(86)	(140)	(151)
Acquisitions of businesses†	(87)	—	(87)
Cash requirements	$(651)	$(974)	$(629)
Net increase in debt‡	585	948	738
Miscellaneous cash flows§	5	8	(16)
Change in cash‖	$ (62)	$ (18)	$ 93

*Exhibit 14-7.
†Exhibit 14-9.
‡Exhibit 14-11.
§Aggregation of "other" cash flows and effect of exchange rate changes (all from Deere cash flow statements).
‖Deere cash flow statements.

"long-term borrowings" footnote indicates that $342 million ($122 million equipment + $220 million credit) of debt is due within one year.

Dividends on preferred shares may also, under some circumstances, be considered required payments. For example, failure to pay dividends may trigger default provisions or grant preferred shareholders voting rights. Some acquisitions or investments may be required under existing contracts or to maintain the company's competitive position.

No adjustment for these factors has been made in the case of Deere. It is important to remember, however, that free cash flow is not the result of a clearly defined calculation. The term itself is subject to a number of definitions. Bernstein[19] computes free cash flows after deducting dividends, whereas Copeland et al.[20] calculate free cash flows before deducting dividends but after deducting all capital expenditures, including those required for growth. The analyst must use judgment to compute a free cash flow figure that accords with the facts and circumstances of the firm under study as well as the purpose of the analysis.

In Exhibit 14-13, cash flow from operations, less the investment in marketable securities and capital expenditures, has been labeled *free cash flow*. The investment in marketable securities is considered a required operating outflow related to Deere's insurance business. Absent further information, we treat capital expenditures as required to maintain the existing business. Thus neither of these outflows can be considered discretionary and must be deducted from CFO to compute free cash flow.

Dividends and acquisitions have been treated in Exhibit 14-13 as discretionary payments. After subtracting them from free cash flow, we arrive at "cash requirements." This is as close to a "bottom line" as cash flow analysis provides. The next step is to see how Deere generated the required cash.

The answer is simple: Deere increased its borrowings. Using the adjusted change in debt, Deere increased its debt by a total of nearly $2.3 billion over the three-year period. This large increase in debt is the next focus of attention.

During the three years ended October 31, 1991, Deere's stockholders' equity rose by $380 million, mainly due to reinvested earnings. Exhibit 14-14 compares Deere's capitalization at October 31, 1991, with the corresponding amounts three years earlier:

No adjustment has been made for the off-balance-sheet obligations of the company; such adjustments for 1988 would complicate the analysis. Generally speaking, however, adjustments such as those in Exhibit 14-1 should be part of this analysis.

Exhibit 14-14 shows that Deere's capital structure has become increasingly debt heavy. Equity as a percentage of total capital has declined from 41% to 33% in three years; debt has increased by 58% while equity has risen by only 15%. The causes for the increase in debt have been already discussed.

Summing up, this analysis confirms Deere's continuing need for capital to finance its normal operations. Additionally, there is cause for concern regarding the credit risk inherent in the assets that ultimately provide protection for Deere's creditors.

---

[19]Leopold A. Bernstein, *Financial Statement Analysis,* 4th ed. (Homewood, Ill.: Richard D. Irwin, 1988) p. 443.

[20]T. Copeland, T. Koller, and J. Murrin, *Valuation: Measuring and Managing the Value of Companies* (New York: John Wiley and Sons, 1990).

EXHIBIT 14-14. DEERE
Comparison of Capital Structure, October 31, 1988, versus October 31, 1991
(in $ millions)

	1988		1991	
	Amount	% of Total	Amount	% of Total
Short-term debt	$2197	36%	$3471	41%
Long-term debt	1394	23	2206	26
Total debt	$3591	59%	$5677	67%
Stockholders' equity	2456	41	2836	33
Total capital	$6047	100%	$8513	100%

II. ACCOUNTING- AND FINANCE-BASED MEASURES OF RISK

OVERVIEW

An important objective of the ratios and analytic techniques discussed in Chapter 3 and in the earlier part of this chapter is an analysis of the risk inherent in a firm's operations. Although liquidity, solvency, and profitability analysis implicitly address the probability that a firm's cash will fall below some level, the ratios commonly used do not directly measure this uncertainty. A large body of research has been devoted to an examination of the utility of accounting-based measures in risk evaluation and prediction. The research can be classified into three broad categories of risk:

1. Risk of financial failure or bankruptcy
2. Debt risk as measured by a firm's bond ratings
3. Equity risk as measured (generally) by the firm's "beta" or systematic risk

The risk levels indicated by these categories lie along a continuum relative to the probability of the firm attaining a specific level of profit or return commensurate with risk.

The risk of bankruptcy is one level of risk—it is the risk that the firm will not be able to continue operations, as its financial condition may fall below some minimum level.

Bondholders face uncertain returns. The level of uncertainty is not (directly) related to the firm's expected return; rather, the level of uncertainty is related to a minimum level of return, that is, the risk that the firm's profits will not be large enough to avoid default on principal and interest payments.

The equity investor takes on more risk than an investor in government bonds or, for that matter, an investor in the debt securities of that same firm and expects a commensurately higher return. The equity investor's risk relates to the uncertainty of achieving the firm's expected return.

Research in these areas typically involves two phases. The first measures the association between the risk measure and a set of financial ratios. The second attempts to exploit this association to evaluate its contribution to the prediction of risk. A result of this research is often an equation of the form

$$Y = w_0 + w_1 X_1 + w_2 X_2 + \cdots + w_n X_n$$

which measures the relationship between the dependent variable Y (e.g., beta, bond rating, or bankruptcy) and the independent variable X_i's (financial ratios or, more generally speaking, accounting-based measures of risk). Discussions of this research are provided throughout the chapter.

Part II is divided into three sections corresponding to each of the risk categories. Each section will contain a brief discussion of the relevant financial risk measure(s) as well as the accounting-based measures of risk used to forecast the financial risk measure. Exhibits 14-15, 14-16, and 14-17 present summaries of the explanatory independent variables (financial risk measures) used in key studies in each of the three areas. Some of these measures and their classifications are familiar. The other, new indicators are primarily explicit measures of the firm's earnings variability. These measures and theoretical justification for their use in the prediction and evaluation of risk are presented below.

Earnings Variability and Its Components

The variance of a firm's earnings is a direct measure of the uncertainty (risk) of its earnings stream. It is surmised that a smooth earnings stream is deemed to be desirable by firms, their creditors, and the financial markets.

Box 14-2 presents a theoretical justification for and a suggested ratio incorporating the variance of a firm's cash flow from operations. This ratio is expressed in terms of CFO and is equal to

$$\frac{\text{Cash Balance} + \text{E(CFO)}}{\text{Standard Deviation of CFO}}$$

where E(CFO) equals expected CFO. The higher the ratio, the less likelihood there is of the firm's cash balance falling below a certain level. The intuitive result emanating from the ratio is that levels of CFO cannot be analyzed alone. Consideration must be given to the variance of the cash flows. Similar implications hold for other financial variables such as earnings. To the extent that accounting earnings mirror a firm's economic well-being, the variance in that measure would be expected to measure a firm's risk.

Variance is often measured in terms of

1. The actual level of earnings, or
2. Year-to-year change in earnings, or
3. Year-to-year percentage change in earnings.

EXHIBIT 14-15
Independent Variables used in Bankruptcy Prediction Models

	Ohlson (1980)	Altman et al. (1977)	Deakin (1972)	Altman (1968)
Activity			Four asset categories divided by sales: (1) Current assets (2) Quick assets (3) Working capital (4) Cash	Sales to total assets
Liquidity	Current ratio	Current ratio	Current ratio	
			Quick ratio	
			Cash ratio	
			Four asset categories divided by total assets: (1) Current assets (2) Quick assets (3) Working capital (4) Cash	
	Working capital to total assets			Working capital to total assets
Leverage and Solvency	Liabilities to assets	Equity (market) to capital	Debt to assets	Equity (market) to debt (book)
	Funds from operations to total liabilities	Times interest earned	Funds from operations to debt	
	Dummy variable indicating if net worth is negative			
Profitability	Return on assets	Return on assets	Return on assets	Return on assets
	Dummy variable indicating if net income was negative in last two years	Retained earnings to total assets		Retained earnings to total assets
Earnings Variability	Percentage change in net income	Standard error of return on assets		
Size	Total assets	Total assets		

EXHIBIT 14-16
Independent Variables used in Bond Ratings Prediction Models

	Belkaoui (1983)	Belkaoui (1980)	Kaplan and Urwitz (1979)	Pinches and Mingo (1973)	Pogue and Soldovsky (1969)	Horrigan (1966)	West (1966)
Activity and Liquidity	Current ratio	Current ratio				Working capital to sales	
						Sales to equity	
Leverage and Solvency	Long-term debt to capital	Long-term debt to capital	Long-term debt to assets	Total debt to assets	Debt to capital	Equity to debt	Debt to equity (market values)
	Short-term debt to capital	Short-term debt to capital	Long term debt to equity				
	Fixed charge coverage	Fixed charge coverage	Times interest earned	Times interest earned	Times interest earned		
	Cash flow to investment in fixed assets and inventory plus dividends		Cash flow to debt				
Profitability			Return on assets	Return on assets	Return on assets	Operating profit	
Earnings Variability			Accounting beta	Years of consecutive dividends	Coefficient of variation − ROA		Coefficient of variation − net income
			Coefficient of variation − net income				
Size	Total assets	Total assets	Total assets	Issue size	Total assets	Total assets	Bonds outstanding
	Total debt	Total debt	Issue size				
Subordination	0–1 dummy	0–1 dummy	0–1 dummy	0–1 dummy		0–1 dummy	
Market Based	Price to net book value	Price to net book value	Market beta				
Other			Coefficient of variation— total assets		Industry dummy variable		Period of solvency

EXHIBIT 14-17
Independent Variables used in Beta Prediction Models

		Predictive and Explanatory			Explanatory			
		Hochman (1983)	Rosenberg and McKibben (1973)	Beaver, Kettler, and Scholes (1970)	Mandelker and Rhee (1984)	Bildersee (1975)	Lev (1974)	Ball and Brown (1968)
Earnings Variability	Operating risk†	Accounting beta (operating income)	*		OLE	Accounting beta	Variable cost % (v)	Accounting beta
	Financial risk†	Debt to capital			FLE	Debt to equity Preferred equity to common equity		
	Total risk†			Standard deviation earnings/ price		Standard deviation earnings/price		
Growth		Dividend yield		Asset growth				
Dividends				Dividend payout				
Liquidity						Current ratio		

*See Exhibit 14-29. †Earnings variability can be measured as the sum of operating risk and financial risk.

There are a number of factors that contribute to the variability of a firm's earnings. These components are presented schematically in Figure 14-1.

Earnings variance is related primarily to the underlying uncertainty of demand for the firm's output, the *variance of its sales*. The extent to which the variability of sales impacts earning variability is dependent on the firm's *operating and financial leverage*. In addition, earnings variability is affected by uncertainty regarding the prices of outputs and inputs.

Using identical arguments made with respect to market returns, sales and earnings can be said to depend upon general economic conditions as well as firm-specific policies. Thus earnings variability has a systematic as well as an unsystematic component. The systematic component of earnings (as well as the systematic component of sales) is referred to as the *accounting beta*[21] ($B_{earnings}$ and B_{sales}), which can be defined as the relationship between the firm's operating results and general economic factors.

[21]In order to differentiate between accounting betas and market betas, throughout this chapter we will denote the former as "B" and the latter with the Greek symbol β.

BOX 14-2
A Probabilistic Measure of Liquidity

Emery and Cogger (1982) framed liquidity in the following theoretical framework. Letting L equal the liquid reserves (e.g., cash)* at the beginning of the period and C equal operating cash flow during the period, insolvency or lack of liquidity is defined as occurring when additional financing is required, that is, when

$$L + C < 0$$

The analytic question becomes one of determining the probability that the foregoing will occur. Assuming that C is normally distributed, the probability† can be found by looking at the normal distribution table for the standardized value

$$-\frac{L + u_C}{s_C}$$

where u_c and s_c are the mean and standard deviation of the operating cash flows. Since this measure is related to the probability of insolvency, Emery and Cogger suggest this as a useful and relevant liquidity ratio. It combines the stock of cash with the flows and the variance of those flows.

---

*The analysis need not be confined to defining L as cash, but it can be extended to include other liquid reserves (such as working capital, and accounts receivable) with appropriate definition of terms.

†This measure will be an upwardly biased measure as it ignores the probability of falling below zero before the period ends. However, as Emery and Cogger point out, in short intervals the bias will be small.

Many of the models utilize the components of variability, that is, operating and financial risk, instead of (or in addition to) overall earnings variability. These components are discussed in greater detail below.

Operating and Financial Risk

Operating (OLE) and financial (FLE) leverage indicate the extent to which a firm's income varies as a result of variations in sales. *Operating leverage* is the percentage of fixed operating costs, and *financial leverage* is the percentage of fixed financing costs in

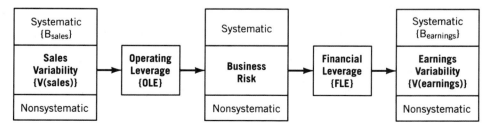

FIGURE 14-1 Relationship of Components of Earnings Variability

a firm's overall cost structure. The higher the percentage of fixed costs, the greater the variation in income as a result of variation in sales.[22]

It is important to distinguish between the concepts of operating leverage and *operating risk*. The existence of operating leverage does not, by itself, mean that earnings are unpredictable. If a firm's sales are predictable, then leverage does not create uncertainty. If, on the other hand, a firm's sales are uncertain, high leverage increases operating risk and the variance of income. Operating risk is, therefore, a function of operating leverage and sales variance:

$$\textbf{Operating risk} = f\{\textbf{OLE, variance (sales)}\}$$

Operating risk is also referred to as *business risk* as it represents the underlying risk of the firm's operations in the absence of financing. When financial leverage is also considered, the total risk of the firm can be expressed as

$$\textbf{Variance (income)} = \textbf{Total risk} = f\{\textbf{FLE, operating risk}\}$$
$$= f\{\textbf{FLE, OLE, variance (sales)}\}$$

There is a clear parallel between this expression and the formulation (given in Chapter 3) for the *total leverage effect* (TLE):

$$\textbf{\% Change in income} = \textbf{TLE} = \textbf{FLE} \times \textbf{OLE} \times \textbf{\% Change in sales}$$

Thus it would be incorrect to say, unequivocally, that two firms having differing levels of leverage differ in terms of risk. The difference would depend on the underlying uncertainty of their sales. Leverage and risk are directly associated only for two firms having the same level of uncertainty with respect to sales. The one with the higher leverage will be the riskier of the two.

Measures of Financial and Operating Leverage

As fixed and variable costs are generally not disclosed, the measurement of the degree of leverage often requires the use of surrogate measures. This is less of a problem for financial leverage where direct measures such as the ratio of interest expense to total expense or earnings before interest and taxes (EBIT) to earnings before taxes (EBT) are available from the financial statements. Nevertheless, some researchers use debt/equity, debt/assets, or debt/capital as surrogate measures of financial leverage, where the higher ratio implies greater financial leverage. The rationale behind the use of these surrogates seems to be reasonable, since higher debt would be expected to result in higher fixed interest charges.[23]

Measuring operating leverage is somewhat more difficult. Appendix 3–A shows how one can estimate a firm's fixed and variable costs using regression analysis. A

---

[22]These concepts were explained in greater detail in Chapter 3.

[23]It is, however, somewhat mystifying as to why some researchers resorted to the surrogate measures and did not use the direct measures of financial leverage.

common measure used to estimate operating leverage is the coefficient, v, derived from the regression equation,

$$TC_t = F + vS_t$$

where TC_t and S_t are the firm's total costs and sales, respectively, in period t and F and v are regression estimates of the firm's fixed and variable costs (the latter as a percentage of sales), respectively. The lower the coefficient v, the greater the operating leverage, as fixed costs are relatively higher.

Another surrogate for operating leverage is the ratio of fixed assets (property) to total assets. The rationale behind this measure is that fixed costs (e.g., depreciation) are associated with capital-intensive industries. Therefore, the higher capital intensity increases operating leverage.

An important question is whether the two measures of risk, financial and operating leverage, are independent of each other. Watts and Zimmerman (1986) take the position that the two should be highly (positively) correlated. They posit that capital-intensive industries (and firms) have higher operating leverage. To finance fixed assets (which determine capital intensity), therefore, more debt is required, increasing financial leverage.

> We expect firms' capital structures and operating leverage to be associated (Myers, 1977). Firms with more fixed assets are able to obtain lower-cost, longer term financing and hence will be more highly levered.[24]

Others argue (see Mandelker and Rhee, 1984) that, in general, the amount of total risk a firm should undertake is fixed, commensurate with its expected return. Therefore, if it increases operating risk, it should compensate by cutting back on financial leverage.[25]

> By changing from a labor-intensive manufacturing process to a capital-intensive one, a significant change would occur in the cost structure of a firm. A rise in fixed costs and a simultaneous decline in variable cost per unit increase the degree of operating leverage and thereby increase the relative riskiness of common stocks. However, the firm's decision on the operating leverage can be offset by its decision on its financial leverage. To save portfolio revision costs to the stockholders, the two types of leverage can be chosen so that changes in the level of beta are minimized.[26]

---

[24]Watts, Ross and Jerold L. Zimmerman, *Positive Accounting Theory* (Englewood Cliffs, New Jersey Prentice-Hall 1986) P. 120.

[25]In fact, as we note in Chapter 3, in the late 1980s a number of firms with high operating leverage proceeded to take on a great deal of debt. When the economy took a downturn, the combination of financial and operating leverage was too much for many of these firms. They were forced into default or major restructuring to survive.

[26]Gershon M. Mandelker and S. Ghon Rhee, "The Impact of the Degrees of Operating and Financial Leverage on Systematic Risk of Common Stock", *Journal of Financial and Quantitative Analysis* (March 1984), pp. 45–57.

This would argue for the two risk measures to be *negatively correlated*. Using regression estimates of both financial and operating leverage, Mandelker and Rhee report a significant negative correlation (approximately -0.3) between operating and financial leverage, indicating that firms tend to balance the two sources of risk. More interesting, perhaps, is their finding that the degree of trade-off between the two risk sources is not uniform across all firms. Rather, firms that tend to be riskier (as measured by their systematic beta (β) risk measure) "engage in trade-offs more actively than firms with low betas."[27]

Accounting Beta

Earlier it was noted that the variability in a firm's earnings can be broken down into two components: one due to (systematic) industry and economywide factors and another to (nonsystematic) firm-specific factors. The systematic factor reflects the degree to which the earnings of the firm vary with the earnings of other firms in the economy. Its empirical measure is the "accounting beta," $B_{earnings}$, the regression coefficient derived from the following equation,[28]

$$E_t = a + B_{earnings}\,ME_t$$

where E_t is the firm's earnings for period t and ME_t is an index of "the market's earnings for period t. When earnings are defined as operating income, then the corresponding $B_{earnings}$ measures the systematic component of operating or business risk.

Different indices can be used to measure market earnings. One may be the average earnings of the Standard & Poor's 500; others include earnings of another broad stock market index, corporate earnings calculated by the Labor Department, or an index created by the researcher (e.g., the average earnings of a random sample of firms). Since the purpose of the index is to provide a measure of general economic conditions, measures of GNP may also be used. The overall objective is to derive a $B_{earnings}$, that best measures the degree to which a firm's earnings (co)varies with general economic conditions. The higher the $B_{earnings}$, the greater the level of systematic risk.

$B_{earnings}$ will, of course, be affected by the variability of sales or more precisely the systematic portion of sales variability, B_{sales}. Thus, just as we have expressed a firm's earnings variability as a function of FLE, OLE, and variance (sales), we can also express its systematic component as a function of FLE, OLE, and the systematic portion of variance (sales).

$$B_{earnings} = f\{FLE,\ OLE,\ B_{sales}\}$$

We will return to these measures and their use in risk prediction during the discussions of bankruptcy, debt, and equity risk.

---

[27]Ibid., p. 55.

[28]For statistical purposes, this model is often expressed in terms of changes in earnings ($E_t - E_{t-1}$) and changes in the earnings index ($ME_t - ME_{t-1}$).

THE PREDICTION OF BANKRUPTCY

Usefulness of Bankruptcy Prediction

The ability to predict which firms will face insolvency in the near future would benefit both potential creditors and investors. When a firm files for bankruptcy, creditors often lose a portion of principal and interest payments due; common stock investors usually suffer substantial dilution of their equity interest or lose all their investment. In addition, bankruptcy imposes significant legal costs and risks on its investors and creditors as well as the firm, even if it survives.

For these reasons, there has been considerable research into the use of ratios and cash flow data to predict bankruptcy. Before reviewing this research, however, we must discuss the appropriate measurement criterion to use in assessing the efficacy of bankruptcy prediction models.

Using the total percentage of correct predictions to evaluate a predictive model is not a sufficient criterion. The evaluation of any predictive model is not complete unless the relative costs and benefits of being correct versus being incorrect are considered. As Exhibit 14-18 indicates, errors of misclassification can be of two types:

1. *Type I error* refers to misclassifying a firm by predicting nonbankruptcy when in reality the firm goes bankrupt.
2. *Type II error* refers to misclassifying a firm as bankrupt when in reality the firm is solvent.

The cost of the two types of error differs. This is especially true for a bankruptcy prediction model where the costs of incorrectly classifying a firm as solvent when in reality it will go bankrupt (Type I) are much larger (Altman et al., (1977), estimate Type I errors to be 35 times as costly as Type II errors) than if the firm is incorrectly classified as insolvent (Type II).

In the first case, the creditor will extend a loan and potentially lose 100% of the

EXHIBIT 14-18
Types of Misclassification Errors in Bankruptcy Prediction

	Actual Outcome	
Predicted Outcome	Bankrupt	Nonbankrupt
Bankrupt	Correct	Error: Type II Cost: Small 0% to 10%
Nonbankrupt	Error: Type I Cost: Large Up to 100%	Correct

investment. In the second case, a loan will not be extended, but the extent of the loss can be measured as the spread between the rate the (incorrectly) rejected firm would have paid and the rate actually earned. This could range from zero if an equivalent debtor were found, or, if no alternative debtor were found (worst case), it would be the spread between the foregone rate and the risk-free rate.

To put these arguments in perspective, consider a strategy of forecasting nonbankruptcy for every firm. Since on average, for established firms, the rate of bankruptcy is only 5%, such a prediction would have a 95% success rate. The problem with this strategy, obviously, is that it would misclassify every bankrupt firm, and it is precisely this type of costly error one would like to avoid. Taking the other extreme and predicting bankruptcy for every firm avoids the potential losses associated with lending to a bankrupt firm, but is tantamount to ceasing business as a creditor.

Thus, given the relative magnitudes of the cost of the two error types, one should be willing to make the following trade-off: lower the accuracy of correctly predicting solvent firms for better accuracy in the prediction of bankrupt firms.[29] (Figure 14-4, from Ohlson (1980), presented later illustrates this trade-off.) In evaluating (and designing) a bankruptcy prediction model, therefore, the percentage correctly classified should be delineated both in terms of the percentage correctly classified as bankrupt and the percentage correctly classified as nonbankrupt.

Model Results

The early studies of bankruptcy prediction date back to the late 1960s. Beaver (1966) examined patterns of 29 ratios in the five years preceding bankruptcy for a sample of failed firms and compared them with a control group of firms that did not fail. The purpose was to see which ratios could be used to forecast bankruptcy and how many years in advance such forecasts could be made.[30] Exhibit 14-19 presents the ratios used by Beaver, classified according to six categories. Figure 14-2 presents the pattern over time of the ratios that performed the best within each of the six categories.

The "cash flow"/total liabilities proved to be the best predictor overall.[31] Its performance is summarized as follows:

---

[29]It is interesting to note that bankruptcy models have also been used in other contexts where it can be argued that the relative costs of the different type of errors are radically different. Antitrust laws forbid mergers of certain companies unless one of the companies is deemed to be "failing." Blum (1974) reports a case where a bankruptcy prediction model was used. By the philosophy underlying the antitrust laws, it might be argued that allowing the merger when the firm is not bankrupt (predicting bankruptcy when the firm is solvent—Type II error) is more costly to society than stopping the merger even if the firm is failing (but the model incorrectly classified it as nonfailing—Type I error).

[30]The procedure involved ranking the ratios of the bankrupt and nonbankrupt firms and finding the optimal cutoff point that delineated between the two groups. This cutoff point was then tested against a holdout sample of companies.

[31]We place "cash flow" in quotations as, consistent with the definition used at that time, the measure actually reflects funds flows.

| Years Prior | Error Rate | | Overall |
to Bankruptcy	Type I	Type II	Correct Classification
1	22%	5%	87%
2	34	8	79
3	37	8	77
4	47	3	76
5	42	4	78

Source: Beaver, William, "Financial Ratios as Predictors of Failure", *Journal of Accounting Research* (Supplement 1966), Table 6, P. 90 (Adapted). Reprinted with permission.

Overall, in the first year prior to bankruptcy, this model had a 13% misclassification rate. The distribution of errors between Type I and Type II errors, however, was not

EXHIBIT 14-19
Ratios used in Beaver's Univariate Study

Group I (Cash flow ratios)
  1. Cash flow to sales
  2. Cash flow to total assets
  3. Cash flow to net worth
  4. Cash flow to total debt
Group II (Net income ratios)
  1. Net income to sales
  2. Net income to total assets
  3. Net income to net worth
  4. Net income to total debt
Group III (Debt–to–total assets ratios)
  1. Current liabilities to total assets
  2. Long-term liabilities to total assets
  3. Current plus long-term liabilities to total assets
  4. Current plus long-term debt plus preferred stock to total assets
Group IV (liquid assets–to–total assets ratios)
  1. Cash to total assets
  2. Quick assets to total assets
  3. Current assets to total assets
  4. Working capital to total assets

Group V (liquid assets–to–current debt ratios)
  1. Cash to current liabilities
  2. Quick assets to current liabilities
  3. Current ratio (current assets to current liabilities)
Group VI (Turnover ratios)
  1. Cash to sales
  2. Accounts receivable to sales
  3. Inventory to sales
  4. Quick assets to sales
  5. Current assets to sales
  6. Working capital to sales
  7. Net worth to sales
  8. Total assets to sales
  9. Cash interval (cash to fund expenditures for operations)
  10. Defensive interval (defensive assets to fund expenditures for operations)
  11. No-credit interval (defensive assets minus current liabilities to fund expenditures for operations)

The components of the ratios are defined in the following manner: cash flow—net income plus depreciation, depletion, and amortization; net worth—common stockholders' equity plus deferred income taxes; cash—cash plus marketable securities; quick assets—cash plus accounts receivable; working capital—current assets minus current liabilities; fund expenditures for operations—operating expenses minus depreciation, depletion, and amortization; and defensive assets—quick assets.
Source: Beaver, William, "Financial Ratios as Predictors of Failure", *Journal of Accounting Research* (Supplement 1966), Table 1, P. 78. Reprinted with permission.

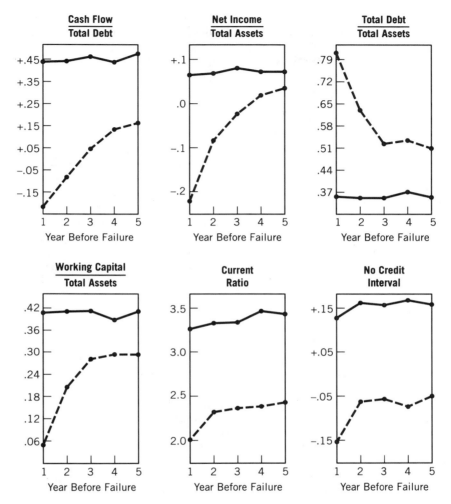

FIGURE 14-2 Ratio Patterns in Years Preceding Bankruptcy
Source: Beaver, William, "Financial Ratios as Predictors of Failure", *Journal of Accounting Research* (Supplement 1966), Figure 1, P. 82. Reprinted with permission.

uniform. There was a greater frequency of Type I errors relative to Type II errors as it was more difficult to classify bankrupt firms correctly. This difficulty increased dramatically with the prediction horizon. Given the greater costs associated with Type I errors, these results underscore the importance of presenting and evaluating each type of error separately.

Beaver's approach was "univariate" in that each ratio was evaluated in terms of how it alone could be used to predict bankruptcy without consideration of the other ratios. Most work in this area, however, is "multivariate," wherein predictive models based on a combination of ratios are used to forecast bankruptcy.

Exhibit 14-15 presents the variables used in four such studies. Note that (in terms of frequency of ratios used) liquidity and solvency ratios figure most prominently followed by profitability and activity ratios. The best known of these studies is Altman (1968), which yielded the "Z-score" model to predict bankruptcy. The Z-score was the value resulting from the following discriminant analysis equation:

$$Z = 1.2 \times \frac{\text{Working capital}}{\text{Total assets}}$$
$$+ 1.4 \times \frac{\text{Retained earnings}}{\text{Total assets}}$$
$$+ 3.3 \times \frac{\text{EBIT}}{\text{Total assets}}$$
$$+ .6 \times \frac{\text{Market value equity}}{\text{Book value of debt}}$$
$$+ 1.0 \times \frac{\text{Sales}}{\text{Total assets}}$$

If the Z-score for a firm was below (above) the critical value of 2.675, it signaled bankruptcy (solvency). Analysis of the misclassifications resulting from this critical value resulted in a more intuitively appealing dichotomy:

> it is concluded that all firms having a Z score of greater than 2.99 clearly fall into the "non-bankrupt" sector, while those firms having a Z below 1.81 are all bankrupt. The area between 1.81 and 2.99 will be defined as the "zone of ignorance" or "gray area" because of the susceptibility to error classification."[32]

Altman et al. (1977) refined and updated the original model replacing it with their ZETA™ model. However, as they sensed that there was money to be made in bankruptcy signaling, the parameters and design of the model were not disclosed and remain proprietary. The explanatory variables used were, however, disclosed. Although no theoretical bankruptcy model was envisioned in designing this model, Scott (1981) showed that the variables used by Altman's ZETA™ model are consistent with parameters relevant for a theoretical bankruptcy model. Details of this relationship are presented in Box 14-3.

Figure 14-3 presents the pattern of ZETA™ scores for bankrupt and nonbankrupt firms for the five years leading up to bankruptcy along with information as to the range of the bankrupt, nonbankrupt, and overlap zones.

---

[32]Edward I. Altman, "Financial Ratios, Discriminant Analysis and the Prediction of Corporate Bankruptcy", *Journal of Finance* (September 1968), pp. 589–609. Also see, Edward I. Altman, *Corporate Financial Distress and Bankruptcy,* John Wiley & Sons, Inc. 1993.

BOX 14-3
ZETA™ and a Theoretical Bankruptcy Model

Scott (1981) demonstrates a relationship between a theoretical model of bankruptcy and the variables used in Altman et al.'s ZETA™ prediction model. In Scott's model, debt (interest) payments (R) can be made from current earnings before interest and taxes (EBIT) or from the firm's equity. This equity is defined as the present value of the firm's future dividends and is symbolized by S. Thus bankruptcy* occurs when

$$R > \text{EBIT} + S$$

or, alternatively, bankruptcy is defined as

$$\text{EBIT} \leq R - S$$

Letting u_{EBIT} represent the expected (average) EBIT and s_{EBIT} the standard deviation of EBIT, the equation can be standardized, and (as in the Emery and Cogger model of Box 14-2) the probability of bankruptcy will be related to

$$\frac{\text{EBIT} - u_{\text{EBIT}}}{s_{\text{EBIT}}} \leq \frac{R - S - u_{\text{EBIT}}}{s_{\text{EBIT}}}$$

Dividing the numerator and denominator of the right-hand side of this equation by total assets (TA) and rearranging terms yields

$$\frac{\text{EBIT} - u_{\text{EBIT}}}{s_{\text{EBIT}}} \leq \frac{\left[\left(\dfrac{1}{u_{\text{EBIT}}/R} - 1 \right) \dfrac{u_{\text{EBIT}}}{TA} - \left(\dfrac{S}{TA} \right) \right]}{s_{\text{EBIT}}/TA}$$

Scott points out that although the functional form differs, all the ratios in the right-hand side are represented (exactly or in surrogate form) in ZETA™.

ZETA™ Variable	Bankruptcy Model Variable
Times interest earned	u_{EBIT}/R
ROA	u_{EBIT}/TA
Standard deviation of EBIT over TA	s_{EBIT}/TA
Common equity to total capital	S/TA

*To ease the already cumbersome notation we have dropped the tax term. With a corporate tax rate equal to t the model becomes

$$R \geq \text{EBIT} + \frac{S}{(1 - t)}$$

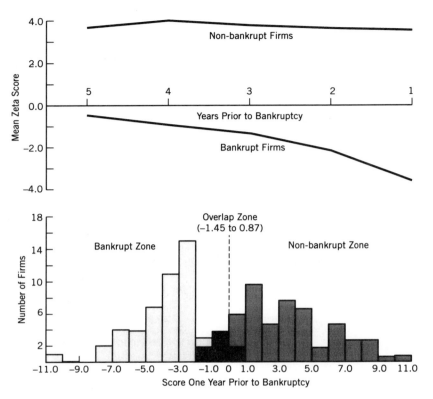

FIGURE 14-3 Zeta Scores in Years Preceding Bankruptcy
Source: Altman, Edward I., Robert G. Haldeman and P. Narayann, "ZETA™ Analysis: A New Model to Identify Bankruptcy Risk of Corporations", *Journal of Banking and Finance* (June 1977), Figures 1 & 2, P. 49

The classification errors for the two Altman models are as follows.

Years Prior to Bankruptcy	Original Z Model Classification Errors		ZETA™ Model Classification Errors	
	Bankrupt (Type I)	NonBankrupt (Type II)	Bankrupt (Type I)	NonBankrupt (Type II)
1	6%	3%	4%	10%
2	18%	6%	15%	7%
3	52%	NA	25%	9%
4	71%	NA	32%	10%
5	64%	NA	30%	18%

NA – Not available.
    Source: Altman, Edward I., Robert G. Haldeman and P. Narayanan, "ZETA™ Analysis: A New Model to Identify Bankruptcy Risk of Corporations", *Journal of Banking and Finance* (June 1977), Table 5, P. 41 (Adapted)

The predictive accuracy of each model is about equal in the year immediately preceding bankruptcy. Similar to Beaver, classifying bankrupt firms proved to be more difficult than classifying nonbankrupt ones. In addition the longer the time period preceding bankruptcy, the less accurate the results. Notwithstanding the foregoing, the ZETA™ model is a major improvement over the old as it is far more accurate in years 2–5 preceding bankruptcy. The original model produces Type I errors over 50% of the time, whereas the accuracy of the ZETA™ model is closer to 70%.

An interesting element of the ZETA™ model is its treatment of accounting data. The data are not taken at face value, but rather adjustments to the following elements (among others) are made:

Off-Balance-Sheet Debt: All noncancelable operating and capital leases are added to firm assets and liabilities. In addition, finance and other nonconsolidated subsidiaries are consolidated with the parent company.[33]

Intangible Assets: Capitalized items such as research and development, interest costs, goodwill and other intangibles are expensed.

These adjustments, while not comprehensive, are certainly a step in the right direction as the results seem to confirm. Dambolena and Khoury, however, downplay the importance of these adjustments.[34] They argue that Altman's results do not demonstrate that his adjustments caused improvement:

What would constitute a proof is running a Zeta model without lease capitalization and observe whether the predictive power of the model decreases significantly.[35]

Ohlson (1980) approached the problem from a different perspective. His used probit analysis, which does not specify a cutoff point delineating a firm as bankrupt or nonbankrupt. Rather, it assigns to each firm a *probability of bankruptcy*. The user of the model can then choose a comfort level in terms of how high a probability he or she is willing to tolerate. The higher (lower) the probability cutoff, the greater the chance of misclassifying a (non)bankrupt company. These trade-offs[36] are illustrated in Figure 14-4. At a cutoff probability of approximately 1%, no Type I error occurs, but the Type II errors equal 47%. At that low level, essentially all firms are classified as being bankrupt. Moving the cutoff probability upward increases the chances of making a Type I error (misclassifying a bankrupt company) but lowers the Type II error. At 3.8% the overall classification errors are minimized with 12% Type I errors and 17% Type II errors.

---

[33]Altman's work preceded SFAS 94 (1987) that required consolidation of all subsidiaries.

[34]Also see Elam (1975), who found that lease capitalization did not enhance a model's predictive ability.

[35]Ismael G. Dambolena and Sarkis J. Khoury, "Ratio Stability and Corporate Failure", *Journal of Finance* (September 1980), pp. 1017–1026.

[36]The reader who goes to the original source should note that Ohlson reverses the nomenclature and calls Type I errors Type II and vice versa.

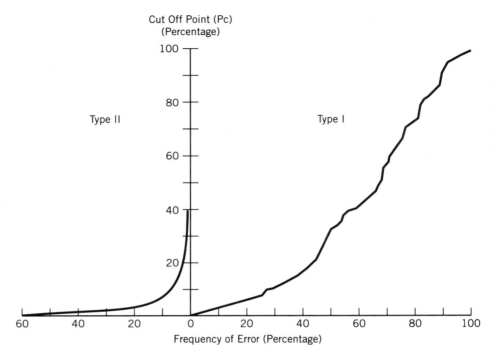

FIGURE 14-4 Trade-offs in Classification Errors in Bankruptcy Prediction
Source: Ohlson, James A., "Financial Ratios and the Probabilistic Prediction of Bankruptcy", *Journal of Accounting Research* (Spring 1980), Figure 5, P. 127. Reprinted with permission.

Bankruptcy Prediction and Cash Flows

Gentry, Newbold, and Whitford (1985) and Casey and Bartczak (1984, 1985) examined whether the use of cash (or funds) flow variables would improve the performance of bankruptcy prediction models. Both studies concluded that *overall* they did not.

Gentry, Newbold, and Whitford found that funds from operations and working capital changes (tested separately) did not aid bankruptcy prediction. Dividend flows were the most significant variable; capital expenditures and debt financing were among the variables which were not significant. As dividends are usually a function of cash available from operations after reinvestment (i.e., free cash flow), one measure may subsume the other.

Casey and Bartczak's study and conclusions serve to put the whole bankruptcy classification issue in sharp focus. A careful examination of their results indicates that an approximation of CFO (which was not reported during the period studied) clearly aids in the prediction of bankrupt companies. In the five years prior to bankruptcy, CFO correctly classified bankrupt firms from 83% to 92% of the time (depending on the time period). In contrast, accrual accounting measures correctly classified bankrupt companies only 30% to 83% of the time. On the other hand, CFO did not do as well as accrual measures in predicting non-bankrupt firms as it classified too many of them as bankrupt (47% incorrectly classified one year prior). Given the relative costs of these errors, however, it is the former type of error that must be avoided. The CFO measure, contrary to the authors' conclusions, does therefore seem to be useful for bankruptcy prediction.

Casey and Bartczak argued that the misclassification of nonbankrupt companies results from ignoring companies' ability to stay alive, in spite of lengthy periods of negative CFO, by renegotiating credit terms with creditors or selling assets to raise cash. We do not dispute this point. However, staying alive by selling assets or renegotiating ("restructuring") debt is not necessarily a sign of success.[37] Creditors and stockholders may suffer large losses even though bankruptcy has not occurred.

Moreover, we question the focus of these models on the event of bankruptcy alone. Bankruptcy is a legal, not an economic phenomenon. It is fraught with political and other nonmarket considerations. A better focus would be on whether the company is "healthy" or "sick," or on whether financial statement information and ratios allow users to forecast future investment performance. From that perspective, CFO is a good indicator of financial distress, raising the question of whether the firm's creditors will be repaid.

Concluding Comments

The evaluation of bankruptcy prediction models requires consideration of two related issues. First, the research may be directed at the wrong question: there are different degrees of and criteria for "failure." Indeed, many of the studies define the event of bankruptcy differently. Second, the variables used in the empirical models are not built on an underlying theoretical framework but, rather, rely on the researcher's intuition. Thus they may be sample or time specific. Notwithstanding the foregoing, Box 14-3 shows that, although the ZETA™ model was not designed in the context of a theoretical model, it includes variables used in such a model.

THE PREDICTION OF DEBT RISK

This section is limited to the evaluation of debt risk using predictions of bond ratings. The research discussed here is primarily applicable to publicly traded debt, although the results may be used to develop analyses of privately held debt.

The Prediction of Bond Ratings

Bond ratings are issued by bond rating agencies, the most prominent of which are Moody's and Standard & Poor's. The ratings attest to the creditworthiness of the firm: the probability that adverse conditions will result in financial difficulties is taken into consideration in assessing the likelihood of the firm defaulting on its interest or principal payments. In addition, the bond indentures and the degree of protection afforded in the event of bankruptcy are considered when the ratings decision is made.

---

[37]In that sense, Ohlson's probabilistic model is useful as the predictive variable is not the ultimate event of bankruptcy but rather a probability of going bankrupt. A higher probability can be used to assess how poorly the company is doing. Burgstahler, Jiambalvo, and Noreen (1989), in fact, used Ohlson's model to assess how changes in the probability of bankruptcy affected firms' equity value.

Bond Rating Classifications

The categories of ratings[38] used by Standard & Poor's along with a brief description of each are presented in Exhibit 14-20. A summary of these ratings along with their Moody's counterparts are presented here.

	Very High Quality	High Quality	Speculative	Very Poor
Standard & Poor's	AAA AA	A BBB	BB B	CCC D
Moody's	Aaa Aa	A Baa	Ba B	Caa C

[38]The ratings are further modified by "+" and "−" designations, permitting a finer gradation in the rating categories.

EXHIBIT 14-20
Standard & Poor's Corporate and Municipal Rating Definitions

STANDARD & POOR'S Corporate and Municipal Rating Definitions

DEBT

A Standard & Poor's corporate or municipal debt rating is a current assessment of the creditworthiness of an obligor with respect to a specific obligation. This assessment may take into consideration obligors such as guarantors, insurers, or lessees.

The debt rating is not a recommendation to purchase, sell or hold a security, inasmuch as it does not comment as to market price or suitability for a particular investor.

The ratings are based on current information furnished by the issuer or obtained by Standard & Poor's from other sources it considers reliable. Standard & Poor's does not perform any audit in connection with any rating and may, on occasion, rely on unaudited financial information. The ratings may be changed, suspended or withdrawn as a result of changes in, or unavailability of, such information, or based on other circumstances.

The ratings are based, in varying degrees, on the following considerations:

I. Likelihood of default-capacity and willingness of the obligor as to the timely payment of interest and repayment of principal in accordance with the terms of the obligation;

II. Nature of and provisions of the obligation;

III. Protection afforded by, and relative position of, the obligation in the event of bankruptcy, reorganization or other arrangement under the laws of bankruptcy and other laws affecting creditor's rights.

AAA Debt rated 'AAA' has the highest rating assigned by Standard & Poor's. Capacity to pay interest and repay principal is extremely strong.

AA Debt rated 'AA' has a very strong capacity to pay interest and repay principal and differs from the higher rated issues only in small degree.

A Debt rated 'A' has a strong capacity to pay interest and repay principal although it is somewhat more susceptible to the adverse effects of changes in circumstances and economic conditions than debt in higher rated categories.

BBB Debt rated 'BBB' is regarded as having an adequate capacity to pay interest and repay principal. Whereas it normally exhibits adequate protection parameters, adverse economic conditions or changing circumstances are more likely to lead to a weakened capacity to pay interest and repay principal for debt in this category than in higher rated categories.

BB, B, CCC, CC, C Debt rated 'BB', 'B', 'CCC', 'CC' and 'C' is regarded, on balance, as predominantly speculative with respect to capacity to pay interest and repay principal in accordance with the terms of the obligation. 'BB' indicates the lowest degree of speculation and 'C' the highest degree of speculation. While such debt will likely have some quality and protective characteristics, these are outweighed by large uncertainties or major risk exposures to adverse conditions.

BB Debt rated 'BB' has less near-term vulnerability to default than other speculative issues. However, it faces major ongoing uncertainties or exposure to adverse business, financial, or economic conditions which could lead to inadequate capacity to meet timely interest and principal payments. The 'BB' rating category is also used for debt subordinated to senior debt that is assigned an actual or implied 'BBB −' rating.

B Debt rated 'B' has a greater vulnerability to default but currently has the capacity to meet interest payments and principal repayments. Adverse business, financial, or economic conditions will likely impair capacity or willingness to pay interest and repay principal. The 'B' rating category is also used for debt subordinated to senior debt that is assigned an actual or implied 'BB' or 'BB −' rating.

CCC Debt rated 'CCC' has a currently identifiable vulnerability to default, and is dependent upon favorable business, financial, and economic conditions to meet timely payment of interest and repayment of principal. In the event of adverse business, financial, or economic conditions, it is not likely to have the capacity to pay interest and repay principal. The 'CCC' rating category is also used for debt subordinated to senior debt that is assigned an actual or implied 'B' or 'B−' rating.

CC The rating 'CC' is typically applied to debt subordinated to senior debt that is assigned an actual or implied 'CCC' rating.

C The rating 'C' is typically applied to debt subordinated to senior debt which is assigned an actual or implied 'CCC−' debt rating. The 'C' rating may be used to cover a situation where a bankruptcy petition has been filed, but debt service payments are continued.

CI The rating 'CI' is reserved for income bonds on which no interest is being paid.

D Debt rated 'D' is in payment default. The 'D' rating category is used when interest payments or principal payments are not made on the date due even if the applicable grace period has not expired, unless S&P believes that such payments will be made during such grace period. The 'D' rating also will be used upon the filing of a bankruptcy petition if debt service payments are jeopardized.

Plus (+) or Minus (−): The ratings from 'AA' to 'CCC' may be modified by the addition of a plus or minus sign to show relative standing within the major categories.

NR indicates that no public rating has been requested, that there is insufficient information on which to base a rating, or that S&P does not rate a particular type of obligation as a matter of policy.

Debt Obligations of issuers outside the United States and its territories are rated on the same basis as domestic corporate and municipal issues. The ratings measure the creditworthiness of the obligor but do not take into account currency exchange and related uncertainties.

Bond Investment Quality Standards: Under present commercial bank regulations issued by the Comptroller of the Currency, bonds rated in the top four categories ('AAA', 'AA', 'A', 'BBB', commonly known as "Investment Grade" ratings) are generally regarded as eligible for bank investment. In addition, the Legal Investment Laws of various states may impose certain rating or other standards for obligations eligible for investment by savings banks, trust companies, insurance companies and fiduciaries generally.

Source: Standard & Poor's *Bond Guide*, November 1992. Used by Permission of Standard & Poor's Corporation. All rights reserved.

The Bond Ratings Process

Ratings are sought by companies from agencies when they issue new debt. The company pays a fee and the agency issues a rating after the agency has examined the "creditworthiness" of the company. The agency will examine the company's operations and personnel, its financial statements, and its pro forma projections as well as other relevant financial and nonfinancial information.[39]

The actual ratings themselves, however, are shrouded in mystery. How each rating agency arrives at its rating and the criteria used are not disclosed. The rating agencies go to great lengths to discourage speculation that the rating process is mechanical and based on some mathematical formula. Rather, they stress that ratings are based on the judgment of their analysts who arrive at their rating after assimilating quantitative as well as qualitative data available to them.

When the ratings are announced by the agency, the firm, if it is unhappy with the rating, may decide to drop the debt offering and search for alternative financing sources, or alternatively, it may decide to appeal the rating. The appeal process may result in a series of negotiations[40] whereby the terms of the offering are changed. These changes may be with respect to the payment terms or the restrictive covenants attached to the offering.

Impact of Ratings

The ratings process exerts a significant influence on a firm's liability position in at least three ways:

1. As Exhibit 14-21 indicates, the higher the ratings, the lower the interest rate associated with the offering. Ratings, therefore, affect real ongoing costs to the issuing firm.

2. The covenants written into a bond agreement are often designed to obtain favorable ratings. As these covenants protect creditors by putting restrictions on the equity shareholders, ratings influence the sharing of risk and reward between equity- and debtholders.

3. Many institutional investors are restricted (legally or by internal policy) as to the type of debt they can hold; that is, the debt must have a minimum rating. Thus the success or failure of an offering (or whether the offering is even made) is often determined by the rating granted the debt issue.

Rating agencies argue that ratings do not cause differential borrowing costs. Rather, they state that ratings and differential borrowing costs reflect the same set of economic conditions indicating the relative risk position of the firm. This argument is not without merit. Others, however, contend that, as with any grading device originally designed to

---

[39]For a more detailed discussion of the rating process see Chapter 1 in Ahmed Belkaoui, *Industrial Bonds And The Rating Process,* (Quorum Books (1983), an imprint of Greenwood Publishing Group, Inc., Westport Connecticut, Reprinted with Permission).

[40]The underwriter will play a major role in these negotiations.

EXHIBIT 14-21
Relationship Between Ratings and Bond Yields

STANDARD & POOR'S CORPORATE & GOVERNMENT BOND YIELD INDEX—BY RATINGS

Weekly Averages 1992	†PUBLIC UTILITY			INDUSTRIAL						†COMPOSITE			U.S.GOVERNMENT			MUNI-CIPALS
	AA	A	BBB	AAA	AA	A	BBB	BB	B	AA	A	BBB	LONG TERM	INTER-MEDIATE	SHORT TERM	
October 28	8.52	8.98	8.97	8.22	8.40	8.84	9.17	9.99	11.41	8.46	8.91	9.07	7.47	6.00	4.13	6.45
October 21	8.54	8.99	8.98	8.25	8.43	8.86	9.18	9.88	11.32	8.48	8.93	9.08	7.48	5.99	4.16	6.47
October 14	8.45	8.95	8.93	8.12	8.30	8.73	9.08	9.84	11.20	8.37	8.84	9.01	7.29	5.74	3.86	6.31
October 7	8.42	8.97	8.93	8.08	8.26	8.70	9.10	10.12	11.03	8.34	8.83	9.02	7.26	5.68	3.73	6.29
Monthly Averages 1992-1991																
October	8.48	8.97	8.95	8.17	8.35	8.78	9.13	9.96	11.24	8.41	8.88	9.05	7.38	5.85	3.97	6.38
September	8.71	8.94	8.91	7.96	8.15	8.72	8.98	10.42	11.04	8.43	8.83	8.95	7.20	5.66	3.78	6.24
August	8.79	8.91	8.92	8.02	8.19	8.85	8.89	10.46	11.37	8.49	8.88	8.92	7.25	5.88	4.14	6.08
July	8.82	9.00	8.97	8.21	8.37	8.98	9.01	10.57	11.71	8.59	8.99	8.99	7.51	6.25	4.37	6.12
June	8.91	9.09	9.11	8.45	8.63	9.18	9.20	10.69	11.58	8.77	9.14	9.15	7.83	6.85	5.08	6.50
May	8.93	9.12	9.15	8.50	8.68	9.22	9.25	10.81	11.67	8.81	9.17	9.20	7.87	7.03	5.23	6.57
April	8.97	9.16	9.23	8.57	8.75	9.28	9.42	10.84	11.69	8.86	9.21	9.33	7.96	7.22	5.52	6.64
March	8.95	9.15	9.24	8.57	8.74	9.29	9.47	10.86	11.71	8.85	9.22	9.35	7.99	7.31	5.85	6.69
February	8.89	9.06	9.13	8.32	8.61	9.12	9.44	10.93	11.86	8.75	9.09	9.28	7.85	6.98	5.45	6.67
January	8.79	8.97	8.98	8.13	8.38	8.90	9.25	11.22	12.09	8.59	8.94	9.12	7.57	6.63	5.23	6.41
December	8.84	9.02	9.07	8.24	8.49	9.07	9.34	11.50	12.91	8.67	9.04	9.20	7.62	6.58	5.27	6.63
November	8.99	9.14	9.25	8.42	8.74	9.27	9.56	11.44	14.68	8.86	9.20	9.41	7.92	7.05	5.79	6.64
October	8.99	9.12	9.22	8.41	8.73	9.24	9.55	11.59	14.99	8.86	9.18	9.39	7.94	7.17	5.98	6.59
Annual Ranges																
1992 High	9.02	9.24	9.32	8.69	8.86	9.38	9.50	11.52	12.53	8.94	9.31	9.39	8.07	7.45	6.03	6.71
Low	8.40	8.88	8.89	7.89	8.08	8.60	8.82	9.84	10.94	8.28	8.78	8.86	7.07	5.53	3.65	5.88
1991 High	9.54	9.75	9.99	9.14	9.55	9.89	11.83	12.58	20.53	9.54	9.80	10.86	8.70	8.13	7.20	7.15
Low	8.77	8.93	8.93	8.05	8.25	8.87	9.13	10.80	12.87	8.51	8.90	9.03	7.36	6.32	5.03	6.50
1990 High	10.17	10.36	10.60	9.76	10.13	10.50	11.48	14.12	19.85	10.15	10.43	10.98	9.32	9.13	8.99	7.56
Low	9.09	9.39	9.68	8.78	9.06	9.55	10.06	11.94	13.80	9.07	9.47	9.87	8.22	7.75	7.22	6.99
1989 High	10.14	10.47	10.56	9.92	10.29	10.70	11.06	12.30	13.95	10.21	10.59	10.81	9.50	9.68	9.97	7.68
Low	8.98	9.28	9.55	8.62	8.91	9.45	9.90	11.20	11.93	8.95	9.36	9.69	7.97	7.71	7.61	6.87
1988 High	10.38	10.65	10.97	9.95	10.33	10.85	11.22	11.35	12.51	10.35	10.66	10.98	9.60	9.24	9.15	8.10
Low	9.27	9.52	9.93	9.05	9.41	9.89	10.44	10.96	11.89	9.34	9.71	10.24	8.44	7.99	7.15	7.41
1987 High	10.96	11.27	11.78	10.74	11.09	11.48	12.06	——	——	11.03	11.37	11.92	10.30	9.89	8.90	9.31
Low	8.59	8.89	9.13	8.37	8.89	8.83	9.52	——	——	8.76	8.88	9.36	7.57	6.90	6.26	6.53
1986 High	10.24	10.69	11.06	9.80	10.41	10.58	11.26	——	——	10.32	10.58	11.15	9.51	9.15	8.44	8.21
Low	8.76	9.05	9.36	8.50	9.18	8.99	9.81	——	——	8.98	9.19	9.61	7.23	6.98	6.27	6.73
1985 High	12.54	12.87	13.24	12.00	12.43	12.50	13.19	——	——	12.48	12.62	13.14	11.84	11.89	10.82	9.93
Low	10.01	10.49	10.93	9.50	10.13	10.20	11.13	——	——	10.07	10.34	11.03	9.24	8.86	8.11	8.41
1984 High	14.45	14.78	15.60	13.66	14.13	14.42	15.12	——	——	14.23	14.54	15.32	13.89	13.79	13.22	11.14
Low	11.94	12.31	12.80	11.40	11.73	12.06	12.78	——	——	11.84	12.18	12.79	11.25	11.30	10.19	9.48
1983 High	13.05	13.14	13.74	12.38	12.62	12.94	13.67	——	——	12.83	13.04	13.63	11.99	12.03	11.26	10.01
Low	10.85	11.10	11.49	10.51	10.72	11.07	11.68	——	——	10.78	11.06	11.58	10.18	9.83	9.21	8.72
1982 High	16.13	16.39	17.14	14.76	15.13	15.57	17.03	——	——	15.63	15.91	17.08	14.32	14.56	14.57	13.34
Low	11.39	11.78	12.68	10.55	10.96	11.75	13.28	——	——	11.18	11.80	13.17	10.18	9.91	9.57	9.16

†'AAA' Public Utility & Composite bond yields discontinued January, 1984.

Source: Standard & Poor's *Bond Guide*, November 1992. Used by Permission of Standard & Poor's Corporation.

measure some attribute, there is often a tendency for the emphasis to shift to the measuring device itself rather than the underlying attribute.[41]

Thus there exists evidence that the ratings themselves can influence bond yields beyond that which may be warranted by the firm's economic position. This may be especially true for adjacent ratings such as, for example, AAA versus AA or Baa versus Ba. This argument is bolstered by point 3, which indicates that certain investment policies are based on the ratings themselves. To the extent that these factors affect the demand for a debt issue, clearly the yield required for its successful sale will be influenced.

Notwithstanding the agencies' claims that ratings are not in any sense mechanically or mathematically derived, researchers have constructed mathematical models to predict bond ratings. The explanatory independent variables, the methodology, and the success rates of some of these studies will be discussed next.

[41] Accounting earnings is, obviously, another example of this phenomenon. A great deal of positive accounting theory is built around this notion. Consistent with the behavior predicted by positive accounting theory as to the existence of incentives to influence accounting numbers (artificially), there is also evidence that firms attempt to cultivate debt ratings agencies to obtain favorable ratings.

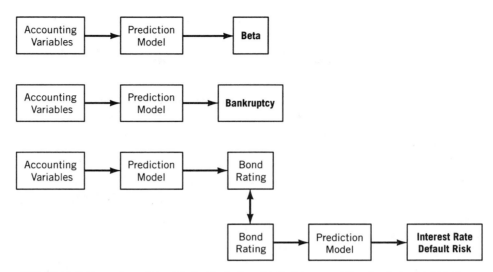

FIGURE 14-5 Comparison of Bond Rating Prediction with Bankruptcy and Beta Prediction (Bold Indicates Variable of Interest)

Usefulness of Bond Ratings Prediction

Figure 14-5 is a schematic representation of the predictive process used in the forecast of bond ratings in contrast to that used in forecasting beta or bankruptcy. The linkages in those models are directly between the accounting variables and the predicted attribute of interest. For bonds, the attribute of interest is the default potential and the required bond yield. The model does not, however, forecast these attributes. Rather, it forecasts another predictor of these attributes.

This raises the following question. If the goal of the mathematical model is simply to duplicate the rating agencies' classification, why bother? Just use the ratings issued by the agency.[42] The responses to this question follow:

1. Some debt offerings (e.g., private placements) are not rated. A mathematical model would, therefore, be useful as a surrogate for the ratings process in determining the appropriate yield and indentures the placement should carry. We have previously suggested using predicted ratings to estimate the appropriate market rate at which to discount debt.

2. Ratings are not continuously revised, and there is evidence of a considerable lag between the time conditions change and when ratings agencies respond by revising ratings. Furthermore, there is conflicting evidence as to the extent to

---

[42]Predicting bond ratings differs from the next section's discussion of the prediction of beta. The object there is to *improve* on the predictions of beta readily available. Further, with respect to the prediction of bankruptcy in the previous section, the object is to forecast the event itself, not duplicate someone else's prediction.

which the market anticipates a rating change. These factors lead to the following interrelated benefits of a bond ratings model:

a. The model can be used to monitor the debt after the original rating is made. This provides a more accurate prediction of the debt's current risk/return characteristics and whether it is over/undervalued.

b. Given that the market may not fully anticipate a ratings change, the model can be used to forecast a ratings change.

3. Firms sometimes undertake large investment or acquisition programs. These programs usually entail changes in the firm's financial (and operating) structure as new debt is required to finance these programs. To the extent that these changes mirror underlying changes in the characteristics of the firm's new and existing debt, the firm's cost of debt capital may change. A ratings model may help the firm (or its investment banker) anticipate these changes in the planning stages of the program.

4. The independent or explanatory variables in a predictive model can shed insight into the important factors that determine the (perceived) riskiness of debt. A firm seeking a favorable rating can take action ahead of time to improve those areas in which it is deficient. This is not to suggest that the firm engage in "window dressing" to spruce up a certain ratio, but rather that it remedy the underlying economic factors that drive the ratio.[43]

5. Finally, as will be discussed in this section, there exists some evidence that ratings at the lower end of the spectrum, especially for subordinated debt, may be inconsistent and "rigid." This evidence may provide some investment opportunities.

Choice of Explanatory Variables

The relationship between financial performance as measured by accounting ratios and bond rating classification is demonstrated in Exhibit 14-22. With few exceptions, the better performers have better ratings. It must, however, be noted that the data in this table are based on a large sample. As will be discussed in further detail shortly,[44] these relationships may not necessarily hold for firms on an individual or small-group basis.

Exhibit 14-16 compares models used to predict bond ratings and the variables in these models.[45] Similar to bankruptcy models, formal theoretical models do not exist.

---

[43]This point is reinforced by recalling that ratios in such models are often used as a surrogate for an overall category or factor (see Chapter 3). Thus the ratio may be masking the actual relationship contributing to the riskiness of the debt.

[44]See the discussion relating to the Ang and Patel paper (1975).

[45]Generally, the variables used are arrived at by first selecting a set of ratios/variables from the ratio classifications described in Chapter 3. The original set is then scaled down, using techniques such as factor analysis, to a subset of ratios capturing the information contained in the full set. The final set of variables then chosen is the subset that provides the best fit in the model's classification (whether regression, discriminant or probit) equation. These best fit results are explanatory in nature as they are based on the same sample companies which were used to develop the models. The model is then tested on a holdout sample to test its predictive ability.

EXHIBIT 14-22
Relationship Between Ratings and Financial Ratios

KEY INDUSTRIAL FINANCIAL RATIOS Three-year (1988–1990) medians	AAA	AA	A	BBB	BB	B	CCC
Pretax interest coverage (x)	11.08	9.43	4.65	3.16	1.91	0.88	0.63
Pretax fixed charge coverage including rents (x)	5.46	5.10	3.00	2.18	1.54	0.94	0.69
Pretax funds flow interest coverage (x)	13.65	11.65	6.65	4.97	3.00	1.59	1.22
Funds from operations/total debt (%)	82.9	74.2	45.6	31.7	18.7	8.4	7.0
Free operating cash flow/total debt (%)	24.8	23.4	8.7	3.4	(0.5)	(3.4)	(4.2)
Pretax return on permanent capital (%)	26.2	21.1	16.7	13.0	11.1	7.4	8.1
Operating income/sales (%)	21.6	15.9	14.9	12.0	12.5	9.3	12.3
Long-term debt/capitalization (%)	12.9	16.6	29.5	39.4	45.7	63.5	79.3
Total debt/capitalization incl. short-term debt (%)	25.1	27.6	37.3	48.0	54.8	73.7	85.5
Total debt/capitalization incl. short-term debt (including 8 times rents (%)	38.2	38.7	50.9	58.6	65.5	78.5	87.2

Source: Standard & Poor's. Used by Permission of Standard & Poor's Corporation. All rights reserved.

Not surprisingly, long-term solvency and leverage ratios feature prominently in these studies. In addition, as bondholders are primarily interested in receiving a (steady) stream of interest and principal payments, variables related to the stability of the firm's earnings stream are included. Similarly, the appearance of "size" variables is explained by the added protection for debtholders, as a result of the endurance of larger firms, in the event earnings take a downturn.

Subordination, as will be seen in the next section, plays a very important role in bond classification. This issue has implications only in the event of financial distress when subordinated bondholders must "wait in line" behind senior claimants. It has no impact on a firm's ongoing interest and principal obligations to the subordinated bondholders.

Model Results

Summary results for five models, and detailed results for two of them, are presented in Exhibit 14-23. Results are presented in terms of the predictive power of ratings for a "holdout" sample.

Generally speaking, the models perform quite well; they average anywhere from 60% to 70% accuracy in duplicating the rating arrived at by an agency. Further, when they are in error, it is usually by misclassifying the rating into the immediate adjacent category. When adjacent categories are "allowed," the "success" rate is over 90%.

Moving from the overall rating to specific categories, the results are not as positive. Both Horrigan (1966) and Pinches and Mingo (1973) find the Baa or BBB classification most difficult to predict. This category is important[46] because it is the rating that

---

[46]For this reason, firms may work harder to retain the higher rating.

EXHIBIT 14-23
Comparison of Bond Ratings Studies

A. Percentage Correct Validation Sample

Pinches and Mingo (1972)	65% and 56%
Horrigan (1966)	59%
West (1970)	60%
Belkaoui (1980, 1983)	66% and 68%

Source: Belkaoui, Ahmed, *Industrial Bonds and the Rating Process,* Exhibit 4.10, P. 106, Quorum Books (1983), an imprint of Greenwood Publishing Group, Inc., Westport, CT. Reprinted with permission.

B. Results of Belkaoui Study
Predicted Category

Number of Observations (and Percentages)
Classified into Groups

From Group Actual Category	AAA	AA	A	BBB	BB	B	Total
AAA	9	8	3	0	0	0	20
	(0.45)	(0.40)	(0.15)	(0.00)	(0.00)	(0.00)	(1.00)
AA	7	62	30	0	0	0	99
	(0.07)	(0.62)	(0.30)	(0.00)	(0.00)	(0.00)	(1.00)
A	0	31	99	10	0	0	140
	(0.00)	(0.22)	(0.70)	(0.07)	(0.00)	(0.00)	(1.00)
BBB	0	0	12	35	3	0	50
	(0.00)	(0.00)	(0.24)	(0.70)	(0.06)	(0.00)	(1.00)
BB	0	0	0	7	18	15	40
	(0.00)	(0.00)	(0.00)	(0.17)	(0.45)	(0.37)	(1.00)
B	0	0	0	0	15	24	39
	(0.00)	(0.00)	(0.00)	(0.00)	(0.38)	(0.61)	(1.00)

Source: Belkaoui, Ahmed, *Industrial Bonds and the Rating Process,* Exhibit 4.17, P. 114, Quorum Books (1983), an imprint of Greenwood Publishing Group, Inc., Westport, CT. Reprinted with permission.

C. Results of Pinches and Mingo Study

Predicted Rating

Actual Rating	Aa	A	Baa	Ba	B
Aa	1	3	0	0	0
A	0	9	0	0	0
Baa	0	2	0	7	0
Ba	0	1	0	15	1
B	0	0	0	3	6

Source: Pinches, G.E. and K.A. Mingo, "A Multivariate Analysis of Industrial Bond Ratings", *Journal of Finance* (March 1973), Table 7, P. 11

has become generally accepted in the investment community as the cutoff between investment and noninvestment grade bonds.[47]

Further, subordination has been found in a number of studies to be the most important variable in the classification model. As the following data, from the Pinches and Mingo study, indicate, the importance of subordination and the difficulty in classifying Baa firms are related.

Classification of Pinches and Mingo (Combined) Sample by Subordination Status

	Aa	A	Baa	Ba	B
Subordinated	0	2	20	60	32
Nonsubordinated	18	33	14	1	0
Total	18	35	34	61	32

Source: Pinches, G.E. and K.A. Mingo, "A Multivariate Analysis of Industrial Bond Ratings", *Journal of Finance* (March 1973), Table 9, P. 12.

Virtually all Aa- and A-rated bonds are nonsubordinated, whereas those rated Ba and B are subordinated. Only at Baa are bonds evenly distributed between subordinated and unsubordinated. Thus the subordination variable by itself[48] can generally provide the initial pass as to which set of ratings the bond belongs to. It, however, provides no discriminating power in the Baa category itself. Thus the poor classification results within the Baa category, where subordination does not play a role, implies that the other variables do not possess strong discriminating power.

The relevance of this point from our perspective is further driven home when we examine the other variables and their relative significance in the classification equations. A size measure (total assets or debt) typically is found to rank second or third. Depending on the study, the other measure in the top three is either debt/capital (Belkaoui) or a measure of earnings stability (years of consecutive dividends in the Pinches and Mingo study). Conventional financial ratios thus generally contribute less than the size or subordination variables:

The results of this analysis indicate that many traditional financial considerations are fairly insignificant in the bond rating process.[49]

---

[47]G. E. Pinches and K. A. Mingo, "A Multivariate Analysis of Industrial Bond Ratings," *Journal of Finance* (March 1973), pp. 1–18.

[48]"If one was only interested in rating bonds as investment quality (Aa, A and Baa) or non-investment quality (Ba and B) the best single predictor is the subordinated status of the bond. Based on this variable alone, correct ratings (investment versus non-investment quality) would have resulted 88.6% of the time for the original sample and 83.3% (40/48) of the time for the holdout sample." Pinches and Mingo (1973), p. 12.

[49]G. E. Pinches and K. A. Mingo, "A Multivariate Analysis of Industrial Bond Ratings," p. 13.

EXHIBIT 14-24
Ratings and Selected Financial Ratios for Small Sample of Firms

	AAA	AA		A	BBB		BB	B
Short-term debt as a percentage								
of total invested capital	5.33	9.00	*	4.35	8.93	*	4.45	6.03
Current ratio	1.65	1.60	*	1.92	1.61	*	1.98	1.89
Fixed charge coverage	19.76	8.75		6.93	4.70	*	5.91	3.79

Source: Belkaoui, Ahmed, *Industrial Bonds and the Rating Process,* Exhibit 4.3, P. 98, Quorum Books (1983), an imprint of Greenwood Publishing Group, Inc., Westport, CT. Reprinted with permission.

	Aa	A		Baa		Ba		B
Interest coverage	1.14	0.61		0.56		0.51	*	0.71
Debt to assets	0.091	0.162	*	0.154	*	0.151		0.215
Return on assets	0.099	0.075		0.066	*	0.075		0.069

Source: Pinches, G.E. and K.A. Mingo, "A Multivariate Analysis of Industrial Bond Ratings", *Journal of Finance* (March 1973), Table 3, P. 7 (Adapted)
*Indicates "break" in expected trend of ratios.

Exhibit 14-24 presents sample means partitioned by rating category for some of the financial variables used in the classification studies. Note that for these samples no clear-cut pattern exists in which higher-rated categories exhibit "better" ratios. This is a further indication that the relationship between ratings and financial variables is weak.

This weak relationship can be viewed in a number of ways depending on one's perspective. One argument would be that financial variables that measure solvency and leverage are not related to the risk of a firm's debt. At face value, this would seem contrary to the thrust of this book and the most fundamental tenets of financial analysis. We shall, however, explore this point later. Ratings agencies would argue, as noted earlier, that although financial variables are relevant, they are so in a way that is more complex than can be captured via a linear weighted summation of them with some other variables. Others, however, argue that the lack of consistency inherent in the fact that firms with similar financial characteristics obtain different rankings is reflective of weakness in the ratings process itself and is precisely why the focus on the ratings process itself needs to be reevaluated.

The Significance of Ratings—Another Look

The explanation offered to justify the foregoing "inconsistency" is that qualitative factors in terms of raters' judgment comes into play. The rating agencies believe this to be a positive factor. However, from our perspective it is not a very satisfactory answer unless there is an objective way of evaluating the efficacy of these qualitative factors.

That is, if the purpose of the ratings is to "rank" the probability of timely repayment of interest and principal, then there needs to be evidence that the differentially rated bonds actually do exhibit different risk characteristics.

The subordination issue mentioned earlier is a case in point. If ratings measure the probability of repayment, then

> *Conventional wisdom suggests that the financial strength of the firm is a better measure of risk than subordination.* However, prior ratings prediction models . . . have identified subordination as an important predictor variable. Such results apparently reflect the actions of bond raters; when a firm has subordinated and unsubordinated bonds, the subordinated issue is invariably rated one grade lower than the nonsubordinated issue. *Apparently, raters automatically downgrade a subordinate bond by one rating.*[50]

Is this downgrading justified? That is, do the financial characteristics of the firm suggest that its two issues be rated differently?[51] If not, then the ratings process is at fault, and if the yield on the subordinated bond is higher as a result of the lower rating, an astute investor can take advantage of the higher return without adding any risk to the portfolio.

Our implicit conclusion is that the focus of the research is misguided. The focus should not be on the relationship of financial variables to bond ratings but rather on their relationship with the actual probabilities of repayment and/or realized yields.[52] Ang and Patel (1975) examined this issue and compared Moody's actual ratings and predicted ratings derived from four[53] statistical bond rating models to actual measures of bond default and loss rate on investment yield (defined as the difference between actual and promised yield). They found insignificant differences between the performance of Moody's and the bond ratings models on an overall basis. In fact, in two of the five years examined, a statistical model outperformed Moody's. This led Ang and Patel to the conclusion that Moody's ratings were inconsistent and should not be relied upon in making long-term bond investments. Investors

> should diversify across all rating groups or even concentrate on lower rated bonds if the analyst is confident that the probability of the firm being solvent in the next few years is high.[54]

---

[50]L. G. Martin and G. V. Henderson, "On Bond Ratings and Pension Obligations: A Note" *Journal of Financial and Quantitative Analysis* (December 1983), pp. 463–470.Emphasis added.

[51]Remember, subordination is an issue only in the case of financial distress.

[52]This, was an early focus of this line of research. Fisher (1959) examined the factors accounting for differences in corporate bonds' risk premia (i.e., excess yield over the risk-free rate). The explanatory variables used by Fisher were the same four used in West's study (Exhibit 14-16). In fact the purpose of West's study was to examine whether Fisher's explanatory variables of bond yields could also be used to explain differences in bond ratings.

[53]Horrigan, West, Pogue and Soldovsky, and Pinches and Mingo's models.

[54]James S. Ang and Kiritkumar A. Patel "Bond Ratings Methods: Comparison and Validation", *Journal of Finance* (May 1975) pp. 631–640.

Ang and Patel's results are interesting insofar as they demonstrated that Moody's ratings did not outperform models designed to duplicate those same ratings in the prediction of default risk and yield. We suggest, however, that a more relevant comparison of Moody's ratings would be to a model specifically designed to examine the relationship between default risk and yield and a set of explanatory variables. Such a model would, of course, be an original ratings model. Unfortunately, the academic community has focused on the less interesting case of models that duplicate already existing ratings rather than design a better ratings model.

Measurement of Financial Variables

Earlier, it was noted that clear-cut distinctions in financial variables did not exist across bond rating categories. One possible explanation lies in how these ratios are measured. For the most part no systematic[55] adjustments for differences in accounting policies, off-balance-sheet obligations, unusual items, et cetera (as suggested throughout this book and summarized in the first part of this chapter) are made to the ratios used in these statistical models. Bond rating agencies may be presumed to consider all the information available that could and should be used to adjust these ratios. Hence the ratios used may be misspecified and in that sense may have little or no discriminating value.

THE PREDICTION OF EQUITY RISK

This section provides a bridge between Chapters 14 and 15. The last measure of risk we examine is the measure of the firm's equity risk. Implicitly, this is tied to a firm's valuation and expected return. A cardinal principle of investment theory is that (expected) returns should be commensurate to the level of risk; the greater the expected risk, the greater the expected return. In the most general sense, equity risk is measurable by the uncertainty of the investment return. However, as discussed earlier, the variance of the firm's returns (and hence the variance of investors' and creditors' returns) is due to a number of factors, such as uncertainty with respect to demand, output prices, input costs, et cetera. These factors themselves are impacted by global and national economic and political conditions, industrywide and competitive pressures, and conditions endemic to the firm itself. Thus risk can be classified by its two sources:

1. *Unsystematic risk:* factors that are specific to the firm
2. *Systematic risk:* factors that are common across a wide spectrum of firms

Modern portfolio theory argues that through diversification, unsystematic risk can be eliminated for the investor. Moreover, it argues that the investor will be compensated only for that level of risk that cannot be eliminated by diversification. Thus *the risk measure that remains relevant is that of systematic risk.*[56] It is for this reason that,

---

[55]We stress "systematic" as there have been some isolated adjustments. Belkaoui, for example, capitalized off-balance-sheet leases and included the resultant debt in his ratios. He did not report on the effects of this procedure as this was not the thrust of his study.

[56]Fama and French (1992) report that beta did not perform as well as other measures in explaining relative returns.

although some studies have examined the overall variability of a firm's returns, most have focused on the systematic risk component and its relationship to accounting-based measures of risk.

As discussed in Chapter 4, both the capital asset pricing model (CAPM), which expresses expected returns as

$$E(R_t) = R_f + \beta_e E(R_m - R_f)$$

or (its empirical counterpart) the market model, which expresses expected returns as

$$E(R_t) = a + \beta_e E(R_m)$$

use beta (β_e), the (standardized) covariance (co-movement) between the returns of a given firm and overall market returns, as a measure of systematic risk.

Importance and Usefulness of Beta (β_e)

Knowledge of beta is important to analysts, investors, and management for a number of reasons:

1. To construct investment portfolios with the desired risk and return characteristics, it is important to know the beta of individual securities.

2. Discounted cash flow valuation models require an estimate of the firm's expected rate of return. With the CAPM formula, beta can be used to estimate that rate (see Chapter 15).

3. Similarly management, in making capital budgeting decisions, needs to know the firm's cost of capital or hurdle rate.

The CAPM formula with beta can provide an estimate of the firm's cost of equity capital.

In all these situations, the ex ante beta, that is, next period's beta, is required. As this value is not directly observable, it must be estimated. One possibility is to use the past history of firm and market returns. This estimate, the historical beta, is generally the ordinary least-square regression (OLS) estimate of beta derived from actual returns in previous periods.[57]

Historical betas, however, are not perfect predictors of future betas, as the regression estimates are subject to measurement error, and the firm's production, investment, and financing decisions change over time. Beta may not be perfectly stable from period to period. Estimating betas on a portfolio basis rather than individually is one remedy for these problems. Additionally, since investors are interested in the systematic risk of portfolios, prediction of portfolio beta rather than individual beta is of primary importance.[58]

---

[57] Alternatively, an adjusted beta is derived by the use of a Bayesian adjustment to the OLS beta estimate.

[58] The problem of measurement error and the benefits of forecasting on a portfolio basis exist not only for forecasts based on historical betas but also when accounting variables are used to forecast beta.

Beaver and Manegold (1975) tested the association between betas in adjacent time periods. They found that betas of one period had a high ex post correlation (45%) with betas of the next period. Thus historical betas could potentially be used in the prediction of the next period's beta. However, that level of correlation means that only about 20% of the (cross-sectional) variation[59] in the second period's betas is explained by the first period's historical beta. On a portfolio basis, the results improve dramatically. For a 5-security portfolio, the correlation is 82% (65% variation explained). At 10 securities the correlation increases to 91% (82% variation explained).

Note that these correlations and percentage variation explained are derived ex post; that is, the "predictive equations" are developed with knowledge of the predicted period's values. In a sense, the equation is developed by asking the following question: "Given the second period beta, what is the best predictive model I can construct using the first period's beta?" The statistics mentioned thus define the degree of association between the two periods and not the degree of predictive power between one observation and the next. Predictive ability, on the other hand, is measured with models that do not use data from the predicted period. They address the following question: "Given *only* the first period's beta, what is the best predictive model I can construct?"

The next section compares the performance of predictive models based on historical betas with those based on accounting-based risk measures. These latter models use accounting measures individually or in conjunction with historical betas in an attempt to improve upon the forecasting ability of models just using historical betas. Exhibit 14-17 presents an overview of the variables used in the studies. Note the emphasis on the *components* of earnings variability discussed at the onset of this chapter.

The approach used in many of the studies is that a more meaningful association between earnings and market returns is found when earnings are also expressed as a return measure. In the discussion that follows, therefore, the term "earnings" encompasses not only its traditional meaning of net income or EPS, but may also include a return measure such as ROA, ROE and/or the earnings/price ratio.[60]

Review of Theoretical and Empirical Findings

The literature in this area is both theoretical and empirical. The theoretical papers attempt to link finance-based measures of risk with accounting measures of risk. Not all measures can be justified on a theoretical basis, and the literature indicates those areas where a theoretical relationship should not exist. Empirical studies test these relationships. We first discuss the theoretical underpinnings of the various risk measures and then provide a review of empirical work.

Theoretical Framework

Due to the nature of the topic the term beta will be used in a number of contexts. The notation and a brief definition of each "beta" discussed is next.

---

[59]The percentage variation explained equals the correlation squared.
[60]When necessary, the exact definition used will be disclosed.

Market-Based Betas

β_e = represents the "classical" beta used in finance to reflect the systematic risk of an equity security. *This is the beta we are attempting to forecast.*

β_a = represents the beta of the equity of a firm that has no debt, the unlevered beta. This beta is a function solely of the underlying systematic risk of the firm's assets, that is, its *operating risk*. It is a theoretical, unobservable construct as few firms have no debt. It is used to demonstrate the contribution of a firm's operating risk to its overall beta.

β_d = represents the beta of a firm's debt. If debt is riskless, β_d equals zero.

Accounting-Based Betas

$B_{earnings}$ = the accounting beta previously defined.

B_{sales} = represents the systematic component of the variability of a firm's sales.

Based on our discussion thus far, it should be expected that the uncertainty of earnings[61] is associated with the stock beta. Thus operating leverage, financing leverage, the variance of sales or earnings, and the accounting beta should be related to the stock beta. A number of theoretical papers, including those of Hamada (1972) and Bowman (1979), have developed these relationships explicitly.

Relationship Among the Stock Beta, Operating Risk, and the Accounting Beta. β_a, the unlevered beta is, as noted, related to operating risk. Clearly, for an unlevered firm, $B_{earnings}$ is also solely related to operating risk. Bowman (1979) has shown that for an unlevered firm the relationship between the stock beta and the accounting beta is

$$\beta_a = \beta_e = \frac{B_{earnings}}{[\text{Relative market value of firm}^{62}]}$$

Relationship Among the Stock Beta, Financial Leverage, Operating Leverage, and the Accounting Beta. Introducing (riskless) debt results in the following relationship:

$$\beta_e = \beta_a + \left[\frac{D}{E}\right]\beta_a$$

Thus the capital structure of a firm (its financial leverage as measured by the debt/equity ratio) increases a firm's systematic risk.

When debt is risky, the relationship can be expressed as

$$\beta_e = \beta_a + \left[\frac{D}{E} \times (\beta_a - \beta_d)\right]$$

---

[61]This, of course, is true as long as they are not solely a result of unsystematic or firm-specific factors.

[62]The relative market value of firm serves the purpose of converting an earnings measure into a return measure. It is the ratio of the firm's market value to the total market value of all firms in the economy.

An obvious parallel to this equation is the equation used in Chapter 3 for the disaggregation of ROE into ROA and the cost of debt:

$$\textbf{ROE} = \textbf{ROA} + \left[\frac{\textbf{D}}{\textbf{E}} \times (\textbf{ROA} - \textbf{Cost of debt}) \right]$$

This similarity is not coincidental but, rather, is a direct outcome of the risk/return trade-off inherent in all investment opportunities. As higher risks require higher returns, it is to be expected that the relationships that determine risk should be similar to those that determine returns.

The foregoing equations imply that equity risk (β_e) is a function of the risk of the underlying assets combined with the risks inherent in financing, that is, the operating and financial leverage notions previously referred to. A more direct description of this relationship is given by Mandelker and Rhee (1984) who derive the following expression for systematic risk:

$$\beta_e = \textbf{FLE} \times \textbf{OLE} \times \frac{\textbf{B}_{\textbf{sales}}}{\textbf{Price/Earnings}}$$

where B_{sales} measures the covariance of the percentage change in sales with the market return (R_m).

Again note the similarity between the foregoing and the expression for total leverage effect derived in Chapter 3:

$$\textbf{TLE} = (\% \textbf{ Change in income}) = \textbf{FLE} \times \textbf{OLE} \times (\% \textbf{ Change in sales})$$

The expressions are parallel except for the price/earnings ratio factor that is needed to effect the conversion from sales to market returns. In the latter expression we are dealing with the returns themselves, whereas in the former we are dealing with the uncertainty of these returns. Hence, "% change in sales" is replaced in the former by its (systematic) risk term.

Relationship Between the Stock Beta and Other Risk Measures. Bowman demonstrates that size, growth, and dividend payout have no theoretical relationship to a stock's systematic risk. In addition, earnings variability is related only insofar as its systematic component is related. Thus, although from a theoretical perspective earnings variability is not directly related to β_e, on an empirical level a relationship will be found to the extent that earnings variability captures the systematic risk component of earnings.

Hochman (1983) lists a number of studies with conflicting views as to the theoretical relationship between β_e and various definitions of growth. Furthermore, Hochman (as will be seen shortly) argues that a dividend yield measure (dividend/market value) would tend to be low for companies with high growth[63] potential. Thus, if growth were to be

---

[63]Higher growth means that income is reinvested in the business; dividends are lower. The high growth would be reflected in higher market value and, therefore, a lower dividend yield.

positively associated with β_e, then (empirically) we could expect a negative relationship between β_e and dividend yield.

Empirical Studies

Given these theoretical relationships, researchers have attempted to use accounting variables and ratios to explain or predict differences in firm accounting betas. By "explain," we mean that the studies examine the historical relationship between β_e and accounting measures of risk to see how much of the variation in β_e can be explained ex post by the accounting risk measures. The predictive studies, on the other hand, attempt to use the relationships derived to predict future period β_e.

It should be noted that some of the relationships tested were ad hoc in the sense that no strict theoretical underpinning existed to justify the relationship. Their inclusion in the models was based on a combination of researcher intuition and "conventional wisdom."

Explanatory Studies. Ball and Brown (1968) found a high degree of association between the accounting beta and the market beta. Depending on how the accounting beta was measured, the correlation between it and the market beta ranged from 39% to 46%. This result was not the main thrust of their study,[64] and they did not attempt to see if they could improve the predictive ability of the market beta by use of the accounting beta.

Lev (1973) examined the association of operating leverage with both the overall risk (total variance) of a firm's returns as well as the systematic risk component β_e. Using firms in three industries (electric utilities, steel manufacturers, and oil producers), he obtained regression estimates of each firm's variable cost percentage v from the equation:

$$TC_t = F + vS_t$$

Lev then proceeded to regress the β_e of these companies against these estimates of v. The hypothesized relationship was negative: the lower the variable cost, the higher the total variance of returns and the higher the beta. The empirical results presented in Exhibit 14-25 confirmed this negative relationship as the regression coefficient on v was negative for all industries and for both risk measures. The equations were all statistically significant. However, the percentage variation explained (R^2) was meaningful only for risk measures for steel manufacturers and the overall risk measure for oil producers. The low R^2 may be due to the fact that Lev (1973) examined firms only on an individual rather than portfolio basis.

Lev did not test for predictive ability. He confined himself to tests of association. Similarly, Mandelker and Rhee examined only the association of beta with OLE and the FLE, not predictive ability. They found that (ex post) OLE and FLE could explain anywhere between 38% and 48% of the variation in beta on a portfolio basis. On an individual basis, only 11% of the variation could be explained.

---

[64]See Chapter 4 for a detailed discussion of the Ball and Brown paper.

EXHIBIT 14-25
Relationship of Risk Measures to Operating Leverage

Industry	Regression of Risk Measure on Variable Cost % (v)	Percentage Variation Explained
Electric utilities*	Total variance $= 0.056 - 0.5v$	$R^2 = 12\%$
(75 firms)	$\beta_e = 0.51 - 6.9v$	$R^2 = 8\%$
Steel manufacturers	Total variance $= 0.162 - 0.11v$	$R^2 = 38\%$
(21 firms)	$\beta_e = 2.28 - 1.34v$	$R^2 = 23\%$
Oil producers	Total variance $= 0.082 - 0.04v$	$R^2 = 31\%$
(26 firms)	$\beta_e = 0.81 - 0.27\,v$	$R^2 = 5\%$

*The equations for the electric utilities had a dummy variable set to 1 if the utility also sold gas and zero otherwise. The coefficient on this variable was $- 0.0017$ in the total variance equation and 0.0422 in the β_e equation.

Source: Lev, Baruch, "On the Association Between Operating Leverage and Risk", *Journal of Financial and Quantitative Analysis* (September 1974), Tables 2 & 3, P. 637 (Adapted)

Explanatory and Predictive Studies. Beaver, Kettler, and Scholes (1970) tested the association as well as the predictive ability of seven accounting risk measures[65] and beta on both the individual security level and the portfolio level for two subperiods (1947–1956 and 1957–1965). The relationship between each of the accounting risk measures and β_e was first tested individually and then in a multivariate context.

The individual results, presented in Exhibit 14-26, indicate that for four of the seven measures, the correlations were significant on an individual and (five security) portfolio level over both subperiods in the direction predicted.

The findings for financial leverage, the accounting beta, and earnings variability are consistent with arguments presented earlier in terms of the predicted association with β_e. The theoretical justification stated by Beaver et al. for the findings with respect to the dividend payout ratio is that, since firms are reluctant to cut dividends, those firms that face more uncertainty (i.e., have higher β_e's) tend to pay lower dividends to start with.[66]

These relationships are all univariate as they measure the correlation between β_e and each of the accounting-based measures individually. Beaver et al. then constructed a multivariate model to be used in forecasting the next period's β_e. The benchmark forecast to be compared against this forecast was period 1's historic (OLS) β_e:

Benchmark forecast of period 2 β_e = Period 1 (OLS) β_e

[65]The accounting risk measures used in all cases were averaged or calculated over five-year periods.

[66]Watts and Zimmermann (1986) use another justification, based on the leverage ratio, to explain the finding. They argue that since empirically it has been shown that firms with more debt tend to pay lower dividends relative to earnings, then the negative relationship between dividend payout and β is just another manifestation of the positive relationship between β and leverage.

EXHIBIT 14-26
Predictive Ability of Accounting Risk Measures

	Predicted Association	Findings Confirmed
1. Payout Dividend/Income	Negative	Yes
2. Growth Assets (year 5)/Assets (year 1)	Positive	Only period 1
3. Leverage (financial) Debt/Assets	Positive	Yes
4. Liquidity Current ratio	Negative	Only period 1
5. Size Average assets	Negative	Only period 2
6. Earnings variability Standard deviation of earnings/price ratio	Positive	Yes
7. Accounting Beta Beta of firm's ratio of earnings/price with market index of earnings/price	Positive	Yes

Source: Beaver, William, Paul Kettler and Myron Scholes, "The Association Between Market Determined and Accounting Determined Risk Measures", *The Accounting Review* (October 1970), Table 5, P. 669 (Adapted).

Using only the accounting-based data from the first subperiod in conjunction with the period 1 (OLS) β_e, the following predictive equation was developed:[67]

$$\text{Period 2 } \beta_e = \text{Fitted period 1 } \beta_e =$$
$$\mathbf{1.016 - (0.584 \times Payout) + (0.835 \times Growth) + (3.027 \times Earnings\ variability)}$$

This model thus uses accounting-based data to modify a market-based measure. Note that the multivariate model does not include the same variables that proved to be significant on an individual basis. This happens often in empirical work as interrelationships between independent variables can alter the ordering found on a univariate level.

The period 2 forecast developed with the foregoing model was compared to the benchmark forecast. The accounting-based forecast explained between 63% and 69% (depending on how the portfolios were constructed) of the variation, whereas the benchmark explained only 37–42%. The benchmark's forecast error was higher than the accounting-based forecast error 54% (57–66%) of the time on an individual (portfolio) basis.

[67]The parameters of the model were developed as follows. First, for each firm in the sample, the historic OLS beta for the first period was found using the market model. This OLS beta was then regressed on the firm's accounting variables. The resultant regression equation was then used to determine the next period's market beta. Since only the first period's data were used, the predicted beta is identical to the first period's "fitted" beta, that is, the beta that falls on the regression line.

EXHIBIT 14-27
Comparison of Forecast Errors

	Benchmark			Accounting Based		
	Individual Security	Portfolio		Individual Security	Portfolio	
		A	B		A	B
% Variance explained	21%	42%	37%	24%	69%	63%
% Times error lower	46	43	34	54	57	66
% Times error lower at extremes	22	12	24	78	88	76
Portfolio A: Constructed on basis of benchmark forecast						
Portfolio B: Constructed on basis of accounting based forecast						

Source: Adapted from Beaver, William, Paul Kettler and Myron Scholes, "The Association Between Market Determined and Accounting Determined Risk Measures", *The Accounting Review* (October 1970), Table 7, P. 677

Generally, when forecasting, it is more difficult to forecast those variables that are "outliers" relative to the mean of the distribution. For market betas, this means it is easier to forecast stocks of average systematic risk (beta approximately equal to 1) than it is to forecast high-beta (extremely risky) or low-beta (low-risk) stocks. The accounting-based model did much better than the benchmark model at these extreme values[68] with smaller forecast errors more than three-fourths of the time. (See Exhibit 14-27.)

Hochman (1983) compared the predictive ability of the historical betas (OLS and Bayesian adjusted) with a beta fitted on the following three risk measures:

1. *Operating risk,* as defined by $B_{earnings}$, where earnings were defined as net operating earnings divided by the book value of capital.

2. *Financial risk,* as defined by the firm's debt to capital financial leverage ratio. (Equity was based on market values whereas debt was based on book values.)

3. *Growth.* Hochman used the firm's dividend yield (dividends to market value) as a surrogate growth measure (see discussion earlier).

Hochman first calculated the historical (OLS) β_e for each firm in the sample over the years 1964–1968. The β_e were then regressed (cross sectionally) on the three risk measures that had also been calculated over the years 1964–1968. This procedure yielded the following equation.

$$\beta_e = 0.81 + 0.03 \; (B_{earnings}) + 0.78 \; \frac{\textbf{Debt}}{\textbf{Capital}} - 86.71 \; (\textbf{Dividend yield})$$

[68]The extreme values were defined as the upper and lower deciles (quartiles) on an individual (portfolio) basis.

The fitted β_e derived from this equation were then used as forecasts of next period's (1969–1974) β_e. The results are presented in Exhibit 14-28A. Note that the fitted beta has the smallest prediction error (mean-square error) albeit the differences between it and the (Bayesian) adjusted beta are relatively small.

A perhaps more interesting result presented by Hochman relates to the property of the various forecasts relative to the actual realization. If one were to express a realization (R) as a linear function of a forecast (F), the expression would be

$$R = a + bF$$

A perfect forecast, $R = F$, would yield $a = 0$ and $b = 1$.

Exhibit 14-28B presents the estimates of a and b for the three forecasting methods. Note how the β_e fitted on the operating risk, financial risk, and growth measures exhibits properties almost identical to those of a perfect forecast with a and b approximately 0 and 1 respectively. The same, however, does not hold for the β_e predictions based upon historical betas.

The most comprehensive attempt at forecasting β_e was carried out by Rosenberg and McKibben (1973) who used a wide variety of accounting as well as nonaccounting variables in their model. Exhibit 14-29 lists the variables tested and those eventually

EXHIBIT 14-28
Comparison of Beta Forecasts

A. Prediction (Mean-Square) Errors

	Historical Betas		Fitted Beta on (1) Operating Risk (2) Financial Risk (3) Growth
	Unadjusted	Adjusted	
Inidividual	0.09713	0.07720	0.07624
Portfolio, size 5	0.03697	0.01720	0.01597
Portfolio, size 10	0.03104	0.008783	0.00790

B. Relationship of Forecast to Realization $F = a + b R$

	Historical Betas				Fitted Beta on (1) Operating Risk (2) Financial Risk (3) Growth	
	Unadjusted		Adjusted			
	a	b	a	b	a	b
Individual	0.39	0.54	0.13	0.84	−0.01	0.96
Portfolio, size 5	0.39	0.54	0.10	0.87	−0.03	0.99
Portfolio, size 10	0.39	0.54	0.10	0.87	−0.03	0.99

Source: Hochman, Shalom, *The Beta Coefficient: An Instrumental Variables Approach in Research and Finance, Volume 4* (Haim Levy, Editor), JAI Press (Greenwich, Connecticut 1983), Table 8, P. 139; Table 9, P. 141

EXHIBIT 14-29
Variables Examined and Used in Rosenberg and McKibben Study

Accounting-Based Descriptors

* 1. Standard deviation of a per share earnings growth measure
  2. Accounting beta, or covariability of earnings with overall corporate earnings
* 3. Latest annual proportional change in per-share earnings
  4. Dividend payout ratio
  5. Logarithm of mean total assets
* 6. Standard & Poor's quality rating
  7. Estimated probability of default on fixed payments
* 8. Liquidity (the quick ratio)
* 9. Absolute magnitude of per share dividend cuts
*10. Mean leverage (senior securities/total assets)
  11. Smoothed operating leverage (fixed charges/operating income)
  12. Standard deviation of per share operating income growth
  13. Growth measure for per share operating income
  14. Operating profit margin (MG)
  15. Retained earnings per dollar of total assets
  16. Growth measure for total assets
*17. Growth measure for total net sales
*18. Growth measure of per share earnings available for common
  19. Nonsustainable growth estimate
*20. Gross plant per dollar of total assets

Market-Based Descriptors

*21. Historical beta, a regression of stock return on market return over preceding calendar years in the sample, assuming alpha equals zero
  22. Standard error of residual risk
  23. Marketability, measured as ratio of annual dollar volume of trading to mean annual dollar volume for all securities
  24. Negative semideviation of returns.
*25. Share turnover as a percentage of shares outstanding
*26. Logarithm of unadjusted share price
  27. Dummy variable equal to one if stock is listed on the NYSE in latest period; equal to zero, otherwise

Market Valuation Descriptors

  28. Smoothed dividend yield
  29. Earnings/price ratio
*30. Book value of common equity per share/price
  31. Estimates of misvaluation based on naive growth forecasts
  32. (G) and (G2)

---

*Indicates "used."

Source: Rosenberg, Barr and Walt McKibben, "The Prediction of Systematic and Specific Risk in Common Stocks", *Journal of Financial and Quantitative Analysis* (March 1973), P. 324

used in their model. Using the criterion of which (predicted) beta best forecast future returns, they tested the predictive power of their beta against a number of alternative (return-based) beta forecasts. They found their model to have the best predictive power. The results were statistically significant albeit in some cases the additional predictive power was marginal (2% increase in R^2). This paper was one of a series Rosenberg carried out (by himself or with others) in an attempt to develop a firm fundamental predictive beta model.

A result of Rosenberg's research was the formation of an investment service company, Barr Rosenberg & Associates (BARRA). The company provides forecasts of betas based on models incorporating accounting-based and other fundamental factors. The actual models used, being proprietary, are not available. This service competes with other investment services that provide beta forecasts based on models incorporating primarily historical stock returns data.

Harrington (1983) tested the forecasting ability of betas provided by such investment services. In all, 12 different predictors of beta were examined. Included in the test were two models based on firm-fundamental characteristics developed by BARRA. The list of beta predictors examined and the results are presented in Exhibit 14-30.

For the industrial companies, one of these fundamental BARRA models had the lowest mean-square prediction error over all four time horizons examined. Their other fundamental model finished second in two of the horizons. For utilities, the fundamental model(s) did not do as well, but as noted in Exhibit 14-30, the model was not designed for utilities. The results also show that it is easier to forecast betas calculated over longer horizons. (In all cases the longer horizons had lower mean-square prediction errors.)

EXHIBIT 14-30
Comparison of Beta Forecasts of 12 Different Models

A. Table II Characteristics of the Beta Predictors

Source	Method	Time Period	Interval	Index	Special Notes	Available From
Merrill Lynch (ML1)	OLS*	5 years	Monthly	S&P 500	Price relatives only	1972
Merrill Lynch (ML2)	OLS/Bayesian adjusted*	5 years	Monthly	S&P 500	Price relatives only	1972
Value Line (Value Line)	OLS*	5 years	Weekly	NYSE Composite	Price relatives only	1972
Drexel Burnham Lambert (Drexel)	OLS/Bayesian adjusted*	8 cycles	8 cycles as defined by Drexel	S&P 500	Sample: 28 utilities, 16 industrials	10/1974
Wilshire Associates (Wilshire)	Fundamental	—	Quarterly	—		1971–77
Barr Rosenberg & Assoc. (RF1)	OLS*	5 years	Monthly	S&P 500	Compound returns	1974

EXHIBIT 14-30. *(Continued)*

A. Table II Characteristics of the Beta Predictors

Source	Method	Time Period	Interval	Index	Special Notes	Available From
Barr Rosenberg & Assoc. (RF2)	Fundamental†	—	—	—	—	1974
Barr Rosenberg & Assoc. (RF3)	Fundamental†	—	—	—	—	1974
Ordinary Least Squares (OLS)	OLS*	5 years	Monthly	S&P 500	Compound returns	NA
Adjusted Ordinary Least Squares (OLSB)	OLS/Bayesian adjusted*	5 years	Monthly	S&P 500	Compound returns	NA
Naive (Naive 2)	β = mean of the sample (utilities or industrials)	5 years	Monthly	S&P 500	Compound returns	NA
Naive (Naive 1)	β = 1	5 years	NA	NA	NA	NA

N/A = not applicable.

*A simple linear regression of historical returns from the stock and the market (usually proxied by the S&P 500):

$$R_j = \alpha_j + \beta_j(R_m) + \epsilon_j$$

where

R_j = **the total returns on a particular security or portfolio**
R_m = **the return on the market**
α_j = **the intercept from the regression**
ϵ_j = **the residuals, or errors**
β_j = **the slope of the regression line**

†A Rosenberg Assoc. spokesman stated that this particular fundamental prediction process is not good for utility stocks. Another method designed to provide better betas for utilities is being developed by them.

B. Table V MSE Results for the Utility Sample

Horizon	Smallest MSE (Source)	Next Smallest MSE (Source)	Mean MSE	Maximum MSE
1 year	0.1560 (V. Line)	0.1617 (Naive 1)	0.2062	0.2857
2 years	0.1005 (V. Line)	0.1071 (OLSB)	0.1324	0.2503
3 years	0.0799 (V. Line)	0.0866 (Naive 1)	0.1166	0.2271
4 years	0.0584 (V. Line)	0.0630 (Naive 1)	0.1098	0.1972

C. Table VI MSE Results for the Industrial Sample

Horizon	Smallest MSE (Source)	Next Smallest MSE (Source)	Mean MSE	Maximum MSE
1 year	0.3572 (RF3)	0.3624 (RF2)	0.4028	0.5644
2 years	0.1879 (RF3)	0.1962 (RF2)	0.2521	0.3941
3 years	0.1399 (RF3)	0.1434 (V. Line)	0.1975	0.3337
4 years	0.1239 (RF3)	0.1323 (V. Line)	0.1098	0.3180

Source: Harrington, Diana R., "Whose Beta is Best?", *Financial Analysts Journal* (July–August 1983), Table II, P. 69; Table V, P. 71; Table VI, P. 71

Summary of Research

The research findings indicate a strong explanatory as well as predictive relationship between accounting-based measures of risk and β_e. Research endeavors in this area have in a sense died out with little or no effort in the past six to seven years. Two areas of criticism and hence room for potential improvements are the following:

1. As in most empirical studies, the accounting ratios used are taken directly from the financial statements without adjustment for differences in accounting policies, unusual items, and off-balance-sheet information. Such adjustments could potentially improve the models. The Dhaliwal study discussed in Chapter 9, for example, found that better predictions of β_e could be obtained if the explanatory variable debt/equity was adjusted to reflect off-balance-sheet pension information.

2. Empirical research by its nature suffers from the problem of omitted variables as the researcher does not know (or cannot obtain data for) all variables that should be in the model. The prediction of β_e is an area of research, however, where the theoretical framework is stronger and richer than most areas of empirical research. Thus it is troubling that certain studies omit explanatory variables that are called for by the theory they use to justify those variables they have included.

Earlier, it was noted that operating and financial leverage by themselves do not define the riskiness of a firm. Risk depends on the underlying variance of the firm's sales. None of the studies that examined the relationship of β_e and leverage (e.g., Lev[69] and Mandelker and Rhee) included sales variance (or its systematic component) as one of the explanatory variables. It could be that firms take on higher operating leverage in inverse proportion to the variability of sales to reach a desired level of risk. Examining the relationship of β_e to leverage under those circumstances could explain the poor results found by these studies.

CONCLUDING COMMENTS

The comments made to summarize the various classification studies are similar in nature. The studies have demonstrated strong linkages between accounting-based measures of risk and various forms of risk facing a firm. What is troublesome is that the major effort in constructing the models has been devoted to the statistical analysis techniques rather than examination of the inputs going into the models.

This criticism takes on two forms. The first deals with the theoretical underpinnings or motivation for the models. It is one thing when the theory does not really exist, as in the case of bankruptcy prediction. It is another when the theory exists but is ignored. The prediction of beta and bond ratings are examples of the latter. In the case of beta prediction, many of the models focused only on one or two variables when the theory

---

[69]Lev's use of data on an industry-by-industry basis could mitigate some of this criticism if one were to assume that firms in the same industry have similar (systematic) variability in sales.

specifies a larger (available) set of explanatory variables. In the case of bond ratings, the research may be focusing on the wrong variable of interest entirely.

The second form of criticism deals with the data used in these models. The research focus is on the tools that measure the data rather than the data themselves. The first part of this chapter demonstrates an analysis for debt. Similar analyses can be carried out for other financial variables related to risk. It is true that there is no clear-cut evidence that these adjustments would improve the models. That is what should make it such an interesting area for research. Ignoring this issue reminds us of the suggestion by Oskar Morgenstern that working with sophisticated statistics and poor data was equivalent to calculating the circumference of a circle by pacing off the radius with one's feet and multiplying by pi taken to the tenth decimal place.

Chapter 14

Problems

1. [Book value per share] Time Warner's shareholders' equity at December 31, 1991, was reported as follows (in $ millions):

Preferred stock, $1 par value, 250 million shares authorized, 124 million shares issued, 123.3 million shares outstanding, $6.256 billion liquidation preference	$ 124
Common stock, $1 par value, 750 million shares authorized, 104 million shares issued, 92.6 million shares outstanding	104
Paid-in capital	9699
Retained earnings (deficit)	(264)
Treasury stock, at cost	(1165)
Total shareholders' equity	$ 8498

Calculate *book value per common share* of Time Warner on December 31, 1991.

2. [Book value per share; 1992 CFA adapted] The equity section of the balance sheet of Bundy Shoe Corporation as of December 31, 1991, was reported as follows:

Preferred stock, authorized 300,000 shares, issued and outstanding 200,000 shares, par value $90, 7% cumulative nonparticipating	$18,000,000
Common stock, authorized 500,000 shares, issued and outstanding 300,000 shares, par value $100	30,000,000
Capital contributed in excess of par value	7,000,000
Retained earnings (deficit)	(10,000,000)
Total shareholders' equity	$45,000,000

The preferred shares have a liquidating value of $95 and are callable at $105. No dividends were declared or paid on preferred shares in 1991. All dividends had previously been paid. Compute *book value per common share* for Bundy on December 31, 1991. Show all calculations.

3. [Adjustments to book value and debt; 1988 CFA adapted] Byron Smart, CFA, a senior portfolio manager with Reilly Investment Management, reviewed the biweekly printout of the equity value screens prepared by a leading brokerage firm. One of the screens used to determine relative value is "low long-term debt/total long-term capitalization ratio." Smart noticed that the ratio indicated for Lubbock Corp. was 23.9%. The Lubbock balance sheet is presented in Exhibit 14P-1.

A. Explain how the information contained in *each* footnote could be used to adjust Lubbock's debt and/or equity. Calculate an adjusted long-term debt/total long-term capitalization ratio. Ignore any potential tax effects.

B. Discuss any tax effects of *each* adjustment made in part A.

C. As a potential investor, Smart should also consider such other financial reporting issues as:

1. The valuation of marketable securities

2. Treatment of deferred taxes

Identify at least *three* other financial reporting issues that Smart should consider. Briefly discuss how *each* of these *five* issues might impact Lubbock's long-term debt/total long-term capitalization ratio.

D. Lubbock has not yet adopted either SFAS 106 on postretirement benefits or SFAS 109 on income taxes. Briefly discuss how each of these reporting changes might affect the debt/equity ratio.

4. [Book value adjustments and leverage ratios; 1986 CFA adapted] Bosworth Oxnarf, CFA, an investment banking analyst with Krayberg and Rabid, has been asked to search for potential leveraged buyout (LBO) candidates. Oxnarf has read that many LBOs occur when the target company has relatively little debt and the ability to tolerate more leverage. New debt is secured by company assets, and funds so raised are used to buy out existing shareholders.

Oxnarf has analyzed the balance sheet of Jersey Products and computed a debt/equity ratio of 26.6%, a debt/assets ratio of 16.6%, and a times interest earned ratio of 3.5X. Earnings before interest and taxes were $350 million, and Jersey's marginal cost of funds is 10%. Upon rereading Jersey's annual report, he found the following footnotes (excerpted):

(1) Actuarial present value of accumulated (ABO) and projected benefit obligation (PBO) for its pension plan at December 31, 1992, was as follows (in $ thousands):

	ABO	PBO
Vested	$450,000	$540,000
Nonvested	25,000	45,000
Total	$475,000	$585,000

EXHIBIT 14P-1. LUBBOCK CORP.
Condensed Balance Sheet, at December 31, 1991 (in $ millions)

Cash and notes	$ 100
Receivables	350
Marketable securities	150
Inventory	800
Other	400
Total current assets	$1800
Net plant and equipment	1800
Total assets	$3600
Note payable	$ 125
Accounts payable	175
Taxes payable	150
Other	75
Total current liabilities	$ 525
Long-term debt	675
Deferred taxes (noncurrent)	175
Other liabilities	75
Minority interest	100
Common stock	400
Retained earnings	1650
Total liabilities and shareholders' equity	$3600

Upon reading Lubbock's annual report, Smart finds the following footnotes:

. . . a subsidiary, Lubbock Property Corp., holds, as joint venture partner, a 50 percent interest in its head office building in Chicago, and ten regional shopping centers in the U.S. The parent company has guaranteed the indebtedness of these properties, which totalled $250,000,000 at December 31, 1991.

. . . the LIFO cost basis was used in the valuation of inventories at December 31, 1991. If the FIFO method of inventory valuation was used in place of LIFO, inventories would have exceeded reported amounts by $200,000,000.

. . . the company leases most of its facilities under long-term contracts. These leases are categorized as operating leases for accounting purposes. The following table summarizes future minimum rental payments as of December 31, 1991. These leases carry an implicit interest rate factor of 10 percent, which translates to a present value of approximately $750,000,000.

1992	$90,000,000
1993	90,000,000
1994	90,000,000
1995	90,000,000
1996	90,000,000
1997–2011	90,000,000 per year

Net assets available for benefits were $425,000.

(2) The firm paid $15,000,000 for postemployment health benefits in 1992; it had not yet adopted SFAS 106.

(3) A subsidiary, Jersey Realty, holds a 50% interest in four Texas office parks. The company has guaranteed half the indebtedness ($150 million) of these properties.

(4) Sixty percent of inventories at December 31, 1992, were accounted for using the FIFO method. If all inventories had been valued on a FIFO basis, inventories would have exceeded reported amounts by $80,000,000.

(5) The company leases several facilities under long-term contracts, reported as operating leases. The following table summarizes the future minimum lease payments as of December 31, 1992:

1993	$ 36,000,000
1994	34,000,000
1995	35,000,000
1996	34,000,000
1997	32,000,000
1998–2012	172,000,000
Total	$343,000,000

Discuss how *each* of the footnotes would affect Jersey Products' leverage ratios. Compute adjusted leverage and times interest earned ratios. What other information, if any, would Oxnarf need to complete his analysis?

Problems 5–7 relate to the takeover by Philip Morris of Kraft and are based on the data in Exhibit 14P-2.

5. [Ratios and bond ratings; 1989 CFA adapted] Philip Morris Companies is one of the world's largest cigarette manufacturers as well as a major producer and distributor of a broad line of food and beverage products. The company has compiled a steady record of growth in sales, earnings, and cash flow.

In October 1988, Philip Morris announced an unsolicited cash tender offer for all the 124 million outstanding shares of Kraft at $90 per share. Kraft subsequently accepted a $106-per-share all-cash offer from Philip Morris.

Kraft's major products include cheese, edible oils, nonfluid dairy products, and frozen foods. Exhibit 14P-2 provides projected financial data for Philip Morris and Kraft individually and on a consolidated basis.

Exhibit 14P-3 reports the median values, according to bond rating category, for the following three financial ratios:

1. Pretax interest coverage

2. Long-term debt as a percentage of capitalization

3. Cash flow as a percentage of total debt (see definition of cash flow in Exhibit 14P-3)

EXHIBIT 14P-2. PHILIP MORRIS COMPANIES, INC.
Projected Financial Data, 1988–1989 (in $ millions)

	1988 Estimate Excluding Kraft	1989 Estimate Before Kraft	Kraft Only	Adjustments	Consolidated
		A. Selected Income Statement Data			
Total sales	$30450	$33080	$11610		$ 44690
Total operating income	$ 4875	$ 5550	$ 1050	$ (210)	$ 6390
As an % of sales	16.0%	16.8%	9.0%		14.3%
Interest expense	(575)	(500)	(75)	(1025)	(1600)
Corporate expense	(200)	(225)	(100)	(40)	(365)
Other expense	(5)	(5)			(5)
Pretax income	$ 4095	$ 4820	$ 875	$ (1275)	$ 4420
As a % of sales	13.4%	14.6%	7.5%		9.9%
Income taxes	(1740)	(2000)	(349)	493	(1856)
Tax rate	42.5%	41.5%	39.9%		42.0%
Net income	$ 2355	$ 2820	$ 526	$ (782)	$ 2564
		B. Selected Balance Sheet Data as of Year-End			
Short-term debt	$ 1125	$ 1100	$ 683		$ 1,783
Long-term debt	4757	3883	895	$11,000	15,778
Stockholders' equity	8141	9931	2150	(2,406)	9,675
		C. Other Selected Financial Data			
Depreciation and amortization	$ 720	$ 750	$ 190	$ 295	$ 1235
Deferred taxes	100	100	10	280	390
Equity in undistributed earnings of unconsolidated subsidiaries	110	125			125

EXHIBIT 14P-3
Median Ratios According to Bond Rating Category

Ratio	AAA	AA	A	BBB	BB	B	CCC
Pretax interest coverage	14.10X	9.67X	5.40X	3.63X	2.25X	1.58X	(0.42X)
Long-term debt as a % of capitalization	11.5%	18.7%	28.3%	34.3%	48.4%	57.2%	73.2%
Cash flow[1] as a % of total debt	111.8%	86.0%	50.9%	34.2%	22.8%	14.1%	6.2%

Source: Standard & Poor's.

[1]For the purpose of calculating this ratio, Standard & Poor's defines cash flow as "net income plus depreciation, amortization and deferred taxes, less equity in undistributed earnings of unconsolidated subsidiaries."

Using the information provided in Exhibit 14P-2 and 14P-3:

A. Calculate the three ratios listed for Philip Morris for 1989, first, using the figures prior to the Kraft acquisition and, second, using the consolidated figures after the acquisition.

B. Compare these two sets of ratios to the medians for each rating category.

C. Formulate and support an opinion as to the appropriate rating category for the new Philip Morris (before and after the Kraft acquisition).

6. [Ratios and bankruptcy prediction] Given the variables used in Altman's two bankruptcy models, discuss the impact of the Kraft acquisition on the probability that Philip Morris will become insolvent. (Use the data in Exhibit 14P-2 as part of your answer.)

7. [Effect of acquisition on beta] Describe the expected effect of the Kraft acquisition on Philip Morris' beta. (Your answer should consider the effects on the "unlevered" beta as well as on the "levered" beta and should distinguish between operating and financial leverage effects.)

8. [Comprehensive financial analysis; 1989 CFA adapted] The Investment Policy Committee of your firm has decided that the soft drink industry, specifically Coca-Cola Company (KO) and Coca-Cola Enterprises (CCE), qualify as potential purchases for the firm's portfolios. As the firm's beverage industry expert, you must prepare an extensive financial analysis of these two soft drink producers.

KO owns the brands included in its broad product line. It plays almost no direct role in the domestic manufacturing and distribution beyond the output of soft drink extract.

The business of CCE is also dominated by soft drinks. CCE, however, purchases extract from KO and transforms it into completed products sold in a wide variety of retail outlets throughout the United States.

Use only the financial information shown in Exhibit 14P-4 in answering parts A, B, and C.

A. Your comparative analysis of these two soft drink companies required calculations of various ratios shown in Exhibit 14P-4D. You have identified four key areas of comparison:

    1. Short-term liquidity

    2. Capital structure and long-term solvency

    3. Asset utilization

    4. Operating profitability

Discuss the differences between KO and CCE in these four areas based on the ratios and the financial statements.

B. Using the information in Exhibit 14P-4A, B, and C, identify the financial statement adjustments required to enhance their comparability and usefulness for financial analysis. (Note: Some of the required adjustments must be deduced from the financial statements as they are not listed in part C of the exhibit.)

EXHIBIT 14P-4. COCA-COLA COMPANY AND COCA-COLA ENTERPRISES
Selected Financial Data (in $ millions)

A. Consolidated Balance Sheets, at December 31, 1988

	Coca-Cola Company (KO)	Coca-Cola Enterprises (CCE)
Assets		
Current assets		
Cash and equivalents	$ 1231	$ —
Trade accounts receivable	627	294
Inventories	779	125
Other current assets	608	69
Total current assets	$ 3245	$ 488
Other investments		
Investments in affiliates	1912	—
Other	478	66
Total other investments	$ 2390	$ 66
Fixed assets (net)	1760	1180
Goodwill	56	2935
Total assets	$ 7451	$ 4669
Liabilities and Shareholders' Equity		
Current liabilities		
Short-term debt	$ 1363	$ 148
Accounts payable	1081	402
Other	425	—
Total current liabilities	$ 2869	$ 550
Long-term debt	761	2062
Deferred income taxes	270	222
Other long-term liabilities	206	27
Shareholders' equity		
Preferred stock	300	250
Common stock	3045	1558
Total shareholders' equity	$ 3345	$ 1808
Total liabilities and shareholders' equity	$ 7451	$ 4669

B. 1988 Consolidated Statements of Income
(in $ millions, except per share data)

	Coca-Cola Company (KO)	Coca-Cola Enterprises (CCE)
Revenues	$ 8338	$ 3874
Cost of goods sold	(3702)	(2268)
Gross profit	$ 4636	$ 1606
Selling, general, and administrative expenses	(3038)	(1225)
Provision for restructuring	—	(27)
Operating profit	$ 1598	$ 354

EXHIBIT 14P-4. *(Continued)*

Interest expense	(231)	(211)
Gain on sale of operations	—	104
Equity in income of affiliates	48	—
Other income	167	21
Pretax income	$ 1582	$ 268
Income taxes	(538)	(115)
Net income	$ 1044	$ 153
Preferred dividends	(6)	(10)
Income available for common	$ 1038	$ 143
Earnings per share	$ 2.85	$ 1.03

C. Data Extracted from Financial Statement Footnotes

Coca-Cola Company (KO)

(1) Certain soft drink and citrus inventories are valued on the last-in, first-out (LIFO) method. The excess of current costs over LIFO stated values amounted to approximately $30 million at December 31, 1988.

(2) The market value of the Company's investments in publicly traded equity investees exceeded the Company's carrying value at December 31, 1988, by approximately $291 million.

(3) The Company is contingently liable for guarantees of indebtedness owed by some of its licensees and others, totaling approximately $133 million at December 31, 1988.

Coca-Cola Enterprises (CCE)

(1) Inventory cost is computed principally on the last-in, first-out (LIFO) method. At December 31, 1988, the LIFO reserve was $2,077,000.

(2) In December 1988 the Company repurchased for cash various outstanding bond issues. These transactiaons resulted in a pretax gain of approximately $8.5 million.

(3) The Company leases office and warehouse space, and machinery and equipment under lease agreements. At December 31, 1988, future minimum lease payments under noncancellable operating leases were as follows (in $ thousands):

1989	$11,749
1990	8,436
1991	6,881
1992	4,972
1993	3,485
Later years	11,181
Total	$46,704

EXHIBIT 14P-4. *(Continued)*

D. Selected Financial Ratios as of Year-End 1988[1]

	Coca-Cola Company (KO)	Coca-Cola Enterprises (CCE)
Return on total assets	0.16	0.06
Total debt to total capital	0.55	0.61
Net income to sales	0.13	0.04
Receivable turnover	13.30X	13.18X
Property, plant, and equipment turnover	4.74X	3.28X
Return on common equity	0.34	0.09
Current ratio	1.13	0.89
Inventory turnover	4.75X	18.14X
Long-term debt to equity	0.23	1.14
Gross profit to sales	0.56	0.41
Acid test ratio	0.65	0.53
Asset turnover	1.12X	0.83X
Times interest earned	7.85X	2.27X

[1]For simplicity, ratios have been computed on year-end data rather than on 1988 average data.

C. For each of the adjustments identified in part B, discuss the effects of these adjustments on your answer to part A.

9. [Deere; fixed income analysis]

A. Exhibit 14-22 presents median values of financial ratios according to Standard & Poor's bond rating categories. Using this exhibit and the financial statements of Deere provided in Exhibit 1B-2:

> **(i)** Compute the corresponding ratios for Deere for fiscal 1991.
>
> **(ii)** Determine the "appropriate" bond rating for Deere.

B.

> **(i)** Using the current cost balance sheet in Exhibit 14-1, recalculate the ratios in part A.
>
> **(ii)** What bond rating category is implied by the adjusted ratios?
>
> **(iii)** Notwithstanding your answer to part (ii), why might these adjustments not make a difference in Deere's bond rating?
>
> **(iv)** Do these adjustments make a difference in assessing Deere's default risk?
>
> **(v)** How do these adjustments affect Deere's bankruptcy risk?

C. Deere's *1992 annual report* (not in text) discusses the potential impact of the company's adoption of SFAS 106 (postretirement benefits). It states that the transition obligation should range from $0.8 billion to $1.2 billion. The incremental annual expense should range from $40 million (if the obligation is recognized in the year of adoption) to $100 million (if the firm chooses to amortize the obligation over 20 years)

Discuss how the adoption of SFAS 106 will affect your answers to part B.

10. [Forecasting bond rating changes] Standard & Poor's Corp. states that it places firms on its *Creditwatch* list when changes in operating profit trends, completed or planned mergers, capital structure changes, or regulatory actions suggest a need for reevaluation of the current credit rating. Listing with negative implications may result in the rating being lowered.

James River is a major manufacturer of paper products. On January 26, 1993, Standard & Poor's Corp. placed James River's debt on *Creditwatch* with negative implications. It cited weak market conditions and James River's deteriorating operating performance. S&P noted fourth quarter operating losses and each segment's lower reported profits. The current debt rating of James River's senior debt was BBB+; its subordinated debt rating was BBB.

Exhibit 14P-5 provides selected balance sheet and income statement data.

A. Using the data in Exhibits 14P-5 and 14-22, evaluate Standard & Poor's decision to place James River on its *Creditwatch* list.

B. What other information would you need to determine whether the firm's debt should be downgraded? Specify financial statement or footnote information and discuss how you would use it.

C. Discuss the limitations of comparing James River's ratios with those in Exhibit 14-22.

11. [Bond ratings] Exhibit 14P-6 contains selected data from the financial statements of Westvaco, a large paper and paperboard producer.

A. Use the data provided to determine the appropriate debt rating for Westvaco. If different from the actual rating (A), discuss briefly.

EXHIBIT 14P-5. JAMES RIVER CORP.
Selected Financial Data, for Years Ended December 31, 1991–1992 (in $ millions)

	1991	1992
Total debt	$1891	$2882
Total equity	2574	2112
Sales	4562	4728
Operating income	244	(62)
Other income	27	24
Interest expense	(138)	(149)
Income (loss) before taxes	$ 133	$(187)
Cash from operations[1]	394	(136)

[1]Computed using Standard & Poor's definition, not that used throughout the text.

EXHIBIT 14P-6. WESTVACO CORP.
Selected Financial Data, for Years Ended October 31, 1991–1992 (in $ millions)

	1991	1992
Total debt	$ 988	$1079
Total equity	1699	1770
Sales	2301	2336
Operating income	326	308
Interest expense	100	102
Income (loss) before taxes	$ 226	$ 206
Cash from operations[1]	338	356

[1]Computed using Standard & Poor's definition, not that used throughout the text.

B. Exhibit 14P-7 contains a comparison of Westvaco with two other paper companies. Using *only* the data in Exhibits 14P-7 and 14-22, evaluate the risk that the debt of the three companies listed will be downgraded.

C. How do the data provided in Exhibits 14P-5 and 14P-6 modify your answer to part B for James River and Westvaco?

D. The years 1991–1992 were ones of recession for the paper industry. How should that affect the evaluation of debt ratings for the three companies?

12. [Effect of different accounting standards on book value] Exhibit 12P-8 contains data from the "Reconciliation to U.S. Accounting Principles" provided by Hanson Industries in its 1989–1991 annual reports. Exhibit 14P-8 contains excerpts from that firm's 1991 financial statements.

A. Compute book value per share at September 30, 1990, and 1991 on the basis of:

(i) U.K. GAAP

(ii) U.S. GAAP

B. Discuss how you would use your answer to either (i) or (ii) and other data to compute a book value per share that best represents the firm's financial status.

EXHIBIT 14P-7
Comparison of Paper Company Debt Ratings (in $ millions)

Company (Rating)	1991			Times Interest Earned		
	Capitalization	LT Debt	Debt/Capital (%)	1989	1990	1991
Westvaco (A)	$2856	$1205	37.8%	4.24	3.09	2.10
James River (BBB+)	4556	1900	43.2	3.15	2.97	1.55
Union Camp (A)	3750	1322	48.9	7.41	3.98	1.95

Source: Standard & Poor's Bond Guide, March 1993.

EXHIBIT 14P-8. HANSON INDUSTRIES
Selected Financial Data, for Years Ended September 30, 1990–1991

	1990	1991
Shares outstanding (millions)	4796	4808

At September 30, 1991, the following were outstanding:

- Executive options to purchase 88.6 million shares at an average price of £1.734 per share
- Warrants to purchase 130.5 million shares at $3.60 per share up to September 30, 1994 (exchange rate at September 30, 1991: £1 = $1.75)
- Warrants to purchase 160 million shares at £3 per share up to September 30, 1997
- £500 million of 9½% bonds convertible into Hanson shares at £2.59 per share until January 31, 2006

Revaluation reserve included in equity of £163 million for both years

Source: Hanson Industries, *1991 Annual Report.*

C. Describe how you would treat *each* of the equity linked securities described in Exhibit 14P-8 when computing book value per share. The closing market price of Hanson shares on September 30, 1991, was 226.50 pence.

13. [Effect of different accounting standards on book value] Exhibit 13P-6 contains a reconciliation from Australian GAAP to U.S. GAAP of stockholders' equity for The News Corporation, an Australian company. There were 384 million shares outstanding at June 30, 1992 (268 million at June 30, 1991).

A. Compute book value per share at June 30, 1991, and 1992 on the basis of:

(i) Australian GAAP

(ii) U.S. GAAP

B. The major difference between U.S. and Australian GAAP for News Corp. is the ability, under the latter, to revalue publishing rights, [book] titles, and television licenses. Discuss the advantages and disadvantages, from the analysis perspective, of including the revalued amounts in the computation of book value.

14. [Effect of different accounting standards on book value per share and credit ratings] Exhibit 14P-9 reports the stockholders' equity of Atlas Copco under Swedish GAAP, U.S. GAAP, and IASC GAAP.

A. Compute book value per share at December 31, 1990, and 1991 on the basis of:

(i) Swedish GAAP

(ii) U.S. GAAP

(iii) IASC GAAP

EXHIBIT 14P-9. ATLAS COPCO GROUP
Shareholders' Equity, at December 31, 1990–1991 (SEK[1] millions)

	1990	1991
U.S. GAAP	6715	6843
Swedish GAAP	6200	6345
IASC GAAP	5901	6046

[1]Swedish kroner.
Source: Atlas Copco Group, *1991 Annual Report.*

There were 35 million shares outstanding on both dates.

B. For 1990–1991 the major differences affecting Atlas Copco among the three sets of accounting standards are:

1. Asset revaluation is permitted only under Swedish GAAP.

2. Under Swedish GAAP (only), investments are carried at cost; the equity method is not permitted.

3. Deferred taxes under IASC GAAP have not been adjusted for changes in tax rates.

4. Under IASC GAAP (only), proposed dividends are charged against retained earnings immediately.

Using the standards differences listed, explain the differences in net worth in Exhibit 14P-9.

C. Discuss how you would use your answer to (1), (2), or (3) and other data to compute a book value per share that best represents the firm's financial status.

15

VALUATION AND FORECASTING

INTRODUCTION

VALUATION MODELS

OVERVIEW OF MODELS

ASSET-BASED VALUATION MODELS

Market Price and Book Value: Theoretical Considerations

Book Value: Measurement Issues

Tobin's Q Ratio

Stability and Growth of Book Value

Earnings Retention

Effect of New Equity Financing

Effect of Acquisitions

Effect of Changing Exchange Rates

Effect of Financial Reporting Choices and Accounting Changes

Restructuring Provisions

DISCOUNTED CASH FLOW VALUATION MODELS

Dividend-Based Models

Estimating r *with the CAPM*

No-Growth–Constant Dividend Model

Constant Growth Model

Earnings-Based Models

Relationship of Earnings-Based and Dividend-Based Models

The Definition of Earnings and the Valuation Objective

No Growth Model

Growth Model

Estimating Growth

Defining and Estimating r*: Return on new equity investment

Estimating k—The Dividend Payout Ratio

The Growth Rate of EPS and Dividend Policy

Alternative Growth Assumptions

Earnings or Cash Flows?

Free Cash Flow Approach to Valuation

Adjustments to Reported Cash from Investment

Dividends, Earnings, or Free Cash Flows?

Valuation: Empirical Results and Additional Considerations

Earnings Valuation and the P/E Ratio
    Growth, Risk and Valuation
    Effects of Permanent and Transitory Earnings
    and Measurement Error
Effects of Nonrecurring Income and Differing
Accounting Policies
    Adjustments to Reported Income

Normalization of Reported Income
Normalizing over the Economic Cycle
Effects of Acquisitions
Impact of Changes in Exchange Rates
Effect of Accounting Changes
Quality of Earnings

FORECASTING MODELS AND TIME SERIES PROPERTIES OF EARNINGS

FORECASTING MODELS

Extrapolative Models

    Permanent versus Transitory Components

Index Models

Forecasting Using Disaggregated Data

    Quarterly Forecasting Models

    Segment-Based Forecasts

    Forecasts Using Income or Balance Sheet
    Components

COMPARISON WITH FINANCIAL ANALYSTS' FORECASTS

Analyst Forecasts: Some Caveats

SUMMARY

APPENDIX 15–A MULTISTAGE GROWTH MODELS

Valuing a Nondividend-Paying Firm

Shifting Growth Rate Patterns

INTRODUCTION

This chapter provides an overview of valuation models. Whether the models are based on assets, dividends, cash flows, or earnings, in a perfect world it can be shown that the various models are identical. However, when this highly stylized environment does not exist, the results of the models can differ. In such settings, the data used in the valuation models represent estimates of expected future values and their measurement as well as predictive ability becomes very important.

The primary focus of the chapter, therefore, is not the theoretical underpinnings of these models but rather on the relationship of their parameters to information obtainable from the accounting system. Throughout the chapter, reference is made to illustrative examples or to Deere in an effort to demonstrate these relationships. Finally, consistent with the forecasting requirements of valuation models, the chapter concludes with a discussion of forecasting and the time series properties of earnings.

VALUATION MODELS

OVERVIEW OF MODELS

The valuation models most commonly used by analysts and investors generally fall into two classes:

1. Asset-based valuation models
2. Discounted cash flow (DCF) models

Asset-based valuation models assign a value to the firm on the basis of the current market value of the individual component assets. To arrive at the (market) value of the firm's equity, liabilities (also at market value) are deducted:

Value = Assets − Liabilities

In *DCF models,* value, at time *t*, is determined as the present value of future cash flows

$$\text{Value}_t = \sum \frac{CF_{t+i}}{(1 + r)^i}$$

where CF_{t+i} represents (expected[1]) cash flows *i* periods from time *t* and *r* is the discount factor or the firm's required rate of return. DCF models come in a number of forms, chiefly varying as to the appropriate "measure" of cash flows, *CF*, which are estimated variously as streams of future dividends, earnings, or free cash flows.

Conceptually, the DCF and asset-based approaches to valuation are related and can be linked via the actual rate of return (r^*) earned by a firm on its equity investment. For an infinite (constant) cash flow stream, using the DCF model,

$$\text{Value} = \frac{CF}{r}$$

But the amount a firm earns, *CF*, is equal to

$$CF = r^*B$$

where *B* represents the book value of the firm. Assuming the firm earns the required rate of return, *r*, ($r^* = r$), then $CF = rB$ and

---

[1]Technically, we should use the expectation operator, $E(*)$, when discussing future period (as yet unknown) cash flows/earnings to differentiate from current period (known) earnings. This would, however, only add needlessly to the notation. From the context, it should be clear that when we speak of future earnings or cash flows, we are talking about their expected rather than realized value.

$$\text{Value} = \frac{CF}{r} = \frac{rB}{r} = B$$

This equation suggests that value can be equivalently defined either in terms of a "stock" of assets or in terms of the flows those assets generate. This equivalence of the two approaches exists within the confines of a highly stylized and perfect world. Such a world also has no need for security analysis as all is known. Security analysis is challenging and interesting, however, in "real"-world settings, with finite knowledge and horizons. There, uncertainty exists with respect to the definition and measurement of the parameters of the model and their actual realizations.

The identity of asset-based and DCF models breaks down in such real world settings, and conflicting valuation results may be obtained. The sources of uncertainty in these models include but are not limited to

- Difficulties in forecasting over a finite horizon let alone to infinity
- The random nature of cash flows and the difficulty in assessing whether cash flows are *permanent* (will persist in the future) or *transitory* (nonrecurring)
- Measurement problems as both assets and *CF*'s can be influenced by selection of accounting policies and by discretionary management policies

Analysts must be able to circumvent the pitfalls introduced by uncertainty and measurement problems. This chapter will discuss these problems in the context of various valuation models.

ASSET-BASED VALUATION MODELS

Asset-based models assign a value to the firm by aggregating the current market value of its individual component assets and liabilities. The previous chapter, in the context of debt analysis, discussed the steps required to formulate an asset-based valuation. Deere's *adjusted book value* on October 31, 1991, was $2375 million, or $31.15 per share, approximately 17% less than the *reported book value* of $2836 million, or $37.20 per share. Both numbers were considerably lower than the closing market price (at October 31, 1991) of $56.00. How should one interpret the discrepancy? Should we expect to see market price equal book value?

To some extent, the possibility exists that the value of the firm should exceed the sum of its parts. Asset-based valuation determines the "sum of the parts." Synergistic effects could then result in a premium ("goodwill") for the going concern. Whether this is true depends on the firm's profitability. There may be other reasons for this discrepancy, including but not limited to the nature of the firm's assets, its operations, management's choice of financial reporting methods, assumptions and estimates, mandatory and discretionary accounting changes, and other problems in the measurement of book value. We will now explore these causes to develop our understanding of the insights they provide and the pitfalls in the use of asset-based valuation models.

Market Price and Book Value: Theoretical Considerations

Earlier we showed that when the actual rate of return (r^*) is equal to the required rate of return (r), then

$$\text{Value} = \frac{CF}{r} = \frac{r^*B}{r} = \frac{rB}{r} = B$$

When r^* is not equal to r, then the equation can be transformed to

$$CF = r^*B = rB + (r^* - r)B$$

and therefore, if

$$\text{Value} = \frac{CF}{r}$$

then

$$\text{Value} = \frac{rB + (r^* - r)B}{r}$$

$$= \left[1 + \frac{(r^* - r)}{r} \right] B$$

$$= B + \left[\frac{(r^* - r)}{r} \right] B$$

Whether a firm's stock price is above or below book value depends on the intuitively appealing factor of how high the firm's expected rate of return is. As we shall see, $r^* > r$, is reflective of a firm having positive growth opportunities leading to market values greater than book value. Thus a firm whose expected r^* is higher (lower) than the required r should be selling at a price above (below) book value. The component,

$$\left[\frac{(r^* - r)}{r} \right] B$$

is, in effect, a measure of the firm's "economic goodwill," the excess of market over book value.

Book Value: Measurement Issues

The determination of Deere's adjusted book value, despite detailed calculations, was relatively straightforward for all liabilities and current assets as much of the required information was available. The major difficulty in applying asset-based valuation is the determination of the market (current) value of long-lived assets such as plant, machinery, and equipment. Because this is generally true for most companies, the relationship between (adjusted) book value and market price is affected by this measurement error.

Reported book value is an "index" against which to compare the market price. Under the assumption that the differential between market price and book value should be similar for firms in the same industry, the analysis turns on whether the relationship for a given firm is "in line" with a comparable population of firms.

When book value is used as an indicator, it is common practice to rely on unadjusted data that are simpler to obtain. The numbers thus generated do not construe value but rather are viewed as benchmarks against which market value is compared. The focus is on how close market value is to book value. If it is very close to book value or below book value, then the firm is a "buy," as the downside risk is viewed as negligible.[2]

This comparison is generally carried out under the implicit or explicit assumption that historical cost–based book value reflects the minimum value of the firm. This minimum value assumption is generally justified by the fact that, since book value is based on historical cost, it does not reflect increases in value caused by inflation. Moreover, when there are adjustments to historical cost, only markdowns not markups (in some cases, markup to original historical cost is allowed) are permitted. Thus the book value is viewed as a conservative estimate of the firm's value.

Notwithstanding the foregoing, firms do trade below their book values. Feltham and Ohlson (1992), for example, note that close to one-third of companies on the COMPUSTAT® tape traded below their book values at some time. The relationship and hence validity of the assumption depend to a great extent on the nature of the firm's assets, its reporting methods, and as discussed earlier, its profitability.

Firms reporting intangible assets such as goodwill can trade below reported book value. Relating this to the theoretical model earlier, if the "economic goodwill" component $[(r^* - r)/r]B$ is less[3] than the recorded goodwill, then a company can trade below its reported book value. For a company that has no recorded goodwill, if its profitability is poor ($r^* < r$), then it is possible for the firm to trade below even its (historical) book value. Such a firm may have more value "broken up" than as a going concern.

The book value is also a function of management's financial reporting choices that affect the allocations of revenues and expenses across time periods and as a result determine reported asset and liability balances. In some cases, these choices result in accounting non-recognition of economic obligations. These choices affect reported book value over time for a given firm, and at any given point in time, they affect comparisons of book value across firms.

A final point relates to restructurings and write-offs. It was indicated in Chapter 6 that the decision to write down long-lived tangible assets is somewhat subjective. Management determines the amount and may accelerate or delay the recognition of

---

[2]Interestingly enough, in a recent article, Fama and French (1992) report that the variables which best explain differential market returns are firm size and the [Book Value]/Price ratio. However, the relationship is opposite to that discussed in the text. Lower book to price ratios were associated with higher returns implying that this ratio may serve as a surrogate risk measure.

[3]This is true even if $r^* > r$.

write-offs and restructurings affecting reported book value and earnings. Thus, if the market anticipates a write-off, the firm's shares could be trading below book value.

Tobin's Q Ratio

The relationship between a company's market and book values is often measured by Tobin's q ratio,[4] defined as the market value of the firm divided by its book value on a replacement cost basis.[5] q values below 1 (price less than replacement book value) imply that the firm is earning a return less than the required rate; a (marginal) dollar invested in the firm's assets does not result in future cash flows whose present value is equal to a dollar. Such firms are poor performers.

However (as discussed in Chapter 12), firms with low q ratios are often seen as prime targets for takeovers. Firms that want to expand find it cheaper to "buy growth" by acquiring a firm already in place rather than constructing the required production/marketing facilities. Implicit in such a takeover is the assumption that the acquired assets will perform better within the new firm due to diversification, synergistic effects, and/or better management.

The assumption of poor management also can provide motivation for takeovers or acquisitions even when the target firm is not in the same line of business and the objective is not expansion. Low q ratios indicate poor firm performance. If this poor performance is viewed as a function of poor management, bidders who feel they are better managers can buy the business at a relatively cheap price.

Stability and Growth of Book Value

The growth of equity capital, the base on which shareholder returns are earned, is an important component of firm value. Even a constant return on equity, if applied to a growing capital base, will result in earnings growth. Thus the trend of book value per share (BPS) is as important as its level, and these characteristics are affected by operating, investing, and financing decisions; management choice of financial reporting methods; and discretionary or mandatory accounting changes. A brief discussion of each of these factors is provided in the paragraphs that follow.

Earnings Retention

For most firms, increases in retained earnings provide most of the growth in book value. That growth is affected by the firm's return on equity (ROE) and by its dividend policy. If the payout ratio (dividend/net income) is equal to k, then the increase in book value (B) will be

$$
\begin{aligned}
B_1 - B_0 &= \textbf{Income} - \textbf{Dividends} \\
&= (\textbf{ROE} \times B_0) - (k \times \textbf{ROE} \times B_0) \\
&= (1 - k) \times \textbf{ROE} \times B_0
\end{aligned}
$$

---

[4]The ratio was developed by the Nobel Prize–winning economist James Tobin.
[5]See Chapter 6, and Appendix 6–C, for a discussion of the concepts of current cost and replacement cost.

where B_0 is the book value at the beginning of the period and $(1 - k)$ is the earnings retention rate. Thus $(1 - k) \times$ ROE is the growth rate[6] of book value per share due to retention of earnings assuming that both k and ROE remain constant.

Effect of New Equity Financing

Another factor affecting book value per share is financing. The sale of new shares at prices above BPS increases that figure, while sales below BPS result in dilution.[7] Similarly, the repurchase of outstanding shares at prices below BPS increase it, while the repurchase of shares above BPS dilute it.[8]

Effect of Acquisitions

When acquisitions are made for stock, book value per share will also be affected. This is true under either the purchase or pooling methods of acquisition accounting (see Chapter 12), although the impact differs.

When the pooling method is used, the newly issued shares are reflected at the book value of the acquired company:

$$\frac{\text{Book value of acquired company}}{\text{Number of shares issued}}$$

If the BPS of the newly issued shares is higher than that of the acquirer, then BPS will be increased. If the BPS of the newly issued shares is lower, the acquirer's BPS will be diluted.

Under the purchase method of accounting, the newly issued shares are recorded at market value. Thus the effect on the acquirer's BPS depends on whether the market price of its shares is above or below its own BPS; it is as if the acquirer sold shares for cash and used that cash to purchase the acquired company.

Effect of Changing Exchange Rates

Changes in foreign currency exchange rates also impact BPS. As discussed in Chapter 13, the net worth of operations in functional currencies other than the reporting (parent) currency are translated at the exchange rate on the balance sheet date. As a result, when functional currencies appreciate, the firm's BPS rises. Similarly, the remeasurement of foreign operations and the translation of foreign currency transactions also affects the BPS and needs careful evaluation.

Effect of Financial Reporting Choices and Accounting Changes

Much of this text has been devoted to analyses of the effects (including those on book value) of financial reporting choices including LIFO/FIFO methods of inventory

---

[6]As we shall see in our discussion of DCF models, this is also one way of estimating earnings growth. We shall also indicate the problems in using these parameters to estimate growth.

[7]A mathematical formulation of this effect can be found in Cohen, Zinbarg, and Zeikel (1987), p. 399.

[8]See, for example, the trend of Merck's BPS in Chapter 3.

valuation, depreciation methods, pensions, other postemployment benefits, leasing policies, and other capitalization versus expensing decisions. Discretionary changes in these policies can also change the level and the trend of growth (or decline) in BPS.

Finally, mandatory accounting changes can have a significant impact on reported book value. In recent years, new accounting standards have had significantly positive (income taxes) and negative (postemployment benefits) impacts on BPS. As noted in earlier chapters, long transition periods and different transition methods, including retroactive or prospective adoptions, affect the level and trend of BPS of a given firm and comparisons across firms.

As a result of Deere's adoption of Statement of Financial Accounting Standards (SFAS) 96, Income Taxes, in 1988, for example, there was a cumulative effect of $29 million ($0.42 per share), increasing Deere's book value by little more than 1%. The adoption of SFAS 106, Postretirement Benefits, however, will have a large negative impact. The estimated transition obligation is approximately one-half of Deere's book value at October 31, 1991, before any income tax offset! Adoption of the new standard will sharply reduce book value unless Deere chooses to defer the transition obligation and amortize it over 20 years as allowed by the standard.

Thus, while the trend of BPS is an important indicator of potential earnings growth, the analyst must be careful to discern whether BPS growth comes from operations (increases in retained earnings[9]) or from the other factors discussed. To the extent that BPS growth comes from nonoperating factors, that growth may be artificial or nonrecurring. Failure to consider the sources of BPS growth can result in erroneous conclusions regarding future earnings trends.

Restructuring Provisions

In recent years, many companies have reported large "restructuring" provisions that have significantly reduced reported BPS. These events can, however, sometimes be anticipated. In the case of Deere, "restructuring" provisions have been small but have recurred with some frequency. The 1988 Management Discussion and Analysis (MD&A) indicates that (after-tax) provisions of $25 million and $58 million were made in 1987 and 1986, respectively. In 1991, the after-tax provision was $120 million. In total these charges have reduced book value per share by $2.80 per share, or 7%. It should be noted that Deere has had repeated LIFO invasions, one of the early warning signals of impairment.

DISCOUNTED CASH FLOW VALUATION MODELS

The parameters that make up the DCF model

$$\text{Value} = \sum \frac{\text{CF}_{t+i}}{(1 + r)^i}$$

---

[9]This source of growth in BPS may also stem from financial reporting choices and the impact of such changes is not necessarily similar to that due to real operating improvements.

are related to risk (the required rate of return) and the return itself (CF). Chapter 14 dealt with the elements of risk and their impact on the required rate of return. This chapter focuses primarily on measurement of the return or CF measure.

The models (emanating in the finance literature) are based on a concept of "economic" income that is very difficult to define, let alone measure. Three widely used alternative CF measures exist: dividends, accounting earnings, and "free cash flows." Just as DCF and asset-based valuation models are equivalent under the assumptions of perfect markets, dividends, earnings, and free cash flow measures can be shown to yield equivalent results as the theoretical models are relatively straightforward. Their implementation, however, is not.

This is due, first, to the inherent difficulty in defining the cash flows used in these models. Which cash flows and to whom do they flow? Conceptually, cash flows are defined differently depending on whether the valuation objective is the *firm's equity*, (denoted as P) or the value of the *firm's debt plus equity* (V).

Assuming that we can define CF, we are left with another issue. The parameters needed in the model are the *future* CF stream. How is that determined from present data? More important, are current and past dividends, earnings, or cash flows the best indicators of that stream? It is these (and other) pragmatic issues that determine which model should be used. Before addressing these issues directly, we will discuss various models based on these measures. Doing so will highlight some of the difficulties inherent in using them.

Dividend-Based Models

The value of a firm's *equity* (P) is equal to the present value of all future dividends paid by the firm to its equityholders:

$$P_0 = \frac{D_1}{(1+r)} + \frac{D_2}{(1+r)^2} + \cdots + \frac{D_n}{(1+r)^n}$$

$$P_0 = \sum_i \frac{D_i}{(1+r)^i}$$

where
P_o = the value of the firms's equity at the end of period o
D_i = the dividend paid by the firm in period i
r = the firm's required rate of return based on the firm's risk class

Since this relationship is independent of the starting point, the value at the end of period 1 equals

$$P_1 = \frac{D_2}{(1+r)^2} + \frac{D_3}{(1+r)^3} + \cdots + \frac{D_n}{(1+r)^n}$$

Combining the equations for P_0 and P_1 yields the following expression for the value of the firm at the end of any period i:

$$P_i = \frac{D_{i+1}}{(1+r)} + \frac{P_{i+1}}{(1+r)}$$

The value of the firm at the beginning of a period is equal to the discounted value of dividends received during the period plus the (discounted) value of the firm at the end of the period. This formulation will now be used to get an estimate of r, the firm's required rate of return.

Estimating r with the Capital Asset Pricing Model

Manipulating the previous equation to get an expression for r yields

$$r = \frac{D_{i+1} + P_{i+1}}{P_i} - 1$$

This is the standard definition of the one-period return on an equity security. As discussed in earlier chapters, the capital asset pricing model (CAPM) defines the expected return of a security (r) to be equal to the risk-free rate (r_f) plus beta (β) times the excess (over the risk-free rate) market return (r_m):

$$r = r_f + \beta \times (r_m - r_f)$$

Thus, by obtaining an estimate of the firm's beta,[10] the risk-free rate, and the (excess) market return, the r to be used in the discount model can be derived directly. Historically, the risk-free rate has averaged 4% and the excess market return ($r_m - r_f$) between 5% and 6%. These long-term average rates change (especially the risk-free rate) periodically due to general market conditions such as inflation rates. Assuming that $r_f = 4\%$ and that $r_m = 9\%$, for a firm whose beta = 1.2, the appropriate discount rate is

$$10\% = 4\% + 1.2 \times (9\% - 4\%)$$

When valuation of equity is the objective of the analysis, the r *obtained with the CAPM is applicable to the dividend discount model and to the other discount models discussed in this chapter.*

While the preceding discussion has made no assumption as to the pattern of dividend payments, different assumptions can be incorporated in the dividend discount models:

No-Growth–Constant Dividend Model. In its no-growth form, the dividend discount model assumes a constant dividend rate equal to the current dividend level and is stated as

$$P_0 = \frac{D_1}{r}$$

---

[10]In Chapter 14 we discuss alternative estimation procedures for beta.

Constant Growth Model. For a firm expected to have a (constant) growth rate of g, dividends in the next period are expected to equal $(1 + g)$ times current dividends, $D_1 = D_0(1 + g)$, and the valuation model becomes:

$$P_0 = \frac{D_0(1 + g)}{r - g} = \frac{D_1}{r - g}$$

Although dividend-based models are easy to use, a conceptual difficulty arises when one considers firms that presently do not pay any dividends.[11] Such firms have value. In fact, firms experiencing high growth opportunities often pay no dividends as they reinvest all funds available to them. In the context of a dividend discount model, firm value depends on the level of dividends the firm will ultimately be able to pay when its growth stabilizes. *Future dividends depend on the earnings stream the firm will be able to generate.* Thus the firm's expected future earnings are fundamental to such a valuation. Similarly, for a firm paying dividends, the level of dividends *may be* a discretionary choice of management that is bounded by or restricted by available earnings.

When dividends are not paid out, value accumulates within the firm in the form of reinvested earnings. Alternatively, firms sometimes pay dividends right up to bankruptcy. Thus dividends may say more about the allocation of earnings to various claimants than valuation. Any assumed (non)growth pattern in dividends is essentially a function of management's discretion and availability of earnings.

Earnings-Based Models

The preceding discussion of dividend-based models highlighted the crucial role of earnings in valuation. We now proceed to a discussion of earnings-based valuation models beginning with an analysis of the relationship between dividend and earnings models. However, one caveat must be noted: the concept of earnings used in these models and the conventional accounting definition of earnings are the same only under very specific simplified assumptions. The notion of earnings in these theoretic models is closer to CFO or free cash flows. For the present, the term "earnings" should be viewed in a very broad sense. We shall expand and clarify this issue as the discussion progresses.

Relationship of Earnings-Based and Dividend-Based Models

An earnings-based model can be derived from the dividend-based model by defining k as dividends/earnings, the dividend payout ratio. That is, if $D_i = kE_i$, then for *the growth case,*

$$P_0 = \frac{kE_0(1 + g)}{r - g} = \frac{kE_i}{r - g}$$

[11]See Appendix 15–A.

As discussed shortly, a firm experiencing no growth in dividends and earnings is (generally) characterized by no new investments undertaken by the firm. Thus all earnings are paid out as dividends. The payout ratio, k, is equal to 1, and the valuation model becomes

$$P_0 = \frac{E_0}{r}$$

The Definition of Earnings and the Valuation Objective

Earnings-based models can be used to value either (1) the equity of the firm (P) or (2) the firm as a whole (V), debt plus equity.

The definition of earnings to be used depends on the valuation objective. When measuring the value of the firm (V), earnings are defined prior to payment of interest, as net operating income. In the valuation of equity, earnings are measured after payment of interest, net income.[12] The definition of such other parameters as the rate of return also differs for each case.

No Growth Model

Using the no-growth case and a simplified income statement (Exhibit 15-1), the appropriate definitions for each case are

Value	= Earnings	/ Rate of Return
Equity P =	Net income	/ Rate of return on equity [e.g., $r = r_f + \beta(r_m - r_f)$]
Firm V =	Net operating income /	Rate of return on debt and equity (weighted average cost of capital)

(1) Equity Valuation. If the valuation objective is the firm's equity, earnings are defined as net income, which is the amount available for distribution to the equity shareholders. Similarly, the required rate of return is the equity rate of return. This rate of return is similar to that used for the dividend-based model and can be estimated by the CAPM. Assuming it is 10%, the value of equity is

$$P = \frac{E}{r} = \frac{\$100}{0.10} = \$1000$$

(2) Value of the Firm. Net operating income (before deduction of interest), that is, the cash available to all providers of capital, is the appropriate measure of earnings when valuing the firm as a whole. Similarly, the rate of return is a weighted average of the required rates of return of all providers of capital. This term is referred to as the weighted

---

[12]This discussion assumes that there is no preferred stock. When preferred stock exists, a third possibility exists, the valuation of total (common and preferred) equity.

EXHIBIT 15-1
No-Growth Model

Income Statement

	All Years
Operating revenue	$ 350
Operating expense	(150)
	200
Depreciation expense	(50)
Operating income before tax	$ 150
Tax @ 20%	(30)
Net operating income	**$ 120**
Interest expense (net of taxes)	(20)
Net income	**$ 100**

average cost of capital (WACC). The weighting is based on the relative proportions of debt and equity.

In our example, if we assume that the firm has a debt/capital ratio of 20% (it finances itself on the basis of four-fifths equity and one-fifth debt) and we further assume that the (after-tax) cost of debt is 8%, then the weighted average cost of capital is:

$$\text{WACC} = (0.8 \times 0.10) + (0.2 \times 0.08) = 0.096$$

and the value of the firm as a whole is

$$V = \frac{\text{Net operating income}}{\text{WACC}}$$

$$= \frac{\$120}{0.096} = \$1250$$

The value of the firm equals the value of the debt plus the value of the equity. The value of the equity, P, can be derived from the value of the firm by deducting from V the value of the debt. Since we have assumed that the (after-tax) cost of debt (interest rate) is 8% and since the (after-tax) interest expense is $20, then the value of the debt must be equal to $250 (8% × $250 = $20). Thus the value of the equity is equal to $1250 − $250 = $1000, identical to the value for equity derived directly.[13]

Growth Model

For a growth model, the relationships between earnings and the amounts flowing to the equity- and debtholders are somewhat more complex. We begin again with the valuation of equity followed by the valuation of the firm.

[13]It should be noted that the $1000 equity and $250 debt are consistent with the debt/capital ratio of 20% based on the *market values* of the debt and equity.

(1) Equity Valuation and Earnings. The firm's net income is assumed to be used either for (1) payment of dividends or (2) investment in new assets.

With k equal to the payout ratio, dividends/net income, then $1 - k$ represents the fraction of earnings reinvested in new assets. Exhibit 15-2A illustrates the allocation of net income between new investment and dividends given an assumed dividend payout ratio of 80%. If these new assets earn a rate of return $r^* = 20\%$, then the pattern of net income and its distribution between dividends and reinvestment, assuming $k = 0.80$ is:

Period	Earnings	= Dividend	+ New Investments
0	$E_0 = \$100$	$= 0.8E_0 = \$80$	$+ 0.2E_0 = \$20$
1	$E_1 = \$100 + (r^* \times \$20) = \$104$	$= 0.8E_1 = \$83.2$	$+ 0.2E_1 = \$20.8$
2	$E_2 = \$104 + (r^* \times \$20.8) = \$108.16$	$= 0.8E_2 = \$86.53$	$+ 0.2E_2 = \$21.63$

The firm's earnings, dividends, and investments are all growing at a rate of 4%. This rate was not specified in advance but as the next table indicates, the growth rate can be measured as the product of the fraction reinvested $(1 - k)$ times the rate of return the firm can earn on the reinvestment (r^*).

Period	Earnings	= Dividend	+ New Investments
0	E_0	$= kE_0$	$+ (1 - k)E_0$
1	$E_1 = E_0 + r^*(1 - k)E_0$	$= kE_1$	$+ (1 - k)E_1$
	$= E_0[1 + r^*[1 - k]]$	$= kE_0[1 + r^*(1 - k)]$	$+ (1 - k)E_0[1 + r^*(1 - k)]$
2	$E_2 = E_1[1 + r^*(1 - k)]$	$= kE_2$	$+ (1 - k)E_2$
	$= E_0[1 + r^*(1 - k)]^2$	$= kE_0[1 + r^*(1 - k)]^2$	$+ (1 - k)E_0[1 + r^*(1 - k)]^2$

Note that the earnings, dividends, and new investment grow each period by an amount equal to $[r^*(1 - k)]$. The firm's growth rate, g, is thus equal to

$$g = r^*(1 - k) = 0.2 \times (1 - 0.8) = 0.04$$

This result is intuitively appealing: a firm's growth rate depends on the level of investment and the return on that investment. Thus a no-growth company is one that has no *new* investment: $k = 1$.

Using the growth formula to find the value of the firm's equity yields

$$P_0 = \frac{kE_0(1 + g)}{r - g} = \frac{kE_1}{r - r^*(1 - k)}$$

$$= \frac{0.8(\$104)}{0.10 - 0.04} = \$1387$$

EXHIBIT 15-2
Growth Model

A. Derivation of Amount Available for Equityholders
for Valuation of Equity

	Year 0
Operating revenue	$ 350
Operating expense	(150)
	$ 200
Depreciation expense	(50)
Operating income before tax	$ 150
Tax @ 20%	(30)
Net operating income	**$ 120**
Interest expense (net of taxes)	(20)
Net income	**$ 100**
New investment (equity)	(20)
Available for equityholders (dividends)	**$ 80**

B. Derivation of Amount Available for Debt- and Equityholders
for Valuation of Firm

	Year 0
Operating revenue	$ 350
Operating expense	(150)
	$ 200
Depreciation expense	(50)
Operating income before tax	150
Tax @ 20%	(30)
Net operating income	**$ 120**
New investment	(30)
Available for debt- and equityholders	**$ 90**
Financing distribution (cash for financing)	
Dividends	$ 80
Interest expense (net of taxes)	20
New debt	(10)
	$ 90

(2) Value of the Firm. We continue with our previous example. In the no-growth case, equity value is related to the earnings available to the equity shareholder, net income. To value the firm (total capital), we used the earnings available to the debt holders and shareholders, net operating income.

In the growth model, to value equity, net income is replaced by the amount available to the equity shareholder after *new investment of equity* (net income − reinvestment of equity). Similarly, when valuing the firm as a whole, we must determine the earnings available to all providers of capital—the debt- and equityholders. This amount equals the net operating income minus *total new investment*. Total new investment is provided by both equity- and debtholders. Given the growth rate of 4% implied by the equity investment of $20, debt[14] must be increased[15] by $10 (4% of $250), bringing total new investment to $30.

The two approaches are contrasted in Exhibit 15-2. We must be careful to distinguish between total new investments and the reinvestment of equity referred to previously. The first refers to the actual investment in new assets made by the firm ($30, in the example). Financing for this investment is provided by the debt- ($10) and equity- ($20) holders. For the valuation of equity, reinvestment refers only to that amount (i.e., $20) provided by the equityholders (that is, net income − dividends).

With new debt of $10, total debt will be $260. The market value of equity, we have shown, is equal to $1387. Therefore, the firm's WACC will equal 9.7%.[16]

Exhibit 15-2 provides year 0 information. For year 1, all values will be higher by 4%. The value of the firm using this approach will therefore be equal to

$$\frac{(\text{Operating income} - \text{total new investment})(1 + g)}{\text{WACC} - g} = \frac{(\$120 - \$30)(1.04)}{(0.097 - 0.04)}$$

$$= \frac{93.6}{0.057} = \$1647$$

The $1647 value of the firm is equal to the sum of the value of the equity ($1387) plus the value of the debt ($260).

Estimating Growth

The firm's growth rate can be estimated in one of two ways:

1. Estimating the individual components, k and r^*, that contribute to growth as $g = (1 - k)r^*$;

2. Extrapolating the historical growth rate to the future.

---

[14]The debt-to-capital ratio of 20% developed for the no-growth case can no longer be maintained. That ratio was based on relative market values. Growth opportunities, however, are "captured" by the equity shareholders, thereby altering the relative proportions of debt and equity. The new proportion is equity of $1387 to debt of $260, which reflects a debt-to-capital ratio of $260/($1387 + $260) = 15.8%. This proportion will now be maintained as both the market value of debt and equity will grow by 4%.

[15]The $10 of new debt is consistent with an assumption of 4% growth in net income. For interest expense to increase by 4%, debt must increase by 4% from $250 to $260.

[16]With debt = $260 and equity = $1387 and the (after-tax) cost of debt and equity equal to 8% and 10%, respectively,

$$\text{WACC} = \frac{\$1387}{\$1387 + \$260} \times 10\% + \frac{\$260}{\$1387 + \$260} \times 8\% = 9.7\%$$

Defining and Estimating r*: *Return on New (Equity) Investment.* The terms r^* and r both represent rates of return for the equity investor. The former represents the actual return enjoyed, whereas the latter refers to the required rate of return. *Growth opportunities exist only when the expected returns,* r*, *are greater than the required rate of return,* r *(i.e.,* r* > r*). When $r^* = r$, then it is easily shown that the growth model reduces to the no-growth model:

$$P = \frac{kE}{[r - r^*(1 - k)]}$$

$$= \frac{kE}{(r - r^* + r^*k)}$$

But $r = r^*$.

$$P = \frac{kE}{(r - r + rk)}$$

$$= \frac{kE}{rk}$$

$$= \frac{E}{r}$$

This formulation does not imply that firms cannot decide to undertake new investments and grow even if $r^* = r$. What it does show is that it does not make a difference whether the firm decides to "grow." The value of the firm's equity will not be affected whether the firm reinvests its net income or pays it out in dividends. Recall our earlier example for the no-growth model in which we found the value of the equity to be equal to $100/0.10 = 1000$. That example assumed all income in future periods will be paid out as dividends. The following table indicates the effect of different dividend payout rates when the remainder is reinvested at the rate $r^* = r = 0.10$.

Payout Ratio k	Reinvested Income $(1 - k)E$	Growth Rate $g = (1 - k)r$	Value $P = kE/(r - g)$
0.75	25	$0.025 = (1 - 0.75) \times 0.1$	$\$1000 = 75/(0.1 - 0.025)$
0.50	50	$0.050 = (1 - 0.50) \times 0.1$	$\$1000 = 50/(0.1 - 0.050)$
0.25	75	$0.075 = (1 - 0.25) \times 0.1$	$\$1000 = 25/(0.1 - 0.075)$

No matter what the firm's dividend policy, the value is not affected.[17]

As r^* measures the actual return earned on (reinvested) equity it is conceptually equivalent to the familiar ROE measure. Using ROE to measure r^* is reasonable if (along with the other assumptions in our simplified world) the firm's new investment opportunities are similar to those experienced to date.

Estimating k—The Dividend Payout Ratio. The term k is often estimated using the current dividend payout ratio. This gives us an estimate of the firm's earnings growth rate in terms of familiar ratios previously used to estimate growth in book value.

$$g = (1 - k) \times r^* = (1 - \textbf{Dividend payout}) \times \textbf{ROE}$$

Use of the dividend payout ratio and ROE to estimate future growth rates requires an assumption of constant levels for these parameters that can limit the usefulness of this technique. For stable growth companies like Merck, k and ROE are relatively constant. For cyclical companies like Deere, they are not. Exhibit 15-3 shows the growth rate estimates computed from 1988–1991 data in the financial summary at the beginning of the 1991 financial statements.

Even excluding 1987, when negative earnings per share (EPS) make the calculations meaningless, and adjusting 1991 to exclude the restructuring charge for the same reason, it is hard to use the growth rate calculations in Exhibit 15-3 with any confidence. Whenever EPS are below dividends per share, the projected growth rate

---

[17]It is not our intention to review all the literature on dividend policy. Modigliani and Miller, in their famous proposition, note that given a level of investment (growth opportunities), dividends are irrelevant as they are readily replaced by external financing. We address this issue in the next section by pointing out that dividend payout must be considered net of the raising of additional capital.

The issue of a firm's dividend policy remains a controversial one in the finance literature. There are those who argue that dividend policy is relevant because investors prefer the security of dividends; others view dividend policy in a "signaling" framework whereby management conveys its intentions and/or forecasts by its level of dividends. These issues are beyond the scope of our discussion. The foregoing argues only that in the context of this model, *ceteris paribus*, dividend policy is irrelevant.

EXHIBIT 15-3. DEERE
Growth Rate Projections, 1988–1991

Year	k	ROE	Growth Rate $(1 - k) \times$ ROE
1988*	0.167	0.138	0.115
1989	0.257	0.155	0.115
1990	0.369	0.148	0.093
1991†	1.526	0.033	(0.017)

*Calculations for 1988 are based on earnings per share of $3.90, excluding effect of adopting SFAS 96 (Income Taxes).

†Calculations for 1991 use earnings per share of $1.31, excluding the restructuring charge.

Source: Data are from Appendix 1-B.

will be negative. While the projected growth rates obtained from 1988 and 1989 data are identical, it is hard to regard that as anything but coincidence, given the differences in k and ROE between 1988 and 1989.

It should also be noted that use of the dividend payout ratio to estimate k is not "correct" from a theoretical perspective. In the development of the models, no distinction is made among dividends paid out, stock repurchases, and issuances of new equity. That is,

$$kE = \textbf{Dividends + Share repurchases} - \textbf{New equity issued}$$

should reflect the net cash flows to and from the equity shareholders, not just the dividends.

Dividend payout measures only one portion of the total flow; it ignores new issues and repurchases and can distort the valuation model. A firm's choice of the form (the mix of dividends and the sale or repurchase of shares) of equity financing should not affect valuation. Thus the more appropriate definition of k is

$$k = \frac{\textbf{Dividends + Share repurchases} - \textbf{New equity issued}}{\textbf{Earnings}}$$

The potential instability of the individual components of growth rates suggests that the historical growth trend should be examined when making growth projections. It is important, however, to note that in a similar fashion, dividend policy can affect the *observed* trend in earnings.

The Growth Rate of EPS and Dividend Policy. Consistent with valuation expressed often in terms of price per share, many models that estimate the trend of earnings do so using earnings per share. A number of factors, not all of them "value" related, can distort the growth rate of earnings per share.

Dividend policy has an important impact on earnings growth. A firm with a low payout ratio grows faster than it would if it paid out most of its earnings since reinvested earnings generate future earnings. This effect of dividend policy is meaningful. However, by choosing the mode of equity financing, that is, trading off dividends and sale/repurchase of equity securities, the growth rate in EPS can be distorted. In Appendix 3-C to Chapter 3 we discussed the adjustment of earnings per share for the effect of dividend policy. Exhibit 15-4 applies that methodology to Deere.

The adjustments shown for Deere are not very large over the 1990–1991 period. However, it should be clear that dividend policy, by affecting the firm's need for external financing, ultimately affects the number of shares outstanding and, as a result, reported earnings per share. Firms with low dividend payout policies should show faster growth in EPS than firms with high payout policies.

Alternative Growth Assumptions. We have demonstrated that the benefits from growth depend on the existence of investment opportunities earning a high rate of return, specifically, $r^* > r$. The valuation formula on page 1104 can be disaggregated into two components:

EXHIBIT 15-4. DEERE
Effect of Dividend Policy on Growth in EPS

This exhibit uses the methodology contained in Appendix 3-C. It is assumed that all earnings are paid out in the form of dividends and that new common shares are sold to account for the increase in retained earnings. As Deere showed a loss for fiscal 1991, the adjustment uses aggregate data for the two years ended October 31, 1991 (in $ millions):*

Net income	$ 391	Total for 1990–1991
Dividends paid	(304)	Total for 1990–1991
Increase in retained earnings	$ 87	Net income less dividends

If Deere distributed its entire net income as dividends, it would need to recover $87 million by selling new common shares. Using the mean price over the two-year period of $58 per share, Deere would have sold 1.5 million shares ($87 million/$58), increasing the number of shares outstanding by about 2% and reducing reported earnings per share by 2%.

This form of analysis can be used in another way. If Deere paid no dividends during the two-year period, it would have an additional $304 million of capital. If shares were repurchased (again using the mean price of $58), Deere would have repurchased 5.24 million shares ($304 million/$58), reducing the number of shares outstanding by nearly 7% and increasing future EPS.

If this analysis were extended over a number of years, the effect would be much greater.

*The data can be obtained from the analysis of retained earnings or from the income and cash flow statements, all contained in Appendix 1-B, Exhibit 1-B2.

$$P_i = \frac{E_{i+1}}{r} + \frac{(1 - k)E_{i+1}}{r} \left[\frac{r^* - r}{r - (1 - k)r^*} \right]$$

The first component is the value of the firm in the absence of growth. The second component is the value of the firm's growth opportunities. Generally, high-return investment opportunities ($r^* > r$) do not exist forever, whereas the models we have used are predicated on the existence of infinite growth opportunities. Variations of (some of) these models using alternative assumptions as to growth are presented in Appendix 15-A.

Additionally, in many cases forecasting is carried out by use of the following relationship:

$$P_0 = \frac{kE_1}{(1 + r)} + \frac{kE_2}{(1 + r)^2} + \cdots + \frac{kE_n}{(1 + r)^n} + \frac{P_n}{(1 + r)^n}$$

Explicit short-term horizon forecasts of earnings ($E_1 \ldots E_n$) for a period of three to five years are made and then a terminal value (P_n) at the end of the period is estimated. This terminal value often incorporates the more general growth assumptions discussed.

Earnings or Cash Flows?

It is clear that the concept of earnings used in these models is more akin to cash flows than GAAP net income. In the theoretical development of these models, earnings are generally defined as the cash flows after the replacement of depreciated assets. Net income, as defined by GAAP, is not the appropriate variable for these models. Only in a very simplified world using stringent assumptions will net (operating) income under GAAP meet the foregoing definition of earnings.

The first assumption required is the equating of funds flows and cash flows. In the highly stylized setting of these models, this can be justified if working capital levels are kept (relatively) constant over time.[18] Generally, however, this assumption does not hold. Moreover, differences between cash flows and income are not solely due to changes in working capital. The second assumption required is that depreciation expense approximates the replacement cost of depreciated assets. This also is generally not true. Furthermore, the choice of accounting methods affects the calculation of income. Thus, as soon as we move away from a simplified world, the use of accounting income becomes more problematic.

Using reported cash from operations (CFO) rather than income may solve some of the problems (funds versus cash flow) inherent in the first assumption. However, as has been shown throughout the book, the distinction among CFO, cash for investments, and cash from financing is also affected by accounting choice. In addition, CFO does not account for the replacement of depreciated assets. Finally, the classification of capital expenditures between investments made to maintain capacity and those made for growth is not directly available in most cases. Thus the use of CFO in valuation models is also fraught with difficulties.

Free Cash Flow Approach to Valuation

The free cash flow (FCF) approach has been suggested by some as a potential solution to the problems just discussed. Free cash flow is defined as the cash available to debt- and equityholders after investment.

Just as we found that the dividend model was essentially equivalent to the earnings model, the FCF model we present is equivalent to the earnings-based model of Exhibit 15-2B where the valuation objective was the value of the firm. To illustrate the free cash flow approach, we return to that example. Free cash flow in that example is equal to 90, derived as follows:

Net operating income	120
Total new investment	(30)
Free cash flow	90

The problem with this definition in the general case is, as previously noted, the breakdown between *new* and *replacement* investment is rarely provided. Only the total cash for investment is given in the statement of cash flows. Upon reflection, however, total investment is really the number we want. There is no need to use depreciation expense, or any other surrogate for that matter, to estimate the cost of replacing depreciated assets. Our objective, in general, is to arrive at the following calculation of free cash flow:

---

[18]Under this assumption, cash from operations and funds (working capital) from operations converge.

Net operating income before replacement of depreciated assets
− Replacement of depreciated assets
− New investment
<u> </u>
= Free cash flow

This is equivalent to

CFO (net operating income plus adjustments)
− Cash for investment (new + replacement)
<u> </u>
= Free cash flow

Note that the CFO is not the same as cash from operations reported in the statement of cash flows. The figures differ with respect to the treatment of interest payments: normal CFO has been reduced by interest payments as required by SFAS 95 while the foregoing measure has not been so reduced.

Exhibit 15-5, column A, presents a SFAS 95 Statement of Cash Flows, for our hypothetical company. Exhibit 15-5, column B, calculates free cash flow in the form used in this section. The difference between them is the treatment of interest and the related income tax reduction.

In column A interest and income taxes are included in the computation of cash from operations. In column B interest and the associated tax deduction ($5 = 20% of $25)

EXHIBIT 15-5
Comparison of Statement of Cash Flows and Free Cash Flow

	A Cash Flow Statement (SFAS 95)	B Free Cash Flow For (valuation)
Cash from customers	$350	$350
Cash for operating expenses	(150)	(150)
Cash for interest (pretax)	(25)	NA
Cash for taxes	(25)	(30)
Cash from operations	**$150**	**$170**
Cash for investment*	**(80)**	**(80)**
Free cash flow		**$90**
Interest (net of tax)	NA	(20)
Dividends	(80)	(80)
New debt	10	10
Cash for financing	**(70)**	**(90)**
Net change in cash	$ 0	$ 0

NA – Not applicable
*Cash from investment is equal to the $30 of total new investment plus the $50 of depreciation that in this simplified example is assumed to be equivalent to the replacement cost of depreciated assets.

have been removed, increasing cash from operations by \$20 (\$25 − \$5). The after-tax interest has been included in cash from financing.

Note that we have assumed no change in cash during the period. If a change had taken place, column B would include the change in cash from operations. By doing so, we explicitly assume that cash is an element of working capital, as is accounts receivable.

Column B calculates free cash flow, which, necessarily, equals cash from financing (CFF). This definition of CFF differs from CFF under SFAS 95 by the inclusion of (after-tax) interest expense. It is this definition of CFF that results from the cash flow discounting model.

The free cash flow approach yields an estimated value for the firm. The appropriate discount rate is WACC. To derive the value of equity, one would subtract the value of debt from the firm value.

The advantages of the FCF approach is that many (but not all) of the issues relating to differences in accounting policies and of income versus funds versus cash flows disappear in this context. Whether the accounting method defines something as CFO or cash from investment (e.g., capitalization versus expense issues) does not make a difference when we focus on the FCF approach. Similarly, whether a cash flow is treated as a principal payment or as an interest payment (see Chapter 8) also does not matter as in this approach any payment to a creditor is excluded from free cash flow.

The problems that remain relate to choices as to whether to treat an item as an operating/investment item versus a financing item. Some potential adjustments follow:

Adjustments to Reported Cash from Investment

- Capitalized interest expense should be removed from cash for investments and added to free cash flow.

- All leases should be capitalized and treated as a reduction in free cash flow at the time the lease is entered into even though no cash has changed hands at that point in time.

- Assets acquired for debt or equity are presently not treated as part of cash from investment or financing. Such transactions are disclosed as "significant noncash investing and financing activities." The relevant amount of the transaction should be deducted from free cash flow.

The free cash flow approach, however, is not without problems. If the objective is valuation, it should not be subject to purely discretionary policies. This discussion assumes that any cash held within the firm is needed as operating working capital. Firms may decide to hold excess cash for other reasons.[19] Moreover, as shown, free cash flow is equal to financing cash flow. As Penman (1991) states,

---

[19]See, for example, the discussion of financial slack in Chapter 9.

Thus the value increment under this accounting regime would represent (be manipulated by) stock and debt issues or repurchases, and, yes, dividends. This is venturing on the absurd. *Free cash flow concerns the distribution of wealth rather than the generation of wealth* (Emphasis added).[20]

Dividends, Earnings, or Free Cash Flows?

All three DCF approaches (attempt to) measure the identical quantity: cash flows to the suppliers of capital (debt and equity) to the firm. They differ only as to how they go about measuring them, with the dividend approach measuring these cash flows directly and the other measures arriving at them in an indirect manner. The free cash flow approach arrives at the term (if the firm is an all-equity firm) by subtracting investment from operating cash flows, whereas the earnings approach expresses dividends indirectly as a fraction of earnings.

This begs the question: If cash flows can be measured directly as in the dividend approach, why use a roundabout approach? The answer to this question relates to the issues of uncertainty and forecasting.

Valuation is a function of future CF, not current CF. The ability of the firm to generate future dividends depends on its ability to generate future earnings. Thus, to arrive at a forecast of future dividends, it is necessary first to forecast future earnings. Similarly, the free cash flow model attempts to "clean up" the measurement problems of deriving dividends as simply a percentage of earnings given the problems with earnings measurement. Nevertheless, to forecast free cash flow the procedure followed is (generally[21]) to first forecast earnings and then adjust the forecasted earnings to generate free cash flow. Additionally, in many applications of the free cash flow model, the following formulation is used:

$$V_0 = \sum_{i=1}^{n} \frac{FCF_i}{(1 + r)^i} + \frac{V_n}{(1 + r)^n}$$

As with earnings, free cash flows are forecast over a short horizon of n years (usually 5), and then a terminal value V_n is estimated. This terminal value, which can contribute over 60% of the total value, is often earnings based.

Thus it is clear that no matter which valuation model is used, an important consideration is the ability to forecast the future earnings stream. When using these models, analysts, as well as academics, often employ accounting earnings for valuation purposes. A case in point is the price/earnings ratio, one of the most widely used measures, which is calculated on the basis of accounting earnings. To a great extent, this is due to the fact that reported earnings are readily available.

Additionally it is conceivable that accounting earnings are a better forecaster of future earning power or cash flows than are historical cash flows. This should not come

[20]Stephen H. Penman, "Return to Fundamentals" University of California at Berkeley Working Paper (November 1991), p. 29–30.

[21]See, for example, Tom Copeland, Tim Koller, and Jack Murrin, *Valuation: Measuring and Managing the Value of Companies,* John Wiley & Sons, New York (1990). They advocate the use of free cash flow for valuation but arrive at that measure by first forecasting earnings.

as a shock. After all, the underlying premise of accrual accounting is just that concept; recording a credit sale (to use one example) provides information as to future cash flows.

Another dimension exists that may make net income a better surrogate for forecasting purposes than cash flows. Period-to-period changes in income and cash flows are random, with some portion transitory and the remainder permanent. For valuation, only permanent earnings are fully capitalized. If cash flow is more subject to random transitory fluctuations due, for example, to timing of payments, then it may be easier to forecast permanent "earnings" using income rather than cash flows.

The next section summarizes some findings as to the price/earnings relationship. This will set the stage for a discussion of the time series properties of earnings and their implications for earnings forecasts and valuation.

Valuation: Empirical Results and Additional Considerations

Earnings Valuation and the P/E Ratio

The price/earning (P/E) is often used to reflect the relative valuation of the firm. This ratio represents the multiple of earnings used by the market to value the firm. Its relationship to our valuation models is straightforward.

For the no-growth case,

$$P = \frac{E}{r}$$

becomes

$$\frac{P}{E} = \frac{1}{r}$$

The P/E ratio in this case is equal to the inverse of the firm's capitalization rate. For the growth case,

$$P_i = \frac{kE_i(1 + g)}{r - g}$$

becomes

$$\frac{P_i}{E_i} = \frac{k(1 + g)}{r - g}$$

Growth, Risk, and Valuation. The preceding formulation implies that the relationship between prices and earnings is a function of the firm's growth rate and the firm's risk (as captured by r).

Beaver and Morse (1978) compared the price/earnings ratios of a sample of firms in an attempt to see whether growth and/or risk could explain the differentials across firms.

EXHIBIT 15-6
Results of Beaver and Morse—P/E Ratio Patterns

A. *Price/Earnings Ratio of Portfolio*

Portfolio	Number of Years After Portfolio Formation						
	0	1	2	3	5	10	14
1	50.0	22.7	16.4	13.8	13.2	13.0	8.3
5	20.8	17.5	16.9	15.9	13.7	11.9	8.4
10	14.3	11.9	11.5	10.3	10.1	9.9	8.3
15	11.1	10.8	10.4	10.0	10.0	8.6	7.1
20	8.9	9.1	9.6	9.4	9.3	9.0	7.7
25	5.8	6.9	8.0	7.9	7.9	7.8	8.9
$\frac{\text{Portfolio 1}}{\text{Portfolio 25}}$	8.6	3.3	2.1	1.7	1.7	1.7	0.9

B. *Cumulative Earnings Growth (%)*

Portfolio	0	1	2	3	5	10	14
1	−4.1	95.3	37.2	28.2	18.9	15.3	11.8
5	10.7	14.9	12.1	13.1	10.9	8.0	18.1
10	9.6	12.9	11.5	12.3	9.2	12.9	29.6
15	10.0	8.8	8.5	8.1	14.3	11.0	33.4
20	10.8	5.2	9.3	12.6	6.0	11.1	18.0
25	26.4	−3.3	7.5	10.8	12.9	16.7	10.1

Source: Beaver, William and Dale Morse, "What Determines Price-Earnings Ratios?" *Financial Analysts Journal* (July–August 1978), pp. 65–76. Adapted from Table 3 (P. 68) and Table 5 (P. 70)

They formed 25 portfolios of firms ranked by P/E ratios and compared the average P/E ratios of these portfolios over 15 years. Parts A and B of Exhibit 15-6 show P/E ratios and average earnings growth rates. Extreme P/E ratios are shown to revert over the period. Note the trend in the ratio of Portfolio 1's P/E to that of Portfolio 25.

Initially, at least, some of the differences in P/E ratios is due to the growth rate in earnings. Portfolios having high P/E ratios had higher growth rates in the first few years. However, their findings indicate (see year 10, for example) that, overall, persistent differences in P/E ratios exist that could not be explained by differences in growth rates.

> Comparing the P/E analysis with the growth analysis, we conclude that some of the initial dissipation of the P/E ratio in the first three years after formation can be explained by differential growth in earnings. Beyond that, however, there clearly exists a P/E differential that cannot be explained by differential earnings growth."[22]

In addition to being unable to explain the long-run differentials using growth rates, they also did not find differences in risk to explain the variations in P/E ratios. Beaver and Morse hypothesized that the long-run differential in P/E ratios was probably due to the effects of different accounting policies.[23]

[22]William H. Beaver and Dale Morse, "What Determines Price-Earnings Ratios?", *Financial Analysts Journal* (July–August 1978), pp. 65–76.
[23]They did not test this hypothesis.

Zarowin (1990) reexamined Beaver and Morse's findings and came to a different conclusion. Using a database[24] in which earnings had been "normalized" in an effort to remove measurement problems resulting from accounting differences, Zarowin found[25] that the differential P/E ratios could not be explained (solely) by differing accounting policies. Even with normalized earnings, persistent differences existed among firms' P/E ratios.

To explain these differences, Zarowin used forecasted growth as a growth proxy. This contrasts with Beaver and Morse who used (ex post) actual growth. *For ex ante valuation purposes, forecasted growth is the more appropriate measure and, as the model predicted, the differences in P/E ratios were attributable to differences in expected growth.* Zarowin argued that Beaver and Morse's nonfindings resulted from using actual growth rather than expected growth rates.

Effects of Permanent and Transitory Earnings and Measurement Error

Beaver and Morse's findings with respect to short-term "growth" rates provide a valuable insight into differential P/E ratios: the filtering by the market of transitory earnings components. In Exhibit 15-6 the high (low) P/E portfolios had low (high) earnings changes in the years the portfolios were formed. Portfolio 1's earnings change in year 0 was −4%, whereas Portfolio 25's was over 25%. The following year (year 1), the high (low) growth experienced is in the opposite direction to the change experienced the previous year. These observations indicate that the actual earnings measure realized when the initial P/E portfolios were formed was abnormally low (high) for the high (low) P/E categories. The next year the situation reversed itself as the firm returned to its normal earnings level. By "ignoring" those temporary changes in earnings, the market factored in the aberration due to the transitory component. That is, the market multiplied normal earnings by a constant. Those firms whose earnings were unusually low (high) appeared to have abnormally high (low) P/E ratios as a result.

On a more general level, academic research has attempted to capture the relationship between prices and earnings by means of the earnings response coefficient (ERC). The ERC measures the change in prices as a result of a change in earnings. If the relationship between prices and earnings is exactly as the simple models suggest, then the ERC would equal (or have the same order of magnitude as) the P/E ratio. Although Collins and Kothari (1989) show that risk and growth explain some of the cross-sectional differences in ERCs, the ERCs generated are typically much lower than expected.

Explanations for these differences relate to the points we have raised earlier. Collins and Kothari note that "persistence" (the extent to which earnings changes carry into the future) also plays a role in the size of ERCs. That is, to the extent there are transitory components prices will not react as much to changes in earnings. More specifically (as Box 15-1 indicates), transitory earnings[26] increase value on a dollar-for-dollar basis,

---

[24]The database used was from Kragg and Malkiel (1982).

[25]In his actual testing procedure, Zarowin used the earnings-to-price (E/P) ratio as the relationship between this ratio and risk and growth is hypothesized to be linear.

[26]An example of a transitory component is a holding gain such as an increase in the value of the firm's inventory. If such increases are not expected to be repeated in the future, then the effect on value should be dollar for dollar: a dollar increase in inventory value would result in a dollar increase in firm value.

BOX 15-1
The Effects of Transitory Components and Measurement Error on Valuation

---

Permanent Versus Transitory Earnings and Valuation

The effects of the permanent/transitory dichotomy on the P/E ratio are described below. The P/E ratio, as we have shown, is consistent with some simplified valuation models. Use of the P/E ratio is meant to be illustrative of the general class of models discussed. The effects are more readily shown on the P/E ratio due to its simplicity.

A firm's permanent earnings are defined as the portion of the earnings stream that is to be carried into the future. For example, assuming a constant dividend model where a firm pays out all earnings as dividends, the firm's expected earnings (dividends) are $5 per share, and $r = 10\%$, the value of the firm would be $5/0.1 = $50. The P/E ratio would be 10.

At the beginning of period 1, suppose it is known that due to some windfall the firm will actually earn $6.10 but after that the EPS will revert to $5. The value of the firm will be equal to $51 derived as

$$P_0 = \frac{E_1}{1.1} + \frac{P_1}{1.1} = \frac{\$6.10}{1.1} + \frac{\$50}{1.1} = \$51$$

The extra $1.10 earned in period 1 was not capitalized (i.e., the value of the firm did not go to $6.10/0.1 = $61). Only the permanent portion of $5.00 was capitalized. The one-shot or transitory portion of earnings entered into valuation only as a one-period adjustment (adding $\frac{\$1.10}{1.1}$ = $1 to value) without any carryover effects. The observed P/E ratio for this firm will be $51/$6.10 = 8.4 even though the firm's "true" capitalization rate is 10.

Would this low P/E ratio indicate that the firm is a buy?* It should not. The potential distortion in P/E ratios can be even greater if we consider measurement error inherent in accounting earnings.

Measurement Error and Its Effects on Valuation

Let E_a represent accounting earnings and E_e represent economic earnings. We will define the difference between them as measurement noise, $M = E_e - E_a$. Further, assume that economic earnings has a permanent and transitory component; that is,

$$E_e = E_{ep} + E_{et}$$

The true relationship between price and earnings will be $P = E_{ep}/r$, with an underlying "unobservable" P/E ratio of $1/r$. The market will fully capitalize only the permanent E_{ep}. Empirically, however, one observes P/E_a, which is equivalent to $P/(E_{ep} + E_{et} + M)$. This observable P/E ratio may be larger or smaller than the "true" P/E_{ep} capitalization rate, depending on the magnitudes and directions of the transitory component (E_{et}) and measurement error (M).

---

*In Chapter 4, we noted that one of the reported anomalies of efficient markets is the abnormal returns that seem to accrue to firms with low P/E ratios.

whereas permanent components increase value by the multiplier effect implied by the P/E ratio.

This is consistent with Kormendi and Lipe's (1987) finding that, the greater the persistence factor, the higher the ERC. Ryan and Zarowin (1993) demonstrate that the measurement error[27] factor also is a contributor to low ERCs. The relationship between earnings and price (as Box 15-1 shows) can be distorted by both transitory noise and measurement problems resulting from choice of accounting policies. Thus it becomes important, when using an earnings-based valuation number, to normalize earnings for nonrecurring items as well as to evaluate the impact of accounting choices, that is, the "quality" of the earnings. The next section discusses the impact of nonrecurring earnings and demonstrates the normalization procedure by applying it to Deere.

Effects of Nonrecurring Income and Differing Accounting Policies

Adjustments to Reported Income

As in the case of book value, reported net income may also benefit from analytic adjustments. The objective is to obtain a measure of operating results that better represents the *earning power* of the firm. The concept of earning power represents the (permanent) net income of the firm, ignoring temporary, nonrecurring, or unusual factors. In theory, the earning power of the firm is stable, but grows at a long-term growth rate. In valuation models, earning power rather than reported income should be the input.

Normalization of Reported Income. In practice, determining the earning power of the firm is difficult, requiring judgment to remove the "noise" that is always present. Part of the difficulty is that one analyst's definition of "noise" may differ from another's. Normalization is the term applied to the process of estimating normal operating earnings.

For noncyclical companies, the normalization of earnings consists mainly of removing nonrecurring items from reported income. Such items may include

- Realized capital gains or losses
- Gains or losses on the repurchase of debt
- Catastrophes such as natural disasters or accidents
- Strikes
- Impairment or "restructuring" charges
- Discontinued operations

The impact of these items may be segregated as a line item in the income statement. Alternatively, in some cases, it may be disclosed in footnotes or in the Management Discussion and Analysis. Sometimes the impact is given on a pretax basis only; other times the after-tax impact on EPS is disclosed.

---

[27]In the literature, the measurement error is referred to as the valuation-irrelevant component. See Ramakrishnan and Thomas (1991).

The analyst should search the financial statements for such items and then remove their effect from net income, *provided they are deemed to be nonrecurring*. When capital gains or losses recur, they cannot be ignored; they should, however, be segregated from operating earnings. Recurring losses from discontinued operations, impairments, or "restructurings" suggest that the company's depreciation or other accounting methods may be overstating reported income. Remember that because "restructurings" consist of past and future expenditures, they reflect on either past income or future income. Such write-offs should be segregated from operating earnings but not ignored.

In Exhibit 15-7 we have "normalized" Deere's reported earnings for the five years ended October 31, 1991, using data from financial statement footnotes and the MD&A. Some of the adjustments were discussed in Chapter 14; we comment briefly on the others.

The effect of the LIFO invasion (reduction of LIFO inventory quantities, see Chapter 5) was to increase 1991 net income by $84 million or $1.11 per share. As we cannot assume that inventories can be reduced continuously, the LIFO reserve reduction should be considered nonrecurring.

Yet Deere has had LIFO invasions in two of the past five years (three of the past six years if 1986 is included). The company has also had restructuring provisions in three of the past six years. How can such items be termed "nonrecurring"?

The short answer is that they cannot. Accounting standards setters have struggled to define such terms as "nonrecurring" and "extraordinary," with a notable lack of success. As users of financial statements, there is no reason to be drawn into this semantic morass. *What should concern analysts is the identification of factors that affect reported operating performance.*

LIFO invasions distort reported gross margins and net income. Restructuring provisions distort the normal pattern of expense recognition. For this reason they must be

EXHIBIT 15-7. DEERE
Normalization of Reported Net Income for Five Years Ended October 31, 1991
(in $ millions)

	1987	1988	1989	1990	1991
Reported net income	$(99)	$315	$380	$411	$ (20)
Effect of nonrecurring items					
Restructuring provisions	25				120
LIFO invasions	(14)				(84)
Cumulative effect of adoption					
of SFAS 96		(29)			
Utilization of tax loss					
carryforwards	18	(45)	(2)	(21)	(2)
Realized capital gains					(8)
Effect of strike	???				
Subtotal	29	(74)	(2)	(21)	26
Normalized net income	$(70)	$241	$378	$390	$ 6

Source: Deere & Company Annual Reports, 1988–1991.

identified so that the analyst can disentangle their impact on reported results of operations. Thus, for the moment, we will consider these items to be nonrecurring. We shall not ignore them, but will return to them later.

Tax loss carryforwards are another recurring "nonrecurring" item in Deere's income statement. In 1987 the company was unable to recognize the full tax effect of its losses in that year. In each subsequent year, some portion of tax loss carryforwards was recognized. (Remember that Deere pays income taxes in many jurisdictions; tax loss carryforwards are determined separately in each.)

It is important to segregate these amounts because they distort the relationship between pretax and after-tax income. Again, we will not ignore tax carryforwards, but will isolate them to identify their impact on both past and future results of operations.

Realized capital gains were reported only for 1991 (they may have been immaterial in prior years). As discussed in Chapter 11, the timing of capital gains recognition is often discretionary. For this reason, it is preferable to replace recognized gains with actual investment performance.

The last item, the effect of a long strike, is the most significant of these nonrecurring items. Yet we have the least information about it. The strike, which started in the last quarter of fiscal 1986, lasted through the entire first quarter of fiscal 1987. Deere reported a loss of $193 million ($2.84 per share) for that quarter, but we do not know how much of that loss was due to the strike. (In reality, nobody knows the answer to that question, although managements sometimes disclose estimates.)

A strike can have a significant effect on reported performance, before, during, and after the event. Production efficiency is often below normal before a strike (companies focus on building inventories rather than efficiency, while workers resist pressures to maximize output) and after (skills have deteriorated). On the other hand, above-normal production runs reduce unit costs by spreading fixed costs over larger quantities. Inventory swings can generate extra storage and transportation costs. For LIFO firms such as Deere, strikes can result in LIFO invasions as decrements cannot be replaced by year end.

Lacking a firm estimate of the cost of the strike, we have recorded the event with a large question mark. Clearly, 1987 was not a normal year for Deere, but we cannot normalize earnings for the effect of the strike.

Subtracting all the "adjustments" from reported net income results in "normalized" earnings. The pattern of normalized earnings is still erratic (Deere's business is, after all, cyclical), but there are some differences. Notice that the 1990 earnings increase is much smaller (3%) after normalization than before (9%).

The five-year total of the "nonrecurring" items is $42 million (excluding the unknown strike effect) or about $8.4 million per year ($42 million/5) per year. How should this amount be handled? One approach would "charge" each year $8.4 million. The argument behind this reasoning is that although a given event may be nonrecurring, on average, some such event does occur and must be accounted for.

Another approach would be to recognize the potential for such events and determine whether they have cash implications. Events expected to recur should be considered permanent in a valuation framework. Recall that the implications for valuation differ if the event is one time or recurring.

Thus, if the analyst were to assume that Deere would incur another LIFO liquidation in 1992,[28] the cash flow implications are higher taxes and lower purchases in that year. The net cash flow from the liquidation should not be considered a part of permanent earnings as Deere cannot be expected to liquidate inventories indefinitely. The liquidation should, therefore, be considered a "one-shot" addition to value after taking into consideration the fact that in the future the firm may have to increase production (lower cash flows) to rebuild inventories. It should also be noted that the LIFO liquidation is nothing more than the realization of price increases which occurred in past years, rather than current period gains.

For the most part, nonrecurring items represent failures of the accrual accounting system. LIFO invasions are the reversal of LIFO reserves added in earlier years (which turned out to be temporary) that reduced reported income at that time.

Restructuring provisions represent either costs of prior periods (underdepreciation of assets, for example) or of later periods (severance and postemployment benefits, lease costs).

To ignore "nonrecurring" items is to permit companies to sweep their mistakes under the rug. The purpose of analysis is to understand, not to forgive.

Normalizing over the Economic Cycle. For cyclical firms, there is another complicating factor. The analyst needs to consider whether operating earnings represent a cyclical high point or low point of the current cycle. This is true whether earnings are sensitive to the general economy or to industry-specific cycles (property and casualty insurance is but one example). Given the varying length of business cycles, the analysis of cyclical firms should encompass a substantial time period—at least one full business cycle. Once these data are assembled, then earning power can be estimated using one of several methods.

One simplistic method is to average operating earnings over the entire cycle and use that average for valuation purposes. A slightly more sophisticated method uses average profitability ratios (such as gross margin or operating margin) or return ratios (return on equity) applied to current period sales or equity to estimate earning power based on the current level of operation.

A better approach involves the creation of an earnings model of the firm based on the economic factors that drive the firm's profitability. For example, industrial production might be an independent variable for a manufacturer of cardboard boxes. Firm sales could then be forecast using regression analysis. That sales forecast, combined with an analysis of the firm's cost structure (see discussion of fixed and variable costs in Chapter 3), could be used to forecast the firm's earnings.

For conglomerates or other multidivisional firms, analysis needs to be done separately for each segment. While segment data are limited (see Chapter 11), they should be used to estimate the future sales and earnings of each line of business. Firm forecasts are arrived at by adding together the segment forecasts and adjusting for corporate overhead (such as debt). We return to these issues in the next part of the chapter, when we discuss forecasting models.

---

[28]Value Line, for example, did make such a forecast for Deere in its March 1992 report.

Effects of Acquisitions. Acquisitions affect reported earnings as the results of the acquired firm are included. The earnings of the acquired firm and the accounting method used must both be examined.

When the pooling of interests method is used, the operating results of the two firms are combined retroactively and prospectively. Thus previously reported earnings are restated. Depending on the profitability of the acquired firm, the growth rate of reported earnings will change in most cases. For example, a firm with a high growth rate (whose shares sell at a high price/earnings ratio), can merge with a low-growth firm (whose shares sell at a low price/earnings ratio). The result will be higher earnings but a lower growth rate.

When the purchase method is used to account for an acquisition, the results of the acquired firm are included only following the merger. Depending on the price paid, the means of payment (cash or stock), the earnings of the acquired firm, and the accounting adjustments required by the purchase method, the acquisition may either increase or dilute reported earnings per share. *The trend of sales and earnings will always be distorted.*

Because the sales of the acquired firm are included only following the merger, reported sales of the acquiring firm will appear to rise, as will expense categories. While pro forma statements (which are required disclosures) may provide some basis of comparison, it is often difficult to separate internal growth from the effect of acquisitions. When there are many small acquisitions, it may be impossible to segregate the impact of each one. Sometimes segment data can help the analyst to track significant acquisitions, if they are maintained as separate segments.

The earnings trend is also impacted, but not in any predictable fashion. The earnings of the acquired firm will be included postmerger. However, these earnings will be offset by the impact of purchase method adjustments and financing costs related to the merger. If the acquisition is partly financed with common stock (directly, or indirectly by selling shares shortly thereafter), then the additional shares will dilute reported EPS.

Impact of Changes in Exchange Rates. When firms operate in foreign countries, changing exchange rates will also affect reported earnings. Translation gains and losses may be included in reported income. More subtle, but no less real, is the impact of translating the operating results of foreign subsidiaries into the parent (reporting) currency. When foreign currencies appreciate, the sales and earnings of operations in those currencies translate into more dollars (or whichever reporting currency is used), increasing consolidated sales and earnings. This phenomenon is illustrated in Chapter 13, using IBM as an example.

Effect of Accounting Changes. Last, but far from least, changes in accounting methods or estimates can have a major influence on the trend of reported earnings. Frequently found examples of voluntary changes include

- Inventory method (Chapter 5)
- Depreciation method or lives (Chapter 6)
- Assumptions used for benefit plans (Chapter 9)
- Accounting method for affiliates (Chapter 11)

Deere's "Pension and Other Retirement Benefits" footnote indicates changes in the discount rate used to account for pension plan benefits since adoption of SFAS 87 in 1986 (1988 for foreign plans), with the rate used to compute pension cost varying from 8.3% to 9.6%. As there has been no clear trend in that rate, the effect has not been systematic, although reported income for individual years has been affected.

Mandated accounting changes also have had significant effects on reported earnings in recent years. Examples include

- Postemployment benefits (Chapter 9)
- Income taxes (Chapter 7)

The adoption of SFAS 106, Postemployment Benefits, will have a significant effect on Deere's future earnings, depending on the method of adoption. If the prospective method of adoption is used, the increase in postemployment benefit cost will be $100 million (see pension footnote), nearly one third of average earnings over the 1989–1991 period.

Deere adopted SFAS 96, income taxes, in 1988; we have previously discussed the impact of this change on reported earnings. SFAS 109, which replaced SFAS 96, was adopted in fiscal 1992 but had no significant effect on reported earnings.

Quality of Earnings

The term "quality of earnings" usually refers to the degree of conservatism in a firm's reported earnings. Indicators of high earnings quality include

- Use of LIFO inventory accounting (assuming rising prices)
- Bad-debt reserves that are high relative to receivables and past credit losses
- Use of accelerated depreciation methods and short lives
- Rapid write-off of acquisition goodwill and other intangibles
- Minimal capitalization of interest and overhead
- Minimal capitalization of computer software
- Expensing of start-up costs of new operations
- Use of the completed contract method of accounting
- Conservative assumptions used for employee benefit plans
- Adequate provisions for lawsuits and other loss contingencies
- Minimal use of off-balance-sheet financing techniques
- Conservative revenue recognition methods
- Lack of "nonrecurring" gains
- Lack of "noncash" earnings
- Clear and adequate disclosures

These issues were discussed in earlier chapters. Indicators listed tend to result in the underreporting of income through a combination of delayed recognition of revenues and accelerated recognition of expenses and losses.

Why is the "quality of earnings" important?

One reason is that companies with high earnings quality are considered to be less risky because these firms have "banked" earnings using conservative accounting policies. Such firms frequently are risk averse in other ways, in their financial structures and business plans, for example. High-quality earnings should be accorded a higher price/earnings multiple (all other things being equal) than low-quality earnings. The higher multiple reflects the lower risk as well as the understatement of reported income.

Alternatively, firms with different degrees of earnings quality can be compared by making adjustments to reported earnings so that the earnings of all firms are based on the same accounting principles and estimates. Techniques for making such adjustments appear throughout the book.

It should be noted that the term earnings quality is sometimes used to denote predictability of earnings. Firms with predictable earnings growth (such as drug and consumer product firms) are sometimes said to have "high-quality" earnings. This usage is, of course, quite different; in some cases predictability is the result of income manipulation, creating low-quality earnings by the definition we have used. Analysts should be careful to determine which meaning of the term "quality of earnings" is intended when it is used.

In our examination of Deere's quality of earnings, we consider the following issues:

1. Deere uses LIFO for 80% of worldwide inventories. The large LIFO liquidation in 1991, however, reduced the quality of earnings in that year.

2. The allowance for bad debts does not appear high (see discussion in Chapter 14).

3. Deere uses straight-line depreciation; there is no indication that lives are especially short.[29] Depreciation for tax purposes is considerably higher than is that for reporting purposes. (This can be seen from the large deferred tax impact of depreciation revealed in the income tax footnote.)

4. Acquisitions have been minimal, with little impact on reported growth. Goodwill is amortized over 25 years, below average for U.S. companies.

5. There is no evidence of capitalized interest.

6. Pension plan assumptions are not abnormal, although the return on assets assumption is above average (see Chapter 9).

7. Deere does use off-balance-sheet financing techniques.

8. No evidence of revenue recognition problems exists, except to the extent that credit receivables may not be collectible under adverse economic circumstances (see discussion in Chapter 14).

9. Deere's disclosures are generally detailed, and the segment disclosures are informative.

Our conclusion is that Deere falls in the broad middle of American business; its quality of earnings is neither particularly high nor especially low.

---

[29]Deere is not required to provide Schedules V and VI in its 10-K. The analysis in Chapter 6 is not possible. There are no data regarding gains or losses on the sale of property. The restructuring provision suggests that the carrying value of some assets may be overstated.

FORECASTING MODELS AND TIME SERIES PROPERTIES OF EARNINGS

As the earlier discussion indicates, the ability to forecast earnings and to filter out its transitory and permanent components is of considerable importance in the context of valuation. A great deal of empirical research has focused on the time series properties of earnings and the development of appropriate forecasting models. The research has generally been based upon income rather than cash flow concepts. In one sense, this is unfortunate. From a practical point of view, however, it may be that earnings work as well as or better than (free) cash flow, for reasons discussed earlier. Moreover, to the extent that evidence exists on the time series properties of cash flows, it indicates little difference between the properties of income and cash flows. The next section reviews some of these results.

FORECASTING MODELS

Generally, two classes of forecasting models exist in the literature: extrapolative models and index models. These are "mechanical" models in that forecasts are made mechanically using the statistical properties of these models without any further judgment on the part of the forecaster.

Extrapolative Models

Extrapolative models use the previous time series of earnings in an attempt to forecast the future level of earnings. That is, the forecast of next period's income defined as $E(Y_{t+1})$ is a function of the past history of earnings.

$$E(Y_{t+1}) = f(Y_t, Y_{t-1}, \ldots, Y_1)$$

Permanent Versus Transitory Components

It is important to separate the permanent and transitory components of a firm's earnings when using time series. The permanent component is expected to carry on into the future. The permanent earnings stream itself can, however, be altered by random events or shocks affecting the firm or its environment. If these random occurrences are of a permanent nature, then they alter the permanent earnings stream.[30] The permanent earnings stream is, thus, a summation of the previous permanent random occurrences.

Nonpermanent, or transitory, random events do not affect the permanent earnings stream. To the extent that transitory random shocks occur, the actual underlying permanent stream is "disguised" and therefore unobservable. The observed income is a summation of permanent and transitory components. Time series analysis is undertaken in an attempt to identify the underlying permanent earnings stream of the firm.

---

[30]For example, an external event may raise oil prices, permanently affecting the earnings of oil producers.

For forecasting purposes, the distinction between permanent and transitory components can be illustrated as follows. Assume that a company in a no-growth environment had expected earnings of $10 but actually realized earnings of $11 in the current period. What is the estimate of the next period's earnings? Maintaining the original estimate of $10 assumes that next period the company's earnings will revert from its present level of $11 to the previous expectation of $10. The $1 deviation ($11 − $10) is treated as a one-time, *transitory,* occurrence that will not be repeated in the next period. In other words, future expectations are not affected by the actual earnings in a given period. Such a process is referred to as *mean reverting,* as the earnings revert to a constant level. In general, for a mean-reverting process, the forecast of next period or, for that matter, any period earnings is a constant, *u.* The estimate of *u* is the mean of all prior period earnings. That is,

$$E(Y_{t+1}) = u$$

where *u* is estimated as

$$u = \frac{1}{t}(Y_t + Y_{t-1} + \ldots + Y_2 + Y_1)$$

If, on the other hand, the $1 deviation is viewed as permanent, then the next period expectation would be $11. Such a process is referred to as a *martingale* or *random walk.* For such a process, the only information needed to generate the next period forecast is the prior period result. All earlier information is irrelevant.

$$E(Y_{t+1}) = Y_t$$

In a martingale process expectations change from period to period based on reported earnings.

The distinction between mean-reverting and martingale processes need not be confined to a no-growth environment. Assume that a company whose income is expected to grow by $2.00 each year had an expected income of $12.00 this year. The actual realization was, however, $11.50, a deviation of $0.50 from expectation. If this deviation is viewed as transitory, then the underlying income of the firm is still assumed to be $12.00. The forecast of next period's income would be $12.00 + $2.00 = $14.00.

$$E(Y_{t+1}) = E(Y_t) + d$$

where *d* represent the growth term.

If the $0.50 deviation is viewed as permanent, then the starting point for the next period growth is the realized $11.50 and the next period forecast is $11.50 + $2.00 = $13.50. Such a process is referred to as a martingale with "drift" or a submartingale and can be expressed as

$$E(Y_{t+1}) = Y_t + d$$

The martingale and mean-reverting processes are two extremes on a continuum. In the first case, the forecast of the next period is determined solely by the current period results. For the mean-reverting process, the current period's results are relevant only to estimate the underlying mean. When choosing between the two extremes of random walk or mean-reverting processes, *the overwhelming empirical evidence indicates that, on average, earnings follow a submartingale process*.

It is, of course, possible that both transitory and permanent components are present in a deviation. Such a process is described in Box 15-2. Forecasting such a time series places one within the two extremes. The forecast would not depend solely on current period but would also depend on all previous reported earnings. At the same

---

BOX 15-2
Description of a Time Series Process Having Transitory and Permanent Components

---

The process is described as

$$X_t = X_{t-1} + v_t$$
$$Y_t = X_t + e_t$$

Therefore,

$$Y_t = X_{t-1} + v_t + e_t$$

Let X_t represent the firm's permanent earnings stream. Then the v_t are the periodic random occurrences that become a permanent part of the firm's earnings.* If there are transitory components, symbolized by e_t, the permanent stream X_t would be unobservable. Instead, one would observe Y_t, which is made up of the permanent and transitory components.† If there are no transitory components, the description of the process would stop at the first equation $(X_t = X_{t-1} + v_t)$, and we would have a random walk process. If, on the other hand, there are no permanent random components, the underlying permanent earnings stream of the firm is a constant, as $X_t = X_{t-1} = X_{t-2}$ . . . and so on. This constant would be the mean, as by definition all random occurrences are represented by the transitory component e_t and the process is mean reverting.

---

*Note that

$$X_t = X_0 + \Sigma v_i$$

That is, this period's permanent earnings is a summation of all previous permanent random occurrences since period 0.
   †Note that

$$Y_t = X_0 + \Sigma v_i + e_t$$

That is, this period's reported earnings is a summation of all previous permanent random occurrences and this period's transitory component.

time, the weights would not be the same for all previous realizations as is the case in mean-reverting models. Typically, the forecast would be a weighted average of previous reported earnings. The *exponential smoothing* model is one such model that uses higher weights for more recent data and lower weights for earlier data. A more complex set of forecasting models used in the literature are *Box-Jenkins models*.[31]

Diagnostic tests, using these models, indicated that, for many firms, the pure (sub)martingale model was not descriptive of the underlying time series. Nevertheless, when forecasting models were designed for these firms on an individual basis, they did not, on average, outperform the (sub)martingale process. The best forecast *based solely on the previous time series* was a (sub)martingale forecast.

The only consistent results that belied this point occurred when the previous year's deviation was abnormally large.[32] Brooks and Buckmaster (1976) found that such very large deviations were typically transitory and that forecasts based upon the exponential smoothing model did better than martingale-based forecasts. The results of Brooks and Buckmaster are in line with those of Beaver and Morse reported earlier.

In a similar vein, Freeman, Ohlson, and Penman (1982) show that forecasts of earnings can be improved by considering the trend in the firm's ROE ratio. Since ROE measures the rates of return on the firm's book value, if the current ROE is "considerably" higher (lower) than its recent mean,[33] it is an indication that current earnings are too high (low) and a reversal can be expected in the next period.

Index Models

The second class of models does not rely on the previous history of earnings but rather makes use of independent variables or indices to forecast earnings. The forecast of earnings is described as $E(Y_{t+1}) = f(Z_{1t}, Z_{2t}, \ldots, Z_{nt})$, where the Z's represent independent variables. The most commonly used model of this sort was described previously (see Chapter 14) in the development of the accounting beta. This model, known as the market model of accounting income, expresses earnings as a function of some overall market index of earnings (ME) such as the S&P 500 earnings index, GNP, corporate earnings, or the average earnings of the sample of firms being examined. Operationally, the model is represented as

$$E(Y_{t+1}) = a + bME_{t+1}$$

---

[31] This class of models is beyond the scope of this book. The interested reader is referred to Box and Jenkins (1976).

[32] There are a number of ways "abnormally large" could be defined. Brooks and Buckmaster for example defined the normalized first difference (nfd) as

$$\text{nfd} = \frac{(Y_t - Y_{t-1})}{\textbf{Standard deviation of earnings}}$$

For large absolute values of nfd, they found exponential smoothing parameters ranging from 0.2 to 0.9 (depending on the sign and magnitude of nfd) to be better predictors than a martingale model.

[33] This result assumes stable book values with no major changes resulting from new stock issues, repurchases, or acquisitions.

where a and b are regression parameters derived using the previous history of earnings and the market index.[34]

Comparisons between this latter model and the submartingale also generally resulted in no preference for this second class of models as the submartingale performed as well. Fried and Givoly (1982), for example, found that over the 11-year period (1969–1979), the index model had an average percentage forecast error equal to 20.3%, whereas the (modified[35]) submartingale's percentage forecast error was 19.3%.

Forecasting Using Disaggregated Data

The models described here all use time series of annual earnings data to forecast annual earnings. The literature has also examined, in varying degrees, the forecasting of annual income by using data disaggregated along three dimensions:

1. By time, using quarterly data
2. By segment, using segment-based data
3. By component using the components of the income statement

Quarterly Forecasting Models

Forecasting models using quarterly data have been those most commonly examined. Although the quarterly models have been used primarily to forecast quarterly earnings, they have also been utilized to forecast annual earnings, such forecasts usually consisting of a summation of the individual quarterly forecasts. These forecasts have been found generally to outperform forecasts based upon annual models alone (see Hopwood, McKeown, and Newbold, 1982). Moreover, as expected, the farther along in the year and the more interim periods that have gone by, the greater the accuracy of forecasts using quarterly reports.

Unlike annual earnings numbers, which seem to follow martingale or submartingale "patterns," quarterly earnings generally are better described by more complex models. The seasonality of certain businesses make the task of designing quarterly models more challenging. Box-Jenkins forecasting techniques, mentioned earlier, are designed to detect seasonality components and have been used with some success in quarterly time series models.

Generally, the extrapolative models for quarterly series tend to find that a quarter's income Q_t (e.g., second quarter of 1992) is "related" to the immediately preceding quarter Q_{t-1} (first quarter of 1992) and the same quarter of the preceding year Q_{t-4} (second quarter of 1991). Three competing models have been put forward as representative of the "average" firm. That is, individually fitted models were not able to improve upon these models in a meaningful way. The models and the researchers who suggested them are the following:

---

[34]As noted in Chapter 14, these models are generally expressed in terms of the relationship between the change in earnings and the change in the index.

[35]The model is referred to as modified because it applied the Brooks and Buckmaster criterion where appropriate.

Model 1: Watts (1975) and Griffin (1977)

$$E(Q_t) = Q_{t-4} + (Q_{t-1} - Q_{t-5}) - be_{t-1} - ce_{t-4} + bce_{t-5}$$

Model 2: Foster (1977)

$$E(Q_t) = Q_{t-4} + a(Q_{t-1} - Q_{t-5}) + d$$

Model 3: Brown and Rozeff (1979)

$$E(Q_t) = Q_{t-4} + a(Q_{t-1} - Q_{t-5}) - ce_{t-4}$$

where a, b, and c are estimated parameters, d is a drift term (the average seasonal change), and e_t (times the respective parameter) represents the transitory portion of a period's Q_t.

Segment-Based Forecasts

The merits of forecasting annual earnings using segment-based data were discussed at some length in Chapter 11. *For time series models,* the potential for improvement was highly dependent on the degree to which the underlying time series behavior of the individual segments differed. If segments, for example, were affected in a similar fashion throughout the business cycle, then the advantage of using segment data was lessened. Moreover (again, for time series models), the improvement of segment-based data over consolidated data seemed not to go beyond the prediction of sales.

Forecasts Using Income or Balance Sheet Components

Studies that use income statement (or balance sheet) components to help in the forecasting of income are few and far between. These models come in one of two forms. The first, similar to segment-based models, generates a forecast of earnings by forecasting individual sales, cost of goods sold, operating expenses, depreciation, and so forth and then aggregating these components to forecast earnings. The results suggest that this form of forecasting is not promising[36] for the same reason discussed for segment-based models. The time series of the individual components are interdependent, which militates against substantial gains in predictive power from disaggregated data.

The second form shows more promise. In these models, interrelationships among income and balance sheet components are modeled explicitly, and a structural model of the firm is constructed. Such "econometric" models were designed by Elliott and Uphoff (1972) and, more recently, Wild (1987). Unfortunately, it is difficult to generalize from these models. Although their results showed improved predictive ability, given the difficulty in constructing such models, studies were usually limited to small samples.[37]

---

[36]See, for example, Fried (1978).
[37]Wild's study, for example, is based on one firm.

A variation of this approach to forecasting is the Ou and Penman (1989) study, which used common financial ratios to improve upon the forecasting ability of a random walk model. They constructed a model that forecast the probability that a firm's earnings change would be positive or negative relative to that forecasted by a random walk (with drift) process. That is, they estimated the probability that a firm's earnings next year (Y_{t+1}) would be higher than a random walk (with drift) forecast of earnings,

$$E(Y_{t+1}) = Y_t + d$$

where d represents the "drift" term calculated as the average change in earnings over the previous four years. More formally, the model generated an assessment of the following probability (Pr):

$$Pr[Y_{t+1} > (Y_t + d)]$$

A set of 68 financial variables and ratios were first analyzed individually to see which were most associated with earnings changes. The analysis was carried out separately for the two subperiods 1965–1972 and 1973–1977. The "best" 18 variables were then incorporated in a multivariate model for each of the subperiods. The resultant models are presented in Exhibit 15-8. Note that not all 18 variables are incorporated in the final model(s) and that the variables incorporated differ from period to period. The model developed over the 1965–1972 period was used to forecast the period 1973–1977, and the model developed over 1973–1977 period was used to forecast the period 1978–1983.

The results of the forecasting model are presented in Exhibit 15-9. At a cutoff of $Pr = 60\%$ the Pr correctly predicted the direction of earnings close to two-thirds of the time. Ou and Penman thus demonstrated that financial ratios could be used successfully to improve predictive power. Their use of ratios, however, was mechanical, in that they did not use any judgment in interpreting the variables they examined. This was driven in part by the nature of the research process and their sample size.

Bernard and Noel (1991) approached forecasting in a less mechanical fashion by using trends in (finished goods and work in process) inventory levels to forecast sales and earnings.[38] As discussed in Chapter 5, they were able to use these variables to aid in prediction. However, in their conclusions, they argued that the nature of the analysis called for a "contextual" approach. That is, changes in inventory may mean different things to different firms. Knowledge of the firm, the industry, and the overall state of the economy at that time was needed before such models could be used to their fullest potential.

Box 15-3 extends the discussion of such models in a different context, that is, in terms of how they perform in forecasting (abnormal) returns.

---

[38]The study by Freeman, Ohlson, and Penman discussed earlier would also qualify as non-mechanical as it combined the relationship of the firm's book value, ROE, and earnings.

EXHIBIT 15-8
Variables Used in Ou and Penman Study

	Included in Model for Subperiod	
Accounting Descriptor	1965–1972	1973–1977
% Δ in current ratio		✔
% Δ in quick ratio		✔
% Δ in inventory turnover	✔	
Inventory/total assets		✔
% Δ in the previous ratio	✔	✔
% Δ in inventory		✔
% Δ in sales		✔
% Δ in depreciation	✔	
Δ in dividend per share	✔	✔
% Δ in depreciation/plant assets	✔	
Return on opening equity		✔
Δ in the previous ratio		✔
% Δ in capital expenditures/total assets	✔	
Previous ratio with a one-year lag	✔	✔
Debt/equity ratio		✔
% Δ in the previous ratio	✔	
% Δ in sales/total assets	✔	
Return on total assets	✔	✔
Return on closing equity	✔	
Gross margin ratio	✔	
% Δ in pretax income/sales		✔
Sales to total cash		✔
% Δ in total assets		✔
Cash flow to debt	✔	
Working capital/total assets		✔
Operating income/total assets	✔	✔
Repayment of long-term debt as % of total long-term debt	✔	✔
Cash dividend/cash flows	✔	

Source: Ou, Jane A. and Stephen Penman, "Financial Statement Analysis and the Prediction of Stock Returns", *Journal of Accounting and Economics* 11 (1989), pp. 295–329. Table 3 (P. 307)

COMPARISON WITH FINANCIAL ANALYSTS' FORECASTS

Earnings forecasting is a prime activity of financial analysts. Such financial analysts' forecasts (FAFs), which are important inputs in valuation models, are usually made within the confines of a contextual approach as such forecasts possess two advantages over those generated by time series models. First, analysts have a broader set of data available upon which to base their forecasts. Extrapolative models use only the past history of earnings; index models are limited to the information contained in the indices chosen.

EXHIBIT 15-9
Results of Ou and Penman Study

Summary of prediction performance of earnings prediction models; earnings changes are predicted one year ahead on the basis of $\bar{Pr}$.*

	Predictions over 1973–1977		Predictions over 1978–1983	
	$\bar{Pr}$ cutoff		$\bar{Pr}$ cutoff	
	(0.5, 0.5)	(0.6, 0.4)	(0.5, 0.5)	(0.6, 0.4)
Number of observations	9138	5791	9640	4779
% correct predictions	62%	67%	60%	67%
χ_1^2 from 2 × 2 table (and *p*-value)	299.94	271.63	387.46	444.54
	(0.000)	(0.000)	(0.000)	(0.000)
% predicted EPS increases correct	62%	67%	59%	66%
% predicted EPS decreases correct	61%	66%	62%	67%

*$\bar{Pr}$ is the estimated probability of an earnings increase indicated by the prediction models.
Source: Ou, Jane A. and Stephen Penman, "Financial Statement Analysis and the Prediction of Stock Returns", *Journal of Accounting and Economics* 11 (1989), pp. 295–329. Table 4 (P. 308)

BOX 15-3
Fundamental Analysis and Valuation: Some Empirical Evidence

In Chapter 4, we noted that accounting research has turned to valuation issues. The objective of the Ou and Penman study, discussed in the chapter, was not "predictive ability" but rather valuation. Their purpose was to see whether a trading strategy* based on their earnings forecasts would prove to be fruitful. It was. The average market adjusted return was 14.5% per annum over a 24-month holding period.†

Holthausen and Larcker (1992) "replicated" Ou and Penman's study with some variation. They did not use the ratios to first forecast earnings and then "trade" based on the expected earnings. Rather, they developed a model to forecast "abnormal" returns directly. Implementation of this model proved to be more successful in earning abnormal returns than Ou and Penman's strategy. Although they found that Ou and Penman's results were sensitive to the time period examined, the excess returns earned by their model were something of a puzzle to them.

we find it surprising that a statistical model, derived without any consideration of any economic foundations, can earn excess returns of the magnitude determined here. Had our trading strategy been based on some new economic insight that others had never considered, or if it had been based upon hours of diligent investigation of annual reports of the firm, its suppliers, customers, the industry, and/or government documents, we would be more convinced that the trading strategy was earning "true" excess returns. As such, we view the results of our paper as something of a puzzle, similar in spirit to other evidence which is inconsistent with joint tests of market efficiency and asset pricing.‡

Both papers have uncovered relationships between prices and financial statement information that go beyond just looking at "bottom-line" earnings. The explanation for their success, as

BOX 15-3. *(Continued)*

Holthausen and Larcker suggest, is not clear. Further, it is implied that even greater returns may be possible if the information was examined in a more analytic fashion.

Lev and Thiagarajan (1991) took a step in this direction. Rather than just allowing statistical models to "select" their predictive variables, they attempted to, a priori, select predictive variables on the basis of those claimed to be useful by financial analysts. The variables they examined included

1. Indications of future growth, for example,
   a. Levels of investment (capital expenditures and R&D)
   b. The percentage change in inventory and receivables relative to that of sales
2. Profitability measures, for example,
   a. Changes in the gross margin percentage
   b. The rate of change in SG&A expenses
3. "Quality" of earnings indicators, for example,
   a. LIFO versus FIFO earnings numbers
   b. Audit qualification
4. Leading indicators, for example,
   a. Order backlog
   b. Change in labor force indicating changes in future costs

Additionally, the authors allowed for the possibility that the effects of these variables might vary (contextual approach) depending on the state of the economy or industry. For example, the impact of changes in inventory levels may depend on whether the firm itself experiences an increase in inventory levels or the economy as a whole is going through such an expansion.

They found that the signals were generally value relevant and could be used to explain and "forecast" abnormal returns. Moreover, varying economic and industry conditions had the desired effect. The interpretation of the financial variables, however, could be quite subtle and situation specific:

The above findings indicate that the valuation-relevance of earnings is assessed by investors within a *broad context* of financial information. Thus, for example, a positive earnings surprise combined with a disproportionate inventory increase, or an order backlog decrease, will have different valuation implications than an identical earnings surprise accompanied by an order backlog increase or a labor force decrease.§

Financial analysis clearly goes beyond the bottom line.

---

*Based on the probability generated by the model, they examined the results of the following trading strategy. If *Pr* was greater than 60%, indicating at least a 60% probability that the earnings change would be positive, a long position in the firm's stock was taken. If the *Pr* was less than 40%, equivalent to saying that the probability is greater than 60% that the earnings change will be negative, a short position in the firm's stock was taken.

†This paper, in effect, was an extension of the Ou paper discussed in Chapter 4. There is much debate (see Ball, 1992) as to whether Ou and Penman's results are an example of market inefficiency as the returns they garnered were "abnormal" or whether their model allowed them to predict better expected earnings relative to the CAPM. We do not intend to enter that debate. What is important is that under either premise, the variables proved to be *valuation relevant*.

‡R. W. Holthausen and D. F. Larcker, "The Prediction of Stock Returns Using Financial Statement Information," *Journal of Accounting and Economics* (1992), pp. 373–411.

§Baruch Lev and S. Ramu Thiagarajan, "Fundamental Information Analysis," Working Paper, 1991, p. 50.

Analysts are not restricted as to the information they can incorporate in their forecasts. Included in this broader set, of course, is the ability to analyze the financial statements and the firm's environment, gleaning information that time series models ignore. Also included are economic forecasts and company disclosures of current business conditions.[39]

In addition, analysts possess a timing advantage in that they can update their forecasts based upon data available after the publication of the annual (or quarterly) report. This information will not be available for time series forecasting until publication of the next report.

Of course, FAFs are much costlier and time consuming to generate than are simple time series forecasts. Bhushan (1989) analyzed analyst services as an economic good by examining the factors that affect the supply and demand for such services. His results are summarized in Exhibit 15-10. These results are only descriptive in the sense that they describe environments that call for more or fewer analyst services. Whether the services provided actually prove to be "useful" was not the focus of Bhushan's study.

For analysts' forecasts to be useful, superiority over time series forecasts must be demonstrated. A number of comparison studies have been carried out.

---

[39]Few firms explicitly forecast earnings. Many will, however, provide "guidance" regarding future operating results to prevent surprises (especially negative ones) when actual earnings are released.

EXHIBIT 15-10
Factors Influencing Degree of Analyst Coverage

Factors Leading to Increased Analyst Coverage

1. *Firm Size*. The larger the firm, the greater the profit that can be earned on any piece of information. This would tend to increase analyst coverage. Additionally, to the extent (brokerage house) analysts are interested in increasing the volume of business for their firms, the larger the firm the greater the potential for transactions business.
2. *Institutional Holdings*. The number of analysts is positively related to both the number of institutions holding shares in a company and the percentage of shares held by institutions.
3. *Greater Return Variability*. The greater the uncertainty associated with a firm, the greater the need for analysts to provide information that may reduce that uncertainty.
4. *Correlation Between Firm and Market Return*. For information relating to macro variables, information acquisition costs are likely to be lower, the more the firm's returns are correlated with the market. This lower cost would therefore increase analyst coverage.

Factors Leading to Decreased Analyst Coverage

5. *Insider Holdings* (Manager Controlled). The greater the percentage of shares held by insiders, the less demand there is for analysts as presumably the insiders have direct access to all the information they need.
6. *Degree of Diversification*. The greater the number of segments, the more complex and costly it is to follow the company.

Source: Derived from discussions in Ravi Bhushan, "Firm Characteristics and Analyst Following", *Journal of Accounting and Economics* (1989), pp. 255–274.

The analyst forecasts used in these studies are generally those that are publicly available and collected by services such as Zacks Investment Research and the Institutional Brokers Estimate System (IBES). These services collect data from a number of analysts. The former provides the individual FAFs; the latter provides data as to the mean and variance of the FAFs. In addition such investor advisory services as Value Line, Moody's, and Standard & Poor's publish earnings forecasts.

The results generally indicate a superiority of analysts' forecasts, albeit not in a dramatic fashion. Givoly and Lakonishok (1984) surveyed studies of analysts' forecasts that compared them to mechanical models. Exhibit 15-11A is adapted from this paper.

> [the table] summarizes the results of the recent studies. Although the magnitude of the errors varied (because of the different treatment of outliers, the different test periods and the fact that Fried and Givoly employed mean, rather than individual forecasts), the common finding is that analysts predict earnings significantly more accurately than mechanical models.[40]

Using quarterly numbers, Brown, Hagerman, Griffin, and Zmijewski (1987a) compared the performance of the three quarterly earnings forecasting models listed with those generated by security analysts (Value Line forecasts) for a sample of over 200 companies. The forecasting ability one quarter, two quarter, and three quarters ahead was compared. The results are summarized in Exhibit 15-11B indicating the superiority of analysts' forecasts. Brown et al. (1987a) examined the reasons for the superiority of analyst forecasts of quarterly earnings and concluded that it was

> due to better utilization of information existing at the forecast initiation date for the TS models, a contemporaneous advantage, and acquisition and use of information after the TS model's forecast initiation date, a timing advantage.[41]

In a subsequent paper, Brown, Hagerman, Griffin, and Zmijewski (1987b) note that analysts' expectations seem to serve as a better surrogate of market expectations than do time series forecasts. Market reaction to earnings announcements is more closely associated with errors in analysts' forecasts than with errors emanating from time series models. The predictive ability of analysts (or at the least the information utilized by them) seemed to be recognized by the market in forming its aggregate expectations.[42]

---

[40]Dan Givoly and Josef Lakonishok, "The Quality of Analysts' Forecasts of Earnings," *Financial Analysts Journal* (September–October 1984), pp. 40–47.

[41]Lawrence D. Brown, Robert Hagerman, Paul Griffin, and Mark E. Zmijewski, "Security Analyst Superiority Relative to Univariate Time-Series Models in Forecasting Quarterly Earnings," *Journal of Accounting and Economics* (1987), pp. 61–87.

[42]Similar findings for annual earnings were reported by Dov Fried and Dan Givoly, "Financial Analysts' Forecasts of Earnings: A Better Surrogate for Market Expectations," *Journal of Accounting and Economics* (October 1982), pp. 85–108. They found that market expectations were more closely associated with analyst forecasts and that financial analysts' forecasts of annual earnings were more accurate due to

> the existence of some timing advantage to forecasts that are made well after the end of the fiscal year and which presumably incorporate more recent information. However, the main contributor to the better performance of FAF is their ability to utilize a much broader set of information than that used by the univariate time-series models. (P. 102)

EXHIBIT 15-11
Comparison of Analyts' Forecasts and Mechanical Models

A. Annual Earnings

Relative Accuracy of Analysts' Forecasts

Mean Relative Absolute Error

	Collins and Hopwood*	Brown and Rozeff†	Fried and Givoly‡
Analysts' forecasts	31.7%	28.4%	16.4%
Mechanical models§	34.1	32.2	19.8%

*Value Line forecasts, 50 firms, years 1970–1974; errors greater than ±300% are equated to ±300%.

†Value Line forecasts, 50 firms, years 1972–1975; errors greater than ±100% are equated to ±100%.

‡Mean forecasts, published in the *Earnings Forecaster,* for 410 firms, years 1969–1979; errors greater than ±100% are equated to ±100%.

§Average result for the competing mechanical models. The three studies used four, three, and two naive models, respectively.

Source: Givoly, Dan and Josef Lakonishok, "The Quality of Analysts' Forecasts of Earnings", *Financial Analysts Journal* (September–October 1984), pp. 40–47. Table I (P. 46).

B. Quarterly Earnings

Mean Percentage Error of Quarterly Forecasts,
Forecasts Carried Out over 24 Quarters, 1975–1980*

Forecasting Horizon	Models			
	TS1†	TS2‡	TS3§	FAF
One quarter	27.3%	29.1%	27.9%	20.7%
	(0)	(0)	(0)	(24)
Two quarters	30.7%	32.2%	30.8%	26.3%
	(1)	(0)	(1)	(21)
Three quarters	33.1%	33.6%	33.1%	28.7%
	(0)	(4)	(0)	(18)

*Numbers in parentheses indicate the number of quarters model has lowest mean.

†Quarterly time series model 1 (Brown and Rozeff, 1979).

‡Quarterly time series model 2 (Foster, 1977).

§Quarterly time series model 3 (Watts, 1975, and Griffin, 1977).

Source: Brown, Lawrence D., Robert Hagerman, Paul Griffin and Mark E. Zmijewski, "Security Analyst Superiority Relative To Univariate Time-Series Models in Forecasting Quarterly Earnings", *Journal of Accounting and Economics* 9 (1987), pp. 61–87. Adapted from Table 1 (P. 67 & 68)

Analyst Forecasts: Some Caveats

Not all the evidence on the issue of analyst superiority is clear cut. Brown et al. (1987b) show that the degree that analyst forecasts outperform time series forecasts as surrogates of market expectation is related to firm size.[43] For smaller firms, it is possible to reduce the measurement error in unexpected earnings proxies by pooling analysts' forecasts with those of time series models. More recently, O'Brien (1988) found that although analyst forecasts are superior to those generated by various quarterly forecasting models,

> Errors from the quarterly autoregressive models, however, appear to be more closely related with excess returns over the forecasting horizon than those of analysts. Because of this anomalous result, it is unclear that analysts provide a better model of the "market expectation" than mechanical models.[44]

Furthermore, some studies indicate that analysts rather than leading the market may in fact be following it. Thus, if the firm is experiencing strong market reaction in a given direction, analysts' forecasts will be revised in that direction.[45] Brown, Foster and Noreen (1985), for example, found that positive (negative) returns precede upward (downward) revisions in analysts' forecasts by as much as 12 months.

Brown, Richardson, and Schwager (1987) examined factors accounting for analyst forecast superiority over time series models. After controlling for the timing effect, they found that analyst superiority was positively related to firm size, which they attributed to the broader information set available with respect to larger firms. On the other hand, they found that the more difficult it was to forecast a given firm in the first place (as measured by the dispersion of the FAF forecasts), the smaller the benefit of using analyst forecasts.

These results are especially interesting in light of Bhushan's (1989) findings reported in Exhibit 15-10. Firm size and earnings uncertainty were two of the factors contributing to increased analyst coverage. For the former, the increased supply seems to be justified. For the latter it does not. This is troublesome as, in precisely the environment (increased uncertainty) where there is a need for analysts' services, the analyst does not seem to outperform time series models.

Additionally, accounting changes, as noted in previous chapters, cause problems for analysts as it takes time for the analysts to learn the effects of these changes. This is true whether the changes are voluntary[46] or mandated.[47]

---

[43]These results are consistent with those of Brown, Richardson, and Schwager (1987).

[44]Patricia O'Brien, "Analysts' Forecasts as Earnings Expectations," *Journal of Accounting and Economics* (January 1988), pp. 53–83.

[45] This result, as Zarowin himself noted, could be an alternative explanation for his finding (discussed earlier) that differential P/E ratios were a function of higher expected growth rates. The expected growth rates used in Zarowin's study were based on analysts' forecasts. Thus, rather than the higher expected growth rate being responsible for the higher P/E ratios, analysts may have forecast such rates on the basis of higher P/E ratios.

[46]See Chapter 5, for example, and the discussion as to the difficulty analysts had with the continuing effects of FIFO/LIFO changes.

[47]See Chapter 13, where we discuss the difficulty analysts have with respect to incorporating exchange rate changes in their forecasts.

These results hold for analysts in general as comparisons are usually done by comparing consensus (average or median) forecasts with those generated by time series models. Such consensus forecasts eliminate the idiosyncracies of individual forecasters.[48]

With respect to individual forecasters, Stickel (1989, 1990) notes that publicly available forecasts are often "stale." Forecasters do not continually update their forecasts but rather tend to wait for events such as interim reports to revise forecasts. Using information from interim reports, Stickel demonstrated that it was possible to anticipate forecast revisions of individual analysts.

Stickel did, however, note that those analysts that had the best forecasting record were those whose forecasting behavior was the most difficult to predict. These analysts were able to add something to simple "extrapolation" of interim results.

SUMMARY

Chapter 15 has two critical objectives. First, together with Chapter 14, it provides both a summation and integration of the preceding chapters by presenting models that use the variables generated by the analysis in those chapters. Equally important, it introduces the final phase in the use and analysis of financial statements: forecasts of the additional variables required for decision making.

These objectives are complementary in that the analyses in the earlier chapters are essential if the variables used in decision models are to reflect the economics of the firm rather than the choice of accounting methods and estimates. Forecasts based on reported data alone, that ignore the database inherent in financial reports are mechanical exercises at best.

The first part of this chapter discussed valuation models based on discounted cash flows, earnings, and net assets. It is not surprising that these diverse models are conceptually equivalent. While reported cash flows and earnings can diverge sharply in the short run (and, as we have shown, there may be some permanent differences as well), they tend towards equality over longer time periods. As net assets include the cumulative impact of earnings, changes in net assets reflect earnings (as well as capital transactions).

The discussion of asset based valuation models includes a reexamination of the impacts on net assets of dividend policy, equity transactions, acquisitions, exchange rate changes, and accounting methods. The discussion of discounted cash flow and earnings models provides a similar reevaluation. These reviews reinforce the view, presented throughout this text, that both economic and accounting factors must be considered when using financial data.

The discussion of valuation models ends with a brief commentary on the three competing valuation bases: dividends, earnings, and cash flows. A separate discussion reviews the impact of non-recurring items and economic cycles on the valuation decision and also describes the sometimes elusive concept of earnings quality.

---

[48]Kirt C. Butler and Larry H. P. Lang, "The Forecast Accuracy of Individual Analysts: Evidence of Systematic Optimism and Pessimism," *Journal of Accounting Research* (Spring 1991), pp. 150–156, for example, present evidence that certain analysts tend to be "persistently optimistic or pessimistic relative to consensus forecasts."

The second part of the chapter is quite unlike the preceding sections of the book in that it describes and evaluates statistical procedures useful in forecasting. Yet it relies on the preceding chapters through reminders that financial data used in forecasting models may require adjustment or evaluation. The discussion of forecasting, as always in this text, is primarily concerned with the rationale for the analytic techniques used rather than the mechanics of forecasting, which is left to technical statistics and econometrics texts.

Chapter 15 closes the cycle which started with the framework for financial statement analysis presented in Chapter 1. Our goal has been to take the reader from the basics of financial reporting through the valuation models which, ultimately, are the basis for investment decisions. The theme of this text has been that the financial analyst, armed with knowledge of the financial reporting system and analytical techniques that exploit the shortcomings of that system, can make better informed investment decisions.

Chapter 15

Problems

1. [Dividend- versus earnings-based models; 1989 CFA adapted] The Director of Research has asked you to recommend whether the Green Fund should add shares of Emfil stock to its portfolio. Apply the following valuation data to Emfil and determine the attractiveness of its shares, using:

(i) Dividend discount model

(ii) Earnings discount model

EMFIL COMPANY
Valuation Data, June 30, 1993

	Amount	Percentage Change from Prior Year
Current price per share	$115	
1992 earnings per share	$ 10.03	28%
1992 dividends per share	4.05	29
Current annual dividends per share	4.50	11
1993 estimated earnings per share	11.40	14
Predicted long-term growth rates		
Dividends per share		15
Earnings per share		14
Discount rate: 20%		

2. [Effect of dividend policy on valuation] The historical earnings per share and dividends per share for the Lo Co. and Hi Co. are as follows:

	1988	1989	1990	1991	1992
Lo Company					
Earnings per share	$1.00	$1.04	$1.08	$1.12	$1.17
Dividends per share	0.200	0.208	0.216	0.225	0.234
Hi Company					
Earnings per share	1.00	0.80	0.64	0.51	0.41
Dividends per share	1.00	0.80	0.64	0.51	0.41

A portfolio manager has just handed you these figures with a perplexed look, stating:

> Look at these numbers. Both companies are in the same industry. Neither has any debt. The EPS of one are obviously growing; the other's are declining. The funny thing about it is that, although the Hi Company's EPS are declining, its market value is identical to that of the Lo Company, and it is constantly able to raise new funds in the equity market. The Lo Company hasn't obtained external financing in years. I just don't get it.

Preliminary investigation indicates that the capital expenditures of both companies are identical each year. Furthermore, you find that the appropriate discount rate for the industry in question is 10%.

A. Based on the data available for the Lo Company, calculate the appropriate price/earnings ratio for that company.

B. Determine the appropriate price/earnings ratio for the Hi Company. (Hint: Compare to p/e of Lo Company.)

C. Complete the following table. To simplify matters, assume that net income was $1000 for each company in 1988 and that any new financing carried out by the Hi Company was effected at the beginning of the year. Further, assume that depreciation expense is sufficient to cover the replacement of assets.

	1988	1989	1990	1991	1992
Lo Company					
Earnings per share	$1.00	$1.04	$1.08	$1.12	$1.17
Number of shares	1000	___	___	___	___
Net income	$1000	___	___	___	___
Dividends paid	200	___	___	___	___
New investment	800	___	___	___	___
Firm value at period end	___	___	___	___	___
Price per share	___	___	___	___	___
P/E ratio	___	___	___	___	___

	1988	1989	1990	1991	1992
Hi Company					
Earnings per share	$1.00	$0.80	$0.64	$0.51	$0.41
Number of shares	1000	____	____	____	____
Net income	$1000	____	____	____	____
Dividends paid	1000	____	____	____	____
New investment	800	____	____	____	____
New financing	800	____	____	____	____
Firm value at period end	____	____	____	____	____
P/E ratio	____	____	____	____	____
Price per share before new issue	____	____	____	____	____
Shares issued	____	____	____	____	____
Price per share at new issue	____	____	____	____	____

Note: Neither company has declared stock dividends or splits.

C. Calculate the growth rate of net income, dividends paid, and firm value for both companies. Explain why Hi Company's earnings per share growth rate is not consistent with these numbers.

D. The P/E ratio is relatively low for both companies. Explain why. What returns do the companies get on new investments?

3. [Valuation with free cash flows, alternate modes of financing] You are considering joining a syndicate of investors in a new joint venture. The venture is expected to have a two-year life. In addition to investor financing, the syndicate intends to borrow $10 million at the current market rate of 10%. There is some debate, however, as to whether the funds should be raised by issuing:

   (i) zero-coupon notes

   (ii) "conventional" notes with annual interest payments. The funds would be borrowed January 1, 19X1 and repaid January 1, 19X3.

   Projected income statements and cash flow from operations under both alternatives are (in $ millions):

	Conventional		Zero Coupon	
	19X1	19X2	19X1	19X2
Earnings before interest and taxes	$20.00	$20.00	$20.00	$20.00
Interest expense*	(1.00)	(1.00)	(1.00)	(1.10)
Earnings before taxes	$19.00	$19.00	$19.00	$18.90
Income taxes (30% rate)	(5.70)	(5.70)	(5.70)	(5.67)
Net income	$13.30	$13.30	$13.30	$13.23
Add: Noncash charges*	0	0	1.00	1.10
Cash from operations	$13.30	$13.30	$14.30	$14.33

*Interest expense on the zero-coupon bond, although not paid, is deductible for tax purposes.

Given the higher cash from operations in both years with the zero-coupon alternative, there is some support within the syndicate for that choice.

A. Calculate free cash flow for each year under *both* alternatives.

B. Calculate the cash flows to/from debtholders for *each* of years 19X1–19X3, under *both* alternatives.

C. How much is available for dividend payments *each year under each alternative?* (Hint: consider where the funds to repay the debt will come from.)

D. Discuss whether the zero-coupon note is the better alternative.

4. [Permanent versus transitory earnings and growth] The CF company, an all-equity company, has a policy of paying out all its earnings as dividends. The company's earnings per share remain constant at $10 per share. CF stock sells at a price/earnings ratio of 12. The company has not issued any shares in recent years.

A. Calculate the firm's cost of (equity) capital.

B. For the most recent year, the firm reports earnings per share of $13. Consider three possible price/earnings ratios (on current year earnings per share):

  (i) Below 12
  (ii) Equal to 12
  (iii) Greater than 12

What does each ratio imply about whether the increase in earnings is permanent or nonrecurring?

5. [Valuation models, calculation of free cash flows] The income statement for the LZ Company for the current year and the forecast for the coming year follow:

	Current	Forecast
Sales	$100,000	$112,000
Cost of goods sold	(40,000)	(44,800)
Selling expense	(25,000)	(28,000)
Operating income	$ 35,000	$ 39,200
Interest expense	(5,000)	(5,600)
Net income	$ 30,000	$ 33,600

The forecast is based upon a projected growth rate of 12% arising from new opportunities facing the company. To simplify, assume that income taxes are zero and that depreciation expense approximates replacement cost. Depreciation for the current year is $8000 and is included in selling expense.

Assume that the cost of equity capital is 15%, the cost of debt is 10%, and the rate of return on the new opportunities facing the firm is 20%.

A. Based on the data provided, calculate the firm's implied dividend payout ratio.

B. Calculate the firm's total capital expenditures (for replacement and new investment) for the current year. How much of the new investment will come from debt and how much from equity?

C. Prepare a statement of cash flows for the current and forecast years.

D. Calculate the company's free cash flow for the current and forecast years.

E. Calculate, as of the end of the current year, the value of:
   (i) The firm
   (ii) Its equity
   (iii) Its debt

6. [Extension of Problem 5, treatment of leases in free cash flow calculations] Use the same basic assumptions as Problem 5. However, assume that the LZ company has decided that, instead of borrowing funds for capital expenditures, it will now lease assets. Assets exceeding those that the company can acquire from internally generated (equity) funds will be leased. The interest rate on leases is the same as for other debt, 10%.

Current and forecast income statements are presented here. Two forecast statements are prepared: one assumes that leases are operating leases; the second assumes that they are capital leases. These statements assume a five-year lease term and, in the case of capital leases, straight-line depreciation. (Note: The assumption that straight-line depreciation for leased assets approximates replacement cost no longer holds.)

| | Current | Forecast | |
		Operating	Capital
Sales	$100,000	$112,000	$112,000
Cost of goods sold	(40,000)	(44,800)	(44,800)
Selling expense	(25,000)	(29,343)	(28,960)
Operating income	$ 35,000	$ 37,857	$ 38,240
Interest expense	(5,000)	(5,000)	(5,600)
Net income	$ 30,000	$ 32,857	$ 33,640

A. Calculate the annual lease payments.

B. Reconcile the forecast income statements under the operating and capital lease methods with the forecast income statement in Problem 5.

C. Prepare a statement of cash flows for the current and the forecast year assuming that the leases are treated as *operating leases*. How is "acquisition" of the leased assets reported?

D. Prepare a statement of cash flows for the current and the forecast year assuming that the leases are treated as *capital leases*. How is "acquisition" of the leased assets reported?

E. Calculate the company's free cash flows for the current and forecast year assuming that the leases are:

    (i) Operating leases

    (ii) Capital leases

F. Redo Problem 5E. Discuss how lease financing affects the value of the firm, its equity, and its debt.

G. Discuss what this problem suggests regarding the treatment of leases in a valuation model.

Problems 7 to 9 are based on the information presented in Exhibit 15P-1, extracted from Value Line's September 1, 1989, report on FAB Industries.

FAB Industries, Inc., is for all practical purposes an all-equity firm carrying minuscule amounts of debt (1% of total capital). Additionally for the past two years the company had begun to repurchase its own shares whenever management felt the stock price was too low. In answering these problems, assume that the risk-free rate was 8.0% and the market risk premium was 6.00%.

EXHIBIT 15P-1. FAB INDUSTRIES, INC.
Selected Financial Data, 1985–1994E
Recent price: $36 per share
Price/earnings ratio: 11.3
Beta: 0.80

A. Annual Rates of Change (per Share)

	Past		Forecast
	10 Years	5 Years	Next 5 Years
Sales	9.5%	7.0%	11.5%
Earnings	11.5	8.0	10.0
Dividends	19.0	15.0	9.5
Cash flow	11.5	10.5	9.5
Book value	16.5	12.5	9.5

B. Earnings per Share Data

	Actual				Value Line Forecast		
	1985	1986	1987	1988	1989	1990	1992–94
Earnings	$ 2.39	$ 2.95	$ 2.94	$ 2.62	$ 3.20	$ 3.50	$ 5.00
Dividends	0.50	0.60	0.60	0.70	0.80	0.90	1.10
"Cash flow"	3.18	3.87	4.13	4.02	4.70	5.10	6.95
Capital spending	1.04	1.71	2.47	0.95	1.15	1.40	2.25
Book value	19.52	21.86	24.70	26.62	28.95	32.30	41.95
No. of shares (millions)	3.63	3.63	3.53	3.43	3.28	3.25	3.10

C. Current Position (in $ millions)

	1987	1988
Cash	$31.9	$32.8
Receivables	25.5	28.5
Inventory (LIFO)	23.7	23.8
Other	2.2	1.2
Current assets	$83.3	$86.3
Accounts payable	9.5	8.4
Other	8.9	8.3
Current liabilities	$18.4	$16.7

Other information:
FAB's P/E ratio is approximately 85% of the P/E of comparable companies.
FAB has no pension liability and insignificant leases.
"Cash flow" is defined by *Value Line* as net income plus depreciation, deferred taxes, and equity in undistributed earnings of affiliates.
Source: Value Line Investment Survey, September 1, 1989.

7. [Comparison of valuation models, estimating growth and growth assumptions; courtesy of Professor Joshua Livnat.]

A. Compare FAB's book value per share with its market price. What is the implication of this relationship for the existence of economic goodwill? Discuss some adjustments to book value per share that might reduce the difference between book value per share and market price.

B. **(i)** Estimate FAB's dividend payout ratio and ROE and use them to estimate the firm's growth rate. Compare this estimated growth rate with FAB's historical and projected (by *Value Line*) growth rates. Discuss the advantages and disadvantages of each of the (three) growth rate estimates.

(ii) How does FAB's share repurchase program affect the three growth rate estimates?

C. Using the data in Exhibit 15P-1, and assuming constant growth, find the value of FAB industries predicted by (1) a dividend discount model; (2) an earnings-based model, and (3) a free cash flow model. How well did these valuation models predict the price of FAB shares?

D. Discuss the effect of FAB's large cash position on the use of a discounted valuation model. Describe how that "excess" cash may explain the discrepancy between FAB's stock price and the results of part C.

E. Redo part C, but this time explicitly forecast the relevant variable (dividend, earnings, free cash flows) through 1991, using a constant growth model thereafter.

F. In the chapter we note that "growth" does not matter for companies whose expected rate of return (r^*) is equal to its required rate of return (r). Discuss whether FAB Industries fit this description. (Hint: What is the value of FAB assuming its dividend payout ratio is 100%?)

8. [Extension of previous problem] When answering the previous problem you relied on your own and *Value Line's* forecasts. Any differences between the value predicted by the respective models and the actual market price may be due to market expectations that differ from those of *Value Line*.

The following table presents the actual results of FAB Industries for 1989 through 1992. Discuss whether having perfect foreknowledge would have improved the performance of the three models.

Per Share[1]	1989	1990	1991	1992
Earnings	$ 3.26	$ 3.24	$ 5.04	$ 5.30
Dividends	0.80	0.80	1.00	1.00
Cash flow	4.64	4.92	6.60	7.30
Capital spending	1.32	2.18	0.98	2.40
Book value	29.12	31.32	35.40	38.70
No. of shares (millions)	3.29	3.12	3.09	3.08

[1]Number of shares and per share data have been restated to eliminate effect of stock split occurring after 1989.

9. [Valuation, effects of leverage] In 1989, FAB's pretax cost of debt was approximately 11%. FAB's tax rate was 34%. Assume that FAB decided to borrow $50 million.

 A. Compute the effect of the new debt on the value of FAB's equity.

 B. Compute the effect of the new debt on the overall value (debt plus equity) of FAB.

10. [Using ratios as forecasting tools, valuation with changing patterns of growth] Exhibit 15P-2 presents comparative income statements (19X1 and 19X2) and comparative balance sheets (19X0–19X2) for the EFF Company. At the end of 19X2, the company forecast a dramatic increase in sales for 19X3, 19X4, and 19X5:

EXHIBIT 15P-2. EFF COMPANY
Selected Financial Data for Years Ended December 31

A. Income Statement		
	19X1	19X2
Sales	$100,000	$110,000
Cost of goods sold	(50,000)	(53,000)
Selling and general expense	(20,000)	(22,000)
Operating income	$ 30,000	$ 35,000
Interest expense	(3,000)	(3,000)
Income before tax	$ 27,000	$ 32,000
Tax expense	(10,800)	(12,800)
Net income	$ 16,200	$ 19,200
Earnings per share	$ 16.20	$ 19.20

B. Balance Sheet			
	19X0	19X1	19X2
Cash	$ 7,000	$ 9,000	$ 11,000
Accounts receivable	8,000	8,500	9,000
Inventory	6,000	6,000	6,000
Current assets	21,000	23,500	26,000
Fixed assets, gross	83,000	94,000	103,000
Accumulated depreciation	(24,000)	(32,500)	(41,000)
Fixed assets, net	59,000	61,500	62,000
Total assets	$ 80,000	$ 85,000	$ 88,000
Accounts payable	$ 8,000	$ 8,500	$ 9,000
Long-term debt	30,000	30,000	30,000
Stockholders' equity	42,000	46,500	49,000
Total liabilities and stockholders' equity	$ 80,000	$ 85,000	$ 88,000

19X3	$150,000
19X4	180,000
19X5	200,000

After 19X5, the company expects sales to stabilize at the 19X5 level.

A. Prepare the statement of cash flows and estimate free cash flow for 19X2.

B. Using the relationships and ratios implied by the financial statements in Exhibit 15P-2, forecast the income statements and balance sheets for 19X3–19X5.

C. Use the forecast balance sheets and income statements to estimate free cash flow for 19X3–19X5.

D. Assuming a cost of equity of 15%, estimate the value of the EFF Company at the end of 19X2.

11. [Valuation; 1989 CFA adapted] Following its announcement (October 1988) that it was prepared to purchase all Kraft's outstanding shares at $90.00 per share, Philip Morris' own shares dropped $4.50 to $95.50 per share. At the time of the announcement, it was assumed that Philip Morris would raise the funds required for the takeover by issuing 11% notes. Prior to the merger, Philip Morris' earnings growth rate approximated 20%; Kraft's earnings growth rate was 8%. Selected financial data follow (in $ millions):

	October 1988	
	Philip Morris	Kraft
Common shares outstanding (millions)	234	120
Price per share (preannouncement)	$ 100	$ 65
Long-term debt	$ 4700	$ 800
Stockholders' equity	7394	1920
Earnings before interest and tax	4340	796
Interest expense	(475)	(81)
Pretax income	$ 3865	$ 715
Income taxes	(1623)	(279)
Net income	$ 2242	$ 436
Cash flow from operations	2974	607
Capital expenditures	850	260
Dividends paid	892	251
Earnings per share	$ 9.58	$ 3.63

A. Using an asset-based valuation approach, and assuming that market prices *prior* to the merger were appropriate, predict the *price change* for Philip Morris shares that should have *followed* the merger announcement.

B. Suggest why the actual decline in Philip Morris shares following the merger announcement was significantly different from your forecast in part A.

C. The discussion of discounted cash flow (DCF) valuation models in the chapter suggests that the models are identical in theory and that the main differences are their ease of application. For *each* of the three DCF models discussed in the chapter,

1. Dividend discount model
2. Earnings-based model
3. Free cash flow model

discuss the difficulties in using the model to predict the change in Philip Morris' stock price following the merger announcement. Describe the advantages that one model may have over the others. (Hint: Focus on the change in value of Philip Morris rather than on the value itself.)

12. [Deere; free cash flows] Use data from Exhibit 1B-2 to answer the following.

A. Estimate Deere's free cash flow for fiscal 1991.

B. Deere's market price as at October 31, 1991, was $56 per share. Compute Deere's total market value. (Chapter 14 contains an estimate of the market value of Deere's debt.)

C. Based on your answers to parts A and B, compute Deere's implied cost of capital. (Hint: First estimate Deere's growth rate and evaluate the recurring/nonrecurring nature of the components of its free cash flow.)

13. [Deere; DCF valuation—extension of Problem 12] The chapter notes that Deere's market price of $56 was considerably higher than the value resulting from asset-based valuation. Make the same comparison for each of the three DCF models discussed in the chapter using the analysis of Deere's earnings and cash flows provided in Chapters 14 and 15. (Note This problem requires you to estimate Deere's cost of capital; *Value Line* estimated Deere's beta at 1.30. The three-month U.S. Treasury bill rate on October 31, 1991, was approximately 5.00%. Assume that the equity risk premium was 6%.)

14. The "Market Place" column of *The New York Times* featured an article on March 1, 1993, by Robert Hurtado entitled "Analysts Urge Investors to Look Beyond Earnings at Cash Flow." The following is excerpted from the article:

> "Analyzing the cash flow, which is generally defined as net income plus depreciation and amortization costs, of a company enables an investor to see beyond the bottom line and unearth hidden values," said Allison Bisno, director of research for Stephens, Inc., a brokerage firm in Little Rock, Ark. "Cash flows often show a company's future earnings potential, which may be more dramatic than the current net income indicates."
>
> To identify bargain stocks on this basis, an investor needs first to calculate the issue's price–to–cash flow ratio. . . . Wall Street analysts say that stocks are now trading at about 11 times cash flow and investors should seek companies whose shares are trading below this multiple.
>
> The best opportunities naturally lie in companies that have strong corporate earnings and good cash flow, along with a low stock price.

Comment on the investment approach advocated by the author of this article. Can you find a theoretical basis for a price to cash flow ratio? Describe the advantages and disadvantages of using such a ratio to select investments as compared with use of the price/earnings ratio.

15. The Institute of Investment Management and Research (IIMR) is a British organization of investment and financial analysts. Exhibit 15P-3 contains an article concerning the IIMR's proposal for disclosure of "IIMR headline earnings." (Note: FRS3 refers to the U.K. Accounting Standards Board's Standard 3.)

   A. Discuss how the "IIMR headline earnings" envisioned in this article is related to *each* of the following definitions of income: operating income, permanent income, sustainable income, and economic income.

   B. The IIMR agrees with FRS3 that "It is not possible to distill the performance of a complex organization into a single measure." Given this statement, what is the purpose of creating IIMR headline earnings? What is the importance of the amounts removed from accounting earnings to arrive at headline earnings?

   C. The article notes that comments on the IIMR Exposure Draft are invited. Prepare a comment letter to be sent to the IIMR. (Be brief and to the point.)

EXHIBIT 15P-3
Measuring Earnings After FRS3

The Institute of Investment Management and Research, formerly the Society of Investment Analysts, has published an Exposure Draft proposing a standardised treatment of a company's trading earnings for use by analysts, commentators and other observers. A shortened version of the paper follows:

THE first sentence of paragraph 52 of FRS3 states "It is not possible to distill the performance of a complex organisation into a single measure". This is manifestly true. The performance of a company is reflected in a complex and interlocking set of figures, which themselves interrelate with the industry and economy.

If FRS3 can begin to unravel the myth that a single number determines share prices, a considerable step forward will have been taken. Nevertheless, there are several reasons why efforts should be made to delineate some clearly acceptable earnings figure (or figures).

First, in evaluating a company the stock market must order published information in some useful way. If this is so, it would be desirable that the information should as far as possible be ordered in that way in the calculations of earnings.

Second, there are a large number of users of accounts who do not have the time or the expertise to make the detailed investigations which are distilled into the final market price.

Whatever other requirement there may be for an earnings figure it is clearly desirable, indeed virtually necessary, to define a figure for the company's earnings for the year which can be used as an unambiguous reference point between users, the press, the statistical services, etc. This raises the possibility that such a figure should also be used in preliminary and interim announcements as a statement of earnings, and how they compare with the previous year.

The figure—to be known as IIMR headline earnings—should for these purposes have certain characteristics.

First, it should be a measure of the company's trading performance in the year, not confused with capital items.

EXHIBIT 15P-3. *(Continued)*

Second, it should as far as possible be robust. That is, the calculation should be one that can be carried through by anyone presented with the building blocks of the calculation.

Third, the figure should be factual, including incomes and costs which actually occurred.

However, headline earnings, because they robustly and factually represent the past, will not necessarily be the best basis for forecasts of future earnings. Such forecasts require a great deal of judgment and this is where individual analysts or research firms can add value on behalf of their clients. The practical usefulness of the headline earnings figure is, however, its justification. No one earnings figure can do everything.

These considerations lead to a standard definition of the headline earnings, calculated for the purposes set out above. It is intended as an additional figure, which can be reconciled to FRS3 figures subject to the points discussed below. (see table). The guiding principles follow.

- All the trading profits and losses of the company for the year (including interest) should be included in the earnings number. Items which are abnormal in size or nature are included.
- Profits and losses on the sale of fixed assets or of businesses should be excluded. This does not apply to assets acquired for resale.
- Profit and losses arising in activities discontinued at some point during the year, or in activities acquired at some point during the year, should remain in the earnings figure. The costs of eliminating a discontinued operation, or making an acquisition, and the profits and losses on any disposals, should be excluded.
- Prior period items, and the effect of changes in accounting policies and of past fundamental accounting errors should not affect the current year's calculation of earnings.
- Goodwill should not affect earnings in any way.
- Variations in pension fund contributions (and other post-retirement benefit provisions if any) should be included in earnings, but prominently displayed if of significant size.
- Capital and trading items which arise in currencies other than the reporting currency should be handled in the same way as the equivalent items arising in the domestic currency.
- The calculation of the headline earnings number should include tax adjustments to reflect the fact that certain items are excluded from the headline figure.
- Apart from these adjustments, the calculation of headline earnings should normally reflect the tax charge as shown in the company accounts.
- Companies should be encouraged to ensure that adequate disclosures are made to enable the effect of minority interests to be calculated on any adjustments that may be made to arrive at the headline figure if these are not already required.

The definition of earnings. Exposure Draft published by the Institute of Investment Management and Research, 211-213 High St Bromley, Kent BR1 1NY. David Damant of Credit Suisse Asset Management, chaired the subcommittee which produced the draft. Comments invited by April 30.

Source: Financial Times, March 5, 1993, p. 28.

Appendix 15-A

Multistage Growth Models

The original formulation of the discounted models discussed in the chapter is presented below.

$$P_0 = \sum_{i=1}^{\infty} \frac{kE_i}{(1 + r)^i}$$

Theoretically, by predicting each year individually, any assumed growth rate of dividends or earnings payout (even zero dividends) can be accommodated. From a practical point of view, of course, one would not attempt to forecast individual periods over a very long horizon.

One palatable approach is to forecast the near future individually and then impose an assumption as to the appropriate valuation after that period. Recall that the preceding expression is equivalent to

$$P_0 = \frac{kE_1}{(1 + r)} + \frac{kE_2}{(1 + r)^2} + \cdots + \frac{kE_n}{(1 + r)^n} + \frac{P_n}{(1 + r)^n}$$

the present value of the dividends over the first n years plus the discounted value at the end of year n.

For example, assume that you forecast a firm's net income over the next three years as year $1 = 100$, year $2 = 120$, and year $3 = 150$. The firm's $k = 20\%$ and its $r = 10\%$. To use the preceding equation, one must derive a terminal value for the firm at the end of year 3. You may at this point decide to make some general assumptions. One assumption might be that from the third year on the firm will experience growth of 8%. The implicit forecast for year 4's earnings is $(1.08 \times \$150) = \$162$, and the terminal value at the end of year 3 (using the constant growth model presented earlier) is equal to

$$P_3 = \frac{0.2 \times \$162}{0.10 - 0.08} = \$1620$$

The value now will be equal to

$$P_0 = \frac{\$100}{(1.1)} + \frac{\$120}{(1.1)^2} + \frac{\$150}{(1.1)^3} + \frac{\$1620}{(1.1)^3}$$

$$= \$91 + \$99 + \$113 + \$1217 = \$1520$$

VALUING A NONDIVIDEND-PAYING FIRM

A firm paying zero dividends can also be modeled along these lines. A firm that pays zero dividends reinvests everything in the firm. Its growth rate is equal to $[1 - k]r^* = r^*$ since $k = 0$. Assume that a firm having an r^* of 25% for the next five years does not plan to pay dividends for those five years. If its present earning level is $10, its earnings in year 5 will equal $10(1.25)^5 = 30.5. From year 6 and on, assume that its r^* will be 20% and the firm will pay dividends at a rate $k = 60\%$. Its growth rate will therefore equal $(1 - 60\%) \times 20\% = 8\%$. Earnings in year 6 will equal $30.5(1.08) = 32.9. The firm's value at the beginning of year 6 will be equal to

$$\frac{0.6 \times \$32.9}{0.1 - 0.08} = \$987$$

The value today will be equal to the $987 discounted (back five years) to the beginning of year 1 or $987/(1.10)^5 = 613.

SHIFTING GROWTH RATE PATTERNS

Variations of this approach assume a certain level of growth over some initial phase and different growth rates after the initial phase (Figure 15A-1).

The *finite growth* model (Figure 15A-1A) assumes that the firm will experience growth of $g = (1 - k)r^*$ for n years. After that point, the abnormal investment opportunities of $r^* > r$ will not exist. The value of equity for such a firm will equal

$$P_0 = \frac{E_1}{r} + \frac{E_1}{r} \left\{ \frac{g - r(1 - k)}{r - g} \left[1 - \left(\frac{1 + g}{1 + r} \right)^n \right] \right\}$$

Other models commonly referred to as *three-phase models* assume (Figure 15A-1B) an initial (phase 1) high abnormal growth rate g_a for a number of years that tapers off (in phase 2) to a long-term (phase 3) normal-growth pattern of g_n. The calculations for these models are somewhat complex. Fuller and Hsia (1984) simplified these models by assuming a growth pattern as depicted in Figure 15A-1C. They start with initial above-normal growth but assume that it converges gradually to a stable long-term growth pattern. Staying with the definitions of g_a as the initial growth pattern and g_n as the long-term growth pattern to be reached within n years, the value of the equity is equal to

$$P_0 = \frac{kE_0}{r - g_n} \left[(1 + g_n) + \frac{n}{2} (g_a - g_n) \right]$$

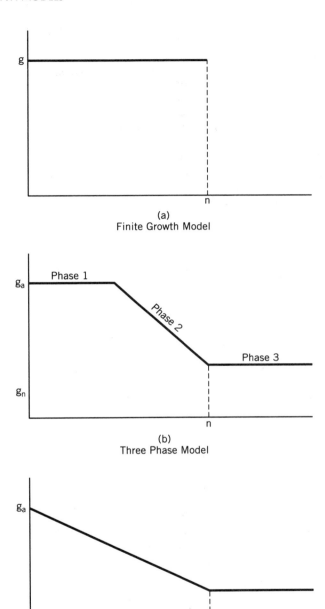

FIGURE 15A-1 (A–C) Simplified Three-Phase Model (Fuller and Hsia, 1984). *Source:* Fuller, Russel J. and Chi-Cheng Hsia, "A Simplified Common Stock Valuation Model", *Financial Analysts Journal* (September–October 1984), pp. 49–56. Figure B (P. 50) and Figure E (P. 53).

GLOSSARY

Accounting Loss:
Loss due to (1) default on a contract by a counter-party (credit risk), (2) change in market prices or (3) theft or physical loss.

Accumulated Benefit Obligation (ABO):
The present value of pension benefits earned to date based on employee service and compensation to that date.

Accumulated Postretirement Benefit Obligation (APBO):
The present value of postretirement benefits earned to date based on employee service to that date.

Anticipated Transactions:
Transactions that the firm expects, but is not obligated, to carry out in the future.

Assumed Per Capita Cost Claims (by age):
Estimated cost of health care benefits at specific ages, based on current costs but adjusted using the assumed health care cost trend rates.

Bargain Purchase Option:
Provision granting the lessee the right, but not the obligation, to purchase leased property at a price that, at the inception date, is sufficiently below the expected fair value of the property at exercise date to provide reasonable assurance of exercise.

Bargain Renewal Option:
Provision granting the lessee the right, but not the obligation, to renew the lease at a rental that, at inception, is sufficiently below the expected fair rental at exercise date to provide reasonable assurance of renewal.

Cancelability:
Lease agreements are considered non-cancelable if cancellation requires lessor's consent, can be effected only when a contingency considered remote at inception occurs, or incurs a cancellation penalty regarded as sufficiently large or punitive at inception to provide reasonable assurance that the lease will not be canceled.

Contingent Rentals:
Changes (normally increases) in lease payments due to uncertain future economic factors (such as lessee revenues). Contingent rentals are included in income as they are earned but are not included in MLPs at inception since the lessor bears the risk that conditions requiring their payment (such as sales of a retail store) will not take place.

Credit Risk:
Possibility that a counterparty may not perform according to contractual terms.

Currency Swap:
An exchange of two currencies as part of an agreement to reverse the exchange on a specific future date. Some agreements may include exchanges of specified currency-denominated interest payments.

Discount Rate:
The interest rate used to compute the present value of the benefit obligation.

Dry Holes:
Wells drilled which do not find commercial quantities of oil or gas.

Estimated Economic Life of Leased Property:
The useful life of leased property estimated at inception under conditions of normal maintenance and repairs. This estimate is not related to the lease term.

Estimated Residual Value of Leased Property:
The expected fair or market value of leased property at the end of the lease term. It is estimated at inception and reviewed annually by lessor; nontemporary declines must be recognized.

Executory Costs:
Insurance, maintenance, and local and property taxes on leased property. Executory costs are not a component of MLPs.

Expected Long-Term Rate of Return on Plan Assets:
The assumed rate of return on pension and other postretirement benefit funds.

Expected Postretirement Benefit Obligation:
The present value of postretirement benefits expected to be paid, including benefits that require further employee service.

Fair Value of Leased Property:
The selling price of the property less applicable trade and volume discounts in an arms-length transaction between unrelated parties, at inception of the lease.

Fair Value of Plan Assets:
Current market value of all plan assets.

Financial Instrument:
Cash, an ownership interest in a firm, or a contract that *both:*

    a. imposes on one entity a contractual obligation (1) to deliver cash or another financial instrument to a second entity or (2) to exchange financial instruments on potentially unfavorable terms with the second entity

    b. Conveys to that second entity a contractual right (1) to receive cash or another financial instrument from the first entity or (2) to exchange other financial instruments on potentially favorable terms with the first entity.

Firm Commitment:
Contractual agreement (generally legally enforceable) where penalties for nonperformance are sufficiently high to make performance probable.

Forward Contract:
Agreement to purchase or sell commodities, securities, or currencies on a specified future date at a specified price.

Full Cost:
Method of accounting under which the costs of unsuccessful exploration efforts are capitalized as part of the cost of producing properties.

Futures Contract:
Exchange-traded contract for future acceptance or delivery of a standardized quantity of a commodity or financial instrument on a specified future date at a specified price. Futures may be settled in cash or (in most cases) by physical delivery at contract expiration. Changes in the market value of open futures contracts are settled in cash daily.

Gain or Loss:
Differences between expectation and actual experience in the investment performance of plan assets or calculation of the benefit obligation.

Health Care Cost Trend Rate:
Assumed inflation rate for health care costs resulting from cost increases as well as changes in utilization and technology.

Hedges:
Instruments for transferring price, foreign exchange, or interest rate risk.

Implicit Interest Rate:
Discount rate, at inception of the lease, equating the lessor's fair value of leased property to the present value of MLPs and unguaranteed residual value accruing to the lessor.

Inception of the Lease:
The earlier of the date of the lease agreement or the date of a signed, written commitment.

Incremental Borrowing Rate:
Lessee's cost of funds if it were to purchase the leased asset under substantially equivalent terms and conditions at inception.

Initial Direct Costs:
Lessor's incremental cost to negotiate and consummate lease. Excludes marketing and administrative costs of leasing activities.

Interest Rate Swaps:
An agreement to exchange variable rate interest payments based on a specific index for a fixed rate or a variable rate stream of payments based on another index. The payments are based on contractual or notional principal amounts but no exchange of principal is involved.

Lease Term:
Fixed, non-cancelable lease period, including bargain renewals, ordinary renewals prior to a bargain purchase option or during which lessee guarantees lessor debt or is a creditor of lessor, and periods covered by penalty provisions.

Market-Related Value of Plan Assets:
A smoothed measure of plan assets that incorporates changes in market values over not more than five years; can be used to compute the expected return on plan assets.

Market Risk:
Possibility that changes in market prices may reduce the value of a financial instrument or make its terms more onerous.

Medicare Reimbursement Rates:
Payments due to retirees from Medicare under current legislation.

Minimum Lease Payments (MLPs):
For lessees, MLPs include minimum lease payments over the lease term, specified penalties, the exercise price of bargain purchase options, all guarantees of residual value, and the purchase price when lessee is required to purchase leased property at the end of the lease term. MLPs exclude contingent rentals, lessee guarantees of lessor debt, and executory costs.
For lessors, MLPs include all the components listed for lessees plus any additional amounts guaranteed by unrelated third parties.

Option:
A financial instrument that conveys to its owner the right, but not the obligation, to buy or sell a security, commodity, or currency at a specific price over a specified time period or at a specific date.

Prior Service Cost:
A change in the benefit obligation due to plan amendment.

Projected Benefit Obligation (PBO):
The present value of pension benefits earned to date based on past service and an estimate of future compensation levels for pay-related plans.

Proved Developed Reserves:
Proved reserves that can be produced without additional major expense; undeveloped reserves require either the drilling of additional wells or major expenditures on existing wells to obtain production.

Proved Reserves:
Quantities recoverable, with reasonable certainty, from known oil and gas reservoirs, under current economic conditions.

Rate of Compensation Increase:
The expected growth rate of employee compensation; used to compute the projected benefit obligation, as well as measures of the postretirement benefit obligation.

Related Parties in Leasing Transactions:
Investor companies and all investees (including subsidiaries, joint ventures, and partnerships) for which the investor exercises significant influence over operating, investing and financing policies.

Service Cost:
The present value of benefits earned during the current period.

Successful Efforts:
Method of accounting under which the cost of dry holes is charged to expense.

Vested Benefit Obligation (VBO):
The portion of the pension benefit obligation that does not depend on future employee service.

TABLE 1 AMOUNT OF 1

$$a = (1 + i)^n$$

(n) PERIODS	2%	2½%	3%	4%	5%	6%
1	1.02000	1.02500	1.03000	1.04000	1.05000	1.06000
2	1.04040	1.05063	1.06090	1.08160	1.10250	1.12360
3	1.06121	1.07689	1.09273	1.12486	1.15763	1.19102
4	1.08243	1.10381	1.12551	1.16986	1.21551	1.26248
5	1.10408	1.13141	1.15927	1.21665	1.27628	1.33823
6	1.12616	1.15969	1.19405	1.26532	1.34010	1.41852
7	1.14869	1.18869	1.22987	1.31593	1.40710	1.50363
8	1.17166	1.21840	1.26677	1.36857	1.47746	1.59385
9	1.19509	1.24886	1.30477	1.42331	1.55133	1.68948
10	1.21899	1.28008	1.34392	1.48024	1.62889	1.79085
11	1.24337	1.31209	1.38423	1.53945	1.71034	1.89830
12	1.26824	1.34489	1.42576	1,60103	1.79586	2.01220
13	1.29361	1.37851	1.46853	1.66507	1.88565	2.13293
14	1.31948	1.41297	1.51259	1.73168	1.97993	2.26090
15	1.34587	1.44830	1.55797	1.80094	2.07893	2.39656
16	1.37279	1.48451	1.60471	1.87298	2.18287	2.54035
17	1.40024	1.52162	1.65285	1.94790	2.29202	2.69277
18	1.42825	1.55966	1.70243	2.02582	2.40662	2.85434
19	1.45681	1.59865	1.75351	2.10685	2.52695	3.02560
20	1.48595	1.63862	1.80611	2.19112	2.65330	3.20714
21	1.51567	1.67958	1.86029	2.27877	2.78596	3.39956
22	1.54598	1.72157	1.91610	2.36992	2.92526	3.60354
23	1.57690	1.76461	1.97359	2.46472	3.07152	3.81975
24	1.60844	1.80873	2.03279	2.56330	3.22510	4.04893
25	1.64061	1.85394	2.09378	2.66584	3.38635	4.29187
26	1.67342	1.90029	2.15659	2.77247	3.55567	4.54938
27	1.70689	1.94780	2.22129	2.88337	3.73346	4.82235
28	1.74102	1.99650	2.28793	2.99870	3.92013	5.11169
29	1.77584	2.04641	2.35657	3.11865	4.11614	5.41839
30	1.81136	2.09757	2.42726	3.24340	4.32194	5.74349
31	1.84759	2.15001	2.50008	3.37313	4.53804	6.08810
32	1.88454	2.20376	2.57508	3.50806	4.76494	6.45339
33	1.92223	2.25885	2.65234	3.64838	5.00319	6.84059
34	1.96068	2.31532	2.73191	3.79432	5.25335	7.25103
35	1.99989	2.37321	2.81386	3.94609	5.51602	7.68609
36	2.03989	2.43254	2.89828	4.10393	5.79182	8.14725
37	2.08069	2.49335	2.98523	4.26809	6.08141	8.63609
38	2.12230	2.55568	3.07478	4.43881	6.38548	9.15425
39	2.16474	2.61957	3.16703	4.61637	6.70475	9.70351
40	2.20804	2.68506	3.26204	4.80102	7.03999	10.28572

TABLE 1 AMOUNT OF 1   **1165**

8%	9%	10%	12%	15%	(n) PERIODS
1.08000	1.09000	1.10000	1.12000	1.15000	1
1.16640	1.18810	1.21000	1.25440	1.32250	2
1.25971	1.29503	1.33100	1.40493	1.52088	3
1.36049	1.41158	1.46410	1.57352	1.74901	4
1.46933	1.53862	1.61051	1.76234	2.01136	5
1.58687	1.67710	1.77156	1.97382	2.31306	6
1.71382	1.82804	1.94872	2.21068	2.66002	7
1.85093	1.99256	2.14359	2.47596	3.05902	8
1.99900	2.17189	2.35795	2.77308	3.51788	9
2.15892	2.36736	2.59374	3.10585	4.04556	10
2.33164	2.58043	2.85312	3.47855	4.65239	11
2.51817	2.81267	3.13843	3.89598	5.35025	12
2.71962	3.06581	3.45227	4.36349	6.15279	13
2.93719	3.34173	3.79750	4.88711	7.07571	14
3.17217	3.64248	4.17725	5.47357	8.13706	15
3.42594	3.97031	4.59497	6.13039	9.35762	16
3.70002	4.32763	5.05447	6.86604	10.76126	17
3.99602	4.71712	5.55992	7.68997	12.37545	18
4.31570	5.14166	6.11591	8.61276	14.23177	19
4.66096	5.60441	6.72750	9.64629	16.36654	20
5.03383	6.10881	7.40025	10.80385	18.82152	21
5.43654	6.65860	8.14028	12.10031	21.64475	22
5.87146	7.25787	8.95430	13.55235	24.89146	23
6.34118	7.91108	9.84973	15.17863	28.62518	24
6.84847	8.62308	10.83471	17.00000	32.91895	25
7.39635	9.39916	11.91818	19.04007	37.85680	26
7.98806	10.24508	13.10999	21.32488	43.53532	27
8.62711	11.16714	14.42099	23.88387	50.06561	28
9.31727	12.17218	15.86309	26.74993	57.57545	29
10.06266	13.26768	17.44940	29.95992	66.21177	30
10.86767	14.46177	19.19434	33.55511	76.14354	31
11.73708	15.76333	21.11378	37.58173	87.56507	32
12.67605	17.18203	23.22515	42.09153	100.69983	33
13.69013	18.72841	25.54767	47.14252	115.80480	34
14.78534	20.41397	28.10244	52.79962	133.17552	35
15.96817	22.25123	30.91268	59.13557	153.15185	36
17.24563	24.25384	34.00395	66.23184	176.12463	37
18.62528	26.43668	37.40434	74.17966	202.54332	38
20.11530	28.81598	41.14479	83.08122	232.92482	39
21.72452	31.40942	45.25926	93.05097	267.86355	40

TABLE 2 PRESENT VALUE OF 1

$$p^n = \frac{1}{(1 + i)^n} = (1 + i)^{-n}$$

(n) PERIODS	2%	2½%	3%	4%	5%	6%
1	.98039	.97561	.97087	.96154	.95238	.94340
2	.96117	.95181	.94260	.92456	.90703	.89000
3	.94232	.92860	.91514	.88900	.86384	.83962
4	.92385	.90595	.88849	.85480	.82270	.79209
5	.90573	.88385	.86261	.82193	.78353	.74726
6	.88797	.86230	.83748	.79031	.74622	.70496
7	.87056	.84127	.81309	.75992	.71068	.66506
8	.85349	.82075	.78941	.73069	.67684	.62741
9	.83676	.80073	.76642	.70259	.64461	.59190
10	.82035	.78120	.74409	.67556	.61391	.55839
11	.80426	.76214	.72242	.64958	.58468	.52679
12	.78849	.74356	.70138	.62460	.55684	.49697
13	.77303	.72542	.68095	.60057	.53032	.46884
14	.75788	.70773	.66112	.57748	.50507	.44230
15	.74301	.69047	.64186	.55526	.48102	.41727
16	.72845	.67362	.62317	.53391	.45811	.39365
17	.71416	.65720	.60502	.51337	.43630	.37136
18	.70016	.64117	.58739	.49363	.41552	.35034
19	.68643	.62553	.57029	.47464	.39573	.33051
20	.67297	.61027	.55368	.45639	.37689	.31180
21	.65978	.59539	.53755	.43883	.35894	.29416
22	.64684	.58086	.52189	.42196	.34185	.27751
23	.63416	.56670	.50669	.40573	.32557	.26180
24	.62172	.55288	.49193	.39012	.31007	.24698
25	.60953	.53939	.47761	.37512	.29530	.23300
26	.59758	.52623	.46369	.36069	.28124	.21981
27	.58586	.51340	.45019	.34682	.26785	.20737
28	.57437	.50088	.43708	.33348	.25509	.19563
29	.56311	.48866	.42435	.32065	.24295	.18456
30	.55207	.47674	.41199	.30832	.23138	.17411
31	.54125	.46511	.39999	.29646	.22036	.16425
32	.53063	.45377	.38834	.28506	.20987	.15496
33	.52023	.44270	.37703	.27409	.19987	.14619
34	.51003	.43191	.36604	.26355	.19035	.13791
35	.50003	.42137	.35538	.25342	.18129	.13011
36	.49022	.41109	.34503	.24367	.17266	.12274
37	.48061	.40107	.33498	.23430	.16444	.11579
38	.47119	.39128	.32523	.22529	.15661	.10924
39	.46195	.38174	.31575	.21662	.14915	.10306
40	.45289	.37243	.30656	.20829	.14205	.09722

TABLE 2 PRESENT VALUE OF 1　　　　　　　　　　　　　　　　　　　　　**1167**

8%	9%	10%	12%	15%	(n) PERIODS
.92593	.91743	.90909	.89286	.86957	1
.85734	.84168	.82645	.79719	.75614	2
.79383	.77218	.75132	.71178	.65752	3
.73503	.70843	.68301	.63552	.57175	4
.68058	.64993	.62092	.56743	.49718	5
.63017	.59627	.56447	.50663	.43233	6
.58349	.54703	.51316	.45235	.37594	7
.54027	.50187	.46651	.40388	.32690	8
.50025	.46043	.42410	.36061	.28426	9
.46319	.42241	.38554	.32197	.24719	10
.42888	.38753	.35049	.28748	.21494	11
.39711	.35554	.31863	.25668	.18691	12
.36770	.32618	.28966	.22917	.16253	13
.34046	.29925	.26333	.20462	.14133	14
.31524	.27454	.23939	.18270	.12289	15
.29189	.25187	.21763	.16312	.10687	16
.27027	.23107	.19785	.14564	.09293	17
.25025	.21199	.17986	.13004	.08081	18
.23171	.19449	.16351	.11611	.07027	19
.21455	.17843	.14864	.10367	.06110	20
.19866	.16370	.13513	.09256	.05313	21
.18394	.15018	.12285	.08264	.04620	22
.17032	.13778	.11168	.07379	.04017	23
.15770	.12641	.10153	.06588	.03493	24
.14602	.11597	.09230	.05882	.03038	25
.13520	.10639	.08391	.05252	.02642	26
.12519	.09761	.07628	.04689	.02297	27
.11591	.08955	.06934	.04187	.01997	28
.10733	.08216	.06304	.03738	.01737	29
.09938	.07537	.05731	.03338	.01510	30
.09202	.06915	.05210	.02980	.01313	31
.08520	.06344	.04736	.02661	.01142	32
.07889	.05820	.04306	.02376	.00993	33
.07305	.05340	.03914	.02121	.00864	34
.06763	.04899	.03558	.01894	.00751	35
.06262	.04494	.03235	.01691	.00653	36
.05799	.04123	.02941	.01510	.00568	37
.05369	.03783	.02674	.01348	.00494	38
.04971	.03470	.02430	.01204	.00429	39
.04603	.03184	.02210	.01075	.00373	40

TABLE 3 AMOUNT OF AN ORDINARY ANNUITY OF 1

$$A_{\overline{n}|i} = \frac{(1 + i)^n - 1}{i}$$

(n) PERIODS	2%	2½%	3%	4%	5%	6%
1	1.00000	1.00000	1.00000	1.00000	1.00000	1.00000
2	2.02000	2.02500	2.03000	2.04000	2.05000	2.06000
3	3.06040	3.07563	3.09090	3.12160	3.15250	3.18360
4	4.12161	4.15252	4.18363	4.24646	4.31013	4.37462
5	5.20404	5.25633	5.30914	5.41632	5.52563	5.63709
6	6.30812	6.38774	6.46841	6.63298	6.80191	6.97532
7	7.43428	7.54743	7.66246	7.89829	8.14201	8.39384
8	8.58297	8.73612	8.89234	9.21423	9.54911	9.89747
9	9.75463	9.95452	10.15911	10.58280	11.02656	11.49132
10	10.94972	11.20338	11.46338	12.00611	12.57789	13.18079
11	12.16872	12.48347	12.80780	13.48635	14.20679	14.97164
12	13.41209	13.79555	14.19203	15.02581	15.91713	16.86994
13	14.68033	15.14044	15.61779	16.62684	17.71298	18.88214
14	15.97394	16.51895	17.08632	18.29191	19.59863	21.01507
15	17.29342	17.93193	18.59891	20.02359	21.57856	23.27597
16	18.63929	19.38022	20.15688	21.82453	23.65749	25.67253
17	20.01207	20.86473	21.76159	23.69751	25.84037	28.21288
18	21.41231	22.38635	23.41444	25.64541	28.13238	30.90565
19	22.84056	23.94601	25.11687	27.67123	30.53900	33.75999
20	24.29737	25.54466	26.87037	29.77808	33.06595	36.78559
21	25.78332	27.18327	28.67649	31.96920	35.71925	39.99273
22	27.29898	28.86286	30.53678	34.24797	38.50521	43.39229
23	28.84496	30.58443	32.45288	36.61789	41.43048	46.99583
24	30.42186	32.34904	34.42647	39.08260	44.50200	50.81558
25	32.03030	34.15776	36.45926	41.64591	47.72710	54.86451
26	33.67091	36.01171	38.55304	44.31174	51.11345	59.15638
27	35.34432	37.91200	40.70963	47.08421	54.66913	63.70577
28	37.05121	39.85980	42.93092	49.96758	58.40258	68.52811
29	38.79223	41.85630	45.21885	52.96629	62.32271	73.63980
30	40.56808	43.90270	47.57542	56.08494	66.43885	79.05819
31	42.37944	46.00027	50.00268	59.32834	70.76079	84.80168
32	44.22703	48.15028	52.50276	62.70147	75.29883	90.88978
33	46.11157	50.35403	55.07784	66.20953	80.06377	97.34316
34	48.03380	52.61289	57.73018	69.85791	85.06696	104.18376
35	49.99448	54.92821	60.46208	73.65222	90.32031	111.43478
36	51.99437	57.30141	63.27594	77.59831	95.83632	119.12087
37	54.03425	59.73395	66.17422	81.70225	101.62814	127.26812
38	56.11494	62.22730	69.15945	85.97034	107.70955	135.90421
39	58.23724	64.78298	72.23423	90.40915	114.09502	145.05846
40	60.40198	67.40255	75.40126	95.02552	120.79977	154.76197

TABLE 3 AMOUNT OF AN ORDINARY ANNUITY OF 1

1169

8%	9%	10%	12%	15%	(n) PERIODS
1.00000	1.00000	1.00000	1.00000	1.00000	1
2.08000	2.09000	2.10000	2.12000	2.15000	2
3.24640	3.27810	3.31000	3.37440	3.47250	3
4.50611	4.57313	4.64100	4.77933	4.99338	4
5.86660	5.98471	6.10510	6.35285	6.74238	5
7.33592	7.52334	7.71561	8.11519	8.75374	6
8.92280	9.20044	9.48717	10.08901	11.06680	7
10.63663	11.02847	11.43589	12.29969	13.72682	8
12.48756	13.02104	13.57948	14.77566	16.78584	9
14.48656	15.19293	15.93743	17.54874	20.30372	10
16.64549	17.56029	18.53117	20.65458	24.34928	11
18.97713	20.14072	21.38428	24.13313	29.00167	12
21.49530	22.95339	24.52271	28.02911	34.35192	13
24.21492	26.01919	27.97498	32.39260	40.50471	14
27.15211	29.36092	31.77248	37.27972	47.58041	15
30.32428	33.00340	35.94973	42.75328	55.71747	16
33.75023	36.97371	40.54470	48.88367	65.07509	17
37.45024	41.30134	45.59917	55.74972	75.83636	18
41.44626	46.01846	51.15909	63.43968	88.21181	19
45.76196	51.16012	57.27500	72.05244	102.44358	20
50.42292	56.76453	64.00250	81.69874	118.81012	21
55.45676	62.87334	71.40275	92.50258	137.63164	22
60.89330	69.53194	79.54302	104.60289	159.27638	23
66.76476	76.78981	88.49733	118.15524	184.16784	24
73.10594	84.70090	98.34706	133.33387	212.79302	25
79.95442	93.32398	109.18177	150.33393	245.71197	26
87.35077	102.72314	121.09994	169.37401	283.56877	27
95.33883	112.96822	134.20994	190.69889	327.10408	28
103.96594	124.13536	148.63093	214.58275	377.16969	29
113.28321	136.30754	164.49402	241.33268	434.74515	30
123.34587	149.57522	181.94343	271.29261	500.95692	31
134.21354	164.03699	201.13777	304.84772	577.10046	32
145.95062	179.80032	222.25154	342.42945	644.66553	33
158.62667	196.98234	245.47670	384.52098	765.36535	34
172.31680	215.71076	271.02437	431.66350	881.17016	35
187.10215	236.12472	299.12681	484.46312	1014.34568	36
203.07032	258.37595	330.03949	543.59869	1167.49753	37
220.31595	282.62978	364.04343	609.83053	1343.62216	38
238.94122	309.06646	401.44778	684.01020	1546.16549	39
259.05652	337.88245	442.59256	767.09142	1779.09031	40

TABLE 4 PRESENT VALUE OF AN ORDINARY ANNUITY OF 1

$$P_{\overline{n}|i} = \frac{1 - \dfrac{1}{(1 + i)^n}}{i} = \frac{1 - v^n}{i}$$

(n) PERIODS	2%	2½%	3%	4%	5%	6%
1	.98039	.97561	.97087	.96154	.95238	.94340
2	1.94156	1.92742	1.91347	1.88609	1.85941	1.83339
3	2.88388	2.85602	2.82861	2.77509	2.72325	2.67301
4	3.80773	3.76197	3.71710	3.62990	3.54595	3.46511
5	4.71346	4.64583	4.57971	4.45182	4.32948	4.21236
6	5.60143	5.50813	5.41719	5.24214	5.07569	4.91732
7	6.47199	6.34939	6.23028	6.00205	5.78637	5.58238
8	7.32548	7.17014	7.01969	6.73274	6.46321	6.20979
9	8.16224	7.97087	7.78611	7.43533	7.10782	6.80169
10	8.98259	8.75206	8.53020	8.11090	7.72173	7.36009
11	9.78685	9.51421	9.25262	8.76048	8.30641	7.88687
12	10.57534	10.25776	9.95400	9.38507	8.86325	8.38384
13	11.34837	10.98319	10.63496	9.98565	9.39357	8.85268
14	12.10625	11.69091	11.29607	10.56312	9.89864	9.29498
15	12.84926	12.38138	11.93794	11.11839	10.37966	9.71225
16	13.57771	13.05500	12.56110	11.65230	10.83777	10.10590
17	14.29187	13.71220	13.16612	12.16567	11.27407	10.47726
18	14.99203	14.35336	13.75351	12.65930	11.68959	10.82760
19	15.67846	14.97889	14.32380	13.13394	12.08532	11.15812
20	16.35143	15.58916	14.87747	13.59033	12.46221	11.46992
21	17.01121	16.18455	15.41502	14.02916	12.82115	11.76408
22	17.65805	16.76541	15.93692	14.45112	13.16300	12.04158
23	18.29220	17.33211	16.44361	14.85684	13.48857	12.30338
24	18.91393	17.88499	16.93554	15.24696	13.79864	12.55036
25	19.52346	18.42438	17.41315	15.62208	14.09394	12.78336
26	20.12104	18.95061	17.87684	15.98277	14.37519	13.00317
27	20.70690	19.46401	18.32703	16.32959	14.64303	13.21053
28	21.28127	19.96489	18.76411	16.66306	14.89813	13.40616
29	21.84438	20.45355	19.18845	16.98371	15.14107	13.59072
30	22.39646	20.93029	19.60044	17.29203	15.37245	13.76483
31	22.93770	21.39541	20.00043	17.58849	15.59281	13.92909
32	23.46833	21.84918	20.38877	17.87355	15.80268	14.08404
33	23.98856	22.29188	20.76579	18.14765	16.00255	14.23023
34	24.49859	22.72379	21.13184	18.41120	16.19290	14.36814
35	24.99862	23.14516	21.48722	18.66461	16.37419	14.49825
36	25.48884	23.55625	21.83225	18.90828	16.54685	14.62099
37	25.96945	23.95732	22.16724	19.14258	16.71129	14.73678
38	26.44064	24.34860	22.49246	19.36786	16.86789	14.84602
39	26.90259	24.73034	22.80822	19.58448	17.01704	14.94907
40	27.35548	25.10278	23.11477	19.79277	17.15909	15.04630

TABLE 4 PRESENT VALUE OF AN ORDINARY ANNUITY OF 1

1171

8%	9%	10%	12%	15%	(n) PERIODS
.92593	.91743	.90909	.89286	.86957	1
1.78326	1.75911	1.73554	1.69005	1.62571	2
2.57710	2.53130	2.48685	2.40183	2.28323	3
3.31213	3.23972	3.16986	3.03735	2.85498	4
3.99271	3.88965	3.79079	3.60478	3.35216	5
4.62288	4.48592	4.35526	4.11141	3.78448	6
5.20637	5.03295	4.86842	4.56376	4.16042	7
5.74664	5.53482	5.33493	4.96764	4.48732	8
6.24689	5.99525	5.75902	5.32825	4.77158	9
6.71008	6.41766	6.14457	5.65022	5.01877	10
7.13896	6.80519	6.49506	5.93770	5.23371	11
7.53608	7.16073	6.81369	6.19437	5.42062	12
7.90378	7.48690	7.10336	6.42355	5.58315	13
8.24424	7.78615	7.36669	6.62817	5.72448	14
8.55948	8.06069	7.60608	6.81086	5.84737	15
8.85137	8.31256	7.82371	6.97399	5.95424	16
9.12164	8.54363	8.02155	7.11963	6.04716	17
9.37189	8.75563	8.20141	7.24967	6.12797	18
9.60360	8.95012	8.36492	7.36578	6.19823	19
9.81815	9.12855	8.51356	7.46944	6.25933	20
10.01680	9.29224	8.64869	7.56200	6.31246	21
10.20074	9.44243	8.77154	7.64465	6.35866	22
10.37106	9.58021	8.88322	7.71843	6.39884	23
10.52876	9.70661	8.98474	7.78432	6.43377	24
10.67478	9.82258	9.07704	7.84314	6.46415	25
10.80998	9.92897	9.16095	7.89566	6.49056	26
10.93516	10.02658	9.23722	7.94255	6.51353	27
11.05108	10.11613	9.30657	7.98442	6.53351	28
11.15841	10.19828	9.36961	8.02181	6.55088	29
11.25778	10.27365	9.42691	8.05518	6.56598	30
11.34980	10.34280	9.47901	8.08499	6.57911	31
11.43500	10.40624	9.52638	8.11159	6.59053	32
11.51389	10.46444	9.56943	8.13535	6.60046	33
11.58693	10.51784	9.60858	8.15656	6.60910	34
11.65457	10.56682	9.64416	8.17550	6.61661	35
11.71719	10.61176	9.67651	8.19241	6.62314	36
11.77518	10.65299	9.70592	8.20751	6.62882	37
11.82887	10.69082	9.73265	8.22099	6.63375	38
11.87858	10.72552	9.75697	8.23303	6.63805	39
11.92461	10.75736	9.77905	8.24378	6.64178	40

BIBLIOGRAPHY

A

Abdel-khalik, A. Rashad, *Economic Effects on Leases of FASB Statement No. 13, Accounting for Leases*. Stamford, CT: Financial Accounting Standards Board, 1981.

Abdel-khalik, A. Rashad, "The Effect of LIFO-Switching and Firm Ownership on Executives Pay," *Journal of Accounting Research* (Autumn 1985), pp. 427–447.

Abdel-khalik, A. Rashad, and James C. McKeown, "Disclosures of Estimates of Holding Gains and the Assessment of Systematic Risk," *Journal of Accounting Research* (Supplement 1978), pp. 46–92.

Abdel-khalik, A. Rashad, Philip R. Regier, and Sara Ann Reiter, "Some Thoughts on Empirical Research in Positive Accounting," in Thomas Frecka (ed.), *The State of Accounting Research as We Enter the 1990's*, pp. 153–189. Urbana-Champaign: University of Illinois, 1989.

Altman, Edward I., "Financial Ratios, Discriminant Analysis and the Prediction of Corporate Bankruptcy," *Journal of Finance* (September 1968), pp. 589–609.

Altman, Edward I., *Corporate Bankruptcy in America*. Lexington, MA: Heath Lexington Books, 1971.

Altman, Edward I., *Corporate Financial Distress*, New York: John Wiley & Sons, 1993.

Altman, Edward I., Robert G. Haldeman, and P. Narayanan, "Zeta™ Analysis: A New Model to Identify Bankruptcy Risk of Corporations," *Journal of Banking and Finance* (June 1977), pp. 29–54.

American Bar Foundation, *Commentaries on Indentures*. Chicago: American Bar Foundation, 1971.

Ang, James S., and Kiritkumar A. Patel, "Bond Rating Methods: Comparison and Validation," *Journal of Finance* (May 1975), pp. 631–640.

Archibald, T. Ross, "Stock Market Reaction to the Depreciation Switchback," *The Accounting Review* (January 1972), pp. 22–30.

B

Baldwin, Bruce A., "Segment Earnings Disclosure and the Ability of Security Analysts to Forecast Earnings per Share," *The Accounting Review* (July 1984), pp. 376–389.

Ball, Ray, "Changes in Accounting Techniques and Stock Prices," *Journal of Accounting Research* (Supplement 1972), pp. 1–38.

Ball, Ray, "Anomalies in Relationships Between Securities' Yields and Yield-Surrogates," *Journal of Financial Economics* (June/September 1978), pp. 103–126.

Ball, Ray, "The Earnings-Price Anomaly," *Journal of Accounting and Economics* (June/September 1992), pp. 319–346.

Ball, Ray, and Philip Brown, "An Empirical Evaluation of Accounting Income Numbers," *Journal of Accounting Research* (Autumn 1968), pp. 159–178.

Barlev, Benzion, Dov Fried, and Joshua Livnat, "Economic and Financial Reporting Effects of Inventory Tax Allowances," *Contemporary Accounting Review* (Spring 1986), pp. 288–310.

Barth, Mary, William H. Beaver, and Wayne Landsman, "The Market Valuation Implications of Net Periodic Pension Cost Components," *Journal of Accounting and Economics* (March 1992), pp. 27–62.

Bartley, Jon W., and Al Y. S. Chen, "Material Changes in Financial Reporting Attributable to the Tax Reform Act of 1986," *Accounting Horizons* (March 1992), pp. 62–74.

Bartov, Eli, and Gordon M. Bodnar, "Firm Valuation, Earnings Expectations and the Exchange-Rate Exposure Effect" working paper, University of Rochester, June 1992.

Bathke, Allen W., Jr., and Kenneth S. Lorek, "The Relationship Between Time-Series Models and the Security Market's Expectations of Quarterly Earnings," *The Accounting Review* (April 1984), pp. 163–176.

Beaver, William H., "Financial Ratios as Predictors of Failure," *Journal of Accounting Research* (Supplement 1966), pp. 71–111.

Beaver, William H., "What Should Be the FASB's Objectives?" *Journal of Accountancy* (August 1973), pp. 49–56.

Beaver, William H., *Financial Reporting: An Accounting Revolution,* Englewood Cliffs, N.J.: Prentice-Hall 1989.

Beaver, William H., Andrew A. Christie and Paul A. Griffin, "The Information Content Of SEC Accounting Release No. 190", *Journal of Accounting and Economics* (August 1980), pp. 127–157.

Beaver, William H., R. Clarke, and W. F. Wright, "The Association Between Unsystematic Security Returns and the Magnitude of Earnings Forecast Errors," *Journal of Accounting Research* (Autumn 1979), pp. 316–340.

Beaver, William H., and Roland E. Dukes, "Interperiod Tax Allocation, Earnings Expectations, and the Behavior of Security Prices," *The Accounting Review* (April 1972), pp. 320–332.

Beaver, William H., and Roland E. Dukes, "Interperiod Tax Allocation and δ-Depreciation Methods: Some Empirical Results," *The Accounting Review* (July 1973), pp. 549–559.

Beaver, William H., Paul Griffin, and Wayne R. Landsman, "The Incremental Information Content of Replacement Cost Earnings" *Journal of Accounting and Economics* (July 1982), pp. 15–39.

Beaver, William H., Paul Kettler, and Myron Scholes, "The Association Between Market–Determined and Accounting Determined Risk Measures," *The Accounting Review* (October 1970), pp. 654–682.

Beaver, William H., and Wayne R. Landsman, *Incremental Information Content of Statement 33 Disclosures,* (Stamford CT: Financial Accounting Standards Board, 1983)

Beaver, William H., and James Manegold, "The Association Between Market Determined and Accounting-Determined Measures of Systematic Risk: Some Further Evidence," *Journal of Financial and Quantitative Analysis* (June 1975), pp. 231–284.

Beaver, William H., and Dale Morse, "What Determines Price-Earnings Ratios?" *Financial Analysts Journal* (July/August 1978), pp. 65–76.

Beaver, William H., and Mark Wolfson, "Foreign Currency Translation and Changing Prices in Perfect and Complete Markets," *Journal of Accounting Research* (Autumn 1982), pp. 528–550.

Beaver, William H., and Mark Wolfson, "Foreign Currency Translation Gains and Losses: What Effect Do They Have and What Do They Mean?" *Financial Analysts Journal* (March/April 1984), pp. 28–36.

Belkaoui, Ahmed, "Industrial Bonds Ratings: A New Look," *Financial Management* (Autumn 1980), pp. 44–51.

Belkaoui, Ahmed, *Industrial Bonds and the Rating Process.* Westport, CT: Quorum Books, an imprint of Greenwood Publishing Group, 1983.

Bernard, Victor L., "Capital Market Research During the 1980's: A Critical Review," in Thomas Frecka (ed.), *The State of Accounting Research as We Enter the 1990's,* pp. 72–120. Urbana-Champaign: University of Illinois, 1989.

Bernard, Victor L., and James Noel "Do Inventory Disclosures Predict Sales and Earnings," *Journal of Accounting Auditing and Finance* (March 1991), pp. 145–182.

Bernard, Victor L., and Thomas Stober, "The Nature and Amount of Information in Cash Flows and Accruals," *The Accounting Review* (October 1989), pp. 624–652.

Bernstein, Leopold, *Financial Statement Analysis*, 4th ed. Homewood, IL: Richard D. Irwin 1988.

Bhushan, Ravi, "Firm Characteristics and Analyst Following," *Journal of Accounting and Economics* (July 1989), pp. 255–274.

Biddle, Gary C., "Accounting Methods and Management Decisions: The Case of Inventory Costing and Inventory Policy," *Journal of Accounting Research* (Supplement 1980), pp. 235–280.

Biddle, Gary C., and Frederick W. Lindahl, "Stock Price Reactions to LIFO Adoptions: The Association Between Excess Returns and LIFO Tax Savings," *Journal of Accounting Research* (Autumn 1982, Part II), pp. 551–588.

Biddle, Gary C., and William E. Ricks, "Analyst Forecast Errors and Stock Price Behavior Near the Earnings Announcement Dates of LIFO Adopters," *Journal of Accounting Research* (Autumn 1988), pp. 169–194.

Bildersee, John S., "The Association Between A Market-Determined Measure Of Risk And Alternative Measures Of Risk," *The Accounting Review* (January 1975), pp. 81–98.

Blum, Marc, "Failing Company Discriminant Analysis," *Journal of Accounting Research* (Spring 1974), pp. 1–25.

Bodie, Zvi, Alex Kane, and Alan J. Marcus, *Investments*. Homewood IL: Richard D. Irwin 1989.

Bowen, Robert M., "Valuation of Earnings Components in the Electric Utility Industry," *The Accounting Review* (January 1981), pp. 1–22.

Bowen, Robert M., David Burgstahler, and Lane A. Daley, "The Incremental Information Content of Accrual Versus Cash Flows," *The Accounting Review* (October 1987), pp. 723–747.

Bowman, Robert G., "The Theoretical Relationship Between Systematic Risk and Financial (Accounting) Variables," *Journal of Finance* (June 1979), pp. 617–630.

Bowman, Robert G., "The Importance of a Market-Value Measurement of Debt in Assessing Leverage," *Journal of Accounting Research* (Spring 1980), pp. 242–254.

Box, G.E.P., and G.M. Jenkins, *Time-Series Analysis: Forecasting and Control*, San Francisco: Holden Day, 1976.

Bradley, J., A. Desai, and E. H. Kim, "Synergistic Gains from Corporate Acquisitions and Their Division Between the Stockholders of Target and Acquiring Firms," *Journal of Financial Economics* (May 1988), pp. 3–40.

Briloff, Abraham J., "Distortions Arising From Pooling-of-Interests Accounting," *Financial Analysts Journal* (March–April 1968), pp. 71–80.

Brooks, Leroy, and Dale Buckmaster, "Further Evidence of the Time Series Properties of Accounting Income" *Journal of Finance* (December 1976), pp. 1359–1373.

Brown, Lawrence D., Robert L. Hagerman, Paul A. Griffin, and Mark E. Zmijewski, "Security Analyst Superiority Relative to Univariate Time-Series Models in Forecasting Quarterly Earnings," *Journal of Accounting and Economics* (April 1987a), pp. 61–87.

Brown, Lawrence D., Robert L. Hagerman, Paul A. Griffin, and Mark E. Zmijewski, "An Evaluation of Alternative Proxies for the Market's Assessment of Unexpected Earnings" *Journal of Accounting and Economics* (July 1987b), pp. 159–193.

Brown, Lawrence D., Gordon D. Richardson, and Steven J. Schwager, "An Information Interpretation of Financial Analyst Superiority in Forecasting Earnings," *Journal of Accounting Research* (Spring 1987), pp. 49–67.

Brown, Lawrence D., and Michael S. Rozeff, "Univariate Time-Series Models of Quarterly Accounting Earnings per Share: A Proposed Model" *Journal of Accounting Research* (Spring 1979), pp. 179–189.

Brown, Philip, George Foster, and Eric Noreen, *Security Analyst Multi-Year Earnings Forecasts and the Capital Market*. Sarasota, FL: American Accounting Association, 1985.

Brown, Robert M., "Short-Range Market Reaction to Changes to LIFO Accounting Using Preliminary Announcement Dates," *Journal of Accounting Research* (Spring 1980), pp. 38–63.

Bublitz, Bruce, and Michael Ettredge, "The Information in Discretionary Outlays: Advertising, Research and Development," *The Accounting Review* (January 1989), pp. 108–124.

Bulow, Jeremy, "What Are Corporate Pension Liabilities?" *Quarterly Journal of Economics* (August 1982), pp. 435–442.

Burgstahler, David, James Jiambalvo and Eric Noreen, "Changes in the Probability of Bankruptcy and Equity Value", *Journal of Accounting and Economics* (July 1989), pp. 207–224.

Butler, Kirt C., and Larry H. P. Lang, "The Forecast Accuracy of Individual Analysts: Evidence of Systematic Optimism and Pessimism," *Journal of Accounting Research* (Spring 1991), pp. 150–156.

C

Canning, John B., *The Economics of Accountancy*. New York: The Ronald Press, 1929.

Casey, Cornelius J., and Norman J. Bartczak, "Cash Flow It's Not the Bottom Line," *Harvard Business Review* (July/August 1984), pp. 60–66.

Casey, Cornelius J., and Norman J. Bartczak, "Using Operating Cash Flow Data to Predict Financial Distress: Some Extensions," *Journal of Accounting Research* (Spring 1985), pp. 384–401.

Chen, Kung H., and Thomas A. Shimerda, "An Empirical Analysis of Useful Financial Ratios," *Financial Management* (Spring 1981), pp. 51–60.

Clinch, Greg J., and Joseph Magliolo, "Market Perceptions of Reserve Disclosures Under SFAS No. 69," *The Accounting Review* (October 1992), pp. 843–861.

Cohen, Jerome B., Edward D. Zinbarg, and Arthur Zeikel, *Investment Analysis and Portfolio Management*, 5th ed. Homewood, Ill.: Richard D. Irwin, 1987.

Collins, Daniel W., "Predicting Earnings with Subentity Data: Some Further Evidence," *Journal of Accounting Research* (Spring 1976), pp. 163–177.

Collins, Daniel W., and Warren T. Dent, "The Proposed Elimination of Full Cost Accounting in the Extractive

Petroleum Industry: An Empirical Assessment of the Market Consequences," *Journal of Accounting and Economics* (March 1979), pp. 3–44.

Collins, Daniel W., and S. P. Kothari, "An Analysis of Intertemporal and Cross-sectional Determinants of Earnings Response Coefficients," *Journal of Accounting and Economics* (July 1989), pp. 143–181.

Collins, Daniel W., Michael Rozeff, and Dan Dhaliwal, "The Economic Determinants of the Market Reaction to Proposed Mandatory Accounting Changes in the Oil and Gas Industry: A Cross-sectional Analysis," *Journal of Accounting and Economics* (March 1981), pp. 37–71.

Collins, Daniel W., Michael Rozeff, and William K. Salatka, "The SEC's Rejection of SFAS 19: Tests of Market Price Reversal," *The Accounting Review* (January 1982), pp. 1–17.

Collins, Daniel W., and Richard R. Simmonds, "SEC Line-of- Business Disclosure and Market Risk Adjustments," *Journal of Accounting Research* (Autumn 1979), pp. 352–383.

Comiskey, Eugene, and Charles W. Mulford, "Investment Decisions and the Equity Accounting Standard," *The Accounting Review* (July 1986), pp. 519–525.

Copeland, R. M., and M. L. Moore, "The Financial Bath: Is It Common?" *MSU Business Topics* (Autumn 1972), pp. 63–69.

Copeland, T., T. Koller, and J. Murrin, *Valuation: Measuring and Managing the Value of Companies.* New York: John Wiley and Sons, 1990.

Cragg, J. G., and B. G. Malkiel, *Expectations and the Structure of Share Prices.* Chicago: University of Chicago Press, 1982.

Cushing, Barry E., and Marc J. LeClere, "Evidence on the Determinants of Inventory Accounting Policy Choice," *The Accounting Review* (April 1992), pp. 355–366.

D

Daley, Lane A. "The Valuation of Reported Pension Measures for Firms Sponsoring Defined Benefit Plans," *The Accounting Review* (April 1984), pp. 177–198.

Dambolena, Ismael G., and Sarkis J. Khoury, "Ratio Stability and Corporate Failure," *Journal of Finance* (September 1980), pp. 1017–1026.

Davis, Harry Z., Nathan Kahn, and Etzmun Rosen, "LIFO Inventory Liquidations: An Empirical Study," *Journal of Accounting Research* (Autumn 1984), pp. 480–496.

Davis, Michael L., "Differential Market Reaction to Pooling and Purchase Methods," *The Accounting Review* (July 1990), pp. 696–709.

Deakin, Edward B. III, "A Discriminant Analysis of Predictors of Business Failure," *Journal of Accounting Research* (Spring 1972), pp. 167–179.

Deakin, Edward B. III, "An Analysis of Differences Between Non-Major Oil Firms Using Successful Efforts and Full Cost Methods," *The Accounting Review* (October 1979), pp. 722–734.

Deakin, Edward B. III, "Rational Economic Behavior and Lobbying on Accounting Issues: Evidence from the Oil and Gas Industry," *The Accounting Review* (January 1989), pp. 137–151.

Devine, Michael, "Using Pro Forma Allocations to Evaluate Business Purchases", *Financial Executive* (June 1981), pp. 15–18.

Dhaliwal, Dan S.. "Measurement of Financial Leverage in the Presence of Unfunded Pension Liabilities," *The Accounting Review* (October 1986), pp. 651–661.

Dhaliwal, Dan, Gerald Saloman, and E. Dan Smith, "The Effect of Owner Versus Management Control on the Choice of Accounting Methods," *Journal of Accounting and Economics* (July 1982), pp. 89–96.

Dieter, R., and J. A. Heyman, "Implications of SEC Staff Accounting Bulletin 88 for Foreign Registrants," *Journal of Accountancy* (August 1991), pp. 121–125.

Dopuch, Nicholas, and Morton Pincus, "Evidence on the Choice of Inventory Accounting Methods: LIFO Versus FIFO," *Journal of Accounting Research* (Spring 1988), pp. 28–59.

Duke, Joanne C., and Herbert G. Hunt III, "An Empirical Examination of Debt Covenant Restrictions and Accounting-Related Debt Proxies," *Journal of Accounting and Economics* (January 1990), pp. 45–63.

Dukes, Roland E., *An Empirical Investigation of the Effects of Statement of Financial Accounting Standards No. 8 on Security Return Behavior.* Stamford, CT: Financial Accounting Standards Board, 1978.

Dukes, Roland E., Thomas R. Dyckman, and John A. Elliott, "Accounting for Research and Development Costs: The Impact on Research and Development Expenditures," *Journal of Accounting Research* (Supplement 1980), pp. 1–26.

Dunne Kathleen M., "An Empirical Analysis of Management's Choice of Accounting Treatment for Business Combinations," *Journal of Accounting and Public Policy* (July 1990), pp. 111–133.

Dyckman, Thomas R., and Abbie J. Smith, "Financial Accounting and Reporting by Oil and Gas Producing

Companies: A Study of Information Effects," *Journal of Accounting and Economics* (March 1979), pp. 45–75.

E

Easman, W., A. Falkenstein, and R. Weil, "The Correlation Between Sustainable Income and Stock Returns," *Financial Analysts Journal* (September–October 1979), pp. 44–47.

Eggleton, Ian R., Stephen H. Penman, and John R. Twombly, "Accounting Changes and Stock Prices: An Examination of Selected Uncontrolled Variables," *Journal of Accounting Research* (Spring 1976), pp. 66–88.

Elam, Rick, "The Effect of Lease Data on the Predictive Ability of Financial Ratios," *The Accounting Review* (January 1975), pp. 25–53.

Elliott, J. W., and H. L. Uphoff, "Predicting the Near Term Profit and Loss Statement with an Econometric Model: A Feasibility Study," *Journal of Accounting Research* (Autumn 1972), pp. 259–274.

Elliott, John A., and Donna R. Philbrick, "Accounting Changes and Earnings Predictability," *The Accounting Review* (January 1990), pp. 157–174.

Elliott, John A., Gordon Richardson, Thomas R. Dyckman, and Roland E. Dukes, "The Impact of SFAS No. 2 on Firm Expenditures on Research and Development: Replications and Extensions," *Journal of Accounting Research* (Spring 1984), pp. 85–102.

Elliott, John A., and Wayne Shaw, "Write-offs as Accounting Procedures to Manage Perceptions," *Journal of Accounting Research* (Supplement 1988), pp. 91–119.

El-Gazzar, Samir M., Steven Lilien, and Victor Pastena, "Accounting for Leases by Lessees," *Journal of Accounting and Economics* (October 1986), pp. 217–237.

Emery, Gary W., and Kenneth O. Cogger, "The Measurement of Liquidity," *Journal of Accounting Research* (Autumn 1982), pp. 290–303.

F

Falkenstein, Angela, and Roman L. Weil, "Replacement Cost Accounting: What Will Income Statements Based on the SEC Disclosures Show? Part I," *Financial Analysts Journal* (January/February 1977a), pp. 46–57.

Falkenstein, Angela, and Roman L. Weil, "Replacement Cost Accounting: What Will Income Statements Based on the SEC Disclosures Show? Part II," *Financial Analysts Journal* (March/April 1977b), pp. 48–57.

Fama, Eugene, "Efficient Capital Markets: A Review of Theory and Empirical Work," *Journal of Finance* (May 1970), pp. 383–417.

Fama, Eugene, and Kenneth R. French "The Cross-section of Expected Stock Returns," *Journal of Finance* (June 1992), pp. 427–466.

Feldstein, Martin, and Randall Morck, "Pension Funding Decisions, Interest Rate Assumptions and Share Prices," in Zvi Bodie and John B. Shoven (eds.), *Financial Aspects of The United States Pension System*. Chicago: University of Chicago Press, 1983.

Feltham, Gerald, and James A. Ohlson, "Valuation and Clean Surplus Accounting for Operating and Financial Activities," working paper, Columbia University, 1992.

Financial Executives Institute, Committee on Corporate Reporting, "Survey on Unusual Charges" (1986 and 1991).

Foster, George, "Accounting Earnings and Stock Prices of Insurance Companies," *The Accounting Review* (October 1975), pp. 686–698.

Foster, George, "Quarterly Accounting Data: Time Series Properties and Predictive-Ability Results," *The Accounting Review* (January 1977), pp. 1–21.

Foster, George, "Briloff and the Capital Market," *Journal of Accounting Research* (Spring 1979), pp. 262–274.

Francis, Jere R., and Sara Ann Reiter, "Determinants of Corporate Pension Funding Strategy," *Journal of Accounting and Economics* (April 1987), pp. 35–59.

Frecka, Thomas J., and Cheng F. Lee, "Generalized Financial Ratio Adjustment Processes and Their Implications," *Journal of Accounting Research* (Spring 1983), pp. 308–316.

Freeman, Robert N., James A. Ohlson, and Stephen H. Penman, "Book Rate-of-Return and Prediction of Earnings Changes: An Empirical Investigation," *Journal of Accounting Research* (Autumn 1982), pp. 639–653.

Fried, Dov, "Aggregation Versus Disaggregation And The Predictive Ability Criterion," Unpublished dissertation, New York University, 1978.

Fried, Dov, and Dan Givoly, "Financial Analysts' Forecasts of Earnings: A Better Surrogate for Market Expectations," *Journal of Accounting and Economics* (October 1982), pp. 85–108.

Fried, Dov, Michael Schiff, and Ashwinpaul C. Sondhi, *Impairments and Writeoffs of Long-Lived Assets.*

Montvale, NJ: National Association of Accountants, 1989.

Fried, Dov, Michael Schiff, and Ashwinpaul C. Sondhi, "Big Bath or Intermittent Showers? Another Look at Write-offs," working paper, New York University, 1990.

Fuller, Russell J., and Chi-Cheng Hsia, "A Simplified Common Stock Valuation Model," *Financial Analysts Journal* (September/October 1984), pp. 49–56.

G

Gahlon, James M., and James A. Gentry, "On the Relationship Between Systematic Risk and the Degrees of Operating and Financial Leverage," *Financial Management* (Summer 1982), pp. 15–23.

Gentry, James A., Paul Newbold, and David T. Whitford, "Classifying Bankrupt Firms with Funds Flow Components," *Journal of Accounting Research* (Spring 1985), pp. 146–160.

Ghicas, Dimitrios C. "Determinants of Actuarial Cost Method Changes for Pension Accounting and Funding," *The Accounting Review* (April 1990), pp. 384–405.

Gibson, Charles H., "Financial Ratios in Annual Reports," *The CPA Journal* (September 1982), pp. 18–29.

Gibson, Charles H., "How Chartered Financial Analysts View Financial Ratios," *Financial Analysts Journal* (May/June 1987), pp. 74–76.

Givoly, Dan, and Carla Hayn, "The Valuation of the Deferred Tax Liability: Evidence from the Stock Market," *The Accounting Review* (April 1992), pp. 394–410.

Givoly, Dan, and Josef Lakonishok, "The Information Content of Financial Analysts' Forecasts of Earnings: Some Evidence on Semi-Strong Inefficiency," *Journal of Accounting and Economics* (December 1979), pp. 165–185.

Givoly, Dan, and Josef Lakonishok, "The Quality of Analysts' Forecasts of Earnings," *Financial Analysts Journal* (September/October 1984), pp. 40–47.

Gombola, Michael J., and J. Edward Ketz, "Financial Ratio Patterns in Retail and Manufacturing Organizations," *Financial Management* (Summer 1983), pp. 45–56.

Gonedes, Nicholas J., "Risk, Information and the Effects of Special Accounting Items on Capital Market Equilibrium," *Journal of Accounting Research* (Autumn 1975), pp. 220–256.

Gonedes, Nicholas J., "Corporate Signalling, External

Accounting and Capital Market Equilibrium: Evidence on Dividends, Income and Extraordinary Items," *Journal of Accounting Research* (Spring 1978), pp. 26–79.

Gonedes, Nicholas J., and Nicholas Dopuch, "Capital Market Equilibrium, Information Production and Selecting Accounting Techniques: Theoretical Framework and Review of Empirical Work," *Journal of Accounting Research* (Supplement 1974), pp. 48–129.

Granof, Michael H., and Daniel G. Short, "Why Do Companies Reject LIFO?," *Journal of Accounting Auditing and Finance* (Summer 1984), pp. 323–333.

Griffin, Paul A., "The Time-Series Behavior of Quarterly Earnings: Preliminary Evidence," *Journal of Accounting Research* (Spring 1977), pp. 71–83.

H

Hamada, Robert S., "The Effect of the Firm's Capital Structure on the Systematic Risk of Common Stocks," *Journal of Finance* (May 1972), pp. 435–452

Hand, John R. M., "Did Firms Undertake Debt-Equity Swaps for Accounting Paper Profits or True Financial Gains?" *The Accounting Review* (October 1989), pp. 587–623.

Hand, John R. M., "A Test of the Extended Functional Fixation Hypothesis," *The Accounting Review* (October 1990), pp. 739–763.

Harrington, Diana R., "Whose Beta Is Best?" *Financial Analysts Journal* (July/August 1983), pp. 67–77.

Harris, Trevor S., and James A. Ohlson, "Accounting Disclosures and the Market's Valuation of Oil and Gas Properties," *The Accounting Review* (October 1987), pp. 651–670.

Harris, Trevor S., and James A. Ohlson, "Accounting Disclosures and the Market's Valuation of Oil and Gas Properties: Evaluation of Market Efficiency and Functional Fixation," *The Accounting Review* (October 1990), pp. 764–780.

Hauworth, William P. II, and Lailani Moody, "An Accountant's Option Primer: Puts and Calls Demystified," *Journal of Accountancy* (January 1987), pp. 87–97.

Healy, Paul M., "The Effect of Bonus Schemes on Accounting Decisions," *Journal of Accounting and Economics* (April 1985), pp. 85–107.

Healy, Paul M., Sok-Hyon Kang, and Krishna Palepu, "The Effect of Accounting Procedure Changes on CEO's Cash Salary and Bonus Compensation," *Journal of Accounting and Economics* (April 1987), pp. 7–34.

Heian, James B., and James B. Thies, "Consolidation of

Finance Subsidiaries: $230 Billion in Off-Balance-Sheet Financing Comes Home to Roost," *Accounting Horizons* (March 1989), pp. 1–9.

Hicks, J. R., *Value and Capital*, 2nd ed. Oxford: Chaundon Press, 1946.

Hirschey, Mark, and Jerry J. Weygandt, "Amortization Policy for Advertising and Research and Development," *Journal of Accounting Research* (Spring 1985), pp. 326–335.

Hochman, Shalom, "The Beta Coefficient: An Instrumental Variables Approach," in Haim Levy (ed.), *Research in Finance,* Volume 4 Greenwich, CT: JAI Press, 1983.

Holthausen, Robert W., "Evidence on the Effect of Bond Covenants and Management Compensation Contracts on the Choice of Accounting Techniques: The Case of the Depreciation Switch-Back," *Journal of Accounting and Economics* (March 1981), pp. 73–109.

Holthausen, Robert W., and D. F. Larcker, "The Prediction of Stock Returns Using Financial Statement Information" *Journal of Accounting and Economics* (June/September 1992), pp. 373–411.

Hong, Hai, Robert S. Kaplan, and Gershon Mandelker, "Pooling vs. Purchase: The Effects of Accounting for Mergers on Stock Prices," *The Accounting Review* (January 1978), pp. 31–47.

Hopwood, William, James C. McKeown, and Paul Newbold, "The Additional Information Content of Quarterly Earnings Reports," *Journal of Accounting Research* (Autumn 1982), pp. 343–349.

Hopwood, William, Paul Newbold, and Peter A. Silhan, "The Potential for Gains in Predictive Ability Through Disaggregation: Segmented Annual Earnings," *Journal of Accounting Research* (Autumn 1982), pp. 724–732.

Horrigan, James O., "Some Empirical Bases of Financial Ratio Analysis," *The Accounting Review* (July 1965), pp. 558–568.

Horrigan, James O., "The Determination of Long-Term Credit Standing with Financial Ratios," *Journal of Accounting Research* (Supplement 1966), pp. 44–62.

Horwitz, Bertrand, and Richard Kolodny, "Line of Business Reporting and Security Prices: An Analysis of an SEC Disclosure Rule," *Bell Journal of Economics* (Spring 1977), pp. 234–249.

Horwitz, Bertrand N., and Richard Kolodny, "The Economic Effects of Involuntary Uniformity in the Financial Reporting of R&D Expenditures," *Journal of Accounting Research* (Supplement 1980), pp. 38–74.

Hunt, Herbert G. III, "Potential Determinants of Corporate Inventory Accounting Decisions," *Journal of Accounting Research* (Autumn 1985), pp. 448–467.

I

Imhoff, Eugene A., Jr., and Jacob K. Thomas, "Economic Consequences of Accounting Changes: The Lease Disclosure Rule Change," *Journal of Accounting and Economics* (December 1988), pp. 277–310.

Ingberman, Monroe and Sorter, George H., "The Role of Financial Statements in an Efficient Market," *Journal of Accounting, Auditing, and Finance* (Fall 1978), pp. 58–62.

J

Jennings, Ross, David P. Mest, and Robert B. Thompson II, "Investor Reaction to Disclosures of 1974–75 LIFO Adoption Decisions," *The Accounting Review* (April 1992), pp. 337–354.

Jensen, M.C. and W.H.Meckling, "Theory of the Firm: Managerial Behavior, Agency Costs, and Ownership Structure," *Journal of Financial Economics* (October 1976), pp. 305–360.

Johnson, W. Bruce, "The Cross Sectional Stability of Financial Ratio Patterns," *Journal of Financial and Quantitative Analysis* (December 1979), pp. 1035–1048.

Johnson, W. Bruce, and Dan S. Dhaliwal, "LIFO Abandonment," *Journal of Accounting Research* (Autumn 1988), pp. 236–272.

Joy, O. M., and C. P. Jones, "Earnings Reports and Market Efficiencies: An Analysis of the Contrary Evidence," *The Journal of Financial Research* (Spring 1979), pp. 51–63.

K

Kaplan, Robert S., and Richard Roll, "Investor Evaluation of Accounting Information: Some Empirical Evidence," *Journal of Business* (April 1972), pp. 225–257.

Kaplan, Robert S., and Gabriel Urwitz, "Statistical Models of Bond Ratings: A Methodological Inquiry," *Journal of Business* (April 1979), pp. 231–261.

Kim, Moshe, and Giora Moore, "Economic Vs. Accounting Depreciation," *Journal of Accounting and Economics* (April 1988), pp. 111–125.

Kinney, William R., Jr., "Predicting Earnings: Entity Versus Subentity Data," *Journal of Accounting Research* (Spring 1971), pp. 127–136.

Kormendi, Roger, and Robert Lipe, "Earnings Innovations, Earnings Persistence, and Stock Returns," *Journal of Business* (July 1987), pp. 323–345.

L

Landsman, Wayne, "An Empirical Investigation of Pension and Property Rights," *The Accounting Review* (October 1986), pp. 662–691.

Largay, James A. III, and Clyde P. Stickney, "Cash Flows, Ratio Analysis and the W. T. Grant Bankruptcy," *Financial Analysts Journal* (July/August 1980), pp. 51–54.

Lasman, Daniel A., and Roman L. Weil, "Adjusting the Debt-Equity Ratio," *Financial Analysts Journal* (September/October 1978), pp. 49–58.

Lau, Amy Hing-Ling, "A Five-State Financial Distress Prediction Model," *Journal of Accounting Research* (Spring 1987), pp. 127–138.

Leftwich, Richard W., "Evidence Of The Impact Of Mandatory Changes In Accounting Principles On Corporate Loan Agreements", *Journal of Accounting and Economics* (March 1981), pp. 3–36.

Leftwich, Richard W., "Accounting Information in Private Markets: Evidence from Private Lending Agreements," *The Accounting Review* (January 1983), pp. 23–42.

Lev, Baruch, "Industry Averages as Targets for Financial Ratios," *Journal of Accounting Research* (Autumn 1969), pp. 290–299.

Lev, Baruch, "On the Association Between Operating Leverage and Risk," *Journal of Financial and Quantitative Analysis* (September 1974), pp. 627–640.

Lev, Baruch, "The Impact of Accounting Regulation on the Stock Market: The Case Of Oil and Gas Companies," *The Accounting Review* (July 1979), pp. 485–503.

Lev, Baruch, "On the Usefulness of Earnings and Earnings Research: Lessons and Directions from Two Decades of Empirical Research," *Journal of Accounting Research* (Supplement 1989), pp. 153–192.

Lev, Baruch, and S. Ramu Thiagarajan, "Fundamental Information Analyis," working paper, University of California at Berkeley, May 1991.

Lilien, Steven, and Victor Pastena, "Determinants of Intra-Method Choice in the Oil and Gas Industry," *Journal of Accounting and Economics* (December 1982), pp. 145–170.

Lindhal, F.W., and W.E. Ricks, "Market Reactions to Announcements of Writeoffs," Working Paper, The Fuqua School of Business, Duke University, January 1990.

Lipe, Robert C., "The Information Contained in the Components of Earnings," *Journal of Accounting Research* (Supplement 1986), pp. 37–64.

Livnat, Joshua, and Ashwinpaul C. Sondhi, "Finance Subsidiaries: Their Formation and Consolidation," *Journal of Business Finance & Accounting* (Spring 1986), pp. 137–147.

Livnat, Joshua, and Paul Zarowin, "The Incremental Informational Content of Cash-Flow Components," *Journal of Accounting and Economics* (May 1990), pp. 25–46.

Lys, Thomas, "Mandated Accounting Changes and Debt Covenants: The Case of Oil and Gas Accounting," *Journal of Accounting and Economics* (April 1984), pp. 39–65.

M

Malmquist, David H. "Efficient Contracting and the Choice of Accounting Method in the Oil and Gas Industry," *Journal of Accounting and Economics* (January 1990), pp. 173–205.

Mandelker, Gershon M., and S. Ghon Rhee, "The Impact of the Degrees of Operating and Financial Leverage on Systematic Risk of Common Stock," *Journal of Financial and Quantitative Analysis* (March 1984), pp. 45–57.

Martin, L. G., and G. V. Henderson, "On Bond Ratings and Pension Obligations: A Note," *Journal of Financial and Quantitative Analysis* (December 1983), pp. 463–470.

Mellman, Martin, and Leopold Bernstein, "Lease Capitalization Under APB Opinion No. 5," *The New York Certified Public Accountant* (February 1966), pp. 115–122.

Morck, Randall, Andrei Shleifer, and Robert W. Vishny, "Do Managerial Objectives Drive Bad Acquisitions?" *Journal of Finance* (March 1990), pp. 31–48.

Moses, Douglas, "Income Smoothing and Incentives: Empirical Tests Using Accounting Changes," *The Accounting Review* (April 1987), pp. 358–377.

Most, Kenneth S., "Depreciation Expense and the Effect of Inflation," *Journal of Accounting Research* (Autumn 1984), pp. 782–788.

Mulford, Charles W., "The Importance of a Market Value Measurement of Debt in Leverage Ratios: Replications and Extensions," *Journal of Accounting Research* (Autumn 1985), pp. 897–906.

Murdoch, Brock, "The Information Content of FAS 33 Returns on Equity," *The Accounting Review* (April 1986), pp. 273–287.

Myers, Stewart C., and Nicholas S. Majluf, "Corporate Financing and Investment Decisions When Firms Have Information That Investors Do Not Have," *Journal of Financial Economics* (June 1984), pp. 187–221.

N

Nakayama, Mie, Steven Lilien, and Martin Benis, "Due Process and FAS No, 13," *Management Accounting* (April 1981), pp. 49–53 .

O

O'Brien, Patricia, "Analysts Forecasts as Earnings Expectations," *Journal of Accounting and Economics* (January 1988), pp. 53–83.

Ohlson, James A., "Financial Ratios and the Probabilistic Prediction of Bankruptcy," *Journal of Accounting Research* (Spring 1980), pp. 109–131.

Ou, Jane A., "The Information Content of Nonearnings Accounting Numbers as Earnings Predictors," *Journal of Accounting Research* (Spring 1990), pp. 144–162.

Ou, Jane A., and Stephen H. Penman, "Financial Statement Analysis and the Prediction of Stock Returns," *Journal of Accounting and Economics* (November 1989), pp. 295–329.

P

Pariser, David B., and Pierre L. Titard, "Impairment of Oil and Gas Properties," *Journal of Accountancy* (December 1991), pp. 52–62.

Patell, James M., and Mark A. Wolfson, "Good News, Bad News, and the Intraday Timing of Corporate Disclosure," *The Accounting Review* (July 1982), pp. 509–527.

Patell, James M., and Mark A. Wolfson, "The Intraday Speed of Adjustment of Stock Prices to Earnings and Dividend Announcements," *Journal of Financial Economics* (June 1984), pp. 223–252.

Penman, Stephen, "An Evaluation of Accounting Rate-of-Return," *Journal of Accounting, Auditing and Finance* (Spring 1991), pp. 233–255.

Penman, Stephen H., "Return to Fundamentals," *Journal of Accounting, Auditing and Finance* (Fall 1992), pp. 465–483 (working paper, University of California at Berkeley).

Pinches, George E., and Kent A. Mingo, "A Multivariate Analysis of Industrial Bond Ratings," *Journal of Finance* (March 1973), pp. 1–18.

Pinches, George E., and Kent A. Mingo, "The Role of Subordination and Industrial Bond Ratings," *Journal of Finance* (March 1975), pp. 201–206.

Pinches, George E., Kent A. Mingo, and J. Kent Caruthers, "The Stability of Financial Ratio Patterns in Industrial Organizations," *Journal of Finance* (May 1973), pp. 384–396.

Pinches, George E., A. A. Eubank, Kent A. Mingo, and J. Kent Caruthers, "The Hierarchical Classification of Financial Ratios," *Journal of Business Research* (October 1975), pp. 295–310.

Pogue, T., and R. Soldovsky, "What's In A Bond Rating," *Journal of Financial and Quantitative Analysis* (June 1969), pp. 201–228.

Press, Eric G., and Joseph B. Weintrop, "Accounting-Based Constraints in Public and Private Debt Agreements," *Journal of Accounting and Economics* (January 1990), pp. 65–95.

R

Ragsdale, E. K. Easton, and George H. Boyd III, "Pension Expense: A Hidden Source of Past Profit Growth is Now Hurting. Kidder, Peabody & Company Quantitative Research Group, August 6, 1990.

Ramakrishnan, Ram T. S., and Jacob K. Thomas, "Valuation of Permanent, Transitory, and Price-Irrelevant Components of Reported Earnings," working paper, Columbia University, 1991.

Rapaccioli, Donna, and Allen Schiff, "Reporting Segment Sales Under APB Opinion No. 30," *Accounting Horizons* (December 1991), pp. 53–59.

Rayburn, Judy, "The Association of Operating Cash Flow and Accruals with Security Returns," *Journal of Accounting Research* (Supplement 1986), pp. 112–133.

Reeve, James H., and Keith G. Stanga, "The LIFO Pooling Decision: Some Empirical Results from Accounting Practice," *Accounting Horizons* (March 1987), pp. 25–34.

Rendelman, R. J., Jr., C. P. Jones, and H. A. Latane, "Empirical Anomalies Based on Unexpected Earnings and the Importance of Risk Adjustments," *Journal of Financial Economics* (November 1982), pp. 269–287.

Richards, Verlyn D., and Eugene J. Laughlin, "A Cash Conversion Cycle Approach to Liquidity Analysis," *Financial Management* (Spring 1980), pp. 32–38.

Ricks, William E., "The Market's Response to the 1974 LIFO Adoption," *Journal of Accounting Research* (Autumn 1982, Part I), pp. 367–387.

Ricks, William E., and John S. Hughes, "Market Reactions to a Non-Discretionary Accounting Change: The Case of Long-Term Investments," *The Accounting Review* (January 1985), pp. 33–52.

Robert Morris Associates, *Annual Statement Studies*. Philadelphia: RMA, 1990.

Robinson, John R., and Philip B. Shane, "Acquisition Accounting Method and Bid Premia for Target Firms," *The Accounting Review* (January 1990), pp. 25–48.

Roll, Richard, "The Hubris Hypothesis of Corporate Takeovers," *Journal of Business* (April 1986), pp. 197–216.

Ronen, Joshua, and Simcha Sadan, *Smoothing Income Numbers: Objectives, Means, and Implications*. Reading, MA: Addison-Wesley, 1981.

Rosenberg, Barr, and Walt McKibben, "The Prediction of Systematic and Specific Risk in Common Stocks," *Journal of Financial and Quantitative Analysis* (March 1973), pp. 317–333.

Roussey, R. S., E. L. Ten Eyck, and M. Blanco-Best, "Three New SASs: Closing the Communications Gap," *Journal of Accountancy* (December 1988), pp. 44–52.

Rue, Joseph C., David E. Tosh, and William B. Francis, "Accounting for Interest Rate Swaps," *Management Accounting* (January 1988), pp. 43–49.

Ryan, Stephen, "Structural Models of the Accounting Process and Earnings," unpublished dissertation, Stanford University, 1988.

Ryan, Stephen, and Paul Zarowin, "Valuation Relevant and Irrelevant Components of Earnings: Implications for Earnings Response Coefficients and Valuation Model R²s," working paper, New York University, 1993.

S

Savich, Richard S., and Laurence A. Thompson, "Resource Allocation Within the Product Life Cycle," *MSU Business Topics* (Autumn 1978), pp. 35–44.

Schiff, Allen I., "The Other Side of LIFO," *Journal of Accountancy* (May 1983), pp. 120–121.

Schiff, Michael, "A Closer Look at Variable Costing," *Management Accounting* (August 1987), pp. 36–39.

Schipper, Katherine, and Abbie J. Smith, "Effects of Recontracting on Shareholder Wealth: The Case of Voluntary Spin-offs," *Journal of Financial Economics* (December 1983), pp. 437–467.

Scott, James, "The Probability Of Bankruptcy: A Comparison of Empirical Predictions and Theoretical Models," *Journal of Banking and Finance* (September 1981), pp. 317–344.

Selling, Thomas I., and George H. Sorter, "FASB Statement No. 52 and Its Implications for Financial Statement Analysis," *Financial Analysts Journal* (May/June 1983), pp. 64–69.

Selling, Thomas I., and Clyde P. Stickney, "The Effects of Business Environment and Strategy on a Firm's Rate of Return on Assets," *Financial Analysts Journal* (January/February 1989), pp. 43–52.

Selling, Thomas I., and Clyde P. Stickney, "Disaggregating the Rate of Return on Common Shareholders' Equity: A New Approach," *Accounting Horizons* (December 1990), pp. 9–17.

Selto, Frank H., and Maclyn L. Clouse, "An Investigation of Managers' Adaptations to SFAS No. 2: Accounting for Research and Development Costs," *Journal of Accounting Research* (Autumn 1985), pp. 700–717.

Servaes, Henri, "Tobin's Q and the Gains from Takeovers," *Journal of Finance* (March 1991), pp. 409–419.

Shevlin, Terry, "The Valuation of R&D Firms with R&D Limited Partnerships" *The Accounting Review* (January 1991), pp. 1–21.

Silhan, Peter A. "Simulated Mergers of Existent Autonomous Firms: A New Approach to Segmentation Research," *Journal of Accounting Research* (Spring 1982), pp. 255–262.

Skinner, R. C., "Fixed Asset Lives and Replacement Cost Accounting," *Journal of Accounting Research* (Spring 1982), pp. 210–226.

Smith, Clifford, Jr., and L. Macdonald Wakeman, "Determinants of Corporate Leasing Policy," *Journal of Finance* (July 1985), pp. 895–908.

Smith, Clifford, Jr., and Jerold B. Warner, "On Financial Contracting: An Analysis of Bond Covenants," *Journal of Financial Economics* (June 1979), pp. 117–161.

Solomons, David, "The FASB's Conceptual Framework: An Evaluation," *Journal of Accountancy* (June 1986), pp. 114–124.

Sondhi, Ashwinpaul C., George H. Sorter, and Gerald I. White, "Transactional Analysis," *Financial Analysts Journal* (September/October 1987), pp. 57–64.

Sondhi, Ashwinpaul C., George H. Sorter, and Gerald I. White, "Cash Flow Redefined: FAS 95 and Security Analysis," *Financial Analysts Journal* (November/December 1988), pp. 19–20.

Sorter, George H., and George Benston, "Appraising the Defensive Position of a Firm: The Interval Measure," *The Accounting Review* (October 1960), pp. 633–640.

Stewart, John E., "The Challenges of Hedge Accounting," *Journal of Accountancy* (November 1989), pp. 48–62.

Stickel, Scott E., "The Timing of and Incentives for Annual Earnings Forecasts Near Interim Earnings Announcements," *Journal of Accounting and Economics* (July 1989), pp. 275–292.

Stickel, Scott E., "Predicting Individual Analysts Earnings Forecasts," *Journal of Accounting Research* (Autumn 1990), pp. 409–417.

Stickney, Clyde P., "Analyzing Effective Corporate Tax Rates," *Financial Analysts Journal* (July/August 1979), pp. 45–54.

Stober, Thomas L., "The Incremental Information Content of Financial Statement Disclosures: The Case of LIFO Liquidations," *Journal of Accounting Research* (Supplement 1986), pp. 138–160.

Strong, John S., and John R. Meyer, "Asset Writedowns: Managerial Incentives and Security Returns," *Journal of Finance* (July 1987), pp. 643–663.

Sunder, Shyam, "Relationship Between Accounting Changes and Stock Prices: Problems of Measurement and Some Empirical Evidence," *Journal of Accounting Research* (Supplement 1973), pp. 1–45.

Sunder, Shyam, "Properties of Accounting Numbers Under Full Costing And Successful-Efforts Costing In The Petroleum Industry," *The Accounting Review* (January 1976), pp. 1–18.

Swaminathan, Siva, "The Impact of SEC Mandated Segment Data on Price Variability and Divergence of Beliefs," *The Accounting Review* (January 1991), pp. 23–41.

T

Thomas, Jacob K., "Why Do Firms Terminate Their Overfunded Pension Plans?," *Journal of Accounting and Economics* (November 1989), pp. 361–398.

Todd, Kenneth R. Jr., "How One Financial Officer Uses Inflation-Adjusted Accounting Data," *Financial Executive* (October 1982), pp. 13–19.

Tse, Senyo, "LIFO Liquidations," *Journal of Accounting Research* (Spring 1990), pp. 229–238.

V

Vigeland, Robert L., "The Market Reaction to Statement of Financial Accounting Standards No. 2," *The Accounting Review* (April 1981), pp. 309–325.

W

Wang, Shiing-Wu, "The Relation Between Firm Size and Effective Tax Rates: A Test of Firms' Political Success," *The Accounting Review* (January 1991), pp. 158–169.

Watts, Ross "The Time-Series Behavior of Quarterly Earnings," working paper, University of Newcastle, England, 1975.

Watts, Ross, and Richard W. Leftwich, "The Time Series of Annual Accounting Earnings," *Journal of Accounting Research* (Fall 1977), pp. 253–271.

Watts, Ross, and Jerold L. Zimmerman, *Positive Accounting Theory*. Engelwood Cliffs, NJ: Prentice Hall, 1986.

Watts, Ross, and Jerold L. Zimmerman, "Positive Accounting Theory: A Ten Year Perspective," *The Accounting Review* (January 1990), pp. 131–156.

West, Richard R., "An Alternative Approach to Predicting Corporate Bond Ratings," *Journal of Accounting Research* (Spring 1970), pp. 118–127.

Wild, John, "The Prediction Performance of a Structural Model of Accounting Numbers," *Journal of Accounting Research* (Spring 1987), pp. 139–160.

Williamson, R. W., "Evidence on the Selective Reporting of Financial Ratios," *The Accounting Review* (April 1984), pp. 296–299.

Wilson, Peter G., "The Relative Information Content of Accruals and Cash Flows: Combined Evidence at the Earnings Announcement and Annual Report Release Date," *Journal of Accounting Research* (Supplement 1986), pp. 165–200.

Z

Zarowin, Paul, "What Determines Earnings-Price Ratios: Revisited," *Journal of Accounting Auditing and Finance* (Summer 1990), pp. 439–454.

Ziebart, David A., and David H. Kim, "An Examination of the Market Reactions Associated with SFAS No. 8 and SFAS No. 52," *The Accounting Review* (April 1987), pp. 343–357.

Zimmerman, Jerold L., "Taxes and Firm Size," *Journal of Accounting and Economics* (August 1983), pp. 119–149.

Zmijewski, Mark E., and Robert L. Hagerman, "An Income Strategy Approach to the Positive Theory of Accounting Standard Setting/Choice," *Journal of Accounting and Economics* (August 1981), pp. 129–149.

INDEX

A

Abdel-khalik, A. Rashad, 359, 373, 375
Abnormal return, 294, 303
Accelerated depreciation methods, 427, 428–429
  inflation compensation effect, 435
  and taxes, 434–435
Accounting beta, *see* Beta
Accounting changes
  exceptions to treatment, 170
  as nonrecurring items, 170–172
  analysis, 177–179
Accounting cycle, 35–36, 41–44
  at business formation date, 37–38
  first year of operations, 39–40
  journal entries and T-accounts, 36
Accounting events, 7
Accounting income, 119–121
  definition, 116–119
  revenue and expense recognition, *see* Revenue and expense recognition
Accounting information, qualitative characteristics, 10–12
Accounting Principles Board, 9
Accounting standards, *see also specific standards, such as IAS and SFAS standards*
  Financial Accounting Standards Board, *see* Financial Accounting Standards Board
  international, 27–30
Accounting theory, *see* Theory
Accrual accounting, 7, 119–121. *See also* Accounting income
  accrual income *vs.* cash flow, 138
  allocation of cash flows, 119
  definition, 116–119
  difficulties with, 138
Accumulated (pension) benefit obligation, 639, 643
Accumulated postretirement obligation, 688
ACME Steel Company, unusual/infrequent items note, 160–161
Acquire, acquisition of Target, 849–851, 854–858
Acquisitions, *see* Mergers and acquisitions

Activity analysis, 198. *See also* Ratio analysis
  example: Merck, 211
  LIFO *vs.* FIFO, 352–354
  long-term (investment) ratios, 209–212
  short-term (operating) ratios, 208–209
  analysis, 209
Actuarial gains and losses, pensions, 645, 650
Additional paid-in capital, 63
Adjunct accounts, 15
Adjusting entries, 36
Advertising costs, capitalization *vs.* expensing, 397, 405–406
Alcan, off-balance sheet financing, 722–723
Alcoa, multinational operations analysis, 982–987
All current rate method, 945–947
Altman, Edward I., 1046, 1050–1053
Amerada Hess
  adjustment of (FIFO) income to current cost income, 348–349
  effective tax rates, 540
  SFAS 96 tax accounting, 524–531
American Depositary Receipts (ADRs), 29
American Institute of Certified Public Accountants (AICPA), Accounting Research Bulletins, 9
Amortization, 424, 433
Analysis, *see* Financial analysis
Ang, James S., 1065
Annual reports, 56–57
  business review, 58
  consolidated income statement, 64–65
  examples: Deere & Co.
    1988 annual report, 68–77
    1991 annual report, 79–112
  financial statements, 58–65
  financial summary, 57
  letter to stockholders, 57–58
  Management Discussion and Analysis section, 65–66
  multiyear summaries, 66–67
  timeliness of, 298–299
Annuity depreciation, 425–426

APB Opinion 8, 637
APB Opinion 9, 164, 172
APB Opinion 11, 510. *See also* Deferred tax method: APB 11
APB Opinion 14, and convertible bonds, 573
APB Opinion 15, 272
APB Opinion 16, 852–853, 898–1291
APB Opinion 17, 910
APB Opinion 18, 785
APB Opinion 20, 170
  depreciation method changes, 439–440
APB Opinion 23, 542–543
APB Opinion 24, 542–543
APB Opinion 28, 362
APB Opinion 30, 164, 167–168
  reporting of impaired assets, 455
Arbitrage pricing model, 302*n*
Archibald, T. Ross, 295, 442
Ashland Oil
  lease reporting, 602–606
  tax accounting analysis, 546–548
ASR 190, 490
Asset-based valuation models, 1095–1096
  book value, 1097–1099
  and market price, 1097–1099
  stability/growth of, 1099–1101
  Tobin's Q ratio and, 1099
Assets
  adjustments for credit analysis purposes, 1016–1017
  classification, 13–14
  current *vs.* noncurrent, 14
  in annual reports, 59–61
  definition in terms of future benefits: problems of, 157–158
  long-lived, *see* Long-lived assets
  productivity of, and acquisition date, 211–212
  receivables as, 158
  relationship to alternate earnings definitions, 115–116, 117–118
  SFAC 6 definition, 13
Assets turnover ratios
  fixed assets turnover, 209–212
  total assets turnover, 212
Auditors, role of, 24–27

Australia, accounting for long-lived assets, 464
Aydin Corporation, minority interest analysis, 805–806

B

Balance sheet equation, 35
Balance sheets, 35–36. *See also* Off-balance sheet financing
adjustments for credit analysis purposes, 1017–1018
analysis example: Thousand Trails, Inc., 157–158
in annual reports, 58–63
assets and liabilities measurement, 14–15
current *vs.* noncurrent assets/liabilities, 14
defined, 6, 12
elements of, 12–13
example: Merck & Co., Inc, 270
foreign currency translation and, 960, 968, 972–978
format/classification, 13–14
impact of depreciation method, 434
inventory information, 335
leveraged buyout effects, 915
long-term debt effects, 568–570
operating *vs.* capital leases, 595–596
post-acquisition
U.S. *vs.* U.K. practices, 890–891, 892
using pooling of interests method, 851, 853–854, 863–866, 875–877
using purchase method, 851, 866–867, 868, 873–877
push-down accounting effects, 912, 914
sales-type leases, 608, 610–611
vs. tax accounting, 511–513
Baldwin, Bruce A., 828–829
Ball, Ray, 297–299, 300–303, 371, 1071
Ball Corporation, unusual/infrequent items note, 162
Bankruptcy prediction, 1037, 1046–1050
cash flows and, 1054–1055
misclassification errors in: types I and II, 1046
probabilistic analysis, 1053–1054
variables used in, 1039
ZETA™ prediction model, 1050–1053
Z-score, 1050
Barlev, Benzion, 356
Barrel of oil equivalent, 472
Barr Rosenberg & Associates (BARRA), 1077
Bartczak, Norman, 1054–1055
Barth, Mary, 660–661
Bartley, Jon W., 338
Bartov, Eli, 995

Bathke, Allen W. Jr., 300
Beaver, William H., 293–294, 296, 299, 302, 438, 538, 660–661, 987–993, 1047–1050, 1068, 1072–1074, 1118–1119
Beecham, merger with SmithKline Beecham, 885–898
Bernard, Victor L., 145, 304, 309, 319, 320, 381–382, 1135
Bernstein, Leopold A., 590, 103
Beta ($B_{earnings}$) [accounting-based], 1045
relationship to other betas, 1069–1070
Beta (B_{sales}) [accounting-based], relationship to other betas, 1069–1070
Beta (β_a) [market-based], 1069
Beta (β_d) [market-based], 1069
Beta (β_e) [market-based]
under capital asset pricing model, 294
in equity risk analysis, 1041, 1067–1068
empirical studies, 1071–1078
summary of forecasts of different models, 1077–1078
and pension liability, 659–660
Bhushan, Ravi, 1139, 1142
Biddle, Gary C., 355, 359, 373, 374–375
Big bath accounting, 176–177
Blanco-Best, M., 27
Block, Frank, 9
BMC Industries Inc., inventory accounting, 380–381
Bodie, Zvi, 235, 312
Bodnar, Gordon M., 995
Bond covenants, 583–586
conformity to GAAP, 587, 588
example: Deere & Co., 587–589, 589
inventory of payable funds, 586
and mergers, 907
Bond Guide, 577
Bonds
basic concepts/ definitions, 564–568
callable, 583, 584
commodity-linked, 724
convertible: debt-with equity feature, 572–574
discount issuance, 567–568
early retirement, 582–583
exchangeable, 725–726
par issuance, 567
par/premium/discount comparison, 565–566
premium issuance, 567
ratings prediction, *see* Debt risk analysis
variable-rate, 572
zero-coupon, 570–572
Bonus plan hypothesis, in agency theory, 314–315

Book value
analysis of adjustments to, 1015–1019
example: Deere and Company, 1027
and asset-based valuation, 1097–1099, 1099–1101
defined, 1015
and market price, 1097
Bootstrapping, 858–859, 908–909
Bowen, Robert M., 145
Bowman, Robert G., 581, 1069
Box-Jenkins models, 1132
Bradley, J., 903
Brands and trademarks, 15
capitalization *vs.* expensing, 412
Brascan, proportionate consolidation method, 812–820
Briloff, Abraham J., 859n
Briloff effect, 310, 311
British Petroleum, inventory accounting, 378–379
Brooks, Leroy, 1132
Brown, Lawrence D., 301, 373, 1134, 1140–1142
Brown, Philip, 297–299, 300–303, 1071
Bublitz, Bruce, 405–406
Buckmaster, Dale, 1132
Bulow, Jeremy, 634
Burgstahler, David, 145
Business combinations, 846–848. *See also specific types of combinations*
accounting method choice criteria
bid premia, 903–904, 906–907
general factors, 900–901, 905–909
income maximization hypothesis, 901–902
market reaction, 903–905
impact of accounting method on ratio analysis, 861–862
international practices in accounting for, 898–899
example: SmithKline-Beecham merger, 885–898
pooling of interests method of accounting, 678, 851, 852–853
APB 16 requirements, 852–853
conditions favoring choice of, 900
example: ConAgra-Golden Valley merger, 863–873
as nontaxable event, 862
problems with, 858–859
purchase method of accounting, 848–851
conditions favoring choice of, 900–901
example: Conagra-Golden Valley, 873–885
example: Acquire and Target, 849–851
example: Georgia Pacific-Great Northern Nekoosa merger, 873–885
as taxable event, 862

Business combinations, *cont.*
push-down accounting, 910–914
example: General Motors-Hughes Aircraft, 911–914
tax implications of, 862
Business review, in annual reports, 58
Business risk, 1043
Business segments, defined, 167

C

Callable bonds, 583, 584
Callable common shares, 480
Canada
accounting for long-lived assets, 464, 465, 466
consolidation practices, 796
depreciation practices in, 425–426
EPS reporting requirements, 283–284
foreign currency transactions, 967
foreign currency translation, 967
inventory accounting practices, 379
lease accounting practices, 615
lower of cost and market method in, 784
multijurisdictional disclosure system agreement, 30
pension plan reporting, 683, 684
proportionate consolidation use, 829
Canning, John B., 291
Capital asset pricing model, 293–294
use in discounted cash flow valuation models, 1103–1104
Capital expenditure ratio, 222–223
Capitalization
of leases, 396n
tables, 219–222
Capitalization *vs.* expensing, 395
advertising costs, 397, 405–406
analytic adjustments involving, 403–405
effects on financial statements, 398–403
income variability, 398
intangible assets, 411–413
interest costs, 409–411
international practices, 464–466
lease *vs.* purchase, 397–398
oil and gas wells, 397, 406
mandated accounting changes and, 407–409
research and development costs, 396–397, 405–406
example: Merck, 403–404
mandated accounting changes and, 407–409
and partnership formation, 413, 479–484
and valuation, 405–407
Capital leases, *see* Leases
Capital markets, role of financial information in, 5–6
Captive credit subsidiaries, 1021
Caruthers, J. Kent, 246, 247, 248

Casey, Cornelius, 1054–1055
Cash cycles
length of, 212–214
manufacturing firms, 214, 215
merchandising firms, 212–213
schematic representation, 213
Cash flow
allocation in accrual accounting, 119
convergence over time with income, 119
free, *see* Free cash flow
vs. accrual income, 145–146
Cash flow from operations ratio, 217
Cash flow statements, 36
in annual reports, 65
classification issues, 132
cash from investments, 133–134
free cash flows, 134–135
interest and dividends received, 135
interest paid, 135–136
noncash transactions, 136
creation, 45–50
defined, 6, 7, 18–19
example: Merck & Co., Inc., comparative, 271
financing cash flows, 19, 49–50
foreign currency translation and, 963–966
impact of depreciation method, 434
investment cash flows, 18, 19, 49
long-term debt effects, 568–570
operating *vs.* capital leases, 599, 601
operations cash flows, 45–48
post-acquisition
using pooling of interests method, 859
using purchase method, 848, 859–861, 878–882
relationship to income statement, 138, 145–146
choice of accounting method, 147–148
going concern assumption and, 145–146
and liquidity, 149
and sales-type leases, 609–610, 611–612
Cash from operations (CFO), 19, 45–48, 133–134
and bankruptcy prediction, 1054–1055
and capitalization *vs.* expensing decision, 403
in credit analysis: Deere example, 1030–1032
effect of reporting method on, 136–137
interpretation, 157n
operating *vs.* capital leases, 599, 601
and sales-type leases, 609–610, 611–612
Cash from operations-to-debt ratio, 223
Cash ratio, 216

Castle Company, A. M.
analysis of depreciation disclosures, 449–452, 454
transactional analysis of cash flow statements, 139–144
Centocor, R&D partnership with Tocor, 480–484
Chen, Kung H., 246
Chen, Y. S., 338
Chrysler Corporation, change from LIFO, 358–359
Clarke, R., 302
Classical approach, to accounting theory, 288, 289, 290–291
Clinch, Greg, 419n
Closing entries, 36
Clouse, Maclyn L., 408
Cogger, Kenneth O., 1042
Cohen, Zinbarg & Zeikel, 1100n
Collins, Daniel W., 409, 827–828, 829, 1121, 1122
Comiskey, Eugene, 791–792
Commercial Intertech, postemployment benefits, 689–690, 691
Commitments, reporting in annual reports, 63
Commodity-linked bonds, 724
Common-size statements, 198, 202–206, 207
industry comparison, 204–206
Common stock equivalents, and EPS calculation, 274, 275, 276
Comparability, of accounting information, 12
Completed contract method, revenue recognition, 125–126, 131
vs. percentage-of-completion method, 126–130
Composite depreciation methods, 430–432
Comprehensive income, SFAC 6 definition, 16–17
Computer software development costs: capitalization *vs.* expensing, 412–413
ConAgra, merger with Golden Valley, 863–873
Consistency, of accounting information, 12
Consolidation, 58–59
Consolidation method, *see* Intercorporate investments, consolidation method of accounting
Constant dollar method, 485, 486–488, 494
advantages/disadvantages, 488
Construction costs, for adjusting assets values for changing prices, 494
Consumer groups, as class of financial information user, 4
Contingencies, disclosures related to, 21

Continental Corporation
  mark to market accounting, 779–782
  off-balance sheet financing, 717
Contingencies, reporting in annual
    reports, 63
Contra accounts, 14–15
Contracting theory, *see* Positive
    accounting research
Contracts, based upon accounting
    information, 6
Contribution margin ratio, 225
  for operating leverage estimation,
    228, 230
Convertible bonds, 572–574
Convertible debt, 13
Convertible securities, and EPS
    calculation, 275
Coors Company, unusual/infrequent
    items note, 163
Copeland, Koller & Murrin, 1117*n*
Copeland, R. M., 176
Copeland, T., 1036
Copyrights, capitalization *vs.*
    expensing, 411–412
Corning Glass, reporting of capitalized
    interest, 411
Corporate annual reports, *see* Annual
    reports
Corridor method, 650*n*
Cost method, *see* Intercorporate
    investments, cost method of
    accounting
Cost of goods sold, 48
  adjustment from LIFO to FIFO,
    344–346
  adjustment to current cost income,
    346–349
  and inventory accounting, 332–334
  recognition, 124
Cost recovery method, of revenue
    recognition, 130–131
Coupon rate, of bonds, 564, 569
Cragg and Malkiel, 1120*n*
Credit analysis, 1014–1015
  book value adjustments, 1015–1016,
    1018–1019
    asset adjustments, 1016–1017
    liabilities adjustments, 1017–1018
  example: Deere and Company
    asset adjustments, 1019–1024
    capital structure analysis,
      1027–1029, 1037
    cash flow analysis, 1029–1037
    liability adjustments, 1024–1027
Creditors, as class of financial
    information user, 4, 5
Credits, defined, 35
Cumulative translation adjustment, 63,
    734, 946, 954–955, 982
Current cost depreciation, 491–492,
    493–494
Current cost method, 488–490,
    493–494
  disadvantages, 489–490

Current ratio, 216–217
Cushing, Barry E., 369–371, 377

D
Daley, Lane A., 145, 660
Davis, Harry Z., 359
Davis, Michael L., 901, 902, 903, 904
Dawson Geophysical, MES accounting,
    769–772, 775
Deakin, Edward B., III, 418–419
Debits, defined, 35
Debt
  defined, 562
  financing of, *see* Financing
    liabilities; Off-balance sheet
    financing
Debt covenant hypothesis, in agency
    theory, 315–316
Debt covenants, 219
Debt ratios, 219–222
Debt risk analysis, 1037
  bond ratings and rating process,
    1056–1059
    significance of, 1064–1066
  bond ratings prediction, 1056–1059,
    1061–1062
    variables used, 1060–1061
  variables used in, 1040
Deere & Company
  annual reports
    1988, 68–77
    1991, 79–112
    discussion, 57–68
  bond covenants, 587–589
  credit analysis, 1019–1037
  Deloitte & Touche audit, 24–25
  equity *vs.* consolidation methods,
    797–804
  market value of debt estimation,
    577–580
  normalization of income for
    valuation, 1123–1128
Defensive intervals, 217
Deferred taxes, *see also* Tax accounting
  analytical issues, 536–538
  effective tax rates, 539–541
    example: Amerada Hess, 540
  equity method and, 788–789
  and liability adjustments for credit
    analysis purposes, 1017–1018
  market valuation, 538
Deferred tax method: APB 11, 510,
    511–514
    deferred tax assets, 514, 516
    deferred tax liabilities, 514, 516, 517
      growth of, 517, 519–520
    example, 515–516
    problems with, 520
    tax rate/tax law changes and,
      516–517, 518
Dent, Warren T., 409
Depletion, 424, 432–433
Depreciation
  accelerated methods (SYD and

DDB), 427, 428–429
    inflation compensation effect, 435
    and taxes, 434–435
  accounting *vs.* economic
    depreciation, 424–425
  amortization, 433
  annuity (sinking fund), 425–426
  changing methods, 439–442
    example: Ford Motor Company,
      441
    example: General Motors, 441,
      443–445
    example: Ratliff Drilling, 445–448
    example: Snap-on Tools, 439, 440
  competition and, 429–430
  current cost, 491–492, 493–494
  depletion, 432–433
  disclosure of method, 433–434
  effect on financial statements, 434
  group and composite methods,
    430–432
    example: DuPont, 431
    example: Georgia Pacific, 432
  inflation's impact on, 435, 437–439
  international practices, 466
  investment disincentives, 437
  number of companies using various
    methods, 433
  salvage value and, 434
  service hours method, 427, 429–430
  straight-line, 425, 426–427, 428–429
  units of production method, 427,
    429–430
Depreciation expenses, 135*n*
  inclusion in cost of goods sold, 48
Desai, A., 903
Dhaliwal, Dan S., 342*n,* 409, 442, 660
Dieter, R., 30
Direct costs, recognition, 124
Direct financing leases, 612
Direct method, for cash flow
    statements, 19
Disaggregation, *see* Ratio analysis,
    disaggregation of ROA/ROE
Disclosures
  of depreciation method, 433–434
  and earnings per share calculation,
    282
  in footnotes, 20–21
  hedging activities, 735–740
  leases
    sales-type, 609, 611
    SFAS 13 requirements, 601
  of market values of financial
    instruments, 7
  oil and gas firms, 419–420, 468–478
  and positive accounting theory, 313
  of ratios, 250–251
  SEC-required, 7–9
  SFAS 87 pension requirements, 637,
    643–644, 647–652
    example: General Motors,
      662–678
  SFAS 109 requirements, 544–545

Discontinued operations, 167–170
Discounted cash flow valuation models,
    1095–1096, 1101–1102,
    1116–1117
  accounting change effects,
    1126–1127
  dividend-based models, 1102–1104
    capital asset pricing model to
      estimate r, 1103–1104
    constant growth case, 1104
    no-growth case, 1103–1104
  earnings-based models, 1104–1105
    growth case, 1106–1113
    no-growth case, 1105–1106
  earnings *vs.* cash flow perspective,
    1113–1114
  empirical studies, 1118–1122
  free cash flow approach, 1114–1117
  measurement error effects, 1121
  multistage growth models,
    1145–1147
  nonrecurring income effects,
    1122–1126
    example: Deere and Company,
      1123–1128
  permanent and transitory earnings
    components, 1120–1122
  price/earnings ratio, 1116–1120
  "quality of earnings," 1127–1128
Disposal date, 168n
Distributable earnings, 116, 117–118
Divestures, 846
  effect on pension plans, 679
Dividends, 135–136
Dodd,, 291
Dopuch, Nicolas, 299n, 349–350,
    375–376
Double-declining-balance method, 427,
    429
Double-entry bookkeeping, 35
Dow Chemical Company, segment data
    analysis, 822–825
Drug companies, *see* Pharmaceutical
    firms
DSC Communications Corporation,
    164, 166
Duke, Joanne, 585
Dukes, Roland E., 299, 408, 438, 538
Dunne, Kathleen M., 908
DuPont, group depreciation, 431
DuPont model, 235
Duracell, leveraged buyout of,
    914–1310
Dyckman, Thomas, 408

E
Earnings
  alternate definitions of, 115–116,
    117–118
  manipulation, 175–179
Earnings per share (EPS)
  adjustments for convertible
    bonds/preferred stock, 275–276
    two-thirds rule, 275, 276, 282

  adjustments for options and warrants,
    276–278
    treasury stock method, 276,
      277–278, 282
  for complex capital structures,
    273–273
  computational issues, 273–275
  definition (APB 15), 272–273
  disclosure requirements, 282
  example calculation, 278, 279
  fully diluted EPS, 274–275
    exceptions to dilution calculations,
      275
  international differences, 283–284
  limitations of calculations, 282–283
  primary EPS, 274
  for simple capital structures,
    272–273
  for two-class securities, 278
    example: Greif Bros. Corporation,
      280–281
Earnings statements, *see* Income
    statements
Earnings variability, 1038, 1041–1045
Economic consequences of accounting
    research, *see* Positive accounting
    research
Economic earnings, 115–116, 117
Economic order quantity, 354–355
ED 32, 28, 784
ED 33, 550
ED 37, 380
ED 39, 465
ED 43, 464, 466
ED 44, 968
ED 45, 465
ED 51, 464
Effective interest rate, of bonds, 565,
    569
Effective tax rates, 539–540
Efficient market hypothesis, 5,
    292–293, 295–297
Eggleton, Ian R., 373
El-Gazzar, Samir, 590
Elliot, John A., 176, 177, 178, 408,
    460–463
Elliott, J. W., 1134
Emerson Electric, spinoff of ESCO
    Electronics, 921–1314
Emery, Gary W., 1042
Empirical research, *see* Market-based
    research; Positive accounting
    research; Research
Employee Retirement Act of 1974
    (ERISA), 635
EQK Realty, zero-coupon financing of,
    571–572
Equity
  classification, 14
  SFAC 6 definition, 13
Equity method, 762, 763, 784–790,
    791–792
  expanded equity method, 808,
    830–831

  and ownership position, 791–792
  vs. consolidation method, 792–793,
    796–797
    example: Deere & Co., 797–804
  vs. cost and mark to market
    methods, 777–778
Equity risk prediction, 1037,
    1066–1067
  beta(s), 1067–1068
    empirical studies, 1071–1078
    prediction models, 1041
    relationship to other betas,
      1069–1071
    summary of forecasts of different
      models, 1077–1078
  empirical studies, 1071–1078
  systematic *vs.* unsystematic risk,
    1066–1067
  theory, 1069–1071
Ettredge, Michael, 405–406
Eubank, A. A., 246, 247, 248
European accounting standards, 29
European Economic Community
    (EEC), 29
  Directives, 29
Exchangeable bonds, 725–726
Exchange rates, *see* Foreign exchange
    rates
Executory contracts, 714–715
Expense recognition, *see* Revenue and
    expense recognition
Expenses
  SFAC 6 definition, 16
  variable/fixed components, 226, 228
Expensing, *vs.* capitalization, *see*
    Capitalization *vs.* expensing
Exponential smoothing model, 1132
Extended functional fixation
    hypothesis, 296n
Extraordinary items, 164–167. *See also*
    Nonrecurring items
Extrapolative forecasting models,
    1129–1132

F
Face value, of bonds, 564
Fact books, 23
Fair value method, *see* Current cost
    method
Falkenstein, Angela, 347n
Fama, Eugene, 292, 1098n
Fédération des Experts Comptables
    Européens, 29
Feldstein, Martin, 660
Feltham, Gerald, 1098
FIFO, *see* First-in, first-out (FIFO)
    accounting
Financial Accounting Standards Board,
    9–10
  conceptual framework of, 10–12
  Statement of Financial Accounting
    Concepts (SFAC), 10–12. *See also*
    specific SFAC statements, i.e.
    SFAC 1

Statement of Financial Accounting
Standards (SFAS), 9–10. *See also
specific SFAS statements, i.e.
SFAS 69*
Financial analysis
implications of research for, 323–324
for investment decisions, 4–5
nonrecurring items and, *see*
Nonrecurring items
ratio analysis, *see* Ratio analysis
role in capital markets, 5–6
Financial leverage, 230, 235n
and beta(s), 1069–1070
risk analysis and, 1042–1045
Financial leverage effect ratio, 230–231
Financial position statements, *see*
Balance sheets
Financial reporting systems
basic financial statements of, 6
differences in, 3
divergence of economic
events-accounting period, 3
Financial services industry, market
value asset reporting, 14
Financial statements, *see also*
Accounting cycle
balance sheets, *see* Balance sheets
cash flow statements, *see* Cash flow
statements
contingency disclosure, 21
in corporate annual reports, 58–65
footnotes, 20–21
general principles and measurement
rules, 6–7
income statements, *see* Income
statements
international standards, 27–30
SEC requirements, 7–9
shareholder's equity statements, *see*
Shareholder's equity statements
summary of types, 6
supplementary schedules, 22
Financing cash flows, 19, 49–50
Financing liabilities, 562–563. *See also*
Off- balance sheet financing
bond covenants, 583–587
conformity to GAAP, 587, 588
example: Deere & Co., 587, 589
current liabilities, 563–564
operating *vs.* financing activities,
563
debt-equity distinction: blurring of,
574–575
effects of interest rate changes,
575–582
leases, *see* Leases
loan impairment, 576
long-term debt
bonds, 564–568
callable bonds, 583, 584
debt-with equity, 572–574
early retirement, 582–583
effects on financial statements,
568–570

perpetual debt, 574
preferred equity, 574–575
variable-rate, 572
zero-coupon bonds, 570–572
market value of debt estimation,
576–577
example: Deere, 577–580
market *vs.* book value, 580–582
empirical studies, 581
restructured debt, 576
Finite-growth model, 1146
First-in, first-out (FIFO) accounting,
60, 333–334. *See also* Inventory
accounting
adjustment of income to current cost
income, 346–349
example: Amerada Hess, 348–349
balance sheet information, 335
income statement information, 336
international use of, 379–380
vs. LIFO: effect on financial ratios,
349–356
vs. LIFO: effects on income, cash
flow, and working capital,
339–342
Fixed assets, *see* Long-lived assets
Fixed assets turnover ratio, 209–212
Fixed charge coverage ratios, 222
Floating rate debt, 572
Flowers Industries, Inc., 164, 167
Footnotes, 20–21
in annual reports, 60
disclosure of change to LIFO, 357
off-balance sheet financing reporting,
716
Ford Motor Company, change of
depreciation method, 441
Forecasting models
extrapolative models, 1129–1132
income or balance sheet-based
models, 1134–1136
index models, 1132–1133
inventory balances as an aid to,
380–382
quarterly models, 1133–1134
segment-based models, 1134–1135
using disaggregated data, 1133–1136
vs. financial analysts, 1136–1143
Foreign affiliates, assets/liabilities
reporting, 15
Foreign currency transactions, as
hedging activities, 733–734
Foreign currency translation, 943,
945–947
all current rate method, 945–947
cumulative translation adjustment,
946, 954–955, 982
functional currency choice, 947–948,
956
example: Alcoa of Australia,
982–985
gains and losses, 943, 945–947
"currency holding gain," 946
historical *vs.* current rate, 943

hyperinflationary economies, 948,
967, 989
example: Alcoa Aluminio,
985–987
non-U.S. practices, 966–968
remeasurement, 955–957
remeasurement *vs.* translation,
948–950
balance sheet effects, 960
cash flow effects, 963–966
income statement effects, 957–960
ratio analysis, 960–963
SFAS 8 requirements, 943–944
SFAS 52 requirements, 944–945,
948
temporal method, 944, 946–947
gross profit margin distortion, 958
use in remeasurement under SFAS
52, 948–949
translation process, 950–954
Foreign exchange rates, 943
interest rate-inflation-exchange rate
relationship, 987–993
valuation effects, 1126
Foreign registrants, SEC requirements
for, 29–30
Foster, George, 300, 829n, 1134, 1142
Fourth Directive, 29
Framework for the Preparation and
Presentation of Financial
Statements, 28
France
accounting for long-lived assets, 464,
465, 466
business combination accounting,
898
foreign currency translation, 966
inventory accounting practices, 379
lower of cost and market method in,
784
pension plan reporting, 683, 684
proportionate consolidation use, 829
segment reporting, 829
tax accounting in, 550
Franchises
capitalization *vs.* expensing, 412
revenues, recognition, 130–131
Francis, Jere R., 636
Francis, William B., 734
Frecka, Thomas J., 251–252
Free cash flow, 134–135, 403n
Free cash flow approach, to valuation,
1114–1117
Freeman, Thomas J., 1132
French, Kenneth R., 1098n
Fried, Dov, 176–177, 356, 359, 458,
460, 1133
Full cost accounting, for oil and gas
exploration, 416–419, 420–424
Fuller, Russel J., 1146–1147
Fully-diluted earnings per share
(FDEPS), 274–275
Functional fixation, 295n, 296n
and LIFO, 371
Funds from operations (FFO), 133

G

General Electric
  LIFO accounting, 361
  postemployment benefits, 691–693
  SFAS 106 adoption (postemployment
    benefits), 696–698
Generally accepted accounting
  principles (GAAP), 3
  and FSAB, 9
General Motors
  change of depreciation method, 441,
    445
  Hughes Aircraft acquisition, 911–914
  pension plan analysis, 662–678
  SFAS 106 adoption (postemployment
    benefits), 696n
General price level accounting, see
  Constant cost method
Gentry, James A., 1054
Georgia Pacific
  composite depreciation, 432
  joint ventures, 725, 726
  merger with Great Northern
    Nekoosa, 873–885
  off-balance sheet financing, 718–720
Germany
  business combination accounting,
    898–899
  consolidation practices, 796
  inventory accounting practices, 380
  lease accounting practices, 615
  long-lived asset accounting, 464,
    465, 466
  lower of cost and market method in,
    784
  pension plan reporting, 683, 684
  proportionate consolidation use, 829
  segment reporting, 829
  tax accounting in, 550
Ghicas, Dimitrios C., 683
Gibson, Charles H., 248–250
Givoly, Dan, 301, 538, 1133, 1140,
  1141
Going concern assumption, 7, 27
  and income and cash flow, 146–147
Golden Valley, merger with ConAgra,
  863–873
Gombola, Michael J., 242, 246–247
Gonedes, Nicolas J., 176n, 299n,
  300–301
Good news/bad news firms
  Ball-Brown study, 297–299, 303
  Ou study, 320–322
Goodwill, 850
  amortization, 433, 910
  analysis of, 909–910
  capitalization vs. expensing, 413
  international standards, 465–466
  "economic," 1097
  international differences in
    accounting for, 898, 899
  in leveraged buyouts, 911
Government, as class of financial
  information user, 4

Graham,, 291, 293
Granof, Michael H., 369
Grant Company, W. T., see W. T.
  Grant Company
Great Britain, see United Kingdom
Great Northern Nekoosa, merger with
  Georgia Pacific, 873–885
Greif Bros. Corporation, two-class
  method illustrated, 278, 280–281
Griffin, Paul, 301, 1134, 1140–1142
Gross change method, 517, 518
Gross margin ratio, 224
Gross pension cost, 657
Group depreciation methods, 430–432
Growth rates, sustainability, 122

H

Hagerman, Robert G., 301, 317–318,
  1140–1142
Haldeman, Robert G., 1046,
  1050–1054
Hamada, Robert S., 1069
Hand, John R. M., 583
Harrington, Diana R., 1077–1078
Harris, Trevor S., 406, 419–420
Hayn, Carla, 538
Health care benefits, 686–687,
  688–689, 699
Healy, Paul M., 315, 439, 442
Hedging activities, 715, 733
  accounting for, 735, 736
    enterprise vs. transaction
      approaches, 735
  disclosures, 735–740
    example: LAC Minerals, 736, 737
    example: Monsanto, 737–738,
      739, 740
    example: Reynolds Metals,
      736–737, 738
  foreign currency transactions,
    733–734
  interest rate swaps, 734
  options, 735
Heian, James B., 716
Heico Corporation, discontinued
  operations disclosure, 168–170
Helmerich and Payne, marketable
  equity securities accounting, 772,
  773–774
Henderson, G. V., 1065
Heyman, J. A., 30
Hicks, J. R., 116, 489
Hirschey, Mark, 406
Historical costs, 7
  and assets/liabilities valuation, 14–15
  relevance of, 11
Hochman, Shalom, 1070–1071,
  1074–1075
Holland, see Netherlands
Holthausen, Robert W., 442,
  1137–1138
Hong, Hai, 903, 905
Hopwood, William, 827, 1133
Horrigan, James O., 244–245, 1063

Horwitz, Bertrand, 408, 829n
Hsia, Chi-Cheng, 1146–1147
Hughes, John S., 789
Hughes Aircraft, acquisition by General
  Motors, 911–914
Hunt, Herbert G. III, 375, 585
Hyperinflationary economies, 989
  example: Alcoa Aluminio, 985–987
  and foreign currency translation,
    948, 967

I

IAS 9, 465
IAS 22, 898
IAS 23, 409, 465
IAS 25, 784
IAS 27, 796
IAS 31, 808–809
IBM
  multinational operations analysis,
    968–982
  SFAS 106 adoption (postemployment
    benefits), 695
  software development cost
    capitalization, 412–413
Imhoff, Eugene A., Jr., 591
Impairment of assets, 454–455
  effect on financial statements,
    458–464
  measurement of, 458
    proposed FASB standard, 459–460
  oil and gas properties: Pennzoil
    example, 455–458
  reporting requirements, 455
  tax implications, 459
  write-downs vs. restructurings, 458
Income
  convergence over time with cash
    flow, 119
  relationship to alternate earnings
    definitions, 115–116, 117–118
Income smoothing, 175–176
Income statements, 36
  analysis of, 120–121
  in annual reports, 64–65
  defined, 6–7, 15–16
  elements of, 16–17
  example: Merck & Co., Inc.,
    comparative, 271
  foreign currency translation effects,
    957–960, 969, 978–981
  format/classification, 17–18
  impact of depreciation method, 434
  inventory information, 335–336
  leveraged buyout effects, 915–918
  long-term debt effects, 568–570
  net income components, 18
  operating vs. capital leases, 597, 599
  post-acquisition
    U.S. vs. U.K. practices, 891–897
    using pooling of interests method,
      858–859, 867–870, 877–878
    using purchase method, 848,
      855–857, 870–871

push-down accounting effects,
912–913
relationship to cash flow statement,
138, 145–146
choice of accounting method,
147–148
going concern assumption and,
145–146
and liquidity, 149
and sales-type leases, 608–609, 611
vs. tax accounting, 511–513
Income taxes, *see* Deferred taxes; Tax
accounting; Taxes
Indefinite reversals, 542–543
Index-based forecasting models,
1132–1133
Indirect method, for cash flow
statements, 19
Inflation, *see also* Hyperinflationary
economies
impact on depreciation, 435,
437–439
relationship to exchange rates, 989
Inflation accounting
adjusting financial statements for,
492–494
constant dollar method, 485,
486–488, 494
current cost method, 488–490,
493–494
historical cost model, 485–486
physical *vs.* financial capital
maintenance, 489
Information content studies, in
market-based
research, 299–300
Infrequent items, 160–163
Ingberman,, 325
Installment method, of revenue
recognition, 130,
131
Institutional Brokers Estimate System,
1140
Insurance companies
market value asset reporting, 14
mark to market accounting, 778–782
Intangible assets, 15. *See also specific
types of intangibles, particularly
Goodwill*
amortization, 433
analysis of, 909–910
capitalization *vs.* expensing, 411–413
Intercorporate investments, 762–763
accounting methods: overview,
762–763
consolidation method of accounting,
762, 763, 790, 794–795
minority interest, 794, 805–806
nonhomogeneous subsidiaries,
795–796
non-U.S. practices, 796
proportionate consolidation, *see*
Proportionate consolidation
vs. equity method, 792–793,
796–804

cost method of accounting, 762,
763–764
analysis considerations summary,
783–784
comparison of methods for MES
vs. non-MES, 766–767
and marketable equity securities
(MES), *see* Marketable equity
securities
non-U.S. practices, 784
vs. equity method, 787–788
equity method of accounting, 762,
763, 784–787, 789–790, 791–792
deferred taxes and, 788–789
expanded equity method, 808,
830–831
and ownership position, 791–792
vs. consolidation method,
792–793, 796–804
vs. cost and mark to market
methods, 777–778
vs. cost method, 787–788
joint ventures, *see* Joint ventures
segment data, *see* Segment data
Interest and dividends
paid, cash flow classification,
135–136
received, cash flow classification,
135
Interest costs
capitalization *vs.* expensing, 409–411
example: Corning Glass, 411
international standards, 465
pensions, 644, 650
postretirement benefits, 698
Interest coverage ratios, 222
Interest expense, defined, 562–563
Interest method, of bond amortization,
567
Interest rates, relationship to exchange
rates, 989
Interest rate swaps, 734
Interindustry factors, in ratio analysis,
242–245
International accounting standards, *see*
Accounting standards, international
International Accounting Standards
Committee (IASC), 28–29
International Organization of Securities
Commissions (IOSC), 28
Inventory accounting
basic relationships, 332–333,
332–334
rising prices, 333–334
stable prices, 333
change of method, 338–339
economic order quantity and,
354–355
example: British Petroleum, 378–379
FIFO/LIFO choice
effects on financial ratios,
349–356
effects on income, cash flow, and
working capital, 339–342
empirical studies, 368–376

overview, 366–368
summary of reasons, 376–377
FIFO method, *see* First-in, first-out
(FIFO) accounting
inventory balances as an aid to
forecasting, 380–382
and inventory holding policy,
355–356
IRS regulations on method/change of
method, 340, 358
just in time, 355
LIFO method, *see* Last-in, first-out
(LIFO) accounting
lower-of-cost-or-market-valuation
basis, 336
manufacturing firms, 337–338
merchandising firms, 337–338
non-U.S. reporting requirements,
379–380
weighted average cost method, 334,
336*n*
adjustment to LIFO, 349
international use of, 379, 380
working capital distortion, 340
Inventory turnover ratio, 200, 208
hybrid, 352–354
problems with, for LIFO firms,
352–353
Investment cash flows, 18, 19, 49
Investment decisions, 4
role of financial information in
capital markets, 5–6
user classes, 4–5
Investments
cash
cash flows from, 133–134
intercorporate, *see* Intercorporate
investments
off-balance sheet financing, 725–726
Investors, as class of financial
information user, 4–5

J
January effect, 309
Japan
accounting for long-lived assets, 464,
465, 466
consolidation practices, 796
foreign currency transactions, 967
inventory accounting practices, 379
lease accounting practices, 615
lower of cost and market method in,
784
pension plan reporting, 683, 684
tax accounting in, 550
Jennings, Ross, 376
Jensen,, 314
Johnson, W. Bruce, 246, 342*n*
Joint ventures, 806–807
jointly-controlled entities, 807–808
off-balance sheet financing, 725
proportionate consolidation method,
see Proportionate consolidation
Jones, C. P., 300, 302
Journal entries, 36

Joy, O. M., 300
Justin Corporation, revenue recognition methods, 127–130
Just in time inventory accounting, 355

K
Kahn, Nathan, 359
Kane, Alex, 235, 312
Kang, Sok-Hyon, 439, 442
Kaplan, Robert S., 295–296, 442, 903, 905
Kenwin Shops, Inc., SFAS 109 tax accounting, 533–536
Kettler, Paul, 1072–1074
Ketz, J. Edward, 242, 246–247
Kim, David H., 993, 994
Kim, E. H., 903
Kim, Moshe, 438
Kinney, William R., Jr., 827
Kohlberg Kravis Roberts & Co., leveraged buyout of Duracell, 914–918
Koller, T., 1036
Kolodny, Richard, 408, 829n
Kormendi, Roger, 1122
Kothari, S. P., 1121, 1122

L
Labor unions, as class of financial information user, 4
LAC Minerals
  commodity-linked bonds, 724
  hedging disclosures, 736, 737
Lakonishok, Josef, 301, 1140, 1141
Landsman, Wayne, 659, 660–661
Larcker, D. F., 1137–1138
Lasman, Daniel A., 356n
Last-in, first-out (LIFO) accounting, 60, 333–334, 359–360. *See also* Inventory accounting
adjustment to FIFO
  cost of goods sold, 344–344
  example: Sun Company, 342–344
  inventory balances, 342–344
balance sheet information, 335
change from, 357–359
  example: Chrysler Corporation, 358–359
  tax consequences, 358
and declining prices, 360–361
  example: General Electric, 361
dollar value methods, 365, 366
extent of adoption by industry, 367–368*table*
income statement information, 336
initial adoption or change to, 357
  example: Quaker Oats, 357, 358
interim reporting and, 361–362
  example: Nucor Corporation, 363–364
LIFO base liquidation, 362
LIFO effect, 346
LIFO liquidations, 359–360
LIFO reserves, 342, 360–361

pooled specific goods method, 364–365
retail method, 365–366
for tax purposes, 340
vs. FIFO: effect on financial ratios, 349–356
vs. FIFO: effects on income, cash flow, and working capital, 339–342
Latane, H. A., 302
Lawsuits, 15
Leases
capitalization, 396n
classification (operating *vs.* capital)
  les*sees*, 592–593
  lessors, 593–594
  incentives, 589–592
    nontax advantages, 591
    tax advantages, 590–592
  les*see* financial reporting, 594–602
    example: Ashland Oil, 602–606
  lessor financial reporting
    direct financing leases, 612
    example: Pillsbury Company, 612–614
    sales-type leases, 606–612
    sales with leasebacks, 614
  minimum lease payments, 593
  non-U.S. accounting practices, 615
  operating *vs.* capital leases, 589
    comparative analysis, 594–602
  vs. purchase, and capitalization, 397–398
LeClere, Marc J., 369–371, 377
Lee, Cheng F., 251–252
Leftwich, Richard, 586–587, 588, 907
Lev, Baruch, 251–252, 301, 409, 1071–1072, 1138
  critical evaluation of market-based research, 303–309
Leveraged buyouts, 582, 846. *See also* Business combinations
  analysis problems, 918–919
  example: Duracell, 914–918
  goodwill in, 911
  zero-coupon bonds and, 570n
Leveraged recapitalizations, 923
Liabilities
  adjustments for credit analysis purposes, 1017–1018
    example: Deere and Company, 1024–1027
  classification, 13, 14
  current *vs.* noncurrent, 14
    in annual reports, 61–63
  from financing, *see* Financing liabilities
  SFAC 6 definition, 13
Liability method, *see* Tax accounting, liability method: SFAS 96
Licenses, capitalization *vs.* expensing, 412
Life insurance, 686, 699
LIFO, *see* Last-in, first-out (LIFO) accounting

Lilien, Steve, 590
Lindahl, Frederick W., 373, 374, 460, 463–464
Lipe, Robert C., 301, 1122
Liquidity, and income and cash flow statements, 149
Liquidity analysis, 199. *See also* Ratio analysis
  cash/operating cycles, 212–214
  defensive interval, 217
  example: Merck, 217–218
  LIFO *vs.* FIFO, 352
  turnover ratios in, 217
  working capital ratios, 214–217
Livnat, Joshua, 145, 301, 356, 716
Loan impairment, 576
Long-lived assets, 395, 396
  accounting for over lifetime, *see* Depreciation
  analysis of disclosures, 448–454
  capitalization *vs.* expensing of, *see* Capitalization *vs.* expensing
  effect of changing prices, 492–494
  estimating age and useful life, 452–454
  impairment, *see* Impairment of assets
  international accounting aspects, 464–466
  off-balance sheet financing, 725
Long-term debt, *see* Financing liabilities, long- term debt
Long-term debt and solvency analysis, 199, 219. *See also* Ratio analysis
  capital expenditure ratio, 222–223
  capitalization tables, 219–222
  and capitalization *vs.* expensing decision, 403
  CFO-to-debt ratio, 223
  debt covenants, 219
  debt ratios, 219–222
  example: Merck, 220–221
  interest coverage ratios, 222
  LIFO *vs.* FIFO, 356
Lorecke, Kenneth S., 300
Lower-of-cost-or-market valuation basis, 336, 764–765
Lys, Thomas, 409

M
Magliolo, Joseph, 419n
Majluf, Nicolas S., 635
Malkiel,, 829
Malmquist, David H., 418
Management discretion, nonrecurring items, 175–179
Management Discussion and Analysis, 7, 21, 22–23
  in annual reports, 65–66
Mandelker, Gershon M., 903, 905, 1044, 1045, 1070, 1071
Manegold, James, 1068
Manipulation
  of earnings, 175–179
  of ratios, 200

Manufacturing firms
cash/operating cycles, 214, 215
common-size statements, 206
inventory accounting, 337–338, 382
typical asset/liability classification,
59
Marcus, Alan J., 235, 312
Margin before interest and taxes ratio,
224
Marketable equity securities, 764
analysis, 769, 775
example: Dawson Geophysical,
769–772, 775
example: Helmerich and Payne,
772, 773–774
operating/investment results
separation, 772, 774
current *vs.* noncurrent, 765–767
effect of classification, 769–772
lower-of-cost-or-market, 764–765
mark to market accounting, 775–776
insurance companies, 778–782
vs. cost methods, 776–778
special industry SFAS 12 provisions,
768–769
unrealized gains/losses, 767–768
Market anomalies, 309–312
Market-based research, 288, 289, 290
critical evaluation of (by Lev),
303–309
current status, 303–309
market anomalies, 309–312
development of, 291–292
earnings-stock returns relationship,
300
accounting variables, 300–302
good news/bad news
parameter-abnormal return
relationship, 303
market-based variables, 302–302
summary of research studies,
305–307table
efficient market hypothesis, 292–293
forms of (weak, semistrong,
strong), 292
vs. mechanistic hypothesis,
295–297
good news/bad news firms:
Ball-Brown study, 297–299
information content studies, 299–300
inventory accounting method
switches, 296–297
market-analyst relationship: do
markets react to analyst's
expectations?, 301, 311
mechanistic hypothesis, 295
vs. efficient market hypothesis,
295–297
modern portfolio theory, 293–295
capital asset pricing model, *see*
Capital asset pricing model
risk classification, 294
social consequences of accounting
alternatives, 299

Market values
and assets/liabilities valuation, 14–15
of debt, 576–580
supplementary disclosures associated
with, 22
Mark to market accounting, 775–782
Martin, L. G., 1065
Martingale processes, 1130–1132
Matching principle, 7
and tax accounting, 510, 511
McGibben, Walt, 1075–1077
McKeown, James C., 373, 1133
Mean-reverting processes, 1130–1132
Mechanistic hypothesis, 295–297
Meckling,, 314
Mellman, Martin, 590
Merchandising firms
cash/operating cycles, 212–213
inventory accounting, 337
Merck & Co., Inc.
activity analysis, 211
balance sheets, comparative, 270
cash flow statements, comparative,
271
common-size statements, 202–204,
206, 207
disaggregation of ROA/ROE, 233,
235, 236, 237
income statements, comparative, 271
liquidity analysis, 217–218
long-term debt and solvency
analysis, 220–221
R&D cost capitalization/expensing,
403–404
Merger accounting (pooling of interests
method), *see* Business
combination, pooling of interests
method
Mergers and acquisitions, 846. *See also*
Business combinations;
Intercorporate investments
for adjusting assets values for
changing prices, 494
effect on pension plans, 678
example: Acquire and Target,
849–851, 854–858
example: ConAgra-Golden Valley,
863–873
example: Georgia Pacific-Great
Northern Nekoosa merger,
873–885
tax accounting, 543–544, 668–669
unfriendly, 853
valuation effects, 1126
Mest, David P., 376
Meyer, John R., 460
Mingo, Kent A., 246, 247, 248,
1063–1064
Minimum lease payments, 593
Minority interests, 794, 805–806
Miscellaneous sources, of financial
information, 23–24
Modified accelerated cost recovery
system (MACRS), 435, 436

Modified liability method, *see* Tax
accounting, modified liability
method: SFAS 109
Monday effect, 309–310
Monopoly industries, ratio analysis,
243–244, 245
Monsanto, hedging disclosures,
737–738, 739, 740
Moody's bond ratings, 1055,
1056–1059
Moody's Industrial Manual, 586
Moore, Giora, 438
Moore, M. L., 176
Morck, Randall, 660, 903
Morse, Dale, 1118–1119
Moses, Douglas, 176
Most, Kenneth S., 438
Mulford, Charles W., 581, 791–792
Multijurisdictional disclosure system
agreement, 30
Multinational companies, 942. *See also*
Foreign currency translation;
Foreign exchange rates
analysis examples:
Alcoa, 982–987
IBM, 968–982
basic accounting issues, 943
impact of reporting requirements on
management/investors, 993–995
Multistage growth models, 1145–1147
Murrin, J., 1036
Myers, Stewart C., 635

N
Narayann, P., 1046, 1050–1054
Natural resources, depletion, 432–433
Net change method, 517, 518
Netherlands
accounting for long-lived assets, 465
business combination accounting,
899
foreign currency translation, 966
inventory accounting practices, 379
lease accounting practices, 615
pension plan reporting, 683, 684
segment reporting, 829
Net income, components of, 18
Net realizable value, 458
Neutrality, of accounting information,
10–11
Newbold, Paul, 827, 1054, 1133
Newcor, Inc.
accounting changes reporting,
171–172
income statements, 130
Nexus of contracts, 314
No credit interval, 217
Noel, James, 381–382, 1135
Noncash transactions, 136
Nonhomogeneous subsidiaries, 795–796
Nonrecurring items, 159–160
accounting changes, 170–172
analysis, 177–179
analysis, 174–179

Nonrecurring items, *cont.*
  defined, 121
  discontinued operations, 167–170
  extraordinary items, 164–167
    trends in reporting, 165
  management discretion/earnings
    manipulation involving, 175–179
  prior period adjustments, 172–174
  segregation of, 120
  unusual or infrequent items, 160–163
  and valuation, 1122–1128
Nonsmoothed pension cost, 657
Noreen, Eric, 1142
Notes, 564n. *See also* Bonds
Nucor Corporation, LIFO accounting
  in, 363–364

O
O'Brien, Patricia, 301n, 1142
Off-balance sheet activities
  and liability adjustments for credit
    analysis purposes, 1017
  pension obligations as, 653
Off-balance sheet financing, 714–715,
    715–716
  accounts receivable: wholly-owned
    finance subsidiaries, 716–721
    example: Continental Corporation,
      717
    example: Georgia Pacific, 718–720
  commodity-linked bonds, 724
    example: LAC Minerals, 724
  example: Ashland Oil, 727–732
  executory contracts, 714–715
  fixed assets, 725
  inventories, 721–724
    example: Alcan, 722–723
    example: Reynolds Metals,
      721–722
  investments, 725–726
    example: Panhandle Eastern,
      725–726
  joint ventures, 725
    example: Georgia Pacific, 725,
      726
  noncancellable leases as, 601
Ohlson, James A., 406, 419–420,
    1053–1054, 1098, 1132
Oil and gas companies
  political cost hypothesis and, 316
  supplementary disclosures by, 22
Oil and gas exploration
  capitalization *vs.* expensing, 397,
    406
    example: Pennzoil, 420–424
    international practices, 466
    mandated accounting changes and,
      407–409
    SFAS 69 disclosures, 419–420,
      468–478
    successful efforts *vs.* full cost
      accounting, 416–419, 420–424
  impairment of assets: Pennzoil
    example, 455–458

Oligopolistic industries, ratio analysis,
    244–245
Operating cycles
  manufacturing firms, 214, 215
  merchandising firms, 212–213
  schematic representation, 213
Operating leases, *see* Leases
Operating leverage, 228–230, 1042,
    1043–1045
  and beta(s), 1069–1070
  estimation, 267–269
Operating leverage effect ratio, 230
Operating losses, tax treatment,
    541–542
Operating margin ratio, 224
Operating risk, 1043
Operations cash flows, *see* Cash from
    operations (CFO)
Option pricing model, 302n
Options, 735
  and EPS calculation, 276–277
Other sources, of financial information,
    23–24
Ou, Jane A., 290, 320–322,
    1135–1136, 1137
Overhead, capitalization, 136n

P
Palepu, Krishna, 439, 442
Panhandle Eastern, exchangeable
    bonds, 725–726
Pastena, Victor, 590
Patel, Kiritkumar A., 1065
Patell, James M., 302n
Patents, capitalization *vs.* expensing,
    411–412
Payout ratio, 1105, 1111–1112
Penman, Stephen H., 290, 319n, 320,
    373, 1116–1117, 1132, 1135–1137
Pennzoil
  capitalization *vs.* expensing issues,
    420–424
    SFAS 69 disclosures, 468–478
  impairment of assets, 455–458
Pension plans, 634–635. *See also*
    Postretirement benefits
  analysis of costs/liabilities, 652,
    654–658, 661–662
    importance of assumptions,
      652–654
    market valuation, 659–661
    research studies, 659–661
  analysis of disclosures: General
    Motors example, 662–665,
    677–678
    estimation of pension costs,
      669–670
    estimation of pension status,
      665–668
    future cost estimation, 674–677
    trend analysis, 670–674
  curtailments/settlements, 679–680
    overfunded plan termination,
      680–683

defined benefit plans, 635, 637
  accounting for, 647–652
  accumulated benefit obligation,
    639, 643
  example illustration (fictional
    company), 639–644
  obligations estimation, 638–645
  pension cost computation,
    647–652
  plan assets, 646–647
  plan status, 651–652
  projected benefit obligation, 639,
    643
  vested benefit obligation, 643–644
defined contribution plans, 635, 637
effects of acquisitions/divestures,
    678–679
as "implicit contract," 634, 635
non-U.S. reporting practices,
    683–685
  example: SmithKline Beecham,
    684–685
overfunding/underfunding incentives,
    635–636
SFAS 87 disclosure requirements,
    637, 643–644, 647–652
tax incentives for, 635, 636
trends in income and expenses, 674,
    675
Percentage-of-completion method, of
    revenue recognition, 125–126 *vs.*
    completed contract method,
    126–130
Period costs, recognition, 124
Permanent earnings, 116, 117
Perpetual debt, 574
Petroleum Corp., expanded equity
    method, 830–831
Pfizer, common-size statements,
    202–204
Pharmaceutical firms, *see also* Merck
    & Co., Inc.
  patent capitalization, 411
  R&D cost capitalization/expensing,
    403–404
Philbrick, Donna R., 177, 178
Pillsbury Company, lease reporting,
    612–614
Pinches, George E., 246, 247, 248,
    1063–1064
Pincus, Morton, 349–350, 375–376
Plant closings, 174
Political cost hypothesis, in agency
    theory, 316
Pooled specific goods method, 364–365
Pooling of interests method, *see*
    Business combinations, pooling of
    interests method of accounting
Portfolio theory, 293–295
  capital asset pricing model, 293–294,
    1103–1104
Positive accounting research, 288, 289,
    290, 312–313, 316–319

agency theory, 313–314
  bonus plan hypothesis, 314–315
  debt covenant hypothesis, 315–316
  "nexus of contracts," 314
  political cost hypothesis, 316
  disclosure and regulatory
    requirements, 313
  summary of research studies,
    316–319
Postannouncement drift, 310
Postemployment benefits, 685–686
  accumulated postretirement
    obligation, 688
  forecasting costs, 698–699
  health care benefits, 686–687,
    688–689, 699
  importance of assumptions in
    analysis, 688–693
    example: Commercial Intertech,
      689–690, 691
    example: General Electric,
      691–693
  life insurance, 686, 699
  net benefit cost computation,
    687–688
  non-U.S. practices, 699–700
  pensions, see Pension plans
  SFAS 106 and, 686
  transition methods (to SFAS 106),
    694–698
    example: General Electric,
      696–698
Preferred equity, 574–575
Preserve improvements, 155–156
Press, Eric G., 586
Pretax margin ratio, 224
Price/earnings ratio, low, as a market
  anomaly, 310
Prior period adjustments, nonrecurring
  items and, 172–174
Prior service cost, pensions, 645, 651
Product life cycle, and ratio analysis,
  238–242
Profitability analysis, 199, 223. See
  also Ratio analysis
  and capitalization vs. expensing
    decision, 403
  and cash flows, 226
  example: Merck, 227
  financial leverage, 229, 230–231
  fixed vs. variable operating cost
    components, 226, 228
  LIFO vs. FIFO, 351–352
  operating leverage, 228–230
  return on investment, 225–226
  return on sales, 224–225
Profit margin ratio, 224
Pro forma information, 853, 883–885
Projected (pension) benefit obligation,
  639, 643
Proportionality assumption, in ratio
  analysis, 199–200
Proportionate consolidation, 808–809,
  830–831

example: Brascan, 812–820
non-U.S. practices, 829
Publishers, revenue recognition in, 125
Purchase method, see Business
  combinations, purchase method of
  accounting
Purchasing power accounting, see
  Constant dollar method
Push-down accounting, 910–914

Q
Q ratio (Tobin's), 908
  and asset-based valuation, 1099
Quaker Oats, change to LIFO, 357,
  358
Quarterly corporate reports, 56–57
Quarterly forecasting models,
  1133–1134
Quasi-reorganizations, 922–923
Quick ratio, 216–217

R
Random walk processes, 1130–1132
Rapacciolli, Donna, 175, 176
Ratio analysis, 198–199. See also
  specific defined ratios, i.e.,
  Turnover ratios, Quick ratio, etc.
  and capitalization vs. expensing
    decision, 403
  categories of, 198–199, 206. See
    also Activity analysis; Liquidity
    analysis; Long-term debt and
    solvency analysis; Profitability
    analysis
  cautions
    accounting methods choice,
      201–202
    benchmark choice, 200
    economic assumptions, 199–200
    management manipulation, 200
    negative numbers, 200–201
    timing and window dressing, 200
  classification/partitioning of ratios,
    245–248
  common-size statements, 198,
    202–206, 207
  for competing strategy
    differentiation, 236, 238
  disaggregation of ROA, 232–233
    example: Merck, 233, 234
  disaggregation of ROE, 233–236
    example: Merck, 207, 233, 235,
      236
  disclosure of ratios, 250–251
  empirical studies of, 245–253
  foreign currency translation and,
    960–963
  foreign currency translation effects,
    981
  impact of purchase vs. pooling of
    interests methods, 861–862,
    872–873, 882–883

industry norms as benchmarks,
  251–253
interindustry factors, 242–245
objective, 198
perceived importance of ratios (by
  CFAs), 248–250
post-acquisition, U.S. vs. U.K.
  practices, 898
and product life cycle, 238–242
proportionality assumption, 199–200
push-down accounting effects,
  913–914
ratio composites, 232
ratio interrelationships, 231–232
ROE-ROA relationship, 232–233
as starting point for further analysis,
  202
statistical properties of ratios,
  245–246
Ratliff Drilling, change of depreciation
  method, 445–448
Rayburn, Judy, 145, 538
Real estate sales, cost recovery method
  for, 131
Realization, 14
Receivables, as assets, 158
Receivables turnover ratio, 208–209
Recoveries, 14
Recurring continuing operations,
  predictive ability of, 120
Recurring cost, pensions, 657
Redeemable preferreds, 13
Reeve, James H., 364
Regulated utilities, see Utilities
Regulatory requirements, and positive
  accounting theory, 313
Reiger, Phillip R., 359
Reiter, Sara Ann, 359, 636
Relevance, of accounting information,
  10–11
Reliability, of accounting information,
  10–12
Rendelman, R. J., Jr., 302
Reorganizations, 846, 847, 922–923
Replacement cost, 491
Replacement cost method, see Current
  cost method
Reporting systems, see Financial
  reporting systems
Representational faithfulness, of
  accounting information, 10
Reproduction cost, 491
Research, see also Market-based
  research; Positive
  accounting research
  "classical" theory, 288, 289, 290–291
  current directions in, 290, 319–320
  good news/bad news firms: Ou
    study, 320–322
  implications for analysis, 323–34
  overview, 288–290
Research and development costs
  capitalization vs. expensing,
    396–397, 405–406

Research and development costs, *cont.*
  international standards, 465
  mandated accounting changes and,
    407–409
  partnerships and, 413, 479–480
    example: Centocor, 480–484
Residual risk, defined, 198
Restructured debt, 576
Restructurings, 458
  provisions, 1101
Retailers
  common-size statements, 204–206
  inventory accounting, 381
Return on assets, pensions, 647, 650
Return on assets (ROA) ratio, 225, 226
  disaggregation, 232–233
  relationship to ROE, 232–233
Return on common equity (ROCE)
    ratio, 225–226
Return on equity (ROE) ratio, 226
  disaggregation, 233–236
  relationship to ROA, 233–234
Return on investment (ROI) ratios,
    225–226
Return on sales ratios, 224–225
Revenue and expense recognition,
    124–125
  choice of method, and income and
    cash flow statements, 147–148
  completed contract method,
    125–130, 131
  cost recovery method, 130–131
  criteria for, 150
  departures from sales basis, 125
  example: Thousand Trails, Inc.,
    150–155
  importance of in analysis, 159
  installment method, 130, 131
  percentage-of-completion method,
    125–130, 131
  summary of methods, 131
Revenues, SFAC 6 definition, 16
Reynolds Metals
  hedging disclosures, 736–737, 738
  off-balance sheet financing, 721–722
Rhee, S. Ghon, 1044, 1045, 1070,
    1071
Richardson, Gordon D., 408, 1142
Ricks, William E., 372, 373, 374–375,
    460, 463–464, 789
Risk analysis, *see also* Bankruptcy
    prediction; Debt risk analysis;
    Equity risk analysis
  classification under capital asset
    model, 294
  earnings variability, 1038–1042
  operating and financial leverage,
    1042–1045
  overview, 1037–1038
Risk exposures, supplementary
    disclosures associated with, 22
ROA, *see* Return on assets (ROA) ratio
Robinson, John R., 901–902, 908
ROE, *see* Return on equity (ROE) ratio

Roll, Richard, 295–296, 442
Ronen, Joshua, 175, 300–301
Rosen, Etzmun, 359
Rosenberg, Barr, 1075–1077
Roussey, R. S., 27
Rozeff, Michael S., 409, 1134
Rue, Joseph C., 734
Ryan, Stephen, 290, 1122

S
SAB 88, 30
Sadan, Simcha, 175, 300–301
Salatka, William K., 409
Sale-leaseback transactions, 614
Saloman, Gerald, 442
Salvage value, and depreciation, 434
SAS 58, 24–25
Savich, Richard S., 238, 239–241
Schering-Plough, common-size
    statements, 202–204
Schiff, Allen, 175, 176, 360
Schiff, Michael, 338, 359, 458, 460
Schipper and Smith, 921
Scholes, Myron, 1072–1074
Schwager, Steven J., 1142
Scott, James, 1050, 1051
Sears, Roebuck and Co., SFAS 109 tax
    accounting, 533
Securities and Exchange Commission
  form F-6 reporting, 29
  form 20–F reporting, 29–30
  form 6–K reporting, 29
  10–K annual report
    requirements/schedules, 8
  8–K current report, 8
  Management Discussion and
    Analysis requirements, *see*
    Management Discussion and
    Analysis
  multijurisdictional disclosure system
    agreement, 30
  10–Q quarterly report, 8
  regulation S-X requirements, 7–9
  requirements for foreign registrants,
    29–30
  SAB 88, 30
Segment-based forecasting models,
    1134–1135
Segment data, 820–821, 825–826, 826
  example: Dow Chemical Company,
    822–825
  geographic reporting, 821–822
  non-U.S. practices, 829
  uses of, 825–826
    for estimating consolidated
      earnings/risk, 826–829
Selling, Thomas, 235, 238, 242–244,
    245, 989
Selto, Frank H., 408
Servaes, Henri, 907
Service costs
  pensions, 644, 650, 657
  postretirement benefits, 698
Service hours method, 427, 429–430

Seventh Directive, 29
SFAC 1, 4
SFAC 2, 10–12
SFAC 3, 10
SFAC 4, 10
SFAC 5, 15, 124
SFAC 6, 10, 12–13
  revenues/expenses definition, 16–17
SFAS 2, 316, 397
SFAS 4, 164*n*
  and early bond retirement, 582
SFAS 5, 21
SFAS 8, 943–944
  criticism of, 993
SFAS 12
  proposed replacement exposure draft,
    782–783
  requirements for marketable equity
    securities, 764–765
  special industry provisions,
    768–769
SFAS 13, 592
  lease disclosure requirements, 601
  and lease incentives, 590, 591
SFAS 14, 175, 494, 820–821
SFAS 15, 576
SFAS 16, 172
SFAS 19, 416
  suspension of, 407
SFAS 25, 416
SFAS 28, 614
SFAS 33, 291*n*, 438–439
  inflation accounting and, 490–492
  reporting of impaired assets, 455
SFAS 34, 409–410
SFAS 52, 733, 735, 736
  functional currency definition, 948
SFAS 56, 125
SFAS 60, 769, 778
SFAS 66, 614
SFAS 68, 480
SFAS 69, 419–420
  example disclosures: Pennzoil,
    468–478
SFAS 71, 397*n*
SFAS 77, 717*n*
SFAS 80, 733, 735, 736
SFAS 85, 275*n*
SFAS 86, 412
SFAS 87, 25, 30, 64
  SFAS 87 pension requirements and
    analysis, 637, 643–644, 647–652
SFAS 88, 679
SFAS 89, 455
  inflation accounting and, 490
SFAS 94, 58–59, 716, 795
SFAS 95, 18–19, 45, 48, 410
  cash flow classification guidelines,
    132
  marketable securities and, 60
  and W. T. Grant bankruptcy, 147
SFAS 96, 25, 510. *See also* Tax
    accounting, liability method: SFAS
    96